CCCS Selected Working Papers Volume 1

This collection of classic essays focuses on the theoretical frameworks that informed the work of the Centre for Contemporary Cultural Studies at the University of Birmingham, the methodologies and working practices that the Centre developed for conducting academic research and examples of the 'grounded studies' carried out under the auspices of the Centre.

This volume is split into four thematic sections that are introduced by key academics working in the field of cultural studies, and includes a preface by eminent scholar, Stuart Hall. The thematic sections are:

- CCCS founding moments
- Theoretical engagements
- Theorising experience, exploring methods
- Grounded studies

Essays by: Lucy Bland; Eve Brook; Charlotte Brunsdon; Iain Chambers; Phil Cohen; John Clarke; John Ellis; Dan Finn; Johan Fornas; Paul Gilroy; Ann Gray; Michael Green; Larry Grossberg; Stuart Hall; Dick Hebdige; Dorothy Hobson; Richard Hoggart; Richard Johnson; Errol Lawrence; Robert Lumley; Gregor McLennan; Angela McRobbie; Elspeth Probyn; Robin Rusher; Alan Shuttleworth; Phil Slater; Colin Sparks; Allon White; Paul Willis; Janice Winship; Charles Woolfson.

CCCS Selected Working Papers

Volume 1

Edited by Ann Gray, Jan Campbell, Mark Erickson, Stuart Hanson and Helen Wood

LONDON AND NEW YORK

First published 2007
by Routledge
2 Park Square, Milton Park, Abingdon, Oxon OX14 4RN

Simultaneously published in the USA and Canada
by Routledge
270 Madison Ave, New York, NY 10016

Routledge is an imprint of the Taylor & Francis Group, an informa business

Typeset in Baskerville by RefineCatch Limited, Bungay, Suffolk
Printed and bound in Great Britain by
The Cromwell Press, Trowbridge, Wiltshire

British Library Cataloguing in Publication Data
A catalogue record for this book is available from the British Library

Library of Congress Cataloging-in-Publication Data
A catalog record for this book has been requested

ISBN10: 0–415–32440–8 (hbk)
ISBN10: 0–203–35706–X (ebk)
ISBN10: 0–415–41259–5 (2-volume set)

ISBN13: 978–0–415–32440–3 (hbk)
ISBN13: 978–0–203–35706–4 (ebk)
ISBN13: 978–0–415–41259–9 (2-volume set)

Contents

Editorial team

Jan Campbell is senior lecturer in English at the University of Birmingham and a former member of staff at DCSS. Campbell's research focuses on the interface between psychoanalysis and cultural theory, psychoanalysis and film and psychoanalysis and therapy practice (she is a clinical analyst). Her most recent book, *Psychoanalysis and the Time of Life: Durations of the Unconscious Self* is a rereading of Freud in relation to the work of Henri Bergson.

Ann Gray is Professor of Cultural Studies at the University of Lincoln, Editor of the *European Journal of Cultural Studies* and is on the Editorial Board of the *Journal of British Cinema and Television* and *Memory Studies*. Her previous publications include *Research Practice for Cultural Studies: Ethnographic Methods and Lived Cultures* (2003) and *Video Playtime: the Gendering of a Leisure Technology* (1992). She is director of the AHRC project 'Televising History: 1995–2010'.

Mark Erickson is currently Senior Lecturer in the School of Applied Social Sciences at the University of Brighton. He was a member of staff at DCSS from 1996 until its closure in 2001. His most recent book is *Science, Culture and Society: Making Sense of Science in the 21st Century* (2005) published by Polity.

Stuart Hanson is Senior Lecturer in Media Studies at De Montfort University, Leicester. He has previously taught at Wolverhampton University and in the Department of Cultural Studies and Sociology at the University of Birmingham. He is author of a forthcoming book for MUP entitled *From Silent Screen to Multi-screen: A History of Cinema Exhibition in Britain Since 1896.*

Helen Wood is Lecturer of Sociology at De Montfort University. She is author of *Talking With Television* forthcoming, University of Illinois Press, and has published on television, audiences, talk shows, reality television and cultural studies in a number of journals. She is also assistant editor of the journal *Ethnography*. She was an undergraduate student and member of staff in the Department of Cultural Studies at Birmingham.

Preface

Stuart Hall

This is a selection of essays and papers from the less well-known parts of the archives of the Centre for Cultural Studies which have been rescued for publication from the Centre's arbitrary closure by the University of Birmingham, which hosted it for many years (1964–2002). They are published here in two volumes. Among other purposes, they constitute a contribution to the long, much contested and still unsettled history of the Centre and the early years of Cultural Studies before – as Marx once memorably remarked – being abandoned 'to the gnawing criticism of the mice'.

In her Introduction, Ann Gray situates the emergence of the Centre in its wider historical and cultural context. The aim of this Preface is to set the selection of papers in the working context in which they were produced. Volume 1 deals with early theoretical developments, of both a conceptual and more 'grounded' kind. They relate specifically to a particular 'moment' in the history of the Birmingham Centre: from its inauguration in 1964, through the tumultuous 70s, to the beginning of the 80s (the date of the most recent paper included is 1981). In the wider history of Cultural Studies, these were still very early – if heady and exciting – days. The collection thus omits much that subsequently followed – the Centre's work over the subsequent two decades; its many institutional vicissitudes, leading to the University's *coup de grace* in 2002; the expansion of Cultural Studies as a critical intellectual project and field of research, first at other sites in the UK, and then as a global, trans-national 'movement'; the wide-ranging impact of what is now called 'the cultural turn' on many other disciplines in the Humanities. These developments are not only *not* reflected here, but are hardly even hinted at or anticipated.

The selection is drawn from a larger archive of papers informally circulating in this period within the Centre or among readers at its margins. They include some of the originating documents; a selection of papers first circulated in the highly provisional and technologically primitive form of the Stencilled Papers series which are often drafts of things which appeared in expanded and revised form later; papers from the Centre's journal, *Working Papers In Cultural Studies* (*WPCS*), which was launched in this period to raise the profile of the Centre's work (the tentative character of whose title tells its own story); and]extracts from the Hutchinson book series which, although undoubtedly a venture into the wider world and an effort to make the Centre's work available to new audiences, mainly re-printed in hard-back form issues of *WPCS* or papers produced by and debated within the Centre's various working groups.

That this is not a comprehensive or representative selection goes without saying. Some important papers and a few juicy documents – in particular, those from internal Centre debates, with the steam of argument still coming off their surfaces – will probably not now see the light of day (the question of where the Centre's archives should be housed is still, at the time of going to press, unresolved). Others could have been chosen and many will regret that their favourites have not been included. The selection itself – as Ann Gray tactfully hints – provoked argument and debate, between those who wanted the volume to include mainly what still seemed valuable and relevant to present concerns, and those anxious that the selection should reflect the balance and circumstances of work at the time when it was produced. Those who know the history will understand this to be a typical Centre way of proceeding – par for the course! The happy result is the product of a negotiated compromise and aims to satisfy both purposes.

Archival enterprises, while representing themselves as neutral and objective, are often highly contentious exercises. What is selected? Who or what is left out – and why? Is a definitive account – despite assurances to the contrary – being surreptitiously offered? And, if so, whose account is it? What claims are being made – about origin ('this is where it all started'), or authenticity ('this is what really happened') or authority ('we are in a better position to know what cultural studies is than you')? These remain contested issues in the Centre's history, which, as Ann Gray notes, has been haunted by questions of origins despite strenuous efforts to the contrary. This is hardly surprising, given the anti-foundational, anti-essentialist theoretical ethos in which Cultural Studies has matured, its instinctive inclination to critique and deconstruct 'grand narratives'. The volume offers no definitive answer to these questions. Accordingly, this history has been and will continue to be fought over as well as discussed and debated, despite the best efforts of the editors to be inclusive: both by those who were there at the time and have a significant stake in it, but all of whom experienced it differently, from different positions and with different degrees of engagement; as well as by those who were not and who often feel excluded from the project in some way, or resent the authority which 'Birmingham' still seems to exert over the field. In addition there is the difficulty which haunts all archival-based research – making sense of the 'lived experience' of a particular moment when all that remains are the fragmentary traces from which the past has to be re-constructed, re-remembered and re-interpreted.

Throughout these years, the Centre had only a small academic staff – Richard Hoggart, its Director, and myself, first as Research Fellow and later as Director; then, Michael Green from English, and Richard Johnson from Social History; and later Paul Willis when he became a post-doctoral research fellow. All the others, except a small number on funded research projects – and therefore the majority of the contributors – were graduate students: either formally attached to the Centre and registered for MAs or PhDs, often initially on research studentships; or the large diaspora of people 'informally attached', completing theses or regularly 'visiting', many of whose contributions are included here. Since the former were funded fee-paying students and the latter were not, the University made much of this formal distinction but the Centre in its working practice – as this selection shows – did not. Initially, the Centre was one of two research groupings in the English Department where Richard Hoggart was Professor, though subsequently it was given its independence within the Faculty of Arts before being transferred – in varying institutional relationships – to the Faculty of Commerce and Social Science.

These papers are therefore very much early 'work in progress' by everyone involved, whatever their status as staff or students; who, in the spirit of the times (they included the upheavals of '1968') organized themselves as a sort of 'working collective'. They reflect an institutional initiative in its early stages, a field of work in the process of emergence, an intellectual project *in formation*. It is true, as Ann Gray also notes, that many people, including Raymond Williams, have argued elsewhere, that people had been doing kinds of work which we would now recognise as 'Cultural Studies' long before such a field was institutionalized. It could also be argued that an element of 'cultural studies' was implicit in the work of most Arts and Humanities departments, where the literatures, languages, arts, ideas and histories of different societies were studied, and in the Social Sciences, especially in departments of Sociology and Anthropology. However, the concept of 'culture' did not figure largely in these fields as they were constituted at the time in British academic life but had at best a sort of un-acknowledged 'half-life'. I would argue that to name an inter-disciplinary field of work as such, which fore-grounded the concept of 'culture', and to attempt to institutionalize it within a largely indifferent, suspicious or hostile academic environment, represented a transformatory shift, though it did not in any sense constitute an absolute beginning.

However, this institutionalization posed certain practical and conceptual problems. How could this area of study, which had many overlaps into other disciplines, be constituted as a distinctive intellectual field, even if it was not a discipline in the old sense but rather the product of the partial disintegration or reconstitution of the traditional disciplines and the dramatic rise of inter-disciplinarity, which was a feature of academic and intellectual life at the time? How could a coherent intellectual discourse be constructed in which students from very different disciplinary backgrounds could work and research, place their various specific projects relationally, be guided and supervised, argue and innovate, without some sense of shared purpose, conceptual clarity or common intellectual framework? Could work be initiated and supervised in a 'field' which did not pre-exist the research, but was literally being constructed at the same time as people were beginning to produce work in it?

The papers collected here represent the early struggles of the Centre to do just that – to constitute Cultural Studies as a field of critical intellectual inquiry and research. They should therefore be read, less as definitive formulations of a finished body of 'Cultural Theory' (a term almost never used in this period in its imperious, over-arching and capitalised singular) and more as offering a glimpse into the informal intellectual life and practices of a group of students, teachers and researchers struggling to find new ways of working, reasoning and 'theorising' together about the relationship between 'culture and society', the meaning, place and constituitive role of culture itself, and the significance of 'the cultural' in the heady context of rapid post-war social change – the historical conjuncture which shaped the Centre's early work and in which much of its early theorising must be contextualised. They are the traces of an attempt to cohere individual thesis work and research around certain shared themes and concepts, of the struggle to bring into existence a field of intellectual inquiry only just beginning to discover its own methodologies and critical language, its distinctive body of ideas, internal coherence, conceptual frame and paradigmatic issues. Read symptomatically, they provide an insight into some of the formative working methods and practices of an emerging field of critical work – entry points, as it were, for a trip 'below decks' into the 'boiler room' which was to become Cultural Studies.

The work of the Centre in this period is now sometimes referred to as 'The Birmingham School', perhaps in imitation of that other much more famous and distinguished collective, 'The Frankfurt School'. The comparison is both absurd and misleading. The two did share something in common – the project of bringing a wide range of disciplinary approaches and intellectual traditions to bear on a critical reading of recent developments in contemporary capitalist societies and the cultural forms of late modernity. However, Adorno, Horkheimer and the rest were scholars of the highest intellectual distinction, already deeply schooled in German philosophy, European intellectual history and social theory. Those leading the CCCS project had no such philosophical background, no fully formed cultural theory to unfold, no deeply honed intellectual traditions of writing and high speculation in these fields to draw on, especially in terms of theorising culture, relating culture to other practices in the social formation or drawing cultural and social questions into a single framework of analysis. Indeed, we had to make clear to institutions wanting to follow the Cultural Studies track that the particular disciplines represented at the Centre were an arbitrary not a considered assortment and it could as easily develop from a different disciplinary mix – as indeed it did.

The principal intellectual terrain in which some of the issues which confronted the Centre had previously been posed was the school of 'close textual reading' which had developed in literary criticism, most actively represented in the UK by the work of F. R. and Q. D. Leavis and the critics grouped around the Cambridge journal, *Scrutiny.* As Ann Gray reminds us, its approach, which was reflected in the early founding documents of the Centre, was 'critical and evaluative'. In addition to the close reading of literary texts, this group had developed a particular speculative reading and critique of recent developments in English culture, including popular culture. However this work, though influential on the formation of Cultural Studies at the Centre, was of a distinctly conservative cast. Raymond Williams, in a brilliant re-reading, had located the cultural work of *Scrutiny* and the Leavises, among many other writers, in a wider, deeper, more critical body of social and cultural criticism and commentary from the Romantics and the onset of industrial society forwards, which he called 'the Culture-and-Society tradition'. Richard Hoggart, who also came from this literary-critical formation, had offered, in *The Uses of Literacy,* a subtle and profound analysis, not only of how the trend towards a more commercially-driven 'mass culture' was producing profound cultural changes in British post-war society, especially in working class values and attitudes, but also a brilliant methodological demonstration of how these social shifts could be 'closely read' as if they were texts.

These were the tentative traditions of thought – in which, it should be noted, the 'society' side of Raymond Williams' 'culture-and-society' couplet remained very un-historicised and under-conceptualised – on which the Birmingham Centre had immediately to draw. The papers reprinted in the opening sections of this volume are situated on this contested terrain. The Rowntree-funded project, *The Popular Press and Social Change 1945–65,* operating in the Centre at this time – the study of the contrasting popular discourses of the *Mirror* and the *Express* and their relationship to social change in Britain in the post-war period – was specifically devised to test the validity of this method in comparison with more positivistic social-scientific methods; though it is significant that, as the project developed, it was obliged to assume an increasingly historical dimension, mirroring the movement towards a more inter-disciplinary framework for Cultural Studies which was in progress throughout the Centre's work.

In order to create that 'common discourse' referred to earlier, the Centre organised that, in addition to their individual research projects and the weekly public seminar with invited external speakers, all students were required to participate in two other weekly seminars. The first, taken by Richard Hoggart, was based on the 'close reading' method, in an attempt to teach students from different disciplinary backgrounds how to read 'society', social attitudes and social change – as *The Uses of Literacy* had done – from within the texts of literary and popular culture. Early Centre students still have fond memories of these seminars based on a reading for 'tone' and the text's address to its readers, of the opening passages of – among other texts – D. H. Lawrence's *Sons and Lovers*, E. M. Forster's *Howards End*, George Orwell's 'Shooting An Elephant', William Blake's *Tyger, Tyger* and Sylvia Plath's *Daddy.*

In the second seminar, which I took, we read and discussed a range of texts which related to conceptualising the 'society' part of the culture-and-society equation: Leavis, Williams and E.P. Thompson; later, Dilthey, early German social theory and the *geistwissenschaft* tradition; certain founding texts by Marx, Weber and Durkheim; the Sociology of Knowledge and the recently emerging Sociology of Literature; certain key texts in American sociology including Parsons, the Chicago 'school' and the social constructionists; the mass culture/mass society debate. Something of the flavour of this seminar can be found in the 'Hinterland of Science' essay by me which is included in this volume. Later versions of this seminar became the basis of the Theory Seminar from which the Centre's taught MA was constructed. It was principally to this seminar that such figures as Lukacs, Goldmann, Barthes, Levi-Strauss, Sartre, Gramsci, Althusser, Adorno, Benjamin, and later Juliet Mitchell, Kristeva, Freud, Lacan and Foucault, were first introduced.

As active and wide-ranging debate developed around this process of engagement with a range of thinkers and different schools of thought, within and outside the seminars, students and staff, individually and in groups, began to explore more deeply and articulate their critical responses to these authors. As can be seen from the second and third sections of this Volume, many of these ideas began to be taken up and applied in the more experiential and grounded contexts of concrete studies. Out of all this, something like a Centre approach, or rather a set of related approaches, to the question of conceptualising culture began to emerge.

Though it has become convenient retrospectively to summarise the Centre's work in terms of the dominance of a 'Gramscian approach' – and the introduction of Gramsci's work by Lidia Curti, an exchange teacher of language from Naples in the Italian department and a regular participant in these seminars as well as the fierce debates around Althusser's work, did prove to be a critical turning point for some of us – a glance at the range of authors engaged and the variety of positions emerging in these papers demonstrates that no such totalising theoretical Centre orthodoxy ever existed; similarly with the idea that Cultural Studies was at this time, in any simple sense, a 'marxist' centre. It would be more accurate to say that Cultural Studies – from the re-formulations of Williams' *The Long Revolution* onwards – evolved partly on the basis of a long-running 'quarrel' with orthodox Marxism, resistance to its economic reductionism, its teleological character and a strong sense of its inadequacy, in its orthodox forms, to provide the all-encompassing framework in which culture could be adequately thought: a critique only partially overcome for some by the new non-reductive 'marxisms' which emerged in the 70s.

On the contrary the Centre's theoretical work, as it appears in this volume, was less about the production of a substantive orthodox Cultural Theory and more about how to 'go on theorising' the relative autonomy of cultural forms and the relationship between 'the cultural' and other practices in a social formation. Paradigmatically, the work takes the form of 'the critique of positions'. Nevertheless, this was undoubtedly one of the primary sites of that so-called 'theoretical turn' within the Centre's work, which seemed at the time to be following a naturally evolving and uncharted pathway through the 'culture-and-society' question, but has since been seen by some as abandoning the original, more literary, roots of the Centre's early formation.

When the Theory seminar evolved into part of the 'taught' MA, we added a more practical and methodologically-focussed site of collective work in the form of a Work-in-Progress seminar. Here students reported to other members on their individual studies and thesis topics, helping to constitute through discussion, debate and indeed shared writing, a more collective style of research. Work-in-Progress seminars subsequently proliferated into what came to be known as the Centre's Working Groups, the source of many Centre books and of many of the papers selected in Volume 2. However, in its early days, the Work-in-Progress seminar also developed some collective projects of its own, whose joint papers are not represented in this Volume: notably, the study of the Western film *genre*, where structuralist and semiotic analysis first reared its head; a study of the media and the construction of the discourse of social conflict, in the form of an analysis of the press and media coverage of the 1968 Birmingham sit-in; and the study of a magazine for women, *Women's Own*, and its lead story, symptomatically entitled 'Cure For Marriage', with its pre-second-wave feminist and quasi-psychoanalytic methodological analysis focussed on questions of femininity, fantasy and desire.

It is often asked – somewhat wistfully – whether it would be possible to institutionalize a critical research centre of this kind in today's university system. Of course, Cultural Studies has expanded exponentially across the world, taking root in a variety of academic systems, often by grafting itself on to other, well-established disciplines (while, some would add, hollowing them out from the inside!). But I think it would be difficult to establish such an exploratory centre of work, so committed to a critical approach, in today's academic conditions. The university has become so much more marketised and entrepreneurialised, and graduate research – which at the time was very under-developed and un-regulated – has become almost intolerably bureaucratic, in ways which are structurally hostile to the open, interrogative, inquisitive kind of intellectual environment which the Centre attempted for a time to create and sustain. The work represented in this volume must therefore be read as in and of a particular 'moment' – that is conjuncturally located and determinate. Horses for courses. . .

Acknowledgements

We have made every effort to contact all the authors of the enclosed papers and thank those who agreed so readily to have some of their earliest scholarly work published in this collection. Our thanks are also due to former colleagues at the University of Birmingham, especially to Tilusha Ghelani, Barbara Shaw-Perry and Sue Wright who worked on the initial reading and selection of papers and to Michael Green who supported our efforts throughout. Thanks also to Erin Bell and Lynn Johnson at Lincoln for their help in copy editing and producing readable copies of the papers. Rebecca Barden during her time with Routledge never lost faith in the project in spite of quite major set-backs and delays and Natalie Foster picked up the final stages of its production – our thanks to them both.

In memory of

Eve Brook
Ian Connell
Adrian Mellor
Robin Rusher
Allon White

The following articles have been reproduced courtesy of the authors and publishers involved:

Bland, Lucy, Brunsdon, Charlotte, Hobson, Dorothy and Winship, Janice: 'Women "inside and outside" the relations of production', in Women's Studies Group, *Women Take Issue: Aspects of women's subordination*, London, Hutchinson, 1978

Brook, Eva and Finn, Dan: 'Working class images of society and community studies', *Working Papers in Cultural Studies*, Vol. 10, 1977, pp. 127–46

Centre for Contemporary Cultural Studies: 'Scope of research', CCCS first report, 1964

Chambers, Iain: 'Roland Barthes: Structuralism/semiotics', *Working Papers in Cultural Studies*, Vol. 6, 1974, pp. 49–69

Clarke, John: 'Football hooliganism and skinheads', Stencilled Paper No. 42, 1973

Cohen, Phil: 'Subcultural conflict and working class community', *Working Papers in Cultural Studies*, Vol. 2, 1972, pp. 5–52

Ellis, John: 'Ideology and subjectivity', *Working Papers in Cultural Studies*, Vol. 9, 1976, pp. 205–19

The Fieldwork Group: 'A critique of "community studies" and its role in social thought', Stencilled Paper No. 44, 1976

Gilroy, Paul: 'Steppin' out of Babylon: Race, class and autonomy', in *The Empire Strikes Back: Race and racism in 70s Britain*, London, Hutchinson, 1982

Green, Michael: 'Raymond Williams and cultural studies', *Working Papers in Cultural Studies*, Vol. 6, 1974, pp. 31–48

Hall, Stuart, Lumley, Robert and McLennan, Gregor: 'Politics and ideology: Gramsci', *Working Papers in Cultural Studies*, Vol. 19, 1977, pp. 45–76

Hall, Stuart: 'A "Reading" of Marx's 1857 introduction to the *Grundrisse*', Stencilled Paper No. 1, 1973

Hall, Stuart: 'A response to people and culture', *Working Papers in Cultural Studies*, Vol. 1, 1971, pp. 97–102

Hall, Stuart: 'The hinterlands of science: Ideology and the "sociology of knowledge" ', *Working Papers in Cultural Studies*, Vol. 10, 1977, pp. 9–32

Hebdige, Dick: 'Subcultural conflict and criminal performance in Fulham: The wind up', Stencilled Paper No. 25, 1974

Hebdige, Dick: 'The Kray twins: A study of the system of closure', Stencilled Paper No. 42, 1973

Hoggart, Richard: 'Schools of English and contemporary society' in *Speaking to Each Other Volume Two: About Literature*, Harmondsworth, Penguin, 1970

Johnson, Richard: ' "Really useful knowledge": Radical education and working class culture 1790–1848' in Clark, J., Critcher, C. and Johnson, R., *Working Class Culture: Studies in history and theory*, London, Hutchinson, 1979

Johnson, Richard: 'Three problematics: Elements of a theory of working class culture', Stencilled Paper No. 56, 1979

Johnson, Richard: 'What is cultural studies anyway?', Stencilled Paper No. 74, 1983

Lawrence, Errol: 'Common sense racism and the sociology of race relations', Stencilled Paper No. 66, 1981.

Lumley, Robert: 'Gramsci's writings on the state and hegemony', Stencilled Paper No. 51, 1977

McRobbie, Angela: '*Jackie*: An ideology of adolescent femininity', Stencilled Paper No. 53, 1978

Rusher, Robin: 'What is it he's done? Ideology of Althusser', *Working Papers in Cultural Studies*, Vol. 6, 1974, pp. 70–97

Shuttleworth, Alan: 'People and culture', *Working Papers in Cultural Studies*, Vol. 1, 1971, pp. 65–96

Slater, Phil: 'The aesthetic theory of the Frankfurt school', *Working Papers in Cultural Studies*, Vol. 6, 1974, pp. 172–211

Sparks, Colin: 'Georg Lukacs', *Working Papers in Cultural Studies*, Vol. 4, 1973, pp. 69–85

White, Allon: 'Exposition and critique of Julia Kristeva', Stencilled Paper No. 49, 1977

Willis, Paul: 'Symbolism and practice: A theory for the social meaning of pop music', Stencilled Paper No. 13, 1974

Willis, Paul: 'The motorbike within a sub-cultural group', *Working Papers in Cultural Studies*, Vol. 2, 1972, pp. 53–70

Winship, Janice: 'Woman becomes an individual: Femininity and consumption in women's magazines 1954–69', Stencilled Paper No. 65, 1981

Women's Studies Group: 'Trying to do feminist intellectual work', in *Women Take Issue: Aspects of women's subordination*, London, Hutchinson, 1978

Woolfson, Charles: 'The semiotics of working class speech', *Working Papers in Cultural Studies*, Vol. 9, 1976, pp. 163–98

Work Group: 'The Experience of Work', *Working Papers in Cultural Studies*, Vol. 9, 1976, pp. 133–162

Formations of cultural studies

Ann Gray

Ideas for the publication of a collection of Working and Stencilled Papers began, to my knowledge at least, as early as 1990, and quite possibly earlier. The fact that this was always going to be a difficult and contentious task was probably the reason it took so long to happen. Successive colleagues at what became in 1987 the Department of Cultural Studies and later, in 1995, the Department of Cultural Studies and Sociology, whilst acknowledging the importance of getting these papers published, were themselves quite reluctant to embark on the task. Their reasons were not always those of lack of time, but the Department often felt that it lived in the shadow of its former self and many colleagues were happy to move into new territories of exploration, which had opened up since the days of the Centre for Contemporary Cultural Studies (CCCS). It was the sudden and deeply shocking closure of the Department in 2002 that convinced our editorial group that such a published collection would provide a fitting legacy to that early work and would be, frankly, a task upon which we could continue to work together. The rupture to working and personal relations, which were central to the Department and to the pleasure we all took in our academic and intellectual work, was profoundly painful. This project has provided us with a welcome continuity. This collection of Working and Stencilled Papers produced from the Centre between 1971 and 1982 does not purport to present the 'definitive' history or story of CCCS, if such a thing were possible. For the first time, however, readers will be able to see a selection, from the archive, of the fruits of the early work of the Centre, some of which have not previously been published. What I aim to do here is to sketch in some of the background to the CCCS with particular emphasis on its social, political and intellectual formations and its establishment and organisation within an academic institution.

One of the most common ways in which the 'origins' or beginnings of the British version of cultural studies is identified is by reference to four texts written by three scholars. *The Uses of Literacy* by Richard Hoggart (1957), *Culture & Society* (1958) and *The Long Revolution* (1961) by Raymond Williams, and *The Making of the English Working Class* by E. P. Thompson (1963) were all published within a period of 7 years (Hall 1980). The notion of 'origins' is problematic and Williams himself, in his essay 'The Future of Cultural Studies', published posthumously in the collection *The Politics of Modernism*, warns against constructing a history of cultural studies which takes texts as its starting point (Williams 1989: 151–62). Instead, he emphasises the importance of adult education in the formation of what were to become the published texts, arguing that what might be described as 'cultural studies' was already happening in adult education classes in the UK as early as the late 1940s. Hoggart, Thompson and Williams himself taught such classes through the 1950s with the aim of achieving majority democratic education. Here also, courses in visual arts, music, film, the press, advertising and radio, as well as what might come under the heading of 'lived cultures', studies of communities and settlements for example, were delivered in this unprivileged sector of education. By locating *texts* as originators of cultural studies, as it has now come to be known, we gloss over all these years of work with adult students who brought to the classes their ideas and experiences from their own lives. Instead we present, as Williams suggests, 'a very academicized kind of literary or intellectual history' which represents for Williams 'only the surface of the real development' (ibid: 155). This process also denies certain important continuities, as much as it denies the labour of students and tutors in an under-resourced part of the education system. Williams is also critical of the effects of identifying formations that imply the 'newness' and originality of particular work. Clearly this tendency is found in the institutionalisation of intellectual work and the fairly regular attempts to reflect on 'origins'. Handel K. Wright, writing in 1997, argues against such institutional and academic narratives, pointing towards movements and experiments in other parts of the globe that can and should be described as 'cultural studies', providing an important challenge to the Anglo-centrism of accounts of the formation of cultural studies. The title of his paper 'Dare we de-centre Birmingham?' speaks volumes about the unquestioned centrality of Birmingham within the narratives of cultural studies and the mythical reverence afforded to it.

These volumes obviously run the risk of 're-centring' Birmingham, although that is certainly not the intention. Rather, it is to present a selection of research papers which at least complicate a particular version of cultural studies which has become known in much academic literature as the 'Birmingham School'. This version, characterised by a focus on the study of youth and popular culture within a Gramscian framework, ignores not only other topics which formed part of the work of the Centre, but also the process of intellectual production which can be evidenced in this collection.

Whilst taking Williams' warning seriously, there is strong evidence of the importance of the work of Hoggart, Williams and Thompson in the formation of CCCS at Birmingham. This was, after all, the social, political and intellectual milieu of the period and Stuart Hall himself confirmed the importance of these texts for the work of the Centre in his lecture to the Conference on Literature and Society at the State University of New York and Buffalo in the summer of 1967. He said, 'In their very different ways, these books provided anchor points for the Centre's work as an organised enterprise' (Fifth Report 1968–69: 3). The body of work 'expressed, crystallised and attempted to transcend a peculiar "moment" in post-war British society and culture', understood as 'the emergence of post-industrial society and culture, within a network of historical continuities, a structure of values and relationships, inherited from the past' (ibid: 2).

Writing later, in the collection of papers published in 1980 as *Culture, Media, Language*, Hall points out that these texts were also and more importantly 'responses of different kinds to a decisive historical conjuncture'. The authors 'brought disciplined thought to bear on the understanding of their own lives', whilst the texts 'were far from neutral or scholarly: they were cultural interventions in their own right' (Hall *et al.* 1980: 16). It is worth noting here that Hoggart and Williams' works were published in paperback by Penguin Books, who aimed at a much broader readership than the academic imprints of today. However, the books provided 'anchor points' for the methodological moorings of the work of the Centre as the adoption of these texts acknowledged the need for an interdisciplinary approach in addressing questions of culture. Thompson was a historian and Hoggart and Williams came from literary studies. Hoggart, in his study of British northern working class culture, used a combination of literary and sociological modes but also drew heavily on his own memories and experience of growing up in the industrial city of Leeds. Williams also employed autobiographical techniques in later work. Thus all authors were doing cultural analysis on the shared or lived experience of particular classes and social groups which were located and observational. Their work can be characterised as attempts at grasping forms of consciousness, of lived beliefs and modes of expression within particular social and historical conditions. As organic intellectuals they fore-grounded new ways of understanding class in the British context which attended to culture and lived experience as well as the economy. As Hall points out above, they were cultural interventions in their own right and were also texts of dissent within the academy, challenging the orthodoxy of their different intellectual fields and disciplines. This 'structure of feeling', to use Williams' term, can be understood within wider social and political currents of the time.

The wider political context is that of the British New Left which was 'born' in 1956 out of the twin events of the Russian suppression of the Hungarian Revolution and the British and French invasion of Suez. In his reflections on the life and times of the 'first' New Left, Hall asserts that the shockwaves of these events challenged thinking about the dominant political systems of the time. Hungary brought an end to what he describes as 'a certain kind of socialist "innocence"' and Suez 'underlined the enormity of the error in believing that lowering the Union Jack in a few ex-colonies necessarily signalled the 'end of imperialism' (Hall 1989: 13). Within the British New Left there were two main groups. One included former communist party members, amongst whom were Edward and Dorothy Thompson and John Saville who founded the journal *The New Reasoner*, first published in May 1957. At the same time a younger generation of left intellectuals, Stuart Hall, Raphael Samuel, Gabriel Pearson and Charles Taylor, launched *The Universities & New Left Review*. The political and intellectual formations of the two groups were distinct. The 'Old' New Left were of the generation of British intellectuals whose politics had been formed by the dissident Communism of the 1930s and 1940s. Williams, although sharing some of Thompson's politics, had remained relatively independent of the group. The younger generation in *The Universities & New Left Review*, who had cut their political teeth in Oxford in the years immediately prior to Hungary and Suez, sought to find new definitions of politics and ways of doing politics. Whilst they engaged with Marxism, they were also critical of it and were interested in the impact of immanent social change on the lives of 'ordinary' people and in particular at the level of the cultural, which the older guard felt were not important or particularly relevant issues in the political struggle. To a great extent Raymond Williams acted as mediator between the 'old new' and the 'new new' groups. Stuart Hall, supporting himself as a supply teacher in schools, teaching adult education classes and delivering occasional lectures for the Education Department of the British Film Institute, served as editor of *The Universities & New Left Review* from 1957–9 and as editor of *New Left Review*, which emerged from the amalgamation of *Universities & Left Review* and *New Reasoner*, from 1959 to 1961. The significance for cultural studies of these political and intellectual formations is that they provided space, especially through the journals, but also through the 'New Left clubs' which sprang up around the country, for the development of ideas which, in the case of *The New Left Review*, engaged from the start with popular culture, film and television, whilst publishing important academic work.

Grass roots educators in English and film emerged as influential groups in the development of what was to become 'cultural studies'. The journal *The Use of English* established in 1949 by Denys Thompson as a sort of specialised off-shoot of *Scrutiny* which Thompson co-edited with F. R. Leavis, was a significant vanguard in getting the ideas expressed in *Culture and Environment* (1933) into the context of school-teaching. In the 1960s various *Use of English* readers' groups had sprung up who gave their support to Thompson's initiative in the formation of the National Association for the Teaching of English. Although Thompson's philosophy and politics were conservative with his emphasis on the protection of pupils from the declining standards of contemporary culture the movement towards the 'Culture and Environment' tradition within education clearly opened doors to the study of a wider range of cultural forms than previously was the case. Similarly, the British Film Institute's education department, was the driving force behind the 1950 organisation of teachers who set themselves up as the 'Society of Film Teachers', to promote the teaching of film appreciation, mainly in schools, but also in colleges and youth clubs. Their journal *The Film Teacher* ran for only 2 years but was replaced by the cheaper, more effectively distributable *SFT Newsletter*, which had reasonably wide circulation amongst school and college teachers. These developments eventually led to the journals *Screen Education* (1959–68 and 1971–82) and *Screen* (1969–). The Uses of English teachers' groups were the primary audience for Stuart Hall and Paddy Whannel's extremely practical study *The Popular Arts* and Brian Doyle (1981) provides a convincing account of the historical links between the Uses of English group and their work in development 'Culture & Environment Studies' to Richard Hoggart's inaugural CCCS lecture. In the then relatively conservative worlds of theatre and arts similar currents were flowing, which in different ways represented challenges to British post-war culture. Culturally this period was sowing seeds that would fully emerge in the 1960s and beyond. In 1956 John Osborne's play 'Look Back in Anger' was produced on the London stage. London theatregoers were presented with a working class setting, where the central character Jimmy Porter was frustrated by his working class background and denial of opportunities in the rigid class system of Britain. A number of other young dramatists and novelists produced work on the same theme and many were quickly adapted for film. In 1960 the ITV company Granada produced its first soap opera, *Coronation Street*, set in a working class area of north-west England, the opening episode of which featured a young male graduate in conflict with his working class background.

These were reflections of a period of social and cultural change in Britain in the context of the post-war settlement. Whilst the roles of women were still highly prescribed within the context of femininity and domesticity, the arrival of rock music and the emergence of a (rebellious) youth culture loosened the strictures of the grey, conformist and austere 1950s. Moving into the 1960s this change was particularly evidenced in the field of education, in particular further and higher education, previously the privilege of the few. Between 1963 and 1970–71 the total student population in full-time higher education in Britain doubled to 457,000. An important development came in 1964 with the government 'binary policy' for higher education. This represented a division between the autonomous 44 universities and a 'public sector' led by 30 polytechnics. The numbers of students in polytechnics grew to 215,000 in 1970/1. Both universities and polytechnics broadened the class base in higher education, and polytechnics provided fertile ground for the development of 'new' academic subjects. This 'democratising' of further and higher education was coterminous with an intense expansion and development of what Hans Magnus Enzensberger was to call 'the consciousness industries' and, in the British case, the increasing 'Americanisation' of popular culture. The 'swinging sixties', in which London had such a pivotal role, were in part the development of a meritocracy that challenged the establishment, which took a particular conservative form in the UK. The establishment of the CCCS in Birmingham hit the middle of this decade and from its inception engaged with these social and cultural changes.

Richard Hoggart's inaugural address as Professor of English at the University of Birmingham in 1963 set out the parameters of an approach to literature which looked to the present as well as the past, and which he provisionally called 'Literature and Contemporary

Cultural Studies' (Hoggart 1973 [1970]: 239). His motives for attending to the contemporary and especially 'commercial' culture were to find ways of understanding the languages of developing popular media forms; television, magazines and, especially, advertising, which he thought represented an assault on 'the life of language' (234). According to Hoggart, 'So much language is used not as exploration but as persuasion and manipulation' (235) addressing individuals not as whole beings, but 'as bits, bits who belong to large lopsided blocks – as citizens, as consumers, as middle-aged middle-class parents . . . as voters or viewers, as religiously inclined car owners, as typical teenagers or redbrick professors' (236). Clearly Hoggart had in his sights the advertisers, journalists and others working in the rapidly expanding communications media, culprits already named in his *The Uses of Literacy*. But he was also questioning the continuing relevance of Schools of English, which confined themselves to the literary past when the world around them was changing and, what is more, when students of those schools were well versed in the languages of popular culture. The field he mapped out for development of 'possible work in Contemporary Cultural Studies' (239) was divided into three parts: historical and philosophical; sociological; and literary critical. 'History' was to explore the 'culture debate', referring to explorations of culture which had been investigated through most interesting debates about literature and society, inspired, to a certain extent, by the organicism of Leavis and Eliot. The sociology of literature and culture were nascent fields within sociology and Hoggart set out the parameters of further exploration for contemporary cultural sociology with a series of questions. Where do 'writers and artists' come from, who are their audiences, who are the opinion formers, how is production and circulation of contemporary forms organised and how can the interrelations between these actors be explored? Finally he called for the development of a critical practice relevant to what he called the 'mass or popular arts'. He also insisted on more humility about the audience, inviting his fellow academics in the University auditorium to reflect on their own experience:

> It is hard to listen to a programme of pop songs, or watch 'Candid Camera' or 'This is Your Life' without feeling a complex mixture of attraction and repulsion, of admiration for skill and scorn for the phoney, of wry observations of similarities and correspondences, of sudden reminders of the raciness of speech, or of the capacity for courage or humour, or of shock at the way mass art can chew up anything, even our most intimate feelings.
>
> (242 and quoted in Hall and Whannel 1964: 79)

The Centre was formally constituted in the spring of 1964 as one of two research centres in the English Department of the Faculty of Arts at the University of Birmingham under the directorship of Richard Hoggart. Its first full-time appointment – Stuart Hall as Research Fellow – was made in April of that year. Since leaving his editorship of *The New Left Review* Hall had been teaching media, film and popular culture at Chelsea College, University of London and had worked with Paddy Whannel at the BFI, publishing their book *The Popular Arts* in 1964. The scope of research set out in the Centre's first report followed Hoggart's three main areas of study outlined in his inaugural lecture. The Centre distinguished its approach as a '*critical-evaluative* one, with close attention both to the imaginative meanings and social attitudes contained within these forms, and to their aesthetic and cultural qualities' (First Report: 4) from other approaches developing in Britain which took the 'influence and effects' approach to mass media. By contrast the main emphasis of the CCCS was 'upon the critical evaluation of these phenomena, and an understanding of them in their social and cultural setting' (ibid.). The Centre was open to research students registered for postgraduate degrees, but also occasional and part-time students who were self-financing. According to the first Report there were more than forty applications to work at Birmingham, with some twelve students commencing in the autumn of 1964. Other favourable responses to the Centre came in the guise of publishers' donations of books for the new library and free subscriptions to journals, and the funding came from a seven-year grant from Penguin Books, which financed the appointment of the Research Fellow. Other grants came from Chatto and Windus and The Observer Trust. According to the first Centre Report, 'The Formal Life of the Centre' was organised around three occasions. A weekly general graduate seminar was held for Centre students and 'other interested faculty members and research workers.' This included topics of general interest and largely consisted of outside speakers emphasising the importance of interdisciplinarity to the work of the Centre. In addition, a weekly 'closed' seminar limited to workers at the Centre was held. Draft research papers were presented and discussed. The third activity was the formation of 'project groups' and after the first year, time was allocated to fortnightly supervisions. A plan for publications was set out in the form of full-length studies; individual or group and smaller studies and work in progress were to be published directly by the Centre as 'occasional papers'. The significance of the relationship between education and the development of contemporary cultural studies was evidenced in Hoggart's inaugural lecture and the appointment of Stuart Hall, whose book with Paddy Whannel was based on practical engagement in teaching across schools, film societies, teacher training colleges, youth clubs and adult education classes, as well as further and higher education. The Centre at the outset had established links with teachers and lecturers in Adult Education, Teacher Training, Colleges of Art and Further Education and secondary schools.

The speakers at the Tuesday Seminars in the first year covered wide-ranging topics: Common Culture; Theology; Television; Marxism; Psychoanalysis; Aesthetics; Mass Culture; Urban Society; Mass Education; and History; and visiting speakers included Raymond Williams, Hilde Himmelweit, Troy Kennedy Martin (one of the writers on the then new TV police series *Z Cars*) and the historian Edward Thompson.

The first and second Centre Reports emphasised the need to obtain external funding for research projects in the recognition that such focussed projects would 'be so styled as to yield answers to some of the problems of method and interpretation which have arisen during the course of the year. This will have the added effect of drawing the Centre's work together, and giving greater cohesion and direction to its efforts' (Second Report: 14, 1965–66). Two such projects were financed for the third year. The first, funded by the Gulbenkian Foundation for one year, was to explore the links between the public and the providers of television programmes, mounted at the invitation of The Television Viewers' Council. The second, more substantial project, financed for three years by the Joseph Rowntree Memorial Trust, was to look at the role of the press in reflecting, mediating and shaping attitudes. The aim was to examine what is mediated by the press, and not the effect upon audiences. The project was staffed by Anthony Smith, an English graduate but with experience in journalism, Elizabeth Glass (later Immirzi) as Senior Research Associate and Trevor Blackwell as Research Assistant. The joint work first emerged as a research report, 'The Popular Press and Social Change, 1935–1965' and was then one of the Centre's first publications, *Paper Voices* by A. C. H. Smith (with Elizabeth Immirzi and Trevor Blackwell), carrying an introduction by Stuart Hall, published in 1975. The study challenged one of the dominating models of analysis within the social sciences, content analysis, by adopting analysis of the 'language and rhetoric, of style and presentation' (Smith *et al.* 1975: 15) of two examples of the popular press, the *Express* and the *Daily Mirror*. Newspapers were understood not as simple channels for the transmission and reception of news, which was the current sociological understanding of the press, but as 'a structure of meaning'. Methodologically this study challenged questions of 'objectivity' and the scientific nature of social research and marked out the Centre's interest in the production of meaning by asking questions of *how* meaning is conveyed and not simply *what* is conveyed.

In 1966–67 the Centre's Monday seminars devoted themselves to 'bridging the gap between the background training in literary studies common to most . . . of the Centre's students and the literature, methods and problems of the social sciences, especially sociology, social psychology, anthropology and the sociology of mass communications.' This was in order to 'lay proper foundations for interdisciplinary work in cultural studies' (Third Report 1966–67: 24). According to Hall in the 1971 Report this was initiated by experience on the previously mentioned research project into the popular press, which had attempted a liaison with sociologists. This had resulted in reiteration of the distinct boundaries of the literary and the sociological disciplines. 'In short, a fateful rupture had been sealed between positivistic sociological inquiry and the problems central to a serious study of culture' (Sixth Report 1969–71). This encounter with the texts of the social sciences, which Hall described as the Centre's 'middle period', was 'to say the least, a testing time for the Centre'. This was a characteristic strategy by those working at the Centre at this time, and represented an attempt to grasp an enormous terrain of intellectual material in a very short space of time. On looking back at this period in 1971, Hall surmised that their attempt at 'mastering' this body of knowledge might well have foundered had not the assault on the field [of positivistic social science] mounted from outside its walls, been matched by a major 'demarche' within the field itself. This period was seen by Hall and his colleagues, and by others, as a major crisis within sociology from which it has taken a long time to recover.

The Centre's Report for 1967–68 indicates a strengthening of numbers and research staff with the addition of a further externally-funded research project, the 'Content Analysis Study' funded by the Government's Television Research Committee and led by Alan Shuttleworth. There were 6 full-time, 3 part-time and two attached students. Students from Russian Studies, Philosophy and Italian were regular attendees at the weekly Seminars.

The Centre's Fifth Report, 1968–69, seems to represent something of a turning point and Hall himself acknowledges this particular 'moment' as significant in the work of the Centre. The 'disintegration from within of sociology itself in its mainstream form' was taking place alongside the development of a more complex Marxism introduced and made possible through newly available work in English from Goldmann, Benjamin, the 'Frankfurt School' and Sartre. These theoretical and intellectual developments were in dialogue with and shaped by profound changes in society and culture at the time.

The social and political context which marks this shift in the work of the Centre was, in the British case, the challenge of what has been termed the 'New New Left' and international developments. These included the events of May 1968 in Paris, which inspired the student sit-in at the University of Birmingham the following November; the Vietnam Solidarity Campaign; and the Prague Spring. Indeed, the New New Left represented and embraced internationalism in a way that the Old New Left had not. Raymond Williams wrote important essays in the *New Left Review*, for example on Lucien Goldmann (Williams 1971) and Gramsci (Williams 1973). In his seminal article 'Cultural Studies: Two Paradigms' published the year after he left the CCCS, Stuart Hall acknowledged Williams' early and continuing influence on the work of the Centre, especially the constant re-viewing and re-thinking of his project. Williams' work of this period was heavily influenced by the appearance in translation of some of Goldmann's publications and those of other Marxist thinkers who were within a more complex and interesting Marxist tradition than had been available to British intellectuals thus far. Hall also marks out this fusion of social upheaval and the opening up of new work which emphasised the role of culture, ideology and power, as a turning point in the work of the CCCS. The crisis in sociology and its inability to provide any kind of understanding of the rapid social and political changes, as captured in Martin Nicolaus' words 'What is this science which only holds good when its subjects stand still?' (Hall *et al.*: 26) opened up the possibilities of new intellectual work. As far as cultural studies was concerned, according to Hall, '[it] gave us a much-needed theoretical breathing-space' (ibid).

As Larry Grossberg remarks in this collection, the importance of the arrival of translations of hitherto unavailable intellectual work were key to the development and shape of the work at the Centre. The encounters with 'continental' patterns of thought were sudden and provided a heady mix of challenges as well as recuperations. The period from the mid-1960s through to the early 1970s saw the translation into English of key works: in 1969 Althusser's *For Marx*; in 1971, Gramsci's *Selections from the Prison Notebooks* and Lukacs' *History and Class Consciousness* and *The Theory of the Novel*; in 1972 Adorno and Horkheimer's *Dialectic of Enlightenment* and in 1973 Barthes' *Mythologies.*

The availability of these important works definitively shaped the work of the Centre, firstly in the move towards the linguistic model and structuralism. The arrival of structuralisms, according to Hall, interrupted the 'culturalism' of cultural studies exemplified by Williams and Thompson with their humanist ethos and 'experiential pull'. Althusser provided an important re-reading of Marx usefully defining his economic determinism as 'over-determinism'. But it was the work of Gramsci which offered the potential for analysis of a culture as a set of practices, lived and experiential, without losing sight of the structural determinants that became the dominant influence in the work of the Centre. This approach at once remedied the economic determinism of Marx while insisting on historicisation, which was absent in Althusser's formulations.

Arguably the period from post-1968 to the late 1970s was the most prolific and rich in terms of the work of the Centre. Centre Reports from this period have a perhaps surprising air of professionalism, and would gain approval from any bureaucratic university assessment regime today. They also evidence the ways in which isolated and largely unfunded Research Centres were driven to operate within large institutions such as Birmingham. The Centre had to justify its existence by demonstrating evidence of activities, intellectual developments, publications, completed theses and research projects which would not have been expected of conventional academic departments at the time. The plan to publish a Centre Journal, *Working Papers in Cultural Studies*, was a bold move on very limited resources and the first issue appeared in the summer of 1971. This was intended for public circulation and was purchased by libraries and individuals directly from the Centre.

This period also saw a major upheaval in the Centre's life. Richard Hoggart resigned his posts of Professor of English and Director of the CCCS towards the end of 1973 which triggered an inquiry into its future. The Faculty of Arts appointed a working party for this purpose and, according to Stuart Hall, at this point the Centre came close to being shut down.[1] The wide connections the Centre had established with the outside world and its gaining intellectual reputation paid off here as letters to the working party from Asa Briggs, J. D. Halloran and Raymond Williams persuaded them to recommend that the Centre continue. The institution's ambivalence, and often downright hostility, to the CCCS and Cultural Studies continued through the following decades until its abrupt closure in 2002.

Of course the CCCS was not operating in an intellectual vacuum but was often in different kinds of relationships with other developments in related fields. For example, in 1969 *Screen Education* re-launched as the journal *Screen*, which was often seen to be in contest with the focus of the Centre. To what extent this was the construction of 'straw men' on either side is a matter for debate. Also, the Centre for Mass Communication Research at the University of Leicester was a regular sparring partner. The early 1970s saw the publication of a number of works across the arts and humanities, indicative of the intellectual and political concerns of that decade. For example, 1970 saw the publication of Hans Magnus Enzensberger's *New Left Review* article 'The Consciousness Industries', and Sheila Rowbotham's pamphlet 'Women's Liberation and the New Politics'. In 1972 Nicholas Garnham's *The Structures of Television* and Denis McQuail's *Sociology of Mass Communication* marked out the political economy and sociological approach to the media. Challenges to conventional approaches to the history of art came in John Berger's *Ways of Seeing*, Tim Clark's *Image of the People* and *The Absolute Bourgeois* and Nicolaus Hadjinicolaou's *Art History and Class Struggle*, while the women's movement began to find a published voice through Sheila Rowbotham's *Women's Consciousness, Man's World* and *Hidden from History*.

It is clear from some of these collected papers and recollections of members that CCCS was in part characterised by internal contestation and conflict. The relative openness of cultural studies to people from the political and intellectual margins often resulted in deeply held differences which were difficult, if not impossible, to contain. Charlotte Brunsdon cites Stuart Hall's contribution to the 1990 Illinois conference, where he asserted that 'theoretical work at the Centre for Contemporary Cultural Studies was more appropriately called theoretical noise. It was accompanied by a great deal of bad feeling, argument, unstable anxieties and angry silences' (Hall 1992: 278 quoted in Brunsdon 1996: 278). Struggles and disagreements were often about the nature of 'the project'. As evidenced in these volumes, much of the early work of the centre focussed on class; theoretically, conceptually and experientially within a Marxist framework. These were passionately held positions and were the continuities pulled through from the British left and the 'founding' texts. When young scholars arrived whose intellectual, political and experiential formations were different, the certainty of 'the project' was challenged. Brunsdon's account of the struggles around feminism at the Centre in the mid-1970s describes the difficulties of developing an intellectual feminism within a working environment in which other investments and assumptions were not easily shaken. The particular working practice, which had developed a collective approach to theorising (see Larry Grossberg in this volume), meant that there was no hiding place in which the development of different positions could be tentatively articulated. To a great extent the notion of collective theorising assumes, if not coherent positions, then at least that the collective should be heading in the same direction. As Brunsdon reflects on the difficulties of imagining a feminist cultural studies, 'Were there going to be two spheres of cultural studies – "ordinary" (as before, uninterrupted) and a feminine/feminist sphere?' (Brunsdon 1996: 282). In his 1990 paper Stuart Hall also draws attention to 'the question of race in cultural studies' (Hall 1992: 283). He speaks of the profound theoretical struggle of which *Policing the Crisis* is what he describes as 'the first and very late example' of placing the critical questions of race on the agenda of cultural studies. Just as feminist scholars revealed and questioned the patriarchal assumptions of early formations of cultural studies, black scholars struggled 'against a resounding but unconscious silence' (ibid.) to get acknowledgement of the profound Englishness and, indeed, 'whiteness' of the 'foundational' texts of cultural studies (Gilroy 1992). These contestations and struggles resulted in the important collection *The Empire Strikes Back*, published in 1982. Hall himself admits that 'the group of people who produced the book found it extremely difficult to create the necessary theoretical and political space in the Centre in which to work on the project' (Hall 1992: 283).

These were, then, tumultuous times, with the carving out of new areas for study and an intellectually productive spirit of dissent, which characterised cultural studies in this period. It is remarkable, however, that the study of contemporary culture gained an institutional foothold, albeit insecure, at such a relatively early period in its development. In an interview with Kuan-Hsing Chen, Stuart Hall said that the early days of the Centre were like an 'alternative university'. The Centre's new approach to the study of what was previously regarded by the academy as inferior and trivial artefacts and insignificant cultural practices, its openly political aims and its challenges to academic modes of working, led to a grudging acceptance by the University of Birmingham. Its existence was threatened on more than one occasion and it is worth giving a brief account of these moments when the Centre found itself fighting for its life. I have already outlined the 1974 events after the departure of Richard Hoggart for UNESCO. In 1987/8 the Centre was again under threat and eventually, following the closure of sociology at Birmingham, merged with two sociologists and formed the Department of Cultural Studies in the Faculty of Social Sciences. In 1995 once again cultural studies came under the institutional spotlight when Birmingham decided to resurrect sociology. Moves were made to transfer staff specialising in 'race', 'gender' and 'media' back into the Faculty of Arts leaving the way clear to develop a 'mainstream' sociology programme. This was successfully resisted and the Department added sociology to its title and developed an undergraduate programme in sociology with a distinctive cultural bias. In 2001, after the Research Assessment Exercise awarded the Department the status of 'national significance', a long battle began to save the Department involving staff, former and current students and scholars from around the world whose work had been influenced by the work of the CCCS. This ended unsuccessfully with its closure in 2002. Whilst the Centre continued to attract brilliant students, the various regimes at Birmingham never really recognised its significance. This is evidenced in Centre Reports across this period covered by this volume and perhaps can be understood as a simple failing on the part of the University to see the potential of the pioneering work being undertaken. However, this continued throughout the chequered history of cultural studies at Birmingham where the University authorities never acknowledged, or perhaps recognised, the enormous international reputation that the CCCS had won. This was apparent in 2002 when the vice-chancellor received floods of e-mails from all over the world protesting at the closure (Gray 2003).

Turning to the organisation of this volume, as might have been predicted, the task of selecting and organising the papers into two volumes was not smooth nor without its problems. Our rationale, to reveal the range of work and the interconnected levels which the Working and Stencilled Papers evidenced, initially took rather a different shape and one which, as I said earlier, did not claim to construct a 'history' of the CCCS. Of course, all selections shape and impose a version of the object of study but our aim was to present an archive – a body of work – which we, as editors, along with postgraduate students then in the Department, found particularly interesting and relevant to contemporary cultural studies. Our intention was to come at the work with fresh eyes. None of us had been at Birmingham for very long and our routes into cultural studies had been from sociology, literary studies, youth and community studies. The postgraduate students, in particular, came up with some most interesting choices (many of which did not survive into the final version) of papers which had something to say to them. However, as we started to share our plans with others, a debate began about how these volumes would be perceived and what kind of version of the story they appeared to present. Very strong and, eventually, persuasive arguments were made that, whatever our intentions, these volumes would take on the status of, if not the definitive, then at least an authoritative version of the early days of CCCS and, according to our critics, we had not got the story right. After much negotiation the entries and organisation of the volumes were agreed. Perhaps this is another example of the difficulty of positioning and of claiming new positions in relation to versions of the past. We were delighted when Larry Grossberg, Elspeth Probyn and Johan Fornäs agreed to introduce the three sections which form this volume. They each draw out what are the key elements of this early phase of this version of cultural studies, and elegantly provide accounts which have intellectual, personal and political verve.

Larry Grossberg, in his introduction to 'Theoretical engagements', demonstrates through his reading of the papers the place of theory in cultural studies and the practice of theorising at the Centre. He argues that theory was not seen as an end in itself, some esoteric exercise, but rather, was regarded as a toolbox with which to tackle empirical and structural expressions of culture and power. He identifies two problematics which underpin and inform the collective theorising at the Centre as being 'thinking the relationships between culture and society' and one of 'methodology', that is the exploration of the nature of those relationships.

Secondly, the section 'Theorising experience, exploring methods' includes papers which demonstrate how members of the Centre were actively working with new combinations of these theoretical ideas in their attempts to define the problematic and methodologies of cultural studies. Elspeth Probyn, in her reading of Richard Johnson's paper 'What is Cultural Studies Anyway?' is struck by its relevance for the contemporary struggles which she and others are experiencing within the Australian University sector during an intensely conservative regime. She situates herself in her academic role as public intellectual and draws on the early attempts at the Centre to find ways of tapping into lived experience, which might capture complexity of social and cultural determinants.

'Grounded Studies' are perhaps the hallmark of the CCCS and Johan Fornäs observes that intellectual fields emerge through labour. He reminds us how critical studies take hold and are shaped differently in different locations. In this section we can see that 'practice' becomes an important new analytical category through which to engage with theoretical debates about agency, ideology and structure.

Whilst for organisational purposes these three levels have been separated out for this volume it is clear from reading the Working and Stencilled Papers and the Centre Reports that the work cross-fertilised. Doing theoretical work is evidenced in the working sub-groups (see Volume 2) and in the empirical studies undertaken. Conversely, the engagement with specific cases and examples, magazines addressed to young women, popular television programmes, music and lads in school, amongst others, produced questions and challenges for theoretical assumptions and an understanding of the role of theory in cultural research.

However, it is important to recognise just how 'local' and 'specific' much of the early work of the Centre was. As Hall says 'From its inception . . . cultural studies was an "engaged" set of disciplines, addressing awkward but relevant issues about contemporary society and culture' (Hall *et al.* 1980: 17). These grounded and specific studies developed their own methods and drew on relevant and available theories and concepts for interpretation and analysis. This suggests that cultural studies is not merely the study of culture, but rather a drive to understand the place and operation of the cultural in specific contexts. In the British case it emerged from political, social and intellectual change and was grasped within a particular institutional context. Thus cultural studies will be different in present and future specific and distinct political, historical, social and institutional contexts.

Bibliography

Adorno, T. and Horkheimer, M. (1972) *Dialectic of Enlightenment* (translated by J. Cumming) New York: Herder and Herder

Althusser, L. (1969) *For Marx* (translated by B. Brewster) London: Allen Lane

Anderson, P. (2000) 'Renewals' *New Left Review*, (II) 1 5–24

Barthes, R. (1973) *Mythologies* (translated by A. Levers and C. Smith) New York: Hill and Wang

Berger, J. (1972) *Ways of Seeing* Harmondsworth: Penguin

Brunsdon, C. (1996) 'A thief in the night: stories of feminism in the 1970s at CCCS' in Morley, D. and Chen, K-H. (eds) *Stuart Hall. Critical dialogues in cultural studies* London: Routledge

CCCS (1982) *The Empire Strikes Back* London: Hutchinson

Chen, K-H. (1996) 'The formation of a diasporic intellectual: an interview with Stuart Hall by Kuan-Hsing Chen' in Morley, D. and Chen, K-H. *Stuart Hall. Critical dialogues in cultural studies* London: Routledge

Clark, T.J. (1973a) *Image of the People: Gustav Courbet and the 1848 Revolution* London: Thames and Hudson

—— (1973b) *The Absolute Bourgeois: artists and politics in France, 1848–1851* Greenwich, Conn: New York Graphic Society

Doyle, B. (1981) 'Some uses of English: Denys Thompson and the development of English in secondary schools', General Series: SP No. 64, Centre for Contemporary Cultural Studies

Enzensberger, H. M. (1970) 'The Consciousness Industries', *New Left Review* 6 (41) 13–36

Garnham, N. (1972) *The Structures of Television* London: British Film Institute

Gilroy, P. (1992) 'Cultural Studies and Ethnic Absolutism' in Grossberg, L., Nelson, C., Treichler, P. (eds) (1992) *Cultural Studies* New York, London: Routledge, 187–99

Gramsci, A. (1971) *Selections from the Prison Notebooks* (translated by Q. Hoare and G. Nowell Smith) London: Lawrence and Wishart

Gray, A. (2003) 'Cultural Studies at Birmingham: the impossibility of critical pedagogy', *Cultural Studies* 17 (6), 767–782

Grossberg, L., Nelson, C., Treichler, P. (eds) (1992) *Cultural Studies* New York, London: Routledge

Hadjinicolaou, N. (1973) *Art History and Class Struggle* London: Pluto

Hall, S. (1989) 'The "first" New Left: life and times' in Oxford University Socialist Group (ed) *Out of Apathy: Voices of the New Left Thirty Years On* London: Verso, 11–38

—— (1992) 'Cultural Studies and its Theoretical Legacies' in Grossberg, L., Nelson, C., Treichler, P. (eds) (1992) *Cultural Studies* New York, London: Routledge, 277–294

Hall, S., Hobson, D., Lowe, A. and Willis, P. (1980) *Culture, Media, Language Working Papers in Cultural Studies, 1972–79* London: Hutchinson

Hall, S. and Whannel, P. (1964) *The Popular Arts* London: Hutchinson Educational Ltd

Halsey, A.H. (2000) 'Further and Higher Education' in Halsey, A. H. with Webb, J. *Twentieth Century British Social Trends* Basingstoke: Macmillan

Hoggart, R. (1957) *The Uses of Literacy* London: Chatto and Windus

—— (1973) *Speaking to Each Other Volume One: About Society* Harmondsworth: Penguin

Lukacs, G. (1971a) *History and Class Consciousness* (translated by R. Livingstone) London: Merlin Press

—— (1971b) *The Theory of the Novel* (translated by A. Bostock) London: Merlin Press

McQuail, D. (ed.) (1972) *Sociology of Mass Communication* London: Longman

Morley, D. and Chen, K-H. (eds) (1996) *Stuart Hall. Critical dialogues in cultural studies* London: Routledge

Oxford University Socialist Group (ed.) (1989) *Out of Apathy: Voices of the New Left Thirty Years On* London: Verso, 11–38

Rowbotham, S. (1969) *Women's liberation and the new politics* London: May Day Manifesto Pamphlet 4

—— (1973a) *Women's Consciousness, Man's World* Harmondsworth: Penguin

Rowbotham, S. (1973b) *Hidden from History* London: Pluto Press
Sedgwick, P. (1976) 'The two new lefts' in Widgery, D. (ed) *The Left in Britain 1956–1968* Harmondsworth: Penguin
Smith, A. C. H. with Immirzi, E. and Blackwell, T. (1975) *Paper Voices: the Popular Press and Social Change, 1935–1965* London: Chatto and Windus
Thompson, E. P. (1963) *The Making of the English Working Class* London: Gollancz
Widgery, D. (ed.) (1976) *The Left in Britain 1956–1968* Harmondsworth: Penguin
Williams, R. (1958) *Culture and Society* London: Chatto and Windus
—— (1961) *The Long Revolution* London: Chatto and Windus
—— (1971) 'Literature and Sociology: In Memory of Lucien Goldmann', *New Left Review* (I) 67 3–18.
—— (1973) 'Base and Superstructure in Marxist Cultural Theory', *New Left Review* (I) 82 3–16.
—— (1989) *The Politics of Modernism. Against the New Conformists* London: Verso
Wilson, E. (1980) *Only Halfway to Paradise. Women in Postwar Britain: 1945–1968* London: Tavistock
Wright, H.K. (1998) 'Dare we de-centre Birmingham?' Troubling the 'origin' and trajectories of cultural studies', *European Journal of Cultural Studies* 1: 1, 33–56

Centre reports

First Centre report 1964–65
Second Centre report 1965–66
Third Centre report 1966–67
Fourth Centre report 1967–68
Fifth Centre report 1968–69
Sixth Centre report 1969–71

Note

1 Personal communication from Stuart Hall, August 2006.

Section 1

CCCS founding moments

1 Schools of English and contemporary society

Richard Hoggart

Can one really say anything worthwhile about Schools of English and contemporary society? Doesn't such a title suggest a failure to recognize the 'timeless' nature of the work that should be central to a School of English? Isn't it only another indication that one more teacher has succumbed to the cult of contemporaneity? Won't such an interest distract us from our central, our manifestly proper work?

I know the importance of all these questions. Much of the work of an English School should have little direct relation to the particular forms and fashions of contemporary society. There must be historical, textual, editorial, bibliographical and literary critical research into a thousand years of linguistic and literary change. Here the Schools are repositories of knowledge, and contributors to knowledge about their past. Young scholars have to be trained to take up this advanced work and others trained so that they may go out to teach our language and literature. Here the Schools of English are active transmitters.

One can easily appreciate certain other arguments: that, even if Schools of English may be more relevant to modern society than has been suggested in the preceding paragraph, they will do best not to bother directly about the contemporary world whilst they are at work. That if their students come to grips with *The Canterbury Tales* or *Paradise Lost* or even *Love's Labours Lost*, or with medieval England or Renaissance England as literature reveals them, this will in the long run do more for their understanding of modern society than will a constant reaching after modern instances. That the steps toward a loss of depth, toward the point at which you are satisfied with the glitter of the new and fashionable, are gradual and painless steps, since apologetics are provided – by modern society itself – all along the way. That the real profit of a training in English is a tempering of mind and imagination.

Although I am going to argue that time should be given – more than most Schools give at present – to the study of certain aspects of modern society, I am sure that even this will not be done well unless English Schools keep central to their work those elements I have called fundamental. And those of us who choose to work in this contemporary area will not work well unless we regularly refresh ourselves with traditional work, and remind ourselves that a special occupational risk is loss of balance.

The essential aims of a training in English ought obviously to include the encouraging of a love and respect for language, for its complex relationship with individual and social experience. Most people do not paint or compose music each day or indeed any day, but virtually everybody uses words every day, and uses them not only functionally but emotionally, not just as tools but as ways of expressing his personality. He uses them and misuses them, so that they never remain still or pure (but neither do they set in classic poses). If, as we are often told, music is the purest of the arts, then literature is the muddiest, up to its knees in the mud of life. But, though there may be magic words and sacred words, no words are 'dirty' words in themselves. A writer always wants to pick them up and make them fresh again, by the power of his love. (Sometimes, admittedly, he has to decide that certain of them are past redemption, in his generation at least.)

Whatever else it does, a training in English should bring an increased ability to appreciate the many ways in which the literary imagination explores human experience – ways that range from the directly literal and moralistic to the oblique or apparently irrelevant.

A work of literature may have formal qualities beyond and irrelevant to the needs of meaning and the ordering of experience. A sonnet is not only an exploration and patterning of significant experience; it is also a playful pattern, made for its own sake and enjoyed for its own sake. And some of the deepest meanings of literature may come in the most indirect ways – through the odd, the fantastic, the grotesque. Although in fact the technically fantastic and the apocalyptic vision run right through English literature, Jacobean drama being only the most immediately striking instance, we tend to be uneasy about such elements. When we discuss the novel, in particular, we tend to speak about narrative skill or close moral explorations – even though this may cause us to underread Richardson, to ignore Sterne, to put Emily Brontë in an aberrant corner, and to leave Lewis Carroll to children and psychologists. Today we talk chiefly about, for instance, Angus Wilson's skill as a social satirist whereas he is at bottom a novelist of horror, horror at cruelty and at final meaninglessness. More often than we recognize, English writers see the skull beneath the skin, and can only express their vision by moving outside the more literal conventions.

But I am chiefly concerned here with literature as it deals with what E. M. Forster calls 'the life by values'. It starts in absorbed attention to the detail of experience, in immersion in 'the destructive element', in 'the foul rag and bone shop of the heart'. It, first, 'blesses . . . what there is for being'. It works not by precept and abstraction but by dramatization, by 'showing forth', in a fullness of sense and feeling and thought, of time and place and persons. In ordering its dramas it is driven by a desire to find the revelatory instance, the tiny gesture that opens a whole field of meaning and consequence. It does not do this pointlessly, nor explicitly to reform; it aims first at the momentary peace of knowing that a little more of the shifting amorphousness of experience has been named and held, that we are now that bit less shaken by the anarchy of feeling and the assault of experience. To push for this kind of truth, no matter how much it may hurt, is a kind of moral activity. As Jung says, the poet 'forces the reader to greater clarity and depth of human insight by bringing fully into his consciousness what he ordinarily evades or overlooks or senses only with a feeling of dull discomfort'.

I do not believe that reading good books necessarily makes us behave better – that if we appreciate Jane Austen's *Emma* we will henceforth act with greater self-knowledge. Yet how well would we be able to apprehend, let alone express, the complexity of personal relations, if it were not for literature working as literature? I do not mean that we all need to have read the best books; but what has the fact that they have been read, and that their insights have to some extent passed into the general consciousness, contributed to our understanding of our own experience?

Though literature has to do with meanings it is not primarily analytic or discursive, or it would be something else, something valuable perhaps but not art. Only art recreates life in all its dimensions – so that a particular choice is bound up with space, people and habits. Only here do we at one and the same time see ourselves existentially and vulnerably; and also as creatures who can move outside the time-bound texture of daily experience. The two make up, in Auden's phrase, 'the real world of theology and horses'.

So English studies are important at any time. But it is harder to live up to our own professions than we realize. Those of us who teach in Schools of English assert a case for the importance of great literature and tend to assume that we have thereby made the case for the importance of Schools of English. Which is to assume that our practice as teachers lives up to the challenge of the works we study, and this is not often so.

*

An increased respect for the life of language, and for the unpremeditated textures of experience – how are these qualities, which a training in English ought to encourage, valued in contemporary society? In what ways might a literary person concern himself with them today?

Years ago Ezra Pound wrote a striking rhetorical passage about this:

> Has literature a function in the state, in the aggregate of humans? It has . . . it has to do with the clarity of 'any and every' thought and opinion. It has to do with maintaining the very cleanliness of the tools, the health of the very matter of thought itself. Save the rare and very limited instances of invention in the plastic arts, or in mathematics, the individual cannot think or communicate his thought, the governor or legislator cannot act effectively or frame his laws, without words, and the solidity and validity of these words is in the care of the damned and despised literati. When their work goes rotten . . . by that I do not mean when they express indecorous thoughts . . . but when their very medium, the very essence of their work, the application of word to thing, goes rotten i.e. becomes slushy and inexact, or excessive or bloated, the whole machinery of social and of individual thought and order goes to pot.[1]

Is language neglected and despised today? In one way, certainly not. A BBC current affairs producer, who had spent years in interviewing and reporting, once told me: 'We've talked enough about the "affluent society", "the meritocratic society" and the rest. I propose "the articulate society", the society in which everyone is ready to and feels they ought to speak on invitation about anything. They are often talking nonsense – *but they do it in whole sentences*, and with a vocabulary that would have surprised their grandfathers.'

If language is decaying today, it is doing so not from neglect but from a surfeit of insensitive attentions. The 'Use of English' is one of today's proliferating trades, and any English School could within a year or two treble its size by setting up peripheral agencies – some sensible and useful, some dangerous – from courses in English for foreign students, through courses in English for science students or technical students, or for apprentices or for executives, to courses in 'the prose of persuasion' for advertising men or public relations men or politicians.

We have no equivalent to 'commercial artist' for his counterpart in writing and speech. 'Commercial writer' on a visiting card would be a good deal less 'slushy, inexact, excessive and bloated' than 'creative copywriter'. I wonder whether in any previous period so many words were being used inorganically – not because the writers had something to say about their experience, but on behalf of the particular concerns of others. So much language is used not as exploration but as persuasion and manipulation; so much prose has its eye only slightly on the object and almost wholly on the audience; so many words proclaim, if you listen to them carefully, not 'I touch and illuminate the experience' but 'this will win them over'.

It would be easy to compile a list of words that are by now unusable, until they have been redefined by each writer within each particular context. Not the old words we are all used to laughing about – 'tragedy' for the popular press, or 'magnificent' for Metro-Goldwyn-Mayer: the process goes on quickly and the newer men have quieter voices. So words like 'sincere', 'creative', 'vital', 'homely' and 'love' go out of use. Try writing an obituary notice for a respected old man, or a speech in honour of a quiet, decent life:

> All words like peace and love,
> All sane affirmative speech,
> Had been soiled, profaned, debased
> To a horrid mechanical screech:
>   No civil style survived
>   That pandemonium
> But the wry, the sotto-voce,
> Ironic and monochrome.

The process works at many levels, and at each level the language can seem alive – as in the high nervous pseudo-life of some magazine stories. But the snags and roughnesses of real response have been smoothed away.

Even more: much writing does not address itself to the experience of whole men. It addresses us as parts of men, since on those parts (for one reason or another) pressure has to be brought to bear. So we are addressed as bits, bits who belong to large lopsided blocks – as citizens, as consumers, as middle-aged middle-class parents of one and a half children, as voters or viewers, as religiously inclined car owners, as typical teenagers or redbrick professors.

It is too easy to blame the advertisers and the public relations men for all this. It is part of a larger problem, part of the price of self-consciousness (up to a certain point and of a certain kind), a consequence of the endlessly working, conveyor-belt productiveness of modern communications, and of the increasing centralization and concentration of societies. Governments are under this pressure as much as advertisers – to influence us through words, for limited but urgent purposes.

A way of using language toward people is a way of seeing people, of making assumptions about them. This goes further than seeing them as, say, limited in vocabulary or background; it indicates how much respect we have for them as human beings. In short, changes in contemporary English – Government prose, *Daily Mirror* prose, *Observer* prose, the changing prose of social occasions, of public occasions or of love-making – these are not narrowly linguistic matters but can only be understood socially, psychologically, morally.

Schools of English should obviously be aware of all this. So should any teachers within the humanities, and perhaps all teachers. As it is, too many of us stay most of the time within our well-defined academic areas – but succumb easily to occasional invitations from the world outside. We do not with sufficient confidence separate ourselves from that world nor sufficiently critically engage with it. By insisting on the difficult but responsible life of language, and on the overriding importance of the human scale, we can try to do our part in resisting the unreal, unfelt and depersonalized society.

Yet there is a great deal to be hopeful about: that so many now have the chance to become articulate may mean that self-consciousness will lead to self-awareness – and both are better than dull illiteracy; that so many people are subjected to various kinds of verbal persuasion indicates at least that they have some freedom to choose.

Each year's groups of graduates, presumably with a sound training in English language and literature, leave the universities anxious to communicate their heritage in the schools. They soon find that the voices that most readily speak to their schoolchildren are very different from the voices heard in that high art they are now trained to teach. Jane Austen does not speak with the accents of *Honey*, and *Honey* is much read even in girls' grammar schools. 'Only connect'; how many teachers make sense of this split, although many of them listened to those popular voices before they came to university and some might still do so with some part of themselves? In my experience few resolve the contradictions. They can rarely assert their truths with the assurance of the communicators on the other side of the cultural fence. They are often confused and baffled; they despise without understanding and feel like keepers in the museum of high but irrelevant art, training a few in the next generation to be keepers in their turn.

It would be better if more of us were more informed, if we sought more relevance and connection, if we encouraged a stronger sense that the life of the imagination has always to be fought for. Today especially – when commercial media consume whole areas of artistic possibilities as though working-out an automated mine, when we subject language to elaborate misuse – we need to make these connections. Some secondary schools already attempt it; they do not get much help from university English departments.

Listen to this voice, to this kind of voice:

> We live in the realm of the *half* educated. The number of readers grows daily, but the quality of readers does not improve rapidly. The middle class is scattered, headless; it is well-meaning but aimless; wishing to be wise, but ignorant how to be wise. The aristocracy of England never was a literary aristocracy, never even in the days of its full power – of its unquestioned predominance did it guide – did it even seriously try to guide – the taste of England. Without guidance young men, and tried men are thrown amongst a mass of books; they have to choose which they like; many of them would much like to improve their culture, to chasten their taste, if they knew how. But left to themselves they take, not pure art, but showy art; not that which permanently relieves the eye and makes it happy whenever it looks, and as long as it looks, but *glaring* art which catches and arrests the eye for a moment, but which in the end fatigues it. But before the wholesome remedy of nature – the fatigue arrives – the hasty reader has passed on to some new excitement, which in its turn stimulates for an instant, and then is passed by forever. These conditions are not favourable to the due appreciation of pure art – of that art which must be known before it is admired – which must have fastened irrevocably on the brain before you appreciate it – which you must love ere it will seem worthy of your love.

That paragraph occurs in, of all places, a critical essay on the poetry of Wordsworth, Tennyson and Browning. I do not agree with all its formulations but I admire its boldness in tackling interconnections between history, politics and the aesthetics of popular taste. That kind of voice should be heard more often in Schools of English. But if a teacher were to produce such a paragraph in the middle of an otherwise straightforward critical essay, some of his colleagues would advise him to delete it – on the grounds that it wasn't sufficiently specialist and scholarly, might well make people wonder whether he wasn't 'becoming "journalistic" ', and might even affect his chances of promotion. Actually the passage is about a hundred years old and is by Bagehot.[2]

*

The approach I have been outlining may be provisionally called Literature and Contemporary Cultural Studies. It has something in common with several existing approaches, but is not exactly any one of them. And it has many ancestors; but Dr Leavis in his culture and environment work and Mrs Leavis in her studies in popular fiction are more important than most.

The field for possible work in Contemporary Cultural Studies can be divided into three parts: one is, roughly, historical and philosophical; another is, again roughly, sociological; the third – which will be the most important – is the literary critical.

We need to know more about the *history* of what is called 'the cultural debate'. In *Culture and Society* Raymond Williams did some interesting work in the line from Burke to Orwell, and got praise and punishment from people whose specialist fields he had been bound to encroach on. It would be useful if those others would now make their contributions.

Probably even harder: we need to define the terms of the debate more closely. At the moment they are muddled; more even than is usual, semantic shifts hide confused assumptions. The clash of undernourished generalizations and of submerged apologetics takes the place of what should be a dialogue.

Talk about 'highbrows, middlebrows and lowbrows' continues, although it is now almost entirely useless as critical terminology. The educational press (still following Ortega y Gasset) talks about 'your common man' and 'the masses' as though these were well-defined terms rather than conditioned gestures. Most of the discussion of conformity, status, class, 'Americanization', mass art, pop art, folk art, urban art and the rest is simply too thin.

Or look at the language used in the debate about advertising: the most intelligent and seriously received of the apologists are so high-minded – high-minded but semantically cavalier – that it is painful to read them. And how easily the organs of opinion create new little cultural patterns; the 'Angry Young Man' movement or the 'U and non-U' controversy. The promotion of all such patterns is almost wholly lacking in precision or historical perspective. We have as yet hardly begun to get any of the terms in the debate straight, partly because to do so will require us to reconsider a lot of comforting notions. It would be better if more philosophers came into this field; but until they do literary people will have to try to clear the undergrowth for their own enquiries.

Some students of sociology have worked in the areas traditionally called the sociology of literature or of culture during the last few years and so have some students of literature.[3] But we need much more varied work in contemporary cultural sociology. We need enquiries into such questions as:

(a) *About writers and artists*: Where do they come from? How do they become what they are? What are their financial rewards? (One can, of course, make historical comparisons at any point.)

(b) *What are the audiences* for different forms and what the audiences for different levels of approach? What expectations do they have, and what background knowledge do they bring? Is there such a person as 'the common reader' or the 'intelligent layman' today? What are the ins-and-outs of a line running from Jude the Obscure through Kipps and Mr Polly to Koestler's anxious corporals and the readers of egghead paperbacks?

(c) What of *the opinion formers and their channels of influence* . . . the guardians, the élite, the clerisy (if there is such a body today)? Where do they come from? Who, if anyone, has succeeded the Stephens and the Garnetts? We realize how much could be done here when we remember how exceptional is such a book as Noël Annan's *Leslie Stephen, His Life and Times*.

(d) What about the *organizations for the production and distribution of the written and spoken word?* What are their natures, financial and otherwise? Is it true, and if so what does it mean practically (whatever it may mean in imaginative terms), to say that the written word (and perhaps all the arts) are progressively becoming commodities, to be used and quickly discarded? What, to take a small instance, are the commercial facts, what the pattern and what the significance of 'the paperback revolution'?

What of the rise of reputations? How far are they the creation of commercial forces, seeking concentration and rationalization here as in motor car production, and so tending to give excessive attention to a few and almost wholly to ignore other artists?

(e) Last, how little we know about *all sorts of interrelations*: about interrelations between writers and their audiences, and about their shared assumptions; about interrelations between writers and organs of opinion, between writers, politics, power, class and cash; about interrelations between the sophisticated and the popular arts, interrelations which are both functional and imaginative; and how few foreign comparisons we have made.

Most important of all: the directly literary critical approach in cultural studies is itself neglected. Yet it is essential to the whole field because, unless you know how these things work as art, even though sometimes as 'bad art', what you say about them will not cut deep. Here, we particularly need better links with sociologists. It is difficult, outside a seminar, to use a literary critical vocabulary – to talk about 'the quality of the imagination' shown; or to discuss the effect on a piece of writing of various pressures – for instance, to talk about corner-cutting techniques, or linguistic tricks, or even (perhaps especially) about what tone reveals. All this needs to be analysed more, to be illustrated and enforced – and at all levels, not just in relation to mass arts.

The mass or popular arts about which we know too little and in which there is room for developed critical practice include: film criticism; television and radio criticism; television drama (which tends to be ignored or overrated); popular fiction of many kinds – crime, westerns, romance, science fiction, the academic and academic's detective story;[4] the press and journals of all kinds; strip cartoons; the language of advertising and public relations; popular songs and popular music in all their forms.

Some people say they don't want or need to know more about any of this, that it is all beneath serious critical consideration. The same people will often make sweeping and uninformed generalizations about mass art. A few make handsome exceptions for the *News of the World* or 'Z Cars'.

If only for a start, a little more humility about what audiences actually take from unpromising material would be useful.[5] Perhaps no one should engage in the work who is not, in a certain sense, himself in love with popular art.[6] One kind of 'love' is a disguised nostalgia for mud. Assimilated lowbrowism is as bad as uninformed highbrowism. It is hard to listen to a programme of pop songs, or watch 'Candid Camera' or 'This Is Your Life' without feeling a complex mixture of attraction and repulsion, of admiration for skill and scorn for the phoney, of wry observations of similarities and correspondences, of sudden reminders of the raciness of speech, or of the capacity for courage or humour, or of shock at the way mass art can chew up anything, even our most intimate feelings. All this is related also to hopes, uncertainties, aspirations, the search for identity in a society on the move, innocence, meanness, the wish for community and the recognition of loneliness. It is a form of art (bastard art, often) but engaging, mythic and not easily explained away.

Of course, this art is being increasingly machine-tooled: there are thirteen-week sociological soap operas, with a crisis at every natural break; predigested tales for the women's magazines; the extraordinary sophistication of today's Westerns; the offbeat commercials. But even with these, there are sometimes spaces between the brittle voices in which a gesture sets you thinking in a new way about some aspect of human experience.

We cannot, then, speak of the effects of all these arts as confidently as some social scientists do unless we have a close sense of their imaginative working; we have to recognize the meaningfulness of much popular art. If we do, we shall not be left with that 'passion of awe' which we can find in the best works of art. Nor shall we be left only with contempt. We may more often be ironic than contemptuous; and we may well have moments of awe.

I have admitted the danger of too contemporary a slant in English studies, of too social a slant and even of too 'moral' a slant. If we forget the 'celebratory' or 'playful' element in literature we will sooner or later stop talking about literature and find ourselves talking about history or sociology or philosophy – and probably about bad history and bad sociology and bad philosophy. But that truth has been used by some Schools of English as a shelter. English, once again and finally, has to do with language exploring human experience, in all its flux and complexity. It is therefore always in an active relation with its age; and some students of literature – many more students of literature than at present – ought to try to understand these relationships better.

Notes

1 *Literary Essays of Ezra Pound*, London: Faber; New York: New Directions.
2 From 'Wordsworth, Tennyson and Browning; or, Pure, Ornate and Grotesque Art in English Poetry', 1864.
3 For instance, Professor Altick in the USA, Professor Dalziel in New Zealand and Dr Louis James here.
4 Orwell did some good early work here and a few others have followed him.
5 I was glad to see just this point hinted at by – surprisingly, to me – C. S. Lewis in *An Experiment in Criticism.*
6 Some American critics are very interesting here, such as Benjamin DeMott.

2 Scope of research

First report, September 1964

Centre for Contemporary Cultural Studies

The Centre 1963–4

The Centre for Contemporary Cultural Studies is a postgraduate research centre for the study of contemporary cultural problems, constituted as part of the School of English in the University of Birmingham. Its director is Professor Richard Hoggart. The Centre was formally constituted in the Spring of 1964, and the first full-time appointment – Stuart Hall as Research Fellow – was made in April. Since then, the Centre has been preparing for the full opening of operations with the new university session in October.

There has been a surprisingly enthusiastic response to the Centre's formation. We have considered over forty applications to work here, all of them serious possibilities; and more than a dozen of these people are to join us, on a full-time or part-time basis, in October. They are all people with good academic qualifications who have developed a personal interest in some aspect of this work; many of them have found it difficult to pursue this interest within the established framework of disciplines in the universities, and welcome the opportunity to work here for this reason. We have had enquiries about joint work or affiliation from half-a-dozen bodies in this country, and made contact with as many abroad. We have spent several weeks talking with interested individuals who wanted to know in greater detail what we proposed to do. Almost every publisher approached has given a generous grant of books for the Centre library and workroom; and almost all the periodicals and reviews approached for free subscriptions have agreed. In general, the size and character of the response have been most encouraging.

The Centre has been accommodated by the University in two places. The Director and Secretary are in the English Department wing of the Faculty of Arts building, and the Research Fellow and Centre Workroom are housed in the same building. There are three work-rooms for research students in the house known as 'Westmere', ten minutes walk away from the main campus, where the other graduate centre forming part of the English Department – the Shakespeare Institute – is now located.

The Centre: scope of research

The purpose and scope of the Centre were defined by Professor Hoggart in his inaugural lecture as Professor of English, *Schools of English and Contemporary Society* (February, 1963). Copies of this lecture are available in two issues of the journal, *Use of English* (Winter 1963, Spring 1964).

Professor Hoggart proposed three main areas of study. The first – 'historical and philosophical' – will be concerned with the terms in which the debate about contemporary culture and social change is carried on. It will try to trace climates of opinion, the main movement of ideas, their sources and interaction, and their influence in society over the last fifty or sixty years. For example, one of the first projects will be a study in depth of the period of the 1930s, using Orwell's work as a 'key'. The second area – 'the sociology of literature and the arts' – will try to develop a critical language for dealing with those phenomena which have both artistic and social significance. Here the Centre will try to bring together the disciplines of literary criticism, sociology and social psychology, and social history. It will also be concerned with the nature of different audiences for different kinds of art and literature, with the relationship between different 'kinds' and 'levels' of art, and with the influences of communication upon audiences.

In the third area – 'the critical-evaluative' – studies in depth will be made of mass art, popular art and culture and the mass media. 'Essentially we will be trying to understand *how* the mass arts or the popular arts achieve their effects.' This field includes popular fiction, the press, film and television, popular music and advertising. Projects in these fields will, of course, draw on and be nourished by the disciplines of sociology and social psychology, but the main approach throughout will be the *critical-evaluative* one, with close attention both to the imaginative meanings and social attitudes contained within these forms, and to their aesthetic and cultural qualities.

This question of approach is central to the whole character of the Centre's work. There are few centres concerned with this general area in Britain, and where work of a serious kind is being conducted it is largely in terms of measurable influence and effects. The Centre will, of course, be concerned with questions of influence and effect, but its main emphasis is upon the critical evaluation of these phenomena, and an understanding of them in their social and cultural setting. Its work will, we hope, fall into line with the best critical work done in schools of literature, while at the same time extending this work in scope.

The projects

We have tried, so far as is possible, to group each project around a focus of interest. This has the advantage of promoting group work wherever possible, though it in no way precludes individual research students pursuing a particular aspect or writing up one part of the project, either for an individual study or for presentation as a thesis.

In the main, these are long term projects, conceived as two-year or three-year jobs. We shall also initiate shorter-term studies of our own; and we shall be taking up, jointly with outside bodies, a number of shorter-range special studies.

The range of groupings is already wide. In almost every case more than one person is involved, and we are prepared to be flexible about the degree of looseness permitted within each group. This must be allowed to grow and change with the shape of each project. One of the projects already mentioned – a 'period' study of the 1930s – will be a loosely-knit group, bringing together people of differing ages, with widely different interests, and different academic experience. This group includes two English specialists, one of whom is also a social anthropologist, several literary critics, a political historian and a biographer. The two youngest are in their early twenties, graduates in English from Keele and Oxford respectively. The eldest is a senior lecturer in English in the Training College, himself a man formed by and personally involved with the period itself. One is an American Fulbright scholar.

Some projects will involve a clear overlap with the work of sociologists and social psychologists, and may include careful supporting survey studies. The study being made by two students (with training in the visual arts as well as literature) of domestic art and taste in the home, and the study of pop music and teenage culture will be 'mixed' projects of this kind. The group of three who are working on various aspects of contemporary fiction will also, of course, be concerned with the social background and social attitudes, but this project will be a 'literary' study in the more precise sense. In work done on advertising, domestic art and television and film, particular interest will be shown in the refinement of critical terms for phenomena with a distinctive visual bias. Some projects will span the various channels of communication: the proposed project on sport, for example, will look at the presentation of sport, and its cultural significance, in several of the media, as well as the use made of sport as a theme in serious literature. In other cases – television, for example – the media will be studied in depth.

Several of these projects are still taking shape. Here is a rough listing of the projects which are most likely to be undertaken beginning in October:

1 Orwell and the climate of the 1930s
2 The growth of and changes in the local press
3 Folk song and folk idioms in popular music
4 Levels of fiction and changes in comtemporary society
5 Domestic art and iconography in the home
6 Pop music and adolescent culture
7 The meaning of sport and its presentation

In addition, we hope to make a start on a critical Bibliography of primary and secondary material in the field of contemporary social and cultural criticism. This will be the first indexed bibliography of its kind in the country, and may be offered as a regular supplement to the Centre's publications.

Research students

Some students will be registered for post-graduate Degrees; others will be Occasional Students of the university, engaged on a piece of research but not presenting it for a higher degree. Some students will be working full-time; others will be part-time students, either those already working close at hand who will be joining one of the projects, or those who have taken half-time jobs in Birmingham so as to finance themselves for their research at the Centre. Provided these students make a regular contribution to the Centre and take part in its formal and informal life, no strict distinctions will be made between part-time and full-time work. In some of the projects – Domestic Art in the Home, for example – one researcher is a lecturer in the College of Art and Crafts, the other is a full-time student.

This pattern arises partly from the problem of financing the Centre's work. We have not so far been able to offer direct grants for research to students, and they have had to find ways and means of financing themselves. Some students will be coming on State Studentships; some will be financing themselves by part-time employment; some will be appointed jointly between the Centre and private bodies, on funds raised privately or from foundations; some will pay for themselves.

Formal life of the Centre

In the main, the Centre will have three kinds of 'formal' occasion. On the Tuesday of each week in Term, a general Graduate Seminar will be held for Centre students and other interested faculty members and research workers. Here topics of general interest will be raised in the form of papers presented, largely, by outside speakers. The purpose here is to give every student an opportunity to confront the general social and cultural issues which lie at the heart of this work. This will also provide an opportunity for different approaches and disciplines to be brought to bear on particular topics.

On Monday afternoons, a 'closed' Seminar, limited to full and part-time workers at the Centre, will be held. These will be critical-analytic sessions, in which each member will be invited to participate both by way of contributions to discussion and the presentation of papers. The purpose here is to get close work going on a fairly narrow and clearly-defined topic. 'Evidence' – such as examples, photographs, records or film – will, so far as is possible, be directly presented or available beforehand. The discussion will be as free-ranging and intensive as possible. At a later stage, sections of studies written up, draft chapters or research problems will be presented and discussed at this meeting.

Opportunities will also be available for the individual 'project groups' to meet to discuss their work separately. These will be encouraged, but each group will arrange and manage these sessions for itself, and the frequency of these sessions will depend upon the degree of closeness involved in the particular project.

The Centre has developed a close link with the Department of Sociology. Some students will be registered for a Master's degree in that department, and there might be joint supervisions where necessary. Centre students will also have access to graduate seminars in the Sociology Faculty, as well as to general advice on sociological research methods and problems.

A number of non-Centre people will be invited to the Tuesday Seminars, but the numbers are certain to be restricted. They will be asked to make this Seminar a regular commitment, so that over the year continuity of interest and attendance can be maintained. [. . .]

Publications

The Centre is envisaged as both a publishing and research centre. Full length studies – the result of individual or group work – will be published regularly by arrangement between the Centre and a publisher, as a connected series of studies. Several publishers have expressed an interest in seeing our material. We have agreed with Chatto and Windus that they shall have first refusal of any material which is likely to appear in book form.

Papers, shorter studies, aspects of work written up as articles, or reports on shorter projects will be published directly by the Centre as 'occasional papers'.

On special occasions, the Centre will also offer a contribution to a particular cultural controversy or debate in the form of a specially prepared pamphlet. These are intended as interventions, especially where aspects of the argument are being neglected in the current debate, or where terms and definitions need to be more fully explored or developed.

Discussions about founding a regular journal are under way with some interested organisations.

Links with teachers

The Centre is already in touch with a substantial number of teachers and lecturers who are concerned with the links between research projects and education. These are contacts in Adult Education, Teacher Training, Colleges of Art and Further Education, as well as in secondary schools. An arrangement is being worked out whereby these individuals and their institutions may affiliate to the Centre, make use of its workroom, and receive such occasional publications and information about work in progress as may be of help to them in their work. In a number of cases, linked projects may be set up. The Centre would like to be able to offer more direct teaching assistance and the services of a field-officer to these contacts, but is limited at the moment by lack of funds. There is a growing body of people in education who see the direct connection between our work and their educational concerns, and we shall try to maintain and develop a close liaison with them – in the first instance by arranging occasional conferences.

Over the years, we should like to see the Centre increasingly as a rallying point, both for research work on cultural change and also for those who are engaged in the same field, but express it in the practice of education and teaching at all levels. There is much to be done here, alongside such bodies as The British Film Institute and the Use of English groups, to nourish and strengthen this work on the educational side.

Services

There are other kinds of 'service' which we envisage the Centre providing as it expands. We are already in touch with a number of institutions doing work along similar lines abroad – in the United States and Canada, and on the continent. Again, we should like to provide for regular exchanges of work-in-progress reports, information, published articles and sources between these various centres. We may jointly with them sponsor conferences, here or abroad; at present we are considering just such a proposal for a three-way conference in the summer of 1965 between Birmingham, Utrecht and New York (proposed by the new Professor of English at Utrecht, Professor Seymour Betsky).

We shall occasionally ourselves, and sometimes jointly with other bodies, organise conferences of our own. There might well be a general conference on aspects of popular culture, open to all those interested; or a series of special or specialist conference – e.g. for teachers; or conferences on limited topics, such as television, or regional broadcasting.

Finance

The Centre is self-financing. The University provides accommodation and furniture. Otherwise we are responsible for raising our own funds. At present our income derives from a small number of private grants. The main grant is from Penguin Books, who have generously convenanted the Centre £2,400 a year for seven years. This grant started the Centre and pays for the first Research Fellow and the secretary. Other than this we have two grants of £100 a year for seven years (from Chatto and Windus and The Observer Trust) and a once for all gift of £500 from a well-wisher. This is our total income. It is invigorating that so much can be done on so little. But if the Centre is to match its clear possibilities it must have more money. A number of foundations are being approached for additional grants towards work now being undertaken.

Section 2

Theoretical engagements

Introduction

CCCS and the detour through theory

Lawrence Grossberg

Upon its founding, the Centre was organized around three weekly seminars. Within three years, the less formal Monday morning 'working seminar' had been transformed into the 'Seminar on selected texts,' the aim of which was to 'lay the proper foundations for interdisciplinary work in cultural studies.' (Third Annual Report: 1966–1967: 24). In just a few more years, by the end of the decade, it had, first informally and then formally, become dubbed 'the theory seminar' and everyone understood its task was not merely to fill in the gaps – usually social scientific and social theory – that the majority of students, coming from literary studies, brought to the table of an interdisciplinary cultural studies, but rather, to lay the theoretical foundations for the cultural studies project itself.

It is both appropriate and misleading, then, to begin this collection with a section on theory at the Centre – appropriate because these essays demonstrate how central theory has always been to cultural studies, but potentially misleading because placing them up front may lead some people to assume that theory defines the leading edge of cultural studies, that somehow it is theory that is, at it were, the driving force of cultural studies. Reading these essays, however, should make it clear that while cultural studies is not theory-driven, and it is not about theory per se, theoretical work is absolutely crucial to its project and was central to the development of that project at the Centre. These essays can, if read in their own contexts and histories, give a valuable indication of the place of theory in cultural studies and of the practice of theorizing at the Centre, as it was articulated to and within the project of cultural studies.

These essays make visible some of that history of theorizing; they make it clear that theoretical investigations were inseparable from the Centre's varied efforts to develop and practise cultural studies, even as its participants were struggling to imagine and define what they meant by cultural studies. They make it clear that theory played a key role in the ongoing work of the Centre, which Angela McRobbie has often described as 'making it [cultural studies] up as we went along,' even if they do not always make clear the particular kinds of work organized around theorizing, or the particular kinds of work that theory was called upon to do.

One of the crucial lessons that can be gleaned from these essays, if they are read together and in context, is how very thin the line was, and how very great the distance was, between the dominant way of reading theory and the Centre's practice of theorizing. These represent two ways of relating to and practising theory: on the one hand, the search for the 'right' theory and on the other, the necessary detour through theory and the need, as Stuart Hall famously put it, to go on theorizing. It is easy, following many of the contemporary discourses of theory, to fall into the trap of, to become absorbed into, the never-ending search for the one final correct theory, impervious to criticism, that would provide the answers to the questions that cultural studies poses and thus, in a sense, bring the necessity of theoretical labor to an end. Of course, since this end can never quite arrive, theoretical labour takes on the form of endless theoretical critique, as if the adequacy of theory to fill its place in cultural studies could be worked out entirely in theoretical terms.

The Centre's relation to theory was always more practical; theory was less a sacred object than a toolbox – practical, flexible and contextually specific. Theory is not an end unto itself. Theory in cultural studies, at least as the Centre attempted to practise it, is always deployed in the service of a political project: in the attempt to open new possibilities for transforming the existing context, and to imagine new futures, one has to gain a better understanding of the present context (or what is eventually called the conjuncture). And that better knowledge of the context requires what Marx called a 'detour through theory.' Theory is an absolutely necessary tool (concepts, abstractions) on the way to a different future because theory is a crucial element or practice in the effort to offer a different (and in some ways better) analysis of the present context. But theory's development – its purported 'adequacy' – can never be defined only in theoretical terms; it can only be negotiated in relation to the context to which it is called to respond and, as we shall see, to the particular commitments – e.g., to complexity, specificity and the refusal of reductionism – that partly embody the Centre's understanding of the project of cultural studies. (I will return to these commitments shortly.)

The effort to read these essays as documents of the active intellectual life and work of the Centre must inevitably face some of the limits of what one can glean from the essays themselves. I might start by saying that the essays do not transparently encode their own social relations of production. While people often have celebrated the Centre's commitment to collective work, usually this collective practice is located in the various working groups and research projects. But the most radical moment of the Centre's intellectual practice may have been in its effort to make theorizing into a collective activity in its own right, for generally, in the western academy, nothing is treated as so solitary an activity as theory.

Whether individually or collectively authored, these essays are very much a record of conversations, arguments and collective efforts. In many cases, it is difficult – if not impossible – to specify the actual historical moment of their authorship, in relation to the actual timeline of the ongoing readings (in the Theory seminar) and of the conversations that took place inside and outside the seminar, conversations that were, for the most part, the lifeblood of the Centre. Many of these essays were produced inside or as a result of the work of the theory seminar, and one can sometimes hear the reverberations of the concrete historical moments as if they were ghosts. Yet the essays often fail to inscribe, within themselves, the temporal lines of influence, as well as their relations to other forms and fora of work at the Centre.[1]

A significant part of what haunts these essays, for anyone who cares to listen, is the excitement of discovering new theoretical possibilities. Perhaps this helps to explain the tendency to search continually for and embrace the theoretically new, and sometimes even the theoretical novelty. At the Centre, the excitement of discovering a whole universe of theoretical texts, especially Marxist and structuralist work of the twentieth century, was palpable, for many of the authors and texts discussed in these essays had only recently become available in English. This work of translation was crucial, not only for the Centre, but also more generally for political, cultural and social theory in Britain. And yet it was never about the discovery of the new per se (however old it may have been) that excited the people at the Centre; it was instead about the potential that such new sources offered. It was about what could be borrowed and re-read that would enable them to continue to develop and expand cultural studies itself as a project.

There is a lot more that needs to be said about the social relations of the intellectual production at the Centre, and how it changed over time, that cannot be addressed here. A fuller description would have to address, among other things, the changing interpersonal relationships at the Centre;[2] the changing politics of those relationships; the various conditions of the labour at the Centre; the ways those conditions were lived by specific students at the Centre (many had full- or part-time teaching posts, many commuted to Birmingham from London and other places, etc.). It would also include the evolving relations among the Centre, other departments at the university, and the central administration, and how the Centre attempted to fit into (and was perceived as not fitting into) the pedagogical mission of the university.

These essays make visible at least some of the enormous theoretical diversity that characterized the Centre throughout its career, a diversity and complexity that is often written out of the histories not only of cultural studies itself, but of theory in British cultural studies, as various writers have attempted, whether implicitly or explicitly, and for a variety of reasons, to read it as too linear and homogenous. We should not assume that there was ever a theoretical consensus at the Centre; instead, there were always competing positions around which a number of different competing consensuses were organized – and there was, no doubt, the perception, and perhaps even the reality, organized at various moments, that certain consensual positions came to dominate the Centre's work or at least to represent the Centre to its audiences. Yet much of the real history of theory at the Centre is only visible in the diversity, and in the struggle to produce at least a common set of commitments around the project of cultural studies. I think it is only in understanding the existence of diversity and commonality together, of understanding the diversity in the commonality, that we begin to approach the specifically theoretical contributions of the Centre, and the place of theorizing in cultural studies. At the same time, I do not mean to suggest some sort of idyllic theoretical pluralism in which a thousand positions were nurtured and allowed to bloom. Inevitably, the openness, while real, was also limited, and there were no doubt people who felt (and positions that were) more or less marginalized (and the emotional echoes of this marginalization can be heard in some of the essays collected here). Still, the wide range of theoretical texts and positions that were encountered, read, and discussed, not only in the Theory seminar but also (and in some ways even more importantly in terms of the diversity) in the various working groups, suggests a degree of openness and eclecticism (and a refusal of the demand for 'theoretical correctness' and closure) that is both consistent with the Centre's sense of cultural studies and that stood (and I hope continues to stand) against the spirit of too much contemporary critical theory.

Consequently, we must resist the tendency to generalize from these essays, to read in them a coherent and consensual CCCS position, or a simple linear history of positions. This may be unavoidable and, to different degrees at different moments, it may be more or less valid (at least insofar as it registers the 'hegemony that won,' as John Clarke has put it). The extent to which, for example, Chambers' reading of structuralism in general and of Barthes in particular, or Ellis' reading of Kristeva, or Slater's reading of the Frankfurt School, can be taken as representative of a broader agreement is uncertain. Yet we would be equally mistaken to refuse to acknowledge that they must be representative of something about theory at the Centre and that they were crucial elements of the ongoing theoretical work of the Centre.

These essays exhibit a wide range of voices and modalities. Some are descriptive and presentational, others defensive or argumentative or engaged. These are radically different sorts of essays with different relations to the theories and theorists they talk about. They speak in different tones, and they present different ways of reading, from a relatively – and I emphasize relatively – neutral exposition, to a passionate advocacy, to an argumentative posture in the field of possible foundations for cultural studies. For example both Ellis and White present the substance of Kristeva's theories in very similar ways, yet their tones and implicit purposes are very different.[3] Similarly, both Hall *et al.* and Lumley write about Gramsci – a very similar Gramsci, and yet, again, the tone and the motivations are fundamentally different.

Yet at the same time, the essays seem to share a common effort to fit whatever theory or theorist is their subject into the project of cultural studies. That is to say, they all engage with positions through their own efforts to construct something called cultural studies. For example, Rusher's description of his exposition of Althusser, actually more of an engagement and a critique 'determined by a partisan position adopted within the field of "all possible readings," the position of cultural studies', can be taken, I think, as emblematic of the questions driving all of these essays.

Consequently, I want to read these essays as signposts of the trajectories, the problematics, and the practices of the theoretical work of the Centre. I want to read them as attempts to think through not only the place of theory in the project of cultural studies but also, to use theory to help formulate the project of cultural studies itself. The introduction to the first issue of Working Papers in Cultural Studies (WPCS) gives a good initial sense of how the Centre understood the project: 'The intention was not to establish one more compartment in the already fragmented "map of knowledge", but rather to attempt to view the whole complex process of change from the vantage point of "culture".' Chambers' essay reiterates this in a slightly different but useful way: 'Cultural Studies is to be read not as a discipline in the traditional sense but as a developing problematic,' and the Introduction of WPCS 10 ('On Ideology') explicitly says that ' "Cultural studies" . . . designates descriptively a broad field of interests and not a unified body of theory.'

I want to make use of this notion of the 'problematic,' used in a number of these essays, and introduced by Althusser, to organize my own efforts to navigate a way through them. One might object that even a brief reading of these essays makes it clear that these essays, or at least the theories they read, do not always attempt to answer the same question. Unravelling this paradox requires more than a reminder of Chambers' observation that the problematic is 'developing.' First, we have to understand that a problematic refers not to the content of particular answers, or even to the explicit questions that a particular theory poses, but rather, to the underlying question that makes possible any particular theoretical framing of an answer. Second, we have to understand the trajectory of the Centre's empirical-political work, and of the theoretical conversations that crucially accompanied and articulated that work. I cannot adequately deal with the latter question here, so I will focus on the first issue.

Although I have said that one would be mistaken to impose a singular, harmonious and straightforward narrative on the history of theory at the Centre, there is, nevertheless, a kind of narrative that has to be told. This is a narrative of the Centre's growing explicit effort to embody, in its work, the theoretical commitments that increasingly came to define the project of cultural studies: commitments of contextuality, complexity, contestation, etc. What we can see in the history of theoretical work is the effort to find a theoretical practice capable of founding and grounding a radically anti-reductionist analysis of historical conjunctures.

In order to clarify this argument, I want to make an analytic (and therefore artificial) distinction between two problematics that run throughout these essays, and through the project of cultural studies. In a sense, one might say that these two problematics operate on different levels of abstraction, in different realms. To put it differently, cultural studies, at least as understood at the Centre, shares each of these two problematics with other, and different, bodies of critical work.

The first, which I will call the substantive problematic of cultural studies, might simply be posed, following Raymond Williams (to whom the Centre owed much, as Michael Green makes clear), as the question of the relationships between those sets of relations and practices commonly designated as 'culture' and 'society' or, in another version, 'culture' and power. Cultural studies seeks to analyze the complex connections, homologies, mediations, determinations or articulations (understood conceptually, these are not all necessarily equivalent) between signifying or discursive practices and structures of social life, power and experience. This 'problematic' can be and has been posed in many different ways and broken into any number of questions.

While it may be the case that many of these essays seek to develop a theoretical apparatus, to introduce theoretical concepts and categories, that will enable any particular instance of the question to be 'adequately' answered, we still have to ask how the notion of adequacy functions here or, referring back to Rusher's statement quoted above, what does it mean to read theory, to enter into a conversation and even debate with theoretical texts, from the position of cultural studies? After all, there are other critical practices and critical theories that also seek to examine the linkages between culture and society. Such approaches – including, apparently, given their reception at the Centre, the Frankfurt School and various poststructuralisms – were viewed with suspicion because of what I want to describe (through my own act of abstraction) as a second problematic, which might properly be referred to as meta-theoretical, or what Hall, in his essay on Marx's 1857 Introduction to the *Grundrisse*, refers to as methodological. This involves a set of commitments defining, in somewhat formal terms, the very notion of relationality, as it operates in and develops through the history of the Centre's efforts to pose the substantive problematic of the relations between culture and society/power.

To put it simply, the major trajectories of work at the Centre seemed explicitly to shy away from theories that either made the connections too direct, obvious and simple (labelling them as reductionist, deterministic, essentialist; theories which guaranteed their answers in advance) or that made the connections so distant, hidden and fractured that there appeared to be no way of describing any effective connections at all. Once again, the Centre shared this second problematic – of developing an anti-reductionist and contextualist practice capable of acknowledging the complexity of the conjuncture – with other emergent critical practices that were not necessarily interested in using culture (or signifying practices) as a way into the context or the social totality. There is no reason to assume that intellectuals trying to rethink, for example, the nature and effectiveness of economic or political practices within the conjuncture, even though they may recognize that such realities are partly discursive, necessarily share the first, substantive problematic of cultural studies, although they most certainly should be seen as common travellers and allies who share the second problematic.

Not surprisingly, perhaps, I believe it is the articulation of the two problematics that defines the specificity of the Centre's project of cultural studies.[4] It is also important to acknowledge that most of the essays collected here, as well as the best work in cultural studies more generally, address both problematics simultaneously and, in most cases, the two problematics are never explicitly distinguished. (This is not surprising, since the analytic distinction is mine, not the authors' or the Centre's.) Nowhere is this more clearly seen than in the pieces by Bland *et al.* and Gilroy, which are wonderful embodiments of theorizing at the Centre, as I hope to explain.

Consider what I have called the 'substantive problematic.' The introduction to the first issue of WPCS described cultural studies as the attempt 'to make intelligible the real movement of culture as it is registered in social life, in group and class relationships, in politics and institutions, in values and ideas.' Sparks describes Lukacs' theoretical problematic as 'the relation of the material life of a society to its ideological phenomena, or more precisely, its consciousness.' Chambers describes this problematic as 'an attempt to analyze the pivotal relationships between conscious social experiences, in their various forms, and the profoundly unconscious historical and material constitution of those experiences.' Put in another way, cultural studies

> seeks to grasp the 'logics-in-use', the transformations that operate in this dialectic . . . and to lay bare their specific enunciation in particular practices. . . .This involves analysing the concrete realizations, the objectivation, of 'social knowledge', as found within particular configurations and practices.
>
> (Chambers, in this volume)

His essay presents a 'structuralist' solution, as it were, to the question. Slater elaborates the Frankfurt's School's effort to answer questions that echo the substantive problematic of cultural studies: 'What aspects of the respective social structures find their expression in the individual work of literature?' and 'What are the effects of that work within its society?'

The debate between Shuttleworth and Hall in the inaugural issue of WPCS follows upon the theoretical elucidation of this problematic by Raymond Williams. As Green argues, by equating culture with the relation between the individual and the social, Williams basically set cultural studies upon a conceptual foundation in which equivalence among communication, community, and intersubjectivity defined the theoretical foundation for cultural studies. On Shuttleworth's reading, the question is whether intersubjectivity (and hence, culture) can be understood in purely phenomenological terms (i.e., in terms of the structures of individual consciousness and experience), or does it require a notion of culture as the objectification of consciousness and hence, the production of a 'distinctive notion of the social' that cannot be reduced to individual experience?[5]

Hall (in 'A response to people and culture') argues that the core theoretical task of cultural studies – understanding 'the dialectic between consciousness and social being' (a variant of what I have called the first substantive problematic) requires that we distinguish among private meaning, public meanings and situated meanings; he argues that cultural studies needs to find a way to talk about 'how subjective meanings and intentions, come, under certain determinate conditions, to create and inform the "structures" of social life? And how in turn, the structures of social life shape and inform the interior spaces of individual consciousness.' Rooted in Sartre's *Search for a Method*, Hall draws upon a sociological tradition of theorizing (see Chapter 7 in this volume) in order to argue that the 'dialectic of culture' can only be understood through a notion of culture as the dialectical relation of objectification and internalization. Hall is negotiating his way, in this crucial essay, with the tradition of the 'social construction of reality,' which postulated a notion of social knowledge or 'Weltanschauung' as the necessary mediation between consciousness and social being. Sparks' criticism of Lukacs' failure to explain 'the realization of a world-vision [a particular structure of class consciousness] in literary terms' follows a similar logic. That is to say, in cultural studies' terms, Lukacs failed to offer a sufficiently theorized description of signifying practices as mediations.

Consequently, the Centre's turn to structuralism and semiotics in order to 'get beyond a phenomenological understanding of the social construction of reality' by considering what phenomenology took for granted, the background (knowledge) 'as the site of structuring rules and resistant transformations' (Chambers in this volume) is the continuation of this argument.[6] One might locate a connection between this attempt to theorize the taken for granted and the later turn to a Gramscian notion of common sense. Similarly, both Ellis and White, in their readings of poststructuralist/psychoanalytic theory, and in particular, the theories of Julia Kristeva, can also be seen in part as a response to the inadequacy of phenomenology as a social psychology (because of both its radical separation of individual consciousness from the social, and its denial of the unconscious). They argue that Kristeva provides a very different set of theoretical concepts and relations (including notions of subjectivity-in-process, the unconscious, and a more radically processual understanding of semiotic processes and systems) as the necessary condition for an appropriately complex and anti-reductionist theory of the relations among individual experience (consciousness, subjectivity), culture (semiotic, signifiance) and society (power).

I could go on but I hope it is clear that these – and other versions that appear in other essays – are variations on a theme, or better, on a problematic. In a sense, they all attempt to figure out the question at the heart of cultural studies: How do we inquire into the relations between culture and society? But in these efforts, one can see another discourse, another problematic. For each of these essays seems to engage particular theories with an eye to some notion of adequacy, of what would constitute an adequate theory for cultural studies (e.g., Sparks' critique of Lukacs' failure to recognize 'the complexity of real historical development').

The efforts to theorize this first – substantive – problematic culminated, I think, in the two bodies of work that came to 'represent' British cultural studies to much of the world in the 1970s and 1980s; subcultural studies and encoding-decoding.[7] Interestingly, and absolutely correctly, albeit I fear unintentionally, the work of the Centre was seen not in its strictly theoretical output, but in its contextually grounded empirical work, that embodied the Centre's sense of the necessary detour through theory. (See the last section of this volume and all of volume 2 for examples of this work.) In part motivated by an attempt to understand the role of, and give a place to, lived experience in its analysis, and to acknowledge, in the concrete analysis itself, the agency of the actor and the concrete possibilities of various forms of resistance in the face of the new structures of sociopolitical domination, these two bodies of work were the fruition of the attempt to theorize the relationship between consciousness and social being.[8]

While there are many different readings of the theoretical position of these works (in terms of the first problematic), there are in fact significant differences not only between the two bodies of work but also within each one as well (and the groups: subcultures and media) out of which they emerged. I will, given the exigencies of this introduction, limit myself to subcultural studies here since it was, in many ways, more central both to the future work of the Centre and its theoretical trajectory.[9] My own sense is that the very richness of subcultural theory, as developed in *Resistance through Ritual*, depends on the ambivalence of the position presented, caught as it were at the intersection of Marxist humanism (Williams and a certain reading of Gramsci) and structuralism (through the incorporation of certain crucial arguments and elements of an Althusserean Marxism, rooted also in Gramsci). Yet this ambivalence is also the beginning of an as yet under-theorized – this task would have to await the publication of *Policing the Crisis* – more radically conjuncturalist reading of Gramsci.

Yet even *Resistance through Ritual* was consciously trying to locate itself 'between' the reductionism of certain Marxisms (as a theory of guaranteed correspondence) and the radical rejection of determination or mediation in certain poststructuralist readings of Althusser (which produced a theory of the guaranteed absence of correspondence). This sense of the project defined by the second problematic was further developed in the full-blown model of conjuncturalism that was theorized and deployed in *Policing the Crisis*, which increasingly emphasized the concept of articulation and points, I believe, to the growing self-consciousness of the second problematic (of a radical contextualism as the way to realize anti-reductionism) and to the reformulation of the Centre's understanding of the project of cultural studies.

It is at this point in the history of the Centre that one can see, quite visibly, the effects of the second problematic, although I believe its influence and force had been there all along. This had an immediate and visible consequence on so-called subcultural theory. It emphasized the radically contextual nature of the work of cultural studies. Thus, it is not coincidental that the 'Introduction' to WPCS 6 attempted to locate the Centre's own questions and practices inside the very context of post-war Britain, out of which the Centre's specific research questions (e.g., the political significance of youth subcultures) arose. The introduction glosses it as follows: 'What seemed new in the late 'fifties and early 'sixties was the capacity of the ruling class to dominate and the inability of the working class to resist.' The unsigned introduction goes on to elaborate this situation by talking about the emerging power of the mass media, the resulting appearance of 'cultural domination as a special area of politics'; and 'the emergence of "cultural politics" as a distinctive movement.' And finally, it points to the 'failure of the revolutionary left to take even a minimal cognizance of the political implications of this context.' This was, of course, the period that Hoggart and others had described in part as 'Americanization.' It was also the period of the Cold War, of the beginning of the breakdown of older class-based politics, of the first stirrings of new forms of social movements including CND, the new left, feminism, the civil rights struggle in the US, and of Bandung and the anti-colonial wars of liberation.

In its research on changing relations of class and generation, the subcultures group attempted to concretize the context and capture something of the lived reality of the moment within their work, without defining the project in totally ethnographic terms. They not only attempted to understand subcultures as a response to the changing structural conditions and lived experiences of British youth; they attempted to articulate their own work in that very context. To put it simply, they refused to universalize either their theories or their analysis; and in this way, they gave expression to a second consequence of the second problematic: the demand for concrete complexity led them to critique other (and some of the Centre's own earlier theoretical) efforts as 'idealist,' that is, as embodying a notion of theory as universalizing abstraction.

This radically contextualist practice, linked to the second problematic as I have described it, is given its most explicit and elegant statement in Hall's 'A 'reading' of Marx's 1857 Introduction to the *Grundrisse*.' This piece, and the very explicit statements of the second problematic that it inaugurates, presents Hall's response to what he takes to be the idealist elements of Althusser's reading of Marx, and offers a highly original interpretation of the Marxist dialectic (an interpretation that Hall would ultimately connect to his reading of Gramsci as a radical anti-humanist and conjuncturalist theorist). Hall's essay is a sustained reflection on the Marxist dialectic (a notion which is present in the earliest reflections on theory at the Centre and which, to a certain extent, binds together the two problematics) through a very careful and detailed reading of Marx's text. Hall interprets the Marxist dialectic, contra Althusser, as a methodology rather than an abstract epistemology.[10]

The essay argues that Marx contrasts three models of relationality (or determination, with implications for how one theorizes the totality) in his Introduction: a simple or immediate identification; the mediation of mutual dependence; and the dialectics of 'inner connexion that passes through a distinct process . . . in the real world.' The first, Marx suggests, is an idealist practice of abstraction that moves from the particular to the general by seeking the points of stability and commonality; the second involves mere external juxtapositions. Only the third is truly dialectical, embracing complexity. A dialectical methodology constructs unities and totalities not by abstracting away all the differences and determinations, but precisely by seeing how the differences and determinations articulate a different kind of unity and totality, a complex totality, a differentiated unity.

Within a dialectical methodology, any point of analysis, whether located at the beginning or the end, has to be understood as the result of many determinations. Erasing those determinations, the complexities, does not reveal some hidden true unity, but rather denies the very reality that one is attempting to understand. Thus, Hall reads Marx's effort to think the dialectic as having profound theoretical and methodological resonance, demanding a practice of historical specificity that recognizes the complexity and multiplicity of determinations, without thereby giving up a notion of the structured totality of the conjuncture. Such a practice, Hall suggests, would be, necessarily, radically contextualist.

Johnson in his 'Three problematics' essay brings this argument to bear on the very practice of critique itself, arguing that criticizing a text simply through the identification of some presupposition such as an abstraction like idealism or essentialism is insufficient unless one can 'return to the surface of the text and show the effects of theoretical structures on the detailed treatment of events, the construction of narrative, the portrayal of relations, on the actual texture of the historical account.'

On the basis of this 'methodological' argument (which I am reading as a statement of the second, meta-theoretical problematic), Hall and others at the Centre began to criticize and reject the sociological (and Kantian) work that informed much of the early theorizing of the Centre (again, see Hall's 'Hinterlands' essay, Chapter 7). Such work had too quickly assumed too simple and too immediate a correspondence (homologies) among the domains (culture and society) and levels (measured as it were by degrees of concreteness and abstraction). Instead, cultural studies had to learn to live in a universe of differences and articulations, a world in which the relations are never guaranteed even as they are real. It had to learn to operate on and within conjunctures. This second problematic committed at least some people at the Centre to a radical practice of historical specificity. Its implicit critique of universalizing and abstract theorizing determined one dimension of the debate in the late 1970s and 1980s between the Gramscians at the Centre (particularly the subculturalists and others affiliated with the politics of popular culture) and the poststructuralists (such as Ellis and his partner, Ros Coward, who were indirectly aligned with the journal *Screen*). While the Gramscians at the Centre rightly accused the poststructuralist position of idealism, the poststructuralists somewhat correctly accused the subcultural position of a different kind of idealism, because their analysis continued to assume a universalizing humanism in which subjects had identities outside of discourse.[11]

My construction of a second problematic then points to this notion of a cultural studies methodology that seeks to go on theorizing in ways that avoid any sort of reductionism (that would explain some phenomenon in simple and singular terms) or essentialism (that would abstract some stable common core out of the diversity and complexity of historical realities). Importantly, this project arises not out of any pre-supposed universal epistemology or ontology but out of the political engagement with a material historical reality that defines, at yet another level, the project of cultural studies. Historical specificity is not an epistemology (which then leads to the dilemma of relativism) but the recognition of the need to historicize epistemology itself, that is, the willingness to embrace an 'historical epistemology.'

I believe that key figures at the Centre in the late 1970s and early 1980s articulated this second problematic through a reading of Gramsci's writings as 'geared primarily towards political perspectives and analyses rather than general epistemological principles.' In fact, regarding what I have called the first problematic, they quite explicitly 'make no claim that Gramsci offers us a rigorous theory of ideology, or indeed of anything else' (Hall *et al.* op. cit.)

Let me take a moment to elaborate some of the consequences and determinations of this problematic, emphasizing that it is a problematic and not a theory precisely because it is always a task to be accomplished, a methodology yet to be realized.[12] In fact, this dialectical methodology (eventually the dialectic is emphasized less in the Centre's work in favour of articulation and no guarantees) is itself a complicated, differentiated unity, a contingent articulation of a number of determining commitments and practices.

First, closely linked with its methodological and rigorous anti-reductionism and anti-essentialism is a deep and complex sense of materialism, juxtaposed in the first instance to the abstractness and universalizing tendencies of 'idealism.' But it also involves a real sense of the material conditions of social life, visible in Chambers' critique of structuralism:

> by putting between brackets, or simply failing to acknowledge, the material conditions of the practices they examine, and treating them and society solely as a sign system, structuralism and semiotics have remained caught in the very ideology they claim to have exposed.
>
> (Chambers, in this volume)

Secondly, this materialism goes even deeper, if it is possible to use such a metaphor, for it means that, as Rusher put it, 'the struggle against dominant theory . . . cannot remain, in form or language or impulse, "wholly within theory".' Materialism speaks to the very nature of theorizing itself, which can never remain entirely within the realm of the conceptual, for the task of theorizing is always about 'the grasping of real relations,' and therefore its practice always involves a movement through those relations and practices. Theory is a (necessary) detour in the effort to transform an inchoate (simultaneously simple, structured and chaotic) empirical reality into a conceptualized, complex understanding of 'the concrete.' Reality in all its material complexity is always there, at the beginning and the end, but also in the middle, during the concrete work of theorizing itself, as a (necessary) detour as it were as well. Theorizing is a necessary tool in the effort to work on and through, to transform, the material conditions and forces, the structures of social relations, the organizations of practices, of social life itself.

And finally, the second problematic articulates theory and practice, intellectual work and political work, together. Consider Slater's insightful reading of the Frankfurt School. Not surprisingly, he criticizes its too simple notion of a 'manipulative popular culture.' He criticizes its inability to understand the specificity of the link between consciousness and specific literary forms. But his more powerful critique deals with its failure to 'relate in any real way to . . . what it repeatedly stresses . . . as being the ultimate form of critical activity, namely: revolutionary proletarian praxis.' The Frankfurt School (or at least Horkheimer and Adorno), according to Slater, failed to offer 'any practical-critical theory on the socio-political level.' As a result, they placed all the weight on the radical possibilities of art, but those possibilities – of art's negation – remained ultimately passive.[13] One can also see this commitment to political realities in the important role that both Gilroy and Green, albeit in different ways, want to give to the necessary mediation of 'the actual institutional and organizational forms of struggle' (Gilroy) in the organization not only of social life, but also of the understanding of political possibilities.

This question of the relation of theory and practice, of intellectual work and politics, runs through all these essays. It often seems to drive them and there can be no doubt, as has often been acknowledged in discussions of the Centre, that they saw their research as an attempt to provide the conditions of possibility (as knowledge) that would enable real interventions into the political realities of their context. Again, on this basis, it is not surprising that the dominant and most visible group at the Centre 'arrives' at Gramsci, for whom the political is 'the crucial level of the social formation.'

As I have suggested, the two problematics can have a complicated set of relations to each other and to the theoretical project of cultural studies. The turn to conjuncturalism and the methodological commitments of historical specificity do not, by themselves, answer the first problematic: crudely put, the relation between culture and society or perhaps, more accurately now, the place and effectivity of cultural practices in particular conjunctures or contexts of social life. However, they do set new constraints and open up new possibilities for theorizing, in a specific conjuncture, a response to the contextually specific appearance or articulation of the (first) problematic. It is not coincidental that volume 10 of WPCS revisited the problems of both ideology and subjectivity. Whether considering ideology as the necessary misrepresentation or displacement of real relations (Marx), or as the systems of representation through which people live their relation to their real conditions of existence (Althusser), or as the cement that holds together the structure and the complex superstructure (Gramsci), or as common sense, the accumulation of popular knowledges and logics (Gramsci), the problem of ideology and representation continue to be theorized in these essays but always now within a more explicit context. It is also done without the reductionist assumption that ideology completely covers the domain of culture, or that language and ideology are necessarily equivalent. Rather, the very nature of culture, and the very effectiveness of ideology, can only be understood within the differentiated unity, the balance of forces, of the conjuncture. Similarly, Johnson encourages cultural studies scholars to differentiate among the various moments of cultural processes, including ideology, fantasy and entertainment.

Johnson presents a wonderful rereading, in broad strokes, of theories that have answered to the first problematic, through the lens of the second problematic. He distinguishes three variations of the first (culture and society) problematic. The first 'manifesto' variant simply identifies (through direct processes of causality) economic classes (proletariat as economic class) and political forces (proletariat as revolutionary class). It accomplishes this by assuming that particular common forms of consciousness are essentially linked to particular socio-economic positions. The second 'cultural' variant focuses on the 'actual forms of popular practices and beliefs' but at the same time collapses the very distinction between culture and society by rendering everything into experience, which becomes 'both the object and method of such analyses.' The third (structural) problematic takes up the problem of the complex unity but cannot sustain it, offering little in the way of methodological guidance and thus it commonly falls back into functionalism and relations of external juxtaposition (rather than internal articulation). It fails to understand the processes of social reproduction and change as always 'contested transformations' produced through necessarily contradictory and antagonistic processes. It fails, as it were, to understand theory as a detour through reality and thus fails to make the necessary movement into empirical research, which can call for 'fresh abstractions.'

Johnson proposes a different vision, one based again on a Gramscian reading of the second problematic, of how one might go about studying the relationship of culture and society, built on the need to distinguish between and differentiate within the various levels or instances of the social formation (the political, the economic and the cultural, etc.), on the one hand, and the various apparatuses, institutions or sites of social relations (e.g., schools, family, domestic life, work, etc.) on the other. These two different ways of modelling the social formation define at least two different forms of abstraction and theorizing, enabling Johnson to suggest the possibility of a theory that is capable of describing the complexity of the relations of the cultural and the non-cultural.

We can perhaps see some of the complexity that Johnson describes in the essays by Bland *et al.*, and by Gilroy. It is worth pointing out the obvious here: these essays address matters of gender and race respectively, matters which they clearly are attempting to bring onto the agenda, not only of cultural studies but of the left more broadly speaking. While it is true that in the early days of the Centre race and gender did not have a sufficient place on the Centre's agenda and that struggles to recognize their right of place were often difficult and emotionally charged, too often the fact that questions of gender and race were raised in the Centre earlier than assumed is overlooked.[14] It is also true, as I have tried to emphasize throughout these introductory comments, that these essays, and the claims I am making for them, reflect, in their very effort, a particular moment in the history of the Centre, a moment of both theoretical and political upheaval in the Centre, on the left, and in Britain. They also represent, as is true of the selection of the essays in this section in general, only a partial view of the diverse activities at the Centre and in the various working groups at this or any other moment.

Still, I want to suggest that both of these essays are exemplary instantiations, from different moments and formations, and to different degrees, of the impact of what I have called the articulation of two problematics, and of the turn, with differing degrees of explicitness, to conjuncturalism and historical specificity as a methodological/theoretical project. Both attempt to connect theoretical, empirical and political work. As Gilroy explicitly states, 'our premise is therefore the problem of relating "race" to class, not for sociological theory, but for socialist politics.'

Both essays historicize and contextualize theory and attempt to operate on the 'relations between shifting theoretical emphases and concrete political demands' (Bland *et al.*). In Bland *et al.*, the authors bring their analysis to bear upon what was, at the moment of its production, a recent piece of legislation, arguing for a reading of the law that recognizes it as a complex articulation of multiple determinations and contradictions. The essay approaches the question of women's domestic labour, crucial for the reproduction and sustenance of the labour force; they argue, perhaps surprisingly, that it cannot be considered 'productive labour' (a technical term in Marxist economic theory) precisely because it is always specific and therefore cannot be appropriately incorporated into the category of abstract labour. In fact, women's domestic labour 'cannot be understood without attention to the specific historical and ideological articulations of the sexual division of labour, in relation to particular forms of "the family" through which women's sexuality is organized . . .'. Understanding the specificity, then, of women's subordination requires that we 'attempt to hold, simultaneously, the family and the labour process, *within* an understanding of the contradictory developments of the capitalist accumulation process.'

The authors' demand that we see the concrete forms of the sexual division of labour as 'both the historical *outcome* and *site* of struggle' ties the problematic of the essay to that of Gilroy's essay, which similarly argues that 'the form in which labor power appears in social formations is not determined mechanistically by accumulation, but directly by political struggles.' Arguing against any reductionism, and against any abstract theory (ontology) of classes, Gilroy proposes that we recognize that classes are 'an effect of heterogeneous struggles perhaps premised on different communalities.' In the context of this contingency and indeterminacy, Gilroy offers us a radically contingent vision of race as well:

> It is precisely this meaninglessness [of the biological category of race] which persistently refers us to the construction, mobilization and pertinence of different forms of racist ideology and structuration in *specific historical circumstances*. We must examine the role of these ideologies in the complex articulation of classes in a social formation, and strive to discover the conditions of existence which permit the construction of 'black' people in politics, ideology and economic life. Thus there can be no general theory of 'race'. . . .
>
> (Gilroy, in this volume)

These essays exemplify a different vision of theory, and of how it is practised in cultural studies. They also make their understanding of theory inseparable from their effort, not merely to understand and intervene into a specific conjuncture, but from the ongoing effort to reconstitute the project of cultural studies in relation to the conjuncture and to the task of opening up possible futures (based on present interventions). Nevertheless, it is here that we can begin to understand the theoretical work of the Centre as inevitably articulated to the task of defining cultural studies as an ongoing project.

The necessary openness of the project has to be understood in the light of my effort, however artificial and forced it may seem, to define cultural studies at the intersection of two analytically distinct problematics, one defining culture as the preferred way into the context or conjuncture (and thereby posing all sorts of questions about the nature of culture, of power, etc.), the other defining the practice of a radically contextualist analysis. Each problematic guides, shapes, and even determines the other. At the very least, this means there is no single question that cultural studies asks in every context. The way in which the substantive problematic is actualized cannot be separated from the context in which it is posed; that is to say, the questions cultural studies asks are as much determined by the context in which it operates and to which it responds, as are the theoretical and political elements of its practice. Hence, what cultural studies will or should look like at any moment, in any context, cannot be determined outside of the effort to instantiate a cultural studies practice in the context. Cultural studies has to be both reflexive and self-reflective, and most importantly, it has to be ready to go on theorizing, even as it has to be willing, temporarily at least, to stop theorizing. To go on theorizing is to recognize the responsibility of theory, and the theorist, to a complex political and material reality that is constantly changing (rearticulating the old and the new). It is also to recognize that reality has no obligation to fit the demands of any particular theory. Theory is never, on its own terms and by itself, a sufficient and useful description of the world. In the contemporary universe of theoretical work, too often theory substitutes for the more complex work of conjunctural analysis, for the articulation of theory into historical specificity. This is at least in part the lesson that CCCS brought to the question of the place of theory in cultural studies.

Lawrence Grossberg is the Morris Davis Distinguished Professor of Communication Studies and Cultural Studies, Adjunct Professor of Anthropology, and the Director of the University Program in Cultural Studies, at the University of North Carolina at Chapel Hill. He is the co-editor of the international journal *Cultural Studies*. His books include *Bringing it all Back Home: Essays on Cultural Studies*, and *Dancing in Spite of Myself: Essays on Popular Culture* (both Duke University Press, 1997), *MediaMaking: Mass Media in a Popular Culture* (with Ellen Wartella, D. Charles Whitney and MacGregor Wise, Sage, 2005), *New Keywords: A Revised Vocabulary of Culture and Society* (With Tony Bennett and Meaghan Morris, Blackwells, 2005) and *Caught in the Crossfire: Kids, politics and America's future* (Paradigm, 2005).

Notes

1 Interestingly, an article by McLennan *et al.* on Althusser, published three years later in volume 10 of WPCS, failed even to mention Rusher's earlier effort.

2 One would have to write something about the trajectories of the various participants in these discussions. Some of them have remained active in cultural studies; others have adopted other versions of the project or other intellectual projects. Some have remained in the academy, others have left the academy but remain involved in ongoing intellectual production, and still others have moved into other areas of productive activity.

3 The obvious defensiveness in Ellis' essay has to be understood against the background of an ongoing debate at the Centre between the 'Gramscians' involved in the subcultures and media research groups, and the poststructuralists. See Coward (1977); Chambers *et al.* (1978); Adlam *et al.* (1977); and Hall *et al.* (1979).

4 This may be a way of rethinking Williams' distinction between the project and its formations. Or perhaps more accurately, it adds a third, mediating, term into the analysis. If the project always remains abstract, the formations must always be seen as the actualization of the particular, contextually specific articulation of the two problematics that constitute the project.

5 We should recognize, despite its reduction of culture to phenomenological experience, Shuttleworth's efforts to incorporate a sense not only of the complexity of public culture, but of the need to locate any singular expression in the wider cultural universe. Shuttleworth also gestured to a notion of consciousness that included both bodily experience and emotion, refusing the too common rationalism of much of the phenomenological literature at the time.

6 Additionally, structuralism was adopted as a way to oppose the mystifying intuitive practice of the literary criticism of F.R. Leavis and his followers, who were a major influence on early British cultural studies. As Chambers puts it, it was a 'methodology that breaks with systemic tyranny.' This can be understood in relation to cultural studies' (at least at the Centre) ambivalent relationship to literary criticism. After all, two of the three 'father-figures,' Williams and Hoggart, were deeply rooted in (Leavisite) literary studies, while the third, Thompson, was a historian. In a sense, Leavis was almost alone among British intellectuals in the post-war years in taking culture seriously (as a key element and a key indicator of the health of a society). While his approach was both elitist and untheorized, it pointed to a crisis in the humanities, out of which cultural studies emerged. See Hall (1990) and Anderson (1968).

7 Interestingly, none of this work is included in this theory section, although it most certainly could have been. Some of the relevant essays have been included in other sections of this and the second volume.

8 One must take care not to generalize the particular topographies of any one moment into a universal model of cultural studies. For example, the moment of so-called resistance theory was often characterized by a tension between a sociological and a textual analysis, but we should not assume this tension is constitutive of cultural studies, even at the Centre.

9 The encoding–decoding work, certainly one of the most influential interventions to come out of the Centre, is too often read outside of the larger project and productions of the media working group, and too often disarticulated from the particular problem to which it attempted to respond. The result was, too often, that the work was taken to establish an independent inquiry into

audiences and reception. For a more complicated and conjunctural understanding of this work, see the work of various Centre participants, including Charlotte Brunsdon, David Morley, Janice Winship, Dorothy Hobson, etc.

10 He also refuses to follow other theorists who would make it into an ontology! Hall also refuses to follow Althusser's efforts to expel all traces of Hegel from the dialectic. On the contrary, Hall holds on to Marx's appropriation of 'the rational kernel in Hegel's method.'

11 See Coward (1977); Chambers *et al.* (1978); Adlam *et al.* (1977) and Hall *et al.* (1979). Although continuing some of the same debates, the later debates, such as those between Hall and the editors of *Ideology and Consciousness*, were not quite so straightforward.

12 Much as Raymond Williams defined cultural studies as an impossible project: to study all of the relations among all of the elements in a whole way of life.

13 One should remember that only a limited part of the oeuvre of the Frankfurt School was available in English at the time Slater's essay was written.

14 One might point to the work of Trevor Millum, and to the later work of Ian Connell, as well as to some of Stuart Hall's earlier essays on race and racism in Britain.

References

Adlam, D., Henriques, J., Rose, N., Salfield, A., Venn, C. and Walkerdine, V. (1977) 'Psychology, ideology and the human subject', *Ideology and Consciousness* 1, 5–56.

Anderson, P. (1968) 'Components of the National Culture', *New Left Review* I/50, 3–57.

Chambers, I., Clarke, J., Connell, I., Curti, L., Hall, S. and Jefferson, T. (1978) 'Marxism and Culture: a reply to Rosalind Coward', *Screen* 18 (4), 109–19.

Coward, R. (1977) 'Class, Culture and the Social Formation', *Screen* 18 (1), 75–105.

Hall, S., Adlam, D., Henriques, J., Rose, N., Salfield, A., Venn, C. and Walkerdine, V. (1979) 'Debate: Psychology, Ideology and the Human Subject', *Ideology and Consciousness* 3, 113–27.

Hall, S. (1990) 'The Emergence of Cultural Studies and The Crisis of the Humanities', *October* 53, 11–23.

McLennan, G., Molina, V. and Peters, R. (1977) 'Althusser's theory of ideology', *Working Papers in Cultural Studies* 10, 77–105.

Centre Reports

Third Centre report: 1966–67.

3 People and culture

Alan Shuttleworth

A.S. has been Senior Research Associate at the Centre since 1968, and is the author of *Two Working Papers in Cultural Studies*. His present interest is in the culture of violence in modern society. The paper is an important attempt to define the field of Cultural Studies in a humanist context. Central to the argument is the contention that the culture of a people should always be studied from the point of view of its connection with their personal thoughts and experiences. The essay is followed by a response from Stuart Hall.

The meaning of 'culture'

It is well known that in the last hundred years the meaning of the word culture has been greatly extended. Culture in Matthew Arnold's sense – the best that has been thought and said (and the best that has been painted, sculpted and composed, we should add) – had a very restricted meaning: the word referred to the distinctively intellectual and artistic part of civilisation – the fine arts especially, the humanities, and also, perhaps, the broader, more philosophical aspects of science. Definitely not a part of culture were all the practical, technical, vocational and professional skills, crafts and knowledges. In complete contrast, in the modern anthropological (or sociological) sense of the word, we would be more inclined to say that learned gentlemen have their culture, certainly: but, equally, technicians have theirs. Every group in society, in other words, has a culture. Thus, we can speak of the culture of a whole society or else of the culture, or sub-culture, of a particular section of the society – working class culture, youth culture, and so on. In this modern sense (it is not to be found in the *OED*), culture means something like the way of life of a group in all its aspects, or else all the products of a group, all the thought, speech and writing, actions and artefacts produced by a group of people. From meaning the best that has been thought and said, the word has come to mean everything that is thought and said.

The extension of the meaning of culture has a complicated history, but part of the energy behind the widening has been democratic. The argument here is not that in matters of culture the majority is always right; it is, rather, that everyone always has some right. The core of the argument is that an intellectual and imaginative life is not confined to one group in society alone – those who have been specially gifted or who have been specially trained for it. On the contrary, all human beings have such a life and all social living is informed by the intellect and imagination of its members. There is not a thinking, creating minority and then an inert, mechanical, working mass. Instead, there are many ways of life, each with its own centre of thought, its own characteristic ideas and images, each producing distinctive expressions, products, activities and artefacts.

At one time, only a limited range of expressions – the best of the poetry, novels, drama, 'serious' music, ballet, and works of philosophy of a period – were thought to contain significant intellectual and artistic content. A group of interpretative studies – broadly speaking, the humanities – took those expressions as their field of study. It was an essential part of these disciplines to make qualitative judgements, to sort out the best. The rest, all other human expressions, were not thought worthy of study, were not thought to 'have enough in them' to make the effort of close and extensive inquiry worthwhile. We now shift our ground. We hold that all the thought, and all the speech and writing, actions and artefacts, of all people express interesting, worth knowing, inner life. The interpretative study (struggling into existence of all human expressions) is cultural studies. This inquiry does not only select 'good' expressions for close study: it aims to be able to study any expression. It is an interpretative study in that its main effort is to understand and then state what images and ideas, what values, what mental life those expressions embody.

Thoughts and expressions

We can put our starting position in slightly different terms. Any human activity, individual or collective, is always the product of ideas – at least, in part. A society, for instance, from the Birmingham University Motorbike Club to the Co-op to the nation state, is the embodiment or acting out or crystallisation of a set of beliefs and ideals. Men have ideas and then they act on them: that, in the simplest possible terms, is the story of human activity – at least, as I say, in part. That basic premise – we could call it idealism – inaugurates a whole field of studies: those which try to uncover the ideas behind the actions, to recover the thinking that has gone into making the public scenes that we regularly move among.

Ideas are found in two places: they are thought but not expressed, or they are expressed. On the one hand, a person may reveal his own ideas as little as possible. As far as he can, he may keep his ideas and ideals private, secret inside his own head. He may, for instance, be ashamed of what he thinks, or alarmed by it, or confused by it. That, as I say, may be extreme; but, certainly, no one reveals all his thought to all and sundry: most people are a bit wary about what they say in public. Thus, there are thoughts in people's heads which are not made public: we could call them personal thoughts. On the other hand, some ideas do get made public; they are expressed openly in some form. Some of these expressions are very perishable – talking, gesturing, *ex tempore* little dances, for instance. Other expressions achieve a relatively permanent public form – books, posters, graffiti, statues, gravestones, churches. Thus, ideas may exist as personal thoughts or they may be expressed and made public. The two sets of ideas do not generally coincide. On the one hand, what is commonly said does not straightforwardly reveal what people are really thinking – a lot goes on under the counter. Conversely, much of what people are thinking is not made available for others to share. Many people lead icelandic lives, shut in, unable to speak freely, numbed.

We began by saying that culture was all the products of a group, all the thought, speech and writing, actions and artefacts produced by a people. We are now separating the personal, unexpressed thoughts of a people from the speech and writing, actions and artefacts, that they have produced. We are separating personal thoughts and public expressions. The whole field of inquiries that we are envisaging, that we have called Cultural Studies, could thus be split from the start into two separate inquiries. On the one hand would be the study of personal thoughts. The aim of this study would be to describe, as far as possible, what people were thinking but were not, left to themselves, saying. Its basic method would be the extended interview. Recording how particular individuals see the world, getting down and making public the thoughts that would not otherwise be made known, that would be the sole end-in-itself of the work. Such a study, contrary to many misconceptions, would not, as I understand it, correspond with any branch of psychology as at present constituted. Contemporary psychology either refuses to study consciousness on the grounds that it does not exist or, if it does exist, is unstudiable; or else it studies the unconscious mind; or else it studies the structure, not the content, of consciousness. In any case, scientific psychology will not accept description as an end-in-itself, but insists that it is only with explanation and the study of causes that a science is instituted. Existential psychoanalysis does describe individual consciousness as part of its main effort; their work is very close to what I am proposing. Oddly enough, descriptive sociology quite frequently attempts the description of contemporary personal thoughts (whether of single individuals or of average or typical themes among individuals), but it is only a subsiduary part of sociology and is not wholeheartedly valued by the powerful, scientific movement in the discipline. We can, then, envisage a study aiming to report the thoughts of any individuals, whoever they may be. I cannot, I must confess, think of an appropriate name for such study – unless it were called Humanist Studies! What would be the aim of such inquiry? First of all, simple curiosity. We are, I think, intrinsically interested to a certain extent in how other people see the world, in what it is like to be in someone else's shoes and to look at things the way they do. If not intrinsic, this interest is certainly very widespread: witness the great popularity of biographies and memoirs, documentary TV programmes with this sort of focus, interviews, etc. But such studies, far from being encouraged academically, are dismissed as journalism. Second, such studies directly serve the moral end of treating other people as ends-in-themselves, with thoughts, feelings, beliefs, equal in importance to our own – our basic moral requirement. We cannot treat other people as equal to ourselves in this way by a decision of the will alone, however: it is only when the moral decision is accompanied by active curiosity that we may discover who other people are. It is only by carefully studying the thoughts of others – whether in a special inquiry or in the ordinary round of life – and it is a hard discipline in either case to do it sustainedly – that we can be at all responsive to them in our behaviour. We cannot act humanely without doing, formally or informally, humanist studies. (There are, of course, certain general rules of common decency which we can apply in any situation – but they do not take us far enough without this special effort to understand, begun afresh at each encounter.)

People, then, have their personal thoughts. But there is also a medium of ideas in between people, partially expressing and partially obscuring what they really think. If there is to be one kind of study of the otherwise unexpressed thoughts of individuals, there needs also to be a rather separate study of public expressions, of the ideas that do get expressed openly. We could try to detach the two studies from each other as far as possible and have them as altogether separate inquiries. If we did so, then it is this study of public expressions, I suppose, that should be called Cultural Studies. If we did seek to sever in this way the connections between the two sorts of inquiry we would have one study, Humanist Studies, which would deal only with the personal thoughts of individuals; a quite separate study, Cultural Studies, would deal only with public expressions. Some members of the Centre for Contemporary Cultural Studies favour such a programme of separation and Centre practice has by-and-large been confined to the study of the public medium of ideas. It is one of the main aims of this essay to argue against such a complete severance. I contend that, while personal thoughts do indeed differ from public expressions, while the two things must therefore be studied separately some of the time, the whole point of the study should be to look in the end at the relations between the two. We need, for instance, to be able to compare and contrast what is thought and experienced in a society with what is openly stated. We should study personal thoughts and public expressions separately for a time, in order to look finally at the connections and disconnections between them. I am arguing, that is, for an integrated study of people and culture.

A vast amount of theoretical writing in this century has pointed towards an empirical discipline for the study of culture somewhat separated from the study of individuals. It is now thirty years since Susanne Langer wrote of the new key to the understanding of man that had been discovered:

> . . . symbolism is the recognised key to mental life which is characteristically human and above the level of sheer animality. Symbol and meaning make man's world, far more than sensation; Miss Helen Keller, bereft of sight and hearing, or even a person like the late Laura Bridgman, with the single sense of touch, is capable of living in a wider and richer world than a dog or an ape with all his senses intact.[1]

Since that time the argument has gathered even greater force: it is only because we are born into a culture, into a world of symbols, of public meanings, that each of us develops the distinctively human capacity for thought. Since that book of Susanne Langer, the publication of the later work of Wittgenstein has added enormous force to the point. A new discipline for the empirical study of symbols, of culture, is clearly called for and, equally clearly, has not yet come into being. Such a new discipline would have a great mass of material to study, for there is no existing discipline whose primary aim is the study of the full range of expressions in the contemporary world and of the ideas that they express. We are surrounded by ideas all the time – on billboards, on the radio, in letters, in conversations, in interior decoration, in the fashion in clothes. Public ideas mediate all our relationships to each other: people can only get to know each other through the medium of expressions which exists in between them. But where are these public expressions studied? Sociology, sometimes, as a minor method, studies written documents. There are, of course, also mass media studies; but their attention is not usually strongly focused on the ideas expressed in the media. Some art criticism, some architectural criticism, a bit of linguistics, the odd article in *New Society* all touch on the area. But the great mass of public expressions – the cultural air in which we live and which we breathe – receive no study at all. We need, then, a study of public expressions. We also need a study of personal thoughts. Above all, we need a connected study of both, of people and culture.

A descriptive study

Before pressing on, there is a point that ought to be made, in parenthesis. At various times so far I have said that the aim of the study of ideas, in either of its two forms, is to describe ideas, or to report ideas, or to interpret them. These terms obviously require some clarification. First, I would argue, the study of people's ideas should aim to be descriptive, in the sense of not aiming to be explanatory in the scientific manner, not formulating laws of behaviour, not proving cause and effect. The primary interest of the student in this field should not be to seek to explain why people think or say the things they do, he will rather want to concentrate on describing what their thoughts and expressions actually are. That may seem to the reader an oddly limited ambition. Surely explanation is a much worthier end than description? I feel the need to emphasise the importance of 'mere' description because the merits and benefits of explanation in all fields of study are so often and so exclusively insisted upon that the very real merits of description become largely ignored. First of all, description is a necessary preliminary to any explanation. We can only explain what we have first described adequately. The bane of a great deal of social science and psychology is too great a passion for explanatory theories and too little respect for careful, empirical, real-life description. Second, valid explanations are, in any case, very hard to come by; they are not to be had simply by wishing. We cannot explain in any strict sense nine tenths of what people do around us all the time. If we cannot explain in a causal way why someone is doing what he is doing, we can always improve our description of what he is doing and what his accompanying thoughts and feelings are. Third, there is a powerful argument (which may well be true) that because men possess some free will we will never be able to explain their actions fully: we will always be left in the end describing but unable to explain. Fourth, suppose on the contrary we do not possess free will. The correct explanation of some piece of behaviour might turn out to be biological or chemical. We might discover conclusively, for instance, that some kinds of emotional disturbance are due to a specific chemical imbalance and that a drug therapy will cure them. Nevertheless, while we treat a patient as a body in this way, we should also go on treating him as a person at the same time. Even if his consciousness of the world is only epiphenomenal, even if his feelings and thoughts and fantasies are caused and not causing, it is still *his* consciousness. He may have an objective illness which should and can be cured, but he also lives that illness subjectively. He not only has a body which suffers illness, treatment and cure, he also inevitably tries by himself to make sense of what has been happening to him and to imagine what might happen next. And though it might turn out to be a diseased understanding, it is still *his* understanding. A humane response should respect both elements. A man is a product of factors and also a person who lives for himself there at the end of the causes. Given that we do have a primary curiosity about people, and given also that we have a moral duty to be curious about people, such description is worthwhile as an end in itself.

If our aim is to describe ideas, whether personal thoughts or public expressions, this may be done either by presentation or by interpretation. To begin with, there is the surface level of actual real world events and things. Of course, I am not using the phrase ‘actual real world events and things’ here in the way a behaviourist would. Thoughts and feelings are as real as words, or ink and paper – as I see it. By the phrase I mean such things as the actual thoughts of people in their own words; actual intact graffiti; real stuck-on-the-wall posters. One kind of study aims to discover such material and then present it as far as possible; tries to get as close as possible to putting the actuality down on the page – quoting interviews verbatim, for instance, pauses, ‘ums’ ‘ahs’ ‘you knows’ and all; printing reproductions of posters and collections of rugby songs. On the other hand, there is the deep level of interpretation, of summary, moving from the real world events to the underlying patterns, essences, themes, ideal types. The aim here is to get as compact as possible a statement of the basic ideas which underly the apparent surface variety of what is thought or expressed. The student, instead of quoting the words of the people he is studying, has to formulate their ideas in his own clearer terms. Both methods apply to both of the types of the study of ideas that I have defined: we can present and interpret personal thoughts and public expressions. Of course, pure presentation is not really possible: there must at least be some selection – that should be thoughtful and therefore is, in effect, interpretative. Similarly, unless interpretation is firmly anchored in real world phenomena, it has no point, it becomes mere unattached speculation. In fact, we should always use both methods, moving backwards and forwards between presentation and interpretation. Nevertheless, there is a clear difference between work which tends towards the presentative end of the scale and that which tends towards the interpretative. Both are valuable.

Personal thought

On the one hand, people's actions follow from their thoughts. People enact what they are thinking. Faced with someone whose behaviour seems strange to us, we only come to understand what he is doing by also understanding his thoughts and feelings, his view of the world, which urges him to act in that way. On the other hand, the relationship between thought, word and deed is only very rarely straightforward. More often, thought and expression are disconnected from each other to some extent. What people say and do in ordinary social situations does not, normally, clearly reveal what they are thinking. In turn, the things that people say and the things they do often do not neatly coincide with each other. It is because these gaps exist between thought and expression, word and deed, that there is a problem of understanding people, and that there is need of a special effort, a special discipline, of understanding. If everyone, left to themselves, already explained fully what they were doing, what they felt while they were doing it and what they were aiming at, and if we all listened while they were explaining it, there would be no need for a special study to try to uncover and make public their thoughts. The human world would already be clear enough. It is because there are disconnections between what people think and what they say and do, because personal thoughts and public expressions embody somewhat different ideas, that they must be studied, some of the time, separately.

The elements of consciousness

So far, I have used the word thought to mean everything that takes place in the consciousness of an individual, whether it is openly expressed or not. In this section I will take a closer look at the kinds of thing that go on in people's consciousness and it will become clear that the single word thought is too limiting. My argument will be that any moment of consciousness is always a fusion of four elements:

1 bodily experience
2 emotion
3 individual thought
4 cultural meanings within the individual mind

Any state of consciousness is always a fusion of all four elements. The sort of study of an individual that I am trying to outline sets out to describe what it is like to be in someone else's shoes – to describe, to take one instance, what it is like to be a skinhead on the day of a Cup tie. On such a day, as on all days, his consciousness will be a mixture of his bodily experience (the sights, smells, sounds and touches of the match), his aroused emotions, his own effort of thinking and the cultural images and ideas that he has in mind. It would be the aim of such a study of the Skinhead's day to describe – in so far as it could, and its attempt will always be very incomplete – all four dimensions of his consciousness through the day. (The question at once arises, how can we know what is in his mind, but is not expressed. Clearly, the task is very difficult. Clearly, it can only ever be done with very partial success. But, also clearly, there are ways of finding out some of what people are thinking, some of what they can smell and what preoccupies their gaze, some of what they are feeling. We can find out bits of what is on someone's mind – bits that they would not express if we were not there making a deliberate effort.)

Bodily experience

A man is a kind of animal. We are live bodies in a world of things. We are, for instance, mortal and prone to illness; we have many inborn characteristics; we have eyes, ears, nerves, glands, a brain. As live bodies we are described by biology. Our concern here is not that – we begin with the fact that we are live experiencing bodies. Through our senses, our nerves and our brain working together, we get an awareness of the outside world. We see, hear, touch, taste and smell the things all about us. We also sensorily experience our own limbs and some of our insides. We experience the world through our whole bodies. All our senses are continuously active when we are awake and conscious, registering and responding to the world about us. Any human action is always the action of such a whole experiencing body: in a fight, for instance, we are engaged, bodily quickened and alive in all our senses; we see and hear, we touch, smell and taste; we are balanced; we can feel all the time, without having to look and without having to think about it, where our arms, legs, fists, head and chest are and we move them thoughtlessly; we feel our tendons; we feel pain; we feel in our stomach, in the throat and in the mouth; we may feel we are suffocating; we feel our bladder distending. All these are not just bodily responses; they are bodily experiences. Much more than what I have described is going on in the body during a fight, but we are not aware of it, we do not experience it. Only what we are aware of, what we experience, concerns us here.

Emotion

Feeling is much more extensive than we generally realise or allow. A few of the stronger feelings have acquired names and have been greatly celebrated. As they are the ones we can most easily speak about, we tend to assume that these are all there are. Fear, love, hate, regret, despair, contentment – these and a few others are what we usually think of in connection with the term feeling. We tend to think that an expression of feeling would be an overpowering (and very embarrassing) statement of one of these – 'Oh, it is all too awful! I despair!' In reality, feelings consist of a continuum, a never-ending stream flowing through all our experience, with thousands of appearing and vanishing components. We notice the stronger feelings, because they have a name and because they have an apparent cause and because it may seem to us to be those feelings which impel us to action. We do not recognise much of the rest of the continuously present stream of feeling. Such nuances of feeling always accompany and colour sense impressions. Travelling home from a football match, as evening falls, through the varying areas of the city, some known and some unknown, we see many different kinds of houses, streets and buildings, and the light is gradually changing. We are not neutrally perceiving all this time. Responding to the sense impressions, seeming inseparable from them, will be subtle feelings, perhaps pleasant, perhaps unpleasant, and perhaps so weak and vague as to defy expression, but feelings nevertheless. These emotions do not impel us to action; they merely give a tone to all our experience. Feelings are made of vapour and are hard to describe, they are constantly shifting and often on the borderline of consciousness. But there is a distinct feeling leaving the football ground on a cold winter later afternoon amidst a solid crowd after a middling home win; another feeling when the crowd has begun to thin out and go in different directions, and you are back on the pavement, walking among the rather seedy factories surrounding the ground; another feeling arriving off the bus in the neon-lit, plastic and glass city centre, everyone now separated in ones or twos, other people going home after shopping, going to the pictures after a shopping outing or going out to the pictures, or whatever, making for their various private evenings; another feeling travelling on the train in the dark past the suburban back gardens, looking in at the tellies and arm-chairs and lounges; another feeling arriving back in the familiar, well-known side streets and then home. Feelings make a continuous and subtle commentary all the time on our bodily experience. The sensations by themselves are clear and definite, they could be described, given time, coldly and neutrally in great detail. But that is not the way we normally experience the world; such a description does not capture the way that sensations and feelings are thoroughly mixed. Our usual language for describing such feelings is very thin – lovely, nice, interesting, beautiful, pretty (or their hip equivalents). The tendency is to describe feelings as either pleasant or unpleasant and to let it go at that. At times, feelings startle us with their forcefulness; but normally they seem to disappear from our attention.

Thought

Through our senses we become aware of the world about us. This can be thought of as a wholly inactive, receiving of experience. Things in the world simply present themselves and are seen or heard or touched. Their impressions flood into us and we cannot control their entry. Through our senses we are made to experience the world as it is. This idea has much to commend it. We cannot by thought and will alone create a sensuous world different from the one that we do occupy. When we (or the skinhead) open our eyes, we cannot help seeing things and our sight is always much fuller and more detailed than any preconception about the scene that we had. At the same time, by our thought, we do also partly shape the world we see. Our minds are active in sensual experience, attending, neglecting, patterning, shaping, making some sense of it all. What is seen depends not only on what is there, but also on who is looking and what he is looking for. We look upon the world selectively, looking for the things that matter to us or interest us, and not noticing things that are not important. What we pay attention to, we shape. Thus, each of us may experience the same thing in different ways, from different aspects. We need (and it is very rare) a balanced view here: our sensuous experience of the world is always formed and shaped by our preoccupied, attending, interpreting mind, but experience is never wholly submissive and obedient, taken captive. Though we do generally see what we pretty well knew was there already, and pay no attention to at least nine tenths of what is around us, we still do sometimes see what we did not intend to, what we did not want to, what we had thought could never be there. We are sometimes overtaken by sights and feelings. Occasionally the senses and the emotions do take us beyond the mind's ability to understand – though never quite beyond the mind's effort to understand. We do not simply passively experience the world; nor do we dream it all up out of our heads. Instead, we do both at once: experience and interpreting ideas are always thoroughly intermixed.

Individual thought

The interpreting mind which works over all our experience is in turn, a compound of the individual effort at thought and culturally received ideas and images. The individual effort at thought can be shown in an illustration – it will be clear from this, I hope, that the effort involved is not always very great and the thought not always of a specially high quality. Consider a man sitting in a deck chair in his garden on a summer afternoon. He has been preoccupied with thinking about work, and then his chain of thought comes to an end and he notices the scent from a nearby rose bush. He lingers on the scent because it pleases him. Then his thoughts begin to work again and he remembers the effort he has put into planning and growing those roses over the years. He remembers the strain of moving big stones in the wheelbarrow. He feels a sense of achievement and self-satisfaction: he always wanted a garden of a certain sort and atmosphere and it seems, on afternoons like this, that he has got it and he can enjoy it now. He thinks to himself that he's a pretty contented man, all round. The day also means something to him because it is his wife's birthday – he has cut some roses for the occasion and they are now in a vase on the table in the lounge, which he can see by turning his head and looking through the window behind him. He sees his wife entering the room. She has just had flu and he watches her, anxiously, moving about, opening the sideboard, getting the tea things ready. The experience of that fictional man in a brief segment of his life is being continuously surrounded and framed by his thoughts. Now, clearly, I mean thoughts here in an extended sense – it includes hopes, memories, resolutions, concerns, judgements, decisions and the odd fantasy. There is no thought here in the logical, rational, objective, deductive sense. The mind wanders and ambles about. It is all thought penetrated by emotion. Perceptions arouse thoughts; thoughts evoke moods and emotions which colour the perception; feeling prompts resolution. The mind, it might be said, is merely drifting here, merely idling. Yet it is also doing its work: the man in the garden is forming out of these various odd bits and pieces a view of his life and its elements, an idea of himself and his condition. This is not the detached thought of science – the thought that a few people sometimes practise. It is the subjective thought that we all live by. In this kind of thought, ideas, judgements, moods, desires, and acts of will are thoroughly interwoven in the mind with sensuous experience, and there are many nuances, merging into each other.[2]

Cultural meanings in the mind

Much of the contents of the mind in such a situation do not derive just from the individual activity of thought and the unique individual biography. People's minds are also stuffed full with culturally derived images and ideas. These also frame the experience. A friend at the Centre commented on the illustration I have just offered and extended it in this direction. He writes, 'The scent of roses is of course natural: but the fact that a man has the scent growing in his garden, available to him there, is not "natural" and is not his unique idea either. There are many rose gardens. And the associations of roses derive even more from where he has been, what he has read and seen. The scent of the roses is natural, but the poignancy has been celebrated from Ronsard to Burns to Tamla Motown. His contact with and response to them will be part of his consciousness of the rose, the pure olfactory sensation.' Someone else then remarked that the scent of roses is, in any case, only ambiguously 'natural' these days; the rose as we know it is the product of several centuries of man deliberately working on nature, transforming the given rose into the cultivated rose. Both comments are true and emphasise how much of our 'personal' thought is second-hand; we repeat even in our secret day-dreams, the images and ideas with which we are supplied by others. It is inevitable that this should be so: we can only develop the capacity for individual thought because we are first given thoughts by others. And yet, our ideas are never completely the products of others; the experience of that man in his garden, and his thoughts, are not entirely a product of the rose manufacturers' advertising and publicity departments. Sensuous experience, individual thought and culturally derived images and ideas are always intimately mixed.

The aim in this kind of study is, as far as we can, to stand in other people's shoes, to think their thoughts, see the world with their eyes, discover what the world is like for them. An individual's world is always a compound of four elements – sensuous experience, feelings, individual thoughts and culturally derived images and ideas. I have tried to emphasise the interconnection of these parts of the mind: thought does not normally exist separate from feeling or feeling separate from experience; on the contrary, the four elements of the mind are constantly at work on each other and are not readily separable from their mutual relationships. I wish to resist a study of someone's ideas separate from their feelings, of their feelings separate from their experience, of their culturally received ideas apart from their individual effort of thought turned onto those received ideas. It would be the main task, in a study of the rose-grower of the kind that I am envisaging, to describe as much as it could of all this. (I do not suggest that such a study could transcribe more than a fraction of his inner world, and it could only do that with his sustained assistance.)

The degrees of consciousness

Experiences and thoughts and feelings are tangled together in the mind and any few minutes of consciousness always contains very complicated sequences and mixtures of moods, images, perceptions and thoughts. But a person's mind is not altogether a random muddle, for our thoughts have a certain dominance over the other elements in the mind. By thought we seek to order what would otherwise be an incoherent jumble and to make some steady sense of our experience. Our thought turns on our varied experience in the attempt to make an adequate map of plan of it. Our thought is turned in our experience and makes some sense of it, but yet we never reach a finalised, definitive mapping. Our experience is never completely made sense of – sorted, labelled and put into place – by our clarifying thought: there is always some incompleteness in our understanding of our experience of things. Within each man, thought turned on experience, and yet thought falling short of experience – that is what is being human. If thought fully mastered experience, then nothing would surprise us, our lives would unroll before us like an old movie we had seen many times before. If thought entirely failed in its effort to order, then we would be incessantly surprised: nothing could ever be expected, and nothing that arrived could ever be compared with what was already known. In the next few pages I will try to identify four distinct degrees to which thought may master experience. I call the four degrees:

1 common sense thought
2 articulate thought
3 flow of consciousness
4 power of the senses

Common sense thought

To begin with, the mind does not normally work in an exposed fashion as it shapes and forms sensuous experience. We normally make sense of the world in a routine, habitual way, without noticing what we are doing, without making a special effort at interpretation. Habitually, we sort things into place. We are not normally aware of our interpretations as interpretations; we are not aware that nine-tenths of our surroundings have gone by unnoticed; we think we are merely passively registering what is indisputably there. That is, we have many subjective interpretations which we do not notice are subjective; we have many beliefs which we do not regard as beliefs, but simply as obvious visible facts, common sense, what any reasonable sane man would recognise as such. This kind of interpretation, below the threshold of consciousness, has been called by Alfred Schutz 'common sense thought'. It can be uncovered and revealed (with difficulty, by peculiar methods) as a closely organised collection of beliefs, assumptions, rules and methods. The individual sees it as being, without question, true and shared by everyone normal. Everyday, practical concerns are especially dominated by this mode of thought: the individual gets the things done that he has to and readily makes sense of his ordinary day-to-day experiences. This is our normal mode of thought. We live most of our time immersed in practicalities.

Articulate thought

No one lives all his life as a thing of habit and routine. Sometimes, self-consciously and deliberately, we take thought about our situation. I call this kind of deliberate thought 'articulate' because I think it is always thought in words. It is what some writers call 'inner speech'. In such thinking we may be said to be talking to ourselves. In this way we form projects for the future, we think out our alternatives, we puzzle about a recurrent trait in our character, try to remember more examples of it, think about possible explanations. Such thinking is very conscious of ideals and of how the individual stands in relation to them. It is predominantly, though not entirely turned inwards; it is concerned to develop a theory about the individual's being in the world. At the same time, it is somewhat detached and self-conscious; some times it seems to be we who are thinking, at other times it is like a rather critical, ironic stanger watching us and criticising. This kind of thought could also be called subjective or autobiographical. It is not, I think, the province of the intellectual alone: it is part of the life of everyone.

Everyone makes up an interpretation of his own life, for himself: we all tell ourselves, on occasion, the story of our own life. It deals centrally with personal meanings, those beliefs, plans, ideals, ideas, remembered experiences, which the individual sees as central to the understanding of his own life. Because it is articulate, even if it is never openly communicated to anyone but is kept private and secret, it is nevertheless capable of being communicated.

The flow of consciousness

Everyone has moments when they are not doing anything in particular, when they are neither performing some routine task nor deliberately thinking. We may just day-dream, letting the mind wander. We often occupy a world of struggling, wandering thoughts, wandering into past and future and fantasy. This is, above all, that mental life in which ideas, moods, emotions, experiences, memories, desires are all interwoven. Our primary, sensuous experience of the world is not only constantly dominated and reduced to plan by our interpreting thoughts, it is also often surrounded and played with by a freer, speculating, imagining, remembering, meandering consciousness – mind not tied to immediate perception or practicality or too much sense. And it is here that the mind is, in some ways, most exposed in its peculiar, intimate play with the stuff of the senses. Somewhere near here, I think, we should locate the formation of our ideals. When strong feelings (and not external reality) are in the saddle and they ride our thoughts, then fantasies are generated – images of worlds dominated by single emotions: a perfectly secure, warm nourishing world: or an unendurably stagnant, fetid quagmire; or a world of incessant, tearing, raging, punishing violence. These fantastic images, perhaps, are the source of the real energy behind our ideals. They are formed by the free unrealistic play of the mind on emotions.

The power of the senses

I have been discussing the power of thought to define experience. Perhaps most of the time, the mind sorts experience into place in a routine programmed way. Sometimes, we deliberately strive to make sense of things by an effort of thought. On other occasions, our thoughts unpredictably and intricately wander and flow. In these ways, thought exercises its usual dominion in the mind. And yet the power of thought is incomplete; it is always short of full domination. We must beware, in a discussion such as this, of seeming to dissolve our sensuous experience entirely into our thoughts, of reducing experience to consciousness. Therefore, we must twist round here and insist on the force of our primary sense impressions. The present, as distinct from memory and fantasy, is precisely where consciousness is filled up, flooded by the senses. In contrast to what has been and what may yet be, only in the present is their real fullness of life. This is the sharp, present world, coloured and sounding and smelly sometimes insisting on itself against our preoccupations. We collide against it, we grasp it, it can hurt us. A dull drizzly day in Manchester is a cultural image, a comforting idea to hold in the mind and perhaps laugh about. It can also be a wet reality. This is the character of real experience. This is the character of the world that touches us, is opened to us in its limitlessness, when we are not wholly taken up with our routines, our day dreams or our serious thinking.

We may, then, find ourselves suddenly shaken in body by experiences that we cannot easily assimilate to our normal map of thought. I am unsure of my ground here, but I think that such unassimilated experiences press on us for definition. At least, they press on us for a time until we have become far enough removed to turn our back and walk away. I think that it is perhaps here that differences in talent, differences among kinds of developed intelligence, may be important. By effort, art and intelligence we may learn to encounter more exactly our unassimilated experiences and so attempt to describe them in their very rawness. In that way, we can sometimes communicate something of our primary experience. For example, a man describes the experience of being near to a stabbing:

> No, I know it wasn't Micky Davies. I was right there in that fight, all the time, I was never more than a yard or two away from him. And he didn't have a knife. If he had had a knife, I'd have known. I'll tell you this too. When you've got a knife and you've cut somebody, you know about it. It's like – well, I suppose to someone like you it'd be like when you stepped off the pavement. You know it's happened, you are tensed up, your heart's going bang. It's like that when you've cut someone. You know – and because you know, you know when other people have done it too, it shows, if you're experienced in that sort of thing. And I'll tell you straight: Davies was no boy for the knives, and if he'd just used one I would have known. And he hadn't. He was a bit puffed, and bit out of breath, because he's been doing what he said he'd been doing – having a punch-up. But he'd never been using a knife, I can tell you that, and I was there all the time with him and afterwards too.[3]

There, I suggest, the words are near to touching the experience. Through the words we can sense the moment itself. Alternatively, we may turn away from the effort to put experience into words, we may turn back from such moments to the routine as soon as possible. And so our thought may fail to seize possible grips on our real world, it may lose some of what control it has, become more detached and accustomed to its distance from us, of less real power.

I have been trying, in this whole part of the paper, to define the tasks of a descriptive study of individuals and their personal ideas. The aim is to be able to report the thoughts of other people, whoever they may be. We cannot understand the ideas of individuals in the way that we understand ideas in books of philosophy. Our personal thinking too much exists in its relation to our experience and is not readily detachable from it. There is not just a separate room in the mind, the study, where all the serious thinking is done in proper intellectual isolation. We should, that is, try to describe, not ideas in isolation, but ideas at work on experience. A varying, many-sided inner life is lived by everyone – skinhead, rose-grower and intellectual. (I have been accused of describing only a certain kind of fairly passive, day-dreaming, liberal intellectual, tending his roses, whereas most people live hard, even brutal, lives without the time for self-contemplation and fine smells. That seems to me untrue.) All the elements of consciousness, in their characteristic mixtures, in all men and women – that is the subject-matter for this kind of study.

The argument that I have been putting forward as to what is involved in the study of a person's thoughts has special point in relation to an important school of sociology. These sociologists stress the important part played by people's consciousness in the genesis of their actions. They invoke a person's inner thoughts as a part of the explanation of his outer actions. They stress, for instance, the 'subjective meaning' of the action to the actor, or his 'definition of the situation' or his 'opinions' or his 'attitudes'. It will, I think, be clear that this is the kind of sociology to which I owe most allegiance. My effort in this essay has been to insist on some of the complexities of the mental life referred to by those phrases. A person's definition of his situation is a complicated, many-layered thing. It follows that the proper method for this sort of study is something other than the standard questionnaire; there is more in our minds than can be declared in response to one or two direct questions.

How is it done?

It would take a great deal of space to discuss this question adequately and much more needs saying than I am about to say here. But two questions of method seem to insist on asking themselves at this stage in the argument. I will try to deal with these in a preliminary way and then press on. The problems begin when we recognise that we cannot take the lid off someone's mind and look at his thoughts and experiences and feelings inside, in the way that we can take the top off his head and get to work with probes and knives on the grey brains. We can only know thoughts through the medium of expressions: we can only come to know the inward life that individuals will reveal to us. Two problems of method follow from this recognition that we can never study thoughts directly, that we must always work with expressions, that we must always reconstruct the hidden thoughts from the revealed expressions.

First, are we not, after a long digression about a separate study of personal thoughts, now in fact arriving at the conclusion that that study is impossible? That we can only ever study public expressions? That we can only every study what people say, and what they think is, in consequence, forever hidden. I will be looking at this charge more fully in the next part of the essay, in the section on expressions. I can, however, say here in an interim way that we can and frequently do distinguish some expressions which explicitly aim to state a personal view of the world from others that do not. Some expressions aim to be anonymous and impersonal – income tax forms, mathematical papers, traffic signs, for instance – and we do not look to them to find our their authors' personal thoughts. Other expressions, many of which may never be published in any way, do clearly aim to reveal their authors' inner life – diaries, private letters, secret autobiographical writing are all instances. It is also the case that in extended interviews, people who would not otherwise reveal their personal thoughts may do so to a sympathetic inquirer. The study of personal thoughts is not, then, just equivalent to the study of the dominant public expressions.

Second: if we are relying in our studies on what people openly tell us, does that not mean that we can only ever get to know the level of articulate thought, because it is the only deliberate thought, the only thought a person is fully aware of, the only thought that is in words? Now, by definition, a man cannot 'frankly declare' his common sense thinking, for it is in such thinking that his experience is habitually placed into moulds of thought without his being aware of it. If he becomes aware of what he was hitherto taking for granted, it ceases to be common sense thought – it has become articulate. However, though he does not openly declare his routine assumptions, he may nevertheless reveal them in everything he does and says and makes – reveal them, that is, to someone who is himself sufficiently outside them to notice them. So, an acute observer who looks sustainedly between the lines for what is assumed, taken for granted, implied but never said, may be able to unfathom some of a man's common sense thinking. With articulate thought, such detective work is not necessary. Here we are dealing with the conscious, worked-out thought of people. We need sympathy and tact to discover it much more than forensic skill. We can only come to know someone's autobiographical thoughts if he will openly tell them to us. We can only study such thoughts with the subject's cooperation.

But what of the other depths of the mind? What of the meandering flow of consciousness, the continuous patterns of mood and feeling and what of sensuous experience? Are they not still, despite what has been said, hidden from us? There is, indeed, in the end, a limit here. We are entirely reliant on other people's power to put things into words. It thus becomes a matter of great importance for us that people vary in their power to describe experiences. In some people, articulate wordy thought will be relatively deteached from the rest of their consciousness, from their emotional and sensuous experience, from day dreams and fantasies. When such people explain themselves, they will tend to state opionions and beliefs and theories all the time and will not try to render in words much of the fullness or variety of their intricate inner life. If we want to know what it is like to be in someone else's skin, in the full sense that I have been trying to outline, we become straightaway heavily reliant on those individuals who succeed in putting more of their experience and consciousness into words (or pictures, or sound, of course).

So, if we wish to study people's individual inner lives we have to work with their expressions. There is no direct access to the mind. We will have to sort among expressions to uncover those which are aimed to express personal thought and we will have to encourage people to make new expressions especially for us. Furthermore, we will have to sort among those expressions to uncover the ones that most fully succeed in expressing a complicated mixture of thought and experience together. If we wish to know what it is like to be a skinhead on the day of a Cup tie, what he sees and hears and smells, what his altering feelings are, what he thinks and day-dreams, what cultural images rest in his mind, we are in the end dependent upon his telling us. Our main task is to listen.

Public culture

Because only some expressions – probably, only a few – clearly reveal genuinely personal thoughts, it follows that a study which confined itself in the way I have been proposing to the thoughts of individuals would leave the great mass of public expressions untouched. Since it is rare for an individual to declare at all fully what his varying thoughts and feelings are, much of the public culture of a society as a result embodies ideas which are not the genuinely personal ideas of the people who live in it. (Is that true in all societies? It is certainly true in this one.) We can take a strong but, I think, clear instance of this: the people who are intimately involved in a death, the dying person and the bereaved, are all unquestionably undergoing intense and varied experience; they are deeply feeling a number of contradictory emotions and are thinking deeply in an attempt to grasp hold of themselves. Yet little or nothing of all this may be said or openly expressed in any other way. On the contrary, the participants may try very hard to maintain a public silence over their loud private sounds. Meanwhile, they will fit in with the prescribed hospital routines and all the ordinary politenesses. Later they will follow the available routines of burial and the forms of mourning. Grief and mourning – the individual experience and the public expression – do not readily coincide. As a result, in an adequate inquiry into the culture of death in our society, there would need to be one study of the grief of individuals and then a separate study of the public expressions of mourning available to them. A truly human study, that is, will not be concerned just with the individual inner lives. Precisely because that is its main concern, it will also be concerned with this medium of expressions in between people. For these public expressions embody ideas and definitions and when we maintain our silence, they speak for us.

The public culture of a people is all the expressions used among them. It includes their temporary gestures and their enduring monuments. Expressions are the embodiments of ideas; they are the public form taken by ideas. In our extended, unremitting conversation with each other – a conversation in which we use many other forms than speech – we give and take and deposit (that is, we express) a description of the world, a public version of our experience in it, of our ideals for it. A study of the public culture should be especially interested in uncovering the ordered meanings, the sustained, frequently present meanings or the powerful meanings in the public conversation of a people. There is, surely, always some order within the publicly current descriptions of the world. For instance, if we were studying the public culture of death in this society, we would probably want to note the presence in our public conversation of two major, differing interpretations of the world, of life and of death: a religious interpretation and a scientific-medical interpretation. Such bodies of ideas are not only present among us when they are openly stated; they are also implicit in many of our practices. So that when individuals do maintain their silence through the experience of a death and burial – and which of us ever speaks quite freely? – it is the religious and medical routines which, above all, speak for us. We are, then, interested in the public ordered ideas.

But some order is not the same thing as totalitarian uniformity, and we should beware of adopting a method of study which systematically exaggerates the amount of public order that there is. There is not a fully coherent religious world view, uniformly present and powerful in our society; there are, rather, fragments of a religious view, variably present, only rarely of great power. The scientific-medical view is equally incomplete. 'There is not a creed which is not shaken, nor an accredited dogma which is not shown to be questionable, not a received tradition which does not threaten to dissolve.'[4] As a consequence, many of our expressions, being of some length and quite complex, do not simply state one idea: they may be somewhat ambiguous, they may equivocate, they may reveal a split between two or more opposing ideas. Thus, a typical conclusion of a study of the ideas embodied in our public culture might be that many of our expressions show that such-and-such a theme is present, but to varying extents, coexisting with opposing views, and with some twists.

The process of communication

We are, then, considering how a public culture, embodying the public ideas, stands in between people. All around this culture, making the expressions and receiving them, are the people, each with their own thoughts. And thus, though we are forced to separate for the sake of presentation a study of personal thoughts from a study of public culture, our real overall interest is not so much in personal thoughts alone, nor just in public expressions alone, but in their connections. That is, we are interested in the whole incomplete, partial process of the movement of thoughts through expressions from one person to another. We are really considering communication.

One important kind of interest in the study of the process of communication could be called 'genetic'. By this I mean an interest in how we come to be able to communicate with each other in the first place. Such an approach would be obliged to stress the inescapable inter-dependence of personal thoughts and public culture. On the one hand, it would emphasise that public culture has arisen only because of individuals' innate capacity to think, and as the sum of the expressions of their thoughts. On the other hand, it would also need to emphasise that we each of us only develop our capacity for personal thought because we are born into a surrounding culture. That is, seen in a long enough time perspective, personal thoughts are formed out of the public culture, and the public culture is formed out of the accumulation of the expressions of personal thoughts. My interest in the process of communication, in this essay, is different from that without in any way contradicting it. Granted that personal thoughts and public culture only develop together, in that interwined way, nevertheless, at any one point in time they do not coincide with each other. What a man thinks very rarely coincides fully with what he says at the time, or with what is said on his behalf nearby. The question that I am asking is not: How have the capacities for personal thought and public culture developed? The question being considered here is: What is the connection at this place and time between these people's inner worlds and the outer expressions that they move amongst?

Individuals can only communicate with each other through the intervening medium of expressions. The process of communication involves, on one side, people making partial expressions – they are partial because they do not say nearly all that the people are thinking. On the other side, it involves other people understanding these expressions – though, again, their understanding will probably always be incomplete. On the one hand, people express themselves to some extent. A public world of ideas is thereby created, available to all; it is a common world, common ground amidst different people. On the other hand, people encounter these expressions and partially understand them.

Individuals with their personal thoughts exist on both sides of the process of communication. So far, we have been mainly attending to the way people live with their thoughts before they express themselves and how, by and large, they only very incompletely express themselves. We are now emphasising that people also have to live with their thoughts after they have been talked to by others: they must now respond in their thoughts to the ideas they have encountered in public. We may think here of a hypothetical, completely social man who absorbed the public ideas fully. He has responded to them so well that they have become the thoughts which most intimately frame his own experience of the world; he would feel his own inner experience fully confirmed outside. This individual has entered the public ground and he has there been surrounded by the expressions of others; he has learnt from them the public ideas; he has identified with those ideas so thoroughly that he is shaped by them through and through and there is no part of his inner life that has not passively received their patterning touch; he has drawn the public ideas into himself and has made them entirely his meanings, and his meanings them. That straightforward, complete receiving of what we are publicly given happens to us all, partially. However, a totally socialised individual, one who always subjectively echoes every available public idea, is not possible. It is certainly not possible in our society if only for the reason that the public culture is clearly heterogeneous, containing many contradictions: no man can believe in all available points of view.

The process of communication is always incomplete, from both sides. A man only partially expresses himself and another man only partially takes his meaning in. In our reality, the situation is always that many things are being thought but not expressed; conversely, many things are being expressed that are not the real thoughts of anybody, and many of the things which are expressed are variously and incompletely understood and their receivers respond to them inwardly and do not say what they think.

As a result, we must study the public culture somewhat separately from the personal thoughts of individuals. Our real, overall interest is in the whole process of communication, in the movement from thought to expression and back to thought again: we are interested in the extent to which people make contact with each other. But precisely in order to study that whole process, we must study the available public expressions somewhat separately from the individual personal thoughts – because that is how the public culture exists in reality, somewhat separately, a third party. We need to be able to study all the three moments in the jerking movement from thought to expression to thought. Before we can reconstruct the whole process of communication, we need first to have described its separate parts. Accordingly, we proceed now to look more closely at this intervening public moment – the common ground of expressions between people.

The full range of expressions

We continue now in the effort to clarify this (at least partially separated) study of culture. I wish to establish what an overwhelming amount of culture there is in the world. The country is crammed full and the seams are bursting with the expressions of ideas. At the beginning of this essay I wrote (and it was not an idiosyncratic definition of my own) that culture means 'all the products of a group, all the thought, speech and writing, actions and artefacts produced by a group.' In the meantime, I have been proposing somewhat separated studies of personal thoughts and public expressions – separated for a time in order to bring them back into truer connection later. That is, I have been saying that we should take thoughts out of that list and put it on one side for the moment: we are then left with all the speech and writing, actions and artefacts of a people as their public culture. We are, it should be clear, defining the public culture here in a very wide sense. It is our argument that culture is not only what people write and paint or play on the violin: everything that people make and do is a public expression of ideas. Men and women have a kind of Midas touch: everything we deliberately handle and work over turns into an expression. We all make expressions and we are all surrounded by the expressions of others. Though we may all as individuals keep very quiet, we are surrounded by a thousand objects which speak for us. Cultural studies should be the study of the ideas in all public expressions.

This broad definition of culture is not idiosyncratic. For instance, writers in what Raymond Williams has called 'the culture and society tradition' strived to see all society as a culture, all social life as the enactment of ideas, ideals, images of the good and bad. In scattered writing throughout the nineteenth century, that view of social life was sustained in commentary upon the developing society – the effort was to see the new society, not as the enactment of necessity, economical or technical, but as the product of a choice of values. The men who were building factories were not simply engaged in producing more goods, they were also creating and imposing a limited idea of human needs and experience, an image of nature, a narrow thwarting view of life. The very buildings, the machines, the products, the imposed patterns of life in the factories, all expressed that idea. Whatever the entrepreneurs may have thought to themselves in their secret heart of hearts, these were the things that spoke for them in public. And whatever the personal inner life of the workers, this is what they had to listen to all day in public. Again, in this century, T. S. Eliot stressed the anthropological notion of culture – I will not quote his well known list. F. R. Leavis has had a wide notion of the meaning of culture; he has repeatedly spoken of a 'folk culture', alongside the literate culture, enacted in patterns of speech, crafts, manners of living. Richard Hoggart has studied 'working class culture', embodied in all areas of working class life. In *Uses of Literacy* he looked at such things as orally transmitted phrases and tags; at *Old Moore's Almanac*; at the *In Memoriam* columns of newspapers (you generally choose a message from the selection of printed cards available); the notices on library walls; men's Masonic type organisations; whist drives; and, inside the home, '. . . plastic gewgaws and teapots shaped like country cottages . . . lace paper d'oyleys, complicated lace half-curtains, crocheted table runners, fancy birthday and Christmas cards. . . .' and so on. More recently, the notion of a 'pop culture' or 'youth culture' has circulated widely: such a culture is partly enacted in pop songs, but also in clothes, hair styles, posture and gesture, patterns of speech, styles of relationship and organisations. We derive, I think, from such sources a firm sense of the range of expressions, the overwhelming multiplicity and diversity of the embodiments of ideas that surround us, constituting the atmosphere between us, both joining and separating us.

Recent writers on culture have stressed the contemporary importance of the mass media and it is, of course, quite right that the central place the mass media have in our society should be recognised. Nevertheless, that place can be over-stressed. Important as the mass media are in our lives, people live most of their lives in a world of speech, in buildings of many kinds, amidst traffic signs, notices, instructions, posters, in the live presence of other people who wear clothes and have hair styles, who gesture and talk. This is the primary world of expression. By comparison, we only live a fraction of our lives being addressed by the mass media. It is only by such an extension of our understanding of what our effective public communication is, that we are able to recognise what is perhaps the single most powerful mode of communication in our society. I am thinking, here, of all the expressions of mass administration, whether in words, business letters, duplicated matter, forms, IBM cards, orders, analyses and officialese. It is on communications of this type that all our large-scale organisations depend. It is probably the case in our society that more people communicate more things to more other people in this mode than in any other. These sorts of expressions, I suggest, constitute a very large part of our public culture. A study of the mass media on their own – while it is certainly valuable and it provides a point of entry into the whole field – ought not, I suggest, to be isolated for long from the study of all forms of expression.

Perhaps it will clarify this broad definition of culture, if we distinguish well-known or deliberate forms of expression from less well-known forms of expression. No one doubts, so no one needs to argue, that speaking, writing and blushing are all forms of expression. When we use language, for instance, we intend to express ourselves or to communicate something. Other expressions are not intentional in that way, but are nevertheless well-known. We don't generally intend to blush, for instance, but when we do blush we know that we have 'given ourselves away'. Drawing, painting, making music are also all unmistakably forms of expression. We can go on in this way a little but not much further, naming the forms of expression that are well-known by all their users to be forms of expression or communication and which serve no other clear purpose. However, there are other forms of expression which are not generally recognised to be such, which are often not meant to express ideas, but which are intended to serve other practical ends. On many occasions, when we are going about our business and not thinking of communicating, we are nevertheless unintentionally, unknowingly expressive. All human activity is shaped in its course by the thoughts, feelings and decisions of the actors. Therefore, everything that we make or do, individually and socially, gives some sense of what we have in mind. We communicate far more than we intend to. A woman's gestures, her lined face, her posture, her manners, her clothes, her accent and tone of voice, the type of her house and the way it is decorated inside, the garden, her hobbies, her job and the way she does it, all are expressions: they were not intended to express a state of mind, but they do. Everything that a people does embodies their distinctive public intellectual and imaginative life. The technical expert says of a new bridge that it is a more or less efficient way of getting a specified job done. No, says the student of culture, it is also a way of making a monument to a certain view of the world – and that, let us be clear, is not at all like saying that it is a pretty bridge or an ugly bridge: we are asking, what does the whole conception of the bridge signify? If the reader finds this notion of a bridge signifying something is a strange one, let him think of the various bridges over the Thames in London: all of them are, I trust, efficient – yet what contrasts!

The complexity of the public culture

In the discussion so far of the notion of 'public culture' I have been making two main points. (1) I have been trying to convey a sense of the range of expressions in this society, to indicate how massive and varied our public culture is. My point has been to suggest by the broad use of the term 'expression' that there is a great territory here, largely unexplored, full of things to be studied. (2) I have made it clear from the start that my interest in these expressions is in the ideas embodied in them. We can either present or interpret expressions. When we interpret them, we are seeking to lay bare their underlying ideas or themes or values or meanings. If those two points are taken, it will be clear that they inaugurate a whole new field of studies, for the full range of human expressions are nowhere studied today.

I have just defined the field of Cultural Studies in a very wide sense, yet it is not my intention to argue that all expressions are the same as each other, embodying ideas in the same way, all equivalently meaningful. On the contrary, I wish to emphasise the heterogeneity, the variety, the many-layeredness, the complexity of the public culture. Because there is such a great diversity of kinds of expressions in our society – a much greater diversity than in any hitherto existing society – it is possible for a great diversity of ideas to have expression, to achieve some public presence among us. There are, of course, the very powerful mass media. They have not replaced, but exist alongside, all the modes of face-to-face communication that have existed in all societies. In addition to these two basic modes of communication, there are many other new modes of communication, which are dependent on new technologies but which are not mass media. We have, for instance, the phone-call, the snap shot, the home movie, special blue movies and filthy pictures, the fishing club's duplicated monthly news sheet, the parish magazine, ham radio, the tape recording of the family sent to relatives in Australia as a Christmas present, Christmas cards, silk-screen posters advertising a local dance, shop fronts in neon lights, libraries full of books written all over the world in different centuries, prints for the wall from small editions to The Laughing

Cavalier, film societies, art cinemas, *Black Dwarf*, *The Buddhist Weekly*, photographic society exhibitions, underground tapes of Bob Dylan. I contend, then, that the expressions in circulation in our society are of very diverse kinds and the ideas that they express are also very diverse. If the mass media do dominate our communication with each other, it is not a simple domination. If our culture is one-dimensional, it is not a self-evident, straightforward, one-dimensionality. In other words, the order that does exist exists amidst a great variety.

Order does, however, exist amidst variety. If we do not live in a simple autocracy, we do not live in a simple democracy either. It is not the case amongst us that everybody feels free to use a great variety of forms to express whatever is happening inside them. If that were so, the distinction between personal thoughts and the public culture would be abolished. The nature of the limits on full, open communication become clear if we recognise the importance of two distinctions. First, expressions may be more or less public. Second, expressions may be more or less authentic.

First, we need to make more complex the notions of expressions being public. Once an idea is uttered, written down, painted, or in some other way expressed and published, it does not immediately become directly available to every member of the public. Not everything that is public is equally public. It is not all public in the same way. There are different kinds of publicness and there are degrees of publicness. Some ideas are more public than others.

Second, I am concerned with the notion of expression. When dealing with this term it is essential always to bear in mind the essential paradox involved in the movement from thought to expression. On the one hand, I have said that anything that reveals thoughts is an expression: on the other hand, I have said that expressions do not normally fully reveal thoughts. Expressions, I say, embody ideas: but they do not fully embody the ideas of their expressors. Or, to put the same paradox a third way, we can only understand another person's thoughts by means of his expressions: but, at the same time, understanding his expressions is something different from understanding his thoughts. We only resolve this paradox when we get to a distinction between the authentic part of expressions (that part which does reveal an individual's thought accurately) and the inauthentic part (which does not). If all expressions were authentic, there would be perfect communication and all our personal thoughts would be public. If all expressions were inauthentic, there would be no real communication at all and we would be altogether alien things to each other, no different from natural objects. In actuality, we live in between those two states, veering from time to time towards one pole and then back towards the other. The public culture is the mental air between ourselves and others. Sometimes, perhaps most often, that air is all fog: we can see nothing through it, only the thick obscuring medium itself. At other times, the air becomes clarified and we see, at varying distances from us, other people.

What we most need to avoid here are two contradictory over-simplifications. On the one hand, there is a very powerful sociological/anthropological/political spirit abroad which persuades us that the public realm is the only real one. Man is a political animal. We are thoroughly formed, inside and out, by the culture into which we are born. Our inner selves are either entirely products of the public culture, or else they are unstudiable in themselves, or else they are irrelevant or meandering and unstable. (A propos that last point, Max Weber, despite being the sociological theorist of subjective meaning, considered that people's inner thoughts were too changeable, self-contradictory and ambiguous ever to be properly studied: all we could study, in his view, were the thoughts that men acted on, for then you had proof that they believed in them.) According to this sort of perspective on man, all we can ever know, all we can study, all that is of real importance, is the public life of people. I think I recognise a good deal of truth in that whole intellectual atmosphere – it was the atmosphere my mind was reared in. But it is nevertheless the main aim of this whole paper to argue against what I think has become a characteristic over-emphasis of the view.

The sociological perspective on man is not the whole truth. Man is more than a political animal. Man is, surely, profoundly shaped by his surrounding culture. Yes, he can only be known by way of his public expressions. Nevertheless, people do also have inner, personal lives – a life of the senses, feelings, daydreams, half formed hopes. It is true that most individuals make very little of their inner worlds known to others, but it is possible, by study and effort, to expand the amount of individual thought and experience that is available in public. So, I wish to counteract what I see as a now characteristic sociological over-emphasis.

At the same time, there is an equal and opposite error. The personal may be seen as the only reality and the public world, the world of action, collective life may be dismissed altogether, without qualification, as entirely and uniformly inauthentic. If we follow this line of thought, we come to believe that it is only when we escape inwards, only when we turn entirely around inside ourselves away from others and the narrow public grooves to which they confine us that we become truly individual and alive. That kind of perspective, while it recognises the importance of inner experience, denies any reality to anything else. I am not proposing that view. I would argue that in our personal thoughts and experiences we cannot help being ourselves. We all, inwardly, have the distinct individual lives that we do have. The question is, do we manifest them? The question that a wholly sociological perspective or a wholly subjectivist perspective cannot answer is, what is the connection at this particular time and place between these people's inner lives and the expressions that they move amongst? The public world is not equally, uniformly inauthentic. The distinction between authentic and inauthentic expressions is a distinction between kinds of public life, kinds of public activity, possible social forms.

Kinds of expressions

I suggest, then, that we approach the study of the public culture with the following intentions. (1) We intend to study the full range of expressions. (2) Our aim is to uncover the ideas embodied in them. (3) We then want to establish how large a place in the public realm each of these expressions of ideas occupies. (4) We wish to establish to what extent each of these ideas corresponds to the real experience of anyone in this society. I am proposing those as the four main tasks of cultural studies. Within that framework, I will now proceed with some more distinctions between kinds of expressions in an attempt to further clarify the extent of the range of expressions and also to clarify the ideas of publicness and of authenticity.

Natural and conventional expressions

Natural expressions – such as going white with anger – are instinctual. They occur on the surface of the body and reveal some of our strong emotions. Natural expressions are universal among the species. Conventional expressions – speech and writing, for instance – are all those forms of expression that are not inborn but are acquired in society and they vary, accordingly, from society to society and from time to time. There are very few entirely natural expressions; even when we weep we usually, but not always, hold in our tears with many acquired restraints. The great bulk of human expressions are conventional. In a study of the public culture, we will nearly always be dealing with conventional expressions. However, many expressions which are predominantly conventional nevertheless contain some element of natural expressivity. When we are in the presence of someone and he is speaking to us, his face by its natural expressivity may unintentionally reveal a subtle, qualifying commentary on the expression that he is making in the conventional medium of words. Our interpretation of what he is clearly saying in words may be modified by what he is less clearly revealing, if we care to look for it, with his hands, his eyes, his face. (The reader should beware in the presence of these terms of the ancient confusion of the conventional with the inauthentic. A man's truest statement, *King Lear*, a traffic signal and a bare-faced lie are all conventional expressions. Some conventional expressions are authentic, others are inauthentic; or, perhaps it would be better to say, some are more authentic than others.)

Making unique expressions and exchanging public counters

Consider one of the examples I quoted from *The Uses of Literacy* – that of the *In Memoriam* columns of newspapers, where the individual must choose from among the limited selection of printed cards available at the office. Many conventional expressions are of that type – there is a very restricted set of complete expressions open to us and everyone alike must choose one of the set. This is true, for instance, of anything we buy in a shop – kinds of Christmas cards, kinds of teapot, kinds of motor car – we have to choose from the range displayed. 'I'm afraid that's all we've got in stock, dear!' Some expressions, however, we make for ourselves (whether we use shop bought materials or not). In this case, however poor our invention, there is an infinite range of expressions possible: no two hand-made expressions are exactly alike.

It is now clear that both of these tendencies are deeply built into language. On the one hand, language is so formed that there is no limit to the number of things that can be said in it. (All men could type for ever, not repeat themselves, and not write the works of Shakespeare.) Anyone who knows the language has the capacity to say an infinite number of new things; he has the capacity to make every sentence he uses different from any sentence ever used before. On the other hand, there is a tendency for language to congeal, to become standardised into fixed forms or idioms, so that the individual always uses ready-made sentences for ready-made occasions. 'How are you?' 'Very well, and you?' 'Not too bad.' 'A bit windy, isn't it?' 'Milder than yesterday, though.' Everything has been said before, many times. Language here becomes like the cards in the newspaper office. A great deal of our actual language, spoken and written, consists of fixed routine bits responding in a fixed way to other people's fixed routine bits. At the same time, having acquired this capacity from our society, we also in the same breath acquire the other capacity, to say entirely new things. From a limited stock of public goods, it is nevertheless possible to construct an infinite number of unique new things. What we are given in the speech of others may be mainly inauthentic; but in being given the power of speech by them, we are also given the power to go beyond anything that has been said already. Thus, we all of us, as possessors of language if not in other ways, have some capacity to state a definition of ourselves as ourselves, to go beyond how our world is being labelled by other people and to insist on ourselves, on our own definition of our own experience, in public. Given that power, we may nevertheless settle, in public, for the stock fashions to dress ourselves in, straight off the peg. We may then become used to a state of living where the words we use never really grip our own individual experience, and so can never hold out to others.

Individual expressions and collective expressions

Some expressions are the work of individuals, however socially influenced they may be, acting on their own: for example, speech, informal writing, gesture, doing your own garden, do-it-yourself interior decoration. Other expressions are the joint interactive work of many people: income-tax forms, the Bull Ring in Birmingham, most movies, political demonstrations, the Royal and Antediluvian Order of Buffaloes. (This distinction should not be confused with the previous one: collective expressions may be every bit as unique as individual expressions. There is a common opposition between individual, unique, natural, personal expressions and collective, conventional, stock, public expressions: it is that simple opposition that I am trying to break down here into various parts. All the distinctions that I am now making are amongst expressions – that is, amongst things in the public realm. Individual and collective expressions, unique and routine expressions, natural and conventional expressions, authentic and inauthentic expressions are all forms of public activity. They are all different ways of being in public.) Collective expressions are influenced in their course by many people – I am not thinking of expressions where one creator uses other people purely as a means to obey his commands absolutely. Of course, some people always exercise a bigger influence than others; very few collective expressions are more than a little democratic. But the essential point is that collective expressions do not express the thoughts of any individual in particular; they express the ideas that have happened between people on some occasion.

Fleeting local expressions, the mass media and artefacts

One kind of expression – such as gesture, speech, dancing, action – can only exist in the present moment in the immediate presence of the expressor. Other kinds of expression may reach a larger, more distant audience. Some expressions, that is, are more public, available to more people, than others. Basically, this extension beyond the immediate presence may be done in two ways.

First, in modern times, new techniques have made possible the mass communication of expressions to millions of people in a very short period of time. There may be an audience of hundreds of millions for an expression in the very instant of its delivery! At the same time, a great many of the products of the mass media are very perishable; they do not survive beyond the instant of expression.

Second, other kinds of expression – writing, painting, sculpting, building – result in more-or-less enduring end-products, or artefacts. Once produced, such expressions do not quickly disappear again: they stay, recalcitrant, not to be wished away, perhaps long after the original thoughts and feelings which they expressed have disappeared. Inside his mind, an individual may wander at will: he may hope, wish or remember a multitude of constantly changing things; he can dream of different societies and imagine himself in all sorts of fantastic situations; tomorrow he may think something entirely different from what he thought today. Many of his expressions are just as quickly passing, and therefore changeable: I can take back today a good deal of what I said yesterday. But the objects that people make are much more resistant. Buildings remain, only to be changed with much effort, long after their architects are dead. We are surrounded by expressions that no one any longer means, but which still embody their original meanings. Who now thinks like John Donne? Yet, thankfully, the poems and sermons survive. Who now thinks like the makers of Stonehenge? Yet every one in the country over infancy must have encountered the image, or a reproduction of the image, that they formed. Who now thinks, even, like the designer of the Albert Hall or the rest of our Victorian public buildings? That is, who would now express themselves in that way? And which of us could do so, even if they would? Or, again, many things which are only thought by a few of the people some of the time may be given a massive, monumental enduring form among us all. Does anybody really think the things that the Shell building expresses? And how many think like the Hayward gallery next door? Conversely, much is now thought and experienced by many people that isn't expressed at all. And much that is expressed isn't given a permanent or enduring form. The experience of the time, the thought of a time, the expressions of a time and the artefacts (the monuments) of a time stand in complex relations to each other. There are degrees of publicness. There is not just one public place to which we all bring our thoughts to be made known for ever. There are many public places of varying sizes. What is said in one place may never be said in another.

Situated and unsituated expressions

Some expressions are responses to particular situations; they refer to some actual event and are meant to cope with it in some way; they are not intended to enter general circulation. Other expressions are not tied to local contexts in that sense, but are meant to be widely applicable, available for common use, truly public property. To illustrate the point of this distinction, we can take the example of suicide. To begin with, there obviously are generally circulating ideas about suicide in our society: for instance, there are probably, across the whole length and breadth of the country, a hundred abstract moral arguments a day about whether suicide is ever justified. There are certain words and phrases which crop up again and again in such arguments and in all public references to suicide – 'despair', 'unhappiness', 'life is not worthwhile', 'escape from harsh realities', and so on. In such phrases we see the core of a public idea about suicide. When we are detached, not inside a suicidal situation, we feel that because we have these phrases we know the meaning of suicide; we have a vague image of the event, a rough idea of its main theme.[5] It is not very difficult to apply the vague, abstract language to unreal (not necessarily fictional; unreal to us, distanced) situations. In a newspaper book review, recently I read this sentence (it was all that was said on the matter) about the companion of a famous writer: 'She shared his life for sixteen years, killed herself in despair soon after his death'. We read it, the event makes sense to us, it fits into a pattern, we feel we have understood it, 'how awful life is' we say to ourselves: we pass on. It is, however, very difficult to apply this vague, abstract common language of suicide to actual encounters with suicide. The meaning of particular suicides to those closely involved is not given to them by the public, communicated culture. Because of the inadequacy, the incompleteness, of the general public meanings, those involved experience a loss of meaning, a failure of events to make sense, an inability to come to terms with what is happening. The effort to make sense is, in part, a personal, perhaps private one: the individual must come to some terms with the event himself.

That individual work I have dealt with already. But there is also a *social* effort to understand and that is my main concern here: those who are closely involved, however secretive they may be, must reveal something of their response, they must express themselves in some way. Moreover, the participants must come to some terms with the situation that now faces them as a group. So, those closely involved exchange meanings with each other, however covertly, and by this conversation construct a social, *situated* meaning – the meaning that works among them.

Personal and impersonal expressions

There is an important distinction, often made, between those signs, speeches, writings and drawings which are *expressive* and those which are *objective*. (This distinction, in turn, readily gives way to some of our favourite cultural stereotypes: *emotional, subjective, adolescent, neurotic, feminine* versus *informative, scientific, logical, impersonal, masculine*.) Such a stark opposition between the two modes is, however, unhelpful. We will be misled unless we recognise that the purely expressive and the purely objective are the two end points on a scale that has many intermediate points. A fuller version of the scale would begin by including some of the following types.

There are moments when the primary human emotions (anger, grief, sexual passion . . .) seem to break through to the surface almost unchecked, no longer filtered through the restraints and channellings of the mind. At such moments we lose control. We break down and sob uncontrollably. Or we go white with rage and strike with whatever comes to hand. At such moments we are nearest to being purely *expressive*. We come closest to behaving naturally, pre-culturally.

We are not normally so overwhelmed by major emotions. Rather, all our sensory experience, our thoughts, memories and images, are toned by subtle feelings. This emotional texturing of life, changing and changing from mood to mood, cannot be released by a cry. It can only be expressed by being described. We attempt to *describe our feelings*. That description cannot be completed by sheer, brave self-revelation – though that helps. It requires also a capacity for subtlety, for care and power, in the use of words to match the subtlety of the feelings. Here we are engaged in the very difficult and rare effort to be objective (that is, honest, precise, descriptive) in the public expression of our personal experience.

There is a different kind of mixture of objectivity and feelings. We may set out to describe some situation outside ourselves and yet (intentionally or unintentionally, clearly or unacknowledged) our emotions may flow into the description. We use colourful language and imagery. This is *emotive description*.

Outside the sciences, the effort to erase the individual voice, to rule out all expression of feeling and value, is very common in our civilisation. We are encouraged to adopt the *impersonal voice*. This is the voice of bureaucracy, in particular. It is also the voice of scientism – the attempt to carry the language and stance of science beyond the proper sphere of science into our subjective lives, our acting lives. Value judgements are made but are not stated in an openly evaluative, expressive form: they are stated as the impersonal judgement of an 'exhaustive technical reappraisal'. In *scientific* writing, all that results from individuality and emotionality is systematically erased: not in order to disguise the covert presence of these things, but in order to attain a genuinely impersonal position – the objective truth.

All the points along this scale are expressions, in the sense in which I have been using that term throughout this paper. However, the purely expressive and the purely scientific are on the very margins of the proper concerns of cultural studies. A primary emotion releasing itself from us by its own force, would be pre-cultural: it would still be in the realm of nature. A purely objective truth would be post-cultural: man would have transcended his local or individual, subjective visions and would be returned again to nature, this time reflectively. In the meantime, it is how we express our distinctive subjectivities, and how our activities in the world constantly declare or reveal or partially conceal our subjectivities, that is the central concern of cultural studies.

Conclusion

I am proposing that the basic task of Cultural Studies should be to uncover the ideas embodied in all the various kinds of expression in our society. Of course, expressions do not just state one idea; they are often ambiguous, equivocating between several varying ideas. As a consequence, interpretations will most often be of the form that such-and-such an idea was present in this expression, but waveringly so, in tension with other opposing views. Having done that, we would next proceed, by using categories of the sort that I have just been proposing, to place this expression of an idea within a complexified notion of the public realm. As we did that, we would be moving beyond the study and interpretation of one isolated expression; we would be placing that expression within the context of the extended, unremitting conversation of expressions among people that is the public realm. We would now be dealing with a number of different expressions, comparing the various ideas embodied in them, assessing the differing presence and permanence they had among the public. Finally, we would look at the extent to which each of these ideas correspond to the real experience and thoughts of anyone in this society. We would, that is, assess the authenticity of these ideas. But this, it should be clear, could only be done by comparing these public expressions with the personal thoughts of the people involved. It is at this point that the two, so far separated, studies of people and culture intersect. That is, we return to the study of the whole process of people communicating with each other. Thought to expression to thought is the circle of culture. It is this full, incomplete, partly succeeding and partly failing, movement of thoughts through expressions from one person to another that I am proposing as a focus study. For the sake of presentation, I had to separate the study of personal thoughts from the study of public culture. In actual study, also, they will have to be undertaken separately a good deal of the time. But as a final aim, I suggest, what is wanted is an interlocked study of people and their culture, of people in a very incomplete way speaking to each other.

I will finish off by offering an illustration of what this might mean. Take the case of Western films on television. If we studied them we might be interested in their treatment of violence. Our question would then be: What idea of violence, or what conflict between ideas, do these films portray? But the culture of violence in our society extends far beyond television films and it exists in very many modes. We get a very inadequate idea of the whole culture of violence if we look at TV alone. That whole culture also includes horror films, contemporary cinema Westerns, sado-masochistic pornography, *War and Peace*, editorials in *The Times*, letters to *Any Answers*, pulpit pronouncements of many varieties, judges' summings up, Probation Officers' reports, rugby club male cameraderie, skinhead folklore – the list could go on a long way, but the idea is clear enough already that very different ideas of violence circulate in many different channels in this society. There is, however, some order among this variety: some expressions about violence are more public than others. We would, then, get a clearer picture of the significance of the idea of violence carried by TV Westerns if we saw them in the context of the whole variegated culture of violence in this society. We would, in other words, be putting the voice of the TV Western in its proper place in our extended, continual conversation with each other about violence. But finally, I suggest, our interest in this diverse culture is that people live in the midst of it. This culture is us talking to each other! In the end, then, it seems to me, our interest should return to include the people living in the culture, to their actual varied experience of violence and their thoughts, at many levels, about it. That is the context in which we should locate the culture of violence when we undertake the study of the whole process of people communicating with each other. With this approach, then, the question that we would end up offering an answer to about violence on television would not be: What is its effect? The question that such a study as I have proposed would end up trying to answer would be: To what extent in these programmes are these people succeeding in talking to each other about what they really think and feel, their real experience, of violence?

Notes

1 Susanne K. Langer, *Philosophy in a New Key* (Mentor Books) p. 34.
2 This illustration is not really mine. I found the man contemplating roses in Peter Rickman's introduction to his translations from Dilthey – H. P. Rickman, *Meaning in History* (Allen and Unwin, 1961) pp. 30 and 31. In the succeeding versions of this essay I have steadily altered the man to fit my argument more exactly. Though he is still recognisably Rickman's man, I have played about with him a bit. I would have made up a different example, but other people had begun to offer comments on this one and it seemed better to keep it. In other ways, too, I am indebted to Rickman's book.
3 Tony Parker, *The Plough Boy* (Arrow Books 1969) p. 232.
4 Matthew Arnold, 'The Study of Poetry', *Essays in Criticism*, vol. 2
5 I am drawing here on Jack D. Douglas *The Social Meanings of Suicide* (Princeton University Press, 1967).

A Note on Sources

I think it may help the reader to follow my argument and to place it if I sketch here what I see as the main strands of thought that I have tried to weave together in this essay. First of all, this essay has been written in the course of an extended, still continuing debate at this Centre about what we should be trying to do here. The Centre is, in my experience, rare among academic institutions in the emphasis it gives to debate about its own first principles. I could not have written such an essay as this without the continuous debate here over a number of years. Moreover, many members of the Centre gave a lot of time to the discussion and criticism of an early draft of this essay. In a number of ways, then, I am very dependent on my colleagues here and I am grateful to them, though they will undoubtedly disagree with much that I am saying.

I was awakened to the existence of such a field of study by reading, as a student, Richard Hoggart's *Uses of Literacy* (Chatto and Windus, 1957) and Raymond Williams' *Culture and Society* (Chatto and Windus, 1958) and *The Long Revolution* (Chatto and Windus, 1961). I first read these books round about 1960 when I belonged to the New Left as was and so the issues of *Universities and Left Review* and the early issues of *New Left Review* and Edward Thompson's *Making of the English Working Class* (Gollancz, 1963) were also very potent, connected influences. Following on from Raymond Williams' book I came to read some of the culture and society tradition and Coleridge in particular. The work now being done, in a sort of continuation of that tradition, on the problems of teaching English literature, especially poetry, in schools seems to me to be of great interest. David Holbrook's *English for Maturity* (Cambridge University Press, 1961) and *English for the Rejected* (Cambridge University Press, 1964) are both very good of this kind; so is James Britton's *Language and Learning* (Allen Lane, The Penguin Press, 1970).

At the time I was reading these books, I was also trying to become a sociologist and I have been influenced a great deal by the two grand masters of sociology, Max Weber and Emil Durkheim. If the reader is not familiar with their work, I think he will find their greatest books, Weber's *The Protestant Ethic and the Spirit of Capitalism* (Allen and Unwin, 1930) and Durkheim's *Elementary Forms of Religious Life* (Allen and Unwin, 1915) very illuminating and in many ways complementary to the insights of the English tradition I have mentioned above. I am also a great admirer of Weber's predecessor Wilhelm Dilthey. I don't read German and little of Dilthey's work has been translated into English, but there is an excellent little collection of extracts called *Pattern & Meaning in History* (Allen and Unwin, 1961) translated and edited by H. P. Rickman. There is also a book by Rickman, reworking some of these ideas, called *Understanding and the Human Studies* (Heinemann, 1967) though the second half collapses too much into orthodox divisions of the disciplines for my liking. I have also been influenced by a different sociological school, the symbolic interactionist school founded by G. H. Mead. Howard Becker's *The*

Outsiders (Glencoe Free Press, 1963) offers a good introduction to this work. I have also been very influenced by a brand of anthropology, that which is perhaps best represented by Professor Evans-Pritchard and his books *Withcraft, Oracles and Magic among the Azande* (Oxford University Press, 1937) and *The Nuer* (Oxford University Press, 1940). I became very dissatisfied with a purely sociological approach. This dissatisfaction was crystallised by existentialist writers, especially Sartre's *Being and Nothingness* (Methuen, 1969). My interest in the study of people's emotional life was stimulated by Melanie Klein – see, for instance, *Love, Hate and Reparation* (London, 1953). My thinking about what a descriptive study of the thoughts and experiences of particular individuals would be like has been much stimulated by the books of Tony Parker, such as *The Courage of his Convictions* (Hutchinson, 1962) and *The Plough Boy* (Hutchinson, 1965). John Berger's *The Fortunate Man* (Penguin Books, 1969) could also be taken as an instance of the sort of humanist study of individuals that I have tried to define in this essay.

4 A response to 'People and culture'

Stuart Hall

'People and culture' is an impressive paper, above all, for the consistency of its tone and approach. I assent to many of its original formulations. But I radically dissent from what I take to be its central thrust. This is difficult to pinpoint, since the paper is so comprehensive. I believe, however, that within the fat and rounded argument, there is a smaller argument struggling to get out. My aim is to disentangle – and quarrel with – some central propositions which flow directly from the theoretical heart of the paper. My comments are therefore less than fair to the paper as a whole. The central area of disagreement must be formulated in general terms first.

The paper takes up a position within the 'break' with positivistic types of explanation in the human studies, and makes a decisive stand on the question of meaning and intentional action. I strongly agree with this point of departure. However, the argument seems now to have gone clean through to the other side. 'People and culture' adopts a phenomenological position so radical that for two-thirds of it, virtually everything is bracketed which cannot be directly referred to individual consciousness. Ideas have not only been restored to a prominent place in the scheme of things – they seem altogether to have vanquished the notion of activity, of *praxis*, or of relationship. Individual subjectivity is reaffirmed, but at the expense of any distinctive notion of *the social*.

I do not believe that the idea of culture can be properly conceptualized from this position. The 'methodological individualism' of the paper recreates all the problems of the positivistic approach *in reverse*. The paper has abandoned the struggle to clarify those issues which form the core problematic of cultural studies: the relationship of subject and object; of culture to society; the reciprocity between meaning and structures; the problem of history and historical development; the dialectic between consciousness and social being. Consciousness is given an unproblematic status. The model which links consciousness to culture is essentially linear. It proceeds from the authentic source, in 'personal thought', via expressions, towards the wider, and on the whole more inauthentic, realm of 'public meanings'. The movement is one-way: there is no reciprocal determination. Thus the central issue – that men actively make culture and are then in turn shaped by it – is suppressed.

The perspective adopted in 'People and culture' is fundamentally idealist – 'Any human activity . . . is the product of ideas'. Ideas are not embedded in social situations, in social relationships or experience. They inform situations, but – so to speak – from outside. The process of having ideas and of expressing them is treated as discrete: 'Men have ideas and *then* they act on them' (my italics). A radical break is thus affected between the ideas 'he may . . . keep inside his own head' and their public expression. Throughout subjective meaning is identified with personal thought, and personal though with 'individual consciousness'. The notion that collective patterns of thought exist and have as palpable a reality as the ideas that haunt individual minds is never centrally taken up – not at least until Section 3, when the realm of personal thought has been fully and separately articulated.

But *where* and *how* does individual consciousness, the self, arise except – as Mead put it – 'in social experience', and through the 'conversation of gestures' with significant others? The way to approach that question is not to invert the positivistic paradigm (society-over-self) into its opposite, since both formulations collapse back into that polarity – individual-versus-society – which has been such a profound blockage to cultural studies. The question is, rather, how subjective meanings and intentions come, under certain determinate conditions, to create and inform the 'structures' of social life? And how, in turn, the structures of social life shape and inform the interior spaces of individual consciousness. As R. E. Park remarks: 'man is a creature such that when he lives at all, he lives in his imagination, and, through his imagination, in the minds of other men . . . The consequence is that the individual in society lives a more or less public existence'. Park does *not* mean that only the objective facts of social life are real. Rather, as he says:

> All his acts are anticipated, checked, inhibited or modified by the gestures and intentions of his fellows. It is in this social conflict, in which every individual lives more or less in the mind of every other individual, that human nature and the individual may acquire their most characteristic and human traits . . . We come into the world as individuals, achieve character, and become persons.
>
> ('Human Nature and Collective Behaviour')

What is 'personal thought', then, outside this interior/exterior reciprocity? A richly phenomenological account is offered in Section 2 of the paper; one far more adequate in its complexity than the usual accounts of 'mind' available to us from traditional psycology. But this account itself seems inadequate, because so rigorously sealed off from 'exterior' influences. Take, for example (Section 2) the treatment of 'common sense thought'. 'Common sense thought', incorporated here into 'personal thought' as one of its aspects or 'layers', is conceived in a manner very similar to the way it is defined by Schutz and Husserl: the informal meaning-structures which govern our routine, 'taken-for-granted', social existence in everyday life. 'Common sense thought' (as Schutz, and Berger and Luckmann have argued, and as the paper achnowledges) is 'a closely organized collection of beliefs, assumptions, rules and methods'. But how do such 'beliefs and assumptions' arise, and in what sense are they best defined as *personal*? They are 'personal' because 'below the threshold of consciousness': but they are also massively 'collective' – interpretations, habits, typifications internalized from and exteriorized in our *most publicly routinized social existence*. Common sense thought, far from being a realm of consciousness intelligible in terms of the individual actor alone, arises essentially in *intersubjective* experience. It is one of the provinces of consciousness most thoroughly penetrated by the social. Schutz indeed describes it as the realm, par excellence, of typification, of sedimented social knowledge. The concept seems to me to have been wrenched free of its position in phenomenology. For Schutz, it was the point from which he began to sketch out a 'phenomenology of the social world'.

Here, and elsewhere, it seems as if crucial but complex ideas, which offer the beginnings of an alternative theory of culture, have been pulled up from their moorings in a whole body of thought, and freely inserted into a much simpler schema. The use made of phenomenological concepts throughout the paper is perhaps the most striking example of this. It seems to have been forgotten that Schutz's work, for example, begins with a radical critique of the Weberean notion of 'subjective meaning'. In the *Phenomenology of the Social World* Schutz writes:

> What concerns us is that Weber reduces all kinds of social relationships and structures, all cultural objectification, all realms of objective mind, to the most elementary forms of individual behaviour . . Never before had the project of reducing the 'world of objective mind' to the behaviour of individuals been so radically carried out.

Schutz recognised that the Weberean perspective made it possible to 'disclose the structure of the social world . . as a structure of intelligible intentional meanings' – but *only*, he argued, if the subjective meaning-complex of action is firmly grounded in the intersubjective world. Otherwise, Schutz argued, Weber could not draw any distinction 'between the meaning of the producer of a cultural object and the meaning of the object produced, between the meaning of my own action and the meaning of another's action, between my own experience and that of someone else, between my self-understanding and my understanding of another person'. These criticisms seem to me to apply, *tout court*, to 'People and culture'. If the concept of *culture* is to be clarified within the phenomenological perspective, it requires, at the very least, the decisive shift which Schutz accomplished, against Weber, from 'subjective' to 'intersubjective' meaning: and then the further expansion, via the notions of 'reciprocal perspectives' etc. It was these moves which enabled Schutz to deal 'not only with the single meaningful act and the context or configuration of meaning to which it belongs, but the whole social world in its fully differentiated perspectives'.

For myself, I doubt whether the concept of culture is graspable from the phenomenological perspective alone. This perspective does not allow for the intrinsic double-sidedness of culture on which Berger and Pullberg have remarked:

> The human enterprise of producing a world is not comprehensible as an individual project. Rather, it is a social process: men together engage in constructing a world which then becomes their common dwelling . . . Man the world-builder and man the name-give are possible only as manifestations of man the social being. Every human society can thus be understood as a world-building enterprise, that is, as a world-building activity. The reality of such a world is given neither in itself, nor once and for all. It must be constructed and reconstructed over and over again . . . the world must be confirmed and reconfirmed *by others* . . . Being in the world means, for men, being in the world with others . . . the world is produced by means of a human enterprise that is social in character. As a product this world possesses expressivity, that is, it manifests the intentionality of those who produced it. Because of this, it is possible for others to understand this world, that is, to understand the intentionality of those engaged in building or having built this world.
>
> ('Reification and the Sociological Critique of Consciousness')

This seems to me a more adequate point from which to approach the idea of culture, while holding firmly to the perspective of human agency. I do not mean that it resolves the issues, but it *poses them correctly*. From this position we begin to see the inadequacy of trying to conceptualise culture in terms of the ideas of the individual actor. Berger and Pullberg, and before them, Hegel and Marx, insist that society and culture *begin* with the reciprocal relation of Self/Others. In 'People and culture' 'Others' form a sort of block to the otherwise free transmission (expression) of meanings from their inner source to the outer world.

It is true that 'People and culture' calls, time and again, for 'connected studies', for attention to 'the whole process of communication', for a study of 'the movement from thought to expression and back to thought again'. But the actual thrust of the exposition seems to be moving in a different direction.

The paper treats expressions as the end product of personal thought. But expression is also a form of *praxis*, and praxis is a social not an individual enterprise. It always takes place, not in some ideally free and undistorted realm, but in the real and determinate conditions and quite concrete and specific historical situations. There is no such thing as 'perfectly undistorted, free expression'. To express (i.e. to communicate) at all, ideas pass through the mediations of a social praxis. The so-called 'loss of meaning' is not a special condition but the condition, *sui generis*, of all the real communications which compose the real culture which men 'construct' in circumstances which, though manmade, are not wholly of their making. One crucial form of expression which is dealt with in the paper is expression through language. But language is, through and through, a social praxis – that specially human activity which the French call *signification* and which Lefebvre calls *poesis*. Language, as Marx observed, begins as 'practical consciousness'. In making use of the medium of language, ideas and meanings which appear to have a fundamentally individual root enter a social space, an already-objectivated and unfolding social practice. They enter time, history. They gain a life of their own (objectivation); meanings which, though never separable from the individual project which made them, are no longer reducible to the terms of individual intention. As Sartre suggests:

> Thus significations come from man and from his project, and the significations reveal to us men and relations, but they are inscribed everywhere in things and in the order of things. Everything at every instant is always signifying, and the significations reveal to us men and the relations among men mediated by the structures of our society . . . Our understanding of the Other is never contemplative; it is only a moment of our praxis, a way of living – in conflict or in complicity – the concrete, human relation which unites us to him.

Here, the dialectic of culture is joined: it cannot be torn asunder. The interpreter must not then confuse – as I believe 'People and culture' does – the attempt to recover the praxis behind what appears as a simple process (a project which has to be interpretative because expression is socially mediated, un-transparent) with the dissolution of the mediations. We cannot get round the mediations, as this paper tries to do: nor can we repress them, as both positivism and mechanical marxism, in their different ways, have attempted. We must go through the mediations. But instead of this passage through the mediations 'People and culture' seems to me to erect a simple opposition, counterposing the relative authenticity of individual expressions to the relative inauthenticity of the social world. Expression, not conceived as an activity, is experienced simply as a dehistoricized alienation, attributable to 'the human condition'. The world of culture is thus represented as the sphere of a *general* and permanent impoverishment. Yet this 'loss', this impoverishment, is the medium in which culture is objectivated. Without it culture would not exist.

'People and culture' rightly insists that there are radical disjunctures within any 'whole process of communication'. But the paper locates the disjunctures only at the gap between Self and Others. There is no discussion of the possible disjunctures *within* the self: i.e. between consciousness and the unconscious (in Freud's sense); or between personal consciousness and 'unconscious structures' (in Levi-Strauss' sense); or between our intention to express and the ruling ideas in which often we are forced to communicate (the problem of ideology and 'false consciousness', in Marx's sense). Expressions have been freed, from the notions of repression ideology or power. The public meanings available to us through the agency of men in history, seem in this paper, separate from human agency: they are never the products of former human practices and projects which, as Sartre says, 'address us through them'. There is a persistent failure to deal with the question of collective ideas and meanings. 'People and culture' is correct when it argues that public definitions are not to be *identified with* the subjective meanings individuals have about their experience. In this respect, both the early Durkheimean perspective and the mechanical version of Marxism which has for so long vitiated cultural analysis, are both inadequate. They lack any conception of the dialectic. That is why the recovery of phenomenology, and with it, the restoration of the subject-object problem at the heart of the field, marks a new departure. But 'People and culture' seems now to desert the ground of dialectic on the opposite front.

To take an example from the opening of Section 3 it is true that the public meanings of grief and mourning available to us from the public culture, are inadequate to the individual experience of death. As Douglas argues in *The Social Meaning of Suicide*, many of our crucial meanings are constructed with others in the concrete and immediate situation of facing death – they are 'situated meanings'. The way this 'inadequacy' in the public culture is experienced by an individual is, of course, a perfectly proper kind of study. I am not certain, however, that I would call a study with *this* emphasis 'cultural studies'. Indeed, some confusion seems to arise here, because of an indiscriminate expansion of the scope of what is to be included in 'cultural studies' – an expansion which identifies the field with the study of virtually everything which is 'distinctively human'. This is a too inclusive – even imperialising – a view of 'cultural studies'. For one thing, history is virtually absent from its perspective – surely part of the domain of the 'distinctively human? True, the human studies have been fatally compartmentalised: true the subject matter of the human studies constitutes a single, complex totality. But this totality can and has to be studied from more than one vantage point, without falling into fragmentation. The study of grief and mourning as proposed here is really more a study in what I would call 'existential biography' – not so much psychology as normally understood, but rather what Sartre calls 'improving biography'. This is to approach the problem at the privileged level of the individual life-situation rather than of culture as such. From that perspective, certainly, a 'connected study' would still allow us to see the relation of life-situation to culture but it would not desert its own special point-of-departure out of some mistaken view that everything can be seen from only one point of view.

The study of 'the *culture* of grief and mourning' (my italics) would approach the same subject matter from a different vantage point. It would be concerned with the socially-situated construction of meanings and definitions adequate to the situation of grief, with how men fill the void between inadequate collective representations and imperfect private meanings. How – through what praxis – do men give definition to such experiences, events, etc., which are imperfectly or problematically defined in the public culture? How – in what terms, on the basis of what possible field of meanings – do men handle meaningfully events which seem intrinsically 'meaningless'? Such a study could *not*, by definition, be – as proposed – 'one study of the grief of individuals and then a separate study of the public expressions of mourning' but precisely a study which tried to grasp, as a single intelligible phenomenon, the reciprocity between these two poles in the social construction of death as a meaningful human passage in social life.

In general terms, there is a tendency throughout the paper to polarise the problem in terms of a dichotomy between the inadequately given public meanings (about death or suicide) on one side, and the 'effort of personal thought' on the other. Douglas, who also uses the notion of situated meanings, and on whom much of the argument at this point in 'People and culture' depends, is pointing to a third, if you like, intermediary stage between these two polar extremes; the level at which the actors, together, construct some definition of suicide or death, more adequate to their experience than is available to them *either* at the wholly public *or* the wholly private level. Situated meanings are indeed recognized in the paper as 'the meaning that works among' the participants to a social situation, but the deeply intersubjective nature of this kind of meaning-construction is not, I think, really sustained.

Douglas is not, in my view, altogether clear on the point. But, as I understand him, he argues that, (a) situated meanings are to be distinguished from both private and abstract-public meanings; and (b) that, though we must study meaning construction 'from the clearly observable concrete phenomena upward', yet shared cultural meanings do provide a sort of rough map of 'the possible or plausible meanings of these phenomena (including criteria of various sorts)', which limit and frame, to a degree, which meanings will be constructed through the intentional actions of the individuals involved. In the study of all such ill-defined and problematic areas, there must be a sort of 'double-fitting' between meanings which are generally available, and those which are situationally constructed. Situated meanings are therefore, in Douglas' model, neither wholly determined by the public meanings, nor wholly free of their determination. Here we have the beginnings of a dialectical model of social meaning. How men define death or suicide to themselves in our culture will be neither wholly given nor random. Our ideas about such pivotal experiences and life-crises in our culture are neither the pure reflexions of the 'dominant ideas' (ideology) of our epoch, nor ever free of their constraining and informing power. The degree of 'closure' is, of course, to be empirically determined in each concrete instance – the purpose of such studies being, not to 'dissolve men in a bath of sulphuric acid', but, as Marx once said, 'to rise from the level of the general to the concrete'.

If such a model proves difficult to apply, it remains, nevertheless, the only one which is 'true' to the situation – true, I mean, in the sense of adequate to our experience of the reciprocity of freedom and constraint inside the notion of culture. Edward Thompson, discussing the problem of class-consciousness in 'The Peculiarities of the English', wrote

> The problem is to find a model for the social process which allows an autonomy to social consciousness within a context which, in the final analysis, has always been determined by social being. Can any model ecompass the distinctively human dialectic, by which history appears as neither willed nor as fortuitous; and neither lawed (in the sense of being determined by involuntary laws of motion) nor illogical (in the sense that one can observe a *logic* in the social process)?

Sartre, in *The Question of Method*, is suggesting something of the same kind when he speaks of the 'impulse toward objectification' (the individual project) projecting itself 'across a field of possibles, some of which we realize to the exclusion of others'. Such a method, Sartre insists, must always attempt to 'determine the field of possibles, the field of instruments'; it must 'at once place the agent or event back into the historical setting', not in order to repress human agency, or reduce the specificity of the event, but rather, precisely, to reveal, by 'these procedures – regression and cross-reference . . . the profundity of the lived'. Such a progressive-regressive method – 'determining a biography (for example) by examining the period, and the period by studying the biography' – requires, in its turn, a number of concepts which are, on the whole missing from 'People and culture'. The paper, we argue, lacks any true conception of *praxis*. But it also, more surprisingly, lacks any notion of the *project* (in the sense of a surpassing, by intentional action, of all the determinations, the actor 'going beyond his situation . . . by what he succeeds in making of what he has been made'), or of *determinations* (which is different from determinism; Lefebvre's account in *The Sociology of Marx* is brief, but classic).

'People and culture' affirms that, 'Thought to expression to thought is the circle of culture'. I think the formulation in Sartre is less elegant but truer:

> . . . the joint necessity of the internalization of the external, and the externalisation of the internal. Praxis is, indeed, a passage from objective to objective through internalization. The project, – the subjective surpassing of objectivity towards objectivity, stretched between the objective conditions of the environment and the objective structures of the field of the possibles, represents in itself the moving unity of subjectivity and objectivity, those cardinal poles of activity. The subjective appears then as a necessary moment in the objective process.

My criticism is that 'People and culture' carries a sort of phenomenological reduction to an illogical extreme. In the process the individual, far from being concretised and particularised, comes through as an inactive subject, an abstract property. Correspondingly, in my comments, I have opened myself to the charge of having repressed the individual aspects of culture and exaggerated the social. I can only reply in Marx's own words:

> . . . It is above all necessary to avoid postulating 'society' once more as an abstraction confronting the individual. The individual is a *social being*. The manifestation of his life – even when it does not appear directly in the form of a *social* manifestation, accomplished in association with other men, – is therefore a manifestation and affirmation of *social life*. Individual human life and species-life[1] are not *different* things, even though the mode of existence of individual life is necessarily a more *particular* or more *general* mode of species-life, or that of species-life a more particular or more general mode of individual life. In his *species-consciousness* man confirms his real *social life*, and reproduces his real existence in thought, while conversely species-being confirms itself in species-consciousness, and exists for itself in its universality as a thinking being. Though man is a *unique* individual – and it is just his particularity which makes him an individual, a really individual social being – he is equally the whole, the ideal whole, the subjective existence of society as thought and experienced. He exists, in reality, as the representation and the real mind of social existence, and as the sum of human manifestation of life.
>
> Thought and being are indeed distinct, but they also form a unity.
>
> *Economic and Philosophical Manuscripts*

Note

1 The term 'species' was used by Marx, following Feuerbach, to refer to man's awareness of his general human qualities, of belonging to the 'human species'.

5 A 'reading' of Marx's 1857 introduction to the *Grundrisse*

Stuart Hall

Prefatory note

This is a shortened version of a paper on Marx's 1857 Introduction presented to and discussed in a series of Centre seminars. It has been somewhat revised in the light of those discussions, though I have not been able to take account of some further, more substantive criticisms generously offered by John Mepham, among others. The 1857 Introduction is Marx's most substantial text on 'method', though even here many of his formulations remain extremely condensed and provisional. Since the Introduction presents such enormous problems of interpretation, I have largely confined myself to a 'reading' of the text. The positions taken by Marx in the Introduction run counter to many received ideas as to his 'method'. Properly grasped and imaginatively applied – as they were in the larger corpus of the Grundrisse to which they constantly refer – they seem to me to offer quite striking, original and seminal points of departure for the 'problems of method' which beset our field of study, though I have not been able to establish this connection within the limits of the paper. I see the paper, however, as contributing to this on-going work of theoretical and methodological clarification, rather than as simply a piece of textual explication. I hope this conjuncture will not be lost in the detail of the exposition.

The *1857 Introduction* is one of the most pivotal of Marx's texts.[1] It is also one of his most difficult, compressed and 'illegible'. In his excellent Foreword to the *Grundrisse*, Nicolaus warns that Marx's Notebooks are hazardous to quote, 'since the context, the grammar and the very vocabulary raise doubts as to what Marx "really" meant in a given passage.' Vilar observes that the *1857 Introduction* is one of those texts 'from which everyone takes whatever suits him'.[2] With the growing interest in Marx's method and epistemology, the *Introduction* occupies an increasingly central position in the study of Marx's work. I share this sense of its significance, while differing often from how many of Marx's explicators have read its meaning. My aim, then, is to inaugurate a 'reading' of this *1857* text. It is, of course, *not* a reading *tabula rasa*, not a reading 'without presuppositions'. It reflects my own problematic, inevitably. I hope it also throws some undistorted light on Marx's.

In a famous letter of January 14, 1858, Marx wrote to Engels:

> I am getting some nice developments. For instance, I have thrown over the whole doctrine of profit as it has existed up to now. In the method of treatment the fact that, by mere accident. I have glanced through Hegel's *Logic* has been of great service to me – Freiligarth found some volumes of Hegel which originally belonged to Bakunin and sent them to me as a present. If there should ever be used for such work again, I

> should greatly like to make accessible to the ordinary human intelligence in two or three printer's sheets, what is rational in the method which Hegel discovered but at the same time enveloped in mysticism.

It was not the only time Marx made expressed that hope. In 1843 Marx made notes for a substantial critique of Hegel's *Philosophy of Right.* The *Critique of Hegel's Philosophy As A Whole*, usually printed together with the other *1844 Manuscripts*, also aimed at an exposition and critique of Hegel's dialectic, now in relation to the *Phenomenology* and the *Logic*, though, in the final event, largely confined to the former. As late as 1876, he wrote to Dietzgen:

> When I have shaken off the burden of my economic labours, I shall write a dialectic. The correct laws of the dialectic are already included in Hegel, albeit in a mystical form. It is necessary to strip it of this form.[3]

These hopes were not to be fulfilled, the burden of the economics never laid aside. Thus, we do not have, from the mature Marx, either the systematic delineation of the 'rational kernel', nor the method of its transformation, nor an exposition of the results of that transformation: the Marxian dialectic. The *1857 Introduction*, and the compressed 1859 *Preface* to the *Critique*, together with other scattered asides, have therefore to do duty for the unfulfilled parts of Marx's project. The *1857 Introduction* in particular represents his fullest methodological and theoretical summary-text. Decisive, however, as this text is, we must not handle it as if it were something other than it is. It was written as an Introduction to the Notebooks, themselves enormously comprehensive in scope, digressive and complex in structure; and quite unfinished – 'rough drafts'. Rosdolsky remarked that the *Grundrisse* 'introduces us, so to speak, into Marx's economic laboratory and lays bare all the refinements, all the bypaths of his methodology'. The *Introduction* was thus conceived as a resumé and guide, to 'problems of method' concretely and more expansively applied in the Notebooks themselves. It was not, therefore, intended to stand wholly in its own right. Moreover, the tentative character of the text was signified by Marx's decision in the end *not* to publish it. The *Introduction* was replaced by the terser *Preface*: and some of the central propositions of the *Introduction* are modified, or at least suspended, in the later *Preface*. An immediate contrast of the *Introduction* with the *Preface* (where a classical conciseness is everywhere in play, quite different from the linguistic playfulness and conceit of the *Introduction*) reminds us that, despite its dense argumentation, the *1857 Introduction* remains, even with respect to Marx's method, provisional.

In the *Introduction Marx* proceeds via a critique of the ideological presupposition of political economy. The first section deals with Production. The object of the inquiry is 'material production'. Smith and Ricardo begin with 'the individual and isolated hunter or fisherman'. Marx, however, begins with 'socially determinate' individuals, and hence 'socially determined individual production'. Eighteenth-century theorists, up to and including Rousseau, find a general point of departure 'the individual' producer. Smith and Ricardo found their theories upon this ideological projection. Yet 'the individual' cannot be the point of departure, but only *the result.* Rousseau's 'natural man' appears as a stripping away of the contingent complexities of modern life, a rediscovery of the natural, universal human-individual core beneath. Actually, the whole development of 'civil society' is subsumed in this aesthetic conceit. It is not until labour has been freed of the dependent forms of feudal society, and subject to the revolutionary development it undergoes under early capitalism, that the modern concept of 'the individual' could appear at all. A whole historical and ideological development, then, is already presupposed in – but hidden within – the notion of the Natural Individual and of universal 'human nature'.

This is an absolutely characteristic movement of thought in the *Introduction*. It takes up the 'given' points of departure in Political Economy. It shows by a critique that these are not, in fact, starting points but points of arrival. In them, a whole historical development is already 'summed up'. In short: what appears as the most concrete, common-sense, simple, constituent starting-points for a theory of Political Economy, turn out, on inspection, to be the sum of many, prior, determinations.

Production outside society is as absurd as language without individuals living and talking together. It takes a gigantic social development to produce 'the isolated individual' producer as a concept: only a highly elaborated form of developed social connectedness can appear as – take the 'phenomenal form' of – men pursuing their egoistic interests as 'indifferent', isolated, individuals in a 'free' market organized by an 'invisible hand'. In fact of course, even this individualism is an 'all sided dependence' which appears as mutual indifference:

> The reciprocal and all-sided dependence of individuals who are indifferent to one another forms their social connection. The social bond is expressed in *exchange value*.[4]

This concept – that the capitalist mode of production depends on social connection assuming the 'ideological' form of an individual dis-connection – is one of the great, substantive themes of the *Grundrisse* as a whole. But its working-out also has consequences for the problems of method. For the displacement of real relations via their ideological representations requires, for its critique – its unmasking – a method which reveals the 'essential relations' behind the necessary but mystifying inversions assumed by their 'surface forms'. This method – which, later, Marx identifies as the core of what is *scientific* in his dialectic – forms the master methodological procedure, not only of the Notebooks, but of *Capital* itself. This 'methodological' procedure becomes, in its turn, a theoretical discovery of the utmost importance: in its expanded form (there are several provisional attempts to formulate it in the *Grundrisse*) it constitutes the basis of the pivotal section in *Capital* I, on 'The Fetishism Of Commodities'.[5]

The *Introduction*, then, opens with a methodological argument: the critique of 'normal' types of logical abstraction. 'Political Economy' operates as a theory through its categories. How are these categories formed? The normal method is to isolate and analyse a category by abstracting those elements which remain 'common' to it through all epochs and all types of social formation. This attempt to identify, by means of the logic of abstraction, which remains the core of a concept stable through history is really a type of 'essentialism'. Many types of theorizing fall prey to it. Hegel, the summit of classical German philosophy, developed a mode of thought which was the very opposite of static: his grasp of movement and of contradiction is what raised his logic above all other types of logical theorizing, in Marx's eyes. Yet, because the movement of Hegel's dialectic was cast in an idealist form his thought also retained the notion of an 'essential core' which survived all the motions of mind. It was the perpetuation of this 'essential core' within the concept which, Marx believed, constituted the secret guarantee within Hegel's dialectic of the ultimate harmoniousness of existing social relations (e.g. The Prussian State). Classical Political Economy also speaks of 'bourgeois' production and of private property as if these were the 'essence' of the concepts, 'production' and 'property' and exhaust their historical content. In this way, Political Economy too presented the capitalist mode of production, not as a historical structure, but as the natural and inevitable state of things. At *this* level, even classical Political

Economy retained an ideological presupposition at its 'scientific' heart: it reduces, by abstraction, specific historical relations to their lowest-common, trans-historical essence. Its ideology is inscribed in its method.

On the contrary, Marx argues, there is no 'production-in-general': only distinct forms of production, specific to time and conditions. One of those distinct forms is – rather confusingly – 'general production': production based on a type of labour, which is not specific to a particular branch of production, but which has been 'generalized': 'abstract labour'. (But we shall come to that in a moment.) Since any mode of production depends upon 'determinate conditions', there can be no guarantee that those conditions will always be fulfilled, or remain constant or 'the same' through time. For example: except in the most common-sense way, there is no scientific form in which the concept, 'production', referring to the capitalist mode, and entailing as one of its required conditions, 'free labour', can be said to have an 'immediate identity' (to be 'essentially the same as') production in, say, slave, clan or communal society. Later, in *Capital,* Marx reminds us that this transformation of feudal bondsmen into 'free labour', which is assumed here as a 'natural' precondition for capitalism, has, indeed, a specific history: 'the history of . . . expropriation . . . written in the annals of mankind in letters of blood and fire'.[6] This is one of the key points-of-departure of historical materialism as a method of thought and practice. Nothing in what Marx subsequently wrote allows us to fall behind it. It is what Korsch called Marx's principle of 'historical specification'.[7] The 'unity' which Marx's method is intended to produce is not *weak* identity achieved by abstracting away everything of any historical specificity until we are left with an essential core, without differentiation or specification.

The *Introduction* thus opens, as Nicolaus remarks, as the provisional, extended answer to an unwritten question: Political Economy is our starting point, but, however valid are some of its theories, it has not formulated scientifically the laws of the inner structure of the mode of production whose categories it expresses and theoretically reflects. It 'sticks', despite everything, inside its 'bourgeois skin' (*Capital* I, p. 542). This is because, within it, historical relations have 'already acquired the stability of natural, self-understood forms of social life' (p. 75). Its categories, then, (in contrast with vulgar Political Economy) 'are forms of thought expressing with social validity the conditions and relations of a definite, historically determined mode of production'.[8] But it presents these relations as 'a self-evident necessity imposed by Nature as productive labour itself'. Thus, though classical Political Economy *has* 'discovered what lies beneath these forms', it has not asked certain key questions (such as the origin of commodity-production based in labour-power: 'the form under which value becomes exchange-value') which are peculiar to specific historical conditions (the forms and conditions of commodity-production). These 'errors' are not incidental. They are already present in its presuppositions, its method, its starting points. But, if Political Economy is itself to be transcended, *how? Where to begin?*

The answer is, with 'production by social individuals', 'production at a definite stage of social development'. Political Economy tends to etherealize, universalize and de-historicize the relations of bourgeois production. But what follows if, as Marx does, we *insist* on starting with a principle of historical specification? Do we then, nevertheless, assume that there is some common, universal practice – 'production-in-general' – which has always existed, which has then been subject to an evolutionary historical development which can be steadily traced through: a practice which, therefore, we can reduce to its common-sense content and employ as the obvious, uncontested starting-point for analysis? The answer is, no. Whatever other kind of 'historicist' Marx may have been, he was definitively *not* a historical evolutionist. Every child knows, he once remarked, that production cannot cease for a moment. So, there must be something 'in common', so to speak, which corresponds to the idea of 'production-in-general': all societies must reproduce the conditions of their own existence. This is the type of abstraction, however, which sifts out the lowest common characteristics of a concept and identifies this unproblematic core with its scientific content. It is a mode of theorizing which operates at a very low theoretical threshold indeed. It is, at best, a useful time-saver. But, to penetrate a structure as dense and overlaid with false representations as the capitalist mode of production, we need concepts more fundamentally dialectical in character. Concepts which allow us to further refine, segment, split and recombine any general category: which allow us to see those features which permitted it to play a certain role in this *epoch*, other features which were developed under the specific conditions of *that* epoch, distinctions which show why certain relations appear *only* in the most ancient and the most developed forms of society *and in none in between*, etc. Such concepts are theoretically far in advance of those which unite under one chaotic general heading the quite different things which have appeared, at one time or another, under the category, 'production-in-general': conceptions which *differentiate* in the very moment that they reveal hidden connections. In much the same way, Marx observes that concepts which differentiate out what makes possible the specific development of different languages are more significant than 'abstracting' a few, simple, basic, common 'language universals'.

We must observe – it is a common strategy throughout the *Introduction* – that Marx establishes his difference here *both* from the method of Political Economy *and* from Hegel. The *Introduction* is thus, simultaneously, a critique of both. It is useful, in this context, to recall Marx's earlier procedure in the famous Chapter on 'The Metaphysics of Political Economy', in *The Poverty of Philosophy*, where he, again, simultaneously offers a critique of 'Hegelianised Political Economy' via an attack on Proudhon.

The terms of this critique of Proudhon are particularly germane to this argument against 'abstraction', for they remind us that something more than a methodological quibble is involved, namely the exaltation of mental operations over the content of real, contingent historical relations; it was not surprising that

> if you let drop little by little all that constitutes the individuality of a house, leaving out first of all the materials of which it was composed, then the form that distinguishes it, you end up with nothing but a body; that if you leave out of account the limits of this body, you soon have nothing but a space – that is, finally, you leave out of account the dimensions of this space, there is absolutely nothing left but the quantity, the logical category. If we abstract thus from every subject all the alleged accidents, animate or inanimate, men or things, we are right in saying that in the final abstraction, the only substance left is the logical categories . . . If all that exists, all that lives on land and under water can be reduced by abstraction to a logical category – if the whole world can be drowned thus in a world of abstractions, in the world of logical categories – who need be astonished at it?

Apply this method to the categories of political economy, Marx argues

> and you have the logic and metaphysics of political economy . . . the categories that everbody knows, translated into a little-known language which makes them look as if they had newly blossomed forth in an intellect of pure reason . . . Up to now we have expounded only the dialectics of Hegel. We shall see later how M. Proudhon has succeeded in reducing it to the meanest proportions. Thus for Hegel, all that has

> happened and is still happening is only just what is happening in his own mind . . . There is no longer a history according to the order of time, there is only the 'sequence of ideas in the understanding'.[9]

Marx had long ago noted[10] Hegel's 'outstanding achievement': his recognition that the different categories of the world – 'private right, morality, the family, civil society, the state, etc.' – had 'no validity in isolation', but 'dissolve and engender one another. They have become "moments" of the movement'. However, as we know, Marx radically criticized Hegel for conceiving this 'mobile nature' of the categories as a form of 'self-genesis': Hegel 'conceives them only in their thought form'. Thus 'The whole movement . . . ends in absolute knowledge'.[11] In Hegel, the constitution of the real world becomes 'merely the appearance, the cloak, the exoteric form' of movement and contradiction, which, in the speculative conception, never really deserts the ground of thought. 'The whole history of alienation and of the retraction of alienation is therefore only the history of the production of abstract thought, i.e. of absolute, logical, speculative thought.' This was certainly not the simple, trans-historical, external connections established by vulgar forms of Political Economy, but an equally unacceptable alternative: the ultimate identity of Mind with itself 'only in . . . thought form'. Marx added, 'this means that what Hegel does is to put in place of these fixed abstractions the act of abstraction which revolves in its own circle'. He put the same point even more clearly in *The Holy Family*:

> The *Phenomenology* . . . ends by putting in place of all human existence 'absolute knowledge' . . Instead of treating self-consciousness as the self-consciousness of real men, living in a real objective world and conditioned by it, Hegel transforms men into an attribute of self-consciousness. He turns the world upside down.

And in the *Poverty of Philosophy*:

> He thinks he is constructing the world by the movement of thought, whereas he is merely reconstructing systematically and classifying by the absolute method the thoughts which are in the minds of all.

The core of these earlier critiques is retained by Marx here in the *1857 Introduction*. Hegel *did* understand 'production', he did understand 'labour': but ultimately, it was what Marx called, 'labour of the mind, labour of thinking and knowing'.[12] However dialectical its movement, the historical production of the world remains, for Hegel, 'moments' of the realization of the Idea, the 'external appearances' of thought – stations of the cross in the path of Mind towards Absolute Knowledge. The method which Marx proposes in the *Introduction* is not of this kind: it is not merely a mental operation. It is to be discovered in real, concrete relations: it is a method which groups, not a simple 'essence' behind the different historical forms, but precisely the many determinations in which 'essential differences' are preserved.

Marx ends this argument with an illustration. Economists like Mill start from bourgeois relations of production, and extrapolate them as 'inviolable natural laws'. All production, they assert, despite historic differences, can be subsumed under universal laws. Two such 'laws' are (a) production requires private property, (b) production requires the protection of property by the courts and police. Actually, Marx argues, private property is neither the only nor the earliest form of property: historically, it is predated by communal property. And the presence of modern, bourgeois legal relations and the police, far from indexing the universality of the system, shows how each mode of production requires, and produces, its own legal-juridical and political structures and relations. What is 'common' to production, then, as produced by the process of mentally abstracting its 'common attributes', cannot provide a method which enables us to grasp, concretely, any single, 'real historical stage of production'.

How then, *are* we to conceptualize the relations between the different phases of production – production, distribution, exchange, consumption? Can we conceive them 'as organically coherent factors'? Or simply as 'brought into haphazard relation with one another, i.e. into a simple reflex connection'? How, in short, are we to analyse the relations between the parts of a 'complexly structured whole'? Throughout his later work Marx insists that the superiority of the dialectical method lies in its ability to trace out the 'inner connection' between the different elements in a mode of production, as against their haphazard, and extrinsic 'mere juxtaposition'. The method which merely sets opposites together in an external way, which assumes that, because things are neighbours, they must therefore be related, but which cannot move from oppositions to contradictions, is 'dialectical' only in its surface form. The syllogism is one of the logical forms of an argument by external juxtaposition. Political Economy 'thinks' production, consumption etc. in this syllogistic form: production produces goods; distribution allocates them; exchange makes the general distribution of goods specific to particular individuals; finally, the individual consumes them. This can also be interpreted as almost a classical Hegelian syllogism.[13] There are many ways in which Marx may be said to have remained a Hegelian; but the use of Hegelian triads (thesis, antithesis, synthesis) and syllogisms (general, particular, singular) is *not* one of them. The coherence such syllogisms suggest remains conceptually extremely shallow. Even the critics of this position, Marx adds, have not taken their critique far enough. The critics assume that the syllogism is wrong because it contains a logical error – a textbook mistake. For Marx, the error consists in a taking over into thought of the mystifications which exist in the real relations of bourgeois production, where production, distribution and consumption do indeed, *appear* 'phenomenally' as 'independent, autonomous neighbours', but where this appearance is false, an ideological inversion. Conceptual mistakes cannot be clarified by a theoretical practice alone, 'wholly within thought'.

In *The Critique of Hegel's Dialectic*, Marx had remarked that, in Hegel, the supercession of one category by another *appears* to be a 'transcending of the thought entity'. However, in Hegel, thought treats even the objectively-created moments as 'moments' of *itself* – 'because the object has become for it a moment of thought, thought takes it in its reality to be a self-confirmation of itself'. Thus 'this superseding in thought, which leaves its object standing in the real world, believes that it has really overcome it'. There is no true 'profane history' here, no 'actual realization for man of man's essence and of his essence as something real'.[14] Thus, 'The history of man is transformed into the history of an abstraction'.[15] The movement of thought therefore remains ultimately confined within its own circle:

> Hegel has locked up all these fixed mental forms together in his *Logic* laying hold of each of them first as negation – that is, as an alienation of human thought – and then as negation of the negation – that is, as a superseding of that alienation, as a real expression of human thought. But as even this still takes place within the confines of the estrangement, this negation of the negation is in part the restoring of these fixed forms in their estrangement.[16]

Thus, 'The act of abstraction. . . . revolves within its own circle'. The language here remains headily Hegelian-Feuerbachean . . . How much cleaner the blow is in the *1857* text: 'as if the task were the dialectical balancing of concepts, and not the grasping of real relations'. 'As if this rupture had made its way not from reality into the textbooks, but rather from the textbooks into reality'.[17]

Thus, neither the functional disconnectedness of Political Economy nor the formal supercessions of the Hegelian Logic will serve to reveal the inner connection between processes and relations in society, which form 'a unity' of a distinct type, but which must be grasped as real, differentiated processes in the real world, not merely the formal movement of the act of abstraction itself. It is because, in the 'real relations' of capitalist production, the different parts of the process *appear*, simply, as independent, autonomous 'neighbours' that they appear, in the textbooks, as linked by an accidental connection: not vice versa. But, how then to think the relations of identity, similarity, mediateness and difference which could produce, at the conceptual level, in thought, a 'thought-concrete' adequate in its complexity to the complexity of the 'real relations' which is its object?

The most compressed and difficult pages of the *Introduction*, which immediately follow, provide an answer to this question. This section deals with the relations between production, distribution, consumption and exchange. Start with production. In production, individuals 'consume' their abilities, they 'use up' raw materials. In this sense, there is a kind of consumption *inside* production: production and consumption *are* here 'directly coincident'. Marx seems to have thought this example of 'immediate identity' 'right enough', though – as he says earlier and later of other formulations[18] – 'trite and obvious', or 'tautologous'; true at a rather simple level, but offering only a 'chaotic conception', and thus requiring 'further determinations', greater analytical development. The general inadequacy of this type of 'immediate identity' *is* clearly signalled by Marx's reference here to Spinoza, who showed that an 'undifferentiated identity' cannot support the introduction of more refined 'particular determinations'. However, in so far as 'immediate identities' reign, at this simple level, identical propositions can be reversed: if A = B, then B = A. Marx, then, reverses the proposition. If there is a consumption-inside-production, there is, also, 'immediately', production-inside-consumption. The consumption of food, for example, is the means consumption. The consumption of food, for example, is the means whereby the individual produces, or reproduces his physical existence. Now Political Economy recognizes these distinctions but simply in order to separate out the consumptive aspects of production (e.g. the consumption of raw materials) from production proper. Production, as a distinct category, remains. The 'immediate identity' thus leaves their 'duality intact'. (This type of identity is thus open to the criticism which Marx originally delivered on Hegel in the 1844 fragment on the *Critique of the Hegelian Philosophy As A Whole*: 'this superseding in thought which leaves its object standing in the real world, believes it has really overcome it').

Marx now adds a second type of relation: that of *mediation*: the relation of 'mutual dependence'. Production and consumption also mediate one another. By 'mediate' here Marx means that each cannot exist, complete its passage and achieve its result, without the other. Each is the other's completion. Each provides within itself the other's object. Thus, production's product is what consumption consumes. Consumption's 'needs' are what production is aimed to satisfy. The mediation here is 'teleological'. Each process finds its end in the other. In this mediating movement, Marx later observes,[19] each side is 'indispensable' to the other; but they are not identical – they remain necessary but 'external to each other'.

Marx now expands on *how* this mediation works. Consumption 'produces' production in *two* ways. First, production's object – the product – is only finally 'realized' when it is consumed.[20] It is in the passage of the forms, from productive activity to objectified product, that the first mediating movement between production and consumption is accomplished. Second, consumption produces production by creating the need for '*new* production'. It is crucial, for the later discussion of the determinacy of production in the process as a whole, that what consumption now does, strictly speaking, is to provide the 'ideal, internally impelling cause', the 'motive', 'internal image', 'drive' 'purpose' for *re*-production. Marx stresses '*new* production'; strictly speaking, and significantly, it is the need to *re*-produce for which consumption is made mediately responsible.

'Correspondingly' production 'produces' consumption. Marx notes *three* senses in which this is true. First, production furnishes consumption with its 'object'. Second, production specifies the *mode* in which that object is consumed. But, third, production produces the need which its object satisfies. This a difficult concept to grasp, for we normally think of consumption's needs and modes as the property of the consumer (that is, belonging to 'consumption'), separate from the object which, so to speak, satisfies. But as early as 1844 Marx had pointed to the way in which needs are the product of an objective historical development, not the trans-historical subjective property of individuals:

> The manner in which they (objects) become his depends on the nature of the objects and on the nature of the essential power corresponding to it: for it is precisely the determinate nature of this relationship which shapes the particular, real mode of affirmation. To the eye an object is another object than the object of the ear.

If consumption of the object produces the subjective impulse to produce anew, the production of the object creates, in the consumer, specific, historically distinct and developed modes of 'appropriation', and, simultaneously, develops the 'need' which the object satisfies. 'Music alone awakens in man the sense of music'.

Thus the 'forming of the senses' is the subjective side of an objective labour, the product of 'the entire history of the world down to the present'.[21] 'The production of new needs is the first historical act', he observed in The *German Ideology*. Here, 'the object of art . . . creates a public which is sensitive to art'.[22] Production, then, *forms* objectively the modes of appropriation of the consumer, just as consumption reproduces production as a subjectively experienced impulse, drive or motive. The complex shifts between objective and subjective dimensions which are tersely accomplished in this passage seem incomprehensible without the gloss from the *1844 MSS*, even if, here, the language of 'species being' has altogether vanished.

The general argument is now resumed.[23] There are *three* kinds of identity relation. First, *immediate* identity – where production and consumption are 'immediately' one another. Second, *mutual dependence* – where each is 'indispensable' to the other, and cannot be completed without it, but where production and consumption remain 'external' to one another. Thirdly – a relation, which has no precise title, but which is clearly that of an *internal connection* between two sides, linked by the passage of forms, by real processes through historical time. Here, in contrast with relation (2), production not only proceeds to its own completion, but is *itself reproduced again* through consumption. In this third type of relation, each 'creates the other in completing itself and *creates itself* as the other'. Here we find not only what distinguishes the third type of relation from the second; but also, what permits Marx, on the succeeding page, to give a final determinacy to production over consumption. Production, he argues, initiates the cycle: in its 'first act', it forms the object, the mode and the need to consume: what consumption can then do is to 'raise the inclination developed in the first act of production through the need for repetition to its finished form'. Production, then, requires the passage through consumption to commence its work anew; but in providing 'the act through which the whole process again runs its course', production retains a primary determination over the circuit as a whole. Some of Marx's most crucial and sophisticated distinctions, developed later in *Capital* – such as those between simple and expanded reproduction – achieve a gnomic, philosophic, first-formulation in this elliptical passage. In this third relation, production and consumption are no longer external to each other: nor do they 'immediately' merge. Rather, they are linked by an 'inner connection'. Yet this 'inner connection' is *not* a simple identity, which requires only the reversal or inversion of the terms of the syllogism into one another. The inner connection here passes through a distinct process. It requires what Marx, in his earlier critique of Hegel, called a 'profane' history: a process in the real world, a process through historical time, each moment of which requires its own determinate conditions, is subject to its own inner laws, and yet is incomplete without the other.

Why is relation 3 not an 'immediate identity' of the Hegelian type? Marx gives three reasons. First, an immediate identity would assume that production and consumption had a single subject. This identity of the 'subject' through all its successive 'moments' of realization – a pivotal aspect of Hegel's 'essentialism' allowed Hegel to conceive the historical world as, ultimately, a harmonious circuit. In the real historical world, however, the 'subject' of production and consumption are *not* one. Capitalists produce: workers consume. The production process links them: but they are not 'immediate'. Second, these are not Hegelian 'moments' of a single act, temporary realizations of the march of World Spirit. These are the circuits of a *process*, with 'real points of departure': a process with specific forms through which value is prescribed to pass 'for its realization'. Third, whereas Hegel's identities form a self-engendering, self-sustaining circuit, in which no one moment has priority, Marx insists that the historical process through which production and consumption pass *has* its breaks, its moment of determinacy. Production, not consumption, initiates the circuit. Consumption, the necessary condition for value's 'realization', cannot destroy the 'over-determinacy' of the moment from which realization departs.

The significance of these distinctions is delivered in the closing paragraph – the distinction between a Marxian and a Hegelian analysis of the *forms* of capitalist production.[24] Capitalism tends to reproduce itself in expanded form *as if* it were a self-equilibrating and self-sustaining system. The so-called 'laws of equivalence' are the necessary 'phenomenal forms' of this self-generating aspect of the system:

> this is precisely the beauty and greatness of it: this spontaneous interconnection, this material and mental metabolism which is independent of the knowing and willing of individuals.[25]

But this constant tendency to equilibrium of the various spheres of production is exercised only in the shape of a reaction against the constant upsetting of this equilibrium.[26] Each 'moment' has its determinate conditions – each is subject to its own social laws: indeed, each is linked to the other in the circuit by quite distinct, determinate, forms – processes. Thus, there is no guarantee to the producer – the capitalist – that what he produces will return again to him: he cannot appropriate it 'immediately'. The circuits of capital 'depend on his relation to other individuals'. Indeed, a whole, intermediate or 'mediating movement' now intervenes – 'steps between' – producers and products – determining, but again 'in accordance with social laws', what will return to the producer as his share in the augmented world of production. *Nothing except the maintenance of these determinate conditions can guarantee the continuity of this mode of production over time.*

> Just as the exchange value of the commodity leads a double existence, as the particular commodity and as money, so does the act of exchange split into two mutually independent acts: exchange of commodities for money, exchange of money for commodities; purchase and sale. Since these have now achieved a *spatially* and *temporally separate* and *mutually indifferent* form of existence, their immediate identity ceases. They may correspond or not; they *may* balance or not; they *may* enter into disproportion with one another. They will, of course, always attempt to equalize one another, but in the place of the earlier immediate equality there now stands the constant *movement of equalization*, which evidently presupposes constant non-equivalence. It is now entirely possible that consonance may be reached only by passing through the most extreme dissonance.[27]

It is, in short, a *finite* historical system, a system capable of breaks, discontinuities, contradictions, interruptions: a system *with limits*, within historical time. It is a system indeed, which rests on the mediating movement of other processes not yet named: for example – distribution: production – (distribution) – consumption. Is distribution, then, 'immediate with' production and consumption? Is it inside or outside production? Is it an autonomous or a determinate sphere?

In the first section,[28] Marx examined the couplet – production/consumption – in terms of an immediate Hegelian unity: opposites/identical. He then dismantled the production/consumption couplet by the terms of a Marxian transformation: opposites, mediated-mutually dependent-differentiated unity (not identical). In part, this is accomplished by wresting from apparently equivalent relations a moment of determinacy: *production*. In the second section (p. 94) the second couplet – production/distribution – is dismantled by means of a different transformation: determined-determining-determinate.

In Political Economy, Marx wrote, everything appears twice. Capital is a factor of production: but also a form of distribution, (interest + profits). Wages are a factor of production, but also a form of distribution. Rent is a form of distribution: but also a factor of production (landed property). Each element appears as both *determining* and *determined*. What breaks this seamless circle of determinations? It can only be deciphered by reading back from the apparent identity of the categories *to their differentiated presuppositions* (determinate conditions).

Here, once again, Marx is concerned to established the moments of *break*, of *determinacy*, in the self-sustaining circuits of capital.[29] Vulgar Economy assumed a perfect fit between the social processes of capital. This was expressed in the Trinitarian formula. Each factor of production was returned its just rewards in distribution: Capital – profits; Land – ground rent; Labour – wages. Thus each bit 'appeared twice', by grace of a secret assumed 'natural harmony' or compact with its identical opposite. Distribution appears to be, in common sense, the prime mover of this system. Yet, Marx suggests, behind the obvious forms of distribution, (wages, rent, interest) lie, not simply economic categories, but real, historic relations, which stem from the movement and formation of capital under specific conditions. Thus wages presuppose, not labour, but labour *in a specific form:* wage-labour (slave labour has no wages). Ground rent presupposes large-scale landed property (there is no ground rent in communal society). Interest and profit presuppose capital in its modern form. Wage-labour, landed property and capital are not independent forms of distribution but 'moments' of the organization of the capitalist mode of production: they *initiate* the distributive forms (wages, rent, profits), not vice versa. In this sense, distribution, which is, of course, a differentiated system, is nevertheless 'over-determined' by the structures of production. Before distribution by wages, rent, profits can take place a *prior* kind of 'distribution' must occur: the distribution of the means of production between expropriators and expropriated, and the distribution of the members of society, the classes, into the different branches of production. *This* prior distribution – of the means and of the agents of production into the social relations of production – belongs to *production*: the distribution of its *products*, its *results*, in the form of wages or rent, *cannot* be its starting point. Once this distribution of instruments and agents has been made, they form the starting conditions for the realization of value within the mode; this realization process generates its own distributive forms. This second type of distribution, however, is clearly *subordinate* to production in this wider, mode-specific sense, and must be considered as over-determined by it.

In the third section, on exchange, the demonstration is even briefer.[30] Exchange, too, is an 'aspect of production'. It mediates between production and consumption, but, again, as its presupposition, it requires determinate conditions which can only be established within production: the division of labour, production in its private exchange form, exchanges between town and country, etc. This argument leads, almost at once, to a conclusion – it is a conclusion, not simply to the section on exchange, but to the whole problem posed on p. 88. Production, distribution, consumption and exchange are not adequately conceptualized as immediate identities, unfolding, within the essentialist Hegelian dialectic, to their monistic categorical resolution. Essentially, we must 'think' the relations between the different processes of material production as 'members of a totality, distinctions within a unity'. That is, as a complexly structured differentiated totality, in which distinctions are not obliterated but preserved – the unity of its 'necessary complexity' precisely *requiring* this differentiation.

Hegel, of course, knew that the two terms of a relation would not be the *same*. But he looked for the identity of opposites – for 'immediate identities' *behind* the differences. Marx does not altogether abandon the level at which, superficially, opposite things *can* appear to have an 'essential' underlying similarity. But this is not the principal form of a Marxian relation. For Marx, two different terms or relations or movements or circuits remain specific and different: yet they form a 'complex unity'. However, this is always a 'unity' formed by and requiring them to preserve *their difference*: a difference which does not disappear, which cannot be abolished by a simple movement of mind or a formal twist of the dialectic, which is not subsumed into some 'higher' but more 'essential', synthesis involving the loss of concrete specificity. This latter type of 'non' immediacy is what Marx calls a *differentiated unity*. Like the notion to which it is intimately linked – the notion of the concrete as the unity of 'many determinations and relations' – the concept of a 'differentiated unity' is a methodological and theoretical key to this text, and to Marx's method as a whole. This means that, in the examination of any phenomenon or relation, we must comprehend *both* its internal structure – what it is in its differentiatedness – as well as those other structures to which it is coupled and with which it forms some more inclusive totality. Both the specificities and the connections – the complex unities of structures – have to be demonstrated by the concrete analysis of concrete relations and conjunctions. If relations are mutually articulated, but remain specified by their difference, this articulation, and the determinate conditions on which it rests, has to be demonstrated. It cannot be conjured out of think air according to some essentialist dialectical law. Differentiated unities are also therefore, in the Marxian sense, *concrete*. The method thus retains the concrete empirical reference as a privileged and undissolved 'moment' within a theoretical analysis without thereby making it 'empiricist': the concrete analysis of concrete situations.

Marx gives an 'over-determinacy' to production. But how does production determine? Production specifies 'the different relations *between* different moments' (our italics). It determines the *form* of those combinations out of which complex unities are formed. It is the principle of the formal articulations of a mode. In the Althusserean sense, production not only 'determines' in the last instance, but determines the form of the combination of forces and relations which make a mode of production a complex structure. Formally, production specifies the system of similarities and differences, the points of conjuncture, between all the instances of the mode, including which level is, at any moment of a conjuncture, 'in dominance'. This is the *modal* determinacy which production exercises in Marx's overall sense. In its more narrow and limited sense – as merely one moment, forming a 'differentiated unity' with others – production has its own spark, its own motive, its own 'determinateness' derived from other moments in the circuit (in this case, from consumption). To this argument – the nature of the relations of determinacy and complementarity or conjuncture between the different relations or levels of a mode of production – Marx returned at the end of the *Introduction*. One of its results, already foreshadowed here, is the 'law of uneven development'.

Marx now goes back to the beginning: the method of Political. Economy.[31] In considering the political economy of a country, where do we begin? One possible starting position is with 'the real and concrete', a given, observable, empirical concept: e.g. population. Production is inconceivable without a population which produces. This starting point, however, would be wrong. Population, like 'production', is a deceptively transparent, 'given' category, 'concrete' only in a common-sense way.[32] Already it presupposes the division into classes, the division of labour, and thus wage-labour, capital, etc: the categories of a specific mode of production. 'Population' thus gives us only 'a chaotic conception of the whole'. Further, it triggers off a methodological procedure which moves from the blindingly obvious to 'ever more simple concepts', 'ever thinner abstractions'. This was the method of abstraction of the seventeenth century economists. It is also the 'metaphysical' method of Proudhon which Marx pilloried so brilliantly and brutally in *The Poverty of Philosophy*. Later economic theorists begin with simple relations and trace their way back to the concrete. This latter path, Marx calls 'the obviously scientifically correct one'. This 'concrete' is *concrete* in a different sense from the first formulation. In the first case, 'population' is 'concrete' in a simple, unilateral, common-sense way – it manifestly exists; production cannot be conceived without it, etc. But the method which *produces* the 'complex concrete' is concrete because it is 'a rich totality of many determinations and relations'. The method then, is one which has to *reproduce in thought* (the active notion of a practice is certainly present here) the concrete-in-history. No reflexive or copy theory of truth is now adequate. The simple category, 'population', has to be reconstructed as contradictorily composed of the more concrete historical relations: slave-owner/slave, lord/serf, master/servant, capitalist/labourer. This clarification is a specific practice which theory is required to perform upon history: it constitutes the first part of theory's 'adequacy' to its object. Thought accomplishes such a clarification by decomposing simple, unified categories into the real, contradictory, antagonistic relations which compose them. It penetrates what 'is' immediately present on the surface of bourgeois society, what 'appears' as 'the phenomenal form of' – the necessary form of the appearance of – 'a process which is taking place behind'.[33] Marx sums up the point. The concrete is concrete, in history, in social production, and thus in conception, not because it is simple and empirical, but because it exhibits a certain kind of necessary complexity. Marx makes a decisive distinction between the 'empirically-given' and the *concrete*. In order to 'think' this real, concrete historical complexity, we must reconstruct in the mind the determinations which constitute it. Thus, what is multiply determined, diversely unified, in history, already 'a result', appears, in thought, in theory, not as 'where we take off from' but as *that which must be produced*. Thus 'the abstract determinations lead towards a reproduction of the concrete by way of thought'. Let us note at once, that this makes the 'way of thought' *distinct* from the logic of history as such, though it does not make thought 'absolutely distinct'. What is more, for Marx, the concrete-in-history makes its appearance once again, now as the historical substratum to thought. Though the concrete-in-history cannot be the point of departure for a theoretical demonstration, it is the absolute precondition for all theoretical construction: it *is* 'the point of departure in reality and *hence also* the point of departure for observation and conception' (our italics).

Marx's formulations here[34] are seminal; the more so since they have, in recent years, become the *locus classicus* of the whole debate concerning Marx's epistemology. The 'way of thought', Marx seems to be arguing, must 'lay hold upon historical reality' – 'appropriate the concrete' – and produce, by way of its own distinct practice, a theoretical construct adequate to its object ('reproduce it as the concrete in the mind'). It is important, however, to see that, right away, Marx addresses himself directly to the much-vexed question as to whether this 'theoretical labour' can be conceived of as a practice which 'takes place entirely in thought', which 'is indeed its own criterion', and which 'has no need for verification from external practices to declare the knowledges they produce to be "true" '.[35] Significantly, his remarks here are, once again, embedded in a critique of Hegel, a procedure which appears to warn us explicitly against any final, idealist bracketing. Because 'thought' has its own mode of appropriation, Marx argues, therefore Hegel made the error of thinking that 'the real' was the product of 'thought concentrating itself, probing its own depths, and unfolding itself out of itself'. From this it was an easy step to thinking of thought as absolutely (not relatively) autonomous, so that 'the movement of the categories' became 'the real act of production'. Of course, he continues, thought *is* thought and not another thing; it occurs in the head; it requires the process of mental representations and operations. But it does not, for that reason, 'generate itself'. It is 'a product of thinking and comprehending', that is, a product, rather, of the working-up of observation and conception into concepts. Any theory of 'theoretical practice', such as Althusser's, which seeks to establish an 'impassable threshold' between thought and its object, has to come to terms with the concrete reference (it is not, in our view, an empiricist reduction) embodied in Marx's clear and unambiguous notion, here, that thought proceeds from the '*working-up of observation and conception*' (our italics). This product of theoretical labour, Marx observes now, is, of course, a 'totality of thoughts' *in the head*. But thought does not dissolve 'the real subject' – its object – which 'retains its autonomous existence outside the head'. Indeed, Marx caps the argument by briefly referring to the relation of thought to social being, a reference consonant with his position as previously stated in the *Theses on Feuerbach*. The object, 'the real' will *always* remain outside the head, so long as 'the head's conduct is merely speculative, merely theoretical'. That is, until the gap between thought and being is closed *in practice*. As he had argued, 'Man must prove the truth i.e. the reality and power, the this-sideness, of his thinking, in practice. The dispute over the reality or non-reality of thinking, that is isolated from practice is a purely scholastic question.' There is no evidence here for Marx having fundamentally broken with this notion that, though thinking 'has its own way', its truth rests in the 'this-sidedness' of thinking, *in practice*. In fact, the *1857* text makes the point explicit: 'Hence, *in the theoretical method too*, the subject, society, must always be kept in mind as the presupposition'.[36] On this evidence, we must prefer Vilar's brief but succinct gloss over Althusser's complex but less satisfying ones:

> I admit that one ought neither to mistake thought for reality nor reality for thought, and that thought bears to reality only a 'relationship of knowledge', for what else could it do? Also that the process of knowledge takes place entirely within thought (where else on earth could it take place?) and that there exists an order and hierarchy of 'generalities'

> about which Althusser has had really major things to say. But on the other hand I fail to see what 'astounding' mistake Engels was committing when he wrote (in a letter, incidentally, as a casual image) that conceptual thought progressed 'asymptotically' towards the real.
>
> (*New Left Review* 80)

As Vilar remarks, 'when reading the *1857 Introduction*, if one should "hear its silence", one should also take care not to silence its words' (*New Left Review* 80, pp. 74–5).

Thought, then, has its own distinct, 'relatively autonomous' mode of appropriating 'the real'. It must 'rise from the abstract to the concrete' not vice versa. This is different from 'the process by which the concrete itself comes into being'. The logic of theorizing, then, and the logic of history do *not* form an 'immediate identity': they are mutually articulated upon one another, but remain distinct within that unity. However, lest we immediately fall into the opposite error that, therefore thinking is its own thing, Marx, as we have seen, immediately turned, as if in the natural course of the argument, to the critique of Hegel, for whom of course, the march of the categories was precisely the only motor. In so doing, Marx offered a critique of every other position which would transpose the *distinctiveness* of thought from reality (in terms of the modes of their production) into an *absolute distinction.* His qualifications on this 'absolute' break are pivotal. Thought *always* has built into it the concrete substratum of the manner in which the category has been realized historically within the specific mode of production being examined. In so far as a category already exists, albeit as a relatively simple relation of production, not yet with its 'many sided connections', then that category can already appear 'in thought', because categories are 'the expression of relations'. If, then, turning to a mode in which that category appears in a more developed, many-sided form, we employ it again, but now to 'express' a more developed relation, then, in that sense, it *does* remain true that the development of the theoretical categories *directly mirrors* the evolution of historic relations: the 'path of abstract thought, rising from the simple to the combined', does indeed 'correspond to the real historical process'. In this *limited case*, the logical and historical categories *are indeed parallel.* The notion that Marx has prescribed that the logical and the historical categories *never* converge is shown to be incorrect. It is a matter of cases.

In other cases, however, the two movements are *not* identical in this way. And it is these instances which concern Marx, for this was precisely Hegel's error. Marx's critique of any attempt to construct 'thinking' as wholly autonomous is that *this constitutes an idealist problematic*, which ultimately derives the world from the movement of the Idea. No formalist reduction – whether of the Hegelian, positivist, empiricist or structuralist variety – escapes this stricture. The distinctiveness of the mode of thought does not constitute it as absolutely distinct from its object, the concrete-in-history: what it does is to pose, as a problem remaining to be resolved, precisely *how* thought, which is distinct, forms 'a unity' with its object: remains, that is to say, nevertheless, determined 'in the last instance' (and, Marx adds, in the 'first instance, too, since it is from "society" that thinking derives its 'presupposition'). The subsequent passages in the *1857 Introduction* in fact constitute some of Marx's most cogent reflections on the dialectical relation of thought, of the 'theoretical method', to the historical object of which it produces a *knowledge*: a knowledge, moreover, which – he insists – remains 'merely speculative, merely theoretical' (there is no mistaking that 'merely') so long as practice does not, dialectically, realize it – *make it true.*

If thought is distinct in its mode and path, yet articulated upon and presupposed by society, its object, how is this 'asymptotic' articulation to be achieved? The terms are here conceived as neither identical nor merely externally juxtaposed. But what, then, is the precise nature of their unity? If the genesis of the logical categories which express historical relations differs from the real genesis of those relations, what is the relation between them? How does the mind *reproduce* the concreteness of the historical world *in thought?*

The answer has something to do with the way history, itself, so to speak, enters the 'relative autonomy' of thought: the manner in which the historical object of thought is rethought inside Marx's mature work. The relation of thought to history is definitively *not* presented in the terms of a historical evolutionism, in which historical relations are explained in terms of their genetic origins. In 'genetic historicism', an external relation of 'neighbourliness' is posited between any specific relation and its 'historical background': the 'development' of the relation is then conceived lineally, and traced through its branching variations: the categories of thought faithfully and immediately mirror this genesis and its evolutionary paths. This might sound like a caricature, until one recalls the inert juxtaposings, the faithful tracing out of quite unspecified 'links', which has often done justice for modern instances of the Marxist method. It is crucial to distinguish Marx from the evolutionism of a positivist historical method. We are dealing here neither with a disguised variant of positivism nor with a rigorous a-historicism but with that most difficult of theoretical models, especially to the modern spirit: a *historical epistemology*.

Marx now employs again the distinctions he has made between different types of 'relation': immediate, mediated, etc. Previously, these had been applied to the categories of a theoretical analysis – 'production', 'distribution', 'exchange'. These distinctions are now applied again; but this time to the different types of relations which exist between thought and history. He proceeds by example. In the *Philosophy of Right*, Hegel begins with the category, 'possession'. Possession is a simple relation which, however, like 'production', cannot exist without more concrete relations – i.e. historical groups with possessions. Groups can, however, 'possess' without their possessions taking the form of 'private property' in the bourgeois sense. But since the historico-judicial relation, 'possession', *does* exist, albeit in a simple form, we can think it. The simple relation is the 'concrete substratum' of our (relatively simple) concept of it. If a concept is, historically, relatively undeveloped (*simple*) our concept (of it) will be *abstract*. At this level, a connection of a fairly reflexive kind *does* exist between the (simple) level of historical development of the relation and the relative (lack of) concreteness of the category which appropriates it.

But now Marx complicates the Theory/History couplet. Historically the development of the relation is not evolutionary. No straight, unbroken path exists from simple to more complex development, either in thought or history. It is possible for a relation to move from a dominant to a subordinate position within a mode of production as a whole. And this question of dominant/subordinate is not 'identical' with the previous question of simple/more developed, or abstract/concrete. By referring the relation to its articulation *within a mode of production*, Marx indicates the crucial shift from a progressive or sequential or evolutionary historicism to what we might call 'the history of epochs and modes': a structural history. This movement towards the concepts of *mode* and *epoch*, interrupts the linear trajectory of an evolutionary progression, and reorganizes our conception of historical time in terms of the succession of modes of production, defined by the internal relations of dominance and subordination between the different relations which constitute them. It is a crucial step. There is, of course, nothing original whatever in drawing attention to the fact that Marx divided history in terms of successive modes of production. Yet the *consequence* of this break with genetic evolutionism does not appear to have been fully registered. The concepts, 'mode of production' and 'social formation' are often employed as if they are, in fact, simply large-scale historical generalizations, within which smaller chronological sections of historical time can be neatly distributed. Yet, with the concepts of 'mode of production' and 'social formation', Marx pin-points the structural interconnections which cut into and break up the smooth march of a historical evolutionism. It represents a rupture with historicism in its simple, dominant form, though this is not, in our view, a break with *the historical* as such.

Take money. It exists before banks, before capital. If we use the term, 'money', to refer to this relatively simple relation, we use a concept which (like 'possession' above) is still abstract and simple: less concrete than the concept of 'money' under commodity production. As 'money' becomes more developed so our concept of it will tend to become more 'concrete'. However, it is possible for 'money', in its *simple* form to have a *dominant* position in a mode of production. It is also possible to conceive of 'money', in a more *developed*, many-sided form, and thus expressed by a more *concrete* category, occupying a *subordinate* position in a mode of production.

In this double-fitting procedure, the couplets simple/developed, or abstract/concrete refer to what we might call the diachronic string, the developmental axis of analysis. The couplet dominant/subordinate points to the synchronic axis – the *position* in which a given category or relation stands in terms of the other relations with which it is articulated in a specific mode of production. These latter relations are always 'thought' by Marx in terms of relations of dominance and subordination. The characteristic modern inflexion is to transfer our attention from the first axis to the second, thus asserting Marx's latent structuralism. The difficulty is, however, that the latter does not bring the former movement to a halt, but *delays* or (better) *displaces* it. In fact, the line of historical development is always constituted within or behind the structural articulation. The crux of this 'practical epistemology', then, lies precisely in the necessity to 'think' the simple/developed axis and the dominant/subordinate axis as dialectically related. This is indeed how Marx defined his own method, by proxy, in the second *Afterword* to *Capital*: 'What else is he picturing but the dialectic method?'

Take another case. Peru was relatively developed, but had no 'money'. In the Roman Empire, 'money' existed, but was 'subordinate' to other payment relations, such as taxes, payments-in-kind. Money only makes a historic appearance 'in its full intensity' in bourgeois society. There is thus no linear progression of this relation and the category which expresses it through each succeeding historical stage. Money does not 'wade its way through each historical stage'. It *may* appear, or not appear, in different modes: be developed or simple: dominant or subordinate. What matters is not the mere appearance of the relation sequentially through time, but its *position* within the configuration of productive relations which make each mode *an ensemble*. Modes of production form the discontinuous structural sets through which history articulates itself. History moves – but only as a *delayed and displaced trajectory*, through a series of social formations or ensembles. It develops by means of a series of *breaks*, engendered by the internal contradictions specific to each mode. The theoretical method, then, to be adequate to its subject, society, must ground itself in the specific arrangement of historical relations in the successive modes of production, not takes its position on the site of a simple, linearly-constructed sequential history.[37]

Now Marx defines the articulation of thought and history. The 'most general abstraction' – in the main sense – of general (i.e. many-sided) development appears only when there is, in society, in history, 'the richest possible concrete development'. Once this has happened 'in reality', the relation 'ceases to be thinkable in its particular (i.e. abstract) form alone'. Labour, as a loose, catch-all, concept (such as 'all societies must labour to reproduce') has thus been replaced by the more *concrete* category, 'labour-in-general' (generalized production), but only because the latter category now refers in bourgeois society to a real, concrete, more many-sided, historical appearance. The 'general concept' has, Marx strikingly asserts, 'become true in practice'. It has achieved that specificity, 'in thought', which makes it capable of appropriating the concrete relations of labour in practice. It has 'achieved practical truth as an abstraction only as a category of the most modern society'. Thus,

> even the most abstract categories . . . are nevertheless . . . themselves likewise a product of historical relations and possess their full validity only for and within these relations. (p. 105)

It is for this reason especially that bourgeois society, 'the most developed and the most complex historic organization of production' allows us insights into vanished social formations: provided we do not make over-hasty 'identities' or 'smudge over all historical differences'. For, it is only in so far as older modes of production survive within, or reappear in modified form within, capitalism, that the 'anatomy' of the latter can provide 'a key' to previous social formations.[38] Again, we must 'think' the relation between the categories of bourgeois social formations and those of previous, vanished formations, *not* as an 'immediate identity', but in ways which preserve their appearance in bourgeois society (that is the relations of developed/simple and of dominant/subordinate in which *new* and *previous* modes of production are *arranged* or combined within it). From this basis, Marx can make his critique of simple, historical evolutionism.

> The so-called historical presentation of development is founded, as a rule, on the fact that the latest form regards the previous ones as steps leading up to itself.

This is to regard the matter 'one-sidedly'. This does not however, abolish 'history' from the scheme. If thought is grounded in social being, but not in social being conceived 'evolutionarily' then it must be *present social reality* – modern bourgeois society, 'the most developed and complex historic organization of production' – which forms thought's presupposition, its 'point of departure'. The object of economic theorizing, 'modern bourgeois society', is 'always what is given in the head as well as in reality'.[39] And it is *this point* – it 'holds for science as well' – which is 'decisive for the order and sequence of the categories'.

It has recently been argued that, with this observation about the distinction between the historical and the logical succession of the categories, Marx makes his final rupture with 'historicism'. It is often forgotten that the point is made by Marx in the context of a discussion about the fundamentally relativized epistemological origins of thought itself: a discussion which specifically draws attention to the dependence of the logical categories on the relations, the 'forms of being', which they 'express'. Thus, not what thought produces by its own 'mechanisms' from within itself, but what is concretely 'given in the head as well as reality' is Marx's starting-point here for his discursus on the epistemological foundations of method.

'The order and sequence of the economic categories', then, do not 'follow one another in the sequence in which they were historically decisive': not because – as was true for Hegel – the logical categories engender themselves above or outside the 'real relations', but because the epistemological reference for thought is *not the past but the present historic organization of production* (bourgeois society). This is a quite different argument. Thus, what matters is not the historical sequence of the categories but 'their order within bourgeois society'. In bourgeois society, each category does not exist as a discrete entity, whose separate historical development can be traced, but within a 'set', a *mode*, in relations of dominance and subordination, of determination, and determinateness to other categories: an *ensemble of relations*. This notion of an ensemble does indeed interrupt – break with – any straight historical evolutionism. The argument has then, sometimes, been taken as supporting Marx's final break with 'history' as such – a break expressed in the couplet, historicism/science. Marx, in my view, is drawing a different distinction, signalling a different 'break': that between a sequential historical evolutionism determining thought, and the determinateness of thought within *the present historic organization of social formations*. The relations of production of a mode of production are articulated *as an ensemble*.

There are complex internal relations and connections between them. In each mode, moreover, there is a level of determination 'in the last instance': one specific production-relation which 'predominates over the rest . . assigns rank and influence to the others . . . bathes all other colours and modifies their particularity'.[40] Marx insists that we attend to the specificity of each ensemble, and to the relations of determination, dominance and subordination which constitutes each epoch. This points towards the Althusserean concept of a social formation as a 'complexly structured whole' 'structured in dominance' and to the complementary notions of 'over-determination' and 'conjuncture'. The full theoretical implications of this modal conception take Marx a good deal of the way towards what we may call a 'structural historicism'. But, since thought, too, takes its origins from this 'reality', which is 'always given in the head', it too operates by way of an epistemology determined in the first–last instance by the 'present historical organization of production'.

Marx now develops this argument, again by way of examples. In bourgeois society, 'agriculture is progressively dominated by capital'. What matters for the order and sequence of categories is not the evolution of any one relation – say, feudal property – into industrial capital: though, in *Capital*, Marx does at certain points provide just such a historical sketch. It is the relational position of industrial capital and landed property, or of 'capital' and 'rent', in the capitalist mode as against their relational position in say, the feudal mode, which matters. In the latter 'combination' provides the starting-point of all theorizing. This is 'anti-historicist' if by that term we mean that the method does not rest with the tracing of the historical development of each relation, singly and sequentially, through time, But it is profoundly *historical* once we recognize that the starting-point – bourgeois society – is not outside history, but rather 'the present historic organization of society'. Bourgeois society is what 'history' has delivered to the present as its 'result'. The bourgeois ensemble of relations is the present-as-history. History, we may say, realizes itself progressively. Theory, however, appropriates history 'regressively'. Theory, then, starts from history as a developed result, *post festum*. This is its presupposition, in the head. History, but only in its realization as a 'complexly structured totality', articulates itself *as the epistemological premise*, the starting point, of theoretical labour. This is what I want to call Marx's historical – not 'historicist' – epistemology. However undeveloped and un-theoreticized, it marks off Marx's method sharply from a philosophically-unreflexive traditional mode, including that final reference to the self-generating 'scientificity' of science which indexes the lingering positivist trace within structuralism itself. Colletti has expressed the argument succinctly when he observes that much theoretical Marxism has shown a tendency

> to mistake the 'first in time' – i.e. that from which the logical process departs as a recapitulation of the historical antecendents – with the 'first in reality' or the actual foundation of the analysis. The consequence has been that whereas Marx's logico-historical reflections culminate in the formation of the crucial problem of the contemporaneity of history (as Lukács once aptly said, 'the present as history') traditional

> Marxism has always moved in the opposite direction of a philosophy of history which derives its explanation of the present from 'the beginning of time'.[41]

Marx's 'historical epistemology', then, maps the mutual articulation of historical movement and theoretical reflection, not as a simple identity, but as differentiations within a unity. He retains – in, as it were a displaced form – the historical premise, thoroughly reconstructed, inside the epistemological procedure and method, as its final determination. This is not thought and reality on infinitely parallel lines with 'an impassable threshold' between them. It signifies a convergence – what Engels called an *asymptotic movement* – on the ground of the given: here, bourgeois society as the ground or object both of theory and practice. It remains an 'open' epistemology, not a self-generating or self-sufficient one, because its 'scientificity' is guaranteed only by that 'fit' between thought and reality – each in its own mode – which produces a knowledge which 'appropriates' reality in the only way that it can (in the head): and yet delivers a critical method capable of penetrating behind the phenomenal forms of society to the hidden movements, the deep-structure 'real relations' which lie behind them. This 'scientific' appropriation of the laws and tendencies of the structure of a social formation is, then, *also* the law and tendency of its 'passing away': the possibility, not of the proof, but of the *realization* of knowledge in practice, in its practical resolution – and thus, the self-conscious overthrow of those relations in a class struggle which moves along the axis of society's contradictory tendencies, and which is something more than 'merely speculative', more than a theoretical speculation. Here, as Colletti has remarked, we are no longer dealing with 'the relationship "thought-being" within thought, but rather with the relation *between* thought and reality'.[42]

It is worth referring this methodological argument in the *Introduction* to passages in the *Grundrisse* itself where the distinctions between the 'historical origins' of the capitalist mode, and capitalism as 'the present historic organization of production' are elaborated.[43] The capitalist mode, Marx is arguing, depends on the transformation of money into capital. Thus, money constitutes one of 'the antideluvian conditions of capital, belongs to its historic presuppositions'. But once this transformation to its modern form in commodity production is accomplished – the establishment of the capitalist mode of production proper – capitalism no longer depends directly upon this recapitulation of its 'historic presupposition' for its continuation. These presuppositions are now 'past and gone' – they belong to 'the history of its formation, but in no way to its contemporary history, i.e. not to the real system of the mode of production ruled by it'. In short, the historical conditions for the appearance of a mode of production *disappear into its results*, and are reorganized by this realization: capitalism now posits 'in accordance with its immanent essence, the conditions which form its point of departure in production' – 'posits the conditions for its realization', 'on the basis of its own reality'. It (capitalism) 'no longer proceeds from presuppositions in order to become, but rather it is itself presupposed, and proceeds from itself to create the conditions of its maintenance and growth'. This argument is again linked by Marx with the error of Political Economy, which mistakes the past conditions for capitalism becoming what it is, with the *present* conditions under which capitalism is organized and appropriates: an error which Marx relates to Political Economy's tendency to treat the harmonious laws of capitalism as natural and 'general'.

In the face of such evidence from the *Grundrisse*, and later from *Capital*,[44] it cannot be seriously maintained for long that, with his brief remarks on the 'succession of the categories' in the *1857 Introduction*, Marx wholly relinquishes the 'historical' method for an essentially synchronic, structuralist one (in the normal sense). Marx clearly is sometimes unrepentantly concerned, precisely, with the most delicate reconstruction of the *genesis* of certain key categories and relations of bourgeois society. We must distinguish these from the 'anatomical' analysis of the structure of the capitalist mode, where the 'present historic organization of production' is resumed, analytically and theoretically, as an on-going 'structure of production', a combination of productive modes. In the latter, 'anatomical' method, history and structure have been decisively reconstructed. The methodological requirement laid on his readers is to maintain these two modes of theoretical analysis – a view eloquently endorsed in the Afterword to *Capital I*. This injunction constitutes both the comprehensiveness, and the peculiar difficulty, of his dialectical method. But the temptation to bury one side of the method in favour of the other – whether the historical at the expense of the structural, or vice versa – is, at best, an evasion of the theoretical difficulty Marx's own work proposes: an evasion for which there is no warrant in the *1857 Introduction*. As Hobsbawm has remarked,

> a structural model envisaging only the maintenance of a system is inadequate. It is the simultaneous existence of stabilizing and disruptive elements which such a model must reflect . . Such a dual (dialectical) model is difficult to set up and use, for in practice the temptation is great to operate it, according to taste or occasion, either as a stable functionalism or as one of revolutionary change; whereas the interesting thing about it is, that it is both.[45]

The problem touched on here goes to the heart of the 'problem of method', not only of the *1857 Introduction*, but of *Capital* itself: a question which the *Introduction* throws light on but does not resolve. Godelier, for example, argues for 'the priority of the study of structures over that of genesis and evolution': a claim, he suggests, inscribed in the very architecture of *Capital* itself.[46] Certainly, the main emphasis in *Capital* falls on the systematic analysis of the capitalist mode of production, not on a comprehensive reconstruction of the genesis of bourgeois society as a social formation. Thus, the long section *Capital III* on 'Ground Rent', opens:

> The analysis of landed property in its various historical forms belongs outside of the limits of this work . . . We assume then that agriculture is dominated by the capitalist mode of production.[47]

This does not contradict the centrality of those many passages which *are* in fact directly historical or genetic in form (including parts of this same section of *Capital III*). Indeed, there are important distinctions between different *kinds* of writing here. Much that seems 'historical' to us now was, of course, for Marx immediate and contemporary. The chapter on 'The Working Day', in *Capital I*, on the other hand, contains a graphic historical sketch, which *also* supports a theoretical argument – the analysis of the forms of industrial labour under capitalism, and the system's ability, first, to extend the working day, and then, as labour becomes organized, the movement towards its limitation ('the outcome of a protracted civil war'). Both are modally different from 'the task of tracing the genesis of the money-form . . . from its simplest . . . to dazzling money-form', announced early in the same volume:[48] a genesis which Marx argues 'shall, at the same time, solve the riddle presented by money', but which in fact is not cast in the form of a 'history of money' as such, but an analysis of 'the *form* of value' (own italics), as expressed in the money-form, a quite different matter. And all of these differ again, from the substantive historical material in *Capital I*, addressed explicitly to the question of 'origins' but which Marx deliberately put after, not before, the basic theoretical exposition. None of these qualifications should be taken as modifying our appreciation of the profoundly historical imagination which informs *Capital* throughout. Decisively, the systematic form of the work never undercuts the fundamental historical premise which frames the whole exposition, and on which Marx's claim for its 'scientificity', paradoxically, rests: the historically-specific, hence transitory, nature of the capitalist epoch and the categories which express it. As early as 1846 he had said this to Annenkov, *à propos* Proudhon:

> He has not perceived that economic categories are only abstract expressions of these actual relations and only remain true while these relations exist.[49]

He never changed his mind.[50]

It is certainly the case that, *in extenso*, Capital deals with the forms and relations which the capitalist system requires to reproduce itself on an expanded scale: that is, with the 'structure and its variations'. Some of the most dazzling parts of the manuscript consist, precisely, of the 'laying bare' of the forms of the circuits of capital which enable this 'metamorphosis' to take place. But Marx's method depends on identifying two dialectically related but discontinuous levels: the contradictory, antagonistic 'real relations' which sustain the reproductive processes of capitalism, and the 'phenomenal forms' in which the contradictions appear as 'equalized'. It is the latter which inform the consciousness of the 'bearers' of the system, and generate the juridical and philosophic concepts which mediate its movements. A *critical* science must unmask the inverted forms of the metamorphosis of the structure of capital, and lay bare its antagonistic 'real relations'. The difficult but magnificent opening sections on Commodity-Fetishism (which it is now sometimes fashionable to dismiss as another Hegelian trace) not only lay the base, substantially, for the rest of the exposition; they also stand as a dramatic demonstration of the logic and method by which the other discoveries of the work are produced.[51] Thus, though for Marx one of the truly staggering aspects of capitalism was, exactly, its self-reproduction, his theory transcended Political Economy only in so far as he could show that the 'forms of the appearance' of this structure could be read through, read behind, read back to their presuppositions – as if one were 'deciphering the hieroglyphic to get behind the secret of our own social products'. And one of the sources of these permanent, self-reproducing 'appearances' of capitalism to which Marx drew our attention was, precisely, the 'loss' (mis-recognition) of any sense of its movements as socially-created, historically produced forms:

> Man's reflections on the forms of social life, and consequently also his scientific analysis of these forms, take a course directly opposite to that of their actual historical development. He begins *post festum* with the results of the process of development already to hand. The characters that stamp products as commodities, and whose establishment is a necessary preliminary to the circulation of commodities, have already acquired the stability of natural, self-understood forms of social life before man seeks to decipher, not their historical character, for in his eyes they are immutable, but their meaning.

'So too', he added, 'the economic categories, already discussed by us, bear the stamp of history'. They are 'socially valid and, therefore, objective thought-forms which apply to the production-relations peculiar to this one historically determined mode of social production'.[52] But, this decipherment (which is, in its 'practical state', *his method*: 'all science would be superfluous if the outward appearance and the essence of things directly coincided'[53]) is not *just* a critique. It is a critique *of a certain distinctive kind* – one which *not only* lays bare the 'real relations' behind their 'phenomenal forms', but does so in a way which *also* reveals as a contradictory and antagonistic necessary content what, on the surface of the system, appears only as a 'phenomenal form', functional to its self-expansion. This is the case with each of the central categories which Marx 'deciphers': commodity, labour, wages, prices, the equivalence of exchange, the organic composition of capital, etc. In this way, Marx *combines* an analysis which strips off the 'appearances' of how capitalism works, discovers their 'hidden substratum', and is thus able to reveal how it *really* works: with an analysis which reveals why this functionalism in depth *is also* the source of its own 'negation' ('with the inexorability of a law of Nature').[54] The first leads us to the ideological level, at which the 'phenomenal forms' are taken at their justificatory face-value: they 'appear directly and spontaneously as current modes of thought' – i.e. as the prevailing forms of common-sense perceptions. The second penetrates to 'the essential relation manifested within', to 'their hidden substratum': they 'must first be discovered by science'. Classical Political Economy provides the basis – but only via a *critique* – of this second, scientific level, since it 'nearly touches the true relation of things, without however consciously formulating it'.[55] Marx's critique transcends its origins in Political Economy, not only because it formulates consciously what has been left unsaid, but because it reveals the antagonistic movement concealed behind its 'automatic mode', its 'spontaneous generation'.[56] The analysis of the double form of the commodity – use-value, exchange-value – with which *Capital* opens, and which appears at first as merely a formal exposition, only delivers its first substantive conclusion when, in the Chapter on 'The General Formula for Capital', the 'circuit of equivalence' (M–C–M) is redefined as a circuit of disequilibrium (M–C–M), where 'This increment or excess over the original value I call "surplus value" '. 'It is this movement that converts it (value) into capital'.[57] Thus, as Nicolaus has argued,

> Exploitation proceeds behind the back of the exchange process . . . production consists of an act of exchange, and, on the other hand, it consists of an act which is the opposite of exchange . . . the exchange of equivalents is the fundamental social relation of production, yet the extraction of non-equivalents is the fundamental force of production.[58]

To present Marx as if he is the theorist, solely, of the operation of 'a structure and its variations', and not, also and simultaneously, the theorist of its limit, interruption and transcendence is to transpose a dialectical analysis into a structural-functionalist one, in the interest of an altogether abstract scientism.

Godelier is aware that an analysis of the variations of a structure must embrace the notion of contradiction. But the 'functionalist' shadow continues to haunt his structuralist treatment of this aspect. Thus, for Godelier, there are two, fundamental contradictions in Marx's analysis of the system: that between capital and labour (a contradiction *within* the structure of the 'social relations of production') and that between the socialized nature of labour under large-scale industry and the productive forces of capital (a contradiction *between* structures). Characteristically, Godelier exalts the latter (deriving from the 'objective properties' of the system) over the former (the struggle between the classes). Characteristically, Marx intended to connect the two: to found the self-conscious practice of class struggle *in* the objective contradictory tendencies of the system.[59] The neat, binary contrast offered by Godelier between a 'scientific' contradiction which is objective, material and systemic, and the practice of class struggle which is epiphenomenal and teleological disappears in the face of this essential internal connectedness of theory to practice. Korsch long ago, and correctly, identified the attempt 'to degrade the opposition between the social classes to a temporary appearance of the underlying contradiction between the productive forces and production-relations' as 'Hegelian'.[60] Marx ended his letter outlining the theoretical argument of volume 3 thus:

> Finally, since these three (wages, ground rent, profit) constitute the respective sources of income of the three classes . . . we have, in conclusion, the *class struggle*, into which the movement of the whole *Scheisse* is resolved.[61]

Yet, when Godelier quotes Marx's letter to Kugelmann[62] – 'I represent large-scale industry not only as the mother of antagonism, but also as the creator of the material and spiritual conditions necessary for the solution of this antagonism – he appears unable to *hear* the second half of Marx's sentence at all. Yet, for Marx, it was exactly the interpenetration of the 'objective' contradictions of a productive mode with the politics of the class struggle which alone raised his own theory above the level of a 'Utopia' to the status of a science: just as it was the coincidence of an adequate theory with the formation of a class 'for itself' which alone guaranteed the 'complex unity' of theory and practice. The idea that the unity of theory and practice could be constituted on the ground of theory alone would not have occurred to Marx, especially after the demolition of Hegel.

There remain the extremely cryptic Notes[63] which conclude the *Introduction:* notes on notes – 'to be mentioned here' . . . 'not to be forgotten', nothing more. The points rapidly touched on in these pages are, indeed, theoretically of the highest importance: but there is scarcely enough here for anything that we could call a 'clarification'. They are at best, *traces*: what they tell us is that – significantly enough – Marx already had these questions in mind. What they hardly reveal is what he thought about them. They primarily concern the super-structural forms: 'Forms of the State and Forms of Consciousness in Relation to Relations of Production and Circulation, Legal Relations, Family Relations'. What would the modern reader give for a section at least as long as that on 'The Method of Political Economy' on *these* points. It was not to be.

We can, then, merely, *note* what the problems here seemed to him to be. They touch on the question as to how, precisely, we are to understand the key concepts: 'productive forces', 'relations of production'. Moreover, they specify these concepts at the more mediated levels: the relation of these infrastructural concepts to war and the army; to cultural history and historiography; to international relations; to art, education and law. Two conceptual formulations of the first importance are briefly enunciated. First, it is said again, that the productive-forces/relations-of-production distinction, far from constituting two disconnected structures, must be conceived dialectically. The boundaries of this dialectical relation remain to be specified in any theoretical fullness ('to be determined'): it is a dialectic which connects, but which is *not* an 'immediate identity' – it does not 'suspend the real difference' between the two terms. Second, the relation of artistic development, of education and of law to material production is specified as constituting a relation of 'uneven development'. Again, a theoretical note of immense importance.

The point about artistic development and material production is then briefly expanded. The 'unevenness' of the relation of art to production is instanced by the contrast between the flowering of great artistic work at a point of early, indeed, 'skeletal' social organization – Greek civilization. Thus the epic appears as a *developed* category in a still *simple*, ancient, mode of production. This instance parallels the earlier example, where 'money' makes its appearance within a still undeveloped set of productive relations. Though Marx is here opening up a problem of great complexity – the graphic demonstration of the 'law of the uneven relations of structure and superstructures' – he is less concerned with developing a specifically Marxist aesthetics, than with questions of method and conceptualization. His argument is that, like 'money' and 'labour', art does not 'wade its way' in a simple, sequential march from early to late, simple to developed, in step with its material base. We must look at it in its 'modal' connection at specific stages.

His concrete example – Greek art – is subordinated to the same theoretical preoccupation. Greek art presupposes a specific set of 'relations'. It requires the concrete organization of the productive forces of Ancient society – it is incompatible with spindles, railways, locomotives. It requires its own, specific modes of production – the oral art of the epic is incompatible with electricity and the printing press. Moreover, it requires its own forms of consciousness: mythology. Not *any* mythology – Egyptian mythology belongs to a different ideological complex, and would not do. But mythology as a form of thought (at the ideological level) survives only to the degree that the scientific mastery over and transformation of Nature is yet not fully accomplished. Mythology lasts only so long as science and technique have not overtaken magic in their social and material pacification of Nature. Thus, mythology is a form of consciousness which is only possible at a certain level of development of the productive forces – and hence, since this mythology forms the characteristic content and mode of imagination for the epic, the epic is connected – but by a complex and uneven chain of mediations – to the productive forces and relations of Greek society. Is this historical coupling, then, not irreversible? Do not ancient society and the epic disappear together? Is the heroic form of Achilles imaginable in the epoch of modern warfare?

Marx does not end his inquiry with this demonstration of the *historical* compatibility between artistic and material forms. The *greater* theoretical difficulty, he observes, is to conceive how such apparently *ancient* forms stand in relation to the '*present* historic organization of production'. (Our italics) Here, once again, Marx gives a concrete instance of the way he combines, in his method, the analysis of *concrete instances*, the epochal development of complex structures *through time*, and the structural 'law' of the mutual connection and interdependence of relations *within the present mode of production*. The demonstration, though brief and elliptical, is exemplary. The answer to the question as to why we still respond positively to the epic or Greek drama – in terms of the 'charm' for us of 'the historic childhood of humanity' – is, however, unsatisfactory in almost every respect: a throwaway line. The resolution to these perplexing, (and, in our time, progressively central and determining) theoretical issues is achieved stylistically, but not conceptually.

What light, if any, does the *1857 Introduction* throw on the problem of 'theoretical breaks' in Marx? Marx considered classical Political Economy to be the new science of the emergent bourgeoisie. In this classical form it attempted to formulate the laws of capitalist production. Marx had no illusions that Political Economy could, untransformed, be made theoretically an adequate science for the guidance of revolutionary action: though he did, again and again, make the sharpest distinction between the 'classical' period which opened with Petty, Boisguillebert and Adam Smith and closed with Ricardo and Sismondi, and its 'vulgarisers', with whom Marx dealt dismissively, but whom he read with surprising thoroughness and debated intensively to the end of his life. Yet some of his sharpest criticism was reserved for the 'radical' Political Economists – the 'left-Ricardians', like Bray, the Owenites, Rodbertus, Lasalle and Proudhon – who thought Political Economy theoretically self-sufficient, though skewed in its political application, and proposed those changes from above which would bring social relations in line with the requirements of the theory. The socialist Ricardians argued that, since labour was the source of value, all men should become labourers exchanging equivalent amounts of labour. Marx took a harder road. The exchange of equivalents, though 'real enough' at one level, was deeply 'unreal' at another. This was just the frontier beyond which Political Economy could not pass. However, merely by knowing this to be true did not, in Marx's sense, make it real for men in practice. These laws could only be thrown over in practice: they could not be transformed by juggling the categories. At this point, then, the critique of Political Economy, and of its radical revisionists, merged with the meta-critique of Hegel and *his* radical revisers – the left-Hegelians: for Hegel, too, 'conceived only of abstractions which revolve in their own circle' and 'mistook the movement of the categories' for the profane movement of history; and his radical disciples thought the Hegelian system complete, and only its application lacking its proper finishing touch. Certainly, when Marx said of Proudhon that he 'conquers economic alienation only within the bounds of economic alienation', it was a direct echo, if not a deliberate parody, of the critique he had already made of Hegel.[64]

It is this point – that bourgeois relations must be overthrown in practice before they can be wholly superseded in theory – which accounts for the complex, paradoxical, relations Marx's mature work bears to Political Economy: and thus for the extreme difficulty we have in trying to mark exactly where it is that Marxism, as a 'science', breaks wholly and finally with Political Economy. The difficulty is exactly that which has in recent years so preoccupied the discussion of Marx's relation to Hegel: and it may be that we must tentatively return the same kind of answer to each form of the question.

The whole of Marx's mature effort is, indeed, the *critique* of the categories of Political Economy. The critique of method is positively opened, though not closed, in the *1857 Introduction*. Yet Political Economy remains Marx's only theoretical point-of-departure. Even when it has been vanquished and transformed, as in the case of the dismantling of the Ricardian theory of wages, or in the break-through with the 'suspended' concept of surplus value, Marx keeps returning to it, refining his differences from it, examining it, criticizing it, going beyond it. Thus even when Marx's theoretical formulations lay the foundations of a materialist science of historical formations, the 'laws' of Political Economy still command the field, theoretically – because they dominate social life in practice. To paraphrase Marx's remarks on the German 'theoretical conscience', Political Economy cannot be realized in practice without abolishing it in theory, just as, on the other side, it cannot be abolished in practice until it has been theoretically 'realized'.

This is in no sense to deny his 'breakthroughs'. In a thousand other ways, *Capital*, in the doubleness of its unmasking and reformulations, its long suspensions (while Marx lays bare the circuits of capital 'as if they were really so', only to show, in a later section, what happens when we return this 'pure case' to its real connections), its transitions, lays the foundation of a 'scientific' critique of the laws of capitalist production. Yet it remains a *critique* to the end: indeed, the critique appears (to return to the *1857* text) as paradigmatically, *the form of the scientificity of his method*.

The nature of this 'end' toward which his critique pointed must be spelled out. It was not an attempt to erect a scientifically self-sufficient theory to replace the inadequate structure of Political Economy: his work is not a 'theoreticist' replacement of one knowledge by another. In the aftermath of the 1848 upheavals, Marx's thought did, clearly, increasingly cast itself in the form of theoretical work. No doubt the systematic and disciplined nature of this work imposed its own excluding and absorbing rhythms: the letters eloquently testify to that. Yet for all that, the theoretical labour of which the successive drafts and pre-drafts of *Capital* were the result, had, as its prospective 'end' – paradoxically – something other than the 'founding of a science'. We cannot pretend, as yet, to have mastered the extremely complex articulations which connect the scientific forms of historical materialism with the revolutionary practice of a class in struggle. But we have been right to assume that, the power, the historical significance, of Marx's theories are related, in some way we do not yet fully understand, precisely to this *double articulation* of theory and practice. We are by now familiar with a kind of 'reading' of the more polemical texts – like the *Manifesto* – where the theory is glimpsed, so to speak, refracted through a more 'immediate' political analysis and rhetoric. But we are still easily confused when, in the later texts, the movement of the classes in struggle is glimpsed, so to speak, refracted through the theoretical constructs and arguments. It is a strong temptation to believe that, in the latter, only Science holds the field.

Marx's mature method – we would argue – does not consist of an attempt to found a closed theoreticist replacement of bourgeois Political Economy. Nor does it represent an idealist replacement of alienated bourgeois relations by 'truly human' ones. Indeed, great sections of his work consist of the profoundly revolutionary, critical task of showing exactly how the laws of political economy *really worked*. They worked, in part, through their very formalism: he patiently analyses the 'phenomenal forms'. Marx's *critique*, then, takes us to the level at which the real relations of capitalism can be penetrated and revealed. In formulating the nodal points of this *critique* Political Economy – the highest expression of these relations grasped as mental categories – provided the only possible starting point. Marx begins there. *Capital* remains 'A Critique of Political Economy': not 'Communism: An alternative to Capitalism'. The notion of a 'break' – final, thorough, complete – by Marx with Political Economy is, ultimately, an idealist notion: a notion which cannot do justice to the real complexities of theoretical labour – *Capital* and all that led up to it.

Much the same could be said of Marx's relation to Hegel, though here a substantive 'break' is easier to identify – for what it is worth, it is identified time and again for us by Marx himself. It is the relation to Hegel in terms of *method* which continues to be troubling. Early and late, Marx and Engels marked the thorough-going manner in which the whole idealist framework of Hegel's thought had to be abandoned. The dialectic in its idealist form, too, had to undergo a thorough transformation for its real scientific kernel to become available to historical materialism as a scientific starting-point. It has been argued that Marx and Engels cannot have meant it when they said that something rational could be rescued from Hegel's idealist husk: yet, for men who spent their lives attempting to harness thought to history in language, they appear peculiarly addicted to that troubling metaphor of 'kernel' and 'husk'. Could something remain of Hegel's *method* which a thorough-going transformation would rescue – when his *system* had to be totally abandoned as mystification and idealist rubbish? But that is like asking whether, since Ricardo marked the closure of a bourgeois science (and was a rich banker to boot) there was anything which the founder of historical materialism could learn from him. Clearly, there was: clearly he did. He never ceased to learn from Ricardo, even when in the throes of dismantling him. He never ceased to take his bearings from classical Political Economy, even when he knew it could not finally think outside its bourgeois skin. In the same way, whenever he returns to the wholly unacceptable substance of the Hegelian system, he always pinpoints, in the same moment, what it is he learned from 'that mighty thinker', what had to be turned 'right-side-up' to be of service. This did not make the mature Marx 'a Hegelian' any more than *Capital* made him a Ricardian. To think this is to misunderstand profoundly the nature of the *critique* as a form of knowledge, and the dialectical method. Certainly, as far as the *1857 Introduction* is concerned, time and again, Hegel is decisively abandoned and overthrown, almost at the very points where Marx is clearly learning – or re-learning – *something* from his dialectical method. One of the traces of light which this text captures for us is the illumination of this suprisingly late moment of supersession – of return-and-transformation.

Notes and references

1 I have used the translation of the *1857 Introduction* by Martin Nicolaus, in his edition of *The Grundrisse*, Pelican (1973).
2 Pierre Vilar, 'Writing Marxist History', *New Left Review* 80.
3 *Samtliche Schriften*, vol 1. Translated in Hook, *From Hegel to Marx*.
4 *Grundrisse*, p. 156–7.
5 On the 'real relations/phenomenal form' distinction, Cf. especially, Mepham, 'the theory of Ideology in *Capital*' (below) and Geras, 'Essence + Appearance: Aspects of Fetishism in Marx's *Capital*', *New Left Review* 65.
6 *Capital* I, p. 745.
7 Karl Korsch, *Three Essays On Marxism*, Pluto Press (1971).
8 *Capital* I, p. 76.
9 *Poverty of Philosophy*, p. 118–19, 121.
10 In the *Critique of Hegel's Dialectic*.
11 *Economic & Philosophical Manuscripts*, p. 190.
12 ibid, p. 44.
13 Cf: Marx's ironic use of the terms, *Grundrisse*, p. 450.
14 *Economic & Philosophical Manuscripts*, p. 186–7.
15 *The Holy Family*.
16 *Economic & Philosophical Manuscripts*, p. 190.
17 *1857 Introduction*, p. 90.
18 Cf: *Introduction*, p. 88, 100.
19 *Introduction*, p. 93.
20 Cf: Marx's more developed notion of how the 'activity' of labour appears in the product as a 'fixed quality without motion': *Capital* I, p. 180–1.
21 *Economic & Philosophical Manuscripts*, p. 140–1.
22 *Introduction*, p. 92.
23 *Introduction*, p. 93: the distinctions between the 3 types of identity-relation are not as clearly sustained as one could wish.
24 *Introduction*, p. 94.
25 *Grundrisse*, p. 161.
26 *Capital* I, p. 356.
27 *Grundrisse*, p. 148: our italics.
28 *Introduction*, p. 90–3.
29 Cf: the dismantling of the theory of wages in *Capital* II and of the 'Trinity Formula' in *Capital* III.
30 *Introduction*, p. 98.
31 *Introduction*, p. 100.
32 On Hegel's and Marx's usage of 'concrete', Cf: Kline, 'Some Critical Comments on Marx's Philosophy', in *Marx & The Western World*, ed. N. Lobkowicz, Notre Dame (1967).
33 *Grundrisse*, p. 255.
34 *Introduction*, p. 101.
35 L. Althusser, *For Marx*, p. 42, 58.
36 *Introduction*, p. 102.
37 Marx's discussion of a further example – labour – has been omitted here.
38 *Introduction*, p. 105.
39 *Introduction*, p. 105–6.
40 *Introduction*, p. 107.
41 L. Colletti, *Marxism & Hegel*, p. 130–1.
42 ibid, p. 134.
43 Cf: *Grundrisse*, p. 459ff.
44 Cf: *Capital* I, p. 762ff.
45 E. Hobsbawn, 'Marx's Contribution to Historiography', in *Ideology & Social Science*, ed. Blackburn.

46 Cf: Godelier, 'Structure & Contradiction in *Capital*', in Blackburn, (ed), *op. cit*: and developments of the same argument in Godelier, *Rationality & Irrationality In Economics*, NLB.
47 *Capital III*, p. 720.
48 *Capital III*, p. 48.
49 Reprinted in *Poverty of Philosophy*, p. 209.
50 He quoted his reviewer in the *European Messenger* to the same effect, without demur: in the *Afterword* to the second Edition of *Capital*.
51 For a recent, and striking, reassertion of the centrality of 'Fetishism' to *Capital* from an 'anti-historicist' interpreter of Marx, Cf: the 'Interview with Lucio Colletti', in *New Left Review* 86.
52 The quotes are from *Capital I*, p. 74–5, 169, 42, Cf, also, Engels to Lange, in *M–E Correspondence*, p. 198.
53 *Capital III*, p. 797.
54 *Capital I*, p. 763.
55 On this point, also, Cf: 'Interview with L. Colletti', *New Left Review* 86.
56 *Capital I*, p. 542.
57 *Capital I*, p. 150.
58 In Blackburn, (ed), *op. cit.* p. 324–5.
59 The two strands are beautifully and inextricably combined in passages such as, e.g. *Capital I*, p. 763ff.
60 K. Korsch, *Karl Marx*, p. 201.
61 To Engels: *Correspondence*, p. 245: dated 30/4/1868.
62 Dated 11/7/1868, only three months later.
63 *Introduction*, p. 109–11.
64 *Holy Family*, p. 213.

6 Raymond Williams and cultural studies

Michael Green

> within each of these classes there are a certain number of *aliens*, if we may so call them – persons who are mainly led, not by their class spirit, but by a general *humane* spirit . . .
>
> Arnold, *Culture and Anarchy.* (1868)

> culture is one way in which class, the fact of major divisions between men, shows itself . . . to create public meanings which are authentic for us: to create a society where values are at once commonly created and criticised, and where the divisions of class may be replaced by the reality of common and equal membership. That, still, is the idea of a common culture, and it is increasingly, in developed societies, the detailed practice of revolution.
>
> Williams, *From Culture to Revolution,* (1968).

This article is a very compressed account of Raymond Williams's work over two decades, with an attempt to assess its current value in cultural studies – so it may be useful to begin, for reference, with a review of the issues discussed. Williams, in effect, founded the study of culture, in the early 1960s, from a socialist perspective which saw the general conflict between classes in industrial capitalist society to be located partly in the field of values and meanings. The inherited shape of the English tradition of thought about culture, compounded by his own training and history, led to a concentration upon the case of literature as a site for the general conflict between ideology and consciousness. Literature became a primary object of study, with much less said about other kinds of recorded and lived meanings, or about the institutions and structures of the society. His theoretical concepts, especially in his best-known though often difficult *The Long Revolution*, embody an oscillation between a liberal pluralist and a Marxist conception of history and society, though in later work the Marxist model is explicit. His key terms condense, in a way which is both summary and sometimes confusing, a set of interests central to any study of culture. So, the rich words communication and culture are themselves used at different times in both very wide and quite specific senses; 'social character' is used to mean both a conscious 'ideology' and its lived internalisation as a 'personality'; while 'structure of feeling' tries to capture (in fact too swiftly, in a collapse) both subjective meanings and something of the objective social structures to which they are a response. In his later work, an argument for a hegemonic dominant culture, which seeks through institutions, ideology, and the shaping of lived experiences, to incorporate both alternative and oppositional cultures (themselves present in both residual and emergent forms) sets up what we may expect to be a further phase in his own work and in any cultural studies: less literary, less reformist, less founded in and appealing to personal experience, concerned with the detailed study of hegemony in its various forms (especially ideological forms), with consciousness, and, as:

> crucial to any Marxist theory of culture that it can give an adequate explanation to the sources of . . . practices and meanings.
>
> (*New Left Review* 82, p. 11)

– the study both of a dominant bourgeois culture and of struggles against it.

Williams was born in 1921, the son of a railway signalman on the Welsh borders, studied English at Cambridge and taught evening classes at Oxford before becoming in 1961 a Fellow of Jesus College Cambridge, where he still teaches. Reviewing his own work at a conference in 1967, Williams described his earliest involvement in problems to which the idea of 'culture' first gave him access:

> Culture was the way in which the process of education, the experience of literature and – for someone moving out of a working-class family to a higher education – inequality, came through. What other people, in different situations might experience more directly as economic or political inequality, was naturally experienced, from my own route, as primarily an inequality of culture: an inequality which was also, in an obvious sense, an uncommunity. This is, I think, still the most important way to follow the argument about culture because everywhere, but very specifically in England, culture is one way in which class, the fact of major divisions between men, shows itself.
>
> (*From Culture to Revolution*, p. 24)

The stress on the necessity to make connections between intellectual work and personal experience is important, and had been elaborated in *Culture and Society*:

> To take a meaning from experience, and try to make it active, is in fact our process of growth. Some of these meanings we receive and recreate. Others we must make for ourselves, and try to communicate. The human crisis is always a crisis of understanding; what we genuinely understand we can do.
>
> (pp. 323–324)

This is a chosen emphasis, a way of defining intellectual work, which has been widely attractive and influential in his own work and that of Richard Hoggart and is represented in the early work of this Centre: see, for instance, Alan Shuttleworth's *People and Culture* in our first issue. It connects with a way of writing powerful in a primarily literary tradition of social commentary in England from Coleridge and Wordsworth on, to which Williams himself gave first full acknowledgement. Observed details and an open appeal to the reader's sympathies were used to enforce general arguments, in a way hardly known from European 'sociology' though since, more vehemently and abrasively, well known in Marx. But other connections were to give this way of writing, especially in Hoggart and Williams, its resonance in the 1960s. At a time when many social sciences and, ironically, English itself (now a formidably impersonal 'literary criticism') seemed to consist of shuffled abstractions, a direct commentary on contemporary experience had immense power – while the languages of official 'politics' and of the newer spheres of upper management, and of the media were as remote, as in need of any voice of clear (and perhaps also non-metropolitan) integrity. Most crucially, it was a simultaneous concern of the New Left and of many later groupings (and now Women's Liberation) to insist on the importance of personal experiences and precisely of the effort to understand, so well described in Williams, against authoritarian political hierarchies, and the use of theory as a weapon of defence against new ideas. Hence

Williams has become known as one of the few visibly Socialist intellectuals in Britain, known primarily for the range of his writing on culture and communication over 25 years (see the list at the end of this article) but taken as exemplary also for a stance towards experience and ideas: patient, open, learning with persistence and difficulty, which has contrasted itself tenaciously and deliberately with other modes of thought on the left and in literary studies.

The political difficulty is to move between this responsiveness to lived experiences and the necessary abstraction, and scale, of a theory concerned with the social world as a whole. This involves the effort of understanding involved in the intelligent use of major theories; but then needs to avoid a blanket retreat to unfamiliar European theory as a way in part of avoiding problems in the English situation to hand (for which both Williams and E. P. Thompson criticised *New Left Review* in the late 1960s). In reverse, an openness to the authenticity of personal experience leads to an infinite, and perhaps politically crippling, tolerance; as in Williams's handling of expected opponents in *Culture and Society* where he says that his respect for other writers stems from their making available:

> a special immediacy of experience, which works itself out, in depth, to a particular embodiment of ideas, that become, in themselves, the whole man. The correctness of these ideas is not at first in question . . . If writing is an articulated experience, it has a validity which can survive even the demolition of its general conclusions . . .
>
> (pp. 24–25)

The double commitment to cultural equality and to truth to personal experience then accounts for Williams's distinctive position in his early work. He defines himself in the 1940s against the two main groups concerned with culture not as a static inheritance of certain works of art, but, as the living, problematic and contested field of human thought and values. In the work of Leavis and Eliot it was argued that only a minority, embattled or ascetic, can preserve a deeply felt quality of response to life against the increasing pressures, in their formulation, of a 'mass', 'commercial' society; an argument Williams rightly rejected for its pessimism about potential social change and about the capacities of most human beings, written off as a 'mass' (see his critique, *Culture and Society* pp. 287–301). Second, there was a Marxism as received, defined and practised in England under the shadow of Stalin and within the cold war. (The recovery of some Marx texts in the 1960s, and the growth of new kinds of Marxist theory and practice, were to alter Williams's sense of his own position. Almost none of the history of English intellectuals and their relation to various kinds of Marxism has yet been produced, though Chris Pawling has attempted some of this work in relation to Orwell in his thesis.)

> As for Marx, one accepted the emphases on history, on change, on the inevitably close relationship between class and culture, but the way this came through was, at another level, unacceptable. There was, in this position, a polarisation and abstraction of economic life on the one hand and culture on the other, which did not seem to me to correspond to the social experience of culture as others had lived it, and as one was trying to live it oneself.
>
> (*From Culture to Revolution*, p. 28)

This sums up both Williams's early distrust of and dissent from Marx, and the already mentioned distrust of theory:

> by temperament and training, I find more meaning in this kind of personally verified statement than in a system of significant abstractions.
>
> (*Culture and Society*, p. 18)

So it came about, by what seems in 1974 like a complete misunderstanding, that Williams thought he was writing *against* Marxism in emphasising *connections* between separated areas of social life, and the possibility for men to redefine their lives actively and (a word he often stresses) 'creatively', rather than live out the simple determinism of an economic structure and 'the consequent social relations' (p. 261).

In this spirit, and during the general bleakness of the 1950s for the English Left, Williams set himself to write a group of three books: *Culture and Society 1780–1950* (1958), a tribute to the long tradition of critical responses by English writers to industrial capitalist society: *Border Country* (1960), a novel about a Welsh railwayman and his family between the wars, based on personal experience; and *The Long Revolution* (1961), a set of linked essays on modes and possibilities of communication in Britain over the last two centuries.

Early work: Four Arguments

Williams insists that all human beings, not the cultured minority alone, are continually involved in the testing and exploration of meanings. The *spirit* of this argument, and its insistence that all have the capacity to work out an understanding of the world which does not merely reproduce given ideas, is at once attractive. (See *From Culture to Revolution*, p. 29; *The Long Revolution*, p. 54; revised *Communications*, pp. 18–19). Theoretically, it is supported very unsatisfactorily by a sentence from J. Z. Young's *Doubt and Certainty in Science – A Biologist's Reflections on the Brain:* 'the brain of each one of us does literally create his or her own world'. Whatever shadowy evidence work on the brain provides, or may later provide, in practice Williams proceeds to ignore, almost completely, the actual ways in which individuals receive ideas (through the various practices within family, school, work, such state mechanisms as the legal system, and through the mass media) and then partly individually, partly jointly, and with very different powers of articulation depending on class situation, work through, beyond, or against them. As it stands, the suggestion of *individual* effort to perceive dovetails with the emphasis on the *artist* in Williams's work (though again without much stress on ideas handed down and pre-existing in language, genres and the material conditions of communication), though not with the highly original writing on *collective* working-class achievements in the 'Conclusion' to *Culture and Society*.

Second, it is argued that meanings, values, attempted communications and (in the most elaborated verbal form) ideas are involved in *all* human practices and institutions:

> art is . . . an activity, with the production, the trading, the politics, the raising of families . . . all the activities as particular and contemporary forms of human energy . . . (there are) meanings and values not only in art and learning but also in institutions and ordinary behaviour.
>
> (*Long Revolution*, pp. 61, 57)

It follows that the study of culture is of the meanings in almost any human activity; and in turn that such study will be the work of a group if it is to succeed. Williams's own recurrent working concentration on art and learning is paralleled by the narrowing of focus in Richard Hoggart between *Uses of Literacy* and the later work.

The third argument is political:

> if it is at all true that the creation of meanings is an activity which engages all men, then one is bound to be shocked by any society which, in its most explict culture, either suppresses the meanings and values of whole groups, or which fails to extend to these groups the possibility of articulating and communicating these meanings. This, precisely, was what one wanted to assert about contemporary Britain, even at a point where we were being assured, in the usual kind of happy retrospect, that most of the social problems had been resolved. It was, on the contrary, perfectly clear that the majority of people, while living *as* people, were both shut out by the nature of the educational process from access to the full range of meanings of their predecessors in that place, and excluded by the whole structure of communications – the character of its material ownership, its limiting social assumptions – from any adequate participation in the process of changing and developing meanings which was in any case going on.
>
> (*From Culture to Revolution*, p. 29)

Williams's attack on the 'dominative attitude' provoked at the time, among others, Richard Wollheim's Fabian pamphlet *Socialism and Culture* (1961) and Anthony Hartley's *A State of England* (1963) which argued that 'only by adopting a "dominative attitude" can (intellectuals) do their duty by the society to which they belong' (p. 42). The decade spans Williams's repeated and much attacked argument for a 'common' culture, first put in terms of necessary reforms in press, radio and television, more sharply during the decline of the new Left and in the face of Wilson's second administration, in 1968:

> the struggle to create public meanings which are authentic for us: to create a society where values are at once commonly created and criticised, and where the divisions and exclusions of class may be replaced by the reality of common and equal membership. That, still, is the idea of a common culture, and it is increasingly, in developed societies, the detailed practice of revolution.
>
> (*From Culture to Revolution*, p. 308)

Fourth, various kinds of English writing since the late eighteenth century are examined in detail. *Culture and Society* shows how it is distinctively through moral and social analysis by such men as Ruskin, Morris and Carlyle, and by novelists, that a tradition of intellectual dissent from the suppression of human needs under capitalism has been maintained in Britain. The analysis shows clearly how this tradition can use a combination of precise observation, rhetoric and appeals to a notion of a repressed 'human nature' in assaulting industrialism, while relying on the reader's fellow-feeling to win polemical arguments, and rarely generating precise analysis of the social formation. In this respect the work reviewed has analogies with that of the early Marx, discussed in the book, though it is oddly said that: 'the validity of his economic and political theory cannot be here discussed' (p. 271).

Since *Culture and Society*, European traditions of dissent from capitalism have been intelligently presented in such books as Stuart Hughes's *Consciousness and Society*, R. A. Nisbet's *The Sociological Tradition*, and Anthony Giddens's *Capitalism and Modern Social Theory*. The books have emphasised the general conservatism of the positions adopted, and the conscious construction of a 'sociology' as a way of resisting 'Marxism'. Perry Anderson has argued, in a brilliant essay, that literary men in England, from Wordsworth and Coleridge down to Leavis, Williams and Hoggart themselves, have been forced into a comprehensively intellectual role by other absences in British society:

> The culture of British bourgeois society is organized about an absent centre – a total theory of itself, that should have been either a classical sociology or a national Marxism. The trajectory of English social structure – above all, the non-emergence of a powerful revolutionary movement of the working class – is the explanation of this arrested development . . . it quite literally deprives the Left of any source of concepts and categories with which to analyse its own society, and thereby attain the fundamental pre-condition for changing it.
>
> (*Student Power*, ed. Cockburn and Blackburn, pp. 276, 277)

It follows that in *The Long Revolution* Williams is seeking new theoretical supports, beyond the radically criticised English inheritance, the ambivalently rejected Marxist tradition, and an unfamiliar sociology; with resulting problems to be looked at in a moment. Meanwhile, the book is also concerned to analyse ways in which some particular forms of verbal communication (novels, plays, newspapers) have evolved their own conventions and their own tensions within and against the conventions:

> in the very acts of perception and communication, this practical interaction of what is personally seen, interpreted and organized, and what can be socially recognized, known and formed is richly and subtly manifested . . . the tension can be great, in the necessarily difficult struggle to establish reality . . . in a period of exceptional growth, as ours has been and will continue to be, the tension will be exceptionally high, and certain kinds of failure and breakdown may become characteristic. The recording of creative effort, to explore such breakdown, is not always easy to distinguish from the simple, often rawly exciting exploitation of breakdown. Or else there is a turning away, into known forms, which remind us of previously learned realities and seek, by this reminder, to establish probability of a kind.
>
> (p. 315)

Recurring conventions, and their modification, are related to the social tensions with which the various forms of communication are concerned as their subject-matter, but, as significantly, also to their producers (in pt. 2, ch. 6), their audience (pt. 2, ch. 2) and to the structure of ownership and exchange underlying the changing practices of commercial publication (pt. 2, ch. 3).

To outline in summary form these four arguments, conducted at the time in an almost complete theoretical vacuum, sketches in only the bones of the achievement. Various interests, competing for attention in *The Long Revolution*, make it a hard book to grasp as a whole. The directly political attack on capitalism, on modes of adjustment to it, and on its defensive strategies, 'Britain in the 1960s', which concludes the book, is written with a bite which paradoxically detaches it from the rest. The use of J.Z. Young fits uneasily with the neo-Freudian Erich Fromm's concept of 'social character', discussed in a moment. And growing in all three of these books is the painful subject of his second novel: the cultural choices open to those who have detached themselves from the life and values of their class. Taken up in the review of such middle class rebels as Gissing and Orwell (*Culture and Society*, pp. 178–179 and 280 – Orwell was to be more fully and penetratingly analysed in the later *Orwell*) the subject arises in family conflicts:

> a part of a whole generation has had this. A personal father, and that is one clear issue. But a father is more than a person, he's in fact a society, the thing you grow up into. For us, perhaps, that is the way to put it. We've been moved and grown into a different society. We keep the relationship but we don't take over the work. We have, you might say, a personal father but no social father. What they offer us, where we go, we reject.
>
> (*Border Country*, ch. 9)

A profound crisis is then articulated in Williams's magnificent and almost intolerably painful novel *Second Generation* (1964), which uses a narrative about an Oxford car worker's son, in post-graduate research on 'communities', to explore the chasm (not least in the Labour party) between academic and manual labour, the split in the union movement between economism and radicalism, and the various ambiguities of the 'academic radical'. (It is worth wondering why the novel never achieved paperback publication). As he says of Orwell:

> Part of the England he discovered was a real society, living under and within this order, keeping certain values going. But inseparable from this was the different England created by this order, in prejudices, compromises, adjustments, illusions. To respond to the society would be to distinguish one part from the other, to enter into a necessary conflict, reaching into every area of life.
>
> (*Orwell*, p. 28)

The skill of the book on Orwell is particularly impressive; while the problems of those losing touch with working-class origins have been fairly thoroughly charted in the last twenty years (Williams, Hoggart, Seabrook, observations in McInnes, Lessing and many others), those detaching themselves from middle-class values have expressed themselves only intermittently and indirectly. Rowbotham's *Woman's Consciousness, Man's World* is an exception.

The status of art and literature

But though Williams is himself a very intelligent novelist, the status given to art and literature brings about a primary distortion in the early analytic work. This is not only a matter of emphasis, nor of competence to deal with diverse materials arising from the enclaved specialisms of the contemporary university. In *Culture and Society* he rightly stresses that:

> to the highly literate observer there is always a temptation to assume that reading plays as large a part in the lives of most people as it does in his own . . . the majority of people do not yet give reading this importance in their lives; their ideas and feelings are, to a large extent, still moulded by a wider and more complex pattern of social and family life. There is an evident danger of delusion, to the highly literate person, if he supposes that he can judge the quality of general living by primary reference to the reading artifacts.
>
> (p. 297)

This indication of the need to use other evidence, other methods ('oral history') is undercut when the 'actual analysis' of English culture in the 1840s is given over to fiction and the press, concluding weakly that:

> as we look at the whole period, we recognize that its creative activities are to be found, not only in art but, following the main lines of the society, in industry and engineering, and, questioning the society, in new kinds of social institution.
>
> (p. 88)

which is a very distant account. Even in the discussion of writers themselves, in *Culture and Society*, there is some sense of an abstracted 'Tradition', with only brief reference to the writers' social location; compare the brief but incisive social analysis of Orwell's displaced class identity and resulting personal and fictional consequences, in the *Modern Masters* study. The idea of a tradition, in which all present help 'contribute' to a general 'growth' also blurs the enormous and angry disagreements between some of the writers surprisingly put together in civilised discourse.

Harder still to accept, or understand (except in terms of an influence from Leavis apparently rejected earlier) is what can seem a qualitative preference for art over other human activities, expressed most strongly in his critical writing under pressures during the 1960s:

> while we may, in the study of a past period, separate out particular aspects of life, and treat them as if they were self-contained . . . in the living experience of the time every element was . . . an inseparable part of a complex whole . . . it is from such a totality that the artist draws; it is in art, primarily, that the effect of a whole living experience is expressed and embodied.
>
> (*Drama from Ibsen to Brecht*, p. 18)

Such a claim is linked to his proposal of a new term, *structure of feeling*, to define: 'the particular living result of all the elements in the general organization' (*The Long Revolution*, p. 64).

'Structure of feeling' makes two suggestions at once. One, that ideas in a society are always contradictory and never complete, are always outrun by experience, so that the ways they are 'lived out' never fit properly with the ideas as originally formulated. The lived response: 'has to deal not only with the public ideals but with their omissions and consequences as lived' (*The Long Revolution*, p. 80).

This produces one of the few model analyses we have in English of 'literature and society'; it demonstrates, from novels of the 1840s, the tension of living out social contradictions; characteristic choices by writers within the contradictions; and the use in popular art of fantasy endings, 'magic solutions', to 'postpone the conflict between the ethic and the experience' – where great art tries to move beyond the given, familiar defintions of the problems. But to speak of the novel embodying 'all the elements in the general organization' goes too far, suggests that all the various ideologies and attitudes in a society are simultaneously present, interacting, rather than living under the ideology of a dominant culture, as his later essays rightly argue. So it is part of the generally unresolved conflicting arguments in the book that although conceding such a 'structure of feeling' is: 'not uniform throughout the society; it is primarily evident in the dominant productive group' (p. 80) with the realisation that art carries evidence very largely about the attitudes of a dominant class, he can still make sweepingly larger claims for its value. Thus:

> Sociology can describe social conditions more accurately, at the level of ordinary measurement. A political programme can offer more precise remedies, at the level of ordinary action. Literature can attempt to follow these modes, but at its most important

> its process is different and yet still inescapably social: a whole way of seeing that is communicable to others, and a dramatisation of values that becomes an action.
>
> (*The English Novel*, pp. 58–59)

The difficulty lies in the word 'communicable'.

As, in a genuine paradox, Williams uses 'culture' to refer now to works of art and now to a whole social totality, so also 'communication' assumes a double meaning. Partly it describes the actual communications media, as in the empirical *Communications*, but partly also the family, education, work, even society itself, considered as *unequal exchanges of meaning and value.* Society itself is: 'a process of learning and communication' (*Communications*, rev., p. 19) but the *reverse is also true:* 'if we study real relations, in any actual analysis, we reach the point where we see that we are studying a general organization in a particular example . . .' (*The Long Revolution*, p. 61).

At times this seems to mean, implausibly, that any particular social phenomenon (or perhaps only art, as a 'whole way of seeing', is given this status) can itself be seen as a reliable microcosm of the whole society, or in terms of organic growth metaphors (often used) as a cross-section through the developing whole. More interesting is the realisation, whose genuine difficulty is struggled with in the writing of the book, that whatever exists, and is later analysed, is linked to and shaped by its place in a particular social formation. In *The English Novel* he refers to the romantic writers' perception that society was: 'a process that entered lives, to shape or to deform; a process personally known but then again suddenly distant, complex, incomprehensible, overwhelming . . .' (p. 13).

This means, in his work, not only that part and whole, the practice and the totality, are inextricably involved with each other, but that every apparently independent factor analysed: novel, press, law, union, is 'itself a social relationship'; this quotation is taken from the most sympathetic study of the resulting problems of method, B. Ollman's *Alienation*, ironically a study of Marx.

The mistaken slide in the argument, in my view, is that he goes beyond insisting that communication is one way of understanding all social relationships, that there is therefore no satisfactorily isolable 'discipline' of 'communication' (neatly dismissed as 'scraps of applied psychology and linguistics', *Culture and Society* p. 18) which ignores prevalent patterns of relationship, power, class and so on to say that any real theory of communication is a theory of community (p. 18). Yet if *community* is to have a different meaning from *society*, it presumably involves a sharing of experience and purposes, as a preferred way of life. The recent bandwagon adoption of the word by politicians and broadcasters is now causing Williams to withdraw uneasily from it: 'community is also a real social fact: not an idealised notion but a social system containing radical inequalities and conflicts of interest' (*Television*, p. 149).

In the earlier work it had been widely used, and art, as a form of communication, held to *bring it into being:*

> the arts . . . command very powerful means of sharing . . . The discovery of a means of communication is the discovery of a common meaning . . . It is often through the art that the society expresses its sense of being a society . . . even in our own complex society, certain artists seem near the centre of the common experience.
>
> (*The Long Revolution*, pp. 40, 47)

But in this account there is an undifferentiated 'the' common experience, and an unproblematic account of communication itself, overlooking the varieties of possible readings. The argument, generalised, becomes circular: art=communication=community:

> in this respect the arts of a period . . . are of major importance. For here, if anywhere, this characteristic is likely to be expressed; often not consciously, but by the fact that here, in the only examples we have of recorded communication that outlives its bearers, the actual living sense, the deep community that makes the communication possible, is naturally drawn upon.
>
> (pp. 64–65)

Community becomes especially paradoxical in *The Country and the City*. For even if those who do read the literature of the past today were to read the English novel with Williams's own patience and skill as 'the exploration of community', this 'brings together', in a special way, the differing interests of various writers at various historical moments, presenting them too smoothly as a mutually sympathetic group pursuing continuously the same concerns. *The Country and the City* contains magnificent literary criticism; but its ordered eloquence ('that chained bark') smooths much away, and the study of literature risks becoming 'an action' which conceals some of the struggles it seeks to recover, though this was never the intention.

In summary, the early stress on art's centrality in defining and recording community, needed to give way to the more recent argument that while art still records the way in which a dominant culture is lived and experienced, and the contradictions within it, yet it will at the same time: 'contribute to the effective dominant culture and be a central articulation of it' (*New Left Review 82*, pp. 11,14).

This certainly gives art, in a non-evaluative sense, a unique status. It also starts to open up empirical questions concerning the ways in which art is actually used by different fractions of its audience. Meanwhile 'structure of feeling' and the highly original attempt in that chapter to connect social institutions, ideologies and lived experience, impacts two kinds of inquiries which cultural studies had to go into more deeply before considering whether, in analysis, they could be brought together again: the study of *subjective meanings*, in phenomenology and sub-branches of various disciplines (each with problems of method attached), and the study of *objective social structures*, of production and distribution, of political, educational, familial organisation. As it is, *The Long Revolution* tends to read as though we should study either middle-class feelings or working-class institutions; the feelings of working-class people, and the institutions of the middle-class, are both neglected. And this is connected with his interpreations of bourgeois individualism and working-class solidarity.

Social character, social class

The ending of *Culture and Society* and the opening of *The Long Revolution* present the unresolved argument with Marx in Williams's mind. In the first book, where he says he is 'not a Marxist', his account of a Marxist theory of culture had been sympathetic:

> any formula in terms of levels, as in terms of structure and superstructure, does less than justice to the factors of movement which it is the essence of Marxism to realize . . . A Marxist theory of culture will recognize diversity and complexity, will take account of continuity within change, will allow for chance and certain limited autonomies, but,

> with these reservations, will take the facts of the economic structure and the consequent social relations as the guiding string on which a culture is woven, and following which a culture is to be understood.
>
> (pp. 260, 261–262)

His objection was to the inconsistencies of (English) Marxist practice, where the vehement assertion of positions both crude and mutually incompatible as Marxism went with a general thinness of reference to any actual culture. His own conclusion had neverthless elaborated the ideas of a class:

> 'working-class culture' . . . is not proletarian art, or council houses, or a particular use of language; it is rather, the basic collective idea, and the institutions, manners, habits of thought and intentions which proceed from this. Bourgeois culture, similarly, is the basic individualist idea and the institutions, manners, habits of thought, and intentions which proceed from that.
>
> (pp. 313–314)

He had also noted the effect of bourgeois culture in containing and reducing the idea of solidarity to 'a defensive attitude, the natural mentality of the long siege' (p. 318). The observation was elaborated in Perry Anderson's essay 'Origins of the Present Crisis:'

> the English working-class has since the mid-nineteenth century been essentially characterized by an extreme disjunction between an intense consciousness of separate identity and a permanent failure to set and impose goals for society as a whole.
>
> (*Towards Socialism*, ed. Anderson and Blackburn, p. 34)

In *The Long Revolution* these terms are held at bay: ' "class" carries an emphasis different from "community" or "association", because it is not a face-to-face grouping but, like "society" itself, an abstraction' (p. 95).

Instead, he turns to Erich Fromm (discussed in Phil Slater's article in this issue) and to Fromm's *Fear of Freedom* (1942). In that book Fromm himself tries to produce a social psychology of class, in the same spirit as the Frankfurt School's *Authoritarian Family* or Sartre's attempt at a Marxist psychoanalysis, a materialist psychology, in *Search for a Method*. Fromm argues that a child confronts a particular mode of life, determined by its place in the economic structure of a society, through the medium of a family representing the typical features of a class. This mode of life is internalised as a set of character traits which in turn shape the adult's participation in society; a 'social character'. Williams goes on to use social character to condense severely two lines of thought: one about the internalisation of a cultural formation in a structure of 'personality', the other about the formally held beliefs and values of a class, its ideology; again, two crucial areas are broached, but with a compression which lessens their significance. Combined with this is a straight inconsistency in the book between two models of society. In one version, a society is made up of classes, each with its ideology, but with a dominant class having the power to seek to impose its ideas on subordinate classes, in a process of conflict. In the other, there is a notion of 'alternative social characters' co-existing, while 'all contribute to the growth of the society' (p. 80, a passage on which E.P. Thompson commented in his very important review, crucial to any assessment of Williams, in *New Left Review*). The first model, a Marxist conflict model, and the second, a liberal model of co-existence, exist in unresolved tension, as, less visibly they do in *The Uses of Literacy*, as when speaking of American songs in working-class clubs Hoggart notes they are played: 'so that, though their main lines are kept, they are transmuted into the received idiom. When this act of transmutation has been performed, the new and the old live together happily' (p. 124).

In Williams's work, rural communities are replaced by a commercial, city-led 'society'; in Hoggart's, a working-class culture of poverty, stretching from the late nineteenth century, is replaced by a consumer culture. Both will have permanent value, of course, and present themselves, as substantial accounts of this process rather than as 'theories of culture'.

Political implications

But the movement between co-existence and conflict models is consonant with Williams's leading position in the New Left. In this role, Williams was in the work of the early 1960s appealing quite widely to 'men of good will', hoping for a more democratic socialism, and for changes in the institutions of culture and communication on the basis of reforming intervention; but:

> There was a point, quite evident to me between the publication of *The Long Revolution* and *Communications*, and evident in the most public way in reactions to the Pilkington Report, when a genuine and powerful counter-attack was mounted . . . all the time, beyond this ebb and flow of opinion, the basic character of our major cultural institutions was not only unchanged, but was becoming more settled, more established, and more widely integrated with a whole variety of other activities.
>
> (*Communications*, rev. ed., p. 11)

The dilemmas of the reformist position then combine with the personal crisis analysed in *Second Generation*, and with the explosion of student politics, sexual politics, revolutionary groupings and open class confrontation in the late 1960s, to intensify the contradiction between radical change and human continuity:

> Am I then saying, after all, that the definition of culture as a whole way of life should be replaced by its definition as a way of struggle? No, because . . . struggle . . . is still only part of the process . . . we would be excluding love and comradeship and any possible agreement . . . the isolation of struggle, where this is not merely a rhetorical device, would be empty and even, in certain circumstances, malign.
>
> (*From Culture to Revolution*, pp. 298–299)

It seems worth citing one terse retrospective assessment of the New Left in the period:

> The New Left had begun as a handful of intellectuals: it gained a certain – minority – middle-class audience: it never touched any section of the working-class. Once it had ceased to be a purely intellectual grouping, the hope of becoming a major political movement haunted it, and ended by dissipating its initial assests . . . (this) affected its theoretical work itself. In one crucial field, objective ambiguity became subjective confusion, and, ultimately, evasion. In terms of the sociology of knowledge, the New Left, lacking clear-cut social boundaries, was unable to focus any precise image of

> itself or – by extension – of its society. Its almost complete failure to offer any structural analysis of British society is striking.
>
> (*New Left Review 29*, pp. 16–17)

Structural analysis was in fact impressively provided in the *May Day Manifesto* of 1968.

Recent work

A considerable re-appraisal of position is signalled in a preliminary way in Williams's recent work. One, he has talked of a need to break with ordinary language:

> I think many people have now noticed the long-term effects of the specific social situation of British intellectuals . . . pulled back towards ordinary language . . . in a manner of exposition which can be called unsystematic but which also represents an unusual consciousness of an immediate audience . . . while this group . . . was in effect and detail a privileged and at times a ruling class, this pull towards ordinary language was often, is often, a pull towards current consciousness: a framing of ideas within certain polite but definite limits.
>
> (*New Left Review 67*, p. 4)

Characteristically, his critique of too rapid a movement from this language sees clearly, but retains a sympathy:

> definitions attaining the sudden extra precision of italics . . . A break with the English bourgeoisie . . . seemed to demand these alternative procedures and styles, as one of the few practical affiliations that could be made at once and by an act of will.
>
> (pp. 4, 5)

Two, in his 'Base and Superstructure' he insists on determination within a complex social structure:

> if we come to say that society is composed of a large number of social practices which form a concrete social whole, and if we give to each practice a certain specific recognition, adding only that they interact, relate and combine in very complicated ways . . . we are . . . withdrawing from the claim that there is any process of determination. And this I, for one, would be very unwilling to do.
>
> (p. 7)

He now argues that a dominant class maintains its hegemony, not merely through 'an imposed ideology', but through the living out of class values, informally, unconsciously often, in a variety of social institutions:

> The processes of education; the processes of a much wider social training within institutions like the family; the practical definitions and organisation of work; the selective tradition at an intellectual and theoretical level; all these forces are involved in a continual making and remaking of an effective dominant culture, and on them, *as experienced as built into our living*, its reality depends.
>
> (p. 9, italics added)

He proposes that against the *dominant* culture there are both *alternative* and *oppositional* cultures: 'someone who simply finds a different way to live and wishes to be left alone with it, and someone who finds a different way to live and wants to change the society in its light.' (p. 11) each of which can appear in either a *residual* ('practised on the basis of the residue – cultural, as well as social – of some previous social formation') or an *emergent* ('new meanings and values, new practices') form, and each of which seeks to avoid the increasingly far-reaching attempts at *incorporation* by the dominant class. About the possibilities of an emergent oppositional culture the article ends with a very qualified optimism in which art again has its role:

> the dominant mode is a conscious selection and organization. At least in its fully formed state . . . But there are always sources of real human practice which it neglects or excludes . . . for example, alternative perceptions of others, in immediate personal relationships, or new perceptions of materials and media, in art and science . . .
>
> (p. 13)

It is a list which excludes political groups of any kind!

Conclusion

This article has tried to show why Williams was so much a part of the founding of cultural studies: in his keeping alive a comprehensive interest in all human activities as meaningful, against the widely canvassed Eliot–Leavis preference for a minority culture holding at bay a mass civilisation. In retrospect it seems inevitable (assuming that Perry Anderson's survey sketch of what needs more detailed work) that in England a socialist struggle over the realm of culture should stand in for other kinds of work; and that here, argument began out of literary-intellectual tradition, which Williams was the first to properly record, and whose strengths of moral concern, observation, and appeal to a reader's conscience, he was to share. In his work and Hoggart's, experience generates a powerful survey and analysis of a dominant culture's power to suppress, but the cutting edge is sometimes later lost; Williams's finest piece is perhaps the 'Conclusion' to *Culture and Society*. Later, though there is a long series of intelligent contributions to the study of literature and to the ways in which writers try to see behind and beyond the ideologies of their period, there is uncertainty about the vision of society being offered. While the record of learning in public is valuable, especially among the crisply assured new model Marxisms of the early 1970s, it is a weak ending in 'Base and Superstructure' that: 'the true crisis in cultural theory, in our own time, is between this view of the work of art as object and the alternative view of art as a practice' (p. 15).

Rather, the crisis is the dis-relation between such theory itself and the sources of alternative and oppositional human practice of which the article speaks; and within the theory, the difficulty of combining a sufficiently elaborate general analysis of society with either detailed knowledge of particular areas or the wish to understand and listen to the lived meanings unrecorded in written texts. It would of course be impertinent to think Mr Williams did not have much to say on these issues.

Raymond Williams: major works

Drama from Ibsen to Eliot (1952, London*, and paperback)
Culture and Society 1780–1950 (1958, London, and paperback*)
Border Country (1960, London*, and paperback out of print)
The Long Revolution (London, 1961, and paperback*)
Communications (Harmondsworth 1962, paperback, alternative title *Britain in the Sixties*)
Second Generation (1964, London)
Communications, revised edition (1966, London)
From Culture to Revolution, ed Eagleton and Wicker (1968, London)
May Day Manifesto (1968, Harmondsworth paperback)
Drama from Ibsen to Brecht (1968, London)
The English Novel from Dickens to Lawrence (1970, London*, and paperback)
Orwell (1971, London, paperback)
'From Leavis to Goldmann' *New Left Review 67* (1971)* reprinted as Introduction to *Racine* by Lucien Goldmann (1972, Cambridge paperback)
'Base and Superstructure' *New Left Review 82* (1973)
The Country and the City (1973, London)
Television: Technology and Cultural Form (1974, London, paperback)

* Edition quoted

7 The hinterland of science: Ideology and the 'sociology of knowledge'

Stuart Hall

'Ideology' is a term which does not trip lightly off an English tongue. It has stubbornly refused to be 'naturalised'. English political theory sometimes refers to 'ideologies', meaning simply 'systematic bodies of ideas'. But the concept is largely descriptive – it plays no significant analytic role. Generally, the concept of 'ideology' has never been fully absorbed into Anglo-Saxon social theory. In his important collection of essays published in 1949, Robert Merton included two essays on 'The Sociology of Knowledge' and on 'Karl Mannheim'.[1] In his introduction to this section, Merton self-consciously signalled these pieces as marking the 'rediscovery' of the concept of ideology for American social science. This 'rediscovery' was conducted in the context of a general *contrast* between two radically different styles of thought – the European (where the concept has played a significant role) and the American (where it had up to that point been largely absent). But Merton's opening was not followed by a flood of new studies informed by this concept. What he called 'the sociology of knowledge' has, until very recently, remained a minority interest in American empirical social science.

In his labour of rediscovery, Merton openly acknowledged that 'In this respect, as in others, Marxism is the storm centre of *wissensociologie* [the sociology of knowledge] . . . we can trace out its formulations primarily in the writings of Marx and Engels.' The absence of an interest in the problem of ideology in American sociology thus clearly relates to the absence anywhere in this tradition of thought, until very recently, of any major open confrontation with Marxist concepts. An interesting essay could be written on what concepts did duty, in American social theory, for the absent concept of 'ideology': for example, the notion of norms in structural functionalism, and of 'values' and the 'central value system' in Parsons. Merton's mind had undoubtedly been directed to this absence by the growing body of work in the study of mass communications and public opinion. But the concept of ideology was never rigorously applied to this promising area of work.[2]

Bacon called for a thorough-going investigation and critique of the roots of conventional wisdom – what he called a 'criticism of the idols'. And Helvetius – a favourite of Marx's – made much of the proposition that 'Our ideas are the necessary consequence of the societies in which we live'. But most of the recent 'overviews' of the concept *ideology* agree that the word itself, in its modern meanings, originated with that group of *savants* in the French Revolution who were entrusted by the Convention of 1795 with the founding of a new centre of revolutionary thought – an enterprise which was located in the newly founded Institut de France.[3] It was to this group that the term 'idéologues' was first applied. Their fate constitutes a salutary warning for all ideologues. For a time this group of thinkers constituted the spokesmen for revolutionary ideas – the French Revolution 'in thought'. Their aim was to realise in practice what they conceived as the 'promise' of the Revolution – the freedom of thought and expression. But they were hoisted on the horns of a dilemma which has dogged the concept of 'ideology' from its inception. As Lichtheim points out, they were concerned with 'ideology' in *two* senses, which were logically incompatible. First, they saw the relation between history and thought – the tide of the Revolution and the 'ideas' which expressed it. But they also wanted to advance certain 'true' ideas–ideas which would be true whatever historical conjuncture they were located in. They thus compromised – 'for the sake of ideas' – with that historical agent who they imagined had the power to make their ideas come true: Napoleon Bonaparte. This was an ill-judged faith. Napoleon took them up in 1799, in the 'moment' of Brumaire, in order to win support in the class where the *savants* had greatest influence – the educated middle classes. He even signed his proclamations to the army during the 1798–9 period, 'Général en Chef, Membre de l'Institut'. But by 1803, in the 'moment' of his Concordat with the Church, he abandoned them, deliberately setting out to destroy the Institut's core, the '*classe des sciences morales et politiques*, from which liberal and republican ideas radiated throughout the educational establishment'. 'The story of Bonaparte's degeneration', Lichtheim concludes, 'can be written in terms of his relation with the *ideologues*'.

The interest in ideology did not, however, altogether disappear with the disbanding of this group. Destutt de Tracy inaugurated a 'natural history of ideas', treating the history of the contents and evolution of the human mind as a species of zoology – an enterprise whose warrant he claimed to have found in such sources as Locke and Corrdillac. He called his study *Eléments d' Idéologie* (1801–15). But de Tracy's work was shadowed by the same contradiction as his predecessors'. He wanted to unmask the historicity of ideas – but he also wanted this unmasking to yield a true and universal knowledge of human nature. His 'materialist theme' was 'crossed by a normative purpose'. The contradictory nature of this project revealed its true Enlightenment roots. Even Comte, the direct inheritor of this line of inquiry, did not escape its contradiction. In line with his massive evolutionary schemas, Comte also conceived of a branch of 'positive science' which would be devoted to the evolution of the human mind as a 'social' process. But he too thought that this study would reveal that the social was subject to 'invariable natural laws'. Lichtheim describes this as a 'chilling thought' which, despite itself, aimed 'to sustain reason's faith in itself'. What these and other examples from this period suggest is that, from its modern inception, the concept of 'ideology' has been shadowed by its 'Other' – Truth, Reason, Science.

Whatever else it signals, the concept *ideology* makes a direct reference to the role of *ideas*. It also entails the proposition that ideas are not self-sufficient, that their roots lie elsewhere, that something central about ideas will be revealed if we can discover the nature of the determinacy which *non*-ideas exert over ideas. The study of 'ideology' thus also holds out the promise of a critique of *idealism*, as a way of explaining how ideas arise. However, the difficulty is that, once the study of ideas is placed at the centre of an investigation, an immense theoretical labour is required to prevent such a study *drifting*, willy-nilly, into idealism. This dilemma is clearly revealed in the history of one of the major philosophical currents which has informed the study of ideas and ideologies – the tradition inaugurated by Kant.

Kantianism (with its roots in both Cartesian rationalism and Lockean empiricism) took the abstract Enlightenment notion of 'Reason' and subjected it to a thorough-going critique. Kant asserted the primacy of the structures and categories of 'mind' over matter. It was 'mind' which organized experience into intelligible wholes. Mind 'constructed' reality. The trace of Kantianism is to be found in many of the subsequent theories of 'ideology'; though – because it was itself a critical idealism – it did not promote a study of the *historical* roots of knowledge. The story is not so straightforward with Kant's main rival – Hegel, even though Hegel 'out-idealised' Kant's reluctant idealism. For it was Hegel's aim to heal the Kantian division of the world into the knowledge *of* things, produced by our mental categories, and 'things in themselves', which were radically unkowable. Hegel's method for overcoming this discontinuity was the dialectic. The dialectic proposed a specific conception of the relation between knowledge and the world, between mind and matter, between the Idea and History: the relation of the dialectical supersession of each by the other. Once the Hegelian synthesis had been toppled from its idealist base and inverted – as it was by his radical disciples – it *did* once again produce the problem of the historical roots of knowledge as a theoretical problem. Thus for Feuerbach (who carried through the 'inversion' of Hegel in its most radical form) and in the work of the Left Hegelians who followed him, a task of central importance lay in unmasking the human and sensuous roots of *religious* ideas.[4] Feuerbach's work, Marx observed, 'consists in resolving the religious world into its secular basis'. But

> He overlooks the fact that after completing this work the chief thing remains to be done . . . the secular basis . . . must itself therefore first be understood in its contradiction and then . . . revolutionized in practice.[5]

Here Marx explicitly advanced to a materialist theory of ideology on the back of Feuerbach's inversion of Hegel.

For Hegel, of course, particular knowledges – one-sided knowledge, knowledge at any particular 'moment' – were always partial. Analytic Reason could not overcome this limit. But in Dialectical Reason Hegel glimpsed the possibility of a truly universal knowledge. If one 'moment' consisted of the objectivation of Mind in History, another 'moment' represented the appropriation of History in Mind. Thorough-going idealist as he was, Hegel fixed the final apotheosis in the second of those synthetic leaps – in the disappearance of the 'Real' into the 'Rational'. Then – just like the Revolutionary *savants* before him – he could not resist actually locating this Universal Moment in a particular historical conjuncture. The *savants* chose Napoleon – Hegel chose the Prussian State. This 'concretization' served Hegel no better than Napoleon had served the *savants*.

Hegel recognized that concepts were historical: but, he argued, 'historical concepts possess true generality because they relate to a universal agent that unfolds through the histories of particular peoples and civilizations'. Thus, Marx argued, for Hegel, 'conceptual thinking is the real human being . . . the conceptual world as such is thus the only reality, the movement of the categories appears as the real act of production.'[6] But the Hegelian system, once 'inverted', led to precisely the opposite conclusion: 'the real' – what Feuerbach called 'sensuous human nature', – is the only motor of history; ideas are simply the projections of the essential human nature and human *praxis* which they reflect. It was from this 'inverted dialectic' that Marx proceeded, by a further break, to inaugurate a *historical* materialist theory of ideology. (Though, as we know, his first attempt to do so – *The German Ideology* – still contains traces of the 'inversion' he was breaking from, particularly in its undifferentiated notion of 'human *praxis*'.) It is certainly within this general framework that we must understand Marx's famous assertion that 'it is not consciousness which determines being but . . . social being determines consciousness'.[7] But the materialist theory of ideology must be understood as a *break* with Hegel's system – not merely as setting Hegel's idealism on its materialist feet; since, as Althusser has shown, the inversion of a system is still the system inverted.[8] For Marx, Feuerbach simply resolved religion into its 'human essence'. But the point was to 'rethink' human essence as 'the ensemble of social relations'. Thus, the Left

Hegelians unmasked the 'truly human roots' of religion: Marx unmasked the historical roots of the Left Hegelians. He called this his 'settling of accounts' with his 'erstwhile philosophic conscience'.

The materialist path out of Hegel and Kant was neither the only nor indeed the most dominant residue of this theoretical encounter. In German thought, the problem of ideology is *framed*, for the rest of the century, by a double exposure: caught as Stedman Jones has argued, between the dissolution of the Kantian, and the dissolution of the Hegelian systems.[9] Each leaves its distinctive trace. This circuitous path is not without its surprising short-cuts back to Marxism. We refer here to the line which winds its tortuous way from Hegel through Dilthey, Simmel and Scheler, to Max Weber and the neo-Kantians; and thus to Lukács, Goldmann and Mannheim. The starting point for this line of descent lay in Hegel's conception that, until its final unity with Spirit, Mind was continuously, through the process of the dialectic, *objectivating itself* in palpable forms *in* the world (History). Mind was given what Hegel called 'objective form'. For a lengthy period, the study of ideology is nothing more nor less than a study of Objective Mind.

Though Hegel was no evolutionist, he was not so far removed from the impulse of the Enlightenment as to be incapable of conceiving this endless dialectic as arranged into distinct stages or epochs: the 'age' of Religion, the 'age' of Poetry, the 'age' of Science – crowned, of course, by the Age of Philosophy. These epochs had a shadowy history sketched within them, though they were in no sense precisely rooted in a historical periodization. Indeed, like much Enlightenment thought, they began with what *looked* like a historical moment, but was, in fact, something rather more like the essential moment of genesis of all human history: that is, with the Greeks. It was the neo-Hegelians – Dilthey above all (1833–1911) – who really seized on this notion of Mind objectivating itself through History in a sequence of distinct stages; and who set about constructing both an 'objective social psychology' and an 'objective history' – a history of the stages of human thought – on its foundations.[10] Ideas, Dilthey argued, could be conceived and *studied* as a series of forms, arranged progressively into stages extending through history. Each stage was characterized by its own 'style of thought'. The many different objectivations of each period could be studied as a *whole*, because they all reflected a particular 'outlook' on the world, a world-vision, a *Weltanschauung*. Distinct *Weltanschauungen* could be identified for each period, for each society. Dilthey's notion was thus easily extended into the idea that each nation or 'people' possessed its own distinctive *Weltanschauung* or 'Spirit'. This idea connected with earlier ideas of the '*Volk*', stemming from German Romanticism, and fed into subsequent ideas about the peculiar historical character and destiny of each nation or national culture. A central theme in German thought could thus be plotted in terms of the complex history of this definition of 'Spirit' *(Geist)*, in its successive manifestations through to its debased coinage by fascist ideology in the 1930s. Marx once accounted for the radical etherialization of this whole tradition in terms of the 'over-development' of German theorizing in contrast with the backwardness of its historical and economic development. But the career of the concept of 'Spirit' also reflected to a significant degree the complex and tortuous political history of German unification and the 'peculiar' form in which Germany emerged as a nation state.

The transformation of the problem of 'ideologies' into the study of *Weltanschauungen* constitutes something like the *dominant* tradition in German thought for most of the Nineteenth Century. It displays a complex evolution. It contributes, as we have seen, to the emergence of German nationalism. It fed into the great schools of German 'historicism'.[11] It nourished – through its attention to 'styles of thought' – a distinguished tradition of art history.[12] Its legacy is clearly to be seen in the work of Lukács: in his translation of the

Marxist notion of 'ideology' as 'world-vision', as well as in his use of the concept of *Weltanschauung* to analyse literary texts and periods.[13] Lukács's early works, *The Soul And Its Forms* and the *Theory of the Novel*, are directly Hegelian and Diltheyean in inspiration – especially the former, with its succession of 'forms' – epic, lyric poetry, novel. In his later work, Lukács tried to relate particular 'world-views' to class outlooks, but the underlying notion of *Weltanschauung* is never liquidated. The concept that each nation has its own distinctive 'world-view' is transposed, in *History And Class Consciousness*, into the notion that each *class* has its 'objective' world-view. The lingering presence of this concept thus accounts, in part, for the radical historicism of that text (for a fuller account, cf the following section of this journal, on Lukács).

Via the early Lukács, the tradition passes directly to Goldmann. It forms the whole theoretical basis of *The Hidden God* – Goldmann giving it a further Marxist or socio-historical gloss. But many of the same ideas are present, in a not dissimilar form, in the work of Karl Mannheim, and in what has been called Mannheim's 'bourgeois Marxism'. Mannheim's concern with ideology is, of course, central to his best known work *Ideology and Utopia* – a text in which Mannheim tries out his own resolution to the problem which has dogged this problematic from its inception: if ideas are 'historically relative', where can 'truth' be found? (Mannheim's answer is in the relatively un-relativistic thought of the detached intelligentsia.) But the connections with Dilthey are even more pronounced in Mannheim's earlier studies, for example the essays 'Conservative Thought' (treated as a *Weltanschauung)* and 'On The Interpretation of *Weltanschauung*'.[14] The history of this series of transformations of the elements of the Hegelian system therefore marks out one of the seminal points of confluence between *a certain* kind of Marxism and a *certain kind* of historicism – both deeply coloured by their Hegelian moment of inspiration.

The study of culture as Objective Mind *(Geisteswissenschaft)* and of history as the 'objectivations of Spirit' *(Geistesgeschichte)* also entailed a particular *method* of studying them. Human objectivations required their own distinctive 'mode of knowledge' different from the objects of the natural world. This method required an act of 'understanding' *(Verstehen)* – a reconstruction of embodied meanings through imaginative projection or 'empathy'. This enabled the successive manifestations of Objective Mind through history, and the 'world-views' they expressed, to be grasped as 'wholes'. Particular manifestations had meaning only in relation to the 'wholes' (or totality) which they expressed. Spirit, the essence of history, could thus be seen as this larger pattern or configuration of any epoch, manifested or expressed in each of its forms. The method of studying culture through 'interpretation' was called *hermeneutics*; and the procedure of relating parts to whole and whole to parts in an endless process of 'double fitting' was described as 'the hermeneutic circle'.

The debate between hermeneutics and more positivist methods of analysis came to constitute the site of a major theoretical debate – the 'struggle over method' – to which the sociologist Max Weber made a major contribution. Weber was not a Diltheyean, though the concept of the 'uniqueness' of culture, exemplified in his essays in *The Methodology of the Social Sciences*, is more than fleetingly inflected by historicist formulations. But he did engage with the hermeneutic tradition when he came to formulate his own definition of social action. The argument turned on the question of whether there were, in fact, two sets of 'things' to be studied – the world of Culture (ideas, human actions, Spirit) and the world of Nature: each with its appropriate method of analysis. The cultural world would then require a 'historicist hermeneutics', based on the imaginative reconstruction of the structures of past thoughts and actions; while the natural world would be subject to a positivist or causal-analytic mode of explanation. This debate divided the German intellectual world. Marburg became a centre for the stricter Kantian approach to this question. The figures associated with Marburg argued for a radical split between the two areas and the two methods, with primacy of place being given to positivist approaches, as the truly scientific one. Heidelberg was more 'historicist' in orientation, and thus more receptive to the work of Dilthey and the anti-positivism of the influential sociologist, Georg Simmel. Windelband and Rickert, against whom Max Weber polemicized in his *Methodology* essays, lectured at Heidelberg. So did their distinguished pupil, the philosopher Emil Lask. The group of young European intellectuals much influenced by Lask included Georg Lukács, whose early work, as we have seen, was steeped in the *Geisteswissenschaft* tradition.

Weber, in his search for an adequate sociological method, also addressed himself to the same problems. He attempted to combine the best in each, while more radical Kantians, like Lask, presented the problem as a stark choice. Thus, in the *Methodology* essays, Weber argued that Culture, the product of a historical rather than a natural process, had its own 'uniqueness'; the study of it could not be expected to yield universal laws of the kind which, from a positivist perspective, would have made that study properly 'scientific'. On the other hand, he wanted a more empirical method than that offered by pure hermeneutics. Weber thus settled, methodologically at least, for a compromise position. The building up of heuristic models – ideal types – each of which accentuated a different aspect of a phenomenon (a position which foreshadows Mannheim's *relationism*), was one way of ensuring a more comprehensive, and at the same time more carefully prescribed, view of the phenomenon than a simple empathizing with it could offer. So far as explanation was concerned, Weber argued that cultural objects and historical events required *both* hermeneutic (interpretive) *and* causal-historical understanding. The objective conditions producing an event or a cultural objectivation had to be rigorously constructed, so to speak, from the outside, showing where possible how the causal chain produced the 'result' under analysis in that particular form, rather than any other. But this same path would also have to be traced 'inside' – in terms of the logic of its meanings. Causal-historical explanations, Weber argued, also had to be 'adequate at the level of meaning'. There are many examples offered by Weber in the course of his argument for this methodological compromise in his *Methodology of the Social Sciences*. But the most important fruit of this Weberian synthesis, from our point of view, is certainly Weber's best known contribution to the substantive analysis of an ideology, *The Protestant Ethic and The Spirit of Capitalism*. Weber explicitly counterposed his attempt to reconstruct the 'inner logic' of the relation of Protestantism to the rise of capitalism in Europe against what *he* defined as the one-sidedness of a materialist or Marxist explanation of ideologies. The latter he claimed to understand as a form of economic reductionism. The debate has raged ever since as to whether *The Protestant Ethic* is in fact necessarily contrary to a Marxist theory of ideology. In this study, in typical Weberean manner, both Capitalism and Protestantism are constructed as 'ideal types' – one-sided accentuations. Sometimes Weber appears to be arguing that, of course, Protestantism could be looked at from another angle – a more materialist one: and that that accentuation, too, would reveal its relative truth (though not, as he says Marxism claims, its whole truth). This is not simply a gesture on Weber's part, since his subsequent work on the world religions does examine the religions of Judaism, India and Ancient China in terms of the sociological structures which sustained them. This rather more 'sociological' approach – in the traditional sense, of treating religion from the viewpoint of religious institutions – is, of course, no more 'Marxist' than his method in *The Protestant Ethic*. Elsewhere, in the latter text, Weber does characterize his work as explictly 'anti-Marxist'; and – so far as both method and theoretical emphasis is concerned – this characterization was undoubtedly correct.

The relation of Protestantism to capitalism was not, of itself, a non-Marxist question. Both Marx and Engels and pointed to the connection.[15] It became a favourite theme of inquiry in the German historicist school. In England, the work of Tawney and Christopher Hill shows that it is possible to give this question sustained attention without falling into an idealist problematic about the necessary primacy of ideas in history. Indeed, Hill's work suggests that an attention to the crucial role of ideology and religion is a necessary feature of a Marxist analysis of the transition from feudalism to capitalism in the Seventeenth Century. It could even be argued that it was Hill's decision to treat the religious, ideological and intellectual dimensions of the 'English Revolution' seriously in their own terms – and not simply as a simple reflection of economic forces – which saved his work from its earlier tendency to economic reductionism: saved it, that is, not from but *for* Marxism (Marxism is not an economic reductionism, though, in the period of the Second International, Weber could be forgiven for sometimes thinking that it was). To say this is to say something more than that an attention to 'ideas' ought to be added to an analysis of economic forces. It is to advance a proposition about the Marxist theory of ideology, properly formulated.

Marxism attempts to understand a social formation as a 'complex unity', composed of different levels which exhibit their own 'relative autonomy' while being determinate 'in the last instance'. A particular conjuncture like the Seventeenth Century Revolution is the result of the accumulation of contradictions stemming from each of those levels, and the over-determination of effects between the relatively autonomous instances. It is precisely in giving to any social formation the full complexity of this articulation, and in not assuming a 'given', simple or immediate correspondence between the levels, that Marxism *breaks* with the expressive totality central to – among other traditions of thought – the *Geisteswissenschaft* approach outlined above. The fact that the appearance of the bourgeoisie on the historical stage in the Seventeenth Century took the ideological form of a clash between religious ideologies had – to use a current phrase – *pertinent effects*. The superstructure has its own effectivity, even if Marxism requires us to think it as determined by the economic 'in the last instance'.[16] Ideologies are not self-sufficient; but in the Marxist theory of ideology, they are not empty and false forms, pure figments of the imagination, either. Otherwise they would not constitute an important area of analysis for Marxism. Anyone who seriously attends to the problems of a Marxist analysis of the Northern Ireland crisis would be hard put to it to say that the articulation of class struggle through religious ideologies is not a pertinent feature. In so far, then, as the study of religious ideology constitutes a real, and not merely an 'epiphenomenal', problem for Marxist theory, Weber's work has something of importance on which Marxists can draw. He makes a significant contribution to the analysis of the *internal structuration* of an emergent ideological formation. His radical weakness emerges precisely at the point – a central one for all Marxist theories of ideology – where he is required to show the *articulation between* the ideological instance and other instances. His failure at this point clearly relates to his ideal-typical and nominalist way of defining 'capitalism' (essentially, in terms of rationalised and regulated economic activity), and the absence of a theory of class formations in relation to an analysis conducted at the level of the capitalist mode of production.

The detailed argument of *The Protestant Ethic* – which is, by any reckoning an intellectual *tour de force* – cannot be rehearsed here. But some points which bear more generally on the theory of ideology ought nevertheless to be noted:

1 The essay works by means of what Weber calls an 'elective affinity' between the structure of Puritan ideas (above all, of the Calvinist variant) and the structure of the

rationalization of capital accumulation necessary to the development of capitalism. That is, it opposes any notion that economic change *directly* provides the *content* of capitalist ideas. Instead, it suggests that what is important is the 'homology' between what capitalism needed in order to become a sanctioned system of regulated economic activity, and the impulse to planned and routinized 'activity' in Puritanism. It adds to this a middle, mediating term: the Puritan/capitalist 'character structure'. It is worth noting that the move from content to 'homologies of structures' is the *key* theoretical advance represented in Goldmann's *Hidden God:* and that the attention to 'character structure' is an aspect to which both the 'Frankfurt School' and Reich were, later, to pay considerable attention.[17] This approach, though radically departing from a Marxist theory of ideology, does not contest Marx's proposition (in *The German Ideology*) that 'the ideas of the ruling class are in every epoch the ruling ideas': it suggests, rather, one way in which, historically, this may have come about.

2 Thus, the *Protestant Ethic* suggests one approach to the question of how ideas might work to create in a class that 'inner compulsion' to order its actions in certain ways: it points to the 'psychological' aspect of ideologies, without falling into an individual psychologism. It also suggests how an ideology may serve to break the hold of traditional ideas and give 'new' ideas a compelling force for that class in which they take root.

3 It suggests that, as well as the 'logic' which connects ideologies to economic forces – Puritanism to Capitalism – ideologies have their own, complex, internal articulation whose specificity must be accounted for. In this latter respect, Weber's demonstration is startling: for it turns on the paradox that the most secular, materialist of economic systems – capitalism – emerged at the level of ideology, paradoxically, *not* through the gradual erosion and secularization of Catholicism but through the intensified *spiritualization* of Puritanism. It is only much later, when the transformation has been accomplished, that the religious component – what Jameson once called 'the vanishing mediator'[18] – can disappear. Thus, though ideology and economic development exhibit, in the long term, the same tendential direction, they are articulated through the *differences*, rather than through the correspondences, in their respective logics. Europe becomes capitalist – at the ideological level – not by moving further from God, but by setting everything, including man's worldly activity, directly under His scrutiny. A theory of the 'relative autonomy' of ideology *could*, therefore, be rescued from Weber's work, without doing violence to his argument. It must be added, of course, that this is certainly *not* how Weber himself put it. He did not go on to develop anything approaching a 'regional' theory of ideology. In his later studies, he simply inverted the point of view. He drew no general deductions for theory from this *virtuoso* study. In general terms, Weber remained to the end a 'methodological individualist'. He continued to search for a resolution to the problem of knowledge within the framework of neo-Kantian, not Marxist, theory.

Three other lines of descent from the German tradition we have been examining must be briefly indicated. The first concerns what, earlier, we called certain important short-circuits in the tradition back to Marxism. The paradigm case here is that of Lukács. The most substantive contribution by Lukács to the theory of ideology – that represented by *History and Class Consciousness* – is examined more fully below. But Lukács is important to this part of the story because of his general position at the nexus of two traditions – post-Hegelian idealism and Marxism. Lukács, who is often treated as the perpetrator of a too simple concept of ideologies – as 'world-views' – sometimes also appears as its victim. He fell under the spell of

Geisteswissenschaft as a gifted intellectual in the heady climate of the Heidelberg 'school', as he has himself acknowledged. To escape the lingering strains of positivism he tried to go 'further back' – to Hegel himself *(The Young Hegel)*. In order to escape from Hegel he turned to Marx – but the path from one to the other was ineradicable: the absent-presence of Hegel lay across the route Lukács took to Marx, like the sky trail of a vanished aircraft. En route, he passed by way of the German irrationalists – that final revenge which Hegelian metaphysics wreaked on European thought.

'Irrationalism' constitutes the second line of descent. The 'struggle over method' had polarized into two main camps – positivism and historicism. But historicism was itself a fusion of many different strands. It included German Romanticism, which had never been fully tamed by the efforts of men like Dilthey to make the study of Objective Mind (the 'beyond of Science') orderly, and in its own way, 'scientific'. Mannheim's study of German 'Conservative Thought' brings out clearly its irrationalist roots. And at the end of the century, this impulse surfaced again in European thought – this time in the form of Vitalism. For Nietzsche, who made himself its most forceful spokesman, there was no guiding philosophy or method left at all. There was only the general *debunking* of all ideas, and their savage reduction to the sordid interests masked within their high-flown generalities. 'We live', Neitzsche asserted, 'only through illusions . . . the the foundations of everything great and alive rest upon illusion. The pathos of truth leads to destruction'.[19] Nietzsche believed that the contradiction inside the notion of ideology had at last been dismantled: Reason *was* a ruse: all that was left was the naked power-struggle between illusions, between interests. The most successful illusion was that which evinced the greatest 'will to power'. We know what Hitler and the skilled masters of illusion who gathered around him in the 1930s did with that idea. They translated Nietzsche's fantasy into reality: they set about constructing a *Götzendämmerung*. When the 'Frankfurt School' came, under the circumstances of fully empowered fascism, to examine the problem of 'ideology', they therefore had strong reasons to treat it as requiring not much more than the analysis of the mass manipulation of administered 'illusions'. In their efforts to reconstruct how the Age of Reason had produced, as its result, the Destruction of Reason, Adorno and Horkheimer were forced to look back at the irrationalist element which, they argued, had always been present in the Enlightenment dream: they unearthed what they called 'The Dialectic of Enlightenment'.[20]

The third line of descent really followed on, not from *Geisteswissenschaft* directly, but from Max Weber's measured response to it. Though, in his *Methodology* essays, Weber had entered directly into the debate with *Geisteswissenschaft*, in his general sociology he remained, as we have said, a 'methodological individualist'. This does not mean that he believed all social phenomena could be reduced to the level of concrete historical individuals. He meant that sociological concepts, to be 'adequate at the level of meaning', had to be constructed, *heuristically*, in terms of the *typical* actions, meanings and orientations which could be ascribed to *typical* individual actors. Hence his definition of social action was the ascription of typical motivations to an 'individual' whose actions were oriented to 'the other'. All the sociological concepts which followed on from this were necessarily heuristic devices – second-order constructs. One of the key figures who attempted to develop a more rigorously *sociological* approach, from this Weberian synthesis, was Alfred Schutz.[21]

Schutz was a 'phenomenologist' who left his native Vienna to work as an assistant to the great phenomenologist, Husserl. Schutz accepted the argument of phenomenology that all that could properly be 'known' consisted of the contents and structures of *consciousness*. Whereas Marxism tended to treat consciousness as a realm of 'false appearances' (Marx, of course, added *necessary* false appearances), phenomenology took the opposite position.

Everything outside of consciousness had to be 'bracketed out'. Meaning was the product of intention, and consciousness was the domain, *par excellence*, of intentionality. What could be studied was the intentionality of individual consciousnesses – and the interaction between consciousnesses, the realm of *inter-subjectivity*. In its pure form, certainly, phenomenology was a radical retreat into mentalism. Even that 'drama' in the world of social action which Weber had tentatively grasped was transposed entirely into consciousness and the interchanges between consciousnesses.

Schutz held firmly to this phenomenological perspective. But he believed that it could be developed and extended into a rigorously 'phenomenological *sociology*'.[22] The problem was how to account for phenomena in the 'real' social world from this phenomenological starting-point. Here, Schutz once more made a stealthy return to the terrain of Objective Mind. The intentionality of consciousness was realized – *objectivated* – in the world through activity. Men then had to live in the structures of meaning which they had objectivated: the meanings inside their heads had 'taken form' in the world outside. But these objective 'worlds' were not the product alone of the single intentional consciousness, but of the inter-subjective exchanges *between* consciousnesses. Meaning was therefore produced through this reciprocity – the reciprocity or alignment of perspectives. This 'reciprocity of perspectives' was the foundation – the common ground – for the reciprocal processes of 'meaning establishment' and 'meaning interpretation'. Its most active basis was face-to-face exchange, where each actor is co-present to the other: where they are 'consociates'. They share the same perspectives, the same 'history', and constantly come to 'construct social reality' together. This mutually constructed space constituted the 'lived' inter-subjective world. Through the medium – the store-house – of language and sign-systems, these actors could 'make active' other domains of existence not actually present to them (through the construction of 'typical' constructs). They could also summon up the past. Though the shared ground between 'consociates' constituted, for Schutz, the most massively 'present', the most taken-for-granted, sphere of reality, the whole of social and historical life could in fact be theoretically mapped out in terms of these basic processes of meaning construction/meaning interpretation. Since everything that had ever been in the world was the product of intentional inter-subjective consciousness, everything was *meaning*. Thoughts or references to others not present 'to consciousness' – whether simply absent, or deriving from the past – as well as 'theories' *about* social actions were simply second-or third-order constructs.

Language enabled all the domains not actually present in face-to-face interchange to be preserved, stored, recalled. Constantly repeated or institutionalized actions had the effect of rendering the meanings active in them stable, standardized. The meanings which informed such actions no longer appeared to constitute a domain of meaning at all. Meaning, here, had become standardized, institutionalized, 'backgrounded'. The 'typifying medium *par excellence* . . . is the vocabulary and syntax of everyday life'. These constructs, once the product of intending consciousness, but now lodged 'in the world', achieved a *facticity* of their own. They became objectivated meanings, capable of acting back upon the subjects who inhabited them, as if from the 'outside'. The activity (praxis) of meaning-construction which produced them has been lost to consciousness (alienated). They appeared now to impose their meanings, to constrain and rule men, from the outside. As Sartre, who was powerfully influenced by this general paradigm, put it:

> Thus significations come from man and from his project, but they are inscribed everywhere in things and in the order of things. Everything at every instant is always

> signifying, and significations reveal to us men and relations among men across the structures of our society.[23]

Though the language which Sartre employs here is far removed from the terminology of 'phenomenology', and draws as much from the early Marx as it does from Husserl, it inhabits very much the same paradigm: ultimately, for the purposes of this exposition, this is a problematic rooted in what has come to be called the 'Subject-Object dialectic'. In whatever form it appears, the presence of the Subject-Object dialectic always testifies to the unexorcised 'ghost of Hegel'.

Schutz argued that the many various objectivations in the world correspond to the different levels or layers of consciousness. Reality was structured into different 'regions', each with its appropriate layer of consciousness: the 'multiple realities' of play, dream, trance, theatre, theory, ceremony and so on.[24] As one moved from one realm of social reality to another, so each 'proposed' its own scheme of interpretation: bringing one mode of consciousness to the fore, and backgrounding the rest. The most sedimented region of reality and of consciousness was that sector of reality which men had to take most for granted, since it formed the basis of their everyday, ordinary actions. This was the realm of 'everyday life': and the mode of consciousness appropriate to it was that which was the most taken-for-granted of all the modes: the domain of commonsense. When we operate 'in common sense', Schutz argued, we are hardly aware at all that we are operating in a domain of constructed meanings. We simply take it for granted. Schutz proposed that sociology should concern itself, above all, with 'the structure of the commonsense world of everyday life'.

In the work of Schutz, we see the 'sociology of knowledge' taken to its most extreme point. We are no longer concerned with the relation *between* social knowledge and social relations. Social relations are conceived *as*, essentially, structures of knowledge (provided we treat 'knowledge' in its widest, everyday sense, and do not confuse it with systematic ideas; with 'ideologies' in their more limited sense). Berger and Luckmann, the modern sociologists who, in *The Social Construction of Reality* (1971), have tried to advance this line to its farthest limits, put the point succinctly:

> The social reality of everyday life is thus apprehended in a continuum of typifications . . . Social structure is the sum of these typifications and the recurrent patterns of interactions established by means of them.

It is in *this* form, above all, that the 'sociology of knowledge' has come to exert a powerful influence within the dominant traditions of American sociology. The later schools of 'symbolic interactionism' and of 'ethnomethodology' are direct extrapolations from it.[25]

In general, the sociology of knowledge has a complex position in relation to the theory of ideology. Ideas are no longer treated in terms of their historical roots, the classes which subscribe to them, the specific conjunctures in which they arise, their effectivity in winning the consent of the dominated classes to the way the world is defined and understood by the dominant classes. The relation of the ideological instance to other instances in a social formation has been obliterated. Their specific practico-historical function is lost. Ideas have been given a far wider and more inclusive range: they form the background to *every* social process. Indeed, it would be more correct to say that social processes are treated essentially in terms of ideas. They are pre-eminent because *it is through ideas that we construct social reality itself.* There is no objective reality – and hence there can be no 'scientific' knowledge of it. There are only the different 'takes on reality', lodged in the different perspectives which social actors bring to the world. The area of everyday social interactions only *feels* like a substantial sector of reality, because it is the zone in which the vast majority of individual perspectives overlap.

Thus, whatever insights can be rescued for a Marxist theory of ideology from this tradition, it must be recognised that each is generated by a quite different problematic. Marx wrote *The German Ideology* precisely to show that the historical development of society could not be reconstructed 'from what men say, imagine, conceive . . . from men narrated, thought of, imagined, conceived . . .' phenomenology must assume that there is nothing to historical reality *but* what men say, imagine, conceive . . . (We must add that, if, for Marxism, history does not consist of what men say, imagine, conceive, it is still a problem *for* Marxism to account for why men say, imagine, conceive what they do, where these 'thoughts' arise and what is their degree of effectivity. But this is a different problem.) True, for Schutz, the world is not *wholly* reduced to the thoughts in men's heads; for he was concerned with how thoughts gained an objective facticity in the world, and thus, by shaping human actions, affected how reality was constructed. But this partial dislocation of the 'pure' phenomenological impulse did not take him back to Marx, nor did it point in that direction. It pointed instead to another – and quite unexpected – convergence: a *rendezvous* of phenomenology with the tradition of positive social science as represented by Durkheim and his 'school'.

Durkheim's position on this question was misunderstood in his day and has been much misrepresented since.[26] A major factor in this must be attributed to the selective manner in which Durkheim's work has been appropriated (expropriated might be more accurate) into mainstream American empirical social science.[27] Durkheim is regarded as the 'father' of positive social science *because* he rejected all the Germanic nonsense about ideas, Mind, Spirit. He consigned 'ideas' to a little black box not because they were unimportant but because they could not be analysed. Instead, he determined to treat what *could* be analysed – patterned social interaction governed by norms and channelled by institutional structures. The observable aspects of these had to be treated as if they exhibited the hardness and consistency of objects in the natural world. Hence the famous admonition – to 'treat social facts as things'.[28] Durkheim did believe that social phenomena had a reality of their own – a reality *sui generis*; and that they must be analysed by rigorous and objective methods of study. In all these senses, he stood four-square within the tradition of French Positivism.

What is usually left out of this account is that those famous 'facts' which Durkheim wanted to treat as 'things' were social actions *informed by ideas* – or to put it in more positivist language, action governed by rules and norms – rule governed behaviour. It was the constraining effects of the 'rules of social life' upon individual actions which made 'society' possible for Durkheim – and, at the same time, by making behaviour systematic, constituted it as the possible object of a positive science. Hence Durkheim's concern with method – with things arranged as classifications, with the discovery of 'the rule', with the 'type' and 'rate' of social phenomena. It was because he despaired of the capacity of hermeneutics to give us an adequate knowledge of these things that he turned to the positive method. He was certainly not uninterested in how ideas informed actions. His question was: how do you discover what norms are operating? how weak or strong the norms are (and therefore what the degree of social solidarity is)? how unified or plural, obligatory or optional they are? Rather than ask what was the 'intention' concealed in the mind of the individual actor, Durkheim began at the other end: from the codified legal or moral system of ideas. For these were the 'collective representations' of social relations, and in them, at least, one could find, in a studiable form, those 'rules' which men had thought it worthwhile to embody in the formal system of the Law. In this sense, Durkheimean positivism self-consciously closed itself off from that whole Subject-Object dialectic which Hegel had inaugurated. Positivism chose to start with *already objectivated social reality:* with the factivity which the 'rules' of social life had achieved, and their constraining force over action. It treated the 'knowable' world as, already, a reification. And, despite the very different routes by which they arrived at this point, it did establish a certain common terrain between Durkheimean positivism and sociological phenomenology.

Despite appearances, then, Durkheim belonged to the neo-Kantian tradition. 'Noumenal' reality had to be studied through its forms of appearance – through 'phenomenal' reality. Two related concerns served to inflect this neo-Kantian position in rather different directions – leading to what can only be described as 'two' Durkheims. The first was a classic concern with the nature, degree and types of social solidarity. He followed earlier theorists here in believing that the bonds of social solidarity had been immensely weakened in societies of individual competition (i.e. capitalist market societies). This weakening was, precisely, to be seen in the loosening of the constraining power of 'the rules' over individual behaviour. The condition, typical of such societies, in which actions were insufficiently 'ruled' by norms, he called *anomic*. This is the classic terrain of positivist sociology; and to it Durkheim devoted some of his major work, including *The Division of Labour, Suicide* and the *Rules of Sociological Method*. It was *this* Durkheim which American sociology appropriated.

But Durkheim also believed that social integration depended on *normative* integration – or, as Bourdieu has recently put it, that 'logical integration is the pre-condition of moral integration'. 'Normative' integration depended in turn on the strength or weakness of the norms in society – or what Durkheim called the *conscience collective*. But the source of the norms and rules was *society itself*. Thus logical categories had society as their source of origin. It was 'society' – the source of the normative – which made the rules 'sacred', and therefore binding: 'society' which men worshipped (the central argument of *The Elementary Forms of the Religious Life*).

The seminal text in which Durkheim worked out this part of his theory was that which he wrote with his pupil, Marcel Mauss: *Primitive Classification*. In it Durkheim set out to show how the cognitive categories and mental classifications which 'primitives' used to think their world were in fact modelled on social relations. Society did not – as rather crude functionalists assumed – provide the content of social taxonomies. Rather, Durkheim believed – following Kant – that what society did was to provide the *categories* in which men 'thought' their world. Of course, whereas Kant was concerned with the most abstract categories – space, time – Durkheim was concerned essentially with *social* categories. It was this line of thought which provided Durkheim's main inspiration for his French followers and collaborators, and which distinguished the group of the *Année Sociologique* which he gathered around him.[29]

It is hardly surprising, then, that when Lévi-Strauss succeeded to the Chair of Social Anthropology at the College de France, and delivered the inaugural lecture which declared that the centrepiece of Social Anthropology should be the study of 'the life of signs at the heart of social life', he was able to defend this enterprise as nothing more nor less than the resumption of the 'forgotten part of the Durkheim–Mauss programme'.[30] Levi-Strauss's 'structuralism' was crossed by many paths other than that of Durkheim and his followers. The influences on it included Marx and Freud, Rousseau, the schools of Prague linguistics and Russian formalism to which Jakobson introduced him, and the anthropological linguistics of Franz Boas, the great student of American Indian languages. The latter connected him to that strand in American cultural anthropology which had taken up what is called the 'Sapir-Whorf' hypothesis – that each culture classifies the world differently, and that the principal inventory of these social taxonomies is to be found in the categories of the native language. One way or another it was *linguistics* which gave structuralism its main thrust, as well as providing it with the 'promise' – at last – of a truly 'scientific' study of culture. But it was the inheritance from Durkheim and Mauss which enabled Lévi-Strauss so confidently to claim this new orientation *for* Social Anthropology. Thus Lévi-Strauss's first application of structuralism was made to two classical themes of Social Anthropology: kinship systems (where the relationship between the kin and kinship terminology is crucial) and totemism.[31] French structuralism commenced its work on this classical terrain, before (in *The Savage Mind*) it was applied to a wide range of signifying classifications and, subsequently, to the rich field of myth.

The essential difference lay in the two meanings of the key term, *structure*. By 'structure' classical Social Anthropology understood the observable structures – the institutional orders – of a society. In Lévi-Strauss, the term is closer to the 'deep structure': it means the underlying system of relations between terms, conceptualized on the model of a language. There was no longer any one-to-one, simple correlation between these two levels – the order of classification and meaning, and the order of 'real relations'. The two had to be conceived as articulated through some relation other than that of reflection or correspondence, or even simple analogy. Certainly, this approach cut decisively into any notion that in language men 'named' simple functional objects in the real world. The gulf separating the two approaches is neatly caught in the following distinction: Malinowski believed that primitive peoples classified certain edibles as totems because they were good (or bad) to eat. Lévi-Strauss's response was that they were arranged within totemic systems 'not because they are good to eat but because they are good to think with'. In *Tristes Tropiques* Lévi-Strauss claimed geology, psychoanalysis and Marxism as his 'three mistresses'. Glucksmann is correct when she suggests that this is principally in a *methodolological* sense.[32] What all three had in common with Lévi-Strauss's structuralism was that 'All three showed that understanding consists in the reduction of one type of reality to another; that true reality is never the most objective of realities, and that its nature is already apparent in the care which it takes to evade our detection'.[33] As Marx once said of the vulgar economists, 'it is only the immediate phenomenal *form* of these relations that is expressed in their brains and not their *inner connection*. Incidentally, if the latter were the case, what need would there be of *science*?'[34] The reduction of 'immediate observables' to the level of structure therefore constituted for Lévi-Strauss the heart of a scientific method. But it was especially relevant to how thought, ideas, meaning related to or corresponded with the real world. Men's heads, too, were full of 'ideas', notions, secondary rationalizations and 'explanations' of their actions. These, too, constituted an endlessly open, variable and infinite set of cultural lexicons. Here too, it was necessary to express the variety of observable ideas in terms of the *limit* of their underlying structures, in order to make them amenable to scientific analysis. It was not fortuitous, therefore, that Lévi-Strauss declared his interest as 'the savage *mind*'. It was the impulse of 'mind' ceaselessly to impose forms on contents which marked the origin of thought, as well as the break between Nature and Culture. In the myriad arrangements which this produced in different cultures, Lévi-Strauss identified the trace of a universal activity, common to the primitive *bricoleur* and the modern engineer alike. This was the activity of *making things mean* the collective, unconscious activity of signification. Just to complete – and confuse – the circle, he called this universal faculty 'l'esprit humain'.

The emergence of structuralism constituted a major development in the analysis of the domain of culture and knowledge. Poole, in his admirable introduction,[35] suggests that the transformation which structuralism marked occurs at that point in the dismantling of the problem of totemism where Lévi-Strauss replaces the classic question, '*What is* totemism?' with the structuralist question, '*How* are totemic phenomena *arranged*?'. This represents what some would define as the principal transformation which structuralism as a method effects. It is the shift from contents to *forms* or, as Lévi-Strauss would say, *to structure*. It is through the *arrangement* of its field of significations that the 'logic of totemic classification' relates to or, better, articulates the arrangement of things and objects in the world of the Australian primitive. It is in *the forms of the arrangement* – to which the constitution of a structure gives us a privileged entry – that mental and social categories are related. Thus, discussing an important passage in Evans-Pritchard's study of *The Nuer* concerning associations in primitive thought between 'birds' and 'twins', Lévi-Strauss remarks that 'Twins "are birds", not because they are confused with them or because they look like them but because twins, in relation to other men, are as "persons of the above" to "persons of the below"; and, in relation to birds, as "birds of below" are to "birds of the above" '.[36] The relation between the two levels is *not* one of direct reference, function, reflection, direct correspondence, or even resemblance or analogy. It is the internal arrangement of the field of classifications which has been made to 'resemble' the internal classification of the field of natural objects and men. 'The resemblance is between these two systems of differences.' It is not the 'resemblances but the differences which resemble one another'.

One could therefore only decipher the rules governing culture and knowledge by examining the internal relations through which these fields were produced. Structuralist linguistics (especially Saussure, but also Jakobson's seminal work on the contrastive features of the phonetic system)[37] was of critical value in helping Lévi-Strauss to develop a *method* for 'decoding' their production. The arrangement was an arrangement of things – elements, terms, 'bits' – into categories. These composed the classificatory sets or paradigmatic fields into which the elements of a culture were 'inventoried'. Then you had to know the rules by which certain terms or elements were *selected* from these cultural taxonomies and *combined* with others, to produce any specific cultural 'utterance'. This was the syntagmatic element of cultural articulation. The basic elementary 'move' for structuralism was that which enabled the analyst to express the latter in terms of the former: to transpose a corpus of cultural significations (e.g. myths) into the classifications, the elements and the rules of selection and combination from which they were generated. This was 'the structure' for a corpus of myths – many of them not yet told! The many variants of the myth could then be shown to be generated – like the surface-strings of spoken language – from variations and transformations performed *on the deep structure*. Each variant was constituted by transforming or transposing elements in a given structure. Thus a corpus of myths was nothing but the result (at the surface level of expression) of a structure and its variants. Different 'moments' of the myth, produced at different times and in different places, could therefore all be expressed as variant realizations of the structure. In these ways, what appeared as articulated through time (diachronic) could only be scientifically grasped and studied when it had been re-expressed as a 'structure and its variations' – that is, with time arrested (synchronically). Saussure had argued that the body of real and potential utterances (*paroles*) were not amenable to scientific study, precisely because they did not constitute a closed field. Only 'the social part of language' – what Saussure called *langue* – could be the object of scientific linguistic study. In the same way, for Lévi-Strauss, the endless variety of surface productions of a culture were too amorphous to compose a scientific field of study. That field had first to be subject to the 'necessary reduction' to the elements and rules of its structure to become an object of scientific investigation. Thus, in *Totemism*, Lévi-Strauss proposed

> Let us define the phenomenon under study as a relation between two or more terms, real or supposed; construct a table of possible permutations between the terms; take this table itself as the general object of analysis . . .

Culture was organized 'like a language': hence it could only be studied on the analogy of structuralist linguistics. This brought structuralism directly to the terrain of classifications and codes: 'the analysis of relationships and transformations within symbolic systems'. These relationships were *not* those which we experienced but those which we used to 'think the world with': *concus*, not *vécus*. The aim of the enterprise thus became, not decyphering the social contents locked up or somehow expressed *in* symbolic forms, or examining the relationship between *what* was conceived and *who* conceived it. Its aim was to decypher the internal articulation: to *crack the code*. This is, without any doubt, the moment of the formation, within the sphere of the study of culture and ideology, of a quite distinctive problematic, based on an altogether different notion of causal relationship between social and mental categories: the moment of inception of what has come to be called 'structuralist causality'.

The birth of structuralism as a general theory of culture, and of the structuralist method, constitutes something like a 'Copernican' revolution in the sociology of knowledge; despite its apparently heterogeneous theoretical supports and antecedents. As intellectual fashion has tended to swing away from Lévi-Strauss's work towards other points in the structuralist field, so the seminal character of its intervention, for all that has followed, has tended to be retrospectively repressed. There are at least three 'lines of descent', none of which can be traced here in anything but the most summary fashion, but which must be indicated. The first is the development of a specifically 'Marxist structuralism', marked above all by the work of Louis Althusser. This is fully discussed in another contribution to this journal, and will not be further developed here. It is worth, however, noting that Althusser and his collaborator in his major theoretical work (*Reading Capital*), Etienne Balibar, go to considerable lengths in that volume to mark the distinctions between their 'Marxist structuralism' and that of Lévi-Strauss. In the subsequent volume, *Essays in Self-Criticism*, Althusser acknowledges a number of theoretical debts – including, most significantly, that to Spinoza: but he continues to give little or no weight to the influence of Lévi-Strauss (the relevant section of 'Elements of Self-Criticism' is only five pages). He repeats here what he has elsewhere identified as 'the most important demarcation line': Lévi-Strauss tends to 'the ideal production of the real as an effect of a combinatory of elements', whereas Althusser and Marx do 'speak of the "combination" of elements in the structure of a mode of production. But this combination is not a formal "combinatory" '.[38] Althusser and Balibar made this specific point in *Reading Capital*.[39] However, since both theorists have subsequently acknowledged a tendency to 'formalism' in that work, the differences between a Marxist and a non-Marxist structuralism – not as they are affirmed but as they appear in the actual exposition – is worth examining again with care.

The second important 'line of descent' is constituted by the two applications of the structuralist method to the field of the semiotic: the first most clearly identified with the work of Barthes, the second with that of Lacan and Kristeva. To judge from the *Elements of Semiology* it was principally from Saussure, rather from Lévi-Strauss (that is, from linguistics rather than from anthropology) that Barthes derived the impetus for his work in semiology. Saussure saw the use of all sign-systems as part of the general science of linguistics. Barthes inverted this proposition, declaring that linguistic systems were only one element in a much wider field of sign-systems, the science of which was semiotics. Semiotics was *the* method by means of which the mental and symbolic or signifying systems of a culture could be systematically investigated. But Lévi-Strauss's concern with mapping the inventories of a culture was seminal for Barthes.[40] Unlike Lévi-Strauss, Barthes retained the concept of 'ideology' as distinct from the general concept of *culture*, but it was the latter which constituted the proper object of 'the science of signs'. Ideologies were only the particular 'uses' of particular signification systems in a culture, which the dominant classes appropriated for the perpetuation of their dominance. In the subsequent development of semiotics, Barthes is perhaps the outstanding case of the semiotician who continued to be interested in the interface between signifying systems and 'fragments of ideologies'. On the whole, the dominant tradition in early semiotics was more concerned with identifying the rules by which signification as such took place *at all*. Thus, though semiotics certainly placed on the agenda the possibility of a more systematic and rigorous analysis of specific cultural systems and ideologies, this promise has been largely unfulfilled. Barthes's contribution on 'Myth Today'[41] – despite its tentative nature – remains one of the few seminal treatments of the relationship between signification and ideology in what might be called the first phase of Semiotics. The break with this first phase of semiology and with its directly Lévi-Straussean impetus was made by Lacan. Interestingly enough, Lacan's transformation begins with a 're-reading' of Freud from a linguistic standpoint; and the terms of structuralist linguistics continue to provide him with certain key terms in his conceptual repertoire. Lacan's Freud is the Freud of the language of dreams, and the 'rules' of the dreamwork – condensation, displacement, etc.: the Freud of *The Interpretation of Dreams* rather than of *The Ego And The Id*. Lacan, too, treats the unconscious as if it were 'structured like a language'. Lacan's work, and more especially that of his followers, has also returned to a concern with the question of 'ideology', though this is not the terrain of ideologies arising from specific historical structures and objectivated in social representations and in public languages, but the 'positioning of the subject' *in* ideology, through the mechanisms of the unconscious.

For both Lévi-Strauss and Barthes, what enables us to make a systematic study of sign systems is the fact that men never cease 'to impose forms on contents' – they are constantly 'classifying out the universe'. But whereas, for Barthes, any particular set of significations is historically located, Lévi-Strauss was more interested in the rules of classification and combination themselves – rules which he regarded as synchronic and trans-historical. The comparison of 'primitive' and 'sophisticated' classification enabled Lévi-Strauss to show that every culture employs the same basic mechanisms in order to 'make things signify'. He prefaced *Totemism* with a quotation from Comte to the effect that 'The laws of logic which ultimately govern the world of the mind are . . . essentially invariable'. True, in the *Savage Mind* he described himself as making a modest contribution to 'this theory of superstructures scarcely touched on by Marx'.

> Without questioning the undoubted primacy of infrastructures, I believe there is always a mediator between *praxis* and practices, namely the conceptual scheme by the operation of which matter and form are realized as structures.

These are among Lévi-Strauss's most tantalizingly ambiguous formulations. However, the only characterization which Lévi-Strauss has ever accepted without demur was Ricoeur's description of him as a 'Kantian without the transcendental imperative' (i.e. without God).[42]

It is difficult to know precisely why it is that this Kantian legacy, in its manifold permutations, has continued so persistently to haunt the theory of ideology. One reading suggests simply that *idealism*, in one form or another, constitutes the dominant bourgeois philosophical tradition (apart from a behavioural empiricism which has never been much concerned with the problem of ideas at all); and materialism is constantly in danger of collapsing back into it. Another reading suggests that some variant of the Kant problematic continues to exert its force over this whole field because of the unoccupied spaces, the under-developed nature, of the materialist theory of ideology. The first proposition is certainly true; but the second is not without its pertinence too.

Ideology is one of the least developed 'regions' in marxist theory. And even where it is possible to construct the *site* of ideology, and the general relation of the ideological instance to other instances, the forms and processes specific to this region remain peculiarly ill-defined and underdeveloped. Semiotics has greatly contributed to our understanding of how signification systems work, of how things and relations signify. But – precisely in the hope of constituting a closed field amenable to positive scientific inquiry – it tends to halt its investigation at the frontier where the internal relations of 'languages' articulate with social practices and historical structures. The materialist theory of ideology has considerably advanced our understanding of the nature of the economic and socio-historical determinations *on* ideas – but it lacks an adequate theory of *representation*, without which the specificity of the ideological region cannot be constituted.

Bourdieu has recently advanced this criticism again, in his discussion of two syntheses.[43] The first synthesis is that accomplished by Lévi-Strauss on ground staked out by Durkheim and others. This takes the *internal relations* of a field of classifications as the object of analysis. This completes one line of thought – the Kantian one. Marxism stresses the *political* functions of symbolic systems: it treats logical relations as relations of power and domination. Ideologies, from this standpoint, 'contribute to the real integration of the dominant classes . . . to the fictitious integration of society as a whole, and hence to the demobilization . . . of the dominated classes and the legitimation of the established order by the establishment of distinctions (hierarchies) and the legitimation of these distinctions'. This represents for Bourdieu a second synthesis.

Bourdieu suggests that both as they stand are inadequate. The first makes the study of the *internal* relations of a field of classifications self-sufficient – autonomous: whereas the second collapses the symbolic field of ideology *into* the social field of class relations – it is, he says, reductionist. Bourdieu wants to treat the problem in terms of the mutual articulation of two discontinuous fields. Symbolic relations are not disguised metaphors for class relations: but nor are they 'merely signifying'. It is *because* they do symbolic work of a certain kind, that they can function as the articulation of another field – the field of class relations: and hence also do the work of power and domination.

> It is as structured and structuring instruments of communication and knowledge that 'symbolic systems' fulfil their political function as instruments of domination . . . [Thus] the field of ideological positions reproduces the field of social positions *in a transfigured form*.
>
> (our italics)[44]

We can see at once Bourdieu's own – third? – synthesis in these formulations: his concern with the 'laws' which constitute many different 'fields' as distinct, each reproducing other fields, by reproducing itself – reproducing them, that is to say, 'in a transfigured form'. And this synthesis presents its own order of problems. However there can be no doubt that Bourdieu is trying to 'think' the problematic of the second synthesis (the Marxist) while holding to some of the advances made within the problematic of the first (the structuralist).

For it is a first principle of structuralist linguistics that a sign cannot signify on its own (only within a field of relations to other terms): but also that it does not signify by referring directly to *an object* in the world. As Bourdieu paraphrases Saussure (and Lévi-Strauss, not to speak of Althusser), meaning arises 'in the correspondence between one structure and another (ideological field and social field) or one position and another (within each of these fields) and not between one element and another'. When Lévi-Strauss was discussing the relationship between totemic systems and the natural world, he insisted that we could not take any single term of a totemic classification as directly 'referencing' an object or animal in Nature. It was the relation of one term to other terms within the system which resembled – corresponded, in structure, to – the relation between one animal and another in the species referred to.

Whether or not we try to develop an adequate Marxist theory of ideology from this point, it seems to be the case that the problem of ideology presents us with a paradigm instance of Marxist theory as *such*: what Althusser has called the necessity – and difficulty – of holding on to 'both ends of the chain' at once: the relative autonomy of a region (e.g. ideology) and its 'determination in the last instance' (i.e. the determinacy of ideology by other instances, and, in the last instance, by the economic). It is the necessity to hold fast to the latter protocol which has, from time to time, sanctioned a tendency to *collapse* the levels of a special formation – especially, to collapse 'ideas' or ideology *into* 'the base' (narrowly defined as 'the economic'). On the other hand, it is the requirement to explore the difficult terrain of 'relative autonomy' (of ideology) which has given the field of ideology its awkward openness. It is through this gap – to borrow a recent metaphor of Althusser's – that the 'pup' of semiology continues to 'slip between the legs' of a Marxist theory of ideology . . .[45]

Notes

1 In *Social Theory and Social Structure* (1968).
2 It is not surprising that it should have been Robert Merton who reintroduced the topic to American sociology, since his own early work was concerned with the social roots of the Scientific Revolution of the Seventeenth Century England. cf 'Puritanism, Pietism and Science' and 'Science and Economy of Seventeenth Century England'.
3 The following account is taken from G. Lichtheim's 'The Concept of Ideology', in *The Concept of Ideology and other Essays*. (1974).
4 See, *inter alia*, *The Young Hegelians and Karl Marx* (1969), by David McLennan, and Karl Lowith's 'Hegelian' discussion of these issues in *From Hegal To Nietzsche* (1967).
5 From Marx's 'These on Feuerbach', in *The German Ideology* (1970).
6 The *1857 Introduction* to the *Grundrisse* (1973).
7 One of the best-known formulations of *The German Ideology*.
8 The metaphor of 'inversion' to describe Marx's relation to Hegel is extensively debated by Althusser in *For Marx* (1969).
9 In Stedman-Jones's essay on 'The Marxism of The Early Lukács', *New Left Review* 70.
10 Not much of Dilthey is available in English. But cf *Pattern and Meaning in History*, selected with an introduction by Peter Rickman, and the long, patient exposition of his ideas in *The Philosophy Of Wilhelm Dilthey*, by H.A. Hodges (1952).
11 For an outline of this development, cf Carlo Antoni's *From History to Sociology*.
12 The work of the art critic and historian, Riegl, is a good example. But the influence can be traced in both Panofsky and Gombrich. Cf, for example, Gombrich's *In Search of Cultural History* (1969).
13 Lukács re-examines his relation to Hegel in the 'Preface To The New Edition' (1967) of *History And Class Consciousness* (1968).
14 Cf Mannheim's *Essays on the Sociology Of Culture* and *Essays On the Sociology of Knowledge*.
15 For example, in Engels's *Peasants War In Germany* (1956), and in 'Socialism, Utopian and Scientific' and 'Feuerbach and the End of Classical German Philosophy', both in *Marx–Engels Selected Works* (1951).

16 The most illuminating discussion of 'determination in the last instance' remains Althusser's 'Contradiction and Over-determination' in *For Marx* (op. cit.).
17 The 'Frankfurt School' in their (untranslated) *Studies In Authority And The Family* and in T. Adorno *et al.*, *The Authoritarian Personality:* Reich everywhere, but especially in *The Mass Psychology Of Fascism* (1970).
18 F. Jameson in 'The Vanishing Mediator: Narrative Structure In Max Weber', *WPCS* 5 (1974).
19 For the position of Nietzsche in this constellation, cf Lichtheim, *op cit.*
20 Adorno and Horkheimer argue this case, especially, in *Dialectic of Enlightenment* (1974)
21 Cf. the three volumes of the *Collected Papers* of Schutz (1966).
22 The work of Schutz's which most systematically develops a 'phenomenological sociology' from the critique of Max Weber is *The Phenomenology of the Social World.*
23 From J. P. Sartre's *The Problem of Method* (1963), an essay of 1957 subsequently appended as a prefatory paper to Volume I of Sartre's *Critique of Dialectical Reason.* Sartre, who plays Existentialism off against 'lazy Marxism' in that essay, sets up Kierkegaard as the 'phenomenological pole' of the argument.
24 Cf Schutz's essay on 'Multiple Realities', in *Collected Works*, Vol. I.
25 Schutz and Mannheim's 'documentary method' are the two major supports in the volume which establishes 'Ethnomethodology' as a sociological perspective – H. Garfinkel's *Studies In Ethnomethodology*.
26 Durkheim set about correcting some of the misinterpretations at once: Cf the Second Preface to the *Rules of Sociological Method.*
27 For American sociology, Durkheim's *Division of Labour* provided the basic problematic (the problems of order, social cohesion, consensus), the *Rules of Sociological Method* provided the method, and *Suicide* (read as the correlation of variables) the demonstration. A major simplification was involved at each stage. The actual moment of this expropriation is most clearly exemplified in the 'work' which Talcott Parsons does on Weber and Durkheim to produce the Parsonian synthesis, in *The Structure of Social Action.*
28 The much-misunderstood injunction of *The Rules of Sociological Method.*
29 That work included Durkheim and Mauss's work on Australian totemism, Mauss's essays on Magic and 'The Gift', Hubert and Mauss on Sacrifice, Hertz on the significance of Death and the Right Hand, Granet's seminal analysis of the 'mentality' of Ancient China (one of the sources of this concept, later much expanded by the *Annales* school of French historians), Halbwachs on the categories of Memory and the social psychology of social class, Meillet's structural linguistics. Other seminal figures, less directly connected but very considerably influenced by the work of the *Annales* school include Lévy Bruhl's studies of Primitive Mentality and, of course, Saussure's structuralist theory of language.
30 In *The Scope Of Anthropology* (1967).
31 The two studies are *The Elementary Structures of Kinship* and *Totemism.* But similar themes are extensively discussed in *The Structural Study of Anthropology* and *The Savage Mind.*
32 Cf Miriam Glucksmann, *Structuralist Analysis in Contemporary Social Thought* (1974).
33 From Lévi-Strauss, *Tristes Tropiques* (1965).
34 Marx to Engels, 27 June 1867. In *Marx–Engels Correspondence* (1955).
35 Roger Poole, 'Introduction' to the Pelican edition of *Totemism* (1964).
36 *Totemism*, op. cit.
37 Cf Saussure, *Course In General Linguistics*, (ed. by Bally, etc.) (1960), and Jakobson and Halle, *Fundamentals of Language* (1956).
38 Section 3 of 'Elements of Self-Criticism' in *Essays In Self-Criticism* (1976).
39 Cf the discussion of the combination/combinatory distinction in *Reading Capital*, pp. 215–16 and 226. Also, the first 'reply' by Althusser to the charge of 'structuralism' in his work: the 'Foreword to the Italian Edition', reprinted in the English edition of *Reading Capital* (1970).
40 Cf Barthes's review of Lévi-Strauss's work, 'Sociology and Socio-Logic'; English translation, CCCS. (Birmingham, 1967).
41 In *Mythologies* (1972).
42 The 'Overture' to the *Raw And The Cooked* (1970).
43 For the English translation of Bourdieu's paper 'Symbolic Power', cf *Two Bourdieu Texts*, trans. R. Nice, CCCS Stencilled Papers No. 46. (1977).
44 Bourdieu, *ibid.*

45 The daring metaphor occurs at the end of the 'Science and Ideology' section of Althusser's 'Elements of Self-Criticism', *Essays in Self-Criticism, op. cit.*

Bibliography

T. Adorno and M. Horkheimer (1973) *The Dialectic Of Enlightenment* Allen Lane, Harmondsworth.
L. Althusser (1969) *For Marx* Allen Lane, Harmondsworth.
L. Althusser and E. Balibar (1970) *Reading Capital* New Left Books, London.
L. Althusser (1976) *Essays In Self-Criticism* New Left Books, London.
C. Antoni (1959) *From History To Sociology* Merlin, London.
R. Barthes (1967) *Elements of Semiology* Cape, London.
R. Barthes (1972) *Mythologies* Cape, London.
P. Berger and T. Luckmann (1971) *The Social Construction of Reality* Penguin, Harmondsworth.
P. Bourdieu 'Symbolic Power' CCCS Stencilled Paper No. 46 Birmingham. Destutt de Tracy (1826) *Elements d'Idéolgie* Brussels.
W. Dilthey (1962) *Pattern And Meaning In History* Harper, New York.
E. Durkheim (1964) *The Division of Labour* Routledge and Kegan Paul. London.
E. Durkheim (1964) *The Rules of Sociological Method* Free Press, New York.
E. Durkheim (1952) *Suicide* Routledge and Kegan Paul, London.
E. Durkheim (1961) *The Elementary Forms of the Religious Life* Collier, New York.
E. Durkheim and M. Mauss (1963) *Primitive Classification* Cohen and West, London.
H. Garfinkel (1967) *Studies in Ethnomethodology* Prentice Hall, New Jersey.
M. Glucksmann (1974) *Structuralist Analysis In Contemporary Social Thought* Routledge and Kegan Paul, London.
L. Goldmann (1964) *The Hidden God* Routledge and Kegan Paul, London.
E. Gombrich (1969) *In Search Of Cultural History* Clarendon Press, Oxford.
H. Hodges (1952) *The Philosophy Of Wilhelm Dilthey* Routledge and Kegan Paul, London.
R. Jakobson (1956) *Fundamentals of Language* Mouton, The Hague.
C. Lévi-Strauss (1964) *Totemism* Pelican, Harmondsworth.
C. Lévi-Strauss (1965) *Tristes Tropiques* Athenaeum, New York.
C. Lévi-Strauss (1966) *The Savage Mind* Weidenfeld and Nicolson, London.
C. Lévi-Strauss (1967) *The Scope Of Anthropology* Cape, London.
C. Lévi-Strauss (1963) *Structural Anthropology* Basic Books, New York.
C. Lévi-Strauss (1970) *The Raw and The Cooked* Cape, London.
G. Lichtheim (1967) *The Concept of Ideology and Other Essays* Vintage, New York.
G. Lichtheim (1970) *Lukacs* Fontana, London.
K. Lowith (1967) *From Hegel To Neitzsche* Doubleday Anchor, New York.
K. Mannheim (1936) *Ideology and Utopia*, Routledge and Kegan Paul, London.
K. Mannheim (1952) *Essays In the Sociology of Knowledge* Routledge, London.
K. Mannheim (1954) *Essays In Sociology And Social Psychology* Routledge, London.
K. Marx (1970) *The German Ideology* Lawrence and Wishart, London.
K. Marx (1973) *The Grundrisse* Penguin, Harmondsworth.
R. Merton (1968) *Social Theory And Social Structure* Free Press, New York.
T. Parsons (1968) *The Structure of Social Action* Free Press, New York.
R. Poole (1964) *Introduction* to C. Lévi-Strauss, *Totemism* Pelican, Harmondsworth.
J.-P. Sartre (1963) *The Problem of Method* Methuen, London.
F. de Saussure (1960) *Course In General Linguistics* Peter Owen, London.
A. Schutz (1967) *Collected Papers* Vols 1–3, Nijhoff, The Hague.
A. Schutz (1967) *The Phenomenology Of The Social World* North-Western University Press, Illinois.
M. Weber (1949) *Methodology Of The Social Sciences* Free Press, New York.
M. Weber (1930) *The Protestant Ethic And The Spirit Of Capitalism*, Unwin, London.
M. Weber (1966) *The Sociology Of Religion* Methuen, London.

8 Three problematics

Elements of a theory of working class culture

*Richard Johnson**

This Stencilled Paper is one chapter from a CCCS/Hutchinson volume due to appear in July 1979: Richard Johnson, John Clarke and Chas Critcher (eds.,), *Working Class Culture: Studies in History and Theory*. A list of contents of the book as a whole, and parts of the Preface to the book are included at the beginning of this paper to help readers to see how the arguments of this, the penultimate chapter, fits within the framework of the book as a whole.

I am grateful to Claire L'Enfant of Hutchinsons for permission to publish the chapter in this form.

Both the book and this chapter were written before the publication of E.P. Thompson, *The Poverty of Theory & Other Essays* (Merlin Press, 1978) which deals with many of the issues here discussed. I am grateful to Edward Thompson, however, for his comments on earlier versions of parts of the argument, though I know major disagreements continue.

Richard Johnson, CCCS, 1979

Extracts from preface

This book has an unusual form. It has many authors but aims at a somewhat greater unity than is usual in collections of this kind. It is best to begin by explaining how this comes about.

The book was first planned, in collaboration with the Hutchinson Publishing Group, as a collection of essays on working class culture by members of the Centre for Contemporary Cultural Studies. It was to consist of work already produced or currently in progress, with, perhaps, an initial 'overview' of the field. In planning the volume, however, two facts became obvious. First, the Centre had produced relatively little work that directly followed up one of its founding texts – Richard Hoggart's *The Uses of Literacy*; second, 'working class culture' had itself become much more difficult to define both because of social changes since 1957 and because of intense theoretical debate around the terms 'culture', 'consciousness' and 'ideology'. There *were* relevant studies however, some historical in manner, some the product of a qualitative, observational sociology. Moreover, the importance of the project remained, not least because for the period of the modern working class (in Britain from, say, 1850 or 1880) neither historical nor sociological work was very developed. One consequence, then, is that

* This essay is based in part on a paper given at the British Sociological Conference on Culture (1978) but has benefitted since from criticism from Edward Thompson, Keith MacLelland, Philip Corrigan and Stuart Hall and from discussions in the CCCS History Group. I have also been greatly helped by discussions with John Clarke, author of the companion piece which ends this volume.

most of the pieces published here have been specially written for the collection. This is wholly the case with the critical or 'theoretical' essays in parts I and 3. Most of the case studies in part 2 existed in an earlier form, but all have been extensively re-written. All but one of the authors have worked at this Centre; and the work of Michael Blanch, the exception, was already known to the editors. It was possible, then, to plan a volume that was more than just a collection of essays, more than a set of individual contributions.

The resulting unity, however, remains much looser than in a single-authored, consecutively-written text. For reasons that are explored in the book, it would be difficult at this point in time to produce an adequate or definitive account of post-war working class culture, let alone a history of a longer duration. We emphasize, then, the 'studies' of our title. These are a set of related explorations of a common field – some predominantly critical and theoretical, some more substantive. In particular we have not attempted to *start from* a common theoretical framework to be consistently elaborated in each essay. We start, rather, from *problems* and seek to work through them in different ways and on different materials. Thus the more theoretical essays are largely critical and clarificatory, not, until later in the book, prescriptive.

The first part of the book reviews some of the existing literature. It focusses on two main traditions of writing about the working class: a tradition of empirical sociology and a tradition of history. We have sought to understand these traditions in their own historical time, as an expression, importantly, of the dilemmas of certain groups of intellectuals faced with differing political possibilities and expectations. The first essay examines a cluster of works that belong to the same 'moment', the post-war debate about 'affluence' and its immediate aftermath. It ends, deliberately short of some newer sociologies, with the revival of Marxist analyses and the publication, in 1965, of *Towards Socialism.* The second essay looks at a different but related tradition of the historiography of the working class and of popular histories more generally. It deals with the origins of labour and social history from the 1880s onwards and with the new histories, distinctively cultural in emphasis, of the late 1950s and early 1960s. It ends with some attempt to define the dilemmas of history-writing in the 1970s, noting the relative weakness of studies of working class culture for the post-1850 period, and the complexity of contemporary theoretical debate. Certain ways of working through these difficulties are suggested, to be returned to later in the book.

Part II consists of a set of case studies. Though they do not share a common theoretical position, they represent attempts to work through difficulties in the process of research. In selecting or commissioning these pieces, we had two main considerations in mind. First we wanted to span the whole period of the existence of a working class in any identifiable sense, partly to correct the a-historical character of many sociological accounts. This long working-class history is a unique feature of the British experience. We have, however, placed the emphasis on more recent times: two of the studies deal with the period before World War I, two with the period between the Wars, and two with post World War II developments. Similarly, we have tried to cover the most important spheres of working-class life. Thus Richard Johnson's essay deals centrally with politics, political ideologies and education, Michael Blanch's and Pam Taylor's with aspects of 'youth', Paul Wild's and Chas Critcher's with recreational forms and their relation to capitalist business, Pam Taylor's and Paul Willis' with waged work and with domestic labour. It has not been possible to be comprehensive – we would have liked to have said more, for instance, about forms of the family and the cultural forms of sexuality, though Pam Taylor's and Paul Willis' essays more than touch on these questions. We would also have liked to include a major study of trade unionism as a cultural and political form in some attempt to re-think the central topics of a labour history.

In general, however, we have deliberately sought a broad scope and wide coverage rather than the more usual concentration on a particular theme or period.

In part III we return to some of the dilemmas sketched in Part I. The first essay of this part considers three main ways in which working-class culture may be conceptualised: through the problematics of 'consciousness', 'culture' and 'ideology'. Arguing that each of these paradigms bear the stamp of the moment of their formation, we examine the strengths and weaknesses of each. We point to some elements of a more developed way of thinking about working class culture, appropriate to present conditions. In the concluding essay of the book, we provide some pointers, based upon a theoretical reading of aspects of current research, towards a history of the post-war working class

We expect the book to be used in different ways by different kinds of readers. But we have sought, in general, to break with or to re-form a number of separations of this kind: between 'past' and 'present', between 'history' and 'sociology', between the empirical and theoretical, between the study of cultural and the not-cultural-at-all. In particular, we have sought to make theoretical discussion more aware of its own history and make historical (or 'concrete') studies more aware of theoretical debts and dependencies. Hence our sub-title – 'history' *and* 'theory'.

Introduction

We return now to the more general problems posed at the end of the first part of this book. Do we need new ways of thinking about working-class culture and what should these be? We proceed by identifying three main approaches. We suggest that each is, in some way, inadequate. We end by suggesting pointers to a better practice.

The three main approaches are rooted in the larger tendencies which we discussed in 'Culture and the Historians.' Each employs its own key terms. Within orthodox Marxism the key terms have been 'class' and 'class consciousness'. In the work of Williams, Thompson, Hoggart and others, 'culture' replaced 'consciousness' or forced a re-working of its meaning. 'Culture' and 'consciousness' however, remained closely coupled to 'class'. The term 'working-class culture' lies firmly within this problematic. Finally, in 'structuralist' approaches the consciousness/class couplet altogether disappears. As two not-dissimilar terms in Althusser's work we might choose 'ideology' and 'mode of production' or 'ideology' and 'social formation'. But the truth is that there are no real *equivalents* across these traditions. Each semantic shift represents a major theoretical and political movement.

The notion of 'problematic' and the procedure of 'symptomatic reading' are absolutely indispensable tools of analysis and critique. They inform this essay throughout. 'Problematic' may be defined as 'a definite theoretical structure', a field of concepts, which organises a particular science or individual text by making it possible to ask some kinds of questions and by suppressing others. In 'symptomatic reading' a text is read as much for its 'absences' or 'silences' as for what it more directly 'says'.[1] The problematic(s) of a particular text may be more or less explicit. In works of history the organising ideas and presuppositions may lie very deep. They nonetheless exist. One aspect of critique, then, is to render explicit what is implicit, and to consider the underlying propositions. For Althusser, concerned with historical materialism as the 'science of the history of social formations', intellectual productions in the human sciences are organised around a conception of the relation of 'thought' and other practices (an epistemology) and a conception of the general nature of societies (a sociology). His repertoire of critical terms – 'humanist', 'historicist', 'empiricist', etc. – designate particular faults in either aspect or in both.

The Althusserian 'reading' is inadequate in so far as it stops short at the analysis of 'problematic'. For the appearance of finality in the method is quite illusory. Symptomatic reading provides us with a *description* of a work, or of its main internal structures. The dismissal, at this stage, of a text as 'historicist', 'empiricist' etc. can only rest upon a very formal idea of 'science', in Althusser's case, of 'Marx's Immense Theoretical Revolution'. To stop at this stage is merely to say, 'This is not a Marxist text according to the way I have defined Marxism'.

It is not possible to accept, just like that, Althusser's own definition of Marx's uniqueness and scientific superiority, or his own taking of sides within Marxism as a tradition. Structuralism has certainly recovered *a* Marx; one might be pardoned for doubting whether it recovered *the* Marx. *Reading Capital*'s conception of 'Marxism-as-science' and all else including Marxist heresies as 'ideology' tends to a 'closure', prematurely cutting off that open exploration, which Althusser himself has defined as the key to science. Answers to the question 'What is Marxism' remain far too difficult to be a valid way of closing debates of substance.

Allied to this difficulty is the strongly reductive character of some forms of symptomatic reading. The whole of an account is reduced to its problematic. This is particularly gross when applied to works of great empirical density, to most histories for example. Presuppositions once identified, it is necessary to return to the surface of the text and show the effects of theoretical structures on the detailed treatment of events, the construction of narrative, the portrayal of relations, on the actual texture of the historical account. And there are arguments to be conducted on this level too: 'within this problematic it is not possible to account for this or that phenomenon which other research reveals'; 'the incoherences of that part of the account is related to the failure fully to theorise *these* sets of relations'; 'theoretical rigidity has produced this or that a priorism with no corresponding research'. In other words, the adequacy of a particular problematic can only be assessed at the author's preferred level of analysis. In such a critique, the proposition that 'historicism' (or any other -ism) is, in general, flawed is itself on test.

The third main difficulty is the absence of historical critique.[2] This is allied to the high 'theoreticism' of *Reading Capital*, its stress on *general* epistemological or philosophical questions, its 'speculative' or 'rationalist' character. This old and correct criticism of 'structuralism' has been endorsed by Althusser himself in his *Essays in Self-Criticism*. The corrective is simple; to recognise that every problematic has a history or, as Althusser puts it, 'material, social, political, ideological and philosophical conditions'.[3] The adequacy of a theory cannot be judged outside these conditions, by purely internal criteria.

Finally, in some usages, 'problematic' has a tendency to simplify or homogenise texts or theories.[4] There is a temptation to look for the 'essence' of a text. As essential unities, then, texts or theories may be discarded wholesale. The method adopted here rests on different assumptions. The struggle over definitions depends precisely on the fact that the concepts that constitute a given problematic are not 'all of a piece'. As elements, re-organised, they may constitute the basis for more adequate accounts. Elements taken from different existing problematics may in a new order and constituting a new field, yield us greater explanatory power and political purchase.[5]

In what follows we try to learn from this settling of accounts with our erstwhile Althusserianism. No full history of our three problematics can be attempted; but the historical nature of the ideas we use is fully recognised.

Class and class-consciousness in 'manifesto marxism'

This view of class had its origins in the collaborative work of the young Marx and Engels. It was an attempt to understand their political experiences in the early communist movement and the novel features of English social life, especially of the English 'proletariat'. The key texts are Marx's *Poverty of Philosophy* (1847), *The German Ideology* (1845–46), *The Communist Manifesto* (1848), (both jointly authored) and Engels' own *The Condition of the Working Class in England* (1844), especially the last two. The political and intellectual moment represented by Engels' *Condition* was as important as the departure from philosophical communism represented in the classical work of 'the break', *The German Ideology*. Engels' encounters with English working-class movements and English radical theory, together with his strategic location in Manchester, the 'shock city' of the Industrial Revolution, supplied 'the changing questions which provoked the new theory'.[6] Many of the themes of *The Communist Manifesto* are demonstratively present in Engels' *Condition*; the second text is, in many ways, a working up of Engels' primary insights.

Certain key elements of the classic Marxist view of the proletariat were formed therefore, *before* the emergence of a modern working class. They also preceded Marx's mature understandings of the capitalist mode of production and the character and constitution of classes within this mode. *The Communist Manifesto* view of classes remains somewhat 'philosophical', based upon a generalised view of proletarian destinies (the 'negation' of bourgeois society) rather than a full grasp of capitalism's internal dynamics.[7] The political features of Britain and Europe before 1848 are no less significant. The character of their writing – the feeling of wide-eyed discovery in Engels' *Condition* ('Of the vehemence of this agitation no-one in Germany has any idea'), the assured sweep of *The Communist Manifesto*, the intoxicated polemic against Proudhon's idealism – all testify to the expectancy out of which historical materialism was born. Yet theories generated from the intellectual consumption of very specific events do not always serve well as more generalised truths one hundred and forty years later.

The class and class-consciousness problematic rests on a distinction made explicit in *The Poverty of Philosophy* between two aspects of the proletariat as a class. The proletariat is a class in its relations with ('as against') capital: under capital's domination 'this mass' acquires 'a common situation, common interests'.[8] At the heart of this definition of class is the figure of 'the worker' or 'the labourer': 'a class of labourers, who live only so long as they find work, and who find work only so long as their labour increases capital'.[9] In this first guise the proletariat is understood, passively, as a creation of capital, thrown hither and thither by its movements; only in a second moment does it become active, a collective agency or force 'for itself'. Proletarians acquire the capacity to struggle and to conceive of their place within capitalism and history.

Some such distinction (between economic classes and political forces) is, analytically, indispensable. But these two forms of analysis are also bound, in the original formulation, into a necessary and causative unity: they are stages in one necessary historical process. The grand design of proletarian politics is already present in the economic position of the labourer. The position of proletarians in their relation to capital produces the proletariat as a revolutionary class. Capital produces its own negation, its own 'grave-digger'. In the early texts this doctrine permits of no contingencies. As Stuart Hall has noted, of *The Manifesto*: 'what is so fatally seductive about this text is its simplifying revolutionary sweep . . . above all, its unmodified sense of historical inevitability'.[10]

There are, perhaps, two possible readings of how this argument is actually secured in the early texts. Priority could be given to the stress on class struggle. Though antagonisms are founded in the direct relations of capitalist production, outcomes are not. The proletariat as a political force is 'made' in protracted and repeated struggles; major difficulties, especially capital's tendency to place labourers in competition, must be overcome. One might call this the 'activist' reading of the early texts; it points to the priority of politics developed in later Marx–Engels texts and in Lenin's theory and practice.

But this reading cannot be sustained textually. The various forms of class struggle always appear in the guise of 'phases' or 'stages', 'a growing revolt': individual acts of crime, followed by trade union combinations, followed by Chartism as a political party, followed by a communist-led proletarian movement.[11] The stages themseves are very little explored, even in *The Condition*. There is no consideration of the ways in which these working-class practices (forms of class struggle within capitalism) may actually modify its structure or affect bourgeois strategies, including strategies of accumulation. Engels in *The Condition*, indeed, found trade unionism an index of the English 'social war' and a stage along the road to the abolition of 'competition' but doubted its practical effects in other ways.[12] The whole discussion of 'stages' is organised teleologically, not in terms of particular effects. Attention is drawn forward to the revolutionary future, with little pause for study on the way.

That future, moreover, is given in the character of capitalism itself. The proletariat is the agent of revolution, but its revolt is not merely 'growing', it is also obligatory. E.J. Hobsbaw's summary of the main lines of argument in *The Condition* is quite faithful to Engels' text but reveals a whole theoretical legacy.

> Socially Engels sees the transformations brought about by the Industrial Revolution as a gigantic process of concentration and polarization, whose tendency is to create a growing proletariat . . . The rise of capitalist industrialism destroys the petty commodity producers, peasantry and petty-bourgeoisie, and the decline of these intermediate strata, depriving the worker of the possibility of becoming a small master, confines him to the ranks of the proletariat which thus becomes 'a definite class in the population, whereas it had only been a transitional stage towards entering into the middle classes'. The workers therefore develop class consciousness . . . and a labour movement. Here is another of Engels' major achievements. In Lenin's words 'he was among the first to say that the proletariat is *not only* a class that suffers; that it is precisely its shameful economic situation which irresistibly drives it forward, and obliges it to struggle for its final emancipation'.[13]

The problems are concentrated in the breath-taking sentence: 'the workers therefore develop class consciousness'! But this 'therefore' is plainly present in the texts themselves. It is present in the oft-repeated argument about the massification and concentration of working-class thought.[14] But the most important generator of class consciousness is the sheer force of economic relations. The proletariat is *driven* to revolt. If the bourgeoisie simplifies society, it simplifies the proletarian too. It strips him of all incidentals. He is reduced to economic simplicity itself: to naked necessity and need, pure lack, 'bare existence'. He has 'nothing to lose but his chains'. He is stripped of all illusions, including those of nationality. No mean English bourgeois he, but full of 'passions as strong and mighty as those of the foreigner'.[15] Moreover the relations in which he stands, the cause of his suffering, become more and more visible. In the end the modern labourer has no choice but to 'revolt' while capitalism opens itself to him, as a book. It cannot even guarantee the means of his existence:

> In order to oppress a class, certain conditions must be assured to it under which it can, at least, continue its slavish existence . . . The modern labourer . . . instead of rising with the progress of industry, sinks deeper and deeper below the conditions of existence of his own class . . . And here it becomes evident, that the bourgeoisie is unfit any longer to

> be the ruling class in society, and to impose its conditions of existence upon society as an over-riding law. It is unfit to rule because it is incompetent to assure an existence to its slave . . . because it cannot help letting him sink into such a state . . . Society can no longer live under this bourgeoisie, in other words, its existence is no longer compatible with society.[16]

The historical content of this passage is clear through the 'philosophical' forms. The feeling that capitalist society provided no lodgement for the worker, that the position of proletarian was *simply not habitable*, is a dominant tone of early working-class radicalism. It was based certainly on extreme privations but, as Edward Thompson has stressed, also on a widespread sense of loss. This was the experience of the small-producer-becoming-proletarian, not yet, one must insist, the characteristic experience of the proletarian as such. Of course, the modern working class was to be made and re-made and made again in struggles against capital, but the content of these later struggles was to be more the taming of capital than its abolition. Based upon observation of a particular phase, 'Manifest Marxism' extrapolated its features into a law of capitalism as such.

It is possible to add more 'theoretical' criticisms, based, that is, in a knowledge of subsequent events and of contemporary needs. These points are relevantly made since 'Manifesto Marxism' remains a mid-twentieth century presence. This form of Marxism does not grasp specifically cultural or ideological conditions of oppositional working-class politics. Though Marx and Engels continually argued against early European socialisms, they remained incurious about popular cultural legacies. Engels' portrayal of pre-Chartist popular culture, for instance, is self-confessed guess-work with high comic qualities:

> They could rarely read and far more rarely write; went regularly to church, never talked politics, never conspired, never thought, delighted in physical exercises, listened with inherited reverence when the Bible was read, and were, in their unquestioning humility, exceedingly well-disposed towards the 'superior' classes. But, intellectually, they were dead . . .[17]

His accounts of Chartist culture are, by contrast, full of excitement and particularity. But it is precisely the less overtly 'political' elements of a culture that most need study, since their role in politics is most obscure.

Other criticisms concern the neglect of complexity.[18] Within this problematic internal complexities of the class ('in itself') cannot be grasped. Yet historically the labourer's dependence on capital has taken varied forms. Divisions within the class have been exceedingly complex. 'Simplification' seems always to produce further internal structurations. Similarly, the simple class/party relation gives us little purchase on the complexities of working-class politics and representation. These points will recur later in the argument.

Several commentators have noted important subsequent shifts in Marx's theory of classes. These amount to a profound practical self-criticism of *The Manifesto*. This was necessary to preserve some organic relation between Marxist theory and the train of events in Britain and Europe after 1848. There were, perhaps, two main moments of revision: the first, identified precisely by Gwyn Williams, was the immediate aftermath of the counter-revolution in the late 1840s. Revision followed the disappointment of the expectations of *The Manifesto* and the subsequent political isolation of the Communists. The most important text of this moment is *The Eighteenth Brumaire of Louis Bonaparte*. In this essay, as Hall argues, the faults of *The Manifesto* are transformed, through attempts to understand the complexity of the relations between economic classes and political parties.[19] Fernbach makes a similar point when he argues that in *Class Struggles in France*

> Marx began, for the first time, to develop a systematic set of concepts for coming to grips with the phenomena of a politics which is certainly that of class struggle . . . but which is nevertheless *politics*, practised in the field of ideology and coercion that gives it its specific character.[20]

The second moment of revision, a longer period but still an attempt intellectually to recoup political defeats, is the moment of *Capital* and its preparatory works, the rendering of the historical and philosophical generalities of *The Manifesto* into a much more precise account of the economic position of 'the labourer' under capital. Nicolaus argues that the 'Hegelian choreography' of *The Manifesto* – the 'negation' of bourgeois society by the proletariat – was replaced by categories that allow us to understand the rise of intermediate classes and the complication (rather than the simplification) of the structure of capitalist society.[21]

These revisions certainly provide the *means* for a full recasting of the older problematic. Yet they resemble the more familiar tussles with 'old Hegel' himself in that they were never completed. The earlier simplicities were not replaced by the new complexities – rather the two co-exist, often in the same texts. There are, in Hall's phrase, 'echoes' of *The Manifesto* in *Capital*. The prospect of proletarian revolution, no less inevitable, merely delayed till capital's maturity, remains one organising assumption even of *The Eighteenth Brumaire*.[22] Later commentators have sometimes under-estimated their own roles in teasing out the implications of later formulations for earlier ones. It is not clear that Marx was always so perceptive. For today, it is more important to recover the 'best' Marx, than to continue to chastise the elements of 'economism', 'teleology' or 'class reductionism' in Marx at his worst. But the *historical* significance of the absence of a developed Marxist theory of classes has been immense. Since *The Manifesto* remained the most widely-used agitational text of the communist movement, since *Capital* itself gave warrant to the earlier problematic, and since Engels' interpretative work tended to disguise rather than highlight the revisions of the 1850s and 1860s, the theoretical resources of working-class movements in the period from the Great Depression to the rise of Fascism were severely weakened.

Lenin and Gramsci

It has become a somewhat routine procedure to identify a whole middle period of Marxist theory ('Second International') with various species of 'economism'. Much less understood are the historical conditions of this 'deviation'. No such history is attempted here, but it is important to say that while the problematic of *The Manifesto* became irrelevant in Britain after 1850, it acquired relevance again in late nineteenth-century Europe, whenever large masses of peasants, small producers or semi-proletarians were caught up in industrial transformations similar to those of early nineteenth-century Britain, whenever the subordination of labour to capital was conspicuously deepened and in the times of 'syndicalist' excitement that often accompanied these transformations. Deep and rapid economic change seems often to produce a neglect of political and ideological conditions even in theorists whose thought generally is opposed to this tendency. One thinks of the young Gramsci of the 'Red City' of Turin and of the Factory Councils.[23]

It is to Lenin however that we should turn for the further development of the Manifesto problematic. Lenin developed that side of 'Manifesto Marxism' that emphasised the importance of political struggles in determining outcomes. At the same time he stressed the historic role of the proletariat 'as the builder of socialist society'. This was, indeed, 'the chief thing in the doctrine of Marx'.[24] In effect, then, Lenin grafted a Marxist political theory onto the basics of the Manifesto scheme. His analysis moves constantly between the 'objective' or 'economic' aspect of immediate tactical situations and the 'subjective' features, matters of organisation and consciousness. The economic/political duo is the key structure of his thought. Yet the main themes of Lenin's writing – science and ideology; spontaneity and political consciousness; masses and party – are handled in a way that suppresses the cultural or ideological content or object of politics and obscures questions about popular attitudes and feelings.

This follows, in part, from Lenin's version of the science/ideology divide. Marxism may not be a completed science but it is a science of a very developed order. For most situations it is important to recapitulate the findings of Marx and Engels – Lenin's characteristic polemical mode is precisely to recapitulate thus, confronting 'revisionism' with the findings. Marxism is a 'strikingly integral and harmonious scientific theory' which needs to be applied to new situations, and to be completed, but is not in need of revision.[25] This creates the distinction between science and ideology in its most closed form: true knowledge/the bumbling mistakes of revisionism; proletarian knowledge/petty-bourgeois conceptions; consciousness of class/'deceptions' or 'self-deceptions'. The content of ideology, in a sense, matters little; it may swiftly be reduced to its class character:

> People always have been the foolish victims of deception and self-deception in politics, and they always will be until they have learnt to seek out the *interests* of some class or other behind all moral, religious, political and social phrases, declarations and promises.[26]

In this conception of ideology, not inappropriate certainly for analysing a state with few ideological resources, the main absence is the force of belief or conviction. The models continuously evoked in Lenin's language are those of delusion or corruption. The contents or logic of opposed positions are lost in the pejorative labels: 'revisionism', 'opportunism', 'petty-bourgeois mentality'. It is not, after all, beliefs that move people, but 'interests'.

Much the same could be said of Lenin's understanding of bourgeois strategies, especially in the West. Out of a largely pre-war and then Russian experience, Lenin understood the state mainly in its repressive moment.[27] Where this was not adequate, he used notions of manipulation or top-downward, one-dimensional control, the language of 'bribery and corruption'. As he said of 'labour aristocracy', 'they are bribing them in a thousand different ways, direct and indirect, overt and covert'.[28]

A similar structure is to be found in the spontaneity/politics couplet. The masses learn, to be sure, from their practical activity, and leaders may fall behind as well as lead, but the source of conceptions is a pre-given theory which is developed outside the class and communicated to it.[29] There are 'spontaneous' and 'conscious' elements, a distinction which threatens to become that of thinking head and political muscle.[30] Even 'propaganda' (hardly a nuanced way of thinking how popular conceptions may be changed) is given a heavily organisational emphasis. Lenin's writing on 'party literature' or the need for 'an all-Russia political newspaper' understands such projects as foci for unities, but is silent about the relations to be sought, ideologically, between such productions and their readers.[31]

The obvious comparison is with Gramsci. While the very notion of 'spontaneity' disguises the fact that the masses already have conceptions of the world beyond mere 'force of habit'

Gramsci insisted that 'all men are philosophers', and share in some conception of the world.[32] 'Pure spontaneity' does not exist in history since it would amount to 'pure mechanicity'. It exists only in the fact that conscious leadership is diffused rather than concentrated, or has beliefs that do not transcend 'traditional conceptions of the world'. It follows that there is a need 'to study and develop the elements of popular psychology, historically and sociologically, actively (i.e. in order to transform them by educating them into a modern mentality)'.[33] Much of *The Prison Notebooks* are an elaboration of this point. This project Gramsci found to be 'implicit' in Lenin – 'perhaps even explicitly stated'. Yet despite many similarities and later development in Lenin's own position, their emphases *do* seem dissimilar and lead to different analyses of the relation of party to class. Gramsci was the first major Marxist theorist to take the 'culture of the popular masses' as the direct and privileged object of study and of political practice.

These deficiencies were the reverse side of Lenin's political virtues: his stress on 'concrete' analysis, intervention in immediate political contingencies and impatience, in situations demanding heroic activity, of 'mere words'. These features, aspects of the tightest of theory–practice relations, may distinguish Leninism from its subsequent corruptions in Stalinism where a mechanical notion of Marxism as pre-given 'science' is allied to a rigidly organisational and authoritarian conception of party.[34] But Lenin's legacy had a tendency to relieve Marxism from the concrete study of working-class culture, and to narrow the range of what was considered relevant to political practice.

Later orthodoxies: two examples

Two further extensions of this problematic are especially revealing. These are rather dissimilar examples, but share a historical dilemma and a structure of argument: first, the theory of 'labour aristocracy', casually present in the later Engels, developed in Lenin's writing on Imperialism and Reformism, re-introduced into English Marxist historiography by Eric Hobsbawm and currently the subject of much historical debate;[35] second, the early work of Georg Lukács, whose book *History and Class Consciousness*, is the fullest development of the class/class consciousness position.[36]

The dilemma is that posed in the contradiction between the theoretical destiny of the proletariat and the actual course of Western working-class politics. Marxist theory has worried around the problem of the revolutionary class manqué, not only in the classic debates around 'reformism' or 'labourism' but also in much of the thinking around culture-ideology-consciousness. To speak rather rashly there have been two responses to this situation: to abandon recognisably Marxist analysis or to construct a second level of theory or special explanations, to show why a 'normal' or long-term historical development had somehow been blocked or delayed. These have been commoner responses than attempting to reconstruct the original problematic.

The commonest form of second-order theory has been the recovery of elements absent in the original problematic though often present, in a different, less accented, form in the historical experience which is expressed. These new elements, not theorised as part of the central dynamics of the capitalist mode of production, are then understood as historically contingent factors, features of a particular phase. They are fetters or inhibitions on more organic processes, a belief in the simpler forms of which are thereby preserved. Features central to the constitution of the working class appear in a displaced or marginalised role.

The 'theory' of labour aristocracy is an excellent example. It has been used to explain the 'liberalisation' of mid-nineteenth century Britain, labour 'reformism' and the failure of early twentieth-century working classes to develop a counter-hegemonic strategy. Two kinds of argument are embraced in the same term: the first centres on labour organisation and its partial incorporation within the agencies of the State; the second posits some larger social-structural division within the class itself, commonly between 'skilled' and 'unskilled' sectors.[37] Both arguments correspond to observable tendencies in the post-1850 history of the working class, but also limit the effects of such observations on the fundamental inadequacies of an older orthodoxy. Theories of the incorporation, 'corruption' or detachment of 'leadership' have actually hindered a more fundamental reconceptualisation of the relationship between economic classes and political parties, or a more adequate analysis of the dispositions of the 'rank and file'.[38] Similarly, 'the mid-Victorian aristocracy of labour' may not be a very helpful construction. For it was not just a unique historical phenomenon; but rather a particular *form* of a more general tendency. As Marx discovered in his deeper analyses, the expansion and the movements of capital do not simply unify and massify labour, even in the direct relations of production. Rather, the working class is continuously recomposed around major internal structurations. These internal divisions – within factories, within industries, between occupations, between the sexes and between the employed and the reserve armies – ought to be an object of any primary theory of the working class. We need to start indeed, politically and theoretically, not from the assumption of simplification and unity but from that of complexity and division.[39] These divisions are based on hierarchies of labour modified by the effects of gender relations which are reproduced mainly within the family. These forms of division are, however, also the object of ideological and political practices. A whole politics may be wrought on top of them. Socialist strategies are not at all aided by the rooted belief that such divisions must somehow pass away, or be easily transcended in the name of some essential unity.

Lukács' *History and Class Consciousness*, essays written or revised in the heat of struggles within the Hungarian Communist Party in 1922, share the general features of labour aristocracy theory. For his early project was an attempt to graft a more developed theory of 'consciousness' onto the classical root. The result is a similar hybrid. Lukács was a forerunner of the extreme abstractness of 'Western Marxism' and his borrowings were colossally heterogeneous: a classical Marxist root, a recovery of Hegel and the pre-Manifesto Marx, a debt to Weber and Simmel and a reading of part I of *Capital*.[40]

His starting point was Marx's distinction between the class 'as against capital' and the class 'for itself'. The first characteristic move was to render 'class consciousness' a 'sacred' category.[41]

Despite its 'profane' origin in Chartism and Owenism, it now acquired a wholly theoretical status. It became 'the thoughts and feelings men would have in a particular situation if they were *able* to assess both it and the interests arising from it', or 'rational reactions "imputed" to a particular typical position in the process of production'.[42] How then to explain the distance between such a consciousness and the contents of proletarian heads, this side of revolution?

'False consciousness' has fundamental forms, differently inhabited by the two main classes. (Lukács accentuated the schematism of *The Manifesto* by denying to other classes an effective historical role).[43] These forms had been described by Marx in *Capital* as the mechanism of 'fetishism'. Relations between people acquire, under capitalism, a 'phantom objectivity', appearing as things. By a series of daring homologies, the features of a fetishised consciousness were discerned throughout capitalist society: in its bureaucracy, its sexual relations, its economic ideologies, its jurisprudence and, especially, its philosophy and epistemology.[44]

The bourgeoisie inhabits this world with a necessarily partial vision, having knowledge of practical management but not of the totality of processes nor of those elements that point to future transformations, the tendency to recurrent crises for instance. Faced with the instability of its domination, its objective interests force it to deceive itself. The proletariat has no such interest, but in its immediate perspective, it has its own 'bourgeois' (i.e. 'false') consciousness within which it is held by 'opportunist' politics. But a knowledge of the totality is both possible and necessary – 'a matter of life and death'. Crises force the proletariat to self-realisation. In this moment the duality of class 'as against capital' and class 'for itself', transformed in Lukács' thought into the Hegelian dialectic of subject and object, is resolved. The proletariat becomes the identical subject-object of history.[45]

So questions inadequately treated in earlier accounts return to the tradition with a vengeance. Lukács remains important for his concentration on 'consciousness', for his criticisms of an unreflexive epistemology, and for the attempt to theorise the relation between capital's economic forms and the general features of bourgeois thought. But he is also a classical instance of two recurrent tendencies commoner in sociological traditions: the tendency to see class cultures as straightforwardly and wholly conditioned by social position (for this is the argument, ultimately, about class consciousness); and the tendency to ascribe to whole societies one 'central' or 'essential' modality of thought which enters the consciousness of all classes (for this is the argument about 'false consciousness'). The major fatality, as always in the class/class consciousness problematic, is any concrete, complex account of lived cultures, how they are formed and how they may be transformed.

Origins of the culture problematic

The complicated origins of 'culture' belong to the same history as early Marxist theory. The culture paradigm was formed in the Industrial Revolution, was redefined in the 1880s and 1890s and was recovered as a 'tradition' in the 1950s. Some elements were then worked into a theory of cultural-ideological processes.

Yet the social origin of these two traditions differs very much. Early Marxism was a rendering into theory of the experience of the small-producer-becoming-proletarian. The problematic of culture expressed the dilemmas of some English intellectuals sufficiently removed from industrial capital, in situation or sympathies, to distance themselves from its morality and purposes. Except for three main moments – the 1790s (fleetingly), the 1880s and 1890s and, the 1950s and 1960s – these intellectuals were distanced from popular movements and almost uniformly dismissive of popular moralities. Their 'autonomy' can be seen in the very structure of their thought: 'the emergence of *culture* as an abstraction and as an absolute', as a separate set of moral and intellectual activities, and as 'a court of human appeal', even as 'a mitigating and rallying alternative'.[46] Williams' description of this 'structure of feeling' seems also to spell out the increasingly differentiated functions of intellectual labour (whether of poet, novelist, artist, critic or academic) and the desire to find in specialised pursuits some canon of judgement and behaviour relevant to the whole society. Since this tradition was an overwhelmingly 'literary' one, the debate was evaluative rather than analytic. It concerned appropriate social moralities or what Edward Thompson has called 'the education of desire'.[47]

This long line of 'literary-sociology' has been much discussed. We will mainly concentrate on the post-war advocates of 'culture', and especially upon Raymond Williams and Edward Thompson. Yet these writers seem to have found themselves in some account of predecessors: Williams in a long detour in search of 'a general theory of culture', Thompson in his twenty-year espousal of the ideas of William Morris.[48] Why did they choose to write about their deepest political convictions through the presentation of significant persons, mostly long dead?

Williams' *Culture and Society* constructs a 'tradition' around the history of a word – 'culture' – and a succession of writers who contributed to its sum of meanings. Perhaps the most obvious conclusion of a return to the book is the great variety of this 'tradition'. Yet Williams' sharpest critics have constructed a still more homogenous entity – 'the literary intelligentsia' – and attacked his 'social tradition' as one of 'almost uniform political reaction'.[49] There has even been a tendency to take the 'Culture and Society' intellectuals as typical of English intellectuals as a whole, thereby excluding a whole middle-class radical and liberal tradition from the historical record.[50] Edward Thompson's critique is much more perceptive: there was not one Culture and Society tradition, but several.[51]

A more discriminating history would have to make some distinctions. Though all these writers were distanced from the ruling interests and ideas of their time, their evaluations were more or less interesting or useful to different social classes or groups. Often they were taken up (and thereby changed) by particular parties or movements. On such a basis three main strands might be distinguished among those discussed in *Culture & Society*. The first strand is a Conservative tradition, the ideological *alter ego* of Liberalism: Burke, Southey, Disraeli, Newman, Mallock and Eliot are central here. One distinctive feature is a deep distrust of democracy. If capitalism is opposed, it is because it is a 'leveller'. The social bases of this conservative organicism were the Anglican Church, the Conservative Party and the social order and institutions of an agrarian capitalism. 'Culture' was understood as the repository of traditional social values, whose most important practical function was to distinguish between leaders and led and to defend attendant privileges. Since 1945 it has become difficult, except as an eccentricity, to avow fully hierarchical philosophies; under the pressure of the ideological assumption of 'equality' the Conservative Party has changed its repertoire to a more liberal variant.

Edward Thompson has written the history of the second strand – a Radical Romanticism.[52] The succession runs from the early Romantics (especially Blake, Keats and Shelley) through Carlyle and Ruskin, to William Morris, in whom Romanticism and Marxism are conjoined. There are two points of junction with popular movements: between plebeian radicalism and the utopian intellectuals of the 1790s and with Morris' crossing of 'the river of fire', to take the standpoint of the working class in the 1880s.[53] Later projections of the tradition are not altogether clear: it should include, perhaps, 'Marxisante independents' like G.D.H. Cole and 'ethical socialists' like Tawney or Orwell. It should include perhaps the radical populism of the 1930s and 1940s, without the 'Stalinist pieties'. But the most important test of the organicity of Morris and of the earlier tradition is their reception into working-class traditions of independent socialist education and the continuance of utopian and ethical elements in the British labour movement.[54]

Thirdly, we might distinguish writers whose very lack of an organic connection is their defining feature. They explore the dilemmas of people like themselves, express the viewpoint, for instance, of those Oxbridge-civil-service-literary circles in which Matthew Arnold moved. This thought remains, in Gramsci's word, 'intellectualistic'. One might include here Arnold, the various artistic Bohemias (e.g. the Pre-Raphaelites) and Leavis and the Leavisites, whose dilemmas are very much those of the academic layer in a modern education system. Elements of the thought of such traditional intellectuals may, of course, influence more organic thinkers, as Arnoldian formulations influenced Tawney's thought on education for instance.

It would require a proper history of these traditions to show the force of these categories and to refine them. But it should be clear that wholesale acceptance or rejection of the 'culture' tradition is perilous. It will hardly do to dismiss the whole sequence as one of unmitigated reaction, or to see the idea of culture as 'contaminated' at root. At the very least one must ask *whose* idea of culture? In the end, though, such questions cannot be answered by historical pedigrees, only by modern relevances.

Yet why should it have been so important for certain intellectuals of the left to discover themselves in 'traditions' at all? Some answers have already been given in contextualising the sociologies.

The 1950s were a period of crisis for those who based their politics on a criticism of capitalism and a faith in the mass of the people. The conditions of this decade were particularly testing for the characteristic politics of the English left: strong in popular sympathies and moral sensitivities, weak in the concrete analysis of capitalism and its twentieth-century adaptations. The 'radical populism' of the 1930s and 1940s depended on the crisis-ridden state of the inter-war economy, the immediacies of the fight against Fascism, and opposition to the most overt forms of social inequality and class rule. When these conditions seemed to evaporate, underlying weaknesses were clearly displayed. A generally 'leftist' climate among intellectuals was rapidly dispersed, leaving only a harder contingent. But they could offer, from inherited theoretical resources, no adequate explanation of capitalism's success to place beside the gospels of growth and affluence. So confident were right-wing intellectuals in this period that they even began a re-appraisal of the less 'acceptable' moments in the history of British capitalism, rehabilitating the Industrial Revolution as a moment of 'growth'.[55] A reviving leftism invested the weaker points of this analysis – overwhelmingly, the analysis of culture. One consequence was the reproduction of a persistent dichotomy within English ideologies: between a liberal, utilitarian and 'economist' pole, where the progressive side of capitalism was well but one-sidedly understood; and a romantic, literary and 'qualitative' pole with popular political sympathies but a romantic and equally one-sided view of capitalism's evils.

This pressure was accompanied by major internal stresses. This affected intellectuals in the Labour Party through the party's loss of confidence and the bitter debates about 'revisionism'. Intellectuals to the left of this, in the Communist Party or with a firmer alignment to Marxism, were even more beset, their party paralysed, then split, by the half-revelations of the 20th Congress and the Soviet invasion of Hungary.[56] To judge from the force of the explosion to which they gave rise, the pressures must have been intense. The moment of culture can be understood as an attempt to vindicate critical social thought (from Marxism to Left Leavisism) in an exceptionally hostile climate and in circumstances where even 'the people' seemed content. Every single national resource was important in such an effort. What could English culture offer to stem the tide of 'Progress'? Answer: The Tradition; Answer: William Morris. Answer: The English Working Class in a more heroic phase.

Culture, experience and theory

The culture paradigm is distinguished by an over-riding concern with describing the actual forms of popular practices and beliefs. The manner of this commitment, the sharpness of an accompanying politics, even the key terms of definition, differ very much. The term 'culture' for instance remains central in Williams' cultural theory whether thought of as 'a whole way of life' or in its latest more difficult formulation as 'a constitutive social process, creating specific and different ways of life'.[57] Thompson's concern with culture, values, ideas, and moral evaluations is no less marked; and he defines this as the crucial absence in Marxism.[58] But his solution was less a long meditation on 'culture' and more, in his early work, a re-working of familiar Marxist categories, especially of 'class consciousness'. The engagement with culture or lived experience is secured by insisting that class consciousness is the way in which experiences are 'handled in cultural terms: embodied in traditions, value systems, ideas and institutional forms'. It has a definite history: it is neither an abstraction nor a hopeful projection. It is a category to be made 'profane' again. Any idealist or normative version – of class consciousness 'not as it is, but as it ought to be' – is rejected.[59]

'Experience' defines both the object and the method of inquiry. It is a method in which the author himself, *his* experience, is very intrusive: there is much self-revelation in Hoggart's portrayal of his childhood, in Williams' pursuit of 'the implications of personal experience to the point where they have organically emerged as methods, concepts, strategies',[60] and in Thompson's style of polemical address. The method rejects sociologies in which lived relations are marginalised or over-borne by theory. Part of the criticism of elite cultural theory and of the restriction of creativity to the artist is that it provided a flattened stereotypical view of the life of the 'masses': 'there are in fact no masses; there are only ways of seeing people as masses'.[61] Thompson attacks a whole range of otherwise very dissimilar positions on the same grounds: economistic Marxism, 'ideological' economic history, a 'Platonist' Leninism, structural-functionalism, the construction of abstract typologies in anthropology or sociology and, latterly, a Marxist structuralism.[62] These all have the same moral and epistemological features: 'violent abstraction', the 'imposition' of *a priori* scheme on a living history, the forcing of historical materials into the mould of the theorist's own pre-occupations, speculative or dogmatic. Advocated instead is an explicitly anti-rationalist epistemology in which theory is restricted to critique and hypothesis, and the key moment is likened to listening:

> If you want a generalization I would have to say that the historian has got to be listening all the time. He should not set up a book or a research project with a totally clear sense of exactly what he is going to be able to do. The material itself has got to speak through him. And I think this happens.[63]

Williams argues a very similar position, defining, with great accuracy, common tendencies in both older (base and superstructure) and modern (structuralist) Marxisms:

> The analytical categories, as so often in idealist thought, have, almost unnoticed, become substantive descriptions, which then take habitual priority over the whole social process to which, as analytic categories, they are attempting to speak.[64]

There are immense strengths in this position. Culturalism conducts a profound critique of theory-as-dogma, of a rationalism or a conceptual *a priorism*, in the first place in the name of 'experience', in the second in the name of 'materialism'. This response was first formed against economistic Marxism; but it has an equal force against many forms of the explosion of 'Theory' in the 1970s. If, like Marx, one regards various forms of idealism as the occupational vice of 'the philosopher' (for which read intellectual or academic), the culturalist argument remains immensely important.

But it also has considerable weaknesses. The stress on the privilege of 'experience' leads to an under-developed theoretical enterprise and a tendency to avoid abstract or generalising discourse in itself. There are several aspects of this: the tendency of rejecting analytical distinctions as a matter of principle, the tendency to disguised or un-selfconscious theoretical borrowings, and the failure fully to theorise the results of concrete studies. We might take some examples of each of these. Thompson's *Making of the English Working Class*, for example, an historical masterpiece, remains a work whose findings are seriously under-exploited by the author himself. It is full of profound insights about the relations between the lived, cultural level and transformative ideological practices whether those of methodist preachers or of radical journalists. For such insights to become fully available they would have to be stated more abstractly, or generally. They would have to be abstracted from the particular patterns of 'lived' historical complexity in which they occurred. Their relation to a more general debate about, say, culture and ideology would have to be explored, and a specifically theoretical contribution developed from them. Such abstractions do not have to be thought of as completely general or trans-historical in scope – the historian's nightmare of Theory. A proper use of concepts involves arguments about their historical scope of reference. Still, if such abstractions are not made, findings remain locked up in accounts of specific historical contingencies: they cannot be consumed theoretically, cannot generate parallel questions for other instances, cannot contribute to the development of conceptual tools. In one sense, *The Making* is a very theoretical book: it is organised, very consciously, around a particular problematic and conducts an extended historical critique of other positions. This case, these big bold truths, are mightily made for page after page. Yet, as many readers find, there are great richnesses in the book (and in the history it describes) which are difficult to grasp for want of a more explicit theoretical labour. A work of this stature ought to *produce theory*.

The concluding sections of *Whigs and Hunters*, Thompson's latest major text, illustrate a rather different problem. Here Thompson does generalise from his findings on the subject of class and the law. He conducts an argument against notions of the law as the simple expression of the interests of a dominant class, stressing those features of law as a practice which may limit its use as a class instrument. Yet this very convincing argument is presented as a polemic against 'modern structural Marxists' who, in fact, adopt a very similar view of the juridical as that pressed by Thompson![65]

This is simply a case of inattention to the arguments of theoretical works, an inattention that would hardly be tolerated for the usual order of historical 'sources'. Williams' *Marxism and Literature*, by comparison, represents a very advanced position within the culturalist problematic since it is explicitly a long and challenging theoretical statement based upon more concrete work. In general, however, culturalist premises tend to interrupt the full movements from the concrete to the abstract (and back again) that distinguished Marx's method and which would make possible a continuous revision and development of a theoretical legacy from the products of new research.

The question about analytic distinctions is best illustrated through particular questions: how does culturalism understand the relation of culture to not-culture and, in particular, how is this distinction handled in relation to class? These questions are central to our object, 'working-class culture'.

Classical Marxism handled these problems through the base–superstructure metaphor and the class–class consciousness distinction. Both Williams and Thompson have consistently, in all their work, argued against the base–superstructure formulation. Williams has traced a kind of pathology of the notion from Marx's ambiguous statements to later rigidities, has stressed the tendency to empty the 'superstructure' of any really material force and to compartmentalise areas of social life rather than examine their 'constitutive processes'.[66] Thompson has argued, similarly, that the initial separation out of 'the economic', on which the metaphor is based, was a product of the traditions which Marx contested and that real historical problems are not thinkable in this way:

> There is no way in which I find it possible to describe Puritan or Methodist work discipline as an element of the 'superstructure' and then put work itself in a 'basis' somewhere else.[67]

Both Thompson and Williams attempt to find better ways of thinking about these things. Their solutions differ, however, and have to be treated separately.

Williams and 'culturalism'

Williams has, characteristically, refused to make rigorous or systematic distinctions between cultural and other processes. The following formulations, one from the early works and one from the late, are quite typical:

> The truth about a society, it would seem, is to be found in the actual relations, always exceptionally complicated, between the system of decision, the system of communication and learning, the system of maintenance and the system of generation and nurture. It is not a question of looking for some absolute formula, by which the structure of these relations can be invariably determined. The formula that matters is that which, first, makes the essential connections between what are never really separable systems, and second, shows the historical variability of each of these systems, and therefore the real organisations within which they operate and are lived.[68]

> Orthodox analysts began to think of 'the base' and 'the superstructure' as if they were separable concrete entities. In doing so they lost sight of the very processes – not abstract relations but constitutive processes – which it should have been the special function of historical materialism to emphasize . . . It is not 'the base' and 'the superstructure' that need to be studied, but the specific and indissoluble real processes . . .[69]

The procedure of both these passages is to identify certain distinctions to insist that there can be no adequate general formulation of relations between different spheres, and, finally, to insist on the importance of totalities or 'constitutive social processes' that lie behind the distinctions anyway. In practice this procedure amounts to the collapse of distinctions, since the weight of the argument is always about their essential artifiality. 'Experience', it seems, can always grasp a process that is beyond or beneath analytical distinctions and which they may (perhaps must?) obscure. Collapses of this kind can be seen all the way through *Marxism and Literature.* The distinction between economic production and other practices disappears in the expansion of production as an undifferentiated concept akin to 'creativity'. The term 'material' is applied to all aspects of a social and political order in a parallel expansion.[70]

There are several difficulties in this solution. First, there is the difficulty of arriving at any precise view at all of the characteristics of culture. Such questions are referred back, all the time, to total social process, 'real men' and classes in specific situations. Yet at no moment in the whole Williams *oeuvre* does a clear definition or boundary of culture emerge. Thus 'way of life', as Edward Thompson suggested in 1961, tends to become everyone's shopping list of elements of thought, action, organisation, work or leisure.[71] 'Cultural Studies' tends to inherit and to develop the extreme descriptive heterogeneity of this object. It follows that it is not possible to speak coherently about the relation between culture and other (kinds of?)

practices, except continually to insist that all is part of one totality. A persistent fuzziness must result. But more serious consequences may follow, for a second set of problems concern what relations actually are, in practice, dominant in Williams' accounts of the world: how the failure to specify is actually supplied more pragmatically. As literary critic and cultural theorist, Williams does stress certain kinds of practices, all of them broadly cultural and, within that, mainly literary. Other practices tend to be marginalised or defined away. There is no check on this from theoretical controls. Thus the early works are particularly inattentive to political processes, a tendency which Williams himself has acknowledged.[72] The tensionless 'expansion' of culture replaces struggle over values and definitions. Though some of this is repaired in later work, there is a persistent neglect of the particular character and force of economic relations and therefore of economic definitions in relation to class. This 'culturalism' is described by Anthony Barnett, the most careful of Williams' critics, as a kind of inversion of economism, a reduction 'upwards'.[73] This is the characteristic tendency of 1950s and 1960s texts in both history and 'literary-sociology'. It is very characteristic of Hoggart's *Uses of Literacy*, for example, from which both economic production and politics are literally absent. Even Thompson's work is not altogether exempt from it.

The nature of Williams' culturalism can best be seen in his treatment of class. As others have noted, the category 'class' is hardly present as an active shaping idea in Williams' early work: it tends to emerge in conclusions, especially in the famous passages at the end of *Culture and Society*. But here we encounter a further set of problems. Since culture is an expansive or inclusive term (potentially including everything), the only way to give a coherent account of a particular lived culture is to reduce it to its organising *principles*. It is not the elements of a culture that are important, but the principles or values which, overall it expresses. If no categories (distinctions) of a systematic kind exist with which we can grasp complexities, there is no option but to simplify. One way to simplify is to seek 'essences' or 'principles' and this is very much how, in a classic form of idealist reduction, Williams approaches class cultures. We are offered a simple typology of cultures: bourgeois culture is individualistic but is modified by the idea of service; working-class culture by contrast, revolves around collectivity and solidarity. It then becomes possible to examine the strengths and weaknesses of such principles in a Matthew Arnold-like search for the elements of a 'common culture'. The procedure produces results that are very close to other idealist accounts of class elements in English culture, including those of several historians.[74] But it also produces stereotypes as misleading as 'mass culture' or 'false consciousness'. Is solidarity a *general* feature of working-class culture? Does it apply to *all* the social sites and internal relations of a culture: to relations between men and women and men and children for instance? How powerful have solidarities been outside the culture of the work place? Such compressed descriptions-cum-judgements can hardly hope to capture the complexity of a lived culture, let alone the forces, material and ideological, which form it.

Thompson and socialist-humanist history

Thompson's position often resembles Williams', with a similar tendency to refuse certain distinctions. Relations of production are not only economic but also 'human' relationships. Production *involves* culture. Every mode of production carries with it corresponding modes of culture. 'Economics' and 'culture' are 'two sides of the same coin', or are in a dialectic of interaction. Certain values are 'consonant' with certain modes of production and therefore an inextricable part of them. Relations of production are simultaneously expressed in all areas of social life.[75] More commonly, Thompson has worked with a minimum distinction, taken from Marx, between 'social consciousness' and 'social being'. Social being is understood as the mode of production of material life and 'the human relationships' to which it gives rise. These 'human relationships' include 'exploitation' but also relations of domination and of 'acquisitiveness', knowledge of which we owe not only to Marx but also to Weber, Tawney and Veblen. Thompson has employed this distinction very much as the young Marx did, to attack positions which are seen as idealist. Thompson insists against the early Williams (as Marx did against Hegel or Proudhon) that social being determines social consciousness. This often co-exists with an insistence on 'dialectical interrelationship' of being and consciousness, a formulation which appears inconsistent with the notion of determination. Partly, no doubt, because of these inconsistencies, Thompson's latest position seems to be different again: it is not possible, even for capitalist societies, to maintain the social being/social consciousness distinction as a general guide or control. In studying the folklore or common sense of particular groups within the subordinated classes 'we cannot conceive of social being apart from social consciousness or norms' and it is therefore 'meaningless' to ascribe priority of one over the other.[76]

These shifts indicate difficulties in a position that gives overwhelming priority to the portrayal of 'experience'. Faithfulness to experience, an impulse with moral and literary roots comes into conflict, at a certain point, with what we can only call 'scientific' intentions, using the term in its broader continental uses rather than its narrower English ones. Systematic knowledge and the search for more adequate *explanations* of social processes require developed analytical procedures. Within Marxism as a 'science', abstraction plays a part occupied in other systems by ideal types, model building or the testing of hypotheses. Abstraction precisely depends upon a necessary simplification of 'real history', a presentation of elements in it in a quite formal way. Most of *Capital* as a work is 'abstract' in this sense: theory is derived from the study of the concrete and is used to illuminate particular instances, but in its form and presentation, most of *Capital* does not at all resemble 'real history'. Abstraction is both a condition for thinking clearly about the world and for learning from concrete instances in such a way as to be able to transfer insights or consider them in relation to another case. If we refuse analytical distinctions of the most elementary kind (e.g. culture/not culture) we will not be able to examine that real history whose integrity we aim to preserve. Distinctions like base/superstructure or economic/ political/ideological practices, properly used, are no more than the means with which to grasp 'total social process'. To reject these tools and supply no others is to return us, scientifically, to a radical historical relativism and the denial of any generalising or accumulative intellectual procedures.

Attempts at a proper theoretical enterprise must always, within this problematic be 'guilty' or inhibited, so we ought to turn to Thompson's portrayals of the relation of culture and class in his actual histories. How can we describe the characteristic object of Thompson's history?

All the histories from *The Making of the English Working Class* to *Whigs and Hunters* have shared a common theme: the conflict between two cultural modes.[77] The first mode is rooted in the characteristic relations and values of a society of small producers, artisans and semi-proletarians which existed within cultural and political horizons set by agrarian capital – the first English form of a bourgeois ruling class – and policed, centrally, by law. The second mode includes the cultural world of industrial work discipline, of protestant or puritan notations of time, of the psychic disciplines of methodism, of political economy, utilitarism and the 'Gradgrind school' and of the cultural aggressions associated with the requirements of commercial and especially industrial capital. The conflict of these modes involves a long co-existence that corresponds to Maurice Dobb's long transition in relations of economic production. It is, indeed, the political-cultural expression or aspect of these very same changes: the long transition in culture and politics and in forms of struggle between classes. Thompson's earlier work, especially *The Making* looks at the later points of the transition: the English working class is formed, politically and culturally, out of the collapse of the older moral framework ('paternalism' and 'the moral economy') and through popular opposition to the imposition of the new. If, as was argued earlier, *The Making* recounts the end of a story rather than the beginning of a new one, we can understand why Thompson's trajectory is back into the eighteenth century rather than forward once again to the nineteenth or later. He has developed, once more, the territory opened up by the initial explorations of Dobb and Torr, planning an historical rendez-vous, perhaps, with the work of Christopher Hill. This later work has concentrated on the forms of gentry hegemony and of popular self-assertion, but has never lost sight of the transition in cultural-economic modes. *Whigs and Hunters*, for instance, deals not only with the importance of juridical relations in the eighteenth century, but also with the enforcement of capitalist property rights, over the customary use rights of the foresters.

Before we look more closely at the treatment of class, it is important to note one general weakness of these histories. They rest on a reduction not dissimilar to Williams' 'culturalism'. It is not that economic relations and changes in ways of producing are absent from these histories: their presence is *assumed* all the time. But the changes in economic relations are understood *through* their experiential or political effects, not, for the most part, in themselves. Thus, in *The Making* the transformative character of the Industrial Revolution is grasped largely through the experiences of artisans, weavers and others: the character of this shift in economic social relations is never fully described and is only passively present in the story. The characteristic move is to *assume* the force of economic changes, to insist upon the force of cultural and political processes too, but only to describe the latter in any detailed or active way.[78]

It is very easy to see how this tendency occurred. The problem with existing historiographies, especially of older Marxisms and its assailants in the shape of the economic historians was the absence of any proper consideration of 'values'. *The Making* conducts a powerful critique of both these traditions, rehearsing much of Romanticism's objection to utilitarianism and political economy. The working class is not just made by industrial revolution ('steam power plus the factory equals the working class') but also through political counter-revolution, and a re-working, in the light of new experiences, of inherited cultural traditions. It made much sense, then, to occupy the ground of experience from which to criticise the orthodoxies. All of Thompson's own 'traditions' – Romanticism, the concern with moralities, the literary mode, the historiography of the Hammonds and of Tawney and the Morris-inspired reading of Marx – pushed hard in the same direction. But it is now possible to see that the stress on culture involved vacating the ground of economic relations, leaving the heart of opposing positions untouched and threatening an impoverishment of analysis.

Class, class struggle and class-as-relationship are central categories of Thompson's history. Historical outcomes are the product of class struggles. Even the apparently assured control of the eighteenth-century gentry is secured and 'lived' through conflicts: the challenge of crime or riot; the response of magistracy or law. *The Making* commences with a major re-definition of class which then forms the central argument of the book. This is the emphasis that marks Thompson's history as 'Marxist' and distinguishes it from, say, the early Williams or the passivity of Hoggart's account.

Yet, as we have suggested, 'class consciousness' is re-worked in the light of 'culture'. Retained from the older problematic are all the activist elements: classes as agents, present at their own making, forged in struggles: the stresses of Marx's 'class for itself'. Suppressed or rendered peripheral are the more 'objective' or passive elements in the classic concept: 'class as against capital' in the earlier formulations, developed, in *Capital*, into a profound analysis of the labourer's subordination within capitalist economic relations. Economic class relations are not entirely absent from *The Making*. Some of their force is carried in an extended and much looser notion of 'relationship': classes are groups of people in historical forms of human relationship. A more developed notion of relations of production sometimes seems about to emerge. But, generally, it is the *quality* of human relation*ships* rather than the *structuring* of these through *relations* that is the key concern. One symptom of this is the massive over-loading of the term 'experience'. It is made to carry the full weight of objective determinations but also expresses the relay or relation between 'economics' and 'culture'. Two quotations with rather different emphases illustrate this:

> The class *experience* is largely determined by the productive relations into which men are born – or enter involuntarily. Class-consciousness is the way in which these *experiences* are handled in cultural terms: embodied in traditions, value-systems, ideas, and institutional forms.[79]

> In Part Two I move from subjective to objective influences – the experiences of groups of workers during the Industrial Revolution which seem to me to be of especial significance.[80]

In the first case 'experience' is seen as a relation between productive relations and culture; in the second 'experience' is *identified with* 'objective influences'. In either case, since 'objective influences' are little described, 'experience' is made to carry all their weight. It indicates, at once, the way in which individuals or groups are subject to external or uncontrollable pressures and the most located or immediate of their understandings. In it are contained, in the most compressed form, the unwillingness to distinguish culture and not-culture and many of the difficulties that arise.

Against this it is important to argue for certain minimum distinctions. In the analysis of the major classes of capitalist social formations the distinction 'class as against capital'/ 'class for itself' should be retained. The latter term reminds us that people stand in relations that are independent of their wills and of which they are more or less conscious. These relations do stamp a social character on people, but should not be reduced to relationships between people (of a nicer or nastier kind). The proletarian is not faced, merely, by greedy or exploitative middlemen or millowners, nor, just, by the 'inhuman' doctrines of political economy. Rather, by virtue of occupancy of a particular economic class position, the proletarian is forced to expend life energies under the control and command of capital, in order to acquire the means of subsistence, in order to live. Underneath the cultural handling of this relation (in its particular historical forms) the figure of the 'naked' labourer still moves, according to the fundamental disciplines of the capital relation. It matters, certainly, whether labourers work willingly, or with murder or even socialism in their hearts: but go to work they must or they and their children must starve or sink into still deeper forms of dependency. Since the early nineteenth century, the force of this economic relation has certainly been modified through the active political interventions of the class of labourers themselves. But it is still present and the arrangements which mitigate its severity may always be removed or rendered more oppressive or conditional. This is why it remains possible, in 1979 to speak meaningfully of a working class in Britain, irrespective of the strength or weakness of labour organisation. At one (indispensable) moment of analysis, the class is composed of those who partake in a proletarian relation to capital, are a class 'as against' it. The complexities of this form of class analysis, and the need for research as well as categories, should not lead us to abandon it.

This is of the utmost importance for the general problem raised in this book. Any analysis of 'working class culture' must be able to grasp the relation between economic classes and the forms in which they do (or do not) become active in conscious politics. If the two aspects of class analysis are conflated, this is not possible. If class is understood only as a cultural and political formation, a whole theoretical legacy is impoverished and materialist accounts are indistinguishable from a form of idealism. It may indeed be that the relation between what culturalism calls 'experience' and the marshalling of political forces, or, more correctly, between economic classes and political organisations is never or rarely as simple as 'transitive' or 'expressive' models imply. Economic classes rarely appear as political forces. Most of Thompson's work, for instance, has concerned periods in which the political representation of popular interests has, apparently, been secured with a relative faithfulness. In the period 1790 to 1840, the class character of political and cultural forms is relatively easy to see. Either that, or, as in the work on the eighteenth century, the absence of economic class categories has permitted the presentation of political forces *as* classes. Thompson's 'patricians' and 'plebeians' is a case in point. But whatever happened to small producers, semi-peasants and semi-proletarians? And why must eighteenth-century class borrow the garbs of Antiquity? As soon as we enter a period when formal political arrangements for the 'representation' of working people become more complex and acquire firm institutional continuities, these problems become inescapable. Do the British Labour Party or even British trade unions simply or expressively 'represent' working people? At the very least they define or structure what passes for politics as such, so preventing the representation of some elements and promoting others. These questions cannot even be properly *posed* within the culturalist problematic.

There is one final set of temptations that lie along the route of 'culture'. The one-sided stress on class as a cultural and political formation commits analysis to discover such forms in every place or period. Such searches will never be altogether in vain since the class organisation of society will always find expression of *some* kind. But the temptation is to present such findings as always analogous to a developed and politically conscious opposition. The 'class' is 'struggling' after all. Such a search slips easily into a romantic abasement before every manifestation of 'resistance', however exotic, peripheral, displaced or contained. Edward Thompson retains, perhaps, too conventional a view of what counts as class organisation to fall into this trap: a stress on party, unions and socialist intellectual traditions may, indeed, disguise the elements of 'primitive rebellion' in a modern working class. Yet some tendencies in modern sociology, focussing especially on the symbolic oppositions of groups of young working-class men do parallel Thompson's own stress on crowd actions, rituals of protest and moments of exceptional popular excitement and communal mobilisation. The point is that we can only reach a proper assessment of the character of such moments – then and now – by placing them within a wider analysis of economic and social structures. This requires conceptual tools for a properly historicised analysis of capitalism's continued economic transformations and of the position of groups of men and women in relation to it and each other.

'Structuralism' and 'humanism'

It is neither possible nor necessary to discuss structuralist emphases as fully as the previous problematics. This is partly for pragmatic reasons: the range of structuralist writing on matters that might be judged relevant is immense. An adequate account would have to include work as different as the two quite distinct moments in Althusser's project (the 'theoreticist' phase as well as subsequent self-criticisms), elements in French structuralist anthropology, those (diverse) tendencies summed up in the terms 'semiology' (the science of signs or of signification), the historical analysis of discursive practices in the work of Michel Foucault, and, perhaps, on an outer 'structuralist' limit, French historical traditions, especially the treatment of popular 'mentalité' by the *Annales* historians. The solution adopted here is to concentrate on Althusser's central and symptomatic contribution. In general, however, structuralist contributions are more important for their critical edge than for what they produce as alternative accounts. They have already informed our critique of other positions. In any very direct sense, 'structuralism' has little to contribute to an account of 'working-class culture'. This is not an object recognisable within this problematic. Structuralist theories push into the background the association between culture (or particular ideologies) and class and focus instead on the relation between ideology, as a general feature of historical societies, and mode of production as their determining base. In general, this tendency opposes what is termed a 'class-reductionist' view of culture-ideology. The main purposes of this section are, then, to recapitulate, briefly, some of the elements we take from a structuralist critique of other positions, and to identify the points where structuralism actually falls behind earlier achievements.

Althusser's project was formed under general conditions similar to those that faced the English New Left, but in a society that offered very different intellectual and political materials.[81] It, too, was a response to the crisis of the social-democratic and communist left in Western Europe in the 1950s and early 1960s. The writing of *For Marx* and *Reading Capital* was exactly contemporaneous with the 'culturalist break'. The search for solutions was also conducted within a national tradition in which Marxism was a weak presence, weaker, perhaps, than in England. The elements that were drawn on in the construction of structuralist theory were, likewise, diverse. The chief antagonists were, once more, the Cold War critics: the task to vindicate Marxism, this time as a 'science', against contemporary calumniators and past corruptions. The chief targets within the traditions were, again, 'economism' and 'Stalinism'. Similar situations beget similar solutions. Both the English New Left and the Althusserians took non-economic questions as their central concerns, supplying 'absences' in an existing Marxism: the stress on 'culture' was paralleled by the absorption in questions of 'science' and 'ideology', initially with a strongly epistemological emphasis, latterly with a more general concern with the formation of subjectivities. Similar solutions also begat similar problems: notably in the whole area of the relation between ideology and non-ideological relations.

In polemics between the two traditions these similarities are often forgotten. The differences, however, are also very marked. We might best grasp them by noting one founding divergence: while the English New Left took dominant post-1956 developments in Marxist theory as a source of inspiration, Althusserianism was formed in resolute hostility to them. In the early 1960s, when writing his critique of Williams, Edward Thompson was mulling over 'alienation' and 'the subject-object antitheses', reading early Marx, especially the *1844 Manuscripts*, searching *Capital* for its most 'humanist' moments and eagerly awaiting the publication of works by George Lichtheim and C. Wright Mills.[82] The new history was helped on its way by the discovery of a Marx whose problematic pre-dated that of *The Manifesto* and the encounter with the English working class. Althusser's Marxism was formed *against* these very tendencies. Perhaps this reflected the greater pull of the communist political presence in France compared with the situation of the English 'rebels' and the American Marxists; but it also grew from the desire to establish Marxism as a science, Althusser's most powerful lesson from the emasculation of the intellectuals in the struggles of the day. So Althusser and his colleagues, hostile to 'humanism' and the Hegelian 'taint', returned to Marx in his most 'scientific' mood, in the 'mature' works, especially *Capital.* They constructed from Marx's greatest work a through-going critique of the Marxisms of the moment. So it happened that the Althusserian critique was formed in a double movement: opposition to economism and Stalinism but also to the commoner forms of the 'liberation' of the intellectuals. Indeed, a common intellectual anatomy was discerned in these two opponents: economism and humanism were both understood as forms of essentialism; Stalinism was understood as a combination of economism and humanism.[83]

Many of the strengths of the position derive from this double movement. We might quote two passages that sum up, respectively, the critiques of humanism and economism, and illustrate some basic emphases. Both are taken from *Essays in Self Criticism*, a summation of the position without, it may be thought, many of its earlier difficulties.

1 Against humanism:
Marx shows that what in the first instance determines a social formation . . . is not any chimerical human essence, or human nature, nor man, nor even 'men', but a *relation*, the production relation, which is inseperable from the Base, the infrastructure. And, in opposition to all humanist idealism, Marx shows that this relation is not a relation between men, a relation between persons, nor an intersubjective or psychological or anthropological relation, but a double relation: a relation between groups of men concerning the relation between groups of men and things, the means of production . . . Naturally human individuals are parties to this relation, therefore active, but first of all in so far as they are held within it . . . If you do not submit the individual concrete determinations of proletarians and capitalists, their 'liberty' or their personality to a theoretical 'reduction' (i.e. an abstraction RJ), then you will understand nothing of the terrible practical 'reduction' to which the capitalist production relation submits individuals, which treats them only as bearers of economic functions and nothing else.[84]

2 Against economism:
The capitalist social formation, indeed, cannot be reduced to the capitalist production relation alone, therefore to its infrastructure. Class exploitation cannot continue . . . without the aid of the superstructure, without the legal-political and ideological relations, which in the last instance are determined by the production relation . . . These relations too treat concrete human individuals as 'bearers' of relations, as 'supports' of functions, to which men are only parties because they are held within them . . . But all these relations . . . determine and brand men in their flesh and blood just as the production relation does.[85]

Many of the emphases which have informed our critique so far are stated more generally in these passages: the stress on 'relations' and the abstractions of certain kinds of relations from the social formation as a whole producing the Althusserian 'instances' – economic, political-juridical, ideological. Each of these kinds of relation are held to have their own effects on historical outcomes, though the economic, the capitalist 'production relation' retains an over-arching determination on the forms of struggles between classes. Though the base-superstructure metaphor is retained, the irreducibility, 'effectivity', even 'materiality' of ideology is repeatedly emphasised: No *mere* superstructure.[86] Ideology is so far from being dispensable that it is the medium in which people, in all societies, live their conditions of existence, experience their world. If certain conditions of this kind are not met, on this 'level', societies, including capitalist societies, will cease to reproduce themselves.[87] It follows (it *should* follow – unfortunately it does not always in Althusser's texts) that ideology is an important and necessary site of political struggles, that there is, indeed, a class struggle in ideology.

There is much to say about weaknesses in this way of thinking, but it is important first to stress the advances. As a 'theoretical' intervention, as a criticism of other tendencies at a high level of generality, these 'protocols' retain an enormous force. Paradoxically, in view of the degree of abstraction and the fundamental epistemological difficulties, they represent an advance for concrete historical analysis, chiefly by removing earlier obstructions. It becomes possible to think about a materialist history which is not organised around some unfolding 'essence', whether this is the progress of productive forces, the deepening of alienation or even a simplified view of *the* class struggle as a predetermined battle between two composite historical agents, to the force of which every institution or element of culture must equally and synchronically bend. In other words 'social formations' (historical societies) can be thought with a complexity that approximates to the complications of the historian's sources and of the practices they reveal. It is this step, from essential to complex unity, that contributes most to historical practice.

More pragmatically, the Althusserian 'protocols' (we had better say 'reminders') warn against tendencies we should strive to avoid. They lead us to ask, clearly, whether we are slipping back into a neglect of the cultural-ideological, or are so obsessed with literature, artistic production or human creativity in general that we forget the material conditions from which such creativity is never free. They help us to avoid the conflations of the culture problematic and the reductionism of 'consciousness'.

No supercession: problems with 'structuralism'

The relation between structuralism and earlier problematics is not, however, one of supercession. The sharpest way to demonstrate this is to focus on features that debar it as a basis of alternative accounts. There are three important aspects here: the inhibitions to concrete analysis created by structuralism's major absence – a developed epistemology of historical research; a tendency to functionalist portrayals of the operation of ideological social relations; an alternative tendency to produce accounts of ideology, 'discourse' or 'representation' in which what began as a rational abstraction becomes a complete autonomy. We might call this tendency 'the autonomisation of instances'.

Out of a particular French philosophical tradition, Althusser and his co-workers derived a view of Marx's contribution to knowledge. This 'philosophical' reading was not limited to the discussion of intellectual procedures – indeed, the characteristically philosophical contribution was pursued rather incompletely. *Reading Capital* pronounced too on the character and substance of *historical* materialism. It presented a philosophy with decidedly un-philosophical ambitions – no mere help-meet to 'science' but a fully-fledged theoretical sociology in philosophical disguise, inheritor not of Literature nor yet of History but of Philosophy as the Great Tradition!

This philosopher's reading was, in fact, very selective.[88] It effected a radical simplification of Marx's results and a truncation of his procedures. Simplification is best seen in Balibar's part III of *Reading Capital.* Here Marx's extended three-volume definition of the capitalist mode of production is reduced to some formularies about the invariant elements of modes of production in general, their variant modes of combination, and an account of 'transition' (best compared with the richness of Maurice Dobbs') in terms of the formal principle of non-correspondence.[89] There is no serious consideration here of Marx's 'laws' of accumulation, the existence of counter-vailing tendencies, the possibilities of capitalist 'solutions' to crises and to the declining rate of profit, and the forms of the reproductive circuits – all of which constitute the substance of the description of the capitalist mode. This inattention to the detail of Marx's economic analysis parallels the culturalist absence and has, as we shall see, not dissimilar results.

Marx's procedures are similarly treated, Marxist science, the opening of 'the continent of history' is held to have occurred through a practice which had as its object previous problematics, especially that of political economy. It follows that development within Marxism may occur through critical commentary upon Marx's own categories: the raising of these to full theoretical status, the supplying of silences, the making explicit or uniform implicit new problematics. The value of this theoretical labour has already been acknowledged, along with the need to take Marx's own texts and the work of other historians as its object. But this theoretical enterprise by no means exhausts the whole circuit of knowledge. It by no means describes the whole of Marx's best practice. It says nothing of research of the stages in inquiry which Marx described as 'appropriating the material in detail' and analysing its forms of development and their inner connection.[90] It deals in part with the character of abstractions, but hypostasises 'the concept' as finished knowledge. In particular Marx's own concern with the rush and muddle of observable phenomena is lost in the objections to 'empiricism':

> I should under no circumstances have published the second volume before the present English industrial crisis had reached its climax. The phenomena are at this time singular, in many respects different from what they were in the past. . . . It is therefore necessary to watch the present course of things until their maturity before you can 'consume' them 'productively', I mean '*theoretically*'.[91]

Althusser is right to argue for a non-empiricist mode of working and his texts post important questions. Yet *Reading Capital* is singularly devoid of solutions. The problems, at the end of part I, are simply left in suspension.[92]

Yet this absence – the connection between the investigation of specific situations (the 'English crisis' of 1879) and the development of more general categories (the theoretical consumption) – is the really damaging feature of the Althusserian epistemology. Around this lack, a whole history of post-Althusserian epistemological agonies could be written.[93] In the absence of a model of research, a 'vulgar Althusserianism' becomes a mirror image of the empiricism of the historians. Althusserianism renders 'the appropriation of the real in thought' peculiarly difficult by stressing only one side of Marx's epistemology – the 'rationalist' side, the emphasis on the distinctiveness of thought. Culturalist epistemologies stress only the other side – the 'materialist premise' which insists that these categories always express social relations. *It* 'forgets' that thought does indeed have its own rules, that it proceeds by abstraction. Each represents aspects of Marx's best practice whose organic relation in *Capital* and elsewhere, we are only beginning to understand. At its worst, then, Althusserianism of the theoreticist period does become an 'idealism', the characteristic ideology of the intellectuals. It is easy to see its origin in the protest against the over-politicisation of knowledge in an earlier communist politics.[94]

One consequence of the particular form of abstractness which is a feature of Althusserian philosophy is the failure to realise a theoretical promise in the production of specific histories. For this requires categories – fresh abstractions – at a lower level of generality than those of the abstract social formation. We cannot hope to grasp actual societies only in terms of the dominant mode of production and its ideological and political conditions. We encounter immediately the problem of 'survivals', of un-thought relations that can only be grasped by historical research.[95] And if we attempt to bridge this gulf by simple extensions of Althusser's insights, we risk further failings: especially the use of simplified functionalist models and a neglect of the specificities of economic relations. It is to these failings we may now turn.

Althusser's essay on Ideological State Apparatuses is the classic site of these difficulties. The essay is a series of 'notes' on the part played by ideology and the state in the reproduction of capitalist relations of production. Potentially, this essay is of great value not least to our object 'working class culture'. We might expect it to deliver an account of the forms of class struggle in ideology: the way in which capital and the agencies of the capitalist state seek to secure the reproduction of a working class in a form appropriate to the requirements of accumulation and the way in which, on the basis of their own economic condition of existence, proletarians struggle against this process. We might expect Althusser to have built upon Marx's own account of reproduction, adding a characteristic emphasis on cultural-ideological forms.[96] For in historical reality the working class is never simply reproduced as a 'naked' proletariat, pure bearers of the capital relations. Labour is always reproduced with historically specific habits and 'needs' and within a social and cultural world whose character is never exhausted by the functional requirements of capital.

This essay has been exhaustively criticised and none of the points made here are new.[97] We can therefore, be very brief, recapitulating criticisms germane to our purpose. The essay represents 'reproduction' which, in Marx is a necessary contradictory and antagonistic process, as the functional necessity of a system. Rather than being a process in which the state intervenes in the primary contradictions of economic relations, reproduction is a function performed *by* ideology *for* capital *through* the state. The whole sphere of the ideological – the very processes by which consciousness and subjectivities are formed – is subsumed within this function. Ideology-in-general – the natural culture-bound state of man – is conflated with ideology in another of its meanings, the specific conditions of a cultural kind that prepare labourers and others for the places in the hierarchical division of labour. What is correctly understood as a condition or a contingency becomes, in the course of the argument, a continuously achieved outcome. Dominant ideology, organised especially through apparatuses like schools, works with all the certainty usually ascribed to natural or biological processes. We are returned to a very familiar model of one-dimensional control in which all sense of struggle or contradiction is lost. Althusser's account resembles nothing more than those (unrealised) bourgeois visions of the perfect worker which re-occur across the capitalist epoch, whether images of the sober and prudent aristocrat of labour or those soon-to-be employed young men and women, complete with aptitudes, 'employability' and 'social and life skills' who are the object of the Manpower Services Commission. And all this is achieved, apparently, by and through ideology: no hint of the force of economic relations themselves which in Marx's own account (and an unemployed future) provide the main disciplines. In general, the over-riding concern with outcomes – reproduction – suppresses the fact that these conditions have continually to be won – or lost – in particular conflicts and struggles. Some of these dimensions are supplied by Althusser in a later postscript, but this self-criticism is of a very radical kind, which actually demands a recasting of the argument. The sense in which this falls behind existing accounts might be seen in a comparison with Edward Thompson's 'Time, Work Discipline and Industrial Capitalism', a history of the construction of some of the conditions which the ISA essay takes for granted – and eternalises.[98]

Conclusions: elements of a theory of working class culture

We end by presenting three main arguments. These are offered, not as a finished theory of working-class culture but as indications of how to work towards more adequate accounts. Any fully developed theory, a reconstruction of Marx's original problematic for instance, could not rest on theoretical clarification alone, only on research and fresh abstractions.[99]

First we want to argue a case about the nature and rationality of culture-ideology as an abstraction. This involves a distancing from several positions discussed in this essay (and several more not discussed): from the refusal to abstract at all (Williams); from the tendency to regard culture-ideology or the ideological 'instance' as a concrete set of institutions or apparatuses (some readings of the ISA essay); and from all partial or trivialising conceptions of culture (e.g. its identification with 'leisure pursuits').

Second, we suggest that there is a need to differentiate moments or aspects of cultural-ideological processes. The complexity of this instance cannot be grasped through one term of analysis only, whether culture *or* ideology. One symptom of this is the way each term becomes overburdened with meanings, as if massive terrain could be encompassed by a tiny word. One useful move here is to differentiate the two major terms in use – culture and ideology – and to attempt to define what is specific to each and how cultural-ideological processes might be seen as a unity.

Third, we shall return to the issue of working class culture primarily as an example of how the relation culture to class may be re-thought in the light of earlier discussions.

It is clear from the earlier discussion that the character of the cultural-ideological as such remains persistently difficult to grasp. Culture expands infinitely, a slide indexed by 'whole way of life' or 'constitutive social process'. But there are also problems with 'ideology', whose meanings accumulate through successive usages: ideology as false or inadequate knowledge and as opposed to 'science'; ideology as an instance – a set of practices which occur in all social formations; ideology as a site of conditions which must be met if capitalism as a system is to continue; ideology as a trans-historical ever-present concomitant of human existence, the medium in which men and women live their conditions of existence – 'the representation of the imaginary relationship of individuals to their real conditions of existence'. Althusser's insistence that 'ideology has a material existence' parallels the slide of 'whole way of life'.[100] In the ISA essay ideology as an instance in the social formation seems to be identified with particular institutions or sites, with ideological state apparatuses, especially the family and the school. These different uses are, at the least, very confusing.

One solution is to distinguish very much more sharply between the notion of 'level' or 'instance' and the notion of 'apparatus', 'institution', 'site' or 'sphere' of social relations. The two ideas are different forms of abstraction: the abstraction of instances focuses on practices of a similar kind that occur throughout the whole society and in different concrete locations; the notion of 'site' or 'apparatus' tries to grasp what is specific to a particular sphere or set of institutions – schools, family, the factory. To conflate these two forms of analysis and especially to understand 'instance' in terms of a set of concrete institutions is a serious vulgarisation. It is vulnerable to Williams' strictures on the idealist tendency to make analytic distinctions into things.[101]

We understand the notion of 'ideology' to be an abstraction of the first rather than of the second kind. It does *not* denote specific institutional sites but practices or moments in social processes *that have a distinctive character*. It involves particular kinds of relations and movements. Social formations or processes may be looked at *from this aspect*, with this most closely in focus.

What then is specific to the ideological-cultural aspect? It is important to insist, in a thoroughly 'orthodox' way, on the specifically mental (as opposed to 'material') character of these relations – their equivalence to Marx's general category of 'consciousness' (not the consciousness of class but consciousness-in-general as used by Marx in *The German Ideology*). Consciousness, in this sense, is a necessary but 'simple' abstraction, a feature of human beings as such, evident in all history. Just as men and women have always won a living from nature and sustained their material existence, so also they 'possess consciousness'.[102] This, indeed, is a specific feature of human labour, 'an exclusively human characteristic'. It distinguishes architect and bee.

> At the end of every labour process, a result emerges that had already been conceived by the worker at the beginning, hence already existed ideally. Man not only affects a change of forms in the materials of nature; he also realises his own purpose in these materials.[103]

The characteristic feature of the ideological-cultural instance, then, is the production of forms of consciousness – ideas, feelings, desires, moral preferences, forms of subjectivity. This is fully recognised in Thompson's stress on 'values' and in the Althusserian usage 'imaginary'. It is not so much a question that schools or families *are* ideology, more that they are *sites* where ideologies are produced in the form of subjectivities.

All this is to say, of course, that there is no separate institutional area of social life in which forms of consciousness arise: mentalities and subjectivities are formed and expressed in every sphere of existence. Subjectivities are very powerfully formed, as Paul Willis argues, in processes of economic production. Economic practices – production and consumption – have a cultural aspect, rest on cultural conditions. Concrete political processes similarly always involve an ideological moment. As Foucault puts it, writing of punishment:

> We should admit rather that power produces knowledge . . .; that power and knowledge directly imply one another; that there is no power relation without the correlative constitution of a field of knowledge, nor any knowledge that does not presuppose and constitute at the same time power relations.[104]

Beliefs and preferences are formed and expressed in practices which are not commonly understood as involving signification or representation Perhaps they operate more powerfully there than in practices evidently organised for the production of consciousness: schools, media, art. Yet even these cases show the dangers of collapsing institutions and instances, for a proper concrete analysis of schools or media would involve examination of economic and political conditions as well as ideological effects. The notion of 'instance' in other words is *theoretical* in the strongest possible sense: it is a *means* for analysing concrete situations not a description of a chunk of concrete experience itself. Just as Marx abstracted from a living historical whole those relations most directly implicated in the production of material life (i.e. economic social relations) and left aside concrete human persons in favour of 'personifications of economic categories',[105] so a similar abstraction can be made of those relations most implicated in the production of specific forms of consciousness. Relations having been understood in this way, we may then return to actual history 'but this time not as a chaotic notion of an integral whole, but as a rich aggregate of many determinations and relations'.[106]

The distance between this conception of culture – ideology, and trivialising ones will by now be clear. Such a conception has nothing in common with 'culture' as a residuum when other practices – work and politics – have been subtracted, that is with culture-as-leisure. Nor is it in any way similar to 'culture' as limited to certain specialised activities – writing, reading, consuming films or playing football.

There is an under-developed tendency in both structuralist and culturalist accounts to make some distinctions between levels or moments in the cultural-ideological.[107] Althusser has distinguished between 'theoretical' and 'non-theoretical' ideologies, or 'theoretical' and 'practical' ideologies.[108] More interestingly, there is the distinction, implicit in the description of ideology-in-general, between a lived relation to real relations (what culturalism would call 'experience') and the *representation* of that lived relation. This distinction implies the need to understand both the 'lived relation' itself and the representation of it in ideology. There are not dissimilar distinctions in the culturalist tradition. In Thompson's history, for example, several terms other than culture and consciousness are in play, especially 'values' or 'value systems' and 'ideology'. Value system seems to describe cultural or ideological elements in their most organic relation to a mode of production; ideology, by contrast, has classic *German Ideology* connotations of ideas and idealism.[109] In practice, however, these distinctions are not rigorously used and there is a tendency in the histories for theoretical problems to be solved by a mixture of moral evaluation and political choice: utilitarianism, methodism, political economy, Evangelicalism (each of which may be 'lived' by middle-class people) are 'ideology'; working class radicalism is 'culture' or 'consciousness'.[110]

The most developed distinctions of these kinds are, however, to be found in Gramsci's *Prison Notebooks*. Gramsci employs three key terms of analysis where culturalism and structuralism mainly employ one. 'Common sense' refers to the 'lived' culture of a particular class or social group understood as a complex, located whole. It is the 'philosopher' in every one, carried in language 'good sense' or 'folklore'. It has many of the connotations of 'culture' in the English usage.[111] 'Philosophy' (occasionally ideology) on the other hand, refers to some organised set of conceptions produced by intellectuals (those with the *function* of philosophers) and having a more or less 'organic' relation to social classes and 'the necessities of production'. Ideologies, if 'organic', are understood as essentially active and transformative, transformative especially, of 'common sense'.[112] 'Hegemony', Gramsci's third major term, indicates the state of play, as it were, between the whole compley of class-based 'educative' agencies and ideologies on the one hand, and the common sense or lived culture of the masses on the other. It concerns the extent and the modes by which 'common sense' is made to conform to 'the necessities of production' and to the construction of 'consent' and a political order. Gramsci builds on Marx's realisation of the importance of the cultural conditions of capitalist production – all the moral and subjective aspects of labour power for example[113] – by examining the processes in which such conditions are organised and fought over politically. 'Hegemony' is, in effect, Althusser's 'reproduction', but a reproduction without the functionalism. It incorporates, indeed, a view of the relation between structure and superstructure that is distinctive and, perhaps, unique. The normal state of this relation is far from a meeting of functional requirements: it is a state of massive disjunctions and unevenness. Gramsci describes, in other words, the normality of 'survivals', concrete features of a society that cannot be grasped as the dominant mode of production and its conditions of existence.[114] Hegemony describes the processes by which some greater conformity is sought. 'Reproduction' is, then, a hard and constantly-resisted labour on very obstinate materials indeed.

These ideas are in a 'practical state' in Gramsci's writing. It was indeed the connection with concrete analysis that produced the theorisations in the first place. They are peculiarly pertinent for today. In what follows we indicate some key moments in the study of culture/ideology drawing heavily on Gramsci's categories.

1. The importance of 'culture'

It is important to retain 'culture' as a category of analysis. By culture is understood the 'common sense' or 'way of life' of a particular class, group or social category, the complex of ideologies that are actually *adopted* as moral preferences or principles of life. To insist on this usage, is to insist on the complex recreation of ideological *effects* as a moment of the analysis of consciousness. The effects of a particular ideological work or aspect of hegemony can only be understood in relation to attitudes and beliefs that are already 'lived'. Ideologies never address ('interpellate') a 'naked' subject.[115] Concrete social individuals are always-already constructed as culturally class-ed and sex-ed agents, already have a complexly formed subjectivity. Outside some structuralist texts, the 'lonely hour' of the unitary, primary, primordial and cultureless interpellation 'never comes'. Ideologies always work upon a *ground*: that ground is *culture*. To insist on this is also to insist on 'history' and to enter a protest against large parts of the Marxist tradition for its neglect of the ground of *its own* political practice too.

The retention of elements of a cultural analysis is also important for checking tendencies to functionalism. It is genuinely difficult to disengage the notion of ideology from a mode-of-production analysis in which all ideologies are seen as functionally related to the conditions of production. There *are* ideological conditions for a given mode; but these by no means exhaust the whole sphere of the cultural-ideological in any concrete society. There are cultural elements to which capitalism is *relatively* indifferent and many which it has great difficulty in changing and which remain massively and residually present. Similarly it is not easy to think the forms of cultural resistance to capitalism and to its particular re-structuring of patriarchy, within this frame of reference. Cultural analysis, especially in the form adopted by Edward Thompson may attach cultural struggles too closely to class, but guarantees thereby that struggles within culture will not be ignored.

The second major check to functionalism is the culturalist insistence, derived from the heart of the culture tradition, on the production of self or self-making. We have already noted the dangers of a theoretical humanism that ignores the conditions under which 'choices' are made, moral preferences formed. But to neglect the *moment* of self-creation, of the *affirmation* of belief or of the *giving* of consent would, once more, return us to 'pure mechanicity'. It is clear that one specific feature of processes within consciousness is exactly this 'cultural' moment. *It is what distinguishes the force of ideological social relations from relations of political coercion or economic necessity*. Outcomes in ideology or consciousness are not determined *in the same kind of way* as in economic or political relations.

2. *The heterogeneity of cultures*

It is an error, certainly in modern capitalist conditions, to view working class culture as 'all of a piece'. The degree of homogeneity (and of distinctiveness) is undoubtedly historically variable. It is probable that working-class culture from the 1880s to the 1930s was more homogeneous and distinct than in any period before or after. Yet, all notions of cultures as coherent value systems tend to mislead; Gramsci's stress on the radical heterogeneity of (even) peasant culture is a better general guide.[116] We have already noted many of the forms of internal difference: those organised around geographical unevenness and the social and sexual divisions of labour, and the divisions into sites or spheres of existence, products of ideological work, economic development, and legally-enforced institutional separations. We have noted too specific forms of hierarchisation (e.g. 'aristocracy of labour'; the de-politicisation of the role of women) that are secured on top of these divisions. If there are features in the position of the 'labourer' that are common to a whole working class, there are a myriad features that are not. These may always become objects of political practices seeking greater division or a unity. It follows that there can be no simple or 'expressive' relation between economic classes and cultural forms, and that we should start any such analysis by looking for contradictions, taboos, displacements in a culture as well as unities. This is one way of breaking from the bad 'romantic' side of 'cultural studies'. Another very important way is to recognise the gender-specific elements in any class culture and the ways in which the subordination of girls and women is reproduced, in part, within the culture itself.

3. *The place of the analysis of ideologies*

More generally, the heterogeneity of a lived culture is an index of the effects of hegemony. One classic form of heterogeneity is that described by Gramsci thus:

> The active man-in-the-mass has a practical activity, but has no clear theoretical consciousness of his practical activity, which nonetheless involves understanding the world in so far as it transforms it. His theoretical consciousness can indeed be historically in opposition to his activity. One might almost say that he has two theoretical consciousnesses (or one contradictory consciousness); one which is implicit in his activity and which in reality unites him with all his fellow workers in the practical transformation of the real world; and one, superficially explicit or verbal which he has inherited from the past and uncritically absorbed.[117]

Gramsci goes on to argue that such 'verbal' conceptions have their consequences, especially in inducing passivity by contradicting a more 'lived' impulse. The political problem, for Gramsci, is to develop critical forms of theoretical consciousness that actually engage with practical activity, develop it and give it a sense of its own historicity, and its ability to change the world.

Cultural contradictions of this kind are the product in part of ideological work. Against the humanist view of 'self-making' it is important to stress that what is affirmed or assented to has its own particular origin and history. The model of culture as a working up of 'experience' lacks one vital element – the instruments of labour themselves, in this case the conceptions, categories and preferences already present. As we have seen 'experience' as a term conflates the raw materials (the way, especially, in which capitalist economic relations impinge on human beings) with the mental means of their representation (the existing cultural repertoire). It is by supplying conceptions where none exist (or merely aiding in the reproduction of old) that ideology operates on culture to hold it below the level of 'critical', 'historical' or 'hegemonic' understanding.

There is an important role, then, for the analysis of ideologies in a developed cultural studies. These may take altogether more abstracted forms than the study of a class culture. In the case of culture the most 'lived' conceptions are closely tied into practical activity; it is necessary to describe the physicality of labour in order to grasp its cultural significance. It is possible on the other hand to examine ideologies in terms of 'fields' and 'discourses' which, in their own internal structures, position of address (ideal) 'subjects'. This, perhaps, is the predominant form of ideology – analysis within the structuralist tradition, resembling, more than anything, a literary model of investigation that treats ideologies as a 'text'.[118] This form of analysis has an important part to play in discerning the logics and internally-generated pressures of particular ideologies or ideological fields; but we will still need to know the effects of such discourses on actual already-acculturated subjects. Ideology-analysis of this kind, in other words, does not replace, though it should certainly supplement, a more 'historical' analysis of lived cultures. Without this the origins and effects of ideologies, in the common sense of classes and the labour of intellectuals, will remain obscure.

4. Culture and class

We have noted the structuralist tendency to detach the analysis of ideologies from classes and class struggle, and the value of this as a critique of expressive and economistic formulations. The relation between the economic conditions of existence of a particular class and its culture *is* a problematic one. Yet it is absurd to believe that there is *no* relation between ideological and political forms and economic classes.

There are two main ways of understanding this connection for working class culture. The first concerns the material conditions of the class itself and the sense that is made of these. The second concerns the particular relation to capital and capital's need continuously to transform the cultural conditions of labour.

Particular economic relations have a particular salience for particular classes. The economic form of the wage is, for example, a salient relation for the proletarian, just as the rate of profit has a special importance for the capitalist. Such relations become a focus for more symbolic processes; they are the raw material of culture. The sense that is made of, say, dependence on capital, the probability of unemployment, or relative poverty depends, of course, on the conceptions that are available or may be worked up from existing class practices. There is nothing in these relations themselves that produces a particular form of understanding of them, no automatic relay between class and class consciousness. Yet to have any purchase on the culture of a class, new ideologies must address salient relations of this kind. It is only in that way that ideologies, including socialism, can become principles of life. The conditions of existence of classes profoundly shape class cultures, less by specifying 'interests' more by supplying a kind of agenda with which the culture must deal. It is a matter of historical record that working class culture has been built around the task of making fundamentally punishing conditions more inhabitable.

We must end, however, by looking at this process from the viewpoint of capital. Though this is stressed, by Althusser, to functionalist excess, capital *does* have certain requirements in relation to the reproduction of labour power.[119] Though working-class culture cannot be seen as having a simple functional relation to capital's needs, capital certainly has a *stake* in the forms of working class culture. Minimally, it is a stake in labour's availability, willingness to labour under conditions rational for the production of surplus, and a suitable level of skill and aptitude. More particular conditions require historical specification, but from this viewpoint 'working class culture' is *the form in which labour is reproduced*. In this respect capitalism is far from being a self-policing system; far from labour continually being reproduced in appropriate forms, these processes require continual management. Moreover, capital's requirements are frequently themselves undergoing transformation. This process of 'reproduction', then, is always a *contested transformation*. Working class culture is formed in the struggle between capital's demand for particular forms of labour power and the search for a secure location within this relation of dependency. The outcome of such necessary struggles depends upon what ideological and political forces are in play, and, ultimately, upon the existence of socialist organisation with an integral relation to proletarian conditions and working-class cultural forms.

Notes

1 Althusser & Balibar, *Reading Capital*, esp. pp. 13–30.
2 I am especially grateful to Keith MacLelland for arguing this point with great force.
3 *Essays in Self Criticism*, p. 124.
4 See, for example, Rosalind Coward, 'Class, Culture and the Social Formation' and the response from Ian Chambers *et al.*, *Screen* (Spring 1977 & Winter 1977–8).
5 For a more rigorous exposition of a similar view see Ernesto Laclau, *Politics and Ideology in Marxist Theory*, New Left Books, 1977, esp. pp. 1–13.
6 Gareth Stedman Jones, 'Engels and the Genesis of Marxism', NLR, 106, p. 103.
7 Martin Nicolaus, 'Hegelian Choreography and the Capitalist Dialectic: Proletariat and Middle-class in Marx' in *Studies on the Left*, VII (1976), pp. 22–49.
8 *Poverty of Philosophy* in Marx & Engels, *Collected Works*, Lawrence and Wishart, 1976, vol. 6, p. 211
9 *Manifesto of the Communist Party*, *loc. cit.* p. 490.
10 Stuart Hall, 'The "Political" and the "Economic" in Marx's Theory of Classes' in Alan Hunt (ed.), *Class and Class Structure*, Lawrence and Wishart, 1977, p. 20.
11 Similar sequences are portrayed in Engels, *The Condition of the Working Class in England*, Panther edn., 1969, pp. 240 ff., in *The Manifesto* and in *The Poverty of Philosophy*.
12 Engels, *Condition*, pp. 243–54.
13 *ibid.*, editor's introduction, p. 10.
14 e.g. *ibid.*, p. 152.
15 *ibid.*, p. 239.
16 *Manifesto of the Communist Party*, *Collected Works*, vol. 6, pp. 495–6.
17 Engels, *Condition*, p. 39.
18 For an elaboration of these points see Hall, *op. cit.* (note 10 above).
19 *ibid.*, pp. 39–50. See also Gwynn Williams, 'France 1848–1851', Open University (A 321 Units 5–8) 1976.
20 Marx, *Surveys from Exile*, Penguin, 1973, editor's introduction, p. 9.
21 Nicolaus, *op. cit.* (note 7 above).
22 Most strikingly in the 'old mole' passage – *Surveys from Exile*, pp. 236–37. I am grateful to Greg McLennan for discussions about these elements in *The Eighteenth Brumaire* and other conjunctural texts.
23 For an interesting discussion of Gramsci's early economism see Robert Lumley, 'Gramsci's Writing on the State and Hegemony, 1916–35: A Critical Analysis', *CCCS Stencilled Paper*, No.51 (1978). For a fuller contextualisation see G. Williams, *Proletarian Order*, Pluto Press, 1975.
24 'The Historical Destiny of the Doctrine of Karl Marx', *Selected Works*, Lawrence & Wishart, 1971, p. 17.
25 'The Three Sources and Three Component Parts of Marxism', *Selected Works*, p. 21. For characteristic attacks on revisionism see 'The State and Revolution', *loc. cit.* pp. 264–351.
26 'The Three Sources', *Selected Works*, p. 24.

27 See for example the stress on 'special bodies of armed men', 'the rapacious state power', the state as 'a special organisation of force' etc. in 'State and Revolution' and other Lenin texts. There is nothing surprising in this emphasis given the historical circumstances of 1911 to 1919! For interesting comparisons with Gramsci see Perry Anderson, 'The Antinomies of Antonio Gramsci', *NLR*, 100, esp. pp. 49–55.
28 'Imperialism: The Highest Stage of Capitalism', *Selected Works* p. 175.
29 This is a basic argument of *What is to be Done*; see also 'A Talk with the Defenders of Economism', *Selected Works*, pp. 44–49.
30 *ibid.*, p. 47.
31 'Party Organisation and Party Literature', *Selected Works*, pp. 148–53.
32 *Prison Notebooks*, p. 323.
33 *ibid.*, pp. 196–7.
34 See for example, Stalin's essay on 'The Foundations of Leninism'.
35 For a summary and critique of the debate see H.F. Moorhouse, 'The Marxist Theory of the Labour Aristocracy', *Social History*, vol. 3. No.1 (Jan. 1978).
36 Georg Lukacs, *History and Class Consciousness: Studies in Marxist Dialectics*, Merlin Press, 1971.
37 Examples of the first form of argument include John Foster, 'Imperialism and the Labour Aristocracy' in J. Skelley (ed.) *The General Strike*, Lawrence and Wishart, 1976; examples of the second include John Foster, *Class Struggle and the Industrial Revolution*, Methuen, 1977, esp. Ch.7, and R.Q. Gray, *The Labour Aristocracy in Victorian Edinburgh*, Oxford University Press, 1976.
38 See the interesting criticism of common sense views of the corruption of leadership or bureaucracies in Tony Lane, *The Union Makes Us Strong*, Arrow, 1976.
39 Some of these points are made in relation to *Capital* in Hall, *op. cit.* (note 10 above).
40 For the character of Lukács' early thought see Gareth Stedman Jones, 'The Marxism of the Early Lukács', *NLR*, 70, (Nov–Dec.1971).
41 Paradoxically Marx's distinction between 'sacred' (i.e. idealist) and 'profane' (i.e. materialist) categories and histories is made in the course of his dispute with Proudhon, the source too of Lukacs' founding definitions of class. See esp. Marx to P. V. Annenkov, 28 Dec. 1846, in Marx & Engels, *Selected Letters*, Progress Publishers, 1975, esp. p. 31.
42 *History and Class Consciousness*, p. 51.
43 'We cannot really speak of class consciousness in the case of these classes (petty bourgeoisie and peasantry) . . . for a full consciousness of their situation would reveal to them the hopelessness of their particularist strivings in the face of the inevitable course of events' *ibid.*, p. 61.
44 Most of the essay 'Reification and the Consciousness of the Proletariat' is concerned to establish these homologies.
45 *ibid.*, esp. pp. 197–8.
46 Raymond Williams, *Culture and Society 1780–1950*, Penguin, 1961, p. 17.
47 E.P. Thompson, *William Morris: Romantic to Revolutionary*, Merlin Press, 1977 edn., p. 791.
48 *ibid.*, p. 810.
49 See esp. Perry Anderson 'Components of the National Culture' in Cockburn and Blackburn (ed.), *Student Power: Problems, Diagnosis, Action*, Penguin, 1968, pp. 214–84 and Terry Eagleton, 'Criticism and Politics: The Work of Raymond Williams', *NLR* 95, (Jan–Feb. 1976) esp. p. 9.
50 For a development of this point see Richard Johnson, 'Barrington Moore, Perry Anderson and English Social Development', *Working Papers in Cultural Studies*, 9, esp. pp. 25–26.
51 E.P. Thompson, 'Review of the Long Revolution', *NLR*, (May–June & July–August 1961).
52 *ibid.*, but see also Thompson, *Morris*, Chs. 1 & II and Part Iv.
53 For the second see ibid., Ch. VII; for the first see *The Making* esp. pp. 50–52, 162 & 415.
54 For these indications see, mainly, E.P. Thompson, 'The Peculiarities of the English' *Socialist Register*, 1965.
55 The classic polemical text of this tendency was the volume edited by F.A. Hayek, as *Capitalism and the Historians* (1954). But see also the works of T.S. Ashton, W.W. Rostow and R.M. Hartwell. Latterly this enterprise has been extended to other periods, notably the 1930s.
56 For accounts of this period see the essays in *Socialist Register*, 1976; Thompson, 'Review of the Long Revolution' and Raymond Williams, *Marxism and Literature*, pp. 1–4.
57 Williams, *The Long Revolution*, esp. Ch.2; *Marxism & Literature*, Ch.1; Raymond Williams, *Keywords: A Vocabulary of Culture and Society*, Fontana, 1976, pp. 76–82.
58 e.g. 'Interview with Edward Thompson', *Radical History Review*, vol. 3, No.4, p. 23.

59 The fullest statement, from which these quotations are drawn is the preface to *The Making*.
60 Eagleton, 'Criticism and Politics', p. 9.
61 Williams, *Culture & Society*, p. 289.
62 *Making*, esp. pp. 195, 120, 10–11; 'Interview with Edward Thompson' pp. 4–5; 'Anthropology and the Discipline of Historical Context', *Midland History* vol. 1, No.3 (Spring (1972)) pp. 41–55; 'Measuring Class Consciousness', *Times Higher Education Supplement*, 8.3.1974 (Review of John Foster, *Class Struggle and the Industrial Revolution*).
63 'Interview with Edward Thompson', p. 15.
64 *Marxism and Literature*, pp. 80–81.
65 *Whigs and Hunters*, pp. 258–69.
66 *Marxism and Literature*, Ch. on 'Base and Superstructure'.
67 'Folklore, Anthropology and Social History', *The Indian Historical Review*, vol. III, No. 2 (Jan.1978) p. 262. I am grateful to Edward Thompson for drawing my attention to this article.
68 *The Long Revolution*, p. 136.
69 *Marxism and Literature*, pp. 81–82.
70 *ibid.*, Ch. on 'Productive Forces'.
71 'Review of the Long Revolution'.
72 'There is no alternative, from any socialist position, to recognition and emphasis of the massive historical and immediate experience of class domination and subordination, in all their different forms'. This option is stressed against 'the alternative language of co-operative shaping'. *Marxism and Literature*, p. 112.
73 Anthony Barnett, 'Raymond Williams and Marxism: A Rejoinder to Terry Eagleton', *NLR*, 99 (Sept–Oct 1976) p. 56. Barnett's criticism of Williams closely parallels my own comments on Thompson in Johnson, McLennan & Schwarz, 'Economy, Culture and Concept'. Actually they apply most accurately to Williams. I now favour the more careful formulations about Thompson that follow below.
74 *Culture and Society*, pp. 307–24 and c.f. the treatment of class 'ideals' in H. Perkin, *Origins of Modern British Society*.
75 For these formulations see 'Interview with Edward Thompson'; 'Review of the Long Revolution'; 'Folklore, Anthropology and Social History'.
76 *ibid.*, p. 265. This particular article contains many of the most interesting formulations on these questions, suggesting considerable movements in Thompson's position which are parelleled by the practice of *Whigs and Hunters*.
77 The following typifications are based on a reading of all of Thompson's published historical work – it is difficult to cite particular sources.
78 This point is argued at greater length for particular chapters in *The Making* in Johnson, McLennan and Schwarz, 'Economy, Culture and Concept'.
79 *The Making*, p. 10.
80 *ibid.*, p. 12.
81 For Althusser's own account of the context of his project see 'To My English Readers' and 'Introduction: Today' in *For Marx*, Penguin, 1969.
82 All this can be seen in 'Review of the Long Revolution' (1961).
83 *Essays in Self-Criticism*, editor's introduction, esp. p. 32.
84 *ibid.*, pp. 201–2.
85 *ibid.*, pp. 203–4.
86 For these formulations see esp. 'Contradiction and Over-Determination' in *For Marx*.
87 See esp. 'Ideology and Ideological State Apparatuses' in *Lenin and Philosophy and Other Essays*, New Left Books, 1971.
88 For the general character of the 'reading' see Althusser & Balibar, *Reading Capital*, pp. 1–30.
89 See esp. the reductions involved in the very formal account of 'Elements of the Structure', esp. p. 225.
90 Postface to the Second Edition of Capital, *Capital*, vol.I (Penguin edn.), p. 102.
91 Marx to Danielson, 10 April 1879, *Selected Letters*, p. 296.
92 *Reading Capital*, p. 69.
93 One post-Althusserian path can be traced through B. Hindess & P. Hirst, *Pre-Capitalist Modes of Production*, Routledge & Kegan Paul, 1975 and the same author's auto-critique – *Mode of Production and Social Formation*, Macmillan, 1977.

94 It is not possible to pursue these issues of method further here since this would take us even further away from 'working-class culture'. The comments here and in the section on 'culturalism' will, however, be developed in later CCCS publications.

95 This point is developed more fully in 'Histories of Culture: Theories of Ideology' in the BSA 1978 Conference volume.

96 The most important discussions of 'reproduction' in *Capital* include vol I, Ch. 23 'Simple Reproduction' and Appendix to vol I (Penguin), esp. pp. 1060–65. For a brief reading of these and other aspects of Marx's treatment of reproduction see Johnson, McLennan and Schwarz, 'Economy, Culture and Concept' pp. 40–41.

97 Criticisms of the essay include: P. Q. Hirst, 'Althusser and the Theory of Ideology', *Economy and Society*, vol. V No.4; M. Erben & D. Gleeson, 'Education as Reproduction' in Young & Whitty (eds.), *Society, State and Schooling*, Falmer Press, 1977: *Ideology and Consciousness*, No.1 (1977).

98 E.P. Thompson, 'Time, Work-Discipline and Industrial Capitalism', *Past & Present*, 38, (1967).

99 The main theoretical resource in what follows is Gramsci's *Prison Notebooks* and a return to those parts of *Capital* where Marx deals with the cultural conditions of production and with the problem of the relation between the 'phenomenal forms' of capitalist relations and the character of bourgeois ideologies. But there has already been, in this essay, quite enough of the exposition of positions, so the form of what follows is prescriptive or argumentative rather than expository. For the sources of many of these arguments see, however, the notes that follow.

100 Both quotations above are from the ISA essay.

101 *Marxism and Literature*, pp. 80–81.

102 Marx & Engels, *The German Ideology Part One* (ed. C.J. Arthur), Lawrence & Wishart, 1970, p. 50.

103 *Capital*, vol. I, Penguin Edn., pp. 283–84.

104 Michel Foucault, *Discipline and Punish: The Birth of the Prison*, Allen Lane, 1977, p. 27.

105 *Capital*, col. I, Penguin Edn., p. 92. For an extremely telling elaboration of this point see Victor Molina, 'Notes on Marx and the Problem of Individuality', in CCCS, *On Ideology*, Hutchinson, 1977.

106 David McLellan, *Marx's Grundrisse*, Paladin, 1971, p. 45 (from 'the 1857 Introduction').

107 This is in addition to any (useful) tendency to distinguish 'regions' or 'sub-ensembles' of ideologies, a contribution especially of Nicos Poulantzas.

108 e.g. *Essays in Self Criticism*, p. 37, note 3.

109 See, especially, 'Review of the Long Revolution' and 'Folklore, Anthropology, and Social History'.

110 'Folklore, Anthropology and Social History' marks an advance on this, but I think that in most of Thompson's work this is the characteristic solution.

111 See esp. *Prison Notebooks*, pp. 323–43, 418–424.

112 See esp. *ibid.* pp. 330–335, 375–77, 390–93, 404–5, 407–8 and the essay on 'The Intellectuals'. It is important to remember that Gramsci understood Marxism, 'the philosophy of praxis', also as a transformative *ideology*.

113 e.g. *Capital*, Vol. I, Penguin Edn., esp. pp. 275, 719–23, 615–17 & 620–21. The meat of Gramsci's view of hegemony is to be found in the notes on 'The Modern Prince' and 'State and Civil Society'.

114 This is especially plain in the notes on 'Americanism and Fordism'.

115 'Interpellate' is taken from the ISA essay. For an interesting and historically-usable development see Laclau, *Politics and Ideology in Marxist Theory*.

116 *Prison Notebooks*, esp. pp. 826, 333 & 419.

117 *ibid.*, p. 333.

118 The classic case is the analysis of film in *Screen*, but there are elements of the 'reading of ideologies as a text' in Foucault's approach to discursive practices and in Laclau's treatment of specific ideologies. There is a problem in these approaches of remaining locked into the ideological forms themselves and *inferring* effects.

119 A fuller account should also consider capital's requirements in relation to consumption and the reproduction of the relations within which generational reproduction takes place.

9 The aesthetic theory of the Frankfurt School

Phil Slater

Phil Slater's article, produced after three years of research on the Frankfurt School, begins with an account of the critical theory of society. This theory involves a critique of ideological formations, of the objective forces that give rise to them, of the ways they are internalised by individuals, and also the question of an alliance with the most progressive socio-political groups to change these conditions. The article shows the flaws in the conceptualisation of this alliance, and highlights the distortions which they produce in the School's 'aesthetics'.

'Aesthetics' is here used in its broadest sense, as the analysis of art in its variously mediated social forms; the article covers the problems associated with 'affirmative culture', the 'culture industry', and 'art as negation'. While stressing the positive contributions of the School's theory, the article tries to situate it in its crucial position, at once critical of the official Communist Party line and its major theoretician Lukács, yet unable to accept the practice of Brecht or the theory of Benjamin. By analysing the notion of art as 'struggle' the article moves towards a metacritique of Frankfurt School theory. This involves the use of many lengthy quotations from the School's work (Horkheimer's important manifesto of 1937, for instance) here appearing in English for the first time.

While such a metacritique necessarily precedes any study of the School's later work, in for example Marcuse's writings of the 1960s, this is not an exhaustive analysis either of the School's aesthetics or of its general development. Much of the Frankfurt School's work has recently been translated and republished in England, because of its seminal role in various debates in the 1930s in Germany. On art, the School's writing constitutes a very major contribution to a Marxist theory and practice in superstructural forms. In another area, questions of a historical materialist psychology are again being faced by Roland Barthes, Julia Kristeva and others in Paris and for example, Juliet Mitchell in Britain. We hope to return to this in a later issue. Meanwhile the School's work remains to be situated, assessed critically and used, in ways that this article begins to suggest.

Introduction

The term 'Frankfurt School' is used widely, but loosely to designate both a group of intellectuals and a specific social theory. The intellectuals concerned were associated with the Institute for Social Research, which was established in Frankfurt in 1923 with money donated by Felix Weil and his father, Hermann. Felix (born 1898) was at this time a student at Frankfurt University and a close friend of Max Horkheimer (1895–1973). It was only after the appointment of Horkheimer as the Director of the Institute in 1930 that the basis was laid for what has come to be known as the Frankfurt School. Horkheimer, Professor of Social Philosophy at the University, gathered together a team over the next few years, including such famous figures as Herbert Marcuse (born 1898), the philosopher and later ally of the student anti-authoritarian movement; Theodor W. Adorno (1903–1969), philosopher, sociologist and outstanding aesthetic theoretician; and Erich Fromm (born 1900), the psychologist of international repute.

Despite the role of other figures in Horkheimer's team (such as Friedrich Pollock, Leo Löwenthal, Karl August Wittfogel), it is essentially the work of Horkheimer, Marcuse, Adorno and Fromm which constitutes the 'classic' Frankfurt School. However, a crucial, if controversial figure for an understanding of the Frankfurt School is Walter Benjamin (1892–1940), a theoretician who greatly influenced Adorno, did some work for the Institute, but also, largely due to the influence of his close friend, Bertolt Brecht, kept a critical distance from the Institute's mainstream activity. The precise relationship between Benjamin and the Institute cannot yet be fully established, due to the secrecy surrounding the Institute's files, which are kept in Montagnola. But in any case, a discussion of Benjamin's work throws a great deal of light, much of it critical, on the Frankfurt School as a whole.

The Institute's personnel had to emigrate after Hitler's rise to power, since they were all clearly left-wing and many of them were of Jewish origin. After various detours, the team finally assembled in New York, where, in a building donated by Columbia University, they continued their studies of society until the early 1940s, when for financial as well as personal reasons the team split up. It was during this period that the Frankfurt School really took shape and produced its most significant work on the question of a critical social theory.

The term 'Frankfurt School' is largely interchangeable with the concept of 'critical theory of society'; which is the label consciously chosen by Horkheimer's team to designate their work. This term was established in Horkheimer's 1937 essay 'Traditionelle und kritische Theorie', which was complemented in the same year by a joint essay from Horkheimer and Marcuse on the relation between critical theory and philosophy. These essays were not, in fact, a radical new departure; rather, they served the purpose of systematising the previous attempts at a social theory into a coherent, explicit methodology, the socio-political function of which was now stated programmatically.

The term 'critical' was explicated with direct reference to Marx's critique of political economy. Thus, although the Frankfurt School consistently failed to produce any analysis of the economic base of monopoly capitalism, they did produce a large number of highly significant critical analyses of the ideational representation of that society, just as Marx's analysis had been a critique not only of liberal capitalist economy, but also of political economic *theory*. Simultaneously, 'critical theory of society' was articulated by explicit reference to Marx's critique of dialectical idealism and it seems certain that the label 'critical' was chosen so as to demarcate Frankfurt School theory from the theory and praxis of 'orthodox Marxism–Leninism', which, in the Frankfurt School's eyes, had lost the full humanist dialectic of Marxian theory. Thus, the Frankfurt School were in many ways the heirs of the work of Georg Lukács and Karl Korsch in the early 1920s.

Certain people who had dealings with the Institute in the 1930s have related that the term 'critical theory of society' was used as a tactical euphemism for 'Marxism' so that the Institute could correspond with colleagues still in Europe without endangering the latters' lives. Also, it cannot be denied that the choice of this concept made life much easier for Horkheimer and his colleagues in America. This coincides with Felix Weil's admission that he always envisaged his Institute as an 'Institute for Marxism', a title that was only dropped in the interest of achieving formal academic respectability. But the full significance of the term 'critical' remains locked away in the files of Montagnola.

Since this article attempts not merely to fill out the present picture of the Frankfurt School in England, but also to assume a critical position vis-à-vis the Frankfurt School, it should be emphasised that this is not a 'purely theoretical' critique. In fact, a fundamentally critical appraisal is possible only due to the *practical* critique the Frankfurt School underwent at the hands of the student anti-authoritarian movement. While using certain Frankfurt School texts as handbooks, this movement was nonetheless immediately and necessarily involved in a critique of the whole Frankfurt School, whose distance from radical praxis was not the reflection of an objective diminution in revolutionary class praxis but actually revealed fundamental flaws in the conceptualisation of the theory–praxis nexus. Thus, the emerging critical praxis of the late 1960s brought forth only an abstract condemnation from the Frankfurt School (with the significant exception of Marcuse).

Fortunately, an extensive debate on the Frankfurt School has been underway in the English speaking world for some years now, and a critique does not have to begin *ex nihilo*. The most important publication to date is Martin Jay's *The Dialectical Imagination* which presents an invaluable biographical and institutional history of the Frankfurt School up to 1950, as well as delineating their major areas of research. However, Jay's study avoids the task of a metacritique of their conception of the theory–praxis nexus; instead, Jay both justifies and simplifies the situation:

> The critical edge of intellectual life comes largely from the gap that exists between symbol and what for want of a better word can be called reality. Paradoxically, by attempting to transform themselves into the agency to bridge that gap, they risk forfeiting the critical perspective it provides. What usually suffers is the quality of their work, which degenerates into propaganda . . . It will be one of the central contentions of this work that the relative autonomy of the men who comprised the so-called Frankfurt School of the *Institut für Sozialforschung*, although entailing certain disadvantages, was one of the primary reasons for the theoretical achievements produced by their collaboration.[1]

Jay does not really justify his contention; significantly, he fails to operate with any systematic, concretised notion of 'propaganda', and he also fails to specify the materialist dimension of the 'disadvantages' of the Frankfurt School's 'relative autonomy'.

Lastly, a word should be said about the contribution made by *New Left Review* to the reception of the Frankfurt School. It has featured several serious discussions, as well as presenting translations of some highly pertinent material from the Frankfurt School's own pen. In particular, *New Left Review* has focused on the specific question of cultural analysis, especially as regards the crucial exchanges between Adorno and Benjamin, and Benjamin and Brecht. However, the commentaries to this material have not pinpointed the central problem of the theory–praxis nexus, although it might be appropriate to add that even in Germany the systematic critique of Frankfurt School aesthetics has yet to be done. This article attempts to outline the basic categories for such a critique.

Critical theory of society

'Critical theory of society' can best be explicated by outlining those aspects of Marx's critique of Hegel's dialectical idealism which the Frankfurt School stressed as crucial in the genesis of an adequate social theory. Marx maintained that Hegel, thanks to his dialectics, had evolved a critical method which served to uncover and express certain fundamental social contradictions, but also that because of his idealist distortions, he had mystified these contradictions as 'spiritual' and 'resolved' them by philosophic fiat, (that is without resolving them in their material reality). The historical materialist critique of political economy de-mystified the analysis, de-absolutised the role of theory and consciously aimed at promoting revolutionary social change as the only means of solving the problems of both theory and social reality. At the same time, the critical force residing in dialectical philosophy was saved not only from stultification in its own, idealist hands, but equally from an abstract abolition at the hands of positivism and reaction.

'Critical theory of society' worked out its method and categories in the 1930s and Horkheimer stressed in the 'manifesto' of 1937 that the term 'critical' related essentially to the Marxian critique of political economy.[2] The nature of this relation, and of the role of philosophy, is perhaps best introduced by Marcuse's *Reason and Revolution*, which, written in 1941, as the first major period of Frankfurt School production draws to a close, is dedicated to Horkheimer and the Institute of Social Research. Marcuse explains in the introduction:

> Philosophy reaches its end when it has formulated its view of a world in which reason is realized. If at that point reality contains the conditions necessary to materialize reason in fact, thought can cease to concern itself with the ideal. The truth now would require actual historical practice to fulfil it. With the relinquishment of the ideal, philosophy relinquishes its critical task and passes it to another agency. The final culmination of philosophy is thus at the same time its abdication . . . Critical thinking does not cease, but assumes a new form. The efforts of reason devolve upon social theory and social practice.[3]

But the term 'critical', in the sense of the Marxian critique, has the complementary significance of being critical not just of objective social reality, but also of ideological expressions of that reality. This ideology–critique concerns not just Marx's critique of Hegel, as well as of political economists; it also concerns the constellation of consciousness in contemporary society. This is a concern fundamental to the Frankfurt School's entire production. Unlike the ultra-left tendency simply to 'expose' and 'denounce' all ideological strains not immediately subsumable under a Marxist critique, the Frankfurt School endeavoured to show the *necessary* contradictions within ideological thought, and, in particular, to reveal how certain metaphysical and generally mystifying trends of thought were a reflection of, and in their own way, a critical response to, the weight of economic manipulation; for example, Horkheimer states:

> The turn against rationalism in impressionist literature and painting, as also the philosophy of Nietzsche and Bergson, reveal the insecurity of the bourgeoisie in its humanist heritage, but at the same time this turn expresses the protest against the fettering of individual life under the increasing concentration of capital.[4]

This is intended not as an abstract apology, but as part of a struggle for the rationalisation of all such mystified protests and for a practical activation of these protests, not only to forestall their perversion into elements of totalitarian demagogy, but also to underpin these protests in their struggle with positivism:

> The type of man in whom a clear understanding of the present form of society really asserts itself as a force to reckon with, alters the significance this understanding had in the

> sceptical thought of the disillusioned bourgeois individual. Now, in this new, coherently critical type, the knowledge becomes a progressive force, pushing ever forward.[5]

Complementary to this theoretical clarification is the theory–praxis nexus; the Frankfurt School, particularly in the 1930s (and in Marcuse's work up to this very day), repeatedly stated that 'the value of a theory is determined by its relation to the tasks that are taken up, at the given moment in history, by the most progressive social forces'.[6] What is aimed at is the correct subjective reflection of the objective social reality:

> The antagonistic nature of society as a whole in its present form develops, in the case of the subjects of the critical position, to the point of a conscious contradiction.[7]

However, this remains very abstract in its failure to specify the precise relationship between the correct consciousness and the 'most progressive social forces'. It is unclear whether the 'subjects of the critical position' are the political *avant-garde* or the critical intellectuals. And in fact, the lack of clarity already reveals something of the flaws in the conception.

In his most explicit statement ever on this question, Horkheimer reveals, significantly, that he sees the source and stronghold of the 'critical position' as an ill-defined, but explicitly independent group of oppositional intellectuals:

> If . . . the theoretician and his specific activity in conjunction with the oppressed class is viewed as a dynamic unity, so that his presentation of the social contradictions appears not merely as an expression of the concrete historical situation, but equally as a stimulating, active factor within that situation, then the function of critical theory becomes apparent. The course of the debate between the advanced elements of the class and those individuals who pronounce the truth about the former, and, further, the debate between these most advanced elements, together with their theoreticians, and the rest of the class, must be understood as a process of action and reaction in which consciousness unfolds not only its liberating force, but also its inciting, disciplining and violently practical force. The trenchancy of consciousness reveals itself in the ever present possibility of a tension between the theoretician and the class which his thought concerns.[8]

This passage, central to all Frankfurt School theory, suggests a kind of extended, differentiated Leninism, such that Lenin's distinction between the lower level of consciousness among the mobilised masses and the coherent socialist theory of the *avant-garde*, is taken one step further, separating out on the one hand, the practical *avant-garde* (with it *own* theoreticians), and, on the other, the 'individuals who pronounce the truth'. Everything thus hinges on the ability of these individuals to mediate 'the truth', via a meaningful 'debate' with the political *avant-garde*, to the proletariat as a whole.

Horkheimer emphasises that the agitational force of 'critical theory of society' has a direct practical effect: 'The theory . . . that pushes towards the transformation of the social totality has as its immediate result a sharpening of the struggle with which it is linked.'[9]

However, with the exception of Marcuse's work since the late 1960s, Frankfurt School theory has consistently failed to relate in any real way to the concrete constellation of what it repeatedly stresses (at least in it general epistemological and methodological discussions) as being the ultimate form of critical activity, namely: revolutionary proletarian praxis. Such is the ultimate failing of the main body of Frankfurt School theory, the limit to their sublation of philosophy and ideology, and the limit to their historical materialism. Hans-Jürgen Krahl, Adorno's brilliant student, and ardent critic of the entire Frankfurt School, has expressed this in a manner as yet unsurpassed.

> Critical Theory benefitted from the tradition of the German Idealists in that its intellectual activity was fitted out against positivism with the mediating reason of dialectics. Critical Theory was able to recognise a concept of totality – and, in reflection upon the critique of political economy, this was an anti-metaphysical concept of totality – but Critical Theory was nonetheless unable to grasp this totality in its concrete expression as class-antagonism . . . The practical class stand-point, to put it crudely, did not enter into the theory as an active constituent of that theory.[10]

Thus, the fundamental methodological premises of 'critical theory of society' assume metacritical significance for the Frankfurt School's actual analyses. Only a metacritical perspective of this nature is adequate to the task of an evaluation of their aesthetics.

The Frankfurt School's 'aesthetics': changing role and object

Horkheimer's inaugural lecture of 1931 focuses on the question of 'the relationship between the economic life of society, the psychic development of the individuals and the changes in the cultural spheres (in the narrower sense)'. Specifically included in the latter is art.[11] Thus, the first issue of the Frankfurt School's main theoretical organ, the *Zeitschrift für Sozialforschung*, includes the first systematic utterance on art by Horkheimer's team. The essay, by Leo Löwenthal, emphasises the necessity of an overall theoretical frame of reference: 'To concern oneself with literary history, means to explain literature historically and the possibility of such an explanation presupposes an articulate theory of history and of society.'[12]

Significantly, Löwenthal adds:

> In the social illumination of the superstructure the concept of ideology assumes a decisive position. For ideology is an element in consciousness which has the function of concealing social antagonisms and replacing an understanding of these antagonisms with the illusion of harmony. The task of literary history is largely the analysis of ideologies.[13]

This theory, which anticipates the subsequent critique of affirmative art, pinpoints two major questions: firstly, what aspects of the respective social structures find their expression in the individual work of literature? Secondly, what are the effects of that work within its society?[14] In his actual analyses, however, Löwenthal concentrates exclusively on the former question; the latter question is not seriously taken up, and the question of an agitational art, relecting society *critically*, aiming at a specific audience and at furthering revolutionary social praxis, is not even posed. Later in this article I shall pose that very question as the central guide to a metacritique of Frankfurt School aesthetics.

Before proceeding, however, it is necessary to understand that the relative role of aesthetics within 'critical theory of society' has not been constant. In the 1930s, the concern with a historical materialist psychology was much greater than the concern with art. Horkheimer, in his inaugural lecture, his editorial preface to the *Zeitschrift*, and in his articles in the first issues of the *Zeitschrift*, stressed that the articulation of a social psychology adequate to the needs of the historical materialist analysis of society, was a foremost task. This job was undertaken by Fromm, who published several methodological essays in the *Zeitschrift* and wrote the social-psychological section of the collective production entitled *Studien über Autorität und Familie*. These *Studien*, which are not available in translation (apart from Marcuse's contribution) mark one of the Frankfurt School's outstanding achievements, and this mammoth work was reprinted, in a pirate edition, as a handbook of the student anti-authoritarian movement in Germany in the late 1960s.

Fromm, with Horkheimer's support, evolved his categorial apparatus from a positive – critical discussion of Freud's work, which owing to the stress on the historical interchange between the individual and his social context, had done much of the preparatory work for a historical materialist analysis of the problem of ideological consciousness and irrational behaviour in the socio-political sphere. However, the significance of social psychology for 'critical theory of society' underwent a radical qualification, even before the 1930s were out. The *Studien* had been launched in the early days of Horkheimer's directorship and the collective discussions had occupied a central place in the Institute's work. With the emigration to America, the work was interrupted and the *Studien* were published, unfinished, in 1936. Further work on a comparable scale was announced, but never materialised.

This was due, in part, to the departure of Fromm in the late 1930s (amidst an atmosphere of mutual resentment, the reasons for which are still not fully clear). But far more important was the radical shift in the Institute's object of study. In the U.S.A., the Frankfurt School were confronted with an advanced monopoly capitalist stae, with an equally advanced network of non-Fascist, but nonetheless manipulative popular culture. They no longer saw the family as the decisive agent of socialisation; on the contrary, they perceived a dissolution of the family, and thus a drastic qualification of the significance of Freud's model of id, ego, superego. The psychological component as a whole gradually became subsumed under a broader socio-political analysis of the production, distribution and consumption of popular culture. The notion of 'culture industry' will be discussed at length below; for the present, it is enough to understand the shift in the Frankfurt School's attention from the analysis of the family to the more complex study of the mass media. Marcuse's *One Dimensional Man* is representative as an account of this shift and its reasons:

> Introjection . . . implies the existence of an inner dimension distinguished from and even antagonistic to the external exigencies – an individual consciousness and an individual unconscious *apart from* public opinion and public behaviour. Today this private space has been invaded and whittled down by technological reality. Mass production and mass distribution claim the *entire* individual, and industrial psychology has long since ceased to be confined to the factory. The manifold processes of introjection seem to be ossified in almost mechanical reactions.

Marcuse adds that the family's role as an agent of 'socialization' has been increasingly taken over by 'outside groups and media'.[15] These media formed the focal point of the last issue of the *Zeitschrift* (by then entitled *Studies in Philosophy and Social Science*) and have become infamous under the label of *Culture Industry: Enlightenment as Mass Deception*, a title taken from Adorno's and Horkheimer's joint work, *Dialectic of Enlightenment*.[16]

Lastly, it must be appreciated that not only the relative role of Frankfurt School aesthetics, but the object itself of that aesthetics is a historically determined and thus changeable quantity. Adorno's definitive statement on aesthetics explains, by way of introduction:

> The definition of what is art is initially guided by what it once was, but legitimates itself only by relating to what it has become and by keeping itself open to what it is trying to become and perhaps can become.[17]

Frankfurt School aesthetics is the analysis of art in its dynamic tension with the socio-historical totality, of its revolutionary struggle against, and victory over, feudalism, its heyday and subsequent decline, its denigration in 'culture industry', as well as the question of art's continued, precarious existence as a critical social force.

Art as affirmation

Apart from the work of Walter Benjamin (a marginal figure of the Frankfurt School whose theories will be discussed later), the most advanced position on art ever assumed by the Frankfurt School is the critical notion of 'affirmation'. This notion was given its clearest expression by Marcuse in 1937:

> By affirmative culture is meant that culture of the bourgeois epoch which led in the course of its development to the segregation from civilization of the mental and spiritual world as an independent realm of value that is also considered superior to civilization. Its decisive characteristic is the assertion of a universally obligatory, eternally better and more valuable world that must be unconditionally affirmed, a world essentially different from the factual world of the daily stuggle for existence, yet realizable by every individual for himself 'from within', without any transformation of the social reality.[18]

Since this judgement is, in fact, the Marxian critique of dialectical idealism, transposed into the sphere of aesthetics, it is not surprising that this critique is no mere denunciation: Marcuse stresses that this very culture, despite, or, perhaps, because of, its idealism, was an expression of the dissatisfaction with a world pervaded by blind economic determinism. Art of the liberal bourgeois era strove to reveal the human nature and human relationships behind the reified screen of commodity-production, thereby indicting economic fetishism. However, the materialist criticism of 'affirmative culture' still stands':

> Affirmative culture uses the soul as a protest against reification, only to succumb to it in the end. In the form of existence to which affirmative culture belongs, 'happiness at being alive . . . is possible only as happiness in illusion'. But this illusion has a real effect, producing satisfaction. The latter's meaning, though, is decisively altered; it enters the service of the status quo.[19]

Thus, 'affirmative culture' is doomed to impotence, argues Marcuse, by its very medium of existence. This, in the context of aesthetics, is a forceful demand for the theoretical and practical supersession of idealism.

The question emerges of a sublation* of this culture: that means not merely a critical

* 'Sublation' is a makeshift translation, actually used by the Frankfurt School in their English publications, of the dialectical concept *Aufhebung*. Hegel explains the concept as follows:

> That which is sublated, does not thereby become Nothing; Nothing is *unmediated*, whereas something that has been sublated is *mediated*. It is the Non-Being which is the *result* of the action of a Being, and as such it still

reflection upon it, but also, and above all, the commitment to rescue the oppositional forces expressed in art, and to rescue art itself from the distortion of idealism. The task presents itself of evolving a critical aesthetic theory and praxis, which, aware of the materialist dimension of 'truth' and 'freedom', and free of any idealist absolutisation of 'Mind' or 'Spirit', or 'Art', can constitute itself as a coherent oppositional force within society, linking concretely to the needs, goals and perspectives of critical social praxis as a whole. It is precisely at this juncture, however, that Frankfurt School aesthetic theory retreats in a maze of unmastered contradictions.

However, before examining the precise nature of the Frankfurt School's inability, in aesthetics, as in their theory as a whole, to assume what Krahl terms 'the practical class stand-point', it must be clearly understood that the ambivalence in the critique of 'affirmation' is not without some justification. In the face of the new socio-political constellation of monopoly capitalism, fascism and 'culture industry', the evaluation of liberal culture has to be modified. The 'affirmative' culture of *laissez-faire* capitalism assumes the retrospective significance of a subversive force, by virtue of not being one-dimensional. This theory is well known from *One Dimensional Man*, but it also figures in Marcuse's 1937 essay on 'affirmation':

> The critical and revolutionary force of the ideal, which in its very unreality keeps alive the best desires of men amidst a bad reality, becomes clearest in those times when the satiated social strata have accomplished the betrayal of their own ideals.[20]

The weakness of this evaluation is that the 'critical and revolutionary force of the ideal' is merely reinstated, not sublated into a commitment to working out a concrete critical aesthetic praxis adequate to the needs of the class-struggle in the new socio-historical context. The 'critical and revolutionary force' does no more than become clear, and the passivity of this stance is evidenced by the assurance that 'even keeping alive the desire for fulfilment is dangerous in the present situation'.[21] The transition from this 'danger' to critical praxis, in society as a whole, and in art as an integral aspect of the latter, is not discussed. However, any discussion of this critical praxis will remain abstract until the nature of 'cultural industry', of contemporary ideological manipulation through popular culture, is grasped. This task faces the critical intellectual today, just as it faced the Frankfurt School. And if the task today is well in hand, it is thanks in large measure to the work of the Frankfurt School in this area.

Art as manipulation: 'culture industry'

The Frankfurt School framed their critique of cultural manipulation as an attack not merely on fascism (as if one some 'thing in itself'), but also, and above all, on all monopoly capitalism. Marcuse, in the essay on 'affirmative' culture, begins with an outline of the *inner* 'freedom' of liberal capitalism, and then introduces the historical dialectic:

---

carries with it the determination of whence it came. Sublation has the double meaning, in German, of preserving, i.e. *retaining*, and, at the same time, causing to cease, i.e. *ending* . . . Thus, that which has been sublated has also been preserved; it has lost its immediacy, but has not thereby been destroyed. (G.W.F. Hegel, 'Wissenschaft der Logik, Erster Teil', in *Hegel, Werke*, Vol. 5, Suhrkamp, Frankfurt am Main, 1969, pp. 113–114.)

The Marxist use of the concept, as of all dialectical concepts, is such as to reject any 'systematic' simplification of the historical process, thus materialising it. In addition, Marx speaks of a 'sublation' of Hegelian dialectics into the theory and praxis of scientific socialism. It is in this sense that this article raises the question of a sublation of affirmative culture's protest into a practical-critical aesthetic praxis.

> Changes occur as soon as the preservation of the established form of the labor process can no longer gain its end with merely partial mobilization (leaving the individual's private life in reserve), but rather requires 'total mobilization', through which the individual must be subjected in all spheres of his existence to the discipline of the authoritarian state . . . Total mobilization in the era of monopoly capitalism is incompatible with the progressive aspects of culture centred about the idea of personality.[22]

This perspective gives rise to a concept of totalitarianism which cannot be used for the ideological defence of non-fascist monopoly capitalism; *One Dimensional Man* states:

> In this society, the productive apparatus tends to become totalitarian to the extent to which it determines not only the socially needed occupations, skills and attitudes, but also individual needs and aspirations.[23]

Whereas Marcuse's theory was sustained, and actually radicalised in later years, Horkheimer's notion of totalitarianism became less anti-capitalist, in line with his general alienation from a fundamental critique of capitalism. The following discussion focuses on the earlier work of the Frankfurt School since it was this work (which Marcuse still affirms) that helped lay the ground for a systematic analysis of 'culture industry'.

The notion of a manipulative popular culture is stated by Horkheimer in the last issue of the *Zeitschrift:*

> 'What today is called popular entertainment is actually demands evoked, manipulated and by implication determined by the cultural industries.'[24]

As this theory was developed, the dichotomy of 'high' and 'low' art assumed a central significance:

> Light art has been the shadow of autonomous art. It is the bad social conscience of serious art . . . The division itself is the truth: it does at least express the negativity of the culture which the different spheres constitute. Least of all can the antithesis be reconciled by absorbing light into serious art, or vice versa. But that is what the culture industry attempts. The abolition of educational privilege by the device of clearance sales does not open for the masses the spheres from which they were formerly excluded, but, given existing social conditions, contributes directly to the decay of education and the progress of barbaric meaninglessness.[25]

The categories of the Frankfurt School's critique of 'culture industry' owe most to Adorno, who moved to America in 1935 to work on the Princeton Radio Research Project. In his 'intellectual autobiography' he explains how his opposition to positivism caused friction between himself and his colleagues on the project, and he sums up his own position as follows:

> I opposed the procedure of merely substantiating and measuring effects without relating these to the respective 'stimuli', i.e. the objective reality of what the consumers of culture – industry (in this case the radio listeners) were actually reacting *to*. To me, the procedure, axiomatic in orthodox social research, of beginning with the reaction-patterns of the subjects under scrutiny, seemed far from immediate and far from unproblematical.[26]

To establish an adequate method and categorical apparatus, Adorno produced the vital essay on musical fetishism which appeared in the *Zeitschrift* in 1938. This complex essay situates the critique of popular culture within the context of the Marxian critique of commodity – fetishism:

> Marx designates the fetishistic character of the commodity as the veneration of what one has oneself produced but which, as exchange-value, is alienated from both producer and consumer ('man') . . . This 'secret' is also the true secret of success and fame. It is the mere reflection of what one has paid for the product on the market: the consumer really does worship the money that he has paid out for his ticket to the Toscanini concert. He has, quite literally, 'made' that success, which he reifies and accepts as an objective criterion without recognising himself therein.[27]

The critique is thus not an abstract rejection of mass-distribution, but a dialectical critique of popular culture in its socio-historical complicity with capitalism.

The last issue of the *Zeitschrift* contains a follow-up essay by Adorno, entitled 'On Popular Music', where the basic categories are further articulated and concretised. The analysis begins with the phenomenon of 'standardisation':

> The most successful hits, types and 'ratios' between elements were imitated, and the process culminated in the crystallization of standards. Under centralized conditions such as exist today these standards . . . have been taken over by cartelized agencies, the final results of a competitive process, and rigidly enforced upon the material to be promoted.[28]

Linked to this is the phenomenon of 'pseudo-individualism': the standardised production provides its 'alibi' by allowing, and actually encouraging, 'deviations' from the norm, thus being 'stimulating':

> By pseudo-individualization we mean endowing cultural mass production with the halo of free choice or open market on the basis of standardization itself. Standardization of song hits keeps the customers in line by doing their listening for them, as it were. Pseudo-individualization, for its part, keeps them in line by making them forget that what they listen to is already listened to for them, or 'pre-digested'.[29]

In this way, standardisation of the norm enhances a dynamic, but manipulated standardisation of its own deviation.

This standardised music requires a technique of enforcement all its own, and this, Adorno continues, is plugging:

> Plugging aims to break down the resistance to the musically ever-equal or identical by, as it were, closing the avenues of escape from the ever-equal. It leads the listener to become enraptured with the inescapable. And thus it leads to the institutionalization and standardization of listening habits themselves.[30]

This plugging involved not just the repetition of certain records, but the false glamour surrounding the whole industry (e.g. drum-rolls and fanfares before the 'latest release' is played on the radio), as well as the plugging of personalities who, largely due to their public appearance, function as would-be refutations of the fetishism that pervades the entire industry.

As to the socio-political reasons for the public's acceptance of 'culture industry', Adorno maintains that the praxis necessitated in the reception of what he terms 'good serious music' is blocked by the rigours of alienated social labour:

> The consumers of musical entertainment are themselves objects or, indeed, products of the same mechanisms which determine the production of popular music. Their spare time serves only to reproduce their working capacity. It is a means instead of an end. They want standardization and pseudo-individualization, because their leisure is an escape from work and at the same time is molded after those psychological attitudes to which their workaday world exclusively habituates them.[31]

Dialectic of Enlightenment points out, forcefully:

> The effrontery of the rhetorical question, 'what do the people want?' lies in the fact that it refers, as if to active thinking subjects, to those very people who the culture industry actually serves to relieve of any such active thought, feeling or response.[32]

However, it must be clearly understood that this 'service' is not viewed by the Frankfurt School simply as a 'fascist conspiracy'. The relationship of 'culture industry' to fascism is one of a highly mediated, precarious balance. Although false consciousness is generated 'systematically', this does not necessarily imply a conscious plan; on the contrary, it may reflect an unconscious determining force operating rather like the 'blind' economic determinism of capitalist society. People behave, in plugging, for example, in a manner one would expect of them only if they were bribed to do so; of course, bribing does go on, but this harmonises with the 'normal' manner of presentation. The significant point is that the manipulations involved in the production of 'culture commodities', though aiming primarily at profitable consumability rather than ideological effect, can, in specific situations, readily be combined with deliberate political manipulation. Hence, the role of radio in the transition to fascism is emphasised by Horkheimer and Adorno:

> Chesterfield is merely the nation's cigarette, but radio is the voice of the nation. While bringing cultural products wholly into the sphere of commodities, radio actually foregoes any attempt to present its culture products to the public as commodities. In America it collects no fees from the public and so has acquired the illusory form of disinterested, unbiased authority, which suits Fascism perfectly. In the latter case, radio becomes the universal mouthpiece of the Führer.[33]

The analysis of 'culture industry', of the manipulative employment of the new means of communication within the relations of production of a class-society, raises the question of the non-manipulative even critical employment of those means of communication. But before that question can be examined, the general notion of a 'critical' art has to be established. This is the notion of art as a part of the struggle for radical social change. It is the question, to borrow Adorno's phrase (from a different context), of what, confronted with its denigration in 'culture industry', art is striving to become and 'perhaps can become'. But it is this very question that pinpoints the major failing of Frankfurt School aesthetics, as this article will demonstrate. For this reason, the concept of art as 'struggle' will have to be broached, in the first instance, by a brief discussion of the historical materialist attempt to conceptualise a critical aesthetic praxis. The discussion of Lenin, Lukács and Brecht is not an exhaustive analysis of that attempt, but merely a convenient way of introducing, concretely, the method and categories which the Frankfurt School repudiate.

Lenin and Trotsky

Lenin, in 1905, asserted that 'freedom' in literature was at best a delusion, at worst a hypocritical rationalisation for the artist's lack of commitment to the cause of humanity. To this he counterposed a literature that consciously allied itself to the proletariat, 'enriching the last word in the revolutionary thought of mankind with the experience and living work of the socialist proletariat'.[34] Lenin even subjected this partisan art to the demands of organisation; although he could, in 1905, only make plans for party literature, he later, in the period of socialist construction, insisted that all art be 'imbued with the spirit of the class-struggle being waged by the proletariat for the successful achievement of the aims of its dictatorship', announcing that the Communist Party would guide this work.[35]

Two factors are, however, crucial to an understanding of how Lenin conceptualised the evolution of such an art. Firstly, in 1905, he emphatically stated that proletarian partisanship would not block, but actually encourage greater scope for 'personal initiative, individual inclination, thought and fantasy, form and content'. He concluded thus: 'Far be it from us to advocate any kind of standardised system, or a solution by means of a few decrees. Cut-and-dried schemes are least of all applicable here.'[36]

Secondly, in the 1920 text, he significantly criticised the abstract notion of evolving a 'directly' proletarian culture without recourse to the cultural history of mankind:

> Marxism has won its historic significance as the ideology of the revolutionary proletariat because, far from rejecting the most valuable achievements of the bourgeois epoch, it has, on the contrary, assimilated and refashioned everything of value in the more than two thousand years of the development of human thought and culture.

Lenin concluded that socialist construction, including the struggle for socialist culture, could only mean 'further work on this basis'.[37] This precept is identical to the Frankfurt School's general concern with a dialectical sublation of ideological consciousness. How far Lenin's actual evaluations of specific movements in art lived up to his methodological goal, cannot be discussed here. (In fact, he was almost totally negative on the artistic *avant-garde*; but ample evidence of such hostility will be found in the subsequent discussion of Lukács.) The main concern is to examine how this dialectical concern manifested itself, in specific discussions, in the work of the Frankfurt School on art.

The debates on art in the Russian Communist Party after Lenin cannot be discussed in any length, but one aspect of the controversy must be mentioned, since it is explicitly raised by Adorno. It concerns Trotsky's contention that bourgeois art can only be superseded by a socialist art; such, Adorno relates, was the nature of Trotsky's polemic against the nation of 'proletarian culture'.[38] Trotsky's actual words may be recalled:

> . . . as the new regime will be more and more protected from political and military surprises and as the conditions for cultural creation will become more favourable, the proletariat will be more and more dissolved into a socialist community and will free itself from its class characteristics and thus cease to be a proletariat.[39]

However, this is not a repudiation of partisanship in art. Trotsky is speaking here of art's position in the socialist dictatorship, and not of art's potential role as a weapon in the class struggles of a capitalist country. Significantly, Adorno does not allude to the very passage in Trotsky's work which bears most on the constellation to which he should be turning his attention; Trotsky states unequivocally:

> Socialism will abolish class antagonisms, as well as classes, but the revolution carries the class struggle to its highest tension. During the period of revolution, only that literature which promotes the consolidation of the workers in their struggle against the exploiters is necessary and progressive. Revolutionary literature cannot but be imbued with a spirit of social hatred.[40]

Lukács

In the early 1930s, as Horkheimer gathered his team together, the official Communist Party line on art was represented, in Germany by Georg Lukács. Lukács too was concerned with the critical appropriation of bourgeois culture, but, in his case, this took a very narrow form. His main argument was that a would-be oppositional novel (the genre appropriate to that era) which presented only a voluntaristic 'message or 'tendency', fell behind the achievements of such great realists as Balzac and Tolstoy, in whose works the power of realism had countered their subjective, even reactionary 'tendency'. Explicitly quoting Engels' letter to Miss Harkness of April 1888 (where Engels discusses the question of a novel with a 'tendency') and in conjunction with Lenin's epistemology, Lukács develops the theory of a reconciliation, through historical materialism, of personal interest and the partisanship of reality, thereby erasing all traces of an abstract, subjective 'tendency', of the revolutionary, historical materialist novelist. Lukács says:

> He does not bring to bear upon his forming of reality any demands 'from without', for the simple reason that his forming of reality must itself contain the fate of those demands which grow, concretely and physically, out of the class struggle, and he must present these demands as integrating moments of the objective reality, in their genesis, evolution and effect upon that reality; otherwise, he will not portray it correctly – dialectically.[41]

This concept of realism already contains the second major element of Lukács' theory, namely 'forming', or 'fashioning', *Gestaltung*. Although reality itself is partisan, the fetishism of economic life hides this partisanship and this fetishism can only be overcome, in art, as in political economy, via the critical force of abstraction. Quoting once more from Engels' letter, Lukács proceeds to distil the essence of socialist realism:

> In the forming of reality, the individual and his fate must appear as a type, i.e. must contain the respective class-characteristics of that individual. The concrete totality of the formed world of art can only accommodate such individuals who, acting and reacting upon one another in the dynamic reality of social intercourse, serve to illuminate and fill out both their own character and each other's, so that, firstly, those individuals become intelligible, and, secondly, their individual relations among themselves make the overall picture typical.[42]

Only thus can society appear in its essential nature as relations between human beings in a class-society.

Adorno certainly concurred on the need for forming the respective subject of the artistic work. As early as his professorial dissertation of the early 1930s, he wrote:

> Wherever aesthetics relies on the dualism of form and content, and fails, in the concrete analysis of forms and contents, to reveal their mutual self-conditioning, the primacy of the formal principle will assert itself in the theory as a whole . . . Content – aesthetics turns formalist in the light of the 'magnitude' of the objects.[43]

But the concept of socialist realism was anathema to Adorno, and he later accused Lukács of being 'culturally conservative',[44] particularly in his predilection for the bourgeois novel:

> Lukács thinks in a manner totally alien to the nature of art when he counterposes typical, 'normal' works to a-typical and thus deviant works . . . And his claim that the work of art is the given unity of the particular and the general, is nothing but a dogma, repeated parrot-fashion from Idealism.[45]

Here, Adorno touches on a massive deficiency in Lukács' theory, namely the failure to relate to the *avant-garde*. The question of such a relation is, of course, bound to be central in the 'critical theory of society' of the Frankfurt School.

Lukács' inability to appreciate the *avant-garde* in art, reveals itself in his critique of expressionism. Lukács states that this movement had no connections with the working-class:

> Basically, this fault lay with the expressionists themselves, in whom the process of bourgeoisification had advanced so far that even in their oppositional efforts, they raised their 'social' questions to the level of a mystical objective idealism, thus losing all possibility of achieving any understanding of the social forces of reality.[46]

Lukács goes as far as to accuse expressionism of being 'one of the many bourgeois ideological currents that later flow into fascism', and thus of having a 'role in the ideological preparation for fascism'. He concludes:

> Fascism, as the composite ideology of the most reactionary bourgeoisie of the post-war period, inherits all those currents of the imperialist epoch which manifest decadent-parasitic traits; that includes all pseudo-revolutionary and pseudo-oppositional movements.[47]

Lukács fails to question whether these 'pseudo-oppositional' and 'pseudo-revolutionary' movements have any practical significance, and, in particular, whether they have evolved any artistic productive forces capable of sublation into a *coherently* oppositional and revolutionary aesthetic praxis. Instead, for Lukács, the label 'decadent. – parasitic' says it all.

The significant factor in the Frankfurt School position is that their highly differentiated debate on the non-socialist *avant-garde* is shot through with an unmistakable rejection of the practical notion of art as a revolutionary weapon. The former aspect constitutes one of the Frankfurt School's positive contributions to aesthetic theory; the latter defines its limits. Adorno reveals this ambivalence when he claims: 'Art does not mean pointing out alternatives, but by its very existence, resisting the course of the world, which continues to hold a pistol to man's breast.'[48]

'Engagement' is rejected for an art which is socially critical, not despite, but precisely because of, its refusal to frame itself as articulate agitational communication, or as articulate, coherent communication of any sort:

> Closed aesthetic images criticise the status quo far more determinedly than do those works which, for the sake of intelligible social criticism, go to great pains to achieve a formal conceptual coherence and thus tacitly recognise and acknowledge the all-pervasive and flourishing machinery of communication.[49]

This theory relates, implicitly, to the Marxian critique of commodity-production and commodity-exchange (as presented in Volume One of *Capital*), but this relation is a highly idiosyncratic one. Adorno stresses that art restores what functionalist cognition excludes.[50] However, the restoration concerned encompasses the 'non-identical', that is, that which repudiates the identity based on abstract labour and exchange-value, and Adorno's theory actually rejects *all* identity in the aesthetic sphere. Art cannot 'represent' classless society, the struggle for that society, nor any aspect of that struggle; art's critical force resides precisely in its repudiation of any 'standing for something else'. Instead, the work of art is *itself*: 'We have reached a point where the work of art can only suspend empirical reality (the abstract function-nexus) any longer by not taking anything specific as its content.'[51]

Thus, art's critical consciousness of its social context results in an 'oppositional' stance synonymous with its own autonomy:

> Art's social character is its immanent movement against society, not any manifest pronouncement on that society. Its historical gesture repels the empirical reality, even though works of art are, as things, part of that reality. In as far as one can predicate a social function of the work of art, it is its functionlessness.[52]

This theory, a kind of reflected Kantianism, though aiming at the abolition of economic enslavement, cannot mediate that aim to the needs and goals of actual social struggle. The 'practical class stand-point', to use Krahl's phrase, is absent.

Adorno is, of course, correct to reject any dogmatic exaggeration of the significance of art's 'manifest pronouncement', which would obscure the question of the dialectical relationship of form and content. But given the practical sterility of his conclusions as regards the critical role of art, it is crucial to consider whether an art can be envisaged which, firstly, like Lukács and Adorno, rejects any forced 'tendency', which, secondly, like Adorno but unlike Lukács, succeeds in observing the oppositional productive forces (hitherto mystified) in the *avant-garde*, but which also, finally, avoids Adorno's hypostatisation of these forces in their 'natural' state. This question demands a more precise analysis of the *avant-garde*. And the precise question of the practical significance of the latter leads directly to the figure of Bertolt Brecht. It is the Brecht–Adorno polarity that, more than anything else, reveals the failings of Frankfurt School aesthetics.

Brecht's praxis: 1) theatre

Brecht's theory and praxis, while accepting the epistemological notion of 'objectivity as partisanship' and rejecting any abstract 'tendency', and while, further, accepting the precept of a critical realism that shows up the essential class-constellation,[53] remained highly critical of Lukács' conception of how this was to be achieved. Brecht repeatedly stated that writing a realistic novel did not mean writing in the style of Balzac or Tolstoy, but giving the reader a clear picture of the nature of his specific social reality. Since this reality was itself constantly changing, any 'norms' of realism, established by reference to specific realists, resulted in formalism. Brecht maintained that whereas the bourgeois revolution could, in accordance with its specific character, be represented through 'great' individuals, proletarian class-struggle was, by contrast, the self-activation of the majority of society. Any realistic portrayal would have to do justice to this difference:

> . . . it is a waste of time for the author to so simplify his problem that the massive, complicated life-process of men in the era of the final struggle between the bourgeoisie and the proletariat can be 'used' as a 'plot', a landscape, a 'backcloth' for the formation of great individuals. The individuals can scarcely be accorded more space, and certainly no other space, in books than is accorded them in reality.[54]

And it is precisely this concept of realism, and of the changing needs of critical art, that provided Brecht with the key to the artistic *avant-garde*.

The best way of approaching this problem is by looking at the writings of Ernst Bloch. In his crucial book of 1935, *Erbschaft dieser Zeit*, (whose very title, *Legacy of this Time*, reveals the dialectical intention of the analysis), he asked whether the bourgeoisie did not, in its decline, throw up a dialectically serviceable legacy in the form of the manifold elements which its own decomposition set free. Replying in the affirmative, Bloch polemicised against Lukács:

> . . . perhaps Lukács' reality, the reality of the infinitely mediated cohesion of the social totality, is not so objective after all; perhaps Lukács' concept of reality still contains certain traits of the system of classical philosophy; perhaps the true nature of social reality is also interruption. Because Lukács has an objectivist, closed conception of reality, he turns, in the face of expressionism, against all artistic attempts to break up the ideational picture of a world, even if it is the picture of the capitalist world. This is why, when confronted with an art that exploits real dislocations in the superficial cohesion of society and that tries to reveal something new in the cavities, Lukács can see only subjectivist, arbitrary dislocation; and this is also why he equates the experiment of breaking up with the state of decay.[55]

This perspective has a clear affinity to the methodological precepts of the Frankfurt School. However, the elucidation of this theory in Bloch's work on the one hand, and in the Frankfurt School's work on the other, is totally different. And this difference is nowhere clearer than in the respective evaluations of Brecht.

Brecht upheld the maxim of 'not linking to the good old traditions but to the bad new ones'.[56] And in a fragment written between 1937 and 1941 he reveals a strong Blochian influence in his hostility to Lukács' isolation of the collapse of bourgeois literature from the rise of a proletarian literature:

> In reality, the decline of the bourgeoisie reveals itself in the miserable hollowness of its literature (which remains formally realistic), while the works of people like Dos Passos, despite, or, rather, precisely by, shattering the realistic forms, show the breakthrough of a new realism, made possible by the rise of the proletariat. This is not merely a process whereby one tendency relieves the other of its duties, but a constellation of active and dialectical struggles.[57]

Brecht conceded that expressionism did not reveal the essential nature of monopoly capitalism, but he emphasised that the same applied to the 'realistic' works of Thomas Mann. Equally, the opposition contained in expressionism was not an adequate liberation from capitalist ideology, but Brecht refused to put an undialectical and static stamp on this movement. Instead, he focused on the relation of the new productive forces and the needs of a dynamic realism:

> Certainly, Kaiser is . . . an individualist. And yet there is something in his technique which doesn't suit his individualism, and which, therefore, does suit us . . . For example, Kaiser's technique, foregoes the great Shakespearean device of suggestion . . . Kaiser directs himself to man's reason . . . For a time, he made possible in the theatres that revolutionary new stance on the part of the public, that cool, analytic, interested stance which is the stance of the audience in the scientific age.[58]

Thus Brecht's theatre attempts to continue the development outlined and realise the full critical potential of anti-empathising dramatic communication; the theatre of alienation (*Verfremdung* as distinct from *Entfremdung*, which is the Marxian term expressing economic alienation) divests the world of its appearance as something natural, normal, self-evident, and, instead, arouses surprise and curiousity about it. Unlike Adorno's 'total' repudiation of reified society, Brecht's alienation technique is the dialectical representation of the latter: all relations, all values are historicised and de-fetishised. And the result is a coherent discursive cognition: 'What was formerly taken for granted is, in a certain sense, made incomprehensible, but this happens only in order to make it, subsequently, all the more comprehensible.'[59]

What was formerly just known (*bekannt*) now becomes recognised (*erkannt*), and this discursive communication has a direct agitational value; Brecht says of the audience: 'The theatre lays the world bare before them in such a way that they, in turn, can lay hands upon it.'[60]

In this way, Brecht's aesthetic theory leads to a *specific* negation of capitalist society, and this specific negation is the bridge between art and general ideological struggle.

The Frankfurt School evaluation of revolutionary theatre was almost totally negative. Horkheimer, in an early work entitled *Dämmerung* made a generalising and wholly pessimistic assertion as to the prospects of a would-be revolutionary dramatic praxis; writing between 1926 and 1931, he states:

> The reason why a continuing revolutionary effect of the theatre is out of the question today, lies in the fact that this theatre turns the problems of class-struggle into objects of communal contemplation and discussion, thereby creating in the sphere of aesthetics that very harmony which, as it manifests itself in the consciousness of the proletarian, must be smashed; this is one of the foremost tasks of political work.[61]

This assessment (which, with its stress on proletarian class consciousness, and its critique of affirmative art, constitutes Horkheimer's most radical attitude on the question of ideological struggle) is a distortion because it fails to reflect on Brecht's work. Brecht did aim precisely at smashing any illusory harmony and undifferentiated unity among his audience. But even after Brecht explicitly formulated his intention to split his audience and unite only the working-class component,[62] the Frankfurt School held to the accusation of a neutralising harmony in all *engagé* literature. For example, Adorno wrote in the early 1960s:

> Literary realism, no matter of what variety, whether it calls itself critical or socialist, is much more readily reconciled to the attitude of hostility towards all that is new and strange, than are those images which, without swearing an oath to any political watchwords, suspend, by their mere appearance, the rigid coordination system of those people who submit themselves to authoritarian rule.[63]

In a word, Brecht's aesthetic praxis is, for Adorno, 'positivistic'.[64]

Adorno's own use of the concept of alienation (and he usually refers to *Entfremdung* not *Verfremdung*) is far less specific than is the case with Brecht; Adorno says: 'Form acts as a magnet, so arranging the elements of empirical reality as to alienate them from the relationship of their extra-aesthetic existence, thus and only thus, enabling them to master that existence.'[65]

This is why Adorno's aesthetic theory features Kafka among the privileged, and tiny, elite of 'critical artists' not proceeding beyond a passive eulogy, whereas Brecht's admiration for Kafka (as an exponent of alienation in art) is a dynamic concern to sublate that productive force into mass ideological struggle.

The Adorno–Brecht polarity is further exemplified by their attitude to the progressive technique of montage. Brecht claimed that Lukács rejected montage as 'decadent' because it tore asunder the supposed 'organic unity' of the work:[66] this argument against Lukács' realism was identical to Bloch's, which, in turn, seemed to be in agreement with the Frankfurt School's general position vis-à-vis culture. But Bloch explicated the technique of montage with specific reference to Brecht's dramatic praxis, where montage meant:

> . . . extracting a man from his previous situation and re-programming him, casting him into a new situation; or, alternatively, taking a code of behaviour that is the product of a certain set of conditions and trying out this code in a radically different context. The montage-type experiment is not abstract, nor is it a 'dislocating' encroachment into an otherwise closed, inherently coherent reality; rather, reality is itself shot through with interruptions.[67]

Such a specific employment of montage was alien to Adorno, who explicated his own conception of montage, in the essay on fetishism in music, with reference to Mahler:

> Everything he operates with is already there. He takes it up in its depraved state of existence; his themes have been disappropriated. Yet not one sounds as we are accustomed to hearing it; each one is as if deflected by a magnet. And precisely those chords which have been worn out and played to death, yield to the hand of improvisation, thus gaining a second life, as variants.[68]

In Frankfurt School aesthetics, montage, in line with the abstract conception of artistic alienation, plays the role not of practical class-agitation, but of a general de-ideologising 'negation'. 'Negation' is, in fact, the Frankfurt School's substitute for 'struggle'. This concept can now be summarised.

Art as negation

The Frankfurt School's abstract concern with art as 'negation' rather than as concrete 'struggle' focuses not merely on the work of art, but also on the artist, the producer. But in this theory, the producer is not the producer for the receiver, but is viewed far more as the main subject of the 'anti-discursive' aesthetic experience (Adorno's term for art that does not aim at 'formal conceptual coherence', but 'suspends', by its 'mere appearance', the 'rigid coordination-system of those people who submit themselves to authoritarian rule'). Adorno concedes that art is 'partisan' (although he uses the term *parteisich* rather than the recognised socialist term *parteilich*):

> Partisanship, the virtue of works of art no less than of people, resides in the depth in which social antinomies become the dialectic of artistic forms: artists, in helping these contradictions to the level of speech via the synthesis of the image, are doing their bit socially.[69]

And this theory actually extends to the effect of the work of art, which seems to have a role in ideological struggle: 'In the world of alien administration, the only adequate form in which works of art are received is as the communication of the incommunicable, the smashing of reified consciousness.'[70]

But in reality, the repudiation of discursive communication in Frankfurt School aesthetics precludes any concrete agitational struggle for correct consciousness. Indicatively, instead of putting the question of *mass* ideological struggle in art, Adorno puts the question, rhetorically, as the vulgar question of *cui bono?*, which he then dismisses as 'instrumentalist', that is 'one-dimensional'.[71]

Again, at times, the materialist awareness of art's isolation does assert itself, but the problem is expressed (via hypostatised terms) is such a way that art's elitism is vindicated: 'The only spirit [*Geist*] that respects man is the spirit which instead of pandering to him as society has fashioned him, immerses itself in the cause which, unbeknown to him, is his own.'[72]

The scurrilous reverse of this perspective (according to which, art's non-comprehensibility is due to its faithfulness to its very nature, which is negation – a theory running through Adorno's aesthetics from beginning to end)[73] is the claim that the masses do, in fact, know full well why they reject the *avant-garde*: because it challenges their security in their manipulated existence. Horkheimer claims:

> Yet every new work of art makes the masses draw back in horror. Unlike the *Führers*, it does not appeal to their psychology, nor, like psychoanalysis, does it contain a promise to guide this psychology towards 'adjustment'. In giving downtrodden humans a shocking awareness of their own despair, the work of art professes a freedom which makes them foam at the mouth.[74]

The masses are viewed as totally manipulated and as one with the alienated world that art 'negates'. Although art is not all that it would wish to be, it can do no more than defy and 'negate' the one-dimensional society of which it is a part; Adorno explains:

> It is true that art remains tied up with what Hegel calls the World Spirit, and thus art too carries some responsibility for this world; however, it could only escape this complicity by abolishing itself, and if it did that, it would really be aiding and abetting actively the alien and speechless domination of man, and thus yielding to barbarism.[75]

While the critical notion of art as 'affirmation' has not been totally lost, the question of a sublation into practical–critical struggle has.

This aesthetic theory throws some light on the basic tenets of 'critical theory of society'. Horkheimer's 'manifesto' outlined a 'dynamic unity' of proletariat and intelligentsia, wherein the critical theoretician, in a constant 'tension' with the class his theory 'concerns', was nonetheless 'linked' to the class-struggles actually underway. Evolving 'the truth', he was to mediate it, through a debate with the political *avant-garde*, to the struggling masses, thereby 'sharpening' those struggles. But in reality, this 'truth' became, in the work of the Frankfurt School, totally isolated; Horkheimer, in the late 1930s, related:

> Under the conditions of late capitalism, with the impotence of the workers in the face of the authoritarian states' machinery of oppression, truth has fled to small groups, worthy of admiration, who, decimated under the reign of terror, have little time for the sharpening of theory.[76]

Here the Frankfurt School's absorption of the experience of fascism reveals its weakness: the view of the masses as being totally manipulable means that with the return to a non-fascist monopoly capitalism, the 'truth' of 'critical theory of society' cannot relate to class-struggles with any notion of a continuing confrontation between wage-labour and capital. The 'truth' is so immediately 'total' in its opposition to class-society, that anything less than total revolution with a perfect mass class-consciousness is, for the Frankfurt School, hopelessly caught up in the very essence of the world that must be smashed.

Given the absence of any practical-critical theory on the socio-political level, attention is diverted to the 'radical' praxis of art. To complete the vicious circle, however, art's 'negation' is passive and waits impotently for the real negation in revolutionary praxis. Adorno's theory of art is both élitist and pessimistic:

> . . . art is more than praxis because, turning its back even on praxis, art equally denounces the limitations and falsity of the practical world. Praxis can perhaps have no direct cognisance of that fact as long as the practical rearrangement of the world has not yet succeeded.[77]

Critical even of the concrete struggle to achieve a non-alienated society, Frankfurt School aesthetics nonetheless waits tensely, passively and impotently for that struggle to succeed and realise concretely the 'negation' that at present necessarily resides in art alone.

However, Frankfurt School aesthetic theory does seem at times to sound an optimistic note, and, in particular, the analysis of 'culture industry' stresses, if only in isolated passages, that 'something dialectical' is happening. Adorno's essays in the *Zeitschrift* often end on such a 'dialectical', and thus hopeful note. Martin Jay, who correctly states that Adorno never abandoned his 'cultural elitism',[78] but who fails to concretise this notion, relates that 'as in the case of jazz, Adorno felt there might still be an isolated element of negation in popular music'.[79] This, again, is correct, but Jay fails to ask after the materialist dimension of this 'negation'. If, by contrast, one does pose this very question, then the usual weaknesses of Adorno's position emerge yet again. This is Adorno's argument:

> Enthusiasm for popular music requires wilful resolution by listeners, who must transform the external order to which they are subservient into an internal order. The endowment of musical commodities with libido energy is manipulated by the ego. This manipulation is not entirely unconscious therefore . . . But the closer the will decision, the histrionics, and the imminence of self-denunciation in the jitterbug are to

> the surface of consciousness, the greater is the possibility that these tendencies will break through in the mass, and, once and for all dispense with controlled pleasure.[80]

This 'possibility', which gives no real guide as to an active heightening of ideological struggle, serves to justify once again the élitism and esotericism of the *avant-garde* in art; Horkheimer, for example, wrote, in conclusion to his penultimate essay in the *Zeitschrift:*

> One day we may learn that in the depths of their hearts, the masses, even in fascist countries, secretly knew the truth and disbelieved the lies, like katatonic patients who make known only at the end of their trance that nothing has escaped them. Therefore it may not be entirely senseless to continue speaking a language that is not easily understood.[81]

Here is the suggestion that the masses are *not* totally manipulable. Yet the conceptualisation of any concrete relation of critical art to the weaknesses of 'culture industry' is not only weak, but non-existent. It is thus crucial to put now the question of the possibility of critical work in popular culture; this is the question of the progressive employment of the advanced means of communication. This question leads once more to the figure of Brecht. But before that, it will be useful to discuss briefly the work of Walter Benjamin; Benjamin's theoretical work was largely an attempt to systematise and propagate the praxis of Bertolt Brecht, and this constitutes one of Benjamin's lasting contributions to aesthetics. First, however, it is informative to consider some basic differences between Benjamin and the Frankfurt School.

Walter Benjamin's theory Brecht's praxis: 2) radio and agitation songs

The difference between Benjamin and Adorno can be summarised as the differing levels of concretion in their respective work. Adorno's aesthetics reveals a high level of hypostatisation, generalisation and even unintelligibility; the most blatant example of which is the following passage from the *Asthetische Theorie:*

> It is dubious whether works of art intervene politically; if they do, it is usually peripheral to the respective works; and if they strive to, they usually fall short of their own concept (*Begriff*). Their true social impact, or effect, is highly mediate; it is participation in that spirit (*Geist*) which contributes in subterranean processes to the transformation of society and which is concentrated in works of art.[82]

Benjamin, on the other hand, might be considered to have forestalled, and repudiated, this very passage in a lecture of 1934, where he said:

> The mind, the spirit that makes itself heard in the name of fascism, *must* disappear. The mind which believes only in its own magic strength (a strength it opposes to fascism) *will* disappear. For the revolutionary struggle is not fought between capitalism and mind. It is fought between capitalism and the proletariat.[83]

This perspective was, in Benjamin's case, not just an epistemological imperative of a stated methodology (as it was with the Frankfurt School), but actually permeated his analyses of concrete cultural phenomena.

Like Adorno, Benjamin was interested in the *avant-garde*, but he avoided Adorno's passive, uncritical stand. This was largely due to the influence of Brecht, who, while repudiating Lukács' undialectical attack on the *avant-garde*, nonetheless emphasised that it *could* become unrealistic: 'It can march so far ahead that the main body of the army cannot follow it, loses it from sight, and so on.'[84]

Benjamin followed this lead, and in his discussion of the affinity between the anti-mechanistic force of surrealism and the struggle for classless society, he gained a critical perspective through a set of materialist categories:

> as Berl puts it, 'even if he has revolutionised art, the artist is not thereby any more revolutionary than Poiret, who, for his part, revolutionised clothing-fashions'. The most advanced, most adventurous products of the *avant-garde* in all arts have had as their only public, in France, as in Germany, the upper bourgeoisie. This fact contains, if by no means the judgement as to its value, nonetheless a clue to the political uncertainty of the groups behind these manifestations.[85]

Anticipating the later concept of 'one-dimensionality', Benjamin succeeded in revealing the specifically materialist problematic:

> For we are confronted with the fact that the bourgeois apparatus of production and publication is capable of assimilating, indeed of propagating, an astonishing amount of revolutionary themes without ever seriously putting into question its own continued existence or that of the class which owns it.[86]

Thus, Benjamin explained the rational use of montage in terms of Brecht's epic theatre, where montage did not have the force of titillating the senses, but had an 'organising function'.[87] This organising function was not merely the mental labour of artistic 'negation' (as it was with Adorno's Mahler), but aimed, by linking to the 'realities of class-struggle through discursive communication, at organising a listening-mass'.[88] In addition, Benjamin's categories of production, distribution and reception have metacritical significance for the Frankfurt School's theory of 'culture industry'. And in this, again, Benjamin's work is largely the theoretical reflection of Brecht's actual praxis: in this case, his involvement in the sphere of popular culture.

Whereas the Frankfurt School's first theoretical involvement with the new means of communication (i.e. after the emigration to America) resulted in a subsuming of these means under the critical notion of 'culture industry', Brecht had been involved with them since the late 1920s, attempting to use them in a progressive manner. Brecht refused to be passively critical:

> Those people who advise us against using these apparati confirm the right of these apparati to work badly; these people lose themselves in their 'pure objectivity', for they resign themselves to the principle that only rubbish can be produced for these apparati. But they thereby immediately deprive us of the very apparati that we need for our production . . .[89]

Brecht's view was that the new means of production, distribution and consumption should not be supplied, but 'functionally transformed', or 'subverted' (*unfunktioniert*) in the interests of proletarian communication. Apart from demanding actualisation, Brecht propagated a radical change in the sender–receiver relationship:

> Radio would be the greatest apparatus of communication imaginable for public life, a massive network, that is, it could be, if it could see its way clear to not merely transmitting, but also receiving, making the listener not just listen but actually speak, thus not isolating him as a passive object, but putting him in active contact with other listener-speakers. Radio, according to our conception, should become more than a supplier: it should organise the listener as a supplier.[90]

Benjamin, for his part, stressed the significance of the Brechtian notion of 'functional subversion',[91] and, in his essay 'The Work of Art in the Age of Mechanical Reproduction', he explained that precisely because of the loss of the work's 'aura' in the age of technical reproducibility of art, the work of art was definitively emancipated from its 'parasitical dependence on ritual'.[92] This positive evaluation provoked Adorno to a critical reply, and the essay on musical fetishism was written, in part, to fulfil this very purpose. This essay was a passively sceptical reflection on Benjamin's essay, which, Adorno later explained, assessed the new media undifferentiatedly and undialectically.[93]

However, Adorno's own analysis was undialectical, in that it failed to question whether the new techniques of production could not function differently in a different social context (i.e. in different production-relations) and whether those media could not be subverted now, as part of the struggle for social change. And in addition, Benjamin, and Brecht, were far from undialectical in their analysis. Benjamin actually anticipated Adorno's critique of pseudo-individualisation and personality-plugging, as well as analysing the fascist abuse of film.[94] And Brecht's repeated tactic of appealing to the radio-authorities did not testify to any political naivety, but was intended as a means of giving a public *exposé* of his own conception of how the media should operate, and thus challenging the authorities to comply with the conception which, so Brecht claimed, was in the best interests of the majority. Brecht emphasised simultaneously that any progressive stand by the radio personnel would provoke repressive radio-laws, and that, as a result, only mass working-class support would win the fight. The non-manipulative implementation of the means of communication presupposed a proletarian dictatorship. Thus, the whole debate was both a theoretical anticipation of, and a propaganda-campaign for, a society where these means would realise their full potential.[95] Any optimism on Brecht's part was not passive (as was Adorno's pessimism) but the enthusiasm of somebody actually involved in concrete struggles.

In addition, Brecht tried to use the medium of radio for direct Marxist propaganda, the classic example being the *Flug der Lindberghs*, later re-titled *Der Ozeanflug*. Here, the dramatic representation of a historic one-man flight aimed at activating the audience, who became the main speakers; the radio transmitted the various background-voices, while the audience, school-children, recited the lines of the pilot and become 'the pilots'. In the section entitled 'Ideology', the pilots' text juxtaposes technological progress and socio-political chaos, both real and ideational:

> In the cities god was created by the chaos
> Of social classes, because there are two sorts of people
> Exploitation and ignorance, but
> The revolution will wipe him out . . .
> So join
> In the struggle against all that is primitive
> In the liquidation of the 'Beyond' and

In the banishing of each and every god wherever
He appears.[96]

In this way, the school-children become the subjects of the action, subjects linked in a group-ego, subjects of a socialist struggle.

This attempt to create, via critical aesthetic praxis, an active, socialist group-ego was, in fact, taken over from the example of workers' songs and choruses, a major aspect of the class-struggles in the Weimar period. Lenin, who had no productive relationship to the *avante-garde* (admitting that he was an 'old fogey'), had emphasised that the evaluation of the *avant-garde* was, in fact, of secondary importance: 'Art belongs to the people. Its roots should be deeply implanted in the very thick of the labouring masses. It must unite and elevate their feelings, thoughts and will.'[97]

These words are significant, not for the dogmatic assertion of the 'orthodox Leninist' position, but because Lenin succeeds in pinpointing a crucial aspect of critical aesthetic praxis, namely the strengthening of the will of the masses. And Lenin explicitly referred, in 1913, to the 'hearty proletarian song about mankind's coming emancipation from wage-slavery'.[98] This art-form emerged, in Weimar Germany, as a highly successful method of uniting and strengthening the will and solidarity of the anti-fascist workers.

Brecht wrote numerous agitational songs with Hanns Eisler in this period; an example is the 'solidarity song', the chorus of which runs as follows:

Onwards and no retreating,
Our strength lies in unity!
When we're starving and when we're eating
Onwards and no retreating
In solidarity.

The final chorus is modified:

Onwards, never retreating
And asking defiantly
When we're starving and when we're eating
'Whose tomorrow is tomorrow?
Whose world is the world to be?'[99]

This song links directly to the class-struggles of pre-fascist Germany, where mass-immiseration, of an absolute, and not merely relative, nature marked the realities of working-class life. Thus, 'When we're starving' was no anachronistic reference to a stereotyped image of the workers' lot, but was a desperately pressing issue that mobilised the masses in a potentially revolutionary, but, unfortunately, disunited struggle.

The presentation of the song should be an infectious, but jagged fusion of chanting and singing. Brecht emphasised that the correct presentation was, quite simply, the one that accommodated the current expressions of the class-struggle, which are harsh, rough and aggressive. Regular rhythms with uniform intonation, by contrast, 'do not bite sufficiently', and require circumscriptions.[100] Thus, Brecht's repudiation of 'affirmative' art had quite definite practical consequences.

At times, Adorno praises Brecht for 'brushing taste against the grain', for recognising the complicity of richness in expression with the poverty of reality.[101] However, Adorno questions the efficacy of broken style in an agit-prop chorus of the early 1930s (although the scepticism is 'purely' aesthetic), stating that 'it was always dubious whether the artistic attitude of roughness and growling actually denounced, or identified with, these forces in their social reality'.[102] Thus, Adorno's position remains one of 'total negation' of reification, and precludes concrete agitational struggle. Brecht, by contrast, retained the materialist perspective of the theory–praxis nexus, and stressed the relation of critical theory (and art) to an addressee:

> You cannot just 'write the truth'; you have to write it *for*, and *to* somebody, somebody who can do something with it. You must address yourself not merely to people of a certain disposition, but to those people who this disposition befits on the basis of their social position.[103]

To this, Adorno replied by applying to Brecht's work the Anglo-Saxon label of 'preaching to the saved'.[104] This reveals Adorno's ignorance of the complex, dynamic nature of class-consciousness. For Brecht, there was no clear line of demarcation between those who were 'saved' and those who weren't. Rather, revolutionary art was the art of a period when the masses were already being mobilised on a considerable scale and with a progressively critical consciousness; and revolutionary art directed itself to these people in order to carry out the vital task of *strengthening* their will and *clarifying* their consciousness. Brecht explained: 'The workers' agitational song can have a powerful political effect in periods when . . . the masses are mobilised on a large, but disunited scale. The agitational song can help to drive on, deepen and organise the movement.'[105]

Adorno's idealist perspective reveals itself once again in his discussion of the crucial question of the potential mediation between art's 'negation' and critical social praxis. Although he states, quite correctly, that the practical impact of any specific work of art is not determined exclusively by the work in itself, but by the historical context, Adorno proceeds to explicate this idea with reference to Beaumarchais' political effect (adding that Brecht was 'socially impotent'). And Adorno then maintains, of works of art in general:

> The effect that they would wish to have is at present absent, and they suffer from that absence greatly; but as soon as they attempt to attain that effect by accommodating themselves to prevailing needs, they deprive men of precisely that which they could (to take the phraseology of needs seriously, and to use it against itself) give them.[106]

To link art, via discursive communication, to actual socio-political struggles, would mean, Adorno believes, abolishing art altogether, not as a sublation, but as a concession to barbarism. Meanwhile, 'true' critical art 'gives' us only necessarily incomprehensible works.

Conclusion: aesthetic elitism and class-praxis

If we now look at the various historical contexts through which the Frankfurt School have passed during their productive lives, then it must be admitted that the preceding quotation does deserve some sympathy: after all, it was written in the 1960s, when no mass revolutionary consciousness existed among the working-class. Equally, the article on 'Engagement' was written in 1962, with the Cold War at its height, with the depressing sight of the degenerate workers' state in the Soviet Union, and with the traumatic memory (particularly for the intellectual of Jewish origins) of Nazi barbarism. Fascism had been defeated in Germany, but the capitalist base that had spawned it was thriving, and no serious anti-capitalist movement was evident among the masses.

However, Frankfurt School aesthetics, distilled in Adorno's *Ästhetische Theorie*, is far more than a response to post-war Europe. Their theory has spanned several decades, and during this time has revealed a remarkable consistency. So far, this article has concentrated on giving a clear outline of that theory, and thus has neglected many of the different historical constellations amid which this theory asserted itself. However, having achieved a basic understanding of Frankfurt School theory (and in particular, of its hostility to the theory and praxis of a figure like Brecht), the article can now focus on an essay of 1932, written by Adorno when the class-struggles of Weimar Germany were at their highest intensity, and when the idea of revolutionary art was no longer merely theoretical but actually an extensively developed aspect of historical praxis. An analysis of this essay will prove, once and for all, that Frankfurt School aesthetics as a whole is critically deficient in regard to the crucial question of the theory–praxis nexus.

In the essay concerned, entitled 'Zur gesellschaftlichen Lage der Musik', (which appeared in the independent, and ideologically progressive *Zeitschrift*, edited by Adorno's close friend and colleage Horkheimer), Adorno had a perfect opportunity to express his views on critical art without consideration for the restraints of institutionalised academia. However, the essay provided not a single constructive suggestion for furthering class-struggle. He maintained that the prevailing consciousness, even the class-consciousness of the proletariat, was deformed because it bore (necessarily) the scars of class-society; and this attitude determined Adorno's aesthetics: 'Just as theory as a whole goes beyond this prevailing consciousness of the masses, so too must music go beyond it.'[107]

But, like 'critical theory of society', Adorno's aesthetic theory, and the praxis it eulogised, went so far beyond the prevailing consciousness that, to use Brecht's expression, even the most advanced sections of the workers were bound to 'lose it from sight.' This was due to Adorno's formalistic criteria:

> Here and now, music can do no more than to present, in its own structure, the social antinomies which, amongst other things, carry the responsibilities for music's isolation. It will succeed all the better, the more deeply it manages to form, within itself, the force of those contradictions and the need to resolve them in society, and the more precisely it expresses in the antinomies of its own language and forms, the miseries of the status quo, emphatically calling, through the ciphered language of suffering, for change.[108]

Paradigmatic is Arnold Schönberg, whose technical solutions in music are, despite their 'isolation', nonetheless 'socially of consequence'.[109] As to the concrete consequence of this esoteric music for social praxis, Adorno is silent. Thereby, his correct materialist awareness that music's isolation can be resolved 'not in an inner-musical struggle, but only socially, i.e. by transforming society'[110] eventually locks him in a vicious circle, upon which his dialectical thought can reflect only as a pessimistic resignation.

Adorno actually discusses Eisler's agitational music. To Brecht, Eisler was the most fortunate of the Weimar Republic's revolutionary artists: in possession of a highly developed technique, acquired as a pupil of Schönberg, Eisler freed this technique from its élitism and placed it in the service of the mobilised masses, who now became the producers.[111] Such an activation of the masses as self-conscious producers would seem to satisfy, on the aesthetic level, the Frankfurt School's demand that 'in the struggle for classless society . . the masses must first organise themselves and transform themselves from a mere object into the active subject of history, thereby throwing off their character of being masses once and for all'.[112] But, as it turns out, Adorno accuses Eisler's praxis of absolutising the prevailing consciousness, which is deformed:

> . . . those very criteria which this production orientates itself to, singability, simplicity, collective effect as such, are necessarily tied up with a state of consciousness which is so weighted down and shackled by class-domination – nobody formulated that more extremely than Marx – that this consciousness, if it is to become the one-sided criterion of production, becomes a fetter on the musical productive force.[113]

Adorno gladly concedes that the agitational value in proletarian music is indisputable, and that it would be 'utopian' and 'idealist' to replace this music with one 'which was inwardly more appropriate to the essential function of the proletariat, but which was unintelligible to that class'. But Adorno's concept of an adequate *aesthetic* praxis 'transcends' proletarian music in the direction not of a higher mass ideological struggle, but in the direction of the bourgeois *avant-garde*. Thus, Adorno says of proletarian music:

> As soon . . . as this music leaves the front of immediate action, reflects and posits itself as an art-form, it becomes patently obvious that the products cannot hold their own against the advanced bourgeois production . . .[114]

The analysis of the *avant-garde* is therefore, no sublation, and the critical art of class-struggle loses all significance for Adorno's aesthetic theory. Thereby, Adorno's theory loses all significance for concrete critical aesthetic praxis.

Notes

1 Martin Jay, *The Dialectical Imagination*, Little, Brown and Co., Boston-Toronto, 1973, pp. xiv; 4.
2 Max Horkheimer, 'Traditionelle und kritisch Theorie' in *Zeitschrift für Sozialforschung* Vol. 6 (1937), Librairie Felix Alcan, Paris, p. 261.
3 Herbert Marcuse, *Reason and Revolution*, (1941), Routledge and Kegan Paul, London, 1969, p. 28.
4 Max Horkheimer, 'Zum Rationalismusstreit in der gegenwärtigen Philosophie', in *Zeitschrift für Sozialforschung* Vol. 3 (1934), Librairie Felix Alcan, Paris, p. 5.
5 Ibid, p. 32.
6 Ibid, pp. 26–27
7 'Traditionelle und kritische Theorie', op. cit. p. 262.
8 Ibid, p. 269.
9 Ibid, p. 272.
10 Hans-Jürgen Krahl, *Konstitution und Klassenkampf* (Schriften, Reden und Entwürfe aus den Jahren 1966–1970), Verlag Neue Kritik, Frankfurt am Main, 1971, p. 289.
11 Max Horkheimer, 'Die gegenwärtige Lage der Sozialphilosophie und die Aufgabe eines Instituts für Sozialforschung', in *Frankfurter Universitätsreden* Vol. 37 (1931), Englert und Schlosser, Frankfurt am Main, p. 13.
12 Leo Löwenthal, 'Zur gesellschaftlichen Lage der Literatur', in *Zeitschrift für Sozialforschung* Vol. 1 (1932), Hirschfeld, Leipzig, p. 92.
13 Ibid, pp. 94–95.
14 Ibid, p. 93.
15 Herbert Marcuse, *One Dimensional Man*, (1964), Sphere, London, 1970, p. 25.
16 Max Horkheimer and Theodor W. Adorno, *Dialectic of Enlightenment*, (1944) translated by John Cumming, Allen Lane, London, 1973, pp. 120–167.
17 Theodor W. Adorno, *Ästhetische Theorie*, Gesammelte Schriften Vol. 7, Suhrkamp, Frankfurt am Main, 1970, pp. 11–12.

18 Herbert Marcuse, 'The Affirmative Nature of Culture', (1937), in *Negations*, translated by Jeremy Shapiro, Penguin, Harmondsworth, 1972, p. 95.
19 Ibid, pp. 108; 121.
20 Ibid, pp. 102–103.
21 Ibid, p. 131.
22 Ibid, p. 124.
23 *One Dimensional Man*, op. cit. p. 13.
24 Max Horkheimer, 'Art and Mass Culture', in *Studies in Philosophy and Social Science* Vol. 9 (1941), Published by The Institute of Social Research, Morningside Heights, New York, pp. 302–303.
25 *Dialectic of Enlightenment*, op. cit. pp. 135; 160.
26 Theodor W. Adorno, 'Wissenschaftliche Erfahrungen in Amerika', (1968), in *Stichworte*, Suhrkamp, Frankfurt am Main, 1969, pp. 118–119.
27 Theodor W. Adorno, 'Über den Fetischcharakter in der Musik und die Regression des Hörens', in *Zeitschrift für Sozialforschung* Vol. 7 (1938), Librairie Felix Alcan, Paris, pp. 330–331.
28 Theodor W. Adorno (with the assistance of George Simpson), 'On Popular Music', in *Studies in Philosophy and Social Science*, Vol. 9, op. cit. p. 23.
29 Ibid, p. 25.
30 Ibid, p. 27.
31 Ibid, p. 38.
32 *Dialectic of Englightenment*, op. cit. pp. 144–145.
33 Ibid, p. 159.
34 Vladimir I. Lenin, 'Party Organisation and Party Literature', (1905), in *V.I. Lenin On Literature and Art*, Progress Publishers, Moscow, 1970, p. 26.
35 Vladimir I. Lenin, 'On Proletarian Culture', (1920), in *V.I. Lenin on Literature and Art*, op. cit. p. 154.
36 'Party Organisation and Party Literature', op. cit. p. 24.
37 'On Proletarian Culture', op. cit. p. 155.
38 *Ästhetische Theorie*, op. cit. p. 251.
39 Leon Trotsky, 'Literature and Revolution', (1923), excerpts in *Leon Trotsky on Literature and Art*, Pathfinder, New York, (1970), p. 42.
40 Ibid, p. 60.
41 Georg Lukács, 'Tendenz oder Parteilichkeit?', (1932), in Georg Lukács, *Schriften zur Literatursoziologie*, Luchterhand, Neuwied, 1961, p. 118.
42 Georg Lukács, 'Reportage oder Gestaltung?', (1932), in *Schriften zur Literatursoziologie*, op. cit. p. 128.
43 Theodor W. Adorno, *Kierkegaard*, (1933), Suhrkamp, Frankfurt am Main, 1962, pp. 34; 39.
44 *Ästhetische Theorie*, op. cit. p. 213.
45 Ibid, p. 147.
46 Georg Lukács, 'Zur Ideologie der deutschen Intelligenz in der imperialistischen Periode', (1934), excerpts in *Schriften zur Literatursoziologie*, op. cit. p. 321.
47 Ibid, p. 324.
48 Theodor W. Adorno, 'Engagement', (1962), in Theodor W. Adorno, *Noten zur Literatur* Vol. 3, Suhrkamp, Frankfurt am Main, 1965, p. 114.
49 *Ästhetische Theorie*, op. cit. p. 218.
50 Ibid, p. 87.
51 Ibid, p. 203.
52 Ibid, pp. 336–337.
53 Bertolt Brecht, '(Der Weg zum zeitgenössischen Theater)', (1927–1931), in *Bertolt Brecht, Gesammelte Werke*, Suhrkamp, Frankfurt am Main, 1967, Vol. 15, p. 225.
Bertolt Brecht, '(Uber den Realismus)', (1937–1941), in *Gesammelte Werke*, op. cit. Vol. 19, p. 326.
54 Ibid, p. 310.
55 Ernst Bloch, *Erbschaft dieser Zeit*, (1935), Gesamtausgabe Vol. 4, Suhrkamp, Frankfurt am Main, 1962, pp. 270–271.
56 '(Uber den Realismus)', op. cit. p. 298.
57 Ibid, p. 317.
58 '(Der Weg zum zeitgenossischen Theater)' op. cit. pp. 152–153.
59 Bertolt Brecht, '(Neue Technik der Schauspielkunst)', (1935–1941), in *Gesammelte Werke*, op. cit. Vol. 15, p. 355.

60 Bertolt Brecht, 'Über eine nichtaristotelische Dramatik)', (1933–1941), in *Gesammelte Werke*, op. cit. Vol. 15, p. 303.
61 Heinrich Regius (pseudonym of Max Horkheimer), *Dämmerung*, Oprecht und Helbling, Zürich, 1934, p. 108.
62 Bertolt Brecht, 'Anmerkungen zur Mutter', (1932 and 1936), in *Gesammelte Werke*, op. cit. Vol. 17, pp. 1062–1063.
63 'Engagement', op. cit. p. 112.
64 *Ästhetische Theorie*, op. cit. p. 152.
65 Ibid. p. 336.
66 Bertolt Brecht, *Arbeitsjournal 1938–1955*, Auf- und Abbau- Verlag, Peking–Moskau–Havanna–Berlin, 1973, p. 19.
67 *Erbschaft dieser Zeit*, op. cit. p. 253.
68 'Über den Fetischcharakter', op. cit. p. 354.
69 *Ästhetische Theorie*, op. cit. p. 345.
70 Ibid, p. 292.
71 Ibid, pp. 182–184.
72 Ibid, p. 217.
73 Theodor Wiesengrund-Adorno, 'Zur gesellschaftlichen Lage der Musik', in *Zeitschrift für Sozialforschung* Vol. 1, op. cit. p. 106.
Theodor W. Adorno, 'Voraussetzungen', (1960), in *Noten zur Literatur* Vol. 3, op. cit. pp. 136; 139.
74 'Art and Mass Culture', op. cit. p. 296.
75 *Ästhetische Theorie*, op. cit. p. 310.
76 'Traditionelle und kritische Theorie', op. cit. p. 288.
77 *Ästhetische Theorie*, op. cit. p. 358.
78 *The Dialectical Imagination*, op. cit. p. 23.
79 Ibid, p. 192.
80 'On Popular Music', op. cit. pp. 45; 47.
81 'Art and Mass Culture', op. cit. p. 304.
82 *Ästhetische Theorie*, op. cit. p. 359.
83 Walter Benjamin, 'The Author as Producer', (1934), in Walter Benjamin, *Understanding Brecht*, translated by Anna Bostock, NLB, London, 1973, p. 103.
84 '(Über den Realismus)', op. cit. p. 302.
85 Walter Benjamin, 'Zum gegenwärtigen gesellschaftlichen Standort des französischen Schriftstellers', in *Zeitschrift für Sozialforschung* Vol. 3, op. cit. pp. 73–74.
86 'The Author as Producer', op. cit. p. 94.
87 Ibid, p. 100.
88 Walter Benjamin, 'What is Epic Theatre?' (First Version), in *Understanding Brecht*, op. cit. p. 10.
89 Bertolt Brecht, '(Über Film)', (1922–1933), in *Gesammelte Werke*, op. cit. Vol. 18, p. 156.
90 Bertolt Brecht, '(Radiotheorie)', (1927–1932), in *Gesammelte Werke*, op. cit. Vol. 18, p. 129.
91 'The Author as Producer', op. cit. p. 93.
92 Walter Benjamin, 'The Work of Art in the Age of Mechanical Reproduction', (1936), in *Illuminations*, translated by Harry Zohn, Collins/Fontana, London, 1973, p. 226.
93 'Wissenschaftliche Errahrungen in Amerika', op. cit. p. 117.
94 'The Work of Art', op. cit. pp. 233; 243.
95 '(Radiotheorie)', op. cit. pp. 121–122; 133–134.
96 Bertolt Brecht, 'Der Ozeanflug', (1929), in *Gesemmelte Werke*, op. cit. Vol. 2, pp. 576–577.
97 Cf Clara Zetkin, 'My Recollections of Lenin', excerpts in *V.I. Lenin On Literature and Art*, op. cit. p. 251.
98 Vladimir I. Lenin, 'The Development of Workers' Choirs in Germany', (1913), in *V.I. Lenin On Literature and Art*, op. cit. p. 79.
99 Bertolt Brecht, 'Solidaritätslied', (1932), in *Gesammelte Werke*, op. cit. Vol. 8, pp. 369–370.
100 Bertolt Brecht, '(Anmerkungen zur literarischen Arbeit)', (1935–1941), in *Gesammelte Werke*, op. cit. Vol. 19, p. 403.
101 *Ästhetische Theorie*, op. cit. pp. 60; 66.
102 Ibid, p. 341.
103 Bertolt Brecht, '(Kunst und Politik)', (1933–1938), in *Gesammelte Werke*, op. cit. Vol. 18, p. 230.
104 *Ästhetische Theorie*, op. cit. p. 360.

105 '(Anmerkungen zur literarischen Arbeit)', op. cit. p. 405.
106 *Ästhetische Theorie*, op. cit. p. 361.
107 'Zur gesellschaftlichen Lage der Musik', op. cit. p. 106.
108 Ibid, p. 105.
109 Ibid, p. 111.
110 Ibid, p. 104.
111 '(Über den Realismus)', op. cit. pp. 336–337.
112 Max Horkheimer, 'Montaigne und die Funktion der Skepsis', in *Zeitschrift für Sozialforschung* Vol. 7, op. cit. p. 42.
113 'Zur gesellschaftlichen Lage der Musik', op. cit. p. 123.
114 Ibid, p. 124.

10 Georg Lukács

Colin Sparks

Recently, a series of translations and reprints have made available to the English reader a wide range of the works of the Hungarian critic Georg Lukács. The exceptional range of his learning, his obvious intelligence and critical acumen, and the differences between his work and that of other schools of Marxist critics, have made his works very popular. However, the underlying theoretical positions and methods with which he worked have excited less interest than some of his specific judgements, and the attempts at theoretical critiques have tended to concentrate most heavily on his political and philosophical contributions,[1] to the detriment of his literary works. The efforts of empirically minded British critics have been largely devoted to 'disproving' his concrete judgements, without seriously examining the foundations of these.[2]

We shall argue later that an understanding of Lukács' general positions is of vital importance in understanding his literary works, but it is simply not possible to reduce the one into the other. It may as well be stated that, considered politically, Lukács' career was one of almost uninterrupted disaster: he managed to be wrong on every major topic of politics from 1917 to his death, both in the eyes of the Leninists and of the Stalinists. With this unique talent, he also combined the attributes of a 'marxist' Vicar of Bray, changing his public utterances to suit the current needs of the Russian, and later Hungarian, bureaucracy, with an uncanny facility. This political servility, which never seemed quite to satisfy his masters, is a very important element in understanding the structure and judgements of his literary works.[3] However, it does not settle the matter of his importance as a critic. The consistent thread running throughout Lukács' whole writings, as much in his pre-Marxist days as later, is the attempt to grapple, at a whole number of levels, with the problem of the relation of the material life of a society to its ideological phenomena, or more precisely, its consciousness. The reformulation is of importance in understanding the nature of Lukács' answers to the problem, because the term 'ideology' has been frequently used to describe crystallised and static products of consciousness, and the central point of Lukács' case is that to examine the problem of consciousness in general implies a further study of the factors which determine the particular structures which that consciousness takes, at particular times, and with particular social classes.[4]

In 1914, before he came to a Marxist position, Lukács had posed the problem of the general historical periodisation of literature. In *The Theory of the Novel* a schema is elaborated which links the epochal development of history with the evolution of literary forms in the widest sense (i.e. the succession of epic, tragedy and novel). Literary form, in this case, as with aesthetics in general, is determined by ethics. The change of the relation between conscious subject and objective world (in terms of an increasingly radical breach between 'self' and 'world') results in a structural reproduction of that relationship in the forms of literature. The epic is the form of unconscious identity, the tragedy that of unconscious non-identity, and the novel of conscious opposition. This general periodisation, recast in terms of material production and social relations, remains with Lukács in his Marxist writings, and it is at this level that a determination model can be seen to operate.[5]

The general level of historical periodisations is quite inadequate for the detailed problems of aesthetic judgement, and at this level, Lukács adopts a more complex method which follows on from that already used. 'Marxist Orthodoxy' had posed the problem of consciousness, part of the general category of the 'superstructure', as the evolution of the ideas of a class resulting from an objective, pre-existent development of the productive forces. From this followed a necessarily reductivist approach to the problem. The relation of base to superstructure was itself one of material, logical and historical dependency; the superstructure reflected *passively* the developments of the economic base.

In *History and Class Consciousness* Lukács advanced the position that class consciousness, properly considered, did not represent the mechanical product of the position of a class within society, but was the active product of the possibilities open to that class in a given historical situation. Hence the decisive factor in the consideration of consciousness is shifted from those elements which are a reflection of a pre-existent material reality to those elements which represent the possibility of the transformation of that material reality. Consciousness is not the dead epiphenomenon of an 'objective' material reality, but the central factor in understanding real historical development. All of the dangers of mechanical materialism, and its logical concomitant of idealism, which are concentrated in the simple reflection model, are removed if consciousness is grasped as conscious historical action-praxis.

Lukács goes on to make an important distinction within class-consciousness. The formation of consciousness is located by Lukács in the total social activity of the class under consideration. In general it is not the relation of the individual components of any given group to the productive life of society which gives the characteristic form to the consciousness of that group, for such an analysis could only lead to a subjectivist analysis of consciousness in terms of the conscious response of the individual to a situation. The group itself, however, stands in an objectively defined relation to production, and it is that relation which determines its consciousness *as a group*. Historical action, the decisive events of historical development which lead to the transformation (or the failure to achieve the transformation) of a mode of production are the consequences of the action by social classes, acting on the basis of this objectively determined consciousness. The relation of a class to the mode of production is quite distinct from the relation of those individuals who constitute that class – an example can most easily be given from Marxist economics, where the problem of surplus value, the exploitation of labour by capital, cannot be understood from the standpoint of the *individual* capitalist opposing the *individual* worker in production, but only from the point of view of the relation of the two classes.

From this follows Lukács' second point: that the consciousness possessed by any individual, or objectified by him or her in, for example, a novel, may be a closer or more distant approximation to the consciousness of the class which has determined his or her consciousness, but need not in any particular case actually correspond to the consciousness of that class:

> Now class consciousness consists in the fact of the appropriate and rational reactions 'imputed' to a particular typical position in the process of production. This consciousness is, therefore, neither the sum nor the average of what is thought or felt by the single individuals who make up the class. And yet the historically significant actions of the

> class as a whole are determined in the last resort by this consciousness and not by the thought of the individual – and these actions can be understood only by reference to this consciousness.[6]

Lukács' theory of consciousness therefore operates at two levels. Consciousness is determined by the development of the productive forces in that the particular characteristic features of a given consciousness correspond to the forms of life peculiar to particular classes, and the relations of contending classes – in the last instance a productive relationship – determine the historical situation of class consciousness. But class consciousness itself remains undetermined at a second level, in that it constitutes the category of *objective possibility*. This category is by its very nature both determined and indeterminate, in that its objective nature is the consequence of historically antecedent developments in production, while its status as the historically unrealised makes it of necessity contingent. This formulation is of extreme analytic power, and marks a definite advance on the theories previously held by the followers of Marx; its limitations will have to be taken up below.

The theory entails two additional points which are of considerable importance. The empirical consciousness of the members of a class may correspond more or less closely to the 'imputed' consciousness of the class. However, just as the nature of class consciousness is determined by the relation of the particular class to the mode of production, so also are the forms of class organisation which correspond to the possibility of reaching 'imputed' consciousness. These will be different for the different classes. To take an obvious example, proletarian class-consciousness is possible only through the medium of the democratic-centralist party, whereas for the bourgeoisie no such definite form of organisation is required. The consequence of this is that the analysis of a given type of consciousness requires not only a study of the specific feature of the class under study, but also of the forms of class-organisation which it has thrown up.

The second consequence of the theory is that while the 'imputed' consciousness of the class represents the consciousness which guides its ideal and rational actions, it does not follow that the consciousness of any class therefore represents an objective, scientific characterisation of the totality of society. The degree to which even the 'imputed' consciousness of a class corresponds to the structure of society as a whole is itself determined by the position which that class has in the productive process. The peasantry, in Marx's example,[7] are a case in point; because of their particular, isolated, individual, mode of production, they are incapable of a generalised class-consciousness which rises to the level of society as a whole. Their consciousness remains fragmented, individualised, and local. Social classes historically antecedent to the proletariat are of necessity unable to reconcile even their 'imputed' consciousness with the nature of historical reality. Even the class whose mission it is to create for the first time a universal market, (and thus to transcend the limitations of geography which the peasantry labour under), the bourgeoisie, are incapable of developing a scientific consciousness of history. A scientific grasp of history would imply theoretical self-abnegation, which is absolutely precluded by their position within the productive process: '. . . the bourgeoisie was quite unable to perfect its fundamental science, its own science of classes; the reef on which it foundered was its failure to discover even a theoretical solution to the problem of crises.'[8]

Works of art undoubtedly are objectifications of consciousness (the special mode of objectification we shall examine shortly), and therefore represent to a greater or lesser extent the 'imputed' consciousness of a given class. Some may actually contain that historic consciousness in its entirety; others may operate so far within its limits as to be entirely trivial in this respect. Such a proposition, which flows directly from the distinctions possible within Lukács' theory of class consciousness, is by definition evaluative, and therefore provides a scientific basis for discrimination between works of art.[9] This is a fundamental point for the understanding of Lukács' aesthetic work, which seeks, through the mediation between art and production by way of class consciousness, to include an aesthetic (i.e. a descriptive and evaluative theory of art) within the historical science elaborated by Marx.

The 'imputed' consciousness of a class defines the historical framework within which it is possible for that class to act. It therefore consists of an ordered and structured representation of the reality of the world which confronts that class – at all levels from the materially productive to the philosophical. However, as we have seen, it is not possible for a class other than the proletariat to have a fully coherent consciousness. All other consciousnesses are of necessity partial and problematic. The more coherently a given objectification of the consciousness of a class represents the historical situation of a class, the more sharply in relief will appear the limits of that consciousness. The historic limitations of a given class come to be more and more the central problematic of that representation. The economic science of the bourgeoisie represented a significant achievement the more nearly it approached the unattainable holy grail of a satisfactory analysis of the labour theory of value, and sank into vulgarity once it abandoned this quest. Similarly, the art of the bourgeoisie gained its aesthetic value the more it attempted to grapple with its own insuperable problems, themselves artistic representations of the fundamental economic and social contradictions of its own class life.[10]

To provide a solution of the relation of art to social life hardly solves the problems which Lukács set himself. The second and equally important pillar upon which his literary work rests is the specification of art within the general category of consciousness. As Marx observed, the explanation of the material conditions which give rise to a particular art-work in no way explain the continuing artistic validity of such a work in a different historical epoch.[11]

The explanation of this problem advanced by Lukács is substantially the same as that advocated by Marx in his fragmentary studies of the question. The history of social development itself represents a development of previously non-existent qualities within man as a socially defined subject. These characteristics are not those of the structure of an isolated personality considered from the 'psychological' standpoint, but the subjective expression of an objective complex of social relations determined by the character of production in a given society. The nature of historical development is such that although succeeding modes of production 'negate' previous modes, they do not do so in the sense that the objective complex of production begins again from an entirely new basis; the negation is an Hegelian negation which implies the preservation of the previous developments at a new level and in an altered form. Consequently, the artistic achievements of a previous society remain available to the developed aesthetic sense of a later society in so far as the development itself presupposes both a continuity and discontinuity in the aesthetic sense.[12]

To speak of an 'aesthetic sense' in this context does not imply a reversion to the earlier Kantian model. The aesthetic sense is here a qualitatively distinct attribute of human development which is the result of a development of the objective relations between man and the external world mediated by labour.[13]

The proposition of special and defined aspects of the basic sensual relations of man to the world – eye, ear, hand etc. which have the character of aesthetic senses provides Lukács with his point of departure for the analysis of the category of aesthetics within the general category of consciousness. Special senses, embodied in objective social structures (e.g. schools of music), without which the idea of musical instrument, let alone the concept of music, is unthinkable, imply the development of a qualitatively distinct relation of subject to object:

> It is a fundamental thesis of a dialectical materialism that any apperception of the external world is nothing but the reflection of a reality existing independently of the consciousness, in the thoughts, conceptions, perceptions, etc. of man . . . As a mode of reflection of the external world in human consciousness, artistic creation is subsumed under the general epistemology of dialectical materialism. However, because of the peculiar character of artistic creation, it is a particular, special, part often with distinctive laws of its own.[14]

If the concept of an aesthetic is brought into a close relation with social life in general by the first aspect of Lukács' theory, then this second aspect specifies its relation to other aspects of consciousness. The science of aesthetics is the study of these 'distinctive laws'. It is in the elaboration of this field that Lukács' most important contribution to Marxism is located. It had been implicitly stated by Marx that consciousness implied a structure of consciousness, but in general the theoreticians of Marxism had only elaborated this at the political and economic level. Lukács developed the structure in the realm of the aesthetic.

From these two points, most of Lukács' methodological points flow. We do not propose to deal here with the question of realism nor with the category of the type. Both of these have been extensively, if inadequately, examined elsewhere.[15] However, a number of important points remain to be given their full weight, and a brief exposition of the chief ones will provide us with a starting point for a critique of the limitations of Lukács' position.

The method of literary criticism

It is clear from the above analysis that the aesthetic character of a work of art, while representing a distinct area of consciousness with its own internal laws, gains its decisive contours from the character of the total historical situation. The category of objective possibility, the determinant of the historically significant character of a work of art, is not inherent in the internal structure of that work. The category arises from the objective social situation which generates it. Thus any analysis of a work of art in relation to 'imputed' consciousness presupposes an analysis of the objective, material conditions under which any given work is produced. Only when that task is completed is it possible to determine the nature of 'imputed' consciousness, and hence to examine the degree to which a given art-object approximates to that.

> The method employed . . . is a very simple method: it consists in first of all examining carefully the real social foundations upon which, say, Tolstoy's existence rested, and the real social forces under which the human and literary personality of this author developed. Secondly, in close connection with the first approach, the question is asked: what do Tolstoy's works represent, what are the real spiritual and intellectual contents and how does the writer build up his aesthetic forms in the struggle for the adequate expression of such contents. Only if, after an unbiased examination, we have uncovered and understood these objective relationships, are we in a position to provide a correct interpretation of the conscious views expressed by the author and correctly evaluate his influence on literature.[16]

Personality and influence

The staple of literary scholarship – the hunting down of 'influence' and 'parallels' receives short shrift from Lukács. While not doubting the value of this empirical work, it is central to Lukács' argument that the decisive question in the study of any given author is his consciousness as determined by the historical situation in which he lives. The consciousness of a writer is formed by the multitude of personal and social relations into which he must enter in order to live. The idea of the noble literary savage ready to form his whole literary consciousness from his readings is absurd. Although the actual texts which any given author chooses to study may be determined either by a conscious plan or by a range of personal and psychological factors, the way in which those works are approached and the extent to which they are ordered and assimilated in the literary consciousness is not determined by their literary logic. The consciousness which appropriates a literary tradition is defined by social life, and can only be understood in relation to that life.[17]

Psychology of the writer

The formation of consciousness is not undertaken by the individual artist, but by the social class which he or she represents ideologically. Consequently, the study of the individual writer, from a biographical or psychological standpoint, cannot take us to the core of what that writer is expressing in the objectification of the historical consciousness of a class. The importance of personal quirks will increase the further the work in question is removed from historic consciousness. Similarly, the conscious intentions of the writer may well lead to certain definite artistic ends, but the structure of the work as a whole depends upon a reality greater than the individual writer's grasp of his or her historical situation. What the individual psychological constitution of the writer can show is the process by which he or she comes to reach the limits of the consciousness of his or her class. It cannot either describe that consciousness or become a substitute for it:

> Of course, Flaubert's position in this process [a change in the conception of history on the part of the bourgeoisie – C.S.] is not an average one. His literary greatness is expressed in the fact that the general tendency of the times appears in his work with an honest, passionate consistency. While in most other writers of the time, a negative attitude towards the contemporary prose of bourgeois life was simply a matter of aesthetic amusement, or, frequently, of reactionary feeling, in Flaubert it is an intense disgust, a vehement hatred.[18]

Politics and literature

One of the chief merits of Lukács' theory is that it avoids the common trap of hunting down the 'progressive' writer, and adulating him or her for the overt political content of a work. How far this is true of the actual practice of criticism by Lukács is another matter. As the quote on Flaubert shows the question of the overt intentions of a writer is of importance, but it is secondary to the objective changes in the consciousness of the class. Thus it is possible to give artistic recognition to a writer whose overt politics are not at all 'progressive' (Balzac is the classic case), and to deny it to those whom Lukács would consider very 'progressive' politically (e.g. the doyens of Socialist Realism').

A different order of question is the relation between the literary consciousness of a class and its consciousness as a whole. Here art is necessarily subordinate to politics. The historical existence of a class presupposes its material practice before its intellectual:

> It would be altogether superficial and wrong to suppose that, when a class turns its back so radically upon its earlier political aims and ideas, the spheres of ideology, the fates of science and art can remain untouched.[19]

Content, form and style

Much contemporary bourgeois criticism has concentrated its attention on the questions of artistic form and style. This procedure supposes a conception of the work of art which allows it an internal development according to artistic laws independent of the historical situation. This of course is a position which Lukács is bound to reject. All aspects of the work of art are subordinate to the historical situation. Consequently the starting point of literature is not literature itself, but a completely 'external' reality, and formal considerations are materially, logically and artistically dependent upon this:

> The distinctions that concern us are not those between stylistic 'techniques' in the formalist sense. It is the view of the world, the ideology or **Weltanschauung** underlying a writer's work, that counts. And it is the writer's attempt to reproduce this view of the world which constitutes his 'intention' and is the formative principle underlying the style of a given piece of writing. Looked at in this way, style ceases to be a formalistic category. Rather it is rooted in content; it is the specific form of a specific content.[20]

It might appear from this quotation that the relation of form to content is the simple one of unidirectional determinance. In most of the book *The Meaning of Contemporary Realism* the analysis ignores entirely the questions of form and style. This emphasis is only partly due to the needs of polemic, but it does represent an oversimplification of the position advanced by Lukács at other times.

In the first place, we have already seen that it is central to Lukács' overall position that the general categories of form – epic, novel and drama, arise as structural reproductions of the material life of historical epochs, and thus have rather more than a 'specific' significance.

The more developed aspects of Lukács' analysis of form arise from his conception of the nature of the artistic mode of grasping reality. It is quite obvious that no literary work can reproduce the totality of human experience. Any given work of art represents only elements of the concrete world. However, the elements, if they are to appear not simply as *fragments* require a unifying principle which can transform them from abstractions to representations of concrete experience. Form, for Lukács, provides exactly this unifying principle. It is the relation of the contents of a work of art which allow the disparate elements of real life, torn from their complex living relationships with each other, to come together again at the level of art, to form a new totality. It is only in so far as the material which the artist abstracts from experience is unified by means of an adequate form, that art gains the specific nature which differentiates it from simple 'documentation':

> The task of art is the recognition of the concrete – in the Marxist sense – in a direct, perceptual self-evidence. To that end those factors must be discovered in the concrete

> and rendered perceptible whose unity makes the concrete concrete. Now in reality every phenomenon stands in a vast, infinite context with all other simultaneous and previous phenomena. A work of art, considered from the point of view of its content, provides only a greater or lesser extract of reality. Artistic form therefore has the responsibility of preventing this extract from giving the effect of an extract and thus requiring the addition of an environment of time and space . . .[21]

The strengths of Lukács' theory and method, which we have here attempted to sketch, are self-evident. However, the weaknesses are equally apparent. These are usually presented in different ways, depending upon the theoretical position adopted by the critical investigator, but seem to me to arise from a central limitation in Lukács' theoretical stance.

The most obvious difficulty is that which naive young Marxists encounter when they come across a passage such as this:

> The real dilemma of our age is not the opposition between capitalism and socialism, but the opposition between peace and war. The first duty of the bourgeois intellectual has become a rescue operation for humanity rather than any breakthrough to Socialism.[22]

For those of us who, in trust and innocence, followed Lenin in believing that Imperialism leads necessarily to war, and that the only way to prevent war is through the overthrow of capitalism, a passage such as this is, to say the least, embarrassing if we wish to claim Lukács for Marxism. It is not enough to record that the cloven hoof of Stalinism is here clearly visible, for this passage is not a chance quotation, but is actually the formative principle of the influential book *The Meaning of Contemporary Realism*. We cannot accept the conclusions of such a book and ignore its central theme. Nor can we simply assume that a correct theory has been 'misapplied'. It is blatantly obvious that we must examine the theory itself to see how this unpalatable conclusion has come about.

Other, perhaps differently motivated, critics, discover in Lukács remarkably little treatment of stylistic and formal problems. This is not just the result of the above-stated location of the role of form, but a consistent failure to apply this position with any rigour. While Lukács provides an alternative tradition and method to bourgeois criticism in his work, he does not provide the weapons to meet the bourgeois critics on their own ground, and consequently seems to require 'supplementing' from from a hostile tradition.

A third difficulty is probably shared by almost everybody who studies Lukács. While we may rejoice in the devaluation of Kafka and Joyce, and agree that Naturalism represented a decisive retreat from the artistic achievements of Classical Realism, it is a little difficult to accept that bourgeois literature has stuttered fitfully since 1848. For example, the discussion of Conrad in *The Meaning of Contemporary Realism*, while correctly pointing to the limitations of *Lord Jim* and *Heart of Darkness*, ignores a work of the scale of *Nostromo*. Lukács' argument is that Conrad is essentially a short story writer because his ideas did not enable him to go beyond the 'exclusively personal, moral conflicts' of his heroes and locate them in the concrete social problems of his day. This is a remarkably accurate characterisation of Conrad, up to a point. It reveals at once the appalling weaknesses of *The Heart of Darkness*: the ludicrously inflated subjectivity of Kurtz, and of the narrator, arise simply because the social significance of the human brutality and degradation of Belgian Imperialism is not admitted by Conrad, and cannot be accommodated in the short story form. But *Nostromo*? Of this book, an English Marxist critic has written '. . . the whole process and consequences of imperialist exploitation, [are] so richly and concretely and humanely illuminated throughout the length of the book . . .'.[23] He is undoubtedly right against Lukács. The theoretical equipment, whatever its overall power, is quite unable to come to terms with the real evolution of the bourgeois novel.

The common root of these failures lies in the nature of Lukács' original analysis of class consciousness. In the passage quoted from *History and Class Consciousness*, we saw how Lukács posed the interpretation of the historically significant actions of a class in the light of its 'imputed' consciousness – the objective possibility which the situation gives it. This argument has a great degree of truth, and provides valuable insights. But it remains essentially one-sided. What is at stake in any historical study is not the historical possibilities open at any given stage in history but the real, objective actions taken by classes. It is true that these can only be understood in the light of 'imputed' consciousness, but this is only the beginning of comprehension. The real movement of history is located in the *relation* of the 'imputed' consciousness of a class to its actual empirical consciousness. Any given historical event in the class struggle can only be analysed by examining these relations in terms of concrete social forces – the relative weight of different class organisations within a class, the extent to which any one of these possesses a hegemony *within* a class as much as over other classes.

Stated politically, the problem is as simple today as when the leaders of the Comintern took up the struggle against the proponents of these theories. According to Lukács, the problem of class consciousness is resolved to the extent that the 'imputed' consciousness of the proletariat is realised in the revolutionary party. The conquest of state power is prepared by the elaboration of the party as the living social embodiment of the categories of Marxism. The leaders of the Comintern replied to this that the problem was not solved by the existence of a revolutionary party. The conditions for the resolution of the struggle for state power were *both* the existence of a class-conscious vanguard party *and* the real existence of that party as the leadership of the majority of the working class. The 'putschist' disasters which followed from Lukács' theoretical position are well attested.[24]

Translated into literature, the question for Lukács is equally simple: at what date did the bourgeoisie cease to play a historically progressive role? The answer: 1848. Consequently, the objective possibility for the bourgeoisie, at that point and subsequently, was only that of counter-revolutionary consciousness. It was therefore forced to shut itself off from whole areas of the reality of its own existence. Ergo, its literary productions could not reach the heights they did in the preceding period.

Now it is at once obvious that the bourgeoisie has managed not only to survive since 1848, but also considerably to expand the productive forces. Hence, by the most rigorous objective text, its role has not in reality been simply that of reaction. If it is the case that the objective pre-requisites for Socialism have existed since 1848, it is also the case that in 1973, we do not live under Socialism. Literary works reproduce not the 'imputed' consciousness of a class, but the real historical consciousness of that class. This consciousness may or may not be the 'imputed' consciousness of the class depending upon the real social forces at a given time. The argument that the bourgeoisie can no longer play a progressive role on the world scale and must therefore of necessity cut itself off from some aspects of social life is not at all relevant. On Lukács' own argument, the consciousness of the bourgeoisie, even in its revolutionary phase, is of necessity unable to provide a total world picture. The real case which can be argued from this point is that the bourgeois class was unable, on a world scale, to carry out any significant advances upon its theoretical or artistic achievements before 1848. The recognition of this fact in no way implies that a given bourgeois writer, in definite historical circumstances, might not raise his own work to the level of the masters.

In fact, his concern for literature forces Lukács to recognise this. Unfortunately, he is unable fully to integrate this realisation into his theoretical position because of the parallel notion of historical development which he holds. On the one hand, he advances the abstractly correct statement that 1848 marked a turning point for the bourgeoisie. On the other hand, he puts forward the theory that, in certain national instances, the bourgeoisie was capable of a historically progressive role.

What is lacking is the notion of combined and uneven development. This is one of the fundamental theories of Marxism, developed most fully by Trotsky, but for obvious historical reasons, it was one which Lukács was unable fully to accept. The basis of the theory is that the development of capitalism on a world scale, particularly in its imperialist phase, produces in 'underdeveloped' countries the co-existence of the most advanced and most backward forms of production. An example is Russia, which accommodated both the most modern factories in the world and vast feudal estates. Its argument can be extended to explain the development even of 'advanced' capitalist countries, for it is evident no national capitalist state encompasses within itself a single uniform level of development, and that consequently the real movement of social forces is a complex of interacting factors.

Lukács does at times approach a position of recognising the complexity of real historical development.[25] On the other hand, the theoretical model with which he operates remains very simple. The central argument of *The Historical Novel* may be reduced, without excessive distortion, to the following proposition:

> For the countries of Western and Central Europe the revolution of 1848 means a decisive alteration in class groupings and in class attitudes to all important questions of social life, the perspectives of social development. The June battle of the Paris Proletariat in 1848 constitutes a turning-point in history on an international scale.[26]

The abstract truth of this statement is an exact parallel to the proposition on class consciousness. The proletariat and the bourgeoisie remain as theoretical entities opposing one another on a world scale. The historical development of the two classes in relation to the productive forces is not admitted. Within the real movement of history are the interrelations of different layers and groups which make up classes, each with its own organs and interests. These are the material for the scientific historian: if it was just us and them, we would have won years ago.

When Lukács does address the problems of culture, he argues that works of 'great realism' were produced after 1848, but in countries other than those of western and central Europe:

> . . . the true heirs of the French novel, so gloriously begun early in the last century, were not Flaubert and especially Zola, but the Russian and Scandinavian writers in the second half of the century.[27]

The theory of uneven development is present here only in its truncated, 'Bukharinised' form, as the uneven development *between* national states. This is undoubtedly one of the aspects of the theory, but without the concept of uneven development *within* these states, it is inadequate to the point of falsity. Without this theory, it is impossible to present an adequate analysis of the development of the culture of any country in the 19th and 20th century.

For example, in the instance of English culture, it is one of Lukács' great achievements to have rescued Scott from oblivion, but if we pass beyond 1848 we find a number of novelists whom it is hard to fit into a pattern of continuous decline. We have already glanced at the example of Conrad, but Eliot and Hardy are immediate examples upon which Lukács' method enforces silence. The gaps cannot simply be attributed to an inadequate knowledge of English literature. It is rather that the theory has already defined a set of problems, which do not include these writers. Certainly any theory defines its problems, but what is at stake here is the inadequacy of a particular theory and, in that the abstract categories of thought are more 'real' than the material reality which generates them,[28] Lukács' is a 'Hegelian' theory.

If the conception of history admits, in theory, only two possible world-visions in the epoch of declining capitalism, then the study of the differing intellectual currents within a class becomes of secondary importance. The theory is capable of accounting for fully elaborated and systemised views of society, but as far as less developed positions are concerned there is no adequate explanation. The precise social mechanism which lead different writers to quite contradictory positions within one general ideology is dealt with simply in personal terms (e.g. the quotation on Flaubert above), as examples of degrees of 'artistic' talent. Any oversimplified view of materialism leads to idealism.

The point was made long ago by Marx[29] that the problem of the literary 'representatives' of a class was not to be sorted out by a process of sociological identification. The tradition of this activity was one against which Lukács specifically forged his theory. Yet he provides no adequate alternative.

We cannot here elaborate such an alternative except in so far as to state its main postulate. What is required is an analysis of the 'intelligentsia' as a distinct and defined social group, not as some 'free-floating' privileged class, but as a social stratum subordinated *of necessity* to the main classes in society. The complex forces which drive this and that section to different positions are located outside of that stratum itself. For the representatives of the intelligentsia, these forces appear as the internal problematics of their own concerns – for example their relation to a literary tradition.[30] A theory which is restricted to analysing the formation of world-visions by the main classes can provide considerable insights into the structure of that world-vision. Linked with a theory of artistic modes of grasping reality it can show us how, in a particular case, that world-vision is given a concrete artistic form. Its limitation is that it cannot explain that realisation in literary terms. The argument is conducted from the world-vision to its literary realisation. No account is given of the 'weight of past generations' in terms of the available literary modes and the writers artistic relation to them. Although Lukács' concept of consciousness is a structured one, it remains insufficiently structured.

Hence the noted underemphasis on the question of literary form arises. The internal relations of a work of art, and its development out of previous works are problems specifically of ideology and its structure. Lukács' conception of aesthetics provides the tools to analyse this structure, but the vital mediation between this literary analysis and the sociology of the world vision remains absent. The disjuncture between the two aspects of the theory is papered over, simply by failing to develop the second with any rigour. In this sense, Lucien Goldmann is a true interpreter of Lukács when he ignores the problem of aesthetics in its entirety. The original starting point does not provide space for the analysis of the intelligentsia which could alone provide the mediating factor which can link the two halves of the theory.[31]

In conclusion, it may be said that Lukács' literary criticism and aesthetic writings represent a considerable development of the Marxist method over that practised in the preceding epoch. Their limitations are set precisely by the character of the Marxism which Lukács evolved in his early period of 'leftism'. The flaws in the theoretical and political model pervade the literary analysis of many of his best-known works. To the extent that he represents a major step forward from the simple sociological approach, it constitutes a significant achievement. To the extent that it fails to provide a fully elaborated theoretical system for the study of literature, it requires a serious development.

Notes

1 The best of these is to be found, of all places, in Belazs Nagy, *Georgy Lukács: A Political Itinerary*, Fourth International, Vol. 7, nos. 2, 3, 5, (continuing). G. Stedman Jones' contribution in *New Left Review*, 70, Nov. – Dec. 1971 adds little to the discussion except to emphasise the continuing debt of *NLR* to the work of George Lichtheim. His short book on Lukács, *Lukács* (Fontana, 1970) is very hard reading, but combines the usual blend of brilliant scholarship with vitriolic anti-communism.

2 A case in point is A. G. Lehmann, 'The Marxist as Literary Critic' in G. H. R. Parkinson, ed., *Georg Lukács: The Man, His Work, and His Ideas* (Weidenfeld, 1970). Lehmann claims, at the end of his analysis of Lukács' handling of Scott that: 'The texts of Scott are devoured by a mind ready with the schemata, and this means that the real historical canvas (the historiographical background of Scott) is not considered at any point. On the other hand, though the texts of Scott, being approached for the purpose just mentioned, *cannot be allowed to speak for themselves, fully, at leisure, and with their own equilibrium so to speak* . . .' (p. 185. My emphasis). In so far as this means anything at all, it is simply an expression of a naive and cheerful empiricism at its most insensitive. What Lehmann is actually saying is that there is a discrepancy between his judgement of Scott and that of Lukács. His, being his own and arrived at by his method, he prefers. Hence Lukács is wrong.

3 For example, the whole of the last section of *The Historical Novel*, trans. H. S. Mitchell (Penguin, 1969) is devoted to justifying the cultural hangers-on of the Popular Front.

4 Lukács defined his own contribution to Marxist criticism in terms of a sharp and conscious opposition to the 'vulgar sociology' which had previously dominated the field. The theoreticians of the Second International who had worked in this field, even such dissident figures as Lenin and Rosa Luxemburg, had carried their marxism only as far as the analysis of the sociological origins of a given work. For a writer like Kautsky, this provided the sum total of the analysis, but in the cases of Plekhanov and Mehring, both very distinguished critics, there remained the glaring problem of what it was that made a work of art special and distinct. They themselves could only resolve this problem by means of a quasi-Kantian formulation in terms of a special aesthetic sense with its own, quite distinct, laws which it was impossible to subordinate to the historical analysis to which the other aspects of a given work were subjected.

5 See for example, the discussion in *The Historical Novel* pp. 103–22.

6 *History and Class Consciousness*, trans. R. Livingstone (Merlin 1971) p. 51.

7 Marx discusses the peasantry in *The Class Struggles in France* and in *The Eighteenth Brumaire*, both in K. Marx and F. Engels op. cit. Vol I. The position is summarised by E. Hobsbawm in his essay 'Class consciousness in History' in I. Mezaros ed. *Aspects of History and Class Consciousness* (R. K. P. 1971).

8 *History and Class Consciousness* pp. 53–4.

9 This is of course L. Goldmann's position, for an exposition of which see A. Mellor's article in this journal.

10 This very important position seems to me fundamental to understanding Lukács' aesthetic works. It could be argued in detail that it permeates his critical practice, but it is true that it is very rarely stated explicitly. One of the few direct statements is in *Goethe and His Age*, trans. R. Anchor, (Merlin, 1968) pp. 39–40.

11 For example '. . . the difficulty is not in grasping the idea that Greek art and epos are bound up with certain forms of social development. It lies rather in understanding why they still constitute for us a source of aesthetic enjoyment . . .' from the 'General Introduction to the "Grundrisse"' in D. McLellan ed., *Marx's Grundrisse* (Macmillan, 1971) p. 45.

12 Ibid, pp. 45–6.

13 See K. Marx, *Economic and Philosophical Manuscripts of 1844*, trans. M. Milligan (Progress, Moscow, 1959) pp. 100–01.

14 G. Lukács, *Writer and Critic*, trans. A. Kahn (Merlin, 1970) pp. 73–4.

15 See the essays by Parkinson and Pascal in Parkinson *op. cit.* Also E. Bahr and R. G. Kunzer *Georg Lukács* (Ungar, New York, 1972); this book is a good introduction to Lukács as a literary critic.

16 G. Lukács *Studies in European Realism*, trans. not named (Grosset and Dunlap, New York, 1964) p. 16.

17 See the study of Scott's conception of history and its parallels in *The Historical Novel* pp. 15–69.
18 Ibid pp. 219–20.
19 Ibid pp. 202–3.
20 G. Lukács, *The Meaning of Contemporary Realism*, trans. J. & N. Mander (Merlin, 1962) p. 19.
21 *Writer and Critic*, p. 47.
22 *The Meaning of Contemporary Realism*, p. 92.
23 A. Kettle, *An Introduction to the English Novel* II Vols (Hutchinson 1969) Vol II p. 72
24 Rudolf Schlesinger's unfinished and fragmentary essay 'Historical setting of Lukács' "History and Class Consciousness"' printed as an Appendix to *Aspects of History and Class Consciousness* is one of the few attempts to explore the theoretical debate seriously. See also B. Nagy, op. cit.
25 See the isolated passage pp. 112–13 of *The Historical Novel.*
26 Ibid, p. 202.
27 *Studies in European Realism*, p. 5.
28 See McLellan op. cit. pp. 33–5.
29 In a famous passage in the 'Eighteenth Brumaire'. See K. Marx and F. Engels, op. cit. Vol. I, p. 424.
30 The groundwork of this theory was outlined by Gramsci. See *The Modern Prince and other writings*, trans. L. Marks (International New York, 1957) pp. 118–25.
31 In that part of the *Ontology of Social Being* which is available, there is a significant development of Lukács' position. In the discussion of the relation of labour and more developed forms of practice, Lukács introduces the conception of the original teleological project of labour as the direct transformation of material objects. In developed social labour, the teleological projection implies projections with respect to the practices of other groups of men. The increasing social and technical division of labour therefore provides the basis for the evolution of teleological projects whose relation to the material practice of labour is highly mediate. Taking this as a starting point, it is possible to see how the argument would proceed with respect to art. See *The New Hungarian Quarterly* 47, Vol XIII, Autumn 1972, pp. 6–43.

11 Roland Barthes

Structuralism/semiotics

Iain Chambers

He's a walking contradiction
Partly truth and partly fiction.
Kris Kristofferson

Introduction

In setting forth the general aims of this paper a couple of points need to be borne in mind. Firstly, that the original impetus of structuralism has today been largely incorporated within the more fashionable discipline of semiology or semiotics.[1] Secondly, and more importantly, cultural studies is to be read not as a discipline in the traditional sense but as a developing problematic. A problematic whose centre is held by an attempt to analyse the pivotal relationship between conscious social experiences, in their various forms, and the profoundly unconscious historical and material constitution of those experiences. Put in another way, cultural studies seeks to grasp the 'logics-in-use', the transformations that operate in this dialectic (the space of ideologies) and to lay bare their specific enunciation in particular practices.

This involves analysing the concrete realizations, the objectivation, of 'social knowledge' as found within particular configurations and practices. Ideologies are the 'assembly' areas where fragments of social reality are brought together, transformed and integrated in an ongoing legitimizing process to produce a coherent explanatory map of the social world. The ideologies produced in these particular practices whilst seeking to validate 'reality': the status quo, should in no way be conceived of as static. They are constantly re-vamped and extended to incorporate new areas and situations. The interpretation of this problem is thus too complex to be caught in mechanistic metaphors or formalist models.

Theoretical knowledge is only a very small part of what passes for knowledge in society. Therefore a critical study must not restrict its objects of study to the processes whereby such knowledge is legitimized, such as the media and, at a more 'rarefied' level, such practices as literature and film. Analysing these particular processes should not blind us to the central core of the struggles waged in the ideological universe: the understanding of why such legitimation is required in the major meaning constellations of contemporary society; class, work, the family, leisure, youth cultures. 'For the revolutionary struggle does not take place between capitalism and the intellect, but between capitalism and the proletariat.'[2]

It was in the attempt to probe beyond a phenomenological understanding of the 'social construction of reality' that structuralism initially intervened in cultural studies.[3] It was principally through a study of Lévi-Strauss's work that the debate moved from considerations of individual interactionism against a pluralist background, to considering that background itself as the site of structuring rules and resultant transformations. Structuralism was able to postulate the logical scaffolding, the schema for interpretation for members of a particular society. It began to locate the unwritten rules of social knowledge that are sedimented not only in traditions and institutions but also in the subjects of a society. This shifted attention from considering the individual as the repository of cultural 'meaning' to the social totality.

However, it is the intent of this paper to demonstrate that the very formalism of the structuralist and now the semiotic activity, and the idealism it has engendered, has resulted in a skewed analysis of that totality and its particular practices. This paper makes no attempt to examine these skewed 'totalizations' as found in Lévi-Strauss, Foucault and Althusser, but will restrict itself to examining the ramifications of such skewing for particular practices.[4] I intend to demonstrate that by putting between brackets, or simply failing to acknowledge, the material conditions of the practices they examine, and treating them and society solely as a sign system, structuralism and semiotics have remained caught in the very ideology they claim to have exposed.[5]

It was precisely this idealized and 'one-sided' explanation that Marx criticized whereby the 'puzzling forms' assumed by social relations between man and man are ascribed to a conventional origin:

> But if it be declared that the social characters assumed by objects, or the material forms assumed by the social qualities of labour under the regime of a definite mode of production, are mere symbols, it is in the same breadth also declared that these are arbitrary fictions sanctioned by the so-called universal consent of mankind.[6]

Structuralism, semiotics and linguistics

Historically, structuralism is both a school and a method. It emerged, principally in France, in the wake of structural linguistics as inaugurated around the late nineteenth century by Ferdinand de Saussure, and continued in the Prague Linguistic Circle and through Hjelmslev's work in Copenhagen. Under the structuralist banner various attemps were increasingly elaborated to applying the formalist methodology of structural linguistics to other fields, notably social anthropology and literature, and in more recent years to history, psychoanalysis, film and throughout the 'human sciences'.

Saussure located his work beneath the heterogeneous level of speech (parole) in order to uncover the site (langue) that generated individual speech acts. In this way he revealed the constitutive social rules and logic that lies beneath the apparent spontaneity of individual speech. In a similiar fashion structuralism seeks the logic behind phenomenal performances. It seeks the coherent, regulatory and transformational rules and forms that exist behind and structure such performances as kinship systems, myths, literary narrative, psychological disturbances etc. It finds the sense of analysis not in the 'content' but in the 'form', or rather it supersedes that traditional debate by examining not entities but the relations that structure the material. It replaces atomism with structures and individualism by universalism. It is an attempt to unearth unconscious structuring rules and is crucially dependent upon the linguistic finding that the infinitude of manifest utterances are generated by a very small number of constitutive relations.[7]

Reacting against the dominant linguistic methodology of the time which studies languages in an evolutionary and historical framework, Saussure was more concerned to study the relations that existed within the linguistic totality at any one time. This *synchronic* study was pursued in order to capture in a single projection the 'frozen' logic, the generative grammar, that binds together co-existing terms to form the linguistic system. It must at this point be clearly stated that Saussure's study of the synchronic was a tactical move against the prevalent study of the developmental nature of language. He wrote: 'the synchronic law is general but not imperative.'[8]

However, in being appropriated by structuralism the synchronic law *has* become an imperative. Although the problem of history has received a lot of attention within the structuralist debate it has not been confronted head on, and this is symptomatic of a basic methodological flaw in the structuralist enterprise. Sometimes the problem is circumvented by relocating history in the diachronic nature of the narrative, thus turning it side on and slipping it into a series of static synchronic structures and relations.[9] The analytical knife of structuralism cuts across the movement of history but becomes so engrossed in tracing the relations and rules within the resultant segment as to forget that that segment has also a diachronic axis; that it was constituted in a historical process.

Despite Lévi-Strauss's stricture of 1960, against ignoring the historical dimension and thus being satisfied with an impoverished sociology in which 'phenomena are set loose, as it were, from their foundations', he was forced to admit in a seminar three years later that diachrony presented too many problems for structuralism at the present time and was therefore to be put to one side.[10] Thus the constitutive forces that resulted in a certain state of relations at any one time are given such a mediated determinacy that they almost disappear in many structuralist analyses. This recasting and ontologising of synchrony following its appropriation from linguistics has become the formal linchpin of structuralism whose methodology can be correspondingly abbreviated to

$$\frac{\text{synchrony}}{\text{diachrony}}$$

where diachrony is relegated to a subordinate and highly mediated position.

In identifying the relations within the linguistic totality Saussure located what he considered to be a determinate moment in that system: the linguistic *sign*. The linguistic sign is composed of a sound image, *signifier*, and a concept, *signified*. The Janus-like composition of the sign established a double thrust in Saussure's work. In cutting up the linguistic totality into constitutive units he was dealing with matters of language, but in the same operation these units were contextualized, as chains of signs, *signification*, in the matrix of social life as a sign system. The latter movement constituted a new discipline: semiology or semiotics.

However, the dialectic between the systemic nature of signification (the coupling of signifier and signified in a sign chain) and its ultimate referent (the object that remains in the world outside the system of signification) in the social materiality of the world in which that signification is but a particular practice, is a dialectic with which semiotics has rarely been concerned. Such blindness has resulted in the construction of systems and structures operating only in the domain of signification; that is, within the self-referring terms of the particular system's internal organization. The fact that these signifying practices, be they literature, music, film or architecture, exist in the sensuo-physical materiality of the social and historical world, is put in parenthesis. The resulting 'one-sided' analyses examine emasculated objects ripped from their genesis and relations in a mode of production, and analysed in the closed universe of a self-reflexive totality.

Roland Barthes: the sign meets the sign

> *. . . the more exactly he knows his position in the process of production, the less he will be tempted by the idea of passing for an intellectual.*
>
> *Walter Benjamin*, The Author as Producer.

I will concentrate on the two texts of Barthes that have proved most pertinent to cultural studies: 'Myth Today' in *Mythologies* (1957) and *Elements of Semiology* (1964). These two texts, in differing degrees, represent a methodology that has been seminal for semiotics and has been put into practice in varying fields, not least by Barthes himself. Barthes has continued to flesh out his original intentions and to consolidate the practice from whence he originally emerged: literature, with *S/Z* (1970) and *Le plaisir du texte* (1973) being the latest marks along that route. These latter two works will also receive some general attention.[11]

The problem of appropriating Barthes's work in this country is compounded by the fact that his latest book to be available in English, *Elements of Semiology*, was in fact written over ten years ago.[12] Another problem is the traditional British scepticism towards Continental theorizing, in this case generated in the conservative bastion of the British literary tradition. Thus the importance of Barthes's later work in which he examines literary practice and firmly seeks to establish the text as the moment of semiotic analysis and which has important ramifications for the study of expressive practices in general, has, as yet, received scant attention in this country.

In the preface to *Mythologies*, Barthes defines his intention as the construction of a 'general semiology of the bourgeois world'. Semiology becomes an instrument for collating the psycho-social symptoms, the *representations*, of the bourgeois world. In a series of brief essays, Barthes examines some of these representations in their varying forms: wrestling, the face of Garbo, striptease, the new Citroen. In the 1970 preface to the volume Barthes wrote:

> I had just read Saussure and as a result acquired the conviction that by treating 'collective representations' as sign systems, one might hope to go further than the pious show of unmasking them and account in detail for the mystification which transforms petit-bourgeois culture into a universal nature.[13]

However, these essays, written at least fifteen years earlier, while acknowledging Saussure as their mentor, make very cavalier use of linguistic terms and read more as examples of literary intuition than of an applied methodology.

In dealing with wrestling, for instance, the collapsing of the wrestling spectacle into a linguistic communication is simply presented as a non-contestable a-priori category. Barthes fails to question whether or not it can be considered as a linguistic communication at all.[14] There is a general semiological assumption that everything must pass through language. It results in semioticians talking of the 'languages' of systems rather than talking of systems directly.

> . . . to perceive what a substance signifies is inevitably to fall back on the individuation of a language: there is no meaning which is not designated, and the world of signifieds is none other than that of language.[15]

Barthes's ambiguous use of the term 'language' only adds to the confusion. Whether such 'languages' are linguistically based or not is never really resolved. It is certainly the case that the analytical procedures of signification require language but it does not necessarily follow that a process of signification such as a blush or a smile has to pass through language (in the ordinary sense of the term). If the latter were the case, then it would presuppose that the mind thinks in terms of linguistic organisation. However, since this has yet to be demonstrated, a reduction of systems of signification to a linguistic model is a hypothetical programme and closure for what basically remains an open question.[16]

What needs to be firmly established is that a communication is *denoted* in accordance with a signifying system. For analytical purposes *all* communication has to pass through written or verbal language. *Connotation* emerges from the particular signifying practice and operates *within* a *meaning* system. This last point will be taken up and elaborated below.

Barthes's rather woolly formulations are again heavily in evidence in 'Myth Today', where he again refers to Saussure as the prophet of 'this vast general science of signs'. Barthes's confusion when using linguistic terms in this essay resides in his employment of the word, *sign*. Within the linguistic system the sign, according to Saussure, was arbitrary.[17] In 'Myth Today' Barthes is aware of this arbitrary quality when he talks of the 'double articulation' of the *semiological sign*. The second articulation lies over the arbitrary linguistic articulation. In the ordering of the linguistic sign 'roses' to the further level of connotation 'roses' + 'passion' = 'passionified roses', the arbitrary quality is shown not to be operative at the second level. This clearly establishes the *intentionality* of the connotative sign (which in being decoded in a systemic analysis becomes a semiological sign) as a psycho-social representation of the dominant meaning system: the myths that constitute bourgeois ideology.

Therefore, the connotative sign is of a different order and must be clearly separated from the systemic organization of the linguistic sign. Although Barthes clearly sets forth this distinction he then goes on to collapse it. In the process the 'logics-in-use' behind the intentionality of the connotative sign are decontextualized in the reductionist movement back to the linguistic model.

> This is why the semiologist is entitled to treat in the same way writing and pictures: what he retains from them is the fact that they are both signs, that they both reach the threshold of myth endowed with the same signifying function, that they constitute one just as much as the other, a language object.[18]

The point to note here is that Barthes equates all signs with language objects. Even if all systems of signification are 'languages' (the 'language' of film, the 'language' of dance) there is still a reductionist argument at work here. If pictures and writing are to be treated without distinction equally as signs, constituting 'one just as much as the other', then the specificity of the practices that produced them is lost. Associated with that loss, the intentionality inscribed in those practices, as they exist within the universe of practices, is bracketed out under the blanket phrase: 'bourgeois ideology'.

Returning to the connotative plane and its associative signs that Barthes examines in *Mythologies*, we discover that in fact what Barthes is describing, if he is remaining loyal to the linguistic model, are not Saussurian signs, but what Saussure defined as a *symbol*; something that is not wholly arbitrary.

> . . . there is a rudiment of a natural bond between the signifier and the signified. The symbol of justice, a pair of scales, could not be replaced by just any other symbol, such as a chariot.[19]

I would quarrel, however, with Saussure for calling the bond 'natural'. The symbol is socially motivated and is thus a cultural convention. The bond has become sedimented in the logically taken-for-granted scaffolding of the world, it has become *naturalized*.

In Saussure's terminology, Barthes in studying connotative signs, is studying symbols. The 'natural' bond of the symbol owes its efficacity to its 'openness'. Being iconic such signs are open to multiple interpretations. It is this iconic factor which is of primary importance in allowing it to escape the 'closure' of natural language with its captive linguistic signs. The more arbitrary the system, the more 'closed' it is; thus the 'language' of film is more open than verbal or written language. Similiarly, the iconic symbols, the 'signs' of *Mythologies*, operate with an 'openness' that breaks with the arbitrary closure of the linguistic sign, and thus clearly operate with respect to an extra-linguistic referent.

Therefore, the correct interpretations of these symbols or connotative signs cannot be a linguistic one, it requires a *decoding* of a different order. This is not to deny the crucial mediation of language that Barthes points to in the Introduction to *Elements of Semiology*. For the working up of materials into concepts depends upon the basic premise of language. The decoding of these symbols via the *relay* of language needs to respect both the extra-systemic referent of the symbol and the mediation of language. Despite Barthes's attempt in *S/Z* to conceptualize an idealized 'scriptible' text there can be no 'writing degree zero'. These considerations call for an epistemology that locates its positivity within the social material conditions in which these representations ('mythologies') emerge and exist.

In *Elements of Semiology*, Barthes makes a considerable effort to systematize the method towards which he was groping in *Mythologies*, in a more rigorous manner. In the Introduction Barthes puts forward the claim of semiology to take in all sign systems with linguistics as the parent model, thus reversing Saussure's formulation and thereby making semiology a branch of linguistics. 'Finally, and in more general terms, it appears increasingly more difficult to conceive a system of images and objects whose signifieds can exist independently of language.'[20]

However, on the next page Barthes admits that the semiotic activity is rash because semiotic knowledge at that time could only be a copy of linguistic knowledge. Rash, because this knowledge must be applied to non-linguistic objects. On the previous page he had already written that 'every semiological system has its linguistic admixture'. This can be read in two ways: either that linguistics as realized in language is the relay for all semiotic systems, or in the more closed sense of linguistics being the master pattern for all semiotic systems. Two pages further on Barthes writes, 'not that semiology will always be forced to follow the linguistic model closely'. This last point is explicitly taken up by Barthes when he later makes the distinction between the linguistic sign and the semiological sign.[21] But, just as in 'Myth Today', the aegis of an overarching linguistic model results in a collapse into a homogeneous system.

In this pioneering work the collapse takes the form of a confusion between *signification* and *meaning*. This is a confusion that is not peculiar to Barthes but is found, with one or two exceptions, in linguistic research in general. The linguistic consideration of meaning (semantics) has usually concluded that meaning resides completely in language. In *Semantics*, Ullmann defines meaning as a 'reciprocal and reversible relationship between name and sense'. Leech in his recent book also entitled *Semantics*, writes of semantics as follows: 'Our remedy, then, is to be content with exploring what we have inside the room: to study relations within language.'[22]

In a similar vein in *Semantic Theory*, Katz opens with the statement: 'Semantics is the study of linguistic meaning'. He then goes on to complete the circular closure of his theory by saying that the question 'What is meaning? is a request for a semantic theory'.

In discussing *Mythologies* it was noted that the connotative plane lying atop the linguistic plane required a decoding of a different order from that pertaining to the linguistic plane. The introduction of the term 'intentionality' into the second plane was not to suggest that language, owing to its arbitrary nature, is pure and unintentional. Rather, the term intentionality was referring to the implications of the open nature of the connotative sign. That is, although the more open the system the greater the number of different 'readings' that can be generated; this fact, paradoxically, allows an understanding that can lead, albeit unconsciously, to a directing of readings towards an intentional end. The giving of 'passionified roses' to a woman has the intentional reading of love and passion. A dominant reading that has culturally and socially won consensus. But it could also be read as effeminate, romantic in a pejorative sense, or even an insult in the context of some sectors of the Women's Movement.

The difference between the linguistic and the connotative sign is not between 'intentional' and 'non-intentional', but a difference founded on the varying degrees of 'openness' operating in the different plane's systemic organisation.[23] It is *not* a difference of different epistemological configurations, for both are clearly dependent upon the same epistemological consideration. They are both dependent upon awareness of the extra-systemic referent to which both systems ultimately refer in the decoding of their respective signs and the realization of the *meaning* of those signs.

Between language and the extra-linguistic referent, there exists a dialectical relationship. The concrete object (i.e. a kitchen sink) which is translated into the 'concrete-in-thought' ('sink') remains outside the head and cannot be collapsed into the latter. Saussure wrote: 'The linguistic sign unites not a thing and a name, but a concept and a sound image.'[24]

The concrete object also exists within a system, a set of material relations: a sink refers to a kitchen range and other kitchen systems such as cooking vessels, cutlery, et al. Meaning is thus *produced* in the dialectic between that particular system and the linguistic system, with signification being the formal denotation of that dialectic. Neither Barthes's work or semiotics in general has recognized this series of relations in the production of meaning.

At the end of the section on the signifier and signified in *Elements of Semiology*, Barthes writes:

> . . . language is the domain of articulations, and meaning is above all a cutting out of shapes. It follows that the future task of semiology is far less to establish lexicons of objects than to rediscover the articulations which men impose on reality.[25]

But meaning is not the cutting out of shapes! On the previous page Barthes quotes Saussure's example of simultaneously cutting out the two 'floating kingdoms' of ideas (signifieds) and sounds (signifiers) as though two sides of a sheet of paper. This is not the realization of meaning but of *signification* in the form of linguistic signs. The *value*, as Saussure terms it, of these signs arise in their linear relationship with each other in the linguistic system, and the *meaning* is produced in the practice of language in the materiality of social existence.

The point is that it *does not* follow that the future task of semiology is to rediscover the articulations which men impose on reality (these *articuli* being the linguistic signs). Barthes is here reducing reality to ideas and collapsing the extra-linguistic referent, which as Saussure noted continued to exist outside the language system, into the concept or signified of the linguistic sign.

In the last section of *Elements of Semiology*, Barthes returns to the methodological propositions he set forth for examining ideology (myths) in 'Myth Today'. Explicitly drawing upon the work of the Danish linguist Louis Hjelmslev, Barthes sets forth the formal mechanisms of ideology and the method whereby these mechanisms are revealed (semiotics) in a diagrammatic manner. If we fill in the connotative model (the plane of ideology) with Barthes's example in 'Myth Today' of the photo of a black soldier saluting the French flag we get the following:

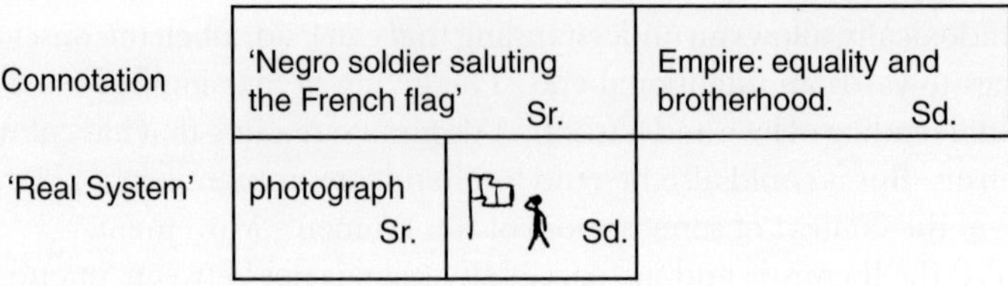

Now the first question such a model raises is the nature of the origin of the connotative signified. Where does the myth's signified, the ideological concept come from? Out on a limb like this it suggests ideology to be a corrupt appendage imposed upon the purity of the first system. As well as implying a conspiracy theory of mass manipulation, it also seems to point to the objects of the first system (the photograph of the black soldier) as being somehow pure, prior to the ideological intervention. Symptomatically, Barthes calls this first system the 'real system'. Despite the fact that Barthes carefully points out that semiology is a 'science amongst others, necessary but not sufficient', he often seems perilously close to turning objects and social instances into an ontology: '. . . semiological research centres by definition round the signification of the objects analysed: these are examined only in relation to the meaning which is theirs.'[26]

Barthes admits that other factors are excluded; so what sort of 'meaning' are we left with? We are left with a semiological meaning, a self-reflexive methodology that becomes an ontology in which the 'sign meets the sign' (J. Kristeva). The object or referent is *prematurely* defined in the closure operated by the hegemony of the linguistic model.

If we now return to Barthes's formal schematization of ideological mechanisms as set forth in the connotative model we can briefly sketch in an alternative description that hints at the complexities that the formal schematization fails to capture. Firstly, I would suggest it to be extremely naive to understand ideology as something imposed from above. Ideology has to negotiate a path through the differential social totality in order to win consensus, and it arises *within* social relationships and particular practices. For instance, whilst waiting at the barber's I am given a copy of *Paris-Match* to read. This is not a 'pure' moment, but occurs in the 'common-sense' world of everyday experiences that forms the framework for my interpretations. My perceptive and cognitive faculties, which are not neutral, but socially and culturally acquired, recognize a black soldier saluting the French flag.[27] Thus my perception of that photograph is grounded in norms of societal expectancies. Secondly, my 'reading' of it is further demarcated. It is not any photograph but the cover of *Paris-Match*; a specific practice with its own ideological configurations ('newsworthiness', captions, touching up photos etc.). It is in the space between the sedimented perceptual appropriation and the contextualized reading that the hegemonic ideology passes 'as though behind men's backs'. In the *space between* the 'common-sense' world of everyday experience (ideology in Barthes's 'real system') and the cover of *Paris-Match* (the signifier of the ideological instance that Barthes locates in the connotative signified) passes the 'truth' that is the cohesive 'cement' of hegemonic ideology.[28]

Barthes's model of ideology sets forth the space between the specific practice and the social totality but he sees the movement as a movement from pre-ideological meaning to ideological form:

> Truth to tell, what is invested in the concept is less reality than a certain knowledge of reality; in passing from meaning to form, the image loses some knowledge: the better to receive the knowledge in the concept.[29]

However, the formalism of Barthes's model means that even this skewed recognition of the ideological inscription is not really contextualized but remains an abstracted movement of terms and concepts in the 'language' of the system under consideration.

The rationale behind Barthes's de-contextualization of objects is to be found in the work of the phonologist who 'examines sounds only from the point of view of the meaning they produce without concerning himself with their articulated nature'.[30] But second order systems of signification, whether we call them myths or ideology, do not exist independently of their material socio-historical context. They are *material* signifying practices. This is not only the materiality of articulated sounds in the relay of language but also the materiality of the fluted metal of the Citroen or the wardrobe of the stripper.

Thus Barthes's conception of what constitutes the material of the first system is an idealist one. In looking for a zero-degree, non-ideological language Barthes refers to ideology as 'larcency':

> From the point of view of ethics what is disturbing in myths is precisely that its form is motivated. For if there is a health of language, it is the arbitrariness of the sign which is its grounding.[31]

But language does not consist of arbitrary signs bumping into one another but of a high degree of organization. In this organizing the signs are put into linear 'syntagms', whose meaning is produced between their systemic origins and their daily existence in the complex social totality, the locus of ideology. In other words there is no neutral language, only discursive enunciations in and through the mediating relay of language.

In this same last section of *Elements of Semiology*, Barthes goes on to deal with the formal method whereby the mechanisms of ideology and its representations are revealed. This introduces a third plane into the real system-ideology model: the plane of *metalanguage*. A metalanguage is a language that is able to talk about languages. Semiotics is a metalanguage since it is able to talk about what it signifies. The plane of metalanguage is therefore also the plane of analysis, and therefore only exists as a potentiality: 'In fact what allows the reader to consume myth innocently is that he does not see it as a semiological system but as an inductive one.'[32]

This model remains extremely mechanistic, especially in its postulation of the 'purity' of the 'real' system. Even to arrive at the 'real' system is, as was noted in the reading of *Paris-Match* at the barber's, a far more complex process, involving crucial mediations, that such a schematization as above is unable to fully account for it. Also, such a model in no way accounts for the positivity of semiotics as an analytical intervention. It is precisely as a methodology that breaks with systemic tyranny that allows it to have critical leverage upon analysing ideology. And it is precisely the question of the positivity of this extra-systemic analysis that is crucial in generating knowledges about ideological representations (myths).

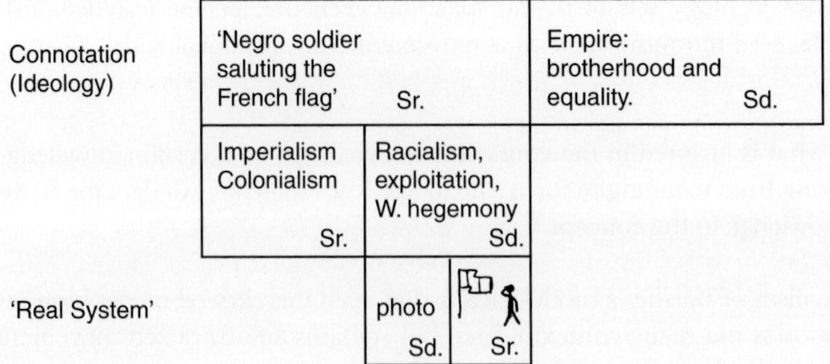

Moving now to a brief glance at some of Barthes's work in literary studies some of the implications of his more theoretical work can be further concretized. The noted collapse of the connotative sign into the decontextualized linguistic model, is a reductionism also in evidence in Barthes's literary analyses. The nature of the literary process of production is collapsed into the linguistic sign in the text. In *S/Z*, Barthes delineates five codes structuring the text. Codes, like ideas, do not drop from the skies, they arise within the material practices of production. However, Barthes reduces that production to a single moment in the process: the Text; and turns that *moment* into a self-reflexive totality divorced from its material existence. The codes become 'structurations' weaving through the 'infinite perspective of citations'. Perspectives for whom and what? A perspective, albeit unconsciously, is grounded in history, classes, in society. A perspective not so grounded leads to idealism and the reproduction of the relations of cultural capital. The implications of this 'tendency' in Barthes's work is of crucial significance for any appropriation of his work.

Barthes's conception of meaning is similiarly predicated upon such idealism: 'The pleasure of a reading guarantees its truth'. To the hegemony of traditional criticism Barthes offers the *subject* in his pleasure; the text being what I should have desired to have written, a desire expressed in the subject's inscription (re-writing) of the text; his reading. Barthes takes no account of the social context of such readings. The fact that an individual can share and enjoy such a practice only to the extent that he shares (is subjected) in the culture of domination, is completely ignored by Barthes.[33]

The 'competence' of individuals to read the 'language' of literature, to read *S/Z*, is not a social constant but is dependent upon the distribution of that 'competence' in class society. As Jacques Lacan has striven to prove, the emergence of consciousness is the entrance of the individual into language. Language is a skill not given but acquired in the educative sites of class, family, schools, work-place, sub-group etc.[34] Therefore, the 'competence' and ensuing pleasure is produced in these various social configurations. The 'truth' of a reading is not an essentialist one but is produced in the dialectical nexus between the reader's 'competence' and the text.[35] As Lacan puts it: truth is that in which the subject recognizes himself. In his attempt to understand the 'meaning' of a particular practice (literature) Barthes has failed to perceive human activity as objective. Instead, he has formally divided reality (conceived as an object) from human activity and arrived at a truncated analysis.

In order to avoid this error it is necessary to discover the nature of the practice and its conditions of existence. Specific practices exist within society, there is not a relation *between* a practice and society. It is just such a distinction that results in the fetishism of any knowledge produced in that practice, as Barthes's work clearly demonstrates.

These considerations lead to the conclusion that Barthes's work in literature does not represent an 'epistemological break' in literary theory but what Bachelard referred to as an 'intra-ideological rupture' or 're-vamping' that serves to refurbish elitism and hegemony.

Conclusion

Looking back over this essay a series of points have coalesced that can be clearly set forth. These relate both to Barthes's work and semiotics in general, although the latter would have to be demonstrated. Set out below are a series of major considerations that any genuine critical work on semiotics would have to acknowledge. Such work is of crucial importance given the seductive, but misplaced, tendency to be found in the vanguard of semiotics (J. Kristeva, U. Eco) where the semiotic programme has been 'dialecticized' in the pursuance of a formal scientism. As of yet, both in France and Britain, a critical evaluation of this work awaits to be carried out.

i Semiotics puts reality (historically defined social practices in the material world) in brackets.[36]

ii It does this by treating social life as a sign system, and *only* as a sign system, and thus reduces the heterogeneity of human existence to the systemic organization of signification: 'languages'.

iii Any analysis that divorces itself from the material conditions in which it practises, and constitutes its objects of study by a reductionist movement to formalism, can only be 'one-sided': that is it remains a systemic analysis of phenomenal forms and is therefore idealist.

iv The critical positivity of such analyses therefore remains locked within the discourse and ideological field it claims to be exposing and is thus a philosophy.

v Semiotics in delineating codes operative in the 'empire of signs', delineates corresponding systems of psychological expectancies in societal consumption. But semiotics remains a closed, self-reflexive contemplation to the degree that social 'reality' and the constitution of the subject in the multiple ideological instances of representation is treated as unproblematic.

vi Practising psychoanalysis reveals the site of individual illness in a displaced manner (the socially decontextualized 'individual') in order to re-equip the patient to return once again to full subjectivity in the 'empire of signs'. In the same manner, structuralist and semiotic practices as long as they remain one-sided only serve to re-vamp the areas and disciplines within which they locate themselves. Such practices ensure the reproduction of the relations of production in academia and the attendant fetishism of knowledge.

vii Any genuine analysis 'should start from reality and not definitions'. It must cross the ideological line of 'naturalization' to symptomatically read the 'texts' in their social existence.[37]

viii Such 'texts', established in the *moment* of formal analysis by semiotics, must be located in specific modes of production and in production in general.

ix This is not to argue for economism. The specificity of production must be respected: it has its own history. The text will not necessarily directly reflect the sociological, technological and technical determinants, which in turn are determined by a 'structure in dominance', in its specific configurations. However, such a practice does not exist in a vacuum. The socio-historical determinants will be refracted in a displaced and condensed manner through the levels and specificity of textual production: external causes become operative through internal causes.[38]

Notes

1 In *The Scope of Anthropology*, Cape 1967, we find Lévi-Strauss, the most prominent figure in structuralism, defining social anthropology in the following terms:

> No one, it seems to me, was closer to defining it – if only by virtually disregarding its existence – than Ferdinand de Saussure, when, introducing linguistics as part of a science yet to be born, he reserved the name of semiology and attributed to it as its object of study the life of signs at the heart of social life. (p. 16)

2 Walter Benjamin, *The Author as Producer*.

3 See *Working Papers in Cultural Studies 1* for Alan Shuttleworth's phenomenological approach to cultural studies and Stuart Hall's reply.

4 See Robin Rusher's article on Althusser in this issue.

5 Naturally this would have to be demonstrated. The people I have in mind here are Michel Foucault, Jacques Lacan and Christian Metz. For instance, Lacan fails to locate the psychic reality in material existence. His analyses are left suspended in the play of language and abstract exchange. As Deleuze and Guattari point out in *Capitalisme et Schizophrénie: L'Anti-Oedipe*, Seuil 1972, desire is not repressed because it is desire for the mother and hate for the father. It is the repressive domestication of sexuality that makes it take an incestuous form. Repression operates under the social codification of desire. The family exists not in a vacuum but in society. It is a functive in the means of production, an agent *not the site* of repression. It ensures the reproduction of the means of production by ensuring the reproductive forces: labour power.

6 *Capital*, vol 1, Lawrence and Wishart 1970, p. 94.

7 In *Elements of Semiology*, Barthes gives the example of Spanish-American with 100,000 significant units (words) created by 21 different phonemes (sounds).

8 See E. Ardener, *Social Anthropology and Language*, A.S.A. Monograph no.10, Tavistock 1971; and A. Wilden, *System and Structure*, Tavistock 1972, especially ch.XI: 'The Structure as Law and Order: Piaget's Genetic Structuralism'.

9 One of the most recent examples of this appeared in *Working Papers in Cultural Studies 5*, in an article by Fredric Jameson, 'The Vanishing Mediator: Narrative Structure in Max Weber'. Here a highly mediated history filters into the semantic oppositional spiral of Weber's individual psychology and leads to the postulation of the almost autonomous existence of Weber's work.

10 1960 was the inaugural lecture for the Chair of Social Anthropology, Collège de France, printed as *The Scope of Anthropology*, Cape 1967. The seminar in 1963 was organized by the French review *Esprit* and is reprinted in *NLR 62*.

11 *Mythologies*, Paladin 1973; *Elements of Semiology*, Cape 1967; *S/Z*, Seuil 1970; *Le plaisir du texte*, Seuil 1973.

12 See *Signs of the Times*, Granta 1971, for an interview with Barthes where he talks of a 'break' in his work on literary semiotics as occuring between *L'introduction à l'analyse structurale des récits* and *S/Z*.

13 *Mythologies*, p. 9.

14 See Georges Mounin, *Introduction à la sémiologie*, Minuit 1970.

15 *Elements of Semiology*, p. 10. Thus in his book on fashion, *Système de la mode*, Seuil 1967, Barthes ends up talking not about fashion but about the 'language' of fashion. See J. Kristeva, 'Le Sens et la Mode' in *Séméitokê: Recherches pour une semanalyse*, Seuil 1969.

16 But see Lévi-Strauss's work and also that of Chomsky with their concepts of 'l'esprit humain' and the 'transcendental ego' and accompanying universalist structures of the mind.

17 More recent linguistic research has suggested that a better term be 'unmotivated'.

18 *Mythologies*, p. 115.

19 *Course in General Linguistics*, McGraw-Hill 1966, p. 68.

20 *Elements of Semiology*, p. 10.

21 Within the semiological sign Barthes further distinguishes the *sign-function*. It is a sign whose origin is utilitarian and functional: food, clothing.

22 G. Leech, *Semantics*, Penguin 1974, p. 5. However, this book does contain some useful openings for beginning to deal with the extra-linguistic referent; see ch. 14.
23 This is not to suggest that language cannot be manipulated. See H. Marcuse, *An Essay on Liberation*, Pelican 1972.
24 *Courses in General Linguistics*, p. 66.
25 *Elements of Semiology*, p. 57.
26 ibid., p. 95.
27 See Umberto Eco on the nature of the iconic sign which is recognized by reproducing certain conditions of culturally learnt perception, 'Articulations of the Cinematic Code', *Cinemantics* no. 1.
28 See S. Hall, 'The Determinations of Newsphotographs' in *Working Papers in Cultural Studies 3*.
29 *Mythologies*, p. 119.
30 *Elements of Semiology*, p. 95.
31 *Mythologies*, p. 126.
32 ibid., p. 131.
33 See N. Poulantzas, *Political Power and Social Classes*, N.LB., ch. 2 'The Capitalist State and Ideologies'.
34 See L. Althusser, 'Ideology and Ideological State Apparatuses' in *Lenin, Philosophy and Other Essays*, N.LB, 1971; and P. Bourdieu 'Cultural Reproduction and Social Reproduction' in R. Brown (ed), *Knowledge, Education and Cultural Change*, Tavistock 1973.
35 This is an area that is only just beginning to be explored. See D. Hymes 'On Communicative Competence', *Sociolinguistics*, Penguin 1972, for criticisms of Chomsky's idealist conceptualization of 'competence'. Also see W. Labov, 'The Logic of Non-Standard English', *Language and Social Context*, Penguin 1972. This also introduces the debate over Bernstein's 'elaborated' and 'restricted' codes, see *Class, Codes and Control*, Paladin 1973; for criticisms of Bernstein's work see H. Rosen, *Language and Class*, Falling Wall Press. A brief survey of this field can be found in D. Holly, *Beyond Curriculum*, Paladin 1974.
36 For instance, see U. Eco's 'A Semiotic Approach to Semantics', *VS 1*, and 'Introduction to a Semiotic of Iconic Signs', *VS 2*, where he attempts to eliminate the concept of the referent from the semiotic foundation of meaning. Also see J. Kelemen, 'The Semiotic Conception of VS' in *Semiotica* 11:1, 1974.
37 Mao Tse-Tung, *Talks at the Yenan Forum on Literature and Art*, Peking Press, p. 21.
38 See Mao Tse-Tung, *On Contradiction*, in *Collected Works*, Peking Press, 1971.

The Semiotic Activity: Bibliography

Despite their age the two introductory texts remain 'Myth Today' in *Mythologies*, Paladin 1973, and *Elements of Semiology*, Cape 1967. In order to unravel the conflated and complicated presentation of semiotics in the latter book it is necessary to examine semiotics' linguistic roots, and in particular the work of Ferdinand de Saussure, *Course in General Linguistics*, McGraw-Hill 1966.

Lévi-Strauss's collection of essays in *Structural Anthropology*, Penguin 1973, is a good example of semiotics' more immediate predecessor: structuralism, in which are related linguistic and semiotic models to analysing the structure of the expressive forms of social totalities. E. Leach's *Lévi-Strauss*, Fontana 1970, is a good, brief, critical introduction to Lévi-Strauss's work. For a more recent exposition on the structuralist method by Lévi-Strauss, see the Ouverture to *The Raw and the Cooked*, Cape 1970. For further critical elucidations see F. Wahl, *Qu'est-ce que le structuralisme?*, Seuil 1968, and L. Sebag, *Marxisme et Structuralisme*, Payot 1964.

For literary semiotics, ch.1 of S. Heath's *The Nouveau Roman*, Elek 1972, provides a useful introduction to the work going on in Paris. Again, Barthes's *Writing Degree Zero*, Cape 1967, still remains the best introduction to this particular field. For a useful but uncritical exposition of Barthes's work over the last two decades see S. Heath's *Vertige du déplacement*, Fayard 1974. For those desiring a heavier immersion in literary semiotics see Heath, McCabe (eds), *Signs of the Times*, Granta 1971, for an Anglicized version of *Tel Quel*'s work in

Paris, in which are set forth some formal analytical devices after the manner of Barthes's *S/Z*. J. Kristeva's *Sémiotikê: Recherches pour une semanalyse*, Seuil 1969, is a collection of essays from *Tel Quel*, and offers probably the best example of 'dialecticized' semiotics and the formalism of 'scientific' rigour. Jean-Louis Baudry's 'Writing, Fiction, Ideology', *Afterimage*, no. 5, Spring 1974, is a brief translated essay that can serve to forewarn a prospective reader of what he has to face in engaging the work of the *Tel Quel* group.

For semiotic work in other areas probably the largest corpus of work is that which has been undertaken by film theorists. For the problems created by treating the 'language' of film as being reducible to the formalism of structural linguistics see C. Metz, *Essais sur la signification au cinéma*, Klincksieck, vol. 1 1968, vol. 2 1972. In the later *Cinema and Language*, Mouton 1974, Metz circumvents the problems of such formalism through employing a more 'open' understanding of language that draws upon the concept of codes. For further work on the semiotic analysis of the codification of the visual see Barthes's 'Rhetoric of the Image', *Working Papers in Cultural Studies 1*, and U. Eco's 'Towards a Semiotic Inquiry into the Television Message', *WPCS 3*. Also see Eco's 'Articulations of the Cinematic Code', *Cinemantics 1*.

Although there has been some critical work done on some semiotic practices, especially cinema and the work of Christian Metz, see summer and autumn issues of *Screen* 1973, critical work on semiotics in general has hardly begun. Georges Mounin's *Introduction à la semiologie*, Minuit 1970, is a critical evaluation of semiotics with essays on Barthes, Lacan and Lévi-Strauss, from a strict linguistic angle. Also, see A. Wilden, *System and Structure*, Tavistock 1972, which, despite the convoluted language of information theory and cybernetics, and its radical 'chic-ness', opens up some critical avenues.

12 Gramsci's writings on the state and hegemony, 1916–35

A critical analysis

Robert Lumley

The rise of Eurocommunism in the last few years has put the problems of a Marxist analysis and political strategy in relation to State and class hegemony at the centre of current debates. Gramsci, the first Marxist theorist to systematically attempt to distinguish the different structures of class rule in East and West, and therefore to pose the need for a revolutionary strategy specific to the Western capitalist states, has been the magnatic pole of reference for the contending analyses.

Interpretations have frequently used Gramsci as ammunition for political polemic with scant respect for his writings. In Britain this exchange, of recent origin, sees the confrontation between pro-Italian Communist Party interpreters and various Trotskyist tendencies. With the exception of Perry Anderson's contribution in *New Left Review 100*, the debate is singularly arid. There is an abyss between the really productive interpretation of Gramsci by intellectuals, especially historians, in a more strictly academic field, and his use for more direct political analysis.[1] It is a small indication of that separation between Marxist intellectuals and the working class movement that has perpetuated 'academicism', on the one hand, and 'workerism' on the other.

In Italy Gramsci has sadly suffered the same fate, only there the battle over his soul has raged for longer and has a much more tangible importance at a political level.[2] The papal succession from St. Peter is paralleled by the PCI's succession from St. Antonio, and many are the heretics, agnostics and unbelievers who contend its legitimacy or value. In the current period, Gramsci's writings are used ever more in the name of '*raison d'état*' as the PCI identifies the interests of the working class with the defence of the democratic State.

This is not the place for detailed analysis of how Gramsci has been used and interpreted since the time of the publication of the *Notebooks* in the 1950s, but it might be useful to briefly summarize the key points of contention over the questions of the State and 'Hegemony'. Firstly, in relation to the State the differences centre on whether Gramsci's analyses conceived the democratic State as a means for the achievement of socialism in the West, and hence as a structure in which the parliamentary organs could be given a new content, or whether his conception of socialism necessarily involved the destruction of the existing State and the construction of a new one on entirely different premises. Secondly differences have emerged on what Gramsci meant by the necessity for the working class to be hegemonic before taking power; and whether the concept itself is applicable only to the rule of the bourgeoisie in a capitalist society. However, needless to say, the problem is infinitely complex. In this contribution some indications are made in relation to these general political issues, though its nature is much more a reading of Gramsci than a systematic treatment of the various interpretations of his work.

The following piece on Gramsci's writings originally written as an MA dissertation in August 1976 and subsequently revised, is an attempt to trace the development of his concepts of 'Hegemony' and the State from his early writings through to the *Prison Notebooks*. These writings are grouped in 4 sections: Gramsci's early intellectual formation, the *Ordine Nuovo* articles, Gramsci on fascism and the revolutionary party, and finally the *Prison Notebooks*. This set of divisions corresponds to a periodization in relation to Gramsci's political activity – as propagandist for the Socialist Party (1916–18), the promoter of the factory councils movement (1919–20), as member and then leader of the Communist Party (1921–26), and lastly as 'full-time theoretician' in prison. In each of these periods Gramsci's writings take a different form – from a series of articles in the papers of the PSI, through '*Ordine Nuovo*' (a paper partly founded by himself), to the internal documents, letters and reports required by the PCI and the Third International (on top of articles in *Unità*), to the more theoretical and analytic *Notebooks*. However, the shifts and breaks in Gramsci's thinking do not mirror this periodization, and they are analysed in this piece as they are registered in his concepts. It should be made clear, and this is also a confession of a profound limitation, that this article is a textual reading, rather than a comprehensive historical enquiry, and is largely restricted to Gramsci's own works.

An outline of Gramsci's intellectual formation – 1916–19

Gramsci's early intellectual formation, before the *Ordine Nuovo* writings, was shaped by a strongly Italian interpretation of two mainstream European traditions – Idealism and Marxism – through the writings of Benedetto Croce and Antonio Labriola, who were the respective protagonists of these traditions. His commitment to them was not simply intellectual: the dominant theoreticians of the socialist movement, the German social democrats, had led their party into the war and the whole European working class into its deepest crisis, and this was seen by Gramsci as a sign of theoretical as well as political failure. Gramsci rebelled against a Marxism which made men the passive agencies of economic laws, and proclaimed the freedom of the will. In his famous article greeting the Bolshevik revolution, 'The revolution against "Capital"', he affirmed his faith in Idealism and refutation of the Marxism of the 2nd International:

> They [the Bolsheviks] are not 'Marxists'; they have not compiled from the works of the Masters an eternal doctrine of dogmatic assertions. They live the Marxist thought which will never die, and which is the continuation of Italian and German idealist thought, which in Marx was contaminated with positivistic and naturalist encrustations. This thinking poses always Man, and the society of men, as the chief maker of history, and not ugly economic facts.[3]

A key Crocean text for Gramsci was 'Teoria della storia della storiografia', which rejected any conception of history claiming to relate the 'facts' as objectively and scientifically validated for all time (Positivist school of history). Croce proposed that history was produced according to contemporary levels of knowledge, and that it was subjectively appropriated by each generation. The conclusion that Gramsci drew was that history was therefore no longer an external determinant but a means of understanding and emancipation. His article 'Socialismo e Cultura', published in *Grido del Popolo* in January 1916, is marked by this Crocean historicism:

> Man is above all spiritual, that is to say a historical being, and not a natural creation; and again 'to know oneself, which is to be in control of oneself, to distinguish oneself, to emerge from the chaos, to be an element of order, but of an order and discipline proper to an ideal.'[4]

It is through history that Man appropriates self-knowledge by locating himself in time and space.

As the above quotation indicates, Gramsci conceived the process of 'emancipation' in this period as an aggregate of individual actions which continually multiplied. This perspective, however, was not purely personal or Crocean; it expressed the Socialist Party's position on political propagandizing as a process of conversion of the masses (later referred to by Gramsci as 'evangelism'). In 'Socialismo e Culture' (*Il Grido del Popula*, 29 January 1916) Gramsci goes on to find forerunners to the socialists in the Enlightenment intellectuals, who through 'critical work' and 'cultural penetration', prepared the way for the French Revolution, the seizure of power itself. His own political activity 'lived' this vision of educating the masses through newspapers, meetings, educational circles and so on. Gramsci, as full-time journalist for *Avanti* (with his personal column, 'Sotto la mole') and for *Grido del Popolo*, wrote about everything under the sun in his attempt to challenge the totality of life under capitalism (a thief who stole papers from a ministry is applauded as the only real reformer of bureaucracy, and the Italian 'sport' of cardplaying is compared unfavourably to British football because it is a source of factional politics rather than two party democracy). After he got his job on *Avanti*, he argued, in a series of important articles, that 'the problem of education is the most important class problem' and that 'the first step in emancipating oneself from political and social slavery is that of freeing the mind'.

Gramsci's conception of political struggle as struggle on several fronts, cultural and social, underwent several changes as he became more critical of the PSI tradition, but the importance he attached to the problems of long-term cultural transformation remains a hallmark of his writings. This comes over clearly in an article for *Ordine Nuovo* in January 1921 entitled 'Marinetti rivoluzionario?'.[5] In it, the Futurist movement is very positively assessed by Gramsci, taking his lead from Lunacharsky on this occasion, as a relentless attack on bourgeois traditions in music, painting and even in language and everyday behaviour. He sees it as opening the breach which the working class should enter in order to develop its own autonomous culture. This is a possibility before the taking of political power, because the capitalist 'spiritual hierarchy' prejudices, idols etc., can be destroyed even though the factories must not be. The Futurists, writes Gramsci,

> had faith in themselves, in the impetuousness of youthful energies; they had a clear conception that our epoch was the epoch of big industry, of tumultuous and intense life which had to have new forms of art, philosophy, customs and language. They had this clearly revolutionary and absolutely Marxist conception, while the socialists did not think about such things.

This uncritical enthusiasm for the Futurists should certainly be treated with suspicion. Walter Benjamin in his 'Work of Art in the Age of Mechanical Reproduction' (*Illuminations*, Fontana, London 1973, p. 244) laconically points to one of the aspects of Futurism: 'This is the situation of politics (the exaltation of war), which fascism is rendering aesthetic. Communism responds by politicizing art.' The Futurist movement's Bergsonian philosophy of continuous change was far from being Marxist. It can be said that Gramsci was carried away: a young intellectual in Turin, who had just escaped the stagnant culture of rural

Sardinia, he shared some of the Futurists' infatuation with industry and technology, and their total scorn for the Italian 'character' (i.e. a nation of third rate Puccinis). Trotsky was shrewd in observing that Futurism arose in those countries that combined uneven development, both feudal modes of production and the most capital intensive, modern industry. Gramsci shared that cultural milieu with the Futurists.

The important point to make, however, is that Gramsci is here again proposing an offensive against the 'spiritual hierarchies' of the bourgeoisie prior to the seizure of power by the working class. This does not mean 'instrumentalizing' the artist and laying down norms for socialist culture, as Zhdanov was later to do, but directing artists through the very process of forming a new culture and ethics. Nor is there an idea of culture suddenly reflecting the changed relations of production of a socialist society. There is a disjuncture between the levels of economics and artistic production because works of art cannot be made to order like the commodities of a factory.

Gramsci's conception of politics as cultural propaganda and agitation, formed under the influence of Croce cannot be conflated with his idea of 'hegemony' as elaborated in the *Prison Notebooks*. Here it is more like a Hegelian notion of 'Weltanschauung'. This conception was, in effect, transformed in relation to the workers' movement in Turin in 1919–20, and in the face of Bordiga's interpretation of Marxism and political practice. As early as 1912, when he had already developed the outlines of a theory of a revolutionary party nearer to Lenin's than to the PSI, Bordiga rejected the politics of cultural messianism: 'The need for study should be proclaimed in a congress of school-teachers, not socialists. You don't become a socialist through instruction but through experiencing the real needs of the class to which you belong.'[6] Whilst Gramsci moved closer to Bordiga's idea of culture learnt through struggle, he did not accept that it arose spontaneously and only in response to particular conjunctures. In *Ordine Nuovo* and his political work from 1919, he developed a conception of cultural struggle that combined the acquisition of practical skills and of the knowledge required for the attainment of a full 'humanity'.

Ordine Nuovo *writings*

Before 1919 Gramsci had already taken a clear position of opposition to the war and hence on the class nature of the Italian State. On the outbreak of war he had condoned Mussolini's interventionism in an article in *Avanti* which his enemies subsequently used against him, but he quickly realized his mistake. It is not until his writings in *Ordine Nuovo*, however, that he really grappled with the problem of the State. The overthrow of the Italian State, itself, seemed to be on the agenda and it was vital for the PSI to develop its leadership of the working class to this end. Two approaches to the problem of state power emerged in the PSI in opposition to the PSI leadership of Serrati: that of the '*Ordine Nuovo*' group and Gramsci in Turin, and that of Bordiga and his sympathizers in Naples. They both revolved around the duality of the process of destroying the existing state and constructing the new worker's state.

Bordiga stressed the necessity of the act of destruction prior to the formation of organs of workers' self-government, whilst Gramsci pressed for the formation of workers' government at the base as part of the process of destroying the State and as the guarantee of the survival of those organs. It was through this heated debate within the PSI that the fraction, which founded the Communist Party, was formed.

Gramsci's conception of revolution centred on the duality of the process of destruction/construction and its dialectical unity. He wrote in *Ordine Nuovo* in July 1919:[7]

> The formula 'conquest of the State' must be understood in this sense – the creation of a new type of State generated by the collective experience of the working class, and its replacement of the democratic–parliamentary State.

and again a year later

> To the extent that it is possible to achieve this by the action of a party, it is necessary to create the conditions in which there will not be two revolutions, but in which the popular revolt against the bourgeois state will find organized forces capable of beginning the transformation of the national apparatus of production from an instrument of plutocratic oppression into an instrument of communist liberation.[8]

Gramsci is never in any doubt about the necessity of destroying the state apparatus as a whole, but this task tends to be displaced by the preoccupation with forming the new State. The reasons for this can be found in the 'catastrophism' theories widespread among revolutionaries during the 'biennio rosso' (1919–20), in the preoccupation with the experiences of the German and Hungarian soviets and in a theoretical approach that still contains currents of economism of the 2nd International and Hegelian conceptions of consciousness.

The revolutionary hopes of the immediate post-war years were made up of a religious belief in chiliasm, in the death-throes of the capitalist regimes. Economic slump and the international upturn in class struggle seemed to signal the presence of the objective conditions for revolution and the subjective readiness of the working class to take power. Gramsci wrote on May Day, 1919:

> Among the workers and peasants internationally is found the reborn youth of human civilization . . . bad cannot prevail . . . The world is saving itself from itself with its own energies that, in sorrow and desperation, are born with a richness of moral character and an unprecedented potentiality for sacrifice and seriousness. One society, the capitalist one, is collapsing, and a revolution, the communist one, is coming at a forced march. Death seeks to infect the living, but the triumph of life is by now as secure and certain as destiny . . . The working class is assuming its form of power which is already the revolution in action . . .[9]

The political crises of the bourgeois regimes were seen as the reflex of the crisis in production, and charges of Menschevism levelled at those who predicted further capitalist development.

> The Italian State does not function politically, because the apparatuses of industrial and agricultural production which are the substance of the political State, no longer function.[10]

This 'economism' in Gramsci's writings, the reduction of the political to the economic level, may seem surprising in view of Gramsci's battle against the determinist ideas of the 2nd International, but what in effect he is doing is turning economism into a theory justifying immediate revolutionary action.

It is most evident in *Ordine Nuovo* of 1919 where the growth of the consciousness of workers seems to be immanent in and developing through the very relations of production:

> Closely associated in the community of production workers are automatically drawn to

> express their will to power in terms of principles inherent in the relations of production and exchange. All the utopian, religious and petty bourgeois ideologies will collapse; communist psychology will rapidly and permanently be consolidated, constantly sparked by revolutionary enthusiasm, and will show the tenacious perseverance of the iron discipline of work.[11]

Gramsci visualizes a linear development of consciousness which necessarily grows in the worker who conceives himself as a producer and hence as a maker of history:

> Moving from this cell, the factory, seen as a unity and as the creative act of a determinate product, the worker rises to the understanding of always vaster units up to the level of the nation which is in its totality a gigantic apparatus of production.[12]

The consequence of this vision of the formation of consciousness was an orientation to workers which limited their political role to the point of production. The worker was fantastically idealized:

> the working class remains alone in its love of work and of the machine. Today the working class dominates production and is the boss of society . . . because it is the only heroic force of production that can infuse it with life . . .[13]

Moreover a dangerously reformist politics can insert itself within this scheme. The State's role as the organizing force of the bourgeoisie is seen as an epiphenomenon of its economic organization, and hence a seizure of the economic infrastructure will determine the collapse of the bourgeois superstructure. The working class therefore must organize itself primarily in the productive apparatus, in councils because such organization is enforced by the process of production itself. It is therefore contractual and necessary, whereas other organizations like the political party and the union are only voluntary associations.

In making these distinctions between the 'contractual' and the 'voluntary' organizations of the working class, Gramsci was taking up the analysis of the syndicalists, only replacing the union with the council. Largardelle, in 1911, spoke of the 'lien de necessité' and the 'lien de volonté'.

Implicit in this formulation was the conception of revolution as a process growing within the bourgeois regime, in which councils formed a counter-power of proletariat-producers. At its worst this led to a productivism at the service of the bourgeoisie, as part of a campaign to demoralize the bosses.

> To those who object that in this way one is collaborating with our adversaries, with the owners of the factories, we reply that instead this is the only way to make them hear in fact that the end of their domination is near, because the working class now conceives the possibility of producing by itself and of producing better; thus, it acquires every day a clearer certainty that it alone is capable of saving the whole world from ruin and desolation.[14]

Gramsci's willingness to promote innovation and technical development when production was still under the control of the bourgeoisie even when workers' sacrifices were involved stemmed from his infatuation with modernism mentioned previously. His view of the forces of production as autonomous from the relations of production, as neutral in themselves, and as simply held back from full development by the capitalist organization of society, stems from the Marxism of the 2nd International.

This conception was the commonsense of the epoch for Marxists and bourgeois theorists alike. Petri, an anarchist, who wrote articles in *Ordine Nuovo* on Taylorism in October–November 1919, shared Taylor's idea exactly, that 'techniques of work, like machines, are invariant in relation to types of society'. Except that under communism, the productivity of labour would increase because external discipline would be replaced by voluntary co-operation – 'Communism, which is at the heart of the worker, can revive the perfect mechanism constructed by Taylor, and the council is the fundamental unit in which the consciousness of the producer is formed'.[15]

The theoretical weakness of revolutionaries in this post war period is understandable given the conditions of mass poverty and unemployment when the crucial problem was to increase production. Gramsci went a long way in tackling the issue of control, and this had political effects on the development of the struggle itself – for instance, involvement of non-union workers in the voting for the factory delegates, and in *Ordine Nuovo*'s successful demand for the collectivization of piece-rates as a means of reducing divisions between workers. However, since Agnelli's (the owners of Fiat) strategy was to increase productivity via the intensification of 'relative exploitation' (Taylorisation) within the new 8 hour day, the absence of a counter-strategy precisely in relation to the comprehensive policy of de-skilling (i.e. the elimination of craft elements of workers' control) meant that there was the absence of an intermediary level between wage struggles of the union and the occupation of the factories under the councils.[16]

Criticism of this aspect of Gramsci's early writings on the factory councils, has sprung up in Italy in the wake of the Chinese cultural revolution which was widely seen on the left as re-posing the problem of the 'capitalist forces of production' as well as the relations of production. Adriano Sofri of Lotta Continua analyses Gramsci's error of understanding in this context.

> The workers at the factory are producers in as far as they co-operate; they are organized for the preparation of the product according to a method/mode exactly determined by the industrial technique, which is, in a certain measure, independent of the mode of appropriation of the values produced.[17]

He comments that this amounts to a notion of 'capitalism without the capitalists' and

> based on this conception, councils adhere organically to the factory, overcoming by the sheer fact of their existence, the limits imposed by the persistence of the class system, whilst the party and unions are excluded because they are relevant only to a class divided society.[18]

Such an analysis, Sofri maintains, led to a virtual abolition of political organization and political rupture.

Before the defeat of the council movement in April 1920, Gramsci is certainly guilty of an underestimation of the forces of the State outside the factory. He counterposed the disciplined organization of the workers in the factory to the chaotic fragmentation of the State. Whilst the entrepreneur and 'captain of industry' played a vital role in the production process of competitive capitalism, in the monopoly phase he was excluded from the factory:

> The working class has acquired the highest degree of autonomy in the field of production because the development of the industrial and commercial technique has suppressed all the useful functions inherent in property, in the person of the capitalist.[19]

Strangely enough, where Marx saw the reduction of autonomy of the worker as the production process was continually revolutionized, tending to make the worker subservient to his machine and reducing his skills, Gramsci thinks the opposite . . .

> technical innovations taken to their height by machines have changed his [the worker's] relations with the technician; the worker has less need than before of the technician, of the maestro d'arte, and has therefore acquired a greater autonomy, and can discipline himself by himself.[20]

Not only has the entrepreneur disappeared from the factory, but the technician, who was previously the disciplinarian of the capitalist, has become a producer 'connected to the capitalist by the naked and crude relations of exploited and exploiter'. Hence the technician's psychology too has lost its 'petit bourgeois incrustations' and become fully revolutionary. Meanwhile the capitalist becomes a 'mere police agent' and puts his 'rights' immediately into the hands of the State. By a sleight of hand, Gramsci then asserts that

> The state thus becomes the sole owner of the means of labour, assumes all the traditional functions of the owner, becomes the impersonal machine that buys and distributes raw materials, plans production and buys and distributes the products.[21]

The result is chaos because the State is made up of petty politicians, adventurers and good-for-nothings.

His identification of 'healthy' capitalism with its classic nineteenth century *laissez faire* form in which the entrepreneur is active in the production process means that he does not grasp the reality of capital in its increasingly abstract forms. The worker does not need the presence of the capitalist to make him work because the machine itself and related methods of payment do that job. The absence of the capitalist and the increasing domination of finance capital are therefore aspects of a higher stage of capitalist development which Gramsci can only analyse with moralism.

By effectively collapsing the domain of the State and the economy, describing not monopoly capitalism, but state monopoly capitalism, Gramsci brings the problem of politics back to the factory in itself which is now the unit of the whole of society. Conclusion: 'The factory council . . . is the solid basis of the process that must culminate in the dictatorship, in the conquest of the power of the state . . .'[22] Gramsci's thinking is here characterized by the most extreme schematism and disregard for the specific historical conjuncture.

Gramsci's comments on the nature of the State have here reached the point of meaninglessness. It was impossible for him to retain such abstract notions in the conditions of daily revolutionary struggle, and his writings reveal an intimate relationship to the political conjunctures in which they were produced. In addition greater familiarity with Lenin's work stimulated reflection. Gramsci complained about the PSI failure to introduce its membership to the Marxism of the 3rd International, and strongly recommended 'State and Revolution' to his readers (in May 1920). His own analysis of the State was indeed based on the 3rd International's characterization of the epoch as the imperialist monopoly stage of capitalism, its highest and therefore final stage of development. The form of State corresponding to this economic stage was conceived as a concentration and centralization of the repressive military and bureaucratic apparatuses. It was not a question of any particular State being highly industrialized but of the overall balance of forces in the world:

> Italy has not reached the fullness of development of capitalism in the sense that the production of goods is not intensely industrialized. But the fact that the world is subjected to a monopoly of economic exploitation and to an uncontested political and military predominance has determined that in Italy also the same rigid conditions of life exist. The Italian situation is thus peculiarly revolutionary for being backward and poor in its economic structure. Italy today can be compared to the Russia of Kerensky.[23]

Gramsci pressed this parallel between Russia and Italy in his fight against the determinist conceptions of the 2nd International which located the likelihood of revolution only in the capitalist metropolis where the economic conditions were most fully developed. These conceptions were still strong in the PSI, and also in the 3rd International itself which waited eagerly for the outbreak of revolution in Germany:

> The reformists and the whole band of opportunists, are right when they say that in Italy the objective conditions for revolution don't exist: they are right in as far as they think and speak as nationalists, in as far as they conceive of Italy as an organism which is independent of the rest of the world, and of Italian capitalism as a purely Italian phenomenon. But they don't have any idea of internationalism as a living reality in history as much for capitalism as for the proletariat.[24]

In other words, Gramsci is saying that the possibility for revolution did not exist taking Italy as a self-contained unit, but only in as far as it was part of a world capitalism in crisis.

In assimilating the Russian and Italian situations, Gramsci went overboard to the point of eliminating the points of difference. Hence the Italian parliamentary tradition, which in fact took root after the Risorgimento, and had its origins in the French revolutionary tradition, is treated as less authentic than the Russian Duma.

> The judiciary does not exist in Italy as an independent power; the repressive apparatus is not under the control of the judiciary; parliamentary power does not exist, and legislation is trickery. In reality and in terms of rights, there is only one power – that of the executive and of the propertied class that wants to be defended at all costs.[25]

Since the reformists in the PSI based their strategy on an Italian road to socialism via parliament, Gramsci went to extremes in his polemics against their 'nationalism' and in one article in *Ordine Nuovo*, proposed that the Italian State itself was 'dead' and was merely a 'sphere of influence, a monopoly in the hands of foreigners'.

> The whole world is a trust in the hands of a few dozen Anglo-Saxon bankers, shopowners and industrialists. The conditions for international communism are totally realized.[26]

Gramsci was not one to go half-way in his arguments.

For all this abstract internationalism, Gramsci was sensitive to the peculiarities of the Italian situation. He had an intimate knowledge of the comings and goings of the politicians and the class fractions they represented in their politicking.

Whilst international capital appeared to be all-embracing and unified, the nation-state was threatened by fragmentation. Whilst the government in Rome represented servitude to the international capital, the bourgeoisie was split so that 'each act of bourgeois indiscipline . . . of "reactionary" insurrection against the actual government finds adherents'.[27]

According to Gramsci, Giolitti was the 'only individual capable of taking up the interests and aspirations of the entire property-owning class', and his success depended on the special conditions that the war had destroyed. His method of government was based on the extra-parliamentary organizations of the bourgeoisie, 'the system of subterranean forces that really dominate the country outside and against parliament' – the banks, Freemasonry, the '*stato maggiore*', the church hierarchy, the Neapolitan '*camorra*', the *Confederazione Generale del Lavoro* – and operated through agreements with the hierarchy of the workers' movement. The economic crisis removed the basis of the labour aristocracy which formed the linch-pin of Giolitti's system. Gramsci concluded that reformism no longer had any basis for existence and hence the crisis which divided the ruling classes would unite the working class. Again Gramsci's analysis was formal and deterministic – reformism was reduced to a mere epiphenomenon emitting from material benefits; but in this he shared the company of the 3rd International leadership, which later judged this analysis to be ultra-left and proposed the 'united front' strategy of a return to mass work as a means of combating reformism as an organized form of ideology that was widely accepted in the European working class.

Gramsci pointed to the role of the State in articulating this reform only in a contemptuous passing comment –

> the multiplicity of States constituted by all the capitalist factories are united in the bourgeois State, which maintains discipline and obedience from the have-nots, giving them the fiction of power and calling upon the people every 5 or 7 years to nominate deputies for Parliament.[28]

This fiction, he claimed, had been destroyed by the factory councils.

References in Gramsci's writings on the State in the 1919–20 period frequently speak of its dissolution, and the moral and political bankruptcy of the bourgeois class. The class which founded the Italian State for the purposes of forming a united market is portrayed as destroying that unity in the pursuit of egotistic gain. Articles regularly conclude on a fanfare to the proletariat's national mission. 'Only the working class, the proletarian disctatorship, can today arrest the process of dissolution of national unity . . .' This triumphalism certainly did not arm the workers mentally for what turned into a disastrous defeat for the Turin working class at the hands of the army. However, Gramsci was alive to two crucial developments in the Italian State: the organization of 'reaction' outside of the formal democratic apparatuses, and the deepening of the economic, social and political division between North and South.

In an article in *Avanti* in October 1920, in the wake of the defeat of the Turin occupations, Gramsci pointed to the danger of 'La Reazione'. He did not locate the threat in any class or fraction, but rather in the 'nature' of the system of private property. Yet this 'reaction' is seen by him not only to be aided and abetted by the State, but to contain the possibility for a *coup d'état*.: 'In the present period, terrorism wants to pass from the private to the public arena. No longer satisfied with the impunity granted by the State, it wants to become the State.'[29]

Whereas previously Gramsci assumed the inevitability of revolution in the proximate future, the change in the balance of class forces made him pose the alternatives – revolution, or the barbarism of national war and repression. The specific features of the fascist movement were barely discernible at this stage, but he was the first to see them, and it is extraordinary that he should already have understood it as a force that aimed at state power.

The other of Gramsci's major insights into the Italian State came in his analysis of the relationship of the South and North. The Northern bourgeoisie, in his eyes, had organized the systematic exploitation of the peasants of the South by making an alliance with the Southern middle class, who were thereby able to maintain their position of feudal domination vis-à-vis the peasantry. The South was a colony in relation to Northern capital.[30] Already before the formation of the PCI, Gramsci and the '*Ordine Nuovo*' group insisted on the need for a worker-peasant alliance to combat the oppressive bloc, whereas the Bordigists were preoccupied with establishing a purely proletarian party, and the PSI largely ignored the peasantry.[31] Gramsci's analysis of the bourgeois State, and specifically the Italian State, was narrowly confined to its repressive aspect, for all his insights. In contrast to this, his conception of the formation of the workers' State concentrated, not on its task of smashing the State, but on the necessity of erecting a proletarian hegemony. Some of the shortcomings of his approach have already been pointed out but justice must be done to the originality of his contribution.

What the theory and practice of the councils movement did was challenge the central tenet of the politics of the 2nd International – the division between economic and political activity. This tradition continued in the PSI, for all its adherence to the 3rd International, and during the factory occupations of Turin it was ratified in a pact between the CGL and PSI. For Gramsci, the factory was not simply a unit of production and hence the region for limited economic struggle, for trade unionism, but also a structure that undertook the reproduction of the social conditions of production, where a set of ideological and political relations of domination and subordination were active as in the 'superstructure'.

If Gramsci misconceived the relation between the factory and the State by tending to reduce the latter to the former in his early writings, he had made the vital advance of understanding the factory in itself as a form of government that had to be totally transformed along with the State. In the chapter in Marx's *Capital*, 'Machinery and Modern Industry', there are numerous passages on the operation of discipline and control in the production process. For example, he writes that in factory regulations 'capital formulates, like a private legislator, and at his own good will, his autocracy over his workpeople';[32] and it is this understanding of the factory that Gramsci grasps. He likens the forms of organization of army and factory:

> In the capitalist army there is the same form of organization as in the capitalist factory, where the property-owning class . . . has the function of despotic rule, where the proletariat is the passive mass of infantrymen, and where the petit bourgeoisie has the role of subaltern command.[33]

The capitalist's authoritarian regime is necessary in the factory because it is the point at which the workers potentially have the most power. In the process of increasing exploitation the capitalist organizes, disciplines and unites a great mass of workers. What Gramsci proposes for the foundation of the socialist State is to make the factory the centre of social and political, as well as economic life, and thereby to destroy capitalist relations of production at their roots. He envisages the construction of a new order that recomposes society in the single unity of the citizen-producer, and that opens the way for the realization of man's creative potentialities. In this vision he was close in spirit to Marx who above all saw human liberation in the act of unalienated work. The image of unity of the single producer is the very antithesis of the worker under capitalism, who is a slave at work and yet, as a citizen, is formally equal to his capitalist neighbour.

However, Gramsci breaks with the old socialist concept of politics that combined an everyday economic realism based on a minimal programme with the vision of a promised land of equality and plenty. He stresses the necessity for the acquisition of 'practical' and 'critical' skills by the working class that will enable it to think as a ruling class.[34] The capacity of the working class to take power is, therefore, not political in the narrow sense, but involves extensive cultural preparation that starts from a detailed understanding of the production process itself. When Gramsci writes that the 'conquest of social power' can only be conceived as 'the dialectical process in which political power makes possible industrial power and vice versa'[35] he intends it in this sense. Gramsci noted himself in 1926, that the 'Turin communists had concretely posed the question of proletarian hegemony, that is the social base of the dictatorship of the proletariat and the workers' State'. The notion of 'hegemony' as inclusive of a whole cultural dimension of class struggle that is elaborated in the *Notebooks* was already present in the *Ordine Nuovo* writings in relation to the tasks of the worker's vanguard. Just as it is necessary to trace back Gramsci's conception of hegemony to his formulations on the factory council, it is equally true that his ideas on 'corporate' or 'hegemonized' consciousness need to be related to his analyses of trade unions. In a certain sense, in 1919–20 Gramsci identifies the unions as the major obstacle to revolution. The power of the ruling class in terms of the State is reduced to a technical problem of physical force. It is an external constraint. The unions, on the other hand, provide the critical bridge between the interests of labour and capital. The unions are a constituent part of the capitalist system because they are based on the logic of the market; they represent workers as the sellers of labour power not as the 'producers of wealth'. Whatever its political colouring the union is objectively subordinate to capital in that its very existence is predicated on the wage relationship that is also bound into the legal system. Moreover, the union mediates workers' interests through its structures. The bureaucracy's very *raison d'être* is based on making agreements, and the officials have an interest in the steady, regular functioning of negotiations which makes them the upholders of industrial legality. All those characteristics that Gramsci identifies in the union makes it the bulwark of the system and the negation of proletarian hegemony to which the councils aspire. When Tasca proposed to base the councils on the union structures, Gramsci savaged him in the following polemic:[36]

> With the gloss of revolutionary and communist phraseology, he has come to the aid of the opportunists and reformists who have always tried to emasculate the factory council, which has tended to carry the class struggle beyond the terrain of industrial legality, by calling for bureaucratic 'discipline', that is, acting as the guardians of an industrial legality that means the codification in the factory of the relations of exploiter and exploited.[37]

However, history was on Tasca's side. The councils vanished and the unions survived. The councils were the first victims of the defeat of 1920. If the unions themselves played an important role in undermining them first by refusing to generalize the workers' struggles beyond Turin and by sabotaging council initiatives, the army did the rest. The councils also disappeared from Gramsci's writings. In his article entitled 'The Communist Party', published in September, the party assumes in full the function of realizing class autonomy.

> This is the miracle of the worker who daily conquers his own spiritual autonomy and his own liberty to build in the realm of ideas, struggling against the weariness, the boredom, the physical monotony which tends to mechanize and even kill his inner life, this miracle organizes itself in the communist party.[38]

This disappearance of the councils that followed a series of workers' defeats internationally was registered in the reinforcement of 'centralist' elements in communist organization and political theory. Gramsci's own development towards a party-centred view of revolutionary strategy and organization was common to a whole second generation of revolutionaries. Whereas Lenin revised his rigid conception of the party and class consciousness of 'What is to be done' under the impact of the 1905 experience, his successors increasingly relegated the significance of the soviets and factory councils. In Gramsci's case the council remained as a political proposal in an emasculated form. Rethinking the Turin experience led him to conceive a more complex idea of the party in relation to the class rather than to a reconsideration of the specific role of the council and the various relations of the organs of class struggle. Objectively the conditions for the creation of councils and soviets did not exist in Italy in the 1920s and 1930s, but the failure to keep alive this vital aspect of the first wave of communist struggles was a serious one that was not recuperated until 1968. Stefano Merli polemically takes Gramsci to task for his responsibility in this respect:

> Of the experience of the factory councils he remembers and values the rank and file only as the mass base of the party and not the concept of the council-soviet . . . The institutions of Gramscian politics . . . had only to fulfil the function of the mass base for the slogans of the Anti-parliament and the Constituent Assembly, that is, the means for pressing for legalistic ends, elements of a political game that had their objectives outside and distinct from working class autonomy.[39]

When Gramsci refers to the factory council experience in the *Notebooks*, it is in connection with the problem of 'spontaneity' and 'leadership' and the need for the party to establish a correct relation between the two.

Writings on fascism and the communist party

In the period of the 'biennio rosso' Gramsci was more preoccupied with the nature and formation of the workers' State than that of the bourgeois one. The defeats of the Italian proletariat, and of the soviets in Germany and Hungary, changed his perspective. Problems which Gramsci began to look at in the summer of 1920 – the relationships of the working class and the party, of fascism to the State and the Southern peasantry to the Northern workers – were to figure centrally in his writings as a member of the PCI. His treatment of them differed not only from Bordigas, but from the dominant theses of the 3rd International after Lenin's death. The key concepts, like 'hegemony', and analyses of the specific national/social formation are outlined, prefiguring their elaboration in the *Prison Notebooks*.

Gramsci's achievement as a theoretician of the communist movement cannot be fully grasped unless it is understood as a continuous contestation with the Marxism of the 2nd International. Lenin had fought a similar battle, but Gramsci was to fight it within the 3rd International itself, and nowhere was this more urgent than in relation to fascism.

Analyses of fascism began in the 3rd International with its IV congress, in the light of theories of capitalist collapse, which reduced the conjunctures of class conflict to epiphenomena of the 'economic' crisis. Theories of the crisis turned what Marx understood as 'tendencies' into laws: hence the fall in the rate of profit was seen as irreversible, rather than a tendency that was subject to counter-tendencies, such as an increase in the rate of exploitation. There was therefore no comprehension of the way politics could act back on the 'economic', how the relations of production could be re-constructed by a 'revolution' within regime of the factory (Fordism) or by the state 'nationalizing' the workforce to sell to the capitalists (fascism). The operation of this law was within the overarching contradiction that developed between the forces of and relations to production. At the IV congress of the International the 'Resolution on Tactics' contained this statement: '. . . Capitalism, having accomplished its mission of developing the productive forces, has fallen into contradiction with the needs of historical evolution . . . The collapse of capitalism is inevitable'.[40]

And when the 3rd International revised its analysis to account for an intermediate periodization of the crisis it was in the notion of 'stabilization', understood in a limited economic sense; this was the case at the IV congress.

This deterministic analysis of the crisis of capitalism entailed a series of erroneous analyses of fascism. Fascism was initially underestimated cf. the Rome theses of 1922 which referred to it as 'in reality, a result of the ineluctable development of the capitalist regime', and then by Bordiga at the V congress, as simply 'a change of the government personnel of the bourgeoisie'.[41]

Poulantzas proposes that the 3rd International's analyses stemmed from a linear/evolutionist conception of history which prevented it from understanding conjunctures and hence 'periodizing', except in terms of stages. The variant theses on fascism as the phenomenon generated by the big landowners in 'backward' countries, and fascism as the 'last card' of 'advanced' monopoly capital both derive from this conception.

In the PCI, the first thesis, launched by Zinoviev at the IV congress, was initially adopted by Gramsci, whilst the latter thesis, which subsequently dominated the Comintern, was held by Bordiga and the majority of the PCI. However, the inadequacy of both positions lay in their failure to grasp the specific and mobile set of relations between the two fundamental classes, their class fractions and the intermediate strata as a contradictory unity. The fascist State was seen as the 'instrument' of monopoly capital, and only in its restricted function as an arm of violent repression (Bordiga assimilated this violent aspect of fascism to the 'white guards' of earlier years in Russia and Germany).

Gramsci's writings on fascism sometimes show affinities with the dominant interpretations of the 3rd International. From the founding of the PCI he did not disagree with Bordiga until late 1923.[42] In April 1921 Gramsci wrote in *Rassegna Communista*

> If the bourgeoisie goes to the limits and through the white reaction destroys social democracy, it will be preparing . . . the best conditions of its rapid defeat by the revolution . . . perhaps when the fascist gladiator will have just felled his adversary, his patron, the bourgeois State, will stop the delivery of the *coup de grace* with a nod, and extend a hand to the fallen . . .

Spriano calls this the classic formulation of the theory of fascism: fascism as the inevitable prelude to revolution and as the mere instrument in the hands of the bourgeoisie. Again in a letter to Zino Zini from Vienna in April 1924 – 'Fascism has truly created a permanently revolutionary situation as Tsarism did in Russia'.

If this is a crude and early example of Gramsci's 'determinism', it is also found in his analyses of fascism after the Matteotti affair when he was leader of the PCI. In his

'Examination of the Italian Situation'[43] given to the Central Committee in early August 1926, Gramsci suggests that another economic crisis is more than likely to bring a democratic republican coalition to power. Given that the Matteotti crisis had put Mussolini on the spot, Gramsci's analysis is understandable. However, his examination refers to the contradictions developing in the Farinacci wing of fascism between the petty bourgeoisie and the agrarian/industrial bloc purely in economic terms, and tends to assume that the political developments will be a reflex of this. Hence Gramsci foresees either an immediate passage to the dictatorship of the proletariat, or, more likely, a democratic phase, and not the possibility of the strengthening of the State through an intensified ideological and political offensive on the part of monopoly capital.

In conditions of massive repression revolutionary militants tended towards what Gramsci spoke of as the religious appropriation of Marxism, and Gramsci himself was not immune to that belief that history was on the side of the revolution. (He wrote later in the *Prison Notebooks*: 'When you don't have the initiative in the struggle, and the struggle itself becomes identified with a series of defeats, mechanical determinism becomes a tremendous force of moral resistance'.) However Gramsci did not get into a rut, unlike Bordiga who clung to his original thesis that fascism represented a simple continuity with previous bourgeois governments. At the Congress of Lyons Bordiga maintained:

> . . . in Fascism and in today's general bourgeois counter-offensive we don't see a break in the politics of the Italian State, but the natural continuation of a method that was applied before and after the war – that of 'democracy'. We don't believe in the antithesis between democracy and fascism any more than we have believed in the antithesis between democracy and militarism.

Gramsci contested this reductionist view with a mind to the dialectical relation of theory and practice and to future political strategy: he replied that fascism imposed a situation in which the Party had to organize itself, whereas democracy allowed the Party to organize the masses for insurrection.

Gramsci's analyses of fascism developed in relation to the movement itself. His caricature of it as the revelation of the 'cruelty and absence of human feeling of the Italian people'[44] in April 1921 was a polemical response which saw only mindless violence. By the summer he pointed to two fascisms in an article with that title – an urban fascism based on the petty bourgeoisie and ex-combatants with a parliamentary leadership, and a rural fascism consisting of the armed gangs of the latifundists.[45] The parallel he drew was with the Kapp putsch and the Hungarian reaction, respectively the movements of ex-soldiers and the peasantry.[46] It was his idea of the dominance of the rural interests that brought him close to Zinoviev's analyses, but by 1926 Gramsci gave equal weight to industrial capital. What emerges from all these analyses is that for Gramsci fascism could not be understood as bearing a one-to-one relationship with a class or with the State. As a movement it had formed autonomously from the State, and its activists were not agents of monopoly capital, but petty bourgeois elements who pressed for their own specific interests, whilst objectively creating the conditions for the expansion of big capital by subjugating the working class.[47] Gramsci recognized the special importance of the petty bourgeoisie in fascism without falling into the social democratic theories which made it the 'third class'. The characteristic fact of fascism consists of having succeeded in constituting a mass organization of the petty bourgeoisie. 'The originality of fascism consists in having found the form of organization adequate for a social class that has always been incapable of having a framework and military ideology – this form is the militia'.[48] Gramsci mocks the ideology that the petty bourgeois did have as a farcical version of French romanticism.[49]

Once installed in power, wrote Gramsci, fascism 'actuates the programme of the plutocracy' and the contradictions within the regime are progressively heightened.[50]

Although Gramsci differentiated fascism from previous programmes of conservatism because of its 'diverse mode of conceiving the process of the unification of reactionary forces' through the formation of 'organic unity of all the forces of the bourgeoisie' which organized the party, government and State as a single centralized unit in the place of 'tactical agreements and compromises', all too little is said in his writings about the coherence of the forces in operation. Gramsci tended to refer to the State as about to collapse because of internal economic contradictions, and the forces of the working class and the peasantry about to combine because of the hegemonic politics of the PCI. The State and hegemony are thought separately. It is not until the *Prison Notebooks* that the two are thought together as integral to the relation of the two classes and their class fractions.

Whilst an implicit notion of the conquest of 'hegemony' appears in the *Ordine Nuovo* writings as realizable through the councils, subsequently its realization was assigned to the political party (initially the 'reformed' PSI and then the PCI). This change was not purely organizational. It represented a reassessment of the whole experience of the Russian revolution which was formalized in the 21 conditions of membership to the 3rd International in 1921; it also represented Gramsci's initial subordination to Bordiga's particular interpretation of the Bolshevik model. But the problem of winning hegemony was compounded, not resolved, by the founding of the politics of the PCI. The winning over of the maximalists was postponed for several years and the politics of the PCI were based on continuous differentiation from the left of the PSI, who were regarded by Bordiga as greater enemies than the fascists.[51] When Gramsci began to organize an alternative leadership within the PCI it was on the basis of Lenin's united front tactic which the PCI under Bordiga had continually opposed. It was from the conceptions behind the united front tactic that Gramsci later developed his concept of hegemony. In the *Prison Notebooks* Gramsci acknowledges his debt: 'it is here (in the "theoretical-practical principle of hegemony") that Ilich's greatest theoretical contribution to the philosophy of praxis should be sought'.[52]

Underlying Gramsci's adoption of the 'united front' was Lenin's understanding of the non-reflexive relationship of the economic and ideological levels, and hence the need for long-term work by revolutionaries in winning away the masses from social-democracy. Gramsci accused Bordiga of making a false distinction between the Russian and European situations: 'in these latter countries the historical mechanism functions according to all the Marxist rules, whereas the determinism is lacking in Russia, and hence the pressing task must be to organize a party in itself and for itself', and proposed an alternative analysis. In this he wrote that the development of capitalism in the West had enabled the formation of a labour aristocracy, TU bureaucracy and social democratic parties that had never really occurred in Russia, and that the tactic of the united front was a crucial way of breaking the hold of reformism.[53]

Moreover Gramsci held to Lenin's conception of the united front as combining economic and political struggles under the command of politics. The Comintern broke from this conception by returning to the same organizational structures as social democracy – that is to the party (the political organization) and the TU (the economic organization of the masses) – and attempting to give the party a 'mass base' through the unions (i.e. 'mass work' = economic) either via party fractions or, post 1928, via Red Unions[54] Bordiga also adhered to this radical distinction between the fields of political and economic intervention, as he had done during the 'biennio rosso'; and the PCI consequently refused to participate in the formation of the Arditi del Popolo,[55] the only viable means of counter-attack, which was formed by ex-combatants of the Left. He rejected participation in any military organization that was not controlled by the PCI. The one aspect of the united front that Bordiga was prepared to accept was in economic struggles where Party members worked with the rank and file members of the PSI, but his conception of that work was limited to the economic, to trade union activity.

Gramsci's own leadership of the Party, although based on the united front tactic, showed some confusion. At the height of the Matteotti crisis, the PCI programme for common action with the parties of the Aventine opposition contained a call for the formation of a constituent assembly based on committees of workers and peasants. As Trotsky pointed out at the time, this implied the subordination of workers' organizations to a bourgeois institution on the fall of the fascist regime, instead of the autonomous organization of the working class through its own organs. However his strategy as leader of the PCI is certainly not assimilable to the 'Popular Fronts' of the 1930s when alliances with bourgeois democratic parties prevented the development of an autonomous revolutionary politics that worked for hegemony over the anti-fascist movement. He opposed working with the Liberal Party in an article in *Unità* in October 1926 on the grounds that class struggle should not deviate from the struggle against capitalism in order to purge Italian society of its 'secondary' contradictions, its 'vecchiumi'.[56]

The problem of the relationship between the working class and the poor peasantry was crucial to Gramsci's thinking on the united front, and in his essay 'On the Southern Question' of 1926 he goes into a discussion of the formation of intellectuals and the dissemination of ideology among these classes. The outline of Gramsci's future elaboration of the concept of hegemony as the class rising out of its sectional and corporate consciousness to lead the peasant masses is visible.[57] The essay challenges the adequacy of the term 'alliance' to account for the hierarchy of relations between classes; because of its everyday use as the joining of material interests (in the 'dirty Jewish' sense), and stresses the power of ideology in cementing the social system. It is here that Gramsci introduces the 'intellectual'[58] as the creator and reproducer of ideologies. Prior to this, Gramsci had thought of the problem of 'intellectuals' in a prescriptive way, in *Ordine Nuovo* and then in the PCI education programme;[59] and he was concerned to create a nucleus of workers with the skills of a ruling class. Now, Gramsci retains this prescription, but goes on to develop a concept of the intellectual in the whole field of class relations with extensive and perceptive reference to the intellectuals of different strata and classes. Gramsci then posed a strategy for the Party that aimed not only at winning the leadership of the peasantry, but of the intellectuals that helped keep it in subjection;

> [The Party] will succeed to a more or less large extent in this obligatory task [of destroying the agrarian bloc] according to its capacity to break up the intellectual bloc which forms the flexible but resistant armour of the agrarian bloc.[60]

Unfortunately Gramsci never completed this piece of writing; nevertheless it marks a shift in his thinking towards a reassessment of the problem of ideologies.

Not only did the poor peasantry preoccupy Gramsci's thinking because of its seeming impenetrability to a new ideology, reinforced by its incapability of producing its own 'intellectuals'. In the *Notebooks* Gramsci begins to tackle this problem in his analyses of commonsense which use material largely relating to the rural world.

State and hegemony in the *Prison Notebooks*

It is quite right to point out, as John Merrington does, that the *Prison Notebooks* should not be divided from Gramsci's earlier writings because he conceived of them as a continued engagement with problems of revolutionary practice.[61] This is perhaps manifested in the 'note form', indicating Gramsci's predominantly journalistic conciseness, and his love of polemical encounters with even the most bankrupt fascist reviews and mindless anthologies of 'folklorists'.

In the *Notebooks* Gramsci reconsiders the problems that faced him as a militant and leader of the PCd'I in the 1920s, but from the lonely vantage-point of defeat and isolation. He had now to explain the durability of bourgeois regimes that survived the economic crises that he had previously predicted would rupture the internal unity of the ruling bloc and destroy the material bases of reformism. The bourgeoisie had shown a remarkable ability to mobilise rapidly and reconsolidate their rule through the State structure, whilst the workers' movement vainly tried to emulate the October revolution in very different conditions. Through a series of discourses on the Italian historical experience and on the political theories of Machiavelli and Croce, Gramsci obliquely addressed himself anew to the debates of the Comintern.

The concept of the State as a military and bureaucratic apparatus, which he had shared with the other leaders of the 3rd International from Lenin to Stalin, was no longer sufficient to explain the continuity of bourgeois governments either in fascist Italy or in the liberal democracies. The concept of 'hegemony' was produced by Gramsci precisely to analyse this problem. It is not new to his own writings; it is implicit in his *Ordine Nuovo* writings and in a more developed form in his article on the 'Southern Question', and, as Anderson amply demonstrates, 'hegemony' was a key term in the theories of the revolutionary movement in Russia from the 1890s and in the 3rd International.[62] But in the *Notebooks*, Gramsci formulates 'hegemony' with bourgeois rule as its specific object, and, moreover, that rule understood in the broadest sense of cultural and ideological rather than narrowly political sense.

The most significant continuity in Gramsci's application of hegemony is in relation to the creation of workers' power. The idea of the factory council as the 'school' for the training of the workers as the new ruling class is taken on by the revolutionary party, and the 'united front' theory of the 1920s, reappears in the *Notebooks* in the form of the Jacobin alliance of bourgeoisie and peasantry.

The interpretation of hegemony as working class dominance in civil society as the precondition to the 'seizure of power' (hegemony itself being the real seizure of power) has been a major source of reformist readings of Gramsci. Nowhere has this been more the case than inside the PCI. Luciano Gruppi, representative of the mainstream of the party, interprets hegemony in the sense of the transformation of the State apparatus through parliament. According to him, Gramsci 'enriches the Leninist concept of the State inasfar as the State is no longer considered only as a machine to be destroyed', and without this concept 'the Italian road to socialism would be inexplicable . . . In fact the whole strategy and tactics of alliance would collapse.'[63]

The space for this reformist reading of Gramsci is found in the texts. Gramsci tends to prescribe bourgeois models of hegemony for the working class. The Reformation and the Enlightenment are posited as classic examples of totalizing intellectual and cultural movements that destroyed the dominant value systems of the old ruling class from within. They are paradigms of bourgeois achievement that the Italian bourgeoisie hopelessly fell short of, and of which only Marxism is capable of paralleling. Such a model, however, leads to a false analogy that is essentially idealist because the working class is deprived of economic power in the capitalist system, unlike the bourgeoisie within feudal society, and hence is incapable of imposing its hegemony. Even after the seizure of political power, the hegemony of bourgeois ideology lives on and has to be systematically rooted out through a revolutionization of the culture itself.

Poulantzas counterposes the positions of Gramsci and Lenin on the question of hegemony:

> Lenin stressed the necessity for the autonomous ideological organization of the working class, but only as one of the aspects of its political organization. 1) ideological organization has nothing to do with the proletariat's conquest of ideological domination before the taking of power, and 2) ideological organization is even systematically conceived as being directed against the dominant ideology: even after the conquest of power this dominant ideology continues for a long time to remain bourgeois and petty bourgeois.[64]

However, the concept of hegemony in the *Notebooks* is used primarily to explain the ways in which the ruling bloc maintains its power. The concept of hegemony enables Gramsci to re-think the capitalist State in terms which break not only from many of his earlier formulations, but those of the 3rd International and of Lenin himself. These formulations centred on the State apparatuses of domination and repression, and tended to reduce the State to being an instrument in the hands of the bourgeoisie. For Gramsci this model only held for ancient and medieval forms of government which comprised a mechanical bloc, whilst 'the modern State substitutes for the mechanical bloc of social groups their subordination to the active hegemony of the directive and dominant group'.[65]

In the modern State the ruling classes exercise power through the combination of hegemony and dominance, and a typology of regimes can be constructed according to the relative use of hegemony or repression in the maintenance of power.

Hegemony, however, cannot now be equated with ideology, and with the propagation of ideas, as was the case in his essay 'Socialism and Culture'. Gramsci in the *Notebooks* includes the economic in the process of hegemonizing.

> Undoubtedly the fact of hegemony presupposes . . . that the leading group should make sacrifices of an economic-corporate kind. But there is also no doubt that such sacrifices and such a compromise cannot touch the essential; for though hegemony is ethical-political, it must also be economic, must necessarily be based on the decisive function exercised by the leading group in the decisive nucleus of economic activity.[66]

Hegemony is precisely articulated through a combination of relations, economic, political and ideological, but it is characterized by the subordination of economic interests both on the part of the exploiters and the exploited. The hegemony of a class is maintained through constraining the dominated classes to sectional and corporate forms of consciousness based on immediate economic interests.[67] At the same time these forms of consciousness are not, therefore, purely illusory: they relate to a material relationship between the classes. But, of course, hegemony is exercised by the ruling bloc in accordance with 'the essential', that is the reproduction and expansion of the capitalist mode of production. The ideological component of hegemony is understood by Gramsci in an exacter sense than 'world views' or 'systems of thought'. 'Systems of thought' structure the ideological domain, but they do so in a problematic relation both to the economic, which, following Engels, he sees as determinant only in the last instance, and to the level of ideologies where 'men become conscious of conflicts in the world of the economy'.[68] Consciousness is not a simple reflex of the economic, for 'popular beliefs' and similar ideas are themselves 'material forces', and moreover, consciousness is by no means uniform. Gramsci accepts that the 'systems of thought' of the dominant class act on the subordinate class, but this is far from a process of saturation or monolithic control.[69] Rather hegemonic ideas set external limits to the bounds of popular thinking without controlling its internal elaborations – '. . . limits the original thought of the popular masses in a negative direction, without having the positive effect of a vital ferment of interior transformation of what the masses think in an embryonic and chaotic form about the world'.

Hegemony is nonetheless exercised because popular thought is restricted to forms that are equivalent to sectional and corporate consciousness in the economic field, in that they are partial and parochial. But whereas, sectional and corporate consciousness can be understood as representations of lived experience, as 'men's real relation to their conditions of existence in the form of an imaginary relation'[70] many forms of popular consciousness (and here Gramsci is thinking particularly of folklore) include sedimentations of 'prejudices from all past phases of history at the local level'. This peculiar form of ideology is more like an imaginary relation to an imaginary world of the past; it is 'fossilized and anachronistic'.[71]

Gramsci conceives of ideologies not as ideas interacting autonomously, nor as simple expressions of social classes, but as organized and reproduced by various agencies and institutions, with varying degrees of relative autonomy from the classes; his premise for this is that 'every man is a philosopher'; even in Fordized factories the worker cannot be reduced to a 'gorilla' whatever the phantasies of Frederick Taylor. However, Gramsci rejects out of hand the classical economists' idea of individuality and freedom of thought:

> In acquiring one's conception of the world one always belongs to a particular grouping which is that of all social elements which share the same mode of thinking and acting. We are all conformists of some conformism or other.[72]

What interests him is the process of organization and dissemination of ideas, and how precisely ideas become material forces. The cellular concepts Gramsci introduces to analyse these movements of ideologies are the 'traditional' and 'organic intellectual', which he relates to the organizations of the party, church, State and so on.

The two types of intellectual are well defined by Gramsci's English translators –

> In the first place there are the 'traditional' professional intellectuals, literary, scientific and so on, whose position in the interests of society has a certain inter-class aura about it but derives ultimately from past and present class relations and conceals an attachment to various historical class formations. Secondly, there are the 'organic' intellectuals, the thinking and organizing element of a particular fundamental social class. These are distinguished less by their profession, which may be any activity characteristic of their class, than by their function in directing the ideas and aspirations of the class to which they organically belong.[73]

Out of the *Prison Notebooks* it is possible to construct sets of relations between groupings of 'traditional' or 'organic' intellectuals and the classes of society. Gramsci writes specifically of the idealist philosophers, the Catholic Church, the revolutionary party, and the State, and their role in the maintenance of creation of hegemony over the classes.

On idealist philosophers Gramsci's formulations are somewhat contradictory; he describes Benedetto Croce as 'a kind of lay pope and an extremely efficient instrument of hegemony, even if at times he may find himself in disagreement with one government or another'.[74]

Yet elsewhere he says the ideas of Croce have probably never been heard of by the mass of the population, let alone understood by it,[75] and that this failure to create a national-popular ideology is characteristic of Italian bourgeoisie from the Renaissance onwards. Perhaps this disparity can be resolved by proposing that the hegemony of Croce was in relation to the other philosophies current among the class fractions of the ruling bloc, but Gramsci does not do so. The important point is that idealistic philosophy is propagated by 'traditional' intellectuals who sustain the illusion that ideas are completely autonomous from class practices, and that both its strength and extreme limitations flow from this conception.

More interesting is Gramsci's analysis of the ideological functioning of the Catholic Church. The church is a sort of collective 'traditional' intellectual, and yet it exercises a hegemony over the masses. It does this not because of its power to constitute and develop an intellectual order; on the contrary it does so because religion is 'an element of fragmented common sense',[76] and the organization of religion holds back both its intellectuals (priests, theologians) and its congregations from philosophical enquiry. Gramsci writes:

> The strength of religions, and of the Catholic church in particular, has lain, and still lies, in the fact that they feel very strongly the need for the doctrinal unity of the whole mass of the faithful and strive to ensure that the higher intellectual stratum does not get separated from the lower.[77]

The church maintains hegemony by fostering disfunctional modes of thought, and keeping commonsense in its state as an aggregate collection of ideas. It deliberately blocks the potential within commonsense to rise to levels of ordered thought and self-activity by sustaining a fatalistic conception of the world, which is implicit in a consciousness that is haunted by the dead 'knowledges' of the past. And more than this, the Church structures a whole world of practices; it forms religion as a 'cultural movement', an ideology which 'is implicitly manifest in art, in law, in economic activity and in all manifestations of individual and collective life'.[78] Gramsci's conception of ideology here included not only the everyday thinking but the complex of feelings and sentiments, which the Church mobilizes through the use of liturgy and the cults, and despite his insistance on the superior power of 'systems of thought', he still concludes that 'in the masses as such, philosophy can only be experienced as faith'.[79]

In considering the role of the revolutionary party, the collective 'organic' intellectual, the 'philosophy of praxis' (Marxism), as a creator of hegemony, Gramsci compares its functioning to the Church. Religion, for him stands as the paradigm of a hegemonic form of ideology, and the achievements of the 'new order' have to be measured against it. Socialism can be formed as a total social system if the superstructures are entirely reformed, and if religion and the Church are abolished (that is rooted from men's minds). Whereas the Church serves to 'cement and unify' the ideological unity of the social bloc by preventing the masses from achieving systematized thought, the 'philosophy of praxis' opens the proletarian road to 'critical' understanding. 'The philosophy of praxis does not tend to leave the "simple" in their primitive philosophy of common sense, but rather to lead them to higher conceptions of life.'[80]

The 'philosophy of praxis', however, is not totally antithetical to commonsense, because commonsense is itself contradictory. It is true that commonsense as a progressive force (as in the seventeenth and eighteenth centuries when it was part of the philosophical battle against 'metaphysical mumbo-jumbo') is seen by Gramsci to have exhausted most of its subversive potential, yet within the fragmentary consciousness are found elements of 'good sense'. The starting point for the 'philosophy of praxis' is precisely from within commonsense: 'It is not a question of introducing from scratch a scientific form of thought into everyone's lives, but of renovating and making "critical" an already existing activity'.[81]

The 'making critical' for Gramsci means developing an historical class consciousness. In opposition to commonsense that is characterized by total subjection to history, to fatalism and to a notion of the social order as 'natural', 'critical' consciousness understands society as itself a product of history, the sum of individual human activities, and hence as open to further transformations. Gramsci radically interprets 'historical materialism' as an 'absolute historicism': 'It has been forgotten that in the case of a very common expression one should put the accent on the first term, "historical", and not on the second, which is of metaphysical origin'.[82]

Yet Gramsci is never in doubt about the severe limitations of commonsense. His respect for Sancho Panza is mixed with the scepticism of an intellectual who thought in international terms. A primary stage in the creation of hegemony by the revolutionary party is seen to be the 'nationalization' of culture, the teaching of a national language in place of the dialect, which forms the linguistic base for the politics of 'campanilismo'. In effect the scepticism goes further. Gramsci even doubts whether the masses are capable of determining their activity through rational choices. The Party has to shift faith away from the Church towards the social class by exercising its moral authority, and by appealing to class solidarity. Meanwhile the Party itself contains an intellectual elite that must develop the theoretical knowledge that is the prerequisite for correct political action, and which cannot spring from the masses. Within the Party itself, then, there is ideological hegemony being exercised. The necessity for this is indicated by the capacity of commonsense to suck Marxism into its boggy depths. Gramsci points out: 'the philosophy of praxis has itself become "prejudice" and "superstition" as it is assimilated to popular notions of materialism'.[83]

Gramsci's analysis of the function of the Marxist party in the transformation of working class consciousness has, therefore, a certain ambiguity. It breaks from the early Leninist model in which revolutionary theory and practice are embodied in the party. Theory consciousness is injected from outside the class by the intelligensia. The notion of 'good sense' as the spontaneously revolutionary thinking of the proletariat is profoundly democratic to the point of dissolving Marxism as a science and making it the systematizer of class consciousness. On the other hand, Gramsci continually reaffirms the leadership role of the party which involves a charismatical function of winning the loyalty and faith of the masses. His regular use of military metaphors and his insistence on discipline and organization reveal a preoccupation with unity and centralization.

These democratic and centralist tendencies do not need to be in contradiction, but there are extreme dangers in a lack of clarity on the issue. The problem needs to be articulated in the relations of party, mass working class organizations and the working class and poor peasantry so that democracy is not an abstraction. Gramsci largely fails to come to terms with the problem. As a revolutionary leader in the 1920s he oscillated between emotional sympathy for the Left Opposition based on a recognition of its past contribution to the revolutionary movement, and an acceptance of the majority Stalinist line of the Comintern. In practice he opted for a conception of unity and discipline which identified the interests of the Soviet State and the 3rd International, and actively repressed the Bordigist opposition within the PCd'I as 'nationalist' and 'factionalist'.[84] What this entailed was the exclusion of dissent from within the party. It could be said that in his political isolation in prison Gramsci was the victim of his own politics.

Gramsci's politics in the 1920s cannot, of course, be automatically projected forward to the *Notebooks* as an explanatory key. However the problem of the relations between party and membership and party and class is not tackled adequately, because they are not clearly distinguished.

The consequence of the elision is that the form of democratic centralism which involves rights of internal opposition, full political discussion before decision-making etc., is not present in the *Notebooks*.

In the *Prison Notebooks*, it is in relation to the State rather than to the revolutionary party that Gramsci develops his concept of hegemony. It is through the State and political parties and press in civil society, that the ruling class in capitalist society organizes its hegemony. The Church is but one of the organs of civil society used towards this end, and one which figures less in the *Notebooks* than those created in the process of the bourgeois revolution.

The Church's propagation of religious ideology is largely negative vis-à-vis the masses since it attempts to keep their minds stagnant, and as such its operations conform better to a feudal order even though it remains a vital ideological force. Although the capitalist State can take advantage of the fatalism of commonsense thinking, on the other hand, it also has a positive, dynamic conception of hegemony in that it works at all levels to bring the masses into conformity with the needs of expanding forces of production.[85] It is primarily in this field that Gramsci formulates the concept of hegemony.

A key passage in the *Notebooks* highlights the role of apparatuses of the State in organising hegemony:

> Every State is ethical in as much as as one of its most important functions is to raise the great mass of the population to a particular cultural and moral level, a level (or type) which corresponds to the needs of the productive forces for development and hence to the interests of the ruling classes. The school as a positive educative function, and the courts as a repressive and negative educative function, are the most important State activities in this sense: but in reality, a multitude of other so-called 'private' initiatives and activities tend to the same end – initiatives and activities which form the apparatus of the political and cultural hegemony of the ruling classes[86]

Here Gramsci's analysis of the State makes an important shift away from the current Marxist tradition which identified the State with the military-bureaucratic apparatuses, and examines the 'normal' functioning of the State as the means of organization and diffusion of the dominant ideology. In doing so he does not produce a simple binary model, repressive and ideological apparatuses, but carefully notes the ideological functions of the repressive organs. Moreover, he distinguishes between the State itself and private bodies, whilst recognizing that the bourgeoisie operates through both 'towards the same ends'.

At the same time, Gramsci calls into question classical political economy's distinction between the spheres of 'State' and 'civil society'. The pregnant 'so-called' indicates that Gramsci saw the division as real, since the different organs of State and civil society corresponded to specific modes of hegemonic activity (these are developed by him with particular reference to intellectuals); but that both are fundamentally united in their function of maintaining class rule, and that the abstraction of civil society as an aggregate of individuals disguises the class structure of society. Elsewhere in the *Notebooks* the separation of State and civil society is openly rejected:

> It is asserted that economic activity belongs to civil society, and that the State must not intervene to regulate it. But since in actual reality civil society and the State are one and the same, it must be clear that laissez-faire itself is a form of State regulation, introduced and maintained by legislative means.[87]

However, as Anderson has demonstrated with great lucidity, the *Notebooks* include a variety of contradictory formulations both on the relations of State and civil society and of the terms themselves. Despite Gramsci's polemical refutations of the concept of civil society, Anderson maintains that the dominant tendency is for its retention, but that three different models of State–civil society can be constructed out of Gramsci:[88]

(a) The predominance of civil society and the virtual marginalization of the State
(b) An equilibrium between State and civil society
(c) State as enveloping and absorbing civil society.

However, in Gramsci's analyses rather than in his explicit formulations, the distinction State–civil society is always held. This enables him to distinguish regimes of the capitalist form of State.

Whereas Bordiga assimilated the fascist and democratic regimes, content to describe them as capitalist, and the social democrats saw the regimes as polar opposites in every sense, Gramsci developed the means for analysing the specific articulation not only of the fundamental classes but their fractions that gave rise to the different regimes. Within the authoritarian type of State he distinguishes Bonapartism from fascism as a 'catastrophic equilibrium' between class fractions as opposed to between fundamental classes as in the latter. Each regime is characterized by a different relation between the State and civil society; for example, the fascist regime by the massive intervention of the State that attempts to eliminate civil society as a relatively autonomous sphere, and the democratic State that at any rate formally respects the freedom of movement of private bodies in civil society.

Gramsci points out that the class nature of a State is never simply deducible from the class composition of its functionaries, but via an analysis of the relation of class forces within the State itself and between the State and civil society. Thus the fascist regime owes its shape to the direct political intervention of the petit bourgeoisie, but it functions according to the interests of the 'agrarian–industrial' bloc. In the case of nineteenth century England, the aristocratic 'caste' held the key posts in the army and civil society.[89]

The balance of forces between the classes and class fractions is established throughout the mechanisms of domination and hegemony through the State and civil society. Gramsci generally couples domination with the State apparatuses and hegemony with the organs of civil society, but never in any absolute sense. The methods of class rule have always to be verified according to the specific historical situation. The normal means with which the bourgeoisie organizes its rule are the educational and legal apparatuses and private bodies in civil society, but they are ultimately backed by the coercive power of the State. In moments of crisis it is the coercive apparatuses that predominate:

> These situations of conflict between 'represented and representatives' reverberate out from the terrain of the parties (the party organizations properly speaking, the

> parliamentary electoral field, newspapers) throughout the State organism, reinforcing the relative power of the bureaucracy (civil and military) . . . . and generally all bodies relatively independent of the fluctuations of public opinion.[90]

Hegemony is not uniform within the State itself.[91] Whilst the coercive apparatuses and the bureaucracy are firmly under the control and supervision of the bourgeoisie, and the least open to outside intervention (the permanent structures with their own esprit de corps), parliament itself has essentially the hegemonic functions of articulating consensus, and is therefore more sensitive to the effects of class struggle. This very persistence of contradictory elements within the State allows for a political strategy designed to heighten the contradictions, and make parliament itself a part of the battleground, but always as the platform for the struggles in the workplace and civil society. Gramsci's perspective was the overthrow of the institutions of bourgeois democracy because he understood them to be irrevocably part of the capitalist order. For him, unlike his latter-day followers in the European Communist Parties, the idea of the working class taking over the existing structures was the fundamental characteristic of the social-democratic parties that had made it necessary in the first place to form communist parties in the West as in the East.[92]

Conclusion

The development of Gramsci's thinking on the problems of the State and hegemony is in no sense a unilinear progression. It is a process involving not only the acquisition of new insights and the production of new concepts, but the loss of certain critical elements. A reassessment of Gramsci's contribution to Marxism must re-establish the place of the factory councils in the politico-theoretical heritage of the revolutionary workers' movement in the light of their defeat. Clearly the limitations of the *Ordine Nuovo* conception of the councils lay in a schematic and teleological idea of class consciousness that identified the factory as the determinant area of class struggle, and hence treated the State as an epiphenomenon of this reality. However, the shift of Gramsci's attention to the problem of bourgeois class rule through the State and to the party as the form of working class organization for the political overthrow of that rule meant that he ceased to see the need for a specific organ of class struggle capable of destroying and replacing the economic and political hegemony of the capitalists in the factory.

However, the experience of defeat that led most of Gramsci's generation to find refuge in myths and dogma, and to develop elitist ideas of the revolutionary party that showed a loss of faith in the possibility of winning the masses to socialism, led Gramsci himself to a profound reconsideration of the mechanisms of class rule. In the place of the various theories that explained the continued survival of the bourgeoisie in terms of their control of the bureaucratic/military apparatuses and of their deceptive cunning (bribery and corruption of a section of the working class), he reinterpreted these elements of analysis in the concepts of domination and hegemony. They ceased to be 'instrumental' and became operable according to the specific relation of class forces. Moreover, Gramsci reworked the global terms of Marxist analysis that had become hackneyed jargon and introduced his own elaboration of them. Class, ideology and the State, to take three, were considered in all their complexity of stratification and articulation. The concept of hegemony itself was produced by Gramsci to conceive class relations as an ensemble of mechanisms of economic, ideological and political domination and subordination, that, taken independently, had led to the crudely idealist or determinist thinking that he himself had been responsible for in the past.

An examination of Gramsci's ideas over the timespan of 33 years reveals the way in which at an early date they were full of important insights that he worked up later into theoretical concepts, but it also shows the radical nature of his break with his own past and with the dominant thinking in the contemporary communist movement.

Comments on Anderson's 'The antinomies of Antonio Gramsci'

After the publication of *NLR* 100 any readings of Gramsci on the problems of State and Hegemony have to confront the seminal contribution of Perry Anderson's 'The Antinomies of Antonio Gramsci'. Anderson's piece combines extensive scholarship with a precise political intervention. He locates Gramsci's *Notebooks* in the debates of the 2nd and 3rd Internationals (from the exchanges of the Bolsheviks and Mensheviks through to the struggle of the Trotskyist and Bordigist oppositions), thereby stripping bare the myths of 'originality' that have enclosed his writings. The ciphers and blurred imprints of the historical moment are decoded in masterly fashion to reveal the meaning of Gramsci's reflections in his own time. Anderson has carefully followed his own dictum 'a scientific solution . . . is only possible through historical enquiry'. But Anderson locates Gramsci's work historically in order to critically reappropriate its insights for contemporary political analysis.

'The Antinomies' is directed against reformist readings propagated by Eurocommunist intellectuals. It is not, however, a counter-reading that unearths appropriately revolutionary statements made by Gramsci to prove that he believed in revolutionary insurrection. Anderson registers two vital responses to the Eurocommunist interpretation of Gramsci. Firstly that the texts themselves leave openings for a reformist interpretation. For example, Gramsci's formulation of the predominance of civil society in the West over the State is cited as the inspiration of the 'Illusions of Left Social Democracy' (the illusion that the central problem was the 'conditioning' of the masses before the elections, and hence that the adequate strategy was winning hegemony in civil society by de-conditioning educative activity).[93]

Secondly, Anderson recognizes in the spread and resiliance of democratic ideology espoused by the European Communist Parties the overarching function of parliamentary democracy itself in the maintenance of bourgeois hegemony. In other words, Anderson proposes a reading of Gramsci as a starting point for a re-examination of the problem of parliamentary democracy as the paradigmatic form of bourgeois rule in advanced capitalist countries not as an academic exercise, but because the mass adhesion to the Eurocommunist parties has made it a key problem for Marxists. Those parties gain their strength through their capacity to interpret the working class's self-recognition in the structures of the capitalist State. That democratic structure is not limited to parliament itself, writes Anderson, but 'the parliamentary state . . . constitutes the formal framework of all other ideological mechanisms of the ruling class. It provides the general code in which every specific message is transmitted'. Moreover 'the code is all the more powerful because the judicial rights of citizenship are not a mere mirage: on the contrary, the civic freedoms and suffrages of bourgeois democracy are a tangible reality, whose completion was in part the work of the Labour movement itself, and whose loss would be a momentous defeat for the working class.'[94]

Gramsci, according to Anderson, did not grasp the key structuring role of parliamentary democracy, and his analyses of the capitalist state concentrate on its educational and legal institutions.

He goes on to explain this as the result of the inherent instability of economic improvements: 'its very dynamism is thus potentially destabilising and capable of provoking crises when growth fluctuates and stalls.' By contrast the parliamentary State is more stable.

Anderson is right to attack the determinist notions current on the Left which predict a mortal crisis in reformism as an automatic effect of material cuts in the standard of living. But by simplifying and making a comparison of explanations of reformism (the 'ideological' and the 'material'), Anderson misses the intermediary mechanism of the articulation of reformism at its political and economic levels. Moreover, the 'material component' of which he writes is not just higher wages or social benefits, but the specific forms of class organization and ideology created in the struggle for them. The 'material component' might be an unstable element, but the significance of the trade union as a potent vehicle of class consciousness has an everyday reality which is often highlighted in moments of economic crisis when the material efficacy of the representative party and therefore of parliament as a means of securing economic and even civil rights objectives is also in crisis. The greater responsiveness of the trade union to its membership and its structural position on the boundary of production and the market, places it at the nodal point of the capitalist system. The trade union is at once the interpreter, arbiter and legimater of the wage relationship which is the defining relationship of capital itself.

The problem, therefore, is to analyse the articulation of parliamentary democracy as the characteristic form of bourgeois hegemony keeping in mind the structures consequent to the decisive division of the economic and the juridico-political which includes the trade union, political parties and parliament. When Anderson footnotes that the completion of bourgeois democracy was 'historically in part the work of the labour movement itself', he gives an indication of the necessity of capturing the nexus of relations, but his own one-sided analysis makes for a fatal weakness vis-à-vis his reading of Gramsci in the perspective of re-posing the 'united front' as the revolutionary strategy appropriate in the contemporary West. The 'united front' was developed by Lenin, Trotsky and then by Gramsci precisely as the means of overcoming the 2nd International's structure and strategy which remained dominant in the interwar period (and subsequently), namely the division of competences between party and trade union, and the division of corresponding maximal and minimal programmes. Gramsci in *Ordine Nuovo* and then in the *Notebooks* wrestled with the problem of breaking with this tradition that he analyses as functional to capital.

Any reconsideration of the 'united front' today has to come to terms with the very same problems that are rearticulated in present day capitalist society. Only a concrete historical materialist analysis will produce a scientific understanding of the contemporary conjuncture, but a starting point is the contradictory relation of the 'stable' ideological and parliament-centred element and the 'unstable material component' of parliamentary democracy. In Britain the current crisis between and within the Labour Party and the trade unions is the terrain on which the 'united front' has to be worked out in theory and practice.

Notes

1 In the NLR debate centred on the 'Origins of the Present Crisis' (*NLR* 23, Jan–Feb 1964), the use of Gramsci has been justly accused of schematism (see E. P. Thompson's 'Peculiarities of the English', *The Socialist Register* 1965; and recently Richard Johnson 'Barrington Moore, Perry Anderson and English Social Development', *Cultural Studies* n9, Birmingham Spring 1976); Anderson refers to E. Hobsbawm, *The Age of Capital*, London 1975, pp. 249–50, and E. P. Thompson, *Whigs and Hunters*, London 1975, as good examples of a developed use of Gramsci's concepts. A

case of a more direct confrontation of the problem of power and culture is Thompson's 'Patrician Society, Plebian Culture' *Journal of Social History* 1974.

The other side of the coin is the mechanical mobilization of the terms 'corporate and hegemonic' in Martin Jacques' essay, Consequences of the General Strike, in *General Strike*, ed. J. Skelly, London 1976. A brief comparison would be revealing of the way in which the latter author tends to take the passages where Gramsci is most explicit and least subtle. Instead of exploring the complexities of, say, 'corporate culture', it is reduced to Lenin's concept of 'Trade union consciousness'. (Martin Jacques, in fact, writes about 'these *stages* (of consciousness)' as a 'useful *framework*'. (pp. 375–6))

2 In Italy the debate on Gramsci has a much longer history, but it is a history that reveals more about the politics of Gramsci's interpreters than about Gramsci's theoretical contribution. From the time of Bordiga's opposition to the Leadership of the PCd'I, and Gramsci's postwar canonization by Togliatti, the *Ordine Nuovo* writings and *Notebooks* have been raided and reconstructed from all sides. The dominant interpretation has remained that of the intellectuals of the PCI, and the historiography of the modern period is choked by re-elaborations of Gramsci's schemes.

Tendencies in Gramsci's own work, 'over-politicization' resulting from a history of parties and a failure to articulate analysis of the 'superstructure' with a structural and conjunctural analysis of the economy, are painfully reproduced. But whereas Gramsci was aware of the limitations imposed on him by imprisonment, his followers accentuate 'Jacobinical' traits to write bureaucratic histories.

The anti-Gramscian current originating in Della Volpe's work has probably been more fruitful both in the field of history and philosophy, and in the political terrain. This current consciously returned to Marx's *Capital* in an attempt to exorcise the Crocean tradition and to enter European debate from which the 'Gramscians' were cut off in a provincial limbo. Raniero Panzieri and the collective of '*Quaderni Rossi*' 'discovered' Marx's *Grundrisse* and the chapter of *Capital* on Machinery and Modern Industry, thereby finding a path through theory which combined with a realisation that the whole structure of class composition in Italy was being transformed. In this way, the Gramsci of notes on 'Americanism and Fordism' sprang to life. In the 1960s the *Ordine Nuovo* writings also took on a new significance as the affirmation of workers' autonomy from below.

The renewed interest in early Gramsci was reflected within the Communist Party itself where the left wing represented by figures like Ingrao and Bruno Trentin took up the theme of conciliarism. The debate on Gramsci then saw a series of interpretations which 'proved' the 'continuity' or 'rupture' between *Ordine Nuovo* and the *Notebooks* (see M. Salvadori 'Gramsci e il PCI: due concezioni de egemonia', *Mondo Oparaio*, Nov. 1976). From a position of total hostility towards Gramsci, the 'New Left', in the process of massive diversification, developed a whole series of analyses varying from Manifesto's championing of Gramsci to continued critical hostility on the part of the founders of Rivista Storica del Socialismo to iconization by some M-L groups. Today the situation is as confused as ever on the New Left, and significantly the open forum issue of *Quotidiano Dei Lavoratori* (paper of Avanguardia Operaia and PDUP) on the 40th anniversary of Gramsci's death, produced a series of conflicting viewpoints. A reading has still to be made that recognizes the contradictions within Gramsci instead of simply instrumentalizing his ideas.

3 A. Gramsci, 'La Rivoluzione contro il "Capitale" ', *Scritti Politici* (Turin 1973) p. 131.
4 A. Gramsci, 'Socialismo e Cultura', ibid pp. 68–9.
5 A. Gramsci, 'Marinetti rivoluzionario?', *Socialismo e Fascismo*.
6 A. Davidson, 'Gramsci and Lenin, 1917–22', *Socialist Register* 1974 p. 127.
7 Gramsci, 'La conquista dello Stato', *L'Ordine Nuovo*, 12 luglio 1919 (*L'Ordine Nuovo*, Turin 1955. Henceforth referred to as ON).
8 Gramsci, ON 3rd July 1920 (quoted G. Williams, *Proletarian Order*, London 1975 p. 225).
9 ON, 'Uno sfacelo ed una genesi', 1 maggio 1919 (ON, 1955) p. 218.
10 *Avanti*, 29 novembre 1919 (ON) p. 54.
11 ON, 'Lo sviluppo della rivoluzione', 13 settembre 1919 (ON) p. 30.
12 ON, 'Sindicalismo e consigli', 8 novembre 1919 (ON) p. 46.
13 ON, 'Tradizione monarchica', 21 febbraio 1919 (ON) p. 327.
14 ON, 'ai commissari di reparto delle officine Fiat Centro e Brevetti', 13 settembre 1919 (ON) p. 34.
15 M. Salvadori, *Gramsci e il Problema Storica della Democracia*, Einaudi, Torino 1970, pp. 59–60.
16 V. Castronovo, *Agnelli*, Torino 1970, Chapter 3.

17 A. Sofri, 'On workers' delegates (trans)', *Les Temps Modernes* no 335, June 1974.
18 Ibid.
19 ON, 'Lo strumento di lavoro', 14 febbraio 1920 (ON) p. 83.
20 ON, ibid, p. 81. Before unqualifiedly casting Gramsci in the role of Dr Ure, it should be made clear that Marx himself in 'Capital' saw not only the destructive and de-humanizing force of technological development, but also its liberatory potential. Gramsci does tend to stress the latter aspect and to attribute the modernization of the labour process to the workers themselves. Thus, in his essay 'Americanism and Fordism', Gramsci writes: 'A careful analysis of Italian history before 1922, or even up to 1926 . . . must objectively come to the conclusion that it was the workers in fact who brought into being newer and more modern industrial requirements and, in their way, upheld these strenuously'. (Gramsci, *Prison Notebooks*, London 1971, p. 292.) However, in the same essay, Gramsci is acutely aware of the process of 'breaking up the old psycho-physical nexus of the qualified professional worker' as a brutal transformation.

A very different perspective on the relationship of the working class to changes in the labour process comes from the work of Italian Marxists like Sergio Bologna. In his view, it is the organized resistance of the workers that the capitalists seek to destroy by re-organizing the labour process; i.e. technological 'advances' are carried through in the face of workers' opposition in defence of their skills and the particular labour processes that require them. Bologna has interpreted the council movement in post-First World War Germany in this light (S. Bologna: 'Class Composition and the theory of the party at the origins of the council movement'; *CSE Pamphlet* 1,1976). It would be very interesting to see a similar analysis made of the council movement in Italy. Unfortunately Gramsci seems to overlook the particular sectional differences in the working class, and perhaps underestimates the artisanal nature of the engineering industry in this period.
21 ON, 'Lo strumento di lavoro', 14 febbraio 1920 (ON) p. 83.
22 ON, ibid; p. 84.
23 ON, 'Ritorno all liberta', 26 giugno 1919 (ON) p. 252.
24 ON, 'I rivoluzionari e le elezioni', 15 novembre 1919 (ON) p. 308.
25 ON, 'Lo stato italiano', 7 febbraio 1920 (ON) p. 74.
26 ON, 'L'unita del mondo', 15 maggio 1919 (ON) pp. 227–8.
27 ON, 'L'unita nazionale', 4 ottobre 1919 (ON) p. 277.
28 ON 'Domenica rossa', 15 settembre 1920 (ON) p. 164.
29 *Avanti*, 'La reazione', 17 ottobre 1920 (ON) p. 351.
30 *Avanti*, 'La tradizione monarchica', 14 marzo 1920 (ON) p. 329.
31 G. Williams, *Proletarian Order*, p. 30.
32 K. Marx, *Capital*, London 1970, p. 524.
33 M. Salvadori, op. cit. p. 94.
34 ON, 'Partito di governo e classe di governo', 28 febbraio 1920 (ON) p. 95 and ON, 'Cronache dell'Ordine Nuovo', 12 luglio 1919 (ON) pp. 446–7.
35 ON, 'Due rivoluzione', 31 luglio 1920 (ON) p. 139.
36 See G. Williams, *Proletarian Order*, pp. 116–120; pp. 216–219.
37 ON, op. cit. p131, quoted M Salvadori, op. cit. p. 138–9.
38 G. Williams, op. cit. p. 228.
39 S. Merli, Gramsci, *Giovane Critica*, autunno 1967.
40 Poulantzas, *Fascisme et Dictature*, pp. 247–9.
41 Ibid p. 45.
42 Spriano dates the first sign of Gramsci's disagreement with Bordiga's leadership from a letter to the Executive of the PCI sent from Moscow on 12th September 1923.
43 Gramsci, 'Un esame della situazione italiana', *La Costruzione del Partito Comunista* (Turin, 1974) pp. 116–120.
44 ON, 'Forze elementari', 25 aprile 1921, *Socialismo e Fascismo*, p. 151.
45 ON, 'I due fascismi', 25 Agosto 1921, Ibid, pp. 297–9.
46 ON, 'Colpo di Stato', 27 luglio 1921, Ibid, pp. 157–9.
47 ON, 'La caduta del fascismo', 15 novembre 1924, *Costruzione del PC*, p. 209. Gramsci wrote: 'At the basis of everything is the same problem of fascism, a movement which the bourgeoisie held to be a simple "instrument" of reaction in its hands, and which, instead, once evoked and released, is worse than the devil. It no longer allows itself to be dominated, but goes forward on its own behalf.'

48 ON, 'La crisi italiana', 1 settembre 1924, *La Costruzione*, p. 28.
49 *L'Unità*, 'Gioda o del romanticismo', 28 febbraio 1924, *La Costruzione*, p. 367.
50 Congresso di Lione, *La Costruzione* p. 497.
51 Bordiga wrote in *Il Soviet*, 15th May 1921: 'The fact that fascism and social democracy take converging routes today may seem a paradox to many . . . but it will be confirmed in the future . . . Fascism and social democracy are two aspects of the same enemy of tomorrow.' (Quoted by Poulantzas, *Fascisme*, p. 245.)
52 A. Gramsci, *Prison Notebooks* (London, 1971) p. 365 (The *Prison Notebooks* are hereafter referred to as PN)
53 Spriano Gramsci's of February 9th 1924 from Togliatti's '*La Formazione del PCI*' p. 196.
54 Poulantzas, *Fascisme*, p. 250.
55 See Spriano, *Storia del PCI* Chap. 9.
56 Gramsci, 'Noi e la Concentrazione Repubblicana', *Unita*, 13 ottobre 1926, *La Costruzione* p. 349. Gramsci did foresee the probability of the fascist regime giving way to a bourgeois democratic one rather than immediately to a socialist state. However he rejected an alliance with the Aventine parties, that is he rejected unity at the leadership level based on a strategy of restoring the democratic status quo in favour of unity at the base on a revolutionary programme. Interpretations of Gramsci that regard him as the theoretician of the alliance of 'progressive forces' (including sections of the bourgeoisie) against the latifundists do have some openings provided in his texts; for example Gramsci talks of the alliance of the industrialists and big landowners of the feudal South as the co-existence of separate economic structures (see Il Congresso di Lione, *La Costruzione* p. 491). His failure to grasp the relationship as unequal, as structured in dominance by monopoly capital opened the way for reformist readings of Gramsci, which theorize a strategy based on separate 'stages' in the revolutionary process – the democratic revolution against 'feudalism', followed by the socialist. Gramsci himself, however, never deviated from the strategy of building a worker–peasant alliance against the entire agrarian-industrial bloc. For Gramsci's relation to the Popular Fronts, see Lucio Coletti's 'Gramsci and the Italian Revolution' *New Left Review* 1971.
57 'They (joiners, builders etc) must think as members of a class which alone aims at leading the peasants and intellectuals, of a class which can conquer and building socialism only if aided and followed by the great majority of these social strata, who in Italy represent the majority of the population. If it does not do this, the proletariat does not become a leading class, and these strata remain under bourgeois leadership.' (A. Gramsci, *The Modern Prince and Other Writings* (NY, 1970) p. 36.)
58 'The Italian situation is characterized by the fact that the bourgeoisie is organically weaker than in other countries and maintains itself in power only in as far as it succeeds in controlling and dominating the peasants. The proletariat must struggle to break the peasants from the influence of the bourgeoisie and put it under its own political leadership. This is the pivot of the political problems that the party must resolve in the near future.' (Ibid. p. 51).
59 'One cannot expect every worker to have a complete awareness of the whole complex of functions that his class must develop in the process of the development of humanity; but that must be asked of every member of the party' (*La Costruzione* p. 53–4) 'Introduzione al primo corso della scuola interna del partito', aprile-maggio 1926.
60 A. Gramsci, *The modern Prince and Other Writings*, p. 51.
61 J. Merrington, 'Theory and Practice in Gramsci's Marxism' *Socialist Register* 1968.
62 P. Anderson, 'Antinomies of Antonio Gramsci', *New Left Review* 100 Jan 1977.
63 L. Gruppi, 'Il Concetto di Egemonia', in ASVV, Prassi Rivoluzionaria e Storie in Gramsci, *Critica Marxista* (Quaderni) n3, 1967 cited by M. Salvadori in 'Gramsci e il PCI: due concezioni dell 'egemonia', *Mondo* Operaio nov 1976 p. 61.
64 Poulantzas, *Political Power* p. 205.
65 PN p. 54.
66 PN p. 161.
67 PN p. 181–2.
68 PN p. 162.
69 Many commentators on Gramsci have, albeit unconsciously, assimilated his concept to a Marcusean model of one-dimensionality. For example, Gwyn Williams writes: '. . . one concept of reality is diffused throughout society in all its institutional and private manifestations,

informing with its spirit all taste, morality, customs . . .' (G. Williams, 'Gramsci's concept of hegemony', *Journal of the History of Ideas*, 1960)

70 Poulantzas, *Political Power* p. 207.
71 PN p. 324–5.
72 PN p. 324.
73 Introduction to *Prison Notebooks* by Q. Hoare and G. Noel Smith p. 3.
74 PN p. 56.
75 PN p. 329.
76 PN p. 325.
77 PN p. 328.
78 PN p. 328.
79 PN p. 339.
80 PN p. 332.
81 PN p. 330–1.
82 PN p. 465 Althusser in *Reading Capital* discusses Gramsci's 'historicism' as a polemical means of insisting on Marxism as a lived intervention in history, and also as inadequate theoretically. His primary objection to 'historicism' is that it collapses the levels of the superstructure.
83 PN p. 396.
84 Gramsci wrote: 'In the ideology and in the practice of the opposition bloc, the whole socialdemocratic and syndicalist tradition that has prevented the Western proletarian revolution is reborn'; see M. Salvadori, *Gramsci e il Problema Storica della Democracia*, op. cit. p. 38. Salvadori gives one of the clearest expositions of Gramsci's relation to the political struggle within the 3rd International. He points out the way in which Gramsci writes of ideology and theory as interchangeable. Whilst disagreeing with Althusser's conception of theoretical practice as undertaken outside the superstructures, it is right to say that Gramsci fails to grasp the theoretical break between Marx and previous thinkers because he sees Marx as the last of the great political economists, different from his predecessors chiefly in his idea that capitalist society was itself a historical stage and not the final and 'natural' form of society.
85 In 'Americanism and Fordism' Gramsci writes about the creation of a new form of hegemony within the capitalist mode of production; the new hegemony is 'born in the factory', that is to say, social customs and ways of life, including sexual practices are forced to conform to the needs of production in a more direct form. This is done at the level of the enterprise (Ford's instillation of production-line discipline) and through the State (Prohibition legislation). Fordism is described by Gramsci as but the latest episode in the 'continual struggle against the element of "animality" in man', in which coercion is succeeded by interiorization of norms as new forms of behaviour become 'second nature' (see PN p. 298). Here the hegemony of one class over another is shown to reach down to the fundamentals of human existance, and to those areas deemed most 'private' by bourgeois political theory – the sacred preserves of the individual where the State must not tread.

Unfortunately Gramsci does not include workers' reactions to Fordism within the scope of his analysis, except in as far as they become more 'disciplined'. Yet Gramsci regards the new form of hegemony as reproducing not only the conditions for expanded production, but also the contradictions inherent in the capitalist mode of production. The hegemony is never complete because it is externally imposed:' 'Puritanical' initiatives simply have the purpose of preserving, outside of work, a certain psycho-social equilibrium which prevents the physiological collapse of the worker, exhausted by the new method of production. This equilibrium can only be something purely external and mechanical, but it can become internalized if it is proposed by a new form of society, with appropriate and original methods!. That hegemony is further weakened when it ceases to be the lived ideology of the ruling classes; Gramsci suggests that in America this breakdown between the dominant ideology of Puritanism and the practice of its propagators had been initiated by the petty bourgoisie, fractions of the ruling class and among the womenfolk of even the sternest pioneering capitalists, and that this was likely to have serious consequences for the maintenance of working class subordination; 'These phenomena proper to the ruling classes will make more difficult any coercion on the working masses to make them conform to the needs of the new industry.'

It should be noted that Gramsci is returning to preoccupation in the *Ordine Nuovo* period with the increasing irrelevance of the bourgeoisie to the production process and the acceleration of its moral depravities in conformity with its role of financial parasitism. However, in the *Notebooks*, Gramsci grounds his analyses in empirical observations rather than in the rhetoric of denunciation, and examines the processes whereby the working class is 'hegemonized' rather than simply provided with the objective conditions for its subjective leap to revolutionary consciousness.

86 PN p. 258.

87 PN p. 160.

88 P. Anderson, op. cit., The whole article revolves around the analysis of these terms.

89 PN p. 83 and p. 115.

90 PN p. 210.

91 '. . . however much the ruling class may affirm to the contrary, the State, as such, does not have a unitary, coherent and homogenous conception, with the result that intellectual groups are scattered between one stratum and the next, or within a single stratum.' (PN p. 342).

92 M. A. Macciocchi takes Luciano Gruppi to task (quite rightly) for acting as an intellectual apologist for the contemporary PCI. She writes that his understanding of hegemony as including the concept of domination is open to the same attack as Gramsci made on Croce for 'putting stress only on the aspect of consensus', and that it leads to his conclusion that 'the State can no longer be conceived only as an instrument of oppression that one must smash' and that therefore it must be reformed. (M. A. Macciocchi, *Pour Gramsci*)

If the reformist reading of Gramsci finds some footholds in his writings, they do so through their narrow partiality and blindness to the passages that contradict their preconceptions. In fact the gap between the ideology of the PCI and Gramsci's theories have appeared so glaring that 'revisions' are taking place. The incompatibility of Gramsci's ideas on the party with democratic pluralism has meant that some are now considered to be 'dated'. However, the following passage in the *Notebooks* remains holy writ: 'A social group is dominant over enemy groups which it tends to "liquidate" or subject with armed force, and is directive over affinal or allied groups. A social group can, and indeed must, be directive before the conquering of government power (this is one of the many conditions for the conquest of power itself); afterwards, when it exercises power and keeps it firmly in its grasp, it becomes dominant, but also continues to be "directive" '.

Anderson offers a reading that turns a reformist reading on its head: 'Gramsci here carefully distinguishes the necessity for coercion of enemy classes, and consensual direction of allied classes. The "hegemonic activity" which "can and must be exercised before the assumption of power" is related in this context only to the problem of the alliance of the working class with other exploited and oppressed groups; it is not a claim to hegemony over the whole of society . .'

93 P. Anderson, op. cit. pp. 27–29.

94 Ibid, p. 28.

95 Ibid, p. 28 footnote.

96 Ibid, p. 30.

97 Marx, op. cit., p. 424.

98 Ibid, p. 354.

99 For a discussion of the significance of the wage relation in the construction of bourgeois ideology, see Hall, Lumley and McLennan, 'Politics and Ideology'. *Working Papers in Cultural Studies* 1976 10, Birmingham

100 P. Anderson, op cit., p. 29.

Bibliography

A. Gramsci

Scritti Politici, Editori Riuniti, Roma 1973

Socialismo e Fascismo, Einaudi, Torino 1972

Ordine Nuovo, Einaudi, Torino 1955

La Costruzione del Partito Comunista, Einaudi, Torino 1971

Modern Prince and Other Writings, International Publishers, New York 1970

Prison Notebooks, Lawrence and Wishart, London 1971

'Letters from Prison', *New Edinburgh Review* Special Editions 1974

Other books and articles

L. Althusser, *Reading Capital*, New Left Books, London 1970
P. Anderson, Antinomies of Antonio Gramsci, *New Left Review* n100, Jan 1977
C. Boggs, *Gramsci's Marxism*, Pluto Press, London 1975
J. Cammett, *Antonio Gramsci and the Origins of Italian Communism*, Stanford University Press 1967
V. Castronovo, *Agnelli*, Torino 1970
A. de Clementis, *Bordiga*, Einaudi, Torino 1971
L. Colletti, 'Antonio Gramsci and the Italian Revolution', *New Left Review* 1971
L. Cortesi, 'Alcuni problemi della storia del PCI', *Rivista Storica del Socialismo*, 24, 1965
CSE Pamphlet 1, 'Labour Process and Class Strategies', Conference of Socialist Economists 1976.
A. Davidson, 'Gramsci and Lenin, 1917–22', *Socialist Register* 1974
A. Davidson, 'Antonio Gramsci', *Australian Left Review* 1968
R. Debray, 'Schema for studying Gramsci', *NLR*, 59, 1970
G. Fiori, *Antonio Gramsci – Life of a Revolutionary*, NLB, London 1970
Carter Goodrich, *Frontier of Control*, London 1975
Luciano Gruppi, Il Concetto di Egemonia, in AAVV, Prassi rivoluzionaria e storicismo in Gramsci, *Critica Marxista* n3, 1967
Hall, McLennan and Lumley, 'Politics and Ideology' . . . *Working Papers in Cultural Studies* Spring 1977 n10
L. Magri, 'Via italiana e strategia consiliare', *Il Manifesto*, Quad.2, Alfani, Roma 1974
M.A. Macciocchi, *Pour Gramsci*, Seuil, Paris 1974
S. Merli, 'Gramsci', *Giovane Critica*, autumo 1967
J. Merrington, 'Gramsci's Marxism – Theory and Practice', *Socialist Register* 1968
N. Poulantzas, *Fascisme et Dictature*, Seuil/Maspero, Paris 1974
N. Poulantzas, *Political Power and Social Classes*, NLB, London 1975
M. Salvadori, *Gramsci e il Problema Storico della Democrazia* Torino 1970
M. Salvadori, 'Gramsci e il PCI: due concezioni dell 'egemonia', *Mondo Operaio* Nov 1976
P. Spriano, *Storia del partito comunista italiano*, vol 1, Einaudi, Torino 1967 vol 2, Einaudi, Torino 1969
P. Spriano, *Occupations*, Pluto Press, London 1975
A. Sofri, 'On workers' delegates (trans)', *Les Temps Modernes*, 335. June 1974 (An issue on *Lotta Continua*)
Ibid, 343, February 1975 (An issue of writings on Gramsci)
G. Williams, *Proletarian Order*, Pluto Press, London 1975
G. Williams, 'Gramsci's concept of hegemony', *Journal of History of Ideas* 21, 1960

13 Politics and ideology

Gramsci

Stuart Hall, Robert Lumley, Gregor McLennan

Introduction

There is no systematic theory of ideology in the work of Antonio Gramsci, though it is certainly true that there are many extremely suggestive passages and comments. It is only possible to produce a reasonably coherent account of these many and varied insights to the question providing we call to mind the densely interwoven character of Gramsci's major concepts. The task of theoretical abstraction should not be allowed to mask that hallmark of his thought. The first section of this paper will therefore be an outline of the Gramscian problematic, a problematic which, it will be argued, is geared primarily towards political perspectives and analyses rather than general epistemological principles. Concrete, historically specific study is of the highest importance in Gramsci's writings. With respect to our present topic, the basis of such specificity is indicated by Gramsci's injunction that ideology should be studied as a *superstructure*.[1] Now the latter task cannot be undertaken outside an understanding of a Gramscian approach to the structure/superstructure complex, the basis of which is formed by the concepts of *hegemony, civil society, the State, the party*, and the *intellectuals*. Without these concepts, ideology as Gramsci might have conceived it could not be 'thought' at all: it occupies its extremely important position only if subordinated to the political conceptions around which Gramsci's thinking is oriented.

We have suggested that those who seek a 'philosophy' in Gramsci will be disappointed. Yet it is well known that he speaks of marxism as the 'philosophy of praxis', and devotes the last third of the *Prison Notebooks* to philosophical questions. This apparently strange juxtaposition of claims is based on an assessment of Gramsci's so-called 'historicist' tendencies, and the general problem of historicism will be approached in later sections through a specific analysis of the way in which Gramsci is appropriated by Louis Althusser and Nicos Poulantzas. Their 'structuralist' perspective seems to offer an epistemological position in opposition to Gramsci's more 'organicist' moments, yet it is clear that they acknowledge the latter to be a theoretical figure of a quite different stature from the much-maligned doyen of historicism, Georg Lukács. Yet another contradiction, it seems.

We will argue that, particularly in the case of Poulantzas, these writers are less than open about a substantive debt to Gramsci for concepts central to their own theoretical projects. We will also suggest that the problem of historicism in Gramsci is in no sense a clear-cut issue. It is certainly true that in some of his *philosophical* generalisations Gramsci tends to reduce or imply a reduction of ideologies as 'conceptions of life' to fundamental classes which are organically linked to some long-term historical goal. It is also plausible to say that Gramsci tends to relativise the criteria of theoretical validity to their historical conditions of approval.

These 'fallacies' seem to fulfil the main charges levelled against historicism by Althusser and Poulantzas. Yet Gramsci's unrivalled sense of the *material* forms and production of ideology and political struggle, the anti-psychologistic stricture that ideology is an epistemological and structural matter,[2] and the lasting value of his own specific concepts (at the very least as they occur in their 'practical' state): these realities ensure the complexity, the partial nature of Gramsci's historicism. If, in addition, it can be shown that Gramsci's concepts lie behind some of the main points of the Althusserians' analyses, a useful anti-reductionist task will have been achieved. In this sense we hope to help re-establish the seminal character of Gramsci's central ideas. That said, we make no claim that Gramsci offers us a rigorous theory of ideology, or indeed of anything else. In particular, the whole question of marxism as a science (or an ideology), and the delicate issue of Gramsci's relevance to communist strategy in Western Europe today, to state but two pressing theoretical and political problems, remain open and urgent.

The conceptual matrix of the *Prison Notebooks*

In the *Prison Notebooks*, Gramsci rarely uses the term ideology itself, but rather a range of terms that serve, more or less, as equivalents – 'philosophies', 'conceptions of the world', 'systems of thought' and forms of consciousness. He also employs notions such as 'common sense', which though not equivalent to ideologies refer to their substrata. These terms have distinct applications and frames of reference, from the all-inclusive Weltanschauung to the very particular form of consciousness. Gramsci's complex conception of ideology has to be reconstructed out of these, and it has to be placed in the whole field of concepts that he uses to analyse the social formation. It is precisely here that he makes his major contribution to marxist theory through his introduction of concepts like 'hegemony', and 'organic intellectual', and his reconceptualisation of others, particularly 'State' and 'civil society'. Ideology is given a new significance in his writings as a 'material force' in history, far removed from the 2nd Internationalist theory of ideology as a simple reflection of the economic base, but at the same time Gramsci explores the specific forms of the organisation and propagation of ideology and culture as an aspect of the class struggle.

Structure and superstructure

The starting point for Gramsci's exploration is given for him by the fundamental marxist model of structure and superstructure. In his writings, the structure, the 'world of economy', is always present; its movements set parameters for the developments in the superstructure, but it is only the 'mainspring of history in the last instance'.[3] Gramsci's analyses of the relationship of structure and superstructure owe little to marxist political economy. His debt is to Marx, the historian of the *18th Brumaire*, rather than to the Marx of *Capital*. Gramsci uses terms of 'historico-political analysis', such as 'historical bloc' and 'organic' and 'conjunctural' movements. However, they do not refer simply to the superstructural level. The 'historical bloc', for example, refers both to the structure in which classes are constituted at the economic level (on this basis Gramsci distinguishes between 'fundamental' classes and class fractions), and to the political level in which classes and class fractions combine.[4] Similarly Gramsci uses 'organic' and 'conjunctural' to distinguish movements in the superstructure according to the degree to which they have a basis in the transformation and reorganisation of the mode of production.[5]

It is often said that Gramsci inquires into the formation of the superstructures alone, and gives entirely politico-cultural analyses of history.[6] Whilst it is true in terms of emphasis, Gramsci's project is to break with both the culturalist/idealist tradition represented by Croce, and with the economic determinism of the 2nd International. A series of concepts employed in the *Prison Notebooks* cut across the simple topographical model of base and superstructure (e.g. historical bloc, hegemony), and open the way to an understanding of the complex articulations of the social formation. One of the key concepts is 'civil society'.

Civil society is a difficult concept to pin down, and Gramsci is more than usually elusive in his use of it. For example, in a section on intellectuals, civil society is called a 'level of superstructure',[7] whilst in a number of other instances the term refers also to the structure.[8] The English translators of the *Notebooks* admit to some bewilderment over Gramsci's diverse usages.[9] A useful way of understanding civil society is as a concept that designates the intermediary sphere that includes aspects of the structure and the superstructure. It is the area of the 'ensemble of organisms that are commonly called "private" '; hence it includes not only associations and organisations like political parties and the press, but also the family, which combines ideological and economic functions. Civil society, then, in Gramsci's words 'stands between the economic structure and the State'. It is the sphere of 'private' interests in general. But this notion of civil society cannot be assimilated to that of 18th century political theorists, who thought of it as entirely separate from the State. When Gramsci uses the formula 'State = political society + civil society' he is indicating the real relation between the formally 'public' and 'private'. This leads him to break down the abstract ideas of Politics and Law. In the case of the latter, Gramsci writes that the ruling bloc has to subordinate the other classes to the requirements of the productive process not just by issuing decrees, but through an ongoing transformation of moral values and customs in civil society.[10] Hence civil society is the terrain in which classes contest for power (economic, political and ideological). It is here that hegemony is exercised, and where the terms of the relations of the structure and superstructure are fought out.

Politics, itself described by Gramsci as a 'level of the superstructure', is the key moment in the relations of structure and superstructure. It is the 'purely political moment' that 'marks the passage from the structure to the sphere of the complex superstructures',[11] and where the nature of class relations is ultimately constituted and contested in a continuously shifting relation of forces. Gramsci's project in writing the *Notebooks* is a theorisation of the political level through reflection on his own experience and on Italian history. For him, the political level has its own laws, distinct from the economic, and its own 'incandescent atmosphere',[12] and it is through an analysis of the political that he conceives of ideology.

In this context, ideologies are not judged according to a criterion of truth and falsehood, but according to their function and efficacy in binding together classes and class fractions in positions of dominance and subordination. Ideology serves to 'cement and unify' the social bloc.[13] Gramsci makes two related distinctions concerning ideology. The first distinction is between systematic ways of thinking ('philosophy' and 'ideology', in his usage) and aggregated and internally contradictory forms of thought ('common sense' and 'folklore'). The second distinction is between organic, semi-organic and non-organic ideologies; that is; according to the degree to which ideologies correspond to the potentialities and movement of fundamental classes in history, and to their capacity for concrete analyses of situations. The 'truth' of an ideology, for Gramsci, lies in its power to mobilise politically, and finally in its historical actualisation.[14]

The theoretical inadequacy of this conception which tends to pragmatically assimilate historical materialism to other ideologies will be dealt with in the next section. But here it should be noted that Gramsci is breaking new ground vis-à-vis marxist understanding of ideology, which had stood still with the famous formulation of *The German Ideology*: 'The ideas of the ruling class are in every epoch the ruling ideas; i.e., the class which is the ruling material force of society is at the same time the ruling ideological force.'[15] Gramsci maintains Marx's important conception that the dominant bourgeois ideology presents itself as universal. Any stains of 'rank and station' that presuppose any inherent inequality between men are washed away; the ruling bloc's power to speak in the name of the 'people', the 'nation', 'humanity' and so on is a precondition of the founding of its own state and the guarantee of its survival.[16] However, Gramsci breaks with the conception of ideology as a simple reflection of relations at the economic level, and as the uniform expression of the ruling class. Whilst the dominant ideology is necessarily systematised and presents itself as universal, it does not spring automatically from the ruling class, but is usually the result of the relation of forces between the fractions of the ruling bloc.[17] Hence Gramsci conceives of the differential appropriation of the dominant ideas within the ruling bloc itself and within the dominated class. The first has its basis in the fractioning of the ruling bloc and in a division of labour between broadly intellectual and more practical functions; the second, in the complex process of assimilation, transformation and rejection of the dominant ideas by the subordinate classes.

Hegemony

This leads us to Gramsci's concept of hegemony. Recent usages of the concept have tended to assimilate it to 'ideological domination' and to instrumentalise it by suggesting a simple mirror relation of domination and subordination;[18] it should therefore be made clear that hegemony, for Gramsci, includes the ideological but cannot be reduced to that level, and that it refers to the dialectical relation of class forces. Ideological dominance and subordination are not understood in isolation, but always as one, though crucially important, aspect of the relations of the classes and class fractions at all levels – economic and political, as well as ideological/cultural. The concept of hegemony is produced by Gramsci to analyse these relations within classes and between classes. It involves the organisation of 'spontaneous' consent which can be won, for example, by the ruling bloc making economic concessions that 'yet do not touch its essential interests', combined with other measures that foster forms of consciousness which accept a position of subordination (what Gramsci refers to as sectional and corporate consciousness).[19] The concept allows an analysis that keeps the levels of the social formation distinct and held in combination; hence Gramsci uses 'political hegemony'[20] or 'hegemony in philosophy'[21] to indicate the dominant instance of that hegemony. This more specified use of the concept is not theorised by Gramsci, though he opens the way for a more complex and articulated notion of hegemony.

Gramsci acknowledges Lenin to be the originator of the concept of hegemony,[22] but the latter's idea of it is far more restricted to the political level. Lenin defined it in terms of the leadership of the proletariat in its alliance with the poor peasantry. Gramsci maintains this usage, as can be seen in his Leninist approval of the Jacobins, but broadened its scope because for him hegemony had to be fought for on the terrain of civil society. Gramsci's frequent reference to 'ethico-political hegemony' indicates its breadth; the hegemony of the ruling bloc is seen not simply at the political level, but as affecting every aspect of social life and thought.

Gramsci has neither a theory of ideology as imposed by the ruling class, nor a spontaneous, immanentist one, like Lukács. He combines elements of both, but does so by working in a different problematic from that of the simple totality. Where the majority of theorists of ideology think only of systematic thought, or do their best to systematise forms of ideology to bring out their coherence, Gramsci is acutely aware of the way in which ideology is a 'lived relation'. His own experience of the peasant culture of Sardinia[23] and as a revolutionary organiser in the 1920s taught him the importance of grappling with the problem of how ideas are appropriated and the relation between those ideas and forms of action and behaviour. He is perhaps the first marxist to seriously examine ideology at its 'lower levels' as the accumulation of popular 'knowledges' and the means of dealing with everyday life – what he calls 'common sense'.

Common sense, intellectuals and the Party

Common-sense thinking for Gramsci is both a historical formation and specific to each class. This is evident in his account of the development of the concept from a term of the 17th and 18th century empiricist philosophers battling against theology, to its subsequent usage as a confirmation of accepted opinion rather than its subversion.[24] However, Gramsci's brief notes on common sense consist largely of general observations on a way of thinking. He characterises it as inherently eclectic and disjointed. Because common sense is not systematic and does not make explicit its own mode of reasoning, it can combine ideas that are contradictory without being aware of that fact. As a consequence, it builds up a storehouse of 'knowledges' that are drawn from earlier ideologies and from a variety of social classes:

> (Common sense) . . . is strangely composite; it contains elements from the Stone Age and principles of a more advanced science, prejudices from all past phases of history at the local level and intuitions of a future philosophy which will be that of the human race united the world over.[25]

Gramsci identifies the absence of a 'consciousness of historicity' and hence of self-knowledge as the principal feature that condemns common-sense thinking to a position of dependence and subordination. Popular notions such as 'human nature' effectively discount the possibility of change and 'naturalise' the social order.[26] The 'naturalisation' process, which for Marx was central to bourgeois Political Economy, is regarded by Gramsci as a key mechanism of common-sense thought. It is precisely in the 'materiality' and the matter-of-factness that has gathered around the notion of 'human nature' that we can see the intimate articulation of the 'structure in dominance' of the 'higher' and 'lower' realms of ideology.

The relation between the dominant ideology and common sense is not, however, hierarchically fixed, but driven by the class contradictions within it. The former can intervene in popular thinking 'positively' in order to recompose its elements and add new ones, or 'negatively' by setting boundaries on its development, whilst leaving it the restricted freedom of internal elaboration.[27] The terms of these relations are often affected by other factors such as language, which can itself become a means of self-defence and proud self-assertion on the part of the masses. Thus a dialect functions both as the infrastructure for folklore and parochialism, and as a means of resistance, which can be called the negative and positive poles of corporativism.[28] Nevertheless, the contradictions between the modes of thinking remain and are manifested within common sense itself between ideas borrowed from ruling ideologies and those spontaneously generated through the experience of class solidarity. In moments of open conflict those contradictions open up a gap between 'the superficial, explicit or verbal consciousness' and the consciousness 'implicit in activity'.[29] These moments often signal a crisis in the hegemony of the ruling bloc.

Whilst the dynamic of ideologies is affirmed by Gramsci through its positioning as a level of the superstructures, it is never free-floating. He introduces the category of 'intellectual' to designate those with the task of organising, disseminating and conserving skills and ideas associated with mental rather than manual labour. To analyse the formation of ideology and culture in relation to classes, he distinguishes between 'organic intellectuals', who have functions firmly based on the interests of a fundamental class, and 'traditional intellectuals', who belong to classes and strata remaining as remnants of a previous social formation.[30] The two categories do have a different conceptual value in that the 'organic intellectual' refers to a definite class affiliation, whilst the 'traditional intellectual' suggests a lack of that affiliation. The key issue is one of function in the system, but Gramsci is sensitive to the differential relation of levels of the superstructure to the structure, and hence to the significance of sub-ideologies that he sees as particularly important among 'traditional intellectuals'. It accounts for a degree of affiliation to a group or organisation that can come into conflict with allegiance owed to a fundamental class. Referring to the Church (the locus classicus of the 'traditional intellectual'), he writes of the 'internal necessities of an organisational character' and that

> if for every ideological struggle one wanted to find an immediate primary explanation in the structure, one would really be caught napping.[31]

The category of the 'intellectual' in Gramsci enables him to analyse the organisation and production of ideology as a specific practice that is not reducible to the classes to which the intellectuals are linked. Hence ideas are not expressive of classes, but comprise a field in which class conflict takes place in particular forms. Through organisations like the Church, the press and political parties (organs of civil society) and through the State (for the ruling bloc) the intellectuals play a leading role in the battle to gain spontaneous support for one of the fundamental classes.[32]

In the organisation of hegemony in capitalist society, the ruling bloc mobilises the organs both of civil society and of the State. Gramsci drew attention to the aspects of class rule that are non-coercive, whereas previous marxists, including Marx himself and Lenin, regarded the State largely as the organised violence of the ruling class. Gramsci writes of the 'positive educative' influence of the schools and the 'repressive and negative educative' influence of the courts.[33] The vital relation, however, for Gramsci, is between the State and civil society; that is, to what extent the ruling bloc can keep civil society under its hegemony. Ultimately the ruling bloc retains power because of its control of the repressive apparatuses (police and army), which enable it to keep other classes in subjection even when it has lost hegemony over them.[34] Hence the 'war of movement', the seizure of State power, is an imperative corollary to the 'war of position' in which classes move to take the vantage points in civil society. However, the central position of the State in the maintenance of class rule is radically reconceived by Gramsci. The crucial development of civil society in the West, for him, changes the relation of the State to the rest of the superstructure so that it becomes merely the 'outer ditch' of the defences. This is because civil society makes up the 'system of fortresses and outworks' that provide the long term guarantee of stability for the ruling bloc.[35] This leads Gramsci to reconceptualise a strategy for the revolutionary party based on winning political hegemony prior to the seizure of power.[36] Since the ruling bloc determines the political terrain and organises its hegemony increasingly in civil society, the party has to explore the terrain and construct a strategy accordingly. Central to this is the development of organic intellectuals by the party and the detachment of traditional intellectuals from the ruling bloc

Hegemony is based on voluntary and spontaneous 'consent', but takes different forms according to the relationship of classes which it embodies. For example, the Church maintains its hold over the masses through external impositions – by clamping down on the freedom of thought of its intellectuals, and by the masses themselves from rising out of the mish-mash of common-sense thinking to more systematic forms of thought. In contrast, the revolutionary party's struggle for hegemony marks a break with previous forms of hegemony. Marxists seek to raise cultural levels, and to break down the cultural oppression institutionalised in the rigid division of mental and manual labour in capitalist society. Gramsci proposes that the party does not act mechanically on popular thinking from outside, but enters the mind of common-sense thinking in order to open up its contradictions:

> It is not a question of introducing from scratch a scientific form of thought into everyone's lives, but of renovating and making 'critical' an already existing activity.[37]

The relationship of the party to the masses is not that of a one-way relay mechanism, but a dialectic between leadership and spontaneity. Because Gramsci does not work with a true/false consciousness or science/ideology model his thinking is directed towards the contradictory possibilities within spontaneous, non-systematised forms of thinking and action. (And here he makes a positive evaluation of appeals to emotional and moral attitudes, and rejects a rationalist notion of persuasion by pure logic.[38]) In itself, he sees spontaneity as doomed because riven by internal contradictions and incapable of producing a systematic account of the world, but when 'educated and purged of extraneous contradictions' that spontaneity is, for Gramsci, the motor of revolution.[39]

Ideology as conceived in the *Prison Notebooks* is bound to the political; it is through politics that the 'relation between common sense and the upper level of philosophy is assured',[40] and politics is essentially concerned with conceptions of the State. Gramsci's analyses of sectional/corporate consciousness and common-sense thinking are aimed at revealing their inability to understand the role of the capitalist State, and hence their failure to grasp the political as the crucial level of the social formation. Corporate consciousness and common sense share a ground of thought which is specifically non-theoretical, and often anti-theoretical. Here 'feeling', 'personal experience' and immediate empirical perception are dominant. Gramsci's comments on peasant 'subversivism' highlight these features as a 'negative' class response:

> Not only does that people have no precise consciousness of its own historical identity, it is not even conscious of the . . . exact limits of its adversary. There is a dislike of officialdom – the only form in which the State is perceived.[41]

There are, nevertheless, 'positive' aspects to corporate consciousness and common sense (Gramsci refers to the element of class solidarity, and to the 'earthy suspicion' involved in popular anti-clericalism). However, they remain necessarily subordinate and defensive.

The whole force of Gramsci's work is to insist on the importance of theory for the analysis of social formations, precisely because the non-theoretical cannot go beyond immediate appearances, and therefore cannot identify the 'enemy' except in a vague way. Marxism is, for Gramsci, in an important sense unlike any other ideology because it enables an understanding of the terrain on which class struggles take place. The *Prison Notebooks* are remarkable as a work of theory which polemically engages with the persistent hold of the dominant ideology on parts of the workers' movement; in so doing, he re-poses the whole question of ideology in relation to the political level.

Ideology and the problem of historicism

Gramsci's conceptions of politics and the social formation in general, we have tried to indicate, are attempts to explain *complex* objects. It is important to keep in mind that his work is directed against a mechanistic or economistic marxism, and ideology, correspondingly, can for Gramsci in no sense be reduced to an irrelevant epiphenomenon. Nor can it be interpreted in a psychologistic fashion as a search for the 'dirty-Jewish' interests of individuals of particular (ruling) classes.[42] Fatalism and conspiracy theses play no part whatever in his work. Correspondingly, for Gramsci, there are no pregiven 'interests' for the working class either. While acknowledging the moral comfort which a fatalistic economism can offer to the masses in politically adverse periods, he constantly points to the need for a general political perspective – one which necessarily involves a recognition of the importance of ideology. His specific concern with common sense as the substratum of ideologies, reveals an analysis quite opposed to any simple dichotomy between 'ideas' and the economy. The repeated stress on the complex unity of structure and superstructure makes clear that Gramsci (correctly in our view) rejects any simple unilinear causal hierarchy. The economistic standpoint itself has its roots in practical experience, is a material consequence of the daily struggle of wage labour with and under capital, and it is a paramount task of the marxist party to overcome the dualities and sectionalisms of what Gramsci terms 'corporate' consciousness. Ideology is not a 'trick' imposed by a ruling class in order eternally to deceive the workers, and thus prevent the class from achieving its (supposedly) predetermined historic role. Ideologies have their ground in material realities and are themselves material forces. Nevertheless, materially based working-class outlooks are not inevitably condemned to remain corporate. Common sense and practical experience can and must be worked on. They contain elements of 'good sense' and class instinct[43] which can be transformed into a coherent socialist perspective because that day-to-day corporate struggle, however characterised by relations of domination and subordination, is itself a contradictory phenomenon.

Ideology, then, for Gramsci, has, like the social formation of which it is a necessary part, a complex and contradictory identity. Unlike Althusser, for example, Gramsci does not offer an epistemological definition in addition to an explanation of ideology's material social role. Ideologies *qua* ideologies, for Gramsci, are neither true nor false, though they can certainly be coherent to a greater or lesser degree. Ideology is principally regarded as the 'cement' which holds together the *structure* (in which economic class struggle takes place) and the realm of the complex superstructures. Yet whether and to what extent ideologies succeed in performing this role is never pre-given. There is, it follows, always a certain openness in the ground of ideology, and, in particular, with regard to common sense. This openness constitutes the space in which the communist party works: to break with the theoretical limitations of corporate consciousness (under which the masses necessarily 'borrow' their conceptions of the world from the dominant class),[44] in order to achieve the required level of coherence and political-cultural breadth for the exercise of hegemony. Only when this is obtained – and it can only be the product of the differential unity of political, economic, and intellectual practices – can the conception of life concerned be said to be genuinely 'organic'. Ultimately, therefore, mass adhesion is the 'validation' of an ideology. But Gramsci's argument about the objective intellectual function of certain 'technical' strata organic to modern capitalism, and his repeated suggestion that these must be won over by the political party, are significant. They militate against any explanation of mass adhesion by recourse either to spontaneism or to the *a priori* notion of a privileged class-subject. It is interesting to note that whenever Gramsci refers to the 'psychological validity' which mass adhesion confers upon an ideology, his account is couched in metaphorical rather than literal terms.[45] The recognition that the party itself must function analogously to a 'collective intellectual'[46] in order to become adequate to the complexity of the structure/superstructure bloc sharpens his keen sense that history is never made other than in concrete historico-political situations.

It is relevant at this point to raise again the problem of Gramsci's 'historicism', for the above formulation of 'mass adhesion' suggests the kind of concessions to relativism which Althusser and Poulantzas, amongst others, see as characteristics of the historicist tendency. Briefly, to recapitulate, historicists are accused of reducing the complexity of a social totality to a simple, uniform essence, and of reducing the validity of theoretical positions to the historical conditions of the period which the ideas are said to 'express'. Now this concept entails an *a priori* collapse of base and superstructure (or levels of a social formation) into an 'expressive unity' which can be either economically, culturally or spiritually defined. For example, the 'essence' of a period or process might be taken to be the *level of the productive forces*, which according to a teleologically defined schema, sets the pace for a series of 'progressive' historical stages. And we have seen in the previous section how a 'culturalist' appropriation of Gramsci – in contrast to the 'economistic' position – is achieved. However, being diametrically opposed to that of economism, the culturalist appropriation is excessive in just the opposite way. Alternatively, history might be seen as a movement in which the most progressive class is that which is potentially capable of the greatest degree of self-realisation in history. Thus, for, say, Lukács, the proletariat is the first class capable (in socialism/communism) of total *self-consciousness* and thus self-realisation in history, for history is nothing other than the expressive unity of consciousness and practice. Formally opposed to economism, this conception self-evidently shares with the other two an essentialism which defies rational verification. It is the fundamentally abstract, and even mystical, nature of these ideas of processes, essences, ends, and class subjects which troubles the theoretically 'rigorous' French schools of marxism. There is no room in a science for irrationalist conceptions, however politically or morally 'progressive'.

Now, undoubtedly, Gramsci tends at times to express himself in historicist terms. In the next section of this paper, that problem is given greater textual elaboration in response to certain structuralist constructions of Gramsci's positions. It should suffice here to indicate the existence of that problem and to suggest the basis or elements of an assessment of it.

Ideologies are, we have seen, 'conceptions of life'. This is a concept, it could be argued, which is close to Lukács's notion of 'world-view' or 'class consciousness' Furthermore, Gramsci argues that organic ideologies are those linked to 'fundamental classes' and mediated by (another example of a 'bloc') a political party.[47] Indeed at one point Gramsci suggests that there is a party for every class: something which allows the political level little autonomy. Now clearly there is a position here which might be interpreted as involving self-moving class 'subjects' each having their own historically sequential organic ideas. The necessity of ideologies is then justified by their expression of and *as* the essence of the historical process itself. We have said that Gramsci's main reflections are premissed upon the idea that the social totality is complex, but doubt appears to be thrown on that assertion when the above thesis is accompanied by a selection from Gramsci's philosophical comments. For example, Gramsci asserts that the activities of economics, politics, and philosophy 'form a homogenous circle'.[48] This could be taken to imply a pregiven harmony between social levels, and seems to undermine the claim for any real or theoretical complexity. The notion of an essential unity between history and human praxis is taken further in arguments of which the following are representative examples:

> It might seem that there can exist an extra-historical and extra-human objectivity. But who is the judge of such objectivity? . . . Objectivity always means 'humanly objective' which can be held to exactly correspond to 'historically subjective': in other words objectivity would mean 'universal subjective'.
>
> We know reality only in relation to man, and since man is historical becoming, knowledge and reality are also a becoming and so is objectivity.[49]

Clearly, in the light of these Hegelian and somewhat mystifying remarks, marxism itself could not be expected to escape relativistic criteria:

> But even the philosophy of praxis is an expression of historical contradictions.[50]
>
> Hegelian immanentism becomes historicism, but it is absolute historicism only with the philosophy of praxis – absolute historicism and absolute humanism.[51]

The problem, then, of whether marxism is a science or an ideology is one of the thorniest in Gramsci. The difference between (social) science and ideology seems not to be a qualitiative one. (The case of the natural sciences is more problematic.) Thus there is no explicit sense in which marxism as a conception of life is any different from, say, Calvinism. Indeed, genuinely organic ideologies (and marxism seems to be numbered amongst them) appear to differ only in the historical circumstances upon which their mass adhesion rests.

We can begin to throw doubt on the 'historicist' accusations by first of all calling to mind other of Gramsci's general pronouncements, and, more importantly, by arguing that his major concepts are unintelligible if those accusations are correct.

> The claim, presented as an essential postulate of historical materialism, that every fluctuation of politics and ideology can be presented and expounded as an immediate expression of the structure must be contested in theory as primitive infantilism.[52]

Even Gramsci's philosophical comments are not theoretically uniform. For example, there is no doubt that he allows considerable autonomy to the sciences,[53] and his argument against Bukharin is not, as is sometimes claimed, a rejection of scientificity. Rather, in denouncing the latter's mechanicism, Gramsci argues that each science is specific and that it is therefore impossible to generate a general, normative, model of scientific practice. A positivist criterion such as Bukharin adopts in fact hinders that which it is meant to facilitate: an account of the intrinsic 'method' of science. Gramsci concludes that what in later discourse has become known as 'science-in-general' is a metaphysical or *philosophical* notion, and that it can no more cover differences *within* the individual natural sciences than it can those *between* natural and social sciences. Gramsci maintains that an irreducible difference in method and and object separates the latter. Those familiar with Louis Althusser's recent self-criticism (for more of which see the conclusion to this article and the separate paper on Althusser in this journal), will be struck by its intriguing resemblance to these ideas of Gramsci.

However, it is above all to Gramsci's substantive concepts of historical materialism that we should turn for a less simplistic picture of his historicism. This argument will be elaborated in a moment. Similarly, Gramsci's stress on the material forms of ideology, its lack of uniform content, and, above all, its social *production* (the intellectuals) directs us once more away from simple (general) philosophical positions.

It is the insistence on historical specificity (and *not* historical relativism) which militates against any blanket categorisation. This is not to dispute – especially with regard to his philosophical remarks – that Gramsci adopts at times positions akin to humanism and even pragmatism.[54] Yet in fairness it should be pointed out that the best examples of this tendency occur in a polemic against positivism and theoretical economism within marxism. To speak of the unity of the levels of a social formation in this context is entirely justifiable, though Gramsci's own term of 'homogenous circle'[55] is certainly an overstatement. In general, Gramsci never questions the complexity of unified social levels.

The perspective which the identification of hegemonic classes, parties, and ideas offers has absolutely no implications of a prior teleology. Rather, those conceptions facilitate a material and theoretically consistent analysis of what is specific about historical conjunctures, and therefore the relation of a marxist party to that practical situation. It is crucial here to point out that an account of factors 'relative' to a conjuncture implies no necessary relativisation of the concepts used in such an analysis. The concepts, of course, are *general* ones, but they do not refer to general *entities*. For Gramsci, ideology-in-general does not exist. There are only conceptions whose political roles depend on the material effect they carry in specific situations. He is not interested in the 'arbitrary elucubrations of individuals'[56] but in the social and political role which ideas play. If this is the case, it would seem more accurate to claim that Gramsci deals with the practico-social function of ideologies at the expense of philosophical theses, rather than to somewhat misleadingly seek a unity between his philosophical speculation and his contribution to the substantive work of historical materialism. This concern with specific analysis of ideologies – their relation to economic class formation and the existence and degree of hegemony exercised in a conjuncture – is considered by Gramsci to be a theoretical precondition for practical interventions by marxists. Such a position cannot be reduced to the fallacies of historicism (humanism, and especially economism), for it explicitly and convincingly advances upon them.

The structuralist appropriation of Gramsci – Althusser

We have already referred to the complex nature of Gramsci's 'historicism'. This question is further compounded when we come to examine the relation to Gramsci of the 'structuralist marxists' (referring here specifically to Althusser and Poulantzas). Structuralist marxism is diametrically opposed to – indeed, is constructed on the back of a systematic dismantling of – 'historicism'. Gramsci's relation to 'historicism' is exceedingly complex: as we have suggested, in many important ways, he is not a 'historicist' at all, if we have someone like Lukács in mind as a representative figure of that tendency. Hence, the relationship of Althusser and Poulantzas to Gramsci must be anything but straightforward.

Gramsci frequently referred to historical materialism as a 'philosophy of praxis'. He clearly took this designation seriously – the reference cannot be wholly explained as a euphemism for 'marxism' adopted by Gramsci to evade the prison censor's eye. Thus, when the structuralists come to deal with Gramsci at this general philosophical level, he is the object of their sharp criticism. However, even here Althusser draws some critical distinctions. He is always at pains to 'except' Gramsci from the *general* critique of historicism such as he levels at Lukács, Korsch and Sartre. He also takes great care to distinguish Gramsci's position on the status of 'historical materialism' as a 'philosophy of praxis', from the latter's substantive concepts, which are singled out for favourable and positive attention. These distinctions are of great importance in defining some of the parameters within which the structuralist encounter with Gramsci has been conducted. But, over and above any specific references to Gramsci or direct acknowledgements of his contribution, it can be plainly seen that Gramsci has played a *generative* role and occupies a pivotal position in relation to the work of structuralist marxism as a whole.

The relationship between Gramsci and the structuralists reveals, however, a significant unevenness. A sort of 'graph' could be drawn, which would not only plot this relationship more accurately, but would go some way to explaining *when* and *why* Gramsci's work has a particular pertinence for the structuralists, and when it does not. Plotting the relationship in this way also helps to establish the main points of convergence and divergence between the two positions. In his early, seminal, essay on 'Contradiction and Over-determination' (in *For Marx*, 1969), Althusser is concerned with defining the nature of 'contradictions' within a social formation. His argument is that a social formation is not a simple 'expressive totality': contradictions do not necessarily arise at all levels of the social formation at the same time, or flood all the levels simultaneously from some 'principal contradiction' lodged in some simple way 'in the (economic) base'. Contradictions have their own specificity. The point of importance is how contradictions which arise from 'absolutely dissimilar currents', to use Lenin's phrase, can effectively 'merge' or fuse into a major ruptural unity, and thus constitute the site of a decisive political conjuncture. This question is 'thought' by Althusser principally with reference to Lenin and 1917.[57] But the terrain of concerns is not at all foreign to that which Gramsci explored in his writings in the *Prison Notebooks* – for example, his discussion of how to distinguish between 'organic' and 'conjunctural' features of a crisis in the relations of class forces in 'The Modern Prince'.[58]

As Althusser advanced into the period of *Reading Capital*, he became preoccupied by a different set of questions – not unrelated, but posed with a significantly different theoretical emphasis. Here he was concerned with identifying the nature of 'Marx's immense theoretical revolution' in *Capital*. This question is 'thought' with the aid of a distinctive set of concepts; the distinction between ideology and science; the nature of 'theoretical practice'; the role of philosophy in providing the epistemological guarantee of the 'scientificity' of marxism; the theory of 'structuralist causality'. Many of these concepts are developed in direct contestation with the conceptual terrain of 'historicism'. At this point, Althusser is at his farthest distance from Gramsci. Though there is, as we shall see in a little more detail in a moment, no blanket condemnation, the critique of Gramsci's 'historicism' constitutes a central strand in the long and important essay in *Reading Capital* devoted to the proposition that 'Marxism Is Not A Historicism'.[59]

There have been two significant developments in Althusser's work since that point. The first is the important 'ISAs essay', in which Althusser turned his attention once more to the concrete analysis of the ideological instance, and to the function of the 'ideological state apparatuses' in reproducing the hegemony of a dominant ideology in particular social formations.[60] The second is that remarkable labour of self-clarification and modification represented by the essays in *Essay In Self-Criticism* (1974). Full justice cannot be done to the latter volume here. But it is important to note the following: Althusser has much modified the simple ideology/science distinction established in his earlier work; he has admitted the 'theoreticism' of some of the positions adopted; he has abandoned the idea of a self-sufficient 'theoretical practice'; philosophy is now defined, not as an 'epistemological guarantee' but as an intervention in 'the class struggle in theory'. Whilst the scientific status of Marx's theoretical breakthroughs cannot be reduced to the historical conditions which made them possible, those conditions are no longer considered irrelevant to when and how such 'breaks' are made. Althusser has continued to insist that these modifications – not all of them securely founded – have not touched the essential points in his critique of humanism and historicism.

But the shift of emphases and the substantial reassessments *have* had the effect of, once again, lowering some of the barriers between 'structuralist marxism' and Gramsci's work. For example, they have made it possible for the structuralist theorists to acknowledge what those critics who were critical of Althusser's 'theoreticism' have always argued: that in Gramsci's attention to the specificity of 'the political', his attack on all forms of economic reductionism, and his insistence on the necessary complexity of the structure-superstructure complex, we *already find traversed* – albeit in terminology very different from that of the structuralists – precisely those questions about 'relative autonomy' and the 'ever pre-given complex unity of a social formation' which are, rightly, believed to constitute *Althusser*'s 'immense theoretical revolution'. Thus, whether Gramsci is a 'historicist' or not, *something* led him, in the *Prison Notebooks*, to register, with remarkable force, clarity and consistency, his necessary break with a marxism conceived *either* as an economic reductionism *or* as a theory of social formations as 'expressive totalities'. And this was a break with what Althusser defined as the essence of 'historicism' – as well as of its mirror-image, economism.

To put the matter summarily, if Gramsci remains a 'historicist', then his is a historicism which *broke* with what the structuralists have defined as the essence of the problematic of historicism. It is therefore a 'historicism' with which the structuralists are obliged to come to terms – to reckon with, not simply to dismiss. Gramsci constitutes *the limit case* of 'historicism' for structuralist marxism.[61] Far from this being now a closed matter, it remains an open and unconcluded encounter – one of the most important encounters in the field of contemporary marxist theory. Objectively, this is the *position* in which the problematic of Gramsci and that of Althusser and Poulantzas stand to one another. How Althusser and Poulantzas have actually negotiated their own particular positions within this theoretical conjuncture at different points in their work is a matter for more detailed tracing.

There are only scattered references to Gramsci in Althusser's early essays (*For Marx*). They all signal his importance, often in direct contrast with Lukács, the arch-historicist. Gramsci is 'of another stature' (p. 114). This is acknowledged specifically in relation to Gramsci's awareness of the need for an 'elaboration of the particular essence of the specific elements of the superstructure'. 'Hegemony' is also specifically cited as a new concept, a 'remarkable solution'. In the later essays in this collection, Althusser begins to develop a theory of ideology – first through the ideology/science distinction, then in terms of 'the way men "live" the real relations of their conditions of existence', or as an 'imaginary relation to the real relations of existence': here 'ideology' is being 'thought' by Althusser largely without the benefit of Gramsci's work.[62] Gramsci's 'great theses on Marxist philosophy' are, again, identified in *Reading Capital* as of considerable significance. He is, of course, identified with those marxist theoreticians – Lukács, Luxembourg, Korsch – who contributed to the development of marxism as a 'revolutionary humanism and historicism', affirming that it is 'advancing "men" . . . who always triumph in the end' (p. 120). Althusser acknowledges that some support for this reading can be discovered in Marx's own work. But he insists that Marx must be read 'symptomatically' – attending to the changing problematics which inform different periods of his work, and the 'epistemological ruptures' which mark one period off from another. However, as we might predict, it is just here that the major critique of Gramsci is launched. Althusser's tread is a cautious one – lest his 'necessarily schematic remarks may disfigure the spirit of this enormously delicate and subtle work of genius' (p. 126). He distinguished Gramsci's 'historicist' view of dialectical materialism and of the role of philosophy in marxism, from his 'discoveries' in the field of historical materialism. The distinction leads Althusser to call for a 'symptomatic reading' of Gramsci *too*. His humanist statements are 'primarily critical and polemical' (p. 127). The work on ideology is positively exempted. The aspect commented on here – Gramsci's attention to the role of ideology in 'cementing and unifying' a whole social bloc, preserving its 'ideological unity', and his rooting of ideology in the superstructures – points forward to the ISAs essay, and to Poulantzas's *Political Power and Social Classes* (1973). But still, Gramsci's stress on the *historical* side of 'historical materialism' is unfavourably compared with Marx's stress on the *materialist*. This is the *nub* of the critique of a philosophy of praxis: that it conflates knowledge and 'the real' – thus Marxism becomes, not scientific knowledge but simply another of the great, organic ideologies.[63] Gramsci's problematic is crossed by more than one path: but when historicism crosses it, everything else in the argument 'submits to its law'.

There is one additional point about the treatment of Gramsci in *Reading Capital* which requires further comment. In a criticial footnote, Althusser attacks Gramsci's use of the concept 'civil society', and declares that it should be struck from the Marxist theoretical vocabulary (p. 162). Later, Poulantzas is to be even fiercer about it. But, as we have seen, the concept 'civil society' is of central importance to Gramsci – a matter made more difficult because of the ambiguity of some of his formulations of it, and the difficulty of locating it precisely in Gramsci's structure/superstructure topography. More than a mere disagreement is signalled here; hence it is worth pursuing somewhat further, not only for the light it might throw on Gramsci but for what it reveals about Althusser and Poulantzas.

There is no mystery to the hostility with which the Althussereans regard the concept of 'civil society'.[64] It played a prominent role in both classical Political Economy and 18th-century political theory, but more significantly in Hegel. All three use it to refer to the sphere of bourgeois 'individualism' *par excellence* – the terrain of possessive individualism, of market relations of contract between 'bare individuals', of individual bourgeois 'rights and freedoms', above all, the terrain of economic needs and of economic man *(homo economicus) per se*. The Political Economists regard it as the arena of economic life as such: Hegel regarded it as that 'egoistic' sphere of particularity which had to be raised to a wider universality – that of political citizenship – by the State. Marx frequently engaged with *all* the themes posed by this problematic. His frequent critique of Political Economy is that it treats market relations as the sum of capitalist economic relations, ignoring the *production* of surplus altogether: it is *this* concept which confined classical Political Economy, in Marx's eyes, to its 'bourgeois skin'. The 'naturalization' of the market is dismantled in some of Marx's most ironic remarks in *Capital* about an economic theory based on the model of Robinson Crusoe. He directly confronted Hegel's use of the concept in, *inter alia*, the *Critique of Hegel's Philosophy of Right*. He assailed the notion that the dismantling of capitalism could be regarded as a struggle for 'bourgeois political rights' alone – in *On the Jewish Question*. In the *German Ideology* we still find Marx using the concept, but now with a more inclusive meaning of his own:

> This conception of society depends on our ability to expound the real process of production, starting out from the material production of life itself, and to comprehend the form of intercourse connected with this and created by this mode of production (i.e. civil society in all its various stages, as the basis of all history).[65]

The structuralists want to insist – it seems to us correctly – that the Marx of *Capital* had left this problematic behind. They want to expunge it from the marxist theoretical vocabulary because to preserve it is to sustain, inside the marxist discourse, the 'humanist' echoes of a reference to the sphere of 'the needs of human subjects'.[66] Marxism, they argue, is a 'theory without a subject'. The presence of 'civil society' in Gramsci's work is therefore taken as an implicit index of his lingering 'humanism' (though this attribution is not, in our view, sustained by any of the *uses* of this concept which Gramsci actually makes). But if it no longer preserves its 18th-century meaning in Gramsci, what is it referencing? We tried, earlier, to say how the concept appears to us to function in Gramsci's discourse. Here we want to indicate why we would also want to say that this is not incompatible with Marx's problematic in *Capital*, even if Gramsci does not use the concept in exactly the same way.

Explicitly, in *Capital I*, Marx advances on classical Political Economy by insisting on going behind the exchange relations of the market to the 'hidden abode' of capitalist production, where surplus value is generated and labour power exploited. He does not, of course, totally excise the moment of market relations and of 'exchange'. In the *Grundrisse* and again in *Capital I* he demonstrates how capital reproduces itself at an expanding rate and realizes itself through the long circuit of capital accumulation – one which requires the articulation between different 'moments', between different *forms* of capital, including the 'dependent' sphere of circulation and exchange. Having established the primacy of the determination of production over the whole circuit of capital, he takes up again in *Capital II* the key questions of circulation and reproduction. Relations of circulation and exchange are capitalist relations too – necessary, though not determining. The sphere of exchange is articulated with the sphere of production, not loosely and fortuitously, but by specific mechanisms. It is in the sphere of circulation that commodities become 'exchangeable' through the 'passage of forms' into the most abstract and universal of commodities – the commodity which has the ability to mediate all commodity exchanges – money. It is through this 'metamorphosis' – 'C – M – C' – that commodities find their 'equivalent' expression in money terms – prices. But it is also in this sphere that capital hires 'free labour', through the mechanism of the labour market (i.e. where it purchases that valuable commodity which it must set to work in production – labour power). And it is also in in this sphere that capital pays the individual labourer the means of his subsistence, the cost of the reproduction of his labour power. Both these absolutely vital functions for capital are paid out of capital – they are the 'variable part' of capital, produced by labour power, which capital *advances* for the reproduction of labour power. But this 'variable part' appears in the sphere of exchange (again through the mediation of money) in the form of a particular economic relation – the wage relation – capital in the 'wage form'. In so far as capitalism is a mode of production founded on 'free labour', distributable to the branches of production only through the means of the market, and is a mode of economic production in which the labourer is separated from the means of existence, it *requires* a sphere of exchange, even though that sphere is dependent on capitalist production relations. The relations of exchange are, thus, the 'phenomenal forms' of the 'real relations' of production. Marx goes through this argument time and again in *Capital*, but the reference we have specifically in mind here is the Chapter on 'The Buying and Selling of Labour Power' *Capital* I, (Part II, Ch.6). Marx may no longer use the term, 'civil society' to designate this phase of the circuit of capital: but he certainly thinks its relation as a part of the economic relations of capitalism, and he retains, if not the term, then the conceptual space which it designated.[67]

But Marx says several other important things about the relations characteristic of this sphere of circulation and exchange. He suggests that it has the *ideological* function of concealing its real foundations – the generation and expropriation of the surplus in production. The 'noisy sphere' of exchange disguises the 'hidden abode' of capitalist production. You have to abandon the former and penetrate the latter in order to 'force the secret of profit making' (p. 176). This is not simply because the former suspends over the latter the forbidding sign, 'No admittance here except on business'. A specific ideological mechanism is involved. This is the mechanism of representation or re-presentation. For the exchanges of the market *appear* to the agents involved as 'free and equivalent' exchanges. They appear to exchange 'equivalent to equivalent'. Thus if, both in economic theory and in 'experience', the labourer 'lives' his relation to capitalism exclusively in the terms and categories with which he is presented in the sphere of the market, the source of his exploitation (in production) will be rendered invisible. He will 'live' – experience – the exploitative relations of capitalist production *as if* they were 'exchanges between equivalents'. If and when these 'free exchanges' become the object of class struggle, they will, of course, be confined to attempting to 'restore to their proper equivalence' relations which, in reality, are non-equivalent, exploitative in their very foundations. Such struggles Lenin called 'economist' and Gramsci called 'corporatist' – they do not, Gramsci said, 'touch the essentials'.

But Marx says something more about this sphere. From it, he says, there arise the principal relations of the political and juridical superstructures of bourgeois society, as well as the key ideological themes and discourses. This sphere 'is in fact a very Eden of the innate rights of men. There alone rule Freedom, Equality, Property and Bentham'. This arises precisely from the fact that this 'noisy sphere' *is* the (dependent) sphere of individual exchange – and hence the seat and origin of the 'possessive individualist' political and juridical freedoms of bourgeois society (all of them predicated on the individual subject) and of those ideologies of individualism which characterise bourgeois 'common sense'. Thus,

> 'Freedom, because both buyer and seller of a commodity, say, labour power are constrained [i.e. *appear* to be constrained] only by their own free will . . . the agreement they come to is but the form in which they give expression to their common will. Equality, because each enters into relation with the other, as with a simple owner of commodities, and they exchange equivalent for equivalent. Property because each disposes only of what is his own. And Bentham because each looks only to himself.' (p. 176).

In short, to adopt a phrase from Althusser himself, this 'noisy sphere' provides the basis for those superstructural practices and ideological forms in which men are forced to 'live an imaginary relation' of equivalence and individualism to their real (non-equivalent, collective) conditions of existence. This is not only the site of one of the very few passages in *Capital* where Marx explicitly marks the articulation between the economic, politico-juridcal and ideological levels of a social formation. It is also the place where, far from simply *abandoning* all that Hegel, Locke and Adam Smith referenced in the term 'civil society', he takes it up, and by thinking it through again, now on the transformed conceptual terrain of capital and its circuit, *produces a new concept of it.* It is no longer the seat and source of individualism. It is simply the individualising sphere of the circuit of capital's path to expanded reproduction. 'Individualism' is thus not the origin of the system – either in fact (Robisonades) or in theory. It is what capital produces as one of its necessary 'phenomenal forms' – one of its necessary but dependent effects. What most distinguishes Marx's designation of this new theoretical space is his use of it as a concept with which to reference some of the complex relations between base and superstructures. To identify the 'immediate forms' of capital at this point in its circuit, is to begin to trace what Gramsci called the 'passage' from base to the 'complex sphere of the superstructures'.

Althusser sometimes appears to be on the threshold of grasping this, but pulls back at a critical point. If we retain the concept 'civil society' he says, we must recognise that it has no economic existence, but is only a 'combined effect of law and legal political ideology on the economic'. This reading cannot be squared with Marx's in the chapter quoted above. Poulantzas follows Althusser in this – again by identifying it with the level of the juridico-political and the ideological only. But Marx is clearly demonstrating the accumulation of effects – economic, politico-juridical, ideological – in this single instance.

Gramsci, as we have already seen, makes a quite distinctive use of the concept 'civil society'. First, without its being precisely the same as Marx's just outlined, he *does* appear to hold quite closely to Marx's provisional formulation: at least in the sense of regarding 'civil society' as a concept which marks the *coupling* effect of base and superstructure. But Gramsci also employs it in a second sense, which is broader in conception, less directly attributable to Marx's formulation in *Capital*, and belonging more unambiguously to the concepts developed by Gramsci to 'think' the specificity of the political instance, and to articulate the concept of hegemony. Gramsci makes a critical distinction between the 'domination' of a ruling class alliance over a social formation, by force and coercion; and the 'direction' or leadership of such an alliance, by consent. The latter moment is that for which he reserves the term 'hegemony'. It is characterised by the capacity of a dominant bloc to extend its sphere of leadership and authority over society as a whole, and actively to *conform* economic, civil and cultural life, educational, religious and other institutions, to its sway. Many of these spheres are apparently far removed from the direct authority of the State, political society and the economy. In his second usage, these are some of the areas Gramsci includes under the loose designation, 'civil society'.

Now the function of the dominant ideology and of the ideological state apparatuses in 'cementing and unifying' a social formation under the hegemony of a particular class alliance *is* a question to which Althusser directed his attention in the ISAs article. But his dislike of the civil society/State distinction leads him to jettison it, declaring the distinction to be a purely legalistic one under capitalism, not of substantive importance. This obliges him to designate all the 'ideological apparatuses' as *state* apparatuses: he calls them 'Ideological state apparatuses'. He argues that it is of no consequence that some of these are directly organised by the State, and others are privately organised, since all of them function 'beneath the ruling ideology'.[68] This definition is tautologous. It also serves to mask certain critical distinctions. There *are* differences between apparatuses directly coordinated by the State and those which are not. These differences matter – they affect how such apparatuses function, how they are articulated *with* the State; they can also provide the basis of significant internal contradictions between different apparatuses within the complex of the State and the ruling bloc. For example, in the British case, the functions of the press (privately owned) and of television (indirectly coordinated with the State) are different because of their different modes of insertion; and these differences have *pertinent effects* – for example, in the manner in which different aspects of the class struggle are ideologically inflected in each. The ideological role of the Church, for example, differs depending on whether or not it is the organisational basis of a 'state religion' – as Gramsci's concern with Catholicism in Italy clearly revealed. The complex position of the trade unions is also not resolved by simply designating them, for all practical purposes, as 'state apparatuses'. For this masks the 'work' which the State has to do, and do ceaselessly, actively, to *hegemonise* the corporate, defensive institutions of the working class. Thus, too swift a designation of the trade unions to the sphere of the State blurs the critical question of the articulation between modern capitalism and Social Democracy. The same, from a different angle, could be said about the family. Those moments when functions for the reproduction of capital and of labour power, hitherto performed by the family as a 'private' institution, are taken over for the State are pivotal moments of transition, and require careful analysis. Althusser has always insisted on the need for specificity as part of the 'necessary complexity' of the marxist concept of totality. But the opposition to the concept of 'civil society' has the theoretical effect, here, precisely of leading us to abandon specificity for a rather too convenient generalisation. Again, Althusser insists on the primacy of 'the concrete analysis of a concrete situation'. But it is Gramsci's use of the distinction between State and civil society, and between different moments and types of combination within the different forms of hegemony, which has the real pay-off for the analysis of specific conjunctures.

We have identified one of the problems which beset Althusser's ISAs essay – the dissolving of the public/private distinction, the too swift absorption of all apparatuses onto the terrain of the State, and the tendency then to see the 'reproduction' functions of the State for Capital as too unproblematic. (A problem of a rather similar kind can also be identified in Poulantzas's *Political Power and Social Classes*, which follows on closely from Althusser and which also shows a tendency to absorb everything under the umbrella of the capitalist State.) Yet, at a more general level, the seminal ISAs essay seems to us unthinkable without benefit of Gramsci's work. Here, the whole problem of ideology appears to have been re-thought with Gramsci's categories very much in mind. Althusser's list of ISAs is a direct borrowing from Gramsci's *Notebooks*. Ideology is thought, less in terms of its contrast with science, more in terms of its practico-social effect in cementing a ruling bloc beneath a dominant ideology. This is a very Gramscian conception. Althusser defines the whole terrain introduced in this essay as that of 'reproduction' – the apparatuses which serve to 'reproduce the relations of production'. But this is not far from Gramsci's notion that the superstructures serve to 'conform' society to the long-term needs of Capital. The centrality given by Althusser to the educational system as an ISA – with the family, the *key* ISA couple, replacing the Church-family couple – corresponds to Gramsci's discussion of the role of the school and the educational system in elaborating the various categories of intellectuals.[69] Both give education a central place in the complex nature of the superstructures in modern capitalism – and, later, Poulantzas relies centrally on the education system as an ISA in reproducing the pivotal distinction between mental and manual labour.[70] 'Gramsci,' Althusser acknowledges, 'is the only one who went any distance in the road I am taking . . .' Unfortunately, 'he did not systematise his institutions . . .' The first half of the ISAs essay could be represented as an attempt to carry through that 'absent systematization' of Gramsci. Althusser undertakes this, not by directly extrapolating from Gramsci's 'intuitions', so much as by *relocating* Gramsci's concepts on the firmer structuralist terrain of 'reproduction'. This relocation of Gramsci undoubtedly lends systematisation and rigour to Gramsci. It also, sometimes, tends to make the work of the ISAs on behalf of Capital more unproblematic than it is in Gramsci, more of a necessary, functional, effect. And, in general, it centres the argument more in a 'general theory' of ideology, and less in the analysis of particular historical conjunctures. In this work of transformation and transposition which Althusser undertakes, there are both gains and losses. Perhaps the single, most significant point of convergence between the Althusser of the ISAs essay and Gramsci is the rooting of the concept of 'ideology' firmly in the practices and structures of the superstructures. Gramsci appears always to think the problem of ideology in this way. For Althusser, it represents a shift of emphasis – and a commendable one – in comparison with some of his earlier positions. The argument here is not undertaken so as to prove or disprove a direct theoretical line of descent, or to plot overt 'influences'. The point is to demonstrate the close convergence of the two problematics. To put the point metaphorically, when the shift of emphasis with respect to 'ideology' takes place in Althusser's work, Gramsci is clearly, theoretically, 'close at hand'.

In sum, then, we would say that if the Althusser of *Reading Capital* and *For Marx* is always respectful and positive in his appreciation of Gramsci's 'brilliant insights', the Althusser of 'Ideological State Apparatuses' is working on terrain very much first staked out by Gramsci's concepts; even though his treatment of the problem differs from Gramsci's in the manner of theoretical formulation and in the direction (very much towards Lacan and 'the constitution of the subject in ideology' – the subject of the second half of the ISAs essay) towards which one element of Althusser's discourse points.

The structuralist appropriation of Gramsci – Poulantzas

Poulantzas is dealt with at length at another point in this review. Hence his relation to Gramsci is more summarily treated here – principally in terms of the text where this relation is of central importance, Poulantzas's *Political Power and Social Classes*. This work aims to apply a general marxist-structuralist framework derived from Althusser to the development of a 'regional' theory of the political instance and the capitalist State. Its central preoccupation, therefore, is with the 'relative autonomy' of the political, types of political regime, the relation between classes and the State, questions concerning hegemony and the dominant ideology. These are, of course, the matrix of problems to which Gramsci's work is also addressed. Moreover, the ways they are formulated by Poulantzas reveal the seminal impact of Gramsci. Thus, for example, Poulantzas draws on the distinction between the 'fundamental classes' and the different class alliances which dominate the State – one which Gramsci also elaborates.[71] Both do so by drawing heavily from Marx's analysis of Britain and from the *18th Brumaire* and *Class Struggles in France* (some of the very few Marx texts Gramsci seemed able to quote from and remember in detail in prison). Poulantzas is the first marxist theorist after Lenin and Gramsci to give the concept 'hegemony' a central position in his theory of the State. He also shares with Gramsci (and, we have argued, with the later Althusser) a preoccupation with the 'cementing' function of the dominant ideology in a social formation.

The many overlaps and convergences, then, are clear. Of course, as Poulantzas notes, Gramsci's theorising is far less systematic than his. Gramsci never makes what Poulantzas calls the full advance to the theory of 'structuralist causality'. For Althusser, this means abandoning the notion of a causal chain, and trying to 'think' the relation between the different levels of a social formation in terms of 'a cause immanent in its effects, in the Spinozist sense of the term . . . the whole existence of a structure consists of its effects' (*Reading Capital*, p. 189). Poulantzas defines it as the necessity to theorize 'the specific autonomy of instances of the capitalist mode of production' (*Political Power and Social Classes*, p. 139). Gramsci certainly never uses this 'structuralist' language. He does not think a social formation in the formal terms of relations between 'specifically autonomous instances'. Therefore he has no developed theory of the different *regions* of a social formation, and thus of the theories appropriate to each as constituting 'regional' theories.[72] But he does, throughout his writings, insist on the 'relative autonomy', the specific effectivity, of the political and the ideological; and he rigorously opposes all forms of reductionism of superstructures to base, whether of the expressive, economist or spontaneist kind. He also, in the *Prison Notebooks* – like Poulantzas in *Political Power* – gives extensive attention to politics and the State. Thus it is difficult to think of the theoretical structure of Poulantzas's book except in relation to terrain which Gramsci was instrumental in opening up, even when we acknowledge that Poulantzas's mode of theorising this space is not Gramscian but rigorously Althusserean in character, and his tone is rigorously Leninist in inspiration. The problem, then, is that Poulantzas is, throughout, far less sympathetic to Gramsci than Althusser is: far less generous in acknowledging his theoretical debt. His attack on Gramsci's 'historicism' is far more *purist* than Althusser's.[73] And he goes to far greater lengths to distinguish his work from any Gramscian taint.

Some of these distinctions are real and fruitful. Others appear to be distinctions without real theoretical differences. An example of the first is the debate about 'Caesarism' and

'Bonapartism' (it is even more fully developed in Poulantzas's subsequent study, *Fascism and Dictatorship*). These are terms which Gramsci employs when he is discussing different types of political resolution to moments of crisis and rupture – non-hegemonic resolutions, or 'exceptional' forms of the capitalist State. Gramsci defines them rather loosely: Poulantzas, correctly, subjects them to a more systematic scrutiny. Poulantzas argues that Gramsci's concept of 'Caesarism' refers to that exceptional moment when neither of the fundamental classes can rule – when there is an equilibrium of power, a stalemate. Fascism, however, is *not* the result of a stalemate between the classes, even though, under Fascism, the capitalist State does exhibit certain features of 'autonomy' which Gramsci identified with a 'Caesarist solution'.[74] This allows Poulantzas to distinguish between different types of the exceptional State more carefully than Gramsci does. It is, therefore, a useful and generative distinction.

The case is rather different with 'hegemony'.[75] Poulantzas claims to use 'hegemony' to refer to 'how a power bloc composed of several politically dominant classes or fractions can function'. And he distinguishes it from Gramsci's usage. The distinction seems a false one: surely this *is* one of the ways in which Gramsci employs the concept? Poulantzas objects to the fact that Gramsci also uses 'hegemony' to apply to the strategies of the *dominated* classes. Now this problem of whether a class which does not possess State power can be 'hegemonic' has presented problems for the use of Gramsci's work before. In his famous exchange with Anderson, E.P. Thompson *also* questioned this usage of the concept – paradoxically adopting there Poulantzas's position. But the question has been posed in a more urgent and practical form by the whole strategy of the Italian Communist Party, and its aim to achieve a social 'hegemony' – for example through the 'Historic Compromise' with Christian Democracy – *before* it grasps State power: a strategy in the construction of which, moreover, Gramsci's name has been constantly invoked. Whether any of these applications can really be sanctioned by reference to Gramsci's work is open to question. But certainly, in his delicate distinction between a 'war of manoeuvre' (a frontal assault on State power) and a 'war of position' (occupying and infiltrating the outer trenches and fortifications of civil society) Gramsci does envisage the party of the working class as, at least, requiring a 'hegemonic strategy'.[76] Poulantzas, however, argues, with Lenin, that the dominated classes 'cannot win ideological domination before conquering political power' (p. 204). Now the difficulty is that Poulantzas is not content with reaffirming this more classical Leninist position. He goes on to ascribe what he sees as Gramsci's error to Gramsci's historicism. Though, he says, Gramsci's problematic 'is on the face of it opposed to the Lukácsean thesis' – the rising proletariat as a class subject, the bearer of a universal 'world view'. This appears to collapse the many real, substantive *differences* between Gramsci and Lukács. As Poulantzas himself elsewhere acknowledges, Gramsci does deal theoretically with the 'dislocation between a dominant ideology . . . and the politically dominant class'.[77] Indeed, this attention to 'dislocations' is what grounds, theoretically, Gramsci's attention to the specificity of the political, and his refusal to tolerate any collapse or simple identity between base and superstructure. This is the site of a *major and irreversible theoretical difference* between Gramsci and Lukács. Poulantzas has been driven in his urgency to attack 'historicism' in all its guises, to reduce this difference – and thus to give a distorted impression of Gramsci's distinctive theoretical contribution.

It is *not* a Lukácsian view of class subjects and ascribed world views which is at issue here. It is an enlarged concept of *hegemony*. Gramsci *does*, as we have tried to show, use 'hegemony' in an enlarged and encompassing sense. He uses it – albeit 'untheoretically' – to deal with a major issue in marxist theory: the question of the complex and often indirect means by which the whole fabric of capitalist society is drawn – often by means of what Althusser has called a 'teeth gritting harmony'[78] – into conformity with the long-term needs of Capital. As we have already argued, this is Gramsci's way of opening up the question which Althusser has posed in terms of 'reproduction'. As we have also noted, the moment Althusser advances to this question, he is obliged to give Gramsci his full measure. Poulantzas uses a more restricted definition of 'hegemony'. He tends to limit it to the terrain of the *political*, and to the ideological in so far as it flows from the political and from the State. It is this more restricted treatment, coupled with the compulsion to attack 'historicism', which produces Poulantzas's 'misrecognition' of Gramsci's problematic.[79]

This then ties in with certain other features of Poulantzas's work in general. His tendency to 'over-politicise' the problems concerned leads him to neglect Gramsci's use of the concept 'civil society' (also dismissed here as 'historicist': see the earlier discussions of this point). And that, in turn, tends to lead Poulantzas (as we have argued it also led Althusser) to draw everything on to the terrain of *the State*. (We say this while fully recognising the major contribution which Poulantzas has made to our conceptualisation of the capitalist State.) It may also have something to do with another feature of Poulantzas's work in this book: a certain 'functionalism' in his treatment of the State and of ideology. When Althusser exposed himself to the same problem, he tried to remedy it by invoking the 'class struggle': but in the ISAs essay, this is primarily in footnotes, asides and in the Postscript: it is not centrally woven into the problematic of his text. The appeal to the 'class struggle' plays a far more central role in Poulantzas's work – it is everywhere and generally invoked. But there remains a sense in which it is – to use an Althusserean metaphor – gesturally, rather than theoretically present in Poulantzas's discourse. Now, though the term itself is not always present in Gramsci's writing, the concept of it is never absent. For Gramsci there is *no* state or moment of 'hegemony' which is not contested; none which is not the result of the ruling class alliances *mastering* the class struggle; no 'hegemony' which does not have to be won, secured, constantly defended. And this is so even when the site of that class struggle is apparently far removed from the terrain of the economic and the direct confrontation between the fundamental classes. It is something of this kind which leads Gramsci to speak of the need for a hegemonic practice even by the political organisations of the dominated classes; which leads him to identify the continuing struggle for 'hegemony' even when the proletariat can only struggle on unfavourable terrain – in the 'war of position'. He may, then, be wrong to speak of the 'hegemony' of the dominated classes – strictly speaking, in his own terms, it is a contradictory concept. But he is *not* wrong to employ the concept 'hegemony' in this enlarged sense, or to see it as a struggle to win over the dominated classes in which any 'resolution' involves both *limits* (compromises) and *systematic contradictions*. Poulantzas does tend to treat 'hegemony' as a 'functional effectivity' of the domination of the class alliance in power – i.e. to treat it unproblematically. This Gramsci is never guilty of.

Hence, whereas for Poulantzas 'hegemony' appears as a more or less guaranteed feature of the domination of the capitalist state by a ruling class alliance, Gramsci tends to treat the concept in a more contested, more conjuncturally located manner. For Gramsci classes *can* 'rule' for long periods without being 'hegemonic': the example of Italy was paramount in his mind here. There can be 'crises of hegemony' which do not result in a breakdown of the system. There can be shifts within the mode of hegemony – moments when 'coercion' outdistances 'consent', or vice versa. Indeed, this further distinction which Gramsci draws between 'hegemonic' and 'non-hegemonic' forms of domination enables us more precisely to *periodise concretely* different moments and forms of the capitalist state, and different phases within any one form. This leads us directly to what Gramsci conceived of as constituting, *par excellence*, the specificity of the marxist theory of *politics*: the analysis of particular conjunctures, of particular moments of 'hegemony', and of the relations of class forces which sustain one kind of 'unstable equilibrium' or provoke a rupture in it. It also led him to consider what was the nature of the 'compromises' which enable a ruling bloc to consolidate its rule by winning subaltern classes to its side; and to examine not only any particular 'equilibrium of forces' but what the prevailing *tendency* in such an equilibrium consisted of – whether producing favourable or unfavourable terrain for the conduct of class struggle, and thus defining the strategy for the Party of the proletariat. Far from this constituting, for all practical purposes, a Lukácsian approach, with its ascription of a particular form of 'class consciousness' to an undifferentiated class-subject, Gramsci's concepts here seem to point us *directly* to the terrain of Lenin: the 'concrete analysis of concrete situations'. Their application to the analysis of a whole variety of political conjunctures appears to us to hold a rich promise – and to have hardly been begun.

It is not surprising, however – given what we have argued – to find that Poulantzas *also* disagrees with Gramsci's distinction between 'hegemony' and 'domination' and attacks Gramsci for reserving the term 'hegemony' for those moments when consent prevails over coercion. Poulantzas objects to this distinction – a central one for Gramsci (caught in the couplets coercion/consent, domination/direction, etc.). He criticizes Gramsci for saying that there is always a 'complementarity' between those two elements of political or state power. The state, he argues – in addition – cannot be 'hegemonic'; only the dominant classes can be 'hegemonic'. With respect to the first objection, we can only say that there *is* a complementarity between coercion and consent, and the distinction is a fruitful one. And we note how useful Althusser himself found it, when, in the ISAs article, he demonstrated how apparatuses of consent also work by coercion (e.g. censorship in the media) and apparatuses of coercion require consent (the concern of the police for their public image). With respect to the second objection, it seems true that the State, as such, cannot be 'hegemonic'. But the State plays a pivotal role in raising the domination of a particular class alliance over a social formation *to the level of consent*. This captures precisely the concept of how the State functions to maintain 'hegemony' by winning, securing and cementing the 'consent' of the dominated classes. This is also Marx's concept of the State as the site of 'universalisation' – the legitimation, the rendering invisible, of class rule, through the giving of the form of the 'general interest' to what are in fact the interests of particular class fractions. Poulantzas himself has fruitfully explored and developed just this argument.[80] But by collapsing the two 'poles' of State power – coercion and consent – and by restricting 'hegemony' to the dominant classes only, Poulantzas appears to neglect what at other points he is at pains to underscore: namely, why the capitalist State, based on universal suffrage, is *par excellence* the necessary site for the generalisation of class domination. Thus, in his haste to distinguish himself from Gramsci, Poulantzas appears to neglect arguments, implicit in Gramsci and often quite well developed, which actually support his own theoretical position. Poulantzas certainly recognises the importance of 'consent' for the normalisation of domination in the capitalist state, but he sometimes seems to take it for granted. Gramsci's treatment of the problem of the capitalist State as, above all, an exercise in winning and keeping the consent of the dominated to their own domination, does not allow us for a moment to neglect this central feature of class struggle *and* state power.

It is certainly true that, as Poulantzas argues, Gramsci's 'insights' are provisional and unsystematic. (Althusser calls them 'brilliant' – echoing a term which Marx used of an early essay by Engels which had greatly influenced him; Althusser's reference can be seen as an implicit acknowledgement of a theoretical debt.[81]) Poulantzas and Gramsci here exhibit opposite strengths – and weaknesses. What Gramsci lacks at the level of systematic theorisation, he gains at the level of conjunctural analysis. What Poulantzas gains by his theoretical rigour, he lacks at the level of the specific and the concrete – the source of his residual functionalism. Gramsci's references to class struggles and to specific conjunctures – and the movement between conjunctures – are always detailed, illuminating particular social formations. Poulantzas tends to draw on particular conjunctures 'illustratively' (at least in this book) and to be better at dealing with systematic features and functions, less attuned to 'moments in the relations of forces'. We might want to say that Gramsci's concepts are *always conjunctural* – there are no 'general' concepts or 'general' functions. This is both a strength and a weakness. Poulantzas has a more developed theory of regions – of regional instances, and of the specific autonomy of levels of a social formation. Gramsci works with a more fused or *coupled* concept of structure-superstructure. The former is certainly clearer, more rigorous. The latter is more dynamic, less fixed in the form of a combinatory of instances.

It is not, then, a straightforward matter of a theoretical choice *between* Gramsci and Poulantzas. If, as we have argued, Gramsci constitutes something like the *limit case* for the structuralist marxists, this is an uncompleted theoretical encounter, as Althusser's *Essays in Self-Criticism* all too clearly reveals. The problem is rather that Poulantzas tends to *foreclose* on this theoretical debate. And he does this by means of the mechanism – one is almost tempted to call it a compulsion – not only of attacking 'historicism', but of eliding all 'historicisms' into the figure of one, general, theoretical Enemy; to reduce them all to their 'historicist' elements, their logic; and then to attack the historicist problematic whenever and wherever it raises its head. It is this which leads Poulantzas to *over-exaggerate* his differences with Gramsci, and to simplify the nature of Gramsci's marxism in the process.

The consequence of this reductionist procedure, and the theoretical 'purism' which informs it, is that it leaves Poulantzas in a position where he is not free to acknowledge his intellectual and theoretical debt to Gramsci. He presents Gramsci as a more reduced figure than does his great mentor, Althusser. In this sense, he out-Althussers Althusser. This tendency is discernible elsewhere – for example, in the rather mechanical 'Althusserian orthodoxy' of the opening section of *Political Power and Social Classes*. Such orthodoxy is particularly difficult to sustain since Althusser himself insists on constantly re-examining and redefining his own position – always, of course, with its own kind of polemical certitude. Generally, there is a striking contrast between Poulantzas and Althusser in the manner in which they have 'appropriated' Gramsci. In this exercise, it is Althusser who has come closer to giving due recognition to the *necessary complexity* of Gramsci's work. The fact that Gramsci has survived this appropriation, and retains his independent position, is a testimony to his countinuing stature as a marxist theorist and militant.

Conclusion

This paper has undertaken two tasks which, we hope, will contribute to the current and widespread discussion about Gramsci. First, an account was given of how the concept 'ideology' relates to and is taken up in the theoretical matrix of the *Prison Notebooks*. Secondly, the idea that Gramsci was a historicist in a strong and simple sense was rejected. Whether and to what extent he was a historicist in any sense is a question which raises as many problems about the scope of the concept of historicism as it does about Gramsci.

It was argued, with respect to the first task, that there is no 'obvious' theory of ideology in Gramsci's writings. Although such a theory can be constructed from its 'practical state' in the *Notebooks*, the concept only becomes meaningful insofar as it is subordinated to Gramsci's general, and politically-inspired, corpus of concepts. At the centre of that corpus are the notions of 'hegemony', 'common sense' and the 'intellectuals'. Now, these concepts exist for Gramsci in order to examine specific, historical conjunctures; or, to put it more politically, to analyse the balance of forces within specific conjunctures. They are therefore concepts of historical materialism. Consequently, it is not surprising that Gramsci is more concerned with specific ideologies than with the question of ideology-in-general. This is not to say that the concepts of ideology or hegemony are not general concepts which can be defined at a general level (if – for Gramsci – they are of limited value at that level). It is, however, to insist that they do not refer to general entities. Ideology-in-general is not, for Gramsci, a legitimate object of inquiry. And since he does not accept a division between marxism as historical science and as philosophy (dialectical materialism),[82] it could not be recognised as a legitimate object for marxism. Therefore, although he cannot be regarded as a relativist over the status of theory (concepts are not wholly reducible to the historical situations to which they refer), it is certainly true that marxism, for Gramsci, is *at one and the same time* a philosophical and historical theory of specific, and only specific, phenomena. Ideology is no exception.

It has also been argued in this paper that Althusser and Poulantzas, despite their critique of historicist forms of marxism (and Gramsci's is numbered amongst them), owe a greater theoretical debt to Gramsci than they (and particularly Poulantzas) are prepared to admit. This is especially so with regard to questions concerning the role and relative autonomy of politics and the State. The relation of theorists such as Althusser to the complex 'historicism' of Gramsci becomes compounded when we consider the propositions put forward in Althusser's recent *Self Criticism*. We therefore conclude this article with an outline of that position. We have said that Gramsci does not comfortably 'fit' the historicist criterion. If, in the light of *Self-Criticism*, that criterion itself appears less sound than was once believed, then not only does Gramsci's work escape blanket condemnation from the anti-historicist quarter; it can be restored to a central place in serious discussions of those theoretical questions of marxism which remain inadequately dealt with.

The critique of historicism was largely based on the arguments of *Reading Capital*.[83] For our purposes, the most important of these is the claim that marxism provides a scientific and unique epistemology; one which definitively separates marxism from any form of empiricism or idealism. Historicism of course, contains elements of both. If the scientificity of marxism can be shown in general theoretical terms, it would follow that all forms or elements of historicism have nothing whatever to do with marxism. It should be made explicit here that such an argument relies on the notion that marxist philosophy is alone capable of such distinctions of scientificity. Historical materialism, in contrast has a quite different object: the analysis of concrete conjunctures. (Some of the other problems of *Reading Capital* are indicated elsewhere in this journal and are therefore omitted here.)

Althusser's self-criticism rejects the idea of a scientific philosophy. He reasserts the proposition, implicit in more 'orthodox' marxism and explicit in Gramsci, that there can be no such thing as science-in-general, and no such discipline as philosophy insofar as the latter claims to be the logical guarantor of 'Science'. Despite the claims in *Reading Capital* to the contrary, Althusser argues, a procedure of this kind cannot escape the (bourgeois) 'problems of knowledge'. Now in the earlier text, ideology (in general) is defined in logical opposition to science (in general). Against this 'speculative' position, Althusser now maintains that science should be understood as 'the *minimum of generality* necessary to be able to grasp a concrete object'.[84] This conceptual generality, moreover, is to be placed *within* historical materialism.[85] If Althusser's self-criticism is correct, then the generalised divorce between science and ideology as an *epistemological* proposition ceases to be a tenet of marxism, and with its demise fall arguments which depend on it. At least a part of the argument against historicism comes under this category. For historicism involves opposition to the separation of dialectical from historical materialism, and concentrates purely on reducing the contents of theories and ideologies to the 'expression' of their historical conditions and effects – features which would certainly have come under the axe of philosophical marxism. Is it then the case that the historicists are, after all correct?

Fortunately, things are seldom quite so simple, and theoretical debates are no exception. In defending what we see as the central concepts of Gramsci, we do *not* imply that the critique of historicism is mistaken. Neither do we suggest that there can be a return to an 'innocent' reading of Gramsci in the light of the structuralist intervention. Rather, we have argued that it involves a danger of bringing genuine concepts of historical materialism under that generalised category. There is thus a need to re-examine, for example, the idea that there is a theoretical equivalence between *reducing* theories and ideologies to their historical conditions of existence, and *relating* theories and ideologies to such conditions. The latter, it seems to us, is a proposition of marxism; the former is not. Similarly, Althusser himself remains intransigently opposed to historicism, empiricism, and idealism, and to that extent the problem is not easily resolvable. Specifically, the *Self-Criticism* involves a rejection of only *some* of the features of the problematic generated in *Reading Capital*. Indeed, it could be plausibly argued that the latest position is internally inconsistent (or at least is a 'transitional' work awaiting fuller treatment), and that consequently a uniquely marxist theory of knowledge and ideology-in-general is still required. Philosophy, certainly, continues to play, for Althusser, a special (if demoted) theoretical role in relation to the sciences.

These important issues cannot be appraised here. What can be asserted is that advances are still to be made in the domain of the self-definition of marxism. Whatever the problems in Althusser's shifting theoretical perspective, his claim that the concepts of science and ideology must be subsumed under historical materialism and not philosophy cannot easily be dismissed. It is a claim that was put forward consistently and persuasively by Gramsci in the elaboration of his scientific (as opposed to philosophical) concepts. It is a contribution which should be openly acknowledged.

This essay went to press before the appearance of Perry Anderson's lengthy study of Gramsci in New Left Review *100. There has therefore been no opportunity to include any discussion of Anderson's interpretation of Gramsci in this essay.*

Notes

1 Gramsci, 1971, p. 376.
2 1971, p. 164–5.
3 1971, p. 164.
4 1971, p. 60.
5 1971, p. 177.
6 According to Norbeto Bobbio (*Gramsci e la Concezione della Società 'Civile'*, Feltrinelli, 1976), Gramsci's usage of 'civil society' marks a radical break with the Marxist tradition. Whereas Marx uses the term to designate the 'whole complex of the material conditions of life' (i.e. as an aspect of the base), Gramsci lifts 'civil society' into the superstructure. On the basis of this interpretation, Bobbio makes a reading of the Prison Notebooks in which the determination of the base on the supestructure is reversed, and 'objective' conditions are turned into the potential instruments of class subjectivity. The poverty of the reading becomes apparent when he comes to identify Gramsci's analytic usage of 'civil society' in his historical work as simply a means of identifying 'progressive' and 'reactionary' blocs. Bobbio is trying to fit Gramsci back into the historicist mould, and succeeds in making his writings very similar to those of Lukács.

7 Gramsci, 1971, p. 12.
8 1971, p. 52.
9 1971, p. 208.
10 1971, p. 265.
11 1971, p. 181.
12 1971, p. 139.
13 1971, p. 328.
14 1971, p. 376–7.
15 Marx, 1970, p. 64.
16 1971, p. 78.
17 1971, p. 83.
18 Carl Boggs (Boggs, 1976) tends to do both these things. In his attempt to refute the economism of the 2nd International, he reproduces the other side of that same problematic, namely 'historicism'. For example, his explanation of hegemony is in terms of 'permeation' of value systems: 'Hegemony in this sense might be defined as an "organising principle" or "world-view" . . . that is diffused by agencies of ideological control and socialisation in every area of life.' Gramsci's concept of hegemony is thereby collapsed into a Marcusean model of social control. Charles Woolfson (Woolfson, 1976) in his article on the 'Semiotics of Working-Class Speech' is clear that 'any hegemony in a class society is necessarily limited and incomplete, and exists in tension'; however, he conflates hegemony with ideological domination and subordination.
19 1971, p. 161.
20 1971, p. 57.
21 1971, p. 442.
22 1971, p. 357.
23 This becomes particularly evident when reading Gramsci's *Letters from Prison* (New Edinburgh Review Special Editions, 1974).
24 1971, p. 348.
25 1971, p. 324.
26 1971, p. 355.
27 1971, p. 420.
28 1971, p. 325.
29 1971, p. 333.
30 1971, pp. 14–15.
31 1971, p. 408.
32 1971, p. 12.
33 1971, p. 258.
34 1971, pp. 275–6.
35 1971, p. 238.
36 1971, p. 57.
37 1971, p. 331.
38 1971, p. 339.
39 1971, p. 198.
40 1971, p. 331.
41 1971, pp. 272–3.
42 1971, p. 165.
43 1971, p. 197, p. 331.
44 1971, p. 328.
45 1971, p. 377.
46 1971, p. 152.
47 1971, p. 152–3.
48 1971, p. 403.
49 1971, pp. 445–6.
50 1971, p. 405.
51 1971, p. 417.
52 1971, p. 407.
53 1971, pp. 432–40.
54 1971, pp. 446–7.

55 1971, p. 403.
56 1971, p. 376.
57 The whole of Althusser's essay 'Contradiction And Over-determination' is relevant here, but especially pp. 98–101.
58 See, especially, the section entitled 'Analysis of Situations, Relations of Force', in 'The Modern Prince' essay, *Prison Notebooks*, pp. 175–185.
59 Chapter 5 of *Reading Capital.*
60 'Ideology And Ideological State Apparatuses: Notes Towards An Investigation' in *Lenin and Philosophy and Other Essays*, New Left Books, 1971. Hereafter referred to as 'the ISAs essay'.
61 Althusser calls Gramsci's case a 'limit-situation', in 'Marxism is Not a Historicism', p. 131.
62 The first formulations of ideology as 'imaginary lived relations' is in Section IV of Althusser's essay on 'Marxism and Humanism', in *For Marx*. These are subsequently developed in *Reading Capital*, but especially in the ISAs essay.
63 'Finally, as well as his polemical and practical use of the concept, Gramsci also has a truly "historicist" conception of Marx: a "historicist" conception of the *relationship between Marx's theory and real history*'. Althusser in 'Marxism is Not a Historicism', p. 130.
64 The first critical assault by Althusser on the concept of 'civil society' is launched in the context of a discussion on 'the ghost of the Hegelian model again' and Marx's so-called 'inversion' of Hegel. See the 'Contradiction and Over-determination' essay, pp. 108–11; and *Reading Capital*, pp. 162 ff.
65 Since the term 'civil society' appears here in what, for this text, must be considered a seminal formulation, Althusser's reading of it appears forced: 'Of course, Marx still talks of "civil society" (especially in the *German Ideology* . . .) but as an allusion to the past, to denote the site of his discoveries, not to re-utilize the concept'. It is more accurate to say that, here, Marx *does* 'utilize' the concept, in a *transformed* way, *thereby* indicating the site of his discoveries . . .
66 Althusser's argument is that the reference to 'the society of needs' disappears from Marx's discourse: *hence* he did not merely invert, but broke with, Hegel. However, theoretical discoveries cannot be limited to 'making old concepts disappear', but must also include retaining them, but in a transformed position within the discourse: or designating the theoretical space which they referenced differently. Althusser knows this well – for both Marx and Hegel use 'the dialectic', though, as he shows, they mean different things by it. Whenever Althusser deals with the question of the 'inversion', he seems compelled to force distinctions, which are correct and necessary, to an absolute point. This stems from too fixed a use of 'epistemological rupture' – a point now acknowledged by Althusser himself in *Essays in Self-Criticism.*
67 Cf: Marx to Engels, April 2nd, 1858: 'Simple circulation, considered by itself – and it is the surface of bourgeois society, obliterating the deeper operations from which it arises – reveals no difference between the objects of exchange, except formal and temporary ones. This is the *realm of freedom, equality and of property based on "labour"* . . . The absurdity, on the one hand, of the preachers of economic harmony, the modern free traders . . . to maintain this most superficial and abstract relation as *their* truth in contrast to the more developed relations of production and their antagonism. (On the other hand) the absurdity of the Proudhonists . . . to oppose the ideas of equality, etc. corresponding to this exchange of equivalents (or things assumed to be equivalents) to the inequalities etc. which result from this exchange and which are its origin.' For a much developed exposition of the same argument, see Chs. 48, 49, 50 of *Capital III*, Part VIII.
68 Unexpectedly, Althusser finds a warrant for this collapse in *Gramsci*: 'As a conscious Marxist, Gramsci already forestalled this objection in one sentence. The distinction between the public and the private is a distinction internal to bourgeois law, and valid in the (subordinate) domains in which bourgeois law exercises its "authority".' 'Ideological State Apparatuses', p. 253.) Althusser is, of course, correct to see that the public/private distinction is principally one enforced by bourgeois law, and that therefore the boundary between them *is constantly being shifted.* But he is wrong if he is arguing that where, at any specific historical moment, this boundary was drawn was regarded by Gramsci as irrelevant. As Althusser notes, without comment, in a previous footnote (footnote 5), when Gramsci had the 'remarkable idea' of adding 'Church, the Schools, trade unions, etc.' to the Repressive State apparatuses, 'he included . . . a certain number of institutions from *civil society*'. Thus for Gramsci, the public/private distinction remained significant, though not determining 'in the last instance'.
69 See Gramsci's essays on 'The Intellectuals', 'On Schools' and 'Americanism and Fordism', in the *Prison Notebooks.*

70 This argument is most fully developed in Poulantzas, *Classes in Contemporary Capitalism*, 1974.
71 See, especially, *Political Power and Social Classes*, pp. 227–252.
72 On a 'regional structure as an *object of science*', see *Political Power*, pp. 16–18.
73 For example, *Political Power*, pp. 137–9.
74 The passages concerned with 'Caesarism', 'Bonapartism' and 'Fascism' are mainly to be found in *Political Power*, pp. 258–62.
75 The concept of 'hegemony', and the difference between his and Gramsci's use of the concept are most fully discussed by Poulantzas, in *Political Power*, pp. 137–9, 204–5.
76 Gramsci elaborates on the distinctions between 'war of position', and 'war of manoeuvre' in 'Notes on Italian History', pp. 108–110, and in 'State and Civil Society', pp. 229–235. Both in *Prison Notebooks*.
77 *Political Power*, p. 204.
78 The phrase is form the ISAs essay, p. 257.
79 The following passage is a good example of what we mean by 'reduction'; 'To grasp the relation between these two "moments" ["force" and "consent"] he [Gramsci] uses the significant term "complementarity". From this stems a confusion of the areas in which hegemony is exercised . . . according to which, force is exercised by the state in "political" society, hegemony in "civil society" by means of the organization usually considered to be private . . . This distinction is the key to the model with which historicism apprehended the relations between the economic and the political: it saw the political (the class struggle) as the motor, the force, of the "economic laws" conceived in a mechanistic fashion; in other words, politics is conceived as the motor of economic "autonomism".' (*Political Power* p. 26).

The 'complementarity' between the moments for force and consent is, certainly, Gramsci. He does not, however, assign the former to political society and the latter to civil society in that simple way. Hence it does not follow that Gramsci thinks the relation of the political to the economic in a historicist way. It would certainly be difficult to reconcile any reading of Gramsci as regarding politics as the motor of automatic economic laws 'conceived in a mechanistic fashion'. The final move in this reductionism, moreover, appears to operate on the back of a pun – on the word 'force' – which cannot be supported from a reading of Gramsci (i.e. he nowhere uses the 'moment of force' to refer to politics as 'the force' of automatic economic laws). In short, the more the argument advances, the more clearly 'historicism' emerges as a theoretical deviation – but the farther we get from a reading which refers in any recognisable way to Gramsci's work.
80 Particularly in *Political Power*, pp. 210–28 ('Bourgeois Political Ideology and the Class Struggle'), and pp. 274–307 ('The Capitalist State and the Field of the Class Struggle').
81 See *Pour Marx*, Maspero 1965, p. 78 n. and p. 114 n. *Génial* in French, but 'brilliant' in English, rather than the 'genial' of *For Marx*, p. 81 n. and p. 114 n.
82 1971, pp. 38, 434–5.
83 See the Althusser article in this journal.
84 Althusser, 1976, p. 112 n., emphasis original.
85 Ibid., p. 124 n.

Bibliography

A. Gramsci, *Selections from the Prison Notebooks*, ed. Hoare and Nowell Smith, Lawrence and Wishart: London 1971.
L. Althusser, *For Marx*, Allen Lane: London 1969. *Reading Capital*, New Left Books: London 1970. *Essays in Self-Criticism*, New Left Books: London 1976.
N. Bobbio, *Gramsci e la Concezione della Società 'Civile'*, Feltrinelli 1976.
C. Boggs, *Gramsci's Marxism*, Pluto: London 1976.
G. Lukàcs: *History and Class Consciousness*, Merlin: London 1971.
K. Marx: *Capital*, Vol. I, Moscow, 1966. *The German Ideology*, Lawrence and Wishart, 1970.
N. Poulantzas, *Political Power and Social Classes*, New Left Books: London 1973. *Fascism and Dictatorship*, New Left Books: London 1974.
C. Woolfson, 'The Semiotics of Working-Class Speech' in *Working Papers in Cultural Studies 9*, Birmingham 1976.

14 What is it he's done?

The ideology of Althusser

Robin Rusher

> But it would be wrong to see Althusser's work as simply a piece of hackwork in the service of revisionism. On the contrary, its interest lies in the fact that it reproduces the spontaneous discourse of metaphysics, the traditional position of philosophy with respect to knowledge.
>
> Rancière: 1969

> Hegel is the paragon of the self-sufficient professional thinker whose real existence is looked after by the State and is therefore meaningless to him. He puts an historical halo upon the lecture platform: the absolute spirit is nothing more than the absolute professor.
>
> Feuerbach: 1860

The aim of this paper is to present a critical exposition of the work of Louis Althusser, an exposition determined by a partisan position adopted within the field of 'all possible readings', the position of cultural studies. The paper makes specific criticisms (and acknowledgements) of the contribution of Althusser to any Marxist theory of culture and ideology. It is a matter of making a critical approach to certain specific problems which a study of Althusser from this position must tackle; predominantly, those concerned with the nature of ideology in societies under the capitalist mode of production (CMP). However, in order to get at these, it is necessary to discuss the frame within which these problems are constituted by Althusser.

I have made use of many footnotes in this paper, both to suggest the implications of my criticisms for discrete problems in Althusser's work which I have not the space to analyse in full, and also to give explanations of some of his terminology, which would otherwise interrupt the line of the argument. The structure and style represent in part an attempt to point the reader outwards, from the text to the footnotes and references, to oblige a *total* examination of Althusser, rather than either a partial reading or a reading in Althusser's own terms. I hope that the language is not needlessly difficult or obscure. It is best to refer to the Glossary in *For Marx* for the approved definitions of key terms. The main texts that I shall be referring to are *For Marx* (especially the essays 'Contradiction and Overdetermination' ('C & O'), and 'On The Materialist Dialectic' ('OTMD'), *Reading Capital* (especially pts 1 & 2) and *Lenin and Philosophy and Other Essays*.

The urge to refurbish Marxism in the way that it is signalled in Althusser is symptomatic of a major change both in the development of the class struggle (internationally and in France) and in the position of the French CP, moving through the 1960s and 1970s into an increasingly reformist parliamentarianism. (There is, I believe, real substance to the charges of 'pluralism' against which Althusser tries to defend himself in 'C & O'.) There is also the important (and extremely difficult) question of the universities. 1968 did not merely happen, without long rumblings of preparatory militancy both in the university and in the factory, and the critiques of 'practices' formed part of them.

A central lesson to be drawn from the period is that 'ideology-critique' cannot be sufficient unto itself: the struggle against dominant theory, theory which supports the rule of Capital, can not remain, in form or language or impulse, 'wholly within theory'.

1. Althusser: man, myth and magic

Althusser is a professional philosopher and a longstanding member of the French Communist Party. His declared intellectual activity is thus as a Marxist philosopher. Not only the difficulty of reading, but also many of the most difficult theoretical problems, arise in his work as a result of the aim to investigate the 'specific nature of the principles of science and philosophy founded by Marx',[1] pursued from this position. His work is peculiarly shaped by the pressures of French philosophy; the way in which he has attempted to demarcate the region and role of Marxist philosophy (dialectical materialism) has led at times to positions which he himself has since acknowledged to be 'theoreticist' or, more bluntly, idealist.[2] I shall deal later with some of the particular distortions which this tendency has produced in his work. For now, the point in mentioning this is not merely for the sake of some reassuring contextualisation. He has himself sketched the problems and tendencies against the background of which he was writing, and sums up the central theoretical tendencies that he was opposing as Hegelianism, Humanism and Historicism, especially as they shaped interpretations of Marx both in politics and theory.[3] The philosophical frontier which he attempts to erect against these, marks them off as forms of Idealism, against the revolutionary philosophy of dialectical materialism. (It is not merely paradoxical to note that they also entail forms of reductionism, a feature which characterises much of Althusser's own theorising).

However, although the form of his activity is necessarily related both to his position as an academic philosopher and as a Party member in France, two warnings from his mouth against collapsing his work into its time, leaving no trace. Firstly, that 'Marxism works because it's true, not the other way about',[4] and secondly, that: 'In the reduction of all knowledge to the historical social relations a second underhand reduction can be introduced, by treating the *relations of production* as mere *human relations*.'[5]

Reading Althusser, then, is a strenuous activity of appropriation: I hope that this paper will provide a clearly argued approach to this (I think necessary) activity. Methodologically, I follow the procedure outlined by J-L Comolli in his critique of André Bazin *Cahiers du Cinéma no. 229:*

> . . . the coherence is only gained at the expense of a number of distortions of the argument which we will read as symptoms of contradictions when we come to them. The action of these contradictions is both to undermine the discourse and at the same time to produce its other side, hence to subvert it. Clearly, such subversion only comes into play when the discourse which experiences it (but also sets up the preconditions) demonstrates some theoretical force.

In England, the level of Marxist analysis of ideology is symptomatically low, and the theory of culture, for example, is only just emerging from the long shadows of liberal humanism. I believe that there are important lessons to be learnt, but warily, from Althusser in the struggle against reactionary and reformist ideology.

And two dangers to avoid, already fallen into by some. The first is the obscurantist, self enclosed mystification of merely playing with the all too seductive categories and language of Althussereanism (see the English magazine *Theoretical Practice*). The real potential value gets undercut by the distorted rationale by which such activity is justified.

The second is the eclecticism to which I feel the English academic *demi-monde* is prone, especially when confronted with work from such a different intellectual and political context. The important point is that both of these tendencies are not merely accidental, but find some root in Althusser's work. The first tendency is merely an embodiment of the potentially *wholly* autonomous 'theoretical practice' which founds much of Althusser's work (see section 7). The eclecticism is, I think, in part an available option in view of the very fundamental disjunctions and confusions in his work, which are concealed by an *apparent* rigour. It is necessary to try to grasp the core of his work: not in an essentialist fashion, but in order to tie down the underlying contradictions within the theory (—ies), to make it possible for the reader to get a grasp on the separate elements and on the work as a whole; and also, crucially, to allow this analysis to be thought through in terms of the political position that the theory asserts. It's impossible to ignore the link between theory and practice when it is precisely this link that receives a novel and challenging treatment by Althusser. In part, the question must be why this needs to be done by him; and accordingly, what is it he's done?

The 'reading' that I make of Althusser is not merely critical; it is, in its most basic orientation and mode an essentially different kind of reading from that offered by Althusser, the protocol of which is *Reading Capital.* It is a fundamental point, not a mere distinction. I believe that Marx's proclamation of the end of 'philosophy' for a practice of philosophy to change the world can not be recouped to theoretical practice without a dangerous degree of self illusion. So there can not be a 'scientificity' by which one can extrude the political/ theoretical truth of a text by means of internal exegesis and development. The truth is a practical one, respecting the specificity of theory as a 'level' which does not necessarily imply the sacred centrality that Althusser's work gives to 'theoretical practice'. Althusser's work derives from and implies more than merely itself, and this in itself is a part of the argument of my article.

2. The social formation

The core of every social theory, according to Althusser, lies in its particular conception of the nature of the social totality. The two conceptions which he rejects appear at first to be polar opposites, but are in fact merely mutual inversions. On the one hand, the Hegelian 'expressive' totality ('the unity of a simple essence manifesting itself in its alienation');[6] and on the other, the mechanistic economic determinism of the Second International. On the one hand, a theory of society and of its laws of development as the 'alienated development of a simple unity, of a simple principle, itself a moment of the development of the Idea', (6); on the other, society as an epiphenomenon of the Iron Laws of Economics. The same principle of a single, simple essence expressing itself in the form of the social formation is common to both: it is at this essentially philosophical level of abstraction that Althusser counters these conceptions with his own, elaborated from Marx, Lenin and Mao. (It must be emphasised, though, that these conceptions are essentially political, in that each embodies and describes a certain tendency). I shall sketch this here, though it is best derived from reading 'C & O' and 'OTMD'.

In place of an 'original essence' (be it 'Economics' or 'The Idea') Althusser proposes an 'ever pregiven complex whole', a concept of the social formation stripped of teleology or expression. To quote from the indispensable 'Glossary':

> SOCIAL FORMATION (A concept denoting 'society' so-called L.A.) The concrete complex whole comprising economic practice, political practice and ideological practice at a certain place and stage of development. Historical materialism is the science of social formations.

The two core elements to this are firstly, the rejection of the 'myth of origins'; that is, the idea that what determines the nature and significance of a phenomenon at a certain moment is how it began and the path it has travelled, rather than its relation at that moment to other phenomena which determine its significance and are determined by it. And secondly, the concept of 'practice'; again, for the official definition, to the 'Glossary' (the absolute importance of this concept in the Althusserean galaxy demands a full excerpt):

> Althusser takes up the theory introduced by Engels and much elaborated by Mao Tse Tung that economic, political and ideological practice are the three practices (processes of production or transformation) that constitute the social formation. Economic practice is the transformation of nature by human labour into social products, political practice the transformation of social relations by revolution, ideological practice the transformation of one relation to the lived world into a new relation by an ideological struggle. In his concern to stress the distinction between theory and ideology, Althusser insists that theory constitutes a fourth practice, that transforms ideology into knowledge by theory.

The separation between 'economic practice' (which it is implied, is universal, static, discrete) and political and ideological practice, which are defined solely as if tending to socialism, is glaringly apparent.[7] This rigid (rather than rigorous) separation reproduces and grounds Althusser's fundamental separation between 'ideology in general' and 'dominant ideology' that I criticise later (below, section 6).

The determining moment 'in the last instance', is the economic mode of production. This decides which 'practice', which region, shall be dominant at any moment. This concept of determination is 'one end of the chain' in the beginnings of a theory of the social formation that Althusser sees Marx as having inaugurated but not delivered in a fully, theoretically elaborated form. The two ends of the chain are: 'on the one hand, *determination in the last instance by the (economic) mode of production*; on the other, the *relative autonomy of the superstructures and their specific effectivity*.'[8]

This is one of the thorniest problems in Althusser, that of determination, and I shall return to it; here, all I shall say is that in the salutary rigour of his defence of this 'relative autonomy', Althusser has on occasion damagingly tended towards an apparent assertion of the *absolute* autonomy of certain practices, especially that of theory itself (and science), but also in his original formulation of the mode of operation of Ideological State Apparatuses ('ISA's). 'From the first moment to the last, the lonely hour of the "last instance" never comes'.[9] This rhetorical phrase sums up the conceptual relation which Althusser develops between the two ends of the chain, in the term *overdetermination*.

3. Overdetermination: structural causality

Overdetermination is a term borrowed from Freud. In Althusser's usage, it signifies the 'reflexion of the conditions of existence of the contradiction within itself, of the structure articulated in dominance, that constitutes the unity of the complex whole within the contradiction'. That is, no contradiction exists 'simply'; the determination in the last instance by the economic is itself always determined in form by the 'accumulation of effective determinations (deriving from the superstructures and from special national and international circumstances)'. In Freud, the term denoted:

> (among other things), the representation of dream thoughts in images privileged by their condensation of a number of thoughts in a single image (condensation), or by the transference of psychic energy from a particularly potent thought to apparently trivial images (displacement).
>
> (Glossary).

It thus represents in Althusser the result of mutual determinations both *between* specific practices (this relation being determined in the last instance by the economic) and *within* each one as a result of contradictions internal to each practice. In a stable moment of society, the 'essential contradictions of the social formation are neutralised by displacement': in a revolutionary situation however, they may 'condense or fuse into a revolutionary rupture' (Glossary). Practices are thus articulated into the social formation by contradiction.

The introduction of this concept will perhaps be found later to be one of Althusser's main theoretical developments: in the earliest formulations, though (see *For Marx*), it is not without its problems, as acknowledged in 'OTMD', in the opening self criticism:

> . . . that by proposing a concept of 'overdetermined contradiction', I have substituted a 'pluralist' conception of history for the Marxist 'monist' conception. The result: what remains of Marxist necessity, of its unity, of the determinant role of the economy – and in consequence, of the basic law of our age?[10]

problems not fully answered, I believe, in that essay. (See below, on structural causality).

Underlying this concept of the social formation lies, inevitably, the question of history. For the purpose of exposition, I shall take this question along with the development of the implications of the nature of causality and determination entailed by this concept.

At any moment of a social formation (in a 'conjuncture'), the overall result of the overdeterminations in the complex whole is to produce itself as a 'structure in dominance', for example, the dominant element in the analysis by Marx of the 18th Brumaire is the political. Then, the forms specific to the region of political practice enjoy a determinacy granted by the peculiar structure of contradictions within and between itself and the other levels of the formation, determined in the last instance by the economic, in that conjuncture. Althusser refers to Marx: 'In all forms of society, it is a determinate production and its relations which assign to every other production and its relations their rank and influence.'[11]

The kind of determination that Althusser is propounding is thus a structural determinacy, the form of the social formation being determined by a structure (composed of multiple overdeterminations) which is 'present' only in its effects, those effects being the real, phenomenal forms of the society. Yet the structure, while being 'nothing outside of its effects',[12] is itself, simultaneously, absent from those effects, not wholly defined by them. Again, the concept is referred to Freud's 'metonymic causality', 'the effectivity of a structure upon its elements'.[13] The structure theoretically isolated here embodies the real relations of production, and it is only from this point of vantage that the real laws of capitalism can be analysed.

(This distinction is underpinned by the fundamental philosophical distinction between the 'concrete in thought' and the 'real concrete' that Althusser develops from Marx's 1857 *Introduction* to the *Grundrisse.* Again, this problem will be taken up later: I believe that the form in which he develops Marx's distinction is one-sided and tends to idealism, but the necessary emphasis here is on the connections between the key moments of Althusser's definitions of philosophical practice (such as this distinction between the 'concrete=in=thought' and the 'real=concrete') and the specific formulations that he develops.)

This rephrasing of Marx's distinction (between phenomenal forms and the real relations) is in the language of a structuralist epistemology, if not in fully-blown structuralist terms. As in Marx, this distinction does not imply that 'value' or 'surplus-value' are merely metaphysical categories, any more than it makes 'prices' or 'profits' merely illusory epiphenomena of what is *really* going on. For Althusser, 'interiority is nothing but the concept'[14]; that is, the scientific concept is that which grasps the true nature and status of the phenomenon.[15]

It is precisely around this simultaneous absence/presence of the structure that Althusser bases his early opposition between science and ideology: 'Ideology . . . is the overdetermined unity of the real relation and the imaginary relation between (men) and their real conditions of existence.'[16]

Science, on the other hand, is that in which the theoretical, knowledge, predominates over the interests of the 'practico-social'. Thus ideological knowledge is largely external acquaintance of the real, the existent, while (in this scheme) science is the knowledge of the concepts whose 'specifications' are the real, the existent. (Following Marx: 'All knowledge would be superfluous if the outward appearance and the essence of things directly coincided',[17] but in a highly particularised way).

In developing this highly complicated theoretical position (which is especially that underlying the texts under discussion), Althusser also relies on the absolute difference between the real and thought, derived from his analysis of the 1857 *Introduction*, (see below section 7); the polemical thrust being his frontal attack on empiricism. Even in this (highly) simplified form however, I think that I have been faithful to the centrality which Althusser gives to thought itself in the process of analysis as he presents it. The difference between the real relations of production and the phenomenal forms of those relations is *not*, according to Althusser, a 'distinction located in the real';[18] that is, of the kind of 'phenomenon/essence', the inessential (phenomenal) only waiting to be pared away from the real object to reveal its true essence: thus the whole social life becomes 'ideological', and Science alone bears the truth of it. [Again, this formulation demands criticism, (see below, section 6)]. In Althusser's system, a central concern in which, being to demarcate dialectical materialism from, and purify it of, various types of reductionism, the particular form of reductionism in hand is common both to idealism and to vulgar materialism. The real becomes merely thought, or thought becomes nothing more than the real itself.[19]

The relation between the real relations and their phenomenal forms is given in the concept of *darstellung*:

> the key epistemological concept of the whole Marxist theory of value, the concept whose object is precisely to designate the mode of *presence* of the structure in its *effects*, and therefore to designate structural causality itself.[20]

For Althusser, this concept, the 'near perfect' concept to which Marx came in *Capital*, is the basis for a theoretical understanding of fetishism, the 'dislocation in the real',[21] by which relations between men under the CMP assume the form of relation between things, especially things-as-commodities. I shall make three specific criticisms of Althusser's use of the concept of *darstellung* before moving on to the concepts which it founds, since it is strategic to Althusser's theories in relation to the entire problematic of cultural studies.

The first weakness has to do with how it is used within the whole Althusserean philosophical system; it is especially noticeable in the work of Balibar ('Elements for a Theory of Transition' in *Reading Capital*) and Rancière [in *Lire le Capital* but omitted from the English edition partly because of this problem[22]]. It is also indispensable to Althusser himself. I used the word 'system' advisedly above; Glucksmann remarks on this outer boundary to Althusser's work, that it is:

> systematization . . . a grand system which would be as such a system of the whole as the whole of the system – not naively, a system *of* the real, but via dialectical materialism and historical materialism, a systematic theory of the real.[23]

Within this 'grand system' (a stricture on the metaphysical nature of the Althusserean project which applies especially to *For Marx* and *Reading Capital*, produced under the earlier definitions of philosophy) *darstellung* is needed to establish both synchronic analysis *and* the development of concepts in *Capital*, a role which it cannot perform, as Glucksmann points out except by itself *presupposing* analysis of the basic concepts of historical materialism.[24] In particular, its validity rests on the concept of a mode of production as established by comparative analysis. Without this prior analysis, it is impossible to generalise from within analysis of the CMP alone to erect *darstellung* as the key both to structural determinacy *and* to the 'truth of' the relations of production, since this truth is hidden both in and by the *darstellung* itself. The creation of a grand system from a starting point in the process of a dubious abstraction from *Capital* can go no further than its boundaries without collapsing into idealism, or the fetishism of reproducing the structures of the CMP and universalising them as a universal theory of history.

The theory of 'modes of production in general' is elaborated most fully in Balibar's work in *Reading Capital*. Its form raises serious problems as to the status of the historical in Althusser's theory, the main problem being in the attempt at theoretical systematisation of 'all possible modes of production' from a few basic 'elements', for the theory to work must fulfil two quite basic but contradictory functions:

1 the elements must remain invariant, or there is no real significance in calling the same element in different modes of production the 'same'.
2 the elements must assume their significance from their relationships to each other in any mode, and thus cease to be merely a series of invariant elements. This latter is what Althusser says distinguishes the structuralist 'combinatory' from the Marxist 'combination'.[25]

yet

3 the system is at best classificatory, preanalytic – yet can only be founded on analysis of the particular modes in question, not solely on the reading of the analysis of the CMP in *Capital*.[26]

This logical jam is at root the same criticism made by Geras in terms of *history*;[27] although Geras is in fact criticising here one of the *results* of this concept (the derived theory of men as 'bearers' which I shall deal with below), the criticism he makes, that 'what Marx regards as a feature specific to *capitalist* relations of production, Althusser articulates as a general proposition of historical materialism' also finds a butt in the founding concept from which the object of his criticism derives.

The result of these two flaws is to undercut the attempt in Althusser to found a universal science along the lines of a natural science, on the basis of analysis by Marx of the CMP alone.[28] Perhaps the most significant effect of this failure is to return one to an awareness of the importance of Althusser's self-critical redefinition of philosophy. In writing that philosophy is 'political practice in the realm of theory' rather than 'the theory of theoretical practice', he acknowledges that it was precisely this earlier, static form of systematisation that Marx was criticising in the theses on Feuerbach, and criticising as idealist.[29]

4. *Träger*, bearers, supports

However, within the whole of Althusser's work, the purpose of the concept of *darstellung* is to provide the strategic foundation for his theoretical antihumanism, as Glucksmann demonstrates. The nature of this antihumanism is perhaps clearest seen in his reply to criticisms by John Lewis in *Marxism Today*.[30] In reply to Lewis's polemical formulations that 'Man makes history . . . by transcending history' and 'Man only knows what he himself does', Althusser proposes that the Marxist-Leninist formulations of these problems must be that 'The masses make history: Class struggle is the motor of history' and 'One can only know what exists'. History, Althusser says, is 'an immense natural/human system in movement', and men enter into the process, which is itself *subjectless*, as bearers of supports (*träger*):

> the structure of the relations of production determines the *places* and *functions* occupied and adopted by the agents of production, who are never anything more than occupants of these places, insofar as they are the 'supports' (*träger*) of those functions.[31]

This problem is the subject of an article by John Mepham,[32] who characterises the two key positions in the field of play in two formulae. Firstly, the Humanist formula that Althusser is attacking: 'It is *men* who make history albeit on the basis of objective conditions which they have to take as given' and secondly, the significantly different forms of the antihumanist formula:

1 It is the masses which make history. The class struggle is the motor of history.
2 The 'subjects' of history are given human societies.[33] *or*: the true subjects of the practices of social production are the relations of production. Men are never anything more than the bearers/supports/effects of these relations.

It is not the case, in my opinion, that as a result of any of these *definitions* 'The human subject is definitively abolished' as Geras suggests,[34] although I also believe that the definitions are in fact more open than Althusser's analytic elaboration would imply. (A preliminary point made by Mepham will perhaps clear away some of the ground of argument; this is that *For Marx* is less vulnerable to the weaknesses in Althusser's position on this subject than is *Reading Capital*).

To illustrate my point about the distance between Althusser's position as formulated here and his practice in *Reading Capital*, it is worth pointing to the slide made between the social process as a whole (the relations of production) and the totality of human relations in the society, in the following: 'The true "subjects" (in the sense of constitutive subjects of the process) are therefore not these objects or functionaries . . . "real men" – but the *definition and distribution of these places and functions*.'[35]

The ordinary human relations, the 'relations between men and men',[36] are consequent on this definition, are 'defined by the precise relations existing between men and the material elements of the production process'. Thus men are bracketted, are moved away from the limelight that they had been placed in by Sartre, for example, by those tendencies which Althusser refers to as 'petty-bourgeois humanism'. But this displacement is effectively an inversion; 'consciousness', instead of being primary, becomes wholly epiphenomenal to the production process which is the 'essence' of the social process. This represents a form of reductionism even of his own form of structural causality: the 'structure' which is implied by the 'effects' which concrete individuals constitute, must itself be truncated, reduced to being the 'real' shape of the forces of production predominating over the relations of production, which themselves predominate over the human relations which are constituted within them. I shall deal with this telescoping effect more fully in section 6; here, I shall point to two criticisms which Mepham makes of the concept.

The two main problems that Mepham points to in these antihumanist formulae are that firstly, Althusser actually spends very little time discussing how the concept of men-as-bearers should enter into our understanding of history. The only hint is that given in *Reading Capital*, that the problem of 'The individual in history' should be rethought as that of the historic forms of individuality. The second point is that 'the relation between Althusser's various uses of the concept is that they are all in one way or another based on a generalised concept of "practice" as forms of production', a concept which despite its central importance is nowhere discussed in full (see below 7). Mepham points to three distinct meanings-in-use of the concept in *Capital*; the capitalist as personified capital, the internalisation by individual capitalists of the objective basis of circulation, and the result of this, that only insofar as men *do* internalise the objective basis in this way do they enter into Marx's analysis of the CMP. That is, only insofar as they fulfil the roles assigned them by the CMP itself. Now this is not a sufficient basis to generalise this into *either* a fully formed concept in Marx's analysis of the CMP (Capital is an unfinished work) *or* a general law of historical materialism. The concept seems to be inadequate, for example, to analysis of those moments when the political instance is dominant, and perhaps in conjunctural analysis in general. Mepham concludes that in 'Contradiction and Overdetermination', Althusser employs the concept only in the limited sense that men enter into a conjuncture as members of a class:

> But there is all the difference in the world about talking about bourgeois ideology and the personifications of social political relations or whatever. The stronger sense (of the second antihumanist formula) would imply that the structure of class relations could be known with all the precision of natural science and experienced as necessities beyond men's control, but the whole point of revolutionary practice is to know how to act to shift the balance of forces in a conjuncture.

One more general underpinning to Althusser's development in this area is that of structural linguistics. A second subsidiary science that is drawn on to supply the logical ground for the theory of 'consciousness' is that of psychoanalysis. In introducing 'overdetermination' Althusser remarks (it is no more than that) that the establishment of this term in a marxist theory of social formations 'might open up a path to psychoanalytic reality'.[37] By use of these two disciplines (which are taken into the system with far too little discussion of their partial and problematic scientific status) the region of human consciousness is effectively inserted into its 'ground of origin'; the subject is dispersed into a social fabric of language and the unconscious. It is faithful to the implications of this formulation in Althusser to remark, as Vilar does,[38] that the concept of *träger* is derived from the formulation of structural causality as a (simple) logic of positions; although in Marx, social relations are not mere intersubjectivity, since they comprise relations between things and classes, this is not to accept Althusser's wholly 'subjectless reductionism'. The primary inertness attributed to men finds its political and analytic inadequacy in the essay on 'ISAs'.

One of the most biting criticisms to be made of this concept is that made by Glucksmann, in that the concept of *träger* in fact reproduces the form of fetishism under the CMP: 'If the economy is basically not a relation between things but a social relation, this is because the commodity is not the enunciator of the discourse in it. Social classes are thus not *träger* but the subjects of the enunciation.'[39]

This criticism is itself, of course, subject to Vilar's stricture that 'social relations are not mere intersubjectivity, for the very good reason given by Marx':

> If it be declared that the social characters assumed by objects or the material forms assumed by the social qualities of labour under the regime of a definite mode of production are mere symbols, it is in the same breath also declared that these characteristics are arbitrary fictions sanctioned by the so-called universal assent of mankind.
>
> (*Capital 1* p. 94)

Althusser *tends* towards an inversion of this, as I have suggested in relation to his anti-humanism; by repressing the social relations of production within his theory, the social process can be conceptualised as a traditionally 'out-there' object of natural science, in a neopositivist fashion, suggesting, again, that the relations between classes can be known in any conjuncture with the precision of that type of science. This is a dream to which Marx would hardly have assented, since it adopts the form of yet another, sophisticated 'interpreting of the world'. (And necessarily entails some distortion of the political relationship of science to that world, such as that made by Althusser: see below, concluding section).

5. History

1. History and the social formation

In Glucksmann's phrase, it is the 'set of shifters from the register of the economy to the historical/social which organises the incomplete development of *Capital*'.[40] That is, there are two modes of analysis in *Capital*: on the one hand, the analysis of the historical genesis of the categories of capital, and the analysis of their articulation under the CMP; and on the other, the analysis of the CMP itself and of the forms of social life under the CMP, 'forty lines on Class, then silence' at the end of the work. I have already touched on the peculiar form of Althusser's repression of the social relations of production: to turn now to his (equally formalist) repression of history, for which the *locus classicus* of Marx's epistemological propositions concerning the relations of history to analysis is the *Grundrisse* 1857 *Introduction*.[41] The historicism of previous Marxists that Althusser criticises,[42] is mainly at fault, in his view, for its 'linear view of time, susceptible to an essential section into a present at any time'. (This 'essential section' necessarily posits an 'expressive totality' of the Hegelian type, in which each element is effectively a microcosm of the whole). In place of this, Althusser asserts that 'Marxism is not a Historicism':[43] 'since the Marxist concept of history depends on the principle of variation of these forms of combination.'[44]

From his partisanship of philosophy's radical irreducibility, and of the declared primacy of dialectical materialism over historical materialism in the arsenal of analytic weaponry, Althusser also charges this 'historicism' with collapsing philosophy into history as merely the 'direct expression of history'.[45]

In attempting to constitute a fundamentally antihistoricist Marxism, the result is that Althusser writes out history altogether or (what is effectively how he achieves this) envelops history within the conjuncture as a further, static dimension to each relatively autonomous level. Each level of the social formation has, according to Althusser, its own distinct 'time'. In *Reading Capital*, where this concept is introduced, the terms 'time' and 'temporality' are used almost interchangeably. I shall use 'temporality', since that denotes 'rhythms, punctuations, breaks' less obliquely than does 'time'. However, in doing so, it displaces one of the central attacks made by Althusser in this development, the attack on the linear, diachronic clock-time as 'ideological'. Hegelian time, according to Althusser, is merely the 'reflexion of the essence of the social totality of which it is the *existence*'.[46] Its two essential characteristics are its *homogeneous continuity* and its *contemporaneity*, the category of the historical present which makes possible the 'essential section'. What Althusser effectively does is to rupture this singular unity into a four-part stave, but each level of 'practice' (economic/political/ideological/theoretical) retains its own form of self enclosed temporality (though determined in the last instance).

2. *History in analysis*

In place of the category of the 'historical present', Althusser employs 'conjuncture':

> . . . it is only in the specific unity of the complex structure of the whole that we can think the concept of these so-called backwardnesses, forwardnesses, survivals and unevennesses of development which coexist, in the structure of the real historical present – the present of the conjuncture.[47]

As so often in Althusser, the emphasis is important but the form of the assertion demands a fundamental *distortion* of Marx in Marx's name.

The distortion involved here is similar to (and connected with) that noted by Glucksmann, who criticises Balibar's formalist analysis in *Reading Capital* for 'positing capitalism in its simple otherness'. The obverse of this is the role of the Althusserean *combination* in founding his antihistoricism.[48] The movement of Marx's analysis in *Capital*, as it concerns history is, as I have said, *double*. It is both an analysis of the laws of the relations of capitalist production as they are, and the analysis of the history of how they came to be. Without this relatedness, the analysis would fall into the errors of classical political economy. The analysis of the CMP is the only way to understand its transitory nature.[49] The historical in Marx's analysis of the CMP is reconstituted via analysis of the 'synchronic' variation. It is correct to criticise, as Althusser does, a historical teleology, since that functions as an apologetics (cf *Grundrisse* p. 460) for capitalism being here now, by right of its arrivedness, as it were. However, to invert this form of analysis, as Althusser does, and to subsume 'history' into the conjuncture is to forego any active perspective to the future which traverses and works through the present. A long excerpt from the *Grundrisse* makes this point with an urgency which undercuts the apparent rigour of Althusser's antihistoricism:

> On the other side, much more important for us is that our method indicates for us the points where historical investigation must enter in, or where bourgeois economy as a merely historical form of the production process points beyond itself to earlier historical modes of production. In order to develop the laws of bourgeois economy, therefore, it is not necessary to write the *real history of the relations of production*. But the correct observation and deduction of these laws, as having themselves become in history, always leads to primary equations. . . which point towards a past lying behind this system. These indications together with a correct grasp of the present, then also offer a key to the understanding of the past . . . This correct view likewise leads at the same time to the points at which the suspension of the present form of production gives signs of its becoming – foreshadowings of the future. Just as, on one side the prebourgeois phases appear as merely historical, i.e. suspended presuppositions, so do the contemporary conditions of production likewise appear as engaged in *suspending themselves* and hence in positing the *historic presuppositions* for a new state of society.[50]

It may seem at first that this is what Althusser is saying when he posits contemporary society both as a 'result' and as a 'society'.[51] However, the assertion that this is tantamount to a concept of history as being 'dependent on the principle of variation of these forms of combination' in fact makes it clear that the careful separation by Marx of the two categories of analysis has *already* been elided. While avoiding the charge of 'structuralism' as he interprets it; that is, an analysis based on the synchronic extraction of fixed elements-in-relation in an 'essential section' through the social formation; the contortions through which Althusser moves reproduce the terms of the theoretical problems, not breaking with it or developing it. The false historicity is also a false scientificity:

> Decisively, the systematic form of the work (*Capital:* especially Volume II) never undercuts the fundamental historical premise which frames the whole exposition, and on which Marx's claim for its 'scientificity', paradoxically, rests: the historically specific, hence transitory nature of the capitalist epoch and the categories which expresses it.[52]

6. Ideology

It is now possible to turn to Althusser's contribution to the Marxist analysis of ideology, of the 'ideological instance in the social formation'. In the essay on Ideological State Apparatuses (ISAs), most of the flaws that I have pointed to in his work, as well as much of the positive achievement to which I have made less reference, find their expression in a deceptively simple form. As to the positive side, I agree with Karel Williams's verdict, that Althusser offers more a rejection of vulgar Marxism than a worked-out theory of the ideological instance. But the apparent straightforwardness and conviction of the essay belies this.

The ISAs essay is concerned with the question of how the reproduction of labour power is ensured under capitalism. Every social formation, in order to carry on existing: 'must reproduce the conditions of its production at the same time as it produces, and in order to be able to produce. It must therefore reproduce: 1/ the productive forces 2/ the existing relations of production.'[53]

After dealing with the obvious means to reproduction (wage slavery) Althusser goes on to develop the thesis that the simple reproduction of labour power must also, under the CMP, be reinforced by a more complex process of training and rule-instilling in the classes under the ruling class and in that class itself. That is, the labour power must be of a *certain kind*. For Althusser, the answer to the original question (how the reproduction of labour power is ensured under the CMP) will also deliver the secret of the superstructure: 'I believe that it's possible and necessary to think what characterizes the essence of the existence and nature of the superstructures on the basis of reproduction.'[54]

Althusser identifies two fundamentally different agencies which ensure this reproduction. There is firstly the Repressive State Apparatus (RSA) which consists of the Government, Administration, Army, Police, Courts etc., and secondly, the Ideological State Apparatuses (ISAs). The 'ISAs' Althusser notes are the religious, educational, family, legal, political, trades unions, communications and cultural apparatuses. They function predominantly by ideological subjection (rather than by direct violence or the threat of violence) and are plural (as opposed to the unity of the state power in the 'RSA'). Finally, Althusser says that the 'ISAs' are predominantly private rather than public. No State can exist for long solely by means of direct repression, that is, without having some means of control via the 'ISAs'. I shall leave this sketch to develop criticism of it, but one obvious question arises, a question that can only be answered from the position of a fundamental critique: whether the division between the 'RSA' and the 'ISAs' is in fact analytically valid or merely descriptive.

The mode of operation of the ideological apparatuses is to 'interpellate individuals as subjects', that is, to form each individual human being who is born into and shaped by the society. The concrete individual thus functions as a 'support' for the individual *subject*; since everybody in any society is 'ever-already' a subject, there can be no 'individuals' in a society who are not subjects. The mechanism by which the *subjection* of individuals is effected, affirming individuals as subjects constituted in and by 'ideology', is that of 'recognition'. Whenever we cry 'That's obvious', or, literally, recognise a person, our subjection to 'ideology' is re-affirmed.[55] So too, of course, in the inverse process; misrecognition. The existence of ideology is furthermore *material;* that is, it does not exist merely 'in the head' as some cloudy cerebral inversion of what really is, but in fact it is carried and made material in *practices*, in professional and social practices. Thus

1 No practice except in and by an ideology
2 No ideology except by the subject and for subjects.

Poulantzas, whose theory of ideology[56] shares certain of the most distinctive features of Althusser's theory, makes it clear that both posit a *double* nature of ideology in class societies. Firstly, ideology is said to locate individuals as *träger* (since it is *in general* the 'representation of the imaginary relations of individuals to their conditions of existence'). And only secondly, its nature in a class society is overdetermined by the dominant class. The importance of this analysis lies, I believe, in the emphasis (which relies on the earlier introduction of 'over-determination') that men 'live in ideology' which is 'profoundly unconscious'. Consciousness of ideology, indeed, is only possible on condition that it is itself rooted in the unconscious. However, I believe that the most important implication of this is not drawn out by Althusser; that is, the absolute centrality to the entire process of 'interpellation' of the family.[57] It is the prior form of entry of the individual into a class divided society that sets the limits of effectivity of the subsequent 'ISAs'. However, the positive elements in the essay are devastated by a crucially damaging series of connected problems, problems essentially political but articulated in a densely philosophical form in Althusser's work, problems which will be the subject of the final section.

7. Philosophy, ideology, science

In the brief sketch above of the theory of ideology in Althusser, I emphasised especially the *double* nature of ideology in Althusser; its general, universal form, existent in all societies, (which Althusser compares metaphorically, rather than analytically, to Freud's unconscious), and its specific form in class societies. My motive in doing this is to expose the immense danger of this (core) emphasis in the theory, in defining 'the concept of ideology in its generality before the class struggle intervenes'.[58]

Two stratagems are at play here. One I have already mentioned in relation to *träger* (see section 4). This is the suppression of the social relations of production, in order to be able to posit society as a traditional scientific object of analysis. In this case the 'general function of ideology' is that of cohering society, of giving it a unity, and for Althusser, this general form of ideology is a function of the productive forces at their particular level of development. This pseudo-objective entity (it cannot be reduced to a simple 'out-there' object in some pre-political fashion) then appears in the analysis as presenting a transcending demand, for its functions to be filled by functionaries. This can be the only explanation for the static form of the 'ISAs' essay, with its apparently almost wholly autonomous practices attaching to each region. The shape bestowed on society by this entity is articulated in the form of technical divisions of labour. It is only secondarily that this particular (ideological and material) formation is 'somewhat overdetermined' in a class society by the ideology of the ruling class. The bitterness of Rancière's attack on the 'Theory of Ideology (The Politics of Althusser)', while not obscuring his critique, testifies to the 'undesirable effects in politics and theory' of this conception of ideology. The specificity of the Marxist theory of ideologies, as Rancière says, is subsumed under what is effectively a 'general social theory' and only secondly a Marxist theory: 'the "ideological forms" which the *Preface to the Critique of Political Economy* talks of are not merely social forms of representation, *but the forms in which a struggle is fought out.*'[59] And the postscript to the 'ISAs' essay acknowledges this; but the main presuppositions remain printed intact.

The second stratagem involves Althusser's distinction between science and ideology and conjointly, the opposition between science/empiricism (as one form of ideology.) In dealing with this, the fallacious forms of the relationship: between thought and reality that Althusser develops in his exegesis of the 1857 *Introduction* provides a vantage point for grasping his work as a whole.

In Althusser's early definitions,[60] Marxism attained the status of *science* when Marx made an 'epistemological break'[61] with the ideology of Political Economy, and also with Hegel, Humanism and Historicism.[62] By doing this, he constituted the fragmentary map of a new continent of science as had Galileo and Newton for their science-continents. Marxist science, then, becomes a similar thing to natural science, social formations being its 'object'. The emphasis on the irreducibly extrasocial, objective nature of the practice of science is borne within Althusser's early theory in Generality II: the corpus of concepts in a science that operates on the raw material (i.e. the *conceptual* raw material, Generality I). The trouble with this element in Althusser's general theory of scientificity is twofold: both that it is set up as the active subject of the scientific process itself, and yet is simultaneously not subject to the social determinations and political responsibility of any agent in the social formation.[63]

Yet this social nature of the means of production, 'To conceive Marx's philosophy in its specificity is therefore to conceive . . . of knowledge as production',[64] is inevitably 'indexed' in them: 'Instruments of labour not only supply a standard of the degree of development to which human labour has attained, but they are also indicators of the social conditions under which that labour is carried on' (*Capital* I, p. 176–7).

The means by which this Althusserean 'science' ensures its scientificity, ensures that its practice is a true one, then become 'rigorously interior':

> Theoretical Practice is indeed its own criterion and contains in itself definite protocols with which to validate the quality of its own product . . . Revolutionary practice intervened in the development of Marx's thought in the form of objects of experience or even experiment.[65]

To support this radically *subjectless process* ('there can be no subject of science except in an ideology of science') Althusser is obliged to place science 'itself' (whatever that is) outside of the social formation altogether. It becomes a 'practice' of which men are only the supports. The form of all practices in Althusser is derived by a process of dubious abstraction from *Capital*, a process that is basically unargued and unsound, as most critical commentators of Althusser note. Geras, on this point, remarks that the effect of the omission to spell out the determinations *on* this practice of 'science' renders it actually wholly autonomous, while nominally relatively so. I would argue that this pluralism is in fact latent in the definition of practice as it is employed in Althusser's work, rather than specific to scientific practice alone.

The later formulation ('philosophy as the class struggle is the realm of theory') is effectively this earlier position revised under the pressure of events and criticism, as Rancière makes clear; the relation between science and ideology is still seen as one of rupture rather than articulation:

> The dominant ideology is not the shadowy other of the pure light of science, it is the very space in which scientific knowledges are inscribed, and in which they are articulated as elements of a social formation's knowledge. It is in the forms of the dominant ideology that a scientific knowledge becomes an object of knowledge.[66]

Finally, turning to the double relation science/empiricism and thought/reality.

Given the extreme importance (for political reasons refracted in theory, which are outside the scope of this article to discuss) of the science/ideology opposition in Althusser, the science/empiricism distinction follows, since empiricism is arraigned as an ideology. Thus there must be some way in which it is possible to insulate, at root, the practice and status of this 'science' from the taint of empiricism. Althusser attempts this by relocating the fundamental distinction elaborated by Marx between the 'real' and 'thought' to within thought itself.[67] The raw material on which 'science' then works is the *concept* of the real; that which is described as Generality I. Knowledge (that is, scientific knowledge) is conceived of as a product, the result of a process of reproduction excised, in effect, from the relations of production.[68] Marx characterised the dialectical method as the 'working up of observations into concepts', and emphasised both the active practice of this working-up and the need to 'prove the truth, that is the reality and power, the this sidedness of (. . .) thinking, in practice':[69]

> There is no evidence for Marx having fundamentally broken with this notion that, though thinking 'has its own way', its 'truth' – its verification – can only rest in the this-sidedness of thinking, in practice. In fact, the 1857 text makes the point explicit – 'Hence, *in the theoretical method too*, the subject, society, must always be kept in mind as the presupposition.'[70]

The only truth that there can be to thinking rests in the recognition of its limits, not in the assertion of its omnipotence. The process of thought proceeds by working up the determinations which bring 'the subject, society' into being. The real concrete is thus mirrored, but not in a simply reflexive way, in the 'concrete= in=thought'.[71] Thought can not merely lift off from the real and go its own way to produce 'knowledge'. It is here that the importance of identifying both the Hegelian and the Kantian forms of idealism in Althusser is important. The Hegelian elements are relatively simple to pin down: the self-generating nature of 'theoretical practice' that is endemic to a philosopy-as-a-philosophy is subject to the criticisms that Marx made early on in his apprenticeship to Hegel. But the Kantian element is more elusive. Glucksmann elucidates it concisely. The only *guarantee* within this system that the result of 'theoretical practice' will actually correspond to the world 'out there' is that the form of both must be ordained by the transcendental essence of the 'mode of production' which produces 'society' and 'knowledge' alike. Thus, according to Althusser:

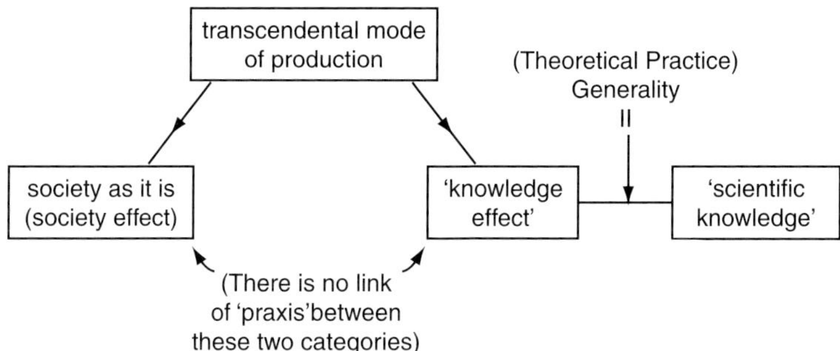

And correlatively, the 'theory of theoretical practice' ensures that through theoretical practice in general, it is possible to reach through to the essence of the development of things in general. (This, it would be correct to add, is the form of determination on the relative autonomy of theoretical practice.)

The persistent, unsolved problem in Althusser's reappropriability to any practical, Marxist analysis of culture and ideology remains here. He himself has acknowledged the failure to solve the problem of the 'knowledge mechanism' (that is, the means by which it is possible within this declaredly 'anti-empiricist' Marxism to make the original observations which are the starting point for 'theoretical practice', are actually got into the brain), and yet, for the sake of his philosophy-as-a-system, can not accept the thesis of John Lewis, that 'man can only know what he himself does'. In other words, for Althusser the truth of theory begins in a mystified form of appropriation of the world and ends in science or the party, rather than in practice.[72] Theory can not be merely a self-constitutive kingdom, as 'theoretical practice' (even if its form of insertion into the world is apparently interventionist, as latterly in Althusser's definitions), it must stand in relation to a real practice outside of itself, in Marx's sense, in the relation *between* theory and practice:

> The neat, binary contrast between a 'scientific' contradiction which is objective, material and systematic, and the practice of class struggle which is epiphenomenal and teleological disappears in the face of the essential interconnectedness of theory and practice.[73]

Finally, I think that it is necessary to assert two points. First, that much of what Althusser says that Marx says is in fact not what Marx says: the most telling example, perhaps, is Marx's endorsement of the writer in the *European Messenger* (Afterword to the Second German Edition of *Capital*) on the nature of the dialectical method. I shall quote some pertinent though disconnected sections:

> As soon as society has outlived a given period of development, and is passing over from one given stage to another, it begins to be subject also to other laws . . . The old economists misunderstood the nature of economic laws when they likened them to the laws of physics and chemistry . . . Nay, one and the same phenomenon falls under quite different laws in consequence of the different structure of those organisms as a whole, of the variations of their individual organs, of the different conditions in which those organs function . . .
>
> The scientific value of such an inquiry lies in the disclosing of the special laws that regulate the origin, existence, development, death, of a given social organism and its replacement by another, higher one.

Marx accepts the comments ('Indeed, what else is he picturing but the dialectical method?') and it is to the double emphasis on interconnections and the political thrust towards a break in history, a revolutionary change, that the entire method is partisan.

Secondly, there is no total epistemology in Marx, precisely the gap that Althusser tries to fill. Yet in view of the reflections in this paper, I feel it is possible to conclude that to perceive this gap is an illusion, the 'total epistemology' is a formal halting of the world: it is not a method *for*, so much as a method *of*, in other words, a metaphysic, an ontology.[74] If I have tended to stress the negative aspects of Althusser's work here, it is not because I believe it is wholly to be rejected, but because the few attempts to learn from it in Britain have been either 'theoreticist' in the worst, most cerebral way or blunt, empirical rejections of a kind that fall far below Marx's rigour, directness and revolutionary truth.

Notes and references

Editions used:			
	For Marx Penguin University Books	*trans* Brewster	1969
	Reading Capital Pantheon/NLB	*trans* Brewster	1970
	Lenin & Philosophy & Other Essays	*trans* Brewster	1971
	Grundrisse Pelican Marx Library	*trans* Nicolaus	1973
	Capital Lawrence & Wishart		1974

1 *For Marx* p. 9.

2 See 'To My English Readers' & 'Introduction: Today' in *For Marx* and foreword to Italian edition of *Reading Capital* (published in English edition).

3 ibid. Whether this is what he is *effectively* doing is another question: rarely does even a whiff of the class-struggle on the ground openly give his work urgency and both the form of the necessary revolutionary organisation and that of post-capitalist society are taken for granted. My own political disagreements with what I take to be Althusser's beliefs on this point enter in mediated form: a thorough critical debate demands a long historical and political argument.

4 Althusser's own.
5 *Reading Capital* p. 139.
6 'On The Materialist Dialectic' ('OTMD') in *For Marx* p. 203.
7 cf Geras's comment on Althusser's concept of fetishism: '. . . Althusser has proposed a reading of fetishism in which, of the two aspects that have been treated, namely, mystification and domination, only the former is treated. The notion of men being dominated by their own products has vanished (almost) without trace. Such an interpretation demands, of course, that the concept of fetishism be regarded as entirely unrelated to, and independent of, that of alienation, and the latter is accordingly dismissed as "ideological" & "pre-Marxist".' (Norman Geras: 'Essence and Appearance: Aspects of Fetishism in Marx's *Capital*' NLR 43)
8 'Contradiction & Overdetermination' ('C & O') in *For Marx* p. III.
9 'C & O' p. 113.
10 'OTMD' p. 163.
11 *Grundrisse* Introduction quoted in *Reading Capital* p. 187.
12 *Reading Capital* p. 189.
13 *Reading Capital* p. 188.
14 *Reading Capital* p. 191.
15 Again, as in section 2, it is necessary to link the one-sidedness of the conceptual distinction in Althusser to its role in establishing a peculiar *double* concept of ideology. (See section 6 and compare footnote 7).
16 *For Marx* pp. 233–4 ('Marxism and Humanism').
17 *Capital*, volume III, p. 797. (See Steve Butters' article in this issue).
18 *Reading Capital* p. 190.
19 The fundamentally unsatisfactory developments of the problems surrounding Althusser's particular formulation(s) of determinacy are the subject of criticisms by Vilar ('Writing Marxist History' NLR 80) and André Glucksmann ('A Ventriloquist Structuralism' *NLR* 64). The latter essay is in my opinion one of the most far reaching critiques to have been made of 'The Althusserean Theatre', of Althusser's work
20 *Reading Capital* p. 188, Althusser's emphases. The problems of a simple translation of this term into English are immense. 'Expression' obviously smacks of Hegel, whereas 'representation' implies little more than a form of expression without an expressing subject. 'Articulation' is perhaps closest, but only because it slides between 'expression' and 'structural form', which is precisely the problem. Despite reservations, I shall use the original term since it at least refers unconfusingly to Althusser's own usage, though that usage may itself be unclear.
21 *Reading Capital* p. 17.
22 cf, the editorial introduction to André Glucksmann's article in *NLR* 64, where it is suggested that the original publication of the articles was partly responsible for alterations in *Lire Le Capital* such as the dropping of Rancière's section.
23 Glucksmann art. cit.
24 Glucksmann art. cit.
25 *Reading Capital*, Foreword to Italian edition printed in English edition.
26 This point is made forcefully and at length by Vilar ('Writing Marxist History'), Geras ('Althusser's Marxism: an account and an assessment' *NLR* 71) and, from the position of a deep-reaching epistemological critique, by Glucksmann (art cit):

'1) It is not proved that *Capital* analyses anything more than capitalist production.
2) It is not proved that the analysis in *Capital* implies a comparative structural analysis, since the terms supposed to articulate this analysis are in fact derived from a developmental analysis of capitalism which *preserves* the existing social relations and keeps its terms.'

27 Geras, *NLR* 43, p. 74.
28 Hall makes this point in his 'reading' of the 1857 Introduction, that Marx's critique of the 'bad abstraction' practised by Bourgeois political economists demonstrates that 'what is *common* to production . . . as produced by the process of mental abstraction of "common" attributes, cannot enable us to grasp, concretely, any single "real historical stage of production".' (my emphasis).
29 Although acquaintance with the reaction of the PCF to the events of 1968 and subsequent criticisms must warn one off from attributing this change to a wholly self-generated process internal to thought, or specifically, to the 'development' of Althusser's thought.

30 *Marxism Today*, October–November 1972.
31 *Reading Capital* p. 180. Althusser's emphases.
32 *Radical Philosophy* 6, 'Who Makes History?', J.K. Mepham.
33 *For Marx* p. 231.
34 *Radical Philosophy* 6 'Proletarian Self-Emancipation', Norman Geras.
35 *Reading Capital* p. 180.
36 *Reading Capital* pp. 174–5.
37 See 'Freud & Lucan', in *Lenin & Philosophy*.
38 *For Marx* p. 206n.
39 Vilar, art. cit.
40 Glucksmann, art. cit.
41 All quotations taken from the Penguin edition ed. Nicolaus.
42 v. Glossary 'Historicism', which mentions Lukács, Korsch, Gramsci, Della Volpe, Sartre and Colletti as all being subject to this criticism.
43 See the chapter of that name in *Reading Capital*.
44 *Reading Capital* p. 177. The 'combination' to which the excerpt refers is that of 5 elements (labour power/objects and instruments of production/appropriation of the surplus labour and the two relations: Relations of production (property relations)/Productive Forces) which together (in articulation or *gliederung*) can constitute a definition of definite, different modes of production. (see 3iii) As Glucksmann notes, the purpose of this *combination* in Althusser is to found anti-Historicism, just as the purpose of *darstellung* is to found anti-Humanism.
45 see *Reading Capital* pp. 131–37, largely on criticism of Gramsci.
46 *Reading Capital* p. 93, Althusser's emphasis.
47 *Reading Capital* p. 106. Also cf 'conjuncture' in Glossary – 'The central concept of the Marxist science of politics (of Lenin's "current moment"); it denotes the exact balance of forces, the state of overdetermination . . . of the given moment to which political tactics must be applied.'
48 The main reference for this must be Hall's paper on the 1857 Introduction, which analyses the crucial differences between Marx's methodology in relation to History and Althusser's account of it.
49 It is interesting to look at one of Marx's suggestions as to what constitutes Marxist 'science' or the 'scientificity' of his analytic activity – 'Insofar as Political Economy remains within that bourgeois horizon, insofar i.e. as the capitalist regime is looked upon as the absolutely final form of social production, instead of as a passing phase of historical evolution, Political Economy can remain a science only so long as the class struggle is latent or manifests itself in isolated and sporadic phenomena.' (*Capital* I p. 24).
50 *Grundrisse* pp. 460–61. Marx's emphases.
51 *Reading Capital* pp. 64–67.
52 Hall art. cit p. 54.
53 'Ideology and Ideological State Apparatuses' in *Lenin and Philosophy* . . . p. 124.
54 'ISAs' p. 131. Althusser's emphasis. All quotes from this essay in this section unless otherwise stated.
55 The term *recognition* is developed from the work of Jacques Lacan, who posits recognition as the fundamental psychic mechanism by which the ego is formed in the mirror-phase. (cf 'The Mirror Phase' *NLR* 51)
56 Nicos Poulantzas, *Political Power and Social Classes*, (NLB 1973), esp. pp. 195–224.
57 cf Pierre Bourdieu, 'Cultural Reproduction and Social Reproduction' in *Knowledge Education and Social Change* ed R. Brown (Tavistock 1973): 'What is measured by the level of education is nothing other than the accumulation of the effects of training acquired within the family and the academic apprenticeships which themselves presuppose this previous training' p. 79.
58 Poulantzas op. cit. Also, for the whole of this section see the paper by J. Rancière: on the Theory of Ideology: (The Politics of Althusser) (1979) *Radical Philosophy 7*.
59 Rancière, p. 18. My emphasis.
60 For newer definitions of the political role of philosophy, see the 'Reply to John Lewis' (*Marxism Today*: May 1972) and the essay, 'Philosophy as a Revolutionary Weapon' in *Lenin and Philosophy*: though I believe that there is an essential similarity in effect between early and new work produced under the different definitions.
61 A concept derived from Bachelard, Foucault and Canguilhem, describing the 'leap from the prescientific world of ideas to the scientific world; this leap involves a radical break with the whole

pattern and frame of reference of the prescientific (ideological) notions and the construction of a new pattern'. (Glossary)

62 NB. That this is nowhere near Marx's expressed notions of science, cf. Marx quoted fn 48, for example, although, as I have said, it is not sufficient to play Marx off against Althusser. It is important, though, to remember that while Marx did not say a lot of what Althusser says, he also said a great deal which Althusser does not say and would rather perhaps have had Marx not say. 'In hearing (Marx's) silences, we must take care not to silence his words', (Geras: *NLR* 71).

63 cf J. Stalin: *Dialectical and Historical Materialism* 'Hence the science of the history of society, despite all the complexity of the phenomena of social life, can become as precise a science, as let us say, biology, and capable of making use of the laws of development of society for practical purposes.' (p. 20)

64 *Reading Capital* see chapter, 'From Capital to Marx's Philosophy'.

65 *Reading Capital* p. 57, Geras makes the interesting point that Althusser ironically makes a very partial reading of the Hobbesian metaphor that he quotes (that 'men tear out their hair or their lives over politics, but are as thick as thieves over the hypotenuse or falling bodies' *For Marx* p. 122), and yet it is precisely a science such as physics or mathematics that he claims to be trying to elaborate!

66 Rancière: art, cit.

67 see *Reading Capital* pp. 105–118.

68 With corresponding effects in the relation of theory to political practice – see the debate between Geras and Mepham in *Radical Philosophy* 6: I think that, the thrust of Althusser's notion of scientists as guardians of scientific truth *must* entail some form of hypodermic relationship of theory to the masses via the Party syringe.

69 *Theses on Feuerbach.*

70 Hall, art. cit. p. 36.

71 cf Ian Chambers's comments on structural linguistics in this journal.

72 cf Rancière's emphasis (1969) on the primacy of the category of *knowledge* over the science/ideology dualism posed by Althusser.

73 Hall, art. cit. p. 59.

74 See Phil Slater's article in this journal on the symptomatic gaps in the work of the Frankfurt School, especially on the omission of the category of the class struggle as effectively *determinant* in both the internal form of their theory and its self-conscious role in society.

15 Exposition and critique of Julia Kristeva

Allon White

L'éclatement du sujet: the work of Julia Kristeva

> How could he say 'I' when he was something new and unknown, not himself at all? This I, this old formula of the age, was a dead letter.
>
> – *Women in Love*

As Plato tells us in the *Cratylus*,[1] the *Sophist*[2] and in *Letter VII*,[3] there is no logos which does not presuppose the interlacing of names with verbs: syntax is the condition of coherence of rationality. Any disturbance of syntactic order or its elements destabilizes the relations of reason and calls into question the fixed boundaries of subject and object, cause and condition. It is on this account that the loss of syntactic coherence has been taken as an indication of insanity.[4] The inability to fix pronouns in place and to keep their designation constant, the inability to follow the grammatical rules for negating, making a phrase passive or conditional, or ordering the unities of subject and object in a sentence, these inabilities token the collapse of mental order and of symbolic control. For our purposes, they also token something more general which pertains even in cases when agrammaticality is not so drastic: any modifications in language, particularly infractions of syntactic laws, are a modification of the status of the subject.[5]

To invoke Plato at the outset is not conventional piety: the philosophic rationalism which begins with Plato and which continues with uneven but massive force through to the present day, has been a dominant and incisive model of what constitutes 'being human', *anthropos* as *logos*. It is the tradition which, present in Aquinas and central in Bacon, Descartes, Locke and Kant, leads through to the philosophic concern of our century with the relation between language and logic. An acceptance of the notion that human understanding and the understanding of the human, must focus its analysis on the interlacing of names with verbs – on language as the bearer of logical relations and hence the articulation of the structure of mind – an acceptance of this notion is the grounding supposition of modern philosophy, particularly logical positivism and its offshoots, but also the phenomenology of Brentano.

The position ascribed to the subject in this tradition, though often left unspoken, is clearly that of a singular, transcendental *unity*. Its clearest expression is perhaps in Kant's *Critique of Pure Reason* when Kant considers the unity of apperception:

> To know anything in space (for instance, a line), I must *draw* it, and thus synthetically bring into being a determinate combination of the given manifold, so that the unity of this act is at the same time the unity of consciousness (as in the concept of a line); and it

> is through this unity of consciousness that an object (a determinate space) is first known. The synthetic unity of consciousness is, therefore an objective condition of all knowledge. It is not merely a condition that I myself require in knowing an object, but is a condition under which every intuition must stand in order *to become an object for me*. For otherwise, in the absence of this synthesis, the manifold would *not* be united in one consciousness.[6]

The identification of consciousness with a synthetic unity of mental action means that the ego constitutes itself as a whole, as a self, which stabilizes the otherwise dispersed and contradictory perspectives of a being which has no fixed or unified position. Modern linguistic philosophy (Frege, Carnap, Russell, Wittgenstein through to Quine and Strawson) explores this concatenation of syntax, logic and reference which unifies, and yet is made possible by, an homogeneous, singular subject. Wittgenstein's double assertion in the *Tractatus* – Die Grenzen meiner Sprache bedeuten die Grenzen meiner Welt: Die Logik erfullt die Welt; die Grenzen der Welt sind auch ihre Grenzen[7] – makes language, logic and the world co-terminous. The limits of my world, of what *is for me*, are made identical to the limits imposed by linguistic and rational order.

This rationalist project, with its attendant notion of the subject as a synthesizing unity, as the unique guarantee of *being*, is as dominant in modern linguistics as it is in philosophy. Nicely marked in Chomsky's *Cartesian Linguistics*[8] by the title of the book itself, Chomsky argues that the supporting subject of syntactic order is in the Cartesian tradition of a unified *cogito*. Again, in post-Saussurian linguistics, Benveniste, writing on the pronominal opposition of Je/Vous, puts it thus:–

> Cette polarité ne signifie ni égalité ni symétrie: l'ego' a toujours une position de transcendance à l'égard de tu.[9]

Thus both the Chomskian and Saussurian conceptions of the subject in language accept the rationalist description of a transcendental ego, and thus both belong in this respect at least, to that philosophic tradition which goes back via Kant and Descartes to Plato. Kristeva calls this conception of the subject *thetic*, since it is characterized by the laying down or setting forth (-Gk. 'such as is placed') of positive statements or propositions. The thetic conception considers subjectivity as a unified consciousness able to produce reason through the propositional structures embedded in syntactic order.

But for at least as long as it has existed, this thetic tradition of high rationalism has been mocked and haunted by alien spirits. From the outset, Plato had to exclude most of music and literature from the realms of *The Republic*,[10] deleting from literature all horrifying and frightening names in the underworld, all gloomy accounts of the afterlife, all laments and unjust misery, all laughter, lies, and intemperate desire for the pleasures of eating, drinking and sex. Madness and the representation of madness were also forbidden, and in music all the modes except two, which represent 'courage and moderation in good fortune or in bad', were likewise forbidden in the kingdom of philosophy. In other words, Plato feels his rational and unified Republic threatened from within by forces, desires and activities which must be censored or ostracized if the rational state is to be maintained. A closer look at the nature of these threatening forces reveals that what Plato has to exclude as dangerous are the desire for sensual pleasure, laughter, the representative of death and of madness, and those two art forms, music and literature, which may express or incite these subversive powers. What are excluded then, are precisely those aspects of human activity which were to become the great themes of freudian psychoanalysis.*

The correspondence is not accidental. The schism which Plato introduced between a harmonious rationality on the one hand, and disruptive forces of passion, wit, death and pleasure on the other hand, has marked every major western conception of the human. Nietzsche, by borrowing the terms Apollonian and Dionysiac, puts the origin of the representation of the schism even further back than Plato, but it is Plato who first begins to theorize the disjunction between them by favouring a dominant rationalism at the expense of these other, potentially disruptive powers. The problem for any thinker who does not merely champion one of these sides in a simple minded way, is to attempt *to think the relations between them*, to comprehend (in both its senses) the rational and the irrational, the sentence and the song.

It is this massive project which Julia Kristeva attempts in *La révolution du langage poétique* (1974). Her work is situated in the dialectic between formalist, passive, 'objective' theories of language and mind on the one hand, and active, psychoanalytical theories of subjectivity on the other, which together are attacked, synthesized and transposed to produce a new concept of subjectivity and its place in language and poetic literature. Poetry is the focus of the work because the space occupied by poetry is poised directly over the schism which Plato opened up, the deep fissure between the thetic and those practices and impulses which threaten the thetic. Literature is the *lieu privilégié* of analysis because it has revealed at certain times, in the practice of its writing, the destruction which is wrought upon the thetic by a number of extra-rational phenomena – the disposition of basic impulses, desires and fears which can be seen only in the degree to which they alter the logical, propositional nature of normal communication.

This tension between the thetic and what for the moment I will term simply the non-thetic, is not an eternal war waged in a vacuum. It has determinate historical and social forms which arise from the particular ways in which the *activity* of writers, caught up in the network of social meaning systems, *transforms* and *challenges* the tradition which fails to contain that subjective activity. Literature, Kristeva argues,[11] not only shows us how language works in disposing of the particular pattern of thetic against non-thetic in a text, it is also an activity which brings the laws of established discourse into question, and thereby presents itself as a terrain where new sorts of discourse may be engendered. And since, as I argued in my first paragraph, a change in discourse is a change in the status of the subject, a radical new poetic discourse may produce a radical new status for the subject. But we must first recover much more of Kristeva's argument before such a statement becomes clear.

Kristeva's first object of attack is the thetic tradition of a single unified subject, embodied in philosophy, linguistics, and also in those types of literature centred on mimetic and narrative representation (which not unnaturally turns out to be most of literature). Of course Kristeva's is only the last in a long line of such attacks, and substantially she is in agreement with both the sociological critique of the thetic (particularly as argued by Marx and Durkheim) and with the psychological critique (as argued by Freud, Lacan, and in some qualified respects, by Marcuse and Reich). In a way it would not be inaccurate to see Kristeva's project as a reworking of both the freudian and marxist notions of an active subject, as revealed in the modernist poetic activity, and mediated by a considerably revised version of modern linguistics.

* Though it must be added that Freud's well known dislike of music led to it being under-represented in his theoretical writings.

The sociological critique of the thetic has become an intellectual reflex of our century. Meaning is not produced *within* a subject, but *between* subjects, in group, class and society. And meaning is not simply given, everywhere and always, in the singular bond between one mind and the world of objects: it is produced, it has a history in the forms of modes of its production, both in the socialization of the child and in the transformations of culture. The cognitions go back at least to Hamann's *Vermischte Anmerkungen*[12] (*Miscellaneous Observations*) of 1761, in which the kinship of linguistic and economic systems of exchange is proposed as a way of explaining both. Production, whether of objects or meanings is social, a *mode* of production, and Kristeva agrees that it was necessary for Marx to emphasize this in iconoclastic opposition to the bourgeois concept of work as purely individual and personal.[13] She quotes Derrida with approval when he writes that[14] –

> L'argent remplace les choses par leurs signes. Non seulement à l'interieur d'une société mais d'une culture à l'autre, ou d'une organisation économique à l'autre. C'est pourquoi l'alphabet est commerçant. Il doit être compris dans le moment monétaire de la rationalité économique. La description critique de l'argent est la réflexion fidèle du discours sur l'écriture.

For Marx, work could only be grasped in the values – of use or exchange – into which it was crystallized. Work represents nothing outside of the values in which it is stored up, for it is only in these values that it can be *measured* and hence enter into society and into theory. Work takes on a determinate form, and thus takes on *meaning*, only when it has already entered the system of exchange as a particular amount of production. Labour itself, anterior to exchange, remains in Marx the foundation of his theory, but unthinkable except as an infinite potential of available physical and mental expenditure. But, Kristeva says, labour itself *has* become thinkable as a concept, even when it is anterior to exchange. For Kristeva, this pure activity of the human body is 'mute' – for it is logically antecedent to exchange and cannot therefore embody value – but must exist as the subject's praxis and expenditure which is taken up by communication, by exchange, by determinate production, by meaning. Work cannot simply be a mode of production, but it must also be, simultaneously, subjective expenditure of effort, working itself through the mode of production. The two aspects have to be thought at once if the subject is not to be left as a blank, a passive, empty bearer of the social processes.

According to Kristeva, it is Freud's concept of work in the *Traumarbeit* which fills this blank and gives us the method to think through this 'production anterior to production', the disposition of subjective expenditure. Freud uncovers production itself as a process,[15] and as a particular semiotic system, a permutation of elements which models production and which is distinct from that of exchange. Kristeva thus wants to take account of Marxist, Logical-Philosophical and Freudian theories of the subject – the sociological, rationalist and psychological – but without collapsing the subject into any one of them. Her description of the subject thus draws on all three, but the central place is undoubtedly that of Freudiansim recaste in the light of Lacan. She conceives this human subjectivity as follows. (All page references to *La Révolution du Langage Poétique* are in brackets).

First of all (both in terms of the child and logically) to be human is to be a psycho-biological entity energized by the movements and rhythms of impulses. The impulses are not only bio-energic charges but also psychic marks (p. 23) and their disposition across the mind and body is called a chora (χώρᾱ – space, room, place, locality).

The *chora* is a non-expressive totality, constituted by the impulses and their stasis in a 'figured movement' which is gradually regulated by the constraints imposed upon the body by family and society. At this rudimentary stage it is hardly anything more than a certain rhythm, and its only analogy is body or vocalic movement. Kristeva follows Melanie Klein[16] in considering the oral and anal impulses the dominant ones, both structured and directed in relation to the body of the mother (pp. 26–27), in a pre-oedipal phase in which boys and girls *alike* view the mother as the receptacle of all that is desirable. The *chora* is the pre-socialized *space of motility* which makes gesture, phonic articulation and chromatic identification possible. Gradually, under the constraints of biological growth and family structure, this chora becomes limited and provisionally fixed (p. 28) into the different semiotic materials – sound, movement, colour and shape – so that it takes on a sort of economy of functions in relation to its contexts. This discharge of energy, which binds and orients the child to the mother, is always double, always both productive and destructive (p. 26) and in its doubleness may be likened to the double helix of the DNA molecule. The *chora* is thus the space of operation of sensory-motor impulses, both positive and negative in the degree to which they settle into a pattern but also destroy the stability of that pattern's new movements (p. 27). Because of this constant movement, there is no subject or personality at this stage, merely an unstable and provisional 'beating out' (frayage) of certain pathways and connections, the establishments of differences, parts of the body, the operation of vocal and anal sphincters, the focusing of the eyes and so forth.

All these processes constitute the basis for language, and form a crucial category in Kristeva's work, what she calls (perversely in view of its many other meanings) the *semiotic*. The *semiotic* is the production of sounds, rhythms, vocal and gestural modulations (such as intonation) *but anterior to meaning*, that is to say before lexical and syntactic organization:

> Ce type de relations nous parait susceptible de préciser le *sémiotique* en tant que modalité psychosomatique du procès de la signifiance, c'est-à-dire non symbolique mais articulant (au sens le plus large du terme d'articulation) un continuum. . . . Tous ces processus et relations, pré-signe et pré-syntaxe, viennent d'être placés dans une optique génétique, comme prealables et nécessaires à l'acquisition du langage avec lequel ils ne se confondent pas.
>
> (p. 28)

The *semiotic* then is the pre-condition for communication and language proper. It is both the ability of the baby to produce movement and differences in voice and gesture, and, more importantly, the rhythmic and phonic modulations which, though chronologically earlier than speech, always accompany speech as its material and psycho-physical grounding throughout adult life. Even in the highest flights of rational thought, this semiotic basis is the necessary accompaniment and continuo. But in dreams and in certain modern literary texts, it actually becomes dominant and breaks through the thetic part of language:-

> Ce n'est pourtant que par la logique du *rêve* qu'ils ont pu attirer l'attention, et ce n'est que dans certaines pratiques signifiantes, comme celle du *texte*, qu'ils dominent le procès de la signifiance.
>
> (p. 28)

Any innate, genetic traits find their place here, in the *semiotic*, the ordering and disposing of primary processes such as displacement and condensation, absorption and repression, rejection and stasis, all the processes which are the innate pre-conditions in the species for the acquisition of language (p. 29). In a sense, this semiotic order is pure musicality. It is rhythm, tonal difference, phonic change, movement of the body and of the limbs. This semiotic area, characterized as enigmatic, indifferent to language, feminine, a semiotic rhythm, is a sort of orchestration of primary movements and functions, what Mallarmé called a 'Mystère dans les lettres' (p. 29). Since it is anterior to signs and syntax – anterior to conscious communication – it is, quite literally, the unconscious, and it is at this point that the link with Freud becomes visible:-

> Notre position du sémiotique est, on le voit, inséparable d'une théorie du sujet qui tient compte de la position freudienne de l'inconscient. Décentrant l'ego transcendental, le coupant et l'ouvrant à une dialectique dans laquelle *son entendement* syntaxique et categoriel n'est que le moment *liminaire* du procès, lui-même toujours *agi* par le rapport à l'autre que domine la pulsion de mort et sa réitération productrice de 'signifiant': tel nous apparait ce sujet dans le langage.
>
> (p. 30)

The reference to the death instinct (la pulsion de mort) is central in Kristeva's thinking on the nature of the *chora* and its *semiotic* expression (even though it must be counted as the most controversial and least supported of Freudian concepts).[17] The *chora* is described as the place of articulation of the death instinct *across* primary narcissism and the desire for pleasure of the subject, this transversality disrupting his identity so that new psychic patterns are beaten out. The death instinct is the tendency of the organism to return to a homeostatic state, rest and equilibrium, whilst the desire for pleasure drives against this stasis. But Kristeva gives a priority to the importance of the death instinct by saying that (footnote to p. 27) pleasure and narcissism are simply provisional positions against which the death instinct pushes, the resulting pressures creating new mental passages. Narcissism and pleasure are thus the 'inveigling and realization of the death instinct'.

Kristeva also links the Freudian idea of a death instinct with a more philosophical conception which she shares with Jacques Derrida.[18] Death is nothing other than a destruction of identity (in both the hegelian and everyday meaning of the word) and is thus *negation* and *difference* with relation to a given subject. Kristeva thus writes about 'la pulsion de mort' as negativity or rejection, any force which tends to *destroy the constituted identity of the subject*, even though this may have only a metaphorical relation to 'death' in the commonly conceived notion of the word.

The *chora* then is the 'space of motility' which engenders the *semiotic*, the grounding of signification in vocalic and corporal movement before it can make signs and sentences. Its nearest representations are the babble of the child and the rhythms of music.

This semiotic layer does not disappear when the child learns to speak, but on the contrary remains as the necessary basis of articulation and sense, it is what drives language on and makes it possible. Language can never be simply a passive set of protocols and structures – though this is usually the way it is envisaged by modern linguistics – but it must be a praxis, an activity and process which is motivated by the psychobiological disposition of the speaking subject.

The next question to which Kristeva addresses herself is how, on the basis of this semiotic chora, the thetic (logical, judging, naming) part of subjectivity may be produced. Kristeva subsumes all the logical, predicative, syntaxic aspects of language under one term which, again demonstrating a wilful perversity in the face of accepted usage she terms the *symbolic*. The *symbolic* is an extension of the thetic discussed above, it is that major part of language which names and relates things, it is that unity of semantic and syntactic competence which allows communication and rationality to appear, Kristeva has thus divided language into two vast realms, the *semiotic* – sound, rhythm and movement anterior to sense and linked closely to the impulses (Triebe) – and the *symbolic* – the semantico-syntactic function of language necessary to all rational communication about the world. The latter, the *symbolic*, usually 'takes charge of' the semiotic and binds it into syntax and phonemes, but it can only do so on the basis of the sounds and movements presented to it by the semiotic. The dialectic of the two parts of language form the *mise en scène* of Kristeva's description of poetics, subjectivity, and revolution.

To even ask the question 'how is the symbolic produced?', one has already delivered a direct challenge to much rationalist-based philosophy. Instead of accepting the thetic notion of subjectivity as a given, defining what may be judged as subjectivity by remaining exclusively in the realm of predication, and analysing its structure, Kristeva displaces it from its accepted centrality, to show that it is a produced stage in the development of subjectivity, bound to, and articulated upon, another stage which makes it possible, and which is neither the realm of objects nor the directly social, but *also* a part of subjectivity. The transcendental ego of Kant and modern logic suddenly finds that it is not alone, nor sovereign, as it had always thought. But this is emphatically not to say that the notion of a transcendental ego may now be jettisoned in favour of an heterogeneous concept of mind. What was wrong was not the argument that a unified subject was necessary to the unity of apperception and hence to the logic of predication: such an argument must necessarily hold true. But it is wrong to make *this* transcendental ego co-extensive with subjectivity as such, rather than a *produced stage* within it. Kristeva does not seek to destroy the philosophic concept of the thetic, nor the weight of logical and linguistic philosophy based upon it, but she seeks to decentre the concept by accommodating it within a subjectivity which has an unconscious, psychobiological drives, and a history:-

> La philosophie moderne est d'accord pour reconnaître que c'est à l'ego transcendental que revient le droit de représenter la thèse instauratrice de la signification (signe et/ou proposition). Mais c'est seulement à partir de Freud que la question peut être posée non pas sur l'origine de cette thèse, mais sur le procès de sa production. A stigmatiser dans le thétique le fondement de la métaphysique, on s'expose à être son anti-chambre; à moins de spécifier les conditions de production de cette thèse. La théorie freudienne de l'inconscient et son développement lacanien nous paraissent, être précisément une mise à jour du fait que la signification thétique est un stade productible dans certaines conditions précises lors du procès de la signifiance, qu'elle constitue le sujet sans se reduire à son procès, puisqu'elle est le seuil du langage.
>
> (p. 43)

Kristeva distinguishes therefore between the *semiotic* (the impulses and their articulation, p. 41) and the domaine of signification, the *symbolic*, which is always a domain of propositions or judgements, that is to say, a domaine of *positions*. This positionality, the ability to take up a point of view, (explored by Husserl in his phenomenological reduction) is what installs the *identity* of the subject and of his objects, identity being a separation which the subject achieves between the image of himself and the image of the world. He becomes conscious of himself as a *self*, and of the world as a world of objects and of other subjects separate from himself. This coming-to-consciousness is actually an identifiable period in the growth of the child, and is signalled by his ability to produce holophrastic utterances, which are probably not always fully formed sentences (NP-VP) as conceived by generative grammar, but differ from the babble of an earlier phase in that they separate out a subject from an object and attribute to it some fragment of meaning (as for example, when the cat goes 'miaow' and all animals are then designated 'miaows').

The mechanisms which produce this symbolic, and hence thetic level of identity and signification, are the *mirror phase* [19] and the *castration complex*.

It is the mirror phase which produces the child's 'spatial intuition' which is at the heart of signification (and which accounts for the fact that the spatial metaphor is the dominant organizing metaphor in language). The mirror phase, taken from Lacan, designates, in a way that is partly literal and partly metaphorical, the point in a child's development when fascinated by its own image in a mirror, it recognizes the reversed image of a self. This visual image of himself is the first time that the child conceives of himself in his imagination as a totality separated from the rest of the world. It is the necessary precondition for the child to be able to say 'me' or 'I', as well as being the visual image which stands as the prototype for the world of objects.[20] The mirror phase inaugurates the position-separation-identification which permits the formation of sentences and propositions.

The mirror phase may be decomposed into three separate moments. At first, the child perceives the image in the mirror as a real being whom he tries to grasp or approach. He reacts to this image by jubilatory mimicry, and what is indicated at this stage is the recognition of the body-image of another *as a whole*. Lacan writes: –

> C'est que la forme totale du corps par quoi le sujet devance dans un mirage la maturation de sa puissance, ne lui est donnée que comme *Gestalt*, c'est-à-dire dans une extériorité, où certes cette forme est-elle plus constituante que constituée, mais où surtout elle lui apparaît dans un relief de stature qui la fige et sous une symétrie qui l'inverse, en opposition à la turbulence de mouvement dont il s'éprouve l'animer.

At first the *gestalt* offers an image of the body which is quite opposed to the 'turbulent movement' which the child himself feels. But before very long the child discovers that the image is nothing but an image. He no longer seeks to seize it, nor does he search for the other behind the mirror, because he realizes that there is *no – body*. Thirdly, the child recognizes, not simply an image but *his* image in the specular reflection of himself. In this moment of recognition he has to a degree which is close to being literal, realized an image of himself, he has grasped his own appearance, the image that he makes for/of himself, as a produced identity, a conquest of his body as a unity and as an image. It is this identification and unification of a self as a self's image, which is important for the generation of a unified consciousness capable of producing speech.[21] Anthony Wilden writes: –

> The central concept of the mirror phase is clear: this primordial experience is symptomatic of what makes the *moi* an imaginary construct. The ego is an *Idealich*, another self, and the *stade du miroir* is the source of all later identifications.[22]

The total image of the body, set over against a realm of otherness, is thus the moment of production and structuration of an identity through the mediation of the body-image. The transcendental ego necessary to logical and rational communication and action comes into play during the mirror phase. Confirmation of this comes from another source, and lends considerable support to Lacan's theory.

The image of the body in bits and pieces, *le corps morcelé*, is one of the most common of dreams, fantasies, certain types of schizophrenia, experience of drugs, art and literature.

The works of Hieronymus Bosch, Salvador Dali and Artaud express the notion clearly. This corporal disintegration is the reverse of the constitution of the body during the mirror phase, and it occurs only at those times when the unified and transcendent ego is threatened with dissolution. The way in which the fantasy of the fragmented body accompanies the breakdown of rational sovereignty is the clear complement of Lacan's idea that the image of the total body is necessary to the creation of rational unity. In each case, the image of the body, of the self, mediates thetic unity and disintegration.

For Kristeva, the fear of castration finished off (parachève) this process (p. 44). The argument becomes a little murky at this point (pp. 45–50) but as I read it, the castration complex has two effects which further the installation of the symbolic. Firstly, the mother, hitherto the receptacle and receiver of every demand from the child, is separated from the child (by (a) the gradual cessation of weaning and (b) the gradual intervention of the father) which has the effect of detaching the child from its dependence and identity with the mother, thus opening up a *lack*, an absence of that-which-is-desired which can only be represented by a figurative substitute, an image or representation. Speech arises as an attempt to fill this lack, this béance towards the absent object (in this case the mother). At the epistemological level, the 'lack of an object' is the gap in the signifying chain which the subject seeks to fill at the level of the signifier.

Secondly, the separation from the mother now makes her into an 'other', someone for whom, and to whom, the speech is made and addressed. The speech is made for her and not for me, and it is thus that the other is established as possessor of, or space of, the signifier: –

> La béance entre l'ego imagé et la motilité pulsionnelle, entre la mère et la demande qui lui est adressée, est la coupure même qui instaure ce que Lacan appelle le lieu de l'Autre comme lieu du 'signifiant'. Le sujet est occulté 'par un signifiant toujours plus pur', mais ce manque à y être confère à un autre le rôle de tenir la possibilité de la signification.[23]

This moment of separation from the mother is a part of the castration complex because Kristeva, following Lacan, makes the mother an identification with the phallus ('c'est dire qu'elle est le phallus' p. 45). The child is 'cut off' from the immediate nurturing contact with the mother hitherto enjoyed with such close physical and mental bonding that there was neither need nor space for the establishment of communication about things. At the same time this period is when the sexuality of the child ceases to be 'polymorphous perverse' (the child as demanding sexual contact and pleasure for all parts of the body and irrespective of incest laws) and becomes specifically genital, the laws of incest, (The Laws) always linguistically structured, are imposed at the same time (p. 45). It is this reference to incest prohibition which completes the oedipal triangle and completes the castration complex. The installation of symbolic language (thetic, naming, propositional) is what allows the imposition of The Law, the interdiction of the Mother as a focus of love through the 'apprehension' (as both fear and learning) of the Paternal order. Lacan writes in his *Rome Discourse*: –

> The primordial Law is therefore that which in regulating marriage ties superimposes the kingdom of culture on that of nature abandoned to the law of copulation. The interdiction of incest is only its subjective pivot, revealed by the modern tendency to reduce to the mother and the sister the objects forbidden to the subject's choice, although full licence outside of there is not yet entirely open.

> This law, therefore is revealed clearly enough as identical to an order of language. For without kinship nominations, no power is capable of instituting the order of preferences and taboos which bind and weave the yarn of lineage down through succeeding generations . . . It is *in the name of the father* that we must recognize the support of the symbolic function which, from the dawn of history has identified his person with the figure of the law.[24]

The mirror phase and the castration complex thus set up the second layer of language, the *symbolic*, which is language as communication proper, which names objects and expresses their relation to one another in the laws of syntax. The symbolic is thus generated by the birth of *desire* as it replaces the simple *demand* of the child and by the birth of *repression* (The Primary Repression of the Oedipal interdiction which prefigures all later repressions) as it replaces simple *rejection*. The two levels of signification therefore, the semiotic and the symbolic, 'correspond' as forms of meaning, to the maternal and paternal functions in the oedipal relation which the child lives through as a condition of his growth. And just as an adult's sexual behaviour is rooted in his own particular experience of the oedipal, his own produced configuration of identification and rejection of the figures of father and mother, so too the adult's particular subjectivity will be rooted in the specific intermixing of the semiotic and the symbolic, the rejection and acceptance of law incessantly weaving the particular dialectic of his personality. Active and passive, submission and aggression, rationality and passion spin out a pattern of loose and now tighter threads which, in their recurrence and repetitions, are the pattern of subjectivity. In other words, it is the *way in which* the semiotic relates to and disfigures the symbolic, as well as the *way in which* the symbolic reasserts its unifying control of the semiotic, which gives us the basis of subjectivity as a process. From the mirror phase onwards the semiotic and the symbolic involve each other in a shifting process of dependence and rejection, the spreading reticulation of synactic and nominal order are informed and sometimes broken, by the power of the semiotic; the signifying power of desire, aggression and pleasure are disposed according to the way the particular person has lived through the oedipal complex and that experience is compulsively repeated in all his later psychic processes.

Kristeva thus reverses the normal way of thinking about the thetic consciousness. It is not some already constituted 'I' which produces coherent sentences about the world: on the contrary, it is the introduction of the child into the world of syntax which permits the development of that child as a unified subject, as a conscious 'I'. The thetic and the syntactic are inseparable and the production of subject and predicate, name and verb, or to take up the terms of Strawson, 'feature concepts' and 'feature-placing statements', the production of the two major syntactic unities (the placed and the placing, the bound and the binding, the modified and the modifier are three ways in which these nominal and predicative functions have been described) enables the subject to achieve a stable position over against the world. The most significant result of this reversal is that *it is only in language that the 'I' exists, but this 'I' is not exhaustive of the subject who is producing the language.* There is always a difference between the subject as expressed *in* a sentence and the subject who *produces* the sentence, the former being a temporary position adopted within the process of the latter.

This distinction, drawing as it does on the familiar linguistic difference between the subject who speaks (le sujet de l'énonciation) and the subject of what is said (le sujet de l'énoncé) is an elegant solution to the dichotomy posed at the outset. These two different subjects correspond to the active, heterogenous subject and the unified, thetic subject respectively, and together make up the process of self-production of subjectivity: – 'Productrice du sujet parlant, cette altération se réalise à condition de laisser hors d'elle, dans l'hétérogène, ce même sujet parlant' (p. 55).

And again, further on in her exposition, Kristeva writes that

> Le sujet *n'est jamais*, le sujet n'est que *le procès de la* signifiance et ne se présente que comme *pratique signifiante* c'est-à-dire lorsqu'il s'absente dans la position à partir de laquelle se déploie l'activité sociale-historique-signifiante.
>
> (p. 188)

If I write 'I sing the sofa', the 'I' of that sentence is not the same as the 'I' who produced the sentence even though it attempts to be so. It is logically impossible that the 'I' who sings the sofa may be coincident with and exhaustive of, the supposedly same 'I' that writes ' "I" sing the sofa'. It must be some other self who is grasping the self as an object to write about, and Kristeva endorses and extends this familiar philosophical paradox by theorizing the mode of production of the first 'I' (the subject of what is said) by the second 'I' (the subject who speaks). The history of subjectivity is never the history of a subject always present to himself, but on the contrary, history of a process of capture and escape, stability and dissolution, an heterogeneous subject which is perpetually displacing its own established positions. The subject which supports syntax and makes it possible is necessarily absent from it, but when it does re-emerge it tends to perturb thetic calm by redistributing the signifying order, by altering syntax and by disrupting nominal groups. This is not to say that the sentence structure is destroyed, but it is pushed into an infinite variety of new forms, forms which Mallarmé, Lautréamont and James Joyce were the first to produce and enjoy. These revolutionary textual forms effected a revolutionary conception of subjectivity which, according to Kristeva (p. 592) embodies a degree of freedom which will require 'at the best several centuries' to be fully realized in practical social terms: –

> Que dans l'art en général, et dans le texte plus particulièrement à partir de la fin du XIXe siècle, se constitue un langage qui parle ces lieux de rupture que la conscience de classe économiste refoule, lieux de rupture propres au désir des masses mais inexprimés et peut-être même inexprimables par elles dans la société capitaliste productiviste en état d'industrialisation, lieux de rupture donc retirés dans l'expérience des élites culturelles et, au sein de ces élites accessibles à de rares sujets chez qui ces ruptures courent le risque et l'avantage de se radicaliser jusqu'à la folie ou l'esthétisme et de perdre ainsi leurs attaches avec la chaîne sociale, – voilà ce que nous voudrions suggérer'.[25]

This claim evidently needs close scrutiny.

The relation of the semiotic to the symbolic is neither facile opposition nor simple dependence, and Kristeva never champions the one at the expense of the other. Though it is the energy, sound rhythm and movement of the semiotic which grounds the word-foundation of the symbolic, the latter is nevertheless the condition of heterogeneity which continues to assure the stable position of the subject and, in deploying his semiotic 'musicality', assures the continuance of the subject as a source of meanings (pp. 62–83). The thetic is the threshold between the semiotic and the symbolic, and the essential point of Kristeva's theoretical position in *La Révolution du Langage Poétique* resides in this: that the modes of infusion between semiotic and symbolic across the thetic give us the forms of subjectivity, and whatever modes these may be, they become particularized and harden out into specific patterns of individuality through the psychic processes discovered by Freud and reformulated by Lacan. The relation to one's mother and father in the realm of the imaginary, fetishism, anal obsession, identification with the law (hysteria p. 329) and rejection of all law (psychosis p. 329); these are all modes through which the thetic may be transgressed to give a distinctive and recognizable type of subjectivity. The mode of transgression, or what Kristeva calls 'forclusion' following Lacan's translation of *Verwerfung* (rejection), is what distinguishes Mallarmé from Lautréamont and determines a particular type of subjectivity. The manifold processes whereby the semiotic may break through the symbolic, or whereby the symbolic assumes control of the semiotic, is transfixed by the forms of movement and displacement which take place across them both.

The role of poetic modernism in this process of subjective creation is paramount, since it is the *practice* of those inner unconscious movements of which *psychoanalysis* is the theory: –

> Alors, dans cet ordre socio-symbolique ainsi saturé sinon déjà clos, la poésie – disons plus exactement le langage poétique – rappelle ce qui fut depuis toujours sa fonction: introduire, à travers le symbolique, ce qui le travaille, le traverse et le menace. Ce que la théorie de l'inconscient cherche, le langage poétique le pratique à l'interieur et *à l'encontre* de l'ordre social: moyen ultime de sa mutation ou de sa subversion, condition de sa survie et de sa révolution.
>
> (p. 79)

'Literature' in the writing of Lautréamont, Mallarmé, Artaud, Roussel and Joyce, has been the refusal to conceal or repress the *signifier*, the material operation of language itself, even though it is the signifier which founds culture and signification. The 'burst unity' (L'unité eclatée) of *Chants de Maldoror* and the *Poésies* of Lautréamont confront (or rather 'affront') the world of discourse in its constitutive laws, subverting its 'normal' and 'established' order, and by disrupting it, opening out a revolutionary possibility for subjectivity within the new significatory processes. Not surprisingly however, Kristeva remains uncertain about the exact nature of the relation between the disruption of normal fictional and poetic practice on the one hand and the political, revolutionary disruption of social relations on the other. In its strong form, Kristeva claims an *active*, determining correspondence between the two, the pleasure and violence which breaks the repressive laws of phallocentric logic at the level of the subject, actively promotes revolutionary social change by 'overthrowing' the ensemblist logic which underpinned the existing society:–

> . . . il y a des textes qui, en introduisant l'infinité du procès dans les éléments constitutifs du système linguistique et dans les énoncés finis du code social (c'est-à-dire dans les idéologèmes qui expriment les rapports de production et de réproduction socialement codés) opèrent aux limites où la logique ensembliste du système social est mise en péril . . . En ce sens, et tout en restant enfermés dans la maison étatique les 'poètes' pour être des 'souverains mineurs' ou des 'enfants de la maison' n'y ajoutent pas moins un rôle subversif radical qu'aucune autre pratique ne peut assumer.
>
> (p. 381)

At other points, Kristeva's description of the role supposedly played by poetry in the transformation of bourgeois ideology is cast differently. She even puts an opposite argument to the one just given and writes that, by an irony of assimilation with which we are all familiar, the avent-garde of the late nineteenth century served the needs of the dominant ideology by acting as a substitute for the repressed subjective praxis that the society itself denied:–

> En abdiquant ainsi le processus social en cours, et tout en exhibant un moment refoulé mais constituant pour autant qu'il exhibe le moment dissolvant toute unité constituée, le texte avant-gardiste du XIXe siècle sert l' idéologie dominante puisqu'il lui fournit de quoi substituer à ses manques, sans mettre directement en cause le système de sa reproduction dans la représentation (dans la signification)
>
> (p. 186)

In another formulation, Lautréamont played a role of passive witness ('témoin') to changes in the subject which 'correspond' (and it is the nature of this correspondence which is precisely in question here) to the social 'éclatement' of the 1871 revolution:–

> Ainsi, *sans dénier l'unité de la raison* (du symbolique et du sujet qu'il pose), mais en *l'excentrant*, en affirmant le sujet comme une contradiction, Lautréamont-Ducasse donne à ses textes une connotation héroique, révolutionnaire, qui témoigne pour le sujet de ce que vont essayer à l'échelle sociale les masses révoltées de Paris en 1871.
>
> (p. 481)

Of the many problems which Kristeva's work raises, the relation between the formal literary 'revolution' of Mallarmé and Lautréamont and social revolutionary practice seems to me by far the most questionable. For Kristeva, the two writers are fundamentally important because they mount attacks, from opposed but complementary directions, on phallocentric logic: Mallarmé, by identification with the mother (and through the form of his verse with the 'maternal', infinite genotext of the semiotic); Lautréamont, by his violent, implacable attack on the father figure, law, and all forms of phallocentric domination. Mallarmé subverts, ruptures and finally destroys the laws of syntax which are the guarantee of the laws of reason, the laws of the father and the laws of the state. Lautréamont, by permuting the shifters of the narrative in *Chants de Maldoror*, breaks up the unity of the subject found in traditional narrative forms with their sustained and clearly distinguished actants (the 'coherent' character of folk-take and realist novel). Thus Lautréamont too, disperses, from a complementary perspective, the unified, transcendent subject which had hitherto always underpinned phallocentric rationality.

However, the step which Kristeva makes from this achieved poetic destruction of masculine rationality to political practice and feminism, seems to me a deft sleight of pen, a merely sophistical linkage. The space between the formal textual innovations which she describes and the radical political practice (feminism) to which she subscribes, is never satisfactorily filled, since the destruction of syntactic order and prominal stability in a poetic discourse, even when it can be appropriated for political use is always and only, a negative politics, an evanescent disruption, incapable of identifying its own political agent (masculine or feminine).

In other words, the destruction of actantial position and pro-position in this poetic revolution can never have a positive vector, a political direction (direction is a function of stable identity), it always remains purified anarchism in a perpetual state of self-dispersal. And in this respect, it reveals its close material relation to the French left-academic context of its own production. Thus the form of *La Révolution du Langage Poétique*, a massive work within the philosophic tradition of the *doctorat d'état*, is evidently in contradiction with the content, a content manifestly hostile to the laws of the discourse in which the argument is caste. This argument is an appeal for an anarchist aesthetics, to displace the traditional sociology of literature across Lacanian psychoanalysis and recognizing in that process the formal novelties of the twentieth century avant-garde as a crucial shift in our understanding of subjectivity.

Upon this theoretical basis, the object of politics in general and feminism in particular, is to follow the lead of this artistic avant-garde and achieve politically the destruction of the old, traditionally unified subject.

Kristeva has recently stated this link between theory and feminist praxis very clearly in an interview which she gave to *L'Espresso*, the Italian communist journal, in April, 1977:–

> Io credo che il problema de movimento femminile è oggi quello di diventare una forma dell'anarchismo che ritraduce in comportamenti e azione il discorso dell'avanguardia storica: la distruzione del soggetto occidentale.
>
> (I believe that the problem of the feminist movement today is that of inventing a form of anarchism which will express in behaviour and in action the discourse of the historical avant-garde: the destruction of the (traditional) western subject).
>
> *L'Espresso*, April 1977, p. 63.

In this interview Céline and Pound are given as examples of what is here meant by the 'historical avant-garde', both, in their own way, having burst open the settled, unified subject underpinning 'masculine' bourgeois thought. Despite their ostensible fascism, Céline and Pound were, for Kristeva, substantially anti-fascist in their formal comprehension of its (psychological) origins ('I discorsi delle avanguardia artistiche sono stati i soli veri discorsi anti-fascisti con conoscenza (inconscia) di causa'). Feminism, according to Kristeva, thus has its political future mapped out along a route which leads back to *The Cantos*, a journey 'au bout de la nuit'. It is for feminists to discuss this project for themselves, and its anarchist grounding in the theoretical work outlined above. For myself, Kristeva's project is a brilliant essay in psycho-anarchic aesthetics, but which replaces a repressive, phallocentric logos by something far worse, a 'new' subject, drifting, dispersed, and as politically impotent as it is ever possible to be. An agent without agency, direction or cohesion, neither *an-sich* or *für sich*, even more vulnerable to the force of social history than Ezra Pound, tearful, in his ward at St. Elizabeth's asylum.

Notes

1 Cratylus 425a *The Dialogues of Plato*, trans. B. Jowett, edited by R.M. Hare and D.H. Russell (London, 1970) Vol. III, p. 176.
2 The '*Sophist*' trans. and introduction by A.E. Taylor, edited R. Klibansky and E. Anscombe (London, 1961) pp. 173–174.
3 'Letter VII', in *Plato, Collected Dialogues*, edited E. Hamilton and H. Cairns (Princeton, 1963) pp. 1589–1591.
4 Aphasia is the traditional testing ground for the study of the inter-relation of syntactic selection and mental malfunction. The most celebrated case was that of 'Schneider' analysed by Gelb and Goldstein in the 1920s later interpreted by Merleau-Ponty. See Gelb and Goldstein, *Psychologische Analysen hirnpathologischer Fälle* (Leipzig, Barth, 1920).
5 J. Kristeva, *La Révolution du Langage Poétique* (Paris, 1974) p. 13.
6 Kant, *Critique of Pure Reason*, trans. Norman Kemp Smith (London, 1929), reprinted 1973, pp. 156–157.
7 L. Wittgenstein, *Tractatus Logico-Philosophicus*, German text with a new edition of the translation by D.F. Pears and B.F. McGuiness (London, 1961) pp. 114–115, proposition 5.6 and 5.61:- 5.6 *The limits of my language* mean the limits of my world. 5.61 Logic pervades the world: the limits of the world are also its limits.
8 N. Chomsky, *Cartesian Linguistics* (New York, 1966).
9 E. Benveniste, 'La subjectivité dans le langage', in *Problèmes de linguistique générale* (Paris, 1966) p. 260.

10 Plato, *The Republic*, translated with an introduction by H.D.P. Lee (London, 1955) pp. 113–138 (literature) pp. 138–141 (music).
11 J. Kristeva, Σημειωτική Recherches pour une semanalyse (Paris, 1969) pp. 7–9.
12 See particularly George Steiner, *After Babel, Aspects of Language and Translation* (Oxford, 1975) p. 77.
13 Σημειωτική, pp. 35–37.
14 J. Derrida, *De la Grammatologie* (Paris, 1967) p. 424.
15 Σημειωτική p. 38.
16 M. Klein, in the French translation used by Kristeva, *La Psychanalyse des enfants* (Paris, 1969, Payot)
17 The Death Instinct was developed relatively late in the works of Freud and was first introduced in *Beyond the Pleasure Principle* in 1920. It has not managed to gain the acceptance of his disciples and successors in the way that his other theoretical concepts have. It unites the fundamental tendency of every living being to return to its inorganic state with the destructive tendency (as revealed for example in Sado-masochism) of the subject. It is this latter link of which Kristeva makes use in considering Lautreamont and Mallarmé.
18 Derrida's course of seminars at the Ecole Normale Superieure for 1975–76 were on the philosophy of life and death, 'La Vie la Mort'. In these seminars Derrida attacked, from a philosophical point of view, the biological writings on the subject, particularly the influential work of the Nobel prizewinner, Francois Jacob. But the linkage of thought on the subject of death between Derrida and Kristeva can best be seen in *L'Ecriture et la différance* (Paris, 1967) p. 301.
19 For the mirror phase, see 'Le stade du miroir' in Jacques Lacan, *Ecrits* (Paris, 1965, p. 95ff). This difficult essay by a notoriously obscure and complex writer can be usefully supplemented by the discussion of the mirror stage in Anthony Wilden's *The Language of the Self* (Baltimore, 1968) to which I am indebted in this section of my exposition. Se also *New Left Review* 51.
20 *Ecrits*, 'Subversion du subject et dialectique du désir', p. 822.
21 *Ecrits*, p. 95.
22 *The Language of Self*, Anthony Wilden (Baltimore, 1968) p. 160.
23 *La Révolution du Langage Poétique* pp. 45–46.
24 J. Lacan, trans. A. Wilden in *The Language of Self.*
25 J. Kristeva 'La Révolution du Langage Poétique' in *Tel Quel*, 56, p. 48.

Translations

p. 327 This polarity does not mean either equality or symmetry: the 'I' always has a position of transcendence with respect to the 'thou'.

p. 329 Money replaces things by their signs. Not only within a society but between one culture and another, or between one economic organization and another. That is why the alphabet is mercantile. It has to be understood in the monetary moment of economic rationality. The critical description of money is the faithful reflection of discourse on writing.

p. 330 This type of relations seems to us to be capable of specifying the *semiotic* as the psychosomatic modality of the process of 'significance', i.e. not symbolic but articulating (in the widest sense of the word articulation) a continuum . . . All these processes and relations, pre-sign and pre-syntax, have now been placed in a genetic perspective, as preliminary and necessary to language acquisition, from which they remain distinct.

p. 330 However, it is only through the logic of the dream that they (these processes and relations) have been able to attract attention, and it is only in certain signifying practices, such as that of the *text*, that they dominate the process of 'signifiance'.

p. 331 It can be seen that our positing of the semiotic is inseparable from a theory of the subject which takes account of Freud's positing of the unconscious. Decentring the transcendental ego, cutting it and opening it up to a dialectic in which its syntactic and categorical understanding is only the threshold moment, itself always enacted by the relation to the author that is dominated by the death instinct and its reiteration which produces 'signifier': that is how this subject appears to us in language.

p. 332 Modern philosophy concurs in recognizing that it is the transcendental ego that has the right to represent the *thesis* which sets up signification (sign and/or proposition). But it is only since Freud that the question can be posed not only as to the origin of this thesis, but as to the process of its production. If one simply stigmatizes the thetic as the basis of metaphysics, one is liable to be merely its antechamber unless one specifies the conditions for the production of this thesis. Freud's theory of the unconscious and its development by Lacan seem to us to be a revelation of the fact that thetic signification is a phase that is producible in certain definite conditions during the process of 'signifiance', that it constitutes the subject without being reducible to its process, because it is the threshold of language.

p. 333 The total form of the body through which the subject overtakes in a mirage the maturing of his potency is only given to him as a *Gestailt*, i.e. in an externality in which, to be sure, that form is more constituting than constituted but where, above all, it appears to him in a relief of stature which fixes it and in a symmetry which inverts it, as opposed to the turbulence of movement with which he feels himself animate it.

p. 334 The gap between the imaged ego and instinctual motility, between the mother and the demand addressed to her, is the very break which installs what Lacan calls the place of the Other as the place of the 'signifier'. The subject is masked by 'an ever purer signifier', but the lack of presence confers on *another* the role of holding the possibility of signification.

p. 335–6 Productive of the speaking subject, this making-other is accomplished on condition that it leaves outside itself, in the heterogeneous, that same speaking subject.

p. 336 The subject never *is*, the subject is only the *process of signifiance* and presents itself only as *signifying practice*, i.e. when it absents itself *in the position* from which social-historical-signifying activity unfolds.

p. 336 In art in general, and in the *text* more particularly from the end of the nineteenth century, there is constituted a language which speaks these sites of rupture which economistic class-consciousness represses, sites of rupture corresponding to the desire of the masses but unexpressed and perhaps inexpressible by them in productivist capitalist society in the state of industrialization, sites of rupture which are therefore withdrawn into the experience of the cultural elites and, within those elites, accessible to rare subjects in whom these breaks incur the risk and advantage of radicalizing themselves into madness or aestheticism and so of losing their ties with the social chain. That is what we wish to suggest.

p. 337 Then, in this socio-symbolic order thus saturated if not already closed, poetry – let us say more precisely, poetic language – recalls what always was its function: to introduce, across the symbolic, that which works on it, crosses it and threatens it. What the theory of the unconscious looks for, poetic language practices, within and against the social order: the ultimate means of its mutation or subversion, the condition for its survival and revolution.

p. 337 . . . there are texts which, in introducing the infinity of the process into the constitutive elements of the linguistic system and into the finite utterances of the social code (i.e. into the ideologemes which express the socially coded relations of production and reproduction) operate on the limits where the ensemblist logic of the social system is put in danger . . . In this sense, and while remaining locked in the house of the State, the poets, though 'minor sovereigns' or 'children of the house', nonetheless add to this a radical subversive role which no other practice can assume.

p. 338 In thus abdicating the current social process, and while exhibiting a moment that is repressed but constituent insofar as it exhibits the moment dissolving all constituted unity, the nineteenth-century avant-garde text serves the dominant ideology since it supplies it with the means of making up for its lacks, without directly challenging the system of its reproduction in representation (in signification).

p. 338 Thus, without denying the unity of reason (of the symbolic and of the subject which it posits), but ex-centring it, affirming the subject as a contradiction, Lautréamont Ducasse gives his texts a heroic, revolutionary connotation, which testifies, for the subject, to what the revolted masses of Paris will endeavour to do on the social scale in 1871.

16 Ideology and subjectivity

John Ellis

Introduction

One development of semiology no longer deals with systems of signs; it deals with the formation of the subject in language, with the internalisation of social contradictions and of their contradiction with the superstructure. It constructs a science of human nature, surpassing the traditional division of Marxism between humanism (those, with Markovic, who believe in a given human nature), and anti-humanism (those, with Althusser, who account for the individual as constructed by ideology and by social structures).

This work is being carried out in various ways by the *Tel Quel* group, Sollers, Kristeva, Barthes and others in Paris, the *Screen* group in England etc. It owes much to Lacan's seminal reading of Freud, which demonstrates the social construction of the individual subject through the crucial medium of language.

It is work that is surrounded by misunderstandings, which this article hopes to dispel. This will be done in three ways, in sections which can be read separately as they tackle the problem in distinct, complementary ways.

First, the misrepresentation and misunderstanding of the work is briefly examined for the ideas and assumptions it mobilises both on the Left and the Right. The way in which these coincide is fascinating; they reveal a common way of reading texts, and of thinking about the subjective, internal, psychological moment of the social process. (The three repetitive adjectives are necessary to show that this is no longer a question of 'subjectivism', 'behaviourism', 'personal politics' etc.; it is a matter of the overdue politicisation of psychoanalysis and equally the encounter of Marxism with the concerns of psychoanalysis.) The normal ways of thinking revealed in this section are ultimately deeply damaging for any Marxist political movement. This the following sections demonstrate.

The second section deals with certain crucial notions of the superstructure and its relation to the base. It takes into account the way in which ideology is concerned with the reproduction of the relations of production; the way in which ideology enters into contradiction with economic and political practices. It then examines the way in which subjectivity is constructed within this process; how external social contradictions articulate themselves internally; and what the effects of this process can be.

The third section takes this awareness and contrasts it to the idea of ideology used by Charles Woolfson in his article earlier in this Journal. It shows how the deficiencies in that theory produce an analysis of a conversation that merely echoes the failed politics of a dogmatic 'politically aware' worker. It argues that his reading of Voloshinov is a return to Russian Formalism; that the politics offered is disastrous; and sketches an alternative analysis and its politics.

Misrepresentation

There are five major themes in the offensive against these recent developments in semiology. The first is to dub it 'structuralism', and then to trot out the traditional criticism which claims that it is incapable of dealing with process, transformation or change (the diachronic). This still happens in the face of almost a decade's work from people like Barthes, Kristeva and Lacan whose project has been to dissolve the distinction synchrony/diachrony (e.g. Barthes's recently translated *S/Z*). But a recent *New Left Review* article still touts this argument:

> Polarisation of the distinction between synchrony and diachrony, and contempt or indifference towards diachronic studies, are essential characteristics of structuralism, which cannot be overcome by any eclectic blending of it.
>
> (S. Timpanaro, 'Considerations on Materialism', *NLR* 85, p. 22.)

Secondly, this system of thought is then seen as anti-humanist, probably because it is considered as dealing with structures at the expense of the human. It will be seen that, far from doing this, the exact value of this 'Marxism of the subject' is to interrogate what hitherto had remained hidden under the category of 'human nature' or had disappeared in accounts of the operation of social structures.

Thirdly, critiques are usually tinged with chauvinism. Woolfson's generalisation about the development of semiology displays it: 'The real danger exists of semiotics acquiring a premature formation in this country, for which the accelerating flow of continental, especially French, studies is largely responsible.'

So far, the examples have been taken from leftwing critiques, but the right mobilises the same themes, as this article in *The New Review* demonstrates:

> 'The most scandalous aspect of Structuralism as a movement,' (Jameson) tells us in *The Prison-House of Language* is its 'militant anti-humanism.' The verdict is reached after a scrupulous examination of the various arguments proposed not only by Barthes, but also by such structuralist figures as Derrida, Greimas, Julia Kristeva [sic] and Lacan, who often differ from him. It is a verdict I find it difficult to resist or refute . . I see the whole thing – though I may well be wrong or oversimplifying – as ultimately only explicable as the loss at the highest level of intelligence of French national *morale*. The French have lost three major wars in succession . . .
>
> (F.W. Bateson, 'Is your Structuralism Really Necessary', *The New Review*, May 1975.)

There is a common problematic here. The same basic way of thinking on the left and right orients very disparate critiques of a semiology that is based at once upon psychoanalysis and upon dialectical materialism. An article in *Encounter* from a literary-critical point of view shows the core of this problematic:

> Is there any substantial connection between Marxism or any other prospect of social change, on the one hand, and the doctrine that fiction can only give an account of itself or of the mind that reads it? . . . The notion that the literary text could ever be shown to have its own structure has now been totally abandoned. A 'text' presents the reader, not with a structure but with a 'structuration' – the process by which the reader persuades himself, no doubt mistakenly, that a structure exists . . . All this looks like a

> curious position for a radical . . . Whether conservative or not in purpose, it is surely conservative in effect.
>
> (George Watson, 'Old Furniture and "Nouvelle Critique" ', *Encounter*, February 1975.)

It is a matter of the old division between subjective and objective. It is not possible according to this thinking to treat both at once. The quotation assumes that the work cannot be Marxist because it deals with the subjective (many Marxists also hold this view, considering the subjective as a mere chimera, constituted entirely of the objective, and insubstantial in itself). It seems more palatable for the left to accept the idea that individuals are caught within structures and simply produced by them (crude Althusserianism), rather than the notion that a person and their unconscious is formed at every point by their history in society, and that this formation – particularly the unconscious – can operate according to its own logic and come into conflict with economic needs. In the West, this problem has been opened up by psychoanalysis in the form of Lacan's reading of Freud, a subject that interests many Marxists including Althusser. In the East, the Chinese have faced this problem during the struggle between two lines and the Cultural Revolution. These two developments are central for any understanding of ideology, its specificity and its power. Without an account of the subjective moment of the social process, Marxism is unable to account for Fascism or political apathy in terms which could prevent the same political mistakes from being repeated.

Unfortunately, there is much prejudice against this work. It has been encountered in the Centre in confused attempts to raise these questions, and this was undoubtedly one element in the process that lead to the rejection of a translation of a Kristeva article for this Journal. However, the major objection to this article revealed a genuine problem that is probably more serious than the other objections outlined here. The article was held to be 'incomprehensible'. This was partly the result of its frame of reference (a critique of phenomenological philosophy and linguistics) which was unfamiliar. For this reason it was probably wrong to propose it as part of an introduction. But some readers experienced a feeling of partial comprehension which complexified on subsequent readings. This is not a normal reading, a reading to consume ideas, but rather to produce them. It revealed the productivity of language, which is repressed in the normal Western style of reading. Our culture prefers a mode in which the reader is placed outside the discourse, picking up, judging, but remaining untouched. This other mode is a more difficult process of throwing into crisis the self as consumer, producing meaning precisely through the interrogation of concepts already known, rather than judging by a comparison of the new against established values. This work compares to that of the Chinese as described by M-A. Macciocchi:

> The language of Mao is not intended to be reducible to a linguistic structure. Its first object is to produce knowledge, imagination, creation . . . Mao is the inventor-creator of revolutionary language, which means that the words of the little red book always represent a concrete object, which then becomes imagination, praxis and finally, revolutionarisation of thought. With us, in the Cartesian mode of thought that is our normal mode – rigorous but preventing imagination – many of the words used by Mao have produced disastrous ambiguities. 'Bombard the headquarters' is a phrase that has been interpreted as an order to begin war, for the artillery to fire . . . The workers we met who were making machines from scrap metal were not Robinson Crusoes abandoned on a desert island. They are inventors, holders of a 'critical thought' which does not refuse,

but *throws into discussion* Western scientific and technical discoveries in order to produce new successes from them. It is the 'political reading of the little red book which has lead them to this inventiveness in their work. Not all of them invent anything important . . . But the mental processes that are born from a simple reading – which stimulates most of the collective to the maximum – becomes a form of creation in the technical production that is indispensible for the new China . . .'

(M-A. Macciocchi, *De la Chine*, Seuil, Paris, revised ed. 1974 pp. 166–8; trans. as: *Daily Life in Revolutionary China*, Monthly Review Press, New York, 1972, pp. 182–4.)

The problem for us is that this reading is anything but 'simple', it is strange, incomprehensible. But it is the only way in which dialectical materialism can solve the problem of the subjective moment in the social process.

The superstructure and the subjective moment

Mao has always been alert to the importance of superstructural forms; indeed, it is the actions that flow from this that define the acute divergences of the Chinese Communist Party from Moscow-oriented parties. However, given the very specific nature of Chinese society and its history, it is necessary to learn from their experience at a certain level of theory (that which sees the unity of theory and practice in the Cultural Revolution, but does not transpose the experience wholesale to a Western advanced capitalist context). The lessons are guides and pointers, needing to be completed by our own experience: in the science of human nature, it is that of Freud and Lacan in psychoanalysis.

The Cultural Revolution is a Revolution 'of men's minds'. It demonstrates the importance of ideology considered not just as a system of ideas, a 'behavioural ideology' or as a 'socialising force', but as the practice that constructs what is often taken as given, that is, human nature. Ideology is seen as a force which enters into the very constitution of the individual and is therefore the area in which changes of attitude are generated. The subjective moment is thus seen as vital for the political struggle. As Mao writes, summing up the various erroneous tendencies in political practice: 'the breach between the subjective and the objective, by the separation of knowledge from practice' ('On Practice', *Four Essays on Philosophy*, Peking, 1968, p. 19) and again: 'External causes are the condition of change and internal causes are the basis of change, and . . . external causes become operative through internal causes' ('On Contradiction' op. cit.p. 28).

These quotations realise the necessity for any successful political struggle to be fought not only on the terrain of contestation of control of social structures, but equally for the collective knowledge and criticism of personality. The importance of the subjective moment is stressed again in Mao's conception of the ideological struggle: 'Ideological struggle is not like other forms of struggle. The only method to be used in this struggle is that of painstaking reasoning and not crude coercion.' ('On the Correct Handling of Contradictions Among the People', op. cit.p. 116.) In Woolfson's tape of the busworkers, examined in the next section, we have an example of a militant who does not heed this advice.

What is at stake in the Maoist understanding of the superstructure? Three things: its sometimes determining role; the need for creative thinking within a party, a movement; a vigilance against a return of attitudes typical of capitalist societies.

The Cultural Revolution is the fruit of Mao's understanding of the role of the superstructure in the social totality. This understanding is vital for a Left movement taken by surprise by the events of 1968, a surprise which is often expressed but rarely learnt from.

> But it must also be admitted that in certain conditions, such aspects as the relations of production, theory and the superstructure in turn manifest themselves in the principle and decisive role . . . When the superstructure (politics, culture etc.) obstructs the development of the economic base, political and cultural changes become principle and decisive. Are we going against materialism when we say this? No. The reason is that while we recognise that in the general development of history the material determines the mental, and social being determines social consciousness, we also – and indeed must – recognise the reaction of mental on material things, of social consciousness on social being and of the superstructure on the economic base. This does not go against materialism; on the contrary, it avoids mechanical materialism and firmly upholds dialectical materialism.
>
> ('On Contradiction', op. cit., p. 58–9.)

The implications for Marxist political practice are clear. Contradictions are produced between the changing nature of the relations of production and language and thought, which often lag behind; these contradictions can become antagonistic, as with the events of May 1968. There is a space, therefore, and a necessity to activate these contradictions within superstructural formations. The need is for a genuine politicisation which acts as a genuine corrective to all forms of leadership. In China, this is achieved by the discussion and utilisation in everyday life of the famous 'little red book':

> The formula 'philosophy in the factory', the combination of these two apparently heterogenous terms, brings us to the heart of the problem: the primacy of the *political* over the *economic*, and a wider sense in relation to the social: it's the key concept in the elaboration of Marxist theory that accompanies the Cultural Revolution. The study of philosophy in the factory . . . is the first qualitative leap of the individual in the revolution of the superstructure. It is what annihilates the 'aristocracy' of philosophic speculation, turning it into a mass science; and above all, through making the masses enter into active political participation in this way, it is a process at the heart of the global task of the political construction of socialist society.
>
> (*De la Chine*, p. 110; trans. p. 136.)

Later in the same book, Macciocchi quotes Mao summing up this thinking of the superstructure, and showing exactly what is being challenged: the habitual attitudes, the self-orientation of ordinary people:

> 'It is thus,' says Mao, 'that the contradiction between the forces of production and the relations of production, and their contradiction with the superstructure will continue to exist in all human societies as long as there exists a mode of production. Inside a mode of production there are reproduced the relations of authority and subjection, of leadership and obedience within which the capitalist relations of production are reproduced.'
>
> (Ibid, p. 352; trans. p. 434.)

A superficial glance might see this as far from the work of Althusser and of people like

Kristeva and Sollers. Their references to the Chinese experience have even been argued as 'assertions, tacked on for rhetoric's sake'. However, this work is absolutely central if the Chinese experience is to be learnt from. For the implications of this attitude for analyses of social structures are very clear: any analysis that is 'characterised by the breach between the subjective and the objective' is inadequate to the political tasks it sets itself. It remains hardly more than a destructive exercise unless completed by an analysis of the mass psychology involved: the psychological processes by which individuals are subjected to the social structures, the drives whose repression these social structures accomplish only to have to deal with their – partial – return.

We see the beginning of the exploration of this process in Althusser's *Lenin and Philosophy*. At least until the late 1960s, he had been very aware of the importance of Mao's work, and in 'Ideology and Ideological State Apparatuses' he begins his notes for an investigation by developing Mao's emphasis on the crucial role of ideology in the *reproduction* of the relations of production: 'Once one takes the point of view of reproduction, many of the questions whose existence is indicated by the spatial metaphor (of base/superstructure), but to which it could not give a conceptual answer are immediately illuminated.' (*Lenin & Philosophy*, Monthly Review, NY, p. 136.)

The essay then goes to deal with the *external* aspects of this reproduction, without however dealing with the *internal* aspects. The question often asked of this essay is 'What is a Subject?'; what constitutes this point (carefully not called person, individual etc.) at which the active production on a day-to-day basis of the structure-in-dominance actually takes place? The answer is not given in this piece, but in a very divergent and in many ways inadequate essay 'Freud and Lacan', which he was 'correcting' whilst writing about ideology. The beginnings of an answer to the problem of the subject come at the end of the essay:

> Since Copernicus, we have known that the earth is not the 'centre' of the universe. Since Marx, we have known that the human subject, the economic, political or philosophic ego is not the 'centre' of history – and even, in opposition to the Philosophers of the Enlightenment and to Hegel, that history has no 'centre' except in ideological misrecognition. In turn, Freud has discovered for us that the real subject, the individual in his unique essence, has not the form of an ego, centred on the 'ego', on 'consciousness' or on 'existence' – whether this is the existence of the 'for-itself', of the body-proper or of 'behaviour' – that the human subject is de-centred, constituted by a structure which has no 'centre' either, except in the imaginary misrecognition in which it 'recognises' itself.
>
> It must be clear that this has opened up one of the ways which may perhaps lead us some day to a better understanding of this *structure of misrecognition*, which is of particular concern for all investigations into ideology.
>
> (ibid.)

In Althusser, the reconciliation of the discoveries of Marx and Freud does not take place: they are marked as parallel, both oriented around a 'decentredness'. His timidity perhaps comes from the outcast nature of psychoanalysis, that he describes at the beginning of the essay. The work which deals with the subject in ideology is to be found elsewhere, in the developments from formal semiology that have taken place since 1966 in Paris. The work has met with exactly the misrepresentation and/or rejection that Althusser describes. In order to explain it, I will use Kristeva's examination of the sensitive point in Marxist theory, the concept of practice.

Kristeva begins by pointing out that Mao's emphasis in his essay *On Practice* is that practice is personal and concerned with direct experience: 'Anyone who denies such (sensuous) perception, denies direct experience, or denies personal participation in the practice that changes reality, is not a materialist.' (Mao, 'Four Essays on Philosophy', p. 9.)

In this light, she then examines the process of generation of new concepts: 'a sudden change (leap) takes place in the brain in the process of cognition' (Mao p. 5). Commonsense describes this as 'It all fell into place', 'It suddenly dawned on me' etc. But a dialectical materialist understanding of the process has to begin from a different point. It is precisely the contradiction between the superstructure and the forces and relations of production that creates the conditions in which this can happen. But the presence of the objective conditions is no guarantee that anything will happen: an account of the subjective moment is needed. However, Marxism usually does not examine this moment, assuming a subject which is unified and outside the objective process:

> By repressing the moment of 'sensuous' and 'immediate activity', the 'practical concept' of Hegel, or *practice* in dialectical materialism, is condemned to a mechanical repetition without modification of the real mechanisms of the material and the signifying, of the objective and subjective. By fixing an opaque reality in an empty-atomic subjectivity, such a conception of practice blocks the very process of practice which aims to 'transform the subjective and objective world' (Mao, op. cit., p. 20). However, in rehabilitating this moment as 'sensuous human experience', dialectical materialism sets itself on the path of what could be called '*the practical analysis* of the impenetrable' and 'atomic' subject who is the bearer of the 'practical concept'.
>
> (Kristeva, *La Révolution du language poétique*, Seuil, 1974 p. 182–3.)

To think the objective without the subjective is to leave the subjective free to reproduce the same old orientations. But the concept of practice that Kristeva is explaining, a conception which pays attention to the 'leap of understanding', can only be grasped using the Freudian notion of the formation of the human subject through the dialectic of drives ('Triebe' more often, and incorrectly, translated as 'instincts') and social constraints. This is not to posit a pre-given 'instinctual' being, since, according to Freud, everything instinctual occurs across social formations. It is a conception, then, which posits a human subject formed by what is refused entry into consciousness; that is, through the formation of the unconscious. A brief exposition of this theory of the construction of the subject will now follow, which can do no more than situate certain features of it.

The human child is not born with a pre-determined sexual identity, according to Freud. 'He found that "normal" sexuality itself assumed its form only as it travelled over a long and tortuous path, maybe eventually, and then only precariously, establishing itself.' (Juliet Mitchell, *Psychoanalysis and Feminism*, Pelican, 1975.)

The child is composed of many diverse drives which could join each other, 'never reach their goal, find another goal, dry up, overflow and so get attached to something quite different' (ibid). This alteration of drives to form the normal 'sexed' infant takes place, according to Lacan, through the dialectic of need, demand and desire. The subject has to find the constituting structure of his desire in the structure of signifiers (language), which are already established in the other person to whom the infant's demand is addressed. In other words *desire* is formed through the subject's relation to language.

> In that language and the symbolic order pre-exist the individual's entry into them, the signifier (language) gives its ratio to the development of demand; and, as demand is always formulated to an Other (that is something or someone in a position of alteriority), and as this Other is represented for the infant by the mother or father who are already constituted as 'sexed' human individuals, then the child must submit to the effects of the signifier. Thus the submission of the subject to the signifier in order to master his dependency in needs through the acquisition of a separate signifying place in language, means submission to the cultural order by which human sexuality is regulated.
>
> (R. Coward.)

Both Lacan and Kristeva take account of the development of modern linguistics, particularly from Saussure, which establishes language as a series of difference. They posit the 'endless tautology' of language, with meaning only established retrospectively: that is, deep structures such as the logical, semantic or intercommunicational are articulated only insofar as language is used by a subject who intends meaning. Meaning occurs only through the function of a subject, not through the fixed position of a sign.

This formulation is not to be interpreted as some form of idealist subjectivism: it proposes *the necessary positionality of the subject to enable communication.* This is close to some of Voloshinov's formulations (see following section). The mechanism by which this positionality occurs is through the refusal of entry into signifying positions of certain signifiers. This is one of the fundamental mechanisms of the unconscious as identified by Freud: metaphor: 'Metaphor must be defined as the implantation into a chain of signifiers of another signifier, by dint of which the one it replaces falls to the rank of the signified.' (Laplanche & Leclaire, 'The Unconscious', *Yale French Studies*, 1965.)

Lacan recognised that this notion of the 'metaphoric' construction of meaning in language is exactly the same model as that of repression.

> We have reason to assume that there is a primary repression, a first phase of repression, which consists in the ideational representatives of the instinct being denied entry into consciousness. With this a fixation is established; the representative in question persists unaltered from then onwards and the instinct remains attached to it.
>
> (S. Freud, 'Repression', *Standard Edition*, XIV.)

Primal repression for Freud exists at the level of the constitution of the unconscious. By this, certain signifiers are barred entry into consciousness and the subject has to recognise himself in the organising structures of the signifier. The unconscious is seen to be constructed in the same process as that by which the individual acquires language: it results from the capture in the web of signifiers of the structuring of need, demand and desire. In Lacanian theory (too complex to be done justice in this space: see the introduction by Lemaire), certain key signifiers organise the structure of the unconscious. These are for example what Lacan calls 'the name of the father' (that is the organisation of desire according to patriarchal social formations in which the phallus is a central term). These signifiers ensure the positions for the reproduction of the species through the establishment of sexual difference. It is not only in these moments that consciousness is constructed out of unconscious formations; the logical structures of language and thought arrange themselves through the same process as the construction of the unconscious. Thus, consciousness itself is affected by the movement in which signifiers are altered, disturbed or put into crisis by the contradictions between the superstructure and the relations and/or forces of production, when they become antagonistic. This experience is one of consciousness encountering an external process which it has not yet organised into language, has not yet symbolised.

> Faced with the laws of a developing historical process, for example with the structure of capitalist society, the rejected drive either invests and recognises itself within these laws, making symbolic theses from them and blocking itself; or, by a violence that no theses can hold back, it rejects all stoppages and produces a symbolisation of the objective process of transformation, according to the constraints which impose themselves on the movement of the drive: it then produces a revolutionary 'discourse', which only testing (c.f. Mao's practice-truth-practice) puts into correspondence with objective movements and necessity.
>
> (Kristeva, op. cit., p. 181.)

It is necessary to explain certain terms: the process of 'making symbolic theses' from a historical process means constructing a conscious understanding in the terms given by the process itself (i.e. in conformity to its ideological practice); this is opposed to an energy which has been constructed in such a way that it can no longer be organised by the web of symbolic theses, an energy which goes on to produce new concepts, whose validity is then shown in practice.

In explaining the way in which this production of new ideas takes place, Kristeva uses the term 'rejection' (*le rejet*) which indicates the drive which meets the external organisation of language, and has to structure itself accordingly, or restructure that external system. The result is an internal disorganisation in which the subject is thrown into process, into questioning and crisis. This state of the subject-in-process comes about because of the impact of social contradictions. The subject, hitherto able to think himself unified, feels disoriented:

> The moment of practice dissolves the compactness and the self-presence of the subject. First, the moment of practice puts the subject in relation to, and so in a position of negation of, objects and other subjects in his social milieu, and he enters into antagonistic or non-antagonistic contradiction with them. Although it is situated outside the subject, the contradiction within social relations ex-centres the subject himself, suspends it and articulates it as a passing-through place, a non-place where opposing tendencies struggle, *drives* whose stases and thetic moments (the *representamen*) are caught as much in the affective relation (parental or loving) as class conflict.
>
> (ibid.)

This describes the way in which social contradictions articulate themselves within the composition of the person, by an investment of drives; but these drives are themselves formed by both social and personal history; and this investment throws into flux – 'atomises' – the composition of the conscious and unconscious. The passage continues:

> Ex- centring the subject, the rejection brings about a confrontation between the atomisation of the subject and the structures of the natural world and of social relations, runs up against them, repulses them and is displaced. At the moment of this rejection, which implies the period of the annihilation of an old objectivity, a linkage component which is symbolic, ideological and therefore positive intervenes in order to constitute in language the new object which the 'subject' in process, whilst rejecting, produces across the moment of rejection. So practice contains, as its fundamental moment, the

> heterogenous contradiction which places a subject thrown into process by a natural or social exterior that is not yet symbolised, in struggle with old theses (that is, with systems of representation which differ from the rejection and blunt its violence).

This describes the way in which the conflict is resolved: the signifying practices intervene to constitute a new understanding. Kristeva expands this in continuing:

> It is *practice* that includes the heterogenous contradiction as motor of infinite dialectical movement in both material and signifying forms. It is in practice that the *process* of signification is realised, since practice is determined by this moment in which the unity of consciousness is atomised by a non-symbolised exteriority, beginning from objective contradictions out of which the rejected drives will create the new object with its determinations objectively existing in the material world outside. The moment of practice is not only an 'appearance' in the presence of consciousness, of the laws of the 'Being' (Hegel). I must insist that there is a logical moment that is *preliminary* to this return of the knowing consciousness, and this is precisely the second term of the movement of practice. I must insist, therefore, on this repressed element in practice, in which, during the passage of the rejection which is always already signifiable but perpetually undermined by what remains outside symbolisation, there takes place the struggle with the properly subjective thesis, with the Unity of consciousness, as much as with every pre-existing systematisation, be it natural, social, scientific or political. The new object is one moment in the process whose struggle is the long process of breaking and renewing. Consciousness has a tendency to repress the stage of this struggle in the heterogenous, which exports the subject into an 'exteriority' that it rejects so as to rethink it in a new way. But this is a struggle which produces what consciousness will think as a *moment* of the 'appearance' of this 'newness'. *Where this struggle takes place*, this 'appearance' *does not exist*, its 'moment' is a 'fiction', for there all sense is ephemeral under the push of the rejection, which for the subject is nothing other than, as Freud indicates, the push of the death or erotic drives.
>
> (op. cit. pp. 179–80.)

It is vital for Marxism to take into account this process of the unconscious whose effects are heard and felt in the conscious. If not, the psychology at work in propaganda and political action remains mechanistic, a simplistic causality. It ignores the process by which social contradictions articulate themselves subjectively, the way in which they can produce a reactionary stance; in short, the contradiction between ideological practice and economic and political practices. In Charles Woolfson's article we have a double example of this: he constructs a theory in which ideology is seen to follow the economic like one sheep after another; he transcribes a tape in which the political consequences of such thinking are clearly demonstrated.

Woolfson formalism and the productivity of language

Charles Woolfson has performed a great service by focussing attention on Voloshinov's work; but he has done it a greater disservice by travestying it. In short, *Marxism and the Philosophy of Language* is a complex book, constituted around a questioning of what was repressed in the project of the Russian Formalists: history and the theory of the speaking subject. Woolfson takes Voloshinov's prevarications and makes them definitive statements. Voloshinov becomes a relatively unsophisticated formalist.

Voloshinov, along with M.M. Bakhtin and P. N. Medvedev, was a member of the 'Bakhtin group', constituted in the late twenties to produce an 'immanent critique' of Formalism. Kristeva reviews Bakhtin's work on literature in an important article in *20th Century Studies*, where she shows that part of the breaking with Formalism was constituted around an enquiry into history, the history of meaning-systems, *genres of discourse.* It is symptomatic that Woolfson's analysis takes no account of the particular form of conversation (as opposed to debate etc.) which 'frames' the interchange he deals with. However, this is the least of the matter. The real point of difference is that his whole reading of Voloshinov excludes the book's fruitful concern with the subjective and ideology, which is expressed in such prevarications as this:

> *Anti-psychologism is correct in refusing to derive ideology from the psyche.* But even more than that is needed: the psyche must be derived from ideology. Psychology must be grounded in ideological science. Speech had first to come into being and develop in the process of the social intercourse of organisms so that afterward it could enter within the organism and become inner speech.
>
> *Psychologism is also correct, however. There is no outer sign without an inner sign.* An outer sign incapable of entering the context of inner signs, i.e. incapable of being understood and experienced, ceases to be a sign and reverts to the status of a physical object.
>
> (Voloshinov, op. cit., p. 39.)

Here, ideology is being treated as a material force in the constitution of the social subject in the first section; yet in the second section, there are distinct indications that this subject could be considered as relatively autonomous (with its own laws and history), and is also in some sense constitutive of the social reality that constructs it. There is, in other words, a sense in which Voloshinov's text tends to treat the subjective moment as by no means entirely subservient to, dominated by, objective forces. But it was not possible for him to go further. Already at odds with Soviet orthodoxy, he also did not have the necessary linguistic understanding of Freud (given by Lacan) in order to read him other than as a biological determinist. As Kristeva puts it:

> The Formalists did not question the assumption that the work must be a system of signs, an objectal surface on which pre-existing elements are combined, a structure in which the transcendental sense is mirrored and maintained by the transcendental consciousness of the ever-present language-users. These were the necessary postulates of a reasoning entrapped in representation. Could anyone go beyond such postulates at a time when the Freudian breakthrough was not an accepted part of language theory, and when linguistics in the process of becoming structural, could not forsee transformational methods? The facts of history show that no-one could.
>
> ('The Ruin of a Poetics', *20th Century Studies*, no.7–8, p. 105.)

The work of the Bakhtin group was precisely in these areas. By studying the history of meaning-systems, they began to break open the transcendental sense. By the attention to the subjective that characterises Voloshinov's book, they began to look at the form of the transcendental subject. But Woolfson's reading ignores this preliminary work, the elements of the critique of Formalism, and merely returns it to the Formalist mould. A set of pre-existing elements are operated by subjects considered as 'outside' (transcending) the system. Voloshinov's attention to the personal and subjective becomes just an emphasis on real physical situations. An extensive analysis of these would just lead to a proliferation of formal models: proxemics etc.

Woolfson's return to the Formalist interests are most clear in his actual analyses: here we have individuals manoeuvering blocks of meaning; both individuals and meanings are fully constituted outside the area of language being analysed. This produces an overall distortion, whose form I shall describe briefly.

In his analysis of U60–84 of the busworkers tape, Woolfson states:

> What W6 does is to take the notion of the parasite and locate it in concrete working-class themes, relating it to the workers' immediate situation as transport employees . . . W6 thereby makes problematic the whole basis of authority and in U80 directly raises the counter-theme of working-class control.

The difference lies in the statement 'makes problematic the whole basis of authority'. W6 is at the weakest making problematic the fact that a particular person should have that position of authority; and at the strongest throwing into question the assumption that the bourgeoisie is 'naturally' fitted to positions of power etc. What he does *not* do is to make the idea of authority itself problematic: he only questions its specific implementations. For the basis of authority is that people can and habitually do act against their material interests *even when they have been made fully aware of them.* This, as Wilhelm Reich points out, was the fundamental mistake of the Left in Germany faced with the rise of Fascism:

> The vulgar Marxist who thinks in mechanistic terms assumes that discernment of the social situation would have to be especially keen when sexual distress is added to economic distress. If this were true, the majority of adolescents and the majority of women would have to be far more rebellious than the majority of men. Reality reveals an entirely different picture, and the economist is at a complete loss to know how to deal with it. He will find it incomprehensible that the reactionary woman is not even interested in hearing his economic programme. The explanation is: The suppression of one's primitive needs compasses a different result than the suppression of one's sexual needs. The former incites to rebellion, whereas the latter – inasmuch as it causes sexual needs to be repressed and anchors itself as a moral defence – prevents rebellion against *both* forms of suppression. Indeed, the inhibition of rebellion itself is unconscious. In the consciousness of the average nonpolitical man there is not even a trace of it.
>
> (W. Reich, *The Mass Psychology of Fascism*, Pelican, 1975, p. 65.)

Though Reich's eventual solution of this problem reflects the mechanistic way in which he poses it, he points well to the fundamental lack in mainstream Marxist politics. Woolfson's tape pinpoints exactly a specific moment in the general process Reich describes. The careful transcript chronicles the failure of a (doubtless well-meaning) Leftist to politicise a group of people into whose conversation he enters. It shows exactly the practical effects of what I have already discussed in theoretical terms: the lack of psychology in politics. Woolfson's analysis is intended to illuminate the neglected problems of the politics of conversation, and his contribution is valuable enough for this alone. But he merely echoes the failed politics of the leftist W6 precisely because he stays locked into the same problematic.

Far from challenging 'the whole basis of authority', W6 rests his whole intervention on himself as authoritative, on conceiving discussion as a matter of winning or losing (an attitude that seems to affect the rhetoric of the analysis at points). Woolfson carefully chronicles the eventual submission of the busworkers to this discourse of authority: 'From this point on, W2 falls completely silent . . . . . . at which point W5 opts out of the confrontation developing a sub-conversation of his own.'

But this discourse is not set up without a challenge. It comes from W5. W6 tries to set up his authority in U62 by introducing the privileged information from the *London Gazette.* W5 twice demands to know (U65 and U67) what the advert is in for, challenging this information and forcing W6 to justify and account for it (U68–76) before he can continue with the point he wants to make. W5 stands out as having a confused grasp of the doubtfulness of W6's methods. Looking over W5's speech as a whole, it becomes clear that his whole orientation is anti-authoritarian in a confused and by no means conscious way. This appears dramatically in his verbal slip in U15 which, though carefully recorded, remains unanalysed: 'workers are their own worst enemies – they expect the union – the eh I beg your pardon – the gaffers you know the employers – to be fair and just . . .'

It's clear that at some level the terms 'union' and 'gaffers' are more interchangeable than he is prepared to admit. He has a profound unease about ideas of authority, which expresses itself consciously in an annoyance with W6, a 'gut' opposition to the display of superiority. This unease (another explanation might call it 'situated consciousness') demands to be politicised. Similarly, his discourse expresses the multi-accentuality of the sign, the *production* of meaning. Look at his conversation with W2 and W4. He produces two themes concurrently: the themes of workers' solidarity against victimisation, and those of each person contributing to a communal effort and not riding on the backs of fellow workers. He is arguing something about the limits and, simultaneously, about the necessity of solidarity. He is working through his own preoccupations and those of the workers he's talking to. In other words, the multi-accentuality of the sign, the actual struggle between ideas and definitions, is expressed more in W5's discourse. Contrary to Woolfson's overhasty qualification of 'hegemonic', many concerns *at different levels* are being expressed, articulated over-and-between each other: solidarity, collective responsibility, attitudes to authority. This is not to put a positive value judgement on W5 as 'confusedly political' or condemn W6 as 'authoritarian' in any simplistic way. It is to propose a different political attitude based on the progressive movements of Voloshinov's critique of Formalism. It shows the points at which W5's conscious confusion (and bloody-mindedness) are the expression of a multitude of contradictions which demand to be politicised. This can be achieved by generalising the themes he situates himself with(in); by producing an awareness of contradiction to enrich his critical thinking. It shows that it is he who holds the idea of authority as problematic, that he has a deep unease in the region where W6 finds a firm basis for his political style (and his positions?) – an aggressively authoritarian stance.

This reading is thus diametrically opposed to Woolfson's. It does not pay attention to the 'manifest content' so much as to its production, the way in which it comes out, the way in which the speakers are orienting themselves. It is an analysis based not on classification but on listening symptomatically, for what is being said underneath what is said. It therefore sees language as an area of *production*, as Kristeva describes:

> While for linguistics, language is a system of signs, for literary science – and for every science of the development of ideologies – language is a practice in which one must take into account the people involved (especially the person addressed), and the way they reorder the sign system. From this comes a second problem: to find a theoretical approach which can eschew both the Form/Content dichotomy and also that of language/ideology, so as to clear the ground for the re-establishment of the word operating

> as a sign in the *language*, and of the ideological function of the specific historical practice which is worked out in that language.
>
> ('The Ruin of a Poetics'.)

Kristeva's careful formulation ('the ideological function of the specific historical practice is worked out in that language') avoids the *confusion* of language with ideology which permeates Woolfson's analysis. It is a matter of the difference between two lines (the echo of China is not unintentional), which needs to be made clear.

Woolfson's use of Vygotsky at the beginning of the article shows that he has nothing to say about the unconscious, about the simultaneous acquisition of language and culture by a child, about the role of ideology in the very constitution of the human individual: 'About the age of two, the curves of thought and speech begin to interpenetrate . . . It is at this crucial stage that the nature of the child's development itself changes from the biological to the sociohistorical.'

To abandon a child's first two years to biology is a crucial underestimation of the dialectical materialist method. The first two years (and the rest) of a child's life are shaped precisely by the complex dialectic between its biological drives and its sociality. It is only this crucial realisation (first expressed by Freud) that makes possible a real understanding of the articulation of the economic, political and ideological practices within a society *and within its individuals*. For Woolfson the question of the constitution of the subject has its solution in the pragmatic statement that: humans are biology which constructs itself through society into a rational form; this rational form is simultaneously alienated by power structures, the dominant relations of that society. The tasks of Marxism are then to convince the working class of their alienation in social structures (the project of Woolfson's piece); to abolish these structures; then to work towards the eventual aim of unalienated man, free to do all things (the millenarian dream of *The German Ideology*). For a Marxist paying attention to the psychological, the constitution of the subect is a vital question. Human beings are composed of shapeless drives which are constructed into sociality by a *necessary* (i.e. it is the prerequisite of social organisation) *repression* (i.e. a shaping whose effect is one of blocking-and-return-elsewhere rather than a mere channelling, as Reich might put it). This means that social structures, particularly as expressed in the family, enter into the very dynamic of the construction of the individual. The individual is not seen as unified, an expression of essence, but as crossed by contradictions (as in Althusser's more mechanistic formulation) and *producing* contradictions. The tasks of Marxism are then to unite the subjective and objective factors to change the material conditions of existence; and afterwards by a continuous criticism to transform self and society in the same movement. Philippe Sollers has summed up the divergences between these two politics:

> Whilst idealism, as Lenin saw, 'develops' the subjective and works on it to the point of drowning in it . . . materialism completely ignores internal causality. Here we see the intersection of a double misrecognition of the dialectical process, whose result is the same refusal of the verifiable workings of psychoanalysis and the politics of passivity. That thinking of the subject that either sees it as diffracted everywhere or denies it does not permit any link between external causality and internal causality, any marking of the aspect of constant transformation, of plurality of contradiction (antagonistic and non-antagonistic contradictions, principle and secondary aspects of contradictions etc.). This situation enables the perpetuation of that greatest of false debates between humanism and anti-humanism, which is completely surpassed by both the Freudian

> perspective and the historical conjuncture; it also provokes the perpetuation of a break between the politics of the subject (to be posed *in* language) and that of the masses.
>
> ('A Propos de la dialectique' in *Psychanalyse et Politique*, Seuil, 1974 p. 28.)

'Cultural studies' should occur at precisely the site of this break between the individual and the masses; its task is to elaborate a theory which overcomes this gaping chasm in our understanding. Failure to do this will leave the Left powerless against Fascism, mouthing some variant of the conspiracy theory of history or the coercive theory of ideology. Our choice is clear: either to be correct dogmatically, or correct historically. We cannot do both.

17 Women 'inside and outside' the relations of production

Lucy Bland, Charlotte Brunsdon, Dorothy Hobson, Janice Winship

Introduction

We have attempted here to work on the articulation of sex/gender and class in an understanding of women's subordination. We have tried to hold on to 'the twofold character' of 'the materialist conception' of the 'production and reproduction of immediate life' which is posed, though inadequately developed, by Engels in his preface to the first edition, 1884, of *The Origin of the Family, Private Property and the State.*

What we have learnt through feminism – particularly in relation to women's position within the patriarchal relations of the family,[1] their 'economic' position as wives and mothers, and ideological position within femininity – sits uneasily with what we know of the capitalist accumulation process. For an adequate analysis we have to work simultaneously with class and patriarchal relations. We have to interrogate the concepts of capital from a knowledge and recognition of women's subordination.

Women's relation to capital is most obvious in their role as wage labourers. However, the specificity of their position economically and ideologically within social production is predicated on women's role as reproducers of labourers, in the family. At the same time, it is this role in the family which limits the extent to which we can *understand* women's subordination *only* through the economic relations of capital. We are, therefore, directed 'outside' the relations of capital to the patriarchal relations between women and men which capital 'takes over', and to the particular ideological constitution of femininity that those relations construct.

We work briefly in three main areas:

1 Women's work in the home.
2 The state's contribution to women's subordination.
3 Women's waged work.

We conclude with a piece on the equal pay and sex discrimination legislation, which seems to us to represent a condensation of the contradictions of women's continuing subordination, and which appears to operate through these contradictions.

Women working in the home

> So Oliver assures Chloe, when she complains about the burden of the children. And who pays, he asks? Not you, but me. Yes, thinks Chloe, in her heart, but your money is easily earned. I pay with my time and energy, my life itself.
>
> Fay Weldon, *Female Friends*

> I have been married for two years this December. My wife is now 19, and I am 20. My problem is that she never does the housework willingly. I have always got to ask her or to tell her to do it, and then she does it with resentment. I have tried many ways to get her to do it, and she still doesn't. I work nights – four out of seven – and my wife works a five-day week, and I always seem to land up doing the housework after a hard night's work.
>
> I don't really mind helping, but she never appreciates it, and never understands how I feel. Our marriage is perfect, apart from this one thing, which we are always quarrelling about.
>
> Letter in the *Sun*, 14 November 1977

Feminists have consistently located the site of what Sheila Rowbotham (1973) calls woman's 'intimate oppression' as her role within the family. As Juliet Mitchell puts it:

> Quite simply, how do we analyse the position of women? What is the woman's concrete situation in contemporary capitalist society? What is the universal or general area which defines her oppression? The family and the psychology of femininity are clearly crucial here. However inegalitarian her situation at work (and it is invariably so) it is within the development of her feminine psyche and ideological and socio-economic role as mother and housekeeper that woman finds the oppression that is hers alone. As this defines her, so any movement for her liberation must analyse and change this position.
>
> (1971, p. 14)

She argues that the key structures of women's situation (which combine to form the complex unity which determines her position within society) are production, reproduction (of children), sexuality and the socialization of children (Mitchell 1971, p. 101). We go on to examine women's production outside the home later in this article,[2] but are first concerned with Mitchell's other three structures, which in our society intermesh in the family, and woman's 'ideological and socio-economic role as mother and housekeeper'.

The early writings of the current (post-1969) women's movement[3] in this area, following the pioneering work of Friedan (1963) and Gavron (1966), had first concentrated on the articulation of the *experience* of housework.[4] The concern was primarily to bring to *visibility* woman's work in the home, and to have it recognized as work, unpaid though it might be, and to challenge the received idea that it was performed easily out of our instinctual desires to nest-make and nurture.

> Isolated, the only adult in a private house, the housewife is yet crowded, by emotional and physical demands of her family, by the unseen pressures of society. But although isolated the housewife is never alone – her domain is the kitchen, the most communal room, and even the possibility of sleeping alone is denied her.
>
> Williams, Twort and Bachelli (1970)[5]

These writings formed the basis for the beginnings of an analysis of women's role in the family from a feminist perspective. Very crudely, these analyses can be differentiated as radical or socialist feminist, depending on the relative determinacy accorded to gender or class.[6] We intend to concentrate on the latter.[7]

Margaret Benston (1969) set out to establish that women as a group have:

> a unique relation to the means of production. . . . The personal and psychological factors then follow from this special relation to production, and a change in the latter will be a necessary (but not sufficient) condition for changing the former. If this special relation of women to production is accepted, *the analysis of the situation of women fits naturally into a class analysis of society*.
>
> [our italics]

While endorsing the necessity of analysing the relationship between women's subordination and the mode of production, we would now argue that to suggest that 'an analysis of the situation of women fits *naturally* into a class analysis' can have a tendency to neglect specific (historically capitalistic, but not *necessarily* capitalistic) determinations of women's situation.

The shift from writing about *being* a housewife/mother developed into an increasing concern with the precise articulation of housework and the capitalist mode of production. As Gardiner, who has been consistently involved in what has become known as the 'domestic labour debate', writes (1975, p. 109):

> The focus of the debate has shifted towards an emphasis on the role of female labour in the family in maintaining and reproducing labour power, since this provides a theoretical link between the family and the capitalist mode of production in which labour power is bought and sold.

This shift in emphasis at a theoretical level was sharpened, within the Women's Movement, by the different political demands that accompanied different analyses. The publication, in October 1972, of *The Power of Women and the Subversion of the Community* by Dalla Costa and James was the first extended argument for the political organization of women in the community, an analysis which later formed the basis for the demand of wages for housework.

There is also the question of the extent to which this shift in emphasis was influenced by the intellectual and political traditions of the British (and American) left. Firstly, in terms of political resistance to the questions raised by Women's Liberation:

> I was just finishing this when my husband came in and asked what I was doing. Writing a paper on housework. Housework? He said. Housework? Oh my God how trivial can you get. A paper on housework.
>
> Mainardi (1970)

Secondly, and this point is rather assertive in a paper of this length, through the economistic tendencies in marxist and socialist analyses which shaped both women's and men's criteria for 'a materialist analysis of women's oppression'.[8] In this case we would argue that this tendency was manifested in a refusal to recognize women's oppression unless it could be grounded in their *exploitation* by capital.[9] These factors, we would argue, must be considered as having some determining effect on the particular form and terrain of what developed into the 'domestic labour debate'. Thus Jean Gardiner's statement (1976, p. 109): 'domestic labour did not even exist as a theoretical category before the current feminist movement made it into an area of theoretical and political debate. . . .' can usefully be considered in conjunction with Maureen Mackintosh's retrospective criticism of the limitations of the debate:

> . . . the women's movement has generated a great deal of debate upon the same theme; the necessity of the family to the reproduction of the capitalist mode of production.

> This debate has made clear to many women – the consciousness has yet to filter down to much of the male left – the inadequacy of an analysis of the family which centres attention on the necessity of housework for capitalism while failing to give an adequate characterisation of the social relations generated by the reproductive role of women.
>
> Mackintosh (1977, p. 119)

Mackintosh here points to the necessity of an analysis of women's work in the home which addresses levels other than that of the *economic* necessity of housework for capitalism. The implications of this passage are not fully examined in this article, but are considered, in differing ways, in other articles in this journal. Here we look briefly at some of the arguments of the 'domestic labour debate'.

One way of approaching the theoretical background to the debate is to see it as an attempt by socialist feminists[10] to 'open up' the question of the maintenance and reproduction of the labour force, which is one element in the reproduction of the forces of production, necessary to the reproduction of any mode of production.[11] Marx: 'The maintenance and reproduction of the working class remains a necessary condition for the reproduction of capital. But the capitalist may safely leave this to the worker's drives for self-preservation and propagation' Marx (1976, p. 718).

The Political Economy of Women Group (PEWG): 'In focusing on domestic labour we are reflecting the view, common to almost all writing on this subject, that women's role in the home is crucial to her subordination under capitalism' PEWG (1975, p. 3).

The maintenance and reproduction of the working class is a condition of the reproduction of capital because of the particular nature of labour, sold as a commodity, labour power, under capitalism: although it can be bought and sold, it cannot be separated from the individual whose ability it is:

> . . . labour power can appear on the market as a commodity only if, and in so far as, its possessor, the individual whose labour power it is, offers it for sale or sells it as a commodity . . . the proprietor of labour-power must always sell it for a limited period only, for if he were to sell it in a lump, once and for all, he would be selling himself, converting himself from a free man into a slave . . . In this way he manages both to alienate his labour-power, and to avoid renouncing his rights of ownership over it.
>
> Marx (1976, p. 271)

Thus, while Marx is concerned at a theoretical level with the commodity labour power, the condition of the appearance of this is the day-to-day and generational reproduction of human beings, as Marx makes clear:

> . . . in the course of this activity, i.e. labour, a definite quantity of human muscle, nerve, brain, etc. is expended, and these things have to be replaced. . . . The owner of labour-power is mortal. If then his appearance in the market is to be continuous, and the continuous transformation of money into capital assumes this, the seller of labour-power must perpetuate himself 'in the way that every living individual perpetuates himself' [sic], by procreation.
>
> Marx (1976, pp. 274–5)

The reproduction and maintenance of the human beings who are the bearers of labour power has been historically accomplished in 'the family', organized through the sexual division of labour, which, under capitalism, takes 'the extreme form of the separation of the general economic process into an industrial and a domestic unit' (Coulson, Magas, Wainwright 1975). The nature of the 'domestic unit', concerned with the reproduction and maintenance of the labour force, which *always* remains a precondition of the reproduction of capital, is partly determined by the absolute separation capital sets up between the worker's individual consumption and her/his productive consumption,[12] and the necessity for the worker to sell her/his labour power to obtain the means of subsistence. The historical 'separation out' of the domestic sphere has been accompanied by, and articulated through, developing, and originally class-specific ideologies of domesticity, femininity, and personal life, which have contributed to the representation and understanding of the home as a private sphere, undetermined by the capitalist mode of production (Hall 1974; Davidoff 1973, 1976; Zaretsky 1976).

In our society, the work involved in 'the maintenance and reproduction of the working class' is done mainly by women[13] as unwaged work in the home, regardless of whether they also do waged work (usually of a similar nature) outside the home. The roles of wife and mother, in relation to the reproduction of capital, are centrally those of the reproduction and maintenance of the labour force. We do the shopping, cooking and cleaning, soothe our husbands and look after the children. The determinations on the domestic by the industrial sphere, which contribute to the reproduction of the specific social relations of the sphere (the relations of subordination of women to men) are central to an understanding of women's position in the home. As Sally Alexander observes, writing of women's work in nineteenth century London:

> But a wife's responsibility for the well-being of her husband and children always came before her work in social production, and in a patriarchal culture, this was seen to follow naturally from her role in biological reproduction.
>
> The intervention of capitalism into the sexual division of labour within the patriarchal family confirmed the economic subordination of the wife. By distinguishing between production for use and production for exchange, and by progressively subordinating the former to the latter, by confining production for use to the private world of the home and female labour, and production for exchange increasingly to the workshop outside the home, and male labour, capitalism ensured the economic dependence of women upon their husbands or fathers for a substantial part of their lives.
>
> Alexander (1976, p. 77)

It is thus argued that the reproduction and maintenance of the labour force is, historically, conducted through specific relations, the particular capitalist articulation of the sexual division of labour and the nexus of relations which construct and contribute to women's 'ideological and socio-economic role as mother and housekeeper'. This is the hidden, and historically specific content of 'the worker's drives for self-preservation and propagation' – and it is in this context that women's role in the home must be considered.

Engels located woman's role in the home as central to her continuing subordination, but understood capitalism to be progressive in this respect:

> The emancipation of women and their equality with men are impossible and must remain so as long as women are excluded from socially productive work and restricted to housework, which is private. The emancipation of women becomes possible only when women are enabled to take part in production on a large social scale, and when

> domestic duties require their attention to only a minor degree. And this has become possible only as a result of modern large-scale industry, which not only permits the participation of women in production in large numbers, but actually calls for it, and moreover, strives to convert private domestic work into a more public industry.
>
> Engels (1972, p. 152)

It has seemed clear to feminists[14] that despite 'the participation of women in production in large numbers',[15] increasing (if fluctuating and at present declining) state intervention, and the penetration of the home by commodities, domestic duties do not yet require women's attention 'only to a minor degree'. Coulson, Magas and Wainwright (1975), and later Adamson *et al.* (1976) have argued: '. . . the central feature of women's position under capitalism is not their role simply as domestic workers, but rather the fact that they are *both* domestic and wage labourers' Coulson, Magas and Wainwright (1975, p. 60).

This has led feminists to try and understand, 'Why have housework and childcare, in modern industrial societies such as Britain, continued to such a great extent to be the responsibility of women, and organised on a private family basis?' Gardiner (1975, p. 47).

Much of the literature has concentrated on the attempt to analyse housework in relation to marxist categories of political economy. There has been extensive interrogation of the adequacy of some marxist concepts to contribute to an understanding of the political economy of women, and the material basis of their subordination. Ann Foreman characterized the main questions that have emerged from this literature as:

> What is the relation of women to the production of labour power? Does the work of women in the home produce value? Is capitalism likely to socialise this work? And what is the significance of the fact that women go out to work as well as working within the home?
>
> Foreman (1977, p. 113)

We now intend first to look briefly at some of the arguments over productive and unproductive labour; the value of labour power; housework in relation to the production of surplus value; then to briefly state how we understand domestic labour, and then to go on to consider the question of the socialization of domestic labour.

The distinction between productive and unproductive labour[16]

Marx uses 'productive' in two senses. Firstly, the more general one of socially useful labour (labour which produces use-values, undertaken in all societies), and secondly, to mean labour that is exchanged against capital rather than revenue.[17] Thus, in the latter sense, the same *kind* of labour can be productive or unproductive. You can peel potatoes at home, in a state school kitchen or in a commercial restaurant. Workers employed by capital, in addition to reproducing the value of their own labour power, produce surplus value – they are productive *from the point of view of capital.* Is housework productive only in the general sense – the production of use-values? (Coulson *et al.* 1975; PEWG 1975; Adamson *et al.* 1976) or does it also contribute to the production of surplus value (Harrison 1973; Seccombe 1974; Gardiner 1975, 1976) or is it directly engaged in the production of surplus value (Dalla Costa and James 1972)?

The value of labour power

Marx:

> The value of labour power is determined, as in the case of every other commodity, by the labour time necessary for the production, and consequently also the reproduction, of this special article. In so far as it has value, it represents no more than a definite quantity of the average social labour objectified in it. Labour power exists only as a capacity of the living individual. Its production consequently presupposes his existence. Given the existence of the individual, the production of labour-power consists in his reproduction of himself or his maintenance. For his maintenance he requires a certain quantity of the means of subsistence. Therefore the labour-time necessary for the production of labour-power is the same as that necessary for the production of those means of subsistence; in other words, the value of labour-power is the value of the means of subsistence necessary for the maintenance of its owner.
>
> Marx (1976, p. 274)

All contributors to the domestic labour debate recognize the historical and cultural determinants on the subsistence level of the working class. The problem arises over whether women's labour in the home – peeling and cooking the potatoes after buying them, or just adding water to a packet of 'Smash' – is taken as a given or not. Is it, and should it be, included within an understanding of the 'labour time necessary for the production, and consequently also the reproduction of this special article'?[18] That is, while all the contributors to the debate *recognize* the necessity of the woman's contribution to the 'means of subsistence', the difference lies in the way this contribution is understood theoretically, which depends partly on whether it is thought that the housewife's private labour in the home can/should be understood through Marx's categories for the analysis of labour exchanged on the market. Here it seems important to stress that labour power as a concept (the ability to labour, sold as a commodity under capitalism) is *not* sexed, just as, in the abstract, capital is indifferent not only to the use values of the commodities which are produced, but also to the sex/gender of its domestic and wage labourers. However, concretely, this is not the case, and there are grounds for arguing that, historically, male and female labour powers have different values (Beechey 1977; Foreman 1977).

Surplus value/surplus labour[19]

The domestic labour debate has partly been 'about' whether and how housework contributes to the production of surplus value (see *Distinction between productive and unproductive labour*, above). It has been argued that the housewife produces surplus value directly, because she produces the value-creating commodity, labour power (Dalla Costa and James 1972). Alternatively, that she contributes to the production of surplus value through her surplus labour in the home, which forms part of her husband's consumption, and thus increases the time he spends in the production of surplus value by lowering the necessary labour time (variously, and in different forms: Harrison 1973; Seccombe 1974; Gardiner 1975).

Within the terms of this debate, we think domestic labour can most usefully be characterized as 'the production of use-values under non-wage relations of production, within the capitalist mode of production'[20] and thus not contributing directly to the creation of surplus value; a private, concrete labour, in the main performed by women, which is essential to the reproduction of labour power under capitalism, concerned as it is with the reproduction and maintenance of the bearer of labour power, the labourer. We find this labour neither productive nor unproductive in Marx's more specific sense because: '[Housework under capitalism] remains a specific labour to which the concept of abstract labour does not apply . . .' Coulson, Magas and Wainwright (1975) '. . . to compare domestic labour with wage labour is not comparing like with like . . .' PEWG (1975, p. 10).

From this 'orthodox' position,[21] the terms of the domestic labour debate as analysis of the relationship between women's continuing subordination and the capitalist mode of production become more explicitly inadequate. For example, Seccombe (1975, p. 89 fn.) argues that he looks at: 'the substantive component of domestic labour, subtracting out the timeless household and child guardian aspects of the housewife's role. This latter aspect is not measurable in terms of labour time or value.'

On one hand, we find this 'substantive component' 'not measurable in terms of labour time or value'. On the other, it is the myth of 'the *timeless* household and child guardian aspects of the housewife's role' that much feminist literature has engaged with (Comer 1974; Oakley 1974b, 1972; Hall 1974; Davidoff, L'Esperance, Newby 1976), arguing for cultural, historical and class specificity. It is the 'timelessness' of women's 'immeasurable' role in the home, and its implied 'naturalness' which has provided its major ideological justification. What Seccombe calls 'the substantive component of domestic labour' is a labour of love precisely because it is performed through 'the household and child guardian aspects of the housewife's role' which have to be considered in conjunction with the particular construction of romantic love between men and women under monopoly capitalism (Millet 1971; Firestone 1972; Greer 1970):

> For a woman's labour in the home typically does not only contain the caring work described above [of children, the elderly, the sick], but also the much less obviously necessary tasks of providing services for an adult male, in a relation of personal dependence upon him.
>
> Mackintosh, Himmelweit, Taylor (1977)

We are thus arguing that women's overall responsibility for the maintenance and reproduction of the labour force cannot be adequately 'thought' through the categories of capital alone. Women's role in the home, from the point of view of capital, cannot be understood without attention to the specific historical and ideological articulations of the sexual division of labour, in relation to particular forms of 'the family' through which women's sexuality is organized for reproductive ends, and the effectivity, in the construction of femininity, of the ideologies of domesticity and romantic love.[22] From the point of view of women:

> Women are trapped into a material dependence upon a man by our lack of access to a decent wage, the absence of services to make full-time waged work and child care compatible, the ideological and social pressures to marry, and the almost complete absence of any alternative to the family as a way of life, a learned sense of inferiority, and the personal effects of isolation and overwork.
>
> Mackintosh, Himmelweit, Taylor (1977)

It is in relation to these points[23] that we want to look at the debate over the socialization of domestic labour. The PEWG (1975) try to 'grasp the fact that the socialisation of domestic labour is necessary in order to permit women to work in wage labour' and argue that there has been a reduction in the time which has to be spent in the home for the production of an acceptable standard of living for the family. That is, although they have rejected the attempt to quantitatively compare domestic labour time with wage labour time, they *are* trying to use some concept of necessary labour time in relation to domestic labour, although they recognize that *actual* labour time varies from home to home:

> By the socialisation of domestic labour we do not necessarily mean *a reduction in the time actually spent on housework by full time housewives* . . . what we mean is the replacement (and at the same time the transformation) of the work done in the home by goods and services produced for the market or provided by the State: laundries and prepared foods, education and health care. [our italics]
>
> PWEG (1975, p. 13)

They understand the limits of this capitalist and state socialization of domestic labour as lying principally in the sphere of market conditions – although they recognize contradictory political and economic factors – and thus the implication of their analysis seems similar to that of Engels, although only likely to be fulfilled under boom conditions: 'Up to now, capital has been unable to overcome the obstacles to complete socialisation of domestic labour' (PWEG 1975, p. 13). Davidoff, considering the rationalization of housework, points out: 'What must be kept in mind is that technical improvements in equipment, such as those exemplified by the use of the small electric motor, are not of the same order as fundamental changes in the organisation or aims of housework' Davidoff (1976, p. 145).

The problem of 'the substantive component' of women's work in the home thus reappears in this analysis,[24] as it does in those analyses which view domestic labour primarily through the necessity under capitalism of individual private, consumption (Coulson, Magas, Wainwright 1975; Adamson *et al.* 1976). 'The enforced privatised consumption of the family could never become optional under capitalism; consequently a residual portion of the work that accomplishes this consumption is structurally necessary . . .' Seccombe (1975)

The limits to the socialization of domestic labour, as argued here, are given in the processes of capital accumulation, the separation of labour power from the labourer, productive consumption from individual consumption. However, it cannot be 'deduced' from the logic of *Capital* (Adamson *et al.* 1976) that the work through which the individual private consumption that is necessary for the reproduction and maintenance of the labour force is achieved, will always be performed by *women*. Contradictory demands are being made on women in a period when 44 per cent of the paid work force is female, a period '. . . of the so-called crisis of the family, epitomised by the legalisation of divorce and the appearance of female sexuality no longer organised solely to reproductive ends' *WPCS* (no. 9, p. 114).

The possibility of the capitalist organization of individual consumption in forms other than a two-parent family must be considered (however unlikely this may seem for more than minority groups of the population). This question is important because it engages partly with the question of how far certain types of feminism can be considered 'a rationalist exigency of capitalism' (*WPCS*, no. 9, p. 114).

The sexual division of labour is taken for granted in a rather different way in the argument for 'wages for housework', which carries an implicit position on the socialization of domestic labour. The argument here is that wages (the 'sign' of value under capitalism) are *due* to housewives, as they are *already* involved in social production: '. . . the family under capitalism is a center of conditioning, of consumption, and of reserve labour, but a center essentially of social production' Dalla Costa and James (1972, p. 10).

The family is the 'social factory' where women produce the commodity labour power: 'What we meant precisely is that housework as work is productive in the Marxian sense, that is, it is producing surplus value' Dalla Costa and James (1973, p. 53, fn 12).

Demanding wages for housework on the basis of this analysis, as both recognition of and recompense for social labour, can be seen as a demand for a sort of 'righting' of the 'phenomenal forms' to fit what are argued to be the 'real relations'. A short-cut to a kind of privatized socialization, which still leaves *women* doing the same work in isolation.[25]

Ann Foreman more suggestively locates women's continuing, though increasingly contradictory, place in the home as partly a result of successful working class struggle for a 'family wage', particularly at the end of the nineteenth and early twentieth centuries: '. . . the growth in strength of the working class movement was pitted towards defining labour power as a male capacity and demanding accordingly that their wage should reflect this fact' Foreman (1977, p. 120; see also Alexander 1976; PEWG 1975).

Here we can begin to see the articulations of the sexual division of labour within the capitalist mode of production as both the historical *outcome* and *site* of struggle. Thus the struggle for a family wage is also the struggle to define women in terms of their reproductive capacity. The benefits to capital of women's role as mother and wife are secured through masculine hegemony[26] which struggles to define women through, and confines them to, these roles. It is through this historically complex and contradictory 'relegation' of women (ideologically, if not always actually) to the 'private sphere' of reproduction – and hence through a recognition of the real divisions within the working class – that the retention of women's work in the home must be considered. 'The family' as the site of women's subordination, and the specificity of women's oppression in her 'ideological and socio-economic role as mother and housekeeper' has to be understood historically through ideological and political determinations which articulate with the benefits to *capital* of the family as an *economic* unit.

The state, reproduction of labour power and the subordination of women

Our concern here is to examine the way in which the state contributes to women's subordination.[27] We would argue that the specificity of this contribution lies primarily in the state's concern with the reproduction of labour power. We take those state apparatuses, legislation and ideological practices which are centrally concerned with the reproduction of labour power to designate a working definition of the 'welfare state'. It is clear that what is commonly conceived of as the welfare state, or welfare aspects of the state, involves more than the reproduction of labour power. However, we wish to centre on this one aspect, thereby also denaturalizing the ideological connotations of the concept of 'welfare'.

From capital's viewpoint there are several aspects to the reproduction of labour power:

1 Capital must be supplied with a continuous source of labour power – a new generation of preferably healthy labourers;
2 capital, being in itself a creative and transformative process, requires in its labour continuous changes of skills and aptitudes/motivation;
3 as a lever of capital accumulation, capital needs an industrial reserve army, in a state of serviceability for capital;

4 capital desires an acquiescent work-force, politically and ideologically,[28] to ensure its continued existence, though this is never achieved unproblematically.

But this is not to view the welfare state as simply acting in the interests of capital; the welfare state's development must also be seen historically as the outcome of class struggle.

If we are taking the welfare state as both concerned with the reproduction of labour power from the viewpoint of capital *and* labour, we must ask what are the consequent implications for women. Under capitalism, labour power is replenished and replaced in the sphere of private consumption, primarily within the family. The family is the site of biological reproduction, but is also the main site for the regulation of sexuality and the acquisition of sex/gender roles, and other aspects of generational and day-to-day reproduction of the labourer. But in relation to the welfare state's concern with the family, it is crucial to bear in mind that both the welfare state's ability to monitor the reproduction of labour power, and the very form of that reproduction, are predicated on relations of domination and subordination between the sexes, power relations, within the reproductive circuit (the circuit of biological reproduction and reproduction of the labourer). State control of the reproduction of labour power has utilized these existing patriarchal relations, thereby reinforcing their pre-capitalist partiarchal nature.

Thus state concern with the reproduction of labour power has centred on women both as biological reproducers and in their wider role within the family. In fact, it is clear that welfare state legislation has largely defined and reinforced women's role as wives and mothers, reproducers of the present and future labour force.

On the other hand, if we see aspects of welfare legislation as 'won' by the working class, we must note that British working class strength and demands for welfare have evolved with an ideology which also centrally locates women within the family. This can be partly linked to the development of a notion of the 'family wage', the defining of labour power as *male*. As Ann Foreman (1977, p. 119) notes, the organized working class 'developed a tradition of values and expectations. Among them, and in pride of place, was the belief that the wage should be sufficient to maintain the worker's wife at home.'

A woman's 'place' also came to involve a view of women as ensuring the sanctity of the home in contrast to the harsh world of labour – the ideology of 'domesticity'. We must remember that: '. . . neither the family nor ideology can be seen as imposed on a passive working class, rather as phenomena it plays a part in forging' Foreman (1977, p. 130).

We would argue that this ideology of a woman's 'place' became crucially incorporated into the ideology of social democracy, with welfare legislation reinforcing its materiality.[29] Again, however, it must be stressed that working class attitudes were and are predicated on relations of domination and subordination between the sexes, which predate capitalism. Thus it is incorrect to see the nature of women's subordination as either determined solely by the economic and political 'needs' of capitalism or the result of class struggle; women's subordination under capitalism lies in the articulation between patriarchal relations and capitalist development.

We shall attempt to show that although the welfare state has encroached on certain functions performed by the family and the neighbourhood, e.g. education, care of the old, disabled, mentally handicapped – developments that appear to have accompanied the shift into machinofacture – in other respects the state has fundamentally shored up the family and women's role as mothers, through various forms of regulated intervention and support.

We shall thus look briefly at three significant historical moments in the development of British welfare legislation:

1 The struggle around the Factory Acts in the mid nineteenth century.
2 The reforms introduced under the Liberal government prior to the 1914–18 war, which created the basic framework of our contemporary 'welfare state' with the introduction of insurance for unemployment, maternity, health, old-age pensions, school meals.
3 The body of ideology and legislation enshrined in the Beveridge Report of 1942, much of which was enacted by the Labour government after the Second World War.

This will be followed by a consideration of women and welfare in the post-war period. It is important to stress that we are not positing a unilinear development of the welfare state. The historical moments delineated are highly specific and represent definite *qualitative* shifts in the nature of welfare, particularly after the Second World War, with the introduction of *universal* provision and the notion of 'social rights'.[30]

The Factory Acts

Marx presupposed the existence of the private sphere of the family, lying outside the circuit of capital, but he was unconcerned with how labour power is reproduced: '. . . the capitalist may safely leave its fulfillment to the labourer's instincts of self-preservation and of propagation' (Marx 1976, p. 718). In fact, even in the heyday of *laissez-faire* in the early nineteenth century in Britain, reproduction was not left to the vagaries of the labourer's instincts of self-preservation: witness the marked moral intervention of the period, the beginnings of state education, state regulation of child welfare, and massive growth of bourgeois philanthropic activities. Marx's comments seem stranger still in the light of his extended account of the struggle around the working day (prior to and during the introduction of the Factory Acts), a struggle which highlighted capital's need for state intervention into the reproduction of labour power.

Until the Factory Acts' restriction on the working day, the main form of exploitation had been the extraction of absolute surplus value: the lengthening of the working day. But capital had used this form to such an extent that it had produced 'the premature exhaustion and death of its labour power', and thus its concern with valorization was ultimately threatening its own existence.[31] The state's enactment of the Factory Acts (and also the Public Health Acts in the same period)[32] can thus be seen as directly benefiting the long-term interests of capital, but, we would argue, also representing gains won by the working class. However, it is debatable whether the Factory Acts can be seen unambiguously as a gain for *women* in terms of their potential for economic independence. The first few Factory Acts applied only to adolescent, child, and female labour, and with their hours thus restricted, women became less attractive employees. This could be seen in one respect as a victory for male trade unionists at the expense of women, in that there was now less likelihood of women's unskilled labour being used to aid de-skilling and to undercut male workers. Further, the Factory Acts extended the definition of a minor to include women, thereby reinforcing the notion of women's dependency on men. However, influences shaping the Acts were more complex than this; as Wilson (1977, p. 9) points out, there were also moral debates on female sexuality concerning, for example, the 'indecency' of women working in the mines. Henceforth, the question of women and children working became seen as a *moral* issue.

The limitation by the state of the extraction of absolute surplus value directed capital to the production of relative surplus value; concern with increasing the intensity and productivity of labour. This shift can be seen as a crucial historical moment in that it represents both the state's first major intervention into the reproduction of labour power, and the first example of any working class agitation resulting in the 'winning' of social reforms.

The Liberal reforms

The welfare legislation in the period before the First World War came in the wake of great concern with national and imperial efficiency. On the one hand, there was the problem of alleged physical deterioration: the Boer War had revealed the British worker's physical puniness (50 per cent of those enlisted were unfit). On the other hand, there was also alarm in relation to the declining birth rate. In response, the Interdepartmental Committee on Physical Deterioration was set up in 1903 and many of its recommendations were enacted in the ensuing legislation.

In addition to the National Insurance Act of 1911 (which applied to few women), measures were introduced to promote the health of mothers and children: the legislation to provide free milk for babies, the beginning of health visiting and midwifery, and clauses relating to parental neglect. Not surprisingly, these measures went hand-in-hand with the promotion of motherhood and denouncement of the 'working mother'. As Booth wrote in his popular *In Darkest England and the Way Out* (1890, cited in Wilson 1977, p. 110):[33]

> The home is largely destroyed where the mother follows the father into the factory, and where the hours of labour are so long that they have not time to see their children. . . . It is the home that has been destroyed, and with the home the home-like virtues. It is the dis-homed multitude, nomadic, hungry, that is rearing an undisciplined population, cursed from birth with hereditary weakness of body and hereditary faults of character. . . . Nothing is worth doing . . . that does not Reconstitute the Home.

As Wilson notes (1977, p. 102) a preoccupation with eugenics was widely prevalent, particularly among the Fabians. In the Fabian tract, *The Decline of the Birthrate*, Sidney Webb recommends state action to encourage the wealthier sections of society to reproduce themselves; it was believed that the poor were breeding at a much faster rate than the rest of the population, thus contributing to national degeneration.

The Liberal legislation also reflected concern with what was seen as a vast undermass of dejected labour, the industrial reserve army. Boards were set up in 1909 to fix minimum wages and maximum hours in sweated trades, thus preventing sections of capital exploiting women workers in particular and attempting the destructive consumption of labour power.

The Beveridge Report

The Beveridge Report (1942) can be seen as the first body of proposed legislation which actually introduced the idea of *planned* reproduction of labour power. But the report must also be seen as a response to economic and political mobilizations of the war, and demands for a reversal of conditions of the inter-war period. Yet such demands came primarily from *male* trade unionists:[34] 'The major demands were for male full employment, an adequate insurance for male workers, for themselves and their families' PEWG (1975, p. 28). Again, women's interests were subsumed to men's, with women relegated to the family as dependants of men.

Wilson sees three basic principles underlying the report: the principles of subsistence income; of insurance; and of the sanctity of the family. A central concern with motherhood was in part a response to (again!) the declining birth rate,[35] and Beveridge's proposal for family allowances was meant not only as a form of income redistribution in addition to a social insurance system (an income redistribution *within* the working class, and not between classes)[36] but also as a material inducement for propagation.[37] Beveridge's position was transparent: 'In the next 30 years housewives as Mothers have vital work to do in ensuring the adequate continuance of the British race and the British Ideals in the world' (Beveridge 1942, pp. 52–3).

The report throughout stresses the importance of the family as an economic unit, with the need to 'treat man and wife as a team' (p. 49). Beveridge erroneously assumed that once the war ended, most married women would cease to be waged workers and would return to the home: 'the great majority of married women must be regarded as occupied on work which is *vital* though unpaid' (p. 49). 'During marriage most women will not be gainfully employed' (p. 50), he argued, which justified the notion that should a married woman take on paid work, she would neither pay contributions, nor receive benefits. Thus married women were assumed to be economic dependants of their husbands and thus their dependence was reinforced. Although Beveridge removed the anomalies concerning single women[38] who, in terms of benefits, were to get the same as men, their contributions were to be lower on the grounds that a man, unlike a woman, was making contributions on behalf of himself *and* his wife. Here we see the implicit assumption of the 'family wage'.

The Beveridge Report also revealed the state's concern with the yoking of sexuality to the family. There was a definite position against 'immorality'; for example, Beveridge recommended a separate allowance for deserted, separated and divorced wives, *only* on condition that they were not responsible for the breakdown of the marriage. Further, there was no provision in the scheme for unsupported mothers.

We have argued that the state's concern with the reproduction of labour power has crucially involved its shaping and shoring up of the family and the woman's location within the family as mother, wife and dependant of her husband. Before turning to a consideration of the central contradiction facing women in the post-Second World War period, it is useful to delineate the different modes of welfare state intervention into the family. This intervention takes the form of a) regulation, b) 'support', c) supercession:

(a) The attempts to regulate the way in which women service the worker and bring up their children in the home are less 'obvious' than the demands of the assembly line, but are for that very reason all the more insidious and mystifying. As PEWG notes (1975, p. 23): '. . . since the war the ideological pressure on women in the home has increased enormously and a veritable army of social workers has been trained in family case work'. Social work 'control' basically involves intervention into families where reproduction of labour power is threatened. In addition, the state, through family law and legislation on matters of sexual morality plays a central role in monitoring and controlling sexual ideology and its relation to the family. The extent of such regulative intervention is often overlooked, since in bourgeois ideology these matters belong *par excellence* to the intimate or private sphere, but the array of legislation dealing with such areas as divorce, separation, adoption, fostering, abortion and contraception, rape, prostitution, homosexuality, etc., belies this.

(b) In its 'supportive' role, the welfare state maintains a family in existence as a unit. The characteristic methods have been allowances, supplements, free school milk, health care, etc. At the ideological level, the ideal of 'motherhood' dominant in much welfare legislation and the practices of welfare agencies, acts to regulate and support women's role within the family as reproducers. Families are almost always ideologically constituted as families-with-children, or families-with-the-function-of-child-care. Yet most families or most people do not have children – they have either never been there, or have not yet arrived, or have left. A woman's sexuality is invariably defined primarily in relation to her capacity to bear children, not as an integral part of her being over which she has control and the right to define as she chooses.

(c) The welfare state's encroachment on certain 'traditional' functions of the family has already been mentioned. Whether capitalism can or will dispense with the existing form of the family remains an open question.

The post-war period

After the war, with the Labour government's commitment to full employment for *men*, married women became the industrial reserve army (see Beechey 1977) and as Wilson (1977, p. 158) notes:

> This period then saw the development of a contradiction between the need to expand the labour force, and the need to raise the birthrate, and tangling with this were the new anxieties about the emotional well-being of children. Women have been the battle ground of this conflict within capitalist society ever since, for what has been attempted is to retain the mother as, in practice, the individual solely in charge of the day to day care of children and yet at the same time to draw married women, the last remaining pool of reserve labour, into the workforce. These demands are not fully compatible.

It is these two aspects of women's lives, their role in production either as members of the work-force or as part of the permanent reserve army, and their role in reproduction or childbearing and child-care, that constitute a major contradiction both for capitalism and for the state, a contradiction that has to be *managed*.[39]

One outcome of this contradiction lies in the predominant post-war definition of a woman's dual role as 'a negative one that sees her mothering function as interfering with her work, and her work function as interfering with her child rearing' (Wilson 1977, p. 151). A 'solution' to this contradiction has been the rise of female part-time work (see *Equal pay* section, pp. 383–7).

However, the welfare state not only attempts to *manage* a contradiction; its provisions have themselves had contradictory outcomes. As the PEWG (1975, p. 26) points out:

> . . . those very services designed to support and maintain the family unit have in many instances provided women with sufficient means to break away from it, to bring up their children independently of their husbands. And the more remedial benefits are introduced, for single parent families, the more parents in unsatisfactory relationships are likely to separate and the weaker men's sense of obligation as breadwinners for their families may become.

Further, through driving away wage-earning children, means-testing has weakened the very family that the state set out to support (see J. Cowley *et al.* 1977).

But it is not simply that welfare policy throws up new contradictions; the ideology implicit in the welfare state is itself in contradiction with structural changes. Most of the patriarchal assumptions enshrined in the Beveridge Report have remained locked into welfare legislation.

Yet, although a woman's financial dependence on her husband is still assumed, the reality of the situation is somewhat different. As H. Land (1975, p. 119) points out:

> At the very least, one in six of all households, excluding pensioner households, are substantially or completely dependent upon a woman's earnings or benefits and the majority of these households contain either children or adult dependants. Among pensioner households a woman is the chief economic supporter in just over half of the households.

The managed contradiction between woman's role as a waged worker and as a domestic worker and reproducer, and the concomitant rise of female part-time work, has itself accelerated militancy among women. The rise of the WLM itself is partly an outcome of this contradiction, and four of the WLM's six demands are directly concerned with reproduction and the relation between reproduction and the state. The limitations of the two demands which do *not* confront this question, the demands for equal pay and equal education and opportunity, are exemplified in the unsatisfactory outcome of the Equal Pay and Sex Discrimination Acts (see below): neither of these Acts questions in any way women's reproductive role, and neither has led to economic equality for women.

This begs the question of how women are to regard welfare legislation and to assess reforms' progressive potential for them *as women*. As has been indicated, the welfare state is deeply contradictory: it is in certain respects 'won' by the working class, but in others, advantageous to the dominant class interests at a certain historical conjuncture. However, as we have attempted to show, its contradictory nature is at its most apparent in relation to women.

The welfare state has undoubtedly led to a rise in living and health standards, but these material improvements have done little to alter the basic dependence of women, whether on their husbands, or on means-tested benefits. As PEWG notes (1975, p. 29), many people feel that the material advantages of the welfare state have been almost outweighed by the repressive ways in which services have been administered, and the social control exerted through them. Certain welfare legislation has had progressive elements, but it has rarely led to any form of democratic control over the *implementation* of that policy, particularly in the case of control by and/or for women. It is obviously crucial to ask why this is the case.

At the conception of the welfare state, the labour movement never really raised the central question of democratic control. This was due partly no doubt to the ideology of social democratic politics in which gains 'won' from the state in terms of welfare were seen *in themselves* as steps to transforming the state. In addition, as PEWG points out, the left has never placed much emphasis on struggle in the sphere of reproduction, either domestic or socialized, which is in part due, of course, to the dominant sexist ideology of a woman's 'place' being in the home, i.e. reproduction is the work and concern of women.

The six demands of the WLM are all at some level demands of the state. These demands must be seen as neither totally separate nor primarily economic; only their *combination* acts to challenge the underlying roots of women's subordination. The fifth demand, the demand for financial and legal independence, appears to make the most direct attack on the patriarchal nature of the state (the ten demands of the Campaign for Financial and Legal Independence all confront those aspects of welfare policy which most centrally define women's dependence on men). However, it must be stressed that the welfare state's ability to create and reinforce this dependency is predicated on women's subordination as biological reproducers. Further, we must struggle not merely for the realization of these demands, but also for control over their implementation (see *Equal pay* section below).

Women in waged work

> I'm a trained machinist, but I can't work during the day because of the kids. I can't afford to have them looked after. I'd rather do day work, but I'd live in poverty if I didn't do night cleaning. People don't do night cleaning for fun.
>
> Wandor (1972, p. 152)

In comparison with other aspects of women's position, women's wage labour most obviously concerns the economic relations of capital. However if, for example, we examine their labour in the post-Second World War period (from which the examples here are drawn),[40] it is impossible to understand the complexities of women's entry and engagement in the labour market through the economic alone, even though it is the processes of capital accumulation that provide the over-reaching umbrella under which women's wage labour takes place.[41] Capital accumulation establishes certain 'needs' in relation to the labour force, economic needs which women primarily come to fulfil for *ideological* and *political* as well as economic reasons. These determining factors concern birth control and associated demographic changes in the family (Titmuss 1963) which also relate to a shifting *ideology* of domesticity: 'a woman's place is in the home' or isn't it?.[42] They include political changes focusing around trade union policies, particularly the predominantly male trade union struggle for a 'family wage' and full employment (for men)[43] and disparate state policies. Here we would consider immigration policy which in the 1950s encourages immigrant labour and then later restricts immigrant entry to create the space in which married female labour can be taken on (Cohen and Harris 1976); the state's underprovision of child-care facilities,[44] and so on (see preceding section on the state).

The specificity of the analysis of female wage labour lies not only in the fact that it is determined by more than the economic. It pertains also to how we conceptualize the economic itself. Female wage labour is always premised on women's position economically and ideologically in the *family*. As we have already argued, it is the patriarchal family in its relations within the processes of capital accumulation which is the site of women's subordination. If we are not to lose the specificity of that subordination in its particular form as wage labour, our analysis must attempt to hold, simultaneously, the family and the labour process, *within* an understanding of the contradictory developments of the capitalist accumulation process. That process has not only at its production 'end' developed new forms of labour in which women have become engaged, but at its consumption 'end' penetrated and altered women's domestic role. That alteration in the post-Second World War period has also been particularly significant for their wage labour.

We can only understand female wage labour then, after we have considered, first, women's patriarchal reproduction of the capitalist commodity, labour power. Second, we must address ourselves to what is, in some of its aspects, integral to that: a woman's involvement at the point of exchange of commodities, i.e. as a buyer of commodities, and her consumption of those commodities, upon which her domestic labour and the family's individual consumption is founded.[45] In addition, we must consider the exchange and consumption of commodities which, while ultimately related to women's position in the family, concern femininity more generally. A woman's femininity is visually constructed from and 'aided' by capitalist commodities, which women *themselves* in part produce and chiefly sell *by means of* their own femininity. It is in this whole area of commodity consumption that we are concerned with capitalist expansion/diversification of commodity production as Marx has detailed it. Only third can we look at female wage labour as overdetermined by these two aspects.

This section on wage labour has two parts: one from the point of view of capital; one from the point of view of women's subordination.

Capital accumulation

Here we want to consider these aspects:

1 Expansion/diversification of consumption of commodities which presupposes production of those commodities and hence, particular forms of labour as well as consumption.
2 Capital's need for cheap labour.
3 Reserve army of labour.

These developments as they affect and include women, i.e. from the *point of view of women's subordination*, not capital, are determined by *patriarchal relations*, within which women are dependent on men: men's dominance as it is structured through what we call the *social relations of reproduction* of the individual sited primarily in the family.

Thus second:

Women's subordination

1 We examine women as a reserve in terms of how, within the capital accumulation process, these social relations of reproduction are determining, and
2 consider how their *sexuality* as structured by those relations of reproduction intervenes in their position as wage labourers.

Capital accumulation

EXPANSION/DIVERSIFICATION OF CONSUMPTION OF COMMODITIES

At the most general level there are two contradictory tendencies of capital.[46] Capital strives to reproduce itself on a constantly expanded scale through the extraction of *relative surplus value*. This results however in a tendency for the *rate of profit* to fall so that capital also sets up procedures to delay that fall.[47] One aspect of capital's expanded reproduction is the tendency for a concentration and accumulation of capital and its tendency towards centralization. Integral to those processes, one of their 'levers' (Marx 1976, p. 779) is *competition* in the production/consumption of commodities to realize the greatest surplus value. Competition and the production of relative surplus value demands widening consumption and circulation, i.e. *more* consumption as well as *different* consumption; hence the *need* to consume in those ways (Marx 1973, p. 93). Corresponding to the production of new commodities, Marx points also to the necessarily increasingly differentiated *division of labour*:

> A precondition of production based on capital is therefore *the production of a constantly widening sphere of circulation*, whether the sphere itself is directly expanded or whether *more points within it are created as points of production*.
>
> Marx (1973, p. 407)

> The production of *relative surplus value*, i.e. production of surplus value based on the increase and development of the productive forces, requires the production of new consumption; requires that the consuming circle within circulation expands as did the productive circle previously. Firstly: quantitative expansion of existing consumption; secondly: creation of new needs by propagating existing ones in a wide circle; *thirdly*: production of *new* needs and discovery and creation of new use values. In other words, so that the surplus labour gained does not remain a merely quantitative surplus but rather constantly increases the circle of qualitative differences within labour (hence of surplus labour), makes it more diverse, more internally differentiated.
>
> Marx (1973, p. 408)

> This creation of new branches of production, i.e. of qualitatively new surplus time, is not merely the division of labour, but is rather the creation, separate from a given production, of labour with a new use value; the development of a constantly expanding and more comprehensive system of different kinds of labour, different kinds of production, to which a constantly expanding and constantly enriched system of needs corresponds.
>
> Marx (1973, p. 409)

Although it cannot be specified by the accumulation process itself, the 'need', while determined by production, is felt within the family. It is the family which consumes more and differently.

On the one hand the family (always the labourer's family for Marx) 'benefits' from a wider provision of commodities while yet being more bound to the capitalist relation.

> Instead of becoming more intensive with the growth of capital, this relation of dependence only becomes more extensive, i.e. the sphere of capital's exploitation and domination merely extends with its own dimensions and the number of people subjected to it. A larger part of the worker's own surplus product, which is always increasing and is continually being transformed into additional capital comes back to them in the shape of the means of payment, so that they can extend the circle of their enjoyments, make additions to their consumption fund of clothes, furniture, etc. and can lay by a small reserve fund of money. But these things no more abolish the exploitation of the wage labourer, and his situation of dependence than do better clothing, food and treatment, and a larger *peculium* in the case of the slave.
>
> Marx (1976, p. 769)

It is within this more extensive relation of dependence that women, particularly as domestic labourers in the home, become enmeshed in capitalist production at the *consumption end*.[48] Their production of use values and their service labour, in the process of becoming commodity production and state servicing respectively, are transformed.

First, for example, the fresh peas grown in the garden become the can of peas, not just to be eaten in season but all the year round, i.e. a quantitative increase of peas eaten and more importantly of commodities consumed. Then the peas become frozen or quick-dried – more expensive – therefore women need to engage in paid work to be able to afford them. While then the new branches of production of domestic goods potentially 'free' the housewife from much domestic labour, at the same time hers and the family's 'needs' become different and greater. She must now shop not simply for the curtains she no longer makes but for cushion covers to match, the lampshade to complement, etc. The ideology of domesticity in play here supports the fulfilling of these new 'needs' yet contradictorily they can only be obtained within the working class by women entering wage labour, a move which the new production and new divisions of labour in part make possible.

Second, however, the family itself becomes dependent, sometimes on market relations, but also on the state for services which women originally performed. The expansion of the welfare state apparatus has contradictorily reinforced women's entrenchment in the home and also required them as wage workers. While relieved of some of their home responsibilities, women come to perform these tasks publicly for a wage. The health, education and social services expansion has relied heavily on women in part-time and full-time capacities.

A third feature of the expansion/diversification of consumption concerns not only the form of labour in the *production* of commodities, but the diversification of the division of labour within the *circulation* process. Expanded distribution associated with the growth of marketing as an important part of the whole process has involved the steady growth across all industries of clerical work (Ministry of Labour 1968); a considerable increase in the number of retail outlets – more sales personnel, mainly women; as well as an increase and transformation of the advertising apparatus in which women sell their sexuality to themselves and men by selling commodities.[49]

We would argue that at least for the post-war period it was principally the production of household commodities – 'labour-saving' devices for the home, together with cheap subsistence commodities previously produced as use values in the home – which contradictorily drew women into social production. It was these 'carrots' which as Wally Seccombe argued, made it economic sense, as well as in capital's interest, for women to take on paid work.[50] These is no similar relation in this period between men's wage labour and the *particular commodity production which capital* carries on. To summarize, for women in the post-war period, that relation is significant at several different levels.

(a) Married women are relieved of some of the burden of domestic labour so have time to do paid work, but simultaneously become *more dependent* on commodities, e.g. food, clothes, by going out to work.
(b) Also, in part, they go out to work for those commodities, i.e. labour-saving devices which are just outside the price range of a single wage. (This is not to suggest that most women do not do paid work to provide subsistence necessities.)
(c) They work in those industries manufacturing such commodities: assembling electrical equipment, in light engineering, as well as in food processing.
(d) For some young, single women – particularly those employed as boutique assistants, receptionists, air hostesses – consumption of certain commodities, i.e. make-up and fashion (in which trades it is again women who are primarily the employees), is essential to the sale of their labour power.
(e) This same group plus other women work in the distribution/marketing apparatus which promotes and sells such commodities.

CAPITAL'S NEED FOR CHEAP LABOUR

While the expansion/diversification of commodity production contributes to capital accumulation, the continuing extraction of relative surplus value which this represents 'founders on the tendency for the rate of profit to fall through the changing organic composition of capital' (Beechey 1977, p. 50). It is also those modes capital adopts to delay that fall which seem particularly pertinent to women's history:

> (a) *By reducing the allotment made to necessary labour* and by
> (b) *still more expanding the quantity of surplus labour with regard to the whole labour employed.* . . . There are moments in the developed movement of capital which delay this movement other than by crises . . .
> (c) *Unproductive waste of a great portion of capital.*
> (d) . . . the fall likewise delayed by *creation of new branches of production in which more direct labour in relation to capital is needed, or where the productive power of labour is not yet developed.* [our lettering and italics]
>
> Marx (1973, p. 750)

(a) Leaving to one side for a moment the first and most important mode in relation to women: 'the reduction in the allotment made to necessary labour', we can see that capital has often taken on women wage labourers within this whole framework of economic terms. Thus:

(b) 'Expanding the quantity of surplus labour with regard to the whole labour employed.' When, as in the post-war period, the ratio of working to dependent population is not growing, when there are checks on immigration, then married women are seen as one of the few available sources to check and possibly increase this balance.[51] An increase in that ratio – more women entering social production – represents more labourers to be exploited, an increase in the working class. 'Accumulation of capital is therefore multiplication of the proletariat' (Marx 1976, p. 764), and therefore represents the necessary expansion of surplus labour. That surplus labour is even further increased because women are paid below the value of the labour power: the value of labour power is spread over husband and wife.

(c) 'Unproductive waste of a great portion of capital'. In particular here the massive circulation processes which do not produce surplus value but on which productive industry is now dependent, constitute such a waste – again a heavy reliance on female labour.

(d) 'New branches of production in which more direct labour in relation to capital is needed'. Labour-intensive industry of which the rag trade is a familiar example predominantly employs married women, either as home workers or in factories. The clothing industry of the 1950s and 1960s rests not on modernization of the technology of clothes production but on such labour-intensive use of female labour.[52]

To return however to capital's attempt to reduce 'the allotment made to necessary labour', i.e. to employ labour as cheaply as possible, it is that tendency which contradictorily catches women whichever way they turn.[53] This reduction is partly achieved by cheapening *subsistence* commodities which the competition between capitals brings about. 'Capital therefore has an immanent drive, and a constant tendency, towards increasing the productivity of labour, in order to cheapen commodities and, by cheapening commodities, to cheapen the worker himself' (Marx 1976, p. 437).

While such a cheapening may potentially mean less housework for women, as the family can afford to buy commodities which previously she would have made, the continual incorporation in the post-war period of *luxury goods* into the means of subsistence of the working class both accentuates and counteracts this cheapening: the value of labour power is increased rather than reduced. With married women becoming more available for work on a much wider scale difficulties and contradictions are set up for capital.

The value of male labour power is premised on the family unit in which women perform domestic labour (Beechey 1977, p. 51). It is generally convenient for capital to maintain this arrangement. At particular times of crisis, e.g. unemployment, it is possible to pay male labour power below its price on the assumption that women in the home will temporarily work harder.[54] Furthermore when women become wage workers the value of their labour power is also premised on the family unit – on them as dependants, receiving part of their means of subsistence from the man's 'family wage'. As Veronica Beechey argues, female wage labour either has lower value than male labour power or is paid at a price below its value. In both cases it represents a depression of the value of society's average labour power.[55]

Capital can only retain these advantages of cheap labour power – unpaid labour in relation to the reproduction of male labour power, and cheap female labour power – so long as women continue to labour in, and have prime responsibility for, the home and child-care. The introduction of part-time work for women would seem to be particularly advantageous to capital in this respect. Even if unions are still fighting for a 'family wage', the practice of both husband and wife working is likely to undermine that, while at the same time: first, women in the family continue to bear the labour of reproduction of labour power; and second the position of responsibility there makes it a 'buyer's' market for their labour power. On all these counts the value of society's average labour power is kept down.[56]

For capital the general resolution to these contradictions has been to constitute women as a reserve army of labour. For women as wives, however, 'they are situated in a state of permanent transition between the two modes of labouring, the capitalist and the family mode' (see Article 9).

RESERVE ARMY OF LABOUR

The creation of a reserve army of labour is one of the features of the contradictory processes of capital accumulation. In general, with technical advances, labourers are 'set free' in greater proportion than they are needed by new production. The growth of the service sector and the welfare state, by providing employment, and trade union activity, in fighting against changes in the labour process which create redundancies, are two ways in which this tendency has been modified. Marx argues that capital needs an industrial reserve army as a lever of capital accumulation: first, as a flexible population entering new branches of production and then being dispensed with as the labour process requires a different labour force; second, to act as a competitive force through 'depressing wage levels or forcing workers to submit to increases in the rate of exploitation and thus increasing the level of surplus value extraction' (Beechey 1977, p. 56).

Women's subordination

WOMEN AS A RESERVE ARMY

Women do not rest easily within Marx's description, although it is clear that they are *as women* a reserve army for capital.

This conceptualization of women as a reserve army, distinctly demarcated as women, must presuppose a *sexual division of labour*. But the concept 'sexual division of labour' neither explains nor is itself explained by the concept 'reserve army'. We have always to explain what kind of division it is, not to leave it as a 'simple category' (Marx 1973, pp. 102–3) which we know commonsensically (as Marx and Engels both do) to be based on sex difference and which we apply across history and culture. As Marx describes with reference to the category of 'production' and 'property' we must reconstruct that apparently general and simple category as contradictorily composed of more concrete historical relations.

> The concrete is concrete because it is the concentration of many determinations hence unity of the diverse. It appears in the process of thinking, therefore, as a process of concentration, as a result, not as a point of departure even though it is the point of departure in reality, and hence also the point of departure for observation and conception.
>
> Marx (1973, p. 101)

The sexual division of labour, as we have already indicated, does not arise as a *sexual* division from capital's own structures. Rather capital has built its own divisions on to already existing sexual divisions. The implications of that however are that, in the sexual division which is our starting point, capitalist and patriarchal structures are *inseparable*. The sexual division of labour structured in masculine dominance is 'colonized', 'taken over' by the structures of capital. That is not to say that it has lost its patriarchal determinations, as the Revolutionary Communist Group pamphlet implies (Adamson *et al.* 1976). Within the dominating structures of capital the sexual division of labour 'arises', as they are correct to say, from the separation of labour power from the labourer, i.e. in the relation between the reproduction of capital accumulation and the reproduction of the individual (labourer or capitalist) who is the necessary agent in the first reproduction. It 'arises' too in the separation of 'production' from 'consumption' (productive consumption and individual consumption) even though capital does not itself stipulate that different groups, let alone different sexes, must be involved at the different moments. As we have described it, the first appearance of the sexual division of labour analytically is in the family: women are domestic labourers, concerned with all the functions associated with bringing up children, *dependent* on men who earn the family wage. We cannot describe that dependent relation as capitalist even if it is supported by state and market intervention as well as overdetermined by capitalist ideologies. Sex/gender identity of women and men, primarily constructed in the family and organized around their respective labours as mothers and fathers, underlies the *transformed sexual division* of labour within wage labour.

It is through a consideration of patriarchal and capitalist relations inseparably structuring the sexual division of labour that we must consider women as a reserve. Economically, for capital they are a reserve like any other; from the point of view of women's subordination, the *specific* characteristics of female labour are, as we shall see, *defined by* women's position as a reserve. Thus the *particular* articulation of women's subordination through their position as a reserve is only a *general* economic benefit to capital. Our interest in female labour as a reserve does not then quite place it within the terms in which Marx defines 'reserve army of labour'. Married women at least do not become a reserve because they are thrown *out* of social production, but *become available* for social production with advances in commodity production and hence consumption. We would argue that the 'full employment' of men in the 1960s has condemned one part of the working class, namely women, not to enforced idleness, but to their overwork as dual labourers – wage labourers and domestic labourers, in their position as an industrial reserve. Veronica Beechey (1977, p. 57) has suggested an important criterion for who is/is not part of the industrial reserve army:

> The preferred sources of the industrial reserve army from the viewpoint of capital are

> those categories of labour which are partially dependent upon sources of income other than the wage to meet some of the costs of the reproduction of labour power.

Married women then 'comprise a section of the working class which is not predominantly dependent upon its own wage for the costs of production and reproduction of labour power but which in addition is not heavily dependent on the welfare state' as are other categories (the elderly, for example). As Beechey goes on to say, they are a particularly advantageous source of industrial reserve army since they are excluded from the social security system except as dependants. They are therefore a pool of unprotected labour which 'can disappear' back into the family without usually appearing in unemployment statistics (Beechey 1977, p. 57).

Beechey is uncertain whether all women's work can be understood in terms of this concept. However the particular characteristic which she selects as constituting married women as a reserve suggests that it can, and indeed, that women's work must be described in this way. If we pay attention to the *movement in and out of the labour market* which women make, we can see that all 'women's work' is of this kind, even when it is not 'women's work' as such, and whether or not women are the 'preferred source' of the industrial reserve army. They constitute a reserve of a 'peculiar type', controlled not so much by the relations of capital production but by the *relations of reproduction in the family* – even when they are not married (ideologically it is expected that they will be).

Marx descriptively details different forms of the industrial reserve army which Beechey considers in an earlier draft of her paper and which we would like to re-examine (Marx 1976, pp. 784–9). His categories are unhelpfully named and perhaps historically specific. Still they do enable us to begin to conceptualize women as a reserve army which is internally differentiated, not just one monolithic grouping. Although in all cases they are a reserve first because of their position *as women* – as reproducers within the family – that determination operates differently for various groups of women. In each case their potential movement in and out of the labour market is distinct; their dependence on men and the family is different; the kinds of work for which they are an industrial reserve shifts and hence their position as an industrial reserve in the overall regulation of wages, and in relation to men's and women's wages separately, must also be differentiated.

(a) *Floating.* Here Marx considers the 'attraction' and 'repulsion' of workers into centres of modern industry, for example, boys who are only employed until maturity. In relation to women, some young women – as sales assistants in boutiques, hairdressers, receptionists, some secretaries – leave their employment at the birth of their first child, at the latest, and tend not to take up the same work it they resume when their children are older. In these jobs their sexuality and their age, i.e. their sexual attractiveness, is all-important: neither men nor older women are eligible. It is also work in which temporary and part-time work are important features. The advantages of the leaving 'of their own accord', in fact because of the contradiction between their social role in production and their 'private' role within the social relations of reproduction, means not just that capital and the state disclaim all responsibility for their 'unemployment', but also:

1. Their wages remain low since their family of origin and then their husband are held partly responsible for their reproduction costs.
2. They are unorganized because their work is 'temporary'.
3. The patriarchal relation is reproduced at work: men don't do secretarial work; sexual attractiveness continues to be a part of what they are selling when they sell their labour

power; men treat them as, and often the work involves them as, 'substitute wives', because there is constantly a further supply of such labour.[57]

4 In relation to wages as a whole the existence of a group of young women prepared to sell their labour power at a price below its value probably means that capital wins both ways, i.e. men's and women's wages, within office work say, negotiated separately because they are performing different work, are settled at lower rates than they might be if assessed together.

5 As an industrial reserve they are not competing for men's jobs.

(b) *Latent.* Here Marx considers agricultural workers who are passing over into a manufacturing proletariat, but who are dependent on the agricultural population – their families (women) – to support them when paid work ceases. This situation is analogous to the position of married women when it is materially and ideologically possible for them to be 'free' from child-rearing for some time, i.e. when it is no longer ideologically taken for granted that they should stay at home to look after their children as their sole occupation, nor economically necessary for them to produce all the family's use values. They become available for paid work when their children are at school, if capital needs them, but can safely be absorbed back into the family if work dries up or the 'dual role' becomes intolerably heavy. These women 'choose' to work and 'choose' to leave. In particular this applies to middle class women whose husbands are more than adequately able to support them and their families. This reserve takes up a variety of jobs – not necessarily 'women's work' – which are united by the tendency to be part-time and of low status within the particular job area, whether professional or other: teaching, nursing, secretarial and factory work. As an industrial reserve it is difficult to generalize about their position. In the present economic crisis part-time teachers and social workers are the first to lose their jobs, while part-time employment in industry is on the increase, though at the expense of full-time women rather than men.[58]

(c) *Stagnant.* This is the group Marx characterizes as working extremely irregularly for a maximum time and a minimum wage. Here we can refer to women-mothers married and unmarried, who for economic reasons are forced to work where and when they can. With no provision for child-care and the state's insufficient support for the very poor there is always a supply of such labour for capital. In the case of home work like sewing-machining, not only is the pay extremely low but the availability of such labour also depresses the wage of machinists who actually work on the employers' premises. Black women, West Indian and Asian, substantially make up this category, typically doing night cleaning, canteen work or home work during 'unsocial hours'.[59]

(d) *Pauperism.* Although the welfare state ameliorates the excesses of poverty to which Marx was referring, nevertheless the women who make up the stagnant reserve – those women often without 'supportive' men, single, looking after elderly parents, unmarried mothers, divorced women, widows, and prostitutes – are all at times likely to be on the verge of destitution.

LABOUR POWER AND SEXUALITY: FEMININITY/MASCULINITY

Conceptualizing women in paid work as a reserve army of labour structured by the social relations of reproduction in the family has already posed a meshing of capital's 'abstract labour' and indifference to gender, with patriarchal relations – in particular femininity. This 'meshing' is invariably contradictory for women. When they enter wage labour there is immediately a contradiction between their position as mothers and wage workers (as well as a contradiction in relation to men). While men are affirmed as men in their double relation as fathers and wage labourers through their role as 'breadwinner' – which is why masculinity as a construct can so often be overlooked[60] – femininity is cast in doubt by such a relation. On the one hand, women's role as mothers is often seen to be in jeopardy; on the other, their femininity carries over into the type of labour they perform: 'women's work', often regarded with derision both by men and women workers themselves. The determination by femininity on women's wage labour is particularly transparent, because waged work in general (despite internal mental/manual divisions) is seen as masculine. This is not relevant simply to the types of job women do, but also to how they carry them out – their consciousness of themselves as workers and men's consciousness of them too.

In this context we have to consider two aspects of the construction of femininity: while we are mothers who serve our husbands and children, we are also the desirable 'sexual object' for men. Both these aspects have been capitalized on in the post-war period: it is through women as *consumers* of certain commodities that capital has intervened in defining the form of femininity – giving children frozen crinkle-cut chips, not home-cut ones, wearing heavy make-up and platform shoes, etc. However the determination by femininity operates at different levels. Here we attempt briefly to separate out these levels in their complex and contradictory articulations with wage relations of capital.

In so far as we sell our commodity, labour power, for a wage as do men, femininity plays no part. Nevertheless the conditions of that sale differ: we are not able to 'freely' sell our labour power on the market because we are not 'the untrammelled owner of our capacity to labour, i.e. of our person' (Marx 1970, p. 168). As Sheila Rowbotham (1973, pp. 168 and 128) argues: 'Within the family the man appropriates the labour power of the women in the exchange of services'; 'Women are thus seen as economic attachments to men, not quite as free labourers.' The sale of her labour power is, then, mediated through marriage: her dependence on a husband and responsibility for family. We have to leave paid work when we have babies or our husbands and children are ill; when our husbands move their jobs to another area; when our husbands express displeasure at our paid work, and so on.

Even when we have seemingly overcome these obstacles and sell our labour power, we are not free of our gender determination. In 'modern industry', where Marx maintains as a tendency that 'natural' differences of strength should no longer be applicable and therefore that men and women should enter on the same terms, the hierarchy of labour which is established follows a sexual division, in so far as the semi- and unskilled work is usually performed by women (Beechey 1977, p. 51). In this way women's labour can be used in the processes of *de-skilling*. However because of the power of the unions – usually male – to resist these processes and women's usually differential place in the labour market, it is not often that women are in competition with men, their unskilled labour replacing men's skills.[61]

In these jobs where women are not doing 'women's work' as such (although it comes to be defined as that) women still, inevitably, live within their femininity at work. It is in the way they are treated by men at work (particular sexist incidents: for flirting with; as strike breakers and/or as workers not to be supported over equal pay strikes); the way they themselves see their work and its role in their lives (secondary to home, its convenience to home in terms of travel, little attention to the interest of the work, temporary, 'nice people,' etc.); their minor participation in union affairs (meetings at times when married women have to be at home 'servicing' the family, or the type of union activity – for better conditions as well as pay – which are gender-determined.)[62] As Audrey Wise (1974, p. 282) writes: 'Women aren't interested just in wages, equal pay is much more than a wage demand. Equal pay is a demand for self-respect, it's more than a demand for equal money, it's hygiene, safety, cold and things like that.'

In other wage labour women take their femininity with them in terms of the *use value* of their labour as 'servers': in the home they serve their families. In paid work they serve 'consumers' in hospitals, canteens, etc. As clerical workers or secretaries they serve men and the company.[63] Or it is the use value of other 'feminine' work in the home that they carry over into paid work, e.g. sewing-machining and detailed handiwork. Inversely, as home workers their femininity confines them to the house as they carry out 'women's work' for a wage, which, because of this 'doubly feminine' wage position, is extremely low, i.e. they are further removed from the masculine bargaining power associated with masculine jobs.

In yet other jobs female sexuality as sexuality on display is part of the *use value of the commodity labour power itself*.[64] For some secretaries, receptionists, boutique assistants, it is essential to be attractively feminine as well as to serve. This particular group of women workers embody a curious contradiction. As Juliet Mitchell describes it they are in the *most advanced* and the *most primitive* sectors of capital. These women are in effect selling their own sexuality in the same way that advertising uses women's sexuality to sell other products. In this position they are 'the subject of the most advanced ideological utilization made by capitalism; its chief ideological means of creating its markets' (Mitchell 1971, p. 143), while at the same time working in 'backwards' areas of capital in terms of how their labour is exploited.

At the ideological level this contradiction extends to all women workers, and in the 1960s was of particular significance to young educated women. This group of women, who experienced an 'equal' education with men, found first that 'equality' was not carried over into the jobs they were able to find (they were expected soon to leave 'as mothers'), but discovered second that they had to live up to both an image of 'equality' with men and of 1960s femininity in which skirts rose startlingly higher each week. While some secretaries, for example, may not experience that contradiction – to them their sexual attractiveness may nurture the illusion of a power and equality at work – it was to this group of young educated women that the contradictory patriarchal relations of sexuality, hitherto private, became publicly visible. It was that bringing-to-visibility of patriarchal structures, now invested with the capitalist commodity form, *in contradiction* to what women believed was their social equality, which played an essential part in the development of the Women's Movement at the end of the 1960s.

> Here they are doing a grand job as teachers, doctors, and barristers, running companies and ministries and banks, just like men and ready for separate tax allowances when suddenly skirts soar up to flash point, somebody opens up Bunny Clubs and the image shatters.
>
> How can you take them seriously after that? Could you ever be sure that inside every bank manager there was not a sex symbol trying to get out?
>
> 'Unfair Comment?', George Newman, *The Times* 31 October 1966

Equal pay

> There are limitations attached to reforms, but reforms also set up new contradictions and new possibilities for struggle. The question we should, therefore, ask is not whether changes in legislation since the '30s or '40s have improved the position of women. Rather we should ask of any particular reform what new contradictions it sets up for women, how these affect their consciousness and the ability to organise.
>
> PEWG (1975, p. 30)

We want to conclude this article through an understanding of the Equal Pay Act and the Sex Discrimination Act[65] as, in part, a condensation of the contradictions of women's continuing subordination under capitalism, which we have already considered. We briefly examine the legislation, which, though proposed in the 1960s, was implemented in the mid-1970s, in terms of its *potential* and *actual* effects on women.

The Equal Pay Act and the Sex Discrimination Act were the legal means by which women should have achieved equal pay by 1976. The Equal Pay Act pertains to women's economic inequality and although it seems to concern the relation of inequality between men and women, it only does so on *capital*'s ground of the value of labour power. Whilst in *theory* the Act should herald at least economic equality for women, the contradiction which prevents this from becoming reality is that it does not consider the position of *structural inequality* in which women are placed before they enter the wage market. It cannot challenge women's inequality before they enter the labour market which is premised on their role in the family. The division of labour which keeps women primarily responsible for the home means that women do not have even the right to equal exploitation in capitalism. To really transform the situation of women, the Sex Discrimination Act would have to confront the deeply embedded ideologies of domesticity and femininity which dominate women's lives.

The introduction of the Equal Pay Act and the Sex Discrimination Act

The history of the political struggle which at last resulted in the Equal Pay Act is itself contradictory. The TUC accepted the principle for eighty years, but only when external pressures demanded active response did it pursue the matter further than an annual or biennial resolution (Pinder 1969).[66] The Act finally takes its place within the context of 'progressive' law reform of the 1960s as part of the movement towards 'equality of individuals' before the law. It was no coincidence that the Act was finally introduced in 1968 – Human Rights Year, and the fiftieth anniversary of the granting of female suffrage. During this year women's organizations and other bodies reviewed the progress made since 1928 and also catalogued the disadvantages still existing in employment, etc. The government's income policy, though making no reference to sex, did ensure that pay problems would receive more publicity than before. The Race Relations Act (1965 and 1968) was understood by some to reveal a situation which put immigrant males in a more privileged position, in some respects, than indigenous females. The publication of the Government Social Survey on women's employment (Hunt 1968) gave more publicity to the problems of working women. This report had much coverage on radio, TV and in the press, calling for an end to all discriminatory practice.

Two events in June 1968 put the question of women's pay to the forefront of the interest of both the public and the employers of large numbers of women. The first was the strike of the women sewing-machinists at Ford's Dagenham plant which, although initially over grading, was taken up by the engineering union, the AEF, as a matter of equal pay. One of the results of the strike was the formation of a national organization of trade union women to campaign for equal rights (Smith 1974). At the end of June, Barbara Castle, Secretary of State for Employment and Productivity, promised to 'put new life' into discussions that her department was having with the TUC and CBI on equal pay, and indicated that it should not take any longer for introduction into the private sector than it had in the public sector.

The Equal Pay Act was introduced by Barbara Castle and brought in by the Labour Government in 1970, but five years were allowed before it was finally operative. During these five years employers were supposed to make plans for the implementation of equal pay within their own wage structures. This period of leeway, in fact, gave employers the opportunity to restructure and redefine jobs, and circumvent the terms of the Act. Under the Act, the Secretary of State was empowered to make an order for women's rates to be raised to 90 per cent or more of men's, if s/he thought 'orderly progress' was not being made, by 31 December 1973. A report published by the Office of Manpower Economics in August 1972 gave evidence of deliberate circumvention of regrading, the separation of men and women workers with union agreement, general lack of progress, and a widespread attitude among employers that they would wait for the Act to be enforced before doing anything (Trodd 1972).

Effects of the Equal Pay Act

Two years after the implementation of the Act, women still lag behind men in wages. Though young men and women who start work in their teens earn about the same, the difference begins to show very quickly. For the highest paid manual workers between 21 and 24, men will average (1976 figures) £80.8 per week while women will average £54. Among the same group of non-manual workers men will earn £74.6 compared with women's £59.1 (Equal Opportunities Commission 1977).

The Equal Pay Act was never meant to give equality to *all* women workers, and indeed, it is impossible for most women to achieve equal pay even within the limited terms of the Act. The Act says that a woman is entitled to equal pay if

1 She is working 'like work' (i.e. the 'same or broadly similar work') with a man, or
2 her job, although it is not the same or broadly similar to a man's, has been rated as of equivalent value to a man's job under a job evaluation scheme.

If a woman's job falls into either of these two categories, and she is not getting equal pay, then she can apply to an industrial tribunal (Coussins 1977).

The Act leaves a tremendous number of women who can make no claim that they are doing 'like' work with men. In the majority of cases, women's work is in a small range of jobs at the lower end of the job market, e.g. secretarial, clerical, service and catering, and in the retail trade, where there is no male counterpart with whom they can claim equality of work. These women could claim on grounds of their job being of 'equal value' with a man's job, but only if a job evaluation scheme has been conducted. The women working in these jobs are often in situations where they do not belong to a trade union, yet they need strong trade union backing if they are to achieve a satisfactory outcome from any job evaluation scheme.[67]

Traditionally women do not do 'like' work with men, and this anomaly is not challenged by the Equal Pay Act. This especially applies to part-time work where women's position is *not* 'equal' to men's because it is premised on their primary responsibility for domestic labour and child-care.

Part-time work – the contradictions

While the Acts appear to provide the opportunity for economic equality, the government has not provided the necessary welfare provisions to enable women to enter the labour market while ensuring that their children are looked after. There has been a decrease in the number of nursery places for the under-fives to a figure less than the 1900 one (Adamson *et al.* 1976). There is no provision for school-age children after school hours and during the holidays, and women with children of school age and under are forced into part-time jobs in order to accommodate their dual role. Part-time work *appears* to and often *does* offer a solution for women in that they can work hours which do not conflict with their domestic role. The increase in part-time work has coincided with the economic crisis for capital, and in this sense part-time work can be seen as a solution for capital.

> In such a situation employers are unlikely to risk heavy investment in highly productive capital-intensive techniques of production which would enable them to employ a high-wage labour force. They are more likely to prefer processes requiring a lot of cheap labour and relatively low capital investment. Women workers, and especially part-time workers . . . provide a suitable labour force in such circumstances, both because they are relatively cheap in employment and because they are more easily and more cheaply displaced when no longer needed. Gardiner (1975, p. 14)

The Equal Pay Act has revealed the contradictory nature of part-time work as a solution for women. Firstly, the existence of part-time 'paid' work is premised on women's primary role within the family and, therefore, *reinforces* the sexual division of labour which means that women have the prime responsibility for the home and children. Additionally, women suffer if they work for less than sixteen hours a week, as they are not covered by the same terms of employment as full-time workers (Campaign Notes 1975). The existence of part-time jobs can catch women in the double bind of the contradiction which forces them into the jobs in the first place.

Patriarchal attitudes at industrial tribunals

The patriarchal ideology and the division of labour which locates women's role in domestic labour and child-care is reflected in the decisions of some chair*men* at hearings of equal pay cases. In some cases reported by the NCCL, the 'given' nature of and the *low status* accorded to women's roles has been used against women at tribunal hearings. The structural inequality of women as domestic labourers can be used to justify their being paid lower wages than men in the labour market. In one case reported by the NCCL an employer's representative tried to justify the lower pay which a woman toilet cleaner received compared to a male cleaner engaged on the same work. He stated that 'a male toilet attendant has to *approach* the job from a labouring point of view and a female toilet attendant approaches it from a housekeeping point of view' [our italics] Coussins (1977, p. 49).

Here 'housekeeping' is accorded lower status than labouring and used as evidence that the work which the female toilet attendant performs is of less value than that performed by a man. The reasoning used is based on the 'approach' of the worker, thereby suggesting that the 'approach' of the woman based on 'housekeeping' warrants less pay than the 'approach' of a man based on labouring!

A further example of the low value accorded to women's role within the family when it is translated into economic terms is revealed in the case of a woman working as a housemother in a school for handicapped children, who lost her claim for equal pay with the housefather. The chair*man*, Sir Martin Edwards, observed in the written decision:

> A housemother is engaged to look after the younger boys and carry out domestic duties. A housefather is engaged to lead the growing boy to a better approach to life and help him in his problems. The roles are largely those of a mother and father in ordinary life; they are both important, but they are different . . . for these reasons, we find that the applicant is not engaged on like work with a man . . . full of admiration as we are for the work which she is doing . . .
>
> Coussins (1977, p. 47)

The decision reveals the tenacity of the ideology of women's subordination in those on whom women must depend for administration of the anti-discriminatory legislation.

This article has attempted to look at the legislation in terms of the new contradictions which it reveals. The PEWG pamphlet suggests that new contradictions will be revealed, but the Acts also highlight *existing contradictions* which remain untouched by the legislation. The supporters of the Acts believe, as did Engels, that women's entry into the labour market would provide the basis for potential freedom for women. However restricted the powers or aims of the Equal Pay Act, they do offer at least the potential for women's independence and the possibility of seeing women as the main wage earner, able to support a family.

It is within the context of the idea of the family wage that the Act has meant that women have found themselves in opposition to male union wage demands. The possibility of equal pay for women is in contradiction with the idea of the family wage traditionally fought for by male trade unions. The idea of the male as bread-winner is a crucial part of the ideology of masculinity. 'The wage packet is the provider of freedom, and independence; the particular prize of masculinity in work. . . . The wage packet as a kind of symbol of machismo dictates the domestic culture and economy and tyrannises both men and women' Willis (1977, p. 50).

The challenge which equal pay poses has to confront the ideology of masculinity as well as the economic level of the wage. The role of the unions and the need for their support to the claims of women under the Equal Pay Act cannot be over-emphasized.

In conclusion, since the terms of reference of the Act do not question the fundamental causes of women's oppression as being located in their reproductive role within the family, the results from these potentially progressive legislations can only be limited. Nevertheless, they do raise women's expectations and self-awareness and thus stimulate pressure for changes which will challenge the ways in which capitalism has exploited women's specific role in production and reproduction. An explanation of women's oppression which addresses the economic level *alone* is too limited, but the contradictions which the Acts reveal point to areas of potential challenge at the economic and ideological level of women's oppression located in their primary responsibility for reproduction.

Acknowledgements

The final draft of this article has been written by only four of us, but it comes out of work started by the Women's Studies Group 1976–7. The original writing group included Rachel Harrison, Val Levin and Roisin McDonough. Our thanks to them for discussing this article with us and particularly to Rachel Harrison who has helped through all the stages of toil.

Notes and references

1 See Article 7, footnote 5 (p. 153), and Article 9, footnote 3 (p. 192).

2 We do not look, in this section, at women's (very underpaid) waged work in the home – as child-minders, home workers, etc.

3 This article mainly draws on British sources, although at points American texts which were central in the debate are used.

4 An early account of housework as *work* can be found in Suzanne Gail (1968). Article 2 examines the concentration on experience in early WLM writing.

5 Their paper, 'Peckham Rye Women's Liberation' was given at the Oxford 1970 Women's Liberation Conference. Now available in M. Wandor (1972).

6 In this distinction, Shulamith Firestone's *The Dialectic of Sex* would be considered 'radical feminist'. See Mitchell (1971, pp. 91–6) for a discussion of this type of distinction.

7 Ann Oakley has substantially developed the sociology of housework. See Oakley (1974a) and with particular relevance to this article the first chapter of Oakley (1974b).

8 Adamson *et al.* (1975), while *recognizing* the importance of the ideological level in an analysis of women's subordination, do not substantially consider this level, and thus underestimate the *reality* of sexual divisions within the working class.

9 Sheila Rowbotham (in Wandor 1972, p. 192): 'The Ford's women also helped to make the question of women's specific oppression easier to discuss on the left. At first the men would only admit that working class women had anything to complain about.'

10 The 1974 Women and Socialism Conference papers have a fairly representative selection of positions, with a clear introduction by Caroline Freeman about the relevance of the debate to feminists.

11 See Marx (1976, pp. 270–80, pp. 709–24, pp. 1060–5); Althusser (1971a).

12 See Marx (1976, p. 717).

13 This article throughout assumes a 'typical' nuclear family. This is not to suggest that (a) we think all women are married, and/or live with men, and/or have children; (b) that women are not the only or main breadwinner in many families; (c) that there are not lots of other exceptions.

14 See Delmar (1976) and Sachs (1974) for feminist critiques of Engels.

15 See Robert Taylor, 'Sex objects: surprise statistics', *Spare Rib*, no. 19, for a summary of 1971 census figures.

16 The following three sections are particularly indebted to the work of the Political Economy of Women Group and to Jean Gardiner's own work.

17 The debate over productive and unproductive labour, and how the distinction is made and used by Marx, is extremely complex. The radical simplification we make, and the limitation of the problem to that of the characterization of housework, is in the context of a summary of, rather than a further contribution to, the debate over domestic labour. In this process, we refer only to elements in individual contributions to the debate, and although we have tried to avoid misrepresentation, this compression may well emerge as that.

18 Thus Seccombe has argued that 'necessary labour time' should be understood to include the wife's domestic labour. Cf. *New Left Review*, No. 83. Gardiner maintained (1975) that 'necessary labour time is not synonymous with the labour embodied in the reproduction and maintenance of labour power once one takes account of domestic labour'.

19 Surplus labour, in any mode of production, is labour performed by the labourer which is in excess of that necessary to ensure his/her survival. In the capitalist mode of production, labour power's unique quality as a commodity is that it creates value. Thus surplus value is the particular form of surplus labour in the capitalist mode of production, and is the basis of capital accumulation.

20 See PEWG (1975) for a summary of the arguments about whether domestic labour should be analysed within the capitalist mode of production, or as a 'client' mode of production articulating with it.

21 See *WPCS* No. 9 for 'orthodox' and 'unorthodox' in terms of the whole debate.

22 Unpublished papers to Birmingham and Coventry Feminist Research Workshop 1976. Catherine Hall, 'The Ideology of Domesticity', and Ray Harrison, 'Romance'.

23 This discussion, inevitably and regrettably through the limitations of our own work, remains at a general level, which is in contradiction with our argument for historical specificity in this area. It is the work of those feminists who have been involved in the domestic labour debate which has made it possible to see its shortcomings.

24 Caroline Freeman (1974) argues: 'We must aim to drive a wedge between the physical tasks of housework and the emotional services wives and mothers are expected to do as *women*.'

25 Freeman (1974) provides an extended criticism of this demand: 'The first defect of this argument is its misrepresentation of the marxist concept of "productive". The designation of housework as "unproductive" is taken as a slur, instead of as a technical concept allowing us to describe the relation between housework and capital. The productive/unproductive distinction does have implications for the sorts of struggle appropriate for different sorts of workers, but it does not *evaluate* their work.'

26 Masculine hegemony: We introduce Gramsci's concept of hegemony in a very condensed way. Another summary: '. . . hegemony, for Gramsci includes the ideological but cannot be reduced to that level, . . . it refers to the dialectical relation of class forces. Ideological dominance and subordination are not understood in isolation, but always as one, though crucially important, aspect of the relations of the classes and class fractions – economic and political, as well as ideological/cultural' (Hall, Lumley, McLennan 1977, p. 48). This concept is developed by Gramsci in the analysis of *class* relations, and there are obvious problems about 'lifting' it into an understanding of the relations of dominance and subordination between men and women (we are not suggesting that women are a subordinate class). We use the concept for two reasons: it 'includes the ideological but cannot be reduced to that level', which seems to us a central element in the way women live their subordination; it also involves the notion of 'consent' to domination by the subordinate group. Rowbotham (1973, pp. 38–9) discusses the use of the concept *male hegemony* (see also Article 7, footnote 8).

27 We would like to acknowledge the help of Richard Johnson, and John Clarke and Roisin McDonough's unpublished paper, 'The Family, State and Reproduction' (1977).

28 See Wilson (1977, p. 40), who notes how early welfare legislation's main preoccupation was with the work ethic.

29 See Greenwood and Young (1976) for a discussion of social democratic ideology in relation to the question of abortion.

30 See 'Out of the people: the politics of containment 1935–45' in *WPCS* No. 9.

31 In fact, not only was capital getting through nine generations of its workers in the span of three generations but, as A. Weir (1975) notes, with widespread epidemics, members of the ruling class were also carried off, e.g. Prince Albert died of cholera in 1865.

32 The Public Health Acts of 1848 and 1875 increased the standards of housing, sanitation and planning in the new industrial towns.

33 In fact the suffragettes themselves did not challenge the ideal of motherhood (PEWG 1975, p. 25).

34 A TUC deputation in 1941 pressed the government for a comprehensive review of social insurance.

35 See the article by A. Scott James in the *Picture Post*, 1943.

36 See Kincaid (1973).

37 A survey by Slater & Woodside (1951, p. 189) found public resentment to such inducement: '. . . they showed indignation that the production of large numbers of children could be expected of them as a duty.'

38 Prior to Beveridge's new legislation, all women, single and married, received lower social insurance and means-tested assistance benefits than men.

39 We are indebted to Roisin McDonough for this point.

40 For the characteristics of women's employment in this period see: Ministry of Labour (1974); Counter Information Services (1976); and Mackie and Pattullo (1977).

In the latter's introduction they ask, 'What is so special about women's work?'

The answer is that women's work is radically different from that done by men. Women workers are paid less than men, they work in a much smaller range of occupations, they do much more part-time work, and, in manufacturing, they tend to work alongside other women, in a small number of industries. Women are not as skilled as men, for a variety of reasons, and they are neither promoted as much as men nor are they to be found in great numbers in the professions and in management jobs.

And we would add that in the post-war period there has been a gradual increase in the number of women, particularly married women, over the age of thirty-five, working. Their work is predominantly in the service sector. They have become increasingly unionized but much less so than men.

41 Braverman (1976, p. 120) makes the following argument about the attention to the processes of capital accumulation:

> . . . household work, although it has been the special domain of women, is not thereby necessarily so central to the issues of women's liberation as might appear from this fact. On the contrary, it is the breakdown of the traditional household economy which has produced the present-day feminist movement. This movement in its modern form is almost entirely a product of women who have been summoned from the household by the requirements of the capital accumulation process, and subjected to experiences and stresses unknown in the previous thousands of years of household labour under a variety of social arrangements. Thus it is the analysis of their new situation that in my opinion occupies the place of the first importance in the theory of modern feminism.
>
> Let me add at once that none of this is said in order to disparage the need for an understanding of the specific forms and issues of household labour, of the working class family and of sexual divisions and tensions both within and outside the family . . .

42 See Bowlby (1951), Myrdal and Klein (1956), Gavron (1966), Fogarty, Rapoport and Rapoport (1972) for examples of shifting attitudes towards women's position in the family.

43 For how policy in relation to women's paid work was explicitly premised on male full employment and the 'family wage' and therefore was directed primarily at encouraging part time work, see Young Fabian Pamphlet II (1966) and Manpower Studies No. 1 (1964).

44 See PEWG (1975), Adamson *et al.* (1976) for arguments and details about the underprovision of child care facilities in this period.

45 See Weinbaum and Bridges (1976, pp. 90–1), who argue that women are 'consumption workers'. While men confront capital in the form of employers,

> . . . in the market for goods and services women confront capital in the form of commodities. . . . The work of consumption, while subject to and structured by capital embodies those needs – material and non-material – most antagonistic to capitalist production; and the contradiction between private production and socially determined needs is embodied in the activities of the housewife.
>
> While they consider the 'contradiction between their work in the market', i.e. their 'work' of buying, and 'their role in the home', using the commodities, they do not take up the contradictions which their position as wage labourers poses.

46 For more adequate accounts of capital's contradictory tendencies, particularly in relation to the labour process, see Braverman (1974), Marx (1976, Chapters 15, 25).

47 Marx's own consideration of women's paid work mainly focuses around an 'earlier' contradiction between the attempt to increase absolute surplus value – which 'founders' on the physical deterioration of the work force and the length of the working day – and the shift to extraction of relative surplus value. See Marx (1976, Chapters 10, 15) and Beechey (1977, p. 50).

48 See also Rowbotham (1973), chapter on 'Imperialism and everyday life'. Also Braverman (1974), particularly Chapter 13, 'The Universal Market', for examination of this whole area.

49 See Braverman (1974), Chapter 15, 'Clerical Workers' and Chapter 16, 'Service Occupations and Retail Trade'. Also Benét (1972) for an account of secretarial work. For general occupational changes see Ministry of Labour (1967), which indicates the importance of women's labour in those changes. On office work, Ministry of Labour (1968).

50 Seccombe (1975).

51 See Manpower Studies No. 1 (1964) and Young Fabian Pamphlet II (1966), which both make such arguments about the need for married women to work in the interest of the economy.

52 A clear indication of the intensive use of women's labour made by the clothes industry providing chain stores is the extent to which home workers are employed. See Hope *et al.* (1976, p. 89).

53 See Beechey (1977, pp. 51–4) to whom we are indebted for much of this argument.

54 See Mackintosh, Himmelweit and Taylor (1977). They discuss both the demand of 'woman's right to work' – the demand for economic independence which means at the same time the right to be exploited, and the work that that ignores: women's work in the home. At times of crises and cuts in services women are vulnerable on *both* fronts, thrown out of jobs *and* forced to do more work in the home.

55 In this context Beechey (1977, p. 53) discusses the relevance to women of the Marxist theory of 'regionalism' of uneven development, i.e. whether married or not, women's position is analogous to that of semi-proletarianized workers on the periphery of capitalist production in the Third

World, whose labour power sells at below its value because their wives are engaged in subsistence production on the land.

56 See Anderson *et al.* (1976) for a discussion of how part-time work has become a 'structural necessity' for capital in the post-Second World War period.

57 See Benét (1972), Toynbee (1977), Korda (1974) for accounts of secretarial work which discuss women's sexuality in their work role.

58 See CIS (1976) which discusses part-time/full-time unemployment in relation to the present economic crisis.

59 On home workers who are an ethnically diverse group see Hope *et al.* (1976), *Spare Rib*, no. 33. On black women, West Indian and Asian (the latter often doing homework) see Amos (1977), who describes how West Indian women – mothers who are often supporting families without a man's financial assistance – frequently take on night and early morning work so that they can look after their children during the day. Also Harris (1972).

60 See Willis (1977), who argues for masculinity as a construct which, articulating with class, *differentiates* men along a manual/mental division which working class men live out as a socially superior masculine/socially inferior feminine divide. It is however working class men's recognition of femininity, as it is lived by their wives, which allows that class division to be constructed through sexuality.

61 See the First World War example in munitions and engineering that Beechey gives (1977, p. 55).

62 See Brown (1976), who considers 'Women employees as a problem' which deals generally with these issues. Also Smith (1976) (in same volume – Barber and Allen 1976), who specifically considers the operation of 'masculine supremacy' in Fleet Street, both in terms of how men see women journalists who work alongside them and how women inhabit that masculine culture of work.

63 Baxandall *et al.* (1976, p. 4) discuss how 'executives object when their personal secretaries are removed to typing pools' because they no longer have their every 'whim' catered for, i.e. the 'serving' role which secretaries perform analogous to that of wives, works against the rationalization of the work process: it is resisted by secretaries *and* executives.

64 'Women do literally sell their bodies – if not as prostitutes, then to the publicity industries, modelling and so on – much as men and women sell their labour power' (Mitchell 1971, p. 55).

65 The Equal Pay Act (1970), as amended, now appears as Schedule 1 of the Sex Discrimination Act (1975).

66 For a fuller discussion of the history, and introduction to the Equal Pay Act, see Pinder (1969).

67 Even when they are unionized, women *rarely* get strong union backing to support them. This article does not attempt to argue the importance of the role of trade unions at *all stages of women's* fight for equal pay. For a more comprehensive argument see Coussins (1977).

18 Steppin' out of Babylon

Race, class and autonomy

Paul Gilroy

The communists have a long time ahead of them before they can do anything for themselves in this country. When they get there we will be for them. But meantime we are for ourselves.

MARCUS GARVEY

Socialism is not a fixed unchanging doctrine. As the world develops, people's insight increases and as new relations come into being, there arise new methods of achieving our goal.

ANTON PANNEKOEK

Even as moribund socialist and Eurocommunist parties cultivate the populist potential in national chauvinism as the answer to their growing marginality,[1] there is a positive side to the political crisis of the European workers' movement. It exists in the diverse attempts to explore the relation between socialism and democracy, to break with reductionist understandings of class relations, and to establish a perspective on social transformation which gives a primary place to the insights and demands of feminism. They are also fruits of that crisis. In place of the totalizing 'zero-sum' view of classes in struggle, which has become an albatross around the neck of socialists who will not turn and face the future, these advances substitute a new dialectic of 'people' and 'power bloc'. Its value is in an understanding of power relations capable of relating political developments in the workplace to those in the home, the neighbourhood and the queue for social security payments. This involves giving due weight to cultural factors, understood neither as purely autonomous nor as epiphenomena of economic determinations. This concluding chapter focuses on the cultural politics of 'black' people in this country, and the implications of their struggles for the institutions and practices of the British workers' movement. It is about *class* struggle. Our premise is therefore the problem of relating 'race' to class, not for sociological theory, but for socialist politics. We will explore the idea that no simple separation of race and class consciousness can be made. Our starting-point is Stuart Hall's observation that in contemporary Britain:

The class relations which inscribe the black fractions of the working class function as race relations. The two are inseparable. Race is the modality in which class relations are experienced.[2]

Race and class struggle – the Eurocommunist version

Unlike the sociologists we looked at in Chapter 2, the British left has been reluctant to approach the Pandora's box of racial politics. They have remained largely unaffected by over sixty years of black critical dialogue with Marxism presented most notably in the work of Garvey, Padmore, James, Wright, Fanon and Cox. The simplistic reduction of 'race' to class, which has guided their practice for so many years, has been thrown into confusion by intense and visible *black* struggles; and, at a different level, by the revival of interest in Marxist theory which has followed Althusser's reading of *Capital*.[3] Recently in a commendable if overdue attempt to confront the specificities of racial politics, sections of the left have reached out to the analyses of independent black political groupings only to dismiss them with a few fashionable insults.[4] These would-be architects of a national 'third way'[5] to democratic socialism, armed with a fervour for cultural politics derived from their idiosyncratic reading of Gramsci,[6] have begun to grapple with the political problems of constructing their version of working-class hegemony over the strategic alliances which their predilection for 'popular democratic' struggle has placed on the historical agenda. Forced back from relating gender to class by the resolutely autonomous politics of women who will not subsume feminism to an unmodified version of socialism,[7] these theorists have made 'race' a prime site on which to establish the value of their break from Stalinist tradition. Race has become important at last, not because of black suffering, but because it can be used to demonstrate the distance Marxists have travelled from economism. Unfortunately, the analysts of 'race' in this influential tendency have expounded the popular and democratic qualities of the struggle for black liberation to the point where its class character has escaped them: 'The struggle for racial equality and racial justice . . . needs to be seen *primarily* as a popular-democratic struggle'[8] (my emphasis).

Though widespread on the left, this position has been most systematically advocated by Gideon Ben-Tovim and John Gabriel,[9] who have acknowledged that it owes a great debt to the important theoretical contributions of Ernesto Laclau.[10] Some comment on their application of Laclau's theses to the theorization of racist ideology and politics is therefore required. His complex positions cannot be rehearsed here in any detail but the basic argument is that the ideological elements, which interpolate individuals and constitute them as subjects in discourse, are not ascribed by class. Discourses, which are not the intrinsic property of any particular class, become articulated to and by conflicting class practices in ideological struggle. They can serve a variety of political ends. His principal examples are the discourses of nationalism and democracy, both of which are particularly pertinent to the study of racial politics and structuration in late capitalist conditions. Drawing his illustration from the debate about the relation of socialism and nationalism in the KPD,[11] Laclau argues that the discourse of 'the nation' may be articulated into struggles where working-class interests are hegemonic, without antagonistic contradiction.[12] Non-economistic socialism becomes compatible with nationalism. He distinguishes thus between the German and British social formations as part of his argument against a necessarily negative character to popular nationalism in the working-class movement: 'In the British case, for example, the nationalist element is far less present – indeed the universalist element is predominant in democratic ideology.'[13]

This statement betrays regrettable ignorance of the unwholesome power of nationalism in British politics.[14] It will take far more than the will to create a 'pluralist national identity' to prise the jaws of the bulldog of British nationalism free from the flesh of the labour movement. It is precisely because the discourses of the British Nation and the British People are *racially exclusive* that a contradiction around race becomes a grave problem for those who adopt Laclau's framework. It may be that the benefits of imperialism have determined that 'the people' will always tend towards 'the race' in this country,[15] at any rate 'The British Nation' and 'The Island Race' have historically failed to, and cannot at present, incorporate black people. Indeed their alienness and externality to all things British and beautiful make it hard to imagine any such discourse which could accommodate their presence in a positive manner and retain its popular character. The popular discourse of the nation operates across the formal lines of class, and has been constructed *against* blacks. 'If increasing segments of the nation come to feel that neither church establishment nor unions care for their sentiments and distress, where may they not turn? The results could be catastrophic for all, not least for the minorities.'[16]

It should be clear that the authoritarian statism that signals the transformation of social democracy in this country has been secured on the basis of popular consent. For us, the racist interpellation of 'the nation' is a prime example of 'social democracy having provided authoritarian populism with popular contradictions on which to operate'.[17] Laclau explains that 'popular-democratic' discourses are constructed on the basis of opposition between 'The People' and 'The Power Bloc'. However, his followers remain unable to face the fact that for Britain in crisis, 'The People' are articulated into a racially specific discourse which has distinctly undemocratic consequences for the blacks whom it excludes. For example, where they follow the Fascist dictum and 'blame the bosses for the blacks', the 'white people' confront an ill-conceived vision of the power bloc, alone in racial purity and for the wrong reasons. This has serious implications for anti-racist practice, as we shall see; it is a concrete illustration of a theoretical point made elegantly by Nicos Mouzellis:

> Certain ideological themes (whether popular or not) can be so incongruent with the structural and *organisational* realities of a class that they cannot become dominant in its discourse. In other terms, if there is no one to one correspondence between classes and ideological themes, neither is there a completely arbitrary relationship between the two . . . once an ideological discourse takes a specific place and form within a concrete social formation, then it too becomes organised and fixed within limits imposed both by *the internal organisation of a class and by the overall socio-political context.*[18]
>
> (my emphasis)

This realization transposes the argument onto the historical plane of the social formation, from where it should be easier to see that the white working class of Great Britain was formed, and has matured, in evolving conditions of imperialist dominance. This historical perspective is yet more important because racial fragmentation is not a permanent or eternal fact. We shall argue later that the politics of working-class youth cultures offers the possibility that 'race', as a source of segmentation, may recede. This must be considered seriously in the wake of recent rioting where black and white youth stood shoulder to shoulder against the police.

Like Laclau, Gabriel and Ben-Tovim move from considering abstract, structural contradictions to examine ideological struggles. They scarcely pause over the concrete reality of the class institutions and organizational forms that comprise the 'mode of class struggle'[19] in which the subsequent articulation and disarticulation of interpellations takes place. They have attempted to address this weakness in recent work on anti-racist struggle and the democratization of the local state,[20] but merely replicate it by failing to come to terms with the lack of accountability and representativeness which they discovered in the 'race relations' agencies of Liverpool and Wolverhampton. What is valuable in their account is deformed by an idealism which cites 'lack of political will' as an adequate explanation of the government's failure to eliminate racial discrimination. It carries the unquestioned assumption that the problem of racial oppression is open to solutions at the level of policy rather than the level of politics. As the institutions of the social-democratic state change, forms of political action predicated on their continued existence must be subjected to rigorous criticism. The expectations which Gabriel, Ben-Tovim *et al.* have of such structures are puzzling, as is their view of them as unproblematically open to infusions of meaningful democratic, anti-racist practice, particularly in the light of the evidence they themselves produce to the contrary. Invoking a concept of democracy in general 'as if it were an ahistorical essence defined by its attributes',[21] they argue for the 'democratization' of these bodies without sensing the obligation to show *why* this has so far failed to develop. For example, it is difficult to disagree with their opinion that poor co-ordination and insufficient integration of the Commission for Racial Equality with other local state agencies has curtailed its efficiency. But the marginal relation of these institutions to the political lives of black communities, and their ubiquitous failure to tackle the problems of racial oppression cannot be seen as an unfortunate accident which can be rectified easily by an injection of ethereal accountability. It need not be reductionist or conspiratorial to enquire whether the popular and structural bases of racism in the 1980s are within the capacity of such agencies to resolve at all. The CRE/CRC complex does not have to be viewed as homogeneous or monolithic for it to be considered essentially irrelevant and intermittently obstructive. We should not be understood to be advocating abstention from these structures which may have valuable, if limited, local roles to play. 'The true question at issue is not the necessity of struggling for the democratisation of the state, both within and outside its limitations, but the scope, modalities and limits of such a struggle.'[22]

We are forced to argue that the authors have muddled the distinction between 'people's democratic rights and freedoms and the institutions of the bourgeois democratic state',[23] and further, that their position is only tenable at the cost of understanding race exclusively as an ideological or cultural issue, shorn of structural determinacy, which only 'subsequently intervenes at the level of the economy'.[24] It is secured by several assertions which fly in the face of historical and political reality.

The authors persistently invoke the possibility of 'broad based political struggles' and 'broad democratic alliances' against racism, though these have failed to materialise on cue. They ignore the inhibitions to the development of political breadth in this area which have crystallised around the pole of nationalism, but more importantly, also fail to examine the character of groups which *have* become involved in large-scale anti-racist mobilizations. Here the most glaring omission is their failure to take account of the experience of white youth and the Rock Against Racism initiative, which leaves a considerable gap in their analysis. However, if the reader is tempted to endorse their convenient vision in spite of these failings, it is well to recall the havoc wrought on the black movement in the United States by the 1935 'popular front' period which is the antecedent of this 'Eurocommunist' intervention.[25] There must be serious debate over whether this broad orientation is desirable or appropriate to the struggle against racism. It should not be emphasized at the expense of a refusal to consider the historic appeal of racist ideologies to the white working class.

Finally, the authors look into the political institutions of the black communities for the mirrored images of their own limited conceptions of political organization.[26] They simply assert that 'Third World ideologies' are 'relatively insignificant in Liverpool' and do not see any need to situate the culture of young Afro-Caribbean people on political terrain. It may be that black youth on Merseyside do not listen to reggae, build sound systems, or wear headwraps, tams and dreadlocks like their sisters and brothers in other parts of the country, but the authors shirk the obligation to make explicit their anxieties over the political limits of these ideologies. Gabriel and Ben-Tovim prefer to discuss the 'black para-professionals' who constitute the locally born black 'leadership', though they never explain who or what this group actually lead. If, as they explain, 'the form of organisation in fact depends on the context and the issue at stake', they give no idea of the issues which have generated an identifiable leadership of the type they have written about. Carchedi's observation that 'immigrant workers . . . have not only participated in existing forms of struggle: they have invented new ones'[27] means that serious analysis cannot take the *forms* of political struggle and organization for granted. The social formation, in which the different political traditions of immigrants and their children confront those of the British labour movement, has constructed the arena of politics on ground overshadowed by centuries of metropolitan capitalist development. But the dominance of these specific institutions and political forms should not be allowed to disrupt assessment of political traditions born elsewhere.

The other influential position that we must note before we proceed, is presented in the sociologistic pseudo-Marxism of Annie Phizacklea and Robert Miles.[28] Here, having advanced a social stratification problematic, the authors argue for a rigid separation of race and class consciousness which they claim to be able to quantify on the basis of questionnaire material. Though we must object to their conceptualization of autonomous black politics as a threat to the working-class movement comparable to that posed by organized Fascism,[29] we will not engage in a detailed critique of their work here because the remainder of this chapter presents our objections in a constructive rather than negative mode. We will attempt to tread a different path from the sociologism of their approach, and the idealism of Gabriel and Ben-Tovim. This involves taking explicit distance from 'race relations'. One or two general remarks about the way we conceive of 'race' and racism are therefore in order.

We are fully aware that the ideological status of the concept 'race' qualifies its analytic use. It is precisely this meaninglessness which persistently refers us to the construction, mobilization and pertinence of different forms of racist ideology and structuration in *specific historical circumstances*. We must examine the role of these ideologies in the complex articulation of classes in a social formation, and strive to discover the conditions of existence which permit the constitution of 'black' people in politics, ideology and economic life. Thus there can be no general theory of 'race' or 'race relations situations', only the historical resonance of racist ideologies and a specific ideological struggle by means of which real structural phenomena are misrecognised and distorted in the prisms of 'race'.[30]

Race, struggle and class formation

The impact of the feminist movement has recently ensured that the status of struggles against patriarchal oppression[31] has been raised as a political and theoretical problem for the versions of 'Marxism' which are also our targets here.[32] We must be wary of overemphasizing parallels between oppression by means of 'race' and oppression grounded in gender difference, yet racist and patriarchal ideologies both 'discover what other ideologies have to construct' in the natural differences they reference. The struggles against the forms of domination they structure suffer a common marginalization by 'sex and race blind' Marxist 'science', which has either ignored or provided reductionist accounts of racial and gender conflict. The way in which racism involves the control of fertility[33] as well as the control of labour power is one of several approaches to thinking about similarities between these forms of oppression. Yet the relation between the ways oppressions work must not be confused with the possibility of political alliances between the movements which struggle to end them. The liberation which these struggles anticipate does not exist in competition with the economic emancipation which may be its precondition, but political organization in these areas can only be built on an understanding of the primacy of racial and sexual determinations in the development of political consciousness, a point well made in a particular context by Richard Wright:

> Negro writers must accept the nationalist implications of their lives, not in order to encourage them, but in order to change and transcend them. They must accept the concept of nationalism because in order to transcend it they must possess and understand it . . . it means a nationalism that knows its origins, its limitations; and is aware of the dangers in its position.[34]

In acknowledgement of this point and armed with a view of the social formation as a contradictory but complex *unity*, our approach seeks to demonstrate the correspondence, connections, ruptures and breaks between capital, patriarchy and their racial structures. It would be wrong to deduce that the recognition of this unity compels its simple transfer into politics. The opposite is true, since our view of the complexity of these relations is such that the autonomy of different political forces in struggle is our premise.

Relations between patriarchal oppression and racisms are most clearly visible where each attempts to ground social differences in a spurious conception of nature. The structures of patriarchy are established in material conditions of a qualitatively different order from the subjugation of peoples who do not have 'white' skin, because political 'races' have no relation to the biology of 'racial characteristics', but we follow Timpanaro[35] in arguing that meaningful materialism must recognize that both have a biological dimension. This resides in the relation of biological determinations to the social construction of their significance. The fact that racisms have often comprised a struggle to establish biological relevance at group level, should not blind us to the 'conspicuous weight [of the biological level] in the determination of individual characteristics'.[36] Skin 'colour' is genetically determined no matter how biologically irrelevant we know it to be. Kate Soper's formulation of 'relatively autonomous biological determinations' sheds some light on a notoriously difficult problem:

> There may be a considerable degree of difference in the extent to which the effects of biological determinations are dominant or subordinate in their 'importance' for the person relative to the effects of other social or less directly biological determinations . . . one might want to suggest that they would be relatively dominant for most women and black persons today.[37]

Discussion of the 'reality' of these differences can rapidly degenerate into an academic issue at odds with materialist explanation, they are clearly real enough to be necessary though not sufficient conditions of existence for the emergence of racist ideologies which are always biologically reductionist. Racist pseudo-materialism must be fought with a scientifically founded materialism.[38]

The significance of these differences is contested in ideological struggle made possible by the contradictory nature of signs themselves, what Voloshinov has termed their multi-accentuality: 'in fact each living ideological sign has two faces like Janus. Any current curse word can become a word of praise, any current truth must inevitably sound to many other peoples the greatest lie.'[39]

He argues that this 'inner dialectic quality of the sign . . . comes out fully into the open only in times of social crisis or revolutionary change' but we want to suggest that this quality is also foregrounded in the struggle to make 'race' meaningful. This should be obvious where anti-racism challenges the status of visible differences designated racial, but is more important where the oppressed negate the very categories of their oppression, revealing that these categories mark sites and boundaries of class struggle in ideology, where they create cultures of resistance.

> Thus black musicians, for instance, had earlier subverted the word bad into its dialectical opposite, a term of approbation: 'Man, that cat is *bad*!' In its jazz usage, funky, obviously enough represented an extension of this tradition. To describe a musician as funky – i.e. unwashed, repellent – meant he was *worse* (that is, better) than just *bad* – he was . . . *funky*.[40]

This is one small illustration of Voloshinov's view of ideological struggle.

> Existence reflected in the sign is not merely reflected but refracted. How is this refraction of existence in the ideological sign determined? *By an intersecting of differently oriented social interests within one and the same sign community, i.e. by the class struggle.*[41]

In this case we are confronted by a class struggle in and through 'race'. The move from 'race' to class becomes crucial at this point because 'The division of humanity into social classes explains its history infinitely better than its division into races or peoples'.[42] However, it cannot be accomplished without reconceptualizing class in opposition to a Marxist orthodoxy which views the working class as a continuous historical subject[43] which, once formed, develops in a linear manner as a political actor. The class character of 'black' struggles in the present conjuncture will remain elusive until the following questions have been answered: 'What brings the particular conflict about? what led the participants to be organised in the particular form? what are the potential outcomes? what are the consequences of these outcomes for future development?'[44]

Prezworski continues:

> All these questions concern objective conditions: the conditions which made the emergence of a particular conflict possible, the conditions which made the particular organisations, ideology, relation of forces possible, the conditions which make particular outcomes plausible or implausible; and finally, but importantly, the conditions which may be created as the result of a particular conflict.

This way of conceptualizing class must be located as part of an attempt to give class struggle a degree of determinacy which it has relinquished in much recent Marxist writing.[45]

Following these methodological guidelines we will establish the boundaries of our concept of class struggle so that it includes the relentless processes by which classes are constituted – organized and disorganized – in politics, as well as the struggles between them once formed. In this way their synchronized movement, no longer pre-given in an ontology of classes, becomes a goal of class struggles themselves. The recent history of the racial segmentation of the British working class[46] readily demonstrates the instability of any view of that class as a continuous or homogeneous subject of history. We have found the idea of 'discontinuous but related histories' a useful way of illustrating the relation of 'black' to 'white' workers, who, though structurally related, were not always geographically proximate.

> If their blood has not mingled extensively with yours, their labour power has long since entered your economic blood stream. It is the sugar you stir, it is in the sinews of the infamous British sweet tooth, it is the tea leaves at the bottom of the British cuppa.[47]

We will also speak of blacks as racially demarcated class fractions in recognition of their power to constitute themselves as an autonomous social force in politics.[48]

In opposition to theorists who reduce race to custom or ethnicity as part of their own parochial battle to maintain the 'sociology of ethnic relations', we must locate racist and anti-racist ideology as well as the struggle for black liberation in a perspective on culture as a terrain of class conflicts. Space does not permit the detailed reproduction of Richard Johnson's important contribution to the theorization of working-class culture,[49] but it indicates the direction of our own enterprise:

> From this viewpoint 'working class' culture is the form in which labour is reproduced. . . . This process of reproduction, then, is always a contested transformation. Working class culture is formed in the struggle between capital's demand for particular forms of labour power and the search for a secure location within this relationship of dependency. The outcomes of such necessary struggles depend on what ideological and political forces are in play, and ultimately on the existence of socialist organisation with an integral relation to proletarian conditions and working class cultural forms.

Having said this, we must be immediately wary of simply tinting Johnson's argument a different shade, by tacking race on beyond the commas of class, and gender. The internalization of blacks by the working class is such that it requires more than that their presence is noted and the multicultural tones of metropolitan class struggle registered accordingly, though this may have polemical value. Marx's famous remark that 'the traditions of all dead generations weigh like a nightmare on the brains of the living' acquires new poignancy as the great grandchildren of martyred slaves and indentured labourers set up home in the land of those who had tormented their progenitors. The mass of black people who arrived here recently as fugitives from colonial underdevelopment, brought with them legacies of their political, ideological and economic struggles in Africa, the Caribbean and the Indian subcontinent, as well as the scars of imperialist violence.

Far from being fixed or unchanging, the accumulated histories of their far-flung resistance have brought a distinct quality to struggle at the cultural level in their new metropolitan home. For as Cabral points out: 'If imperialist domination has the vital need to practise cultural oppression, national liberation is necessarily an act of culture.'[50]

Sivanandan has argued that a disorganic articulation of capitalist relations of production with vestigial political and ideological forms tends to generate a contradiction between:

> The political regime and the people, with culture as the expression of resistance. And it is cultural resistance which . . . takes on new forms . . . in order fully to contest foreign domination. But culture in the periphery is not equally developed in all sectors of society . . . it does have a mass character . . . at the economic level, different exploitations in the different modes confuse the formal lines of class struggle but the common denominators of political oppression make for a mass movement. Hence the revolutions in these countries are not necessarily class, socialist revolutions – they do not begin as such anyway. They are not even nationalist revolutions as we know them. They are

> mass movements with national and revolutionary components – sometimes religious, sometimes secular, often both, but always against the repressive state and its imperial backers.[51]

This passage has been quoted at length not only because it refers us to the people/power-bloc contradiction we shall explore below, but because it hints at the political traditions which the blacks who arrived here since World War II brought with them. The process Sivanandan describes is the dying embers of the furnace in which their now-transplanted political consciousness was forged. They and their British-born children have preserved organic links with it, in their kitchens and temples – in their *communities*. Though their new struggles at the centre are diffused throughout a different structure in dominance, the lingering bile of slavery, indenture and colonialism remains – not in the supposedly pathological forms in which black households are organized, but in the forms of struggle, political philosophy, and revolutionary perspectives of non-European radical traditions, and the 'good sense' of their practical ideologies.

Working-class black communities

Localized struggles over education, racial violence and police practices continually reveal how black people have made use of notions of community to provide the axis along which to organize themselves. The concept of community is central to the view of class struggle presented here. It links distinct cultural and political traditions with a territorial dimension, to collective actions and consciousness[52] within the relation of 'economic patterns, political authority and uses of space'.[53] The idea of a racially demarcated collectivity of this type underlines the fact that community cannot be viewed as either static or given by some essential characteristics of the class or class fractions which come to constitute it. The cultural institutions which specify community have not been a continual feature of working-class life. The history of working-class communities, into which we will introduce the particular experiences of post-war immigrants and their children, is entwined with the processes of industrialization and social discipline[54] which established the city as a site of unique political conflicts. The form and relevance of community have therefore fluctuated with the changing social character of capitalist production which has accorded black labour a specific place, highlighting the means by which 'the dissociation of the upper and lower classes achieves form in the city itself'.[55] Even while the modern proletariat remained immature, the attempt to chart community necessarily required attention to the dynamics of class formation and political organization. The histories of the Minters, the Costermongers, the Scuttlers and their Molls[56] all present the working class organized on the basis of community in urban struggles long before blacks were concentrated as a replacement population in areas which, 'despite the demand for labour power . . . failed to attract sufficient white population'.[57] In an influential discussion which anticipates the direction of our work here, Gareth Stedman-Jones has pointed to a growing separation of the workplace from the domestic sphere as an important determination of the cultural and political patterns of urban workers in late-nineteenth-century London.[58] His example of the disruption of community illustrates how the concept can be useful in the connection of waged and domestic labour space. It is valuable not only where leisure practices impinge on the labour process,[59] but also where political organization forged outside the immediate processes of production (for blacks, with juridico-political apparatuses, organized racists or profiteering ghetto landlords) has effects on the struggle at work, and vice versa.

'The making of classes at work is *complemented* by the making of classes where people live; in both places, adaptive and rebellious responses to the class situation are inevitably closely intertwined.'[60]

Used to cover this connection, the concept denies the hasty separation of the social formation into purified instances. The struggle to construct community in the face of domination makes Eurocentric conceptualizations of 'the political' or 'the economic' hazardous if not misguided. To speak of community is to address complex articulated interests which blur these distinctions. It is to confront the materiality of hegemony and power, not in the abstract but evidenced in definite institutions and structures.

> When I think of the mechanics of power, I have in mind its capillary form of existence, at the point where power returns into the very grain of individuals, touches their gestures and attitudes, their discourses, apprenticeships and daily lives.[61]

Though primarily concerned with the labour-process end of the equation, Michael Burawoy has argued for a reformulation of the relation of politics in production to those outside, on ground afforded by the concept of hegemony.[62] The example of 'homeworking' discussed in Chapter 7 is an illustration of how the experiences of the black communities can make his point in acute form. 'The production of objects is simultaneously the production of relations',[63] and the significant political processes he has discovered in production assume racially specific form. They become articulated to racially bounded struggles, in ways which defy orthodox Marxist wisdom, even as front rooms are daily transformed into machine shops. The interrelation of production and the political space in which community develops is not satisfactorily understood at the level of production's immediate processes. In order to periodize class struggle and relate it to phases of accumulation, it must be remembered that capitalist production necessarily generates surplus labour power. The form in which this labour power appears in social formations is not determined mechanistically by accumulation, but directly by political struggles. 'Processes of formation of workers into a class are inextricably fused with the processes of organisation of surplus labour.'[64]

The place of community in this process will be illuminated in the discussion of black culture which follows, but it should be obvious that the move from full employment to structural unemployment heralds fundamental changes in the way surplus labour power appears as surplus population. We saw in Chapters 4 and 5 that new problems of social control and surveillance have been posed by this development and its context of crisis. It must be understood that the political traditions of black people, expressed in the solidarity and political strength of their communities, have determined a specific *territorialization* of social control; a general tendency noted by Dario Melossi[65] and elaborated in the British context by Lee Bridges[66] in his important analysis of urban social policy. Melossi points out that:

> At this point the discussion of social control becomes the discussion of the state, given that the hegemonic apparatus of the state is the most fundamental vehicle of social control. The struggle for hegemony, therefore, is not a question of more struggle within the institutions or in the localities, generically understood, but the construction . . . of real vehicles of hegemony.

Community is just such a vehicle.

We wish to locate the competing definitions of community, which occur in the struggle to create localized equivalents of the people/power-bloc contradiction, in this context.

Community policing initiatives recognize the political opportunities here in their attempt to organize ideological elements so that community is counterposed to crime, rather than to the police themselves. It should be appreciated that this is an overdue response to the fact that working-class communities have traditionally viewed the officers of the law as representatives of the power bloc.[67] The territorial dimension to social control of urban black communities is presented with startling clarity by the use of 'sus' laws to confine black youth to particular neighbourhoods[68] and by particularly brutal police operations which have become acceptable for black areas.[69] These give credence to the designation of black residential communities as 'colony areas' in which law and order techniques refined overseas can be applied with gusto and impunity.[70]

Ira Katznelson[71] and more recently John Lea[72] have elaborated the patterns of state intervention designed to secure the integration of blacks into the tripartite[73] political apparatuses of the social-democratic state. Their useful accounts are incomplete without some attention to the forms of struggle, organization and political ideology which made this corporatist relation possible. Above all, this requires consideration of the ideology of self-help which fused political representation and state intervention, disorganizing black discontent and channelling it into 'quasi-colonial institutional structures . . . [which would] deal with the issue of race outside traditional political arenas'.[74] If the political consensus over containing the black problem owed something to the colonial period, the black organizations which struggled with it on the terrain of community made this connection increasingly explicit – unfortunately, often in forms which drew the most unhelpful parallels with the situation in the Third World.[75] In a nationalist framework which could do little more than present an inverted image of the oppressor's power, the issue of black control of self-help projects sometimes obscured the nature of the schemes themselves. By restricting their analysis to racial parameters, the nationalist self-help groups became easy meat for state institutions already placing a premium on self-help 'as a response to the threat posed by alienated black youth'.[76] The Community Relations Commission's self-help report for 1976 spells out the limits of their approach:

> Some of the leaders of self-help groups have strong political views particularly with regard to the struggles for freedom for blacks in the USA and Africa. These do not, however, appear to have any significant effect on the work of these organisations.[77]

In both black communities generational conflict expressed deeper debates over political responses, rather than aberrant familial practices. Such conflicts were always premised on the fundamental unity of the community, and conducted within the repertoire of its political traditions, both of organization and ideology. Tension between Asian Youth Movements and the IWA organizations is the clearest example of this process, posing the distinction between corporate and autonomous modes of class struggle in complex fashion, overdetermined by the peasant political traditions from which both have sprouted.[78]

Black people, the power bloc and cultural politics

Though parallel arguments could be constructed from the experience of Asian blacks from Africa and the Indian subcontinent, the remainder of this chapter is focused around the popular culture and politics of Britons of Afro-Caribbean descent. Through their experience we will demonstrate that the mass of blacks in this country are engaged in a complex political and ideological struggle. This is organized through the collective refusal of capitalist domination which they experience in the form of racial oppression. We will explore the basis for a view of their struggles as processes of class struggle, here constituted by and through the dialectical experience of racism. By this, we refer to popular and theoretical racist ideologies, racialist practices and, most importantly, the struggles of the oppressed to contest and transform the categories of their oppression into a source of political strength: their collective refusal of racial domination.

It is necessary to account for the cultural dimension to the political struggles of 'black' people. This involves realizing that the politics of black liberation is necessarily a cultural politics. Coons, Pakis, Nig-nogs, Sambos and Wogs are social constructions *in culture*. Marx's 'On the Jewish question'[79] is relevant to this theme. Towards the end of this notoriously oblique text he attempts to explore the connection between 'Judaism', which for him is the ideology of civil society *not* of the Jews themselves – 'civil society ceaselessly begets the Jew from its own entrails' – and Germany, which requires the 'Jew' at a particular stage of its development. The difficult, and not entirely consistent usage of the term 'Jew', points to the way oppressed people have to locate the ideologies which oppress them historically as the first step to their transcendence. Cedric Robinson[80] has extended Marx's line of thought and demonstrated its applicability to the construction of 'the Negro' in nineteenth-century America. Drawing on C. L. R. James's view[81] of voodoo as the ideology of the Haitian revolution, he speculates that Marx's essay provides a useful means of understanding the complex negation of ideas and images which characterizes the cultural struggles of colonized people. This, if it is to be successful, must move beyond a simple nationalist mirror-image of the colonizer's conquering vision. This nationalist reaction, which has an important place in the recent racial politics of this country, is only a partial and unsatisfactory response to racial domination. Following Robinson, we shall focus on a more profound negation of 'race' and of Europe to be found at the core of the cultural politics of British blacks. It is the key to understanding the relatively recent supersession of nationalist politics by an international revolutionary movement of black people, the most visible manifestations of which are organized popular currents in the Caribbean, America and Britain which have been identified by the dominant ideology as 'Ethiopianism' or 'Rastafarianism'. Horace Campbell[82] and Sebastian Clarke[83] have delivered timely reminders that 'Ethiopianism' is no recent development. There is no space here to consider how the same profound comprehension of the need 'to reverse the ideas, to reverse the values, to reverse even the conceptualisations of movement, causality, forces'[84] links mass organization of African peoples from Chilembwe to Garvey, from Njama and Mwiarma to Omulú.[85] Contemporary Britain is neither Africa nor the Caribbean, but the distinct political traditions of African people must be borne in mind. Contrary to the views of sociologists of 'acculturation' they are present in the practice of black movements today.[86]

This brings us to an examination of what sociological orthodoxy now defines as 'the Rastafarian movement'.[87] Our own view of these phenomena involves considerable redefinition of their contours, boundaries and supposed aims. The critique of sociological theories is set out in Chapter 3; however, it is important to emphasize that we do not consider the sociology of religion as an adequate starting-point for analysis, not least because the pan-Africanist philosophy which characterizes the movement has been in an elliptical and sometimes reluctant dialogue with revolutionary Marxism since the days of Garvey and Randolph.[88] We must also challenge the idea of simple correspondences between the movement in Britain and its forms elsewhere. Though wherever it has taken root, 'Rastafari culture remains an indelible link between the resistance of the maroons, the pan-africanist appeal of Marcus Garvey, the materialist and historical analysis of Walter Rodney and the defiance of reggae.'[89]

We must be careful not to fudge the differences between its political and ideological complexions in Grenada, Dominica and Jamaica let alone amidst the relation of forces in this country where the pertinence of racial politics shifts Rasta struggle into an altogether different mode. The relatively small number of black people here places an immediate limit on the populist appeal of these ideas. The impact of Afro-Caribbean culture in general, and through reggae, Rastafarianism in particular, on the lives and politics of white working-class youth is too often overlooked, but it is the mass character of the movement in the black communities which provides our starting-point.

This means that we take issue with any tendency to define the movement in a crude empirical manner by offering a number of dogmatic tenets to which 'cultists' are subsequently found to subscribe.[90] Instead, we locate the symbols of 'dread', by which researchers have so far identified cult-affiliates, at one end of a broad continuum of belief which spans both age and gender difference. At this extreme, an open signification of 'dreadness' – the wearing of headwraps, hats, dreadlocks, long skirts and Ethiopian colours – merely transposes the *difference* already immanent in the unacceptable attribute of dark skin into open semiotic struggle characteristic of youth subculture.[91] In this case the struggle is against categories associated with the whole racial group. These symbols consolidate the group's collective identity, and become meaningful to those who do not signify their political philosophy in such overt ways. The growing of dreadlocks which draws attention to that least acceptable attribute of 'blackness' – woolly hair – must be seen as superseding the 'afros' and 'naturals' which, once a focus for the redefinition of black as beautiful, faded into the commonplace from the front page of Ebony: 'I and I grow dreadlocks, i.e. uncut and uncombed locks as a symbol of cultural rebellion, since I and I as Africans must establish our own standards of beauty, niceness and discipline.'[92]

Thus the confrontation in style acts as a focal point for dread and baldhead alike, and the scope of the movement must not be underestimated by dwelling on the stylized defiance of its younger and more flamboyant adherents. The second problem with any attempt to approach these struggles through a 'youth subculture' problematic, is its inherent masculinism.[93] Few analysts have perceived that there are female Rastafari. Even fewer discuss their specific relation to the movement. Ernest Cashmore views 'Rasta patriarchy' as a revolt against the supposed matriarchy of the 'normal' West Indian family. For him, as with Dick Hebdige, it appears that youth subculture has provided the perch from which he has been able to engage the young locksmen in conversation. The ideology of the 'queen' in Rasta discourse represents the space from which Rasta women have begun to wage their distinct form of feminist struggle. The cultural offensive represented by reggae music is so central to the political development of the movement that it would be surprising if this trend were not represented at that level. One small but interesting example of the struggle taking place is to be found in the record 'Black Woman' released by Judy Mowatt in the summer of 1979. It formed the basis of several 'Black Woman Experience' stage presentations,[94] and proved so popular during the following eighteen months that a major white-owned record company stepped in to provide a British release for the disc, which had previously only been available through comparatively restricted outlets in black areas. Changes in the packaging and design of the subsequent re-released version are evidence of the impact of the images on the original record sleeve. Mowatt had made 'the queen' the starting point for a redefinition of the Rasta woman, establishing her in an activist role waging struggles distinct from but complementary to those of her brethren. The front was a star of Israel on which a red, gold and green cross had been superimposed. This was divided into five equal squares; in each of the surrounding four was a picture of Mowatt attired as an African queen. In the central square was a very different portrait of her in the male and militant uniform of dread, seemingly prepared to do battle with the forces of Babylon. On the back was a full face view of her, this time with her hair uncovered in explicit defiance of the taboo which some more theologically inclined Rastas have placed on females. The contrasting images posed an explicit challenge to male domination, but in a context which emphasized the continuity of Rasta ideology. The repackaged version disrupted all this with a large 'glamorous' picture of her conventionally attired. Her songs 'Strength To Go Through', 'Slave Queen' and 'Black Woman' were the basis of the record's great popularity at the grass-roots, but it was in 'Sisters' Chant' that Mowatt made her straightforward demand for the validity of 'feminist' Rastafari in language which recalled the nineteenth-century feminists who distinguished between 'man' and 'god'.[95]

Once dread style has been set aside as the essential qualification for 'cult membership', it becomes clear that many older black people share the movement's pan-Africanist sentiments and take pride in its refusal of racial domination. It is often forgotten that blacks arrived here bearing traditions of anti-colonial struggle wherever they set out from. Older West Indians have encountered the discourse of Rasta before, and though sometimes critical of it, many of the first generation we interviewed in preparing this volume were happy to recount tales of their contact with the Garveyites 'at home'. Their sympathy with the movement should be no surprise; the solidarity it provides the whole community appears to offer a refuge from the new pressures of *popular* racism. The formation of parents' groups and defence organizations in both black communities confirms that a high level of state harassment has effected the consolidation of black households across generational lines. Whole families have been drawn into conflict on the basis of immigration laws and police practices which do not differentiate on age lines, but construct black households as special objects of state policy.[96]

The breadth of the Rastas' cultural intervention is also important here. Like the 'Bop' players of the sixties who absorbed black nationalism and Elijah Mohammed alike, reggae musicians have been converted to Rasta in such numbers that it has become impossible to discuss one without the other. Though there are certain styles which appeal more to older people, the universal popularity of Bob Marley is a good illustration of how these different preferences have been spanned. In the West Indian orientation to leisure, the raw material of white youth cultures becomes the background music to an old age pensioner's night out. Closure of shebeens has meant that a growing number of pubs in black areas have opened their doors to reggae music at the weekend. Though these 'hi-fis' are no match for the powerful sound systems of the second generation, they are in many ways a counterpart, catering for the taste of their parents with a selection of 'lovers' ' reggae, soca and the occasional soul record. The popularity of communalist ideology and its implicit politics may also be gauged by the widespread use of Rasta concepts and speech patterns by those who do not wish to express their affiliation or interests more overtly. Such language is able to convey commitment in a selective or intermittent manner, and its racially exclusive mode invites speakers to appropriate the ideas which appeal to them without being pigeon-holed by the oppressor. It is not only that young black people devoid of locks address each other habitually as 'Rasta', though such a group does exist and is far too large to be explained away by Ken Pryce's rather puzzling view of them as 'inbetweeners'.[97] Neither stigmas attached to the wearing of long hair nor the barrier supposedly created by participation in waged labour explain very much. We must resist the equation of Rasta politics with work refusal. Mass unemployment affects dread and baldhead alike, blurring the edges of any simple assessment. (There may be a connection with the reluctance to register with statutory services, but that is an altogether different political struggle.) In truth, the operation of a shared language, far more than the colours and vestimentary codes of dread style, marks the frontiers of a discursive community in which deep disagreement is possible without condemnation or schism. Here, racial interpellations predominate and the contradictions which arise remain in non-antagonistic form. This is a partial explanation of the avowed Rasta's insistence that all black people are Rasta whether they know it or not. This has been a difficult point for some sociologists to digest as the cohesion it invokes contradicts the dominant view of the dreads as a minority within a minority, suffering the resentment of their own people in addition to racial subjugation. This view, which separates the visible Rasta from the whole community, ignores the links forged in sharing language at its cost, a point acutely observed by Joseph Owens:

> It may not always be possible to tell a rasta by his [*sic*] appearance, but in the absence of other signs his speech will frequently reveal his identity. Once two rastas told me that they had been forced out of a job because they were rastas. As they had no locks and could not be visibly identified as rastas, I enquired how the employer knew. They replied: 'By I and I argument. Man know I and I by I and I argument'.[98]

Within this linguistic community the introduction of specifically Rasta concepts is an attempt to bring order to the practical ideology and 'good sense' of the black community. This is:

> not the result of any systematic educational activity on the part of an already conscious leading group, but (has) been formed through the everyday experience illuminated by 'common sense', i.e. by the practical popular conception of the world – what is unimaginatively called 'instinct', although it is in fact a primitive and elementary historical acquisition.[99]

The analytic tendency of Rasta concepts is in opposition to blind acceptance of the world as it appears and the body of ideas which maintain it: 'ism and schism'. Rastas are critical. Coherent explanation that operates at deeper levels is required, and Rastas strive towards a historical theorization of social dynamics – 'overstanding', 'truth and rights' – which is the result of collective processes of dialectical enquiry aptly named 'reasoning'. The Rastas' refusal of complicity with the world creates a distance from which these operations are possible. The philosophical contours of their view of the world are determined by a realism – 'burning all illusions' – and an anthropocentric materialism which not only identifies the present state of oppression as a cohesive human creation – Babylon *system* – but simultaneously acknowledges the potential power of working people to transform it: 'is one ting I say about *any* ghetto, is one ting can solve all ghetto prablem. Togedaness. If de people jus know dat all of us comin off de poorer side a town mus stick togeda as poor people, we mash up anyting'[100] (my emphasis).

This same anthropocentrism points to the conclusion that we are not dealing with a religious movement, but with sophisticated criticism of an oppressed people's paralysing encounter with religion.

> Most people think great god will come from the sky
> take away everything, make everybody feel high
> but if you know what life is worth
> you will look for yours on earth
> now you see the light, you stand up for your rights.[101]

The fact that this criticism appears partially in vestigial religious form should not encourage us to underestimate the extent of the rupture it represents. 'When I look at the photograph of Selassie I, I am not looking at God, nor if I look at Eyesus Christus, these are merely representations for God is I and I and has always been.'[102]

This denial of God, and the rasta insistence that heaven is on earth and nowhere else are the kindling of the process in which, 'The criticism of heaven turns into the criticism of earth, the criticism of religion into the criticism of law, and the criticism of theology into the criticism of politics.'[103]

Even the minority of Rastafari who openly proclaim the divinity of Haile Selassie I are not making simple religious statements. The most theological amongst them will still affirm the primacy of struggle for liberation in the present. Religion has always been a site of struggle for the colonized downtrodden and enslaved. Writing of slave revolts Genovese points out that:

> Until the nineteenth century, and even then albeit with altered content, religion provided the ideological rallying point for revolt. In the Caribbean and in South America religious leaders – Obeahmen, Myalmen, Vodun priests, Nanigos, muslim teachers – led, inspired or provided vital sanction for one revolt after another.[104]

Here, religion became a central pillar in the refusal of servitude rather than 'the sigh of the oppressed creature'. Closer to home, Stephen Yeo has recently demonstrated that the radical potential of religious ideology is not the sole property of African and Asian traditions.[105]

> The 1880s and 1890s were . . . a time of great organisational creativity. This was particularly manifest in the religion of socialism area. Not only was there a Labour Church, but a large number of 'allied social movements' – including Socialist Churches, the Labour Brotherhood, Brotherhood Churches and The Labour Army. . . . Groups gathered to follow prophets – Whitmanites in Bolton, Tolstoyans in Purleigh, Ruskinians in Liverpool – giving a grounding in reality to Katherine Conway's purple vision of a socialist guru in her 'The Religion of Socialism'.

The 'primary semantic function' of the bible in the popular culture of the Caribbean has facilitated an extremely selective and partisan appropriation of it by Rastas mindful of the long and bitter struggles master and slave fought across its pages. The sociologists we looked at in Chapter 3 who view 'religion' as a brake on the development of political consciousness, have not explained the Rastas' disinterest in the New Testament gospels, or their predilection for Psalms, Revelation, and the history of the Children of Israel.

Youth culture and the crisis

The popular character of Rasta politics leads us to the role of music in its dissemination and development. In Britain, the sphere of leisure no less than that of work has hosted the extraordinary encounter between the political traditions of disorganic development in the periphery and the urban working class at the centre. Youth culture has also created an important space for dialogue between black youth from the different communities. Asian youth movements have been inspired by the combativity of Afro-Caribbean young people which has received spectacular press coverage while their own equally tenacious defence of their communities remains concealed behind a stereotype of passivity. At a confrontation in

Coventry in May 1981 which was under-reported for this very reason, young Asians chanted 'Brixton, Brixton' as they charged the police ranks.[106] The youth movements' support for the Chapeltown Rasta Defence Organisation (Leeds) campaign for the reinstatement of Rasta school students suspended for refusing to cut their hair, is a concrete example of how common oppression can generate united black struggle.[107]

The transformation of politics in post-war Britain – the welfare state and changes in production in particular – presaged new kinds of political organization and new sites of struggle. The arrival of black settlers proved to be both catalyst and inspiration to the grandchildren of jingoism who were quick to ape, absorb and adapt the styles and cultural practices which were black relics of a distant colonial engagement with their foreparents. Dick Hebdige has established the connection between white youth cultures and the presence of a black citizenry: 'We can watch played out on the loaded surfaces of the British working-class youth cultures a phantom history of race relations since the war.'[108]

By extending his argument, we can begin to see the fundamental class character of black cultural struggles in a different light, as well as the articulation of 'race' around the contradiction between capital and labour in ways that the dominance of corporatist political representation has obscured. The reification of pleasure in youth cultures has contradictory effects in the struggle for political space and cultural power. The mass mobilizations of white youth it spawned, though always both cultural and political, have not always been anti-racist. There are no guarantees of progressive outcomes even in the fact that neo-Fascists and nationalist interventions in this field identify the political power of black culture as the prime obstacle to success. 'Britain's Youth have had imposed on them, nigger music, nigger culture, jungle standards and jungle culture.'[109]

Regardless of the ultimate direction of the popular struggle of white youth, there are grounds to argue that its form has been prefigured in the resistances of the black communities, in much the same way that the movement of black Americans in the 1960s determined the patterns of autonomous protest which followed it:

> Without Black Brotherhood, there would have been no sisterhood; without Black Power and Black Pride there would have been no Gay Power and Gay Pride. The movement against the abuse of powers of the state . . . derived much of its strength and purpose from the exposure of the F.B.I.'s surveillance and harassment of the Black Panthers and Black Muslims. . . . Only the Environmental Movement did not have the Black Movement as a central organisational fact or as a defining political metaphor and inspiration.[110]

Premised on the now-fading affluence of the teenage consumer and the mass-communications aspect of the leisure industries, the mechanisms of white youth culture provided the means to popularize oppositional ideas forged in the powerlessness of youth.[111] Since the incorporation of reggae into the subcultural repertoire in the late sixties, political themes have begun to displace moral and generational conflict as the raw material of young people's cultural expression. The shift between The Who's 'My Generation', The Sex Pistols' 'Anarchy in the UK' and The Beat's 'Stand Down Margaret' exemplifies this process, which has been fuelled at each stage by youth's own perception of economic crisis and the consequent crisis of social relations. It was in 'punk' subculture that youth's marginality came face to face with these crises. In the realization that 'there's no future, and England's dreaming' the relation of white to black youth took on its most complex form. Hebdige has described this phase as the self-conscious construction of a white 'ethnicity'. The 'disavowal of Britishness' and 'symbolic treason' implicit in 'God Save The Queen', as well as the punks' iconoclastic use of the Union Jack and the Queen's face, are interpreted as a 'white translation' of black subcultural style which the nationalist momentum of Rastafarian self-assertion had placed out of reach. The post-Rasta denial of access to the always-preferable black music, style and leisure pursuits was a severe shock; blacks were not going to lose reggae as they had lost soul to the mods.

> The themes of Back to Africa and Ethiopianism celebrated in reggae made no concessions to the sensibilities of a white audience. Reggae's blackness was proscriptive. It was an alien essence, a foreign body which implicitly threatened mainstream British culture from within, and as such it resonated with punk's adopted values – anarchy, surrender and decline.[112]

This relationship, made concrete in the alliance of punk and reggae musicians under the banner of 'Rock Against Racism', was short-lived. There were contradictions in the nationalist symbols which punks had attempted to subvert, and the decisively working-class character of their movement harked back to an earlier subcultural style from which it had emerged.[113] The realization that black youth would insist on the particularity of their oppression no matter how much the whites identified with Rastafari, precisely because white interest was a threat to the autonomy of the movement, returned white youth to the drab horizons of the skinhead cult with particular bitterness. The familiar 'Crombie' coat and denim jacket returned, this time with Union Jacks and even swastikas stitched neatly onto breast pockets. This is the point at which white youths' culture intersects with the politics of organized Fascism, which acknowledging their experience and their potential power in their own language, speaks to their predicament with a hollow promise of 'jobs for white workers'. The white youth who could accept the racial limitations Rasta placed on their engagement with black culture came to constitute the core of the 'two-tone' subculture which synthesized punk and reggae. Those who were unable to make this adjustment retained their love of reggae – visible in their updating of the sixties skinhead 'ska' cult, constructing a white power ideology from common-sense racism to match the black power which intimidated them. The steady appeal of reggae to white youth throughout the sixties culminated in the skinheads' mass migration to Wembley in the summer of 1969. The success of the Reggae Festival there signified to the leisure industry the promise of mass marketing the music to whites. The independent distributors of reggae had expanded their business on the profits from the inevitably restricted black market to which white companies had little access.[114] They were keen to expand further. The growth of local radio with minority appeal music programming in the 1970–2 period consolidated the black market – once again, making the music available to the white youths, excluded from the clubs they had shared with the 'rudies' three years earlier by their own Powellism and the rhetoric of black power which had crossed the Atlantic to confront it to the strains of 'Young, Gifted and Black'.

The link between the multinational entertainment corporation and the purveyors of reggae to the ghettoes of Britain was secured by a Jamaican exile whose company 'Island Records' is now an appendage of EMI.[115] Island knew that they would have to find the right star to take black music to the white pop fan. Their prototype was Jimmy Cliff, a Jamaican former child star with a substantial following at the roots. Music alone could not transcend the racial hostility that narrowed the market. The company devised a plan to package Cliff and reggae music in an individualistic and romanticized vision of black life in the Caribbean, which posed no threat to the white consumers and was well inside the racist image of blacks as violent, licentious and primitive. The film 'The Harder They Come' starred Cliff as a 'rude-boy' musician turned gunman. The strategy of using film to circumvent the racial hostility of white fans has been an ongoing feature of Island's marketing. 'Exodus' – a film of Bob Marley on stage – and the more contradictory 'Rockers' made filmed live performances available to whites who had neither the inclination nor the opportunity to attend the actual concert hall. The film's initially unsuccessful release in 1972 ironically marks the beginning of the mass movement of black British youth towards Rastafari. It was not Cliff's dated and hopeless hero who captured the imagination of black crowds at The Ace, The Rio and The Kilburn State, but the studied philosophical cool of his dread co-star Ras Daniel Hartman, a well-known artist and poet. The film did not dwell on Rasta, but Hartman's performance whetted the appetites of young black people still hungry from their frustrating encounter with the British black power movement. The leap towards mass internalization of Rasta was not completed until the following year when the activity of 'religiously' inclined Rasta organizations in London formed the backdrop to the release of two LP records by The Wailers. Island pushed 'Catch a Fire' and 'Burning' through both roots and pop distributive networks. Cashmore is correct to situate Bob Marley at the centre of the Rasta movement's growth but the Marley who cranked this historical machinery was not the leather-jacketed pop star who crooned 'No Woman No Cry' two years later. He was the roots politician of these earlier recordings.

> We gonna be burnin' and a lootin' tonight
> (to survive, yeah)
> burnin' and a lootin' tonight
> (save your babies lives)
> burning all pollution tonight
> burning all illusions tonight[116]

These records presented a compulsive unity of populist anti-imperialist politics and Rasta themes which, though lost on the hoped-for white fans, set the black community aflame. Island Records' attempt to build a new market for reggae while retaining contact with roots distributors tempted other companies to try and connect markets. Unsuccessful promotion to whites was a common feature of a crop of releases which only fanned the flames that The Wailers had sparked.[117] When 'The Harder They Come' was relaunched in 1973 the blacks flocked to see it and the whites stayed away. The Wailers were unable to dislodge Johnny Nash from the pop chart, and their dread lyricism remained unpalatable to the white fans. Marley's eventual breakthrough was achieved after the original band had broken up, and he had returned to London as a solo star in the wake of 'Natty Dread'. His transformation from Wailer to superstar was accomplished at the expense of much of his support among the youth. As his long-term project for the internationalism of Rasta took shape, he worked to recover the respect of his first audience. The trail he made has been followed by other performers more skilled in the pedagogy of popular Rasta politics. Their historical researches and political abstractions brought maturity to the new Ethiopianism, simultaneously polarizing the politics of white youth culture.

Bass culture

Many commentators have remained curiously mute on the subject of the music of the black culture they scrutinize. Others who have heard a voice of 'protest' interpret it with bizarre insensitivity. Cashmore contends that the expression of discontent in reggae 'acted to slough off any latent militancy in the black working-class, by translating the hostility into musical form rather than converting it into programmatic proposals'.[118] He is unable to understand that: 'Committed art in the proper sense is not intended to generate ameliorative measures, legislative acts or practical institutions . . . but to work at the level of fundamental attitudes.'[119]

Barry Troyna, whose contemptible methodology has not prevented him from soliciting 'differential commitment to ethnic identity' from the black youth he has 'sampled', believes that the social and political orientations of young blacks may be read off from their musical preferences.[120] His position has been influential and merits detailed examination. The typology of personalities he has adapted from Ken Pryce, is problematic enough, but even this pales into insignificance beside the misconceptions and distortions of black culture which inform his all-too-cosy model. Like Cashmore he locates the 'oppositional element' in reggae at the level of its lyrics, but goes on to divide the music into 'heavy' and 'sweet' categories as a result of the differences he claims to discern in them. Thus on the rare occasion that his 'compromisers' try 'heavy' reggae they are only interested in the music, whereas the 'rejectors' rather conveniently 'insist that the lyrics and not the music form the most important constituent of a record'. Troyna explains that: 'The Rastafarian inspired lyrics inform and help structure their particular perspectives and provide them with their own distinctive and impenetrable group argot.'

While reggae music may be subdivided into 'lovers' and 'roots' styles which echo Troyna's categories, this distinction *does not apply at the level of lyrics*. The contrast relates to different dance styles and the overlapping social relations in which they appear. Roots records usually belong to sexually segregated dancing, and lovers' rock is more often the accompaniment to couples dancing together.[121] The form of reggae music spans the extremities that these styles represent. A particularly resonant lyric or melody may draw temporary attention to one or the other, but this does not alter the need to approach each recording as a complex unity of words and music in its own right. The inept attempt to cast Burning Spear in the role of Joan Baez to the Rasta protest movement closes off the discussion of form and ignores the fact that the dominant form of reggae is Dub.[122] Dub is not a style of music as such, it is a process of enrichment in which music is deconstructed and the meaning of its lyrics transformed and expanded. The Dub process is applied to 'sweet' and 'heavy' reggae alike. The Dub experience is an intrinsic element of the social relations in which *all* reggae reveals its power – in the lounge bar of a pub on Sunday night, or in the heat of a sound-system competition. Only the few reggae records which are aimed exclusively at the white pop market lack a Dubbed version of the same tune on their 'B' side.

In the social context, these two different versions would be played as a pair, the Dub following the un-Dubbed version and forcing the listeners into a critical position by its dismantling of the former piece. A few fragments of the original lyric will have been left intact in the Dub version; these are a springboard for the disc-jockey's own improvised comments on its theme. Thus new meanings are created and the initial meanings modified in a process of selection and transformation which becomes a key source of pleasure for the dancing crowd. The sounds of the instruments in the Dub version are modified by modern sound processing techniques and skilful editing of the tape on which it was recorded. Phasers, Flangers, Delay Lines, Echo, Reverb and the addition of sound effects in particular gunfire, explosions, birdsong, sirens, animals, or even scratches and tape sounds which remind the audience they are listening to a recording, all play their part. Focusing on both the processed and natural sounds of each instrument in turn, and then in a variety of combinations with sound effects mixed in, the Dub engineer is able to expose the musical anatomy of the piece, showing how each layer of instrumentation complements the others to form a complex whole. For example, in the Dub version of the song 'General Penitentiary' by Black Uhuru an insistent syndrum becomes a cell door repeatedly slamming shut, and the only phrase left intact is the line 'down in this dark cell'. A slightly more complex example is furnished by the Wailing Souls whose 'Kingdom Rise and Kingdom Fall' is at the top of the chart as I write. Here, the word 'economy' in the phrase

> Economy has got them in desperation
> Poverty is causing dangerous political tension.

is transformed into the word 'army' by use of an analog delay device.

It is tempting to view the process which lays bare the structure beneath the unified exterior of the whole unmodified version as an expressive homology for the Rasta view of the world.[123] It is certainly articulated to the critical distance from the world of appearances which is the initial impetus for Rasta politics and there are many clues to understanding this in the relation of black music to political struggle all over the new world. The examples of Bebop and Samba generate the most immediate comparisons.[124] This is certainly a long way from musical 'preferences' distinguished by the content of lyrics à la Troyna. Though they may introduce an analytic coherence, political lyrics must be regarded as secondary to the issues implicit in the form of reggae and its consequent exploration in Dub. This may be a difficult point to grasp, but Dubbing is a feature of overtly committed and apparently unpolitical recordings alike. Dub is a bridge between them rooted in their form. This has been explicated eloquently by leading reggae drummer Leroy 'Horsemouth' Wallace.

> I man haffe start play my music in a militant way so we can relate to de people. Cos you can't play a quiet and peaceful music in war time yunno, an dat won serve no purpose because war is going on outside an yu play a lickle quiet violin music! Yu haffe tell de people de right ting whey a gwan inna dem time ya now. Yu ave fe mek *de music* so dread dat a man understan. Until my bredda dem and my sista dem stop suffa me naw go really stop play roots *music*. When me see suffaration stop pan black people me might start play some nice quiet peaceful music. But right now Rasta, a juss some natty music me play as far as me see dis bizniz ya. A de trute deh Iya. Caa tings too dread fe a man out deh now yaa Rasta, fe a man play quiet music.[125]

Wallace's statement illustrates a point made by Armand Mattelart which should serve as a reminder to the Eurocentric sociologist: 'Acquiring and developing class consciousness does not mean obligatory boredom. It is a question of transforming what used to be used exclusively for pleasure and leisure into a means of instruction.'[126]

Reggae is far more than the lullaby of a beleaguered population. In displacing the lyric's 'message' into a secondary place, the Dub movement avoids a trap set for all singers of political songs forced to contend with their art being packaged and sold as commodities. This ensures that: 'for the sake of political commitment political reality is trivialised, which then reduces the political effect.'[127]

Rasta discourse consigns hasty statements of commitment to the realm of 'ism and schism' – the merely 'politrickal' ideologies which suffer by comparison to the total processes of human emancipation involved in social revolution. Many years ago, against Brecht, Adorno argued for the political efficacy of 'atelic, hermetic works of art' in capitalist relations of cultural production. It is on this ground that we have attempted to explore Dub music. Its creators, 'By dismantling appearance explode from within the art which committed proclamation subjugates from without, and hence only in appearance. The inescapability of the work compels the change of attitude which committed works merely demand.'[128]

This music has been dealt with in detail not simply because it is a prime site of cultural struggle by blacks. The popularity of Rasta ideology is in part an unforeseen consequence of the cycles and machinations of the popular music industry. Like the politicization of youth subcultures, permitted by their importation of black styles and forms, which has occurred beyond the limits of any corporatist definition of 'the political', it is one of many new forms of struggle appropriate to new historical conditions: organic crisis at the meeting point of Fordism and neo-Fordism.[129]

Autonomous class struggle

It remains for us to show that black struggles are not merely political in the broadest sense, but approach the task of social transformation not from a transplanted disorganic politics alone, but in ways which relate directly to the historical conjuncture in which they have developed. We focused on Rastafari as one sophisticated expression of the critical consciousness which informs those struggles, commentating on society and state, and extending into an analysis of the post-colonial scene as a whole.

> Africans a bear the most pressure, because you find that the people that are controlling them are the white people them. They try to be superior over black people. Not all of them, but certain of them ones as is gods and seat up in high places; All those system, you just see them big notches who a control. Certain of them captains and them big pirates from long time is them family. Some of them people really have the world in their hands, so them keep up various kinds of isms now. Them stop slaving the Africans alone, but them slaving everyone else still. Is the people them to come and unite now, that's the only way.[130]

We cannot accept that the consciousness of exploitation provoked in the experience of racial oppression, both inside and outside production, typified by this quote, is only some preliminary phase in the development of a mythically complete class consciousness sometime in the future.[131] Though for the social analyst 'race' and class are necessarily abstractions at different levels, black consciousness of race and class cannot be empirically separated. The class character of black struggles is not a result of the fact that blacks are predominantly proletarian, though this is true. It is established in the fact that their struggles for civil rights, freedom from state harassment, or as waged workers, are instances of the process by which the working class is constituted politically, organized in politics. We have distanced ourselves from the view of classes as continuous subjects of history, they are made and remade in a continual struggle. We must also reject the ancient heresy of economistic Marxism which stipulates that the relations of commodity production alone determine class relations. The Marxist concept of class refers primarily but not exclusively to the location of groups in production relations. Capitalism's tendency to generate surplus population structurally excluded from productive employment by the revolutions in the labour process and changes in accumulation should emphasize this point. The composition of this population and the ways it becomes organized politically are determined by class struggles which are not reducible to the objective conditions which delineate the range of possible outcomes. The political organization of surplus population is particularly salient to class segmentation, and therefore to racial politics in the era of structural unemployment. It serves to remind us that the privileged place of economic classes in the Marxist theory of history is not to be equated with an a priori assertion of their political primacy in every historical moment.

> We cannot conceive of the class struggle as if classes were simply and homogeneously constituted at the level of the economic and only then fractured at the level of the political. The political level is dependent – determinate – because its raw materials are given by the mode of production as a whole.[132]

Marx makes it clear that there are periods in which the proletariat is unable to constitute itself as a class in politics even though 'the domination of capital has created for this mass a common situation, common interests'.[133] Recognizing the problems in the effective entry of classes into politics is the first step towards understanding Prezworski's instruction: 'Classes must be viewed as the effects of struggles structured by objective condition that are simultaneously economic, political and ideological.'[134]

These objective conditions change, and the unity between the 'economic movement and political action' of the working class is not the same in 1981 as it was in 1871. The working class is different.

The advent of Fascism, Fordism and Roosevelt's attempt to resolve the 1929 Crash in a Keynesian 'New Deal' all prompted Gramsci to raise the question of whether 'Americanism' could be seen as a new epoch based in capital's passive revolutions, an 'ethical' state and a recomposition of the working class itself: an epoch of social capital.

> In America rationalisation has determined the need to elaborate a new type of man suited to a new type of productive process. This elaboration is still only in its initial phase . . . up to the present there has not been, except perhaps sporadically, any flowering of the 'superstructure'; in other words the question of hegemony has *not yet* been posed.[135]
>
> (my emphasis)

The years since Gramsci wrote these words have seen the question posed with increasing intensity. In these novel conditions the struggle for hegemony cannot be reduced to economic determinations or vulgarized to refer to solely cultural phenomena, and class analysis cannot be restricted to those positioned in the immediate processes of production.

The indeterminacy introduced by a view of class formation as an effect of heterogeneous struggles perhaps premised on different communalities – linguistic, sexual, regional, ecological and 'racial' – is a useful tool against reductionism. It is also a place at which a historical and non-essentialist theory of human needs can be worked into the practice of class politics. The latter is a pressing task, particularly if we understand Fordism to be 'the principle of an articulation between process of production and mode of consumption':[136]

> It is because [the] interaction between needs and products is complex and bilateral, and bears the mark of many determinations other than those stemming directly from economic production and its particular distribution relations, that consumption is both specific to any stage of social development and contradictory in that specificity. The vitality of socialist politics depends on the extent to which it can distinguish between the unnecessary contradiction inherent to a social production that determines use value on

> the basis of exchange value, and the necessary contradiction inherent to any society that has to *plan* to meet needs. Neither contradiction should be seen as an opposition between a brute nature and the manipulations of production; but one is the effect of the dominance of the economic laws of capital accumulation, and the other is the benign index of the dominance of political decision; the latter is not a contradiction to be resolved but rather to be lived.[137]

The politics of need is to the fore in movements for black liberation, as in many of the other autonomous political forces in the ascendant during the last fifteen years.[138]

In our view of class formation, the racist ideologies and practices of the white working class and the consequent differentiation of 'the blacks' are ways in which the class as a whole is disorganized. The struggles of black people to refuse and transform their subjugation are no simple antidote to class segmentation, but they are processes which attempt to constitute the class politically across racial divisions – 'that is which represent it against capitalism against racism'.[139] Like feminist struggles against patriarchal oppression, which have also had side effects on the political formation of classes in the recent period, these struggles do not derive their meaning from the political failures of the classically conceived, white, male, working class. In both cases it appears that autonomous organization has enabled blacks and women to 'leap-frog' over their fellow workers into direct confrontations with the state in the interest of the class as a whole. Responsive and accountable health care raised by the struggle for abortion rights, or democratic and locally controlled police practices demanded by black organization against state harassment are small illustrations of this.[140] The more eruptive forms these struggles sometimes take are not the substitute for a disciplined and tactical war of position, neither are they irreconcilable to one. Both moments have their place in the long struggle to transform society.

> The strategy of 'war of position' (which moreover in no way rules out moments of frontal attack and rupture, if we are not to fall into the most flaccid parliamentary gradualism) is the response to a historical phase marked by a dual tendency: towards the expansion of the state, and towards the passive revolutions of capital.[141]

The crisis in which this confrontation takes place is not yet a crisis of the state form and we must be careful not 'to mistake the appearance for the substance of state power'.[142] The strengthening of repressive apparatuses and functions does not require fundamental change in the institutional structures of the state, which constitute the legitimate arena of politics in relation to their own material existence. The struggles of the dominated masses are now more than ever present inside and outside the state framework, 'whose strategic configuration they map out'.[143] The strategy of 'broad democratic alliances' which perverts Gramsci does have a single virtue in its insistence that the ahistorical fetishization of organizational forms created in previous conjunctures is now a fetter on political progress.[144] These factors, together with the emphasis we have placed on the heterogeneity of class struggle, raise the issue of political organization. This must be considered historically and measured against the tasks of the period in which each specific form arises. In Gramsci's steps we learn that the historical epoch born in the thirties requires new forms of politics and strategy. His 'totalizing' view of the political party's role is rather at odds with this conclusion. It is certainly unsuited to British conditions in which the organization of the working class in politics has a peculiar history of entanglement with the different project of mobilizing electoral support for the Labour Party. Electoral abstention and disinterest are no longer confined to the wards where blacks are a majority, yet the disinterest in 'politics' which they signify is undiscussed from the point of view of left strategy.[145] Organic crisis and the microprocessor revolution demand reassessment of the institutions of political representation. Posing the problem of political organization in direct form is a means to separate corporatist modes of struggle from the diverse attempts to repoliticize the process of class formation in the face of a new imposition of authority, the ideologies of the crisis and the mobilization of the law. Corporatism should be understood as:

> A political structure within advanced capitalism which integrates organized socio-economic producer groups through a system of representation and cooperative mutual interaction at the leadership level and mobilisation and social control at the mass level. Corporatism is understood here as *an actual political structure, not merely an ideology*.[146]
>
> (my emphasis)

We have seen how black political traditions fall outside the 'contradictory unity' of corporatism/parliamentarism. There is also overwhelming evidence to support the view that the institutions of the white working class have failed to represent the interests of black workers abroad[147] and at home, where black rank-and-file organization has challenged local and national union bureaucracy since the day the 'Empire Windrush' docked.[148] We are disinclined to the pretence that these institutions represent the class *as a class* at all. Nor are blacks alone in the marginalization they suffer. The experiences of female, young, unemployed or even unskilled workers present parallel examples,[149] while the growth of rank-and-file organization, and of conflict between shop stewards and the higher echelons of union bureaucracy only hint at the complexity of workplace struggle. The failures of these institutions must be compared to the rapid growth of new movements with an autonomy from capitalist command as well as from the constricting political repertoire of the 'labour movement'. Mass pan-Africanist communalism is but one place among many where the patient listener will discern: 'The dialogue . . . between a young social movement, still searching for its identity, and the movement which preceded it but which is now growing old, dying, or being converted into its own antithesis by becoming an agent of the authorities.'[150]

The tendency in the Marxist movement, best known for its early critique of the articulation of capitalist planning and Soviet statism,[151] is also the place in which a sustained critique of organizational forms has been developed hand in hand with confidence in the capacity of oppressed and exploited people to organize themselves without the mediation of a 'vanguard' on the Leninist model.[152] Though this position has been dismissed by invocation of a mutual exclusion between the concepts of organization and spontaneity, its distinguished advocate C. L. R. James has demonstrated their interrelation and unity. 'You know nothing about organisation unless at every step you relate it to its opposite – spontaneity. It is meaningless without that correlative, its other tied to it, each developing the other.'[153]

James is careful not to oppose organization *per se*; his target is a politics which cannot see beyond 'organisation as we have known it' which 'is now at an end'. For James, the changes Gramsci identified introduced a period in which the recognition of the proletariat's autonomous power would be the basis from which organization would develop. In its prime the working class would find its own methods and forms of organization just as it had done in its infancy. 'New organisations will come as Lilburne's Leveller party came, as the sections and popular societies of Paris in 1793, as the commune in 1871 and the Soviets in 1905, with not a single soul having any concrete ideas about them until they appeared.'[154]

Some of the dangers in this position emerge from critical discussion of the practice of the Italian Autonomists,[155] but none the less it provides a perspective in which we can usefully understand the double articulation of black politico-cultural struggle. This is simultaneously 'disorganic development' come home to roost, and an aspect of autonomous class struggle. Those who doubt that struggles which appear to be organized on the basis of communalities other than class can have effects on the processes of class formation or believe they are unable to transcend a defensive mode, should study the politicization of roots culture, no less than the auto-reduction movements of Turin.[156]

Those who clamour too quickly for 'unified counterhegemonic strategies' under working-class leadership should note that the political discourses of the powerless are subject to connotative resonance, and like the supposedly marginal groups they interpellate, overlap significantly. How *are* we to explain Gay participation in the 'Race Riots' at Brixton?[157] There are many young black women who will make their own struggles against patriarchy and capital which oppress them in racially specific ways. The class consciousness of our epoch is not the sole prerogative of male, white, productive labourers. It remains to be constructed from the potential complementarity of diverse political struggles which constitute the class politically at different levels. It provides a promise of unity which may only be apparent in the rarest moments of revolutionary rupture, where we may catch a fleeting glimpse of the class for itself.

Acknowledgements

Valerie Amos wrote the first draft of one section of this chapter. I would like to say 'thank you' to the various people outside our group who gave detailed and helpful comments during the process of preparation: Veronica Ware, Stuart Hall, Colin Prescod, Sue MacIntosh, Richard Johnson and Robert Lumley. Special thanks to John Solomos.

Notes and references

1 Cathie Lloyd, 'What is the French C.P. up to?', *Race and Class* (Spring 1980). The nationalist bent of The Alternative Economic Strategy is also relevant.
2 S. Hall *et al., Policing the Crisis* (Macmillan 1978), p. 394.
3 S. Hall, 'Race articulation and societies structured in dominance', in *Sociological Theories: Race and Colonialism* (UNESCO 1980).
4 There is a résumé of the contrasting positions of *The Black Liberator* and *Race Today* in the final chapter of *Policing the Crisis*. The disparaging remarks refer to writings by Gideon Ben-Tovim and John Gabriel listed below.
5 See: Colin Mercer, 'Revolutions, reforms or reformulations? Marxist discourse on democracy', in A. Hunt (ed.), *Marxism and Democracy* (Lawrence and Wishart 1980). For an historical account see: Fernando Claudin, *Eurocommunism and Socialism* (New Left Books 1978).
6 Compare: Chantal Mouffe, 'Hegemony and ideology in Gramsci', in Mouffe (ed.), *Gramsci and Marxist Theory* (Routledge and Kegan Paul 1979), with: Henri Weber, 'In the beginning was Gramsci', *Semiotext(e)*, vol. III, no. 3 (1980), *Autonomia Post Political Politics*, and also: Christine Buci-Glucksmann, *Gramsci and the State* (Lawrence and Wishart 1980).
7 Fran Bennett, Beatrix Campbell and Rosalind Coward, 'Feminists: the degenerates of the social', in Adlam *et al.* (eds.), *Politics and Power 3* (Routledge and Kegan Paul 1981).
8 G. Ben-Tovim *et al.*, 'Race, left strategies and the state'; also in *Politics and Power 3* (1981).
9 G. Ben-Tovim, 'The struggle against racism: theoretical and strategic perspectives', *Marxism Today* (July 1978). J. Gabriel and G. Ben-Tovim, 'Marxism and the concept of racism', *Economy and Society*, vol. 7, no. 2 (1978).
10 Ernesto Laclau, *Politics and Ideology in Marxist Theory* (New Left Books 1977); and 'Populist rupture

and discourse', *Screen Education*, no. 34 (Spring 1980). The epistemological position from which my critique proceeds has been outlined with the greatest clarity by: Jose Nun, *Latin America Research Unit Studies*, vol. III, no. 2–3 (1980), pp. 85–145.

11 See: N. Poulantzas, *Fascism and Dictatorship* (New Left Books 1974), footnote on pp. 169–70; 'the error of the Schlageter Line lay elsewhere – to be precise, in the social chauvinist turn of the K.P.D., exploiting in a clearly nationalist way agitation against the Versailles treaty'. Also: Andrew Jenkins, 'Laclau on Fascism', *International*, vol. 5, no. 1 (Autumn 1979).

12 Laclau, *Politics and Ideology*, especially pp. 129–30.

13 ibid.

14 George Bennett (ed.), *The Concept of Empire: Burke to Attlee 1774–1947* (A. & C. Black 1962).

15 Laclau, *Politics and Ideology*, p. 120.

16 Alfred Sherman, *Daily Telegraph*, 9 November 1979.

17 Stuart Hall, 'The legacy of Nicos Poulantzas', *New Left Review*, no. 119 (1978).

18 Nicos Mouzellis, 'Ideology and class politics', *New Left Review*, no. 112 (1978).

19 See: G. Esping-Anderson *et al.*, 'Modes of class struggle and the capitalist state', *Kapitalistate*, no. 4 (Summer 1976), and also A. Markusen *et al.*, 'Typology and class struggle', *Kapitalistate*, no. 6 (1977).

20 Ben-Tovim *et al.*

21 Henri Weber; 'Eurocommunism, socialism, democracy', *New Left Review*, no. 110 (1978).

22 ibid., p. 9.

23 ibid., p. 8.

24 Gabriel and Ben-Tovim, p. 121.

25 Wilson Record, 'The Kremlin sociologists and the Black Republic', and 'Build the Negro People's United Front', in *The Negro and the Communist Party* (New York 1971), Chapters 3 and 4. See also: A. Gayle, *Richard Wright – Ordeal of a Native Son* (Anchor 1980); Claudin and S. Carillo, *Eurocommunism and the State* (1978), Chapter 5.

26 Anton Pannekoek, 'General remarks on the question of organisation', *Capital and Class*, no. 9 (1979), p. 127.

> The adherents of the old forms of organisation exalt democracy as the only right and just political form as against dictatorship, an unjust form. Marxism knows nothing of abstract right or justice, it explains the political forms in which mankind [*sic*] expresses its feelings of political right, as consequences of the economic structure of society.

27 G. Carchedi, 'Authority and foreign labour: some notes on a late capitalist form of capital accumulation and state intervention', *Studies in Political Economy*, no. 2 (1979), p. 50.

28 Annie Phizacklea and Robert Miles, *Labour and Racism* (Routledge and Kegan Paul 1980).

29 ibid., pp. 231–2.

30 See Dominique Lecourt's interesting discussion of this point: *Sociological Theories: Race and Colonialism* (UNESCO 1980), pp. 282–4.

31 Sally Alexander and Barbara Taylor, 'In defence of patriarchy', in R. Samuel (ed.), *People's History and Socialist Theory* (Routledge and Kegan Paul 1981). Veronica Beechey, 'On patriarchy', *Feminist Review*, no. 3 (1979).

32 Heidi Hartman, 'The unhappy marriage of Marxism and feminism', *Capital and Class*, no. 8 (1979).

33 Linda Gordon, 'The long struggle for reproductive rights', *Radical America*, vol. 15, nos. 1 and 2 (Spring 1981).

34 Richard Wright, 'Blueprint for negro writing', *Race and Class*, vol. xxi, no. 4 (Spring 1981).

35 Sebastiano Timpanaro, *On Materialism* (New Left Books 1975).

36 ibid., p. 45.

37 Kate Soper, 'Marxism, materialism and biology', in Mepham and Hillel-Ruben (eds.), *Issues in Marxist Philosophy*, vol. 2: *Materialism* (Harvester 1979).

38 Kate Soper, 'On materialisms', *Radical Philosophy*, no. 15 (Autumn 1976).

39 V. N. Volosinov, *Marxism and the Philosophy of Language* (Seminar Press 1973), p. 23.

40 Frank Kofsky, *Black Nationalism and the Revolution in Music* (Pathfinder 1970), p. 43.

41 Volosinov, p. 23.

42 Timpanaro, p. 43.

43 An important sociological critique of this position is provided by: Alain Touraine, *The Self-Production of Society* (Chicago University Press 1977), especially Chapters 3 and 7.

44 Adam Prezworski, 'Proletariat into a class: the process of class formation from Kautsky's "The Class Struggle" to recent controversies', *Politics and Society*, vol. 4, no. 7 (1977).

45 See Marx's letter to Weydemeyer, 5 March 1852. Though Althusser conceptualizes classes rather differently, he is absolutely correct to insist that:

> For reformists (even if they call themselves Marxists) it is not the class struggle that is in the front rank: it is simply the classes. Let us take a simple example, and suppose that we are dealing with just two classes. For reformists these classes exist *before* the class struggle, a bit like two football teams exist separately before the match. Each class exists in its own camp, lives according to its particular conditions of existence. One class may be exploiting another, but for reformism that is not the same thing as class struggle. One day the two classes come up against one another and come into conflict. It is only then that the class struggle begins . . . you will always find the same idea here: the classes exist *before* the class struggle, *independently* of the class struggle. The class struggle only exists *afterwards*. Revolutionaries on the other hand, consider that it is impossible to separate the classes from class struggle. The class struggle and the existence of classes are one and the same thing. In order for there to be classes in a 'society', the society has to be divided into classes: this division does not come *later in the story*; it is the exploitation of one class by another, it is therefore the class struggle, which constitutes the division into classes. For exploitation is already class struggle. You must therefore begin with class struggle if you want to understand class division, the existence and nature of classes. The class struggle must be put in the front rank.

Louis Althusser, 'Reply to John Lewis', in *Essays in Self-Criticism* (New Left Books 1976), pp. 49–50.

46 Robert Moore, *Racism and Black Resistance* (Pluto 1975); and A. X. Cambridge and C. Gutzmore, 'The industrial action of the black masses and the class struggle in Britain', *The Black Liberator*, vol. 2, no. 3 (June-January 1974).

47 S. Hall, 'Race and moral panics in post-war Britain', in CRE (ed.), *Five Views of Multi-Racial Britain* (CRE 1978).

48 According to Poulantzas' original criteria of 'pertinent effects'. See: *Political Power and Social Classes* (New Left Books 1973).

49 Richard Johnson, 'Three problematics', in Critcher, Clark and Johnson (eds.), *Working Class Culture* (CCCS/Hutchinson 1979), p. 237.

50 Amilcar Cabral, *Return to the Source* (Monthly Review 1973), p. 43.

51 A. Sivanandan, 'Imperialism and disorganic development in the silicon age', *Race and Class*, vol. xxi, no. 2 (1979).

52 Phil Cohen, 'Subcultural conflict and working class community', *WPCS*, no. 2; reprinted in Hall *et al.* (eds.), *Culture, Media, Language* (CCCS/Hutchinson 1980).

53 Ira Katznelson, 'Community capitalist development and the emergence of class', *Politics and Society*, vol. 9, no. 2 (1979).

54 A. Gramsci, *Selections from the Prison Notebooks* (Lawrence and Wishart 1971), pp. 296–8.

55 Lewis Mumford, *The City in History* (Secker and Warburg 1961), p. 370.

56 R. Roberts, *The Classic Slum* (Manchester University Press 1971); E. P. Thompson, *Whigs and Hunters* (Penguin 1975); Henry Mayhew, *London Labour and London Poor*, vol. 1 (Frank Cass 1967).

57 Ceri Peach, *West Indian Migration to Britain* (Oxford University Press 1968), p. 62.

58 Gareth Stedman-Jones, 'Working class culture and working class politics in London 1870–1900', *Journal of Social History*, vol. vii, no. 4 (1974).

59 Paul Willis, *Learning to Labour* (Saxon Hall 1977).

60 Katznelson, p. 232.

61 Michel Foucault, interviews in *Radical Philosophy*, no. 16 (1977).

62 M. Burawoy, 'The politics of production and the production of politics', *Political Power and Social Theory*, vol. 1, no. 1 (1980). See also in the same volume: Adam Prezworski, 'Material bases of consent, economics and politics in a hegemonic system'.

63 Burawoy, p. 272.

64 Prezworski, 'Proletariat into a class', p. 344.

65 Dario Melossi, 'Institutions of social control and capitalist organisation of work', in NDC/CSE (ed.), *Capitalism and the Rule of Law* (Hutchinson 1979).

66 Lee Bridges, 'The Ministry of Internal Security: British urban social policy 1968–74', *Race and Class*, vol. xvi, no. 4 (1975).
67 Phil Cohen, 'Policing the working class city', in *Capitalism and the Rule of Law*. Also: John R. Gillis, 'The evolution of juvenile delinquency in England 1890–1914', *Past and Present*, no. 67 (1975).
68 Clare Demuth, *Sus* (Runneymede Trust 1978), pp. 37–8.
69 *Report of the Unofficial Committee of Enquiry into Events in Southall 23.4.79* (NCCL 1980).
70 John Alderson, *Policing Freedom*, p. 43:

> Colonial governments, never quite sure how the native population will react, equally require repressive police or military services if they are to stay in power against popular sentiment.

71 Ira Katznelson, *Black Men White Cities* (Oxford University Press 1973).
72 John Lea, 'The contradictions of the 60s race relations legislation', in NDC (ed.), *Permissiveness and Control* (Macmillan 1980).
73 Bob Jessop, 'Corporatism, parliamentarism and social democracy', in P. Schmitter and G. Lehmbruch (eds.), *Trends Towards Corporatist Intermediation* (Sage 1979).
74 Katznelson (1973), p. 178.
75 M. Marable, 'Black nationalism in the 1970s – through the prism of race and class', *Socialist Review*, no. 50/51 (1980).
76 Gus John, 'In the service of black youth: a study of the political culture of youth and community work with black people in English cities', National Association of Youth Clubs Special Report Series, *Special Report* no. 2 (March 1981).
77 ibid., p. 142.
78 Resham Sandhu, 'A tentative exploration of events on Saturday and Sunday following the death of Gurdip Singh Chaggar on the night of Friday 4th June 1976 in Southall West London', unpublished conference paper (1977).
79 Marx, *Early Writings* (Penguin 1975).
80 Cedric Robinson, 'Coming to terms: the Third World and the dialectic of imperialism', *Race and Class*, vol. xxii, no. 4 (1981).
81 C. L. R. James, *The Black Jacobins*.
82 Horace Campbell, 'Rastafari: culture of resistance', *Race and Class*, vol. xxii, no. 1 (1980).
83 Sebastian Clarke, *Jah Music* (Heinemann 1980).
84 Cedric Robinson, unpublished early draft of *Coming to Terms*.
85 Tony Martin, *Race First – The Ideological and Organisational Struggles of Marcus Garvey and the Universal Negro Improvement Association* (Greenwood 1976); Colin Henfrey, 'The hungry imagination: social formation, popular culture and ideology in Bahia', in S. Mitchell (ed.), *The Logic of Poverty* (Routledge and Kegan Paul 1981); Donald Barrett and Karari Njama, *Mau Mau from Within* (Monthly Review 1966); Richard Price (ed.), *Maroon Societies* (Anchor 1973).
86 David Dalby, 'Black through white: patterns of communication in Africa and the New World', and 'African survivals in the language and traditions of the Windward maroons of Jamaica', *African Language Studies*, no. 12 (1971). See also: T. Kochman (ed.), *Rappin' and Stylin' out: Communication in Urban Black America* (Chicago University Press 1972).
87 Ernest Cashmore, *Rastaman* (Allen and Unwin 1979); Robert Miles, 'Between two cultures? The case of Rastafarianism', *SSRC RUER Working Paper*, no. 10.
88 Martin, Chapter 10; Manning Marable, 'A. Phillip Randolph, a political assessment', in *From the Grassroots* (South End Press 1980); and Jeff Henderson, 'A. Phillip Randolph and the dilemmas of socialism and black nationalism in the United States', *Race and Class*, vol. xx, no. 2 (1978).
89 Campbell.
90 Cashmore, pp. 129–30.
91 D. Hebdige, *Subculture, the Meaning of Style* (Methuen 1979).
92 *Rastafari Universal Zion*, 18 February 1980.
93 Angela MacRobbie, 'Settling accounts with subculture', *Screen Education*, no. 34 (1980).
94 *Black Echoes*, 16 May 1981.
95 Angelina Grimke, 'Appeal to the Christian women of the south', in A. Rossi (ed.), *The Feminist Papers* (Bantam 1973).
96 London Borough of Lambeth, *Final Report of the Working Party into Community/Police Relations in Lambeth* (London Borough of Lambeth 1980), Section 2 (b).
97 Ken Pryce, *Endless Pressure* (Penguin 1979).

98 Joseph Owens, *Dread* (Sangster 1976), p. 64.
99 Gramsci, pp. 198–9.
100 Burning Spear, interviewed in *Jah Ugliman*, vol. 2 (September 1980).
101 The Wailers 'Get Up Stand Up', and The Congoes 'The Wrong Thing' are two of the best examples. There are many others.
102 E. Cashmore, p. 60.
103 Marx, *Introduction to the Critique of Hegel's Philosophy of Right*. Also in *Early Writings*.
104 E. Genovese, *From Rebellion to Revolution* (Baton Rouge 1979); V. Harding, 'Religion and resistance among ante-bellum negroes 1800–1860', in Meier and Rudwick (eds.), *The Making of Black America*, vol. 2 (Atheneum Publishers 1969); as well as R. Price, ibid.
105 S. Yeo, 'The religion of socialism in Britain 1883–1896', *History Workshop*, no. 4 (1977). We have yet to see how discussion of Rastafarianism is enlivened by comparison with the Owenite movement. In this connection see: J. F. C. Harrison, *Robert Owen and the Owenites in Britain and America* (Routledge and Kegan Paul 1969); and E. Yeo's contribution to Pollard and Salt (eds.), *Robert Owen, Prophet of the Poor* (Macmillan 1971). Logie Barrow's 'Socialism in eternity – the ideology of plebeian spiritualists, 1853–1913', *History Workshop*, no. 9 (1980) is also relevant.
106 Demonstration against racial violence in Coventry, 24 May 1981. See *The Observer, Sunday Times* and *News of the World*, 25 May 1981.
107 *Kala Tara*, paper of Bradford Asian Youth Movement, no. 1 (1979).
108 Hebdige, p. 46.
109 *British Tidings*, paper of the British Movement.
110 David Edgar, 'Reagan's hidden agenda: racism and the new American right', *Race and Class*, vol. xxii, no. 3 (1981).
111 S. Hall and T. Jefferson (eds.), *Resistance through Rituals* (CCCS/Hutchinson 1975).
112 Hebdige, p. 64.
113 Geoff Pearson, ' "Paki-Bashing" in a North East Lancashire cotton town: a case study and its history', in Mungham and Pearson (eds.), *Working Class Youth Culture* (Routledge and Kegan Paul 1976). Also J. Clarke, 'Skinheads and the magical recovery of community', in Hall and Jefferson.
114 Sebastian Clarke, Chapter 7.
115 Island's director Chris Blackwell is a member of the family who own Crosse and Blackwell.
116 The Wailers, 'Burning and Looting'.
117 Big Youth, 'Screaming Target' (TRLS61–1973). I. Roy, 'Presenting I Roy' (TRLS63–1973).
118 Cashmore, p. 104.
119 T. Adorno, 'Commitment', reprinted in Jameson (ed.), *Aesthetics and Politics* (New Left Books 1978).
120 Barry Troyna, 'Differential commitment to ethnic identity by black youths in Britain', *New Community*, vol. vii, no. 3 (1979).
121 *Black Echoes*, 13 December 1980.
122 See: Clarke, Chapter 6. A young Rasta with whom I discussed Troyna's analysis made the following comment: 'Cho, same way bass and drum carry the swing, bass and drum.'
123 Paul Willis's *Profane Culture* (Routledge and Kegan Paul 1978) presents the clearest exposition of this concept.
124 See: A. B. Spellman, *Four Lives in the Bebop Business* (Schocken 1971). On samba see: Marvin Harris, *Town and Country in Brasil* (Norton 1971); and sleeve notes to 'In Praise of Oxala and Other Gods Black Music of South America' (Nonesuch H72036), and 'Folklore e Bossa Nova do Brasil' (Polydor 583–710).
125 Interviewed in *Jah Ugliman*, vol. 2.
126 A. Mattelart, *Mass Media, Ideologies and the Revolutionary Movement* (Harvester 1980), p. 54.
127 Adorno, p. 185.
128 ibid., p. 191.
129 Michel Aglietta, *A Theory of Capitalist Regulation* (New Left Books 1979), pp. 111–15. Also C. Palloix, 'The labour process: from Fordism to neo-Fordism', in *The Labour Process and Class Strategies*, CSE Pamphlet no. 1 (CSE 1976); Mike Davis, ' "Fordism" in crisis', *Review*, vol. II, no. 2 (Fall 1978).
130 Hugh Mundell, *Black Echoes*, 8 November 1980.
131 Phizacklea and Miles, Chapter 7.
132 Stuart Hall, 'The political and the economic in Marx's theory of classes', in Hunt (ed.), *Class and Class Structure* (Lawrence and Wishart 1977).
133 Marx, *The Poverty of Philosophy* (Moscow 1976), p. 160.

134 Prezworski, 'Proletariat into a class', p. 344.
135 Gramsci, p. 286; M. Tronti, 'Social capital', *Telos*, no. 17, p. 197.
136 Aglietta, p. 117.
137 Kate Soper, 'Marxism, materialism and biology', p. 88.
138 Alain Touraine, *The Voice and the Eye: an Analysis of Social Movements* (Cambridge University Press 1981).
139 S. Hall, *Policing the Crisis*, p. 395.
140 See: Trotsky's April 1939 discussions with C. L. R. James in: Breitman (ed.), *Trotsky on Black Nationalism* (Monthly Review 1967).
141 Buci-Glucksmann, p. xii.
142 S. Bologna, 'The tribe of moles', in *Semiotext(e)* no. 9 (1980).
143 Nicos Poulantzas, *State, Power, Socialism* (New Left Books 1978).
144 C. Castoriadis, 'On the history of the workers' movement', *Telos*, no. 30 (Winter 1976–77); C. L. R. James, *Notes on Dialectics* (Allison and Busby 1980), p. 117; S. Rowbotham *et al.*, *Beyond the Fragments: Feminism and the Making of Socialism* (Newcastle Socialist Centre 1979).
145 I. Crewe *et al.*, 'Partisan de-alignment in Britain 1964–74', *British Journal of Political Science*, no. 7 (1976).
146 Leo Panitch, 'Trades unions and the state', *New Left Review*, no. 125 (1981); also 'The development of corporatism in Liberal democracies', *Comparative Political Studies*, vol. x, no. 1 (April 1977).
147 Partha Sarathi Gupta, *Imperialism and the British Labour Movement 1914–64* (Macmillan 1975); and D. Thompson and R. Larson, *Where were You, Brother? An Account of Trade Union Imperialism* (War on Want 1978).
148 R. Miles and A. Phizacklea, 'The TUC black workers and new commonwealth immigration 1954–73', *SSRC RUER Working Paper* no. 6 (1977); and 'The TUC and black workers 1974–76', *British Journal of Industrial Relations*, vol. xvi, no. 2 (1978). See also: *The Times*, 17 February 1954, and *Guardian*, 9 February 1954.
149 A. Coote and P. Kellner, 'Woman workers and union power', *New Statesman pamphlet* no. 1 (1980).
150 Alain Touraine, 'Political ecology: a demand to live differently now', *New Society*, 8 November 1979.
151 C. L. R. James, F. Forest and Ria Stone, *The Invading Socialist Society* (News and Letters Publications 1947; reprinted 1972).
152 Harry Cleaver, *Reading Capital Politically* (Harvester 1979).
153 *Notes on Dialectics*, p. 115.
154 C. L. R. James, *State Capitalism and World Revolution* (News and Letters Publications 1969).
155 Alberto Melucci, 'New movements, terrorism, and the political system: reflections on the Italian case', *Socialist Review 56*, vol. 11, no. 2 (March–April 1981). Robert Lumley, review of 'Working class autonomy and the crisis', *Capital and Class*, no. 12 (Winter 1980–1).
156 Eddy Cherki and Michel Wieviorka, 'Autoreduction movements in Turin', in *Semiotext(e)*, no. 9.
157 *Gay News*, no. 214 (30 April 1981).

Section 3

Theorising experience, exploring methods

Introduction

The politics of experience

Elspeth Probyn

> . . . [S]ubjects *are* contradictory, 'in process', fragmented, produced. But human beings and social movements also strive to produce some coherence and continuity, and through this, exercise some control over feelings, conditions and destinies.
>
> Richard Johnson, 'What is Cultural Studies Anyway?'

'The politics of experience' – it's a phrase that I've grown up with, at least academically speaking. Understanding people's experience of all the facets we call 'the social' and being able to use my own is what got me into academic work. And many of the authors here have been my guides and inspiration, all of which makes writing this introduction rather daunting.

Reading these papers again, or sometimes for the first time, the audacity and the sheer difficulty of the project comes back with urgency. How do you understand individuals' experiences of culture, of family, work life, structures of gender, class, and ethnicity? How do you account for the tension between the individual and the group or collective nature of these experiences? What methods are best deployed? What mode of address – and to whom? How to convey the textures and the haptic realities of moments of life? What of the researcher and her/his relation to the researched, either in the form of living and breathing people or interpreting a broad cultural moment?

To put it mildly, these are tough questions. While we now have much more work to draw on, and a greater institutional legitimacy for different approaches, the fundamental nature of this work remains difficult and of necessity open to revision.

Richard Johnson's key text of 1983, 'What is Cultural Studies Anyway?', makes clear that from the very beginning questions about what is or are cultural studies and how to formulate what he called 'the kind of unity' of different approaches were central to the project of cultural studies. Johnson is at pains to emphasise that critique is a necessary part of the enterprise but that critique must involve 'appropriation not just rejection' (Johnson, in this volume). It is salutary to remember that more than twenty years ago the spectre of codifying cultural studies was an issue: 'cultural studies is a process, a kind of alchemy for producing useful knowledge. Codify it and you might halt its reactions' (Johnson, op. cit.).

As I write in 2006, Johnson's points still have a pressing currency. He was writing in a time of national conservatism, which included 'a vigorous assault on public educational institutions, both by cutting finance and by defining usefulness in strictly capitalist terms' (Johnson, op. cit.). In Australia, we have had ten years of a conservative and mean-spirited government, which has rendered us frighteningly adept at manipulating and working with governmental and institutional constraints in order to survive. This has been particularly acute for my department, which went from Women's Studies to Gender Studies for good intellectual reasons but also because of the necessity of getting more bums on seats. Because the majority of the members of our small department have been deeply invested in cultural studies, over the same time period we have tried repeatedly to have our name changed to Gender and Cultural Studies. A Chancellor who was ideologically against cultural studies first rebuffed this, and more recently it has been blocked by members of other more traditional departments because of proprietorial claims and the desire for what is seen as a 'sexy' and profitable enterprise. Our claims that we are actually invested in cultural studies (for example, in publishing in cultural studies journals and in bolstering our national association of cultural studies) against a marked lack of investment by those wishing to claim the ground, finds succour in Johnson's remarks:

> We need definitions of cultural studies to struggle effectively in these contexts, to make claims for resources, to clarify our minds in the rush and muddle of everyday work, and to decide priorities for teaching and research.
>
> Johnson, op. cit.

If the emphasis back then was on appropriating in creative ways from other disciplines, increasingly the problem is that other disciplines are appropriating from cultural studies for less than salubrious reasons. And as I write this, I am aware how petty these concerns can sound. But that is also why is it so important to remember Johnson's point as well as the tone in which he makes both intellectual and pragmatic arguments. In the cross-national, international and intra-national movements that constitute a loose unity of cultural studies at the moment, it is all too easy to fall into a game fuelled by either envy or resentment at the unequal distribution of resources. This was, for instance, played out recently in Australia when an ex-pat back on a visit from his well resourced position in one of the top American universities railed against what he perceived to be the lack of theoretical and political engagement on the part of his former cultural studies' colleagues in Australia. His comments on the Cultural Studies Association of Australasia's listserve were met with some furious rebuttals, and reminders that staying alive under John Howard's Coalition government required political action that his so-called political colleagues in the USA would never have to imagine. And as with Johnson's remarks, this type of climate perforce changes how one thinks of 'the theoretical' or 'the political', if only by removing the singularising emphasis on 'the' theoretical.

If it's tough, and differently tough within Australia where we have a push to further entrench hierarchies between universities (teaching only versus research), the staggering differences in the material conditions of the production of knowledge at a global level need to be forefronted if we are to have any unity at a larger level. And the differences in the types of theory and research that are considered useful need to be appreciated as the result of the pressures exerted by government but which on the more positive side may render such endeavours more 'worldly', to use Stuart Hall's term. As Johnson puts it, 'If the momentum is to strive for really useful knowledge, will academic codification help this? Is it not a priority to become more "popular" rather than more academic?' (Johnson, op. cit.).

Although we know that 'popular' can have its pitfalls, my energies have been directed to rendering the academic more popular. To illustrate quickly some of the problems of tone, address and reception that this entails, let me recount a recent (failed) moment of CCCS emulation on my part. In addition to my academic job, for the last four years I've been writing a fortnightly column on higher education in our national daily, *The Australian* (owned by News Ltd). It is a privilege to sound off in public about ideas, but, as Murdoch's News Ltd becomes ever more conservative, it also can seem at times like a bit of a chore. Sometimes I feel like I'm scraping the barrel, and I incorporate a lot of whatever I'm doing, reading and hearing when I write.

One particular weekend, what I was doing was reading one of Paul Willis' texts for this collection. This is the beginning of what I wrote:

> *I'm at the beauty and nail salon reading Paul Willis' 'The Man in the Iron Cage: Notes on Method'. Willis is one of the original members of the Centre for Contemporary Cultural Studies (CCCS) at the University of Birmingham, widely regarded as the birthplace of my field.*
>
> *I'm having a pedicure, which leaves my hands free to take notes on Willis' intricate account of the tensions between quantitative and qualitative research methods. His critique of positivism lies in its refusal of any possibility of researching subjective meanings. Willis then turns to participant observation, which he says 'has directed its followers towards a profoundly important methodological possibility – the possibility of* <u>being surprised</u>*; of reaching knowledge not prefigured in one's starting point.'*
>
> *It's a lovely point and I pause on it to open myself up to my surroundings. PT Beauty & Nails is owned by a youngish Vietnamese woman who variously goes by Sabrina or Que. She came over many years ago with her husband who runs the photo developing shop and internet cafe that adjoins the expanding salon. She's won a City of Sydney Business Award, and when I congratulate her she beams. It's not a fancy place but it's hers.*
>
> *The salon is on Redfern Street, a couple of blocks away from The Block.* [For non-Australians, Redfern is the home to the largest urban population of Aboriginal people, who have been coming to the area from outback Australia for over a century, and of course they have been here for some 60,000 years. The Block, a now rundown collection of houses run by The Aboriginal Housing Corporation, is under constant focus by the police and politicians as the site of heroin use.] *Our mayor has promised big bucks to rejuvenate the street. We are to have buried cables, new street furniture and wider footpaths to accommodate her vision of a neighbourhood. So far nothing's happened except for new parking meters.*
>
> *From the salon you get a good view of the street as conversations and arguments walk by. I'm sitting in a chair with a footbath next to an elegant Aboriginal woman. Having a pedicure has to be one of the more intimate things you can do in public. A slight young girl, a cousin of Sabrina, is on her knees shaving off my dead skin. She and the girl doing my neighbour's feet laugh to each other in Vietnamese.*
>
> *PT Beauty does a roaring trade in false fingernails. The other women in the salon are having a tortuous time as the glue of the old nails is ground off in readiness for a new pair. They're white women who probably work in the office towers nearby. They're good talkers and compare their make-up tricks: both have had make-up tattooed on so they don't have to worry about putting any on in the morning. They're regular customers and one of the girls touches up their toe nail polish for free. There's a show of trying to get Hannah to accept the five dollars, which gingerly – because of wet nails – goes back and forth accompanied by a lot of laughter.*

I ended on Willis' central point: that working-class culture is 'richly threaded' but this is 'only the minimum condition of survival, and not a cause for celebration'.

Now as I said, writing an opinion column is a hit or miss affair and I may have missed on this occasion. However, the reason I bring it up is that my editor refused to run it because 'I was patronising to the under-class by inferring that getting their nails done added colour to their lives'.

Talk about being surprised. My immediate impulse was to respond: 'well, they are getting a bit of colour in their lives, you privileged git.' However one doesn't say such things to one's editor, and instead I fumed.

Has so-called political correctness now reached a point where one can no longer even talk about the working class (and if 'underclass' is not patronising, I don't know what is)? The accusation rankles deeply because it goes against, and indeed stigmatises, the desire to describe, to get into the lives of others, in whatever small way; to feel and portray the ineffable webs that tie us together in sociality.

And so I turn back to these founding texts, doubly motivated to glean from them more understanding of how to *do* the politics of experience. I start with the Women's Study Group (WSG), which addresses most directly 'trying to do feminist intellectual work'. The description by the Group of their experience of doing feminist work at the CCCS is an eye-opener. To my generation (which given that Lawrence Grossberg was one of my supervisors, would make it second or third generation), the Centre functions as the antidote to the experience of being the only feminist in a department – as was the case in my first teaching position in a stodgy Francophone department of sociology. As I battled one boringly sexist situation after another, I'd dream of being in the collegial and politically supportive environment that I imagined as the CCCS.

The realities are depicted as somewhat different. As the WSG write, much of their work went into exploring 'the *experience* of the absence of women'. This absence was in terms of the theoretical and empirical material but according to the women, it was also found within the structure of collaboration in the Centre: 'the "neutrality" of intellectual groups in which detached discussion of the *object* of study takes place'. As they further explain, 'It was difficult both to argue among ourselves inside the group and, as individual feminists, to articulate different positions in the wider context.'

By and large, the men at the Centre, at least in their writing, do not appear overly worried about *how* to do intellectual work. Or as the WSG say, they are less concerned about the self-conscious 'use of theoretical language which is one element in perpetuating knowledge as the property of a few'.

This is a rather broad characterisation of the Centre's quite diverse manners of writing and researching. But it is undoubtedly important, and would later go hand in hand with a pronounced feminist care not to use the experiences of women informants for the benefit of researchers and their institutions: or as Angela McRobbie put it a few years later in 1982, 'how to make talk walk'. The question of the appropriate and political relationship to research subjects was to become ever more important throughout the 1980s, with the problematisation of the modes of address, attempts at 'multivocal' authorship of ethnographic work, and a fear of 'speaking for the subaltern'. Equally there would be response on the part of other scholars to the effect that such concerns can become stifling and result in paralysis. Or as Clifford Geertz would say in 1988, *The Anthropologist as Author*, clearly expressing his displeasure at what he perceived as the over-zealous preoccupation with the politics of writing.

One senses that questions of modes of address are only nascent at this moment in the Centre. I laughed reading one manuscript where the author had gone back and laboriously typed in superscript 'she', 'women', 'her' above the previous solely masculine references.

In terms of actual style, there is, in many of the texts, a rather glorious rambling quality that one no longer finds in our tightly restricted journals. For instance, reading Dick Hebdige's account of Fulham, the precise object of analysis is not always immediately clear: there's crims galore, and great depictions of pubs and their illegal activities, wind-ups, fights, drinking and smoking dope. 'The economies of inebriation' (a lovely phrase) segues into discussions about power and its metaphors, Bateson's double bind and schizophrenia.

But Hebdige knows where he going. As he remarks at the end of his essay, 'Hopefully, in the process [of description] "popular culture", which is all too often presented as an amalgam of literary prejudices, or as a figment of the "sociological imagination" was revealed as a heterogeneous complex of shifting relationships'. (Hebdige, in this volume) He does this in ways that, consciously or not, serve as homage and a relocation of Raymond Williams' evocative phrase from 'Culture is Ordinary': 'culture is written on the land'. This time, however, it is written on the smells and tastes of the 'pie-and-mash-and-jellied-eel emporium serv[ing] its doubtful delicacies in an atmosphere of sweat and steam . . . [as] the outside world has come in different ways to Fulham and left its indelible marks across the culture' (Hebdige, op. cit.).

As with Hebdige's remark about literary prejudices and sociological concepts, many of the papers are explicitly working out what was wrong with the then dominant paradigms. Of the papers in this section, this is perhaps the most extended theme. While less entertaining or evocative than the ethnographic work, the need to clear a space was an important feature of cultural studies. It still is but for a variety of reasons – a sense of an existing canon, a less wide-ranging formation which actively engages with more traditional disciplines – it is not as usual as it once was. This is again central to Johnson's chapter, where he stresses the importance of 'reforming the elements of different approaches *in their relation to each other*' (my emphasis).

One can see the worth of clearing conceptual space in the 'Experience of work' Group, as they question deeply the relations between different methods and theoretical perspectives. Their object of critique is mainly mainstream sociology, but along the way they further articulate what they see as the Centre's central theme: 'the subjective meaning complex of action' (Work Group, in this volume). They strive to 'repair the passivity of the subject in Althusserian structuralist Marxism . . . and limit the humanistic indulgence of the subject in bourgeois ethnography'. It's all very complex in the best sense, and as they say, 'it is necessary to detach, straighten out, and project the complex knot of our theoretical uncertainties and differences if we are to conduct an intelligible debate' (Work Group, op. cit.).

Paul Willis' 'The Man in the Iron Cage: Notes on Method' (the piece I was reading while having my toenails done) is even more closely directed to detaching and straightening out the problems of quantitative and qualitative methods and the even knottier ways in which that framing has opposed objectivism and subjectivism. It still stands as a brilliant critique of the problem: as he frames it at the outset, the inability within dominant sociology 'to understand and record human subjectivity' is not helped by strenuously demarcating putatively opposite modes of inquiry: 'now you measure it, now you feel it' (Willis, in this volume).

Willis' short piece hums with energy directed at improving how we understand human beings in their totality. Its theoretical feel and reach recalls earlier attempts by Marcel Mauss and later Georges Devereux to extend sociological analysis to the totality of concrete experience.[1] Willis' piece recalls with force why self-reflexivity is important and how. Instead of a facile nod to the researcher's position (or worse, accounts where panic over the researcher's centrality all but obliterates anything else), Willis defines self-reflexivity in terms of that priceless capacity: 'the possibility of *being surprised*; of reaching knowledge not prefigured in one's starting paradigm'. Following through on this, self-reflexivity occurs when knowledge and experience are challenged, when there are 'areas [that] remain obscure to the researcher'. The 'destructive' moments of reflexivity, the 'unrestrained and hazardous *self-reflexivity*' is prompted by and allows for 'the possibility of a genuine appreciation of another reality . . . another way of seeing the world' (Willis, in this volume).

Another important area of clearing, detaching and sorting was in the area of studies of ethnicity and racism. You can feel the force of what young black scholars and researchers of ethnicity were up against in Errol Lawrence's 'Common sense, racism and the sociology of race relations'. His wide-ranging account of the formation and articulation of common sense around race interrogates Gramsci, the Middle Ages, feudalism, and Enoch Powell before he stages an encounter between, on the one hand, race relations sociology and its then frighteningly close ties to social policy, and on the other, alternative perspectives emerging from Afro-Caribbean culture. Written in 1981, the pall of Thatcherism is in the air. As very real political constraints bear down on the emergent communities of black scholarship, Lawrence writes back about the intricacies of gender and family life, as he tries to dismantle the pathologising strategies aimed directly at differently lived sex/gender arrangements.

Lawrence's conclusion is depressingly familiar to us today. All too often white researchers do not, and seemingly cannot, acknowledge *in productive ways* their/our own racism. In Australia today, the impetus is still on studying migrant communities or Indigenous people, and not white racism,[2] and where and when we have an acknowledgement of white privilege, it is amazing how quickly it turns to 'poor white me'.

Speaking very broadly, at times the view from the present, at least in Australia, is, if possible, even more depressing than Lawrence's account from the 1980s. We now seem to have a robust industry of white (and often feminist) researchers busily decrying white racism without any effect on the politics and realities of those less privileged. And lest we think it's a matter of degrees, we're talking about a twenty-year difference in mortality rates between white and Indigenous people. And speaking of degrees, the numbers of Indigenous lecturers with higher degrees in our universities, along with the mortality rates, should cause all of us within Australian universities to blush . . . and to act daily to advance the possibility of Indigenous students surviving in universities and gaining degrees and meaningful places as scholars in their own right.

The exigency of clearing out space for a different kind of intellectual work is again apparent in the critique of 'community studies' by the Fieldwork Group, and then again in Phil Cohen's argument about 'Subcultural conflict and working class community'. As the Fieldwork Group argues, approaching other paradigms necessitates 'a critique of the whole conceptual basis of an area of study – not a limited borrowing of "hard" data'. They advocate 'a principled attempt to borrow data and evidence from differently constituted academic regions' (Fieldwork Group, in this volume). Their reading of community studies follows through to a more trenchant focus on the policy uses of the research generated by community studies, which enable 'social problems' to be formulated in ways that pathologise working class families and culture. For Cohen, the problem lies in the separation of community from culture at a conceptual level, which then results in very real problems in community life, in which social workers and community activists intervene. By reifying 'community', government agencies '*substitute* the actions and priorities of the social and political work organisations for those of the people they are supposed to serve' (Cohen, in this volume). At the end of his essay, Cohen outlines a new perspective where community and culture come together in practical and democratic ways.

Charles Woolfson's article on 'The semiotics of working class speech' at first seems very far from the pragmatic approach advocated by Cohen. Taking from the then recently translated work of Voloshinov, and arguing against the French interpretation of semiotics, Woolfson attempts to bring a Marxist approach to semiotics. Voloshinov's famous dictum that 'wherever a sign is present, ideology is present' is explained in terms of 'the passage of the sign from material conditions through to its symbolic completion in the superstructure'. In this sense, the sign 'is the ideological refraction of reality in social consciousness' (Woolfson, in this volume). The point taken from Voloshinov is that 'expression is what first gives experience its form'. This is then worked through in an analysis of conversation among transport workers in Glasgow.

In this section there is relatively little about the politics of experience in relation to the media. However, Willis' essay on 'Symbolism and practice: A theory for the social meaning of pop music' advances a broad theoretical agenda for the study of symbolic forms. One can clearly see the influence of Williams in Willis' formulation of the relation of young people to rock music: 'Experience is not atomised and young people live their expressive lives as a symbolic whole . . . a whole way of life interpenetrated by a whole symbolic system.' But one can also see how the study of specific subcultural modes needs to extend on the broader idea of 'culture' as a whole way of life.

Following a critique of positivism and its rather naïve 'trust in the immediate verbal response', Willis proposes a model which integrates analysis of the object or artefact with a broad study of what we now call 'the consumer'. Deploying different methods at various stages of the analysis (group interviews, analysis of technological support – e.g. electrical guitars, television, records, participant observation, etc.) this would yield:

> A total cultural understanding [that] take[s] into account *all* the relationships between a social group and the objects and artefacts around them, *and* the manner in which particularly potent *integral circuits mediate* other relationships, and indeed each other.
>
> Willis, in this volume

Written in 1974 this model begins to suggest the 'encoding/decoding' circuit that Hall would publish in 1980. In some ways, Willis makes more explicit the complex relationships between relations than does Hall's model, although Hall is clearer about the precise stages that production and consumption must pass through to arrive at a 'meaningful' and understood message.

From there to here: what can we take from this broad and rather disparate collection? Thus far I've tried to capture some of the essential thrust of each individual piece. Let us now think about the theoretical ground that they provide. It's clear that much of the work was directed to clearing space for the distinctive analytic projects of the time. In the case of analysing race relations, for instance, the field of sociology and its impacts into social policy had to be sorted out. Or in terms of community studies, attention was given to formulating a way of imbricating theoretical/ideological frameworks with the acknowledgment of empirical realties of actual communities.

In addition to this theoretical specification, there is the productive move to further detach, sort and specify different aspects within culture, understood as a whole way of life. In other words, critique of dominant paradigms proceeded hand in hand with the privileged object of analysis, which in one way or another consistently engaged with what the Work Group called: 'the subjective meaning complex of action'. The subjective versus the objective, the types of methods to be used and the theoretical baggage they bring, the connection between policy and theory – all of these questions continue to be pressing.

What does it mean that we are still grappling with many of the same issues? Should we consider this legacy to be a reminder of the failure of our field? When one thinks of the complexity of the types of questions asked, and the number of levels and interconnections, it is surely not surprising that they haven't been resolved.

However there are glimpses in the material here that suggest ways out of seemingly intransigent and recurring blocks. One involves method and, whether one calls it the ethics or the politics of method, the problems of the subjective and the objective persist. It seems that as a field we have yet to fully follow through on the insights provided by many here, but most acutely by Willis. For me, his challenge reverberates with that issued by Georges Devereux in 1961. In *From Anxiety to Method* he argued that social scientific method serves to distance and protect the researcher from feelings, anxieties and emotions raised in the interrelationship of informant and researcher. It's a false promise, with deleterious effects. Hiding behind method impoverishes the collection of data, its nature and depth, as well as its analysis.

Devereux emphasised 'the difficulty in clearly distinguishing material that comes from the outside (the subject, the field) and from the inside (the researcher's own emotional reaction)' (Devereux cited in Giami 2001). But that blurring was, for him, the site of the richest and most complete data. Devereux's argument about social scientific methods was not to abolish them, but to recognise that they provide only 'the illusion that they abolish all subjectivity and entirely neutralise anxiety' (Devereux 1961: xviii). He issued this challenge: 'a realistic science of man can only be created by men most aware of their own humanity when they implement it most completely in their scientific work' (xx).

Instances of humanity shine through much of this early work in cultural studies. But decades of grappling with post-structuralism and postmodernism have blunted that initial impulse that Willis identifies: that 'unrestrained and hazardous *self-reflexivity*' that allows for 'the possibility of a genuine appreciation of another reality . . . another way of seeing the world' (Willis, in this volume) For all that we have de-centred the human (and certainly many aspects of this were necessary), we have yet to fully rebuild a method of research that effectively grasps networks of human inter- and intra-subjectivity.

To go back to my (failed) portrait of 'the unpleasant work' in a beauty salon, what this demonstrates is the necessity of going beyond thumbnail sketches of people's lives. To properly do justice to the interlocking small pleasures of the customers, the pride of the migrant owners, and the position of the salon in the greater workings of the community would take a lot more work. Understanding the economies of this type of consumption requires in-depth participation, and much more detail on the local and global flows of people, goods and ideas.

It also requires a tone or mode of address that recognises complexity without obfuscation, that acknowledges hardship without being patronising, and that conveys – with purpose – the intricacies and nuances of working class culture as both 'richly threaded' *and* as 'only the minimum condition of survival, and not a cause for celebration'.

The politics of experience remains one of the cornerstones of the project that is cultural studies. To do justice to it requires a constant revisioning of the aims of our research; the necessity of remembering promises to ourselves, our field and to those for whom we do research.

Elspeth Probyn is Professor of Gender and Cultural Studies at the University of Sydney. She has published widely in the area of feminist cultural studies, including *Sexing the Self*, *Outside Belongings*, *Carnal Appetites*, *Sexy Bodies*, *Remote Control* and most recently, *Blush: Faces of Shame* (University of Minnesota Press, 2005).

Notes

1 In my latest book (Probyn 2005) I found it very useful to return to these thinkers for a renewed attention to the study of the total human, and the totality of humanity. See Mauss (1979). I was inspired to return to researching what connects human experience, as well as what differentiates us, by Paul Gilroy's arguments (Gilroy 2000).

2 There are of course many important interventions that do study white racism and more importantly that work with migrant communities and Aboriginal people. It would be unfair to signal individuals out for their contributions; it is also probably unfair to note that critical white studies in Australia have yet to resolve the more than likely unresolvable tensions that arise in the field.

Bibliography

Devereux, G. (1961) *From Anxiety to Method in the Behavioral Sciences*. The Hague: Mouton and Co.

Geertz, C. (1988) *Works and Lives: The Anthropologist as Author*. Stanford, Calif.: Stanford University Press.

Giami, A. (2001) 'Counter Transference in Social research: Beyond George Devereux', *Papers in Social Science Research Methods – Qualitative Series*, no 7. http://www.ethnopschiatrie.net/giami.htm – accessed 7/23/2002.

Gilroy, P. (2000) *Against Race: Imagining Political Culture Beyond the Color Line*. Cambridge: Harvard University Press.

McRobbie, A. (1982) 'The Politics of Feminist Research: Between talk, text, and action. *Feminist Review*, 12, 46–58.

Mauss, M. (1979) *Sociology and Psychology*. Translated by B. Brewster. London: Routledge & Kegan Paul.

Probyn, E. (2005) *Blush: Faces of Shame*. Minneapolis, Minn.: University of Minnesota Press.

19 Symbolism and practice

A theory for the social meaning of pop music

Paul Willis

I The meaning of culture

Rather than approach the cultural behaviour of young people in this country through an empirical listing of new techniques, activities and forms I have chosen in this paper to confront some of the theoretical questions behind the whole category of culture, and to suggest a theory about the relation of social practise and expressive symbolism. Without such a theoretical stance, in my view, there is the danger of our analysis degenerating into a descriptive listing of new phenomena which has no explanatory power at the social plane at all. After establishing the elements of a theory of cultural relation I shall proceed to empirical evidence. This will not, however, constitute anything like a full presentation of the patterns of cultural activity in this country, and will have no quantitative reliability. Furthermore, though the theoretical analysis is applicable to any expressive form, I shall be concerned only with pop music and its surrounding complex of symbolic values and activities. The central assumption of the concluding section, that for most young people in this country, and especially for working class youngsters, the received expressive forms such as theatre, ballet, opera, novels are irrelevant, and that pop music is their only major expressive outlet, will go uncontested. Though it may upset the positivist, such a proposition is taken for granted, and the purpose of the analysis is to investigate the *nature* and *meaning* of the connection between the mass of young people and a widely disseminated, commercially mediated musical form.

First, I would like to examine some of the unspoken theories and theoretical sets behind our discourse on 'culture'. This is the most treacherous of words, and its ambiguous shiftings conceal the precise nature of theories and epistemologies which go under its name. For the use of 'culture' always implies a theory about the role of expressive artefacts in social existence. One inflection of the term pulls with it the meaning of several other terms and categories, so that an apparently isolated and common sense use of the word in fact fixes the whole perspective of an argument, often in a way which passes unnoticed to the reader.

In our current debate there seem to me to be two dominant 'sets' or 'perspectives' lying behind the innocent use of the word 'culture'. Both are damaging to what I take to be a truly social analysis.

Culture as serious art

In the first case culture is used to mean the best of those serious activities separated from everyday life which are meant to express absolute values about the nature of human existence in a medium which is disciplined, self conscious and often difficult to master. This view of culture is a direct descendant of, sometimes even the same as, so-called High Art and its classical Greco-Roman tradition. Even in the more experimental and progressive areas, though the content of the great tradition has been democratized somewhat, and though the scope for experimentation has been widened, and though there is often a self conscious concern with contemporary feelings, the essential assumptions are those of High Art. Art is away from life, judged for itself, autonomous in its functions and values, and ultimately based on detached logo-centric meaning.

The crippling thing about this view of culture, which is also a view of appropriate cultural activity, and a view of the proper scope for cultural analysis, is that it remains analytically blind to its own social placement. From this flows a totally re-ified view of cultural transmission and from this a perpetually outdated perspective on organic or grass root developments in expressive forms.

The integrating belief of culture as separated, heightened, serious activity is the unquestioned value of artistic forms and activities – the supreme placing of Art above the shiftings of whatever social relations exist beneath it. For the adherents of this view Art is classless, timeless and the ultimate touchstone for what is just, human and beautiful. Through shifting sands of circumstance and fortune Art is the only guarantor of worth. Art is the only repository of quintessential human values, the only absolute benchmark in a world of relativism and moral duplicity.

This is a tempting and comforting view of Art, particularly to those for whom the social systems they live under do indeed repress and distort basic human potentiality. Though we may salute these noble cries to heaven we must distrust in serious art any principle which seems to offer an absolute route from bondage and misery. For serious art does not constitute an objective, supra-social, matrix from which poor humans can plot their social development to a more advanced society. For serious art, just as our misery, is a social category. It is constituted, reconstituted and made meaningful at all by a social group. And in all societies this group is the elite. What look like the autonomous all-time absolute values embodied in Art, are in fact chosen quite relativistically by the elite. The great tradition[1] does not select itself, nor autonomously offer its absolute values to save new generations from themselves. Contemporary values select the serious art rather than the reverse, and the selective values are those of the elite. It is true that tradition offers artefacts from the past that are therefore undetermined by the moment, and also true that the moment cannot freely choose to value what does not yet exist in the world. But tradition does not determine the content of serious art, it supplies only the range that contemporary taste can choose from and interpret in its own way. In all the sleeping libraries are ten thousand possible presents. The moving finger is not the value of what exists, but the choice of the living.

It is unimaginable then that a serious art can maintain its own trajectary without being related to a quite specific group. We should be wary of Art as a *deus ex machina* come to right our puny world. All things of this world are ultimately the product of men and women. But the adherents of the view of culture as serious art fail to recognize operationally their art is at bottom an aspect of the social existence of the elites. They see only the salvationary absolutism of the artistic artefact – they re-ify Art. In the sacredness of their abeyance to Art, they miss the profanity of real relations. They spirit away the real nature of serious art – the conflation of an elite with received symbolic values – in their enthusiasm for what they take to be the intrinsic quality of Art.

This re-ification of certain qualities of serious art, the refusal to see the ultimate social base for what they take to be an internal aesthetic, leads to a potential deadness at the heart of cultural activity. The model of cultural transmission is that serious and worthwhile art somehow carries on by itself, and any dialectical connection of form and content to contemporary concerns and feelings is denied. There is the continuous danger of taking what is only the cultural expression of the social position of the elite at one stage in a developing society as the absolute contours of Art, and maintaining this configuration artificially long after its true social congruence to the real living concerns of a group has disappeared.

The elite of course is able to do itself this disservice all the more efficiently because of its privilege and control over resources and institutions. Parallel, though subordinate, cultural configurations amongst the working class have neither the same tendency to internal reification, not the relevant power, to maintain themselves beyond the point of strict, living relevance. In certain respects then working class cultural formations may enjoy real advantages over elitist bourgeois formations. One must not exaggerate this however. The elitist culture is the dominant culture and despite its weaknesses can impress itself across large areas. Besides if the proposition concerning the social basis of cultural forms is right, then it would hold sway even over the reification of serious art, even despite itself, becomes progressively updated. We can expect in this process though, strange and irrelevant displacements, and outdated forms being worked to their last point of decadence and meaningless posture, before being pushed aside by new though still lagged expressive forms.

At bottom serious art is finding it tremendously difficult if not impossible, to break with its long roots in the meaning and logo-centricity of its Greco-Roman tradition. In an age whose wealth, developing social relations, superb technical mastery of nature, might offer qualitively different and hugely relevant expressive forms, serious art even in its non-classical dimensions is still struggling, albeit at its outer fringes, with essentially anachronistic bourgeois expressive forms. Proletarian and mass forms of cultural expression though subordinated and in no sense a true form of mature development, may show us the kindlings of a new and relevant mode of expressing unreified-modern concerns and feelings.

If this line of reasoning has any validity at all we should be particularly alerted by new mass youth cultural forms of expression. In the modern industrial age, where physical and mental maturity occur long before induction in to the bureaucratic/welfare/industrial complex, the teenage interlude is the most important and most problematical period for the reproduction of conventional attitudes, values and practices. In distorted, displaced, exploited and manipulated forms we may see fleetingly the elements of new expressive forms, before the dominant processes of social reproduction at this stage of development close in. A 'cultural' perspective based ultimately though covertly in the perspective of serious art can never hope to pick up these flickers.

The argument here then is that a method of cultural analysis grounded in the unspoken theory of 'culture' as the activities surrounding serious art, is badly equipped to uncover the social meaning of new grass roots cultural activity. Implicitly such a position denies the possibility of the inner *social* connection of an art form to any social group, it restricts the epistomology of enquiry to the modus operandi of elitist culture, it is inherently blind to the possibilities of new and relevant expressive forms. In short such a perspective can only consider modern non-elitist expressive forms as if they were elitist serious forms. It should surprise no one that a shortfall is always found, it has no other measures.

Culture as quantitative relations

The second major perspective lazing innocently behind the use of the word 'culture' is very different. It is a sub-discipline of the much larger and all pervasive academic ideology of positivism. The essential integrative belief of this perspective is that measurement of surface qualities, and correlation of measurements, can reveal real connections. In the field of cultural research this approach is certainly free from elitist overtones, and certainly recognizes the possibility of the connection between social structure and cultural activity. The specific theories are multiform and well represented in the publication from the last conference.[2] American and English media research, statistical breakdowns of audiences, time budgeting research, content analysis of artefacts, are all grouped under the general heading of positivistic research.

Though the role of such work cannot be denied, and though there is still much of a 'factual' nature to be learnt, I want to suggest that such studies can only ever 'point to' a phenomenon. They can chart the extent of particular activities, draw our attention to particular co-variations and connections, expand in the fullest way our essentially *descriptive* knowledge of modern cultural phenomena. What such work cannot do however is to explain the significance, meaning or subjective experience of these phenomena. Positivism in research allows the fullest possible mapping of a culture, but for all that, the culture is still a strange land; we are still no nearer to understanding what it is like to live in, or to understanding why it is like that.

One of the central failings of positivism in social enquiry is its failure to penetrate symbolic, layered systems.[3] A group or a person is never related to a culture in a simple one to one fashion, or in a direct linear fashion. A teenager does not listen to one record in a vacuum, and then to another record, she is not affected by so many degrees immediately by one exposure to a record, or even a type of record. Experience is not atomised in that way, and people live their expressive lives as a symbolic whole. The youth is related at any one time to the whole intricate and complex phenomenon of youth culture. He lives inside this world, is immediately part of this world, lives out its meaning at several levels at different moments. Any one piece or type of music, any one set of experiences, any set of activities, is always taken in the light of her subjective and usually non-verbal understanding of the whole complex of the pop world scene, and its surrounding attitudes, values and symbolic systems. The 'use' made of any particular element in this symbolic whole depends on the rest of the system, and the individual's or group's self recognition of their position within this system. An outside view of the manifest meaning of any particular aspect of this symbolic system, may miss altogether the latent meanings, the reinterpretations, the accepted unspoken meanings that the actors involved may locate in that aspect.

What we are confronted with is a whole way of life interpenetrated by a whole symbolic system, not a series of discrete bits of behaviour alongside a series of discrete cultural artefacts. The meaning of any particular elements of behaviour, or of any isolated expressive work, rests totally on its intricate relations with other parts of the whole integrated cultural system. Even all the constituent parts, assuming one could isolate them, taken separately and only for their manifest qualities, would never amount to the actual culture – they would just be a meaningless random collection of human pieces. In order to see the spirit move in those pieces one has to reach for the central unifying symbolic concepts that are deposited in no single artefact or activity, but only in the dialectical relation of all parts to each other. Positivism, limited as it is to the surface of things, the manifest and the misleading, can never do this, it can only give us the shapes of all the jigsaw pieces, never the picture on them.

Another crucial failure of positivism is its inability to reconstruct, or even register the subjective experience of social actors. Surely a theoretical/intellectual perspective on human behaviour requires a capacity, a potential which need not necessarily be realized, to respond to the raw material of human experience in commensurate terms. Though we may readily agree that a truly social explanation of human activity needs to go beyond the subjective accounts rendered by participant actors, a theory which has no way of accrediting the primary level of human experience – subjective experience – proceeds with a missing centre. The focus of enquiry surely must always be woman/man and his/her sense of his/her relationships to the world. Without this non-quantifiable discipline of *human relevance* – a very much more demanding mistress than mathematical discipline – our studies may as well concern atoms on Mars as humans on Earth.

Looking more closely at the field of rock, those studies which give us the quantitative dimensions of the phenomenon, though useful as a first stage to other kinds of enquiries, for themselves give only a longwinded statement of the obvious, or as they become more ambitious, a huge tautology. We are told in effect that most kids like pop, and they like it because they like it. Without any kind of cutting edge into the subjective plane, and crucially differences between various groups, there is no way of avoiding the view of pop as, both a great monolithic entity – the thing that all those kids like – and, as a totally shallow epiphenomenon – kids like pop because it is simple, bright, colourful or whatever. Only by coming at the subjective experience of real individuals and real groups involved in the music can we break out of these massive simplicities to suggest some of the real and complex bases of connection between the music and the lives of the young people. If we understand some of the central concerns of particular groups, if we have an insight into what they expect from the music, if we can penetrate the symbolic and expressive dimensions of an integrated life experience, then we shall have a base from which to assess the role of pop as a living and dialectically interrelated element of a whole life style. It may well be, of course, that we continue to look at more structural and 'objective' factors in order to come to an appreciation of the totality of the phenomenon, but unless we have proceeded through the located and subjective moment we can never do more than juxtapose life and artefact in a way which is essentially random, and external to the inner connections which should be the business of social enquiry.

Another related weakness of positivistic enquiry is its trust in the immediate verbal response. In the general way we should bear in mind C. Wright Mills' injunction about the discrepancy between 'talk and action' – people's actions often belie their words. In the area of pop music – and cultural phenomena in general – we should be wary even more than usually of the verbal response. I have argued that cultural configurations ought properly to be considered as complex symbolic systems, rather than as atomized conjunctions of bits of behaviour and 'bits of culture' deposited in artefacts. If this is correct, then we should expect the symbolic meanings to be manifested at several levels of social activity, from interaction to bodily expressivity to clothes styles and fashion. There are good reasons to suppose that the self conscious verbal level of expressivity is one of the least favoured modes for the expression of these symbolic values. Self conscious articulate awareness is a characteristic of the dominant strata of society, and is the main instrument of its cultural hegemony[4] over the less powerful groups. Now young people involved in pop culture are excluded from this dominant order in two ways. Firstly the vast majority of young people involved with pop music are working class, and share along with the rest of their class, an inability to articulate their meanings in an abstract verbal manner. Even those individuals and groups with the advantages of a traditional privileged education refuse to mobilize it in the youth cultural context for reasons we shall see in a moment. Secondly, young people are separated off into something like a class which is excluded from the privileges and modes of expression of the dominant class, simply by age. Even though young people are maturing earlier today, the point at which they are being allowed into adult relations of work and consumption is being delayed longer and longer. We should be clear that 'youth' is much more of a social than a biological category. The years, then, between the achievement of adult tastes and motives, and the achievement of the normative and structural outlets for these impulses, represent to some extent a time of cultural oppression and exclusion.

Part of the class and age oppression, as it bites on the young person's world, is the suppression of articulate self consciousness. The symbolic meanings at the heart of the relationship with pop are therefore forced to other media for their expression.

This displacement is not, however, totally the result of coercion, or deprivation. In so far as young people form a distinctive group, whether bounded by age, class or gender they share common concerns and interests which are, to some extent, antagonistic to those of the dominant order. The symbolic expression of their position which achieves any cultural resonance whatsoever will therefore reflect this opposition – it will to that extent be subversive. The dominant order and its modes of cultural control have no reason, of course, to tolerate subversion. Though we need not point to any individual malice or conspiracy there are clear processes (often under capitalism related to commercial rationality) which act either to suppress or to incorporate challenging new forms of cultural expression. Certainly there are those who argue that the process of incorporation of pop is now complete, and that the original spark of rebellion has been inducted as an element of fashion in to a highly successful industry of cultural consumption. At any rate youth cultural forms, in fact any oppositional cultural forms, which can protect their internal workings from the vision of the dominant cultural interests will survive very much longer. Hence we should suspect that the most trenchant and important meanings of youth culture are buried well out of the reach of conventional language – the mode *par excellence* by which the dominant culture penetrates and takes over other cultures. We may expect that really crucial meanings are embodied at non-verbal levels, 'coded' so to speak in such a way that outsiders are unable to interpret. Nor is this coding simply the same message being printed off at another level, it is the symbolization of a totality of experience at several levels – a view of life embedded in a way of life that defies the extraction of its symbolic heart as ratio-scientific meaning.

Positivistic techniques, verbal enquiries, questionnaires, aimed at the verbal level are therefore inadequate. The skill to articulate central meanings does not usually exist in the respondents and even where it does, it is not used. There is every reason for the respondent to deny the invitation to take their experiences out of the totality of their life situations and render them in a diminished and only too appropriable a form.

The lack of articulate response from youth cultural groups has often been taken as proof of the inherent inadequacy and meaninglesssness of the culture surrounding pop music. Certainly to the dominant canons of logo-centric meaning, there is very little to pick up, and the cultural forms are not trying to present themselves as parallel or assimilable forms – to the traditional bourgeois mind much of youth culture really *is* meaningless. However rather than take this as evidence of the non-viability of these cultural forms, we should take it as the *primary* condition for their *social* viability.

I should like now to suggest a theory of 'culture', and an approach to the social meaning of culture, which is based neither on the terms of 'High Art' nor in terms of positivism.

II A theory for the social relation of cultural forms: the case of pop music

The heart of what I understand to be 'culture' is in the *relation* of woman's consciousness, individual and collective, to the objects, and artefacts, both functional and expressive, around her. The study of either of these areas *alone* will not constitute a study of human culture. It does not matter theoretically whether we understand the objects in this relation to be expressive or functional, or indeed whether they are natural or womanmade. The essential and defining feature of culture I take to be the *relationship* of woman to all the objects and artefacts she is consciously involved with. The whole culture of a society or group is the sum of *all* such relationships. Here we are concerned with the relationship of young people to pop music. I suggest that this cultural relation can be understood, and analysed at three levels:–

(a) the INDEXICAL
(b) the HOMOLOGICAL
(c) the INTEGRAL

This approach represents an attempt to honestly recognize, and bridge, the different levels in an interpretative analysis. The *indexical* level of analysis is the least interpretative of all the levels, and can be taken independently of all the other levels. The *homological* and *integral* levels are progressively more interpretative, and progressively further from simple 'objective proof'. They bear witness to the fact that the more explanatory an analysis becomes, the less sure is the empirical grounding of the approach.

1. The indexical level of cultural relation

The indexical level of analysis, and of cultural relation, concerns the degree to which pop music is related to a social group in a general quantitative sense, i.e. for how long a group listens to pop music, where and how often, how much the group spends on pop, what their specific tastes are. The analysis is *indexical* precisely because the interest is in assessing how the artefact is 'indexed' to the life style, how far it is located in a natural human context – a contextualization that the *indexical* stage of the analysis simply recognizes and records, without an interpretative stage intervening to confuse the issue, or to decontextualize the music. This level of analysis can often be presented in the words of the actors themselves and can be uncovered at a verbal level, though clearly observation is an important adjunct to verbal accounts. Positivistic techniques have their greatest appropriateness here.

The *indexical* level of analysis therefore presents in the simplest possible way the minimum case for the existence of a cultural relation between a life style and an artefact. *The indexical* formation of culture is to be seen wherever a human group is in contact with a particular artefact or object. Clearly most of us have an *indexical* cultural relationship with many, many artefacts and objects from houses and cars, to pop music, to Coronation Street, to natural landscapes. The variation of the *indexical* level is a quantitative one. It can record differences in duration and frequency of exposure to music but cannot explain the *significance* of these variations.

2. The homological level of cultural relation

This level of analysis is concerned with the *type* and *quality* of the relationships which the *indexical* stage of the analysis has identified for us. Essentially it is concerned with how far, in its structure and content, the music parallels and reflects significant values and feelings of the particular social group involved with it. Such analysis is *homological* because it investigates what are the correspondences, the similarities of internal relation, between a style of life and an artefact or object. Basic *homologies* are best understood in terms of structure and style, though it may be possible at times to identify *homologies* of content. The essential base of a *homological* culture relation is that an artefact or object has the ability to reflect, resonate and sum up crucial values, states, and attitudes for the social group involved with it. The artefact or object must consistently serve the group with the meanings, attitudes and certainties it wants, and it must support and return, and substantiate central life meanings. One can understand this partly as communication, but much more profoundly it should be understood as a process of cultural resonation, and concretization of identity.

Homological analysis of a cultural relation is synchronic, that is the analysis takes a cross section of the nature of the relationship *at one period in time*. The *homological* notion itself is not equipped to account for changes over time, or to account for the creation, or disintegration of *homologies*; it records the complex qualitative state of a cultural relationship as it is observed in one quantum of time.

An *homological* relationship occurs where a particular group is deeply involved with an artefact or object, and *clearly takes meaning at some level from the artefact or object*, and clearly pursues involvement with it. We are all related to several artefacts and objects at an *homological* level, but it is likely that we will only be significantly related to a few of them, and a *meaningful* relation is more likely with an expressive artefact, than with a functional artefact or a natural object, though this is by no means a consistent rule.

There are two stages of homological analysis, a study of the social group and a study of the music.

(i) The social group

It is here principally that non-positivistic qualitative techniques are required.[5] The aim is to construct the symbolic patterns, attitudes and values embedded in the life style of a group. This task is best approached through a cluster of methodologies. A process of 'triangulation' of the evidence from the different sources gives the maximum possibility of the final phenomenal account of the group's subjective reality being as free from bias as possible. I list the elements of this cluster[6] below and give a brief explanation of what each entails:

CLUSTER OF METHODS

1. Participant observation The act of observing *whilst participating* in the normal round of social and work contacts of the group under study.

2. Observation The distinction between this and the previous technique is that in some situations it is impossible to 'participate' in the full sense of the word, although detailed and careful observation is certainly possible. Simple observation is a crucial adjunct to other methods because only a limited number of meanings are articulated by social groups at a verbal level. Verbal approaches alone to the social group are very limited, and produce evidence only of a verbal kind. Observations of behaviour, style and appearance can go both to cross-check evidence received at a verbal level and to suggest completely *new* areas of the actor's meaning system which are opaque to verbal questioning.

3. Just being around This is the more general process where the researcher, whilst not actually participating in social interaction, is all the same importantly immersed in it. It is not only useful but vital in the early stages of the research, where the researcher is concerned to get a sense of the new frame of reference, without letting his or her own preconceptions obscure the field. It is only after this process of immersion that the researcher can move on to the more detailed, in-close techniques. In many areas it is also the only feasible method of data collection. More generally, the atmosphere and quality of the entire research depends on how well the researcher has felt the whole social ambience of the group he or she is studying.

4. Group discussions Since the group presence is likely to act as a check on the distortion of feelings and experiences, the group discussion is likely to be a privileged source of evidence about group feelings. Furthermore, the most useful data in this kind of research comes from unsolicited statements from subjects, and where a group discussion can proceed without the prompting of the researcher, open-ended discussions can 'take off' and provide data of an unsolicited kind. Discussions constitute the most useful source of detailed and available data about the actor's attitudes and opinions as expressed in the verbal mode.

5. Recorded discussions This has the same advantages as (4) plus the obvious extra advantage of yielding the fullest possible written data about the actors' attitudes and values expressed at the verbal level. The major disadvantage with this technique is that the physical presence of the tape recorder may bring an artificiality to the situation which disrupts the normal ongoing social process. It may also lend an air of formality to proceedings which are basically informal, and need to be informal, for the generation of the kind of data we are interested in. With careful management and appropriate use, however, these dangers can be minimized. The main essentials are that the tape recorder is introduced only when the situation is developing naturally towards some kind of group discussion and is withheld no matter with what impatience, if its introduction would unnaturally affect the course of events.

6. Informal interviews Individual actors are not always involved in ongoing interaction with social groups. During such times, by way of 'just talking', the researcher can gain valuable information about the subject's basic feelings and attitudes. Such data can be used in an important comparative way; it can be placed alongside data covering similar grounds gained in other ways, such as in the group discussion. The course of such interviews should be totally open, and responsive to whatever situation or problem is confronting the subject at the time.

7. Use of existing surveys Wherever possible it is always best to make maximum possible use of existing surveys and reports concerning the specific phenomenon under study, no matter what their theoretical perspective, to 'map the field' and 'cross check' other sources of evidence.

(ii) The music

Broadly there seem to be three possibilities in the analysis of the music appreciated by the social group. It could be argued that the 'value' of the music is *totally* socially given. That is, that the music itself is a cipher, without inherent structures of meaning and value, and that it is the group that reads value into it. There is extreme difficulty, of course, in explaining why it should be pop music, and not some other form, that is specifically taken as the receptacle of socially created meanings and values. One could only explain this in terms of historical accident, by which at a certain point in time in the past the art form is fused with certain values by a certain group. It could be that a certain group is naturally exposed to certain music, so that proximity breeds a relationship which is, in the beginning, accidental in the sense that there is nothing intrinsic in the art form which makes it, and no other form, suitable for a certain group. Once this original point of contact is made, through what I called historical accident, then the process becomes more straightforwardly understandable. Because the original group value the art form, later groups take over what they imagine to be established ways of looking at it and appreciating the form. Accumulation and substantiation through time could develop into what looks like a fully-blown 'aesthetic' of the art form, so that group members themselves would assume values and meanings to be located within the art form rather than in their perceptions of it. Other art forms may be rejected on the apparent basis of their intrinsic inferiority. Values held to be within the art form may be defended as having a substantial and autonomous existence. In fact, those values, and those imagined superiorities, would be nothing more than the accumulated, located reflections of a particular way of life 'read' into the music. In this sense, an art form would be a complex mirror linked to a memory bank, holding but without an intrinsic grasp, valued and significant images, derived in the first place from society.

Such a theory has many advantages of course. It gets over the problem of having to analyse the internal aesthetic of the art form. There would be no reason to attempt an analysis of the internal structure and quality of pop music, and the analysis could proceed totally in terms of the qualities *ascribed* to the artefacts from the outside. That is, the interest would not be in the art form *per se*, but in *how* the art form is received and acknowledged by the significant group. The interest would then be social and cultural, rather than aesthetic; it would fit into other aspects of our analysis without the problems of comparing like with unlike.

This is clearly one extreme approach. At the other extreme would be the view, derived from the 'High Art' perspective, that the value of the art form is totally intrinsic and autonomous. This notion would suggest that an art form would *always* consist of the same immanent qualities, and would keep its integrity no matter what social group was responding to it. The first approach would suggest that different social groupings could see totally different things within the same art form, at least in so far as they had no knowledge of, or no influence upon, each other's tastes. To this extent, the art form would *be* different in itself, to different groups. The second view, then, would see the art form and the social group as totally independent. An analysis of the relationship would proceed through two stages. First, there would be the attempt to evaluate the internal aesthetic of the art form, in its own terms: an aesthetic which would be assumed to be universal. Secondly, there would be the attempt to place this against the life style of the particular group. Such an analysis would assume that the art form would *be* the same, although the profile may alter, no matter what vantage point the critic adopted. In our first approach, the vantage point of the observer would totally determine the art form. In the second case the art form would not mirror back the social and cultural interests of the group related to it, but would stand in its own ground, with a universal, and unchangeable internal relation of parts and feelings. In some senses, it is easier to imagine an art form as having an independent objective existence, quite apart from its social location. This is a common sense view that recognizes the obvious physical separability of cultural artefacts, and accords the artist a distinctive and recognizable role as the creator of something specific, unique and valuable in the world. It would save us from the bottomless relativism of interdependencies, a course which, once started, threatens to challenge common sense meaning. However, there are tremendous problems in the delineation of such a wholly internal aesthetic. The divergence of critical opinions, over time, and even within the same period, demonstrates that immanent qualities are less autonomous and 'there' in the artefact, than this pure theoretical position might seem to suggest. Furthermore, the currency of this analysis is intrinsically set in aesthetic terms. What is assumed to be an intrinsic aesthetic is clearly impenetrable by cultural and social concepts, terms generated from the outside. It can only be penetrated by terms generated from within, which can carry like meaning. Thus, the analysis of the art form producing terms of *internal* significance may be extremely difficult to place against the non-'external' terms of a social analysis. The two may never meet, except in the kind of spurious generalization that characterizes so much writing in the field of cultural criticism.

Finally, one could approach the art form at some point between these two extreme views. This is the position I adopt. My position is that the value and meaning of an art form is given socially, but within objective limitations imposed internally by the art form. Instead of an 'aesthetic' I refer to *objective possibilities* within the art form. Instead of *totally* socially given meanings I suggest that social meanings are returned within certain parameters – fixed by the art form. Thus particular art forms are not seen as having inherent and unchangeable meanings and values; rather they are seen as having the potential *to hold and return a range* of meanings which are, in the first place, socially given. The art form has a certain chameleon quality; it can change according to which group is looking at it, and from where. However, there are limits to the ways it can be perceived, and these are not determined solely by social location and interests of the audience. Some kinds of social meanings for a particular art form will be held and reflected fully within it, others partially, and still others not at all. This kind of limitation will depend crucially on internal structures within the art form; but these internal parameters are not, as it were, always alive and fully operational. They only come alive and become capable of holding meaning when they are rubbed against the real life experience of a particular group. If this life experience is beyond the range of scope of these parameters, then very little will be returned and made socially significant. If the life experience falls *within* the parameters provided by the internal structures of this mark, then the social meanings are held, perhaps importantly modified in a creative relationship with these parameters, and returned to the social group. The parameters themselves, then, do not have meaning in the sense of a fully prescribed content. They both stake out the field of potential meaning and create an ambience in which certain types of meaning from the outside can flourish. The *objective possibilities* are best understood as belonging more to the structure than the content of an artefact. It is the notion that in the design and fundamental orientation of the text certain *categories* or *kinds* of feeling are allowed a scope for meaningful development. (In a sense the *objective possibilities* are the crude outline of a particular 'world view' which can supply the underpinning for more specific context-based meanings.) The notion of an 'aesthetic' places much too unique a construction upon this complex field of forces and would attach the status of meaning to that which is better understood as being capable of holding *several* potential meanings. The notion of 'totally socially given meanings', on the other hand, ignores the objective existence of the artefact with its internal structures, which whilst not capable of generating fully formed meanings, all the same can prevent or encourage *certain types* of meaning.

These *objective possibilities* can be placed against the life style of the groups, or more exactly against the researcher's 'organizing perspective' derived from the empirical evidence of the life style, and the musical tastes of the groups. This comparison is the vital step in *homological* analysis and is the basis for the assessment of the type and quality of the cultural relation between a group and its preferred music.

3. The integral level of cultural relation

This level of analysis is concerned with the degree to which the two elements in a cultural relationship directly influence and modify one another. Integral analysis is likely to apply most fully to human relationships to expressive artefacts and least fully to relationships with natural objects. It is aimed at explaining both the historical generation of basic *homologies*, and the manner of their continued development in the present. Where the *homological* analysis was synchronic, the *integral* level of analysis is diachronic, or more exactly has a theoretical capacity to be diachronic. This third level is *integral* because it investigates the life style and activities of the group, and the music, as they form a whole, or as the elements fundamentally condition each other as part of a tight unitary system.

Firstly, the analysis would investigate the degree to which the music exerts and has exerted a direct creative influence on a life style, that is the way it not only *reflects* central attitudes, values and activities, but actually takes a part in determining the nature of these things. The ways in which the music is capable of this include: the direct intervention of music into action or emotion, i.e. being the stimulus of something new in the behaviour or experience of the listener which would not have occurred without the music; the ability to express blocked personal emotion in a unique way; the ability based on these previous two to directly exert an influence on the shape and form of an individual's or group's sensibilities.

Secondly this analysis would investigate the degree to which a social group exerts and has exerted a determining force on the creation of the music it enjoys and has been able to change the *objective possibilities* of such music. Simply, this would occur where the creative base of the music is and was in the social group, or the extended version of the social group, that the listener is part of.

Now if both these elements were present historically, that is that the music exerted an influence on consciousness, and the social group exerted an influence on the form of the music, then it can readily be seen that a dialectical process will have occurred in which life and music were continually brought closer together in to basic *homologies*. It can also be readily seen that where both of these elements exist in the contemporary situation there will be a *continuing* tightening and substantiation of basic *homologies*.

If determinations flow in only *one* direction then it can also be seen that the process is very much more limited, and is not capable of *continually* developing fuller basic *homologies*. The obvious example here is in the cultural relation of a life style and consciousness to a natural object. There may well be determinations flowing from the object to the life style, but it is difficult to see determinations flowing in the other direction whilst the object is still 'natural'.

Where there *is* mutual determination I call this a process of *integral circuiting*. At a theoretical level I also want to suggest that where there is *integral circuiting* between a life style and an artefact, the power of the relationship will be sufficient to 'drag in' other elements and strongly influence the form of their relation to the central life style of the group. I call this whirlpool effect *integral mediation*, so that for instance the powerful *integral* formation of the motor bike to the motor bike boys powerfully *mediates* many other aspects of the boys' relationship with artefacts and objects, and especially their relationship with pop music. The same is true of drugs in the 'hippie' culture. A total cultural understanding then would take into account *all* the relationships between a social group and the objects and artefacts around them, *and* the manner in which particularly potent *integral circuits mediate* other relationships, and indeed each other.

Just finally, from a theoretical point of view an *integral circuit* should continue to a final and unimaginable collapse of art and life. In fact this point is never reached because of what

I call *integral disintegration*. This is where, for one reason or another, the *integral circuit* goes into reverse and basic *homologies* are slowly unwound. This might be caused by a decisive move of the creative locus of the artefact from the social group which appreciates it, or it might be caused by some kind of collapse of the *objective possibilities* of the music. To generalize, *integral disintegration* would occur, as it were, when one of the poles in the dialectic becomes unresponsive or even repellant to the other.

Clearly this final part of the analysis is the most interpretative of all the modes of analysis I have described. It cannot be approached through the verbal accounts of the actors involved, and has to make the fullest possible use of *every* mode of observation and interaction with the groups the researcher has open to him or her.

III Pop music in England

Before attempting to apply these theoretical concerns to a concrete example I would like to deal briefly and generally with two important areas that impinge directly on pop music and its culture – technology and commerce.

Technology

Firstly as to the role of technology in the production of pop. In terms of the music itself, technical processes have been used as musical resources. The electrification of the guitar was the single most important development for pop, and the pop explosion of the late fifties would have been impossible without it. Amplification of sound generally has been crucial, and some of the more recent groups such as the Who and the Jimmi Hendrix Experience have used *extreme sound* as a musical resource in its own right. In other ways what were once thought of as the costs of using electrified instruments – the best example is feedback – have been creatively adapted to become an internal and *intended* element of the internal musical structure. At the most extreme, such groups as the Pink Floyd make use of electronic equipment almost to the point of leaving behind the traditional instruments altogether. Even during a 'live' performance, of something like 'Atom Heart Mother', the group spend much time at great consoles manipulating sound effects and playing back prerecorded material, as well as 'playing' instruments in the traditional way. In the last few years there has also been an expansion of the media outlets in live performances, particularly into the visual with the so-called 'light show'. Recent developments have been to synchronize the movement of the music precisely with the form and development of the light show. In sum then, pop music is increasingly becoming dependent on certain technological forms, and is moving further from traditional notions of the 'band' playing instruments in a straight forward manner.

Technology is also vastly important on the production side of pop in the way that it has allowed recording of material, and the provision of ready forms of reproduction of the music. It is only fairly recently, with the advent of the 45 rpm. single record, and the 33 rpm. long playing record, that recordings and reproductions have been made of a quality to vie with, and in some cases surpass, the original. It is these developments which have of course allowed the formation and expansion of the vast market for records. The replacement in mass circulation of sheet music by recorded music was one of the crucial stages in the development of pop, and marked the point at which the unique stylistics of particular singers, and the manner of their vocal 'personality', became an important factor in the music – no musical notation could ever reproduce the distinctive brooding quality of Elvis Presley's voice, in the way that a reproduction can instantly. More recently of course with the advent of sixteen-track tape recorders, sophisticated echo effects and stereo recording, the recorded version of a song can be vastly superior (in terms of range and exploitation of effects and resources) to the 'live' version, so that no parallel 'live' version is possible. The Beatles' 'Sergeant Pepper's Lonely Hearts Club Band' took several hundred hours to record, and for the most part could not be successfully reproduced live. The most progressive bands would now regard the recorded artefact as their main medium of expression, and would not attempt to duplicate their sounds in a totally 'live' medium. In this sense then a new technological form has virtually displaced traditional forms, and certain examples of modern music could be said to owe their distinctive internal and aesthetic nature to modern technology.

On the consumption side it is no less clear that technological developments in the mass media have played a powerful part in what we now regard as the phenomenon of youth culture and its involvement with pop music. To sum up many important strands in the telecommunications 'revolution', we can point to a simple phenomenon – the incredible popularity of Elvis Presley in England, *a country in which he has never been present.* Individuals were *known about* outside their own countries in times before the tele-communications revolution, *but never in terms which rested totally on the precise configuration of their personal presence.* Millions of fans in England have the most precise knowledge of Elvis from the particular timbre of his voice, to the oddly self regarding intensity of his eyes. In a crucial sense the telecommunications systems now available to us have transported all but the smell of a man across the Atlantic. Without this incredible technological 'miracle' youth culture and pop music as we know it could *never* have developed.

The importance of these technological considerations for our theoretical approach is that a *new medium* of expression can always be appropriated by an underprivileged group, and it can offer *new* elements of coding in which to express subversive meanings in a way not comprehended by the dominant group. The existing mediums of expression are likely to be controlled and 'policed' by the dominant culture, and are unlikely to provide the basis of a really meaningful cultural dialectic with an oppressed group. New mediums of expression are of course most likely, under normal circumstances, to be taken up by the powerful group, but in certain circumstances the dominant group may not realize the potential of new forms, and may indeed by altogether unaware of the expressive function of the new forms. In such circumstances culturally oppressed groups have a rare opportunity to take possession of a new medium, and of a new code, and to develop them as the basis for their own *integral circuits.* In this way the developing cultural dialectic of those oppressed groups which can appropriate a new form of expression and coding, based on modern technological developments, can be said to be more truly the product of its age, and more truly attuned to underlying social movements than is the dominant cultural dialectic.

Commercial production of pop music

Basically I suggest that where the commercial system of production, advertising, promotion, distribution, market research, intervenes most between the music and the 'consumer' there is least chance of a genuine cultural dialectic developing. Fundamentally this is because the direction of change in the *objective possibilities* of the music will be determined, not by the interests of a living social group, but by the marketing techniques of extrapolation and smoothed averaging. Bureaucratic, mass production commercial bodies don't produce, but only reproduce. Thus, although there might be some dialectical influence of the music on consciousness, there is unlikely to be any meaningful dialectical influence of the life style back on to the music, except as mediated through market research techniques at the service of very different interests. The scope for the development of commercially mediated music is therefore limited by, so to speak, the 'deadening' of one pole of the cultural dialectic.

The case must not be exaggerated here. These comments about the commercial system of production must not be taken as synonymous with the traditional argument about commercial manipulation. Music cannot be 'foisted' upon a group through commercial manipulation alone. There is still the important level of the *homological* cultural relation. Unless commercially provided music has the capacity to hold and return certain values and concerns of its audience it can never be really successful – this condition sets a rigid limit on how far manipulative theories can be taken. Of course the music does, as I have said, have a determining force on life style and consciousness, and it could be argued that this force over time may act to debase sensibility in a manner which makes music, of no matter what standard, acceptable. The case would need to be argued here, but very quickly, I would argue that the determining effect of the music only comes in to real dialectical operation, when the consciousness is already in the grip of a basic *homology*, and that this basic *homology* must, in the first instance, come from the authentic life interests of the actors.

However, in the general case, my argument is that commercial intervention between the performer and his or her audience is likely to act in the direction of limiting the growth of *integral circuits*. This separation of the performer and his or her audience is also likely to have other consequences. There is likely to be a pressure on performers to repeat established and well known successes and the mode of the performer's relation to his or her audience is likely to be of the star system kind. The performer will be distanced from their public, and will be perceived to be from a different and more privileged social group. She/he will also be packaged and publicized by the commercial interests in the way that any other commodity might be. The sum total of these things would be the creation of a 'star', unapproachable and untouchable, *though summing up a lot*, for his or her audience.

In the converse case where the commercial system intervenes least between the performer and his or her audience, there is likely to be the maximum possibility for the growth of *integral circuits*. Real innovation always occurs outside the great commercial blocks. Fundamentally this is because the direction of change of the *objective possibilities* of the music in such outside areas is set, not by marketing techniques, but by the artistic integrity of the performer, who would either know his or her audience very well, or be from the same social group as their audience, and would therefore shape the music progressively to fit the active and dynamic concerns of their audience. Assuming then that the audience is in its turn subject to determinations flowing from the music, we can readily see that the conditions are set for the development of a cultural dialectic to bring basic *homologies* into a tighter relation, and to strengthen cultural identity and confidence. Such processes rely very little on any social category of the 'animateur culturel'. In England the nearest there is to this category, would be the record producer, d.j., or sounds system d.j., who recognizes the importance of a new style or form and gives it wider commercial exposure. As we have seen this may be considered as the beginning of a process of re-ification and stultification of the form.

There is a somewhat special use of the term 'commercial system' here. The suggestion is not that music can be produced totally independently of the 'commercial system'. In a highly complex, post industrial mixed economy, such as in England, it would be virtually impossible to produce and distribute a record on a significant scale without the reliance on some aspects at least of the commercial system. The point at issue is this: to what extent has the commercial system, which must always be involved at some level, enter into the very nature of the music? My suggestion is that where the artists have a free hand in designing their own music, and where they have a better notion of the listening group – because they come from it – than the commercial controllers have, the music though handled, financed, and distributed through a commercial system can be authentically free from that biggest contaminant of commercialism – an internal design determined by quantitative consumerism. Briefly, where the product of a commercial system is responsible to the *real* needs and feelings of its audience, it has escaped total commercial determination, and can enter into *integral circuits* implicitly critical even of the very system by which it was produced. There is a grave danger in regarding the commercial system as a single headed monster with an integrated malicious will. Certain parts of its operation can well be disadvantageous for other parts, and different parts of the system are differentially exploitable.

IV A case study[7]

The essence of this approach to the social meaning of pop music is the identification of a clear social group and the music it enjoys. The group could be as large as the whole of the teenage population of England. However there are severe problems here, and one of the really significant things this approach should alert us to is the danger of referring to 'Youth Culture' as a monolithic entity. Within so-called 'Youth Culture' are several groupings, and each of these is related to its own strand of pop music. Though all of the groups share some common attitudes and feelings, and though all the variant forms of music deserve the common term pop music, an analysis of the macro level would deal only in very basic common denominators. Our task should be to differentiate within 'youth culture' and to begin to build up the contours of its complex internal map, rather than limit ourselves to generalizations.

I would like to present an analysis of one group in England – the motorbike boys. The following is a much condensed version of a section of my Ph.D. thesis.

It should be remembered that the motorbike boys had very clear tastes in music, they liked early rock'n'roll – Chuck Berry, early Elvis, Buddy Holly and the latter music of the Beatles and the Rolling Stones in as far as it was in the same tradition. The *Indexical* and *Integral* levels of an analysis were very much less important than the *Homological.* For convenience here, I'll present only the *Integral.*

The social group

The world of the motorbike boys was above all else concrete and unequivocal. Values and attitudes were so deeply entrenched as to form part of an obvious commonsense reality. There was no abstract dimension to the world, only a straightforward physicality and confidence in things. The touchstone of this world were manliness, toughness and directness of interpersonal contact.

Frankness and directness characterized the modes of group interaction. Formal structures, or considerations of politeness, were not allowed to distract normal on-going life. In this sense, group life was very informal.

This lack of formal respect, and continuous pressure to judge and award status in the here and now, and within the boundaries of their own culture, is also demonstrated by their extreme attitude to the Royal Family. Respect is clearly not given on the basis of a formal, received social deference:

PW: The Queen.
Joe: Oh that silly old cunt . . . She's only there to fucking . . . You know I don't think we

ought to have her there really, she only an ornament, she's an ornament . . . it's all wrong.

June: It doesn't bother me.

Joe: It's all wrong. She's taking all our fucking money.

Fred: I can't see why people should have to pay.

PW: Prince Charles and the Investiture?

Fred: Load of rubbish, they ought to have had a Welshman for it, not a bleeding renegade.

Joe: Yeah, I mean to say, he's fucking Welsh.

Fred: She's German, he's a bleeding renegade, and he's made Prince of Wales – it's a load of rubbish, they hadn't ought to come over here.

Joe: I was gonna say, none of them are fucking English, it should have been all fucking English, the bastards, the Prince ain't fucking English is he?

Fred: No, no his old woman's a German, and he's a Greek. He can't go back to his own country.

This shouldn't be interpreted as iconoclasm, still less as any kind of revolutionary consciousness. It is simply that meanings and values were located in the concrete and lived situations. Formal meanings, or status within an outside hierarchical structure were rejected. They lived in the unalienated world of the present and immediate relations, and would not allow these to be distorted or challenged by definitions from the outside.

Another element of the informality and directness of the world in which they lived was the widespread use of nicknames. These nicknames were partly given by the group and partly adopted by the individual. Once the nicknames were coined they were used universally, and it was difficult to find out what real names were.

Their belief in the strength and control of one's own agency was demonstrated by our group's attitudes towards drugs. They did not see drugs (for instance, as they saw motorbikes) as an access to excitement or glamorous new experiences. They saw them as a threat to the integrity of one's own agency. There is a clear pride in ability to act and make decisions autonomously, and the drug pusher is seen as a threat to this autonomy; it is almost an element of honour, a code of living that distinguishes the motorbike boy; the essential element of this code is self-reliance.

PW: Drugs?

Joe: Oh, fucking drugs, that's stupid . . .

Several Voices: Yeah, it's stupid . . . yeah.

Joe: I've never taken a drug in my fucking life, I'd push the fuck out of the kid who offered me one.

PW: Would you?

Joe: Yeah, I would.

Fred: And I would.

John: They can't be men if they take drugs . . . there must be something wrong with them.

June: Stupid, ain't it?

Joe: If I knew anyone that took them I'd fucking do 'em.

Fred: If I couldn't do anything without a drug in me I wouldn't want to do it at all.

Joe: If I took something to make me fucking do it I wouldn't want to know.

Fred: It's the same as beer isn't it. I mean you get a lot of people, they've got to have a drink before they'll bleeding hit anybody. If I couldn't hit anybody without any beer or drugs . . . I wouldn't be much.

Joe: I know a lot of kids, they go and have a lot of booze, before they go and have a tattoo or something, they're scared of having it, I mean without beer, it's a drug that is, isn't it.

June: It's ridiculous, it's Dutch courage.

Drugs are seen as loosening up the strict relationship between consciousness and reality, between decision and action in the world, between thought and concrete expression. They had never tried 'drugs' apart from alcohol and would not have begun to understand the difference between depressants, stimulants and hallucinogens, and so had no experiential basis for their extreme views. Rather the basis of their feeling was an insubstantial kind of fear. Feeling would have probably been much less intense had soft drugs such as cannabis been tried. Perhaps one can understand the nature of this insubstantial fear as a displaced recognition of a complex truth about themselves. The commonsense and obvious nature of the physical and social world was at once the basis of their reality and the source of ultimate importance in their lives. In the here and now at least they bulked a meaningful presence, they had a dignity. More dissociated views of the world would have threatened not only the way they thought, and the status of their common sense reality, but also their sense of identity and importance within that world. Extinction, or dissolution, of the concrete world was not a matter of philosophic or abstract interest, it was also the dissolution of personality. Of course this is to pitch the argument at too theoretical a level, but the group's violent distrust of drugs, and their rejection of abstract or uncertain, ways of looking at the world, does not suggest a form of recognition of, and avoidance of, zones which were potentially self-destructive to their highly unequivocal concrete world.

The motorbike was a crucial element in their strength of personal identity. Their interest in the motorbike might have been taken as signifying a morbid fascination with death paralleling, in a sense, the search for excitement through drugs youth cultural groups. In my view, this would be to misunderstand their relationship to the motorbike. Firstly, it was *not* the case that they had a simple death wish which the motorbike could efficiently administer to. The notion of skill and experience on the motorbike, which was widely valued, was previously about *avoiding* unnecessary accident. They did not have a submissive attitude to the motorbike, but an assertive attitude that stressed the importance of control over the machine; if the machine won't be subject to the dictates of their will, then it was to be distrusted, not valued:

Joe: No . . . the motorbike don't frighten you.

Jeff: If the bike handles well, the bike will never beat you, if it handles bad, it frightens you, that's all.

PW: Frightens, what does 'frightens' mean?

Jeff: No, scared, I mean. Like if I've got a bike and I don't handle well, I won't go fast on it, but if it'll do everything you want it to, well that's it you know.

Thus the motorbike was not a random source of danger and excitement, but was located well within the commonsense world, and was responsive to ability and coordination in the physical world. I argued earlier that the motorbike was symbolically appropriated into the motorbike world, and this ability to control and master an impersonal technological force was a crucial part of the process. It is precisely the confidence in identity and the controllability, the unequivocality, of the physical world which expands to envelope and control the ferocity of the motorbike. This is quite contrary to the subjective vulnerability of a drug experience. Not only is the ontological security of the motorbike boys demonstrated in their mastery of such an apparently alienative object as the motorbike, but the qualities of the motorbike itself are developed to express crucial aspects of this confidence in identity and unarguable reality. The motorbike responds inevitably and concretely to a subjective will and skill, it accelerates to the point of blowing the rider off at the twist of a wrist. Control decisions are met immediately by the physical consequences of rushing air. The sheer mechanical functioning of the motorbike, with the hardness of metal against metal, the controlled explosion of gases, the predictable power from the minutely engineered swing of machined components, underwrites a positive and durable view of the physical world. The boldness, dash and intimidation of the machine enhance the boisterous confidence in the identity of the rider. In several ways, in its image, in its difficulty of mastery, in its precise functioning, in its predictable response, the motorbike puts beyond doubt the security and physicality of the motorbike boy's world. In its ferocity, and undeniable presence, it contradicts the more abstract and formal structuring of the world.

This care, and ability on the motorbike, did not, of course, eradicate risk. There was danger, and this was accepted, even relished as we saw before. However, it was important that the danger did not come from the capricious tyranny of the motorbike as an object but was the ultimate extension of the qualities of the motorbike into the human zone, and the transcendental symbolic affirmation of those qualities. Danger was accepted for what it was in the scope of a fully-connected consciousness. Death and accident on the motorbike was the culmination of activities that were precisely confident and secure in the tangible world. It was not psychedelic, mind-changing experience, a mystical denouement which undershot the previous existence of things. It was the normal world, with its concrete range of responses pushed to a climax, pushed to the limits but within a secure consciousness, until the sudden bursting through into a transcendence which didn't dissipate identity but substantiated identity even more fully than before, only at a higher and more universal level. At no point is consciousness, of the incontrovertibility of material things, challenged; even in the prospect of death, the risk is met in the confidence and expectation of full consciousness. Death is not an anodyne, but paradoxically, the quintessential recognition of awarencess and personality. The motorbike, at several levels, sums up the confidence and sureness of being-in-the-world of the motorbike boys. In this sense, it was the opposite of what they understood 'drugs' to be and of what they so violently disliked.

The music

One of the interesting things about the motorbike boys' use of pop music was their overwhelming preference for 'singles'. Even here it's possible to see the *objective potential* of the musical artefact! Singles were responsive to the listener in the sense that they only lasted for two and a half minutes. If a particular record was disliked, at least it lasted for only a short time. It could also be rejected from the turntable more quickly without the difficulty of having to pick the needle up to miss a track on the LP and replace it a little further on. Exact selection could also be made so that the order of records was totally responsive to individual choice. To play an LP was to be committed (unless you were prepared to go to a great deal of trouble) to someone else's ordering of the music. By and large, LPs are more popular with an audience which is prepared to sit and listen for a considerable period, and with a certain extension of trust so that unknown material can be appreciated and evaluated. LPs are a cheap way (as distinct from singles) of building up a large collection of songs within particular traditions. Often there will be tracks on an LP, which have never been very popular but which are of interest to the expert, or the devotee, or the technician. LPs tend to serve the interest more of the 'serious' listener, who is concerned to appreciate all the aspects of a particular field, and not simply those to which he is already attracted. Of late, LPs have also been produced which have been conceived as a unit, parallel in a way to the opera or extended musical piece. Dating from approximately 'Sergeant Pepper' by the Beatles, the progressive groups particularly have been concerned to produce LPs imaginatively conceived as a whole in this way, which are meant to be taken as a whole at one sitting. All this implies an audience which is stationary, sitting, not engaged in other activities, and prepared to devote a substantial length of time to the appreciation of the music alone. Of course, there are many exceptions to this, and the whole field of LPs is tremendously varied. An LP of 'Elvis's Golden Hits' for instance is specially produced as a cheap collection of Elvis's singles; the attraction here is specifically based on the attraction of a group of popular singles. However, generally, and especially in contrast to singles, it holds true that the LP audience is stationary and mono-channelled towards the music. This kind of situation is clearly inappropriate to the Double Zero boys. They are usually moving, engaged in other activities, and responsive to music only when it is not boring. Their preference for singles was overwhelming, to the point that, quite apart from inherent musical qualities, the absence of a single version of a song was held as *prima facie* evidence of its inferiority. One can only understand this by appreciating that the connotations of the LP were quite contrary to the fundamental elements of their life style. Here is Joe questioning the value of a Chuck Berry version of a record, which they had just heard and liked by the Rolling Stones on a single, simply because it was 'only on an LP'.

John: The Stones are, well ok, it's not as good as Chuck Berry's then. Have you heard Chuck Berry's?

Joe: Yeah, but its only on an LP, it ain't on a single.

Jeff: It ain't as good as Chuck Berry's, no.

This might be taken as a clottish, obstinate, inflexibility, typical of an uneducated refusal to accept new advances until it is realized that, in fact, the experience of listening to the same track on an LP (as on a single) would not have been so enjoyable for the Double Zero boys precisely because they would have felt a lack of control, an implied seriousness, which would have inhibited the free flow of response. Their preference for singles was simply an honest, logical extension of a coherent set of attitudes, not the random obstinacy of the unimaginative.

Beat and movement

One of the most noticeable things about the kind of music liked by the motorbike boys was the prominence of its *beat*. It is music for dancing to, for moving to, and clearly has the ability to reflect and resonate a life style based on confidence and movement. Elvis Presley was consistently best in his fast-moving beat songs. With his gyrating hips, out-flung arms and coy angling of the head, he altogether did away with the image of the stationary singer. Almost every early record cover shows him *moving*, and of course, his stage name will always be Elvis the Pelvis. Buddy Holly's style too, relied on a strident beat, and the alert quality of his voice was enhanced and projected by the clear beat. For the period and for his colour (white) he was very strongly influenced by black Rhythm and Blues music; this is one of the reasons why he was the only white singer seriously to influence Mick Jagger. The driving dancing rhythm of more traditional Rhythm and Blues comes through in his records time and again. Sometimes, as in 'Not Fade Away', the music is virtually taken over by beat and rhythm, with the melody totally subjugated to a transfixing rhythm pattern. The Beatles, in their early days played a kind of up dated rock'n'roll, which again relied on a fundamental big beat.

In the pre-recording days of the Beatles in Liverpool and Hamburg the big beat was supremely important for two reasons. Firstly, it was vital to provide good dancing music so that people enjoyed themselves and would come again. Secondly, a loud moving beat was likely to pull people off the streets in the first place into the club or bar. The early Beatles records were exact reproductions of their live performances without the aid of any of the studio effects that other singers were using at the time. Consequently they reproduced exactly the same loud clear beat, essentially simple harmonious dancing music, on record, as they did in the live club scene. It was the biggest loudest beat in the pop scene since early rock'n'roll. The progress of the Beatles could be described simply in terms of the loss of this big beat. They became more sophisticated, using melodic asymmetry and complex rhythm patterns. The latter music became very much harder to dance to, especially in the concrete, direct, bopping-to-the-rhythm dance patterns of the early rock era – a style of dancing which had none of the 'freaky' free form movements that later styles developed to match the asymmetry of progressive music. The motorbike boys ranked the early Beatles very highly; they became progressively cooler about the later Beatles; they despised some of their 'really stupid stuff'. To simplify, the process of the motorbike boys' disillusionment was commensurate with the disappearance of the big beat from the Beatles. The Rolling Stones, much more consistently than the Beatles, kept to the strong simple beat of Rhythm and Blues. Of all post-early-rock-music the Stones have kept closest to the elemental function of pop – providing music to dance to. Mick Jagger in performance, with his outlandish talent for movement, mime and gesture, personified in action the movement-potential of his music.

Concreteness and clarity

The preferred music of our group was also hard and concrete, with a clarity of style that made them fairly instantly rememberable. Again, there was a congruence here with a culture that demanded concreteness, unequivocality and instant recognition. Elvis Presley in his early songs, sang in a straight and powerful way dealing with concrete situations. His style was utterly distinctive and one of his records could be recognized from the first syllable of his singing, if not from the atmosphere of the first bar of music. Buddy Holly was not so consistent. Some of his records (mainly on the Coral Label) were soft with a kind of gentle wistfulness; but even here the voice was crystal clear, and the tune simple and rememberable. His records, mainly on the Brunswick Label, were much faster and harder and concrete, with, again, the penetrating clear voice adding a distinctive resonance. The early Beatles' music was simple, and the lyrics direct and concrete about familiar situations. Later the Beatles moved into an exploration of mysticism, one of whose characteristics was the suspension of ordinary language, so that both lyrics and melodies became more abstract, complex and mystifying. It was at this point that the motorbike boys withdrew their warm support of the Beatles, and accused them of deserting the holy torch (my phrase). The Stones, throughout their career dealt in elementary simple harmonics, strong simple rhythms and conventional chord patterns. Throughout, they were direct, forceful and concrete – exactly the *objective potential* that allowed the motorbike boys to gain so much significance from them.

Assertiveness

The aggressive and masculine assertiveness of the motorbike boys also found an answering structure in their preferred music. Elvis Presley's deep brooding voice was full of aggression, unspecified and enigmatic, though always powerful. In the atmosphere of his records, as well as the statement of his words, and his personal image, was a deep implication that he was a man not be pushed around. His whole presence demanded that he should be given respect, though the grounds for that respect were disreputable and antisocial, by conventional standards. Buddy Holly's music was not so aggressive, but it was utterly secure in its own style; it insisted that its range and interests were important and deserving of recognition. The Rolling Stones' music and image has remained entirely 'unrespectable' in its opposition to the adult world, and its espousal of hooliganism and permissiveness. The music was harsh, angry and expressive of cruelty, the violence of the vocal delivery invested the lyrics with meaning far beyond the power of the cold words. There was also, in the Stones' music, an assumed superiority over women, and a denial to them of personal authentic action, which ran very close to the attitudes of the motorbike boys themselves. The Beatles were not aggressive in such an outright fashion, and did not symbolize hooliganism in the same way; but there was a vigorous release of feeling, and an utter confidence in their style of playing which gave the music considerable power and muscular control. In some ways the Beatles' early songs were a 'celebration of youthful confidence', and gave voice to the expectation of being able to control an unalienating world. All this made their music particularly responsive to the special confidence, and rumbustious expectation of success, of the motorbike culture.

Informality

Generally, this music had an informality and frankness that answered to the informal quality of the motorbike boys' life style, with its refusal to let status be judged or imposed by outside hierarchical patterns of any kind. Elvis Presley's voice was spontaneous, informal and direct, there was a palpable sense of an emotional physicality trying to express itself through the music, and define its identity against, and despite of, wide authoritarian and hierarchical patterns and pressures. In this sense, and especially with the confiding tone of the rich voice, the music was very personal and direct, though it avoided the *privacy* of emotion by a denial of indulgence in the lyrics and an overriding strong, extrovert beat. Buddy Holly, in a different way, was extremely informal and direct in his delivery, particularly in the slower, more wistful numbers. He seemed to be speaking straight to the listener, across the gap of – at one level – promoters, commercial companies, show business glitter, at another level, authority, school, police, juvenile courts, bosses . . . The precise articulation of the voice, the frankness of tone, the simplicity, the emotional explicitness of the music, brought it straight through into the concrete everyday world of the young listener. The music was all the same public, and in the shared world, because of the confidence of the music in itself, and the basic dance rhythms present even in the slower tunes. The Beatles' early records, as I said, were exact reproductions of music played in the club situation, and although not so personal, had all the vibrancy of the spontaneous informal action of a lively dance hall. Listening to the early Beatles one can easily visualize figures bounding and shouting around on a packed dance floor.

The stylistic development in the music evidenced in the later Elvis Presley clearly changed the *objective potential* of the music for our group. The motorbike boys' rejection of the later material is entirely consistent. Towards the end of the 1950s Elvis Presley became much more contrived, he dragged his vowels and wallowed in the beat, progressively losing the movement and drive that made his earlier records so distinctive. He tended to exaggerate the importance of himself, to the point of narcissism, and descended into the crooning style of popular songs. The process was confirmed by a record like 'It's now or never' (1960), and records after this date had no relevance for the motorbike boys. The Beatles after the production of 'Rubber Soul', 'Revolver', and 'Sergeant Pepper' (1967), despite a few later flashbacks to an earlier style, progressively lost their big beat, and their immediate contact with spontaneous emotion. Possibly this was through the pressure of production for a seller's market, possibly it was through an internal desire for experimentation in the group. Certainly their developing style was vastly technically superior to their earlier recordings. They manipulated studio effects with amazing virtuosity; but these things took them further from original rock'n'roll and the informality of the live performance. Their lyrics were witty, verbally intricate and allusive, and the music complex and nuanced in a way unknown to earlier pop music; but this later Beatles style had no appeal to the hard non-abstract tastes of our motorbike boys. Possibly it was frustration with this kind of development that moved John Lennon away from the Beatles and to the Plastic Ono Band, the recovery of a big beat. Certainly, the motorbike boys accepted some of the Plastic Ono Band's music and in fact compared it appreciatively to the current Beatle music.

The motorbike boys' preferred music, then, did have immanent qualities and internal dimensions which were *homological* to the particular interests and qualities of their life style. Perhaps most crucially, in terms of the inherent robustness of their culture, the music had an integrity of form and atmosphere as well as an immediate, informal concrete confidence that celebrated movement and masculine assertiveness. It could hold both the claim to belong to the golden age of pop and the claim to be immediately responsive to living concerns, especially those concerns which were about movement, concreteness, confidence, and which were paralleled in the clarity, beat, and confidence of the music. Fundamentally it was because of this dual capacity to answer to the basic ontology, as well as the surface style, of the motorbike culture, that the music was such an important part of the motorbike boys' lives, and could form such a closely sprung *homology* with their life style.

V Conclusion

I am only too aware that this paper has not answered to the six items suggested by the conference organizers. Certainly it's partly through sheer ignorance that I have avoided giving an overall descriptive account of present national developments in England. However, it has also been my project to remind this seminar that a critical review of the terms and concepts we use is a vital preliminary to the empirical stage, and that we should be equipped with an approach to the *nature* and *meaning* of phenomena before plunging in to an analysis. I have attempted to show how one theoretical approach might be applied to a very small segment of the English terrain of 'pop music'. It may serve, however, as a guide to the interpretation and analysis of other areas in the culture of the young. Our long term project should perhaps be to gather work in as many located areas as possible, before launching out on major substantive statements at the macro level concerning new developments in cultural activity.

Notes

1 See R. William's discussion of the 'selective tradition' and elites in *The Long Revolution*, Penguin 1961.
2 I. Bontinck (ed.), *New Patterns of Musical Behaviour*, Universal Edition 1974.

3 For an extremely perceptive discussion of the limitations of positivism see H.P. Rickman, *Understanding and the Human Studies*, Heinemann, London, 1967.
4 For a discussion of hegemony see A. Gramsci, *Prison Notebooks*, Lawrence and Wishart, London, 1973.
5 The best discussion of Participant Observation occurs in J. Filstead (ed.), *Qualitative Methodology*, Markham, Chicago, 1971; G.J. McCall, J.L. Simmons (eds.), *Issues in Participant Observation*, Addison-Wesley, 1969; S.T. Brayn, *The Human Perspective in Sociology*, Prentice-Hall, 1966.
6 The notion of a 'cluster' of methodologies is advanced by B.A. Turner in *Exploring the Industrial Sub-culture*, Macmillan, 1971.
7 This is a much reduced version of a case study to be published soon by R.K.P, London. Other edited versions of this study are to be found in; J. Benthall (ed.), *The Body as a Medium of Expression*, Longmans, 1974; B. Jones (ed.), *Working Papers in Cultural Studies 2*, C.C.C.S., Birmingham 1972; *New Society*, No. 547, March 1973.

Bibliography

Adorno, T.W. 'On Popular Music' in *Studies in Philosophy and Social Science.* in New York, 1941.

Beckett, A. 'Mapping Pop' in *New Left Review.* 54 Spring 1969.

Belz, Carl. *The Story of Rock.* New York: OUP, 1969.

Berg, I. and Yeoman, I. 'Trad' in *An A to Z 'Who's Who' of the British Traditional Jazz Scene.* Foulsham, n.d.

Birchall, I. 'The Decline and Fall of British Rhythm and Blues' in *The Age of Rock.* ed. Eisen, 1973, pp. 94–102.

Chester, A. 'Rock Aesthetics' in *New Left Review.* 59 & 62.

Cleaver, E. *Soul on Ice.* London: Cape, 1969.

Cohn, N. *Pop from the Beginning.* London: Weidenfield and Nicolson, 1969. Paperback ed.: *Awopbopaloo-bopalopbamboom.* London: Paladin, 1970. Also *Rock from the Beginning.* New York: Stein and Day, 1969.

Cole, P. 'Lyrics in Pop' in *Anatomy of Pop.* ed. Cash pp. 9–31.

Ellis, R. *The Big Beat Scene.* London: Four Square Books, 1961.

Ewen, D. *The Life and Death of Tin Pan Alley.* New York: Funk and Wagnalls, 1964.

Fredericks, V. (ed.) *Who's Who in Rock'n'Roll.* New York: Frederick Fell, 1958.

Frith, S. *The Sociology of Pop.* Constable 1974.

Garland, P. *The Sound of Soul.* Chicago: Regnery, 1969.

Gillet C. (ed.) *Rock File.* N.E.L., 1973.

Gillett, C. *The Sound of the City.* New York: Outerbridge and Dienstfrey, 1970.

Gleason, R. *The Jefferson Airplane and the San Francisco Sound.* New York Ballantine, 1969.

Goldberg, I. *Tin Pan Alley.* New York, 1930.

Gosling, R. *Sum Total.* London: Faber, 1962.

Hall, S. and Whannel, P. *The Popular Arts.* London: Hutchinson, 1964; New York: Pantheon, 1965.

Hirsch, P. 'The Structure of the Popular Music Industry' unpublished manuscript, Ann Arbor: University of Michigan 1969.

Herman, G. *The Who.* Studio Vista 1971.

Jones, L. *Blues People.* New York: William Morrow, 1963; London: MacGibbon and Kee, 1965; New York: Apollo, 1965 (pb.)

Keil, C. *Urban Blues.* Chicago: University Press 1966; Phoenix Books, 1968.

Laing, D. *The Sound of our Time.* London: Sheed and Ward, 1969; New York Quadrangle, 1970.

Lomax, A. 'Song Structure and Social Structure' in *Ethnology* I 1962 pp. 425–451.

Mabey, R. *The Pop Process.* London: Hutchinson, 1969.

MacInnes, C. *England, half English.* London: MacGibbon and Kee, 1961; Penguin, 1966.

Marcus, G. (ed.) *Rock and Roll Will Stand.* New York: Beacon Press, 1970.

Mellers, W. *Music in a New Found Land.* London: Barrie and Rockcliff, 1964; New York: Knopf, 1965.

Melly, G. *Owning Up.* London: Weidenfield and Nicolson, 1965; Penguin, 1970.

Melly, G. *Revolt into Style.* London: Allen Lane, 1970.

Meltzer, R. *The Aesthetics of Rock.* New York: Something Else Press, 1970.

Merriam, A. *The Anthropology of Music*. Evanston: Northwestern University Press, 1964.

Mooney, H.F. 'Popular music since the 1920's; the significance of shifting taste' in *The Age of Rock* ed. Eisen pp. 9–29.

Murdoch, G. *Culture, Class and the School Run*. Constable 1974.

Neville, R. *Playpower*. London: Cape 1970; Paladin, 1970. New York: Random House, 1970.

Palmer, T. *Born under a Bad Sign*. London: William Kimber, 1970.

Rorem, N. 'The Music of the Beatles' in *The Age of Rock*. ed. Eisen pp. 149–159.

Roxon, L. (ed.) *Rock Encyclopaedia*. New York: Grosset and Dunlop, 1969.

Rust, F. *Dance in Society*. London: Routledge and Kegan Paul, 1969.

Shaw, A. *The Rock Revolution*. New York: Cromwell-Collier, 1970.

Spaeth, S. *A History of Popular Music in America*. New York: Random House, 1948. London: Phoenix, 1960.

Williams, P. *Outlaw Blues*. New York: E.P. Dutton, 1969; Pocket Books, 1970.

Wolfe, T. *The Kandy-Kolored Tangerine Flake Streamline Baby*. New York: Noonday, 1965; London: Mayflower, 1968.

20 A critique of 'community studies' and its role in social thought

The Fieldwork Group

> . . . the formal groupings of club, band, choir, union, chapel – all the many strands of 'neighbourhood' that reach out to attain 'community'.
>
> Jackson and Marsden 1966 p 19

An important part of the short history of *cultural studies* has been concerned with the level of experience, subjective response, and the texture of the day to day routine amongst particular groups. Partly, and especially in the Hoggartian strands, the interest was in the recording and analysis of cultural activities constituted as aspects of a *whole way of life* rather than as privileged and separate moments relating 'to the best which has been thought and said'.

The Fieldwork Group, as one of the nine current Centre groups, has preserved and developed this line of interest whilst attempting to place it in a more thoroughgoing analysis which both specifies subjective experience more closely, and locates it within a structured social totality rather than in the looser, 'whole way of life'. Our attention has been on the relationship of determining forces – not necessarily recognizably represented in consciousness or practice – and the form, or potential for change, of given experience and cultural activity in a specific zone.

Though there is a body of ethnographic descriptive work developing within cultural studies we thought it vital to review and use work lying in adjacent areas to generate the maximum information possible on the relation between cultural form and determining conditions.

This spirit led us to make a collective reading of the literature within the genre of *Community Studies*. We took CS to be the most massive and continuing attempt within social science to use 'qualitative methods' to record and analyse working class experience in particular located cultural forms.

It soon became clear, however, that it was extremely difficult to define the characteristic elements of such a genre, and that there was no direct *principled* way in which it was possible to borrow evidence directly for our purposes from this source.

We had to proceed via a *critique* of CS. It was necessary to make a careful analysis of the way in which particular CS were bound up quite intimately with the particular social, political, ideological and intellectual conditions of their creation.

This paper is the result of that exercise. It presents a deconstruction of a genre. It attempts to lay bare the connection between presented evidence and underlying pre-supposition. In fact the very completeness of the mediations and necessary connections between these levels severely questioned for us whether it was at all possible to use evidence from CS for other purposes without *also* imparting – perhaps unconsciously – something of its theoretical paradigm. Our project became one then, finally, of a critique of the whole conceptual basis of an area of study – not a limited borrowing of 'hard' data. We believe that this offers a model of the necessarily theoretical work of a principled attempt to borrow data and evidence from differently constituted academic regions.

I

Any account of community studies requires, initially, some definition of the term. As observed elsewhere, and transparently obvious in the above quote, 'community tends to be a God word', and rather than attempt to define it, we are all expected to ascribe to some broad consensual definition of what it means. However, as we have experienced in the group, it is a difficult concept to map out. It appears to contain all or some of the following meanings: a territorial area, a complex of institutions within an area, and a sense of a shared culture.

These vague parameters reflect the diverse traditions feeding into the notion of community studies. Historically, Robert Owen injected 'community' with political connotations when he proposed a living and working community as a solution to the degradation and misery induced by industrialisation. A manufacturer himself in cotton spinning, he saw the effects of industrialisation in long hours, factory employment of women and children and forced emigration of families from the country to the sites of new industry. He wanted not a change in the political and economic system, but a more humane capitalism and a system of working and living in large specially built communities. Ten or twelve buildings were bought or converted between 1819 and 1855 and actually operated. Each community organised its own work (agricultural or craft) domestic work, care of children and schooling. Women would share equally in the economic work with men. A system of pricing goods by the amount of labour involved was tried and markets for exchange of such goods set up. None of the communities was long lived but the fact that they were able to operate at all in a basically 'cut and thrust' economic system is remarkable. The early co-operative movement was formed to raise capital for the Owenite communities.

In 'The Making of the English Working Class', E.P. Thompson uses community in the sense of shared values and mutuality; it is a feeling embodied in the working classes own institutions, the Trade Unions and the Friendly Societies. But he also sees industrial discipline and Methodism as setting out to eradicate traditional or 'community' pleasures. 'The working class community of the early 19th century was a product neither of paternalism nor of Methodism but in a high degree of conscious working class endeavour. In Manchester and Newcastle the traditions and the trade unions and the Friendly Societies with their emphasis of self discipline and community purpose, reach far back into the 18th century' (Thompson 1968 p. 457). Here Thompson means in 'community purpose' a feeling rather than a locality.

A second meaning is given to community by Tory landowning classes; a definition which appears in countless autobiographies and memoirs where country gentlemen or soldiers or diplomats tell of the virtues of their local communities; and of the stirling virtues of the simple and devoted folk whose pleasure it is to serve them as farm labourers, gardeners and domestic servants. In return for this labour, deference and sometimes, votes, the country squire or landowner gives time to serving on local Boards of Guardians, the Bench or to the School Governors. He may support local Church, Church school, give land for playing fields or allotments. F.M.L. Thompson in 'English Landed Society in the 19th century' has a chapter entitled 'Landowners and the Local Community' and he means the village community where much of the employment depends on the local squire, in this case titled aristocrats, whose household records and diaries form much of the evidence for Thompson's book. The system worked because 'each side knew its place and the lower orders recognised and acknowledged their superiors who were superior by reason of their style, authoritative manner, air of gentility and who were acknowledged as such because they claimed the rights of their social position with self assurance'.

Bagehot (1867) portrayed the English as essentially a 'deferential community in which the rude classes at the bottom defer to what we may call the theatrical show of society and by their deference acquiesced in and welcomed the rule of the aristocratic classes'.

Country house living and the income, sports, pursuits and entertaining that went with the possession of land continued, albeit in an attenuated form until 1939. There was a spate of books in the late 1940's and early 1950's eulogising country life and rural communities. As late as 1947 a country squire, Godfrey Locker Lampson, was justifying the existence of himself and his peers in 'English Country Life'. He feared the extinction of the breed with the coming to power of the post-war Labour Government. In Ch. 1, 'The Extinction of the Country Squire' he says 'Before he takes his departure it may not be amiss to render him a passing tribute . . . he may be pictured as having £5,000 of revenue and 2,000 or 3,000 acres. He will have chosen a wife from respectable county stock and be on familiar terms with his fellow land owners within a radius of ten miles. His time will be divided between sport, the management of his estate and local public duties. His sons will be at college and his daughters finishing their education at home. The rest of the household will consist of a butler and footman and perhaps 6 or 7 other servants. There will be a coachman and groom in the stables and 3 or 4 gardeners will prune his lady's roses . . . two estate men will be needed and in addition to these, there will be a couple of keepers to rear five or six hundred pheasants to stock his coverts . . . and to keep poachers and trespassers away'. This author also writes of the 'Old Retainers', 'What pride in the tradition of the Family (note capital F): care for its interests, affection, loyalty, zeal and love untarnished by a thought of gain'.

But this view of community was not only represented by ruling class writers. Far more influential was the literary work done by the representatives of the working class, which has had important repercussions both for English literature and the sociological notion of community. Writers such as George Eliot and D.H. Lawrence perfectly express 'organisistic' ideas of tight-knit communities which display peculiar tensions about the place of the squirearchy. Rulers and leaders of these communities were seen at the same time as necessary and repressive.

Later writers on the working class – especially during the 1950s – returned to the North and Midlands (Sillitoe, Wesker, Waterhouse) as the only place where 'true' working class solidarity still existed.[1]

This is not very different from the idea of community in sociological studies; the talk of simple, face-to-face communities by some sociologists does hark back to rural hierarchical/feudal set ups. The bonds and networks of village and community life were seen as cohesive (not as reactionary and strangling). So, old Tory nostalgic ideas of community did creep into many of the sociological studies.

Not surprisingly, for it was the village community and its attendant relationships which formed the starting point of many classical sociological theories – Durkheim, Simmel, Tonnies, etc. In this sense community was used, not to refer to a situationally specific group of social institutions, or a particular geographical area, rather the concern was with understanding the impact that industrialisation and urbanisation was having on the texture of social relationships and social groupings in a general sense. The basic understanding that fed into mainstream sociology was that industrialisation, or increasing specialisation in the division of labour was leading to new forms of social relationships – away from Gemeinschaft where with 'one's family, one lives from birth on, bound to it in weal and woe', to Gesellschaft, the less overbearing and organic mutual association of individuals. Thus, apart from the writers' concerns being theoretical in intent and practice, this process was seen as largely occurring with the transition from the countryside to the town.

This theme, the transition from rural to urban life, from community to association, was to dominate social theory. However, whereas with Tonnies or Durkheim these concepts were tightly linked to their overall theories of social and historical change, later particularly in the U.S.A. more limited formulations were advanced as attempts to understand and analyse specific and limited aspects of a particular society. It was here that the distinctive form of the community study developed. Stein, in 'Eclipse of Community', analysed many of the early and influential American community studies, and argues to good effect that these studies were looking at specific social processes, such as, bureaucratisation, industrialisation, etc., and that they were really concerned with social change in the city.

Another theme which we wish to identify as feeding into post-war community studies, are the British Social surveys (including official surveys) carried out from the mid nineteenth century onwards. These surveys, particularly those of Booth and Rowntree, aimed not just to measure poverty, but to explain its causes. This involved, of course, not a rigorous analysis of capitalist economics, but individualised explanations in terms of the lack of regular employment, accidents and illnesses suffered by the wage earner, etc.

It was the methods of fact collecting, sampling and evaluation from this tradition, coupled with the observational techniques and functionalism of social anthropology which provided the methodological repertoire utilised by most post-war community studies.

In the preceding discussion we have attempted, as far as it is possible, to identify the heterogeneous traditions and meanings encapsulated within the notion of community and community studies. This preliminary outline is necessary if we are to understand the ambivalence and tensions displayed in the term as it is utilised in post-war community studies. Our concern now is to analyse the post-war development of these studies, by locating them both historically and ideologically, by outlining the central features of their methodology, by identifying their close relationship to social policy, and by examining their understanding of class, particularly as displayed in their analysis of the traditional worker.

Before embarking on the substantive analysis, a note of caution. In dealing with a body of work such as this there is a danger of characterising them as uniform, coherent and lacking in contradictions. It must be remembered that these studies arise from, and reflect, divergent traditions within sociology. The consequences and inconsistencies arising from this have largely been glossed over, not from neglect, but from a concern to come to terms with the field as a genre.

II

Post-war community studies can be seen as a reaction against certain developments in sociology and worries about the direction of social democracy. As with many other developments in the sociology of the 1950s, they can be seen against the background of the proliferation of 'post capitalist society' and 'embourgeoisement' theories, which, however unwittingly, added a new dimension to any discussion of class. To summarise a familiar argument, during the 1950s it was commonly asserted that capitalism as such had ceased to exist and had been superseded by 'post-industrial society'. All the theorists with something in common with the 'post-industrial society' thesis held that old sources of class-conflict were being progressively eliminated or rendered irrelevant and that Western society was being recast in a middle-class style.

These interpretations rested on three basic assumptions. Firstly, that the liberal and social democracies were pluralistic, power now being held by a number of social groups. Secondly, that the substantive inequalities of early capitalism were diminishing and losing their former significance: differentials in income were being eroded and other inequalities were being dealt with by an economy stabilised through the application of Keynesian economic policies; that due to nationalisation there was now a mixed economy and not a purely capitalist one; and most importantly, the post 1945 implementation of the 1942 Beveridge Report had bridged any remaining inequalities through the Welfare State, expressed in Britain through social security, council housing, the N.H.S., and state-funded secondary education. Thirdly, for the above and other reasons, radical dissent had been progressively eliminated or weakened as new patterns of living and aspirations cut across older class-bound horizons: amongst manual workers, it was argued, a faith in collective action was being replaced with a reliance on individual achievement; the old loyalties of class were being replaced with preoccupations of status – the ethos of the middle class.

In its simplest form, the new 'mythology' postulated a continuous tendency towards the reduction of inequality in income distribution, and to a lesser extent, in wealth. Thus, the widespread material poverty characteristic of the 1930s had been overcome, and political debate now revolved around the new problems faced by people living in an 'affluent society'. As far as poverty was seen to exist, it was felt to be a slight social hangover, a problem affecting tiny groups of people who, through their incompetence and inability, were failing to share in the new wealth. This was the heyday of 'you've never had it so good'.[2]

The major ideological impact of these developments was the widely held and potent belief that class was 'withering away' or had disappeared. This utopianism was not just complacency but a diagnosis of something real and important in the 1950s: working-class apathy and lack of enthusiasm for collective ends. In fact, the sheer numbers of writers who espoused the thesis was some sort of evidence that the political apathy of the time was not an illusion – a fact not always recognised by some of its opponents.

The fallacies underlying these conceptions went unchallenged, at least ideologically, until the development of the 'New Left' – arising from disillusionment both with the effectiveness of Labour's social reforms and with the sterility of organised left-wing thought. The thrust of this changing ideological stance was characterised in certain key books – Hoggart's *Uses of Literacy* (1957), Williams' *Culture and Society* (1958). Despite the differences of scope, subject and emphasis, these works stood in one way or another for a favourable evaluation of the meanings of working-class culture, as Hoggart makes clear:

> I think such an impression is wrong if it leads us to construct an image of working class people only from adding together the variety of statistics given in some of these sociological works . . . clearly we have to try to see beyond the habits or what the habits stand for, to see through the statements to see what the statements really mean . . ., to detect the differing pressures of emotion behind idiomatic phrases and ritualistic observances.
>
> Hoggart 1957 p. 17

In the New Left's interpretation of working-class culture, the idea of 'community' plays a pivotal role. 'Community' is important because it allows the Culture/Society question to be thought through in all its dimensions – as a 'totality'. Again, ten years on, it is difficult to appreciate the radical implications of this – but what more than anything else distinguished these literary/cultural studies at this time was their attention to the 'totality': how separate texts/rituals/institutions inter-related in a 'whole way of life'. The idea of community necessarily presupposed an intellectual commitment to go beyond immediate empiricism, the 'obvious', the isolated text, to interpret cultural phenomena in terms of structural relationships or parts of a whole.

These critical developments of Williams and Hoggart were closely linked with a movement in social administration, in which Titmuss (1958) was the leading figure, which stressed the gaps and inadequacies in welfare services, the extent to which working-class material standards remained below those of the middle classes, and argued that political policy rather than individual competence was responsible for these differences.

The theme linking the two areas was the realisation that working-class people had characteristics that were not explicable simply in terms of their financial position, that proposals for change needed to be grounded in a more complex theoretical understanding of working-class life. It is within this context that we find the development of, for example, the Institute of Community Studies and the work conducted by Liverpool University, at a time when more than superficial social research was rare, and where sociology as an academic subject had gained footholds in only a few universities.

Community studies, in fact, very largely ignored the assumptions of the 'post capitalist society'/embourgeoisement thesis, or at best they conceded that higher wages had meant a rise in the standard of living of the working class, but asserted that this had made no real difference and that the working class still existed as a discrete group – on a cultural level at least. Community studies set out to 'rediscover class', and in this sense 'community' carried connotations which can only be described as *political.* There was a kind of smuggling process, whereby the idea of 'community' was identified with the central socialist/social democratic preoccupation with class. Not accidentally, we might add, for it was based in part on real anxieties about Labour's electoral base. It is noteworthy in this context that of the six British studies published in 1957, four had authors with some formal connection with the Labour Party. The notion of 'community' with its overtones of tradition and oppositional culture had an obvious attraction.

So, whilst we can see that the development of community studies was, in part, a reaction to the more vulgar embourgeoisment thesis and a reflection of the concern generated by the apparent erosion of Labour's electoral base, it is apparent that many of the community studies were specifically aimed at the practice of social policy, or directed towards an illumination of those consensually defined 'social problems'. Thus, for Young and Willmott:

> The assumption was that the policy-makers were . . . insufficiently aware of the needs of views of the working class people who form the bulk of the users of the social services, and we hoped that social research might help to provide a more realistic basis for policy.
>
> Young and Willmott 1962 p. 2

Whereas, with Jackson: 'The communal urge could then have been harnessed, for a common good'. He took '. . . the illustration of productivity to show the practical help that can flow from an understanding of the otherness of *working class* life' (Jackson 1968 p. 156).

III

It is important at this point to step back and attempt to understand the position that sociology occupies within bourgeois ideology, and, to explain the phenomenal growth in sociology, both as an academic discipline and as an applied science, during the late 1950s and 1960s. Sociology, as Gouldner (1971) attempts to point out, arises and assumes that economic problems are solved, when economic problems have become transparently social problems which cannot be solved within the framework of bourgeois economics.

> Sociology focuses upon the non-economic sources of social order. Academic sociology polemically denies that economic change is a sufficient or necessary condition for maintaining or increasing social order.
>
> A. Gouldner 1971 p. 4

That is to say, when the social character of capitalist production has become apparent in the oppositional life-style and activities of the chief force of production, the working class, sociology arises as a theory of how to respond to this opposition without abolishing the capitalist mode of production. It recognises the social character of production – only by denying that it is connected with production, which is taken to be the concern of economics. Thus, at one and the same time, sociology is both reformist and repressive. By providing palliatives to real social problems it also, by definition, accrues means of social control.

So, in the boom of social research and sociology, 'social problems', that is, those activities or phenomena which impinge on the interest of capital, are seen to be the result of 'social' life and *not* of economic contradictions. It is no longer the individual 'problem family' that is at fault, it is a lot of 'problem families' living in a 'problem area'. Thus, for example, the incidence of industrial action can now be explained with reference to the community. The work force of industries with few strikes:

> . . . are more likely to live in multi-industry communities, to associate with people with quite different working experiences than their own, and to belong to associations with heterogeneous memberships. In these communities their individual grievances are less likely to coalesce into a mass grievance which is expressed at the job level.[3]
>
> Kerr and Siegel 1964 p. 193

Alternatively, in regard to education, we can now see that it is the community which largely determines educational success:

> What is unchallenged, however, is that the concept of community provides us with an illuminating guide to the expectations and requirements of the population of the school catchment areas, as well as to the prevailing factors in the behaviour of its pupils and teachers.
>
> Eggleston 1967 p. 36

This ideological role is clearly exemplified, for example, in the notion of a 'culture of poverty'. This argues that the poor constitute a distinctive culture or community within society; that the experiences, attitudes and values generated in poor communities are passed on from one generation to the next in a never-ending cycle. Thus, this culture is able

> to perpetuate itself from generation to generation because of its effect on the children. By the time slum children are aged six or seven they have usually absorbed the basic attitudes and values of their subculture, and are not psychologically geared to take full

> advantage of changing conditions, or increased opportunities which may occur in their life-time.
>
> Lewis 1968 p. 60

So it is not unskilled, meaningless, irregular employment, or bad housing, or an irrelevant education that it is at fault – it is 'basic attitudes' that are wrong. This ideological and overtly repressive thesis logically leads to notions of compensatory education which will, no doubt, finally reach down to the foetus, or maybe sterilisation in hopeless cases.

Thus, within the total context of bourgeois ideology, sociology provides important methodological and empirical data for the social policy makers. Because it has no understanding of contradictions within a total structure it is conceptually limited to understanding class conflict in terms either of cultural or individual deprivation, and its policy formulations boil down to 'tinkering with the machine' – never mind the engine.

IV

This inability to understand society as a total structure in the Marxist sense, has meant that sociology in general, and community studies in particular, have automatically limited themselves to the appearance of things, never trying to analyse the relationships latent in the things themselves. It is in this area, and seemingly for this reason, that community studies have drawn on functionalism, particularly as manifested in the work of social anthropolgists. A practice, custom or belief was interpreted in terms of its present and ongoing functions in the surrounding society. But whereas anthropologists within small-scale societies are able to study social life at first hand; sociologists have adopted the same model as if their 'communities' are excused participation in the national structures of class and politics.

In practice this approach leads to a concentration on 'normative' facts ('treat social facts as things') so social structure refers to relations between actual, empirically given social phenomena. These relationships are either given in the facts as directly observed, or arrived at by simple abstraction from the facts. Thus, social structure when used in a functional analysis, refers to no more than the actual organisation of a given social system: 'its all moving wall-paper really'.

From within this perspective social behaviour is seen as determined by norms, enforced by implicit or explicit sanctions. These structure, in a regular and predictable fashion, the social life and relationships of individuals. Thus, to Young and Willmott, the mother/daughter relationship is one where:

> Though they both derive benefit from the relationship, it is far more than a mere arrangement for mutual convenience. The attachment between them is supported by a powerful moral code.
>
> Young and Willmott 1962 p. 193

The analysis focuses on rules of conduct as mechanisms of social control, on the constellations of rules that govern particular forms of social groupings (for example, kinship) and on the consequences which these norms have for the composition of particular social relationships. The meaningful fabric which constitutes social life is therefore found, not in culture, but in institutions considered as regulative social relationships. This largely descriptive approach to social phenomena is given a certain 'dynamic' by the use of the concept of function. Institutions are seen as functioning parts of a social whole, ('the community') and serve to maintain it in a more or less stable condition. The logic of the approach then becomes circular, because insofar as these institutions continue to contribute to the maintenance of the social system, that is, if the system 'works', then they are seen as functional for it. This approach, by definition, leads to a focus on the mechanisms of control that function to ensure conformity to the prescribed normative order.

Thus, many community studies erect a social reality which is taken as given and giving of itself in immediate appearances. A relatively unquestioned reality is reported on relatively unquestioningly.

We are confronted with a single-levelled social totality consisting of attitudes, behaviour, activities and institutions, and the relationships between these things. There is little awareness of *process*, or dynamic relations between different forces and groupings. There is no sense of *levels* within the social whole, and in particular no notion of the relations and mediations between the subjective level of experience, ideology and determining material conditions. In general people are seen as passive with things happening to them, rather than as showing some attempt to create their lives: there is no dialectic between objective and subjective factors.

This single-layered analysis also leads to the abstraction of community from social processes which constitute it *as if* it were a self regulating entity, thus community studies cannot examine the dialectic between local and national factors.

The ideological construction of a world which is self-evident, single-layered and functionally inter-related, in which ideas are just there as they have always been, delivers a specific kind of methodological unconsciousness. Since *one* reality is there for the seeing, there is no more than one way in which to see it – why therefore give the groundings or detail of your observations? It is not a reflexive world so why should your methodology be reflexive? The techniques are 'naturalistic', direct, unproblematic and usually unrecorded. With no clear statement of the paradigms in this work, without any information about research techniques, or how respondents saw the investigator, with no information independently presented both concerning the relationship of the researched to the researcher and concerning the raw data untreated by theories of the writers, it is impossible for us to *triangulate*, to read back along the lines of the prior theorectical predisposition, to deconstruct and reconstruct, to come to our own principled interpretation of the evidence.

CS literature forms the single most massive encounter with the located experience of working-class people, and is the major accredited source of 'qualitative' accounts of working-class culture. As such its text should be 'demystified', and salvaged as sources for our own, hopefully, more reflexive research procedures. As it is 'reading back' from community studies is an uncertain exercise. We are dealing with a peculiarly untheorised, naturalised, impacted problematic which methodologically conceals its own tracks.

Just to give one short example of how this conceptual approach is used in community studies and how it actually obscures that which needs to be explained, we can look at Klein's (1965) use of parts of the Dennis et al. (1956) study dealing with education and mental activity. Parents were asked about their aspirations for their children and the researchers conclude that study, with a few exceptions, is not taken seriously (because 'book learning' is recognised as applying only to careers outside the experience of working people). This they say leads to a general scepticism about theory. Furthermore, the miners are said to have a 'taboo on tenderness' and to regard most forms of mental activity as effeminate (and therefore – since this is a male dominated community – of little value). From this Klein generalises that 'cognitive poverty' – an intellectual incuriosity arising from the strongly conformist pressures of social life – is characteristic of traditional working-class communities. The suggestion here is that anti-intellectualism arises inevitably from the conditions of working-class life – do we detect a note of determinism?

Apart from the very obvious criticism that the dimension of school experience is totally lacking in both the original study and in Klein's reworking of the material, the formulation of the explanation does not explain anything, it leaves us with a necessarily determinist picture: 'That's the way miners are'. The question still to be answered in a meaningful way is 'why are they that way?'

In a sense, this brings us full circle and back to Hoggart who, apart from displaying a peculiar nostalgia for a way of life moulded by insecurity, local seclusion and crude exploitation, at least asks us 'to see through the statements to see what the statements really mean'. However, it would appear that much of the work done in sociology and community studies is ideologically and politically rooted in a conceptual framework which is content to skim the surface of social reality.

V

This paper has taken us a long way from community studies as such, rather we have tried to locate community studies within sociology and use them to say things about sociology in general. We have tried to make plain some fundamental weaknesses which we think are characteristic of the studies we have read. Obviously we have mainly dealt with one particular ideological strand within sociology. We now wish to move on to see how that strand achieves and reflects political expression within social democratic formulations.

We noted the uncritical, and mainly willing acceptance of consensually defined 'social problems' earlier. The construction and perception of these 'social problems' by the State is a complicated process. Suffice it to say that this definition is institutionally reinforced at every level in the academic heirarchy, from term essays to S.S.R.C. projects. We are not suggesting that 'social problems' do not correspond with material ones, simply that the nature of that correspondence is crucially important. In the main, social administration accepts uncritically sociology's definition of 'social problems' and formulates its policy in terms of that acceptance.

It is important to note the institutional (through advisory committees, research etc.), educational (through social work courses, etc.), and cultural links between social policy and research. Thus the aims of the Institute of Community Studies, for example, are reciprocated in full by social administration. Slack maintains that the purpose of social research:

> . . . is to produce factual evidence on which social policy action or reform may be based or evaluated. It could rightly be said of social research workers, as it has been said of sociologists, that their task is to strengthen the case for reform by fuller investigation of the evils needed to be overcome, and to present their results in such a way as to secure greater public attention.
>
> Slack 1966 p. 71

This role, played out in the personal biographies of many social researchers, strictly limits the parameters within which recommendations on social policy can be made – limits of which very few researchers are aware. The understanding of social life generated within this framework tends to take the form of an anaemic cultural pluralism in which to see beyond the habits to what the habits stand for, degenerates into a call to 're-shuffle the pack of cards of cultural values'.

> The aim here was to seek the human detail, the individual situation in a group phenomenon which made some sense of what was happening. And always to raise the old dilemma: Working Class life – listen to the voices – has strengths we cannot afford to lose: middle class life transmits within it the high culture of our society, that must be opened freely to all. That is the problem the planners must solve.
>
> Jackson and Marsden 1966 p. 249

This 'pluralism' provides, and illustrates, one of the crucial linkages between social democracy, public administration and community studies – the linkage being provided by their emasculated understanding of the meaning of class. We do not wish to suggest that there are no important conflicts within social democracy, or within this particular form of sociological practice – what we want to do is to try to outline the relationships that exist between these two bodies of thought in their understanding of the concept of social class.

A crude historical characterisation of the political demands and policies of social democracy enables us to identify an immediate post-war concern with 'equality of provision' – hence the Welfare State, an attempt to establish 'equality of provision' in certain basic welfare services. It was only after these services were attained that the other credo of social democratic thought – 'equality of opportunity' – was able to take its place near the top of the political agenda. Obviously, both these strands were tightly inter-related, but the change in emphasis during the 1950s and 1960s is apparent – particularly, for example, in education: from 'provision' in the 1944 Education Act, to 'opportunity' in the comprehensivisation programme in the 1960's.

The role played by social research in the intervening period was, initially, to provide information outlining the disadvantages still suffered by certain groups, despite ostensible equality of provision. The important finding was not just that certain groups were disadvantaged, but that there was a pattern to the disadvantages, a pattern related to social class. Thus, it is at this stage, that a more complex understanding of working-class life is needed. Statistics demonstrate the existence of deprivations, but deprivations which are no longer simply understandable in terms of inadequate provisions – it is time to 'listen to the voices'.

The whole notion of 'cultural deprivation' or 'working class otherness' as Jackson might say, has been informed and developed by social research. The historical transition from 'controlling the working class', to the 'problem family', to the 'problem community', has significantly altered both the policy makers' conceptions of the problems and the range and type of policy options open to them. Plowden, in this sense, was a 'watershed'. Instead of the 'under-socialised delinquent', we now have the 'cycle of deprivation' which is a 'whole series of interrelated problems'. But because 'social problems' are seen as 'social', and not the manifestations of contradictions, change can only be achieved by changing people, their communal values, and by 'tinkering with the machine'. Thus, education, the social democrats' panacea, is seen as the vehicle for change:

> . . . better educational provision can, by compensating for the effects of social deprivation and the depressing physical environment in which many children grow up, make an important contribution to overcoming family poverty.
>
> D.E.S. Circular 11/1970

To this end we now have Plowden's new policy of 'positive discrimination' (urban aid, nursery education, C.D.P.s, community advice centres, etc.), for areas to be identified by 'the criteria of social deprivation'.

VI

At this point we wish to return to our original discussion of the 'withering away of class', to look at what exactly was being examined under the heading of working-class, both by the 'post capitalist society' theorists and in community studies. The direction which our critical analysis of community studies has taken inevitably leads us into questions about working-class consciousness: where it came from and how it operates – both within local and national class structures.

There has always been a 'two nations' tradition in British sociology and an explicit recognition that British society is the most 'class-bound' in the world. Accent, vocabulary, dress, diet, recreations, and power in the labour market are important components of this traditional view. However, this tradition sees class related economic factors largely in terms of income, not as reflections of a dynamic relationship. The variables are normative or status based, i.e. 'social', and from this is drawn a consensus model of the class structure expressed usually as 'social stratification'. However, this model remains highly problematic because of the obvious differences in the normative factors it considers important *between* classes: to use a Parsonian term there is obviously no 'unitary value system'. Sociology's major conceptual attempt to come to terms with this problem were 'affluence', 'embourgeoisement' and 'convergence' theories. Fifteen years on, these concepts may look more like leaps of faith than theories, but the problem still remains. The major problem posed for sociology by the introduction of a class differentiated view of the normative system is *social control.* If classes differed widely, the dominant class would have to rely heavily on physical coercion as a substitute for moral persuasion – or so it is alleged. Yet this is not necessarily true. As Parkin (1971) points out the main problem with the consensus model is that it fails to make clear the relationship between the normative and factual elements of stratification – i.e. the connection between the distribution of power and the legitimation of values. As Marx pointed out in a celebrated passage 'the ideas of the ruling class are, in any age, the ruling ideas'. The extent to which dominant values are legitimated is largely a function of the institutional power of the dominant class.

However, not every member of the working class endorses the moral order of the ruling class. The 'images of society' held by the working class are anything but homogeneous. As well as the more blatant sectionalism displayed through racism and sexism, and the division between the 'rough' and 'respectable' working class, there is an obvious sense in which the consciousness of a London docker and a Coventry car-worker differ. If the consensual bourgeois values dominant in most institutions were universally endorsed, unselectively, then the regional/industrial variations in working-class culture, central to most sociology, would be non-existent.

Community studies display some strange tensions about class. One major problem is that very often there is no objective definition of class given at all. Yet, at the same time, there is a taken-for-granted postulation of a national, homogeneous class structure on the part of the authors largely based on common-sense notions of 'us' and 'them'. This is evident in the work of Hoggart and Jackson, and Darendorf emphasised (or overemphasised) its significance to support a general theory of class consciousness. On the other hand, the small and often esoteric areas within which the studies were carried out, along with the initial lack of an objective definition leads to a stress being placed on the local experience of being working class and hence, the unique formations of classes in any one area. *Implicit* definitions of class are based on inequality yet dimensions of power and domination are almost entirely lacking. The rich are only different in the sense Hemingway meant – 'they have more money'. The rest of this section seeks to explore how 'class images of society' are created/determined within a particular section of the working class: Lockwood's (1975) 'traditional proletarian' and Parkin's (1971) 'accommodative worker'.[4]

Lockwood distinguishes three different 'class images of society' spontaneously generated through work experience and the values held by the local community. Firstly, the traditional proletarian, typified by miners, dockers and shipyard workers. Secondly, the traditional deferentialist, likely to work in a craft based industry and to have relationships with a paternalistic employer. Thirdly, the privatised worker who is 'instrumental' in his attitude to work and 'privatised' in his home life.

Parkin's categories differ in that they do not refer to spontaneously generated ideologies, but mainly to national ideologies *imposed* by some means or another and to which different sections of the working class place allegiance. Firstly, there is the dominant value system, the social source of which is the ruling class. Typically, it is accepted by the 'deferential' or 'aspirational' working class. Secondly, there is the 'subordinate' value system, the social source of which is two-fold. On the one hand, it is experiential work and community that are of crucial importance. On the other, certain national movements and ideologies – for e.g. trades unionism – impinge on and are transformed by the local class practices. It should be noted that this category collapses two of Lockwood's: the privatised and the proletarianised worker. Thirdly there is the radical value system. This is not the property of the working class since they are incapable of autonomously generating a *systematic* opposition to capitalism – 'the working class on its own can only develop trades union consciousness'. One is left with the feeling that Mannheim's 'free-floating' intellectuals rather than whole social groups generate this value system. The only social base suggested for it is the 'mass political party'. The implication seem to be that only workers who attain a 'state of grace' will actually assimilate these values.

If we take it as axiomatic that people are not simply on the 'receiving end' of their objective class position, then it follows that their actions are partly projected in terms of creative expectations and definitions. Unfortunately, most examinations of this semi-autonomous layer of working-class experience have been within community studies.[5] It is with this imperfect material that arguments about working-class imagery have been carried out.

Lockwood argues that there are two crucial variables in the formation of working-class images of society – work and the local community. There are two basic models for this imagery: a model based on power, conflict and a dichotomy between two classes, and a model based on prestige, status and hierarchy.

The proletarian traditionalist is likely to endorse the dichotomous model. This type of worker is the archetypical subject of community studies: he is the most colourful, romantic and inaccessible representative of his class. The proletarian traditionalist is likely to be male and usually works in a situation of physical discomfort and danger. Nevertheless, he has a high degree of job involvement and a strong attachment to his primary work group. This occupational culture spills over into leisure, facilitated by the fact that most of this kind of work requires an 'occupational community'.

The classic community study in this field is undoubtedly *Coal is Our Life* (1969). This study has shaped a whole generation of academics' perceptions of the miner. The data for this study was collected in the 1950s and it is avowedly a community study influenced by social anthropology. The note of caution this strikes in us seems to be shared by at least one of the authors. Certainly, Henriques is very sensitive to the implications of this approach and method. In the introduction to the second edition he writes: 'By its focus upon the community framework as such, this technique will tend to abstract from the societal framework at every level of social life' (Dennis et al. 1956, p. 7). His example is that whereas relationships between husband and wife or the nature of leisure activity are:

> viewed primarily from the standpoint of grasping their *interrelationships* with the forms of activity and social relations *imposed* by the coal mining work upon which the community is based, this emphasis will tend to obscure the fact that each of these particular sets of relationships is extended beyond the community, in both space and time. By itself, the community study technique provides no way of measuring the significance of its findings against that which may crudely be described as these 'external' factors.
>
> Dennis et al. 1956 p. 7

Ashton miners certainly display dichotomous class imagery – but whether this conforms to Lockwood's model is unclear. It is certainly debatable whether it is spontaneously generated through the social relationships of work and the local community as Lockwood suggests. Apparently Henriques at least agrees that the miners could be drawing on extra-local factors for their class imagery.

The central features of the community life described by Dennis et al., are: recurring domestic conflict; particular attitudes of the miners to their cultural poverty and isolation; the oppression of miners' wives. These are seen as determinants of actual economic relationships and working conditions. Thus a logical connection between the common work experience of the miner and a dichotomous social imagery is posed. But there are many weaknesses here. One problem is the clearly different life experience of women in mining areas. Whilst men have been thrown together by coal, it has exerted the opposite or 'centrifugal' influence on women. There is no paid work for them unless they go outside the area. Nor can they identify very easily through the family – marriage and the family is a battle arena, and seems completely devoid of affection. Men and women are as effectively separated as Eskimos and Africans. In fact, the experience of the sexes is so totally different that one has to make an effort to remember that they live *together* in the same town. As Lockwood is contending that the work and community experience is crucial in the formation of perceptions of class then it is reasonable to expect that the men's and women's images would be different. Unfortunately, this seems never to have been investigated. However, voting returns from mining areas (admittedly vary partial evidence) tend to show that women vote the same way as men, at least suggesting they share the same type of class imagery. This interpretation would tend to favour Parkin's argument rather than Lockwood's, in that far from being spontaneously generated, people are recognising some kind of national ideology and their acceptance or rejection of it is mediated through their local experience and work.

To take a different stage in Lockwood's argument, is the traditional worker the most radical working-class type? For social democrats like Lockwood 'radical' obviously refers to trade-union and Labour Party consciousness. But if we take 'radical' to mean a total and systematic opposition to capitalism, then obviously trade-union and Labour Party consciousness does not go far enough. These types of consciousness are, as Parkin suggests (firmly in the case of trade-union consciousness, more tentatively with the Labour Party), an 'accommodation to capitalism': a cultural transcendence rather than a material transformation. This is reactionary in effect; if not in intent. Far from engendering class-consciousness, in the sense of the awareness of contradictory interests between bourgeoisie and proletariat, the type of community relationships experienced by the proletarian traditionalist brings about the opposite result – a sectionalist, parochial self-interest. In a paper on shipyard workers Cousins and Brown give a good example of what is at stake with reference to the employment market. Favouritism, based on localism and residence, is a factor in gaining employment in an industry and area (Tyneside) where unemployment is a major problem. The daily callstand – a feature of casualisation – encourages localism. Cousins and Brown quote the following case:

> A chargehand from the former Blyth shipyard a little further up the coast and now closed told us 'with us it was always keep the Tynies out'.
>
> Cousins and Brown 1975 p. 58

There are many example of this: the hostility towards women and Poles in Jackson's (1968) Yorkshire mills; the split between newcomers and 'traditionalists' in Stacey's (1960) Banbury; the rich insularity of Hoggart's (1957) Hunslet – the list is endless.

Westergaard has pointed out in numerous articles that localism and parochialism is endemic in the working class, and that this factor inhibits them in the pursuit of their interests. He also makes the interesting point that parochialism is not necessarily a spontaneous creation of the working class, but one influenced and fostered by the ruling class.

A locality consciousness has been imposed in some situations. Victorian reformers always recognised and valued the conservative restraints of parochialism, and feared the radical implications of the absence of those restraints. Westergaard quotes Thomas Chalmers who in 'The Civic and Christian Economy of Large Towns' written in the 1820s advocated a system of localism to break up the large working-class areas of cities into smaller local units.

> His argument was that if working class interests could be turned inward into the locality, then workers would be prevented from forming alliances and loyalties across the restraining boundaries of the locality and the social order would be safeguarded.
>
> Westergaard 1975

According to Lockwood, however, the old working-class traditions of community and collective culture are undergoing a major change. The modern tendency is to break up traditional working-class communities, whether occupational or not, and throw people with little immediately in common together on council estates or low cost private estates. These are the living conditions of Lockwood's 'privatised workers'. However, to return to Lockwood, he argues that there has been an evolution towards a new kind of collectivism which is no longer 'based on instinctual narrower kinship ties', so beloved of traditional social democrats, but 'instrumental', based on a rational calculation of interest. But there is no reason why the second is necessarily narrower than the first. On the contrary 'solidarity collectiveness' based on community and locality is itself a *narrow* form of social consciousness, and can lead to yet more sectionalism in the working class. It is our contention that it is precisely the entrenched, immobile traditional class consciousness of the British working class which holds it back and helps to maintain its most cherished illusions.

Anderson in a rather Hegelian synthesis argues that the advent of 'instrumental collectivism' means for the first time the penetration of reason into the closed universe of the Labour movement – it's still the market rationality of capitalism, but it's a start. Our basic disagreement with this position – on the revolutionary potential of the privatised worker – is reflected in Parkin's collapsing of these two types within the category of 'accommodative' working class. In a sense, they are two sides of the same coin. The traditional worker's locality and work mates easily becomes the privatised worker's family. Nevertheless, the move towards the break-up of traditional working class communities can only be welcomed by the left. In new industries and new areas workers might avoid the stifling parochialism and traditionalism of the rest of the labour movement.

There are, therefore, several problems with Lockwood's formulation of the traditional worker. He has inverted the classical Marxist idea of the proletariat. 'Traditional' and 'proletariat' seem to us to be contradictory terms when applied to working-class consciousness. We would suggest that some of the factors Lockwood associates with traditional community – the existence of face-to-face emotional interaction at work, the localised labour market, and the high degree of job involvement – inhibit the development of proletarian consciousness rather than support it. To this extent (and only this) we would agree with Anderson that Lockwood's 'privatised pecuniary worker' corresponds more closely to Marx's proletariat than the traditional proletariat. As Westergaard points out (1970), the economic developments underlying the cultural response of privatisation are leading to an increasing transparency in the cash nexus, a development not unproblematic for capitalism.

Lockwood also seems to have a deterministic/positivistic idea of consciousness. It is seen merely as a *reflection* of activity at the base. This is surprising in view of the (earlier) Affluent Worker monographs where he insisted that three aspects of working-class activity must be taken into account. These were, in the discussion of embourgeoisement – the economic, the relational, and the normative, all of which had relative autonomy, with the relational acting as a mediation between the other two. In this sense, consciousness could never be just a reflection of what people *do*, since the mediation of *how* they did it, and *with whom* were crucial. In *Sources of Variation in Working Class Images of Society*, Lockwood seems to collapse the levels of the economic and relational, giving us instead a crude base–superstructure formulation with mechanistic determinations. An example of this mechanism is displayed in Lockwood's identification of the proletarian traditionalist as the most class conscious worker. Here is Lockwood's account of their images of the social structure:

> Shaped by occupational solidarities and communal sociability, proleterian social consciousness is centred on an awareness of 'us' and 'them'. 'Them' are bosses, managers, white collar workers and ultimately the public authorities of the wider society.
>
> Lockwood 1975 p. 18

This characterisation displays a crude simplification into a dichotomous imagery, of 'us' and 'them'. Shaped by work and the local community, the proletarian traditionalist sees 'them' in terms of a *hierarchy* impinging on the activities of work and community, a characteristic which is also imputed to the privatised worker. But a dichotomous conception of 'them' and 'us' reflects a power and class relationship with wider ramifications than those within the local community. This point reflects Westergaard's criticism that Lockwood's schema does not allow for a 'radical class consciousness' – i.e. one which transcends occupations and locality and becomes generalised to other sections of the working class. Neither of Lockwood's models display radical overtones and neither represent a dichotomous *class* imagery: they are both hierarchical visions of society.

If 'post industrial society' theorists were taking their typical model of the working class from what Lockwood calls the 'traditional proletariat' and the privatised worker, neither of which, at the moment, poses a particularly substantial threat to capitalism, then it is not surprising that the theories gained a vogue. An important part of the argument was a lack of political mobilisation, and this could be largely due to sectional interests as well as to rising living standards. The fatal flaw in community studies was to oppose the thesis of embourgeoisement with the traditional worker. This meant that instead of coming to terms with new realities, the social democrats fell back on nostalgia and romanticism: a simple minded ahistorical faith that old customs and habits (which had not produced anything spectacular since the middle of the nineteenth century. and the final collapse of Chartism) were still to be the saviour of the Labour Party, and by implication the working class.

The misleading notion of unity implied in this category was compounded, we would argue, by a misuse of the methodological tool of the 'ideal type' in some of the studies we have examined. It was used as a heuristic synthesis of elements in an attempt to show the essence of particular social relationships. But it allowed the assumption to pass uncontested that the social order could be analysed without recourse to the dialectical connection of social forms with production and exploitation. We were given a response to the visible character of capitalist production in the moment that its heart was denied.

We must conclude that workers do not see the class structure in unitary ways, but in different and contradictory ways. The work remains to be done to show their particular forms and inner connections.

Notes

1 However, these works displayed crucial ambiguities, for the working-class life-styles they were describing were changing under the impact of 'Affluence' – particularly these ambiguities were displayed by Sillitoe's anti-hero, Arthur S Eaton: 'All I'm out for is a good time – all the rest is propoganda'. See later discussion.

2 You will be pleased to hear that Sir Keith Joseph, the Conservative 'think-tank', made this precise distinction – between primary and secondary poverty – in a recent policy speech: 'We've got none of the former and too much of the latter'. The mind reels with the impact of the intellectual development of the Conservatives' new policy research committee – from the laissez-faire solutions of nineteenth-century capitalism last year (sterilisation and birth-control) to the penetrative analysis of Butlerism this year: where will it all end?

3 The discussion of whether or not single-industry 'communities' are more or less 'militant' than others is more complex than the above quote suggests. See discussion below.

4 And although all the references shall be to the former, they also apply to the latter.

5 Whilst we have made it quite clear that we disagree strongly with the concept of 'community' as it is usually operationalised, there is a sense in which the concept of 'occupational community' is important. We agree with Salaman (1975) who argues that this concept can be useful: firstly, for the way in which it focusses attention on certain aspects of occupation as subjective collectivities; and secondly, because occupational processes and features are important and significant in our understanding of extra-occupational issues and concerns, for example the development of forms of imagery and processes of change and conflict within the stratification system. We would agree with Salaman that this definition is 'useful' but would see it as an argument for the centrality of work processes, rather than a call for the reintroduction of a reified notion of community.

Bibliography

Bagehot, W. (1867) *The English Constitution*

Cousins, J. and Brown, R. (1975) 'Patterns of Paradox: Shipbuilding Workers Images of Society' in Bulmer (ed.) *Working Class Images of Society* Routledge and Kegan Paul

D.E.S. Circular 11 (1970) *Plowden Report*

Dennis, N., Henriques, F. and Slaughter, C. (1956) *Coal is our Life* Tavistock

Eggleston, S.J. (1967) *The Social Context of the School* Routledge and Kegan Paul.

Gouldner, A.W. (1971) *The Coming Crisis of Western Sociology* Heinemann

Hoggart, R. (1957) *The Uses of Literacy* Penguin.

Jackson, B. and Marsden, D. (1966) *Education and the Working Class* Pelican

Jackson, B. (1968) *Working Class Community* Penguin
Kerr, C. and Siegel, A. (1964) *Labour and Management in Industrial Society* Doubleday
Klein, J. (1965) *Samples from English Culture* Routledge and Kegan Paul
Lewis, O. (1968) *La Vida* Panther
Locker Lampson, G. (1947) *English Country Life*
Lockwood, D. (1975) 'Sources of Variation in working class images of Society' in Bulmer, M. (ed.) *op. cit.*
Nisbet, R. (1967) *The Sociological Tradition* Heinemann
Parkin, F. (1971) *Class Inequality and Political Order* Paladin
Salaman, G. (1975) 'Occupations, Communities and Consciousness' in Bulmer, M. (ed) *op. cit.*
Slack, K.M. (1966) *Social Administration and the Citizen* Joseph
Stacey, M. (1960) *Tradition and Change: A Study of Banbury* O.U.P.
Titmuss, R. (1958) *Essays on the Welfare State* Unwin
Thompson, E.P. (1968) *The Making of the English Working Class* Pelican
Thompson, F.M.L. (1963) *English Landed Society in the Nineteenth Century* Routlege and Kegan Paul
Westergaard, J.H. (1970) 'The Rediscovery of the Cash Nexus' in *Socialist Register 1970* Merlin Press
Westergaard, J.H. (1975) 'Radical Class Consciousness' in Bulmer (ed.) *op.cit.*
Williams, R. (1958) *Culture and Society* Penguin
Young, M. and Willmott, P. (1961) 'Research Report No. 3: Institute of Community Studies: Bethnal Green' in *Sociological Review* July 1961.
Young, M. and Willmott, P. (1962) *Family and Kinship in East London* Pelican

21 The experience of work

The Fieldwork Group

Introduction

This group first came together with two aims and on the basis of concrete overlapping research interests and activities. It did not start with the hope of full collaboration and final collective production, but was seen as a support for individual research projects, as a pool of information and skill that could be used as a resource by individuals, and as an arena for the presentation, critique and development of substantive themes and problems which were common to all our research. The extracts set out below, therefore, are of individual authorship, and relate to separate ongoing research, although they have been selected very much with shared and collective themes in mind.

The two major themes which have occupied us are (a) the problems associated with a qualitative methodology and case-study field work and (b) the possibilities of reproducing in a written account meaning and experience and the status of this category with respect to the 'totality'. We were especially interested in these two questions in relation to wage labour, personal definitions of work, cultures of the work place and the subjective experience of workers. This was partly because many of our research interests overlapped in this area, and also because it seemed to us that work is the crucial area in which a certain subjective orientation amongst those who create value is vital to the whole reproduction of material life and social relations. We felt that it was here that the internal tendency of the qualitative/subjective/meanings perspective towards romanticism and idealization of the individual might be most firmly checked, and made answerable to the obvious external determinations.

Our deliberations on methodology circled around a number of problems. Can we posit the existence of a real 'subject' to our enquiries which is 'out there' existing quite apart from the fact of our enquiry? If such a 'thing' exists, can we ever 'know it' in any direct and 'objective' manner? If, on the other hand, this directness is impossible what is the nature of the mediations through which our 'knowledge' comes to us? Was it possible to discount for the distortions of these mediations and read back to a concrete social reality? Was it sensible, anyway, to talk of a subject 'out there' without immediately linking what we take this to be with our own theoretical and subjective paradigms which were themselves ultimately lodged in an ideological mapping of social reality? Indeed what was the scope for production of 'new knowledge' if all we can discover in our subject is already secretly written into the underside or how we view the problem and ask the questions? What was the ultimate justification of such work and how did we define the nature of our social, moral and political responsibility to those whom we studied? How should language be analysed; in a heuristic mode as a privileged window into a culture, or in a formal linguistic mode as a discourse occupying a discrete level of social reality? What were the connections between a chosen methodology and its anchoring theoretical perspective?

There were differences amongst the group concerning the status and importance of subjective meaning. We also had differences in views of our assessment of the relative space it was possible for the subject – and for that matter the researcher – to hold free from ideology and which could be used for his/her own rational penetration of his/her surrounding conditions, and for the dialectical development of counter and oppositional meanings. There was also a related problem for the group in specifying the degree and tightness of the necessary contact between the underlying theoretical perspective of the researcher and a chosen methodology. There was also a differing degree of scepticism about the capacity of any particular methodology to generate data which could in any basic way reformulate its locating paradigms. Rather than attempt what would be a partial recreation of this debate within the group, we have abstracted below a statement of one member of the group. It is written specifically on the basis of his current practice as a Participant Observer. It is not meant to be representative of the group's feeling, though it certainly deals with and arose from our discussions about, some of the central problems with which we were concerned.

If we *are* able to approach and record subjective meaning systems, what status and importance are we to give to them? How are we to locate this level of interest with respect to the social totality? In particular we were concerned to understand the manner of the connection between the structures and larger determinations within society and individual or group subjective meanings. Were such meanings, and the actions which arose from them, *living* parts of structure, accomplishing what we call 'structure' in their own micro operations or were they basically determined by structures which were in some way quite outside any specific terrain of subjectivity? If the latter was in fact the case, how did the structures efface themselves and deliver to the subject – what would have to be an illusion of – some voluntarism? Clearly this dualism in the group's approach to subjective meaning paralleled differences in emphasis on the appropriate methodology. This risks over-simplification and the suggestion of a polarization, which was not central to our work. We all recognized that a final position would have to chart the dialectical inter-relation between the two positions outlined here. We also thought, however, that the usual dialectical statement of the relationship between the 'real relationships' and the 'phenomenal forms, appearances, ideological forms' often served to *close down* a really honest recognition of an autonomy and power of thought within the subject, or accomplished its resolution, not on the grounds of a genuine demonstration of a dialectical circle between the object and the subject, but upon the literalness of a descriptive middle ground which actually delivers the proper essence neither of the subject or of the object. It would be idle to pretend that the group has resolved its difficulties upon this question, or even that it has posed the question in a proper marxian fashion. In one way we have been trying to accommodate some traditional Centre themes – fundamentally the subjective meaning complex of action – within its contemporary critical marxist perspective on culture and society. It is far from clear yet that the internal contradictions of such a project do not, *ab initio*, prevent the achievement of its stated objectives.

At any rate, we do not attempt to present a final or agreed position on the questions we raise. Rather we have abstracted below three short accounts from the work done by members of the group on their own research projects. Very crudely they lie on points along a kind of spectrum of implicit theories of the subject. At one extreme, subjective experience is seen as the domain where structures through ideology constitute themselves at the level of the subjective in the form of the person, his thoughts and interactions. At the other extreme, subjective experience is seen as the active development of meaning which – though it might be on terms set by structure, and in materials made collectively by other at a different time and place – does precisely have a *creative* element, and is much more than a transference of content to a different form or the reproduction in a given mode of pre-given ideology. At this extreme it is not so much that subjective meaning and its related actions reproduce ideology and the existing social relations of production, so much as that in their *outcomes* these things maintain – indeed are – the fabric of the present structure, but in such a way that, for themselves, they sustain at the same time a real, though usually suppressed, oppositional potential.

There is a danger in misrepresenting what it is that has actually divided the group. Certainly we all share the concern to repair the passivity of the subject in Althusserian structuralist marxism. Certainly we all share the desire to limit the humanistic indulgence of the subject in bourgeois ethnography. On the other hand, it is necessary to detach, straighten out, and project the complex knot of our theoretical uncertainties and differences if we are to conduct an intelligible debate. At bottom the Work Group has been concerned with the possibility of showing the form, type and magnitude of determinations acting upon the individual and the group in our society. This remains a continuing project of the Centre. We hope the brief extracts below show something of the range, quality and nature of the stage at which one group has reached within this endeavour.

The man in the iron cage: notes on method (*Paul E. Willis*)

Mainstream 'positivistic' sociology concedes in the case of method what its nature denies.[1] 'Qualitative' sociology claims for its method what its nature cannot give.[2] We need a sociology which knows itself.

If the 'naturalist'[3] revolt was directed against positivism's inability to understand and record human subjectivity, the latter has nevertheless found it possible to assign Participant Observation and Case Study work a legitimate place in the social sciences.

I shall be arguing that Positivism's unwilling acceptance of 'qualitative' methodology sees more clearly than its own admissions that the emphasis on *methodological* variety may leave the heartland of the positivist terrain untouched. In its recognition of a *technical* inability to record all that is relevant – and its yielding of this zone to another technique – positivism may actually preserve its deepest loyalty: the preservation of its object of enquiry truly as an 'object'.[4] The duality and mutual exclusivity of the over-neatly opposed categories, 'qualitative' methods and 'quantitative' methods, suggest already that the 'object' is viewed in the same unitary and distanced way even if the *mode* is changed – now you measure it, now you feel it.

Still there is much that is valuable in the 'naturalist' revolt. It has certainly disassociated itself from simplistic causal thinking, and it has developed a set of rules and research procedures which do offer an alternative concrete starting point to the positivist methods. This article aims to identify the really central principles of the 'qualitative' method, and to suggest what is worth preserving and what is worth firmly rejecting in a preliminary attempt to outline a method genuinely adapted to the study of human meanings.

The tradition which has most clearly used the 'qualitative' methods under discussion here, was outlined in the last issues of WPCS.[5] The 'Chicago School' of the 1920s and 1930s originated this tradition.[6] W.F. Whyte's work in the 1940s marks a continuance of the tradition into a second phase.[7] The major expansion came in the 1950s and 1960s with the work of Becker, Geer, Strauss, Polsky and others.[8] The tradition crossed to England most clearly when the work of this 'third wave' was taken up by D. Downes,[9] S. Cohen and particularly those associated with the 'sceptical revolution' institutionalized by the National Deviancy Conference.[10] There has been a sporadic but noticeable interest in, and use of, Participant Observation in England which is not specifically in this Chicago-derived tradition.[11] The method itself has been systematized and presented as a 'respectable' methodology in two recent readers.[12]

It may well be that my critique traduces certain texts in the ethnographic tradition. Certainly there are examples where a final account transcends the limitations of its own stated methods. In what follows I have mainly relied on codifications of method, such as those above, which are increasingly accepted as authoritative guides to those wishing to use 'qualitative methods'.

Elements of the qualitative methodology

The manifest posture

The most obvious thrust of 'qualitative' methodology has been *against* traditional sociological theory and methods modelled on the procedures and tests of the Natural Sciences. To simplify, the fear seems to be that a theory can only, ultimately, demonstrate its own assumptions. What lies outside these assumptions cannot be represented or even acknowledged. So to maintain the richness and authenticity of social phenomena it is necessary, certainly in the early stages of research, to receive data in a raw, experiential, and relatively untheorised manner – 'Allowing substantive concepts and hypotheses *to emerge first on their own*'.[13] It is recognized, of course, that there will have to come a time of theoretical closure – that the act of writing cannot draw a map as large as life.[14] It is hoped, however, that the selectivity and theorization of the final work will reflect the patterning of the real world, rather than the patterns of the researcher's head.[15] These 'anti'-theoretical concerns generate a profound methodological stress on contacting the subject as directly as possible. It is as if the ideal researcher's experience can achieve a one-to-one relationship with that of the researched and short-circuit the usual mechanisms. What is held to be the crucial and differentiating hallmark of the method is the attempt to experience the reality of subjective experience.

This conviction, and the general distrust of theory, are most clearly expressed through and by the techniques and methods it is proposed to use.[16] The researcher is to work in the environment of his subjects rather than in the laboratory, and is to enter the field as free as possible from prior theory. He is to participate in the round of activities of his subjects but avoid 'disturbing' the field. He should not question his subjects directly but be as open as possible to the realm of the 'taken-for-granted'. He must take great care to plan his entrance into the field, prepare a feasible role, and assiduously court those who might sponsor his membership in selected social groups.

It is the openness and directness of this methodological approach which promises the production of a final account which, like an icon, will bear some of the marks, and recreate something of the richness, of the original.

The hidden practice

If the techniques of 'qualitative' methodology mark a decisive break from 'quantitative' ones, the way in which they are *usually applied* makes a secret compact with positivism to preserve the subject, finally, as an object. Behind all the concern for techniques, and for the reliability of the data, lies a belief, still common to received notions of 'science', that the object of the research exists in an external world. This implicit positivism is indicated in a number of ways.

The central insistence, for instance, on the *passivity* of the *Participant Observer* in the field conceals a belief that the 'subject' of the research is really an object. Though the stated concern is to minimize 'distortion of the field', the underlying fear is that the *object* may be *contaminated* with the subjectivity of the researcher.[17] Too easily it becomes an assumption of different orders of reality between the researched and the researcher. It can become the technician's devotion to keep the moonrock unsullied.

The insistent, almost neurotic, technical concern with the differentiation of Participant Observation from reportage and Art is also a reflection of the subterranean conviction that PO belongs with the sciences, and must, in the end, respect objectivity.[18] There is a clear sociological fear of naked subjectivity.[19] The novel can wallow in subjectivity – this is how it creates 'colour' and 'atmosphere' – but how do we know that the author did not make it all up? Indeed in one obvious way he did make it all up! If we are to trust Art, it seems, there may be as many social realities as there are imaginations. So the search must be for a unified object which might be expected to present itself as *the same* to many minds. The first principle of PO, the postponement of theory, compounds the dangers of this covert positivism. It strengthens the notion that the object can present itself directly to the observer.

Underneath the technicism of the concern with 'field relations' there is in many studies a strange ambiguity concerning the responsibility of the researcher to the subject. It is here that we find the most unequivocal lead to the text of the hidden practice of the method. W.F. Whyte, for example, gingerly returns to his street corner society half-aware that his exposures may have damaged real individuals. It is with some surprise that he learns that Chick Morelli[20] has his own account of what the exposure meant. What did Whyte expect to find? How would he have felt about an analysis of his University Common Room which characterised *him* as the arrogant ass?

In fact Whyte has transposed the subjective experiences of the street corner boys into a different order of social reality. And whilst they speak in that zone with amazing human likeness, they are not allowed to speak across the gap. They are *objects* of research, to which Whyte only uncertainly and imprecisely attributes real human feelings and responses.

Elements of a critique

On the role of theory

There is no truly untheoretical way in which to 'see' an 'object'. The 'object' is only perceived and understood through an internal organization of data, mediated by conceptual constructs and ways of seeing the world. The final account of an object says as much about the observer as it does about the object itself. Accounts can be read 'backwards' to uncover and explicate the consciousness of the observer. Reading much conventional PO work backwards indicates that the observing consciousness believed itself separate, in a different order of reality, from the 'object' which it observed.

On the other hand, however, we must recognize the ambition of the PO principle in relation to theory. It has directed its followers towards a profoundly important methodological possibility – the possibility of *being surprised;* of reaching knowledge not prefigured in one's starting paradigm. The urgent task is to chart the feasibility, scope and proper meaning of such a capacity. This is the project of formulating a form of analysis, and its appropriate methods, which lies between the theoretical openness of Participant Observation and the closure of positivist reasoning

If we are to recognize the actual scope for the production of 'new' knowledge, we must avoid delusions. We must not be too ambitious. It is vital that we admit the most basic foundations of our research approach, and accept that no 'discovery' will overthrow this most basic orientation. The theoretical organization of the starting out position should be outlined and acknowledged in any piece of research. This inevitable organization concerns attitudes towards the world in which the research takes place, a particular view of the form of the relationship between the subject of research and determining social relationships, and a notion of the analytic procedures which will be used to produce the final account. It would also explain why certain topics had been chosen for research in the first place.

This theoretical 'confession', however, need not specify *the whole* of social reality in a given region, it has merely specified the kind of world in which its action is seen as taking place. It does not include *specific* theories or explanations, nor does it anticipate the particular meaning of the future flow of data.

It is indeed crucial that a qualitative methodology be confronted with the maximum flow of relevant data. Here resides the power of the evidence to 'surprise', to contradict, specific developing theories. And here is the only possible source for the 'authenticity', the 'qualitative feel' which is the method's particular justification. It is in this area – short of any challenge to one's 'world view' – where there is the greatest possibility of 'surprise'.

This is not to allow back an unbridled, intuitive 'naturalism' on impoverished terms. Even with respect to what remains unspecified by the larger 'confession', we must recognize the necessarily theoretical form of what we 'discover'. Even the most 'naturalistic' of accounts involve deconstruction of native logic, and build upon reconstructions of compressed, select, significant moments in the original field experience. There is an art concealing art which precisely obscures the theoretical work that has taken place.

Having recognized the inevitability of a theoretical component, it can be used more self-consciously to probe those areas about which knowledge is incomplete.

We will find in any subjective account a submerged text of contradictions, inconsistencies and divergencies. If we are tuned in to an illusory attempt to represent a single-valency consciousness and subjectivity without interpretative or reductive work upon it, we shall simply reproduce this subtext. We shall also have to admit that to particular actors many areas of their life and experience have the quality of opacity – that is subjective *experience* which is unexplained by subjective *meaning*, or penetrated only by subjectively half-plausible folklore or myth.

There are no obvious virtues in repeating this opacity, especially if there are opportunities – theoretical of course – to draw the opacity back somewhat. Nor is there any loyalty to the subject in concealing things which are genuine and helpful, nor is there a commitment to naturalism in denying the necessary interpretative moments that are necessary to the fullest account. It is necessary to add to the received notion of the 'quality' of the data, an ability to watch for inconsistencies and misunderstandings which provide points for theoretical interpretation. We must maintain the richness and atmosphere of the original experience while attempting to illuminate its inner connections.

And our interpretation of subjective meaning does not amount to a superior theory, quite unavailable to the subject of research. This is precisely to step onto the path of depersonalization of the subject which is the very opposite of our intentions. The interpretation involves the comparison of cases which the subject may not have witnessed, the re-construction in words of what is immediately felt or apprehended. It is the questioning of what is simply assumed, the placing of felt contradictions and disjunctions within a broader picture, the raising of questions about the underworkings of our social life. It is the recognition that rationality may be expressed in behaviour and culture as well as in the written word.

This theoretical work is especially important to a marxist orientation. On the one hand there is an enormous opportunity – the linking of contradictions at the subjective level to the determining structures of society. On the other hand there is a pressing danger – the minimization and objectification of the subject. Certainly, though, the necessary and inevitable level of interpretative theorizing within the method can be used to explicate chosen topics without running greater dangers than are run conventionally in an *unrecognized* way.

So far I have outlined the theoretical 'space' in which the traditional capacity 'to be surprised', might be thought to operate, and have emphasized that the process of 'finding something new' has a definite theoretical edge – it is not 'spontaneous' or 'natural'. However, this is to specify only the form and scale of what might be really distinctive about a qualitative method. To understand the inner process of one's capacity to 'be surprised' we must turn to a critique of the hidden positivism within the existing qualitative method.

On reflexivity: the politics of fieldwork

If we wish to represent the subjective meanings and feelings of others it is not possible to extend to them less than we know of ourselves. What is so often taken as the 'object', and the researcher, lie parallel in their humanity. The 'object' of our enquiry is, in fact, of course a subject and has to be understood and presented in the same mode as the researcher's own subjectivity – this is the true meaning of 'validity' in the 'qualitative' zone. The recognition of this truism is not, however, to declare against all forms of 'objectivity'. We are still in need of a method which respects evidence, seeks corroboration and minimizes distortion, *but which is without rationalist natural-science-like pretence.*

Though we can only know it through our own concepts, and although it must be allowed all the properties of insistent humanity, there is nevertheless a *real* subject for our enquiry, which is not entirely spirited away by our admission of its relativized position. If our purpose is a fuller understanding and knowledge of this subject then we must be concerned with the reliability of the data we use. Furthermore, if our focus is not on the isolated subjective meaning of one individual, but on things which are *shared* between subjectivities, then we will be confronted by symbolic and cultural systems which do have a consistent substance in themselves. It is perfectly justified to use rigorous and logical techniques to gain the fullest knowledge of these things. This is, therefore, to go partly down the road of traditional 'objectivity': many of the techniques used will be the same. The parting of the ways comes at the end of this process. The conventional process takes its 'objective' data gathering as far as possible, and then consigns the rest – what it cannot know, measure or understand – to Art, or 'the problem of subjectivity'. Having constituted its object truly as an 'object', and having gained all possible knowledge about this 'object', the process must stop, it has come up to the 'inevitable limitations of a quantitative methodology'. But it is precisely at this point that a reflexive, qualitative methodology comes into its own. Having never constituted the subject of its study as an 'object' it is not surprised that there is a limit to factual knowledge, or that factual knowledge by no means exhausts all there is to be known about another subjective system. What finally remains is *the relationship between subjective systems.*

The rigorous stage of the analysis, the elimination of distortion, the cross-checking of evidence; etc. have served to focus points of divergence and convergence between subjective systems. Reducing the confusion of the research situation, providing a more precise orientation for analysis, allows a closer reading of separate realities. By reading moments of contact and divergence it becomes possible to delineate other worlds, demonstrating their inner symbolic qualities. And when the conventional techniques retire, when they cannot follow the subjects themselves – this is the moment of *reflexivity*. Why are these things happening? Why has the subject behaved in this way? Why do certain areas remain obscure to the researcher? What difference in orientation lie behind the failure to communicate?

It is here in this interlocking of human meanings that there is the possibility of 'being surprised'. And in terms of the generation of 'new' knowledge, we 'know' what it is, precisely *not* because we have shared it – the usual notion of 'empathy' – but because we have *not* shared it. It is here that the classical canons are overturned. It is time to ask and explore, to discover the differences between subjective positions. It is time to initiate actions or to break expectations in order to probe different angles in different lights. Of course this is a time of maximum disturbance to researchers, whose own meanings are being thoroughly contested. There may be specific occasions when researchers cannot follow subjects in some activity, or when they are explicitly attacked, or criticized, or placed in contradictory, double-binding situations. It is precisely at this point that the researcher must assume an unrestrained and hazardous *self-reflexivity*. And it is the turning away from a fully human commitment, at this point, which finally limits the methods of traditional sociology, and maintains them still within the purview of an iron cage of rationalism.

It is also the destructive moments of this *reflexive* method that there is an opportunity for transcending something of what still remains hidden and self-validating in the the researcher's own paradigm. The possibility of a genuine appreciation of another reality, another set of procedures for the understanding of others, another way of seeing the world, is opened up. It can undercut what the researcher may still assume is an obvious manner of responding to the world unproblematically shared by all. Furthermore, from a more explicitly marxist standpoint, both the conflict between his own meaning system and that of his subjects, and the contradictions within his subjects' experience, picked up by the 'theoretical' edge of the researcher's 'surprise', give the analyst points from which to read 'down' to structural and material determinations, and to the stresses and strains between these, which underlie the domain of subjective experience. These understandings will, of course, be as relevant to a critical explication of the researcher's consciousness and habits of thought – contradictions, opacities and all – as they will be to those of the researched.

On technicism

The notion of a reflexive methodology takes us far beyond a simple concern for techniques of data gathering. It is often stated as a truism that forms of data collection and analytic procedures are profoundly interconnected. And it is precisely a *theoretical* interest which induces the researcher to develop certain kinds of technique, to make comparative forays, to invent or invert methodological canons, to select certain 'problems' for analytical explication. Though techniques are important, and though we should be concerned with their 'validity', they can never stand in the place of a theoretical awareness and interest arising out of *the recognition of one's role in a social relationship*. Without this theoretical quickening the techniques merely poise us on the ledge of an iron cage of rationalism still unable to meet the 'subject' there.

We should resist, therefore, the hegemony of technique. It should be our servant not our master. In particular we should deconstruct the portmanteau notion of Participant Observation and detail its parts along with a number of other techniques, to give us a flexible range of particular techniques to be drawn upon according to our 'master' needs. Within the spectrum as a whole the following techniques can be specified:

Participation
Observation
Participation as Observer
Observation as Participant
Just 'being around'
Group discussion
Recorded group discussion
Unfocused interview
Recorded unfocused interview

These techniques are very different and it is clearly misleading to think in terms of them constituting one blanket methodology. Techniques lower down this list, for example, are more likely to be applied to a phenomenon from the past (cf. the development of 'oral history'). But I believe that all of these techniques are relevant to the principles of qualitative methodology, and each should be rigorously thought through in its particular research context. Clearly the use of tape-recorders is relevant to a quite specific range of data, has its own moral implications, and may have a higher theoretical gearing, coupled with a lower degree of 'surprise' than the more traditional methods of PO.

Conclusion

Traditional sociology then, provides a useful starting point. But we must submit its methods to a rigorous screening, to make explicit the denied theoretical account, and to remove the hidden tendency towards positivism. We must liberate the whole notion notion of 'methodology', and argue finally, for a recognition of the reflexive relationship of researchers to their subjects.

Notes

1 See the ritual acceptance in most mainstream methodology texts of the role of 'quantitative methods' – even if their use is to be limited to 'pilot' or 'descriptive' studies. See for instance Chapter 3, C. Selltiz et al. (eds.), *Research Methods in Social Relations*, Methuen & Co. Ltd., 1966; Chapter 3, J. Madge, *The Tools of Social Science*, Longmans, 1965.
2 See the argument in the previous journal that 'qualitative' sociology has not broken with positivism in any decisive fashion; pp. 243–74, WPCS 7/8.
3 Ibid, pp. 243–4.
4 For a useful discussion on 'objectivity' in positivism see pp. 102–4, A.W. Gouldner, *The Coming Crisis of Western Sociology*, Heinemann, 1970.
5 WPCS 7/8, pp. 243–74.
6 See for instance; C.R. Shaw, *The Jack-Roller*, University of Chicago Press, 1966; W.I. Thomas and F. Znaniecki, *The Polish Peasant in Europe and America*, 1927; F.M. Thrasher, *The Gold Coast and the Slum: A Study of 1,313 Gangs in Chicago*, 1928; N. Anderson, *The Hobo*, 1923; L.W. Wirth, *The Ghetto*, 1928.
7 W.F. Whyte, *Street Corner Society*, University of Chicago Press, London 1969.

8 See for instance; H.S. Becker, *Outsiders: Studies in the Sociology of Deviance*, Free Press, Glencoe 1963; H.S. Becker et al., *Boys in White*, University of Chicago Press, 1961; H.S. Becker et al., *Making the Grade*, John Wiley, 1965; N. Polsky, *Hustlers, Beats and Others*, Penguin, 1971.
9 See D. Downes, *The Delinquent Solution*, Routledge & Kegan Paul, 1966.
10 See S. Cohen (ed.), *Images of Deviancy*, Penguin, 1982; S. Cohen, *Folk Devils and Moral Panics*, Paladin, 1972; P. Rock & M. McIntosh (eds.), *Criminology and the Sociology of Deviance in Britain*, 1974; L. Taylor & I. Taylor (eds.), *Politics and Deviance*, Penguin, 1973.
11 See for instance; Plant, *Drug Takers in an English Town*, 1974; J. Patrick, *A Glasgow Gang Observed*, Eyre-Methuen, 1973; H.J. Parker, *View from the Boys*, David and Charles, 1975.
12 G.J. McCall and J.L. Simmons (eds.), *Issues in Participant Observation*, Addison-Wesley, 1969; W.J. Filstead (ed.), *Qualitative Methodology*, Markham Publishing Co., 1970.
13 My emphasis. B.G. Glaser and A.L. Strauss, 'Discovery of Substantive Theory: A Basic Strategy Underlying Qualitative Research', in W.J. Filstead, *op.cit.*, p. 304 note.
14 See the literature on 'Working Hypotheses', and esp. B. Geer, 'First Days in the Field', in G.J. McCall and J.L. Simmons (eds.), *Issues in Participant Observation: A Text and Reader*, Addison-Wesley, 1969.
15 See H. Blumer, 'What is Wrong with Social Theory', in W. Filstead, op.cit.
16 See McCall and Simmons, *op.cit.*, Chs. 2 and 3.
17 'Contamination' is often referred to; see, for instance, G.L. McCall, 'Data Quality Control in Participant Observation', in McCall & Simmons, *op.cit.*
18 Even when connections are admitted, the concern is specifically to rescue that which is 'scientific' for the sociological method. See McCall & Simmons, p. 1.
19 See for instance the section on 'The Quality of Data' in McCall & Simmons, *op.cit.*
20 W.F. Whyte, *op.cit.*, p. 345.

Subjective experience as a dimension of history (*Pam Taylor*)

In a study of women domestic servants between the two World Wars, I wanted the women's own accounts in their own language to be central; but backed and pointed by statistical and other secondary source material. I collected 17 accounts; some were written but 12 were the result of fairly informal unstructured interviews. I used two autobiographies[1] and accounts in *Useful Toil* reporting experiences of domestic service in the 50 years up to 1920.[2]

While collecting this first-hand evidence I also looked at Census figures, Government Reports, other jobs for women and their pay rates, unemployment, the extent of poverty and malnutrition, newspapers. Very often official or secondary sources would corroborate, emphasize or underline what the women told me in their accounts. The most important fact revealed by Census figures was that well over one million women were still in this underpaid and unregulated occupation between 1921 and 1939. This fact alone colours my evidence, for domestic service was still a widespread and accepted institution.

Surveys in the 1930s by the BMA and by John Boyd Orr[3] revealed that 30% to 35% of the population were undernourished: moreover, this was due not only to unemployment but to low pay for those actually in work.

> Life was wonderful (in a mining area in the Forest of Dean) except for one constant nagging irritation – HUNGER. We knew the wages Dad brought home from the pit were not enough to keep us out of debt, let alone fill our bellies properly.[4]

A woman who had moved from South Wales to Bournemouth said of one job, 'I wished I could have sent home the scraps left on people's plates.'[5]

This remark highlighted the gap between rich and poor or even between comfortably-off and poor.

Even in a small study, correspondences emerged and also, repetitions of experience and attitudes over widely varying situations and areas; this suggests that they might be representative of larger numbers. In the 1920s the number of free places at grammar schools maintained by local authorities was increased, thus enabling poorer children of ability to benefit and to qualify for better jobs. Due to the severe economic depression, there were two unintended consequences to this policy: firstly, girls and boys were leaving school with School Certificate (the forerunner of the GCE O-level) which did *not* give them entry to better jobs because the jobs were not there. Secondly, poorer children, having been selected for grammar school education, could not go because of poverty at home:

> I won a scholarship to the Grammar School but was not able to go for financial reasons. My oldest brother won one as well but he was not able to go either.[6]

> I passed for Grammar School but of course, being number nine in the family I didn't have much chance of going.[7]

In my sample of 19, four girls 'passed for grammar school': three were unable to go because their wages were needed; the one who did go was unable to stay on in the sixth form to get a qualification for teacher training college because her brothers and sisters were out at work:

> My only ambition was to become a teacher and though it must have been a terrible struggle for my mother to keep me in school clothes, books, etc., she still wanted me to return after the holidays and eventually go to a teacher's training college. It wasn't possible in those days to get work in the holidays as the students do today. So there was no way of helping with the financial situation. My eldest brother was only 14 and had just started work in the pit. Naturally, he resented the fact that he had to work while I stayed on at school. I made the decision to leave home and go away to work myself. In the November I went to London [from S. Wales] and became a domestic servant.[8]

Very roughly, two jobs patterns seem to have existed for domestic servants: the country situation, where a local girl would hear of a vacancy at the 'Big House' or with a local family.

> I went to school with the butler's daughter. One day when I was at work at the village shop he went down to see my mother to ask if I'd like to go and work with him for Major and Mrs. Evans who were away on a world trip.[9]

This girl would be working near enough home to go home for her time off. Her parents and the employer would know of each other and the girl would still be in her own neighbourhood.

If girls were living in a country district with no employment or in an industrial area (such as mining) with few or no job opportunities for women, they would have to travel away to work. In effect, they left home and neighbourhood for a completely new and alien environment, a new life style and a job which involved living under the same roof with one's employer. A job, moreover, whose pay and time off did not allow much freedom.

> I really can't imagine what I expected. I only know that my first place was a dreadful shock to me. The advert said 'Lady's Help'. My mother, who'd been a Lady's maid was

> under the impression I would be trained in that kind of work and would travel as she had done. We were completely misled. I was the only servant kept. I felt as though I were in prison. I stayed in my first job 9 months until I had saved enough money to pay my fare home. I longed to see my mother, brother and sisters.[10]

There was a large exodus from South Wales to London for domestic service around 1929. Also from County Durham (another mining area) to London. According to W.H. Coombes,[11] in some mining areas girls were kept at home to help and were supported by the working men of the family. But when the men were out of work the budget could no longer support this arrangement and she would go into service to relieve the family of keeping her. In many cases the girl also sent money home out of her small wage:

> The Nursing Home was owned by three Scottish sisters who paid my fare to Bournemouth (from S. Wales) repayable if I left before three months. I stayed five months. My wages were 10/- a week out of which I sent 7/- home.[12]

> I remembered the time when my brother had fainted and gone into a coma. Dad had run like one gone mad for the Doctor. When the Doctor came he said something about malnutrition and I looked it up in the dictionary at school. Undernourished, that's what it meant. Well, now I would be able to do something about it. Surely I could send home at least a shilling a week. That would pay for three extra loaves.[13]

Hours worked, and kind of work varied from household to household depending on the size of house and numbers of servants kept. A large number of servants meant a division of labour and perhaps less work for the individual. It also meant company. The single servant had a very hard time, often being expected to combine the functions of several servants. She could be lonely sitting on her own in the kitchen in the evenings.

> Loneliness is the greatest of all trials for a girl in domestic service, separated from her home and the cheerful coming and going of family life. Leisure to the solitary occupant of the kitchen can be a dreary affair, especially when through closed doors she can hear echoes of fun and laughter in her employer's parlour.[14]

In spite of long hours, scanty time off and week-end work, domestic service could be a pleasure with a kind considerate employer. It did represent, for some, an escape from poverty and overcrowding.

> There is nothing better for a girl if she is with good, kind, people but nothing worse should a girl find herself in a bad place.[15]

> They were very happy years. I couldn't say that anything went wrong apart from the occasional tiff that you get in any household. They were seven exceedingly happy years. I loved the children and they loved me. I left simply because they would not pay me any more than £24 a year. I did want a little more money as by then Mother was partly dependent on me.[16]

These two remarks highlight the complete lack of legislation over hours, wages, time off and overtime pay (unheard of in domestic service). Time off in all cases reported to me was one half day a week *after* the lunch dishes had been washed till about 10 or 10.30 pm. In addition a half day (or rarely, a whole day) every other Sunday. I did not hear of any living-in servant being allowed to sleep at home on her Sunday off. It seems that in return for board and lodging the servant was supposed to be on the spot *every* morning to do the routine chores before the family rose. This points to the great difference between domestic service as a job and any other job for women: control over the girl's private life was very strong.

Why was such pervasive control exerted not only over work but over life itself? One view is that employers had the role of parents when the servants were young and there is an element of truth in this. But the employers were part of the larger class system that saw the working class as a race apart but necessary to do unpleasant and laborious work essential for their comfort. Normally, the working class lived in different areas and in very different houses. In towns they often lived in ghettoes avoided by the better off. One of the duties of the subordinate class was to 'know their place' and not to overstep the boundary between themselves and 'their betters'. In domestic service the employing upper class was allowing the lower class to step over this barrier and to enter their homes to live and work. Hence it was doubly necessary to define servants' subordinate role and inferiority. Status distinctions were carefully delineated and rigidly enforced. The servants must not be mistaken for kin either in the minds of the employer or of the servant herself or the outsider.

Rules about rising, working, time off, uniform, eating, styles of address and response all served to define the servant as different and having different needs and expectations from women of the family. Even if kindness was shown the control was there and because the girl lived on the job she was more open to this kind of persuasion. Erving Goffman calls this situation a Total Institution or a place where all aspects of behaviour are controlled. There is a set pattern of behaviour already established and it is very difficult not to accept the role defined for you by others. Goffman cites boarding schools, prison, hospitals (where his main work was done).[17]

Remarks made to me do echo some of the ideas contained in this definition:

> I resented the feeling of being owned.[18]
>
> In some ways we weren't much better off than serfs inasmuch as our whole life was regulated by our employers; the hours we worked; the clothes we wore. Even our scanty time off is overshadowed by the thought that we mustn't be in later than ten o'clock.[19]

I have concentrated in this short article on 'extra-work' dimensions of domestic service in its final phase as an accepted institution and major occupation for women.

As academics, we don't quite know how to deal with subjective experience. It has been the novelists' terrain. It doesn't mesh neatly with the rules of positivism which have directed Sociology and, to some extent, History. I have tried to show how secondary source material, correspondences between accounts from different people and theory can interact with reports of individual experience so that this is not viewed 'in limbo' but in the light of the contemporary political and economic system.

Notes

1 Margaret Powell, *Below Stairs*, Pan, 1968; Winifred Foley, *Child in the Forest*, BBC, 1974.
2 John Burnett, *Useful Toil*, Allen Lane, 1974.

3 John Boyd Orr, *Food, Health and Income*, 1936.
4 W. Foley, *op.cit.*
5 Glenys Lowder, S. Wales. Personal account.
6 *Ibid.*
7 G. Evans, Black Country. Personal account.
8 D. Grayson. Personal account.
9 F. Follet, Northants village. Personal account.
10 D. Grayson.
11 B.L. Coombes, *These Poor Hands*, New Left Books, 1936.
12 G. Lowder.
13 W. Foley, *op.cit.*
14 Govt. Report on post-war organisation of private domestic employment, 1944.
15 Govt. Report on the supply of female domestic servants, 1923.
16 L. Rayworth. Personal account.
17 Erving Goffman, *Asylums*, Penguin, 1961.
18 D. Grayson.
19 M. Powell, *op.cit.*

The language of fatalism (*Andrew Tolson*)

There are, according to Alan Dawe,[1] two sociologies. The sociological 'tradition' comprises two distinct ideological paradigms, deriving from the social debates of the nineteenth century (Conservatism vs Enlightenment), and involving diametrically opposed orientations to social theory (theories of 'social order' vs theories of 'social action'). Dawe maintains that these orientations are structurally incompatible – that any attempt at a synthesis results in compromise. Most frequently in sociological theory we encounter the Parsonian compromise: the reduction of action (and subjective meanings) to 'roles' (and objective cultural 'norms'). Here, 'the attempted synthesis subordinates action to system concepts in such a way as to remove the concept of action altogether. Perceptual "orientation" takes its place.'

The 'two sociologies' have, I want to suggest, had a profound influence on the construction of theories of culture. The culture totality is often described in terms of the 'social system' – characterized by an ideological 'consensus', normatively imposed upon, and passively internalized by, its subjects or 'bearers'. This 'consensus' is identified with a ruling class 'hegemony', transmitted by the mass media and the apparatus of the State. On the other hand, there is posited the notion of a 'cultural struggle for control' – through the creation of subjective meanings, oppositional life-styles and group subcultures. Here within the interpersonal milieu of the small group, in the dynamics of social interaction, reified cultural 'systems' can be 'demystified', by reference to their origins in the active, conscious 'projects' of group members.

It is apparent that this sociological approach to cultural studies contains an inherent theoretical problem. In its simplest form, this is the difficulty of understanding the ways in which the 'objective' and 'subjective' orientations – the social system and social activities – *interpenetrate*. On the one hand, it is understood that hegemonic cultural processes, for their vitality and development, must in some way make sense of the immediate interests of social classes, groups, or individuals. Conversely, it is recognized that subjective meanings, must, at some point, pass through institutionalized systems of communication and social control. But the precise relations between the social totality and the local situation, between the 'macro' and the 'micro' levels, the relations of *mediation* – these cannot be clarified, or even conceptualized, from a sociological perspective.

In my own research, I am attempting to reformulate the 'problem of mediations' within the specific social context of the family. My particular focus is *masculinity:* the (principally male) experience of work and home, the definition of 'leisure', and the formation of patriarchal sex-identities. I am trying to show how ideological forms both structure, and are structured by, subjective accounts of social experience. And it seems to me that this 'interpenetration' can be identified within the *language* of social experience. At the level of practical consciousness, I want to claim that the cultural mediations are principally linguistic; that language provides the symbolic structure by which social experience is formulated, and, most significantly, that this symbolic structure has levels which are both conscious and unconscious, and which together comprise the social production of speech.

The following is part of the transcript of a taped interview, made with Bill, who works as a housepainter for the city corporation, painting the exteriors of council houses. He has been in this job for two months, having had a brief period of unemployment, before which he worked as a lorry driver. Here he describes some aspects of the experience of housepainting, and goes on to talk about a previous experience of working (again as a painter) for himself. In the subsequent analysis, I shall try to illustrate the inter-relation, in the text, of conscious and unconscious levels of language. I shall suggest that Bill's conscious description of his experience is 'overdetermined' by unconscious patterns of speech[2] – to produce an overall 'language of fatalism'.

Transcript

U1 A: *Do you think about work when you're not at work, you know?*

U2 B: Oh no, no. No, once I leave work it stops there, you know. I try not to bring it home anyway. I might have a little natter about things in general that's gone on in the day to Jean, and then that's it. But if possible I like to come home from work and leave it there till the next day.

U3 A: *Erm, but things at work don't, never worry you at all, er, I mean don't sort of*

U4 B: Erm, I think probably Andrew it did worry me, let's put it that way. But if I'd let things worry me, they needn't. Like I've been at this trade now a few years. Well to earn a bonus you've got to have a certain amount of speed (*mm*); and if I'd have (inaudible) it working with somebody, thinking that he's faster than me and maybe earning more money – then again he's been at it quite a time, I haven't. Then I – I got over that spell and I think now you know I can, I just plod on, do the best I can, that's it you know. I'm doing my bit so you got to accept that now you know, I don't let it worry me now. I did when I first started.

U5 A: *But that was, er ho-how long ago was that, say fifteen years?*

U6 B: No, no, this job. 'Cause as I say I've been at this trade quite a few years now (*mm*). And er (inaudible) drifting again you know. I mean being at home and doing odd jobs for people it doesn't really keep you in trim. Now and then you need, you know it's like, you acquire a certain speed, you never forget it but, well speed has never come into it till this job (*mm*) being a bonus scheme. Obviously you know I've got to see, think about speed a bit.

U7 A: *This is the first one you've er, you've had that's been a bonus job have you?* (yea, yea, yea). *Erm, I don't know whether you want to say anything about it but erm I'd be interested to know what happened when you were working for yourself. Er why, why you gave that up.*

U8 B: Well, I was working for a firm, Ken Salter's. I enjoyed it there. It wasn't a bad little firm. Anyway we was forever having arguments over little things you know. At the time

I was working on the Yardley Road on backs of houses. A Doctor Mills had a very big house and I had to work with her because of the patients you know *(mm)*. Anyway, I got on very well with her you know, seemed to please her for some unknown reason, and er, she sort of took to me you know. She said 'if you ever went on your own' she said 'I'd find you work'. Well being on me own had never gone through me head; but I had this row one particular day and thought, 'well I've had enough'. And she heard about it and she sent for me and said, 'have you got a job?', I said, 'no'. She said, 'well, have a go on your own'. I said, 'no, got no money, no capital, no kit as kit goes like', you know *(mm)*. 'Oh don't worry about it, 'she says, 'I'll find you plenty of work'. And that's how it started. And the first twelve months I done very well. But then, this is like to me then why I lose faith in human nature and don't really get involved. They seemed then as they got to know me to take a hell of a lot for granted, and they started to bump me. Well you know, it didn't pay *(yea)*. Well, with a wife and family I couldn't stand (inaudible). So I thought, 'well, this is beginning to get a bit of a headache', so I packed it in. But the trouble started after with the tax *(oh, yea)*. You know I'd registered, I'd done everything legal. But the first year like it's like a week in hand. They don't bother you with tax. But they assess your first year the second year. Well, the second year was very, very poor; but the first year as I say was very good. Of course, I got bumped for tax; and the accountant I had apparently didn't seem to know what he was doing you know, and he got thousands of pounds down you know. Anyway they done it for me and when they'd worked it all out and I was earning £14 a week, and er, I owed them a bit of tax and I bumped that at work – you know, I paid sort of £1 a week back and we roughed it a bit like (mm). But we had that straightened out and we had a nice little rebate back. If I'd suffered it I'd have, might have been on me own now.

U9 A: *You would have been?*

U10 B: Probably but, if I could have just suffered that bad patch *(mm)*. But I had no capital Andrew, I had nothing to fall on *(mm)*. You know, if somebody owed me the pay. 'Cause what I used to do, as I said the cash for the materials, as I say me not having capital I couldn't buy the materials. So we'd always agree that they'd pay for the materials straight away. If it was a big job we just used to draw the least we could to live on *(mm)* so that at the end of the job we'd have the lump sum see. We managed quite well like that, and of course we'd get the lump sum. But we moved up here while I was on my own and it seemed to go wrong from there.

Analysis

It is apparent from Bill's intonation patterns and his general self-presentation, that he could be described as a working class 'fatalist'. Such statements as 'I just plod on . . .' and 'I lose faith in human nature . . .' point to an attitude of resignation and hopelessness. But it is important to recognize that this attitude is neither an unconscious reflex-action, nor a conscious form of self-defence. It arises out of a pattern of *contradictory* social experiences, which, according to Bill's (linguistic) frames of reference, can only be made sense of in fatalistic ways. He could not, in any straightforward sense, be 'convinced' otherwise – be argued into taking a revolutionary socialist attitude to his life. For his *consciousness* of social contradictions is *overdetermined* by the *unconscious* structures of his speech, and these are themselves daily reconfirmed by recognisable and immediate patterns of social existence.

Here are two examples of Bill's conscious account of the social contradictions in his life, both to do with the experience of work. Firstly, as he describes his present job, Bill indicates an experienced contradiction between on the one hand, personal rhythms of work (having a background knowledge of a trade, and when unemployed, 'drifting' around doing odd jobs at home) and, on the other hand, the imposed alien rhythms of the bonus scheme (the speed required, the pressure on the informal work group of men being obliged to keep up with each other). Caught between the two – his personal labour-power and the form that labour-power must assume in his job – Bill just 'plods on' and 'does the best he can'. Secondly, as he narrates his previous experience of working for himself, Bill recounts how he was caught between, on the one hand, his responsibility to his wife and family and the personal stress of 'roughing it' to pay back his debts; and, on the other, his former employers, creditors, customers, accountants, tax officials etc., all of whom he feels were out to 'bump him'. He 'loses faith in human nature' and emotionally withdraws from this conflicting experience, because in such situations, as Bill himself states with no prompting from me, he *has no capital* to fall back on. He is inevitably on the receiving end.

From this it is important to note that Bill's fatalism does not arise from an 'incorrect' analysis of the situation, on a conscious level. Perhaps his terminology is not explicitly marxist, but Bill does not need to be told that he is a wage-labourer, that wage-labourers are alienated by work-discipline, and that with nothing to sell but their labour-power they are individually powerless against the forces of Capital and the State (in this case the taxman). Bill knows this well enough, because it is the immediately contradictory structure of his own working life – its overt reality, its manifest content. So if then we are interested in how Bill's interpretation of this experience comes to be *fatalistic*, and not socialist or revolutionary, we are interested in a set of problems which do not arise at a conscious level – a level at which they may be openly debated and challenged.

This consideration leads us, I think, to a different level of analysis, to the *unconscious* structures of ideology. And I am interested in how these structures interact with the conscious narrative to constitute the overall problematic of fatalism. I am suggesting that the unconscious content of ideology is embedded within its linguistic context, and that this context has three primary levels. It is partly (1) a system of individual 'speech genres'; partly (2) a system of inter-personal 'discourse'; and partly (3) a deep-structural relation between class 'codes'. I'll just briefly mention what I mean by these three levels, and try to show how they operate in this transcript.

Speech genres

'Speech genres' are shifts within the structure of individual speech. They express specific types of subjective meaning and point towards recognizable social patterns of inter-subjectivity. I think it is important to emphasize that speech genres, though they are produced by individual speakers in subjective expression, are always oriented towards an audience.[3] A simple example of how speech genres point to patterns in inter-individual speech can be seen in this transcript, as Bill begins to talk about working for himself (UB). Here, he moves quite quickly through three recognizable genres: (1) *The Narrative Genre* (framed by 'Well'), by which he *reports* experience. This is a potentially contradictory experience – for we are told that although he 'enjoyed it there', and 'it wasn't a bad little firm', nevertheless 'we was forever having arguments'. But the potential contradiction in these statements remains unexplained, suspended, as Bill moves to (2) *The Dramatic Genre* (framed in the text by the second 'Anyway'), by which he *recreates* experience, and gives it an immediacy which demands the recognition and assent of the addressee. It is, I would suggest, a particularly pervasive form of working-class speech; and it provides a crucial ideological mediation, so that (a) the experience of social contradictions is represented as a personalized conflict, and (b) idiomatic and proverbial expressions may be introduced into a dramatized world of appearances. The narrated experience of the speaker is thus taken for granted, immediate, obvious and unchallengeable. Finally Bill moves to (3) *The Explanatory Genre* (framed by 'But then'), by which, on the basis of the listener's tacit assent, he *justifies* his actions and offers a generalized conclusion. The form the explanation takes, initially, arises out of the preceding structure of speech genres, especially the dramatic genre. The taken for granted experience of the speaker is here justified in terms of universal categories ('I lose faith in human nature'), appeals to everyday life ('with a wife and family to support'), and commonsense psychology ('the whole thing became a bit of a headache'). And this inherited, unconsciously-generic language mediates Bill's conscious account of his social experience.

Discourse and codes

The inter-individual orientations of speech genres are realized at a second level, in the structures of 'discourse'. Discourse refers to the speech-context created when two or more people are talking to each other; it is the interactive structure of *dialogue*. An analysis of discourse is thus a way of looking at patterned interventions, false-starts, misunderstandings, defensive manoeuvres, evasions, repetitions, etc., which characterize everyday conversations. A discourse analysis may also begin to illuminate the underlying expectations and interpretations of each participant, and the relation between their social and ideological perspectives. It thus points to an analysis, not merely of the 'communicative competence'[4] which a speaker must possess in order to speak at all, but also of the class 'codes'[5] which underpin communications in class societies.

In this transcript for example, a misunderstanding occurs when I assume that Bill's worry about speed (U4), and his ambiguous statement, 'I don't let it worry me now, I did when I first started', refers to when he 'first started' *working*. In fact, as Bill goes on to explain (U6) it refers to when he 'first started' his *present job*, two months ago, for the city council. However, through the ambiguity of 'first started', I have been so misled as to ask (U5) 'how long ago was that, say fifteen years?'. I have taken Bill's earlier statement ('I've been at this trade now a few years') *literally*, thinking that it referred to *time as such* – the length of time Bill has worked as a painter. I have assumed that the later statements ('I just plod on, do the best I can' etc.) are to be interpreted as philosophically-resigned compromises based on *years* of troubling experience. (Thus: 'I'm doing my bit now so you got to accept that' . . . etc.). But as Bill's clarification of his ambiguity makes plain, I have misinterpreted the reference to 'a few years'. This is not an abstract reference to *time*, but a concrete expression of the experience of 'acquiring a certain speed', building up a physical *rhythm*. And this rhythm is contradicted, not by an abstract notion of 'working', but by this particular job for the council. With 'I've been at this trade now a few years', Bill is referring not to time as such; but to the personal, sensuous character of his own labour-power.

I think it is significant that this misunderstanding is not simply 'a mistake'. It does not simply lead to a breakdown in the discourse of the interview. It arises from a specific ambiguity; but the ambiguity is compounded by the fact that I don't immediately grasp the inferential structure of Bill's class 'code' (which is something like: 'understand my statements about time not as abstract philosophizings, but as generalizations from felt experience'). The misunderstanding in the discourse thus indicates the differing relation to wage-labour of the participants i.e. their differing location in the division between mental and manual labour; it shows how these differing relations, manifested in the interactive structure of the discourse, point to underlying class 'codes'; and it illuminates something of the general character of working-class culture – namely that particular experiences are concretely, practically, made sense of through the categories of the class 'code', but that these categories, far from abstract in their foundation, are derived from the practical rhythms and repetitions of working-class existence ('drifting', acquiring 'speed' etc.). I think that this dense, immediate, empirical working-class experience is what often underlies the unconsciously-reproduced, proverbial language of explanatory speech-genres ('so I thought, well this is beginning to get a bit of a headache, so I packed it in'). In working-class culture the coded world is taken for granted because it is concretely lived out in the rhythms of everyday life.

Conclusion

Thus I am saying that Bill's fatalistic ideology is the product of the relation between his conscious perception of the reality of his existence as a wage-labourer and the unconscious speech-genres, structures of discourse, and class codes, which provide the framework for patterns of inference and explanation. These unconscious linguistic structures are themselves habitually reaffirmed in an ideological experience of everyday life – in taken for granted behaviour, immediate social relationships. But it is notable from this transcript that Bill's most fatalistic expression occurs when his account of the rhythms of everyday life comes into *direct conflict* with his conscious perception of his life as a wage-labourer – i.e. when things start to worry him, when people 'bump him', when he and his family have to 'rough it'. Fatalism is thus a way of negotiating the 'lack of fit' between unconsciously reproduced and consciously perceived levels of experience.

And through this kind of linguistic analysis I think we can begin to specify the point at which the 'two sociologies' intersect. Bill's fatalistic negotiation of the contradictions of his experience provides a subjective 'mediation' for the reproduction of the social structures (wage-labour and capital; family and class). The mediation is 'cultural' because it occurs in language, which is a product of the capacity of human beings to symbolise reality. 'Symbolization' is, broadly speaking, the production and communication of *meanings;* it is both an active, conscious ordering of human existence, and an unconscious reproduction, in symbolic patterns, of the human social inheritence. So the site of the cultural 'mediations' may be specified as the 'symbolic order', which constitutes as it were, the 'thread' of the social 'fabric'. And as is implied by the notion of 'meaning', this fabric can only be represented as being continuously, actively, interwoven by new symbolic products – produced out of the conscious/unconscious dialectic in the foundation of the 'symbolic order'.

Notes

1 Alan Dawe, 'The two sociologies', *British Journal of Sociology*, Vol. 21, 1970, pp. 207–18.

2 Here I am using concepts derived from the works of Louis Althusser and Jacques Lacan. 'Overdetermination', as used by Althusser (see *For Marx*, Allen Lane, 1969, pp. 100–101) refers to the simultaneous presence, within a specific social practice, of conditions and effects deriving from other social practices. Each practice, at any given historical conjucture in its development, is thus expressive of its relation to all other 'levels' of the totality. In this instance, I am saying that a particular (conscious) meaning, in the moment of its production, is expressive of its location within the complex, multi-levelled, symbolic structure of language, some aspects of which are unconscious.

I am using the term 'unconscious' in a commonsense way – to describe all linguistic structures which speakers reproduce beneath the level of conscious awareness. Some of these structures may be 'unconscious' in the Freudian sense (i.e. repressed), but within the Freudian framework I think they may be more properly described as 'preconscious' (i.e. subliminal). They relate, I think, to Althusser's notion of 'ideological unconsciousness', by which social structures 'are perceived-accepted-suffered cultural objects and . . . act functionally on men via a process that escapes them' (see *For Marx* p. 233). It is, to quote Lacan, 'a matter of defining the locus of this unconscious'. And Lacan himself provides a salutary reminder:

> The presence of the unconscious in the psychological order, in other words in the relation-functions of the individual, should, however, be more precisely defined: it is not coextensive with that order, for we know that if unconscious motivation is manifest in conscious ones, conversely it is only elementary to recall to mind that a large number of psychic effects which are quite legitimately designated as unconscious, in the sense of excluding the characteristic of consciousness, nevertheless are without any relation at all to the unconscious in the Freudian sense ('The Insistence of the Letter in the Unconscious', in *Structuralism*, ed. Jacques Ehrmann, Anchor, 1970, p. 123).

3 The term 'speech genre' is taken from V.N. Voloshinov (see Charles Woolfson's article in this journal). Voloshinov insists that: '*word is a two-sided act.* It is determined equally by *whose* word it is and *for whom* it is meant. As word it is precisely *the product of the reciprocal relationship between speaker and listener, addresser and addressee.* Each and every word expresses the "one" in relation to the "other" ' (*Marxism and the Philosophy of Language*, New York, 1973, p. 86).

4 cf. Jurgen Habermas, 'Toward a Theory of Communicative Competence', in *Recent Sociology No.2*, New York, 1970. Habermas calls the structures of discourse 'dialogue constitutive universals', property of 'ideal speakers':

> Above all communicative competence relates to an ideal speech situation in the same way that linguistic competence relates to the abstract system of language rules. The dialogue constitutive universals at the same time generate and describe the form of intersubjectivity which makes mutual understanding possible. Communicative competence is defined as the ideal speaker's mastery of the dialogue constitutive universals irrespective of the actual restrictions under empirical conditions (pp. 140–1).

I would want to argue that it is precisely through *misunderstandings* that the social character of discourse rules becomes apparent.

5 The term 'class codes' is taken from Basil Bernstein, *Class, Codes and Control*, Vol. 1, Paladin, 1973. In Bernstein's own work this term remains very slippery indeed – describing on one level, linguistic forms (syntactic structures, hesitation phenomena), on another level, parameters of meaning (specific 'orientations' towards objects and persons), and, on both levels at once, a whole cultural formation. It is significant that as Bernstein has developed his notion of 'code' he has either increasingly focused on *roles* in social interaction (i.e. personal and positional modes of authority in the family), or he has attempted to describe the characteristics of institutional *systems* (the classification and framing of educational knowledge). In other words he has retreated from a unitary definition into the 'two sociologies'. I would want to insist on the importance of class codes which, it seems to me, provide the deep structure of discourse, and which, though not manifest in its surface structure, are indicated at moments of stress or breakdown. Class codes (as Bernstein found with his Post Office apprentices) are indicative of a *failure* to communicate.

Human experience and material production: the culture of the shop floor* (*Paul E. Willis*)

The absolutely central thing about the working-class culture of the shop floor is that, despite bad conditions, despite external direction, despite subjective ravages, people do look for meaning, they do impose frameworks, they do seek enjoyment in activity, they do exercise their abilities. They do, paradoxically, thread through the dead experience of work a living culture, which isn't simply a reflex of defeat. It is a positive transformation of experience and a celebration of shared values in symbols artefacts and objects. It allows people to recognize

* This is an extract from a lecture based on work completed for the SSRC Project: The Transition from School to Work.

and even develop themselves. For this working-class culture of work is not simply a foam padding, a rubber layer between humans and unpleasantness. It is an appropriation in its own right, an exercise of skill, a motion, an activity applied towards an end. It has this specifically human characteristic, even in conditions of hardship and oppression.

What are the elements of this culture? Well in the first place there is the sheer mental and physical bravery of surviving in hostile conditions, and doing difficult work on intractable materials. It is easy to romanticize this element of course, and in one way it is simply charting the degree of brutality a heavy work situation can inflict. But in another way it is the first and specifically human response – the holding of an apparently endless and threatening set of demands by sheer strength and brute skill. Already in this there is a stature and self respect, a human stake on the table against alienation and the relentless pressure of work to be done. Not much you may say, especially if you have never faced the prospect of long punishing labour, but it is the vital precondition of more developed cultural forms, and accomplishes the basic and primitive humanization of a situation. It halts the rout of human meaning, takes a kind of control so that more specifically creative acts can follow. This primitivist base of work experience is also the material of a crude pride, for the mythology of masculine reputation – to be strong and to be *known* for it. Here is a retired steelman describing the furnaces in a steelmaking area of the west of Scotland as they were before the second world war:

> They were the cold metal, hand charging sort and they catered for strong men, only very strong men. About one steel worker in every ten could stand up to them successfully, which was one reason why the furnacemen were looked up to in the world of heavy industry. That they got the biggest pay packets was another reason. They also had the biggest thirsts and that too was a prideful possession in that part of the world [. . .] a legend grew up about the steel smelters. [. . .] The whole district and for miles beyond it was a hotbed of steel works, iron puddling works and coal mines. It was a place given over to the worship of strength and durability. Indeed it needed strength to look at it, and durability to live in it.[1]

In a much less articulate way, but for that perhaps more convincing, the following extract shows the same elemental self-esteem in the doing of a hard job well. It also shows that in some respects the hard environment can become the most natural environment. There is also the grudging recognition of the profound charge this kind of acclimatization can make on a normal social life, *even at the same time* as being one of the major ways in which the hostile work environment is made habitable. The example comes from my own current research and is of a foundry man talking at home about his work:

> I work in a foundry . . . you know drop forging . . . do you know anything about it . . . no . . . well you have the factory you know the factory down in Rolfe St. with the noise . . . you can hear it in the street . . . I work there on the big hammer . . . it's a six tenner. I've worked there 24 years now. It's bloody noisy, but I've got used to it now . . . and its hot . . . I don't get bored . . . there's always new lines coming and you have to work out the best way of doing it . . . You have to keep going . . . and it's heavy work, the managers couldn't do it, there's not many strong enough to keep lifting the metal . . . I earn 80, 90 pounds a week, and that's not bad is it? . . . it ain't easy like . . . you can definitely say that I earn every penny of it . . . you have to keep it up you know. And the managing director, I'd say 'hello', to him you know, and the progress manager . . . they'll come

> around and I'll go . . . 'alright' (thumbs up) . . . and they know you, you know . . . a group standing there watching you . . . working . . . I like that . . . there's something there . . . watching you like . . . working . . . like that . . . you have to keep going to get enough out . . . that place depends on what you produce [. . .]. You get used to the noise, they say I'm deaf and ignorant here, but it's not that I'm deaf like . . . it's that you can hold a conversation better, talk, hear what people say better at work . . . I can always here what they say there, I can talk easy, it's easier . . . yet in the house here, you've got to make . . . pronunciations is it? . . yeah, you've got to like, say the word, say it clearly, and that's hard sometimes . . . sometimes I can't hear straight away . . . they say, 'you silly deaf old codger' . . . it's not that . . it's just . . . well it's just getting used to the noise, I can hear perfectly well in the factory . . . If I see two managers at the end of the shop, I know, like I know just about what they're saying to each other.

It may be objected that the pattern of industrial work has changed: there are no rough jobs today. Besides, it can certainly be argued that there is nothing heroic about the elemental qualities of strength and pride. They are not only made anachronistic by today's technology, but are insulting, oppressive and right at the poisonous heart of male chauvinism and archaic machismo.

Be that as it may, two things are clear. Rough, unpleasant, demanding jobs *do* still exist in considerable numbers. A whole range of jobs from building work, to furnace work to deep sea fishing, still involve a primitive confrontation with exacting physical tasks. Secondly, the basic attitudes and values developed in such jobs are still very important in the general working-class culture, and particularly the culture of the shop floor: this importance is vastly out of proportion to the number of people actually involved in such heavy work. Even in so-called light industries, or in highly mechanized factories, where the awkwardness of the physical task has long since been reduced, the metaphoric figures of strength, masculinity and reputation still move beneath the more varied and richer, visible forms of work place culture. Despite, even, the increasing numbers of women employed, the most fundamental ethos of the factory is profoundly masculine.

Let us go on from this general minimum proposition to look at some of the more specific and developed human patterns of the work place. A clear mark of the lived and contemporary culture of the shop floor is a development of this half-mythical primitive confrontation with *the task*. It is an active *fascination* with the industrial process, and a positive interest in technology. This is not merely a meeting of demands, but a celebration of mastery. Here is a description from a toolmaker of his first day at work.[2] It inverts the usual middle-class account of the dark satanic mill. It is clear that industrialism runs in the blood of this young lad:

> On every piece of open ground lay metal shapes; some mere bars and sheets straight from the steelworks: others gigantic welded constructs covered in a deep brown rust . . . Then I entered the great main workshops. Each chamber, or aisle as they were called, was about one hundred and fifty feet across and anything between five hundred and seven hundred yards long. Several of these great vulcan halls lay parallel to each other [. . .]. Overhead rolled the girdered cranes capable of carrying weights of more than two hundred tons [. . .] one passed over my head. [. . .] My startled attitude to the crane's passage amused the men at work [. . .] a series of catcalls followed my passage down the aisle. Mostly the shouts were good natured advice to get out of the plant while I had the youth to do so. Such advice never even penetrated my outer consciousness, for

how could anyone abhor this great masculine domain with its endless overtones of power and violence.

An element of this absorption in technology is a process of obtaining skills as if by osmosis from the technical environment. There is a profound air of competence in the culture of the shop floor, a competence which is always prior to the particular situation. It is not always based on strict ability, but mixed in with cheek and confidence, it is enough to pull a worker through any number of jobs and problems. Here is a man recorded during my own research talking about his industrial career. He gives us a glimpse of the real paths beaten between different jobs and occupations, the paths which make it sensible to speak of the working class not as an abstract group of those who share similar interests, but as an organic whole with real and used inner connections:

> Well, I've got four trades really, you know I've only been in this job seven weeks. I'm in a foundry now [. . .] on the track you know [. . .]. I was a metal polisher before. It's a dirty job, but it pays good money, and a skilled job, you know, metal polishing. [. . .] Yes and I was a fitter down at drop forgings, as well I mean in the situation today, you've got to go where the money is. Polishing is the best money, but it's up and down, there was four or five months run of work and then it 'ud go dead [. . .] I got out on it didn't I [. . .] Friend o' mine got me a job down at the MMC. [. . .] I've worked in a garage, er . . . I worked for the Council paper hanging and decorating, I worked for a fella . . . chimney-sweeping in the winter, decorating and painting in the summer and all this but I've always took an interest in what I've been doing you know, I mean, I'm pretty adaptable, put it that way you know [. . .] I've always had a motor of me own, and I've always done me own repairs, whenever I've broken me motor, only through experience, doing it meself [. . .]. Paper-hanging, decorating, I've got an in-law, ain't I, that's a decorator, give me a lot of tips you know [. . .] I bluffed me way in to decorating. I said I was a decorator you know, went to work for the council. Actually I subcontracted for the council, and they give an house to do, an empty house, and I done it see. Course the inspector come round from the Council and they was satisfied with the work, you know, so you know if the inspector's satisfied, you're alright see. It's only common sense really.

In one sense this can be seen as a way of exerting some control back on a situation that has been taken from you by the bosses. It is not uncommon now to find very much more massive attempts at direct control of the work process. Short of the more explicit level of plant democracy, sit-ins, or formal worker control, it does happen now that the men themselves actually run production.

This practice rests on what is perhaps the greatest achievement of shop floor culture, its most human achievement and the basic organizational form which locates and makes possible all its other elements. This is the development of the informal group – the fundamental and most basic unit of resistance, and creative extension of control, on the shop floor. It is the massive presence of this informal organization which marks off shop floor culture most decisvely from middle class cultures of work. This informality is not simply neutral – the open ended product of a free association – but is directed *against* the formal. Simply, this is a blanket opposition to the bosses, but it is also a refusal to accept even the idea of acknowledged leadership. It is 'the men' who act as a body, and the actual organizer is recognized only as the symbolic embodiment of 'the men', and is in no way superior or qualitatively different from 'the men'.

If all this seems a little far fetched, consider the following extract. Again from my own research, this is a factory hand on a track producing car engines talking about production in his shop. Note particularly his refusal to let the man who actually organizes the work force be thought of as anything other than a normal worker:

> Actually the foreman, the gaffer, don't run the place, the men run the place. See, I mean, you get one of the chaps says, 'Alright, You'm on so and so today.' You can't argue with him. The gaffer don't give you the job, the men on the track give you the job, they swop each other about, tek it in turns. Ah, but I mean the job's done. If the gaffer had gid you the job you would . . . They tried to do it, one morning, gid a chap a job you know, but he'd been on it, you know. I think he'd been on it all week, and they just downed tools. [. . .] There's four hard jobs, actually, on the track and there's a dozen that's you know, a child of five could do, quite honestly, but everybody has their turn [. . .] That's organized by the men. Especially like the man who, the one who's on the track longest, you know, who knows what rotation it is see.

> PW: *He's the foreman or the supervisor?*
> He's nothing, he's nothing.
> PW: *So why do the men recognize his authority?*
> Well, they don't recognize his authority. They just . . . he's been on the track the longest see, and he knows exactly the rotation, but if try to figure the rotation out, know the rota like, how the men go, I mean I couldn't. I don't know how it works. [. . .]
> PW: *He's not the shop steward or anything?*
> He's nothing. It's the men run that place.

This solidarity, and sense of being a group, is the basis for the final major characteristic of shop floor culture that I want to describe here. This is the distinctive form of language, and the highly developed humour of the shop floor. Up to half the verbal exchanges are not serious or about work activities. They are jokes, or 'piss takes', or 'kiddings' or 'windups'. There is a real skill, which the young worker can take a long time to learn, in being able to use this language with fluency, to identify the points where you are being 'kidded' and to have appropriate response in order to avoid further baiting.

This badinage is necessarily difficult to record on tape or re-present, but the highly distinctive ambience it gives to shop floor exchanges is widely recognized by those involved, and to some extent recreated in their accounts of it. This is again from my current research, a foundry worker talking about the atmosphere in his shop:

> Oh, there's all sorts, millions of them [jokes]. 'Want to hear what he said about you,' and he never said a thing, you know. Course you know the language, at the work like. 'What you been saying, about me?' 'I said nothing', 'Oh, you're a bloody liar', and all this.

Associated with this concrete and expressive verbal humour, is a developed physical humour; essentially the practical joke. These jokes are vigorous, sharp, sometimes cruel, and often hinged around prime tenets of the culture such as disruptions of production or subversion of the bosses' authority and status. Here we have some examples of such jokes described by a worker in a mass production factory. This is again from my current research:

> They er'm play jokes on you, blokes knocking the clamps off the boxes, they put paste on the bottom of his hammer you know, daft little things, puts his hammer down, picks it up, gets a handful of paste, you know, all this. So he comes up and gets a syringe and throws it in the big bucket of paste, and it's about that deep, and it goes right to the bottom, you have to put your hand in and get it out [. . .] This is a filthy trick, but they do it. [. . .] They asked, the gaffers asked to-to make the tea. Well it's fifteen years he's been there and they say 'go and make the teas'. He gus up the toilet, he wets in the tea pot, then makes tea. I mean, you know, this is the truth this is you know. He says, you know, 'I'll piss in it if I mek it, if they've asked me to mek it.' [. . .] so he goes up, *wees* in the pot, then he puts the tea bag, then he puts the hot water in. [. . .] – was bad the next morning, one of the gaffers, 'My stomach isn't half upset this morning.' He told them after and they called him for everything, 'you ain't makin our tea no more', he says, 'I know I ain't not now.'

Always in danger of romanticizing our subject, we should pause now to consider the real status and power of this culture. Given the vivacity and strength of what I am describing, why is it not more visible, why has it not taken over more? Well, as I have argued, it is a subordinate culture and occurs in prior conditions of oppression and dominance, and the whole nature of the system is such that the worker's hands are directed by others than himself, and the product of his hands is taken away: this is the elemental meaning of alienation in work. But there are more complex reasons for the alienation even within the culture of work, and for its inability to challenge the middle-class cultures of work which sit on top of it and obscure it.

Overall, shop floor culture is remarkable for its combination of an extraordinary completeness with a special kind of limitedness. It is complete because it embraces, upon its own ground anyway, several levels of human potential and activity in massive, immediate, day to day detail. There is no concern here for *corporate* aspects of working-class control, and for that, it is free from the reductions and impoverishments of economism, and its forms of consciousness, which dominate the institutional extensions of working-class interests. The complement of this quality of wholeness is, however, the profoundly parochial quality of the shop floor, and its extreme limit of range. Though full of political *significance*, and the only base for a working-class politics, this culture is deeply *unpolitical*. Its rivetting concern for the work place – and specific work places at that – prevents the connecting up of work experiences, issues and social structure; it prevents a true political practice. The inherent and deeply charged contradiction of a culturally threadbare working-class politics having such a richly threaded, but essentially unpolitical base, is right at the heart of the problems facing strategists of class liberation. It is also right at the heart of the ambiguous and troubled relations of Trade Unions to grass roots shop floor culture.

The Trade Union is the institutional extension of the culture of the work place, the form in which the culture and its meanings might have become more visible and the vehicle through which really concrete attempts have been made to transform *symbolic* into *real* control.

By far the most important working-class institution, British Trade Unionism was born through the struggles, over a hundred years, of the world's first industrial proletariat. It was based on, and drew all its meaning strength and loyalty from, the dense culture of the work place. The achievements of the trade union movement are many. They have protected work people in all sorts of ways, and have helped to prevent the relative decline of living standards amongst the working class.

As the main extension of the working-class culture and social organization of the work place, however, trade unionism has many failings. By being, in its own right, a formal structure with narrowly defined ends, it has excluded, to an ever greater degree, the actual informal structure and culture of the work place from which it grew. In becoming a responsible agency on agreed terms set mostly by management – essentially that the bargain is mainly over wages, not over control, and that each party to the bargain must be able to deliver what he promises – the Union has become another authority structure over the worker. It often acts to cut out time-wasting practices – the very ground of the informal culture – and can even put over the management case to the workers in order to carry an agreement it has already made. Here is a lad, again from my current research, talking about the union in his furniture working shop:

> I think our union at work, I think they shouldn't stand for as much as they do off the management, I mean the management do seem to over rule everything although, it's the union what says when to go on strike. [. . .] The management sort of you know, say to the Union, 'Oh, it's a good idea', and they agree with it [. . .] You see they put to us what the management want, and you know the union want it, but the men don't.

Essentially the Trade Union can be seen as a mediation between shop floor culture and the dominant managerial culture. It negotiates the space between them, and in this negotiation, gives up much that is really central to the shop floor for what is often a mere accommodation in managerial interests. The nature of Unionism and its organization is not, however, evenly textured. Whilst the Union bosses adopt a form of managerial culture and join the main industrial establishment,[3] the shop stewards and local organizers are still very much of the local culture. Whilst trying to achieve union and organizational aims, they use specifically shop cultural forms of communication – spectacle, bluffs, drama, jokes, sabotage – to mobilize the men.[4] The Union structure, then, is a complex and varied institution striking different degrees of negotiation, appeasement and settlement at its various levels. The power of shop floor culture determines at least the forms and methods of union activity at the plant level, but the higher administrative level has completely lost that detailed binding in with the lived culture of the work place, which was the original guarantee of true representativeness. To put it another way, the Unions have lost touch with, even betrayed, the real roots of working-class radicalism – the culture of the shop floor.

The lack within the culture of any overall political account – in the sense of connecting up the 'separate' elements of a social structure – aids and is perpetuated by the operation of sophisticated control mechanisms which act decisively to diminish the influence of the culture.

Most insidious of these is the practice of management science and human relations. Under the banner of a humanization of the work process, it has actually been one of the most formidable weapons ever given to the dominant class by 'neutral' academics for use against the working class. Essentially, this whole branch of knowledge and technique rests on a simple and obvious discovery: informal groups exist. Human groups are not fully accounted for in the two dimensional structure of their public face, people exist as well in a private hinterland where they develop relations and language quite unspecified in any formal description of their situation. This is precisely, of course, the area covered by the culture of the shop floor. Hard on the discovery of this territory, came techniques for colonizing it, and, as in all colonizations, for destroying the culture that was already there. It is techniques of 'employee-centred supervision', 'participation', 'job enrichment', 'socio-technical-system analysis', which are penetrating right to the heart of shop floor culture, unhinging its logic of symbolic opposition, unbending its springs of action, flattening it out in the name of ratio-technical advance. The sense of control given to the workers by these techniques is illusory, the basic structures of power remain exactly the same as before, and yet the located, rich, potentially dominating culture of resistance is being destroyed.

Given the hostile conditions in which this culture has grown, given the forces seeking to steal its soul, given the half betrayal of its own strong right arm, it still shows an astonishing vigour. Though in saying this, we are recognizing a creative achievement only within severe and finally neutralizing conditions. Its potential is held as part of the complex balance of forces and tendencies within our modern liberal democratic state; a balance which holds, mediates, and makes possible the apparently free management of our society by consensus. That the work place culture retains, for some its strength for others its virulence, in the face of domination and its own part-submission, indicates its fundamental power, and future potential, as the culture arising from the elemental processes of production – the deep source of *cultural values* amongst the working class, as it is the source of the material conditions of life for us all.

We must not be confused either by a fundamental contradiction lying at the heart of this culture. A result of its success – limited as it is – has clearly been to perpetuate the status quo, and its own expression, by accommodating to, rather than reacting against, its conditions. Though this is evident and though we should not be fooled by this apparent sanction of the status quo, we should not miss the dialectical balance of this contradiction. Though presently distorted and recessive, certain fundamental qualities of shop floor culture must surely be essential to any major political and social development of the working class. Profane testing of the formal, the socialness of relations adapted to production, irreverent humour, a sharp and differentiated consciousness able to judge humanness apart from traditional status or current job title, individuation within a collective solidarity – these cultural qualities arise deep within the materialism of production, and must be both elements of, and internal checks on, the future hegemonic drive of working-class culture.

At the moment, however, we should not romanticize what exists, or be blind. The prospect for most, still, in our society is this: that the products of their hands, the living culture developed with others, the *art* of their daily lives, is stifled, broken and scattered; its remnants returned in unrecognizable dead forms. That this culture ever daily reproduces itself to be daily broken, is *only the minimum condition of survival*, and not a cause for celebration.

Notes

1 *Work 2*, ed. R. Fraser, Penguin 1969, pp. 56–7.
2 Ibid., pp. 22–3.
3 See T. Lowe, *The Union Makes Us Strong*, Arrow, 1974.
4 See H. Benyon, *Working for Ford*, Penguin 1974.

The following code is used in the transcriptions:

= name omitted
. . . = time passing
[. . .] = phrase missed out
[. . . .] = sentence missed out

22 The semiotics of working class speech

Charles Woolfson

Introduction

The present article has as its aim, clarification of the direction which those seeking to develop a genuinely Marxist approach to semiotics might take. The problem of defining semiotics beyond reference to its general concern with the analysis of systems of signs in social communication, indeed dispute over the very term semiotics/semiology, should suggest that as a discipline it still remains unsure even as to its basic conceptual and methodological framework. Nevertheless, the real danger exists of semiotics acquiring a premature formation in this country, for which the accelerating flow of continental, especially French studies, is largely responsible. The kind of semiotic which will be presented here has little in common with such work. It puts forward an object of inquiry which is assigned its theoretical prominence on a basis entirely incompatible with current semiotic practice, and that basis is historical materialism. Our object is the verbal sign; words as spoken by speakers themselves in concrete situations. It is a semiotic that attempts to explore the verbal sign as they key to understanding social consciousness.

In the first section, a brief examination of the role of the spoken word in human development is intended to locate the verbal sign in the forefront of the total repertoire of signs employed in human interaction. The second section elaborates the historical-materialist view of language in terms of the semiotic theory of an early Soviet writer, V.N. Voloshinov, whose seminal contribution has recently been translated into English. In the third section, the semiotic of Voloshinov is applied to transcripts of recorded conversations among workers in the manner of a case study. The final section suggests how this semiotic approach might be refined further to take account of the full complexity of mass social consciousness.

Language and human development

The centrality of articulated speech in human development, ontogenetically and phylogenetically, is the starting point for a historical materialist semiotic. It is with good reason that Soviet psychologists, in advancing the original conception of this problem in the writings of Marx and Engels, have made the relationship between conceptual thought and the spoken word the major concern in their investigations.[1]

The work of L.S. Vygotsky is justifiably the best known, since it was he who provided the current Marxist paradigm of the acquisition of speech and the higher mental processes in the human child.[2] Vygotsky's unit of analysis was word meaning in which thought and speech combine in the complex unity of verbal thought.[3] He refuted the notion that 'pure' thought without linguistic mediation or indeed, the simple identity of thought and language were adequate descriptions. For Vygotsky, the essence of word meaning lay in the fact that each word is a generalisation and generalisation is an act of thought which reflects reality. Following Sapir, Vygotsky suggested that the world of experience must be greatly simplified and generalised before it can be translated into symbols and communicated to others.

> Thus, true human communication presupposes a generalising attitude, which is the advanced stage in the development of word meanings. The higher forms of human intercourse are possible only because man's thought reflects conceptualised actuality.[4]

Vygotsky observed that thought and speech at first develop along separate lines in the child and from the separate points of origin of pre-intellectual speech and pre-linguistic thought. About the age of two, the curves of thought and speech begin to interpenetrate and generate new kinds of behaviour conditioned by the child's discovery of the symbolic function of words.[5] It is at this crucial stage that the nature of the child's development itself changes from the biological to the sociohistorical.[6] The implications of this for the analysis of verbal thought are clear.

> Once we acknowledge the historical character of verbal thought, we must consider it subject to all the premises of historical materialism, which are valid for any historical phenomenon in human society. It is only to be expected that on this level the development of behaviour will be governed essentially by the general laws of the development of human society.[7]

If we accept with Vygotsky, that in articulate speech there is the generalised reflection of social reality in verbal thought, then there is a necessary next step to be taken. The significance of Vygotsky's work for the overall study of social consciousness is his identification of the historical character of verbal thought which allows in principle the class analysis of the verbal signs of language. At the conclusion of his work Vygotsky hinted at the broader relevance of his research with respect to a theory of social consciousness.

> Words play a central part not only in the development of thought, but in the historical growth of consciousness as a whole. A word is a microcosm of human consciousness.[8]

The researches of Vygotsky and those who have followed him, complement the anthropogenetic perspective on the development of human society of both Marx and Engels, particularly in the former's *The German Ideology* and in the latter's unfinished essay on 'The Part Played by Labour in the Transition from Ape to Man'.[9] In these and other writings of Marx and Engels the emergence of man as a social being is predicated upon the evolution of speech integrally linked with socially co-operative labour. Indeed, this was the notion on which Vygotsky based his own work.

> Rational, intentional conveying of experience and thought to others requires a mediating system, the prototype of which is human speech born of the need of intercourse during work.[10]

What is unique to man is the use of tools and language in the labour process to achieve his mastery over nature.[11] Because he possesses language and therefore consciousness, and because he possesses tools with which to effect changes in his environment, man has at his disposal the conceptual categories with which to organise his activity purposively. This interrelationship of verbal thought and labour is described by Cornforth.

> The development of *speech* is an essential part of the development of *labour*. For human labour, unlike the life activity of other animals (including social animals, and animals that build things for themselves or even use objects in a crude way as tools), requires that people should communicate a design . . . should develop means to communicate not only how things are but how they may be changed. Articulate speech is essentially the means of such communication. What distinguishes it from other communication is that it is used not only to signal present perceptions and evoke responses, but to represent possible states of affairs and ways and means to bring about or avoid them – in other words, to make them 'exist in imagination'.[12]

Thus while animals respond to the immediate stimuli of the external environment through their capacity for signality, human beings have developed the more complex intellectual apparatus of symbolic signs. First in importance are the verbal signs which enable men to communicate categories of thought in the purposive organisation of labour.

In tracing the further unfolding relationship between language and labour, only the most tentative suggestions can be made. As Vygotsky recognised, the problem of social consciousness cannot be separated from the historical analysis of verbal thought; as yet, however, this field remains almost entirely unexplored in terms of historical materialism.

What evidence there is implies that at the early primitive communal stage of society, human speech was still largely bound up with the labour process and was at a low level of development. Language attempted, albeit incompletely, to correspond wholeheartedly to the primitive level of social practice in the first efforts of men to dominate nature. Their failure to correctly comprehend the objective necessity of natural laws is suggested by George Thomson as the basis of the poetic magical dimension of language in the early tribes. Deficiency in real technique was supplemented by the illusory technique of magic whereby words themselves were thought to control natural forces.[13] Be that as it may, as societies move beyond the primitive egalitarian communal stage and become class societies in which the mass of men begin to lose control over the product of their labour, over the available surplus they produce, then this organic connection of speech and labour is severed. The spoken word enters a new phase of its life in which its original function in assisting men to dominate nature in relationships of co-operation, is successively overtaken by a new function; the domination of men by each other in relationships of exploitation.

The advent of class societies, with the growth of the division of labour and its accompanying separation of manual and mental activity, imparted a qualitatively new ideological character to language. As Marx pointed out, priests as the first form of ideologists emerged at this point in history and it is not without significance that Marx mentions this immediately following his discussion of the relationship of speech and social consciousness.[14] It could be said that the successive forms of class societies, slave, feudal and capitalist, have each generated ideological superstructures which have turned language into its opposite; from a social effort to comprehend objective reality in the interest of all, into an attempt to obscure it in the interest of the few. Such an attempt, however, can never be wholly successful if only because of the ever-present fact of class struggle. There is a continuing historical reaction against exploitation which imparts its own oppositional ideological evaluation into language. Engels revealed in his account of the German peasant wars how even the language of Christianity which was to become ossified in a powerful ideology of the status quo, could not wholly exclude the popular infusion of a highly critical egalitarian social consciousness into it during periods of mass conflict between social classes.[15] This dialectic of language and social consciousness contains the two opposing poles between which the ideological character of words has fluctuated throughout the history of class societies. As the tension between opposing classes heightens so the ideological flux of words becomes greater and greater. Under capitalism, indeed, where the system of class relations has achieved its most developed antagonistic form, the possibility now exists of a complete perception of social inequality, undistorted by relationships of personal subjugation and dependence. In this sense, language has fully and openly entered into the realm of class relations and class conflict, and with the emergence of the modern proletariat, into the realm of class consciousness. Human speech has assumed a correspondingly antagonistic character. In this sense also, the examination of verbal signs, the degree to which speech contains this potentiality for the social recognition of exploitation, becomes central to the study of social consciousness.

The verbal sign in social consciousness

The question of the verbal sign and social consciousness can only be posed successfully on a philosophical basis that rejects both the inherent dualism of subjective idealist linguistics and the continuing reification of linguistic forms by post-Saussurian linguistics. Since it is the latter trend from which the current practice of European semiology is mainly derived it is necessary to distinguish the weaknesses of this approach. This will be done by reiterating the main outlines of the Marxist critique of Saussure, for it is his writings which have set their stamp on the influential French semiology in particular.[16] The Soviet semiotician V.N. Voloshinov provided the essential elements of this critique which remains as relevant to present day arguments as it ever was. Voloshinov's seminal study, *Marxism and the Philosophy of Language* cleared the way for a Marxist semiotic as long ago as 1930, but has been strangely ignored by those same European semiologists for whom Saussure is the guiding light, despite the availability of Voloshinov's work in translation for some time now.[17] We shall use this critique as the point of entry into a wider discussion of Voloshinov's semiotic of the verbal sign which since it is almost wholly unknown will be freely quoted from in order to make clear the main lines of the argument.

Saussure's model of language in his *General Course*[18] is well known and need not be rehearsed in detail. The governing idea is of language as a system of arbitrary and conventional signs seen to have an objective reality somewhat analogous to Durkheimian social facts. The structure of language is viewed as a system of mutually opposed and interconnected elements comprising a unity existing, as it were, outside the historical process as a self-contained whole. This is the basis of the distinction between the synchronic and diachronic aspects of language. Saussure's main concern is with the former, language as an interconnected structure of forms. The individual speaker is seen as a passive recipient of almost immutable linguistic norms which only if deviated from on a sufficient scale will result in a new synchronic structure. The Saussurian distinction between language as a system of forms, and *parole*, the individual speech utterance, thus allots the latter a residual idiosyncratic role for it is the synchronic dimension which is given theoretical precedence. Therein lies what Voloshinov described as the *pseudos proton* of this trend which he termed abstract objectivism.[19]

By excluding proper consideration of the speaking subject in a false opposition that identifies the language/speech separation with the social/individual separation, Saussure rules out the possibility of an objective sociological theory of the utterance. Abstract objectivism entirely misconstrues the subjective consciousness of the individual speaker with respect to language which is depicted as external to and independent of the speaker. It could be argued that for a member of a given community language may appear as an 'objective' system of immutable norms, fixed and inert, at a particular point in time. In actual fact, however, what is significant for the speaker is not the normatively identical form of language, the signality of words, but their specific and novel meanings in concrete contexts of expression.

> What is important for the speaker about a linguistic form is not that it is a stable and always self-equivalent signal, but that it is an always changeable and adaptable sign.[20]

Here Voloshinov converges with Vygotsky's notion of verbal thought and with the distinction drawn between the sign and the signal in human development in the previous section.[21] Whereas the signal is merely *recognised* as an internally fixed and singular entity, the sign is *understood* in verbal utterances in its specific variability. What abstract objectivism neglects is precisely the sign responsively understood in a particular concrete context.[22]

> The linguistic consciousness of the speaker and of the listener-understander, in the practical business of living speech, is not at all concerned with the abstract system of normatively identical forms of language, but with language-speech in the sense of possible contexts of usage for a particular linguistic form.[23]

The word itself is only relevant to the verbal consciousness of speakers in the context of specific utterances; consequently only in its specific ideological impletion.

> In actuality, we never say or hear *words*, we say and hear what is true or false, good or bad, important or unimportant, pleasant or unpleasant and so on. *Words are always filled with content and meaning drawn from behaviour and ideology.*[24]

To ignore the aims of the speaker's consciousness as does abstract objectivism is to abstractly segregate and reify the linguistic form, from its ideological or behavioural impletion.

Voloshinov shows the roots of the theoretical focus of abstract objectivism to have grown out of the philosophical orientation of early linguistics towards deciphering dead and alien languages preserved in written monuments. From this follows the treatment of the individual utterance as finished, monologic and self-contained, and not as included in actual living generative historical contexts ideologically comprehended. Abstract objectivism is concerned with a purely passive understanding of word meanings and excludes in principle, the active comprehension of the essential contextual multiplicity of word meanings. Language-speech is perceived as an artifact-signal.[25]

> In reifying the system of language and in viewing living language as if it were dead and alien, abstract objectivism makes language something external to the stream of verbal communication. This stream flows on, but language, like a ball, is tossed from generation to generation. In actual fact, however, language moves together with that stream and is inseparable from it. Language cannot properly be said to be handed down – it endures, but it endures as a continuous process of becoming. Individuals do not receive a ready-made language at all, rather they enter upon the stream of verbal communication; indeed, only in this stream does their consciousness first begin to operate.[26]

As with all structuralist systems of thought, the inability of abstract objectivism to reconcile the diachronic and synchronic, introduces inevitable distortions.[27] For Saussurian linguistics it has meant that analysis of the verbal signs of speakers' utterances (*parole*) holds no place in its system. What Voloshinov does in his critique of Saussure is to restore the utterance to the process of social communication in which the verbal sign finds its ideological life.

Voloshinov argues that the sign is, through and through, ideological in character.

> A sign does not simply exist as a part of reality – it reflects and refracts another reality. Therefore, it may distort that reality or be true to it, or may perceive it from a special point of view, and so forth. Every sign is subject to criteria of ideological evaluation, (i.e. whether it is true, false, correct, fair, good, etc.). The domain of ideology coincides with the domain of signs. They equate with one another. Wherever a sign is present, ideology is present too. *Everything ideological possesses semiotic value.*[28]

It follows from this, that if everything ideological has semiotic value, then the content of human consciousness is wholly semiotic, governed by laws of semiotic communication. Thus at the very outset idealist and positivist or physiological approaches to social consciousness are ruled out.

> Signs emerge, after all, only in the process of interaction between one individual consciousness and another. And the individual consciousness itself is filled with signs. Consciousness becomes consciousness only once it has been filled with ideological (semiotic) content, consequently, only in the process of social interaction.[29]

The sign, then, is the vehicle of social communication and permeates the individual consciousness. It is through signs that the individual consciousness and the external environment mutually interpenetrate. Individual consciousness only becomes so in the material of signs. Consequently, consciousness itself is a socio-ideological fact. Indeed, no boundary can be drawn between consciousness and ideology for they share the same material of signs.

Voloshinov shows that it is the sign in the form of the *word* which is of central importance. The semiotic perspective is used to enrich the original conception of speech in Marxism, for it is the word which is the semiotically purest medium of communication. Unlike some symbolic forms, the word is neutral with respect to any particular field of ideological creativity. It can perform its ideological function within the scientific, ethical, religious spheres or whatever, and is not specialised to any given one of these. Moreover, that whole area of communication not specifically linked to any one ideological sphere, the crucial area of behavioural ideology, the nature of which will be examined more closely in our empirical analysis, relies, above all, on the word for its material. Again, it is the word which is at the disposal of the individual consciousness as the vehicle of inner speech. Finally, it is the word in the form of inner speech which always accompanies and comments upon the understanding of any ideological phenomenon, be it pictorial, musical, ritual or whatever. It is the sum of these qualities of the word which make it 'the fundamental object of the study of ideologies'.[30]

By taking this conception of the word as ideological sign, the complex interrelationship of economic basis and superstructures may be clarified. Voloshinov asks how actual existence (the basis), determines sign and how sign reflects and refracts the generative process of existence which comes to completion in the superstructures. In line with this earlier argument about the social ubiquity of the word in human semiotic communication Voloshinov approaches the basis-superstructure problem in the following term.

> Countless ideological threads running through all areas of social intercourse register effect in the word. It stands to reason, then, that the word is the most sensitive *index of social changes*, and what is more, of changes still in the process of growth, still without definite shape and not as yet accommodated into already regularised and fully defined ideological systems. The word is the medium in which occur the slow quantitative accretions of those changes which have not yet achieved the status of a new ideological quality, not yet produced a new and fully fledged ideological form. The word has the capacity to register all the delicate, momentary phases of social change.[31]

Voloshinov is careful to point out that it is production relations and the sociopolitical order shaped by those relations which determine the full range of verbal utterances in society. These in turn condition the actual themes and forms of speech utterances. It is these speech utterances, closely interwoven with concrete situations which 'show extraordinary sensitivity to all fluctuations in the social atmosphere' and it is here 'that the barely noticeable shifts and changes that will later find expression in fully fledged ideological products accumulate'.[32] Voloshinov lists three methodological prerequisites for the study of speech utterances to conform to the requirements of dialectical materialism. First, ideology may not be divorced from the material reality of the sign. Second, the sign may not be divorced from the concrete forms of social intercourse. Third, communication and the forms of communication may not be divorced from the material basis.[33] It is precisely these prerequisites which the contemporary sociology of language and semiotics has failed to meet in its study of the social aspects of language and ideology.[34] The underlying material reality, however, is always reflected in the ideological sign. To become an object of sign formation an item must first acquire social significance at an inter-individual level. But those items which receive the attention of the group, which become objects of semiotic reaction, to some degree have their roots in the basis of the group's material life. It is these items which are socially recognised and evaluatively accentuated, thereby entering into the social purview of the group. Thus the ideological sign comes to life in speech utterances and in its particular socially structured themes, reflects the changing forms of material life.[35]

The sign, however, not only reflects existence but also refracts it. Here the importance of class struggle comes to the fore. Voloshinov describes what he terms 'the inner dialectic motion of the sign' and in so doing throws new light on our problem of the ideological character of words from the semiotic standpoint.

> Class does not coincide with sign community, i.e, with the community which is the totality of users of the same set of signs for ideological communication. Thus differently oriented accents intersect in every ideological sign. Sign becomes an arena of class struggle.
>
> This social *multiaccentuality* of the ideological sign is a very crucial aspect. By and large, it is thanks to this intersecting of accents that a sign maintains its vitality and dynamism and the capacity for further development. A sign that has been withdrawn from the pressures of social struggle – which, so to speak, crosses beyond the pale of class struggle – inevitably loses force, degenerating into allegory and becoming the object not of live social intelligibility but of philological comprehension . . . The very same thing that makes the ideological sign vital and mutable is also, however, that which makes it a refracting and distorting medium. The ruling class strives to impart a supraclass, eternal character to the ideological sign, to extinguish or drive inward the struggle between social value judgements which occurs in it, to make the sign immutable.

> In actual fact, each living ideological sign has two faces like Janus. Any current curse word can become a word of praise, any current truth must inevitably sound to many other people as the greatest lie. This inner *dialectic quality* of the sign comes out fully in the open only in times of social crises or revolutionary changes. In the ordinary conditions of life, the contradiction embedded in every ideological sign cannot emerge fully because the ideological sign in an established, dominant ideology is always somewhat reactionary and tries, as it were, to stabilise the preceding factor in the dialectical flux of the social generative process, so accentuating yesterday's truth as to make it appear today's. And this is what is responsible for the refracting and distorting peculiarity of the ideological sign within the dominant ideology.[36]

This notion of sign is, in summary, as the verbally materialised ideological refraction of reality in social consciousness. This complex dialectical conception of the sign provides a semiotic basis upon which to examine speech forms in class society. It bears important similarities to the work of Antonio Gramsci on the nature of ruling class hegemony, and since the latter notion has achieved some currency in Marxist writings it is useful to draw these together at this point.

Gramsci's investigation of hegemony explores the 'philosophical' conceptions held by the masses, defining the parameters of their consciousness. Gramsci was deeply interested in the way in which a new systematic philosophy of the masses, that is, a unified class conscious ideology, could be created that could decisively challenge the dominant hegemony.[37] In a recent article Raymond Williams provides a definition of hegemony which is helpful here. 'It is', he writes, 'a set of meanings and values which as they are experienced as practices, appear as reciprocally confirming. It thus constitutes a sense of reality for most people in a society, a sense of absolute because experienced reality beyond which it is very difficult for most members of society to move, in most areas of their lives'.[38] Hegemony, then, achieves its force through being embodied in social practices and is experienced as lived reality, in this way suffusing the popular consciousness. But there are important qualifications to the incorporative character of hegemony. Any hegemony in a class society is necessarily limited and incomplete, it exists in tension. Using Voloshinov's notion of the inner dialectic quality of the sign, the contradictions of hegemony can be pinpointed.

Hegemony is above all the province of persuasion rather than force. For its elaboration it relies upon the agencies of social control in civil society, such as the institutions of the church, the school, the mass media and the family unit. All of these attempt to phrase a certain understanding of the world so that any potential challenge can somehow be locked into a purview of continuity. Advanced capitalist hegemony implies winning the belief of the masses that the existing arrangement of affairs in society is socially equitable and just. It is generated in definite stereotyped symbolic forms and slogans of legitimisation. These in turn are conditioned by concretely articulated levels of mass expectations which provide a historical gauge of the balance of the class forces measured in the distribution of social income. Thus certain symbols and legitimising slogans can become historically redundant, from the ruling class point of view, either due to advances won in the class struggle by the working class, or because the ruling class for its part seeks to re-interpret previously socially guaranteed mass expectations in a more restrictive manner, as in moments of crisis. Seen in this way, the task of maintaining hegemony is in a vital respect a linguistic one. The problem is to produce a language fully replete with signs that codify and confirm the overall status quo. Indeed the depth of ruling class crisis is revealed by the degree of difficulty which it faces in producing such a language. As Voloshinov put it, the dominant ideology must strive to impart a supra-class, eternal character to the ideological sign. It must contain the struggle between social value judgements in the sign. Hegemony therefore is neither permanently adhesive nor phrased wholly one-dimensionally. Whilst the hypostasis of signs is always a tendency, it can never be total, for as Voloshinov noted, a sign which crosses beyond the pale of class struggle inevitably loses its force and vitality. Ideological superstructures have to respond actively and accommodate new elements of reality, and thus sign always retain some glimmering of their social multiaccentuality. The ideological sign is always to a greater or lesser degree, in a state of flux. Herein lies the inner contradiction of hegemony; it seeks to deform the ideological sign in a very particular way and in this respect its incompleteness is both its strength and its weakness.

The question of the social multiaccentuality of the sign is the critical one from the point of view of understanding the key problem of how the masses come into possessions of a new ethico-political hegemony which can generate a revolutionary class consciousness. Such a consciousness is articulated at a mass level out of the very signs of language which the existing hegemony is forced to surrender in the moment of global class confrontation – the point at which the existing legitimising slogans and symbols crumble and are then transformed under the pressure of the class assault on state power. This is what Voloshinov meant when he said that the inner dialectic quality of the sign comes out fully in the open in times of social crisis or revolutionary changes. Under these conditions it is the role of the revolutionary vanguard to bring forward the alternative slogans and symbols which encapsulate emerging working-class aspirations within a unifying perspective of radical socialist change. The vanguard acts as the conscious organised agent of change just because the spontaneous or immediate perception of social inequality does not by itself guarantee recognition of the need to secure state power to effect societal transformation. In creating the objective conditions for this process to occur, the chief weapon of the vanguard party is the theory of Marxism which constitutes itself as the opposing pole to the dominant ideology. The perspective and and language of Marxism is the dialectical other face of the ideological sign. It seeks to restore and make explicit the hidden class content of the ideological sign, to de-reify social reality, literally to *disclose* the sign, revealing the disjuncture between surface appearances and the underlying socio-historical determination. By attempting to open up awareness of the gap between contemporary actuality and historic possibility for the class, it poses a threat to the existing structure of domination against which the hegemony must develop an adequate response of its own if it is to be sustained. In day to day terms this is reproduced as an incessant struggle between opposing social value judgements which provides a measure of the tempo of class struggle itself.

The ideological battle is fought out most strenuously among the working class in the dialectical interplay of differing social evaluations. It is registered in the speech utterances of the class, in the language and words, in the themes, which are used as broad evaluations of social reality and as orientations to the contingencies of working-class existence. Voloshinov correctly identified this as the vital realm of behavioural ideology where the as yet unresolved contradiction embedded in the ideological sign achieves its freest play. Behavioural ideology links up, Voloshinov says, on the one side with the underlying soci-economic basis, while on the other it is tangential to the sphere of fully fledged ideological systems.[39] It is distinguished from the established systems of ideology by its unsystemised and unfixed atmosphere. Here the unevenness and diversity of mass consciousness can be charted. The variety of mass sources of experience and the changing impact of material and cultural conditions are made socially accessible in these utterances. Just as the working class is itself in a continuous process of formation as the character and composition of its various strata change, so the various social value judgements in the utterances which make up behavioural ideology are also in a corresponding state of continuous formation and change.

To appreciate this it must be seen that such speech utterances are entirely sociological in nature. The utterance is always to some degree a response to something else. It does not exist in isolation. It is a product of interrelationship between speakers, and its centre of gravity therefore lies outside the individual speaker himself. Situation and audience are what bring the utterance to life. It is not monologic but dialogic in nature. The utterance as a whole possesses a unitary theme in which the meanings of the various words that make it up achieve their coherence. Meaning itself belongs to a word only in its relation between speakers. It becomes meaning only within the concrete theme of an utterance, as part of the process of active responsive understanding. Thus the meanings which are implemented in the theme in their referential denotative aspects are inseparable from evaluative accent. As Voloshinov remarks,

> No utterance can be put together without value judgement. Every utterance is above all an *evaluative orientation*. Therefore, each element in a living utterance not only has a meaning but also a value.[40]

Behavioural ideology is the sphere in which evaluative perception is carried out. Voloshinov argues that for this reason established and already formalised ideological systems must maintain vital organic contact with behavioural ideology, for without living evaluative perceptions, the ideologies would be dead things.[41] It is thus that in the upper levels of behavioural ideology, in its mobile and sensitive speech utterances, the clash of social accents continuously recurs.

From the dominant hegemony ideological themes are presented in stereotypical form in behavioural ideology, for the stereotype as an ahistorical theoretic understanding of problematic areas of social life exactly conforms to the hypostasising tendency of the ideological sign. It seeks to fossilise the sign, to lock it into a framework which blocks out realisation of possible alternative realities. Social stereotypes give utterances a static, blunted character, an evaluative accent with a ring of finality, surreptitiously attempting to foreclose potentially disruptive arguments and information. Adam Schaff has drawn attention to the role of stereotypes in powerfully influencing consciousness, pointing out their suggestiveness, their everyday character and their acceptance as natural.[42] In the formation of social stereotypes the organic connection between the dominant hegemony and behavioural ideology is maintained. The kinds of sectional consciousness which stratify and divide the working class, inhibiting the recognition of its structural subordination feed on authoritative stereotypical formulations. Yet the very incompleteness of the dominant hegemony makes such stereotypes more fragile than sometimes appears.

New and unexpected themes reflecting changing material reality constantly emerge, introducing potential discontinuities in social experience, raising new dimensions of relevance that throw into question taken-for-granted evaluations and mobilise entirely new kinds of evaluation. The development of new themes around structural contradiction at its point of growth is critical to the whole process of ideological evaluation which takes place in behavioural ideology. Such themes are generated at the pole of class consciousness whence they attempt to gain a foothold in mass social consciousness. They are transmitted in utterances that turn their dialectical cutting-edge against the foundations of false consciousness which the dominant hegemony sinks in behavioural ideology. In the speech utterances of behavioural ideology, as Voloshinov says, 'those creative energies build up through whose agency partial or radical restructuring of ideological systems comes about'.[43] It is these which can eventually modify the existing sectional consciousness of the class and by fracturing existing stereotypes permit a unified anti-system ideology to emerge. As the transcript analysis will show, in behavioural ideology there is a battle for linguistic domination, all the more fierce perhaps because every single participant in the conversation has, for the moment, at least, lost the primary battle *as workers* who are objectively subordinated in the relations of production. There is an equality of their participation in conversation which is the obverse of the inequality of their structural location. Although bound by the limitations of its method, this case study is offered as an illustration of some of the possibilities for a concrete study of ideology and social consciousness through the material of verbal signs. In itself, the low level of technique of analysis employed and the limited nature of the generalisation which can be drawn make the case study less than satisfactory. It does however provide a first point of departure, although in the absence of further comparative work it will remain only at such a point. What needs to be examined, and this can only be done empirically, is how speech utterances mediate mass perceptions of social inequality. To concretise this notion of behavioural ideology an emprical analysis of speech utterances from actual discussions among industrial workers follows.

A case-study of behavioural ideology: the Glasgow transcripts

The transcripts of conversations are in the nature of necessary abstractions for analytic purposes from the unending generative flow of utterances which is the social reality of language-speech. In conformity with the whole preceding theoretical outline, each utterance is examined not as monologic and self-contained but as part of a continuing bridging series of reciprocal responses which confirm, question, negate or in some other way qualify the utterances of other speakers. The speakers themselves are in a social situation which itself has a wider historical background and context. Thus the utterances are examined not as idiosyncratic expressions or as externalisation of the unique experience and consciousness of the individual, but as sociologically organised. What is important is not that each individual has his own distinctive set of experiences and consciousness, but that his thoughts and experience, his consciousness, only becomes internally coherent to the degree to which it is given shape and organised in verbal utterances set towards a social audience. As Voloshinov says,

> It is not experience that organises expression, but the other way around – *expression organises experience*. Expression is what first gives experience its form and specificity of direction.[44]

Understood in this way it is no longer possible to view utterances dualistically, as the outward objectification of some inner element or psyche. Thus, while for the individual speaker the utterance may appear as his own possession, in fact, 'word is a two-sided act . . . determined equally by whose word it is and for whom it is meant' that is, the product of a reciprocal relationship.[45]

> Aside from the fact that word as sign is a borrowing on the speaker's part from the social stock of available signs, the very individual manipulation of this social sign in a concrete utterance is wholly determined by social relations.[46]

It is the extent to which the individual is tied into social relationship in particular social collectivities that will determine the degree of ideological clarity and structuredness of his utterances.

> The immediate social situation and its immediate social participants determine the 'occasional' form and style of an utterance. The deeper layers of its structure are determined by more sustained and more basic social connections with which the speaker is in contact.[47]

From this follow several important points of methodology. These recordings were made in the workplace situation where the experience of social collectivity in capitalist society is pre-eminently class-bound in relations of production. The collective nature of shop-floor organisation imparts an ever-present possibility of a specifically *political* coloration of the ideological sign, for here class antagonism can be most keenly felt and immediately perceived. The point of production is the most sensitive point of impact of the wider historical contradictions which can be more readily grasped and given a greater ideological structuredness in verbal utterances. The workplace is a social situation in which overtly political and class conscious as against individualistic or fatalistic forms of expression can gain cognizance. It is precisely the political coloration of the utterance by the more class-conscious workers which sets the ideological sign in a state of flux. The contest of differing social evaluations is then readily accessible in such utterances of workplace conversation. They are samples of the spoken words of behavioural ideology. We are interested primarily in the implementation of ideological themes in these utterances and will attempt to show how the 'immanent' flux emerges in the discourse. The excerpts were selected from the mass of conversational material with this intention in mind. Biographical information on the workers who are the actual participants in these conversations will in no way enhance the explanation of the 'deeper layers' of the structure of the utterance. In his discussion of the utterance in behavioural ideology Voloshinov makes this point,

> In the lower strata of behavioural ideology, the biological-biographical factor does, of course, play a crucial role, but its importance constantly diminishes as the utterance penetrates more deeply into an ideological system. Consequently, while biographical explanations are of some value in the lower strata of experience and expression (utterance), their role in the upper strata is extremely modest. Here the objective sociological method takes full command.[48]

Thus in the analyses of the transcripts no information on the workers themselves is given other than that which emerges contextually in the conversations themselves.

A further methodological point which follows on, is that such contexts must be under the control of the speakers as far as possible. In other words, the conversations should approximate as nearly as possible to the usual kind of workplace discussion using everyday conversational language. The normal methods of participant observation and 'in-depth' interviews are therefore inappropriate in recording the primary conversational data. To be at all useful these conversations had to be recorded in the wholly familiar context of the workplace in which the generative process of verbal exchange was one of co-presence and co-participation of the speakers. The manner of development of particular themes and their actual emergence in conversation could only conform to the usual manner if no 'official arbiter' of speaking turns was present. The presence of the researcher in the recording situation would largely vitiate this requirement since it is exactly this role of neutral arbiter in which the outside observer is generally placed. Critically, any intervention made by the researcher, no matter how 'non-committal', is bound to skew the very conversational process of which he is a part.[49] To overcome this problem the help of two young workers living in the same area of Glasgow was enlisted. These contacts were made during the course of field-work in a council housing scheme. They agreed to take tape-recorders into their place of work after sounding out fellow workers on the idea of making tapes for 'a friend at the University'.[50] Trade union and employer permission was also sought. This proved to be the most satisfactory way of introducing the tape-recorder into the situation in the least threatening manner.[51] A few comments on the workers who collected the tapes should be made although in view of the preceding remarks about the relative unimportance of biographical factors in explaining the sociological structure of the utterance, these need only be brief. One biographical feature which they shared in common, however, doe have some bearing on the material. Both were politically conscious workers who were able to grasp the underlying orientation to language of the project. In the sense that they combat the dominant ideology in their everyday lives and in everyday language they could perceive the importance of an analysis of how language itself is used to convey differing social value judgements geared into opposing ideological frameworks. One criticism which might be made then is that they determined the topics of discussion in some artificial way. In fact, however, although the range of contacts who have made recordings is still rather restricted, and this is a limitation to be overcome in future research, these two workers fully comprehended the importance of not taking a strongly 'directive' role. Indeed, in the first excerpt of transcript analysed, the worker who made the recording does not intervene with a direct verbal contribution at all, which explains the absence of a W1 designation among the participants. No special attempts were made to obtain recordings of 'overtly political' topics. The total corpus of data contains exchanges on a wide variety of subjects and includes speakers of a whole range of views. The particular excerpts analysed here are selected for illustrative purposes but are not discontinous with all the rest of the material which in principle is also subject to analysis on the theoretical basis we have presented. We can now directly confront the problem of the verbal sign and social consciousness.

A. The transport workers

The following excerpt was recorded among Corporation bus crews during break periods of waiting-time between shifts where conversation takes place around tables in a bothy or hut. An extract from ten hours of recordings amounting to some one hundred and sixty pages of typed transcript of recordings was made in the depot over a two week period. The material which follows runs to just over six and a half minutes of continuous conversation amounting to eighty-four utterances numbered sequentially and divided into sections followed by analytical commentary.

By way of introduction it might be useful to make some remarks about Corporation 'green staff', the drivers, conductors and conductresses, so called because of the colour of their uniforms. Working on the buses has traditionally been regarded in Glasgow as a transitional occupation between coming off the dole and finding employment of a kind which does not demand working unsocial hours and a high rate of overtime working. This transitional aspect means that workers of high skill as well as semi-skilled or unskilled workers are employed as drivers or conductors, although obviously the latter categories predominate. Additionally, there are substantial numbers of immigrant Asian workers employed. This means that the garage contains workers from a wide variety of backgrounds. Thus the bothy has a distinctively heterogeneous population of workers within it and is in its way a debating club for the workers. Furthermore, as a group, bus-drivers and conductors come into contact with the general public on a daily basis. The material of human behaviour is thus constantly before them for scrutiny and probably is another factor which enhances the conversational flow that takes place in the bothy. The transcripts as a whole reveal a series of discussions with a fluid membership of anything up to half a dozen participants at one moment or another. These conversations have their own internal momentum and self-consciousness with regard to the presence of the tape-recorder quickly evaporates as the conversations unfold. In addition, the fact that the recordings were made over time by one of their number meant that the workers were familiarised with it and only a few overtly hostile remarks are made made about it in the whole body of transcript.

The transcript begins with a group of three workers discussing the 'work-in' at Upper Clyde Shipbuilders. They are exploring the theme of working-class solidarity of which the UCS experience was an important test. Solidarity is one of the most important and recurrent themes in the evaluative purview of the working class. It falls within the direct experience of most industrial workers and is important precisely because it is a social value judgement about how workers should behave towards each other in the day to day conduct of the class struggle. It is around such questions that the themes of behavioural ideology are constituted in the arena of conversational language.

Transcript: U1–U7

[Key to the transcript is in the Notes]

1. 4W ( ) – and it's up to the union to enlighten them
2. 2W That was a thing in the shipyard – in the UCS – see this work-in – half of them used to go out of the yard in the afternoon – now we were paying them – the actual workers themselves – they were still in employment with the UCS – they were paying that ten shillings every week for to give them wages to keep them supported and yet these guys were going oot – at 11 o'clock and going for a right good bevvy to half past two – coming back in the yerds steaming drunk – and just sittin' playing at cards and playing at dominoes. And then one thing that happened was – one foreman in the yard caught a couple of them drunk on the work-in and he turned round and he says right – the two of yous just get out the yard yous are fired. What happened – the union – right lads just doon tools we're all hittin' the street – if they don't get reinstated. But why should they get oot – if they're in a work-in they should be there for the times/until they (ring the dinner bell)
3. 5W Och aye – but this is this is eh it doesnae matter – I suppose the Paris Commune had its – you know its backsliders and a' the rest I mean every you'll always get that – you know you'll always get the flymen and the so-and-so's and/a' the rest of it
4. 2W OK you get it (everywhere but) – but why should these guys go oot/have a right good bucket and them come back in the yard?
5. 5W Aye – I agree – I agree with you
6. 2W And they come in drunk and everybody's got to go oot on strike just because they come in drunk?
7. 5W Yea well that's up to the men – the men don't – surely to God – now look – surely

the men have got their head on their shoulders – see if somebody got their jotters in here for being drunk – oot on a bus where there's a driver and a conductor and the union says right – strike – if they don't get reinstated – I wouldnae bloody strike/I'll tell you that much

Analysis of U1–U7

W2, it emerged in an earlier part of the tape, had himself been employed in the yards during the work-in and therefore speaks 'authoritatively' about the behaviour of the workers in his opening utterance, U2. What emerges in the first part of the excerpt, between U2 and U7, is a series of dialogic exchanges between W2 and W5. In these an attempt is made to assert the individual against the collective, by defining, negatively, the concrete behavioural limits within which the theme of solidarity should apply. This is done by each cataloguing instances where workers deserve dismissal for falling down on the job in some way. It begins with W2 recounting an experience of the union threatening to mobilise solidarity with two of the UCS workers whose jobs were in jeopardy for a drinking misdemeanour during the work-in. In U3 it appears as if W5 is trying to draw on the theme of the Paris Commune, an essentially heroic act of working-class struggle, to minimise the negative implication of U2 and W3. This, however, does not meet with any more than a tacid nod from W2 in W5's direction in the form of the statement that 'OK you get it (everywhere but)'. However in the greater part of U4 and in the whole of U6, W2 restates his initial theme more strongly as rhetorical questions. By the opening sequence of U7, W5's original theme, that even in the greatest of class battles there will be a few miscreants, has become atrophied into a far less powerful argument that the men have got 'a head on their shoulders' and are therefore not merely mindless sheep who do what the union tells them to. However, in the closing sequence of U7, W5 asserts quite fiercely that he would not respond to the call, 'right, strike, if they don't get reinstated', should a bus crew be dismissed for drunkenness. He takes W2's original words in U2, 'right lads just down tools, we're all hittin' the street if they don't get reinstated', and incorporates them symmetrically in his own words adding a further negative evaluation. The use of the word 'right' by both workers in U7 and U2 is meant to highlight the coercive nature of the operation of union solidarity, i.e., that in any dispute you will do what the union tells you to do. The phrase 'strike, if they don't get reinstated' is a stereotypical representation of union authoritarianism.

Transcript: U8–U15

8. 2W This is it but – it's all mates
9. 5W All mates nothin'!
10. 2W There is – there's a hell of a lot of them – that are all mates; you look at your black squad builders an' that
11. 5W Aye oh aye
12. wt They all stick by each other – but if it was one of them that was drunk
13. 5W Aye – but is it is a good thing?
14. wt It's naw a good thing
15. 5W Naw . . .

Analysis of U8–U13

With the next utterance U8, W2 shifts this theme up a gear by taking a faintly ironical and therefore distanced stance to the proposition that to be 'all mates' is 'a good thing'; again W5 inserts the words 'all mates' into his own speech, likewise negatively evaluated in U9. Here intonational emphasis plays its role in defining the idea against which each is pointing his utterances, i.e., support your fellow worker under *all* conditions. Such intonational nuances are however not easily rendered in the linear form of the transcript but in this case are clearly present in the voices of the speakers on the tape.

Transcript: U15–U19

15. 5W . . . uh you see the thing is – workers are their own worst enemies – they expect the union – the eh I beg your pardon – the gaffers you know the employers – to be fair and just and eh – tae you know – play the ba' play the game wi' the men but the men arenae prepared to play the game – you know. I mean let's face it they're no' – how many strikes have you heard where eh – guys get sacked for skipping away for smokes or extra tea break or that – you know something like that you know – to be fair
16. 4W You get it on the buses
17. 5W You get it everywhere – and the men say if that man's not reinstated we're going on strike. Now why should you go on strike for a person like that – because if he's dodging the work it means that you're daein' his work
18. 2W Aye I know
19. 5W Now I've nai sympathy/for him

Analysis of U15–U19

From U15 the ironical intonational evaluation fades as W5 directly employs hegemonic clichés and stereotypes to develop his position against solidarity. This is the language of the dominant hegemony spreading its roots down into behavioural ideology. It is distinctive in the way in which the fragmentation of the class is confirmed in timeless and immutable signs which convey a sense of unchanging reality. Thus we hear that 'workers are their own worst enemies', that 'the men arenae prepared to play the game', that numberless strikes take place to defend malingering smokers and tea drinkers, each statement interspersed with appeals to reasonableness, the men expect 'the employers to be fair', 'I mean let's face it' and finally once again, 'to be fair'. The following three utterances boost this theme to the level of almost unassailable truth with W4 entering into the discussion with his own bid in U16 which, since all the participants are themselves bus crew members, shows that here a potentially backfiring derogating remark about even their own group can be wholly contained in the context.

This section is an assertion of themes from the dominant hegemony complementing the previous attempt to undermine working-class themes from within, so to speak, by using irony. In turning the evaluative accent of class action against itself, by inverting its solidaristic social accent, the irony of utterances 8, 9 and 10 is inwardly impelled against 'all mates', as it were, against the unity of the class. The attack from above in U15 is a far more explicit form of utterance in which ironical intonations cannot find a place, just because irony emanates potentially subversive impulses. Here the denuding of the theme of solidarity is openly displayed. The words are safely locked into a flat mono-accentual framework. All hint of the multi-accentuality of the sign, as is so characteristic of its hegemonic implementation, is suppressed. In these utterances we see the organic connection of behavioural ideology to the dominant hegemony.

Transcript: U20–U28

20. 4W Yous Yous two are confusing – eh – your your your thing it was called UCS work-in – but as such it wasn't a work-in – they were only there
21. 2W They were just sitting there/aye
22. 4W So eh – that's why we were paying them to be sitting there
23. 5W Aye they occupied the yard
24. 4W To occupy the yards no' eh to work there
25. 5W I can see the eh
26. 4W It was a false eh – false title that was put over it
27. 5W I can see the point there
28. 4W And so this – when eh – John here says that eh they were getting paid to work and they were going oot boozin'
(?W You finished with the paper?)
28. 4W No they were actually just getting that pay to sit there – not really to work
(?W I'll bring it back at eight o'clock)

Analysis of U20–U28

The mono-accentual character of the dialogue is given an offensive or incorporative dimension by W4 in U20. In U20 he takes the notion of 'work-in' and with the collaboration of W2 in U21, actively crushes the working-class content of it, suspending the ideological sign from the generative context of class struggle which produced it. It was not the case, W4 says, that the workers were getting paid to work and were going out boozing, but rather they were actually just getting that money to sit there, as he says in utterances U22, U24 and U28. Thus the work-in, as an attempt to impose a unified demand for 'the right to work' through occupying the yards, is wholly denuded of its ideological challenge and the occupation is posed as a purely passive expression, the men getting paid just to sit. As W4 says in U26, it was a 'false title that was put over it', all hint of counter-evaluation is thereby excluded from the sign.

Transcript: U29–U40

29. 5W Aye but I mean
30. 4W ( ) no' to work in the yard!
31. 5W Aye – but I mean let's face it this is a serious thing – if the work-in hadnae take taken place they were all bein' thrown oot on the street – weren't they?
32. 4W That's quite true
33. 5W That's right – so these men/organised
34. 4W You feel because it was such a serious situation
35. 2W They should have treated it more seriously
36. 5W I think so I don't think – they're no' – they're actually just behaving exactly the same way as they behaved when they were employed – you know jumpin' ower the wa' and goin' oot for a pint when they shoulda been hittin' rivets into a boat or

somethin' like that. That's I mean everybody knows aboot the yards – ma brothers aw worked in the yards – never done a day's work in their puff

37. 4W That's true
38. 5W You know – I mean let's be honest/never done a day's work in their puff these guys
39. 2W When you look at the shipyards aw you see is wee groups of two an' three men staundin' talkin'
40. 5W So they did!

Analysis of U29–U40

In the following utterances, U29 and U33, W5 tries somewhat weakly to assert the working-class content of the work-in as 'a serious thing' which, had it not taken place, would have resulted in the men 'all bein' thrown oot on the street'. However the force of the hegemonic mould is such that W4 and W2 can successfully defuse this by suggesting that the workers should therefore have taken the whole work-in 'more seriously', co-opting this sign for their argument in utterances U34 and U35. Indeed, in utterance U36, W5 quickly reverts to his original theme of U15 only giving it a more intensified one-sided elaboration. He asserts that the workers acted during the work-in just 'the same way' as they always did, 'jumpin' ower the wa' and goin' oot for a pint', generally falling down on the job, in other words. As 'everybody knows', the yard workers 'never done a day's work in their puff'. On this it is worth nothing that yard workers have not made a ship by 'hittin' rivets' for at least thirty years but this elicits no opposing verbal response even from W2. With a further appeal to reasonableness, this time 'let's be honest' and W5 underlines U36 by repeating the identical words of the epithet in U38. In the next utterance U39, W2 who himself worked in the yards at that time is wholly unconscious of the fact that he caricatures himself in his reply that 'when you look at the shipyards aw you see is wee groups of two and three men standin' talkin''. The hegemonic suppression of the inner dialectic of signs is clearly revealed in these utterances of behavioural ideology, acting as they do like blunt weapons with which workers may bludgeon their sensibility of themselves as members of a class with common interests that can only be realised through united action.

Transcript: U41–U84

41. 6W But – why knock – why knock – the working-class parasites?
42. 5W Eh?
43. 6W Why knock the parasites at the bottom of the ladder instead of knocking the parasites at the tap of the ladder
44. 5W I agree with you but we werena talking about the top of the ladder we're talking about the bottom of the ladder
45. 6W But why is it always the bottom of the ladder we always talk about though John?
46. 4W Because
47. 3W Listen
48. 4W It's the bottom of the ladder that we know most/about
49. 5W If you're oot if you're oot on the road. This is where we are – we're at the bottom of the ladder and if you're oot in the road and you've got wan of these parasites driving the bus in front of you/
50. 6W mm hum
51. 5W that lies doon/

52. 6W mm hum
53. 5W kids on he's broke doon
54. 6W Agreed agreed
55. 5W that runs sharp and leaves you to do his work
56. 6W Yea
57. 5W he's the kind of man you're wanting shot of
58. 6W Fair enough
59. 5W I mean it is!
60. 6W But why accept – why accept the parasite at the top of the tree and reject the one/ sitting at the bottom
61. 5W Well I don't think we should accept them but eh – in most cases there isnae very much the ordinary/man can dae about the parasite
62. 6W Do you know – do you know in the *London Gazette* that they had an advert four weeks ago – a new Manager for Glasgow here
63. 5W Aye
64. 6W Six and a half thousand plus – know what it said in the advert – I can show you the advert incidentally. It said – no experience of transport necessary /Is that man no' a parasite?
65. 5W What have they got an advert in for?
66. 6W Is that man no' a parasite?
67. 5W What've they got the advert in for?
68. 6W Because its a public service and therefore/it's got to be advertised
69. 5W The man's been appointed
70. 6W They've still got to advertise it
71. 5W The man's been appointed
72. 6W It's the same wi' you
73. 5W The man frae Edinburgh's been appointed
74. 6W The Glasgow – the Glasgow Corporation darena employ one conductor and one driver without making it publicly known
75. 5W Aye
76. 6W that they want conductors or drivers. It's all got to be gazetted. So why pick the parasites in/Knightswood Garage?
77. 5W Oh aye – no but I'm
78. 6W No experience necessary
79. 4W You don't know nothin' aboot the parasites at the top you can only concern yourself with your knowledge – and your knowledge is near the bottom. And we can only do things – concern ourselves and maintain a good standard down at the bottom* with our knowledge of what's happening there. But we couldn't go into the top bracket and re-organise up there 'cos we know nothin' aboot it
80. 6W How no'? How no'?
81. 4W Cos we don't know nothing aboot it
82. 6W Mr. Du Cann has got a new appointment with the Wages and Prices eh Board right?
83. 4W Right
84. 6W 18,000 a year plus to turn roon' and his job is to turn roon' and say to the nineteen and a half quid a week Gas Board workers – yous cannae get any mair than a poun' and four per cent – the economy cannae afford it.

* [Largely inaudible sub-conversation on Lonrho affair and Duncan Sandys's high paid advisory post.]

Analysis of U41–U84

The intervention of W6 in utterance U41 is like a sharp mental slap to the other participants whose own utterances quickly take on a defensive almost cringing character. W6 is fully able to exploit the inner dialectic of the sign in order to win it back and re-locate it in a working class purview. W6 takes the whole drift of the preceding dialogue and neatly compresses the sum of themes into the notion of 'working-class parasites', the parasites 'at the bottom of the ladder' which he then dialectically counterposes with the parasites 'at the tap of the ladder', who should be the real object of vilification. A new evaluative accentuation is thereby introduced which raises a different set of social significances and points in a different direction. The switch is thrown, as it were, by W6 and the locomotion of hegemonic stereotypes slithers to a halt. From this point on, W2 falls completely silent. W5 after a rather half-hearted restatement of the theme of workers lying down on the job continues by asserting the powerlessness of the 'ordinary man' in U61. However W6 presses in on each utterance W5 makes from U61 and U78 at which point W5 opts out of the confrontation developing a sub-conversation of his own. It is W4 who takes up the self-deprecating theme of the ordinary man in U79 who can only 'do things, concern ourselves and maintain a good standard down at the bottom' since all he possesses is 'knowledge of what's happening there'. While for W5 the 'ordinary man' is powerless, for W4 he is inadequate to the task of controlling his own destiny. In U79 W4 reveals the exact contours of restricted recognition, a self-imposed limitation of horizons attempting to shut out disruptive information about 'parasites at the top' in terms of an unassailable 'top bracket' somewhere up there. It reveals these contours even more sharply because W6 had already demonstrated that he himself has indeed information fully documented in the *London Gazette* about what is happening up there, none of which reflects 'the top bracket' in a favourable light. What W6 does is to take the notion of parasite and locate it in concrete working-class themes, relating it to the workers' immediate situation as transport employees. A parasite is a man who receives a large sum of money in a position for which he has no special qualifications and probably serves no useful function anyway, such as the new transport manager. W6 thereby makes problematic the whole basis of authority and in U80 directly raises the counter theme of working-class control. The final dialectical twist is administered by W6 in U84 where Du Cann's highly paid job is portrayed as simply to tell low paid workers that they cannot increase their standard of living, the totem word 'economy' becoming ironically underlined in this context. In this way W6 matches and tries to overcome the immutable generalised 'truths' of the hegemonic utterances by successfully grasping the inner contradiction of ideological signs. He restores social multi-accentuality to precisely those aspects of reality that the hegemonic utterances of W4 and W5 fail to recognise. The social stereotype these workers present of themselves is that of the ordinary man, destined always to remain on the lower rungs of the social hierarchy, subject to forces which he can neither understand nor control. What we see in the dialogue is how W6 challenges the stereotype with concrete and disruptive information which tries to throw into question the whole immobilising nature of the stereotype. The information W6 presents is like a lever, prising open the trap doors of hegemonic social consciousness, forcing an entirely opposing set of social value judgements into behavioural ideology which imply a recognition of reality that potentially challenges the dominant hegemony. In these utterances the incessant struggle within behavioural ideology attempts to bring new possibilities to the threshold of awareness. The utterances form sequences of rationalisations, articulated affinities and antipathies through which the experience of life in an unequal society is mediated verbally in more or less opaque social formulations. Each of these utterances jostles with the other to achieve some kind of social recognition among their audience and each, in so doing, contributes to the mass of conflicting ideological currents within behavioural ideology.

B. The vehicle production workers

In the following excerpt, the clash of social value judgements does not occur in the same sharp manner as among the bus crews. There is no head-on collision of themes from opposing poles of ideological reference. Nevertheless, an important flux within the ideological sign emerges.

In contrast to the transport workers, who are a heterogeneous group drawn from a variety of skill levels, here we have a conversation among a group of mainly skilled engineers in a vehicle assembly plant with a predominantly semi-skilled workforce. Like the first excerpt, the question of unity in struggle is explored but from a different social location and perspective, that of the skilled workers within the plant.

This is a social location with a corresponding and historically developed sectional identity that generates its own group-specific loyalties, rationalisations and antipathies which linguistically fence off, as it were, one sector of the class in relation to others. Sectional identities possess their own specific creativity producing their own forms of social self-consciousness. They can generate *intrinsic formulations* of particular experiences related to the occupational status of the group which are not shared in common with less skilled sectors of the workforce. Such intrinsic formulations have an important complementarity with hegemonic stereotypes in behavioural ideology with which they co-exist, but less crudely and openly. In a sense they appear to be phrased within an oppositional working-class purview which accepts the need for class struggle whereas, in fact, this is true only to a limited extent. They can reinforce 'false consciousness' all the more effectively because this partial determination has the semblance of a working-class genesis. What we hear in the utterances is how a sectional identity can creatively reaffirm reality in a way that enables the group to maintain its separateness in the working class. The maintenance of a privileged position depends upon a tacit acceptance of the status quo. The utterances are intrinsic responses, less explicit than the overall formulations of legitimacy which imbue behavioural ideology. To 'decode' them, as it were, one has to know something of the way in which sectional identities are sustained in social consciousness and this means looking at the actual content of specific rationalisations, loyalties and antipathies. Indeed, the transcript analysis will show that those areas in which the ideological flux of the sign does become greatest are precisely where the greatest inconsistencies in the sectional identity exist; where in certain important respects its rationalisations no longer correspond to objective changes in the productive forces.

Nevertheless such intrinsic utterances are raw material for behavioural ideology. They also seek to block out recognition of common subordination and exploitation through emphasis upon a differentiated social location. Indeed, as far as the unity of the class is concerned, the ideological haemorrhage is all the more severe where the mediation of inequality is achieved at the deeper and more profoundly damaging level of intra-class antagonism expressed in the language of sectionalism.

There is a group of four workers here, all of whom, except W5 are skilled turners. The conversation is taking place at the end of the night shift for that week beside one of the machines. It is part of five hours of tape recordings made over as many weeks. This conversation lasts eight minutes amounting to 34 utterances. The workers are discussing whether or not a sectional view of trade unionism assists the brotherhood of man.

Transcript: U1–U11

1. W4 That's the employers taking advantage of them – I mean – let's face it/
2. W3 They're taking advantage of a situation
3. W4 Well that's true – deliberately/deliberately engineered
4. W5 Exactly
5. W4 I can tell you another thing – I mean but they do that with a lot of people – they dae it with people that go to – see these government re-training things
6. W5 Uh huh
7. W4 Noo we're led to believe in this society – when there's a scarcity of something up it goes in price – that's what they say – world market shortage – the price of the grub's gone up – you know – that's always their excuse – but when an employer goes down to it – when there when there's a shortage of say – of skills – we'll take turners for instance – seeing as we're all turners – what they do is they open ( ) – open a big training school – noo I've got nothing against people getting retrained for jobs etcetera when their jobs are say redundant – I think it's a great thing – but when it's deliberately engineered to flood the market with the skills that are in demand in order to lower the wages – noo – if we were turners – noo Alec's been in Canada – I believe there are some good wages oot there is that – there's quite a good trade for instance oot there for turners – but in Britain what they dae is flood the market – now they train men to work machines and then they hit the market – it's a pool of labour they can use – Noo I think re-training's great – but I'm no' contra I'm no' gonna contradict myself it's a deliberate policy of the government – I don't see them retraining them to be company directors or lawyers etcetera – but they re-train them to be all sorts of things – turners – for instance . . .
8. W1 What would you say Jim to somebody comes into the factory and operates say a Seven Inch Ward and looks at you operating a Engine Lathe or operating a Montford and says I can dae that how can I no' get on to it – what's the difference between this and a Ward – you know – why are these blokes managed to erect a brick wall you know – between these machines and other machines – do you feel that people should be allowed into other areas apart from Seven Inch Wards etcetera
9. W4 Unfortunate about that is – when you served an apprenticeship – I hope there's no a big wall there – but when we all served our apprenticeship – these boys were all running about on butchers' bikes making a lot mair money than I/was
10. W2 Aye – uh huh
11. W4 Now – I don't see that as a . . . that's no my fault – that's no the bloke on the butcher's bike's fault – that I had to suffer low wages and he didnae – I'm no' making any excuse but – I think when – the thing is – when you start there's nae tradesmen at all in a factory – (when there nane) – usually they start with what you call mobility agreements etcetera and they really destroyed trade unionism – even – it doesnae' matter what trade you want tae point tae – once they pick men aff the street and put them into they places – the employer then – can tell you what tae dae right down the line and they destroy trade unionism – maybe through time these blokes would get organised etcetera and fight against it because they're just the same blokes as I am and it's the same blokes as tradesmen.

Analysis: U1–U11

In U5–U7 we hear W4 arguing that retraining lowers the wage rates of skilled men by increasing the supply of labour. The word 'retraining' is the hinge around which W4's argument swings, that it is something *done to* the working class, 'deliberately engineered to flood the market'. W4 is not repeating hegemonic stereotypes in the same mono-accentual way in which they occur in the early part of the excerpt from the transport workers. He uses such phrases as 'we're led to believe', 'that's what they say', 'that's always their excuse' to take distance from the argument lodged in the framework of 'world market shortages producing price rises in commodities'. He points out that the same logic is not applied to scarcities of skilled labour, for example, turners, as against lawyers and company directors. Thus it is implied that there is a certain class injustice which allows workers to lose their scarcity value and higher wages and not professional ruling groups. This appears to be the assertion of a basic collectivist loyalty which as it soon turns out is no more than a sectional defence. In the following utterances U8, W1 exposes this by questioning the exclusiveness of turners in erecting a 'brick wall' around their particular machines. In the subsequent utterances U9 and U11, W4 lays bare the justification of higher wages for turners, namely that time-served men had to suffer low wages during apprenticeship while unskilled men got a lot more money. This is a key rationalisation of a privileged position and is reinforced by W4 pointing to the dangers of mobility agreements which 'destroy trade unionism' unless there is a group of skilled workers to fight against it. W4 thus identifies the preservation of trade unionism with the skilled workers in the main in contrast to 'men off the street' and by implication therefore the interests of the unskilled, that is unorganised, are also safeguarded in the fight against the employers.

Transcript: U12–U17

12. W1 Look Jim Jim you're talking about destroying trade unionism – there's another attitude that could also destroy trade unionism that's been very very injurious in the past and that's an exclusive craft concept of trade unionism – for example in eh eh this country and in the States and I suppose in other countries – eh eh – craftsmen guarded their privileges very very jealously you know – wouldnae allow anybody in at all to the extent that they wouldn't even let them into the unions because the American Federation of Labour was notorious for that – you know – and people who hadnae served their time werenae gonnae get intae this type of industry

13. W4 (Well)

14. W1 Noo – if you're a trade unionist and you're talking frae a trade unionist point of view which is basically you're talking about the brotherhood of man – do you no' think it's a wee bit contradictory to say well look – I'm no' gonnae let anybody into this this sort of job – another bloke you know. Even if you consider that you're talking about people running about on butcher's bikes there – but I don't know if that's really the reason why some people served their time and others didnae. You know you're making it sound as if other blokes said I don't give a bugger you know – I'm just going to get all the big money when I'm 16 till I'm 21 then I'll go and I'll take advantage of what other people have worked for – whereas you – you know were concerned to learn the trade etcetera you know and you were prepared to sacrifice – I mean I stumbled into an apprenticeship by accident – I know a lot of other people didnae serve their time and the accident – the accidental factor was

just as big – do you no' think it's all that deliberate a lot of people no' giving a bugger and just having a great time enjoying themselves and other people more sensible and intelligent settling doon to learn a trade

15. W4 That's the society we're living in
16. W1 It doesnae help people really you know to develop their ain ( )
17. W4 It's the society we're living in – I mean I wouldnae hide behind a wee bit of paper make myself look a bigger a more intellectual person than somebody else because – say Pete for instance who isnae a tradesman – well he's no' a . . . if you are a tradesman you hold on to your trade – but what I . . . in my experience – when you went into a shop – I've been in two or three shops – I havenae been in a great deal – but where you hid this you had strength in trade unionism – noo what I'm saying is all the people that say – oh well we've complete mobility employers for instance – 'cos it suits them and you can learn this bloke the job – you're a tradesman you can learn this bloke the job etcetera etcetera – they'll no' let anybody in their geme – you've got to wear the old school tie – it's the same as a bit of paper – right so they're telling us that we're wrang – Now come to the trade union point of view which you're trying to cover it's contradictory – I don't think so – it's on the road to good trade unionism – it might sound – it might sound contradictory 'cos we're in the brotherhood of man – but that isnae – that isnae the truth

Analysis: U12–U17

In U12 and U14 W1 clearly suggests that there are contradictions in W4's argument. What W1 does is to broaden the concept of trade unionism to include all sections of the work-force in 'the brotherhood of man', opening up the flux of the ideological sign, as it were, to underscore the narrow sectional basis of W4's utterances. W1 directly counterposes the rationalisation of a low wage apprenticeship by stating that whether a man is 'time-served' or not is merely fortuitous and not a moral criterion of worth and therefore justification for differential reward. W4's reply in U15 and U17 significantly shifts from utterances of sectional creativity, the more elaborated justifications he has previously put forward, to the retrenchment of the hegemonic stereotype which reaffirms the status quo more openly and directly. 'That's the society we're living in' he says but restates his argument that skilled workers provide the 'strength of trade unionism' in a more compressed form and without the moralistic dimension. He says that if it's all right for the bosses to maintain their exclusiveness, 'You've got to wear the old school tie' to get into their game then it's all right for the workers to do the same. W4 while claiming to dislike the rules of this game, he 'wouldnae hide behind a wee bit of paper', in fact makes no suggestion as to how they can be altered and ends up by restating emptily that it still does not contradict the brotherhood of man.

Transcript: U18–U19

18. W1 The old craft concept to a certain extent is outmoded because it was based upon craft and skill and yet there's less and less skill required every year – through the development of new technology – automated machinery – it's gonna be harder and harder to haud on to your machines on the basis of skill because the skill involved is minimal compared to/say 30 40 years ago.

19. W4 Well there's a lot – there's a lot of truth in that – that's quite true – we'll take this factory for instance – 'cos it's the place we're working in – this is the biggest crowd – how it's worked in here – it's worked against and it so happens the skilled turner – that is used against you now – In the works I think there's about 50 turners production oot a machine shop which I think is in the 13, 14 hundreds, right? – I can also say in all confidence that turners put in for a job the noo in here – 'cos I put two men in – I think you put one in Alec's – I know a lot of blokes that arenae time-served getting jobs – Noo if I was gonnae be strictly alang the line that the craftsman starts first – I could take it up because there are district – it's the rules of our union that you don't start a non-time-served man when a time-served man is available and there is time-served men available – so there's definitely discrimination against turners in here – there's no two ways about it – and we're being forced into a position because the machines are simpler – there's nae – they couldnae deny that – of claiming the job rather than the machine. If the job went on to a simple machine we claimed it – but it follows – just to prove that I'm right – that the turners in here – I would say – on average are the best paid tradesmen.

Analysis: U18–U19

It is this fixity of response by W4 that seems to provoke W1 to 'blow the gaff' so to speak, in U18. Considering W5 is present and is not a skilled worker himself, W1 is making a straightforward revelation, saying what probably remains unsaid in other circumstances, in a manner that is potentially extremely disruptive of the kind of sectional utterances of W4. W1 forces the argument by requesting recognition that the 'brick wall' of which he spoke earlier does not rest on a firm foundation any longer. Through the objective development of the productive forces, technological change has in a real sense made redundant many of the technical-vocational skills upon which sectional social consciousness is based. W1 opens up that important area of inconsistency in the 'craft' ideology which no longer corresponds to the realities of the productive process, in short, that skilled workers can therefore no longer claim control over certain types of work because they require special skill levels, since the machines themselves now incorporate many of the skills. In U19 W4 wholly concedes this and indeed articulates the defensive strategy of turners in 'claiming the job rather than the machine', i.e., if the machine can do jobs that the turners formerly did, then the turners would claim that for themselves to keep the semi-skilled men out. What W1 has done is to destroy the basis of W4's previous rationalisations for the privileged position of skilled workers and provoked in response a bald assertion of sectionalism whereby union rules give precedence to time-served men.

Transcript: U20–U34

20. W1 You feel the discrimination is against the turners – you know in the works?
21. W5 No I can't honestly say –
22. W1 Against the skilled man
23. W5 – I can't say that I've found that because I've not been a skilled man Alec – but it's never actually come to my attention you know – that er – it doesn't really affect me and indeed this is the first time I've heard it mentioned by Jim there
24. W4 (wh)

25. W5 But I can see his point – I can see what he's getting at – but nevertheless – at the same time – there's a lot of machines in here which I as a semi-skilled man could operate – which are being operated by turners and time-served men
26. W4 What machine's that Pete?
27. W5 Well this DA's for instance – there are machines that you could put a man on – once again this is going back to your argument Jim – you could train that man and within a space of time he could learn that machine – there's no doubt about it
28. W4 Oh aye – true
29. W5 There's also a lot of things I couldn't do – and which a time-served man couldn't do – such as going into the tool room for instance – certain operations in there which would require time-served men – but once again this is it – where do you draw the line of the brotherhood of man and so on
30. W4 Aye well – what I'm trying to say is – that the basic truth is – that when tradesmen go in and they negotiate something there is a bigger element of solidarity about it
31. W5 Mm uh huhu
32. W4 They're just nae picked aff the streets – noo we'll go back to even the coloured blokes – or – eh it doesnae matter – they're in a position when they've got to earn cash – they're in a strange country maist of them – so they work for under the rate – nobody could argue with that – unfortunately and the employers take advantage of it – that's the facts – but once you've got an element of tradesmen and you've got a wee bit of comeraderie – you can fight for better conditions and the employers know it – the employees know it – if – we've got I think – the only skilled track in Great Britain and that track as far as this division is concerned is the best paid – now that's no' just a coincidence – it isnae a coincidence it's a fact and even in the machine shop – I would say – I know there's men ( ) operators making more money than I do – maybe no' many but by and large the turners in the machine shop are the best paid – noo it's no just a coincidence – the men have fought to get these conditions – it wasnae just because there were a turner on it by the way – and I know there's a lot of turners that don't care either – but still an' all it's no just a coincidence – you take any craft trade – they usually set a precedent for conditions and therefore help the bloke that isnae time-served – where you havenae got the precedent –
33. W5 No that's so – I appreciate that Jim –
34. W4 – Where you havenae got the precedent – I would say for the brotherhood of man at the present time in society they're doing a job by doing that – because experience – if they set up a factory down South they'll be payin' them oot in bunnets eh – buttons – now that's what they'll be doing – and they'll be doing it because – well take Chrysler for instance – they'll no' start them because they know that they might have a wee bit trouble – you know – less mobility and all that carry on – it doesnae suit them.

Analysis: U20–U34

The remaining part of the transcript, following W5's recognition in U29 that as a non time-served man the brotherhood of man is not necessarily all embracing is interesting in the way W4 tries to patch up his previous argument. In U30 and U32 W4 claims that the employers take advantage of the skilled status of the turner but that the skilled workers have more solidarity, 'comeraderie' and can fight for better conditions, hence, it's not coincidental that they are better paid. W4 uses the 'concertina' argument, that the skilled workers by setting a 'precedent' effectively pull up the less skilled behind them. From the sectional perspective this is how W4 sees the skilled man as 'doing a job' for 'the brotherhood of man at the present time in society'. Nowhere in W4's utterances is there a concept of the brotherhood of man which looks beyond the confines of existing sectional division bringing all the workforce into united struggle to change the system. Society is taken as given at the present time. Sectional identities produce utterances which, like those of the dominant hegemony, and complementary to it, restrict recognition of common subordination; in this case by offering a lens through which attacks by the employers, in such forms as mobility agreements, are viewed as encroachments upon particular privileged statuses, rather than as part of a more concerted attack on the working class as a whole. How invidiously the working class divides itself is as important as the divisions which the ruling class seeks to impose on it. This is why it is important to examine these utterances, to try to pinpoint the areas of tension they reveal in sectional identities, to understand the forces that produce these tensions and to spot the points of potential rupture within behavioural ideology as verbally mediated social consciousness.

Proposals for a future Marxist semiotic of social consciousness

In conclusion, some of the more general practical and theoretical problems which are raised by this type of analysis of the ideological nature of speech utterances should be aired. It is important to realise that even the transcripts which were analysed can only be understood within the historical context in which these utterances occurred. Thus, 'a pound plus four per cent', 'the work-in', 'the nineteen and a half quid gas workers' and so on, are all themes located within a specific matrix of historical events from which they obtain this cogency and life. The struggle between social value judgements which was observed in these transcripts might employ a different set of themes were the conversations recorded yesterday or today. In order, therefore, to be able to understand how ideological signs change and develop over time it is necessary to monitor such utterances over a period of months or even years, rather than a few weeks only. In terms of the systematic study of mass social consciousness this work is only a first preliminary scratching at the surface. However the wealth of material that will allow this area to be penetrated is there, and in a real sense immediately available. From such material it should be possible to develop a Marxist discourse analysis that will permit the strategies used in arguments to be closely described.[52] It would be important to know, for instance, the circumstances in which appeals to logic, personal experience or authority seem to prevail. Again the *ad-hominem* nature of arguments, accusations of hypocrisy or inconsistency, diversions by way of humour and the introduction of the sectarian red herring would bear upon the analysis of such data. It might also be useful to involve the speakers themselves, after the recordings have been made, in an analysis of the transcripts. This raises the possibility of constructing a metalanguage out of the speakers' comments on what they said which might be one way of developing the categories of a discourse analysis framework.[53]

To carry this out, a co-operative research effort on a national scale perhaps involving up to half a dozen independent investigators would be required. They would be responsible for recruiting workers to gather conversational data. The work of Mass Observation was an earlier attempt to organise people on a national scale to collect data about their own lives, explicitly attempting to chart the prevailing social consciousness. Madge and Harrison evolved this method to combine anthropology and social psychology in the examination of mass attitudes in complex society. As their original manifesto makes plain, their object was to collect accounts compiled by volunteer observers 'from whose reports a weather-map of popular feeling can be compiled'.[54] The Mass Observation experience does suggest that a wide range of enthusiastic volunteers is not an impossibility. The bulk of their reports of what people are actually saying, however, consists of a surface analysis of isolated comments and phrases noted down by observers.[55] In the opinion of this writer, only the Marxist semiotic can provide the necessary theoretical tools which a proper analysis would require. The object has been to try and show how this approach alone can address itself to the central questions which should be asked about verbal signs and consciousness, since it is the approach which brings the dialectical materialist method to the fore. So that there is no confusion about where we stand in relation to this problem it should be underlined that a study of this sort must be conducted in a way that takes account of capitalist society as a historical system constantly developing in contradiction. From this follows the whole programme of our enquiry.

We are not attempting to discover a working-class culture in a kind of submerged 'oral tradition'. The transmission by word of mouth of stories, songs and jokes forming a stock of knowledge and attitudes passed on from one working-class generation to the next, is not the main substance of the speech utterances of behavioural ideology. Particularly since the second world war, redevelopment of the urban working-class areas and the dislocation of their populations has broken up or severely modified much of the life-styles, behaviour pattern and even local idiomatic speech forms which were thought to constitute a distinctive working-class culture. Over the last thirty years we have seen these older patterns eroded by the partial extension of new styles and possibilities for mass consumption, accompanied by and to some extent fostered within new media of mass communication. The intervention of these media in the context of Keynesian welfare society has actively generated qualitatively new kinds of cultural stereotypes.[56] They bear often only a tenuous connection with cultural responses to the deprivations of working-class life in the inter-war years.[57] It might be suggested that since 1945 there has been, if anything, an important degree of cultural discontinuity, in the way in which the experiences of successive generations of the class have been transmitted. In addition, developments in the productive forces besides reducing the numerical dominance of manual workers in the working class have brought entirely new sections to see their objective links with labour as a whole and with that, further potentialities for class struggle.[58] Though the underlying structure of inequality has altered very little, these developments are necessarily reflected in forms of speech which are responsive to an entirely new set of identities, corresponding to the changing character and composition of the class. Behavioural ideology is the sphere in which these identities are worked out but in very diverse ways. Thus mass attitudes in relation to social class, sexual behaviour and family roles, the various facets of work and leisure, the character of social relations between people in general, all of these are undergoing a continuous evolution and modification in response to changing material conditions and objective pressures. In this respect we are dealing with a most uncertain area and one in which the concept of a working-class culture especially if it is anachronistic, is not particularly helpful. The kind of debate about working-class speech for example, that has emerged as a reaction to the misconceptions of Basil Bernstein's studies lacks coherence precisely because empirically and historically founded conceptions of working-class culture and indeed of speech utterances are wholly absent.[59] What is critically important is to be able to understand ideological signs in their changing content and form and, in particular, in relation to various diverse strata of the working population. At the level of political action, it is the unity of these strata which is the condition for the emergence of a fully oppositional class consciousness, confident in its overall evaluation of the existing structure of society, and prepared to act decisively to realise its own aspirations and objective interests.

What we have tried to suggest is that speech utterances in capitalist society have an ideological nature and that this nature directly stems from the contradictions of that society. As capitalism moves through its phases of crisis new themes develop around structural contradiction as larger and larger numbers of people are pushed into opposition to the system. What we have to be able to specify, and this is why the study of speech utterances is so relevant, are the modifications taking place in sectional consciousness, the development of new forms of struggle and the growth of unified anti-sectional forces in the working class. In terms of the ideological sign these are the points of potential detachment and discontinuity from the dominant hegemony which are revealed in the social multiaccentuality of the sign. Attempts by the ruling class to produce adequate responses to the working-class challenge involve in some way neutralising the perception of social inequality. It is the role of the ideological sign to guard the boundaries of the social recognition of inequality. The importance of stereotypical formulations in speech utterances of behaviour ideology is that they try to mask the incompleteness of the dominant hegemony. They produce the reification of thought and language which corresponds to the fetish commodity character of capitalism as a whole. Finally, we can sum up our argument with a remark once made by Louis Althusser:

> In political, ideological and philosophical struggle words are also either weapons and explosives or tranquillizers and poisons. The whole class struggle can, at times, be encapsulated in the battle for one word against another. Certain words fight like enemies. Others offer the opportunity for vacillation: they are the location of a decisive but as yet undecided battle.[60]

What we must do is to make it our task to find out about these words.

Notes

1 John McLeish, *Soviet Psychology: History, Theory, Content* (London: Methuen, 1975) reviews the achievements of contemporary Marxist psychology in the Soviet Union. On the importance of the question of language and thought for social psychology see pp. 118–19.
2 L.S. Vygotsky, *Thought and Language* (MIT Press, 1970).
3 Ibid., p. 205.
4 Ibid., p. 7.
5 Ibid., p. 43.
6 Ibid., p. 51.
7 Ibid., p. 51.
8 Ibid., p. 153.
9 Karl Marx and Frederick Engels, *The German Ideology* (London: Lawrence & Wishart, 1970). Frederick Engels, 'The Part Played by Labour in the Transition from Ape to Man', in *The Origin of the Family, Private Property and the State* (London: Lawrence & Wishart, 1970).
10 *Thought and Language*, p. 6.
11 Cf. Karl Marx, *Economic and Philosophic Manuscripts of 1844* (London: Lawrence & Wishart, 1970), pp. 113–14.
12 Maurice Cornforth, *Marxism and the Linguistic Philosophy* (London: Lawrence & Wishart, 1971) p. 174.
13 George Thomson, *Marxism and Poetry* (London: Lawrence & Wishart, 1975). See also Christopher Caudwell, *Illusion and Reality* (London: Lawrence & Wishart, 1973).
14 *The German Ideology*, pp. 50–1.

15 Frederick Engels, *The Peasant War in Germany* (London: Lawrence & Wishart, 1969, p. 45). Writing of peasant Christian heresy, Engels says,

> It invoked the 'equality of the children of God' to infer civil equality and partly even equality of property. Equality of nobleman and peasant, of patrician and privileged burgher, and the plebian, aboliton of compulsory labour, quitrents, taxes, privileges, and at least the most crying differences in property – those were demands advanced with more or less determination *as natural implications of the early Christian doctrine.*

Cf. R.M. Hilton, *Bond Men Made Free* (London: Temple Smith, 1973) and R.B. Dobson (ed.) *The Peasant Revolt of 1381* (London: MacMillan 1970). Hilton's important study clearly draws out the potentiality of Christian language to reach well beyond the existing order. See especially pp. 210–13 and pp. 221–30. Dobson shows how the letters and sermons of John Ball injected a revolutionary ideological flux into the Christian message.

16 The work of Roland Barthes is an obvious example here. See especially his *Elements of Semiology* (1967) Jonathan Cape Ltd., London and his *Mythologies* (1973) Paladin, London, to name two of the most familiar works.

One recent popularising exponent of French semiology, Pierre Guiraud, very much in the Saussurian tradition manages to exclude consideration of the place of the verbal sign simply by definition, restricting semiology to the study of non-linguistic sign systems. Pierre Guiraud *Semiology* (London & Boston. Routledge and Kegan Paul, 1975). A brief but adequate refutation of the faulty premises of this kind of misconception is to be found in Adam Schaff 'Specific Features of the Verbal Sign', in A.J. Greimas et al. (eds.) *Sign, Language, Culture* (The Hague, Paris: Mouton, 1970) pp. 113–23.

17 V.N. Voloshinov, *Marxism and the Philosophy of Language* (New York: Seminar Press, 1973).
18 Ferdinand de Saussure, *Course in General Linguistics* (Fontana/Collins 1974).
19 Ibid., p. 61.
20 Ibid., p. 68.
21 Cf. *Thought and Language* p. 146.
22 *Marxism and the Philosophy of Language* p. 69.
23 Ibid., p. 70.
24 Ibid., p. 70.
25 Ibid., p. 73.
26 Ibid., p. 81.
27 Lucien Sève, 'Structuralism' in *World Marxist Review* Vol. 14 No. 5 May 1971, pp. 48–51 and June 1971 pp. 48–50 clearly enunciates the anti-Marxist thrust of structuralism, in particular that of Lévi-Strauss upon whom the influence of Saussure is marked.
28 Ibid., p. 10.
29 Ibid., p. 22.
30 Ibid., p. 15. Cf. Vygotsky's important discussion of inner speech in *Thought and Language*, op.cit.
31 Ibid., p. 19.
32 Ibid., p. 20.
33 Ibid., p. 21.
34 See for example Claus Mueller's tendentious volume *The Politics of Communication: a Study in the Political Sociology of Language, Socialization and Legitimation* (New York: Oxford University Press, 1973). Mueller mechanically uses Bernstein's notion of elaborated and restricted codes to suggest that the working class have been fully ideologically-linguistically incorporated into capitalist society.
35 *Marxism and the Philosophy of Language*, p. 22.
36 Ibid., pp. 23–4.
37 Antonio Gramsci, *Prison Notebooks* (London: Lawrence & Wishart, 1971).
38 Raymond Williams, 'Base and Superstructure in Marxist Cultural Theory', *New Left Review* Vol. 82 November/December 1973, p. 9.
39 *Marxism and the Philosophy of Language*, p. 14.
40 Ibid., p. 105.
41 Ibid., p. 91.
42 Adam Schaff, *Language and Cognition* (McGraw-Hill, 1973), suggests rightly how inadequate the study of this important area has been: 'The study of taboo in primitive societies is certainly much more advanced than the analogous study of stereotypes of behaviour in civilized societies, *especially*

the role of language in such stereotypes' (p. 152 emphasis added). Another way of putting this point might be to say that the stereotype presents linguistic formulations in an artificially imposed *signality*, provoking a one-sided immediacy of response by historically 'decontextualising' the verbal sign. It is this denuding of historicity which gives the stereotype its timeless and immutable character.

43 *Marxism and the Philosophy of Language*, p. 92.
44 Ibid., p. 85.
45 Ibid., p. 86.
46 Ibid., p. 86.
47 Ibid., p. 87.
48 Ibid., p. 93.
49 It is assumed here that wholly 'covert' methods of observation and recording are neither practicable nor ethical.
50 The actual taping was done with a cassette machine relatively compact and unobtrusive, easy to operate and above all, reliable. The cassettes allowed one hour of continuous recording on each side. An omni-directional extension microphone placed by the recording machine picked up most of the utterances although difficulties occurred at the transcription stage when two or more voices occurred simultaneously. This was compounded by inevitable background noise of machinery and so on. A separate high-quality transcription machine was used to try and compensate for the technical deficiencies in sound quality. Even with secretarial assistance in roughing out first drafts the ratio of input was about twenty hours for each hour of recorded material.
51 The original focus of this study attempted to use participant observation techniques to construct an 'ethnography of communication'. Dissatisfaction with this approach which suffered all the limitations in obtaining conversational samples described above as well as the sheer difficulty of gaining access to everyday conversational contexts in the local area where the researcher lived for about a year forced a radical rethink about the research strategy. The suggestion to take in tape-recorders to the place of work first came indeed from one of the workers in the course of a discussion of these problems. In retrospect, it is easy to say that the sphere of production should have been the obvious starting point. This is not meant however to suggest that because participant observation techniques did not allow the particular problem of this research to be tackled that it is not productive in other circumstances. In any event a working point of entry at least was provided by the fieldwork period of participant observation.
52 Sinclair and Coulthard have provided the outlines of a framework of discourse analysis in the formal classroom teaching situation. Their approach to the verbal utterance in contextual terms could be refined and extended in comparative investigations of the more fluid situation of the shop-floor conversation at least in a provisional manner. See J. Mc. Sinclair and R.M. Coulthard, *Towards an Analysis of Discourse: The English Used by Teachers and Pupils* (London: Oxford University Press, 1975).
53 These proposals were made by David Betteridge of the Language Teaching Centre at York in a gratefully received critique of an earlier version of the article.
54 Charles Madge and Tom Harrison, *Mass Observation* (London: Frederick Muller, 1937) p. 50.
55 One exception appears in the *War Factory* report by Mass Observation in which a 'typical' conversation between female factory workers is reproduced but without comment. See Tom Harrison (ed.) *War Factory: A Report by Mass Observation* (London: Victor Gollancz, 1943, pp. 57–60).
56 The whole problem of stereotypes in the mass media has been curiously neglected in terms of the historico-ideological as against the purely cognitive-psychological level. One study that does touch on some of these problems is Paul Hartman and Charles Husband, *Racism and the Mass Media* (London: Davis-Poynter, 1974).
57 Raymond Williams's notion of 'the selective tradition' is apposite here. See Williams op. cit. A good example of how the media intervene in this respect is in the recording of the songs and jokes of Billy Connolly and the strip cartoon characterisation of 'the big yin' in a popular Glasgow newspaper. Connolly's picture of Glaswegian working-class life and attitudes is a subtle blend of outright chauvinism and resigned acceptance, projected in a coherent catalogue of all the self-debilitating incapacities of working-class life. It is tempting to suggest that Connolly has been 'boosted' to the level of Glasgow's 'folk hero' just because of the selective one-sidedness of his 'vernacular' humour. It is also the case, however, that the experiences of poverty and degradation in the inter-war years from which such humour really stems were very widespread, although reaction to them was by no means uniform. These, then, to some extent carried over into the 1950s and so are in the

childhood memory of many of Connolly's audience who grew up in the thirties or the early post-war years. What Connolly's humour does is to provide an antidote to shame in the recollection of such experiences, neatly setting them within a rather cruel love-hate ambivalence that allows people to laugh at themselves and simultaneously renders the experiences harmless by obscuring the systematic causes which produced them. Comparison of the Connolly of *Cop yer whack for this* (Polydor Records) with the work of the 7:84 Theatre Company in John McGrath's plays such as *The Cheviot, the Stag and the Black Black Oil, The Game's a Bogey* and *John MacLean* is instructive as to the way in which a different, far more class-conscious strand of experience can be given a real historical continuity with the present day struggles of the working class.

58 An important series of contributions on this question is contained in *Marxism Today*, the theoretical and discussion journal of the CPGB. See Jack Cohen. 'Some Thoughts on the Working Class Today', *Marxism Today*, Vol. 17, No. 10 October 1973, pp. 293–303, and also T. Timofeyev and A. Chernaev, 'Some Aspects of the Study of the Modern Proletariat', *Marxism Today*, Vol. 17, No.11, November 1973, pp. 329–36.

59 One of Bernstein's most severe critics, Harold Rosen, illustrates this weakness very clearly in the collection of transcripts published as *Language and Class* Workshop 1, February 1974 and Workshop 2, November 1974. See also H. Rosen, *Language and Class: A Critical Look at the Theories of Basil Bernstein* (Falling Wall Press, 1972). It is one thing to demolish theories of 'verbal deprivation' and show the richness and vitality of ordinary speech, but a properly concrete analysis of speech utterances requires more than this.

60 From an interview with Althusser quoted by Maria Antonietta Macciocchi in *Letters from Inside the Italian Communist Party to Louis Althusser* (London: New Left Books, 1973, p. 16).

Key to Transcript

- – Pause in utterance
- [Simultaneous utterance
- / Following utterance begins
- ( ) Empty bracket represents material not transcribable. Where words are given this indicates what seems to be said.

23 Subcultural conflict and working class community

Phil Cohen

Introduction

What I intend to do in this paper is to try to relate some of the theories which have been produced by academic sociologists about the working-class community to some of the concrete problems which people who actually work in those situations come up against day-to-day. It seems to me that the key problem for so-called community activists who are on the whole mostly middle-class or fringe middle-class and are located in a working-class community, especially those communities that are situated in the inner ring of large cities, is that they share an abstract identitive situation with the community but are separated culturally or sub-culturally from the majority of people living in the area. Community organisations that develop tend to be dominated by a combination of socially-mobile working-class people and middle-class drop-outs or the 'rebel' fringe; both those groups are caught in a sort of cultural no-man's land between the two major class formations and they tend to view each other with an incredible degree of suspicion as a result of their respective class origins. This can lead on one hand to a kind of intellectual elitism on the part of the drop-out group who view their own kind of sub-cultural preoccupations as being necessary for access to revolutionary change. And on the other hand it can produce a sectarian localism, a notion that unless you've been born and brought up in an area that you have no right to be there, no right to be involved, and seeing the whole thing in terms of some kind of middle-class intervention from outside. And this is something which has come up recently, when we've been trying to start Project East, which is an attempt at community action in Bethnal Green, a district in the East End of London. One of the problems here is that community struggles don't generate the kind of structural solidarity between activists and rank-and-file which is intrinsic to struggles on the shop-floor. No-one really of the community is in the same situation as a shop steward for example. In terms of factory struggles everyone shares a common and objective position in the production process and this isn't true, on the whole, of community struggles.

This problem leads into the main theme which I want to explore here, which is the relationship between culture and community in the perspective of a class struggle. To what extent do certain community structures generate or mediate cultural or sub-cultural diversity? Under what conditions does cultural diversity tend to generate class-consciousness through community structures with a consciousness which transcends local sectarian community loyalties? To what extent does the breakdown of community structures as a result of re-development for example, generate cultural and sub-cultural conflict? And what possible structures of community action are implied in answering some of these questions? It seems to me that the work of academic sociologists isn't really much help in looking at these questions or in forming them either in theory or in practice, for much of this work separates the problem into two separate fields of study: community studies, Willmott and Young and so on, and cultural studies, mainly the work of Raymond Williams and Richard Hoggart. This separation of what is a single social reality in turn leads to the theoretical production of two hypostasised entities, quasi totalities; firstly, culture, which is subtracted from community, and tends to be reduced simply to ideology or value-systems, and is analysed independently of its embodiment in actual institutions: these institutions are shaped by specific community structures and these structures in turn vary within defined limits according to the historic and socio-economic conditions in which they operate. Secondly, community subtracted from culture tends to lose its class-specificity and can almost become a spiritual value in its own right (a markedly strong tendency among middle-class sociologists discussing community in particular). The working-class community appears as a new kind of transcendental force in history, always the same in time or space; this overview ignores the whole complex of differences within and between specific communities, differences which are determined by macro-social structures, whether they're political, ideological or economic, and the uneven and combined development of the contradictions in these structures. It is this uneven development in particular which produces quite determinate regional variations in the physiognomy of working-class life outside production and this kind of issue is ignored in that separation process I talked about.

From the point of view of community activists then, both these theoretical tendencies fail to pose the thousand-dollar question, which is the relationship between working-class life in the spheres of production, and working-class life in the spheres of consumption, or outside production. A relationship in other words between the issue of workers' control and community control. There are two factors here, and the different sectors of the working-class are involved in each field; those who are most militant and organised at the point of production tend to be the most passive and apathetic in relation to community issues, and equally those groups which are involved in community action tend to be the least politicised in relation to the issues of the work place. I cannot discuss this in detail here, but the sources are complex and it raises quite wide issues about the impact of advanced technology, changes in the structure of the production process and the labour force and the impact of this on the working-class ideology. This we might call the first contradiction. The second one is that institutions in which working-class culture and community organisation are conjointly embodied are extraordinarily resistant to change and are often disjunctive with the changing structures in production: in other words they may correspond to earlier stages in the development of the productive forces. It is the interplay of these two linked contradictions which, to my mind, create the field of force on which any action, any political action, or political movement, has to exist. What I want to do is to explore some of these issues in the context of the East End and to take some of the insights of academic sociologists, whether in the field of community studies or cultural studies, to modify and adapt these in the light of some of the things which activists have worked out, come up with, in the course of actual community action in various situations. I'll start briefly by describing Project East and where it's situated in Bethnal Green.

Friends House, off Bethnal Green Road, which is the location of the project, is a typical settlement building of its period. In the latter half of the nineteenth century the conscience of the middle class was increasingly aroused to the plight of the poor, the victims of industrialism, whose conditions of existence were both a permanent accusation against the system, and a threat to its stability. The East End attracted particular attention; Lord Baden-Powell for instance went on record as to the urgent necessity of establishing the boy scout movement in the area 'lest the youth there become captivated by the dangerous doctrines of socialism and other subversion'. During this period a large number of community settlements took root in the East End, sometimes financed by industrialist philanthropists, more often linked to the great public schools and universities, and run by their progeny. Today many of them still survive, more or less successfully trying to live down the ethos of Victorian paternalism, and adapt themselves to the changed conditions and problems of the modern working-class community. Friends House itself now stands isolated, and somehow awkward amidst the new housing estates and tower blocks which have replaced the nineteenth-century slums. In a way this illustrates the present situation very clearly – the residual problems and attitudes to them inherited from the past, inserted into a whole new complex of problems created by official solutions aimed at a better future, but imposed on the community from outside. The traditional pattern of East End life is undergoing a process of rapid change, and inevitably this has resulted in a period of crisis and social disorganisation, with some alarming symptoms. The purpose of PROJECT EAST is to enable the community as a whole, and particularly vulnerable groups within it to re-organise, to conserve what is functional in traditional working-class life, and to develop new forms of organisation to meet new conditions. But before this is spelt out in more detail let's look briefly at the historical background, and social dynamics of the present crisis.

The past in the present

Since the very beginning of the industrial revolution the East End has provided a kind of unofficial 'reception centre' for a succession of immigrant communities, in flight from religious persecution or economic depression. First came the Hugenots, spinners and weavers, at the end of the seventeenth century, and still today their presence survives in surnames, and place names in the area. Then, throughout the nineteenth century there was a constant immigration of Irish, mostly labourers, and small traders from Central Europe, and in the last two decades of course Pakistanis, and to a lesser extent West Indians and Greek Cypriots. Today the East End is indeed like 'five parts of the world, put in one place'.

Each subcommunity brought with it not just specific skills, but also of course its own traditions, and cultural values. There was no question of assimilation into a dominant indigenous culture – either that of the 'native' dockland community, or of the English ruling class. What in fact happened, until recently, was that each new subcommunity, in turn, and over time became an accepted, but differentiated part of the 'East End' by allying itself with the longer established sections of the community against another, later subcommunity. The outsiders become established, become insiders, by dissociating themselves from an even more conspicuous set of outsiders. Perhaps it is a natural human tendency to draw the line under one's own feet; at any rate in the East End integration has proceeded by means of conflict, rather than by dissolving it.

There are three main social factors underpinning this pattern of integration – the extended kinship structures which regulate socialisation in each subcommunity; secondly the ecological structure of the working-class neighbourhood; and finally the structure of the local economy. In reality these factors interact and reinforce each other – but it is important to understand them, because it is precisely the elimination of these factors, the transformation of these structures which has caused the present state of tension in the area. So let's look at them briefly, one by one.

Extended kinship networks This is a system by which the family of marriage remains linked by an intricate web of rights and obligations to the respective families of origin, and serves as a link between them. Based in the first instance on maintaining the close relationship between mother and daughter, so that when she gets married the daughter will continue to live as close as she can to 'mum', and extending in widening circles to include uncles and aunts, grandparents, nephews and nieces, and their relations, this system virtually turns the family into a micro-community, and in fact provides for many of the functions of mutual aid and support, that are elsewhere carried out by agencies in the community. Obviously such a system makes for cultural continuity and stability; it reduces generational conflict to a minimum – leaving home and getting married do not become life and death issues as they do in the nuclear family. Firstly because the extended family constitutes a much richer and more diversified human environment for the child; secondly children tend to stay at home until they get married, or to put it another way, only leave in order to do so; thirdly getting married does not involve any divorce between the young couple and their families, but rather recruits new members into the kinship network. And although the extended family preserves historical traditions of the subcommunity, handing them on from generation to generation, it does not serve to insulate it from the 'outside world'. On the contrary it serves as the basis for eventual integration. For the family both becomes family anchored in a given locality (matrilocal residence as it's technically called) and the network is continually expanding outwards; the net result is that over time the ties of neighbourhood are extended into ties of kinship and vice versa. If everybody knows everybody else in traditional neighbourhoods it is not because they are related through interlocking kinship networks, but that schoolmates, workmates, pubmates while they may or may not be related to relatives of one's own, will tend to be related to other mates, or mates to other relatives of one's own. But this can't be explained simply in terms of the internal dynamic of kinship, the ecology of the neighbourhood also plays a part.

Ecology of the working-class neighbourhood The close-packed back to backs, facing each other across alley ways or narrow streets, corner shops and local pubs, the turning, all this helps to shape and support the close textures of traditional working-class life, its sense of solidarity, its local loyalties and traditions. And this in turn is underpinned by the extended kinship networks of the traditional working-class family, which have been so well observed in Bethnal Green.

But how does the ecology of the neighbourhood work in practice? Let's take the street as an example. In these neighbourhoods the street forms a kind of 'communal space', a mediation between the totally private space of the family, with its intimate involvements, and the totally public space e.g. parks, thoroughfares, etc., where people relate to each other as strangers, and with indifference. The street, then, is a space where people can relate as neighbours, can express a degree of involvement with others, who are outside the family, but yet not as strangers, it maintains an intricate social balance between rights and obligations, distance and relation in the community. It also serves to generate an informal system of social controls. For where the street is played in, talked in, sat out in, constantly spectated as a source of neighbourly interest, it is also policed, and by the people themselves. Nothing much can happen – however trivial (a child falling, a woman struggling with heavy parcels, etc.) without it becoming a focus of interest and intervention. The presence of corner shops and pubs in the turning, also serves to generate social interaction at street level, as well as providing natural settings for 'gossip cliques', which if they do nothing else constantly re-affirm the reality of neighbourhood ties!

The net result is that neighbours as well as relatives are available to help cope with the day-to day problems that arise in the constant struggle to survive under the conditions of the working-class community. And in many areas, including the East End, institutions such as loans clubs, holiday clubs and the like developed to supplement family mutual aid, and formalise the practices of 'neighbouring'.

The local economy Perhaps the most striking feature of the traditional East End economy is its diversity; dockland, the many distributive and service trades linked to it, the craft industries, notably tailoring and furniture making, the markets. This diversity meant that people lived and worked in the East End – there was no need for them to go outside in search of jobs. The extended family remains intrinsic to the recruitment of the labour force and even to the work process itself; son followed father into the same trade or industry while many of the craft and service trades were organised into 'family concerns'. As a result of this, the situation of the work place, its issues and interests, remained tied to the situation outside work – the issues and interests of the community.

There was a direct connection between the position of the producer and the consumer. The fierce pride of being an Eastender was often linked to the equally fierce pride of craftsmanship and skilled labour. And it was from this section of the working class – sometimes called the labour aristocracy – that the indigenous leadership was drawn; politically conscious and highly articulate in defence of local interest, both at the community level and at the point of production. This elite group was also the most socially mobile, tending to re-emigrate from the East End to the outer ring of the middle-class suburbs; as Jewish people used to put it: the distance from Bethnal Green to Golders Green was two generations. Yet their ranks were continuously replenished as new subcommunities established themselves as part of the respectable working class. There were also those less fortunate who, for a variety of reasons, fell by the wayside, and remained permanent 'outsiders' vis-à-vis the 'established'. They were relegated to the ranks of the labouring poor caught in a vicious circle of poverty, ill health, unemployment and lack of education. This residual group was doubly excluded – unskilled and lacking union organisation they had little or no bargaining power on the labour market; and stigmatised as 'pariahs' by the rest of the community, the scapegoat for its problems, and denied any effective voice in their solution.

At any given time, then, the social structure of the community as a whole, and of the subcommunities within it tended to be polarising into three distinct strata – the socially mobile elite who monopolise leadership, the respectables, who form the 'staple backbone' of the community, and the lumpen (so called) who are often driven to petty criminal activity to survive. And incidentally there is not a better example of the over-riding importance of the extended kinship structure on the pattern of East End life than the fact that when this lowest strata began to evolve a kind of lumpen aristocracy, based on criminal activity, it was the small family 'firm' that was taken as the model for its social organisation!

The future perfect versus the historical present

The social structure we've described held until the early 1950s; and then, slowly at first, but with gathering momentum it began to change, and the pattern of social integration that had traditionally characterised the East End began, dramatically, to break down. Without going into a long argument about cause and effect, it is possible to say that this breakdown concided with the wholesale re-development of the area, and the process of chain reactions which this triggered. The re-development was in two phases, the first spanning the decade of the 1950s, the second from the early 1960s to the present; let's examine the impact of each in turn.

The 1950s saw the development of new towns and large estates on the outskirts of East London, Dagenham, Greenleigh etc., and a large number of families from the worst slums of the East End were rehoused in this way. The East End, one of the highest density areas in London, underwent a gradual depopulation. But as it did so, certain areas underwent a re-population, as they were rapidly colonised by a large influx of West Indians, and Pakistanis. One of the reasons why these communities were attracted (in the weak sense of the word) to such areas is often called 'planning blight'. This concept has been used to describe what happens in the take-off phase of comprehensive redevelopment in the inner residential zones of large urban centres. The typical pattern is that as redevelopment begins, land values inevitably rise, and rental values fall; the most dynamic elements in local industry, who are usually the largest employers of labour tend to move out, alongside the migrating families, and are often offered economic incentives to do so; much of the existing dilapidated property in the area is bought up cheaply by property speculators and Rachman-type landlords, who are only interested in the maximum exploitation of their assets – the largest profits in the shortest time; as a result the property is often not maintained and becomes even further dilapidated. Immigrant families, with low incomes, and excluded from council housing, naturally gravitate to these areas, and their own trades and service industries begin to penetrate the local economy. This in turn accelerates the migration of the indigenous community to the new towns and estates. The only apparent exception to planning blight, in fact proves the rule. For those few areas which are linked to invisible assets – such as possessing houses of 'character' i.e. late Georgian or early Victorian, or amenities such as parks, are actually bought up and improved, renovated for the new middle-class, students, young professionals, who require easy access to the commercial and cultural centre of the city. The end result on the local community is the same; whether the neighbourhood is upgraded or downgraded, long-resident working-class families move out.

As the worst effects of the first phase both on the those who moved, and on those who stayed behind, become apparent, the planning authorities decided to reverse their policy. Everything was now concentrated on building new estates on slum sites within the East End. But far from counteracting the social disorganisation of the area, this merely accelerated the process. In analysing the impact of re-development on the community, these two phases can be treated as one. No-one is denying that re-development brought an improvement in material conditions for those fortunate enough to be rehoused (there are still thousands on the housing list). But while this removed the tangible evidence of poverty, it did nothing to improve the real economic situation of many families, and those with low incomes may, despite rent rebate schemes, be worse off. But to this was added a new poverty – the impoverishment of working-class culture. Re-development meant the destruction of the neighbourhood, the breakdown of the extended kinship network, which as we've seen combined to exert a powerful force for social cohesion in the community.[1]

The first effect of the high density, high rise schemes, was to destroy the function of the street, the local pub, the corner shop, as articulations of communal space. Instead there was only the privatised space of the family unit, stacked one on top of each other, in total isolation, juxtaposed with the totally public space which surrounded it, and which lacked any of the informal social controls generated by the neighbourhood. The streets which serviced the new estates became thoroughfares, their users 'pedestrians', and by analogy so many bits of human traffic, and this irrespective of whether or not they were separated from motorised traffic. It's indicative of how far the planners failed to understand the human ecology of the working-class neighbourhood that they could actually talk about building 'vertical streets'! The people who had to live in them weren't fooled. As one put it – they might have running hot water, and central heating but to him they were still prisons in the sky. Inevitably the physical isolation, the lack of human scale and sheer impersonality of the new environment was felt worst by people living in the new tower blocks which have gradually come to dominate the East End landscape.

The second effect of redevelopment was to destroy what we have called 'matrilocal residence'. Not only was the new housing designed on the model of the nuclear family with little provision for large low income families (usually designated as problem families!) and none at all for groups of young single people, but the actual pattern of distribution of the new housing tended to disperse the kinship network; families of marriage were separated from their families of origin, especially during the first phase of the re-development. The isolated family unit could no longer call on the resources of wider kinship networks, or of the neighbourhood, and the family itself became the sole focus of solidarity. This meant that any problems were bottled up within the immediate interpersonal context which produced them; and at the same time family relationships were invested with a new intensity, to compensate for the diversity of relationships previously generated through neighbours and wider kin. The trouble was that although the traditional kinship system which corresponded to it, had broken down, the traditional patterns of socialisation (of communication and control) continued to reproduce themselves in the interior of the family. The working-class family was thus not only isolated from the outside, but undermined from within. There is no better example of what we are talking about than the plight of the so called 'housebound mother'. The street or turning was no longer available as a safe playspace, under neighbourly supervision. Mum, or Auntie was no longer just round the corner to look after the kids for the odd morning. Instead the task of keeping an eye on the kids fell exclusively to the young wife, and the only safe playspace was the 'safety of the home'. Feeling herself cooped up with the kids, and cut off from the outside world, it wouldn't be surprising if she occasionally took out her frustration on those nearest and dearest! Only market research and advertising executives imagine that the housebound mother sublimates everything in her G-plan furniture, her washing machine or non-stick frying pans.

Underlying all this however there was a more basic process of change going on in the community, a change in the whole economic infrastructure of the East End.

In the late 1950s, the British economy began to recover from the effect of the war, and to apply the advanced technology developed during this period to the more backward sectors of the economy. Craft industries, and small scale production in general were the first to suffer; automated techniques replaced the traditional hand skills and their simple division of labour. Similarly the economies of scale provided for by the concentration of capital resources meant that the small scale family business was no longer a viable unit. Despite a long rearguard action many of the traditional industries, tailoring, furniture making, many of the service and distributive trades linked to the docks, rapidly declined, or were bought out. Symbolic of this was the disappearance of the corner shop; where these were not demolished by re-development, they were replaced by the larger supermarkets often owned by large combines. Even where corner shops were offered places in the re-development area often they could not afford the high rents. There was a gradual polarisation in the structure of the labour force: on the one side the highly specialised, skilled and well-paid jobs associated with the new technology, and the high growth sectors that employed them; on the other the routine, dead end, low paid and unskilled jobs associated with the labour intensive sectors, especially the service industries. As might be expected, it was the young people, just out of school, who got the worst of the deal. Lacking openings in their fathers' trades, and lacking the qualifications for the new industries, they were relegated to jobs as vanboys, office boys, packers, warehousemen, etc., and long spells out of work. More and more people, young and old, had to travel out of the community to their jobs, and some eventually moved out to live elsewhere, where suitable work was to be found. The local economy as a whole contracted, became less diverse. The only section of the community which was unaffected by this was dockland, which retained its position in the labour market, and with it, its traditions of militancy. It did not, though, remain unaffected by the breakdown of the pattern of integration in the East End as a whole, vis-à-vis its subcommunity structure. Perhaps this goes some way to explain the paradoxical fact that within the space of twelve months, the dockers could march in support of Enoch Powell, and take direct action for community control in the Isle of Dogs!

If someone should ask why the plan to 'modernise' the pattern of East End life should have been such a disaster, perhaps the only honest answer is that, given the macro-social forces acting on it, given the political, ideological, and economic framework within which it operated, the result was inevitable. For example many local people wonder why the new environment should be the way it is. The reasons are complex; they are political in so far as the system does not allow for any effective participation by the local working-class community in the decision making process at any stage or level of planning. The clients of the planners are simply the local authority or commercial developer who employs them. They are ideological in so far as the plans are unconsciously modelled on the structure of the middle-class environment, which is based on the concept of *property*, and *private ownership*, on individual differences of status, wealth etc.; whereas the structure of the working-class environment is based on the concept of community, or collective identity, common lack of ownership, wealth etc. Similarly needs were assessed on the norms of the middle-class nuclear family, rather than the extended working-class family etc. But underpinning both these sets of reasons lie the basic economic factors involved in comprehensive redevelopment. Quite simply – faced with the task of financing a large housing programme, the local authorities were forced to borrow large amounts of capital, and also to design schemes which would attract capital investment to the area. This means that they have to borrow at the going interest rates, which in this country are very high, and that to subsidise housing, certain of the best sites have to be earmarked for commercial developers. A further and perhaps decisive factor is the cost of land, since very little of it is publicly owned and land values rise as the area develops.

All this means that planners have to reduce the cost of production to a minimum, through the use of capital intensive techniques – prefabricated and standardised components, allowing for semi-automated processes in construction. The attraction of high rise developments (tower blocks outside the trade) is not only that they meet these requirements, but they allow for certain economies of scale, such as the input costs of essential services, which can be grouped around a central core. As to 'non essential' services i.e. ones that don't pay, such as playspace, community centres, youth clubs and recreational facilities, these often have to be sacrificed to the needs of commercial developers, who of course have quite different priorities. Perhaps the best example of this happening is the notorious St Catherine's Dock Scheme. This major contribution towards solving the East End's housing problem includes a yachting marina, a luxury hotel, luxury apartment blocks, and various cultural amenities for their occupants plus – a small section of low income accommodation, presumably to house the families of the low paid staff who will service the luxury amenities. And lest anyone becomes too sentimental about the existing site, Telfords warehouses etc., it should be mentioned that the original development was by the East India Company in the early nineteenth century, involved the destruction of the homes of thousands of poor families in the area, and met with such stiff opposition from them that it eventually required an Act of Parliament to get the scheme approved!

The situation facing East Enders at present, then, is not new. When the first tenements went up in the nineteenth century they raised the same objections from local people, and for the same very good reasons, as their modern counterparts – the tower blocks. What *is* new is that in the nineteenth century the voice of the community was vigorous and articulate on these issues, whereas today, just when it needs it most the community is faced with a crisis of indigenous leadership.

The reasons for this are already implicit in the analysis above. The labour aristocracy, traditional source of leadership, has virtually disappeared along with the artisan mode of production. At the same time there has been a split in consciousness between the spheres of production and consumption. More and more East Enders are forced to work outside the area; young people especially are less likely to follow family traditions in this respect. As a result the issues of the work place are no longer experienced as directly linked to community issues. Of course there has always been a 'brain drain' of the most articulate, due to social mobility. But not only has this been intensified as a result of the introduction of comprehensive schools, but the recruitment of fresh talent from the strata below – i.e. from the ranks of the respectable working class, has also dried up. For this strata, traditionally the social cement of the community is also in a state of crisis.

The economic changes which we have already described, also affected their position and as it were *de-stabilised* it. The 'respectables' found themselves caught and pulled apart by two opposed pressures of social mobility – downwards, into the ranks of the new suburban working-class elite. And more than any other section of the working class they were caught in the middle of the two dominant, but contradictory ideologies of the day: the ideology of spectacular consumption, promoted by the mass media, and the traditional ideology of production, the so called work ethic which centred on the idea that a man's dignity, his manhood, even, was measured by the quantity or quality of his effort in production. If this strata began to split apart it was because their existing position had become untenable. Their bargaining power in the labour market was threatened by the introduction of new automated techniques, which eliminated many middle range, semi-skilled jobs. Their economic position excluded them from entering the artificial paradise of the new consumer society; at the same time changes in the production process itself have made the traditional work ethic, the pride in the job, impossible to uphold. They had the worst of all possible worlds.

Once again this predicament was registered most deeply in and on the young. But here an additional complicating factor intervenes. We have already described the peculiar strains imposed on the 'nucleated' working-class family. And their most critical impact was in the area of parent/child relationships. What had previously been a source of support and security for both, now became something of a battleground, a major focus of all the anxieties created by the disintegration of community structures around them. One result of this was to produce an increase in early marriage. For one way of escaping the claustrophobic tensions of family life, was to start a family of your own! And given the total lack of accommodation for young single people in the new developments, as well as the conversion of cheap rented accommodation into middle-class owner occupied housing, the only practicable way to leave home was to get married. The second outcome of generational conflict (which may appear to go against the trend of early marriage, but in fact reinforced it) was the emergence of specific youth subcultures in opposition to the parent culture. And one effect of this was to weaken the links of historical and cultural continuity, mediated through the family, which had been such a strong force for solidarity in the working-class community. It is perhaps not surprising that the parent culture of the respectable working class, already in crisis was the most 'productive' vis-à-vis subcultures; the internal conflicts of the parent culture came to be worked out in terms of generational conflict. What I think seems to happen is that one of the functions of generational conflict is to decant the kinds of tensions which appear face to face in the family and replace them by a generational specific symbolic system so that the tension is taken out of the interpersonal context and placed in a collective context, and mediated through various stereotypes which have the function of defusing the anxiety that interpersonal tension generates.

It seems to me that the latent function of subculture is this – to express and resolve, albeit 'magically', the contradictions which remain hidden or unresolved in the parent culture. The succession of subcultures which this parent culture generated can thus all be considered as so many variations on a central theme – the contradiction, at an ideological level, between traditional working-class puritanism, and the new hedonism of consumption; at an economic level between a future as part of the socially mobile elite, or as part of the new lumpen. Mods, Parkers, Skinheads, Crombies, all represent, in their different ways, an attempt to retrieve some of the socially cohesive elements destroyed in their parent culture, and to combine these with elements selected from other class fractions, symbolising one or other of the options confronting it.

It is easy enough to see this working in practice if we remember that subcultures are symbolic structures, and must not be confused with the actual kids who are their bearers and supports. Secondly a given life style is actually made up of a number of symbolic subsystems, and it is the way these are articulated in the total life style which constitutes its distinctiveness. There are basically four subsystems – and these can be divided into the relatively 'plastic' forms – dress and music, which are not directly produced by the subculture, but which are selected and invested with subcultural value in so far as they express its underlying thematic; and then the more 'infrastructural' forms – argot, and ritual, which are more resistant to innovation but of course reflect changes in the more plastic forms. I'm suggesting here that Mods, Parkers, Skinheads, Crombies are a succession of subcultures which all correspond to the same parent culture and which attempt to work out through a system of transformations, the basic problematic or contradiction which is inserted in the subculture by the parent culture. So you can distinguish three levels in the analysis of subcultures; one is historical analysis which isolates the specific problematic of a particular class fraction, in this case, the respectable working class; and secondly a structural or semiotic analysis of the subsystems and the way they are articulated and the actual transformations which those subsystems undergo from one subcultural moment to another; and thirdly the phenomenological analysis of the way the subculture is actually lived out by those who are the bearers and supports of the subculture. No real analysis of subculture is complete without all those levels being in place.

To go back to the diachronic string we are discussing, the original mod life style could be interpreted as an attempt to real-ise, *but in an imaginary relation* the conditions of existence of the socially mobile white collar worker. While their argot and ritual forms stressed many of the traditional values of their parent culture, their dress and music reflected the hedonistic image of the affluent consumer. The life style crystallised in opposition to the rockers (viz the famous riots in the early 1960s) and it seems to be a law of subcultural evolution that its dynamic comes not only from the relations to its own parent culture, but from the relation to subcultures belonging to *other class fractions*, in this case the manual working class.

The next member of our string – the Parkers or Scooter boys were in some senses a transitional form between the mods and skinheads. The alien elements introduced into music and dress by the Mods were progressively de-stressed and the indigenous components of argot and ritual re-asserted as the matrix of subcultural identity. The Skinheads themselves carried the process to completion. Their life style in fact represents a systematic inversion of the Mods – whereas the Mods explored the upwardly mobile option, the Skinheads explored the lumpen. Music and dress again became the central focus of the life style; the introduction of reggae (the protest music of the West Indian poor) and the 'uniform' (of which more in a moment) signified a reaction against the contamination of the parent culture by middle-class values, and a re-assertion of the integral values of working-class culture – through its most recessive traits – its puritanism and chauvinism. This double movement gave rise to a phenomenon sometimes called 'machismo' – the unconscious dynamics of the work ethic translated into the out of work situation; the most dramatic example of this was the epidemic of 'queer bashing' around the country in 1969/70. The skinhead uniform itself could be interpreted as a kind of caricature of the model worker – the self image of the working class as distorted through middle-class perceptions; a metastatement about the whole process of social mobility. Finally the skinhead life style crystallised in opposition both to the greasers (successors to the rockers) and the hippies – both subcultures representing a species of hedonism which the Skinheads rejected.

Following the Skinheads there emerged another transitional form variously known as Crombies, casuals, suedes etc. (the proliferation of names being a mark of transitional phases). They represent a movement back towards the original mod position, although this time it's a question of incorporating certain elements drawn from a middle-class *subculture* – the hippies, which the skinheads had previously ignored. But even though the Crombies etc. have adopted some of the external mannerisms of the hippy life style, viz dress, soft drug use, they still conserve many of the distinctive features of earlier versions of the subculture.

If the whole process as we've described it seems to be circular, forming a closed system, then this is because subculture, by definition, cannot break out of the contradiction derived from the parent culture, it merely transcribes its terms at a micro-social level, and inscribes them in an imaginary set of relations.

But there is another reason. Apart from its particular, thematic, contradiction, every subculture shares a general contradiction, which is inherent in its very conditions of existence. Subculture invests the weak points in the chain of socialisation, between the family/school nexus, and integration into the work process which marks the resumption of the patterns of the parent culture for the next generation. But subculture is also a compromise solution, between two contradictory needs: the need to create and express *autonomy and difference* from parents, and by extension, their culture; and the need to maintain the security of existing ego defences, and the *parental identifications* which support them. For the initiate subculture provides a means of 'rebirth' without having to undergo the pain of symbolic death. The autonomy it offers is thus both real, but partial, and illusory, as a total 'way of liberation'. And far from constituting an improvised *rite de passage* into adult society, as some anthropologists have claimed, it is a collective and highly ritualised defence against just such a transition. And because defensive functions predominate ego boundaries become cemented to subcultural boundaries. In a real sense subcultural conflict (i.e. greasers versus Skinheads, Mods versus rockers) serves as a displacement of generational conflict, both at a cultural level, and at an interpersonal level within the family. One consequence of this is to artificially foreclose the natural trajectory of adolescent revolt. For the kids who are caught up in the internal contradictions of a subculture, what began as a break in the continuum of social control, can easily become a permanent hiatus in their lives. Although there is a certain amount of subcultural mobility i.e. kids evolving from Mods to Parkers, or even switching subcultural affiliations, greasers 'becoming' skinheads, there are no career prospects as such! There are two possible solutions; one leads out of subculture into early marriage, and as we've said for working-class kids this is the normal solution. Alternatively subcultural affiliation can provide a way in to membership of one of the deviant subgroups, which exist in the margins of subculture, often adopt its protective coloration, but which nevertheless are not structurally dependent on it; such groups as pushers, petty criminals, junkies, even homosexuals.

This leads us into another contradiction inherent in subculture. Although as a symbolic structure it *does* provide a diffuse sense of affinity in terms of a common life style, it does not in itself prescribe any crystallised group structure. We believe that it is through the function of *territoriality* that subculture becomes anchored in the collective reality of the kids who are its bearers, and who in this way become not just its passive support, but its conscious agents. Territoriality is simply the process through which environmental boundaries (and foci) are used to signify group boundaries (and foci) and become invested with a subcultural value. This is the function of football teams for the Skinheads, for example. Territoriality is thus not only a way in which kids live subculture as a collective behaviour, but the way in which the subcultural group becomes rooted in the situation of its community. In the context of the East End it is a way of retrieving the solidarities of the traditional neighbourhood, destroyed by redevelopment. The existence of communal space is reasserted as the common pledge of group unity – you belong to the Mile End mob in so far as the Mile End belongs to you. Territoriality appears as a magical way of expressing ownership; for the Mile End is not owned by the people but by the property developers. Territorial division therefore appears within the subculture, and in the East End mirrors many of the traditional divisions of subcommunities: Bethnal Green – Hoxton – Mile End – Whitechapel – Balls Pond Road etc. Thus in addition to conflict between subcultures, there also exists conflict within them, on a territorial basis. Both these forms of conflict can be seen as displacing or weakening the dynamics of generational conflict, which is in turn, a displaced form of the traditional parameters of class conflict.

I want to look briefly at the different kinds of solidarity a working-class community generates and how this relates to what I have said earlier. When we talk about the territorial conflict, when Mile End goes up against Hoxton, for instance, some sociologists have tried to explain this by the concept of the 'urban village'; that the solidarity that characterises traditional working-class communities is very rigid, local and defensive. I don't think this really works however. What is it that is called an urban village then? A village can be defined as a community in which all social activities are equally accessible to all the inhabitants, and institutions are simple undifferentiated structures; although social divisions exist, they remain sublimated to the loyalties to the locality; due to its isolation and low density the village operates a rigidly defensive solidarity, a structured exclusion of anything or anyone outside its immediate perceptions – what does not fit in is simply abolished from its social existence as part of the outside world, which for the village is seen as unknown and uniformly hostile and dangerous. In the early stages of industrialism when the capitalisation of agriculture and the development of factory production drove farm-labourers from the countryside into what were then new towns, they imported with them the community structures of the village as a form of defence against the social disorganisation produced. But the very concentration of the labour force, its separation from the means of production, and its consequent atomisation, generated a new solidarity, a class solidarity which found its organisation expressed in the growth of Trade Unions. Class solidarity at the point of production in turn transformed community structures outside the factory; village consciousness with its narrow loyalties dissolved into wider and more complex forms. Although the term 'urban village' is appropriate for these new towns in the early period of the industrial revolution and still today where you have communities dominated by a single industry composed of a culturally homogenous group drawn from surrounding districts, for example mill-towns and mining villages, it's not appropriate to the vast majority of modern working-class communities and certainly not appropriate to the East End, for the working-class community is defined outside itself by the position of its members in the productive process. It is the mark of this process that it acts completely impartially drawing in widely diverse ethnic and cultural groups considered under the sole denomination as abstract interchangeable units of labour power, so that in major conurbations this results in a highly diverse mixture of social groups and here community structures evolve with particular intensity as a way of negotiating differences between these groups. It's where there's a tendency for these social groups to regress historically back into an early 'urban village' ideology.

At any rate it is in the light of this complex of factors that the recent outburst of 'paki-bashing' by skinheads in the East End has to be understood. There has been a lot of nonsense talked about a 'new Fascist youth group', racism in the working class, interventions by the National Front and the like. Much of this wild talk could be dispelled simply by pointing out that many of the skinhead groups involved in the attacks were in fact led by West Indian kids, and that the music and argot of Skinheads has been positively influenced by the presence of the West Indian community. It is not a question of racial prejudice then, in the simple sense of white against black. In fact it is a question of the discrimination of a white subculture between two different immigrant subcommunities. So what is the specific difference between the West Indian community and the Pakistani vis-à-vis this subculture? Once it is put like this the problem is easy. The West Indian community possess a subcultural identity and status which the Pakistani community do not. They have established their credentials on a number of criteria – through their aggressive rejection of middle-class values and institutions (e.g. the police), their 'machismo'; all this constitutes so many points of contact with the Skinheads. And further, their culture, music, argot etc. is both highly expressive and esoteric, and lends itself to adoption or adaptation by other groups. The parent culture of the Pakistani community, whether from the East or the West, lacks these attributes. It is basically esoteric, centring on religious rituals, food taboos, etc.; and the traditional values system includes a pattern of deference to authority, middle-class aspirations in terms of status etc., and a generally 'entrepreneurial' attitude to the world; the very features which the Skinheads implicitly refuse. To this was added a territorial factor. The Pakistanis moved into the area of the East End previously occupied by the Jewish community. And on certain critical dimensions there is a point by point correspondence between the two cultures. It was not too difficult then for the subculture to carry over the latent hostility of their parent culture to the presence of the Jewish community, (which dated from a period prior to its integration as a component part of East End life) on to a new pariah group. And the original deference of the Pakistanis made them an ideal target for the working out of skinhead machismo. Even more decisively the arrival of the Pakistanis coincided with the large scale redevelopment of the East End, the breakdown of its traditional pattern of social integration. Perhaps it was inevitable that the new arrivals would be blamed by local people as the cause of the destruction of their traditional community, and become the focus of all the secret fears, and resentment this brought about, and also destruction of foci of social interaction between the established and outsiders means that outsiders are reference groups, perceived in terms of social stereotypes. What we have been describing in all this is the formation of a working-class ghetto; the emergence of subcultures was one response to this situation amongst young people. Another, closely allied to it might be called the 'delinquent solution'.

I think it's important to make a distinction here between subcultures and delinquency, for many criminologists talk of delinquent subcultures. In fact they talk about anything that is not middle-class culture as subculture. From my point of view, I do not think the middle class produces subcultures for subcultures are produced by a dominated culture not by a dominant culture. I am trying to work out the way that subcultures have altered the pattern of working-class delinquency. But now I want to look at the delinquent aspect.

For during this whole period there was a spectacular rise in the delinquency rates in the area, even compared with similar areas in other parts of the country. The highest increase was in offences involving attacks on property – vandalism, hooliganism of various kinds, taking and driving away cars. At the simplest level this can be interpreted as some kind of protest against the general dehumanisation of the environment, an effect of the loss of the informal social controls generated by the old neighbourhoods etc. The delinquency rate also of course reflected the level of police activity in the area, and the progressively worsening relations between young people and the forces of law and order. Today in fact the traditional emnity has become something more like a scenario of urban guerilla warfare!

There are many ways of looking at delinquency. One way is to see it as the expression of a system of transactions between young people and various agencies of social control, in the subcultural context of territoriality. One advantage of this definition is that it allows us to make a conceptual distinction between delinquency and deviancy, and to reserve this last term for groups which crystallise around a specific counter-ideology and even career structure which cuts across age grade and often community or class boundaries e.g. prostitutes, professional criminals, revolutionaries; while there is an obvious relation between the two, delinquency often serving as a means of recruitment into deviant groups, the distinction is still worth making.

Delinquency can be seen as a form of communication about a situation of contradiction in which the 'delinquent' is trapped, but whose complexity is ex-communicated from his perceptions by virtue of the restricted linguistic code which working-class culture makes available to him. Such a code despite its richness and concreteness of expression, does not allow the speaker to make verbally explicit the rules of relationship, and implicit value systems which regulate interpersonal situations, since this operation involves the use of complex syntactical structures, and a certain degree of conceptual abstraction not available through this code. This is especially critical when the situations are institutional ones, where the rules of relationship are often contradictory, denied, or disguised, but nevertheless binding on the speaker. For the working-class kid this applies to his family – where the positional rules of extended kinship reverberate against the personalised rules of its new nuclear structure; in the school where middle-class teachers operate a whole series of linguistic and cultural controls which are 'dissonant' with those of his family and peers, but whose mastery is implicitly defined as the index of intelligence of achievement, at work where the mechanisms of exploitation (extraction of surplus value, capital accumulation) are screened off from perception by the apparently free exchange of so much labour time for so much money wage. In lieu of a working-class ideology which is both accessible, and capable of providing a concrete interpretation of such contradictions . . . what can a poor boy do? Delinquency is one way he can communicate, can represent by analogy and through non-verbal channels the dynamics of some of the social configurations he is locked into. And if the content of this communication remains largely 'unconscious' then it's because as Freud would say, it is 'overdetermined'. For what is being communicated is not one, but *two different* systems of rules: one belonging to the sphere of object relations, and the laws of symbolic production, more specifically the parameters of oedipal conflict; the second belonging to property relations, the laws of material production, and more specifically the parameters of class conflict. Without going into this too deeply, I would suggest that where there is an extended family system the oedipal conflict is displaced from the triadic situation to sibling relations which then develops into the gang outside the family. When this begins to break down the reverse process sets in, and is twofold in the study of the structural relations for the emergence of subcultures. One, the changes in the parameters of class conflict brought about by advanced technology where you have a certain class consensus between certain parent cultures and that level of conflict appears to be invisible or acted on in various dissociated ways; and secondly the parameters of oedipal conflict are becoming re-placed into the family context but refracted through the peer group situation. It's a kind of double inversion which needs to be looked at not just in terms of a Marxist theory which would analyse it simply in terms of class conflict and the development of antagonistic class fractions, simply vertically syphoning down into another generational situation; *nor* can it be analysed simply in psychoanalytic terms, through the dynamics of oedipal conflict in adolescence. We need to look at the historical ways in which class conflict and the dynamics of oedipal conflict have undergone transformation and interlock, reverberating against each other.

In delinquency it's a question of a double transgression of the Law, but the difference of these two levels isn't observed in the communication – they are compressed and refracted through each other. All very confusing. And matters aren't helped by the fact that while the delinquent's linguistic code may remain intact, it only serves to inhibit him from assuming and communicating the secret rationality of his actions. Instead his nonverbal behaviour is inserted into quite different communication contexts (court procedures, counselling by social workers etc.) which function either to totally deprive it of rationality (delinquency as madness) or else superimpose a totally false rationality (delinquency as badness). All this adds up to saying that working-class kids are locked in a prison whose walls are invisible because they are made up of institutional processes. Delinquency is both a way of materialising these invisible constraints, and symbolising their invisibility, while simultaneously maintaining their dissociation in consciousness. We might say that the latent function of the police, through their constant presence on the streets, is to become the tangible representation of the very institutional process which the kids cannot focus and resist at their correct (i.e. institutional) level. For the police represent both a direct threat to the territorial integrity of the subcultural group, and the indirect threat of The Institution as such (Approved Schools, Borstals, Detention Centres etc.) which lies behind and supports them, acting at a distance through their presence. For it is these secondary institutions which in our society, formalise and make explicit, the rules and social controls which are elsewhere, in the family, school, work situations implicit and diffuse. But this means that the police themselves are caught up in a situation of contradiction, one which their operating ideology only reinforces, and which the restricted code of the working class recruits who form the lower echelons, and thus confront the kids daily on the street, equally prevents them from perceiving. For the police are neither in or of *this world*, the actual, historical world of the working-class community from which they were originally recruited; nor are they in or of the *other world*, the closed, ahistorical world of The Institution. They belong partly to both and totally to neither; in effect they *mediate* between the two. And if they are the object of such conflicting emotions, at once an abomination and a source of secret fascination, then an anthropologist would say it was because they are by definition an ambiguous social category. But if this is true, it is the effect of a real, objective contradiction in their role. For at one moment they are called upon to perform a community function as a kind of global resource person – directing traffic, providing local information, intervening in everyday emergencies such as lost kids, fires, accidents etc. We might call this their *expressive* function; it derives from the community, and, as we've seen was until recently still partly carried out by local people themselves. But at the next moment they are called upon to carry out what can only be called their *repressive* function – so called law and order, as agents of the State, and of the dominant class whose interests the State protects. In police ideology the first function is mobilised to cover the second; and at the level of popular perceptions this leads to the schizoid idealisation of the 'good cop' e.g. Dixon of Dock Green and the 'bent cop' alias P.C. Pulley. It's easy to see then why the relations between the man on the beat and the kid on the street should be so vicious. Since each for the other is by definition a pariah, an excresence on the community, a social abomination, and each encounter between the two only confirms the perceptions of both. The transactions between them which produce 'delinquency' really do form a system, since it is a question of a two-way process of scapegoating, and at a certain level, not without a degree of (unconscious) collusion. The only difference is that the police have the power to enforce their definition of reality whereas the kids do not.

There are other solutions to the 'ghettoising' process. One might be called the 'academic' solution: the flight of a section of working-class kids from their community through the channels of social mobility organised by the educational system. But this creates its own problems. One of the things this involves is the cultivation of an inviolable inner space from which to organise the rejection of the social space dominated by working-class subculture, and the adoption of an alternative social space, that of the educated middle-class, as the locus of identity. But this is a very precarious operation. For the working-class kid who makes it to the grammar school, or the academic stream of his comprehensive may find himself caught between two irreconcilable worlds – on one side his family and the friends he grew up with, and on the other the school. It's not just that the language, culture, values and so on of both are contradictory, but that he may become radically estranged from both. He is no longer at home with his parents or the local gang; but he is not quite the same as the other middle-class kids at school or the teachers. There can be a cross tug of loyalties both in relation to adult models, and to his peers. Perhaps the situation is most intense within the family itself. For at one level, his parents may be sending across messages saying how proud they are of him, how he must struggle to do even better etc.; and at another level they may be saying 'you are no longer our son since you went to that school, you look down on us, after all we've done for you etc.' etc. These messages don't of course have to be verbal or explicit and they can always be denied. The potentialities for games of emotional blackmail, double binding and the like, in such a situation don't have to be stressed. And if, surrounded by ambivalence on all fronts, the kid himself starts to 'underachieve' (current euphemism for the failure to compete successfully!) then the spiral of incrimination and recrimination may get even tighter. Parents and teachers may blame each other or the kid, the kid may blame himself exclusively or everyone but himself etc., etc. At the worst the kid may retreat totally into the inner sanctum of his ego, and renounce any purchase at all on social space. And/or he may resort to isolated acts of rebellion at home or at school. In any event whether he has an official breakdown or not, he is likely to drop out of school at 15 or 16. However, and especially if he is at a comprehensive, there is a happier solution. He may well gravitate to a 'hippy' subculture within the school, which will provide a viable social space, outside the culture of both family and school, where he can begin to get some purchase on his own identity as well as break out of his social isolation. While this may well mean that he becomes permanently estranged both from traditional working-class culture, and from middle-class aspirations, and in fact encourage him to drop out of school, at least if he does, he has an alternative to drop out into.

There are other retreatist solutions associated with working-class kids who for various reasons become isolated from their peers – notably entry into deviant groups; for example homosexuals and junkies, despite their pariah status within the working-class community can achieve a certain measure of security in such groups. Perhaps it is not surprising that the last five years has seen the emergence both of a flourishing gay scene and of hard drug addiction in the East End. We are not implying a causal relation – a lot of people have suggested that the junkies may be repressed homosexuals, but no-one has so far suggested that gay people are repressed junkies! – but it is interesting that kids from high communication backgrounds and families in flight (i.e. socially mobile) are over-represented in both these groups. And there is evidence that when the extended family 'goes nuclear' it does tend to give rise to the type of oedipal constellation which is likely to produce a narcissistic crisis in the child, which in turn motivates the kind of self consciousness which is likely to enlarge his powers of communication; this in turn orients the child toward academic success in school, further isolating him from his peers, and causing the kind of stress we've already described. As a result he may gravitate toward a dropout culture, where of course deviant groups, such as junkies and gays, are both tolerated and accessible, and there in late adolescence he may find the solution which answers to his original object choice.

Perhaps such trajectories should be called not 'retreatist', but revenge solutions. This is certainly no simple causal chain; rather as a result of a complex social and historical process (the initial situation of the child in the family, of the family in its community, of the comunity in the overall class structure, and ultimately of the political economy of the society in the world system) a human child is inserted into an unconscious problematic, whose dynamics in turn generate a series of secondary social processes, which, meshing in with the first, progressively narrows down his real life options. But if prediction at an individual level is impossible, prevention at a social level is not.

So far we've described the kinds of solution which young people in the East End have tended to adopt. However, the parent culture has also taken up positions. The first certainly qualifies as retreatist and has been too often described to need much comment – family centredness, the withdrawal from public involvement into areas of purely private concern, more personal investment in children, growth of hobbies, domestic status symbols and so on. What has been less noticed is the counter movement to all this – the growth of the tenants association movement. A tenants association is by definition an extended network of families. It is an attempt to redevelop involvement in community politics, even if this remains limited to domestic issues; it is a way of transcending the family while remaining within it. And although the movement has so far been unable to break out of this contradiction, and become – dare we say it – the democratic base of decision making in the working-class community; still its very existence is a hopeful sign for the future.

In this section we've described some of the attempts by East Enders to improvise solutions to the spin off problems created by official solutions to the endemic poverty of the area. We have criticised the official approach as being largely symptomatic, and in certain respects creating more problems than it solved. Nevertheless we don't want to counterpose to this a romantic image of the good old days, when everyone spoke cockney, wore cloth caps, ate pies and mash twice a day and spent their evening doing knees up mother brown in the local pub. The East End community grew out of the desperate struggle to survive the most brutalising conditions, and many of the responses were equally brutal. The strengths of the East Ender could also be weaknesses, an insularity, a narrow sectarian loyalty, which precluded any wider solidarity. And recently as the traditional community structures began to disintegrate we have seen the re-assertion of some of these more reactionary traits in a form of negative militancy. Many of the spontaneous solutions *were* clearly self-defeating. But some of them, and anyone who reads between the lines can guess which we mean, do seem to contain, at least in embryo the real and only solution: a greater degree of autonomy in the hands of the working-class community. And it may well be that in the long term, the irruption of macro-social forces into the community will give rise to a wider and more politically articulate consciousness, and to organisations, which while still rooted in the local situation are also responsive to national issues. However there are also forces which militate against this. For as the new problems began to emerge, both as a result of re-development, and of the communities' response to it, so a whole new series of interventions were consciously evolved to deal with them. And in the next section we are going to examine some of them briefly, to see how far they represented part of a possible solution, and how far they merely aggravated the existing problems.

Some interventions

Interventions broadly fell into two categories – political work and social work; let's look at each in turn.

Political work itself breaks down into two sub-species. The first of these is the avowedly reformist parliamentary approach, which in the East End is represented by the Labour Party, with the CP trailing a bad second. Whether the ruling ideology is Fabianism or neo-Stalinism the result is the same in both cases – a programme of rule by enlightened bureaucrats coupled with a trade union consciousness which confines the struggle to purely defensive positions within the existing framework of capitalist society. The Labour Party and CP do occasionally attempt to mobilise local people on community issues, but only in so far as this serves the national electoral interests of their respective organisations. Once the votes are in, the local militancy which has been generated is carefully diffused. The only historical exception to this rule was possibly the early period of George Lansbury's career in the East End, although his subsequent career, and that of the local Labour Party shows that the exception proves the rule. It should no longer perhaps be surprising that the Labour council (and the CP) should back a re-development scheme such as the one at St. Catherine's Docks, or that they should refuse to negotiate with family squatters. There is no better evidence of the local inertia created by the Labour Party organisation in the area, than the fact that, although Tower Hamlets is one of the safest parliamentary seats for Labour in the country, it has the record for the lowest percentage turnout at local elections of any borough in London.

The other wing of political work is avowedly 'revolutionary'; it consists of a number of small competing vanguard sects – maoists, trotskyists, leninists, who have all rejected the 'parliamentary road to socialism' and all claim to be the authentic voice of the working class. But despite the revolutionary fervour of their manifestoes, their programme in practice appears suspiciously similar to those of the reformist organisations they so bitterly denounce. They also stir up local issues, not of course to collect votes, but to collect supporters for their particular brand of the 'correct line'. And again once roused local militancy is quickly channelled off into organisational rituals; concrete action is postponed until 'after the revolution' or such time as the 'objective situation', as defined by the party, is right. If any spontaneous movement does develop, then it is encouraged as long as it can be manipulated and controlled by party members. It is hard not to be bitter when one sees the ruthless cynicism and blind stupidity with which such policies of so called entrism are pursued. To take one example. Over the last couple of years a strong tenants' movement developed in the East End triggered by the GLC rent increases. A particular trotskyist group decided to move in; within a month they had succeeded in infiltrating and winning the majority of associations over to their political line. This was purely legalistic, and involved fighting a number of test cases through the courts. It was a strategy, of course, which as middle-class intellectuals they had the knowledge and the resources to direct and pursue, whereas local people did not. The test cases took two years to fight through all the courts. During this time a halt was called to any further action, or development of the movement. Inevitably the situation went cold. When the court case was finally lost, the whole movement literally disintegrated. Having seen their line fail, and the movement die on them, the trotskyists then pulled out condemning the tenants' leaders for a 'lack of political consciousness'! Unfortunately this cautionary tale could be reproduced many times over.

In fact political work in the East End has invariably produced the reverse effect to what it intended. Instead of making local people more politically conscious of the issues around them, it has actively *de-politicised* them; time after time the most militant among the local people become disillusioned, and withdraw into private areas of involvement, family life etc. For despite their different aims and ideologies, both the parliamentary and the vanguard parties are appealing to an abstract collectivity – the working class, the proletariat, or even the 'masses'. If they never get any real support, perhaps it's because no-one likes being treated as the symbol of someone else's myth! It's not just that their strategies of intervention fail to relate to the everyday problems of ordinary people in the community, but that from their position they do not, and cannot understand what the community itself is all about. They see it as an undifferentiated whole, whereas, as we've seen from the inside, it is a highly complex structure, made up of a number of subcommunities, each with its own history and divided, not just against each other, but within themselves. The working-class community becomes a community to the extent it *becomes* working class. But this unity has to be constructed in practice – it is not something that can be assumed in theory.

In a way the very failures of political work provided the ground for the development of social work in the area. For what is social work about if it is not caring for the individual needs and problems of the people, which political workers neglected. If one concentrates on attacking the political and economic causes of social problems, then the other concentrates exclusively in treating the ideological effects. It could be said that both have got hold of different ends of the same wrong stick. Historically though current social work developed in the context of the post war welfare state. Just as the British economy underwent modernisation during and after the war, so too did the political structures. There emerged what might be called the economic and ideological branches of the State apparatus. Taking shape during the emergency conditions of state control during wartime, they only began to bear fruit in the early 1950s. The state educational system and the new statutory social and welfare services must be considered part of this development, as agencies of social control, whose function is partly economic, but chiefly ideological. It was inevitable that much of the theoretical training which the new generation of teachers and social workers received, reflected at its own level and applied to their own particular fields, the kind of bureaucratic rationality which regulates all branches of the state apparatus. Whatever the idiom – whether one tested or adjusted to reality, tried positive or negative reinforcement, deferred gratification or socially integrated – the message was basically the same – in the red corner the 'individual' who was plastic, or unstable, and in the blue something called 'Society' which was a stable self-regulating system. Successful socialisation simply meant going from one corner to another – the 'individual' becoming 'society'. Voluntary agencies, although at first they resisted this trend, eventually followed suit and adopted the new 'professionalism' and the magic battery of techniques which went with it. And it is true they had a new job to do. For as the institutions of mutual aid and informal social control, organic to the traditional working-class community (neighbourhoods, extended family, etc.) began to crumble, the professional agencies with which they initially equipped themselves could not have been better calculated to complete the process of demoralisation.

All this is most clearly seen in the earliest of the social work enterprises which dominated the field until the early 1960s – casework – and group counselling. It is hard to describe these techniques without making them sound like something out of Alice in Wonderland. Basically the trained caseworker (or group counsellor) was equipped with two main weapons – a log book of interpretations derived from a mishmash of ego psychology, group dynamics, popular sociology and naive common sense, and a vocabulary of attributions about the client (e.g. as socially inadequate, lacking insight, coping, problem family, drifting, delinquent, immature, etc., etc.) which were really old fashioned value judgements dressed up in pseudo scientific objectivity. In casework, the communication context itself becomes an explicit agency of social control. In this the caseworker is by definition the exclusive source of legitimate interpretations; the client's perceptions, in so far as they conflict with those of the caseworker, remain invalid. Now these 'interpretations' are a special kind of communication or rather meta-communication, which is intrinsic to the restricted code of the working-class client. For interpretations are simply verbally explicit statements about interpersonal rules of relationship; as we've seen meta-communication for the working-class client will be structured through quite different channels – through non-verbal analogic language. But in the context of casework this will simply be interpreted as 'compulsive acting out', a further symptom of the client's problem. Given the fact that the caseworker's style of communication is predefined as therapeutic and the client's as disturbed, it is possible that the client is only confirmed as 'gaining insight' to the extent he successfully alienates himself from his own culture. This can only happen because the initial context of the client/worker relationship, despite its subjective immediacy, is essentially *abstract*. Consider the following (real) exchange:

CLIENT: Mr Smith, can you lend us some money to help out with the gas bill. The Social Security people won't help and me old man says he dunno what to do about it. It's driving me frantic what with the worry and it's beginning to affect the kiddies.

WORKER: You know, Aileen, I can't give you money. It's your way of asking for the love you feel you didn't get as a child, or now from your husband. And perhaps behind this you feel guilty about your own inadequacy as a mother, your husband's failure to provide for the family. Perhaps we should try to work through this . . .

CLIENT: (getting angry, banging the table) I don't come here to be insulted or me old man by the likes of you. I'd like to see your wife manage on what I get for housekeeping, and with four kids and all.

WORKER: You must feel what I just said has some truth in it, or you wouldn't be trying to deny it so strongly.

Later at a case conference, involving four other agencies on this 'problem family' the worker explained that he had been trying to help his client work through her manic-depressive position, and by offering her interpretations rather than money to help her to integrate her internalised good and bad objects. The comments of the client herself are not, unfortunately, recorded. What happens in the face to face relationship is really an abstracting of a whole series of social processes which bring these two people together in the first place – abstraction of an individual from the family, of the family from the community, of the community from the class structure. All this suddenly becomes concrete in the 'problem' which appears as if locked inside the individual client or vice versa. Since the 'problem' cannot in fact be solved in the imaginary space of the casework situation, but only by acting in and on the real world it is difficult to see what useful insight the client can actually gain – apart from learning to 'tolerate the intolerable'. Despite, or perhaps because of its highly personalised approach, casework ends up by underpinning the impersonal norms of bureaucratic society. Although some caseworkers tried to get over this by becoming more 'client centred' they could not break out of the basic contradictions of the approach.

As a result in the early 1960s a counter movement developed among social workers which stressed the very dimension of social reality which casework had ignored – namely *community* work. But this approach, like its predecessor, was largely vitiated because of its false working assumption. For the 'community' which was invoked as the new solution, was in practice co-extensive with the local 'establishment' which included the council, various branches of local government, and other statutory bodies, the church and so on. Now whether or not it ought to be the case, it is a sociological fact that the interests, values, and priorities of this 'official' community are different from, and sometimes openly in conflict with, those of the actual working-class community which it claims to represent, but which remains submerged beneath it. And when the official leaders appeal to 'the interests of the community' then we can be sure that they are really appealing to the particular interests of their own party or class, just as in the same way politicians appeal to the national interest. While this sleight of hand is relatively easy to see through at a national level, it is more difficult locally. And the various species of community work serve to mediate this confusion. Community service is the longest established form of community work and for good reasons. In many ways it simply represents a jazzed-up version of straightforward charity. But although it involves the traditional effort – privileged groups (e.g. students) doing good works for 'those less fortunate' it is now also used as a form of therapy for the dispossessed: whether voluntarily or compulsorily working-class kids (especially the bad boys) are co-opted to help those less fortunate etc., in the hope that through contact with the other (middle-class) volunteers, some of the virtues of the model citizen may rub off on them. Of course this doesn't often work, and it may go the other way – recently for example a group of student volunteers were caught with a group of local skinheads, nicking lead off a warehouse in Stepney! From the point of view of local authorities perhaps the advantage of this kind of community work is that it relieves them of additional expenses in certain fields of social welfare, notably for the aged. While it may give the volunteers the illusion of doing something useful, those on the receiving end tend to be more sceptical about its value. As one old lady put it, commenting on her outing to the country which had been organised by one such organisation 'it was very nice, and I'm very grateful, but it's not the same as when we all used to go – you know the whole street. They're not like . . . your own kind of people, you know, somehow they're different'.

A more sophisticated approach to the whole problem has emerged in the last few years, which goes under the name of *community development*. This approach is highly sensitive to the complex structures of the working-class community, and particularly to the relations between subcommunities. The strategy consists of developing community projects and other forms of aid, and encouraging the emergence of indigenous leadership groups. But the two are tied together in a special way. It might be called a carrot and whip approach. Grants and facilities are made available to local grass roots organisations, on condition they become 'responsible', and responsibility is defined in terms of co-option of their leaders into the official community. Thus by way of informal contact, and membership of committees, it is hoped that over time the hard edge will be rubbed off the local militants, and they will begin to appreciate the official viewpoint on the community's problems, as well as the advantages of their new position both for themselves and for their people. It is then hoped that this viewpoint in turn will filter down through them to the grass roots. A similar strategy is used to deal with conflict between subcommunities – as for example with the establishment of Community Relations Councils where it is hoped that harmony between representatives of each community at the top will somehow filter through to the streets. The success of community development largely depends on local conditions – the strength of grass roots organisations, their degree of militancy, the political integrity of their leaders. If the co-option is successful, and popular leaders become less militant in their overall demands in return for minor concessions from the local establishment (more playspace, another youth centre, etc.) then likely as not they will find themselves discredited among their own people, accused of selling out and the rest. Their usefulness to the official community, as sergeant majors to damp down possible unrest in the ranks, therefore declines in proportion as their respectability grows. However if they stick to their guns and refuse to compromise on their demands, then a confrontation can only result in which the official body itself becomes discredited, either demands are refused, producing mass resignations, or else the whole operation has to be quietly shelved. The story of Community Relations Councils, Neighbourhood Councils and the like amply illustrate the predicament of this approach.

There is one final branch of social work which is relevant to consider – youth work, which has developed alongside case work and community work and reflects them in its methods. The field that particularly concerns us is detached youth work, which emerged when it became apparent that the new subcultures were a more potent source of involvement for working-class kids than the traditional youth club. And this provides the operational set for this kind of youth work. A worker is detached from a given agency of social control – youth club, school, social work agency, attaches himself to a group who are 'unnattached' to any such agency, and through the contact and trust he establishes, tries to detach them from their present milieu and re-attach them to a milieu of social control e.g. by persuading them to go back home, or give themselves up if they are on the run, or get a job, join a youth club. If the worker's approach is casework-oriented, he will concentrate on an individual kid and in the context of a supportive relationship try to draw him away from the 'dangerous' milieu of the subculture, and into a 'healthier' company. In America, as we'd expect, they've got this down to a fine art. The technique is called 'stripping the onion'; the worker starts with the outer fringes of the gang, those least committed to it, and works inwards, peeling off members as he goes, through a variety of ploys. Finally he attacks the inner core, the leadership; having seen the whole group, which was the focus of their existence, crumble invisibly around them, these kids not unnaturally tend to blow up or break down. Their behaviour can then be seen, in retrospect, to have been the pathological cause of the whole group's existence, and a justification of the measure taken against it. Sociologists, since Merton, have a name for such methods – a self-fulfilling prophecy!

If the approach is community-oriented, and in this country after Seebohm, this is what it is officially supposed to be, then the working method is the opposite of the above. The worker makes contact with the leaders of the group first, and through them tries to draw the group as a whole off the street and into some kind of 'constructive' activity.

The last sentence contains the key to the whole enterprise. The anxiety which the 'unclubbables' arouse is due largely to the fact that more than other groups in the community, they tend to *hang about, doing nothing*, on the street. Thus in one stroke, they precipitate two of most secret paranoias induced in people who have had a middle-class upbringing (and this includes most social workers of course): 1) hanging about, doing nothing is something totally incomprehensible to many people, and a clear sign that There is Something Wrong; it's really just a variation on the old theme of The Devil mades Work for Idle Hands. But what appears to outsiders to be just mucking about, to the kids themselves is a natural and not unenjoyable way of spending the time, at least not as boring as school or work; in fact the kind of interactions which go on in these situations are more creative than is often supposed. 2) being out on the street has for some people all kinds of 'bad' connotations – prostitutes in doorways, tramps etc.; the street is seen as an alien, hostile environment, the world of the stranger and the lonely crowd. But for working-class kids, as we've seen, the street is a natural habitat, somewhere to play, meet friends, stop for a chat.

The police, unfortunately, share middle-class prejudices. Such groups of young people quickly become the focus of police activity. They are invariably seen as potential troublemakers, and hence continually moved on, stopped and searched, cautioned, and, at the first sign of resistance i.e. check, arrested. And the increasing delinquency rate which results merely endorses the official image of them as troublemakers. As a result such a group may find itself excluded from cafés and pubs in the area and resort to various forms of revenge which of course only tightens the net around them. It is their situation on the street which is their real 'crime', which makes them at once such a threat to the official community, and so vulnerable to attack from it. The spin off from this only confirms the orthodox youth service viewpoint – that kids must be as far as possible kept off the streets and given some kind of occupational therapy – in the form of canoe building, weight training, mountain climbing or the Duke of Edinburgh Award Scheme. It's not that there is anything wrong as such with these activities, but that they simply beg the question. Recently some detached workers have begun to realise this and to develop alternative environments – cafés, resource centres, which while less vulnerable than the street corner, fulfill many of its social functions. Unfortunately many of these projects turn into rather more informal situations of social control; by providing an artificial version of their natural habitat the hope is that the kids will become more accessible to social work techniques, and needless to say such projects are controlled by the social workers, rather than run by the kids themselves. Underlying even the most experimental of these projects is the notion that somehow subculture is a pathological phenomenon. The knots that some of them get into is well-illustrated in the following quotation, taken from the report of a project dealing with beats:

> The club is the first to use jazz and blues as a therapeutic agent. Although to its members it is just another jazz club, to the workers themselves, who all have a social work training, it is the therapeutic function which is the main concern!!!

On the whole detached workers have been unable to break out of this kind of contradiction, which is endemic to social work; they are caught in the middle between the conflicting interests and needs of their employers and their so called clients. If they appear to identify too much with one side, they lose the trust of the other; the best they can hope to do, as mediators, is to modify the attitudes and behaviour of both towards some kind of compromise or local detente; but given the basic imbalance in the situation, where one side – the employers – have the power of the official community behind them, whereas the other –

the kids, have no bargaining power at all except their nuisance value, such a solution inevitably tends to strengthen the position of the former; since with their nuisance value eliminated, the kids actually have lost the only card in their hand.

To sum up, both political and social work, despite their competition for the same clientele have more in common that their proponents would care to admit. And this is due to the fact that the position of both has remained essentially extrinsic to the working-class community, their solutions to its problems grafted on from outside. Both approaches are dominated by implicitly middle-class assumptions about the world, which are taken for granted to be either co-extensive with those of the working class, or the normative goal of its development. The effect of this in and on practice, is to *substitute* the actions and priorities of the social and political work organisations for those of the people they are supposed to serve. They remain agencies of social control in so far as their programmes are pre-emptive or preventive of the solutions improvised by the working-class community to its own problems. People are offered the spectacle of participation, the illusion of decision making in certain marginal details of their daily life, but no effective control over the major forces, and institutions which shape it.

In the last few years the limitations of both political and social work have become more and more apparent; and a new movement has begun to emerge – community action. Community action derives many of its methods from the respective strengths of the two traditional strategies, while it has also learnt from their respective failures. The movement is characterised by its stress on the collective self activity of the working class community, as the means to solve its problems; by the insistence that grass roots organisations should be democratically controlled, and that community leaders should be directly accountable to the people they represent; and finally by their willingness to challenge the legitimacy of the solutions proposed by the official community, and to contest its monopoly of power. In the bargaining process, the community activist sees himself more in the role of a shop steward, than a foreman (the social worker) or a trade union official (political worker). In fact there are certain similarities, both in means and ends, between the rank and file movement for worker participation in industry, and community action. The new community activists tend to be ex-political or social workers, or people who have been involved in the peace movement or so-called 'underground', and instinctively distrust the elitism of other approaches. As an example of the 'conversion process' perhaps we can cite the story of a probation officer in a busy department in East London. He notices that a number of his clients who were young mothers, with several children, came to him complaining of tiredness or depression. Several of them had previously been involved in shoplifting offences, when they were feeling down. But instead of spending six months working through 'intrapsychic dynamics' as a good caseworker should, he saw that the root of the problem was the lack of playspace in the area. They weren't anxiety neurotics, so much as housebound mums.

Note

1 I think perhaps I've overstated the extent to which the community structures have broken down, as this paper was originally the basis of a proposal for funding the Project.

24 Subcultural conflict and criminal performance in Fulham

Dick Hebdige

Introduction

Fulham is a small borough situated in South West London on the north bank of the Thames. It forms a kind of no man's land bounded in, on the one hand, by the wealthy and fashionable areas of Kensington, Putney and Chelsea, and, on the other, by the traditionally working-class boroughs of Wandsworth, Battersea, Shepherds Bush and Hammersmith.[1] For its size, it contains, therefore, a surprisingly diverse population and an extremely complex and varied culture. It is one of those uncertain cosmopolitan areas which only flourish in the decaying inner rings of Britain's big cities. Thus, the *Sunday Times* could refer in a comparatively recent article (January 25, 1970) to the 'slums of Fulham' and in a subsequent issue could carry a report of Prince Philip's latest game of polo in Hurlingham Park. The situation has been further complicated by two recent and conspicuous waves of immigration into the borough: the first was a result of the extensive redevelopment of the East End, undertaken after the war, which involved a major rehousing project in the new council estates of South London. The second came more recently as a result of exorbitant rents in the adjacent areas of Chelsea-end Kensington, which encouraged the more adventurous members of the professional classes to buy houses in Fulham's working-class communities and carry out extensive conversions. In addition to these influences, the West Indian community based in nearby Notting Hill has, since the early 1960s, contributed another more anomalous strain to this cultural polyphony. The effects of successive waves of immigration have registered subtly in both the changing physical appearance of the borough and in the transformed image it projects to the outside world. More disturbing still (for the local inhabitants at least), the changes resonate at the deeper cultural level.

The Fulham community is traditionally working-class, introverted and self-sufficient. The borough itself was famed for its market gardens which at least up until the 1920s provided the densely packed stalls of the street market at North End Road with a ready supply of vegetables. Even now, the occasional octogenarian is quoted in the *Fulham Chronicle* recollecting the Golden Age of Fulham when green fields were always within walking distance. Only the few narrow allotments which are still kept up in Bishops Park remain to testify to the continuance of this tradition. But if the fields have disappeared, then the market still thrives and the borough retains its fiercely independent character. The pubs still proliferate, the billiard hall stands lavatorial in green tiles, unregenerate and vaguely infamous at the foot of Putney Bridge and a pie-and-mash-and-jellied-eel emporium still serves its doubtful delicacies in an atmosphere of sweat and steam to the lunchtime clientele at Fulham Broadway. But, of course, the old patterns have been disrupted, and despite the cultivated insularity of the local residents, the outside world has come in different ways to Fulham and left its indelible marks across the culture.

Firstly, the two principal 'invasions' require separate considerations. A large number of the East Enders who were dispersed throughout South London during the 1950s found their way to the new high rise estates of Fulham and its environs. On the nearby Alton Estate in Roehampton where there was a ratio of 100 people per acre, families converged from as far afield as Paddington and Stepney, Shepherds Bush and even Scotland, all speaking their slightly different languages, all carrying their slightly different cultures on a microcosmic scale inside the family itself. In the final analysis, these influences were assimilated without too much difficulty, the East Enders and the Fulhamites proving reasonably compatible. Nonetheless, there were times when relations were a little more strained.

In September 1969, a group of boys from the Alton Estate beat a homosexual to death on the edge of Wimbledon Common. During the controversy which followed (over the 'skinhead-menace' and the problems of high rise living), the relationship between the new council estates and the older, more established working-class community was reviewed critically. An article appeared in *The Sunday Times* (February 7, 1971)[2] which more or less debated the proposition put forward by Ken Patridge, one of the L.C.C. architects responsible for Roehampton's 'concrete jungle', that: 'If Roehampton Lane had been the Fulham Road this may not have happened'.

Mr. James Hammond, the father of one of the boys involved, pointed out that eleven of the fourteen boys who had been implicated in the incident came from 'that side of the estate' which contained a large contingent from the East End. He recalls the arrival of the East Enders with a kind of subdued distaste and implies that they are at least partially to blame for his son's conduct:

> A thing I'll always remember was when one block had moved in and on the patio at the bottom was a group of old dears with caps and shawls and the old boys with braces because they had no front steps to sit on. They were alright . . . But we didn't see them when we came here.

Indeed, the Alton Estate had always been viewed with a certain amount of suspicion and fear by the inhabitants of Fulham and Putney. There was an alarming tendency amongst the 'hard mods' and skinheads who 'ruled' the estate to escalate from a dependency on amphetamines, to heroin addiction; and the tales of beatings, and knifings (even shootings) which filtered down from Roehampton to find their way into the local teenage folk-lore gave the Estate a formidable reputation for toughness throughout South West London. How much of this can be attributed to the influx of families from the East End, and how much to the alienating effects of environment is of course problematic. Certainly, estates inside Fulham itself which, for the most part, served to rehouse local people did not have appreciably lower rates of vandalism or delinquency.[3] The same basic problems were most probably amplified at Roehampton, blown up onto a gargantuan scale by the huge size of the estate. Moreover, although the East Enders had a longer and more spectacular history of lawbreaking behind them, Fulham was not without its own deeply rooted criminal tradition. I shall try later on to establish at what points these two traditions converged, here I should merely stress that generally the two communities coexisted without overt conflict. Moreover, the East Enders confirmed the 'cockney feel' of Fulham and ultimately enriched its culture.

This cannot be said of the second wave of 'immigrants', however. The housing shortage and the accompanying boom in land values in Central London during the late 1960s meant that even the more dilapidated properties became attractive investments for those with money and an eye to a quick profit. Situated ideally in the Thames Valley within easy reach of both the busy West End and the quieter residential areas of Richmond and Kew; served equally well by bus and by tube, Fulham provided the perfect target for the property speculators and was soon subjected to the largely unwelcome attentions of prospective middle-class buyers. Along the Kings Road and the Fulham Road, the inevitable erosion of the old class boundaries began in earnest. In the mid 1960s the Labour Council had announced its first General Improvement Scheme and had bought up several crumbling terraces which were earmarked for demolition. In 1968, the newly elected Conservatives sold them off instead to owner-occupiers, and declared a modified policy of limited clearance designed to improve the aesthetic quality of the surroundings in which the new residents were situated. The Council was merely adjusting its priorities to meet the new situation – it was improving the 'look' of the borough, assisting in the timely destruction of what was after all an anachronistic way of life etc. – and the fact that it was making a lot of money in the process was, of course, neither here nor there. In fact the intrusion of large numbers of smart middle-class families was bound to produce considerable tension. In an article which appeared in *The Daily Telegraph Magazine* (January 7, 1972)[4] Bel Mooney investigates the reaction of the local community to the sudden appearance of these newcomers in one Fulham street (Maxwell Road). The gulf between the two cultures – one of 'the street and the garden fence', the other of 'the drawing-room with its tinkling silences' has merely been accentuated by the arrival of the 'new people'. It is literally there to be seen in the contrasting styles in which the houses are decorated ('all glass and steel and white sofas' v the 'slightly tatty' armchairs and the 'comfy' settee). One side of the road falls quietly apart through lack of funds and a sense of insecurity, the other is torn to pieces, pulled apart and reconstructed with the confidence that only comes with money and a promise of more in the form of a council grant for improvements. Predictably, Mrs. Faulkener, the 'rough diamond' of Maxwell Road, with her folded arms and voluminous paisley apron adopts an aggressive stance in her doorway, and issues an open challenge to the council to try and move her, pointing in disgust at the 'bloody toffee noses' opposite with their 'bloody (unwashed) curtains' and 'their dustbins full of wine bottles'.

Of course, this response has its sequel in the arrogant declarations of Dr. Sandford across the street who even claims a philanthropic interest ('I suppose you could call it a sophisticated method of slum clearance with private money') and who recognises in the interviewer a fellow professional and takes him into his confidence: 'Let's face it, they were living like pigs. No bathrooms.' Dr. Sandford's dismissal of the local residents is echoed even more jarringly in the comments of his neighbours:

> Surely it is to their benefit to move into a flats' community where, not to be snobbish, they are still with their own type . . .

But not all confrontations are so clearly defined, and Mr. Mooney's article is itself symptomatic (for all its good intentions) of a whole range of less obtrusive though equally unsettling pressures which bear upon the working-class community in Fulham. The article concludes with a sympathetic look at 'the real old-fashioned thing' and Mooney pens an epitaph to a passing way of life ('the texture, the variety, the evidence of time spent' etc.). But for all his sensitivity, and concern, Mooney merely publicises the problem and increases the already morbid curiousity of the liberal middle classes. He is himself an outsider – and that most insidious of creatures, the man from the media, and it is the media's excessive interest in the 'folksy' aspects of Fulham life which ultimately threatens local culture with circumscription and gradual suffocation. For the intrusion was accompanied by the usual over-exposure on the media (the vanguard of the middle-class invasion in London seems to be comprised largely of scouting parties for the B.B.C. – script-writers, actors, editors, etc.). At the moment of writing, however, the influx of an alien class is probably stimulating a revival of old London working-class 'mores'. There is a renewed interest in rhyming and even backwards slang which is used to exclude unwanted newcomers and to reestablish local identity. Even this outwardly favourable development is merely another desperate step in the race against the camera and the microphone. And nowhere do the irruptions of the media have more unsettling effects than in the area of deviant culture. For as the first wave of immigrants, the East Enders had swelled the criminal and delinquent populations, so the second wave has produced films about them. *Poor Cow* appeared in 1967 with Carol White (whose father actually owns a scrapyard in Fulham) as a local girl made bad, and the 'colourful-slice-of-life' London genre was launched. *Up the Junction*, shot in Fulham and nearby Battersea, told a similarly sordid story and by the late 1960s the London gangster film was becoming popular. Again, *Get Carter*, *Villain* and *Performance* were shot, at least in part, on location around Fulham and dervied much of their potency[5] from the shrewd use which was made of Fulham characters and local folk-lore. Television has followed suit, and in 1972, I.T.V. ran a series called *Budgie* introducing an attractive young Fulhamite (played by Adam Faith) with villainous ambitions and a heart of gold.[6] Fulham, in many instances, then, provided the backdrop against which the British media played out its vicarious fantasies of violent crime in the 1960s, and the local population was not unaffected. Perhaps it would be overstating the case to say that, as a result, local people became more aware of themselves *as actors* (or even more ominously, as extras) but it is certain that the repeated imposition of external definitions altered patterns of behaviour and self-perception inside the community. A study of such patterns should help us to evaluate the significance of aesthetic determinations, and to elucidate the ways in which they are mediated to a working-class community.

The cultural crises which had pertained to many of London's working-class boroughs since the war were presented quite literally in dramatic terms in the Fulham of the 1960s, and those crucial moments when choices were made (to capitulate to outside definitions or to evolve one's own) were that much *more* crucial in the case of Fulham. The community as a whole faced peculiarly complex problems of self-definition, but solutions to these problems were most urgently required inside the deviant group which had to draw up fairly rigid lines of demarcation between itself and the outside world between acceptance and denial if it was to retain any clear sense of identity at all. Unless the contract between the criminal actor and his public was continually ratified in his everyday interactions with 'straights' and 'fellow crooks' nothing could make sense and the credibility of his performance was thrown into jeopardy.

Thus, I have chosen to concentrate my study on the pub as it provided the principal arena in which these contracts were drawn up, in which those crucial choices were made, and more important still, were *seen* to be made. A closer examination of how the criminal behaves in the pub is likely to show, then, how an essentially underground deviant culture reacts when it receives concentrated attention from 'intruders', how it seeks and shuns the light, how it evolves its own ingenious techniques of evasion, and its equally sophisticated techniques through which meanings can be appropriated.

But before I proceed to such a study, I would like to make some more general remarks about Fulham's involvement in crime and the dispersal throughout the community of values which are officially designated 'criminal'. Ironically, these observations would seem to parallel those made by Walter Miller in his article 'Lower Class Culture as a Generating Milieu of Gang Delinquency'. But the two approaches remain diametrically opposed: I would claim that the values crystallise and cluster on the 'deviant perimeter' and are perpetually transmitted albeit in a diluted form, throughout the community (i.e. through a process of centripetal dissemination) whereas Miller argues an opposite tendency concentrating upon the *immanence* of those values within working-class culture as a whole (i.e. he implies a process of centrifugal dissemination). The significance which can be attributed to the deviant group (and therefore to the study of the deviant group) varies according to where one places the emphasis.

1. Straight crooks and crooked straights: the problem of working-class legitimacy in Fulham

The crepuscular nature of working-class legitimacy has never been adequately researched. It would certainly seem that those lines which theoretically separate the 'lumpen criminal' from the 'respectable artisan' tend to dissolve on closer inspection.[7] In Fulham at least, this seems to be the case. Every job has its dubious 'perks', every factory its sharp operators, its very own 'fence', who, with a wink and a whispered caution keeps his pockets lined and his friends supplied with cheap stockings for the wife and perhaps a few valuables which fall, with miraculous regularity, off the back of passing lorries. In some of the smaller workshops and warehouses and most of the big building-sites, the 'fiddles' have been formalised. Even the foreman plays his part in shifting stock off the premises. There is even evidence of systems of stealing where everyone gets his 'cut' and every 'cut' is graduated according to job-status.[8] Blind eyes are turned in every direction and blindness is endemic at half past five.

Every week, the columns of the local paper are filled with stories of employees who have slipped, fallen and 'betrayed the bosses' confidence'. Whilst cases of armed robbery dominate the front page and capture all the headlines, pages 2 and 3 monotonously tell the same old tales of stolen lead, and missing stock, embezzled cash and shoplifting. To take one case amongst many, the 'Woolworths' on North End Road has an extremely rapid turn-over of staff and every other week the *Chronicle* reports the appearance in the dock at the West London Courts of some weeping former shopgirl who pleads domestic pressures, and promises never again to deviate from the 'straight and narrow'. Of course, it is difficult to estimate the extent of this type of petty pilferage and the number of unrecorded misdemeanours which escape the attention of the courts and the papers is probably incalculable. Moreover, I am not so much interested here in assessing the actual volume of crime in Fulham, as in determining how far criminal values are endorsed by the community at large. To do this, I shall have to resort to a good deal of personal recollection, but I hope to avoid too much shapeless reminiscence by concentrating principally upon material gathered during a recent term of jury-service where the situation itself was sufficiently controlled and self-contained to allow a relatively formal analysis to be made.

In May 1974, I served on three juries at various Crown Courts in London.[9] The other members of the juries were mainly working-class people drawn from South and East London (the women seemed to come mainly from Stepney and Poplar, the men from Fulham, Muswell Hill, and Brixton). The central topic of conversation for two weeks was inevitably crime and punishment and the extraordinary circumstances in which we were all placed militated against the normal inhibitions. Confronted with the awesome machinery of British justice with its impenetrable language and its stilted demeanour, jury members tended to evolve a counter-culture fairly rapidly.[10] This culture was naturally marked by a heightened sensitivity to the distribution of power both inside and outside the courts, and generally served to enhance class loyalties. Again, a situation of crisis, where traditional working-class values are threatened can be seen to define those values more clearly, so that they can be realised, and articulated, and hence, protected and preserved. And jury-service constitutes a major crisis for many working-class citizens. The double-bind is there in the phrase itself, and the conflict between class and civic duties itself defines the crisis.

Moreover, the status of the juror in the courtroom is ambiguous at the best of times. The judge smiles indulgently and defers to him with silent irony from his elevated throne. The Defence and Prosecution Counsels go through their tragi-comic repetoire of grandiose gestures and inflexions of the eyebrow for his benefit alone and while he is flattered he is hardly convinced. In fact, he is often a little insulted. The police witnesses refuse to acknowledge his presence and address the judge instead; and the ushers and the underlings are at once matey and officious, determined to exercise to the full the only authority permitted them, and yet never quite sure how to go about it. In a word it is a pecking-order and there is never any real doubt as to who is at the bottom. The juror sits invisible but necessary, the dispensable decision-maker whose decisions have already been made for him. In fact, he is probably closest to the defendant who is also insecure, bewildered and sometimes paranoic, who is also fallible, vulnerable and all too human (unbewigged, unbegowned). One gets the impression that the courts could function far more smoothly without jurors and defendants.[11]

If the juror is working-class, all these contradictions are accentuated. The bonds which tie him to the defendant are strengthened and the pressures which alienate him from the process in which he is supposed to be involved are intensified.[12] He is likely to speak the same language as the defendant, to share the same problems, whereas the verbal gymnastics of the Prosecution Counsel, which might well earn the mute applause of his 'learned colleague', are likely to leave the juror cold. He does not use language, as the court does, as an end in itself, he does not love it intrinsically *for what it is*, and therefore he does not place so much faith in its power. Ultimately, he does not really trust it and by refusing to acknowledge the rules (the rules of rhetoric, the rules of the Debate), he places himself outside the game, sits back and waits for the 'reasonable doubt' which will stop the whole painful process. Thus the basic criteria which the judge uses to assess the 'truth' of a given testimony are often not shared by the jury. Other factors are likely to influence the final decision and not least among these is an overriding sympathy for the underdog. For instance, the Prosecution Counsel in one case attempted to establish the defendant's guilt by proving that he was a 'liar'. He drew attention, during cross-examination, to the criminal argot which abounded in the verbal statement allegedly made by the defendant to the police. The aggressive tone of his questions (backed up by meaningful glances at the jury) implied that to admit one knew the meaning of such words was tantamount to admitting one's guilt. The defendant was understandably edgy, and fell into the trap, denying all knowledge of such terms. The Prosecution concentrated upon one word: 'dipping':

> What about this word here . . . 'dipping'? I don't suppose . . . (here a laugh) . . . I don't suppose you meant you were . . . (here another laugh) . . . having a dip in the sea, did you?

The defendant, obviously confused, replies that he might have meant that if he had said it but the Prosecution pursues the point, until eventually the defendant is made to look ridiculous and contradicts himself. At this point, the Prosecution Counsel rallies on his prey, turns to the jury, hands clasped triumphantly on his lapels, and declares that he has proved the defendant a 'liar'. The fact that the defendant has flatly denied saying the thing in the first place is tactfully ignored; and the jury is obviously meant to be swept away by the Prosecution Counsel's sheer mastery of language. It is a moment which Edgar Lustgarten might have made much of – one of those 'historical moments' which demonstrate the barrister's skill and vindicate the British system of Justice.

Except that it fails to impress the jury; for when we adjourn to consider our verdict, it becomes immediately apparent that the Prosecution Counsel has seriously misjudged his audience. One juror opens by criticising the statements of the 'Old Bill'[13] and a man from Fulham relates a long story about the police planting firearms on a young man ('not unlike yourself' he says to me sensing a willing audience 'about your age') who lives down his street. This triggers off a wave of approbation and a chain of confirmative personal experiences. The majority agree that the police are, on occasion, prone to 'do things' like doctoring evidence ('We all know it goes on, don't we?'). By the time we came to consider the Prosecution's moment of triumph, a consensus has been reached (although two people refuse to subscribe to it) that the police are corrupt. This predetermines our response to all the prosecution evidence. When we consider the defendant's statement, most jurors agree that he has probably been 'verballed up'. One man points out that a 'bloke who's obviously a villain (though that doesn't mean he's guilty, here, does it?)' who, in addition seems exceptionally circumspective under pressure, would never have made such a damning statement. Furthermore, it conspires that everybody is familiar with the criminal argot, and some jurors doubt that certain terms (namely 'dipping' and 'pusher') are still used in the underworld and suggest more modern equivalents. One man points out that the defendant is Scottish and that 'dipping could mean anything up there', and everybody agrees that he was doubly disadvantaged by his accent and his inarticulateness. Finally, a juror (another Fulham man) identifies explicitly with the defendant.

> You've got to remember that it could be any one of us up there, you know.

Many jurors nod in agreement; a vote is taken and the defendant is acquitted by a majority verdict. A precedent has been set (everyone having declared himself) and subsequent discussions (and verdicts) follow more or less the same pattern. Once a consensus had been established, the tension lifted noticeably. Jurors began to relax, and over the two weeks, several admitted that they were naturally predisposed to a not-guilty verdict (though many said that they would consider a case involving violence more carefully). Many of the older men became frankly conspiratorial, winking and chuckling over their lunchtime pints in the pub nearby.

Ironically, the Prosecution regularly appealed to the 'common sense' of the jury (whereas the Defence was inclined to place its confidence in the jury's 'logic and sense of fairness'), and 'worldly wisdom' was instead enlisted in support of the defendant. During the initial debate, rules of conduct which would normally operate at a subconscious level (i.e. at the level of 'common sense') were drawn out and articulated. This was essential if the challenge to communal life which the court represented was to be met and overcome. The formalised legal language and the predetermined nature of the court's responses required a parallel codification at the jury's *own* values. Thus, that which was potential became apparent, and the values which emerged can be said to reflect, on a micro level, the priorities of the working-class community in South London.[14] These can be expressed thus: property is less important than life, and life is more complex than the court allows. No one is perfect, and laws are made to be broken ('Who wouldn't have pocketed the bloody thing? Let's face it, you see something like that lying in the road, you're not going to walk past it, are you'). Thus language is deceitful, even treacherous, fostering dangerous illusions of certainty ('They can do anything with words – it's their job'). Everyone agreed that 'truth' was rather less accessible than language,[15] and that 'real life' was fluid and open to an infinite variety of interpretations: ('it all depends how you see it' . . . 'it could mean anything' . . . 'you've got a right to your opinion' . . . 'your opinion's as good as mine' as [to the two jurors who persisted in the belief that the defendant was guilty].) Obviously, it could be argued that any jury, irrespective of its class background, might come to similar conclusions, and a middle-class juror is just as likely to allow compassion to influence his verdict. But it is doubtful that his interests and those of the defendant will ever coincide sufficiently for him to be able to completely transfer his allegiances from the Bench to the Dock. And it is exactly this shift of sympathies which encourages the working-class juror to make his larger criticisms (of language, of the police, of authority in general) so that a normally latent system of values can be crystallised and allowed to surface. It also gives him the means with which to enlarge his definition of what constitutes a 'reasonable doubt' so that he can, in most cases, 'give the bloke the benefit'. The working-class juror, then, can reconcile the contradictory pulls of class and civic loyalties, simply by voting the defendant not-guilty.[16]

It would be hard to find a more reliable indicator of working-class 'respectability' than membership of a jury.[17] And yet we find jurors from South and East London, not only identifying openly with defendants and tempering their judgements accordingly, but actually transcending[18] the concept of guilt itself, by subscribing to a set of values which are officially defined as 'anti-social' or 'criminal'. If the constrictive atmosphere of the court is thought to introduce a whole range of extraneous factors which are not specifically relevant to this study, I would merely point out the chief advantage of constraint – namely that it solves problems of presentation enabling material to be contained within a reasonably fixed and comprehensible framework (i.e. form does have its uses!)

One has only to turn from the closed and ordered discourse of the courtroom to the looser structures of the street to appreciate the magnitude of those problems. A permeance defies precise definition and it seems impossible to convey the subtler nuances of crime unless one resorts to evocative words like 'texture' and 'colour'. And yet the hints are there on every street corner in the pubs (packed even at lunch time), and the betting shops (packed from the time the pubs close to the last race at Aintree), in the scrapyeards and the junkshops (now called 'antique markets' to exploit the new trend). Industry in the area seems to be very light indeed, and work does not, on the whole, constitute the major commitment in people's lives. In fact it rarely seems to matter at all, and money tends to be transmuted into 'pleasure' buying instant gratification in the form of drink and food, clothes and two weeks in Spain rather than the more sober reassurances of durable items. Moreover, the injection of capital into the area which followed the property boom did stimulate certain sectors of Fulham's economy. The influx of middle-class families, intent on converting neglected houses into ideal homes gave the building trade a considerable boost and the self-employed builders, the painters, and decorators, and demolition men all thrived visibly.

Thus, in certain pubs, the more expensive tastes are regularly indulged and spirits flow as freely as mild ale. Consumption can take place on a colossal scale, is always conspicuous, often spectacular, and a drink can be used to define identity more adequately than a job, and allows for that magical margin of doubt. Thus, at closing time at three o'clock, everyone seems to work for himself and further enquiries are met with an enigmatic silence and a sapient smile. To further complicate the issue, criminal associations tend to cluster around certain jobs and the lines between fact and fiction, legality and lawbreaking are even more confused in these cases. Some occupations are obviously eligible (i.e. the used-car salesman, the mini-cab driver[19]) but others are less likely. For instance, window-cleaning seems to be a profession which has its fair share of ex-cons, and window-cleaning rounds change hands only at a price, and even then are only available to those 'in the know'. Of course, myth and ritual are mystifiers, and conventions have been established which channel expectations. Thus a mini-cab driver is expected to be a 'heavy character' perhaps, and a 'sharp customer' certainly, but there is no way of determining how much of his demeanour derives from a 'real' involvement in crime and how much from less tangible sources. I would suggest that a recognition on his part of the expectations of his audience might encourage him to realise a group fantasy.

To turn from one doubtful area to another, it would be difficult to ascertain how far criminal values are endorsed and supported by working-class women in Fulham. Generally, the pub does not play such a central role in the woman's social life, and consequently she has less access to the attitudes which circulate most readily in a pub-environment. Furthermore, until recently at least, 'respectable' working-class women were particularly susceptible to the conformative pressures of a patriarchal society to submit to authority at home and at work. These pressures were presumably responsible for larger deferential patterns (in relations with the law, in attitudes to Royalty, etc.), but it seems just as probable that communal loyalties would take pride of place over all other considerations at times of crisis (i.e. when a member of the family, or a neighbour clashes with the law). Certainly, a stolen article is not necessarily less attractive because it is stolen; on the contrary, it would seem that there are times when the appeal is positively enhanced by the extra element of the forbidden and the dangerous which knowledge of theft bestows. Thus, a man who set up a makeshift stall on the North End Road openly advertised the fact that his goods were stolen and the crowd, which mainly comprised women, grew visibly as he became more and more outspoken about the nature of his 'nightwork'.

> I work nights . . . an hour and a half every other night without fail . . . me and me two brothers . . . sorry, I mean one brother . . . the other left the firm a bit sudden last Tuesday fortnight . . . he's now on holiday at Her Majesty's expense . . . in Brixton . . . etc. etc.

Though this 'spiel' was basically designed to attract attention and keep the crowd amused, the vendor was also inviting his audience to participate vicariously in the original theft. Speed is essential in transactions such as these, and a speedy sale can be guaranteed if the goods are known to be 'hot' (because stolen goods must go at bargain prices). But the vendor not only managed to escape apprehension by adopting this approach, he also introduced excitement and risk into what was otherwise a thoroughly ordinary exchange and the purses which he was offering up for sale became that much more desirable.[20] His entire stock was snapped up within minutes and he had disappeared before the police arrived on the scene to investigate the obstruction.[21]

Moreover, when the activities of the more ambitious protagonists of Fulham's criminal culture attract the attentions of the national media, all the defence mechanisms of the local community tend to become operative, and men and women close ranks against the press and the police. After the Great Train Robbery, at least, this was the case. The widespread support and sympathy which the Robbers received was naturally reinforced by local ties, and there were plenty of these. Two of the Robbers (Gordon Goody and Roy James) drank regularly in

Fulham pubs and were widely respected figures in the underworld of South West London, and another, William Beal, actually lived in the area. In one case that I know of, sympathy was extended into actual assistance. A woman who lives near the flat[23] in which Ronald Biggs stayed after the crime, told me that everyone locally knew that he had been involved and that he was living there. Information was withheld not through fear of possible reprisals but as a gesture of solidarity with the wanted man. Subsequent police enquiries met with the customary conspiracy of silence.

Some local people, not themselves totally immersed in the underworld, will allow communal allegiances to outweigh all other considerations, even the the case of the most violent crimes. Judgement is held in reserve, and criticisms can be qualified if the criminal 'looks after his mum', or is 'good with the kids' and generally shows 'that he's not *all* bad'. For instance, after an attempt had been made on the life of a Fulham betting-shop owner who had testified for the Prosecution in the Kray case, a local man, who had had the occasional drink with the terrified bookie said:

> I don't understand it . . . you couldn't hope to meet a nicer bloke. Why, he wouldn't even land one on you unless he was paid to do it!

But this is an example of extreme indulgence and is in no way representative of the community as a whole. There are usually quite definite limits to local tolerance, and the sensational case of Tony Lawrence and 'Ba Ba' Elgar exposes those limits. As the case also takes us to the centre of that confined yet chaotic universe of criminal violence and fantasy which we have already examined in relation to the Krays, I feel it requires a more detailed analysis. The following account should serve as a transitional passage which closes the discussion on 'mainstream working-class legitimacy' and reunites us once more with the 'deviant periphery'.

2. A few of the performers – very 'Ronnie' indeed

> 'There was disagreements, but most of them trivial. It's ego, a lot of it. Private, you know.'
>
> Ronnie Kray quoted in *Sunday Times*, Oct. 19, 1969.

> 'I don't know why he came to my yard. That's a logical question but you can't discuss Lawrence logically, he doesn't do logical things. I think I was to be an example to others'.
>
> Jim Sullivan quoted in *Sunday Times*, January 25, 1970.

> 'Lawrence definitely wanted to be the bigshot, the number one.'
>
> George Marshall quoted in *Sunday Times*, January 25, 1970.

On February 11, 1968 the London editions of the Sunday newspapers carried reports of a gun battle which had taken place the night before in Hazelbury Road, Fulham. A local scrap merchant had been seriously injured and his foreman killed. Hysterical editorials warned of 'Chicago-style gunmen' and the facts were promptly adorned with the usual fabrications. Thus, it was rumoured in the press that two young 'professionals' had been 'brought in from outside' and given £1,500 to murder a rival. Final paragraphs referred darkly to the boom in the copper market precipitated by the Rhodesia crisis, and spoke of 'Al Capone type business methods'. Other reports tripled the number of suspected men and stressed their ruthless professionalism: 'Six men who sat round a table to discuss murder were being hunted by detectives etc.'. The following Friday, the *Fulham Chronicle* glumly announced in its headline: 'No one is talking in Hazelbury Road', and proceeded to quote verbatim the wordless responses of the neighbours. After two columns of carefully chronicled head-shaking and closely observed slamming doors, the 'feature' ended with the customary footnote about 'fear on Fulham's streets' and 'threats of gangland reprisals'.

The facts which lie behind the incident are somewhat less spectacular and rather less lucid than these early reports suggest and the case of 'Ba Ba' Elgar looks a little ridiculous inside its mythical pinstriped suitings. The Chicago model can only be invoked ironically in this instance, and the Cagneyite ambitions of Tony Lawrence who was indirectly responsible for the death of his own foreman, seem to tower hopelessly above his actual performance. For Lawrence's 'rise to power' was hardly meteoric, and, though the person he presented to the outside world seems to have blended the basic characteristics of Charlie Richardson and Ronnie Kray, something essential was conspicuously absent. In short, Lawrence lacked originality, his aspirations seem doubly derivative, his actions twice circumscribed, and where Kray appears to parody, Lawrence merely mimics.

The comparisons suggest themselves immediately: Lawrence was born in 1935, one year after Charles Richardson, and two years after Ronnie Kray. Family (in particular fraternal) bonds were taken very seriously indeed and we shall see how the original incident which provoked the major hostilities leading up to Elgar's death was largely an affair of family honour. In 1951, at the age of 16, Lawrence left school, and, in the same year, was convicted of stealing a small quantity of lead (cf. Charles Richardson) for which he was put on probation for 12 months. By 1956, his criminal career had taken a more serious turn, for in that year he took part in an attempted raid on a sub post office, and was found guilty of assault with intent to rob. He was committed to Rampton high security 'special hospital' for 'patients of dangerous, violent or criminal propensities'. Like Ronnie Kray, he found himself faced with the prospect of being committed for life, and, in 1959, the year in which Kray made his ingenious escape from Long Grove Prison Hospital, Lawrence engineered his own release from Rampton. Just as Reggie had been instrumental in Ronnie's escape, so Lawrence was assisted by his parents who wrote a letter to Michael Stuart, Fulham's M.P., maintaining that their son was sane. In 1962, however, Lawrence returned to prison with a four year sentence for abducting, assaulting and robbing a local florist. He was released in 1964, having earned full remission, and promptly moved himself and his family, which by now comprised a wife and two children, from a council flat in Fulham Court to a newer flat in Barclay Close. He began to take an interest in the scrapmetal business and was soon renting a site in Waterford Road, close to Fulham's gas works. On September 5, 1966 Tony Lawrence received his licence from Hammersmith Council, and he was soon running a highly profitable business concentrating particularly on the copper market which was proving extremely lucrative at the time. Gradually, the yard was transformed into something of a fortress, guarded by two ferocious Alsations, and Lawrence began to surround himself with younger local men like Terry Belding and Elgar who were in their early twenties and John Terry who was only nineteen. The consolidation of power followed the pattern which Charles Richardson had already established in South East London, and Lawrence began to accumulate the symbols through which the gangster communicates his intentions to the outside world. Thus, the walls of Lawrence's flat were hung with fighting swords and he cultivated a certain fastidiousness in matters of dress, acquiring several dozen suits and sometimes bathing and changing his shirt three or four times a day.[25] In fact, Lawrence recreated with meticulous care, the vain and violent image of Ronnie Kray[26] and the petty feuds and rivalries which dissipated the energies of the Fulham criminal reproduced on a miniature scale, the larger disputes which occupied the Krays and the Richardsons elsewhere in London.

The incident which sparked off all the trouble was, in itself, remarkably trivial. At lunchtime on Boxing Day 1966, Lawrence was drinking in the public bar of the Queen Elizabeth in Bagley's Lane, Fulham, with his father and his two brothers Kenny and Johnny. After the last bell had been rung, Tony Lawrence asked the landlord, Michael Ahearne for a gin and bitter lemon but was refused. As Ahearne walked back into the saloon, a bottle was thrown which narrowly missed his shoulder. Lawrence came through the bar and smashed another bottle over Ahearne's head. As Kenny and Johnny Lawrence began to beat Ahearne also, a customer, Thomas McGowan attempted to go to his assistance. McGowan was dragged outside and kicked to the ground, and Jim Sullivan, another Fulham scrapdealer and friend of the Lawrence family, intervened and stopped the brothers inflicting any further injury. By the time the police arrived, the Lawrences had left the scene.

The tension between the four conflicting codes of honour which are in evidence here (one of the family, one of the friend, one professional (i.e. of the landlord) and one which can, perhaps, be best described as 'personal') is ultimately irreducible and those who participated in the original incident were trapped in a conundrum. The various lines of action adopted by the central protagonists can be interpreted as strategic attempts to restore some kind of equanimity, to vindicate one or more of the codes, and thus to escape the conundrum. The violent initiative taken by Lawrence sprang from both personal and family codes and was designed to punish an imagined infringement of the code of friendship. The landlord's resolve to prosecute was hardened by a desire to validate personal and professional codes. As we shall see, Sullivan's position was particularly problematic and the final resolution depended ultimately on which options he took. The moment when Sullivan agreed to appear as the main Prosecution witness in the Lawrence trial represents a resolution and a transcendence of all four codes, and can be said to define the larger collective ethos of Fulham's working-class community.

Despite three convictions for receiving stolen metal, the last conviction fetching a 2 month prison sentence, Sullivan was generally considered 'straight' or at least not overtly criminal and existed in that no-man's-land between legality and lawbreaking, which, as I have tried to indicate, appears to be quite densely populated in Fulham at least. But if his relationship with the law was somewhat equivocal, then his private friendships were to prove even more divisive. Sullivan's loyalties were split between Ahearne the 'straight' landlord and Lawrence, the crooked fellow scrap merchant. Sullivan had helped Tony Lawrence to start his scrap business and had acted as guarantor when he bought his scales from Avery's. The two became confirmed friends, and at one time, had even considered opening a yard in South London together. But Sullivan had also grown to like Ahearne who had given Sullivan a crucifix when the scrapdealer's three year old son had died of a throat infection. Sullivan's first resolution appears to have been fairly smoothly accomplished, nonetheless. When Kenny and Johnny Lawrence were arrested on charges of wounding, assault, and making an affray, they asked Sullivan to appear for the Defence. Notwithstanding the pressure which had been brought to bear on Ahearne to withdraw (threatening phone calls, offers of a bribe), Sullivan agreed to make a vague statement for the Defence which nevertheless did not help the two brothers who received 12 and 18 month sentences respectively. Sullivan had committed perjury but the crucial choice between law and crime, landlord friend and scrap merchant mate had been taken and apparently without too much difficulty.

However, when Tony Lawrence himself was arrested on May 7, 1967, and was charged with making an affray, assaulting Ahearne and McGowan and causing them grievous bodily harm, a state of moral emergency was declared once more, and this time a different decision was taken. Lawrence obviously required a more committed statement from Sullivan, if he was to avoid the fate of his brothers, and, as a close friend, he expected Sullivan to co-operate and perjure himself more thoroughly on his behalf. When Lawrence was unexpectedly granted bail on June 2, he sought out the other scrap merchant and stated his position. Sullivan only agreed to consider Lawrence's request and Lawrence asked him to bring two other men who had been in the Queen Elizabeth on the day of the incident to his house for further consultation. When they refused to come, Lawrence grew furious and the two men's cars were later found damaged. On July 2, Sullivan's yard in Garratt Lane was damaged (though not very badly) by a bomb thrown from a passing car, and if this was intended to force a decision, it certainly succeeded. For Sullivan was sufficiently alienated to refuse to offer any statement whatsoever in Lawrence's defence. Still, the idea of contacting the police was never seriously entertained, and though Sullivan grew apprehensive, he declined to acknowledge that war had been declared, hoping that his discretion would mollify Lawrence and enable him to avoid more disastrous confrontations.

But for Lawrence the vendetta was merely postponed and during the summer he made contact with two Coldstream Guards, Wayne Crofts and Michael Melaney who began to supply him with arms stolen from the nearby Chelsea barracks. By September, he had built up a sizeable armoury which included several pounds of plastic explosives (which were very difficult to get from underworld sources at the time) a number of hand grenades (which were well nigh impossible) and a Belgian high velocity rifle which he stored in the dog's kennel on the scrapyard in Waterford Road. Meanwhile, relations between Lawrence and Sullivan's foreman, Charlie Jennings, had deteriorated to the point where open conflict seemed inevitable. Jennings was a large belligerent man who, like his boss, occupied an uncertain position on the borders of crime, but unlike Sullivan, he was willing to force a showdown with Lawrence. As summer moved into autumn, the tension reached breaking point and, in the afternoon of November 29, two men burst into the Garratt Lane shop, threatened Sullivan's eldest son, Larry with a gun and proceeded to shoot Jennings in the legs. Eventually, Jennings' left leg was amputated but he resolutely refused to identify his attackers. Despite the apparent failure of Sullivan's policy of appeasement, he continued to try to effect a reconciliation and at Christmas sent the Lawrence family a large gift of food.

But Lawrence showed no signs of forgiving and forgetting and he began to turn his attention toward Ahearne, the offending landlord, who, as far as Lawrence was concerned, had precipitated the whole disastrous affair. On 29 December, Lawrence, Elgar and John Terry arrived at Sullivan's yard and peremptorily demanded a length of copper tubing. This was used as the casing of a bomb which was placed outside the Queen Elizabeth public house the following night. The explosion blew in the wall of the public bar and glass shattered across the street. On the night of January 11, the saloon bar was partially destroyed by a fire bomb which was thrown through the window. Having merely strengthened Ahearne's determination to see him convicted, Lawrence turned once more towards Tooting and finally managed to provoke Sullivan beyond endurance.

On the night of January 22, whilst Sullivan was presiding over a benefit social in aid of the injured Jennings at the Britannia pub in Fulham, a hand grenade was thrown into the office of the yard in Garratt Lane. Large pieces of shrapnel actually penetrated the floor of the flat above which had been rented to a young family. Both Jennings and Sullivan were openly appalled by this action and interpreted it as a transgression of the family code's most inviolable clause which dealt with the sanctity of innocent life. Obviously, the threshold of Sullivan's tolerance had been reached and all hopes for any possible reconciliation in the future were discarded. At this point, Sullivan decided to redefine his relationship with the law and went to the police. He was wholeheartedly supported in this by Charlie Jennings who was apparently prepared to overlook his own disablement, but could not permit this new outrage to go unpunished. He explained his reaction to the *Sunday Times* reporter Peter Gillman:

> I've been a thief, I've never been a police informer, but I'll never condone this involving women and children.

Sullivan is similarly disgusted and admits that the fact that Lawrence's henchmen had threatened his son a few months earlier 'had really decided me'.

> A man could steal the Crown Jewels and I wouldn't care. But if he attacks innocent people whose only crime is that they live above my property etc. . . .

Finally, Jennings explains how the 'twilight zone' which he inhabits is lit by certain constant lights at least, and how any attempts to extinguish these lights amounts to an act of betrayal. Jennings implies that without these transcendent laws, life would be impossible outside the Law itself:

> Straight people say that the people who are beneath the law live in the jungle. But there's a law of the jungle. It's like a religious code. If you are involved in the twilight zone there are certain rules laid down, and you abide by them.

Thus, Lawrence's excesses had finally broken the moral deadlock in which Sullivan had found himself and had recommended a specific course of action once more. The personal code of honour which had compelled Sullivan to defend Thomas McGowan against the blows of the Lawrence brothers had been suspended whilst loyalties were allowed to untangle and declare themselves. This code could only come into operation again if a new order could be established and Lawrence's transgressions made such an order possible. Ultimately Lawrence had forfeited his friendship by challenging the sacred principles upon which the wider community depended for its very survival, and Sullivan, for his part, could interpret his 'betrayal' of a friend as an act of self-sacrifice undertaken to protect that community. So Sullivan went to Earlsfield Police Station and related the story of the copper tubing and the bombing of the Queen Elizabeth.

A fruitless search of Lawrence's flat produced one result at least – it alerted Lawrence to the new initiative which Sullivan had taken and Lawrence, like Jennings, found betrayal unforgiveable and demanded retribution. Early on Saturday, February 3, 1968, he called on an old friend, Georgie Marshall, at his home in Halford Road, Fulham. A thief by profession, Marshall was in his mid thirties and had worked with Lawrence before the era of the scrapyard in Waterford Road. Lawrence asked Marshall to kill Sullivan and he accepted on condition that he could do the job with a friend called Ian Horton. Lawrence agreed and Marshall and Horton promptly decided to work a confidence trick which though somewhat risky, seemed likely to succeed.

The events which followed bear a remarkable resemblance to the Jack 'The Hat' episode which had taken place one year earlier in the East End. Like McVitie who had failed to carry out Ronnie Kray's commission to kill Leslie Payne, Marshall found it difficult to take the idea of assassination seriously. The provocation which Sullivan had offered seemed negligible, and out of all proportion to the punishment which Lawrence sought to impose. However, Marshall did not hesitate to accept an advance payment of £190 for a job which he had no intention of doing. It seemed probable that Lawrence would be in prison before the end of the week as his case was due to come up for trial on February 8, and Horton and Marshall were convinced that the whole affair could be quietly forgotton with Lawrence out of the way. However, Marshall had underestimated his 'mark', and the con, as in the case of Jack 'The Hat' was to misfire and end in death. On the afternoon of February 3, Marshall and Horton drove over to Sullivan's yard and warned him of Lawrence's plans. Sullivan, acting in accordance with his new resolve, contacted the police who assured him that Lawrence would be behind bars before his injunction could be carried out. However, Lawrence's trial had not been concluded as quickly as Marshall had anticipated and the two would-be assassins were forced to enlist all their powers of ingenuity to combat Lawrence's rising suspicions. When Lawrence confronted Marshall during a lunchtime drinking session on February 10, Marshall prevaricated once more but Lawrence had obviously grown impatient. That night Elgar drove Lawrence and the two assassins to Horton's flat in Hazelbury Road, where there was to be a discussion of various strategies which Marshall and his accomplice could adopt for the murder. An argument suddenly developed as Lawrence produced the Belgian rifle which he had acquired in the summer. As is usual in such matters, the exact point at which the atmosphere of mutual suspicion was replaced by one of open hostility is in doubt. It transpires that both Horton and Marshall were armed and Marshall implies in his statement to Peter Gillman, that Horton fired the first shot.

> Lawrence was rucking with Sailor [Horton] but I knew Lawrence and it's the way he performs. It's very hard to describe a fight. It just happens. If we'd stopped still he would have shot us both.

In the exchange of fire which followed Elgar received a fatal wound in the back and Lawrence was hit in the face and the neck. Horton and Marshall quickly made themselves scarce and the police arrived soon after they had fled. At this point, Lawrence allowed his desire for personal vengeance to lead him into his second major violation of the all-important communal code. When asked by the police if he knew who had shot him, he replied: 'It was Horton and Marshall . . . and Jimmy Sullivan.'[27]

When Marshall gave himself up a week later, he soon realized that Lawrence had incriminated him deliberately and was suitably outraged:

> I thought he'd say (the guns) went off by accident. It's the way you work. If you get nicked together, you don't give names.

Thus, Marshall and Horton (who was arrested in Bolton) felt justified in telling the police the whole story and were ultimately acquitted of murdering Elgar. Their disclosures contributed to Lawrence's second conviction, and his infringement of the code of silence was repaid in kind.

On February 28, Lawrence made a last dramatic public appearance at Elgar's funeral. Photographs appeared in the press showing Lawrence dressed in a black overcoat and dark glasses brooding inscrutably over the flower-covered coffin of his former henchman. He was arrested soon afterwards, and, on May 16, he appeared at the Old Bailey on the three charges relating to the original incident which had taken place at the Queen Elizabeth in 1966. Ironically, Sullivan did not give evidence for either the Defence or Prosecution in this trial, and Lawrence was found guilty of causing an affray and assault. He received a three year prison sentence.

The major trial, which dealt with the more serious offences, opened on June 12. Crofts and Melaney, the two guardsmen who had supplied Lawrence with the rifle and explosives were dealt with first. It is hardly surprising that the judge, Mervyn Griffing-Jones, should take this opportunity to deliver a lengthy harangue against declining standards of discipline in a 'civilised' society which is 'struggling . . . with so much gangsterism increasing'. Crofts was sentenced to ten years in prison, Melaney to eight. The trial of Lawrence and Terry followed. Sullivan appeared as the chief prosecution witness and identified the piece of copper tubing which had been found after the explosion at the Queen Elizabeth as the one taken from his yard on December 30th. But in the event, Sullivan's appearance was somewhat overshadowed by the testimony delivered by Terry Belding. Belding confirmed that Lawrence had indeed received the stolen rifle from Crofts. Despite the fact that he had been intimidated by various 'heavies' before the trial, he had been determined to make his statement, and explained why he had decided to turn on his former associate:

> It did me barmy when Baba got shot . . . If it wasn't for Lawrence, Baba would still be alive today.

Belding's appearance in court finalised that process of rejection whereby Lawrence was steadily denied the protection of the community. When Lawrence himself took the witness stand, he adopted the well-tried tactic of denouncing all the Prosecution witnesses as 'liars' and labelling their allegations 'ridiculous'.[28] Lawrence became particularly incensed over Sullivan's statement and moodily invoked his old friendship making clear his sense of betrayal: 'I used to go all over the place with him. We was *like brothers*.'

Lawrence's bitter denunciation can be read back to the original incident and helps to explain the intensity of Lawrence's hatred for Sullivan. Sullivan had not pledged himself wholeheartedly to the Lawrence family cause in the Queen Elizabeth that day. Instead, he had defended a stranger who had come to the landlord's assistance, and by refusing to ally with the family, he had, at last, declared his true colours. Lawrence's original judgement was confirmed by Sullivan's refusal to make a more useful statement on his behalf at the subsequent trial. To sum up, Sullivan had been 'a brother' only up to a point, and, in the opinion of Lawrence who was perpetually at war with the outside world, this was just not enough. Lawrence was found guilty and sentenced to 14 years; John Terry, who was acquitted of receiving a hand grenade knowing it to be stolen, was sentenced to 5 years for his part in the bombing of the Queen Elizabeth.

I have presented a detailed account of the events which took place in Fulham between December 1966, and February 1968, because I feel that such detail is absolutely necessary if we are to appreciate the complexity of the relationship between Fulham's 'subworld' (somewhere between the underworld and the surface!) and the law, and the density and diversity of criminal interactions in the area as a whole. At various points throughout the narrative, a differential commitment to criminal values was in evidence and as the events unfolded, the conflict between the two central characters (Sullivan and Lawrence) began to revolve increasingly around the question of this commitment. Ultimately, the dispute forced the two men to adopt extreme positions, so that the terms of the original conflict could be transcended. Sullivan, the scrapdealer with criminal connections turned to the police (the 'straight' solution); Lawrence, the criminal with a scrap yard turned to violence (the 'criminal' solution). To explain how this polarisation had come about, I postulated the existence of four separate codes of honour which had dictated the initial choices made by the actors involved in the Boxing Day fracas. Some of these codes were complementary, others contradictory, and the relationship between them was kinetic so that action depended upon which code took precedence at any given time. The various actors organised these codes in hierarchies which correspond to their needs at the moment of crisis. *Taken absolutely* (i.e. not in the spirit in which they were intended), the choices made at this moment also indicated the intensity of the actor's commitment to criminal values and *ideally* defined his relationship with the law. What Lawrence did was to freeze and prolong the moment of crisis and demand that the implications of those original choices be drawn out to their 'logical' conclusions. Lawrence had intersected the *diachronous* line along which choices are made at a point which was arbitrary to all but himself (i.e. he had initiated the conflict) and had replaced a situation of moral flux by one of moral fixity.

For Sullivan this was peculiarly painful, for his allegiances were distributed equilaterally and thus no one code could take precedence. He was morally neutralised (petrified in more ways than one) until that moment when Lawrence had completely realised the implications of his original choice and had exploded the protagonists *back into time* by instigating a new crisis.[29] It was only when Lawrence had broken the spell which he himself had originally cast, that Sullivan could act once more with conviction. In short, Lawrence had created a claustrophobic situation by arresting these processes which allow one individual to accommodate to another; he had introduced the concept of finitude by replacing relativities with absolutes, and the account of his vendetta with Sullivan demonstrates what happens when a system of closure is implemented in everyday life.

Lawrence had reduced the game of gangsterism to its barest essentials, to a point where the power drive functioned undisguised. No attempts were made to displace power into profit, and with Lawrence there were no protection rackets, and no financial interests in clubs. He was a gangster without purpose (which presumably is as bad as being a cowboy without a horse, i.e. one can't really get anywhere); to John McVicar he was just a 'mug', and his criminal career performs the dubious services of a bad 'B' movie – it exposes the conventions of the genre. At the risk of pushing the cinematic metaphor beyond the pale as it were, I would suggest that the story of Tony Lawrence can be represented as the low-budget version of the Kray Twins' major epic.

Nonetheless, as far as the 'respectable' sections of the media were concerned, the 'remake' appears to have been rather more acceptable, and certainly more accessible than the 'original' had been. In fact most of the information used in the preceding account was taken from a lengthy article by Peter Gillman which appeared in the *Sunday Times Magazine* (January 25, 1970). This article was presented in a way which one suspects was designed to appeal to a somewhat sordid voyeuristic interest in a series of events which might indeed have taken place next door but which were, in every other way, inalienably foreign. The cover of the magazine consisted of one of those photographs which I have already mentioned which showed Lawrence all broad shoulders and his wife in leather gloves paying their last respects at the grave of 'Ba Ba' Elgar. This was surrounded by two inches of menacing black border and a headline, self-consciously sensational in lurid red, was placed diagonally across the right hand corner proclaiming 'SCRAPYARD KILLING: NOW IT CAN BE TOLD'. With a touch of irony and a trace of kitsch, the reader is thus introduced to the fascinating side of Fulham's working-class culture, and, over cornflakes and a piece of toast, crime is commuted into pleasure – committed by proxy.

Neither the Kray nor Richardson cases had received such detailed coverage in the 'respectable' Sundays, which as has been so often pointed out, provide a fairly accurate reflection of the preoccupation of the educated middle classes. The very fact that the article could be written betrays the relative vulnerability of Fulham's subculture to penetration from outside and its appearance in the *Sunday Times Magazine* as the main feature marks the arrival of the middle classes. It is a fair example of the 'immigrant' literature, to which I have already alluded, which threatened in the late 1960s to bombard the indigeneous population with alien definitions and to kill local culture albeit through kindness.[30] The extent to which Fulham has been 'infiltrated' can be most clearly expressed in a concrete example. The principal incidents in the Lawrence affair were confined chiefly to the Sands End area of Fulham which is hemmed in on the one side by the New King's Road and Chelsea and on the other by Wandsworth Bridge and the river. Sands End is traditionally 'rough', notorious for its street fights, and was recently described by a local police chief as a 'hot bed of delinquency'. Hazelbury Road, where the killing took place, is in the heart of this district, is dominated by the grim presence of Fulham power station and is permeated by the fumes of the local gas works. And yet, earlier this year, the *Fulham Chronicle* could proudly announce that Lady Jane Wellesley, whose friendship with Prince Charles was, at the time, causing a furore in the press, had taken up residence opposite the very house in which Elgar had been killed. The 'Chelseafication' of Fulham, currently underway, could not be made more immediately apprehensible than in Hazelbury Road's two contrasting claims to local fame, and I shall now turn to consider how the problems of self-definition and self-determination which the middle-class invasion exacerbated, were dealt with in the central arena of the public house.

3. The pub and the performer

> There must surely come a point at which unwilling consumers will resist unwelcome change.
>
> Christopher Hutt in *The Death of the English Pub*

The scene in which the original drama which Lawrence had initiated had taken place, was significant enough in itself, and the confrontation between a scrap merchant and a publican provides an appropriate introduction to the study of criminal interactions in Fulham. For the pub is the single most important area of play available to the working-class individual in this country. It is generally more spacious and less inhibiting than home itself; it embodies a collective past, promises a shared future, and somewhere in between the optics and the pumps it offers some kind of sanctuary from work and television. In Fulham, where play tends not to be taken lightly (in that 'subworld' at least), the pub can dictate a whole lifestyle and embrace a whole world supplying a complex of social and economic needs. It provides the chief locale for meeting friends and doing business; making contacts, and settling feuds, and, as such, it occupies a central position in many people's lives.

The way in which power is distributed inside a pub is therefore absolutely crucial to the 'regulars' who frequent it, and yet even the relatively formal relationship between the customer and the publican is fairly flexible, and is open to a variety of interpretations. The landlord is the salaried host, the benefactor who depends on the good will of his customers and, in the pub, the counter which separates the seller of goods from the public which he serves invites an even greater ambiguity than it does in the market or the small local grocery. The landlord can be the customer's friend, sometimes his enemy, sometimes his accomplice.

More frequently, he can be the agent of unwanted change, a minor cog in the machine which is disrupting local life, the anonymous official in the bureaucracy of the big brewery.

To understand this new development, we must first consider the transformed economics of inebriation. The 'Big Six' breweries who own approximately 80% of Britain's locals have inaugurated a policy of 'systematic rationalisation' which is designed to streamline and modernise all aspects of the industry. This has had profound effects on the structure of the pub at all levels. Basically, it has served to reactivate the controversial question of the diminishing control exercised by local people over communal institutions and the environment in general. In practical terms, the new directive from the breweries has involved a fundamental redefinition of the relationship between landlord and customer. Firstly, the old tenant landlords who were permanently attached to one particular pub so that a reasonably amicable dialogue with the customer was generally possible, have been supplanted in many cases by the breweries' own managers who receive a fixed salary and are moved regularly from pub to pub so that no equivalent rapport can develop. This innovation, traumatic enough in its effects, has often been accompanied by equally disastrous changes in the physical environment of the pub; changes which are often deeply resented by the clientele who are never consulted beforehand and are rarely considered by the architects who perch them on precarious stools and take away their dartboards. The 'regulars' sit amidst the formica and the chrome, and, naturally, frustration is displaced into anger, and anger is directed at the 'brewery's man', the faceless official who never seems able to break the ice, the brand new 'gaffer' who hasn't actually earned the title.

At least, this would seem to be the case in several Fulham pubs and is certainly true of one local pub – the 'Durrell Arms'. The Durrell, situated on the corner of Munster Road and Fulham Road, until fairly recently comprised a saloon bar which was roomy, comfortably seated and dimly lit and a public bar complete with dartboard and quiet corners. This was replaced in 1970 by one large, flashily decorated bar with mock-Victorian light-fittings, blue and red wallpaper and plastic furniture. The dartboard and public bar prices[31] vanished along with the elderly customers who had quite literally sat with their backs to the workmen whilst the conversion was being accomplished. Visually, the new Durrell was strong to say the least, even, in places, a little surreal. The old glass and woodwork which had survived the transition clashed violently with more recent innovations and a window vainly promising 'Billiards' was set in a freshly painted bright red wall. The lights were pure music hall and the mirrors reflected row upon row of 'tasteful' prints arranged in severe symmetries after the fashion of the 'classical' living room. Cut loose from its past, for all its burlesqued history, and uprooted from the communal experience despite its heavy 'common touch', its studied jocularity, the Durrell seemed to drift in a dimension of unspecified fantasy. Like a set from a Hollywood period drama, the pub showed signs of heavy expenditure and was filled with a mass of misconstrued detail which somehow did not quite add up, and the Durrell no longer appeared to be situated anywhere in particular. Moreover, all the dark corners were now brilliantly illuminated and the jukebox joined with the garish visuals to drive away the quieter regulars (including the more discreet hustlers; conmen and thieves, etc.). A more boisterous atmosphere began to prevail and the clientele generally became younger and more extroverted.

However, this new regime was only gradually established, and whilst the old landlord remained a certain amount of continuity was automatically assured. Though not a particularly gregarious man, he had won considerable respect and it was generally agreed that he 'knew how to run a good pub'. He had, moreover, been resident at the Durrell for several years, was familiar with the local customs, catered to the local tastes and had been more or less absorbed into the community. The pressures of adjustment were further alleviated by the landlord's tactful handling of the situation. Thus, when Ted, a powerfully-built regular in his early forties stole some of the prints from the wall in full view of the assembled company, the landlord simply asked him to return them when he had sobered up. The threat of the 'bar' (being excluded) was enough to encourage Ted to comply with the landlord's request.

However, when a new manager took over in 1971, the tension which had been accumulating since the conversion could no longer be contained and complaints about the poor quality of the beer, the short measures, the garish decor, the bad service, etc. became more frequent and more audible. Relations with successive landlords have continued to deteriorate, and, from March 1973 to April 1974, the Durrell has had three new managers none of whom have managed to overcome the initial antagonism of the regulars. Whereas the old landlord was often and quite good naturedly referred to as a 'moaney old bastard', the new manager is immediately called a 'cunt', which is a word which usually denotes a real antipathy[32] and is short and sharp enough to allow for a venomous delivery. At certain times, the conflict between the publican and his clients has been conducted on an epic scale. For instance, when the manager inisted on introducing 'live' entertainment, the reaction of the customers was so fierce that one regular tried to organise a mass exodus to the nearby Wheatsheaf and actually succeeded in leading an expeditionary party to the new pub. During the subsequent hostilities, several people were 'given the bar' and fights began to break out regularly inside the pub itself.[33] Bottles and glasses were thrown across the crowded bar and one man threw a bottle at the optics and was later arrested. Furthermore, aggression began to focus specifically around the bar itself. A soda siphon was thrown at a barman who had spoken tersely to a customer and another younger man, Barry, who boasts a series of convictions for 'G.B.H.' (Grievous Bodily Harm) has been involved in a protracted feud with the present manager. In April of this year, the battle between the brewery and the customers actually reached the pages of the *Fulham Chronicle* when one regular was fined £100, at the West London Courts, for assaulting the landlord.

Obviously, it would be simplistic to attribute all these incidents *directly* to the transformation of the Durrell's interior, or even to the reorganisation of the pub's management. The acrimony has no doubt been increased by the incompatibility of certain individual customers and certain individual landlords; and tardy and inefficient service had been known to produce violent reactions in the past. Nonetheless, violent responses became far more frequent after the conversion, and aggression generally tended to flow through more open and immediate channels. Moreover, though the 'new look' had attracted a large contingent of volatile young men, they could not be held exclusively responsible; for many of the older customers were drawn into the hostilities. It seems more likely that the manager's relative impuissance – his subordination to a higher authority – was made more apparent after the pub had been physically altered by an edict issued from the omnipotent brewery. As the obedient lieutenant of some higher power, he was firmly situated in the world outside the community – the world of inflexible hierarchies, and was associated with all those impersonal, external forces which were becoming increasingly intrusive and oppressive. As an obvious outsider and a newcomer (the present 'gaffer' is Irish), his presence was doubly provocative, and consequently his autocracy was repeatedly challenged. The degree to which the landlord is now grouped with the official organs of authority (the police, the boss etc.) can be gauged by the following exchange which took place in December 1973 between Barry and the landlord.

Barry, who had been 'barred' from the Durrell the night before, made an ostentatious appearance during the Saturday lunchtime session. As he did not attempt to get served, the landlord hesitated for a few minutes and then confronted the younger man. Conversation in the vicinity of the two combatants was suspended, and the regulars watched this new episode with obvious interest:

LANDLORD: I've warned you . . . now get out!
BARRY: Alright, alright. I heard you.
LANDLORD: I won't say it again. Now be on your way!
BARRY: (aware of his audience) I said alright. I heard you the first time.
LANDLORD: Now listen, I'll phone the police if . . .
BARRY: (mimicking with obvious contempt) 'I'll phone the police!' . . . you wanker!
LANDLORD: What did you say? What was that again?

Barry moves forward, the landlord wavers between the bar and the staff door, determined not to lose face and yet anxious for his personal safety. Suddenly, Barry darts forward and punches him in the face. Barry leaves, with the landlord declaring publicly: 'That's it! That's it!' as if he had, at last, been compelled to abandon restraint and was now a force to be reckoned with. He phones the police and, despite Barry's lack of popularity with the older regulars ('he thinks he's Jack the lad'), many of them smile and shake their heads as though their low opinion of the landlord has been confirmed. The incident has been decided by the landlord's identification of his own interests with those of the police, and Barry translates this into a confession of weakness and a demonstration of the 'gaffer's' dependence on external supports.

It is through confrontations such as these that authority-structures inside the pub are regulated and hypotheses about the nature and extent of instituted authority can be tested. Thus, the conflict is not confined to the customer and the landlord, and when other representatives of officially sanctioned power are located inside the pub, similar patterns of challenge and withdrawal can be observed. For instance, when a group of men drinking at the bar were recognised as off-duty members of the police force, people began to gravitate towards that end of the pub which was furthest away from the offending party. Some people used grandiloquent gestures to publicise their antipathy – scowling and turning their backs squarely to the bar. Others sought to undermine the confidence of the policemen by quietly ridiculing them. The police reacted by contriving to present a united front of aggressive joviality in order to combat the cold shoulder. Normally, these ritualistic displays of mutual antagonism would have sufficed to restore order, and the evening would have passed without further incident. However, one regular, a man in his thirties, whom I shall call Alan, became somewhat obsessive, and, as closing-time approached, he became openly abusive, claiming that the 'gaffer' was giving the pub a 'bad name' and exhorting the police to 'fuck off and find (their) own pub'. After a time, the police could no longer tolerate this provocative behaviour, and one of their number was delegated to silence the malcontent. Alan was told that he had 'gone too far' and that the police were 'now out to get (him)'. He immediately became more subdued, and, fearing that the police were planning to plant drugs on him, he asked a young friend to act as intermediary so that the disaster of arrest could, at least for a time, be averted. This young man had recently served a prison sentence for theft and was familiar with some of the policemen present; and his penitent approaches succeeded in stabilising the situation. Whilst Alan did not apologise directly, his conduct was taken as a recognition of the ultimate power of the police, and thus both parties could retreat without losing too much dignity. The customary compromises had taken place behind the bar and the landlord had incurred strong criticisms by fraternising with the police, sharing the occasional joke and generally ensuring that the privileged guests received prompt service. Once more, traditional antagonisms had been expressed and the pulse of deference and defiance had been maintained. Once more, the protagonists had exhibited a heightened sensitivity to relationships of power which seemed to have stemmed from the ambiguous 'leisure' context in which the pub is placed (e.g. policemen out of uniform and working-class customers 'subordinated' to the doubtful authority of the landlord).

Though the reorganisation of the pub seems to have exacerbated tension between the working-class customer and authority in general, the types of conflict which I have described are by no means peculiar to the Durrell Arms. Certainly questions of *ownership* have been raised in the Durrell by the introduction of unpopular managers – questions which have remained unasked in those pubs where more suitable candidates have been chosen for the job or the old tenant landlord has been retained. Nonetheless, the pub is, by definition, one of those borderline areas (cf. the betting-shop) which hover uneasily between business and pleasure. It is a weak link in the economic structure and the sanctions and controls which normally regulate supply and demand, and determine the consumer's passivity simply do not apply. Inside the pub, order can only be established by perpetual conflict along the boundary which the bar represents and controls can only be tentatively introduced and are subject to constant testing and revision. The pub provides a space which is never *possessed* in an absolute sense by either landlord or customer,[34] and the claims of both parties are paradoxically incontrovertible. In fact, it is *disputed territory*, and the stereotypes of the consumer, the shopkeeper and the boss are inevitably confused and often discarded. The dissolution of these stereotypes conspires with the theatrical setting which the pub provides to allow problems of self-presentation to be focussed more clearly than in the mundane surroundings of home and work where roles are relatively fixed. I shall now go on to consider the various ways in which these problems are dealt with and shall try to differentiate between approaches to role-playing which merely embrace and confirm dominant definitions and those which strive to subvert or even transcend them. I shall start with the performance itself.

3. The performance[35] and the law of diminishing outrage

> No more self-defeating device could be discovered than the one society has developed in dealing with the criminal. It proclaims his career in such loud and dramatic forms that both he and the community accept the judgement as a fixed description. He becomes conscious of himself as criminal, and the community expects him to live up to his reputation, and will not credit him if he does not live up to it.
>
> Frank Tannenbaum – *Crime and Community*

> Nature
> This passionless spectator this unbreakable iceberg-face
> that can bear everything
> this goads us to greater and greater acts
> Marquis de Sade in *Marat-Sade* by Peter Weiss.

All the violent confrontations which take place over the bar and elsewhere inside the pub involve an aggressor, a victim (this role is only occasionally alternated – the original terms are usually respected) and a silent third party – the audience. In fact, the audience deserves as much attention as the two central contestants, for the confrontation will achieve nothing unless it is witnessed, verified, judged and acted upon. If we turn back to the fights which took place at the Durrell, the stimulative effect of the spectators can be appreciated immediately because in this particular situation, the performers tended to articulate an aggression which was widely felt but was generally repressed. When fights broke out, the younger men would leap onto seats and some would peer over the partitions which section off parts of the bar in order to get a better view. After one particular feud between two rival groups had resulted in several of the pub's most pugnacious characters being given 'the bar' on the same night, many of the regulars became excited and exhilarated, and several minor unconnected scuffles broke out at a private party, after closing time. The following lunchtime saw the pub packed with expectant regulars, anxious not to miss any new developments and speculating as to whether or not any of the barred men would put in an appearance and force a further confrontation with the management. In all these incidents, the relationship between the assailant (the performer) and his audience can be said to be symbiotic. He can champion the group to which he is affiliated, defend its rights or establish its ascendancy over other groups. The other customers and the bar staff will be compelled to adjust to his new status and will therefore feel involved in the actual confrontation: group myths will be nurtured, confirmed or refuted. The recipient is equally conscious of his public and will attempt to extricate himself with as little injury as possible. He is aware at all times that he is participating involuntarily in a public spectacle and must vindicate his honour and preserve a maximum of self-esteem if he is to maintain any prestige inside the pub. This triangular relationship pertains to most conflict situations which proceed as far as actual physical violence, but if the bonds which unite consumers at the Durrell are felt to be unusually strong (thus upsetting the balance of this triangle) I shall move across the river to another pub – The Bricklayer's Arms – to analyse the relationship more closely.

The Bricklayer's Arms is a very small one-bar pub, situated on the towpath just beyond Putney Bridge. Unlike the Durrell, the Brick has not been affected by the breweries' policy of modernisation, and the tenant landlord has been retained. The pub's 'authenticity' has become a positive asset and a 'Bohemian' image has been so successfully projected that the Brick recently received a favourable mention in the *Good Pub Guide* for its 'colourful qualities'. The interior, in direct contrast to the 'smart' Durrell, is overgrown with the tarnished grotesquerie of successive generations of drinkers: jazz posters of the beatnik era, photographs of boxers, lithographs of Dickensian characters, a battered moose's head and several pairs of antique skating boots are just some of the relics which litter the walls and hang from the ceiling. The limited space remaining is packed nightly with an assortment of self-styled artists, actors, criminals, survivors from the drug culture of the 1960s, and spectators drawn from the wealthy area of Putney nearby. The Brick has a visible history, plenty of dirt and a perpetually postponed demolition order – all the ingredients of a pub with 'character'.

The ratio of group to group within the pub is by no means static and the landlord, unlike the Durrell's manager, is not forced to rely on regular custom. But despite the fluctuating composition of the clientele, certain general trends are detectable. Basically, the influx a few years ago, of a group of garrulous, and extroverted 'heavies' encouraged many of the quieter customers to move away for good. It seemed that the less boisterous criminal, who lives more by his wits than his muscle and to whom anonymity is essential, had been frightened off by too open a discussion of trade secrets which had led to more concentrated attention from the police; and too much performing before people whom he could not take seriously. Certainly the pub had its fair share of performers, and there was always a large receptive audience ready to watch and listen, applaud and give credit where credit was due. Again, the violent encounter can be interpreted as a spectacle mounted for the benefit of the onlookers – it is their presence which necessitates a dramatic resolution of conflicts – and the performer often seems more concerned with the psychological impression he is making on his audience, than the physical impression he is making on his opponent. The following is an example of such a situation. A short, extremely muscular middle-aged man came into the Brick with a woman who was obviously 'rent'.[36] A younger man, aged about 19, made a derogatory remark about the woman which everybody in the vicinity heard, whereupon the other man picked up a bottle and smashed it on the table directly in front of the boy, shouting: 'I'll have your bleeding ears off son – I'm not afraid of Uncle Bill (the police) – the old Bill don't worry me' etc. This went on for about five minutes until the landlord confiscated the bottle and the boy left. It was because the boy had refused to respond, and had remained silent throughout, that a physical fight had been avoided. The performer had been able to castigate his opponent, vindicate his challenged virility and defend the woman's name without recourse to further violence and beyond this, he merely had to wait for the landlord to intervene. Victory had been conceded by default and the champion received the muted recognition of the rest of the patrons. Once again, the ritual was enacted so that a clear decision could be made and a rank order could be established inside the pub.

If a dominant position is achieved, new problems of self-clarification emerge. The reputation which the 'heavy' criminal has acquired demands constant confirmation in his everyday demeanour; and his role becomes increasingly constrictive, dictating his responses, and conditioning his reflexes. He must maintain a high profile at all times, he must allow no slight to go unpunished, no challenge to go unanswered; but most of all he must keep his audience in awe, for if he loses his status he loses everything. He pays for his power with his personality, and buys a desperate kind of freedom by sacrificing the freedom to say no, and he can never afford the luxury of compromise. Erving Goffman diagnoses his condition when he comes to examine the transformation of a 'private person' into a 'public figure':

> Where an individual has a public image, it seems to be constituted from a small selection of facts which may be true of him, which facts are inflated into a dramatic and newsworthy appearance, and then used as a full picture of him.[37]

This is certainly true of Frank, who was probably at one time the most feared man in the Bricklayer's Arms. Frank had built up a formidable reputation over the years, and, in the late 1960s, he had actually succeeded in becoming a household name. He was swamped in myth and celebrated in a mass of anecdotes which were all the more disturbing because dates and scenes were never specified and circumstances were always somewhat vague. His history had been constructed in retrospect, and, using Goffman's words again: 'He (was) anchored as an object for biography'. Thus, at school he was alleged to have been 'a vicious little bleeder', during adolescence he had been a 'young thug' ('He was tooled up (carrying a gun) before he was 20') and at 30, he was a 'real villain'. He had reputedly carried off some very big jobs and was currently running a protection racket extorting money from the local bookies and publicans.[38] Moreover, myth (and dramaturgical metaphors!) are unavoidable in Frank's case for he had invested in his own alienation, and had appeared in several films (*Poor Cow*, *Get Carter*, and *Performance*) and in various television programmes (e.g. *Z Cars*, *Special Branch*) as a stock criminal character, and, of course there was no real transition to be made from the street to the screen. In fact, on or off the film-set he was exactly what he seemed and the two media (the cinema and the saloon bar) crossfertilised and produced the immaculate image – the gangster par excellence. Frank's name was associated with those celebrities whom the press affectionately term the 'hell raisers' and every exploit was eminently newsworthy. He always appeared at the 'Brick' surrounded by an entourage of 'heavies' (some of whom had thick Glaswegian accents which amplified the menage), and, however outrageous or exhibitionist his behaviour, it always met with instant applause and approval, even when it involved actual damage to the property of his audience. For instance, when Frank picked up a large tin drum which he had been rolling around outside the pub at closing time and rammed it through the windscreen of a parked car, no complaints were made and his followers were positively congratulatory.

Of course, the dynamic relationship between the actor and the gallery demanded escalation, and crime was displaced into purer forms of drama and lost its initial rationale. As his actions became more extravagant and dangerous, his audience became increasingly difficult to impress, and, ultimately, Frank was eclipsed by his own performance. After a time, it was generally agreed that he suffered from a 'death-wish' and his doom was prematurely sealed in the stories which began to circulate in the Brick which told of Frank's 'last' exploit. It was said that his arms had been broken by big East End villains, that the tendons in his legs had been cut and he was confined to a wheelchair, crippled for life. But the audience was denied its catharsis and Frank merely faded away from Fulham. Eventually he was absorbed into the world of films and he was paradoxically removed from the community at the very moment when he became the official representative of Fulham's criminal culture.

Frank may seem to constitute a special case,[39] but his situation is symbolic of the predicament in which many violent criminals find themselves. The 'performer' defines himself against the reaction of his public – he *is* only in so far as he is *seen to be* and he must find his self image reflected in the eyes of his spectators. Like the moral entrepreneur, the violent criminal thrives on outrage and is likely to be faced with a similar dilemma. For outrage is an exhaustible resource; it must be perpetually recycled, and if the 'heavy' is to survive in a form which he can recognise (i.e. if he is to remain finite) he must move with his audience. A kind of brinkmanship develops (with the camera, with the audience) which forces the violent criminal into ever greater excesses, into ever more contorted and stylised postures, and, ultimately, the audience manipulates him as much as he controls his audience (a fatal symbiosis!). In fact, the spectacular 'disaffiliate' (one who 'voluntarily acts irregularly and somewhat rebelliously') or 'social deviant' (who 'temporarily refuses to accept his place') threatens to decline to a point where he *serves* his audience as a mere entertainer, and 'performs the clownish functions' of the 'in-group deviant' who, like the 'village-idiot, the small-town drunk and the platoon clown' acts as a communal 'mascot' and dances on the end of strings which he no longer holds.[40] When the criminal tries to avoid the intolerable fact of his own expendability by performing for the crowd, he is no longer in full possession of himself and he is, at least partially, *owned* by his audience.

The 'heavy' image is basically a distancing device allowing the criminal to differentiate himself from the 'straights' who surround him. It is designed to take him *above* the crowd, presumably to an area no longer accessible to dominant definitions where he can relax, expand and be *himself*. Instead, it merely confirms dominant expectations, renders behaviour more predictable (and more visible) and the 'heavy' dwindles inside his role until the image takes over completely. His statements are direct and unambiguous and therefore comprehensible (i.e. assimilable). He remains inside the game, and he is as subject as the 'nobodies' and the 'straights' to external determinations. Indeed, his movements are, in many ways, more restricted than those of 'private persons', and the options open to him are severely limited. In short, his world has been closed and Frank, like Tony Lawrence, can be described as very 'ronnie' indeed.

To examine other more sophisticated distancing devices which seek to transcend or subvert the game itself, and to break the rules of social interaction at a far deeper level, I shall turn to a group of rather less ostentatious deviants. As this group maintains certain connections with the West Indian underworld of South London, I shall be punctuating the following sections with the occasional references to the relevant Jamaican subcultures.

4. Some teaheads and a rule of silence

The ability to adopt a certain role, to play a part or tell a story convincingly, is perhaps the most important skill those involved in various forms of non-violent crime can possess. The confidence trickster is not the only criminal who depends upon his acting ability to make a living. A thief must be able to talk himself out of a difficult situation if he is to avoid arrest for any length of time. In a more abstract way, the criminal often seeks to evade or deflect inquiries and undertakes to escape classification for its own sake.[41] His determination to work outside any code or framework, however sympathetically constructed, which is imposed from outside indicates an extreme individualism and he often validates this by adopting an anarchist position.[42] If the only certainty upon which one can depend is to know what one is not, then those who presume to define what one actually is are going to be greeted with considerable suspicion, and the best way of staying unknown is not to say anything at all. A specific example will illustrate how the rule of silence operates.

Before the Durrell had been redecorated it had served as a convenient meeting-place for various hustlers and villains who were attracted by the pub's discreet atmosphere. The heavy curtains and the dimly-lit corners promised enough privacy for the shadiest of transactions, and drugs, amongst other things, could be bought and sold without too much difficulty. William Burroughs' description of 'teaheads' applies equally well to a certain group who regularly used the Durrell: 'They were gregarious, they were sensitive, and they were paranoic', and Burroughs found them 'unfathomable'.[43] Aged between 30 and 40, they belonged to a kind of first generation of marijuana users and were probably more culturally affiliated to the groups which Becker describes in *The Outsiders*, than to the hippie-groups which were receiving enormous publicity at the time. In fact, some were jazz musicians and many showed an interest in the more esoteric modern jazz and commonly used the distancing techniques which Becker describes ('straight' v 'cool' etc.). But the group derived its singular identity from more local sources and the black immigrant community in nearby Notting Hill and Ladbroke Grove had exerted a considerable influence.[44] Both the marijuana and the music had provided bonds of interest which had drawn the two groups together. Firstly, in the early 1960s, the smoking of 'grass' had been confined mainly to the West Indian community in London, and, as the market had been controlled by black dealers, a certain amount of contact between immigrant subcultures and white groups who sought access to the drug was inevitable. This commercial transaction often led to exchanges at a cultural level and music began to pass along the same subterranean channels which linked the two communities. Thus, black and white jazz musicians would 'jam' together and influence each other's styles; reggae rhythms began to provide the percussive bass and the jazz took on an 'Afro' feel.[45] Other meanings were of course transmitted; contained within the music and wrapped around the 'charge'[46] and these registered at levels less susceptible to analysis. Suffice it to say, that speech patterns, argot and the complex of rituals and taboos which surround smoking were surreptitiously passed back and forth between the two subcultures and formed another basis of communication. It can be reasonably assumed that amongst those subtler decantations, the various techniques of distancing, of limiting access, and controlling the flow of information to the outside world (i.e. the *form* of that social interaction) were also invisibly exchanged; and the first rule is, of course, the rule of silence.

Thus, conversation in the Durrell was conducted in an atmosphere of perpetual understatement and meaning was intimated by gesture and glance. One learned to listen for the significant pause, to read between the spoken lines and fill in the omissions, and information could only be accumulated very gradually indeed. For instance, the abrupt disappearance of Nick, a formerly popular regular failed to attract any comment whatsoever, and direct enquiries were swiftly deflected. Eventually, I was able to piece together a tentative picture of what *appears* to have happened. It transpired that Nick had been arrested for possession of drugs, and had received an unusually heavy sentence (this itself was the subject of a humourous anecdote about Nick and a crusading lawyer from Release). Nonetheless, his appeal was immediately successful and he was free again before the end of the month. This seemingly inexplicable sequence of events represented a riddle which was finally solved for me by Terry, another group member with a talent for equivocation, who said cryptically 'Let's just say that, at that time, a lot of heads started to roll that shouldn't have'. No more was said – I was left with just enough information to make the correct inference and the subject was promptly dropped.

It is only by supplying the missing pieces that episodes such as these can be rendered comprehensible. But absences, though eloquent are never unambiguous, and the authorised version of the story of Nick's betrayal can never be written. Refracted through time and the group perspective, fact has modulated into memory, even mystery; and, in the final analysis, interpretation is a matter of belief. The sentence of silence (i.e. expulsion from the group) is passed in silence and Nick has quite simply ceased to exist for Terry. However, Terry, though circumspect to the point of paranoia, has provided a key and the episode unfolds itself elliptically. Certain other members of the group have evolved more elaborate screening devices, and have extended that margin of doubt upon which communication depends into a whole system of discourse.

I shall now analyse that system and see how it is used to discriminate against outsiders and to mislead public interest.

5. The wind up – rather 'Rasta'

> No Moroccan will ever tell you what he thinks, or does, or means. He'll tell you some of it and tell you other things that are completely false and then weave them together into a very believable core which you swallow, and that's what's considered civilized. What's the purpose of telling the truth? It's not interesting generally. It's more interesting to doctor it up a bit first of all, so it's more decorative and hence more civilized. And besides, how could anyone be so idiotic as to open himself up to the dangers involved in telling the unadorned truth to people?
>
> Paul Bowlos quoted in *Rolling Stone* (May 23, 1974).

> Give me the facts, ma'am, just the facts.
>
> Detective Jack Friday in American T.V. series *Dragnet.*

If Terry demonstrates how silence can be made to communicate then the wind up shows how verbal communication can be used to preserve silence – to prevent anything 'real' being disclosed to the outside world. For the wind up is the game of fabrication, formalised and played at various levels for amusement and for profit, and, as a kind of in-group anastrophe, it implicitly distinguishes the 'straight' from the 'crooked' initiate. Thus, when Billy who is definitely a jazz musician, probably a thief, and perhaps a pornographer is introduced to a new face, he will immediately proceed to wind the stranger up by relating a series of personal exploits which become progressively less credible as the conversation goes on. At some point in this spiral, the 'victim' will realise he is being duped and can either beat an embarrassed retreat or engage in the game itself, but, whichever option he chooses, he can no longer ignore the fact that alien frames of reference are being used which invalidate the normal rules of discourse. At one sweep, the wind up dispenses with the fundamental conventions of verbal interaction and breaks the tacit agreement which, under normal circumstances, unites two speakers by *openly* declaring its commitment to *untruths*. In this way, the wind up performs an inherently subversive function, and, even if the 'straight' victim accepts the terms of the game, he cannot translate his 'findings' back into a more familiar language because a totally different epistemology is governing the exchange. He has forfeited his control of the meanings generated within that exchange and can only transcend his original status as victim if he is prepared to abandon his position in the 'straight' world (i.e. if he takes to crime like Laing to madness). The wind up is therefore used to ward off undesirable outsiders who are reluctant to make this crucial transition and the 'intruders' provide a constant source of amusement and an occasional source of income for the criminal using the wind up technique. To take an example, Billy told me how he had carved a 'primitive' figure in wood, covered it in black boot polish and taken it to a newly opened antique shop on the Fulham Road. He claimed he was given £30 for what the owner had believed to be a valuable African piece and Billy ended his account by drawing his own moral: 'Those geezers don't know nothing'. This comment simultaneously closed the narrative and completed the wind up sequence by undercutting the story which had preceded it and intentionally diminishing the speaker's own credibility. With a purposefully prolonged glance into the eyes of his audience, Billy intimates that no one is exempt from the wind up – that the wind up itself, could be a wind up, and with all the details thrown into doubt, only the initial motivating contempt for the outsider is unequivocally communicated.

All conversations with wind up artists are liable to the sudden 'double take' and the even terrain of conventional pub discourse is discarded for a more unsettled sphere where 'reality' is constantly being questioned, disproved and reevaluated. Indeed, many of the criminals employing the wind up technique have experimented with L.S.D. which has radically affected their ideas about perception and has enhanced the importance of subjective observations.[47] Thus, certain members of the group seem to live on manifold planes of fiction, which they are constantly shifting to amuse each other and confuse onlookers, and these shifts are automatically accomplished by the magic words 'wind up'. Meanings are therefore extremely motile and a stable consensus cannot be established inside the group because these meanings are subject to abrupt and apparently random falsifications. As personal disclosures by individual members of the group can only receive a temporary and cautious ratification, and can, at any time, be repudiated by any other member, relationships inside the group are characterised by distance and unanimity can never be assured. Perhaps it cannot even be considered, and, as there is no standard by which to gauge the verity of a statement or the sincerity with which it is given, opinions tend to aggregate instead of cohering in a 'group perspective'.

Just how complicated such an anarchic situation can become is, perhaps, best illustrated by an account of a brilliantly sustained and thoroughly bewildering wind up conducted in August 1969 by two criminals, Bernie and Den. Both men are professional criminals, have been convicted several times for offences involving theft and violence and have both 'done plenty of porridge'.[48] Bernie is a stocky 40 year old who cultivates a 'bizarre' image, and claims to have worked in an obscure capacity for the Krays. His head is sometimes shaved and he talks in quick staccato bursts, using a curious mixture of beatnik and criminal argot which he intersperses with the occasional Jamaican swear-word. He has spent several years in a mental institution being treated for a schizophrenic condition,[49] and has taken L.S.D. frequently. Den is a small wiry thief and driver, renowned for his uncontrollable temper and his 'colourful' language. The long and bitter experience of prison is indelibly written across his face, and although about the same age as Bernie, he looks at least ten years older. The wind up began in earnest when Den was driving Bernie, myself, and another passenger to a wedding reception after the pub had closed. Den's driving suffered from the effects of the gruelling session which had just been completed at the Durrell, and he also claimed to have been 'swallowing' (i.e. taking amphetamines) since early evening. The following is an approximate transcription of the conversation:

BERNIE: Cool it, Den, nice cool ride – let's have a nice cool ride.

DEN: Alright, alright. I know how to fucking drive.

BERNIE: Your driving's cool, y'know – (*turning to us*) – this cat's a good driver – y'know? He drove for Joe Bananas once – You know Joe? A big hood up the West End – a cat with some muscle up there – but not so good with his eyes – very shortsighted y'know? Well, Den's driving Joe round the Elephant[50] and Den wants to stop and post a letter – y'know? Well, he stops the wheels at the lights – sees a post box – jumps out and posts the letter – comes back, sits down – Joe taps him on the shoulder – says 'Who wuz that flash-looking guy in de red suit you wuz talking to?'

(*Much laughter. The car stops to allow Den to sober up a little*).

BERNIE: I'd like a spliff[51] – There's two cats here would like a draw. They're cool; they're cool (*looks at Den then at us*). I would rather turn on two cats like you than lay a virgin. Can I have the gear, Den?

DEN: You've got it, you cunt!

BERNIE: I have no shit, Den – It's gone – I swear, I have no gear.

DEN: You lying bastard – you've got your own smoke and you've nicked mine out of me pocket – you fucking cunt!

BERNIE: Leave it out, Den, leave it out. Would I do that? You're a brother. Straight up. I dropped the gear in the Durrell and the scene was such that I couldn't pick it up – The cat behind the bar had his bins[52] on me – I could not recapture it.

DEN: Bollocks! Fucking bollocks! You lying bleeder – you've had my smoke!

BERNIE: Would I do that? (*Stops to appeal to us*). The scene was such that . . .

DEN: You mean bastard. I know you.

BERNIE: On my two babies' lives, I did not touch that gear and Eddy and his friend here would like a smoke and all you can think about is keeping your gear to yourself, and other such aggravation.

(*Gives Eddy the cigarette papers with which to start 'building' the 'spliff'*).

DEN: What you wanna nick off a mate for, eh? What you wanna nick off me for? You cunt!

BERNIE: Come on, Den – I haven't touched your lousy gear – now let's turn on these two nice cats and leave all this nonsense out of it.

DEN: Right, we won't have none . . . (*the car shoots forward and snakes off dangerously*).

BERNIE: Nice cool ride, nice cool . . .

DEN: Shuddup!

BERNIE: I must apologise for this cat, y'know? – Too much acid screwed up his head.

DEN: Don't come all that bollocks – I'm alright – It's you who's got to worry. You're a bleeding maniac, you and all that with Rene.

BERNIE: We're friends, Den – right? Brothers.

DEN: Yeah, yeah – but what you have to kill her for? There was no need to fucking kill her.

BERNIE: Cool it, Den – that's all in the past and you're there dragging it all up again (*starts shaking Den to make him change the subject, but also affects his already unsteady driving*).

BERNIE: Now let's get to this gaff – nice cool ride, nice cool ride.

DEN: Shut your fucking mouth – you, and your nice cool ride, nice cool ride – Why don't you get out and fucking walk?

We arrive at the reception, but the argument continues and becomes more and more vociferous until the other guests separate and allow the protagonists to 'take the floor'. Den confronts Bernie in the centre of the room and repeatedly accuses him of theft. Bernie makes silent appeals to his audience, raising his arms in an exaggerated fashion and generally inviting the other guests to join him in deprecating his companion's unreasonable behaviour. As the drama shows signs of losing its initial impetus, Bernie introduces a new theme and announces that he knows a place in Ladbroke Grove where he can 'score' some more 'smoke'. He goes round collecting £1 from each person to pay for the 'gear' but a new argument develops over who is going to drive Bernie to Ladbroke Grove. Den refuses to allow anyone else to use his car, and Bernie, for his part, points out that Den is unfit to drive. This continues for about five minutes until Den eventually concedes defeat and reaches into his pocket for his car keys. At this point, Bernie leaps forward and slaps Den in the face with the pound notes he has just collected chanting 'Bread! Bread! Bread for your head!' Den pushes him off and the two men begin to grapple, knocking into the furniture and the other guests. Locked in an embrace, they stagger across the room and fall to the floor. They are separated, apologise to the bridegroom for making the bride cry and leave. After their departure, conflicting explanations of what had already happened are discussed by the remaining guests, and, for a while at least, the wedding is eclipsed by this new dramatic incident. I left the reception soon afterwards and saw the two men in Den's parked car quietly enjoying a smoke together.

This episode contains a whole complex of interrelated wind ups which systematically undermine each other and overwhelm the observer. Each moment denies its predecessor, and, though there is a sequence, there can be no pattern for, in the last moment (when Den and Bernie share a smoke) all previous moments are atomised and the wind up dismantles itself in retrospect. Moreover, the sequence was not initiated by a signal so we can assume that Eddy and myself merely intersected a continuum and though we constituted the original victims, the relationship between the two central protagonists is itself by no means unambiguous (in fact we can say that the wind up revolved around this central ambiguity).[53] The humourous 'gangster' anecdote about Joe Bananas, and the 'murder' of Rene were most probably introduced to wind up the audience, but the alliance between Bernie and Den was itself supremely unstable and it is highly likely that the two criminals were winding each other up either to see what they could get out of each other or to avoid sharing their hash with too many people. Alternatively, we could see the whole event as a ritual contest inaugurated by the two criminals so that they could test their skill at the game; but as the 'game' itself hovers alarmingly between 'play' and 'not-play' (i.e. it is almost *about* playing games) it would be more meaningful to say that Bernie and Den were *testing the distance* which separated them in the real world rather than *using the symbolic distance* of ritual to protect themselves from the normal implications of their actions. The problems of interpretation remain insoluble, the motives of the protagonists inscrutable. The only thing that is certain is that the incident constitutes a spontaneous performance, enacted by two mutually suspicious criminals.

The wind up is characterised precisely by the unpredictable quality of the performances it produces and if we turn back to the scenarios into which Frank wrote himself, we can begin to assess in what ways and to what extent it is innovative. Whereas Frank habitually fulfils the expectations of his audience, Bernie and Den manipulate and falsify those expectations in order to achieve a measure of freedom from those external controls, which an audience normally impose. Once more, the forms of social interaction have been subverted (cf. Rasta language/perception) and this subversion is accompanied by a disaffiliation from the goals of the society in which the protagonists are situated. Bernie and Den are both extremely hostile towards any 'straight' organisation and welcome their deviant status resisting any attempts by 'normals' to colonise the outlands which they inhabit. The wind up artist, in general, regards the media as a gigantic conspiracy designed to stultify the 'straights' and simplify experience and he responds aggressively to the interest he arouses in the media. Consequently, he attempts to ridicule and mislead as much as possible and the wind up acts as the convenient smokescreen behind which he can live out his life unmolested. In effect, he is waging war on the Word,[54] and it is at the level of linguistics that a fuller exposition of the wind up is now most appropriately directed.

Language as a transformed commodity

'You'd really hate an adult to understand you. That's the only thing you've got over them – the fact you can mystify and worry them.'

16 year old Mod from South London quoted in *Generation X*

When we attempt to describe the wind up as a particular type of speech event we are faced with what appear to be insuperable difficulties. The wind up does not declare itself as ritual. It is remarkably flexible and can fluctuate from one semantic level to another. It is at once a game and not a game and it is designed specifically to elude definition. It can even deny its own existence in the perplexing tautology: 'The wind up itself is only a wind up'.[55] To appreciate the magnitude of the problem, we need only invoke William Labov's rules for ritual insults which are used to describe 'sounding' – an overtly similar type of discourse. Sounding is a competitive game of ritual (i.e. impersonalised) insults played by members of adolescent negro gangs in urban America. Each player takes his turn and one sound is built on another e.g.

ROGER: 'Your mother got a .45 in her left titty.'
MONEY: 'Your mother got a .45 degree titty.'
BOOT: 'Your mother got titties behind her neck.'

Improvisation is strictly limited within this framework and Labov manages to formulate a fairly rigid international structure, arguing four basic properties:

1 A sound opens a *field*, which is meant to be sustained. A sound is presented with the expectation that another sound will be offered in response and that second sound may be built formally upon it. The player who presents an initial sound is thus offering others the opportunity to display their ingenuity at his expense.

2 Besides the initial two players, a third person is necessary.
3 Any third person can become a player, especially if there is a failure by one of the two players then engaged.
4 *Considerable symbolic distance is maintained and serves to insulate the event from other kinds of verbal interaction.* (my italic).

Now, whenever the word 'sound' occurs in rule (1), the words 'wind up' can be substituted, and the other two rules require no modifications at all. However, the last rule cannot be transferred so easily, for the wind up is characterised precisely by the absence of such *symbolic* distancing, and in so far as a wind up sequence is not openly initiated by an identifiable signal (of 'Your mother' . . .) it cannot be differentiated from the welter of discourse which surrounds it. It can inform the exchange *invisibly* (i.e. as a set of expectations) or it can be used to reclassify a previously 'straightforward' exchange (i.e. 'You're winding me up' . . . 'This is a wind up'). That is to say, the wind up can either organise the perceptions of the speakers *in time* and remain unacknowledged, *or* it can work backwards *through time* having been made apparent by one of the speakers. To use Korzybski's distinction[56] the wind up is, at any one time, either all *map* or all *territory* and the two are never allowed to coincide (i.e. it would not be possible to say: 'This is a wind up – Do you want to play?') Certainly, the event has formal aspects (it has a name) and knowledge of the event is shared, but the wind up is used to differentiate between individuals inside the group as well as to define the group itself against the outside world. Conspiracy is, so to speak, the name of the game (i.e. A + B v C), but, as we have seen, it is possible for one conspirator to wind up a co-conspirator whilst still subscribing to the initial compact (i.e. [A v B] v C). As the symbolic distancing which is achieved in a clearly signalled ritual is absent in the wind up, the players are not insulated properly from the normal world and this can result in severe dislocations within both the group and the individual (i.e. real symbolic distancing). Labov defines a ritual as a 'sanctuary' in which the actors 'are freed from the personal responsibility for the acts' in which they are engaged but the safeguards which usually bracket off the ritual exchange from other types of discourse are absent in this case and the wind up does not even qualify as ritual in Labov's sense of the word. And, as all discourse can be negated in retrospect by any group member, Labov's first rule can no longer be used to describe the wind up (because *all* discourse is potential field), and the task of definition remains as forbidding as ever.

Gregory Bateson's theory of the Double-Bind can perhaps be applied to the wind up with rather more success. In his famous series of essays,[57] Bateson demonstrated that play, fantasy, art, poetry and schizophrenia are all 'trans-contextual syndromes' which develop in response to experienced breaches in the weave of contextual structure (i.e. in response to double-bind situations). Russell's discovery concerning the exclusive nature of Logical Types was used as the epistemological base for Bateson's own communications theory which revolved around an examination of the relationship between contrasting levels of abstraction (object: sign: context: mode) as used in ordinary verbal interactions. Each message was contained in and defined by a larger message which Bateson called a 'metamessage' and conventional communication was said to depend upon the correct (i.e. consensual) identification and decodification of these metacommunicative signs (i.e. signs about signs e.g. 'This is play'). These metacommunicative messages corresponded to psychological frames which served to locate the whole message within a context and therefore to give it meaning. The frames were designed to avoid the paradoxes of abstraction by containing them. Thus the frame which corresponds to the metamessage: 'This is play' contains the Epimenidean paradox: 'These actions in which we now engage do not denote what would be denoted by those actions which these actions denote'. This was expressed diagramatioally thus:

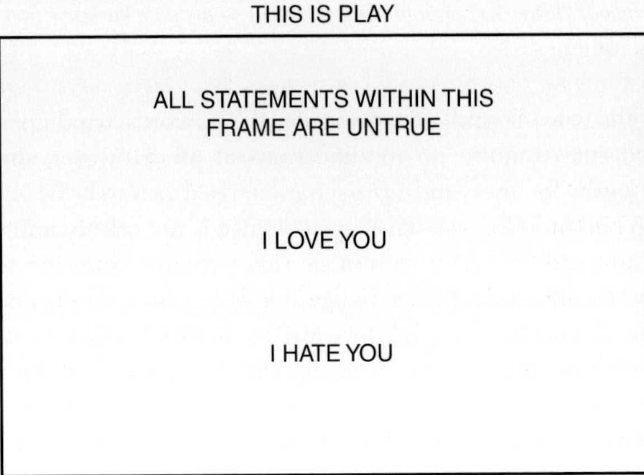

Figure 1

The first statement within this frame is a self-contradictory proposition which carries all the other statements with it for the message or signals exchanged in play are not 'really' meant and denote something which does not 'really' exist. The 'trans-contextual syndromes' mentioned above represented the various responses to 'metacommunicative tangles' – those moments when the mode of the message was confused. Thus, if the signals which identified the mode of the message (i.e. which established whether it was literal or metaphorical) were *involuntarily* misinterpreted, the individual could become severely disturbed and a schizophrenic condition could develop. The schizophrenic's 'word-salad' of unlocated metaphors was attributed to the patient's inability to surround the verbal message with the appropriate frame. Ultimately, the schizophrenic's verbalisations can be said to *meta*communicate the end of communication (i.e. 'There is no relationship between us') and can be said to mean that meaning is impossible. In effect, the paradoxes are no longer contained and have become *themselves* the subject of the communication.[58] Bateson argued that normal discourse, on the other hand, is conducted at multiple levels of abstraction and non-psychotic individuals were credited with considerable dexterity in dealing with sudden shifts in the various levels at which a message could be located. Humour, for instance, often compelled our evaluation of earlier signals and mode-identifiers were deliberately falsified in certain instances (e.g. the confidence trick). Communication between two individuals can therefore be said to depend precisely upon the synchronous discrimination and labelling of the mode in which that communication is cast.

Obviously, we have now encountered a language which can be used to describe quite adequately that class of discourse of which the wind up is a member. It seems strange that Bateson himself did not undertake such a description. Instead, he merely mentioned in passing that another and 'more complex form' of interaction based around the question 'Is this play?' could be identified, and it is to this category that the wind up can be most appropriately assigned. I would maintain that this form deserves far more attention than it has been accorded in the past *because it actually bridges the gap between normal and pathological responses to metacommunicative tangles* (i.e. between creativity and schizophrenia). We have argued that communication between two speakers depends upon correlated frames of reference being used simultaneously by those speakers, and without a high degree of congruence at the various levels of abstraction from which these frames are constituted, communication is itself impossible. Thus, we can say that the function of communication is to provide *answers* (i.e. to establish relationships between things). Now, if the exchange is framed by a question (e.g. 'Is this play?') this cannot be accomplished properly because a question does not allow for the kind of stability which meanings require. The context *itself* is *unlocated*, and as the forms alternate between the mutually exclusive contexts of play and not-play, the paradoxes are multiplied and the frame threatens to disintegrate exposing these paradoxes and exploding communication. The frame (that is to say the metacommunication) only exists to be seen and when it is obscured – (i.e. when it is quite literally *in question*) there is an automatic regress towards the first available context which can be used to define the meaning of the messages which are being exchanged. This, the second frame (or metametacommunication) of that discourse which the question 'Is this play?' has failed to contain, corresponds to the metacommunication (or first frame) of the schizophrenic's verbal 'exchanges' which can be formulated axiomatically thus: 'There is no relationship between us'.

To sum up, I have argued that a frame which is a question is a contradiction in terms. I have attributed the ambiguity of the messages exchanged within a wind up sequence to the fact that they are constructed around the question 'Is this play?'. As they are framed by a question, the forms generated within the exchange are inconclusively located and are therefore extremely insecure. When the paradoxes prove unmanageable, the frame collapses and 'entropy' or 'negative feedback' can be said to occur in the communication system. We are now acquiring a fuller understanding of the implications of the wind up and related forms and we can summarise our discoveries in the following diagram:

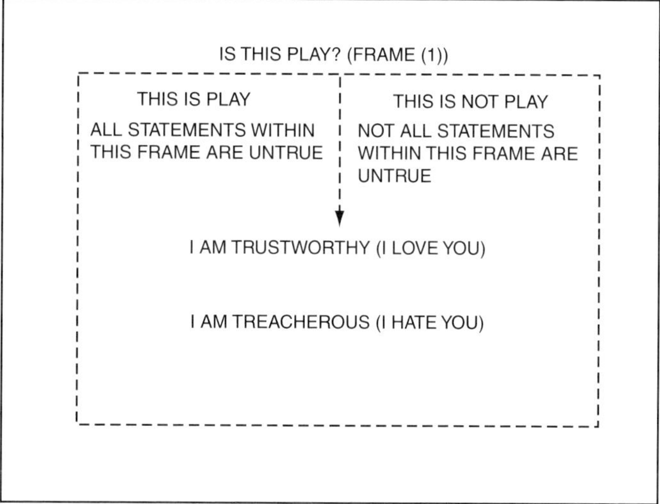

Figure 2

Now, although the paradoxes of abstraction are theoretically contained by the question 'Is this play?' they are never effectively framed because the messages cannot be decisively located in either context (This is play/not play). In other words, the frame cannot resolve itself and, as the paradoxes multiply and accumulate along line (a), frame (1) can no longer contain them. Thus, at certain key stages in that sequence which is the wind up, frame

(1) splits temporarily and is replaced by frame (2). 'Negative feedback' occurs at these crucial points and meaning itself is in the balance for the duration of these crises (i.e. until frame (1) is stabilised once more.)

To understand this process more thoroughly, we need only invoke the experience of the schizophrenic. We can use the mutually double-binding relationship which exists between the therapist and his patient as a model for the relationship between the 'social deviant' (the criminal who embraces an outlaw status) and the 'interested straight'. The therapist requires the patient to discard his own epistemology so that the schizophrenic's world can be discussed and the unlocated metaphors which characterise that world can be firmly situated inside the therapeutic context (i.e. so that the words 'as if' which the schizophrenic has forbidden can be interpolated into the exchange). As the therapist's approach denies the *meta*meaning of the patient's verbalisations (i.e. 'There is no relationship between us'), the schizophrenic responds to his enquiries by becoming more and more evasive and a complementary schismogenesis develops.[59] In the same way, the 'social deviant' is convinced that there can be no congruity between himself and the straight world and the approach of the 'interested straight' is interpreted as an attack on the epistemological foundations of his 'crooked' system. In Goffman's words, he knows that even 'where placement is favourable', he is still going to be placed in someone else's context, and is likely to be defended 'in terms of his stigma'.[60]

It is through the wind up that such placement can be avoided and the threat which the intruder represents can be neutralised. Thus, the wind up constitutes a group strategy which parallels the individual schizophrenic's tactics of consistent evasion. However, it occupies a completely different category precisely because it is a *group* response (i.e. there *can* be 'communication' about the impossibility of 'real' communication). Whilst the wind up could, perhaps, be described as *tactics one stage removed from madness*, that distance between the two responses must always be maintained. For those actively involved in a wind up merely debate the proposition which the schizophrenic lives out, and though the validity of psychological framing is brought into question (because the frame *itself* is a question), the matter is never conclusively decided one way or the other. This can be demonstrated if we refer back to figure 2. Although frame (1) is permanently on the brink of disintegration, it is never dispensed with entirely. Instead, it merely lapses temporarily at these crucial points in the wind up sequence which I have already indicated (i.e. when the paradoxes prove unmanageable and the wind up is registered in the 'victim's' responses). Nonetheless, at these points, entropy does occur, and once the wind up has been recognised as an immanence in the communication system, the stability of that system is jeopardised and all previous communication is seriously devalued. The wind up, then, is integrated into the structured discourse of the pub and yet it can be used at any time to undermine that structure of which it is a part. Ironically, it is the inapplicability of Labov's rules which tells us most about the wind up, for the 'social reality' which Labov explores is a communicable reality – a reality of relationships, and the wind up artist is continually questioning the validity of these relationships and denying their existence. And if language provides an essential matrix for the relationships which pertain within a given society, then the wind up is intrinsically 'anti-social' because it challenges the principle of pattern itself by actively dwelling upon the disjunction between those contrasting levels of abstraction upon whose harmonious interplay communication depends.

In this section, I have argued that the wind up can be located somewhere in between those 'trans-contextual syndromes' which are 'normal' and those which are officially defined as 'pathological'. I would now assign the Rastafarian mythology to the same intermediate category. For the metaphors which abound in reggae are at once located and unlocated and the dubious area in between is the medium through which 'dread' can be communicated (Rollston Kallyndyn defines 'dread' as that 'incommunicable point between the Rude Boy and the Law'). The cult of Ras Tafari itself rests on ambiguity (is the 'as if' clause omitted on purpose?) and retains its diabolical connotations by continually shifting the modes in which its messages are placed. We can distinguish similar patterns of assimilation and inversion, acquisition and denial in the creation of both the Rasta mythology and the wind up technique. Both the Rastaman and the wind up artist embrace their outlaw status, refusing to be drawn away from the fringes of the societies in which they are situated and both publicly declare their disaffiliation from the goals and norms of those societies. This antagonism towards dominant values permeates every level of subcultural meaning and has dictated innovations in the infrastructure – at the levels of language and perception. To understand how those innovations were accomplished, we need only turn back to the Mods and to the transformation of the commodities which they took to themselves. Just as the Mods appropriated those commodities by redefining their use-value (i.e. by disrupting or at least rearranging the syntactical relations which pertain between the consumer and the commodities he consumes), so the wind up artist and the black subscribing to the Rasta mythology transformed language by first taking it and then turning it back upon itself so that it came to perform a profoundly subversive function. The reallocation of meanings at this level amounts to the final act of appropriation open to the deviant subculture which is sufficiently alienated from the dominant system to make an ideological break with that system, but which finds itself unwilling or unable to engage in 'straight' oppositional politics. And it was the failure of the mod movement as a whole to make innovations in the infrastructure which accounts for its ultimate exploitation and assimilation during the mid-1960s.

I shall now go on to finish that task of comparison and contrast which I outlined in Part 3, and shall attempt to differentiate between the various responses to public interest exhibited by the deviant subcultures in Fulham. At the same time, I hope to clarify those descriptive categories ('ronnie', 'rasta') which I have been using throughout this section, and to focus on the problematic area of aesthetic determinations once more, so that some of the questions raised during this study of subcultural conflict can be resolved.

7. Who's directing this film? – the wind up as falsified performance

I have punctuated the preceding account of subcultural styles in the 1960s with repeated references to the popular cinema and the archetypes which that cinema generates. Film recommended itself as a peculiarly accessible medium to both the student and the subculture, and, by identifying two totally different responses to a specific genre, I hoped to delineate as large an area of subcultural meaning as possible. I went on to argue a correspondence between the aesthetic parameter and other adjacent dimensions, and suggested, in particular, that a graduated commitment to dominant forms of expression could indicate a parallel commitment to the status quo. Hopefully, in the process, 'popular culture', which is all too often presented as an undefined amalgam of literary prejudices, or as a figment of the 'sociological imagination' was revealed as a heterogeneous complex of shifting relationships. Thus, we could talk of cinema dictating style and meaning; creating expectations; organising perception; even, finally, reaffirming the conditions of its own production.

These observations were underpinned by the premise that the cinema provides an ideal medium through which the dominant ideology can be unobtrusively transmitted, and that film can therefore be used to represent those concealed channels through which dominant definitions are mediated to members of the working class. As form and content literally pass through the same nodal points in that lens-system which *is* cinema, it was necessary to introduce a term which would at once suggest a simultaneous and congruent causality, and, therefore, I referred to a whole set of intermediary aesthetic determinations (the word 'determination' being used as an ideographic sign for itself).[62] We can now define role as the means through which these two parallel functions are realigned within the individual consciousness (i.e. a role is a determination in practice). The ways in which the various subcultures attempted to deal with aesthetic determinations, the ways in which they appropriated the meanings of the relevant genres which had provided them with their 'styles' were consequently absolutely crucial and could be said to define the value systems which the respective subcultures were ultimately to adopt. Hence, the binary opposition which was set up between the Kray/Gangster and Rasta/Rude Boy styles simultaneously symbolised the distance between two contrasting responses to a formative genre and two totally different ideological systems (i.e. a system of closure and a system of transcendence/ detachment).

When we came to consider the context in which subcultures were evolved in the Fulham of the 1960s, the cinematic metaphor proved particularly appropriate, and the importance of aesthetic determinations could be immediately appreciated. For, as I have already pointed out, the middle-class 'invasion' of Fulham coincided with (perhaps even directly produced) an intensification of the media's interest in the 'colourful' local culture and the resulting conflict between dominant and subterranean definitions was literally projected onto the cinema screen. Consequently, problems of self-determination and self-presentation were exacerbated and made immediately and dramatically apprehensible. Resolutions were required with a greater urgency than is, perhaps, usual. The tension thus created was most noticeably registered in the pubs which provided arenas in which these conflicts were acted out before an audience whose keen interest was often translated into actual involvement (e.g. at the Durrell). I would argue that the lines of demarcation which separated the 'crooked' performer from his 'straight' audience depended not only upon the outcome of these confrontations but also upon the manner in which the performances themselves were undertaken. To demonstrate this, I shall merely elaborate upon the distinction which has already been made between the straightforward response to outside interest exhibited by the performer (e.g. Frank) and the devious and ambivalent reaction to the same interest exhibited by the wind up artist (e.g. Bernie).[63]

When describing the performances in which Frank involves himself, I explained how he scrupulously preserves the ritual distances which separate him from both his victim and his audience and attempts (albeit unsuccessfully) to transcend dominant definitions whilst still fulfilling the expectations of his public. Bernie, on the other hand, adopts a totally different approach, and deliberately plays with appearances, confusing the relations which pertain within that triangle which encompasses the performance; and subverts the game itself by falsifying those expectations. We can say that whereas Frank rises to the occasion and, in a sense, 'loses himself', Bernie only appears to do so, and, by undermining the communication process, he manages to remain 'private' and inscrutable. In practice, this means that Frank acknowledges his public and gives more daring performances for its gratification, whilst Bernie misleads that public and moves secretly behind the impenetrable wall of the wind up. We can now complete that diagram (figure 1) from which were derived the two descriptive categories which were originally used to differentiate between the performances of Bernie and Frank (and the influences which bore upon them), by postulating a parallel polarity between those two responses along the parameter of the London 'villain' genre:

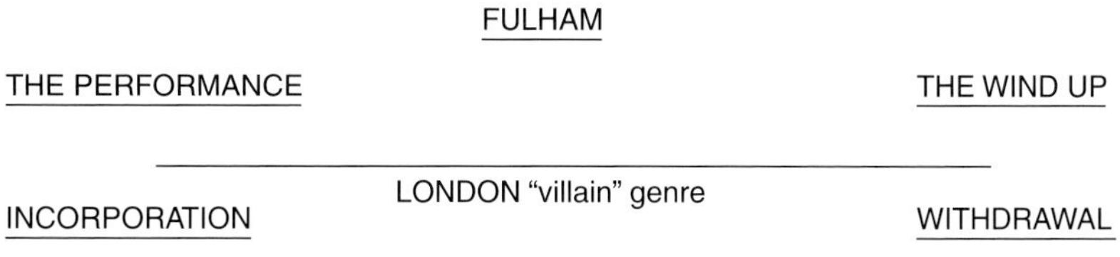

Figure 3

The difference is basically one of *control*,[64] and though both modes of interaction result in patterns of complementary schismogenesis being set up, one proceeds *against the will of the principal protagonist* (i.e. Frank is manipulated by his audience) and the other is *deliberately initiated by the principal protagonist* (i.e. Bernie positively seeks the breakdown in the communication system which schismogenesis inevitably produced and the audience is manipulated by him). In effect, the wind up falsifies the performance by negating all those meanings which 'normals' attach to it and shifts the onus of definition back onto the subject once more. Bernie can thus become at once actor, dramatist, director (and critic!), and is able to avoid the constraints usually contingent upon public performance by making redundant the whole concept of role.

To return yet again to a source which I have already plundered to an unwholesome degree, Goffman suggests in the final chapter of *Stigma* that: 'In theory, a deviant community could come to perform for society at large something of the same functions performed by an in-group deviant for his group.'

In many ways, Fulham's criminal community was made to perform precisely that function during the 1960s, and the performer and the wind up artist chose to respond to the demands of public performance in ways which are diametrically opposed. Whilst the performer capitulated to those demands, the wind up artist consistently refused to play the game. Instead of performing the 'clownish functions' to which he was assigned, he sought to preserve his status as a 'social deviant'. Perhaps, considering the avant-garde forms to which he aspired in his music and which he attempted to carry over into his everyday life, it would be more accurate to say that the wind up artist created his own category becoming a 'deviant deviant' – one whom I would define as a permanent and unrepentant exile from that larger society to which he no longer seeks access. Moreover, if we consider the pressures which have impelled the wind up artist to elaborate this, his most intricate distancing device, I feel that any attempts at further definition would not only be inappropriate but would also be highly presumptuous, and I shall therefore abandon this consideration of the wind up forthwith.

To conclude, in this final section on Fulham, we have been examining a situation of extreme subcultural conflict which was created, in the late 1960s, by the influx into the area of large numbers of 'immigrants' from an alien class. The threat to the indigenous community which these 'immigrants' represented, was countered by a more rigid demarcation of the lines which separated local deviants from local and 'imported' straights, and by the codification of those values in the working class culture as a whole, which are officially defined as 'criminal'. Both these processes were assisted by the absorption into Fulham's criminal community, of meanings generated within two other deviant subcultures with which that community had had considerable contact over a period of years. The first set of subcultural meanings was brought over from the other side of London by the large numbers of East Enders who had settled in Fulham and the adjacent boroughs after the war and the second from the Caribbean, and more specifically, from Jamaica, by the black immigrants who converged upon South London during the 1950s and 1960s. This triadic constellation of influence and meaning can be said to represent the various options open to Fulham's working class community and can be used to situate the culture of that community in the following way:

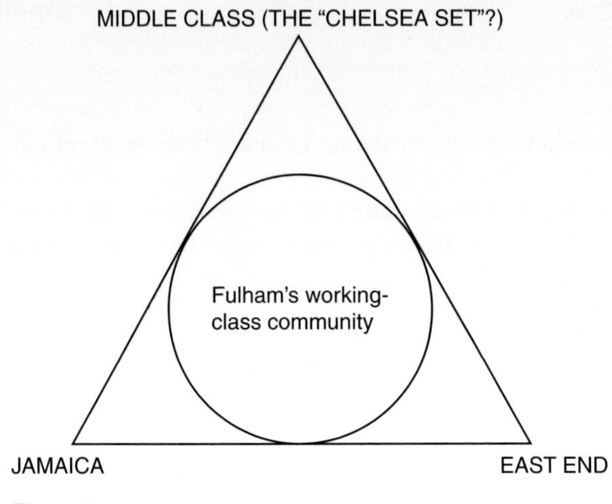

Figure 4

As far as the deviant sections of Fulham's population were concerned, the meanings which clustered along the base of the triangle in figure 4 were used to combat the threat contained within its apex. In other words, the tactics which the indigenous criminals had learnt from the subcultures, brought into the borough by two successive waves of immigration, were used to counteract the threat constituted by a third group of 'immigrants' from an alien class.

Obviously, there is a risk here of reducing what is, after all, a highly complex process of selective assimilation to its lowest common denominator, and, consequently, of circumventing rather than clarifying the problems of interpretation with which the student is faced. Certainly, the importance of direct lines of communication can be easily overstressed (because a subculture is not a 'tabula rasa'), and, so, I established a second scheme of indirect references which was designed to *evaluate* the various responses of Fulham's deviant group as they were encountered according to the semantic differential theory put forward by Osgood and Tannenbaum in *The Measurement of Meaning*. The responses were thus projected onto a sealed parameter set up between two disparate subcultural systems which corresponds to the base of the triangle in figure 4. The system which I have used could therefore be described as *anastomotic* having *collateral* channels which link a real situation of culture contact and subcultural conflict to an ideal sphere where exclusive categories pertain and relationships can be clearly discerned. In this way, the phenomena under consideration in this final section can be read back through the regress of contexts available within this thesis, and, at the same time, those phenomena already studied can be brought forward and made to bear adjectivally upon the data collected in the study of Fulham's subcultures. Bilateral organisation is, of course, by no means unique to this work, but, although the anastomotic system possesses some structuralist aspects, it retains, in marked contrast to conventional structuralist techniques, a commitment to qualitative and evaluative distinctions (i.e. a moral commitment), and, to the extent that it uses scaling procedures, it remains undisguisedly subjectivist and is therefore ultimately fallible. Indeed as I have not eliminated the 'I' from this thesis, my 'findings' are deprived of the magical auspices of 'scientific validity'. However, though I see no virtue in making a flag of fallibility, I can see no point in postulating a 'scientific base' for a work of this nature. And it was by dealing directly with the question of aesthetics, that I hoped somewhat paradoxically to prevent this thesis from degenerating into the aesthetic game towards which the 'science' of structuralism seems naturally inclined. The aesthetic parameter along which the various polarities were organised was therefore designed not only to represent a specific dimension of meaning in a 'scientific' system of subcultural semantics, it was also meant to be concerned *directly* (i.e. to be *about*) the problem of meaning which the phenomenonological study of subcultures habitually raises.

Notes

1 In fact, Fulham has technically ceased to exist. In the recent reorganisation of local borough boundaries in London, Fulham has been incorporated into Hammersmith. Nonetheless, it retains its distinctive quality and still manages to arouse a protective loyalty in its more established residents.

2 *The Queer-Bash Killers* by Peter Gillman.

3 At Lillie Road, Sullivan Court, Lancaster Court, Clem Attlee Court, Wandsworth Bridge Road etc. the older estates at Vanston Place and the Prison block Guiness Trust Buildings.

4 'When fashion moves in, brown paint and memories go' by Bel Mooney (the title tells the story).

5 Except that *Villain* could never, by any stretch of the imagination be called 'potent'. It was a crass and bungled piece of cinema which starred Richard Burton as a rather unlikely gangster and a totally unconvincing Cockney. His accent slips from Merthyr Tydfil to Bethnal Green and he does a kind of low-key Richard III on Ronnie Kray.

6 This has been replaced by *Thick as Thieves* which portrays the farcical exploits of two Fulham crooks.

7 This is perhaps more true of the South where the Puritan tradition of honesty and industry which Hoggart describes in *The Uses of Literacy* never did catch on in quite the same way.

8 The Heathrow car park racket which I mentioned in relation to the Richardsons was operated in this way.

9 One in St. James's Square, two at Basil Street in Knightsbridge.

10 This was already in evidence at the very beginning of the proceedings. Throughout the rather patronising introductory speech given by a barrister to the assembled company, a group of women jury-members from the East End maintained a voluble conversation and would occasionally interject with an audible 'Up Yours!' or would complain to men standing nearby: 'They're trying to turn the whole East End straight.'

11 The equivalent status perhaps accounts for the rumour which was circulated amongst the jurors that one of their number had fallen asleep and was fined for contempt of court. The rumour is apparently generated spontaneously within each new group of jurors and, discounting the possibility that it originates in the judge's chambers and is designed to keep us on our toes, I would suggest that it betrays secret Kafkaesque feelings of guilt and is an expression of solidarity with the defendant.

12 The two middle-aged women from the East End were so alienated that they said they found *Crown Court* (the T.V. series) 'more real'!

13 i.e. the police.

14 The jury comprised 11 men and one woman. All the men came from South London except one who came from Hampstead. The woman came from Stepney.

15 The jury's lack of confidence in the transforming power of language and the efficiency of debate was most in evidence when we failed to reach a decision. After a period, the judge summoned the jury into court, where he urged them to try to reach a unanimous verdict, and then stated the majority he would accept in the absence of such a decision. Rather than reopen the issue, jurors preferred either to sit in silence or to conduct private conversations until a 'respectable' time had passed (about 20 minutes) and a majority verdict could be given.

16 The large number of 'sympathy verdicts' has recently alarmed Sir Robert Mark who urges an end to the jury-system.
17 Picked at random from the electoral roll, the juror must satisfy only one requirement (apart from age) namely that he or she has never been convicted of an indictable offence.
18 'Transcend' might be a bit strong, perhaps he or she only dispenses with the idea of guilt.
19 The mini-cab firms in South London are notorious for their sharp practice and rivalries tend to escalate into open warfare (petrol bombs etc.). Ben, who had been a driver for a local mini-cab firm, told me that within a week of working there he had been given the phone number of a 'heavy' who lived in South London. If he required this man's services he could get them at a specially reduced rate. He claimed he could have someone shot in the legs for as little as £20.
20 The sexual implications don't really need drawing out. I would merely point out that the dilatory way in which the hawker told his story was designed to titillate his audience – a kind of verbal 'striptease'.
21 I actually witnessed this incident. I was told another story about a woman who was asked to act as 'lookout' whilst her husband burgled a local warehouse. Apparently, as soon as he had broken into the premises, she telephoned the police and had him arrested. However, I think this throws more light on matrimonial conflicts than on women's attitudes to crime in the area!
[. . .]
23 This was actually in the adjacent borough of Wandsworth.
[. . .]
25 All this information and most of the facts about the Elgar shooting have been taken from an article in the *Sunday Times* (January 25, 1970).
26 Ronnie Kray had lived for a time in Chelsea and it was not unknown for him to spend an evening in certain clubs down the Fulham Road. Even those only marginally involved in the London underworld of the mid-1960s would be thoroughly familiar with the name of Kray. Some local villains could boast a modest acquaintanceship with the man himself; some even did the 'Colonel' the occasional favour, and one Fulham betting-shop owner, as we have seen, got rather heavily involved.
27 Sullivan's alibi proved watertight.
28 This word crops up again and again in the statements made in court by Reggie Kray, Charles Richardson, and 'Mad Frankie' Frazer. It seems to be an appeal to the outraged 'common sense' of the straight audience, an articulation of its imagined response.
29 i.e. a violation of the communal code.
30 Despite any appearances to the contrary, I am not biting the hand which feeds me my material. The article itself was well researched, and well written; I am merely criticising *the context in which it appeared.*
31 The public bar has since been reopened minus the dartboard.
32 Especially when it is unqualified by 'daft' or 'silly'.
33 Prior to the conversion, people who intended to fight usually went outside into the street.
34 i.e. it is owned by the brewery.
35 I should perhaps mention here that 'performer' means violent criminal in underworld argot.
36 i.e. a prostitute.
37 'Stigma: Notes on the Management of Spoiled Identity'.
38 It is difficult to confirm this but it does seem likely.
39 [. . .] In fact, he may not be so extraordinary – a report appeared in the *Fulham Chronicle* (Feb. 9, 1973) recording the appearance in court of an actor who had appeared in the T.V. series *The Villains.* He was accused of taking part in a shotgun raid on a local bingo club.
40 These categories are Goffman's (see *Stigma*).
41 See Archie in Tony Parker's *Frying Pan.*
42 See Bert in Tony Parker's *Frying Pan.*
43 William Burroughs: *Junkie.*
44 Now there is a fairly large West Indian community in Fulham itself, and a controversy was raging throughout January and February 1973 about the influx of black families into Fulham Court. As usual, they were blamed for the deterioration of local 'amenities' and a fair amount of racial tension developed and was concentrated particularly upon the record shop which serves the residents at Fulham Court and deals exclusively in reggae.
45 A song which is still sung at parties attended by members of this group, shows how the two central

influences have been synthesised. Several people join arms and whilst one keeps up a simple scat which sets the rhythm (chikka chick-cha-cha etc.) the rest sing:

> 'Maroo . . . maroo ana
> Maroo . . . maroo ana
> I like marooana, you like marooana, me like marooana too'.

46 i.e. marijuana.

47 When working in the cloakroom of a Birmingham discotheque, I witnessed an exchange between a student and an 'acid-head' which closely resembled a wind up sequence. Huwie, a young thief and notorious 'head-case' presented the student with a riddle as the latter combed his hair in front of the mirror:

> 'What colour is that mirror?'

The student hesitated, but, as Huwie has a certain intimidating presence, he attempted to find the right answer ('It's yellow (the colour of the wall behind) . . .' 'It's whatever colour it reflects' etc.). Huwie rejected each one of these replies and added to the student's obvious discomposure by openly taunting him. ('Come on, you stupid sod, you're supposed to be clever. . .' 'My kid sister knows the answer and she can't even write' etc.). Finally the student was forced to accept defeat and Huwie disdainfully solved his own riddle: 'It's the colour of water'. There had been an in-built bias in Huwie's favour throughout, and the student had never really been given a chance to seize control of the situation. Although it is a more openly aggressive, and crudely rigged tactic than the wind up, Huwie's insoluble riddle does serve a similar function, asserting the importance of non linear meanings and questioning the validity of 'straight' definitions.

48 i.e. spent a lot of time in prison.

49 The circumstances in which he came to be hospitalised are not without interest. He insists that he only *pretended* to be insane to avoid the 10–15 year prison sentence he would have otherwise received after having been arrested for armed robbery. He maintains that his only problem is that he can't stop acting the part!

50 Elephant and Castle (an area of South London).

51 A cigarette rolled with marijuana.

52 Spectacles.

53 The ambiguity is summed up in the contrast between Bernie's remark 'We're brothers' (cf. Tony Lawrence's complaint against Sullivan 'We was like brothers') and the behaviour of the two men.

54 See William Burroughs for a radical critique of the Word.

55 In fact, the wind up is no longer acknowledged by the group who originated it (although it is still used) because access to the technique is no longer restricted, and the words 'wind up' have passed into the general vocabulary of the Durrell.

56 A. Korzybski argued in *Science and Sanity* that the following equation pertained – map: territory: word: object. If we say the words 'wind up', we immediately translate territory into map etc.

57 See *Towards an Ecology of the Mind* selected essays, Gregory Bateson.

58 Laing, of course, went on to explore the implications of Bateson's theory and the 'unremittingly incomprehensible' 'gambits' of Smith and Jones which are used to introduce the discussion of 'The Schizophrenic Experience' in *The Politics of Experience* demonstrate how completely the paradoxes stand exposed in schizophrenic 'conversations':

> Jones: A lot of people talk that way, like crazy, but Believe it or Not, Believe It or Not, but we don't have to believe anything unless I feel like it.
> Smith: What do they want with you and me? How do I know what they want with you? I know what they want with me. . . etc.

59 Bateson created this category in *Culture Contact and Schismogenesis* and developed the theory of schismogenesis in *Naven*. It refers to 'all those cases in which the behaviour and aspirations of the members of 2 groups are fundamentally different'. For example, if Group A exhibits patterns O, P, Q in dealing with Group B, which group replies with patterns U, V, W and this continues unrestrained a complementary schismogenesis can develop which leads to 'a progressive unilateral distortion of the personalities of the members of both groups, which results in mutual hostility between them and must end in the breakdown of the system'.

60 From *Stigma* Goffman goes on to quote a criminal who distrusts the interest he arouses in 'normals': 'I always feel this with straight people – that whenever they're being nice to me, pleasant to me, all the time really underneath, they're only assessing me as a criminal and nothing else.'

[. . .]

62 i.e. a determination is at once a force and a velocity (or a pressure and the direction in which that pressure is exerted).

63 Alternatively, it could be summed up in the contrast between Billy's adroit manipulation of the antique-shop owner and Barry's blunt 'handling' of the manager of the Durrell.

64 Though there is, in this case, a literal dimension as well. Frank is a professional film actor, whereas Bernie distrusts the media and satirises cinematic archetypes (see his Damon Runyan type delivery of the Joe Bananas story).

25 Common sense, racism and the sociology of race relations

Errol Lawrence

Introduction

This thesis concerns itself with what could be referred to loosely as the 'sociology of race relations'. The arguments presented here are not arguments that have been arrived at as a result of an individualised pursuit of knowledge or academic excellence but have rather emerged out of the collective process of group discussion of Race and Racism.[1] Neither are the arguments, in terms of their political and theoretical trajectory, particularly new. For example, way back in 1971 Robin Jenkins was criticising Rose and Deakin's *Colour and Citizenship* for being 'not scientific but ideological'. The knowledge contained in it, he had argued:

> made the power elite more powerful and the powerless more impotent. He warned blacks not to submit themselves to the scrutiny of white researchers who, in effect, acted as spies for the government. They should be said, be told to 'fuck off'.[2]

Jenny Bourne who describes the circumstances in which Jenkins' paper was produced, points out that his critique 'opened up a major debate as to the whole direction of race relations research and provided a catalyst in the struggle to transform the Institute (of Race Relations) itself'. A struggle which was but a reflection of the struggles of black people outside, against racism. She informs us further, that by 1972 when the dispute in the IRR finally came to a head, the debate had shifted far beyond Jenkins' initial critique.

> where the fundamental problem lay was now the issue. It was not black people who should be examined, but white society; it was not a question of educating blacks and whites for integration, but of fighting institutional racism; it was not race relations that was the field for study, but racism.[3]

Bourne's article goes beyond the local struggle within the IRR to look into the historical development of race relations research. Her criticism was not so much that researchers were focusing upon the cultures and organisations of black people rather than white racism, but that such research sought to influence the policies of governments (both Labour and Conservative) who were already inclined to view racism as a consequence of the number of black people in England. The 1968 and 1971 Immigration Acts, the one enshrining the racist partial/non partial distinction in Law; the other bringing all primary immigration to an end and converting black Commonwealth citizens to 'rightless gastarbeiter' marked not just the end of capital's need for black settler labour,[4] but also the point at which the policy-makers – caught up in a situation where popular racist solutions to Britain's economic and social ills were being advocated – became 'a part of the problem'. This last point requires further elaboration.

Race and the crisis

The notion that the question of race is essentially an 'external' problem, 'foisted on English society from outside'; was as Stuart Hall argued an ideological response to the 'End of Empire'. It entailed an erasure of England's imperial past and, consequently, a refusal to make the connections between that past and the black immigration of the 1950s and 1960s. It is here that he locates the 'moment' of a new form of indigenous racism:

> paradoxically, the native, home-grown variety of racism begins with this attempt to wipe out and efface every trace of the colonial and imperial past from official and popular recall.[5]

The space provided by this 'collective amnesia' for the growth of a new racism, became apparent during the 1964 General Election when Peter Griffiths conducted his campaign in Smethwick around the slogan: 'if you want a nigger for your neighbour, vote Labour.' This was also the period during which the boom – 'you've never had it so good' – years, gave way to the slump. The uneasy political truce that had existed between classes and which had been cemented by the ideology of affluence, cracked apart; revealing the real inequalities between classes; the still existing poverty in Britain's urban centres and the gathering economic crisis.[6] When Enoch Powell made his now infamous speeches (1968/69) about the radical and alien 'enemy within' threatening the very fabric of society, he touched the raw nerve of popular and official feeling about the deepening crisis. However, the crisis he perceived was not a crisis of race relations, nor yet a crisis in the economy, but a crisis of social authority.

It is not possible here to go into the particular reasons for the structural crisis of British Capitalism or to enter into a discussion about why successive governments have been unable to overcome it, but it is worth noting that the present Crisis takes shape during the 'energy crisis' of 1973/74 and the confrontation between Heath's government and the miners in the same period. These events (and the subsequent 'Balance of payments crisis' 1975/76) threw into sharp relief what had really been clear since Wilson had propounded his plans for a 'New Britain' to be born out of and 'forged in the white heat of the technological revolution' . . .

> . . . that the resolution of the economic problems in Britain hinged on a more fundamental restructuring of capitalist production at both a national and international level.[7]

The failure to resolve the structural problems necessitated that the state also manage the effects of the crisis at the level of social relations. As Lord Hailsham put it . . .

> Gentlemen, we live in grave times. The symptoms of our malaise may be economic, may show themselves in price rises, shortages and industrial disputes. But underlying the symptoms is a disease which has destroyed democracies in the past, and the causes of that disease are not economic. They are moral and political and constitutional, and in order to cure it we must recognise them as such.[8]

The means of 'crisis management' have been in part institutional and partly ideological. At the institutional level the important trend has been towards a strengthening and centralisation of the mechanisms of control and the means of state violence and the undermining of the representative institutions of political democracy. The Trilateral Commission's report on *The Crisis of Democracy* anxiously notes this trend.

> Everywhere one discovers a complete dissociation between the decision-making system, dominated by traditional and often quite rhetorical political debate, and the implementation system, which is the presence of administrative systems quite often centralised and strong. This dissociation is the main cause of political alienation amongst citizens. It continually nourishes utopian dreams and radical postures and reinforces opposition to the state.[9]

The shift towards more and more unmediated forms of control is underpinned in one of its crucial dimensions by a growth in state racism – particularly at the legislative and juridicial levels, but also within the 'caring' institutions.[10] At the ideological level the convergence of key themes from the 1960s (violence, moral turpitude, youth) with the theme of Race – particularly noticeable in the construction of 'The Mugger' – cements these developments. It is not that Race, *per se*, is the 'problem' but rather that race comes to signify the crisis. Hall states the articulation of race and crisis succinctly.

> In one of its principal dimensions, this crisis is thematised through race. Race is the prism, through which the British people are called upon to 'live through' to understand, and then deal with crisis conditions.[11]

Hall's argument here is not simply that race expresses the crisis but that racism, within the present context, constitutes 'a vital set of economic, political and ideological practices' which structure the ways in which the crisis is experienced. In this connection the development of racist ideologies which intersect and re-organise the common-sense racism of the white working class, around the themes of 'The Nation', 'The People', and 'British Culture', has been of fundamental importance. For this popular racism has succeeded not only in displacing 'the existing ideologies of class – of economic demands and of class struggle . . .'[12] thereby strengthening the mechanism whereby the working class is reproduced as a racially structured and divided working class; it also combines with the institutionalised racist practices of the state in such a way as to place 'induced repatriation'[13] on the political agenda. As Paul Gilroy remarks

> Repatriation is the British solution to the 'race-relations' problem, an alien problem which, being essentially external to Britain, will vanish with the blacks. It is also the means by which consent for political power may be preserved or won anew in the face of crisis.[14]

The developments briefly outlined above form the background context in my assessment of 'race-relations' sociology. The argument proceeds in three stages. Firstly the contention of this thesis is that the very terrain upon which racist ideologies work, that is the terrain of 'common sense', forms the cornerstone of much of this 'race-relations' sociology. Indeed in many ways it is precisely these common-sense images which are being theorised so as to produce a pathological picture of black family life and black culture. For this reason I have felt it necessary to make a theoretical detour in order to explain how my understanding of common sense differs from popular usage. Following on from this I give a brief description of some of the common-sense images through which blacks are seen and then try to show how these have been taken up and articulated within racist ideologies. In the last section I deal with race-relations research proper and attempt to demonstrate the similarities between common-sense racism, racist ideologies and race-relations research.

Part I Common sense

The term 'common sense' is generally used to denote a down-to-earth 'good-sense'. It is thought to represent the distilled truths of centuries of practical experience; so much so that to say of an idea or practice that it is only common sense, is to appeal over the logic and argumentation of intellectuals, to what all reasonable people know in their 'heart of hearts' to be right and proper. Such an appeal can act at one and the same time to foreclose any discussion about certain ideas and practices and to legitimate them.

Common sense has not always occupied such a pre-eminent position, neither has it always been so easily equated with good-sense. In his *Prison Notebooks*, Gramsci traced its development as a concept from a term particularly favoured by 'the 17th and 18th century empiricist philosophers battling against theology, to its subsequent usage as a confirmation of accepted opinion rather than its subversion'.[15] He characterised common-sense thinking as 'eclectic and unsystematic' in the way in which it accumulated contradictory knowledges within itself. Common sense he argued:

> . . . is strangely composite; it contains elements from the Stone Age and principles of a more advanced science, prejudices from all past phases of history at the local level and intuitions of a future philosophy which will be that of the human race united the world over.[16]

The contradictory nature of common sense means that it should not be thought of as constituting a unified body of knowledge. It does not have *a* theory underlying or 'hidden beneath' it,[17] but is perhaps best seen as a 'storehouse of knowledges' which has been gathered together, historically, through struggle.[18] As a way of thinking and in its immediacy, common sense is appropriate to 'the practical struggle of everyday life of the popular masses'. It is one of the contradictory outcomes of the divisions between mental and manual labour under Capitalism. Yet, while common sense embodies the practical experience and solutions to the everyday problems encountered by the 'popular masses' throughout their history, 'it is also shot through with elements and beliefs derived from earlier or other more developed ideologies which have *sedimented* into it.'[19] The practical struggle of everyday life refers not simply to that 'perennial struggle against nature' but to class struggle. The struggle to decide – in the present conjuncture for example – where the social costs of economic recession are to be borne. The new restrictions on organised labour; the deliberate creation of unemployment and the other attempts by the present government to re-organise the production process, are not polities that can be pursued willy-nilly. Consent for them has to be continually won. It is within the process of winning consent and in the decomposition and re-composition of alliance between the ruling bloc and 'sub-altern classes'[20] by the granting of economic concessions to those classes, (which do not however touch the essential interests of the ruling bloc), that the subordination of the 'popular masses' is ideological and practically secured. The securing of 'Hegemony' by the ruling bloc though, is not a once and for all victory. The situation is rather, a 'negotiated truce' between the hegenomic cultures of the ruling bloc and the 'corporate' cultures of the subordinated classes.[21] While the general ideas of the society are defined within the hegemonic cultures and form the horizon of thought about the world, this does not mean that the thought of the subordinate classes is wholly given over to ideas derived from elsewhere. Common sense also contains 'more contextualised or *situated* judgements' which are the product of their daily lives. The sometimes oppositional and always contradictory nature of this thought is captured quite neatly by Stuart Hall *et al.* when they point out that . . .

> . . . it seems perfectly 'logical' for some workers to agree that 'the nation is paying itself too much' (general) but be only too willing to go on strike for higher wages (situated) . . .[22]

This subordination as has been mentioned already is not merely a mental subordination: the ideas of the hegemonic culture are also embodied within the dominant institutional order since this is controlled by the ruling bloc. The subordinated classes will, then, be 'disciplined' in *practice*. Their actual experience will reflect their subordination, and it is the massive presence of these ideas as they are inscribed within the social relations of everyday life, that gives common sense its 'taken for granted' nature.

The fact that common sense is the product of historical struggles is, to a large extent, obscured by the pre-eminent position within it of an essentialist and static view of 'human nature'. The notion that human beings possess unchanging 'instincts' which profoundly shape human motivations and actions, works on our daily experience of life in such a way as to erase or gloss over the historical class and other struggles which have led to the present configuration of social forces. It also operated to 'effectively discount the possibility of change and to "naturalise" the social order'.[23] Through the mechanism of this 'naturalisation process' the *social* construction of, for example, gender roles is collapsed into the biological differences between the sexes. In common-sense thinking, historically and culturally specific images of femininity and masculinity are rendered as the 'natural' attributes of females and males.

Familial common sense

We will come later to the way in which this particular notion of human nature is mobilised as a sanction for racism but for the moment I intend to look at the common-sense image of the family, since it is seen as the crucial site for the reproduction of those correct social mores, attitudes and behaviours that are thought to be essential to maintaining a 'civilised' society. As such the 'family' is one of those images through which blacks are viewed and by which blacks are compared and contrasted with that society. It is in the domain of the family that children first learn 'right from wrong'; the basic do's and don'ts that will inform their future behaviour. It is here also where girls first learn the duties and functions associated with womanhood and motherhood and where boys learn the responsibilities and privileges accruing to the 'man of the house'. The family then is seen as the site in which self-discipline and self-control are learned and in which relations of authority and power are first internalised. It is important to recognise that the common-sense image of the kind of family which is to fulfill these tasks is that of the nuclear family, where Father 'works' while Mother attends to her household 'chores' and looks after the children. This view of the family's natural structure and role, has particular consequences for the assessment of the conduct of both individuals and groups of people. Where the 'normal' family will generate the correct 'moral social compulsions' and 'inner controls', immoral/sinful behaviour will be seen as the outcome of an abnormal family life or an inadequate upbringing. Criminality or permissiveness, for example, would be traceable in this scheme of things back to the family. Of course it is just this kind of common-sense thinking that informs the present government's suggestions of 'making punishment fit the parent'. The idea is that to make parents liable to pay any fines their children might incur will 'encourage them to exert their responsibility and to provide the guidance and care needed to help keep their children out of trouble'.[24]

Within this notion of the family we can detect the contradictory, inconsistent and ahistorical characteristics that we noted earlier to be the principle features of common-sense thinking. The family here is seen as the 'natural' outcome of the biological differences between the sexes, men and women were quite literally 'made for each other'. Monogamous marriage, as encapsulated in the favourite movie image of primeval man and his mate, is similarly seen as arising out of these natural differences as indeed are the familial roles of mothering and fathering. However, as Michelle Barrett has recently pointed out, this particular arrangement is the specific *historical* achievement of the bourgeoisie. The fact that this view of family life is popularly accepted as the 'natural form of household organization', simply attests to the bourgeoisie's success of securing at an ideological level,

> . . . a hegemonic definition of family life: as 'naturally' based on close kinship, as properly organized through a male breadwinner with financially dependent wife and children, and as a haven of privacy beyond the public realm of commerce and industry.[25]

While the sedimentation of this piece of ideology into common sense has as Barrett argues had obvious benefits for capital through providing a 'motivation for male wage labour and the male "family wage" demand', it is also evident that few working-class households are organised in this way.[26] As we have already argued though it makes sense within common-sense thinking for working-class women to subscribe to this image of the family and yet still acknowledge that they also work outside of the home and that their 'family' extends outside of the nuclear family's orbit.

Common sense and Black Cultures

The connections that are made between the 'Family' and 'Culture' are of particular importance here. For while the 'family' is seen to reproduce culture, specific cultures are also seen to have an important influence on the arrangement of household. A common multi-culturalist argument that flows from this is that a degree of ethnocentrism has led many English commentators to misunderstand certain aspects of black cultures and, therefore, to misinterpret black family life. There may be something in this but it is not, in any simple sense, my argument. The hegemonic definition of family life that has been secured by the bourgeoisie was not organised simply around themes 'internal' to England. This definition, like other notions about what it means to be 'English', was 'forged in relation to the superiority of the English over all other nations on the face of the globe'.[27]

The argument here is that the 'ethnocentric' inflexion of English culture is shaped by England's imperialist expansion into and colonial domination of Africa, Asia and the Caribbean. Clearly there is ample evidence to support this view but it would be wrong to conclude that racism was, therefore, absent from English society before these imperial adventures.

Winthrop D. Jordan in 'White over Black', argues that the literary evidence from a period before any contact with Africa, shows a clearly delineated 'colour symbolism'.

> Black was an emotionally partisan color, the handmaid and symbol of baseness and evil, a sign of danger and repulsion.[28]

The opposition between Black (evil) and White (good) was not merely a poetic device but, suggests Jordan, was actually an integral part of their view of themselves, though it is not clear in his account how far this was a common theme outside of those involved in the production and reproduction of the literate culture.[29] Again from the journals that have been left by those literate people involved in the first excursions to the west coast of Africa, it was the fact of blackness that was the salient feature of Africans and even though further contact revealed differences in complexion between Africans, it was the idea of black Africa that filtered back to and became established in England. Jordan argues, though, that it was not simply that the white English had met their 'negation' in the black African that led to a particular racist conception of Africans. The linkages that were made between evil blackness, 'disobedience' (to God) as a reason for the 'curse' of blackness; and 'carnal copulation' as evidence of a fall from grace, represented a projection onto the African of their own anxieties about their role as entrepreneurs in the burgeoning capitalist developments that threatened to disrupt their social order.

> It was the case with English confrontation with Negroes then, that a society in a state of rapid flux, undergoing important changes in religious values, and comprised of men who were energetically on the make and acutely and often uncomfortably self-conscious of being so, came upon a people less technologically advanced, markedly different in appearance and culture. From the first, Englishmen tended to set Negroes over against themselves, to stress what they conceived to be radically contrasting qualities of color, religion, and style of life, as well as animality and a peculiarly potent sexuality.[30]

While this psychologistic explanation of the genesis of racism may indeed have some validity, it certainly should not be accepted as the whole story. Cedric Robinson, in a recent essay in *Race and Class*, reminds us of what Jordan has left out of his account. In tracing the emergence of capitalism in Europe, Robinson argues that there was a radical discontinuity between the bourgeoisies of the sixteenth century and the earlier bourgeoisies associated with the merchant towns of the Middle Ages. The new bourgeoisies, he argues, 'were implicated in structures, institutions and organisations which were substantively undeveloped in the Middle Ages'.[31] These 'structures, institutions and organisations' were arrangements associated with the development of the modern state and it is here in the 'interstices of the state' that the new bourgeoisies begin to gather. The importance of this for our purposes is that the argument depends on a view of capitalism as not so much breaking the fetters of feudalism, as being an extension of certain feudal social relations; that is to say they are preserved and transformed under capitalism.[32] Such an analysis may go some way towards explaining the persistence of patriarchy under capitalism and also gives a clue about the reasons for the particularistic and 'national' character of the sixteenth century bourgeoisies. The fact that the various bourgeoisies were bounded by and worked within the political economies of specific states, had a profound influence on the way in which they conceptualised the world and their position in it. As Robinson argues, 'the bourgeoisie perceived what later analysis argues in retrospect is the beginnings of a world system as something quite different: an *international* system. The bourgeoisies of early modern capitalism were attempting to destroy or dominate each other.'[33] (my emphasis).

It is important to realise here, that the political economies by which the bourgeoisie were bounded, were not the economies of nations as such. The bourgeoisies were not drawn from the same ethnic and cultural groups as the peasantry; the emerging proletariat were drawn as much from other lands as from the rural parts of the particular state; the standing armies (mercenaries) were also recruited from abroad or else from 'backward areas'; while the slave labour force was brought from 'entirely different worlds'.[34] Indeed, Robinson reminds us that

> In the Middle Ages and later the nobility, as a rule, considered themselves of better blood than the common people, whom they utterly despised. The peasants were supposed to be descended from Ham, who, for lack of filial piety, was known to have been condemned by Noah to slavery.[35]

The enslaving of Africans and American Indians, the use of Asians as indentured labour and the particular forms of racism that were constructed to rationalise such activities, were not peculiar to capitalism but rather have their roots firmly embedded in earlier forms of organisation of labour with European societies. While the connections between these forms of organisation and the images of blackness remain to be spelt out, it seems clear that racism cannot be explained simply by reference to coincidence.

Although racist ideologies were a feature of European societies from an early period in Europe's history, it is still necessary to explore the specific nature of such ideologies today. It is obvious, for example, that few people at the present time would refer to biblical stories as a sanction for their racist attitudes and practises. Nevertheless, it is evident that certain elements of earlier racist ideologies have become embedded in the common sense of the English working and other classes. Blackness is still the signifier par excellence of all things alien and as such is at the centre of the common-sense view of black peoples and black cultures. Gathered around it are a cluster of other images and ideas, some held more strongly than others by different people at different times which, even though they are cross-cut by other ideas such as the essential equality of all people, nevertheless tend to pull public opinion about blacks towards racist interpretations and rationalisations of particular events and circumstances. One important image here, is the image of black cultures as essentially primitive when compared to the sophistication, complexity and civilised nature of England. This does not mean that the different cultures are viewed as being the same. Asian culture is at least permitted a degree of development and cohesiveness as opposed to Africans who are thought not really to have had a culture as such, that is until the English came along and 'civilised' them.

Perhaps the best way to illustrate the common-sense view is to say that within this body of knowledges, Africans were still in a state of 'childhood' while Asians might at best be credited with emerging into a state of 'adolescence'. This relative primitiveness of black cultures is not viewed as the outcome of a certain stage of development of the respective societies, a development which has been suspended and retarded by imperialism and colonialism, but rather is seen to be the natural expression of an inferior intellect. The *naturalisation* of the differences between these cultures and English culture helps to 'explain' why Asians adhere to 'backward' religions and 'barbaric' customs and the 'superstitious' and atavistic beliefs of Africans: in common-sense terms they are simply not capable of any thing else. These congenital disabilities, however, are also felt to be evident in the different characteristics of black peoples. While Asians may possess a certain native cunning, their basic deceitfulness and dishonesty makes them incapable of achieving the European values of intellectual exellence and moral rectitude. The African on the other hand is so stupid and childlike that any orders or requests need to be phrased in the simplest possible terms lest they fail to be understood, at the same time their innate laziness requires constant supervision. (This is at least an advance on the whip!) The view of the African as sexuality personified is of course well known, indeed both James Walvin and Jordan note that this particular element of common-sense racism has been associated with Africans in the English mind since the 1400s.[36] Obviously for those early European gold-hunters who were members of a culture within which the human body signified the temptations of lust, the sight of scantily clad Africans must have conjured up all of the Catholic horrors of sin and depravity; hell and damnation. In any case it seems to have been but a short step from this original vision to a view of Africans as being akin to wild animals in terms of their sexuality. The very fact that they appeared to be unashamed about their nudity merely reinforcing that view. The persistence of this image of Africans, despite the increased contact with other African societies where nudity was not so taken-for-granted, has much to do with the construction of racist ideologies in justification of the later practices of slave-trading and colonialism, though it remains as a popular image up to the present day. Even the supposedly impartial cameras of the B.B.C. unerringly find their way to the quaint and exotic ceremonials where they can get their close-up of the naked bosoms of African women. Of course this view of Africans has reached its fullest and most vicious expression in the U.S.A., where the sexual potency of African males – potent because bestial – is coupled with their supposed predilection for the most brutal forms of repression. At the same time the rape by slave-owners of their female slaves has prompted the elaboration of the myth of the African woman as always ready and willing to satisfy the carnal longings of men, especially if they're white men. This view has not necessarily reached the same heights of elaboration in England, though the idea of the wanton West-Indian woman and the promiscuous West-Indian male is nevertheless a common one; serving not only to fuel a preoccupation with the size of the male's penis and the rhythmical quality of the woman's love-making, but also acting as a means of 'explaining' the incidence of single mothers amongst the West-Indian population. Alternative explanations such as the high level of unemployment and the difficulty of finding suitable accommodation are in this scheme of things almost automatically ruled out of court.

The common-sense view of Asian sexuality does not question their humanity as it does with Africans and would appear at first sight to contain more obvious contradictions. The association that is made, for example, with the 'exotic' sexual practices contained in such works as the 'Kama Sutra' would seem to cut across the deeply held view of the passive Asian woman walking three steps behind her domineering and sometimes brutal 'lord and master'. However this very passivity is thought to be a reflection of her upbringing which is geared towards her learning to accommodate and please her future husband. This image working in conjunction with the absolute power of the male to elicit her compliance and mediated through the image of the lithe and sideway gyrations of the 'belly-dancer' works so as to produce the composite vision of a smouldering sexuality 'full of eastern promise', waiting only to be fanned into flames by the most potent masculinity.

These ideas, though, are closely associated with the perceived organisation of the Asian household which we will be dealing with in more detail a little further on. What I want to go on to discuss at this point are the contradictions that exist in the common-sense view of Asians and West Indians which is thrown into sharp relief when common-sense thinking attempts to *distinguish* between the two.

As we have said Asian humanity is not questioned in the same way as is the humanity of Africans and by association West Indians. Yet of the black communities settled in England it is Asians who are seen as the most alien! Of course there is a sense in which West Indians are viewed as having been 'given' the culture of the English even though their congenital deficiencies are thought to have undermined and debased that culture. Indeed it is perhaps this partial and hazy memory of British Imperialism that allows common-sense thinking to recognise certain similarities. (It is well known, for example, that even the well-educated sociologists, politicians etc. of an earlier period entertained the idea that West Indians were 'essentially' British.) This together with the image of West Indians as 'happy-go-lucky' has promoted the idea of West Indians as 'willing to mix' as opposed to Asians who are seen as being hidden behind cultural barriers. The full weight of Asian alien-ness comes out in ideas about food, not just the way in which food is prepared and cooked but also what is (thought to be) eaten. The stories from white neighbours about the 'constant smell of curry' emanating from next door are well known, as is the peculiarly British distaste for the smell of garlic. But it is the association in the popular mind between the Indian (and Chinese) restaurant and the disappearance of the neighbourhood cats that prompts particular feelings of horror.

Language, however, is the key element in lending coherence to the various other images. While it has taken the English a long time to recognise that West Indians do speak a language of their own and not merely a form of 'bad English', no such tardiness was possible with regard to the Asian communities. The important point here though, is not that Asians speak languages that are dissimilar and were unfamiliar to the English, but the fact that this is perceived as evidence of inferiority. Common sense tends to make the leap from a recognition that English is not their first language to the feeling that they can't speak English. Can't because they are incapable! This is brought out quite clearly in the popular practice of speaking to 'foreigners' in a way that suggests that they are children or imbeciles or both; as though speaking to them in pidgeon-English somehow aids understanding!

Common sense and the black family

The importance that common sense attaches to the family as the site of the reproduction of culture, in particular the transmission of the 'correct values and norms', tends to situate the 'problems' that black people have in the organisation of their households. The difficulties that are thought to flow naturally from these arrangements are seen to be further exacerbated by their coming into contact with the more civilised English culture. We should point out here that while, as we have said, the common-sense images of black peoples are forged in the furnace of British Imperialism and colonial domination, their knowledge of this aspect of their history has been distorted where it has not been erased.[37] The notion of the 'white man's burden' effectively dilutes Britain's imperial past and allows resistance to be portrayed as 'terrorism' and black people generally as being ungrateful for the good services of the British in bringing them out of darkness and into the white light of civilisation. There is, further, no knowledge of Britain's continuing economic domination of the former colonies, which lends credibility to the myth that blacks chose to come here. Listen to the *Sun*:

> Many of the black people who have *chosen* to build their future in Britain *accept* bad housing, poor education, unemployment and insults. They regard it as the price they pay for coming here. Some of them are even grateful. But young blacks are not. They did not choose to be born in Britain.[38]

Once here however, the black family is measured against the white family and found wanting. To begin with there is the fact that black families tend to be larger than the *average* white family. This of course is only natural given the Afro-Caribbean's bestial and spontaneous sexuality and the power that Asian men wield over Asian women. Further neither group bothers to use contraception, either because they don't understand or because religious strictures and taboos forbid such practices. The fact that Asian women have been making their own contraceptives for centuries is conveniently ignored here. Thus the real problem of poor and inadequate housing – a product of racist practices – is seen as self-induced and is summed up in that popular slogan 'they breed like rabbits'. For the Asian community, this is thought to be further compounded by their extended family/kinship system. Here over-crowding is seen as a direct product of their predilection for being together!

As we said earlier the meeting of the cultures is thought to put undue 'pressure on the (black) family'. The problem here is that British culture, particularly its perceived permissiveness is thought to be undermining the 'traditional ways' of black families. Asians face the 'gentle revolt of their children' against, among other things, arranged marriages.

> Asian girls want to uncover their legs and wed boys they choose, not partners arranged for them by their families.[39]

This patronising homily adds another layer of respectability to William Whitelaw's claim to 'have had many letters . . .' and serves to underpin the portrayal of the present government's stance on the finance issue as being on the side of the girls against their religious and tyrannical parents.[40] West Indian children, on the other hand, want the same freedoms as their white peers and are thus revolting against their parents' strict stance. This kind of notion contains the implicit assumption that West Indian children fail at school because, being unused to the permissive regime of British schools, they 'run wild'. Their rebellion against the racist practices and pedagogy of their educators is portrayed as the result of something else. However, the fact of a small percentage of unmarried mothers in the West Indian community which might be thought to contradict the image of traditionally strict parents is dealt with by reference to the West Indian woman's sexuality. Their parents are not worried because '. . . traditionally a West Indian girl proved her womanhood in this way.'[41]

The common-sense image of the Asian mother views her as having and posing particular problems. She is portrayed as isolated from the beneficial effects of English culture, because her movements are circumscribed by custom and she therefore invariably fails to learn English. She is viewed as particularly prone to superstitious beliefs and, being more traditional than the other members of her family, is also more 'neurotic' in her new urban seeting. This is shown clearly in a description of 'an imaginary family of Bradford Pakistanis' carried a few years ago by Bradford's *Telegraph and Argus*. The author characterises her as

> . . . never (having) walked more than 20 years in Bradford after dark . . . and fears that all sorts of terrible things of happen at night.[42]

As was pointed out by Pratibha Parmar at the time she was of course 'quite right not to walk alone after dark because "terrible things" do happen at night';[43] the spate of beatings up and murders perpetrated by racist thugs on the black community are brutal testimony to that. The journalist responsible for this series, a certain John Salmon, can only see the fascist organisations as the lunatic fringe of British politics. In this he is locatable firmly within common-sense thinking, which simply dismisses the 'power crazed nazis' and fails to acknowledge their physical attacks upon the black communities. Furthermore, these communities are discouraged from organising collectively in self-defence, since 'stone throwing Asians and West Indians hardly improve race relations'. The fact that 'race relations' have been visibly deteriorating for many years now, goes by the board and in his myopic view of the situation stone throwing as a means of self-defence is simply 'illegal'.[44]

We should note here that this tendency to characterise black action as illegal is part and parcel of the common-sense image which portrays blacks as inherently violent. As we have seen the West Indian family is viewed as being unable to contain the wilder impulses of its children, particularly since their parents' efforts at control have been undermined by British permissiveness. In this view the fact that West Indians are unused to such laxity produces children who are undisciplined; with little respect for authority and particularly prone to extreme violent emotions and behaviour. This, and the popular image created by the media of W.I. youth as 'muggers', serves to legitimate police repression of the West Indian community in the public mind.[45] Asian crime is seen as being much more internal to the community, either in the form of violence in the family – a product of the male's tyrannical power – or else in the harbouring of 'illegal immigrants' within the extended family/kinship network. All Asians are therefore 'suspect', a view which sanctions 'fishing raids' into their communities and places of work.

Common-sense racism then, articulated through the ventriloquism of the popular media, provides fertile ground both for the legitimation of repressive measures directed toward the black communities and for the growth of racist ideologies. It is to the connections between the latter and common-sense racism that we now turn.

Part 2 The new racism

> They (the wets) don't seem to realise that the *barbarians* are at the gates . . . and that if the Tory Party don't do the job and legitimise the *instincts* of the people, within ten years it'll be a choice between the National Front and the extreme Left.[46]
>
> (my emphasis)

This section will not deal with the racist ideologies of the organised Fascist movements. This is not because I regard them as a 'lunatic fringe' with little support in the country and no connections with the 'powerful'. On the contrary, their ideas on 'race' do have popular appeal and their connections with sections of the command structure of the armed forces and with the Tory Party, for example, have been well documented elsewhere.[47] They have also succeeded to a large extent in defining the terms of debate about immigration and 'race-relations'.[48] But in this section I will be more concerned to look at another racist ideology emanating from the so called more 'respectable' quarters of society. This new racism can be heard being propounded in Parliament and on T.V.; it can be read in the 'quality' press but it seems to have escaped any close scrutiny until very recently. Indeed, for the most part it hasn't even been recognised as racism but has succeeded in passing itself off as 'common sense'.

The lines of its development into a coherent racist ideology can be traced back, as has been said, to the attempt at the 'End of Empire' to erase (or at least obscure) the historical connections between England and her Colonial Empire. As Hall puts it, the fates of

> . . . the labouring classes of the satellites and the labouring classes of the metropolis . . . have long been indelibly intertwined. The very definition of 'what it is to be British' –

> the centrepiece of that culture now to be preserved from racial dilution – has been articulated around this absent/present centre, if their blood has not mingled extensively with yours, their labour-power has long since entered your economic blood stream. It is in the sugar you stir: it is in the sinews of the infamous British 'sweet tooth': it *is* the tea-leaves at the bottom of the 'British cuppa'.[49]

At another level the impetus for the elaboration of a new racism can be found at the point where the Butler/Gaitskell consensus cracks to reveal not 'One Nation' working together so as to expand the 'economic resource-pie', with everyone getting a larger share; but an increasing chasm between rich and poor.[50] Martin Barker explains:

> The Tory Party has had to sell its ideology of limitless human wants and the need for economic growth. But when the crucial prop of that One Nation stance was kicked away by recession, the liberal Tory ideology went into crisis.[51]

The form of Conservatism that emerged out of this crisis contains a particular view of 'race' as one leading component. Why 'race' should occupy such a leading role, apart from its obvious ability to mobilise the 'people' involves a long and complex argument which I cannot go into here.[52] Instead, I will content myself with a look at the content of the new racism; since even though this will not explain why 'race' becomes important in the 1970s, it may go some way towards explaining why this racist ideology is popular.

A question of culture

So far I have been referring to this particular racist ideology as 'new' but its novelty has been not so much in the newness of the ideas as in where the emphasis is placed. The current crop of racist ideologues are concerned to distance themselves from any notions that blacks might be inferior, though they do not always find this easy; as we shall see. Alfred Sherman, for example, who as the *Daily Telegraph* explains 'sees mass immigration as a symptom of the national death wish', argues that even while 'at considerable cost' Britain was trying to cater for her own 'disadvantaged',

> . . . it simultaneously imports masses of poor, unskilled, uneducated, *primitive* and under-urbanised people into the stress areas of this country where they are bound to compete with the existing urban poor for scarce resources.[53]
>
> (my emphasis)

A little later he tells us that 'immigration was bound to *import* problems'[54] (my emphasis). Sherman is one of the more hard-nosed of the ideologues and his evident disdain for black people is likely to show through from time to time, but the important point here is the suggestion that the blacks brought the 'problems' with them. His argument is not that they came into the most run-down areas and worst paid jobs, but that because of their cultures they are not able to surmount these initial 'difficulties'. Indeed their cultural practices actually generate more problems.

We can understand this shift in emphasis better if we go back to one of Powell's early speeches. As far as he was concerned, the problem was not the alleged 'harassment' of whites by their black neighbours – of which he gave vivid examples; neither was it their high birth-rate. These things were merely symptomatic. The real problem was the growth within English society of *alien* communities with *alien cultures*.

> . . . to suppose that the habits of the mass of immigrants, living in their own communities, speaking their own languages and maintaining their native customs, will change appreciably in the next two or three decades is a supposition so grotesque that only those could make it who are determined not to admit what they know to be or not to see what they fear.[55]

According to Powell, the 'rivers of blood' will flow not because the immigrants are black; not because British society is racist; but because however 'tolerant' the British might be, they can only 'digest' so much alienness. This rather cannibalistic metaphor is instructive for (at least) two reasons. Firstly, it fits in well with the assumptions of assimilation. If blacks could be 'digested' then they would disappear into the mainstream of British society. They would no longer be visible or different and therefore, no longer a problem. On the other hand there is also the inference – given the context in which such language crops up – that this alien food will not agree with a British stomach used to less 'exotic' fare. Consequently we can expect the violent ejection; the 'vomiting' up and out of 'all those ethnic lumps of Empire which Mother England agreed to bring home and swallow'.[56] This idea, that the black cultures are not just different but so very foreign as to cause much discomfort in 'Mother England's' digestive tract, is one point at which this racist ideology intersects with common-sense racism. Blacks are alien, aren't they? and because they are alien it is only common sense that Britain can only assimilate a small number.

I said earlier that the current racist ideologues are concerned to distance themselves from notions of racial superiority, and it is true that such notions slip into the argument only infrequently. At one level this is because such talk is not necessary. Once the argument has been couched in terms of 'alien cultures', common-sense racism can be relied upon to provided the missing inflexions. At the more 'abstract' level, however, the ideology is not at all secure at this point. It needs other ingredients. Ivor Stanbrook M.P. gives us a clue:

> Let there be no beating about the bush. The average coloured immigrant has a different culture, a different religion and a different language. This is what *creates* the problem. It is not *just* because of race.[57]
>
> (my emphasis)

Most of this is familiar by now, but while it may not be 'just because of race' it seems clear that 'race' does have something to do with it. A little later Stanbrook lets the cat out of the bag.

> I believe that a preference for one's own race is as *natural* as a preference for one's own family.[58]
>
> (my emphasis)

'It's only natural'

In the section on 'common sense' I argued that the idea of 'human nature' held an important place in common-sense thinking generally and, in particular, I pointed to the bourgeoisie's success in securing, ideologically, the notion of the nuclear family as the only 'natural' unit of household organisation. I also suggested that these ideas and ideas about 'race' were linked only tendentially within common sense, since this mode of thinking is inherently eclectic, unsystematic and contradictory. (One can see for example, in the aphorism that 'variety is the spice of life', a point at which the idea that different household organisations are 'natural', could begin to be elaborated.)

The new conservative ideology 'rediscovers' these ideas about human nature, the 'natural' family and so on, and represents them as the key to a resolution of The Nation's problems.[59] Here, what are only tendential links within common-sense, are argued for as being necessarily connected. They form an organic unity. Barker's work is useful in this respect. He argues that while the 'New Toryism' is strongly individualistic in that it 'demands a new contract between the individual and the nation', we must be wary of equating it simplistically with liberalism. Liberal individualism and the new Tory individualism are not the same thing. He explains thus:

> To be strictly accurate, it is not individualism. It is 'familyism'. Commitment to the family is essential to social cohesion, it is regularly said, for the family is seen as the transmitter and regenerator of traditions, it is the source of order and the sense of responsibility, it is the focus of loyalties below the nation; and all these are 'natural' and the embodiment of Toryism's primary values.[60]

He goes on to point out how these ideas have been harnessed to underpin the present government's monetarist solutions.

> Thatcher herself blamed the decline in just about all standards one could name on 'our having stripped the family, the *fundamental unit of society*, of so many of its rights and duties'.[61]

It is possible here to see connections between this view and the current redefinitions of sexuality in particular (e.g. in the anti-abortion movement[62]) and morality in general (e.g. Mary Whitehouse's 'moral crusade'). It is also possible, needless to say, to see the connections between these developments and the elaboration of the new racism.

The family is seen to transmit traditions and generate loyalties (amongst other things) at least within the immediate family and it is the family's role in reproducing a certain sort of culture, a certain 'way of life' that makes it 'the fundamental unit of society'. Not only is the 'family' structure of the black communities seen to be different; it also, as Powell and others tell us, reproduces different cultures. Blacks are different and recognised as such not just (or even) because they have different features and/or complexions, but primarily because they have different cultures; different 'ways of life'. R. Page tells us what this means:

> It is from a recognition of racial differences that a desire develops in most groups to be among their own kind; and this leads to distrust and hostility when newcomers come in.[63]

Groups then, develop a racial consciousness based upon their racial similarity (defined as shared 'way of life' which is akin to a 'herd instinct'). What is more, like the family or rather through the family, this racial consciousness generates loyalty to the herd and distrust of and hostility towards other 'Herds'. The important point to note here is that this 'herd instinct' is presented, as we saw in Ivor Stanbrook's speech earlier, as a 'natural' evolutionary development. Thus far we have been furnished with reasons for initial antagonisms between groups, but we may even at this late stage want to argue that surely it's only a matter of time before familiarity leads to 'understanding' of each other's cultures and the peaceful-co-existence of the different cultures in a 'multi-cultural' society. Looking through the various writings and speeches of the ideologues, though, it does seem that they have seen this argument coming. What gives this ideology its particularly nasty twist is the yoking of the cart of biological culturalism to the rogue horse of the 'nation' and 'Nationhood'.

The 'Alien Wedge'

The links that have been made between 'human nature'; the family; Culture and the Nation have not been forged without much 'ideological work'. As Barker puts it 'that requires some re-writing of history', it also requires that class and gender division are obscured. Thus Norman St. John-Stevas argues for a thousand-year continuous and uninterrupted development of the 'dominant culture';[64] a notion which erases the history of myriad peoples who have invaded or migrated to Britain at the same time as it ignores class exploitation and the subordination of women. Powell appears to be equally ignorant.

> The Commonwealth immigrant (he argues) came to Britain as a full citizen, to a country which *knew no discrimination* between one citizen and another[65]
>
> (my emphasis)

The importance of the ideological construction of an 'homogenous' nation and national culture, is made clear by Sherman who, given current events, not even Powell can match for sheer audacity.

> The United Kingdom is the national home of the English, Scots, Welsh, Ulstermen (and those of the Southern Irish who *retained British identity* after their fellow-Irish eventually rejected it).[66]

Here, England's domination and suppression of neighbouring peoples is transformed into something that approximates to a family quarrel. Whatever one may think of the methods of struggle adopted variously by the Scottish Nationalists, Plaid Cymru and the IRA (or earlier, the 'Southern Irish') it does not appear convincing to describe these struggles for a measure of independence as exercises in retaining or rejecting 'British identity'. Nevertheless it does give us a clue to the particular form of Nationalism being propounded by these ideologues. Sherman says it best. He argues that 'nationhood . . . remains together with family and religion man's main focus of identity, his roots.' At this point the 'herd instinct' of the group becomes a national consciousness and produces a particular 'national character',

> . . . reflected in the way of life, political culture and political institutions no less than in culture. The difference between the social and political institutions in this country and those in the Indian sub-continent, the Caribbean or Africa – or for that matter Russia or China – reflect this national character among other things.[67]

'National consciousness' forms the basis of an 'unconditional loyalty' to and 'personal identification with the national community'.[68] As we have already seen the blacks are 'alien', they have a different 'national character' and it flows from this that they can never attain the crucial element of a British National consciousness. Their loyalty to Britain, then, is suspect and this makes them a threat. To the British, as Sherman defines them, Britain's 'History, institutions, landmarks are an *essential* part of their *personal identity*'[69] and it is this umbilical cord that makes Britain not just a 'geographical expression' that can be wished away, but 'the national home and birthright of its indigenous peoples'.[70] The territory of Britain is as much a part of the British as their culture; indeed their culture appears as a kind of dialectical relationship between the 'herd' and its territory; their defence of this space is in this scheme of things only 'natural'. It is in this context that we can begin to understand the metaphors of warfare that riddle much of the writings of the ideologues. Powell, for example, argues that the black communities are not merely 'numbers' of people but, 'detachments of communities in the west Indies, or India and Pakistan encamped in certain areas of England'.[71]

These military metaphors, as with the metaphors of consumption we looked at earlier, suggest their own solution – repatriation; but the ideologues do not stop here. They go on to give reasons as to why this is the only tenable solution. On the one hand, if the British have this peculiar relationship to their territory then it follows that the blacks must have a similar relationship with their 'natural environment'.[72] It would then be in *their* interests to send them back. On the other hand their presence is experienced as an attack upon the very person of the British, an attack upon their 'national identity'. That is why they have 'genuine fears'[73] about their culture; their 'British character (which) has done so much for democracy, for law, and done so much throughout the world;'[74] being 'swamped' by people with alien cultures. Should these 'genuine fears' not be assuaged, then the 'Dunkirk spirit' of the 'herd' will reassert itself with disastrous consequences.

> National consciousness like any other major human drive – all of which are bound up with the instinct for self-perpetuation – is a major constructive force provided legitimate channels; thwarted and frustrated, it becomes explosive.[75]

This gives the 'peculiarities of the English' a distinctly new and gruesome twist. More to the point repatriation is the 'natural' solution to a 'natural' problem.

The 'self-destructive urge'

I have tried throughout this section to indicate specific points at which the new racism intersects with common sense. I have also stressed its connections with other aspects of a new conservative philosophy. I would like to conclude this section by pointing to one final 'site' where the new racism intersects with common sense and where its implications are broader than its immediate threat to the black communities.

The specific 'site' I am referring to here is the relationship of dominance and subordination mentioned earlier. The 'anti-intellectualism' within working class common sense which, Hall *et al.* argue, is a recognition of that relationship, is represented in the new racism as

> . . . the conflict between the instincts of the people and the intellectual fashions of the establishment where British Nationhood is concerned.[76]

The ideologues do not seek to shatter the relationship of dominance and subordination for all their appeal to the 'people' and their common sense. Rather they aim to harness that common sense and win popular support for their particular political project. Sherman, for example, wants to single out those intellectuals who have 'studied the pseudosciences of sociology and economics, mainly stemming from America' rather than 'classical and European history and languages'.[77] This needs to be set next to Powell's earlier prognostications. He was concerned more with the location of the 'problem' intellectuals, than with their intellectual origins. They were he said:

> . . . a tiny minority, with almost a monopoly hold upon the channels of communication, who seem determined not to know the facts and not to face the realities and who will resort to any device or extremity to blind both themselves and others.[78]

The ground has shifted considerably since Powell's remarks. It is now necessary to be a little less woolly about who this tiny minority are and why they appear to be so 'wilfully blind'. Again it is Sherman who provides the crucial motivation behind the actions of the 'immigrationists' as he calls them.

> I can see no other answer than the self-destructive urge identified so scathingly by Orwell, three decades back, when be lumped together Russophilia, 'transposed colour feeling', inverted snobbery, a craving for the *primitive*, and anti-patriotism on the part of the intellectuals, as expression of disaffection, alienation and self-hate.[79]
>
> (my emphasis)

The assertion that those whites who oppose racism have been unduly influenced by an *alien* system of ideas together with the extreme biologism of the new racism, prepares the ground for dealing with this 'tiny minority'. They are going against the instincts of the 'herd'. According to the racist ideologues, it is only 'natural' that the British should be racist; obviously then, those British people who are anti-racist (and it should be said those who support feminism) must 'logically' be *unnatural*. Something has gone wrong, they do not have the correct (natural) 'national identity'; they are filled with 'self-hate'.

The 'crime' that this 'tiny minority' have committed is of course to allow blacks into the country. In this connection, it is worth noting once again the changes that have taken place between Powell's earlier utterances and those of Sherman and others more recently. Powell argued that black immigration was a consequence of foolhardiness. The 'visible menace' which he sighted way back in 1966[80] was due largely to 'the legal fiction of commonwealth citizenship' which allowed an 'alien element' to be introduced into Britain. By 1976, Sherman is talking of 'Britain's urge to self-destruction',[81] the implications of which are far more sinister.

> The imposition of mass immigration from backward alien cultures is just one symptom of this self-destructive urge reflected in the assault on patriotism, the family – both as conjugal and economic unit – the Christian religion in public life and schools, traditional morality, in matters of sex, honesty, public thrift, hard work and other values denigrated as 'middle class', in short, all that is English and wholesome.[82]

By 1979 he is talking of 'jet-age migrants' for whom Britain is 'simply a haven of convenience where they acquire rights without national obligations', and where they are '*encouraged* to see immigration restrictions as something to be circumvented'.[83] In Sherman's hands immigration becomes a deliberate invasion. The 'barbarians' are no longer 'at the gates', they are within the city itself. The 'tiny minority' of pseudoscientists are to blame for this. It is no longer enough to blame a few 'blind' politicians. The 'genuine fears' of the people have been raised but the 'tiny minority' refuses to listen. Indeed they will not listen because they have an 'evil intent'; they are subversive. Barker indicates the consequences of this line of argument.

> . . . the logical outcome of this failure of the nation to protect itself is that the minority who press for these self-destructive actions must be purged. If they do not see the error of their ways, they put the pack at risk. How exactly they are to be dealt with is of course open to doubt. But the theory, with its semi-biological orientation, would make easy space for the idea that those who support immigration, those who attack the family, and so on, are biological failures.[84]

The new racism forms an important part of the context for a discussion of race-relations sociology. I have of course emphasised the coherence of this ideology and have tried to point to its logical conclusions. It is clear that not all members of the Tory party hold such a coherent view but the difference between the 'wets' and the 'hards' is one of degree rather than anything else, as the opening quote to this section indicates.

Furthermore it is possible to argue that the Labour Party's thoughts on immigration and 'race-relations' share some common assumptions with the new racism.[85] Lastly, it is not difficult to see how the new racism follows similar contours to the racist ideologies of the organised fascist movements. The Tory 'hards' may not at the moment be prepared to openly share the same bed as the Fascists but they are not above stealing their sheets.

Part 3 Race-relations sociology

One aspect of the earlier discussion was the way in which the question of black cultures was dealt with in common-sense thinking and how this shaped a certain view of black people. An attempt was also made to demonstrate how these notions have been taken up and given more systematic treatment within the new racism. In the light of what has been said already and bearing in mind the policy orientation of much 'race-relations' research, it will be instructive to see how far the sociologists have been able to get behind common-sense racism.

The sociologists I concern myself with here have all made recent contributions to the field of 'race-relations' and can roughly speaking be divided into three categories. Firstly, there is the 'Ethnicity Studies' school, who adopt a 'cultural pluralist' framework for their researches. The people whose work I look at closely are Verity Khan, Catherine Ballard and Peter Weinreich, all contributors to the volume *Minority Families in Britain: Support and Stress*, although I also cite the work of others within this school of thought. Secondly there is the work of John Rex and Sally Tomlinson which approaches 'race-relations' from a 'left Weberean' perspective.[86] Lastly there are the more eclectic and idiosyncratic works of Ken Pryce (a strictly 'sociological' ethnography); Ernest Cashmore (a phenomenological approach) and Len Garrison, whose theoretical framework it is difficult to pin down.

Black cultures

A useful place to begin this discussion is with a look at how black 'culture' is viewed, if for no other reason than because there is such an extraordinary degree of consensus amongst the authors on this point; despite the fact that they are working within different problematics. The starting point for them, the place where they would all agree, can be encapsulated in the twin concepts of a 'strong' Asian culture and a 'weak' West Indian culture and in this they do not differ from the common-sense images we have been discussing. They are, as we would expect, more sophisticated and advance a theoretical justification for this view, which pivots around a certain, truncated historical knowledge of the two peoples. The key term here is 'acculturation' which refers to the 'culture stripping' or 'cultural castration' of Africans during slavery and the fact that they were subsequently 'forced into accepting British Culture along with their servitude'[87] (Rex, Fryco). Asians, however, did not undergo this traumatic process of acculturation, at least not to any significant degree. Their languages, religious institutions and family-kinship system remained intact. Indeed there is a sense in which their cultures and traditions, steeped as they are in the history of the Asian sub-continent, are thought actually to have ameliorated the worst effects of colonial subordination and neo-colonial dependence; though this has to be inferred from the work of the ethnicity studies school since they make only fleeting reference to Britain's imperial past.

> Village life in the Indian sub-continent is neither isolated nor static. The gradual adaptation in past decades indicates the strength of traditional institutions rather than the absence of outside influence.[88]

These twin conceptualisations have important consequences for their view of the organisation of black households, particularly with respect to the role they see the family-kinship system playing in the socialisation of children. The traditional Asian household, circumscribed by religion and custom provides the structured and cohesive atmosphere wherein all members of the household are made aware of their roles, rights and obligations not only to other members of the household but also towards members of the wider kinship group. This arrangement promotes a 'certain stability and psychological health' in all individuals.[89] The view of the Afro-Caribbean household presents a stark contrast to that of the Asian family/kinship system. Pryce argues that the family in Jamaica with its proliferation of common-law unions and high rates of illegitimacy among the 'lower class folk', is an inherently unstable institution; and locates the 'peculiarities of family life in the West Indies' as stemming 'directly from the institution of slavery, which was responsible for the total destruction of *conventional* family life among *slaves*'.[90] We will come back to what he means by conventional in a moment but for the time being it is worth noting that according to Pryce, these 'peculiarities' are wholly part of a 'complex of causes responsible for his [sic] inability to establish a firm, rooted sense of identity'. These 'other causes' include an 'excessive individualism' which though a part of the Afro-Caribbean's European heritage, is exacerbated by their economic position. Thus the kinship system has to remain fluid in order to 'permit individuals to *abandon* family obligations and migrate at short notice to take advantage of economic opportunities overseas'.[91] If this were not enough, the Afro-Caribbean is also seen as being dogged by a 'negative self-image' which is induced by them having internalised a European culture which is fundamentally at odds with their blackness, which downgrades black people. The weakness of the family and culture generally, can do nothing to overcome this 'self-doubt', but more particularly the family fails to instil a sense of fatherly responsibility in the Afro-Caribbean male and fails also to control its members. It is from this perspective that Ernest Cashmore is able to argue that the involvement of Afro-Caribbean youth with the British police and the 'emergence [among them] of subterranean values as dominant motivating vectors of social action', has to do with 'the lack of social control exerted by the West Indian family, due historically to the framentation of family structure in slavery'.[92]

Thus far the Asian household appears to have fared quite well in comparison to that of the Afro-Caribbean community, but this is not actually the case. The very strength of Asian culture is seen to be a source of both actual and potential weaknesses. It is not clear how much this has to do with the failure of students of ethnicity to erase their own ethnocentrism and how much it has to do with their pluralist perspective which tends to obscure relationships of power and to treat the topic as a question of a meeting of cultures on equal terms. In any case Khan argues that the hierarchical structure of Asian households promotes 'stress-ridden relationships' particularly between sisters-in-law. Furthermore, while the family/kinship system promotes a healthy psyche, it does not 'prepare the members for change beyond that of the natural development cycle of the family'. The strength of 'traditional relationships' is thought to determine 'the skills and *handicaps* the migrant brings to his [sic] new situation in Britain', one of these no doubt being the way in which the 'severe reprimand or control' of deviant members of the community is exercised in the maintenance of group *izzat*.[93]

Given our scholars' propensity to discover and tackle any 'problem' it would seem, except the burning problem of racism, it should not come as any surprise to find that the 'migration process is a major source of stress in itself',[94] though what the stress is and who suffers it is subject to a degree of variation. For Pryce, who is seeking to establish a basis for the 'teenybopper' problem which he wants to deal with later, it is the children left behind in the Caribbean who experience the 'stress'. Since family obligations are 'devoid of any formal or binding significance', the child is open to neglect or else finds it 'easy to evade the discipline of guardians'. Furthermore,

> The absence of a viable supportive culture that is independent and capable of tightening family relations to help the West Indian poor carry the burden of their deprivation and impoverishment . . .[95]

is a cause of the psychic and cultural confusion that the youngsters experience once united with their parents. At the same time, the 'mutilating colonial heritage' and 'inferior educational upbringing and colonial origin' mean that the Afro-Caribbean child is unable to cope with the 'demands made on him [sic] by the British school system'.[96] Khan on the other hand sees the greatest source of 'stress' as being on the male Mirpuri 'migrant'. Here the familiar notion that Afro-Caribbeans came to England because England was the 'Mother country' is transformed into the Mirpuri villager's supposed perception of England as 'a land of promise and a way to solve all one's problems'. The stresses here turn on the movement from a 'backward' rural to an advanced industrial urban setting and his separation from and obligation to his family back in the village.[97]

Of these two accounts, it is difficult to assess which is the most damaging. Pryce absolves the racist structures of the English education system by defining the Afro-Caribbean child's struggle against it as 'maladjusted behaviour'. He then locates this maladjustment in the Caribbean family structure which he sees as pathologically reproducing 'failure'. Khan on the other hand, and after the sociological preliminaries, highlights the '*many* migrants' who 'obtain false documentation'; characterises Asian women as *wives* who, circumscribed by traditional customs, remain tied to the house unable to make 'contact' with her white neighbours because she doesn't speak English. Then she argues that the arranged marriage causes greater stress where it is the 'newly married men joining their wives'; since the wives' greater familiarity with England will conflict 'with the established pattern of public male authority and knowledge of the outside world . . .'[98]

These comments would appear to concede ground to the new racism, but they are not the only hostages Khan gives to fortune. In her committment to 'alternative perspectives' on stress, she suggests that any 'problems' Mirpuris might experience in Britain miraculously disappear once they visit urban Pakistan on one of their (frequent she would have us believe) return trips home. Here they will realise that the urban middle class in Pakistan are facing many of the same stresses. Whereas

> In Britain they tend to interpret the problems and stresses experienced as a direct result of life in Britain, and not as an *inevitable* feature of an urban society under rapid social change.[99]

Once again her failure to recognise the systematic workings of racism and the way in which it locates black people in a subordinate position at all levels of the social formation, has led her up a cultural cul-de-sac.

Where Khan has led, others have not been slow to follow. As Jenny Bourne has noted, Khan's propensity to treat relationships of power as 'cultural relations' enables her to suggest that the 'cultural preferences and patterns of behaviour' of the various ethnic minorities, may actually *interact* with 'external determinants'.[100] Brooks and Singh use this idea to argue that while racism placed blacks in specific occupations to begin with, 'their own distinctive traditions and their ethnic identities . . . in turn influenced their occupational and industrial distribution'. Wallman goes one step further . . .

> The effect of their ethnicity is . . . dependent upon the state of the economic system and on their bargaining strength within it. Conversely they will not see, will not accept, will not succeed in the opportunity offered if it is not appropriate to their choice of work and their cultural experience.[101]

to which Bourne adds wryly, 'now we know why black teachers became bus drivers and skilled black workers prefer to do unskilled jobs'.[102] What are we to make though of John Rex's contribution to this area? Although he would claim to be antipathetical to an approach which seeks to understand the position of black people in Britain through their ethnicity, he nevertheless seeks to relate the kinds of work they do here with their previous experience of work in their countries of origin.

> For many immigrants, manufacturing employment is a new experience and they have, on the whole, gone into jobs requiring the lower grades of skill.[103]

He follows this up with the argument that whites hold a higher class position because '44% (of his sample) had *fathers* who had been in manufacturing employment' and that this entailed a 'larger family experience' of this type of work.[104] Now while there is evidence to suggest that fathers are often able to recruit their sons into the same line of work and that such practices can serve to keep blacks out, unless he is arguing that the ability to do such work is hereditary, there is no reason to suppose that the fact that one's father did a particular job, gives the son any innate capacity to pursue that line of work. Further, given the extent of massification and de-skilling that has taken place in manufacturing industries, it is not clear that the level of skill required is that great.[105] This and his other notion that Asians are 'committed permanently to being a migrant', while nearly all West Indians want to return to the Caribbean, suggest that Rex is closer to the cultural pluralism of the ethnicity school than he would care to admit.

Alternative perspectives: Afro-Caribbean culture

I would agree with the general proposition that the experience of Asians and Afro-Caribbeans under colonialism were not the same, and that slavery in particular did operate so as to 'rupture and transform' the cultural practices of Africans in the diaspora. Nevertheless, some points need to be made about the way in which their histories and struggles have been appropriated by the researchers in question. Obviously slavery was a brutal and brutalising experience, but we need not accept that a recognition of this requires the construction of a theory that discovers the traumatic effects of this still existent today. Further, there is a growing body of evidence to suggest that the attempt to eradicate the African slaves' cultural heritage was not entirely successful, if we still find echoes of Africa in their religious institutions and modes of worship, in their language but above all in their music. What marks out the blues, ragtime, jazz, be-bop, soul, funk and gospel music as distinctive is precisely the fact that the theme of Africa is constantly played out within it. This is an important point, for where most commentators would agree that this music is an expression of the Afro-American's experience of and opposition to subordination and racism, the fact that the music is based in African themes and rhythms, remembered, is all too often forgotten. Needless to say, the inspiration provided by current African and Asian music is rarely even acknowledged.[106]

It is important to remember then that what we are talking about is *degrees* of acculturation not a total acculturation. Certainly it would be difficult to maintain that the 'Afro-Brazilians' have lost their culture, given the high degree to which they have not only preserved many of their cultural forms, but in religion, music and dance have also established a cultural supremacy.[107] As far as the Caribbean is concerned, Stuart Hall has already argued the case

> . . . the culture and institutions of the slave population are rigidly differentiated from that of the 'master' class; and African 'traces' enter into the structure of these institutions.[108]

The preservation of 'Africanisms' and the development of Afro-Caribbean cultural forms took place, it is true, within the context of slave society and was locked into a subordinate position vis-à-vis the European culture of the dominant 'master' class; both forming 'differentiated parts of a single socio-economic system'.[109] Having said this however, it is crucial that we realise that the African slaves and their Afro-Caribbean descendants were by no means the inactive victims of slavery and passive recipients of European culture, that is often the implicit assumption of the way in which the notion of acculturation is used. Caribbean peoples have a long and distinguished history of struggle and rebellion against European domination, both in colonial and neo-colonial times and it is evident that the successful revolutions in Haiti, Cuba and recently in Grenada will not easily be forgotten. Of interest here is the role of the peoples' cultures as the repository of an alternative and oppositional ideology.

A claim that is often made to support the argument that Afro-Caribbeans have a form of European culture is that the slaves from similar 'ethnic groups' were deliberately separated from each other. This is thought to have facilitated the acculturation process, though it is by no means clear that the different 'cultures' were so radically dissimilar. Indeed as C.L.R. James pointed out many years ago it was Voodoo – not a 'pure' African religion to be sure but a coming together of different African elements nonetheless – which served as the ideology of the Haitian revolution.[110] Moreover, Deren argues that not only can the various

Voodoo Gods be traced back to still existing religions in Africa, but that the religious ideas of the remaining Caribbean 'Indians' were also incorporated under the hegemony of the African forms. Obviously then in the struggle against oppression cultural difference is not necessarily a barrier.[111] Lastly it is worth pointing out as Sivanandan has already done that Afro-Caribbeans did not simply copy their language from their European masters. Theirs was an active appropriation and subversion of that language. They literally 'blackened' it.[112] That this is so needs no real demonstration, we merely need to remember those white teachers who found it impossible to understand the 'patois' of their 'British born' black pupils! We may want to argue about degrees of acculturation and about just how 'African' Afro-Caribbean culture is, but one thing is clear and that is that it is not a European culture.

The Afro-Caribbean household

I have argued that Afro-Caribbean cultures cannot be described simply as derivatives of European cultures but on the contrary have been actively constructed by Caribbean peoples. Using memories, knowledge and the 'symbol' of Africa together with their historical experiences, they have managed to subvert and in a sense overthrow European cultural dominance. (As Robinson puts it 'the first attack is an attack on culture'.) At this point it is possible to turn to the view of the family/kinship system as so weak that it reproduces pathological personalities. I noted earlier that Pryce measured the Afro-Caribbean family as it is now, against 'conventional family life' and saw it as having certain 'peculiarities' which blocked its proper functioning. What he means by *conventional* here, is obviously the common-sense image of the English family with father, mother and 2.2. children, where father is the breadwinner and mother nurtures the children. As we have already seen, this is not the 'natural' form of household organisation but rather the specific achievement of the European bourgeoisies. Further, its universal applicability is more a 'fact' of a certain 'familial ideology' than a fact of life.

The particular household organisation of certain sections of the Afro-Caribbean peoples can only be viewed as inherently 'unstable' if one holds to the view of a 'father figure' as an absolute necessity and if one holds the sexist view that women are not capable of rearing children without a male presence. Such a view though posits women as given quantities with certain natural attributes and capacities and fails to take into account their ability, individually and collectively, to manipulate their environment. Since Pryce recognises that this is what has actually happened in his (mistaken) characterisation of the family of the subordinate Jamaican classes as 'matriarchal', it can only be his uncritical acceptance of an ideological conception of the family that leads him to see this family system as unstable and pathological. Cashmore also fails to question the patriarchal ideology that sees the fatherless households as a problem. For him the creation of a matrifocal family and its reliance on women has led Rastafarians to usurp motherhood; assert a 'new male identity' and 'create for themselves a father-image and God in Haile Selaisie'.[113]

Gayle Rubin in her illuminating discussion about sex/gender systems and their corresponding empirically observable manifestations in differing kinship systems provides useful guidance here. She defines a sex/gender system as

> . . . a set of arrangements by which the biological raw material of human sex and procreation is shaped by human, social intervention and satisfied in a conventional manner, no matter how bizarre some of the conventions may be.[114]

and argues that the social construction of sexuality and gender informs both the type of kinship system and the position of women, often though not necessarily, subordinate, within that system. Important here, also, is her awareness that sex/gender systems are culturally and historically specific. To use a model drawn from one sex/gender system to talk about or measure another, will produce an ideologically distorted picture but hardly aids understanding.

A second point I would make here derives in part from my first. I agree with the race-relations sociologists that Afro-Caribbean societies' sex/gender systems are different but I cannot agree that this difference is pathological. We need to remember here that their view of the family is not simply the ideological view of the white bourgeoisie, it is also a view forged historically within a white patriarchal society. It is only from this position that race-relations sociologists have been able to launch their attacks upon what they see as either a 'black matriarchy' or the black 'matrifocal' family.[115]

Asian cultures

If we turn now to a consideration of what Khan and others have had to say about the cultures of the Asian sub-continent, the most striking feature is their failure to comment upon the impact of European Colonialism in that part of the world. What is implied though if this is not taken into account is that, culturally at least, the Asian sub-continent enjoyed uninterrupted development. Such an omission is to say the least misleading and can only serve to fuel the commonly held belief that the poverty, and hardships of these 'under-developed' nations, is the result of their 'backward' and 'rigid' cultural forms and institutions. The truth is, however, that colonialism has had as profound an effect – economically, socially, politically – on this part of the world as it has had elsewhere. Although the difference in technological development between Asia, Africa and Europe was not originally as great as is often assumed, Europe did enjoy a superiority in some spheres (particularly shipping). Indian cloth, for example, was much preferred to the English variety such that 'in the early centuries of trade, Europeans relied heavily on Indian cloth for resale in Africa, and they also purchased cloth on several parts of the West African coast for sale elsewhere.'[116] However, Europe's control of the sea trade routes together with the capacity of their cloth industry to 'copy fashionable Indian and African patterns' in large numbers, enabled them to swamp these countries with their own (European) cloth and therefore to retard and eventually destroy the emerging Asian and African cloth industries. As Walter Rodney acerbically puts it:

> India is the classic example where the British used every means at their disposal to kill the cloth industry, so that British cloth could be marketed everywhere, including inside India itself.[117]

The full impact of British colonialism was more far-reaching than this. The 'legal and institutional changes in land and revenue systems' that were introduced by the British had the effect of transferring land from the 'rural magnates (tuluqdars) and small landholders to urban trading and money-lending castes' thus dispossessing the peasantry in much the same way as they had already 'displaced' the weaver. Indeed this was the root cause of the 1857 rebellion which seriously threatened 'the continuation of British rule in India'. Iftikhar Ahmed notes that this rebellion evoked a change in British policies towards India . . .

> The intensive penetration of traditional society was replaced by *cautious preservation* of the pre-existing social order. It seemed more sensible to take Indian society as it was, to concentrate on administration and control, and to shore up the landed aristocrats, who came to be viewed as the 'natural leaders' best suited to the 'oriental mind'.[118]

Verity Khan notes that 'the political instability of Azad Kashmir has also affected its economic development and future prespects',[119] but says nothing about the causes of that political instability. Since the development of the Asian sub-continent's political institutions was determined by the interests of British capital, it seems likely that this instability is another feature of Britain's 'under-development' of India, Pakistan and Bangladesh. Further we should not forget in this connection that these states are still locked into a world economic system in a position of dependence.[120] To the extent then that cultures develop together with the mode of production, we should expect these Asian cultures to have been affected in some way, though the changes that have taken place remain to be specified and linked to other changes.

We do know that in the pre-colonial mode of production weaving was largely the preserve of women. There is also evidence to suggest that women held land in their own right, which would of course have given them a certain degree of power and autonomy from men. The changes noted earlier however – the destruction of India's cloth industry and the changes in land and revenue systems – hit women particularly hard, displacing them as weavers and weakening generally their bargaining position. Further, this and the introduction of work (designated as men's work) in the urban centres, served to strengthen the position of men and certain aspects of the traditional patriarchal structures of the Indian social formation. Gail Omvedt notes that where in 1901 '30% of all workers were women, . . . only 20% are women today'.[121]

While the very fact that women in India do go out of the home to work serves to undermine the image of the 'passive Asian woman', the kinds of work they do betrays the fact that like women elsewhere they occupy a subordinate position in the economy. Nevertheless their very awareness of the sexual division of labour through which they are exploited at work and the sexism that oppresses them in the home, has propelled them to the forefront of their people's struggles.

> 'Women were the most militant' they said. 'It was not only these particular leaders of the local Lal Ilishan (Red Flag) party who said it, but other organisers also . . .'. Women are the most ready to fight, the first to break through police lines, the last to go home.[122]

It would be wrong to make a too easy correspondence between the Indian women who Gail Omvedt speaks to and Verity Khan's Mirpuri women, but it does seem necessary to reiterate the point that these women are not given quantities. Khan comes to the rather dubious conclusion, that Asian women don't identify 'freedom with self-assertion'.[123] Yet, given the 'self-assertion' of Asian women in India, Pakistan and Bangladesh in their various liberation and revolutionary struggles and the 'self-assertion' of Asian women under our very noses at Grunwicks and Chiz; it is not at all clear why Mirpuri women should not be equally capable of organisation and 'self-assertion'.

Between two cultures

The danger of the race/ethnic relations approach, is well illustrated in their theorisation of the experiences of black youth. Thompson's *The Second Generation . . . Punjabi or English*? and

Taylor's *The Half Way Generation*, pointed to the fact that Asian youths' attenuated connection with their parents' culture was proving to be a source of family conflict. This theme was seized upon by the C.R.E. who popularised it in their publication *Between Two Cultures*, which begins

> The children of Asian parents born or brought up in Britain are a generation caught between two cultures. They live in the culture of their parents at home, and are taught a different one in school, the neighbourhood and at work . . . parents cannot fully understand their children, children rarely fully understand their parents.[124]

The children's exposure to British values, norms and attitudes, was thought to undermine their parents' traditional authority and caused the youth to question certain aspects of their parents' culture. For the girls in particular this revolved around the issue of arranged marriage, while Asian youths' militancy in response to the racist murder of Gurdip Singh Chagger was seen to further widen the generation gap.

For West Indian youth who had always been noted for their aggressive behaviour the problem was to explain their failure at school and their increasing penchant for taking on the 'boys in blue'. John Brown's *Shades of Grey*, redolent with the common-sense rationalisations of the Handsworth police and his own colonial memories, located the problem much as Pryce was later to do in the family life and inadequate schooling in the Caribbean. This 'bad start' he saw as merely having been exacerbated by the higher standards of English schools, which led to a subsequent failure to find a job and the inevitable drift into crime.

> Deprived and disadvantaged, they see themselves as victims of white racist society, and attracted by values and life style of alienated Dreadlock groups, drift into lives of idleness and crime, justifying themselves with half-digested gobbets of Rastafarian philosophy.[125]

Brown's formulations which purported to show a split between the law-abiding West Indian community and the religious Rastas on the one hand and the 'criminalised dreadlock subculture' on the other, managed to set the parameters of future race-relations research even though some of the academic contributors protested that he had given all Rastas a bad name. It is not clear whether it is their sympathy for Rasta which prompted these protests or their need to keep the West Indian community 'open' as an object of study.[126] In any case their theorisation does not derive so directly from the mouths of the police.

Len Garrison argues that because the majority of West Indian parents came from a rural background characterised by low living standards, lack of education, limited employment prospects and therefore low expectations of the future, they were prepared to make sacrifices in order to establish themselves in Britain. Their children however either born or largely reared in Britain, in an urban and secular environment, exhibited a 'new defiant attitude' in their rejection of both racism and their parents' religious 'humility'. The generational conflict then revolves around the differences between parent/rural culture and youth/secular culture.[127] Cashmore on the other hand in his attempt to approach an understanding of Rastafari through a mobilisation of some of the concepts borrowed from the 'sociology of religion', suggests that the conflict really has to do with differing religious perspectives. Where the parents because of their 'limited cultural resources', had attempted to transcend the harsh realities of life in Britain by a headlong flight into Pentecostalism thereby 'opting out of the race for conventional rewards', their sons and daughters having been educated along with whites saw themselves as equals and insisted upon equal treatment.[128] The expectation that the children, through the medium of education would be able to enter into and participate in the mainsteam of British society; and the apprehension that these expectations 'were not going to be met', adds further to family tensions as the parents begin to blame the children for failure.[129] If this were not enough, the shattering of certain illusions about British 'fair-mindedness' and associations of whiteness with 'wealth and prestige',[130] only adds fuel to the fire and plunges West Indian youth into an 'identity crisis'.

Garrison links this to the way in which the child's experience of school undermines a confidence which is already low, since they are members of a minority that has a 'less well defined culture'; their parents' negative self-image adds to this, representing 'part of the complex problem the black child will have to overcome in order to arrive at his [sic] own *essential* personality'[131] (my emphasis). West Indian youth are, in his view, suffering from 'personality dislocation', while for Cashmore these conditions precipitate the need for 'discrepancy reduction' and for Pryce they represent a 'psychic disorientation'. John Rex and Sally Tomlinson present their own particular variation on this theme, for they seek to locate the reasons for the supposed differences in performance between the two communities in their respective personalities.

> If the West Indian is plagued by self-doubt induced by white education, and seeks a culture which will give him [sic] a sense of identity, the Asians have religions and cultures and languages of which they are proud and which may prove surprisingly adaptive and suited to the demands of a modern industrial society.[132]

It is no doubt the Jewish future they see for Asians and the Irish route they see West Indians taking that fuels a recognition of Asian cultural and political traditions while at the same time denying those same traditions of West Indians, though they are not averse to suggesting that Asian youth are caught 'between two cultures' and that they suffer – along with West Indian youth – 'considerable uncertainty about ethnic identification'.[133]

The interesting thing here is that while the ethnicity school initially took up these themes, they have both in their unfortunately titled *Between Two Cultures* and their latest *Minority Families in Britain*, tried to challenge the ways in which their earlier work was taken up. Catherine Ballard, in her recent contribution argues that the talk about 'culture conflict' merely serves to reinforce the common-sense perceptions of practitioners and 'sets young Asians apart as a "problem" category'.

> More seriously, it assumes that cultural values are fixed and static and that there is no possibility of adaptation, flexibility or accomodation between one set of values and another.[134]

Having thus argued, however, she then persists in trying to explain 'the strange half-British half-Asian behaviour of the children', illustrating 'the kinds of inter-generational conflicts which may occur', and assessing the 'usefulness of the popular concept of *culture conflict*' which she has just argued is a damaging and erroneous concept (my emphasis). She tramples across the same dreary terrain of the *inevitable* 'gulf' between generations which 'sharpen' as the children get older; and dredges up the idea that they have never experienced their culture 'in the totality of its original context', in support of what is basically a between two cultures argument. This can, perhaps, be explained by her 'professional' interest. But, in the pursuance of that interest, she first of all falls back upon the fact of the parents' 'linguistic handicaps' and then begins to explicate the 'extreme case'. This is odd since she had only just criticised the 'sensationalist media' for the same thing.[135] Even here in one of the 'extreme' cases she cites she erases the possibly obstructive role of the practitioners involved, who 'could not understand what her parents' position might be', by arguing that the girl is to blame.

> Finally it became clear that their involvement was worsening the situation by making it possible for the girl to sustain and exaggerate her problems, and particularly the Asian aspects of those problems, while continually passing the responsibility for solving them to outsiders.[136]

Unable to find any conclusive evidence to suggest that conflict within the Asian family is any more likely than in any other family Ballard proposes the notion of 'reactive ethnicity', whereby Asian youths' response to racism is to close ethnic ranks and maintain 'contact with the sub-continent and familiarity with Asian social and cultural norms'. This is to be their 'ultimate security'. Somehow I do not feel that the Asian youth who have organised so as to make sure that racist attacks upon their community do not go uncontested, would agree with her designation of their activities as an exercise in 'reactive ethnicity'.

Her colleague Peter Weinreich's concern is to replace 'the loose and ambiguous term "identity conflict" with the concept of "conflict in identification with another".' The latter term he feels can be made more concrete since it refers us to 'specific "identification conflicts" with particular others', which can be measured empirically through the modified application of 'Kelly's theory of personal constructs'.[137] The assumption of his paper is that the process of identity development is something which is common to all adolescents and in this connection an 'individual's conflicts in identification with others' are regarded as 'an important psychological impetus for personal change'.[138] This allows him to argue that such conflicts are more often than not a *resource* rather than a liability, an argument which undercuts the view held by the other theorists we have been looking at and is supported by his results which 'demonstrate that ethnic identity conflicts do not generally imply self-hatred.'[139]

The study itself, though, is not as unproblematic as Weinreich implies. Quite apart from the considerable violence he does to his respondents' 'specific value connotations',[140] his assumption that their 'contra-value systems' can be read off simply from their 'positive-value systems' is in itself misleading. The reader will remember that in the earlier arguments about common-sense thinking, it was argued that even though the dominant ideology formed the parameters for common sense, it did not necessarily involve 'conflict' for people to hold contradictory ideas (general vis-à-vis situated judgements). Weinreich's 'bipolar constructs' though do not enable him to recognise this. For him 'believes in law and order' must necessarily contrast with 'each man for himself', though it is by no means clear why the individual should not mobilise 'law and order' in furtherance of an individualistic objective. This points to a fundamental weakness in Weinreich's concepts. They can deal only with individuals who as he says have already been 'socialised', but they cannot grasp the social context within which the individual's 'identifications' – conflicted or otherwise – have been formed; thus stripping those 'identifications' of their pertinence and effectivity. This comes out quite clearly in his uncritical acceptance of the conclusions of Parker and Kleiner, that ambivalence in identification patterns is 'realistic and adaptive for the Negro'; and that 'it is the polarisation of racial identification or reference group behaviour that is *psychopathogenic*'[141] (my emphasis). It is as well to remember here that when Parker and Kleiner were making their study Afro-Americans were engaged in yet another struggle against the racist structures and oppressions which have been grinding them down for centuries. In this context Weinreich's eulogising of those males who seeing themselves as 'black British' 'will be realistic about colour prejudice' and 'their female counterparts [who] are likely to proceed towards potent conceptions of themselves as black British',[142] is slightly suspect. Especially so when those with a 'consciously defined ethnic conception' who identify with Africa or the Caribbean must by inference be associated with their 'psychopathogenic' sisters and brothers in America.

This goes together with the rather dubious notion that it will be the retention, by Asian youth, of their 'ethnic distinctiveness' which will cause them to 'remain apart from native whites and, in this sense, not assismilate to them'.[143] Both formulations could be seen as betraying Weinreich's concern that blacks should not go too far in their struggles to transform the capitalist racist structures of British Society. His view of a 'multi-ethnic' society, is one in which the 'self-concepts' of blacks are 'interactive with the values of the broader community'[144] rather than one in which the structures and practices that subordinate blacks have been overturned.

The 'identity crisis' and criminality

What I want to do now is to draw out the connections, via the work of some of our other theorists, between the idea that 'Negroes' who show no ambivalence in identification patterns are 'psychopathogenic' and Brown's claim to have discovered a 'criminalised Dreadlock sub-culture' in Handsworth. Cashmore, for example, tells us that during the 1960s young blacks at odds with an English culture that degrades their blackness, drifted into a 'rude boy' gang structure where; 'Flitting between the white squares of [their] parents background and the black of his gang enterprise',[145] they derived 'gratification from non-instrumental violence'. This formation of gangs was in the first place facilitated by 'familial fragmentation', the peer-group becoming the major socialising agent and it is here that the 'subterranean values' we heard tell of before lead him and her into an involvement with the police. Garrison agrees:

> Failure in the education system, poor employment prospects, homelessness, bring many youths into contact with the police.[146]

and so does Pryce:

> How divorced from the security and protection of the parental home, the would-be teenybopper, finds it difficult to go straight and remain law abiding. After the loss of his first one or two jobs, the drift into a life of petty crime and homelessness becomes steadier and steadier as his unemployability militates against a conventional life style.[147]

Cashmore goes on to argue that these gang structures were 'inherited' by younger blacks (in the 1970s) where they acted as '*breeding* grounds of Rastafarian themes'.[148] Thus, even Rastafari, which is seen variously as providing a 'new and independent channel of expression' (Garrison) or 'new conceptual maps' (Cashmore) or giving West Indian youth 'a culture which could unify them in their daily struggle with white society', cannot escape the taint of youthful criminality. For Garrison it is a vehicle which is being: '. . . exploited by some black youngsters who use it as a fashionable outlet for their frustration and aggression'.[149]

And Cashmore who criticises Brown's spurious formulation of 'true Rastafarians' and the 'criminalised Dreadlock subculture' cannot help but fall into that self-same dichotomy. Rastafarian beliefs, symbols etc. are he feels being used as a 'sanction for criminal behaviour, or alternatively Rastafari is a "Pandora's Box" of symbols and (no doubt) dangerous ideas'.[150]

Rex and Tomlinson, in their commitment to objectivity, actually go to check the police side of the story after hearing the horror stories of the West Indian youth who graced their sample. This, as Paul Gilroy recently observed, is

> . . . a picture so chilling in its absurdity that it is only matched by their verification of the number of unemployed West Indian youths by a visit to the local Careers Office.[151]

They suggest that 'the police take Rastafarian symbols as signs of truculence and are more likely to stop and question a youth dressed in this way' and argue that West Indian youths' involvement in crime is 'natural' given the level of unemployment. Gilroy remarks:

> This is not one of Rex and Tomlinson's more rigorous formulations. It is remarkable for two reasons. First it accepts police assumptions as legitimate and fails to associate them with 'the problem', which is instead defined in terms of black youth and secondly, it views these racial problems as the natural consequence of non-racial phenomena: youth unemployment and absence of a 'feeling' of legitimacy of police authority.[152]

The above accounts tend to absolve the racist structures and practices of British society and locate the 'problem' in the black family and black consciousness. The popular association of Rastafarians – replete with woolly hats – and crime is not subjected to any scrutiny; indeed the tendency is to actually strengthen that association by locating the appeal of Rastafari in the 'identity problems' of Afro-Caribbean youth. Such theorisations reproduce 'common sense' at a theoretical level, and succeed at the same time in erasing the history of Afro-Caribbean struggle. Horace Campbell is good on this point. He argues that the 'Ethiopianist' thrust contained in Rastafari occupies an historic place in Afro-Caribbean cultures.

> Rastafari culture remains an indelible link between the resistance of the maroons, the pan-africanist appeal of Marcus Garvey, the materialist and historical analysis of Walter Rodney and the defiance of Reggae.[153]

Young Afro-Caribbeans in Britain have been formed in circumstances that differ considerably from those in the Caribbean. They have in fact been subject to conditions similar to those that have given rise to the post war white working-class youth subcultures, but they have experienced those conditions through the mechanism of racism. To them British Capitalism works in a racist way.

> The *class relations* which inscribe (the black fractions of the working class) function as *race relations*. The two are inseparable. Race is the modality in which class is lived. It is also the medium in which class relations are experienced.[154]

The emergence of a British variant of Rastafari must be seen then as a part of the process of class struggle that black people have been engaged in since the 1950s. Afro-Caribbean youth did not take up Rastafarian themes in order to solve their supposed 'identity crisis'. Rastafarianism organised resistances and oppositional values, that were already in existence, in a new way. The mass of Afro-Caribbean youth have taken up its themes and reorganised them in the light of their specific concerns and circumstances.

The mass appeal of Rastafari in the Afro-Caribbean community has not been the starting point for any of the researchers we have looked at. Instead, as Gilroy argues, there has been a

> . . . tendency to define the movement in a crude empirical manner by offering a number of dogmatic tenets to which 'cultists' are subsequently found to subscribe . . . (but) the symbols of 'dread', by which the researchers have so far identified 'cult affiliates' are found at one end of a broad continuum of belief which traverses both age and gender difference.[155]

This brings us abruptly to the fact that Rastafari has been viewed generally as a youth sub-culture and the analyses of it have been correspondingly masculinist in focus.[156] None of our researchers, except Cashmore, has been able to perceive that there are female Rastafari; let alone discuss their relationship to the movement. Even Cashmore can only see Rasta patriarchy as a revolt against Afro-Caribbean matriarchy, a view which effectively blocks any discussion of the ideology of 'The Queen' in Rasta discourse. Thus he implicitly denies the existence of a space from which Rasta women are even now engaged in their distinct form of feminist struggle.[157] These all too brief remarks should go some way towards suggesting that the designation of Rastafari as a 'millenarian cult' with psycho-pathogenic adherents, addicted to crime and violence; is not the best vantage point from which to understand the movement.

Conclusion

One criticism that may be levelled against this thesis is that I have not dealt with the specific paradigms within which each researcher writes. Such a criticism would be valid but it would also be to miss the point. This has not been that kind of critique. I have attempted to demonstrate that common-sense racist ideology, the more 'theoretical' racist ideologies and race-relations research, share common assumptions about black culture and that in the case of race-relations sociology this has resulted in a theorisation of black family life as pathological. In a sense, I have been arguing that Britain now has its own version – diverse and scattered as it may be, of the American Moynihan report.[158]

But this is not all. As we have have noticed, the tendency within race-relations research has been to study black people rather than white racism. This raises specific problems both in terms of the information the researchers can expect to glean from their respondents and for the interpretation of that data once gathered. While some of the researchers do actually recognise this problem, their acknowledgement of it is all too often subsequently suppressed. Cashmore's work is a good case in point.

At the beginning of his book, *Rastaman*, he tells us that his initial attempts to engage Rastas in conversation about, what he calls, their 'new perception of reality', floundered on their refusal to be his guinea pigs. It was only after going away and familiarising himself with the context and content of Rastafari and then approaching the more conciliatory members of the Ethiopian Orthodox Church, that he was able to effect an entry into the Rasta community in Handsworth.[159] His initial difficulties were no doubt compounded by what he describes as the 'cultivation' by Rastas of 'an diosyncratic mode of thought' and a 'brand of patois' designed to stake out a 'social gulf between themselves and the rest of society'.[160] An already problematic situation must have been further complicated by the Rastas' insistence that theirs was not simply a *version* of reality as he constantly sought to imply.[161] Cashmore does indeed warn us that his account is unavoidably 'coloured by [his] own perception' and that many of the categories and formulations by which he describes Rastafari would be unrecognisable to them.[162] Yet throughout the remainder of his book the problematic nature of his encounter with Rastas is given no theoretical weight and is reduced in importance to a mere methodological note.

Again Catherine Ballard acknowledges that 'the outsider who attempts to help with an intergenerational crisis in an Asian family is faced with serious difficulties'. They may well find themselves 'handicapped by a lack of understanding of the cultural factors involved' and might therefore end up doing more harm than good.[163] Yet she fails to make explicit her own 'handicaps' in this regard, suggesting instead that her five or six years working on and researching in this community somehow makes her relationship to it less problematic.

Similar queries could be raised about the relationship of other researchers to the researched. The argument here is not so much that white bourgeois sociologists should not study black proletarian people – though the results of such 'interaction' may incline one towards such a view. The more important question is how much, or whether, these researchers take into account the extent to which their relationship to their respondents may be structured by racism. Generally, they fail to acknowledge the extent to which the replies they get may actually be determined by their positions as white 'authority figures', in a situation where power relations are reproduced in and through racism. The implication of this for their research is far reaching and has to do with their position in a social formation that is structured through and through by relations of 'dominance and subordination'.[164] This is not simply a black and white issue. Feminists have also long recognised the culpability of sociology in reinforcing the subordinate position of women by the way in which it ignores or marginalises them. Dorothy Smith, for example, has argued that 'women appear only as they are relevant to a world governed by male principles and interests'. She goes on to warn that:

> To the extent that women sociologists accept that perspective, they are alienated from their own personal experience. They speak a language, use theories, and select methods in which they are excluded or ignored.[165]

There are obvious parallels here with the black experience of sociology, for sociology has traditionally operated within a white patriarchal paradigm. It focuses upon white masculine concerns. What happens when black researchers accept such a paradigm is well illustrated by Pryce's work. Black women appear in his book as excessively religious wives and mothers ('saints') or as prostitutes. (It is worth noting here that the fleeting glimpse of relationships between black women and white men in his book is of the prostitute/customer variety, while white women/black men appear as prostitute and pimp. One wonders what this vision does for 'race-relations'.) To reduce their lives and experiences to these common-sense notions is, as Colin Prescod argued at the time, 'to be unable really to distinguish between bad race relations and rampant racism'. Pryce's work was hailed as a 'milestone' in race relations research. Prescod felt that it was more likely to prove a 'millstone' around the necks of the black communities. It highlighted the sort of research we could expect from future black academics:

> . . . primed to produce 'outstanding works of empirical sociology' . . . a euphemism for

> work that is low on critical knowledge and wisdom but high on information. Information which cannot be gathered as easily by white researchers. Information organised in categories which reinforce stereotypes.[166]

This brings us full circle back to Jenkins' criticisms, since it appears unlikely that the research we have been considering will actually benefit the 'powerless'. To be sure the designation, for example, of Asian and Afro-Caribbean youth as suffering an 'identity crisis' as a result of their being 'Between two Cultures', is the consequence of a partial recognition that blacks are capable of resisting racism. The overwhelming tendency, however, has been to confine this resistance to a few hot-headed male youths. In part we can trace this back to the closure that has been effected around the history of black struggles in Asia and the Caribbean and a seeming ignorance about the struggles the 'first generation' of black people in Britain. This has prompted a recognition of the current struggles of black youth as being 'radically different' from that of their parents. The radical difference is theorised in terms of 'changes' in attitudes which culminate in 'ethnic redefinitions', and is rarely recognised as the response to 'radically different' structural forces.[167]

The nature of the present crisis and the way in which the 'management' of it has borne down upon black people, has demanded a response by all sections of the black communities. If the response of certain sections of black youth has been particularly militant, then this is because they have, up till now, been the ones who have been affected most intensely. To represent these responses in terms of the 'cultural'/'identity' problems of black people themselves is to actively obscure the issue. As Gilroy puts it:

> It is not simply that the 'theories' of pathological black family life, identity crises, acculturation, generational conflict and crimogenic multiple deprivation fail to break free of the shackles of common-sense racist thinking. It is important to understand that these same ideas and images albeit in their 'untheorised' form, are to be found at the base of a new popular politics tailored by crisis conditions.[168]

It is clear that under these conditions, race-relations sociology has assumed a new relevance for the state. Wherever one looks within the various state apparatuses one can find the same images and assumptions underpinning their practices. The police, for example, are increasingly aware that the situation they are being asked to 'police' has its origins in 'social conditions' which they cannot change.[169] They are aware also that,

> The paramount need is that [they] should retain public support during a period of what may be intensifying social crisis.[170]

Under these conditions and facing an increasingly militant black community whose militancy they are required to contain, the police have not been slow to utilise sociological theories which 'blame the victim'. The sub-divisional commander of Handsworth has recently argued thus:

> The need to persuade West Indian parents to relax strict discipline code [sic] which leads to strife within the family group and the consequent break up of homes is an important factor in creating future stability. Stabilising the home surrounds and drying up the flow of youngsters moving towards squats and Rastafarianism is of paramount social importance.[171]

We would perhaps expect such a convergence here but the recent revelations contained in the Brent Community Health Council's *Black People and the Health Service* shows that even the softer 'caring' agencies are imbued with cultural explanations for the ill-health of their black patients.[172] In schools these theories have precipitated the search for ways of giving black children a 'positive image' of themselves. In practice this has meant the crumbs of a 'black studies' course and having more books with black faces in them.[173] The Youth Service,[174] Social Services,[175] and the C.R.E.[176] also base their policies and practices towards black people, upon similar assumptions and find theoretical justification in the work of race-relations sociologists.

This is not to say that these sociologists have been reduced to simple state functionaries, though some of their connections may cause one some concern.[177] Neither is it to deny that anyone's work can be used in ways one did not intend. Further, I am not arguing that individual practitioners in the various state agencies necessarily harbour an evil intent. What is being argued is that the state agencies are operating racist programmes and that the 'theories' of race-relations sociology lend themselves, by the way the issues are posed, to incorporation into the ideologies of these agencies. In this sense, the race relations sociologists have also become a 'part of the problem'.

Notes and references

1 This thesis forms the basis for one chapter of a book, currently titled *The Empire Strikes Back*, by the Race and Politics Group, CCCS, Birmingham University, Hutchinson

2 Robin Jenkins, *The Production of Knowledge in the I.R.R.* (London 1971). Quoted in Jenny Bourne, 'Cheerleaders and Ombudsmen, The Sociology of Race Relations in Britain', *Race and Class*, vol XXI, No. 4, 1980, p. 338

3 J. Bourne, ibid. p. 339

4 See A. Sivanandan, *Race, Class and the State: The Black Experience in Britain* (Race and Class Pamphlet No.1, London 1976)

5 S. Hall, Race and Moral Panics in Post War Britain (B.S.A. Public Lecture May 2, 78) p. 2

6 See Hall and Jefferson (eds.) *Resistance through Rituals* (Hutchinson, London, 1976)

7 J. Solomos: part of Chapter for Race & Politics Group, op.cit.

8 Lord Hailsham, *The Times*, 1976. Quoted by Bob Findlay: part of chapter for Race and Politics Group, op.cit.

9 Trilateral Commission. *The Crisis of Democracy*. Quoted in Solomos, op.cit.

10 See for example Brent Community Health Council's *Black People and the Health Service* (London 1981)

11 S. Hall, op.cit. pp. 5/6

12 Ibid., p. 9

13 See A. Sivanandan, *From Immigration Control to Induced Repatriation. Race and Class*. Vol. XX, No. 1 (London 1978)

14 P. Gilroy, 'Managing the "Underclass": a further note on the sociology of race relations in Britain': *Race and Class*. Vol. XXII, No. 1 (London 1980) pp. 47/48.

15 S. Hall, B. Lumley, G. McLennan, 'Politics and Ideology: Gramsci' (in *On Ideology*: Working Papers in Cultural Studies, 10, CCCS, 1977) p. 49

16 A. Gramsci, *Prison Notebooks* 1971, p. 324. Quoted in Hall, Lumley, McLennan op. cit. p. 50

17 Cf. M. Barker, *Racism – The New Inheritors* p. 3 where he argues that,

> If it were not for the presence of a theory behind the racist 'common sense', the obvious lacunae and untested assumptions of its approach would not so easily escape scrutiny.

I would argue racism *is* elaborated in 'Common-sense' assumptions which are already 'taken for granted', and where it gains popular support and acceptance.

18 Hall, Lumley, McLennan, op.cit. p. 49

19 S. Hall *et al. Policing the Crisis: Mugging, the State and Law and Order* (London 1978) p. 154

20 See Gramsci op.cit. on 'The war of manoeuvre and the war of position'

21 Hall *et al.* op. cit. p. 155
22 Ibid., p. 155
23 Hall, Lumley, McLennan, op cit. p. 50
24 *Guardian*, 2.6.80
25 M. Barrett, *Women's Oppression Today: Some Problems in Marxist/Feminist Analysis* Verso (London 1980)
26 Ibid., see chapter 6. Also J. Donzelot's *The Policing of Families*, Hutchinson (London 1980) for a history of the changing nature of working-class households in France
27 Hall *et al.* op cit. pp. 146/7
28 W.D. Jordan, *White over Black: American Attitudes Toward the Negro 1550–1812* (Maryland 1969) p. 7
29 Jordan refers to the fact that whiteness

> . . . carried a special significance for elizabethan Englishmen; it was particularly when complemented by red, the colour of perfect human beauty, especially female beauty.

and also remarks upon the practice of whitening the skin still further at the 'cosmetic table', p. 8. However his examples are drawn from middle English and Elizabethan literature and since we know that the rate of illiteracy was high at that time it makes it difficult to know how much these were merely the ideas of the ruling bloc and how much they were the general ideas of English people. Even the argument (taken up also by James Walvin) that Shakespeare 'was writing about his countrymen's feelings concerning physical distinctions between kinds of people' . . . and that 'his audience could not have been totally indifferent to the sexual union of "black" men and "white" women' (pp. 37–8) does not necessarily help us unless we know more about the social composition of the audience.

30 Ibid. p. 43
31 Cedric Robinson, 'The emergence and limitations of European radicalism' (*Race & Class*, Vol. XXI No. 2, Aug. 1979) p. 156. Robinson argues that the idea of 'evolution' suggested by the phrase 'the rise of the middle class' is in fact an illusory image 'unsupported by historical evidence'; which suggests that the focus of trade shifts from the Mediterranean and Scania to the Atlantic.

> The city, the point of departure for the earlier bourgeoisies and their networks of long-distance travel and productive organisation proved incapable of sustaining the economic recovery of those bourgeoisies. . . . The absolutist state, under the hegemony of Western European aristocracies, brought forth a new bourgeoisie. (p. 157)

32 Robinson notes that the practice of drawing army volunteers 'from the least "national", most nondescript types, the dregs of the poorest classes', was not something peculiar to the military. This is merely the 'best documented form of a more generalised pattern of structural formation and social integration', which extended to 'domestic service, handicrafts, industrial labour, the ship and dock workers of merchant capitalism, and the field labourers of agrarian capitalism' (p. 160). He suggests that the fact that the significance of migrant immigrant labour has not been better understood is largely to do with an uncritical use of the 'nation' as a unit of analysis – a tendency promulgated by the 'language of error' of evolutionary theories. Further,

> The tendency of European civilisation through capitalism was thus not to homogenise but to differentiate – to exaggerate regional, subcultural, dialectical differences into 'racial' ones. (p. 162)

The development and character of capitalism is, therefore, determined by the social relations and ideological 'compositions' of a civilisation that assumed its fundamental perspective during feudalism p. 162.

33 Robinson, ibid., p. 158
34 Ibid., p. 162
35 Ibid., p. 158
36 J. Walvin, *Black and White: a study of the Negro and English Society* (1555–1945). Allen Lane (London 1973)
37 See earlier discussion, p. 3.
38 The *Sun*, 11.11.80
39 Ibid.
40 This role as the girls' saviour is not uncommon in schools; though there are cases where the girls have made a collective decision to wear trousers, even where the parents themselves are ambivalent.

41 The *Sun* op.cit.
42 *Telegraph and Argus*, 12.7.78
43 P. Parmar, 'Tackling Salmon' in *Bradford Black* (July 1978)
44 *Telegraph and Argus*, 15.7.78
45 See Hall *et al.* op. cit.
46 Quoted in M. Barker, 'The Rebirth of Conservative Ideology', p. 14 (Chapter 4 of forthcoming book). I owe much of the information for this section to Martin Barker's two chapters.
47 See D. Edgar, 'Racism, fascism and the politics of the National Front', *Race and Class*, Vol. XIX, No. 2 (London 1977)
48 As argued in A. Sivanadan, *From Immigration Control to Induced Repatriation*, op.cit.
49 Hall, op. cit. p. 2
50 See M. Barker, 'The Rebirth of Conservative Ideology', op. cit. for useful discussion of the ideology of 'Butskellism', pp. 4/6
51 Barker, ibid. p. 6
52 This question is given sustained attention in the Race & Politics Group's book (forthcoming); but see also *Policing the Crisis*, Hall *et al.*, op.cit. Chapters 8–10
53 A. Sherman, 'Britain's urge to self-destruction' *Daily Telegraph* 9.9.76
54 Ibid.
55 E. Powell, *Freedom and Reality* (Surrey 1969) p. 307
56 G. Brook-Shepherd, 'Where the blame for Brixton lies', *Sunday Telegraph* 19.4.81
57 I. Stanbrook, Hansard, p. 1409. Quoted in M. Barker, *Racism – The New Inheritors*, op.cit. p. 4
58 Ibid., p. 4
59 In this connection it is worth remembering Marx's remarks about the nature of bourgeois ideology.

> In this society of free competition the individual appears free from the bonds of nature, etc., which in former epochs of history made him part of a definite, limited human conglomeration. To the prophets of the eighteenth century . . . this . . . individual, constituting the joint product of the dissolution of the feudal form of society of the new forces of production . . . appears as an ideal whose existence belongs to the past; not as a result of history, but as its starting point. Since that individual appeared to be in conformity with nature and corresponded to their conception of human nature, he was regarded not as developing historically, but as posited by nature. (p. 346)

60 Barker, 'The Rebirth of Conservative Ideology', op.cit. p. 13
61 Ibid. p. 13.
62 Ibid. p. 13/14
63 R. Page, 'To Nature, race is not a dirty word', *Daily Telegraph*, 3.2.77. Quoted in Barker, *Racism – The New Inheritors*, p. 4
64 N. St John-Stevas, BBC 1. 2 March 1978. (Barker, ibid. p. 5) As Barker observes:

> This idea of a 1,000-year continuous development is either sheer fiction, or it is so all-embracing that there is no reason why it shouldn't continue developing happily even if blacks became 75% of the population overnight.

Of course Barker is right but it's worth recalling here the work of Walvin and Jordan on the early presence of blacks in Britain.
65 Powell, op.cit. p. 285. Powell is indeed ignorant of British History. He argues, for example, that Guyana was a 'fragment of the large and miscellaneous spoils of the Napoleonic wars . . .' (p. 246) acquired almost by accident and nothing to do with Britain's Imperialist expansion. But see Tom Nairn, *The Break-up of Britain*, NLB, on this point.
66 Sherman, 'Britain is not Asia's fiancee', *Daily Telegraph*, 9.11.79
67 Sherman, 'Why Britain can't be washed away', *Daily Telegraph*, 8.9.76
68 Sherman 9.11.79 op.cit.
69 Ibid.
70 Ibid.
71 Powell, op.cit. p. 311
72 See Barker, *Racism – The New Inheritors* p. 5
73 Ibid. Barker argues that the evocation of 'genuine fears' is an important mechanism here.

74 M. Thatcher front page, *Daily Mail*, 31.1.78. Quoted in Barker, ibid. p. 4
75 Sherman, 9.9.76 op.cit.
76 Sherman, 9.11.79 op.cit.
77 Ibid. Obviously no-one has told him of the European origins of those 'pseudo-sciences'!
78 Powell, op.cit. p. 300
79 Sherman, 9.9.76, op.cit.
80 Powell, op.cit. pp. 246/52. A reproduction of his speech at Camborne, 14 Jan. 1966 on the 'myth' of the Commonwealth.
81 Sherman, 9.9.76 op.cit.
82 Ibid.
83 Sherman 9.11.79, op.cit.
84 Barker, *Racism – The New Inheritors* p. 6 He argues that there is a 'conceptual connection' between the new racism, its 'theory' (i.e. socio-biology) and the 'idea of a strong state and a nation founded on organic blood-relationships' (Fascism). His section on 'The New Philosophy of Racism', pp. 8/17, dealing with socio-biology, makes these connections more explicit. See also Barbara Chasin, 'Sociobiology: A sexist synthesis' (May–June 1977); Freda Salzman, 'Are sex roles Biologically Determined?' (July–Aug 77) and Richard Lewentin, 'Biological. Determinism as an Ideological Weapon' (Nov–Dec 77). All in editions of *Science for the People* Ann Arbor & Boston U.S.A., for how socio-biology has been taken up in U.S.A.
85 See, for example, R. Jenkins' speech Hansard 5 July 1976 pp. 973/74 (Quoted in Barker, op.cit.) and R. Hattersley's opinion quoted in *Colour and Citizenship* that 'without integration limitation is inexcusable; without limitation, integration is impossible'.
86 For discussion of Rex's paradigm see S. Hall Race, 'Articulation and Societies structured in dominance', *Sociological Theories: Race and Colonialism* 1980. Also R. Wilson, unpublished paper for Race and Politics Group, CCCS, 1979.
87 J. Rex and S. Tomlinson, *Colonial Immigrants in a British City: A Class Analysis* (London 1979) p. 291. See also K. Pryce, *Endless Pressure* (Penguin Books 1979) p. 291; also p. 3 where he argues that the African slaves had no option but to learn their 'master's language and to ape his values and his institutions'.
88 V. Khan, 'Migration and Social Stress: Mirpuris in Bradford', in *Minority Families in Britain: Support and Stress*, V. Khan (ed.) Macmillan Press Ltd (London 1979) pp. 40/41.
89 Ibid. p. 44
90 Pryce, op.cit. p. 16
91 Ibid. pp. 108/9
92 E. Cashmore, *Rastaman*, Allen & Unwin (London 1979) p. 139
93 V. Khan, op.cit. pp. 42/45.
94 Ibid. p. 46
95 Ibid. p. 112
96 Ibid. p. 120
97 V. Khan, op.cit. p. 46
98 Ibid. pp. 49/51
99 Ibid. p. 48
100 V. Khan, 'The Pakistanis: Mirpuri Villagers at home and in Bradford', in J. Watson (ed.) *Between Two Cultures* (Oxford 1977).
101 D. Brooks and K. Singh, 'Pivots and Presents'; and S. Wallman (Intro.) in S. Wallman (ed.) *Ethnicity at Work* (London 1979) quoted in J. Bourne, op.cit. pp. 343/4.
102 J. Bourne, ibid. 1.344
103 Rex and Tomlinson, op.cit. p. 80
104 Ibid. p. 80
105 See H. Braverman, *Labor and Monopoly Capital: The Degradation of Work in the Twentieth Century*, Monthly Review Press (U.S.A. 1974).
106 See F. Kofsky, *Black Nationalism and The Revolution in Music*, Pathfinder Press (New York 1970)
107 'Supremacy' is probably not the right word here. What I am trying to point to is the extent to which 'African survivals' suffuse Brazilian culture; as revealed in Jeremy Mare's documentary about Brazilian music in The World About Us, Feb. 1981.
108 S. Hall, 'Pluralism, race and class in Caribbean Society' (UNESCO 1977), p. 161
109 Ibid. p. 162

110 See C.L.R. James, *The Black Jacobins*, Allison & Busby (London 1980)
111 M. Deren, *The Voodoo Gods*, Paladin (Herts 1975)
112 A. Sivanandan Rana, *Class and The State*, op.cit.
113 Cashmore, op.cit. p. 78
114 G. Rubin, 'The Traffic in Women: Notes on the "political economy" of sex', *Towards an anthropology of women*, R. Reiter (ed.) Monthly Review Press (New York 1975) pp. 165/9
115 This may also throw light on Rex and Tomlinson's view that the African slaves were 'culturally castrated'.
116 W. Rodney, *How Europe Underdeveloped Africa*, Bogle-L'Ouverture (London 1972) p. 113
117 Ibid. p. 113
118 I. Ahmed, 'Pakistan: Class and State Formation' *Race & Class* Vol. XX11 No.3 (London 1981) p. 243
119 V. Khan, 'Migration and Social Stress', op.cit. p. 44
120 See Rodney op.cit. Also R. Brenner, 'The Origins of Capitalist Development', *New Left Review* No.104 July/August 1977
121 G. Omvedt, *We Will Smash This Prison: Indian women in struggle*, Zed Press (London 1980) p. 11
122 Ibid. p. 2
123 V. Khan, 'Purdah in the British situation', *Dependence and Exploitation in Work and Marriage*, D.L. Barker and S. Allen (eds.) Longmans (London 1976)
124 Commission for Racial Equality, *Between Two Cultures: A study of relationships in the Asian Community in Britain* (London 1976)
125 J. Brown, *Shades of Grey: Police/West Indian Relations in Handsworth*, Cranfield Police Studies (1977) p. 8
126 For example, Cashmore records the renewed suspicions about his work after the publication of *Shades of Grey*.
127 L. Garrison *Black Youth, Rastafarianism, and the identity crisis in Britain* (London 1980)
128 Cashmore, op.cit. pp. 39/42
129 Ibid. p. 85
130 Ibid. see chapter 5
131 Garrison, op.cit. p. 11
132 Rex and Tomlinson, op.cit. p. 237
133 Ibid. p. 228
134 C. Ballard, 'Conflict, Continuity and Change: Second-generation South Asians', *Minority Families in Britain*, op.cit. p. 109
135 The media, she says, 'sensationalise only the casualties among them; those who run away from home, who have attempted suicide' etc., ibid. p. 109. But see p. 119 where, after talking about one father who had been 'verbally abusing his family' and resorting to 'sporadic outbreaks of great violence', she remarks that 'such cases are rare . . .'
136 Ibid. p. 121
137 P. Weinreich, 'Ethnicity and Adolescent Identity Conflicts', *Minority Families in Britain* op.cit. pp. 90/93
138 Ibid. p. 89
139 Ibid. p. 89
140 Ibid. p. 93/4. Weinreich tells us that,

> Their constructs were elicited during semi-structured probing interviews which ranged across various areas of life experience . . . Notes were made of all significant others mentioned.

But it is by no means clear, just who thinks the 'others' are significant. It appears as though the constructs are made up of 'others' who Weinreich feels are (or should be) significant.

141 Ibid. pp. 98/9
142 Ibid. p. 104
143 Ibid. p. 101
144 Ibid. p. 105
145 Cashmore, op.cit. p. 88
146 Garrison, op.cit. p. 13
147 Pryce, op.cit. p. 133
148 Cashmore, op.cit. p. 56

149 Garrison, op.cit. in section on 'image building'.
150 Cashmore op.cit. p. 143
151 P. Gilroy, 'Managing the "Underclass"', op.cit. p. 53
152 Ibid. p. 55
153 H. Campbell, 'Rastafari: culture of resistance' *Race & Class* Vol XXII No.1, op.cit. p. 2
154 Hall *et al.* op.cit. p. 394
155 Gilroy from chapter of Race group book op.cit.
156 See A. McRobbie, 'Settling accounts with sub-cultures', *Screen Ed.* Spring 1980
157 Gilroy from Race group book op.cit.
158 D.P. Moynihan, *The Negro Family: The Case for National Action*, Office of Planning and Research U.S. Department of Labour (Washington 1965). Moynihan argued that,

> In essence the Negro community has been forced into a matriarchal structure which, because it is so out of line with the rest of American society, seriously retards the progress of the group as a whole and imposes a crushing burden on the Negro male . . . Obviously not every instance of social pathology afflicting the Negro community can be traced to weaknesses of family structure . . . (but) once or twice removed, it will be found to be the principal source of most of the aberrant, inadequate, or anti-social behaviour that did not establish, but now serves to perpetuate the cycle of poverty and deprivation.

Quoted in M. Wallace, *Black Macho and the Myth of the Superwoman*, John Calder (publishers) ltd., (London 1979) p. 109. Wallace argues that the policies derived from this report had the effect of increasing the prospects and opportunities for some black men at the expense of black women. Those black families with a female head of household were neglected, and indeed became poorer. The already low income of black women, 'increased only slightly' during this period (1965–1976). Further,

> Jobs for black men did not translate into more financially secure black families with male heads . . . The black males who were given access to employment and educational opportunities did not, for various reasons, automatically connect such opportunities with the imperative of family building. (see pp. 109/16)

159 Cashmore op.cit. pp. 1–14
160 Ibid. p. 57
161 Ibid. p. 5
162 Ibid. p. 11
163 Ballard, op.cit. pp. 109/10
164 Hall, 'Race, Articulation and Societies structured in dominance', op.cit.
165 D. Smith, 'Women's perspective as a radical critique of sociology', *Sociological Enquiry* No.44 (1974) pp. 7/13
166 C. Prescod, 'Black Thoughts (A review of Endless Pressure)', *New Society* 3.5.1979
167 Rex does talk about the 'dependence of . . . belief systems on underlying structures', but he can only equate 'social structures' with empirical 'inter-subjective relations'. Straight away then the distinction between 'belief systems' and 'structurs' collapses, with the result that it is by no means clear how the structures can any longer be 'underlying'. See J. Rex, *Race Relations in Sociological Theory* p. 9 (I owe this insight to R. Wilson, Race and Politics Group op.cit.)
168 V. Amos, P. Gilroy, E. Lawrence, 'White Sociology, Black Struggle', Paper presented to the B.S.A. conference on Inequality. 8.4.81 p. 27
169 In *Policing the Crisis*, Hall *et al.* refer to 'a special report (never fully released to the public) on street crime in South London, prepared by Scotland Yard and passed to the Home Secretary' (p. 330). The report is said among other things to have argued that 'soaring street crime' was not a 'policing problem' . . . 'it is caused by widespread alienation of West Indian youth from white society' (p. 331; the quote is taken from the *Sunday Times* 5.1.75). See also Amos *et al.* op.cit. p. 31
170 T.A.Critchley, *A History of Police in England and Wales* 2nd edition (1978) p. 329. Quoted in Amos *et. al.* p. 31
171 Superintendant D. Webb, *Policing a Multi-Racial Community* (forthcoming) p. 11. For context of report see Amos *et al.* op.cit. p. 34
172 Brent Community Health Council op.cit.

173 See H. Carby, *Multicultural Fictions*, Occasional Paper No. 58.CCCS 1980. Also in *Screen Education* No. 34 (Spring 1980)

174 See for example critical articles by M. Cross and G. John in *Black Kids, White Kids, What Hope*, papers presented at two symposia organised by the Regional Training Consultative Unit at Brunel University, M. Day and D. Marsland (eds.) National Youth Bureau (December 1978)

175 See for example A. Jansari, 'Social Work with Ethnic Minorities: A review of Literature', *Multi Racial Social Work*. No. 1 (London 1980)

176 For recent CRE pronouncement see: *Youth in a Multi-Racial Society: The Urgent Need for New Policies: 'The Fire Next Time'*.

177 Note, for example, the connections between the Home Office and the SSRC Research Unit on Ethnic Relations. Home Research Unit director explains:

> While the Home Office is interested in policy-oriented research, it is of course far from being the principal executant or initiator of such research. The largest single body of recent published academic research on ethnic relations which bears on issues of social policy is that undertaken by the SSRC ethnic relations unit, the directorship of which has just passed from Professor Michael Banton at Bristol to Professor John Rex.

A few pages on Rex added that the Unit's work 'will also form an essential and complementary background to the work carried on for immediate policy and political purposes by the Home Office'. *Home Office Research Bulletin* No.8 (1979), quoted in Gilroy, 'Managing the "Underclass" . . .' op.cit. p. 58. It is also worth noting that some of the 'Ethnicity Studies' researchers, were members of the Unit when Professor Banton held the directorship.

Bibliography

Ahmed, I. 'Pakistan: Class and State Formation' in *Race and Class* Vol. XXII, No. 3. Institute of Race Relations (London 1981)

Amos, V., Gilroy, P., Lawrence, E. 'White Sociology, Black Struggle'. Paper presented to the *British Sociological Association* on 'Inequality' 8.4.81

Ballard, C. 'Conflict, Continuity and Change: Second-generation South Asians' in *Minority Families in Britain: Support and Stress*, V. Khan (ed.) Macmillan Press Ltd. (London 1979)

Barker, M. *Racism – The New Inheritors and the Rebirth of Conservative Ideology*, Chapters 2 & 4 of forthcoming publication

Barrett, M. *Women's Oppression Today: Some Problems in Marxist/Feminist Analysis*. New Left Books (London 1980)

Bourne, J. 'Cheerleaders and Ombudsmen, The Sociology of Race Relations in Britain' in *Race and Class*, Vol. XXI, No. 4, IRR (London 1980)

Braverman, H. *Labor and Monopoly Capital: The Degradation of Work in the Twentieth Century*. Monthly Review Press (U.S.A. 1974)

Brenner, R. 'The Origins of Capitalist Development: a critique of Neo-Smithian Marxism'. *New Left Review* No. 104 (London 1977)

Brent Community Health Council. *Black People and the Health Service* (London April 1981)

Brooke-Shepherd, G. 'Where the blame for Brixton Lies'. Article in the *Sunday Telegraph*, ,19.4.81

Brookes, D. and Singh, K. 'Pivots and Presents' in *Ethnicity at Work*. S. Wallman (ed.) (London 1979)

Brown, J. *Shades of Grey: Police/West Indian Relations in Handsworth*. Cranfield Police Studies (1977)

Campbell, H. 'Rastafari: Culture of Resistance' in *Race and Class*, Vol. XXII, No. 1, IRR (London 1980)

Carby, H. *Multicultural Fictions*. Occasional paper No. 58, CCCS, Birmingham University. Also in *Screen Education*, No. 34, Spring 1980

Cashmore, E. *Rastaman*. Allen and Unwin (London 1979)

Chasin, B. 'Sociobiology: A Sexist Synthesis' in *Science for the People*, Ann Arbor, USA, (May/June 1977)

Clarke, J., Hall, S., Jefferson, T., Roberts, B. 'Subcultures, Cultures and Class: A Theoretical Overview', in *Resistance Through Rituals: Youth subcultures in post-war Britain.* S. Hall and T. Jefferson (eds.), Hutchinson (London 1976)

Commission for Racial Equality. *Between Two Cultures: A Study of Relationships in the Asian community in Britain.* Community Relations Council (now CRE) (London 1976)

Youth in a Multi-Racial Society: The Urgent Need for New Policies: 'The Fire Next Time'. CRE (London 1979)

Critchley, T.A. *A History of Police in England and Wales.* Constable (London 1978) – a revised edition.

Cross, M. 'West Indians and the Problem of the Metropolitan Majority' in *Black Kids, White Kids, What Hope.* Papers presented at two symposia organised by the Regional Training Consultative Unit at Brunel University. M.Day and D. Marsland (eds.), National Youth Bureau (December 1978)

Deren, M. *The Voodoo Gods*, Paladin (Herts 1975). First published by Thames and Hudson Ltd. (1953)

Donzelot, J. *The Policing of Families*, Hutchinson (London 1980)

Edgar, D. 'Racism, Fascism and the Politics of the National Front' in *Race and Class*, Vol. XIX, No. 2. IRR (London 1977)

Garrison, L. *Black Youth, Rastafarianism, and the identity-crisis in Britain.* ACER (London 1980)

Gilroy, P. 'Managing the "Underclass": a further note on the sociology of race relations in Britain' in *Race and Class*, Vol. XXII, No. 1, IRR (London 1980)

Gramsci, A. *Selections from the Prison Notebooks.* Lawrence and Wishart (London 1971)

Hall, S. 'Pluralism, race and class in Caribbean Society' in *Race and Class in Post-Colonial Society*, UNESCO (1977)

Hall, S. 'Race and Moral Panics in Post War Britain', BSA Public Lecture (2.5.78) Published in *Five views of Multi-Racial Britain* CRE (1978)

Hall, S. 'Race, Articulation and Societies structured in dominance' in *Sociological Theories; Race and Colonialism* UNESCO (1980)

Hall, S., Critcher, C., Jefferson, T., Clarke, J., Roberts, B., *Policing the Crisis: Mugging, the State and Law and Order.* Macmillan Press Ltd (London 1978)

Hall, S., Lumley, B., McLennan, G., 'Politics and Ideology: Gramsci' in *On Ideology: Working Papers in Cultural Studies*, 10, CCCS, Birmingham University (1977) *Home Office Research Bulletin*, No. 8, (1979)

James, C.L.R. *The Black Jacobins.* Allison and Busby (London 1980)

Jansari, A. 'Social Work with Ethnic Minorities: A Review of Literature' in *Multi Racial Social Work*, No. 1. (London 1980)

Jenkins, R. *The Production of Knowledge in the IRR.* Paper presented to BSA Conference 1971

John, G. 'Present and Future Police for Black Youth' in *Black Kids, White Kids. What Hope.* Papers presented at two symposia organised by the Regional Training Consultative Unit at Brunel University, M. Day and D. Marsland (eds.) National Youth Bureau (December 1978)

Jordan, W.D., *White over Black: American Attitudes Towards the Negro 1550–1912* (Maryland, USA, 1969)

Khan, V. 'The Pakistanis: Mirpuri Villagers at home and in Bradford' in J. Watson (ed.) *Between Two Cultures: Migrants and Minorities in Britain.* Blackwell (Oxford 1977)

Khan, V. 'Migration and Social Stress: Mirpuris in Bradford' in *Minority Families in Britain: Support and Stress.* V. Khan (ed.) Macmillan Press Ltd (London 1979)

Khan, V. 'Purdah in the British situation' in *Dependence and Exploitation in Work and Marriage*, D.L. Barker and S. Allen (eds) Longmans (London 1976)

Kofsky, F. *Black Nationalism and the Revolution in Music.* Pathfinder Press (New York, 1970)

Lewentin, R. 'Biological Determinism as an ideological Weapon' in *Science for the People* (Ann Arbor, USA, Nov/Dec 1977)

McRobbie, A. 'Settling accounts with sub cultures' in *Screen Education* (Spring 1980)

Marx, K. *The Grundrisse, Karl Marx: Selected Writings.* D. McLellan (ed.) Oxford University Press (1977)

Moynihan, D.P. *The Negro Family: The Case for National Action.* Office of Planning and Research, U.S. Department of Labour, (Washington 1965)

Omvedt, G. *We will Smash This Prison: Indian Women in Struggle.* Zed Press (London 1980)

Page, R. 'To Nature, race is not a dirty word'. Article in *The Daily Telegraph*, 3.2.1977

Parmar, P. 'Tackling Salmons' in *Bradford Black* (July 1978)

Powell, J.E. *Freedom and Reality*. Paperfront (Surrey 1969)
Prescod, C. 'Black Thoughts' in 'A review of *Endless Pressure*' in *New Society* 3.5.79
Pryce, K. *Endless Pressure*. Penguin Books (Middlesex 1979)
Race and Politics Group. *The Empire Strikes Back: Racism in the 1970s*. Hutchinson (London 1982)
Rex, J. *Race Relations in Sociological Theory*. Weidenfeld and Nicolson (London 1970)
Rex, J. and Tomlinson, S. *Colonial Immigrants in a British City: A Class Analysis*. Routledge and Kegan Paul (London 1979)
Ritchie, J. 'Black Britain'. Feature Article in the *Sun*. 11.11.80
Robinson, C. 'The Emergence and Limitations of European Radicalism' in *Race and Class* Vol. XXI No. 2, IRR (London 1979)
Rodney, W. *How Europe Underdeveloped Africa*. Bogle-L'Ouverture (London 1972)
Rubin, G. 'The Traffic in Women: Notes on the "political economy" of sex' in *Towards an Anthropology of Women*. R. Reiter (ed.) Monthly Review Press (New York 1975)
Salmon, J. 'The fears of a lonely mother'; 'The hard fact: walls are not lined with gold'; 'Why Ayesha cried after her arranged marriage'; 'An appalling barrier for Maruf and his English girl'. A series of four feature articles in *The Telegraph and Argus*, Bradford, 12/15. July 1978
Salzman, F. 'Are Sex Roles Biologically Determined?' in *Science for the People*, Ann Arbor, USA, (July/August 1977)
Sherman, A. 'Why Britain can't be wished away', (8.9.76); 'Britain's urge to self-destruction', (9.5.76); 'Britain is not Asia's Fiance', (9.11.79) Feature articles in *The Daily Telegraph*
Sivanandan, A. *Race, Class and The State: The Black experience in Britain*. Race and Class Pamphlet No. 1 IRR (London 1976)
Sivanandan, A. *From Immigration Control to Induced Repatriation*. Race and Class Pamphlet IRR (London 1978)
Smith, D. 'Women's perspective as a radical critique of sociology' in *Sociological Enquiry*, No. 44 (1974)
Trilateral Commission. *The Crisis of Democracy: Report on the governability of democracies*. B. Crosier (ed.) (1975)
Wallace, M. *Black Macho and The Myth of the Superwoman*. John Calder (Publishers) Ltd., (London 1979)
Wallman, S. Introduction to *Ethnicity at Work*. Wallman (ed.) Macmillan (London 1979)
Walvin, J. *Black and White: A study of the Negro and English Society, 1555–1945*. Allen Lane (London 1973)
Webb, Superintendant D. *Policing a Multi-Racial Community*. (Forthcoming)
Weinreich, P. 'Ethnicity and Adolescent Identity Conflicts: A Comparative Study' in *Minority Families in Britain: Support and Stress*. V. Khan (ed.) Macmillan (London 1979)

Miscellaneous speeches

Hattersley, R. (M.P.) Speech to the House of Commons 1965. Quoted in Rose, E. and Deakin, N. *Colour and Citizenship*. O.U.P. (1969)
Hailsham (Lord) Quoted in *The Times* 1976
Jenkins, Roy. Speech to House of Commons. *Hansard* 5.7.1976
St. John-Stevas, N. (M.P.) BBC 1. 2.3.1978
Stanbrook, I. (M.P.) Speech to the House of Commons. *Hansard* p. 1409
Thatcher, M. (P.M.) Front page of *The Daily Mail* 31.1.1978
Also 'Make punishment fit the parent'. News item in the *Guardian* 21.5.1980
'The World About Us', 8.2.1981. Film Documentary by J. Marre

26 Trying to do feminist intellectual work

Women's Studies Group

The book from which this chapter is taken has been produced by a group of nine women and two men, some of whom have previously worked together in the Women's Studies Group (WSG) at the Centre for Contemporary Cultural Studies (CCCS). This is a post-graduate research centre where students and teachers, as well as conducting individual research, work collectively in groups organized around areas of shared interest – for example, education, media, women's studies. This form of work allows groups to define their own area of study without the formal division teacher/taught or the constraint of examinations. There is also usually some continuity in group membership which makes it possible to attempt extended and continuing collective work. This work is annually presented to the whole of the department in the summer term and has formed the basis for issues of the journal, *Working Papers in Cultural Studies*.

When we decided to do this book we thought we were deciding to produce the eleventh issue of *Working Papers in Cultural Studies*.[1] Ten issues, with only four articles concerning women – it seemed about time. Women's continuing 'invisibility' in the journal, and in much of the intellectual work done within CCCS (although things are changing), is the result of a complex of factors, which although in their particular combination are specific to our own relatively privileged situation, are not unique to it. We want here to outline some of the problems the Women's Studies Group has faced, in a way which gives this book some sort of history, but also attempts to deal with the more general problems of women's studies and trying to do feminist intellectual work.

Our situation, as a group of research students, may seem very removed from that of women trying to introduce non-sexist teaching materials in schools, running women's studies (WS) courses on a shoe-string or trying to do feminist research alone in an unsympathetic department or at home with kids. We think, however, that the very different problems of each specific academic environment in which we try to work as feminists are informed by broadly the same basic issues and needs. We are all involved in some way in challenging both the existing understanding of society, and the role and construction of sex/gender within this, and the ways in which this understanding is achieved and transmitted. It is through the questions that feminism poses, and the absences it locates, that feminist research and women's studies are constituted as one aspect of the struggle for the transformation of society which would make 'women's studies' unnecessary.

Working as a group in an academic context raises in a particular way the problems of the relationship between intellectual and political practice. Our relationship to the Women's Liberation Movement (WLM) *as a group* has been ambiguous. For some of us the WSG is our closest contact with the WLM. Others are more active in relation to women's liberation outside an academic context. This topic, and our disagreements over what our practice should be, dominated our early discussions about taking the journal on. The questions this raised became the problem of whom to address in our writings: how far could we assume our readers to be Marxists, or feminists, or both, or neither? We also had to try to be self-conscious about the use we made of theoretical concepts to help us to understand women's subordination more precisely; to avoid a general tendency in CCCS towards an *un*self-conscious use of theoretical language which is one element in perpetuating knowledge as the property of a few. We do not think that we were, by any means, always successful in distinguishing these uses.

Women's studies in academic institutions

The difficulty with writing this type of account is partly that our own rather limited experience is only one example of the way feminists have worked together since the beginnings of the WLM in the late 1960s. One thing to arise from the diverse practices and perspectives of the WLM was women organizing together both to share experiences, and work collectively towards a knowledge of them, and to interrogate and appropriate 'knowledge' and skills which exclude or ignore women. This both preceded and continues to accompany the establishment of WS courses in academic institutions.

We concentrate on our own experiences as a group in an academic institution not because we consider it the more important but because it is in this way that we have experienced problems concretely. We would argue that these problems are partly constituted through the contradictions of women's studies as an academic field.

The Manchester Conference on Women's Studies in December 1976 identified two major problems confronting women's studies in Great Britain. One was the division between academic and non-academic women's studies, the other the 'amorphous nature of women's studies'. The organizing collective understood the problem of the 'amorphous nature of WS' as largely determined by an underlying academic versus non-academic conflict concerning both the structure and content of the conference and the participants to whom it was directed.

We agree that this can contribute to a problem of definition for WS in general but think that it also relates to the considerable diversity, in aims, methods and contents, between WS courses *within* various academic institutions. What the organizing collective define as WS's 'amorphous nature' has also to do with WS in itself being a potentially subversive non-academic set of practices. The established structures of learning are continually challenged in the attempt to construct objects of knowledge and to devise ways of learning that are radical alternatives to the institutions within which they exist. Women's studies, like black studies, as a subject or discipline, has political not academic roots,[2] and is constituted through the recognition of economic, ideological, sexual and political subordination and exploitation of a social group. Its political origins mean that it neccessarily exists in many different forms, and that its every appearance within an academic context is both the *result* and the *occasion* of struggles inside and outside that context.[3]

We have to learn as women together, in many different ways and on many different fronts, often drawing on the collective knowledge of the WLM in areas ranging from self-help, health care, aspects of legal and financial (in)dependence and so on, right through to various 'academic' courses.[4] WS courses have to fight for recognition and at the same time guard against the inroads of academic respectability, viability and fashionability which incorporate and politically neuter them. We would argue that there are inherent contradictions between the political origins and objectives of WS in the WLM and the academic space that these WS courses occupy. As Hartnett and Rendel (1975) put it:

> In essence the dilemma for WS is one of maintaining its own integrity within an educational system having (certain) characteristics while trying to infiltrate and leaven all knowledge.

Moreover the divisions do not work only at the level of 'content', as the Women's Report Collective (1975) point out:

> We should be asking what we want from WS. Is it to raise consciousness – to provide ammunition – to change the education system – to produce feminists – or all of these? or none of these?

We deal with this point partly in relation to our own work but first we make four necessarily interrelated points about WS within academic institutions. Firstly, taking a WS option or course can act as a form of consciousness-raising particularly as it is mainly women who take these courses. The content of WS courses consists of material with a personal relevance for the women involved. The course can therefore provide a forum in which to explore issues about, for example, sexuality, as they relate to individuals, and enables the participants both to dispel the neurosis-producing 'it-only-happens-to-me' complex, and to situate personal experience and their subjectively registered responses to them in a sociological and historical context. Secondly, WS courses take a different starting point in specific disciplines – that of women. This takes the form either of the discovery of new empirical material or the privileging of already existing material. It takes women's sphere of activity, previously marginalized, and places it centrally. Thirdly, WS provides a critique of sexism and chauvinism in existing theories, texts and courses. This often arises as part of, and along with, the previous two aspects. This is because working from the point of view of women reveals that there is a systematic absence of this viewpoint, and the *presence* of whole sets of assumptions about women (and, usually, their place in the family). It is thus necessary to begin to formulate an explanatory theory which rests on some notion of women's *structural* subordination.

This in turn leads to the need to develop conceptual tools for feminist analysis. This may mean using already existing, but neglected or taken-for-granted concepts like the 'sexual division of labour'. It may also mean the separation of concepts like 'sex' from 'gender' as Oakley (1972) does, and the development of new concepts with specific meanings – for example the usage of relations of reproduction in Article 8 in this book [this refers to the original publication]. These concepts are developed and explored in the attempt to understand the material processes which constitute a social formation structured into division and conflict on the grounds of gender as well as class. The struggle for new ways of understanding the social formation[5] means that a 'feminist perspective' in existing disciplines cannot consist of just a token acknowledgement, somewhere, of women. We would argue that society has to be understood as constituted through the *articulation* of both sex/gender and class antagonisms, although some feminists would accord primacy to sexual division in their analyses.

In relation to our own work, one of our main intellectual and political difficulties has been making effective interventions in work that was going on in CCCS. *How* does WS or feminist research transform existing research and knowledge? Where should we start in the attempt to analyse a social formation as structured through *both* class antagonisms and sex/gender? How do we carry out our work without being sucked into the intellectual field as already constituted, i.e. gaining legitimation at the expense of our feminism, losing sight of the informing politics of our work?

To intervene effectively as feminists in other group areas of interest it seems we would have to conquer the whole of cultural studies, in itself multi-disciplinary, and *then* make a feminist critique of it. Or, the alternative we tended to adopt, we could concentrate on what we saw as the central areas of research *within* the *WSG*, and thus risk our concerns remaining gender-specific – our own concerns: the 'woman question' claimed by, and relegated to, the women. Sporadic attempts to argue against the 'hiving off' of the woman question from this seemingly snug corner were viewed as double-binding other CCCS members – either we had something to say and we should say it, or else we didn't, and so we should stop making everyone feel guilty.

The problems will be familiar to feminists. It is only *if* the problem of women's subordination is recognized, politically, that questions about, for example, sex-differentiation, the invisibility of women, the consideration of gender at a structural level, the sexual division of labour, the role of the family arise at a theoretical and intellectual level. However, these questions do not follow automatically from this political recognition, particularly when the focus of study is the general area of, say, 'Education' and not 'Women and . . .' or 'Women in . . .'. The political/theoretical recognition that women have always already been 'left out' (that the field of study will have been constituted through the taken-for-grantedness, and hence, invisibility, of women's subordination) is only the pre-condition for a feminist critique, and subsequently for feminist research. Thus even if a group consciously make a decision, as the media group did, to move into an area of study more obviously related to feminist concerns – in this case from the study of 'hard' current affairs television to a family programme within the same spectrum, BBC's *Nationwide* – there is no guarantee that the resulting work will be 'feminist'. In this case, the research material *reproduced* traditional biases, with some updating. Thus, for example, the gender of interviewers in relation to the type of interview had not been routinely recorded, except in the case of *obviously* sexist items. Our work always confronts the disparity between the sophistication of analyses of the social formation in terms of class, and the relative under-development of work on the structures of sex/gender. We have tended as a group to address ourselves to the problem of the articulation of these two areas at a theoretical level, and are thus constantly undermined by the lack of specificity in our work. It is this necessity – to do concrete, historically specific research from a feminist perspective – which could be described as the most important thing that we have learnt from our last few years.

Establishing the group

The group started in October 1974. Until that time we had been just two or three individual women amongst about twenty men at CCCS. We had worked in various sub-groups, none of which had a serious concern for women as a focus of study, and found ourselves in isolation interrogating text after text for this major absence. The structured absence of women from most theoretical and academic texts poses acute problems when trying to work with this material through insights from the WLM, and alongside material from the WLM, some of which is in many ways antagonistic to theoretical/academic work *per se*. We were constantly trying to understand the *experience* of the absence of women, at a theoretical level (there must be more to this than meets the eye . . .) – to see how gender structures and is itself structured. Although in some areas, at one level, it is a question of the *absence* of empirical material – for example, there is more data available about *boys* at school than about girls – this absence is always already structured. We can't just say 'what about women?' when the answer to this question involves thinking differently about the whole field or object of study.

Because women's lives are structured through their subordination, absent data about women cannot simply be filled in – you cannot just add girls' experience of school to boys' experience of school, because the determinants of this experience are *different*, and have to be understood as such before even the question about girls' experience at school can be asked (see Article 5 [this refers to the original publication]). However, at this stage, we didn't even raise the question of 'what about women?'. We found it extremely difficult to participate in CCCS groups and felt, without being able to articulate it, that it was a case of the masculine domination of both intellectual work and the environment in which it was being carried out. Intellectually, our questions were still about 'absences'. Socially, but inseparable from our intellectual presence, as one woman put it at the time, we could either strive for a sort of 'de-sexualized' intellectual role, or retain 'femininity' either through keeping quiet, or in an uneasy combination with being 'one of the lads'. These problems could only be seriously discussed in a small women's group, a solution which came directly from the WLM. In part, however, it was the influx in 1974 of several more women intending to work on women that finally precipitated the move to set up a WSG – originally only two of us had a thesis topic on women. When it was set up, the WSG was open to both women and men. This is necessarily the case with most WS courses inside academic institutions. However, it was not until the second term of 1975 that one man joined us. The group was, until then, as self-selective in terms of sex-origin as most WS courses.

Unlike other CCCS groups, the WSG had a supportive function for us as women, analogous to consciousness-raising groups in the WLM, and this to some extent gave it an ambiguous function and status in the CCCS. Again in common with many WS courses we were both a *woman's group* and a *women's studies group*. But this political aspect can create problems (which are perhaps more apparent in a research group with a fairly constant membership than, for example, one-year courses) both in terms of our work, i.e. a support group carrying on academic work and, related to this, in the *way* we carried it on. As women, we are inevitably the subject and object of our study. This creates a tension which at one level delivers the political power of our own work, and at another delivers a particular kind of humour, mode of working and an understanding of the uncertainties we all encounter in our work as women. It is based on the recognition of our common experiences of *femininity*. These considerations and their implications resulted in us being split over the question of whether the group should be *explicitly* closed (to men) in the same way that WLM small groups are. We consequently gave out rather contradictory messages to the rest of the CCCS.

It was in an attempt to deal directly with some of these problems that we proposed, in June 1976, to set up a women's forum (WF), a closed women's group, open to all women at CCCS. We hoped in this way to allow the WSG to continue its intellectual project, while discussion of more general feminist issues at CCCS would take place in the larger group. We also saw the WF as fulfilling wider supportive functions for women at and around CCCS. This group was to be the one through which we could organize as women in a more direct relation to the WLM. The proposal provoked lengthy discussion in a meeting at which it originally seemed that no one opposed it. We would now see this in many ways as the beginnings of a more open discussion of the implications of feminism for the CCCS as a whole.

Work in the Women's Studies Group

In the first term the WSG undertook the task of examining 'Images of Women in the Media' for a BSA Women and the Media Conference in December 1974 (see Volume 2, Chapter 24). The project not only began to spell out for us the complexities of femininity that underlie any simple use of the descriptive noun 'woman' – what kind of woman (mother, career woman, virgin, etc.), what bit of woman (her face, her hair, her body, etc.) – but plunged us as a group into both the difficulties of collective work and the problem of who to address in our writings. The problem of who to address is still with us, and we have had lengthy debates over it in the production of this book.

These problems have increased since the 'Images' paper, as our work has subsequently been more theoretical. Nevertheless coming together as a group was exciting as well as difficult. Meeting other people in different parts of the country over the 'Images' paper was an enjoyable and useful learning process. The paper wasn't collective because of the time limit on the project and our unfamiliarity with working in this way. But, more importantly, it was probably our different understandings of what we were studying that worked decisively against the possibility of such collective work. Our work in this project was informed in an unrecognized way by different theoretical positions. The 'Images' paper, whilst essentially descriptive, relied implicitly on a theoretical understanding of women's position while not actually being grounded in any such analysis. Then, as now, there was a tendency to either collapse political, intellectual and theoretical differences into emotionally loaded personal differences or to not acknowledge them.

The shift to the 'domestic labour debate' in our next term was a response to what we understood as the lack of 'theory' in the 'Images' paper, and followed the attention given to the debate at the 1974 Women and Socialism Conference in Birmingham. More particularly, this shift was seen as an attempt to consider the relation between class and women's subordination at a theoretical level. But in some senses it was a direct next step from the 'Images' paper. Alongside woman as sex object, it was woman as mother and housewife who we had found to be the primary and determining image of the media. More generally this work represented an educative engagement with the difficult economic categories of Marxism. It also marked the beginnings of our group's attempt to develop a marxist-feminist analysis of women's subordination (see WPCS no. 9).

However, the analysis of women's work in the home seemed incomplete. We wanted to understand how the ideological construction of femininity articulated with the analysis of women's labour in the home. In response to this, we turned to Juliet Mitchell's *Psychoanalysis and Feminism* (1975), but were left in the impasse of the dualism Mitchell's work poses between patriarchy and capitalism (see Article 6). Thus our continuing problem was how to attempt the articulation of sex/gender with class, and the relevance of this for political struggle. Our work on particular texts of feminist theory had noted how the existing separation between sexuality and class was reproduced. For example, the analysis of domestic labour had to some extent been incorporated within existing theories of 'orthodox' Marxism with the continuing exclusion of the specificities of sex and gender. It was precisely because of that separation within theory that we next tried to understand the contradictions of femininity as 'lived' (at the same time holding to class specificity) through a study of the particular historical conjuncture which saw the emergence of the Women's Liberation Movement.

However this proposed project on the 1960s eventually collapsed. The reasons for this were complicated, and we do not really agree as a group about their relative importance. We look here at two aspects: the relations within the group, and the relations of the group to CCCS as a whole – because these have become foci of our intellectual and political differences. Firstly, our need for solidarity in relation to CCCS became confused with a supposed collective feminist intellectual position which individuals felt they could not argue against because it was 'individualistic' or anti-feminist. It was difficult both to argue among ourselves inside the group, and, as individual feminists, to articulate different positions in the wider context.

Secondly, the setting up of the Women's Forum in this year (1976–7) meant that the WSG was no longer 'the women's group'. The increasing attention generally – under feminist pressure – to areas where women are central, e.g. the family and the welfare state, led to a large mixed group in 1976–7. This caused a superficial return to the 'neutrality' of intellectual groups in which detached discussion of the *object* of study takes place. New problems emerged, which we would now trace to our failure to recognize the very different ideas we had about what the group should be doing. We were not self-conscious, in a way that could be discussed, about the different attitudes we had to women's studies, both as women and men, but also as women who had had differing contact with the WLM. Instead, we assumed an illusory shared feminist position, which gave us little purchase *as a group* on new work, and meant the atmosphere was rather tense, although still much easier for women to work in than other CCCS groups. All of the men, and some of the women, left the group. It was the residue of this group which returned to early feminist texts, in particular Rowbotham (1973) and Mitchell (1971), in order to establish some common ground from which to work. We soon shifted to what emerged as an underdeveloped theoretical concern for us – the understanding of women's subordination at 'the economic level', i.e. women's position in relation to the processes of capitalist accumulation. Without work in that area the sixties' project, and any other conjunctural/empirical analysis, would be likely to flounder. This area of study was pertinent to us in terms of individual thesis work – outside the group in the local Feminist Research Workshop to which most of us belonged – as well as of interest to some sections of the WLM. But it was also important in terms of arguments we were having at CCCS. It was a level of theoretical engagement which, in using marxist economic concepts to understand women's subordination – even if not straightforwardly slotting women into an already worked-out framework – appeared to engage more directly with other work in CCCS. This became particularly clear when we 'presented' the work to CCCS as a whole at the end of the year.

It was during this period that discussion about this book, in which we had to argue our case in CCCS to write and edit it, began. Over this issue the WSG and some of the Women's Forum came together to form the basis of the editorial group. What finally made the CCCS let us do this book was not just that we had 'proved' ourselves in relation to our theoretical work on the economic level in our presentation (see Article 3 which was written up from that work [this refers to the original publication]); it also had to do with playing the tapes of women speaking about their lives as housewives (see Article 4 [this refers to the original publication]), a forceful demonstration of women's oppression, and of the political object of our intellectual work. What had started off that year as a disparate group uncertain of its aims had, during these struggles within CCCS, developed a solidarity and purpose which has continued to be worked at during the production of this book.

Conclusion

The difficulties we have found in writing this article emerged most clearly when we came to writing its conclusion. There is a real sense in which this book has been produced by, and written out of the contradictions we have tried to locate in this article. We are a group of women and men who came together to produce this book with differing understandings of what feminist intellectual work is, and should be. This depends partly on how we understand both 'feminism' and 'intellectual work' as political practices and their relation. We all think that feminist intellectual work is both an intellectual and *political* engagement within intellectual work. But we differ on whether this is in itself an adequate political practice, *and* whether political adequacy is a relevant criterion in a direct way for intellectual work. We have different approaches to the relationship between Marxism and feminism in terms of political practice. We differ over what feminism *is* in terms of whether *men* can *be* feminists. Further we differ on whether we should be *primarily* addressing women or men, and whether it is possible to address both simultaneously, in the same terms. We find that we have obscured many of these differences in an attempt to produce an account of where this book came from. This means that we disagree, differently, with the emphases of this article.

We have found producing this book to be a process of political and intellectual education both for ourselves and for some other CCCS members. Our initial reason for wanting to produce the book was fundamental: the continued absence from CCCS of a visible concern with feminist issues. The process of the book's production has involved other members of CCCS in the areas of study and interest we have been working on and has contributed towards making feminism more 'acceptable' within the department. It remains a responsibility for us to ensure that feminism's developing presence as an area of debate and discussion retains and increases its political force. Editorial work has been a unique politicizing experience for us. The hours we have spent together, and the extent to which our consciousness of each other, as women, as feminists, and as men working with women on a feminist project, has been increased, would have seemed impossible this time last year. Having completed the book we do not think that the problems of the group's internal or external relations (to CCCS and the WLM) have been solved in any way.

We can only return to what we see as the central issues. One of the things we want from WS is work which contributes to a feminist analysis of 'how things are' – critiques of existing understandings, the discovery of new material and new questions, and the development of a theoretical understanding of women's subordination under capitalism. It is towards this that we have worked in this book, although we understand the struggle to conduct this work differently, and relate differently to the WLM. We also perceive differently the nature of the contradictions in gaining recognition for the validity of feminist intellectual work, within an academic context, and the terms in which this recognition is granted. These political differences make it impossible for us to agree on a conclusion.

Notes and references

1 *Working Papers in Cultural Studies* was published by CCCS. This book, along with future collections of CCCS work, is being published by CCCS in association with Hutchinson.

2 To our knowledge, there are as yet no *courses* in academic institutions which take the oppression of gay people as their starting point. The oppression of gays features in some WS courses and, for example, courses concerned with, broadly, 'sex, gender and society'. The seminars held at the National Film Theatre in London in the summer of 1977, in conjunction with the 'Gays in Cinema' season could be seen as one of the beginnings of such a focus on gay oppression.

3 The early composition of the WLM, with its tendency to attract young white middle-class women, can be seen as having a direct effect on the establishment of WS courses, and on feminist critiques of existing courses. As many of these women were already involved in education, either as students or teachers, the institutions they were already within presented themselves as obvious sites for the political and ideological struggle that the establishment of women's studies courses represent. These struggles continue, and can be related to the introduction, and attempts to introduce, some form of women's studies or at least non-sexist practice and materials, in junior, primary and secondary schools.

4 Hartnett and Rendell (1975) survey existing WS courses, as do Beardon and Stevenson (1974), who also comment on WS as a field of study. The 1976 Manchester Conference on Women's Studies has produced a report on the discussions at the conference. There is now a WEA Women's Studies Newsletter, available from Croft Cottage, 176 Hagley Road, Stourbridge DY8 2JN. Discussion articles on WS include: 'Should Women Study W-S', *Women's Report* Vol. 4, no. 2, and 'W-8', *Catcall* no. 4 (Sept/Oct 1976). The Women's Research and Resources Centre, 27 Clerkenwell Close, London ECI, keeps an index of feminist research.

5 We are here dependent on Althusser's use of the concept 'social formation', first developed in *For Marx* (1969). Broadly, this conceptualizes 'society' as complexly and contradictorily structured through class divisions at specific levels (economic, political and ideological), each of which possess their own particular history, their own internal laws and dynamics. In that reading, the economic is seen as *determinate* within every social formation, but not always as *dominant.* (In the capitalist social formation the economic level is both determinate and dominant.) It is precisely the difficulty of using Marxist concepts in the analysis of *women's* subordination that we would see this journal as being partly concerned with.

Bibliography

Oakley, A. *Sex, Gender and Society* Maurice Temple Smith (London 1972)

27 What is cultural studies anyway?

Richard Johnson

Introduction [1]

I do not want to attempt a definitive answer to my question. And I do not see myself as 'the Director' bringing orders from Rome to an unruly part of an empire. Nor is my question a true inquisition – which you must answer correctly. Instead the question should be asked musingly, with a slight air of bafflement: what *is* cultural studies – anyway?

It may even be as well to correct the grammar: what are cultural studies? This has the merit of admitting a plurality of answers from the different centres, not the single Centre. In Britain, cultural studies is now a movement or a network. It has its own first degrees in several polytechnics [2] and its own journals and meetings.[3] It exercises a larger influence on academic disciplines, especially on English studies, sociology, media and communication studies, linguistics and history. So it is important that the different centres communicate about their problems and that is what I want to do today.

In the first part of the paper, I want to consider some of the arguments for and against the academic codification of cultural studies. To put the question most sharply: should cultural studies aspire to be an academic discipline? In the second half of the paper I'll look at some strategies of definition short of codification, because a lot hangs, I think, on the *kind* of unity or coherence we seek. Finally, in by far the longest part, I want to try out some of my own preferred definitions and arguments.

The importance of critique

I want to put the arguments against academic codification first, because in any academic context they are the ones most likely to be missed. A codification of methods or knowledges (instituting them, for example, in formal curricula or in courses on 'methodology') runs against some main features of cultural studies as a tradition: its openness and theoretical versatility, its reflexive even self-conscious mood, and, especially, the importance of critique. I mean critique in the fullest sense: not cricicism merely, nor even polemic, but procedures by which other traditions are approached both for what they may yield and for what they inhibit. Critique involves stealing away the more useful elements and rejecting the rest. It involves appropriation not just rejection. From this point of view cultural studies is a process, a kind of alchemy for producing useful knowledge. Codify it and you might halt its reactions.

The history of cultural studies can certainly be written from this point of view, though I have only time to illustrate this with some key cases. The earliest encounters were with literary criticism. Raymond Williams and Richard Hoggart, in their different ways, developed the Leavisite stress on literary-social evaluation, but turned the assessments from literature to everyday life.[4] The application of literary concerns to texts and practices well outside the conventional literary range has been a well-trodden route to cultural studies ever since, whether via the sociology of literature or art, or via film and media studies, or via a concern with language or Marxist critical theory. Williams' own journeys represent the exemplary odessey here, not least for their political consistency.[5] Thus the appropriations from literary studies have been deep, formative and recurrent – a theme I will return to later.

Similar appropriations have been made from history. The first important moment here was the development of the post-war traditions of social history with their focus on popular culture, or the culture of 'the people' especially in its political forms. The Communist Party Historians' Group was central here, with its 1940s and early 1950s project of anglicising and historicising old Marxism. In a way this influence was paradoxical; perhaps that is why it was rather later and less direct than, say, Hoggart's. For the historians were less concerned with contemporary culture or even with the twentieth century, putting energies instead into understanding the long British transition from feudalism to capitalism and the popular struggles and traditions of dissent associated with it. It was this work which became a second matrix for cultural studies. One strand in our recent work has been to study this earlier project in 'popular memory' as part of a larger appropriation of social-historical approaches.[6]

Central in both literary and historical strands was the critique of old Marxism. The recovery of 'values' against Stalinism was a leading impulse of the first New Left, but the critique of economism has been the continuous thread through the whole 'crisis of Marxism' (as it is called) which has followed. Certainly cultural studies has been formed on this side of what we can also call, paradoxically, a modern Marxist revival, and in the cross-national borrowings that were so marked a feature of the 1970s. These patterns of neglects and importations are themselves a facinating topic. For the moment, it is important to note what different places the same figures have occupied in different national routes. The take-up of Althusserianism is incomprehensible outside the background of the dominant empiricism of British intellectual traditions. This feature helps to the appeal of Philosophy, not as a technical pursuit, but as a generalised rationalism and excitement with abstract ideas.[7] Similarly, it is important to note how Gramsci, a version of whose work occupies a place of orthodoxy in Italy, was appropriated by us as a critical, heterodox figure. He provided mighty reinforcements to an already partly-formed cultural studies project, as late as the 1970s.[8]

Some students of culture remain 'marxist' in name (despite the 'crisis' and all that). It is more interesting, however, to note where cultural studies has been Marx-influenced. Everyone will have their own checklist. My own, which is not intended to sketch an orthodoxy, includes three main premises. The first is that cultural processes are intimately connected with social relations, especially with class relations and class formations, with sexual divisions, with the racial structuring of social relations and with age oppressions as a form of dependency. The second is that culture involves power and helps to produce asymmetries in the abilities of individuals and social groups to define and realise their needs. And the third, which follows the other two, is that culture is neither an autonomous nor an externally determined field, but a site of social differences and struggles. For me, this by no means exhausts the elements of Marxism that remain active and alive and resourceful in the existing circumstances, provided only they, too, are critiqued, and developed in detailed studies.

Other critiques have been distinctly philosophical. Cultural studies has been marked out, in the British context, for its concern with 'theory', but the intimacy of the connection with philosophy has not been obvious, at least to me, till recently. Yet it is plain that there is a very close cousinhood between epistemological problems and positions (e.g. empiricism, realism and idealism) and the key questions of 'cultural theory' (e.g. economism, materialism, or the problem of culture's specific effects). Again, for me, a lot of roads lead back to Marx, but the appropriations need to be wider ones. It is interesting, for example, how much cultural studies as a project depends upon the critique of empiricism as a culturally-reductive theory, and how much we have absorbed all (or many) of the anti-empiricist currents of the last twenty years: hence the critique of positivism in social science, of empiricism in history and of models of 'bias' or 'distortion' in leftish media critiques; hence also the fairly temporary attractions of the phenomenological sociologies of the 1960s and the rationalism of the 1970s,[9] hence even the long indecisive tussle with English notions of 'experience', often using these tools.[10] Latterly there have been attempts to go beyond the rather sterile opposition of rationalism and empiricism in search of a more productive formulation of the relation between theory (or 'abstraction' as I now prefer) and 'concrete studies'.[11]

There have been tussles with sociologies of different kinds as well. The relation of cultural studies to 'social science' is a pretty ambiguous one. We have learned from sociology's concern with social theory and have taken many sociologists' topics, but we have tended to refuse sociology's methods and some features of its (more official) outlook. There are two main exceptions: the adoption of 'qualitative methods' into what I will later call a structural ethnography; and an intimate relation with certain specialist sociologies, especially crime/deviancy, education, and the sociology of sexual divisions.[12] As importantly, cultural studies has deeply influenced many sociologists so that, with the disintegration of sociology as a unified discipline, the two approaches are often indistinguishable.[13] Cultural studies can often rely, however, on the whole-hearted opposition of a quantitative, policy-related and officially-funded sociological mainstream, attached as it is, to very conservative agenda of research.

More important in our recent history have been the critiques deriving from the women's movement and from the struggles against racism.[14] These have deepened and extended the democratic and socialist commitments that were the leading principles of the first New Left. These focussed primarily on class issues, whether from the point of view of scholarship boys and girls or a middle-class dissidence. If the personal was already political in the first phase of CND, it was oddly ungendered. The democratic foundations of the early movements were therefore insecurely based as a new form of politics. Similarly there were (and are) deep problems about the ethno- and anglo-centricity of key texts and themes in our tradition.[15] The contemporary salience in Britain of a Conservative-nationalist and racist politics means these flaws are all the more serious. It is incorrect therefore to see feminism or anti-racism as some kind of interruption or diversion from an original class politics and its associated research programme, on the contrary, it is these movements that have kept the New Left new.

The specific results for cultural studies have been no less important.[16] Much more has been involved than the original question – 'what about women?' Feminism has influenced everyday ways of working and brought a greater recognition of the way that productive results depend upon supportive relationships. It has uncovered some unacknowledged premises of 'left' intellectual work and the masculine interests that held them in place. It has produced new objects of study and forced a rethink of old ones. In media studies, for example, it has shifted attention from the 'masculine' genre of news and current affairs to the importance of 'light entertainment'. It has aided a more general turn from older kinds of 'ideology critique' (which centred on maps of meaning or version of reality) to approaches that centre on social identities, subjectivities, popularity and pleasure.[17] Feminists also seem to me to have made a particular contribution to bridging the humanities/social science divide by bringing literary categories and 'aesthetic' concerns to bear on social issues.

I hope these cases show how central critique has been and how connected with political causes in the broader sense. A number of questions follow. If we have progressed by critique, are there not dangers that codifications will involve systematic closure? Anyway, are there not enough important objects of study irrespective of general definitions? Why not carry out raids from existing work rather than formalise achievements? Why not continue to work freely across disciplinary boundaries, rather than erect new ones? If the momentum is to strive for really useful knowledge, will academic codification help this? Is not the priority to become more 'popular' rather than more academic?

These questions gain further force from immediate contexts. Cultural studies is now a widely taught subject, especially in tertiary education, though not always under this name. Unless we are very careful students will encounter it as an orthodoxy, especially, perhaps, where teacher attachments to the subject are pragmatic. In any case, students now have lectures, courses and examinations in the study of culture. In these circumstances, how can they occupy a critical tradition critically? The problem is especially acute when the impulses that made us critics may be no longer immediate to our students. These are not insuperable problems but they need constant discussion and experimentation. There is no better illustration of a general point – that cultural studies has to be associated with educational innovation, not as an optional extra, but as an integral part of the practice itself.

This is reinforced by what we know – or are learning – about academic and other disciplinary dispositions of knowledge. Recognition of the forms of power associated with knowledge may turn out to be one of the leading insights of the 1970s. It is a very general theme: in the work of Pierre Bourdieu and Michel Foucault,[18] in the radical philosophers' and radical scientists' critiques of science or scientism, in radical education philosophy and sociology and in feminist critiques of the dominant academic forms.[19] There has been a marked change from the singular affirmation of science in the early 1970s (with Althusser as one main figure) to the dissolution of such certainties (with Foucault one point of reference) in our own times. Academic knowledge forms (or some aspects of them) now look like part of the problem, rather than part of the solution. In fact, the problem remains much as it has always been – what can be won from the academic concerns and skills to provide elements of useful knowledge?

Pressures to define

Yet there are important pressures to define. There is the little daily politics of the college or the school – not so little since jobs, resources and opportunities for useful work are involved. Cultural studies has won real spaces here and they have to be maintained and extended. The context of ('big') politics makes this still more important. We have a Conservative Counter-Reformation in Britain too. One manifestation is a vigorous assault on public educational institutions, both by cutting finance and by defining usefulness in strictly capitalist terms. We need definitions of cultural studies to struggle effectively in these contexts, to make claims for resources, to clarify our minds in the rush and muddle of everyday work, and to decide priorities for teaching and research.

Most decisively, perhaps, we need ways of viewing a vigorous but fragmented field of study, if not as a *unity* at least as a *whole*. If we do not discuss central directions of our own, we will be pulled hither and thither by the demands of academic self-reproduction and by the academic disciplines from which our subject, in part, grows. There is a welcome tendency for cultural practitioners (media workers, designers, artists, photographers etc.) to look to cultural studies to help with problems of practice, but most students of culture learn their skills from adcademic practices. Academic tendencies, then, tend to be reproduced on the new ground: there are distinctively literary and distinctively sociological or historical versions of cultural studies, just as there are approaches distinguished by theoretical partisanship. This would not matter if any one discipline or problematic could grasp the objects of culture as a whole, but this is not, in my opinion, the case. In my view each approach tells us about a tiny aspect. If this is right, we need a particular kind of defining activity: one which reviews existing approaches, identifies their characteristic objects and their good sense, but also the limits of their competence. Actually it is not definition or codification that we need, but pointers to further transformations. This is not a question of aggregating existing approaches (a bit of sociology here, a spot of linguistics there) but of reforming the elements of different approaches in their relations to each other. I hope to make this very general statement more concrete in what follows.

Strategies of definition

There are several different starting-points. Cultural studies can be defined as an intellectual and political tradition, in its relations to the academic disciplines, in terms of theoretical paradigms, or by its characteristic objects of study. The last starting-point now interests me most; but first a word about the others.

We need histories of cultural studies to trace the recurrent dilemmas and to give perspective to our current projects. But the informed sense of a 'tradition' also works in a more 'mythical' mode to produce a collective identity and a shared sense of purpose. And I do believe that there are some very powerful continuities to be defined. To me, a lot of them are wrapped up in single term 'culture', which remains useful not as a rigorous category, but as a kind of summation of a history. It references in particular the effort to heave the study of culture from its old inegalitarian anchorages in high-artistic connoisseurship and in discourse, of enormous condescension, on the not-culture of the masses. Behind this intellectual redefinition there is a somewhat less consistent *political* pattern, a continuity that runs from the first new left and the first Campaign for Nuclear Disarmament to the post-1968 currents. Of course there have been marked political antagonisms within the new left and between new left politics and the intellectual tendencies it has produced. The intellectual detours have often seemed politically self-indulgent. Yet what unites this sequence is the struggle to reform 'old left' politics. This includes the critique of 'old Marxism' but also of old social-democracy too. It involves a constructive quarrel with dominant styles within 'the Labour Movement', especially the neglect of cultural conditions of politics, and a mechanical narrowing of politics itself. This is a loose and a variable political connection, but it is a real one, sometimes investing in autonomous political forms, sometimes forced into intellectual isolation, sometimes finding in Labour, Communist or other radical parties a useful sphere of action.

It is this sense of a connection that has been so important for cultural studies. It has meant that the research and the writing has been 'political', but not in any immediate pragmatic sense. Cultural studies is not a research programme for a particular party or tendency. Still less does it subordinate intellectual energies to any established doctrines. It has quite enough to do to hold together its own immediate constituencies.

This political-intellectual stance is possible because the politics which we aim to create is not yet fully formed. Just as the politics involves a long haul, so the research must be as wide-ranging and as profound, but also as politically-directed, as we can make it. Above all, perhaps, we have to fight against the disconnection that occurs when cultural studies is inhabited for merely academic purposes or when enthusiasm for (say) popular cultural forms is divorced from the analysis of power and of social possibilities.

I have said a lot already about the second definitional strategy – charting our negative/positive relation to the academic disciplines. I just want to stress the key point. Cultural processes do not correspond to the contours of academic knowledges, as they are. No one academic discipline grasps the full complexity (or seriousness) of the study. Cultural studies must needs be inter-disciplinary (and sometimes anti-disciplinary) in its tendency. I find it hard, for example, to think of myself as a 'historian' now, though perhaps historian-of-the-contemporary is a rough approximation in some contexts. Yet some 'historian's' virtues seem useful for cultural studies – concerns for movement, particularity, complexity and context, for instance. I still love that combination of dense description, complex explanation and subjective even romantic evocation, which I find in the best historical writing. I still find most sociological description thin and obvious and much literary discourse clever but superficial. On the other hand the rooted empiricism of historical practice is a real liability often blocking a proper cultural reading. I am sure it is the same for other disciplines too. Of course, there are lots of half-way houses, many of them serviceable workshops for cultural study, but the *direction* of movement, to my mind, has to be out, and away, and into more dangerous places.

Our third definitional strategy – the analysis and comparison of theoretical problematics – was, until recently, the favourite one. I still see this as an essential component in all cultural study, but it has some difficulties as the main definitional strategy, especially as a starting-point. The main difficulty is that abstract forms of discourse disconnect ideas from the social complexities that first produced them, or to which they originally referred. Unless these are continuously reconstructed and held in the mind as a reference point, theoretical clarification acquires an independent momentum. In teaching situations or similar interchanges, theoretical discourses may seem, to the hearer, a form of intellectual gymnastics. The point appears to be to learn a new language, which takes time and much effort, in order, merely, to feel at ease with it. In the meantime there is something very silencing and perhaps oppressive about new forms of discourse. I think that this has been a fairly common experience, for students, on the new cultural studies programmes, even where, eventually, 'theory' has conferred new powers of understanding and articulacy. This is one set of reasons why many of us now find it useful to start from concrete cases, whether to teach theory historically, as a continuing, contextualising debate about cultural issues, or to hook up theoretical points and contemporary experiences.[20]

Some theoretical issues of the 1970s also seem less pressing. This is partly a criticism of the rationalist mode in which they are posed, but also a reflection of the working through of theoretical difficulties themselves. For me, for instance, the 'culturalist'/'structuralist' opposition is no longer the inhibiting 'impasse' it was four or five years ago. This is because, with different people, I've worked through the range of difficulties posed in that form and in the oppositions structure/struggle, culture/ideology, theory/concrete studies etc.[21] I see the outcome as a strengthened tradition of cultural analysis – of our tradition in the sense sketched above – and one that has taken note of and incorporated the full weight of structuralist critique. This does not mean, of course, that there are no theoretical problems left. There are many, especially in the broad realm of what I would call post-structuralist theories of subjectivity. But they no longer have the same inhibiting force or urgency and seem best worked through in particular projects rather than big 'in-general' debates.

Simple abstractions: consciousness, subjectivity

I have suggested already that 'culture' has value as a reminder but not as a precise category. Raymond Williams has excavated its immense historical repertoire.[22] There is no solution to this polysemy: it is a rationalist illusion to think we can say 'henceforth this term will mean . . .', and expect a whole history of connotations (not to say a whole future) to fall smartly into line. So although I fly culture's flag anyway, and continue to use the word where imprecision matters, definitionally I seek other terms.

My key terms instead are 'consciousness' and 'subjectivity' with the key problems not lying somewhere in the relation between the two. For me cultural studies is about the historical forms of consciousness or subjectivity, or the subjective forms we live by, or, in a rather perilous compression, perhaps a reduction, the subjective side of social relations. These definitions adopt and gloss some of the Marx's simple abstractions, but value them also for their contemporary resonance. I think of 'consciousness', first, in the sense in which it appears in *The German Ideology*. As a (fifth) premise for understanding human history, Marx and Engels add that human beings 'also possess consciousness'.[23] This usage is echoed in later works too. Marx implies it when in *Capital*, Volume I, he distinguishes the worst architect from the best by the fact that the architect's product has 'already existed ideally' before it is produced.[24] It has existed in the consciousness, the imagination. In other words, human beings are characterised by an ideal of imaginary life, where will is cultivated, dreams dreamt, and categories developed. In his earliest work Marx called this a feature of 'species being',[25] later he would have called it a 'general-historical' category, true of all history, a simple or universal abstraction.[26] Although the usage is less clear (and I need to do more work on it) Marx also habitually refers to the 'subjective side' or 'subjective aspect' of social processes.

Of course, all the Marx passages carry colossal incrustrations of commentary and meaning. In Marxist discourse (I am less sure of Marx) 'consciousness' has overwhelmingly cognitive connotations: it has to do with knowledge (especially correct knowledge?) of the social and the natural worlds. I think Marx's consciousness was wider than this. It embraced the notion of a consciousness of self and an active mental and moral self-production. There is no doubt, however, that he was especially interested in conceptually-organised knowledge, especially in his discussions of particular ideological forms (e.g. political economy, Hegelian idealism etc.). In his most interesting text on the character of thinking (the 1857 Introduction to the *Grundrisse*) other modes of consciousenss, the aesthetic, the religious etc, were bracketed out.[27]

In any case, both terms must be read with specifically modern preoccupations in mind. 'Subjectivity' is, especially here, challenging the absences in 'consciousness'. Subjectivity includes the possibility, for example, that some elements or impulses are subjectively active – they *move* us – without being consciously known. It highlights elements ascribed (in the misleading conventional distinction) to aesthetic or emotional life and to conventionally 'feminine' codes. It focusses on the 'who I am' or, as important, the 'who we are' of culture, on individual and collective identities. It connects with the most important structuralist insight: that subjectivities are produced not given and are therefore the objects of inquiry, not the premises or starting-points. If, therefore, I were forced to choose, I would prefer the more modern term, especially if the full force of possible collective identities (implicitly in 'consciousness') were preserved.

In all my thinking about cultural studies I find the notion of 'forms' also repeatedly recurs. Lying behind this usage are two major influences. Marx continuously uses the terms 'forms' or 'social forms' or 'historical forms' when he is examining in *Capital* (but especially in the *Grundrisse*) the various moments of economic circulation: he analyses the 'money form', the 'commodity form', the form of abstract labour etc. Less often he used the same language in writing of 'consciousness' or subjectivity. The most famous instance is from the 1859 *Preface*:

> a distinction should always be made between the material trans*form*ation of the economic conditions of production, which can be determined with the precision of natural science, and the legal, political, religious, aesthetic or philosophic – in short, ideological *forms* in which men become conscious of this conflict and fight it out. (underlining supplied).[28]

The passage has been much discussed – for Marx's scientism, for the base/superstructure metaphor and for a different more expanded notion of ideology than the negative or critical one which Marx usually employs. What interests *me* about it is the implication of a different parallel project to Marx's own. His preoccupation was with those social forms through which human beings produce and reproduce their material life. He looked at social processes as a whole, but from this point of view. He abstracted, analysed and sometimes reconstituted in more concrete accounts the economic forms and tendencies of social life. It seems to me that cultural studies too is concerned with whole societies (or broader social formations) and how they move. But it looks at social processes from another complimentary point of view. *Our* project is to abstract, describe and reconstitute in concrete studies the social forms through which human beings 'live', become conscious, sustain themselves subjectively. This includes the 'ideological forms' which Marx lists but also, of course, such everyday phenomena as the stories or projections which you or I tell ourselves when we get up of a morning, which help us to get up and get going – or send us crawling back under the bedclothes.

The stress on 'forms' is reinforced, for me, by some broad structuralist insights. These have drawn out the structured character of the forms we inhabit subjectively: language, signs, ideologies, discourses, myths. They have pointed to regularities and principles of organisation – of form-fulness if you like. Though often pitched at too high a level of abstraction (e.g. language in general rather than languages in particular), they have strengthened our sense of the hardness, determinacy and, indeed, actual existence of social forms which exercise their pressures through the subjective side of social life.

This is not to say that the description of form, in this sense, is enough. It is important to see the historical nature of subjective forms too. 'Historical' in this context means two rather different things. First, we need to look at forms of subjectivity from the point of view of their pressures or tendencies, especially their contradictory sides. Even in abstract analysis, in other words, we should look for principles of movement as well as combination. Second, of course, we need histories of the forms of subjectivity where we can see how these tendencies are modified by the other social determinations, including those that work through material needs.

As soon as we pose this as a project, we can see how the simple abstractions which we have so far used, do not take us very far. Where are all the intermediate categories that would allow us to start to specify the subjective social forms and the different moments of their existence? Yet I hope that what I have said so far may distance us from all the partial and trivial views of cultural studies which, despite the original redefinition of culture, tend to return. Given this definition of 'culture', we cannot limit the field to specialised practices, particular genres, or popular leisure pursuits. *All* social practices can be looked at from a cultural point of view, for the work they do, subjectively. This goes, for instance, for factory work, for trades union organisation, for life in and around the supermarket, as well certainly for obvious targets like 'the media' (misleading unity') and its (mainly domestic) modes of consumption.

Circuits of capital – circuits of culture

So we need, first, a much more complex model, with rich intermediate categories, more layered than the existing general theories. It is here that I find it helpful to pose a kind of realist hypothesis about the existing state of theories. What if existing theories – and the modes of research associated with them – actually express different sides of the same complex process? What if they are all true, but only as far as they go, true for those parts of the process which they have most clearly in view? What if they are all false or incomplete, liable to mislead, in that they are only partial, and therefore cannot grasp the process as a whole? What if attempts to 'stretch' this competence (without modifying the theory) lead to really gross and dangerous (ideological?) conclusions?

I certainly do not expect immediate assent to the epistemological premises of this argument. I hope it will be judged in the light of its results. But its immediate merit is that it helps to explain one key feature: the theoretical and disciplinary fragmentations we have already noted. Of course these could be explained by the political and social and discursive differences we have also considered: especially the intellectual and academic divisions of labour and the social reproduction of specialist forms of cultural capital. But I find it more satisfactory to relate these manifest differences to the very processes they seek to describe. Maybe academic divisions also correspond to rather different social positions and viewpoints from which different aspects of cultural circuits acquire the greatest salience. This would explain not merely the fact of different theories, but the recurrence and *persistence* of differences, especially between large *clusters* of approaches with certain affinities.

The best way to take such an argument further would be to hazard some provisional description of the different aspects on moments of cultural processes to which we could then relate the different theoetical problematics. Such a model could not be a finished abstraction or theory, if such can exist. Its value would have to be heuristic or illustrative. It might help to explain why theories differ, but would not, in itself, sketch the ideal approach. At most it might serve as a guide to the desirable directions of future approaches, or to the ways in which they might be modified or combined. It is important to bear these caveats in mind in what follows.

I find it easiest (in a long CCCS tradition) to present a model diagrammatically, then explain it further.

The diagram is intended to represent a circuit of the production, circulation and consumption of cultural products. Each box represents a moment in this circuit. Each moment or aspect depends upon the others and is indispensable to the whole. Each, however, is distinct and involves characteristic changes of form. It follows that if we are placed at one point on the circuit, we do not necessarily see what is happening at others. The forms that have most salience for us at one point may be very different from those at another. Processes disappear in results.[29] All cultural products, for example, require to be produced, but the conditions of their production cannot be inferred by scrutinising them as 'texts'. Similarly all cultural products are 'read' by persons other than professional analysts (if they weren't there would be little profit in their production), but we cannot predict these uses from our own analysis, or, indeed, from the conditions of production. As anyone knows, all our communications are liable to return to us in unrecognisable or at least transformed terms.

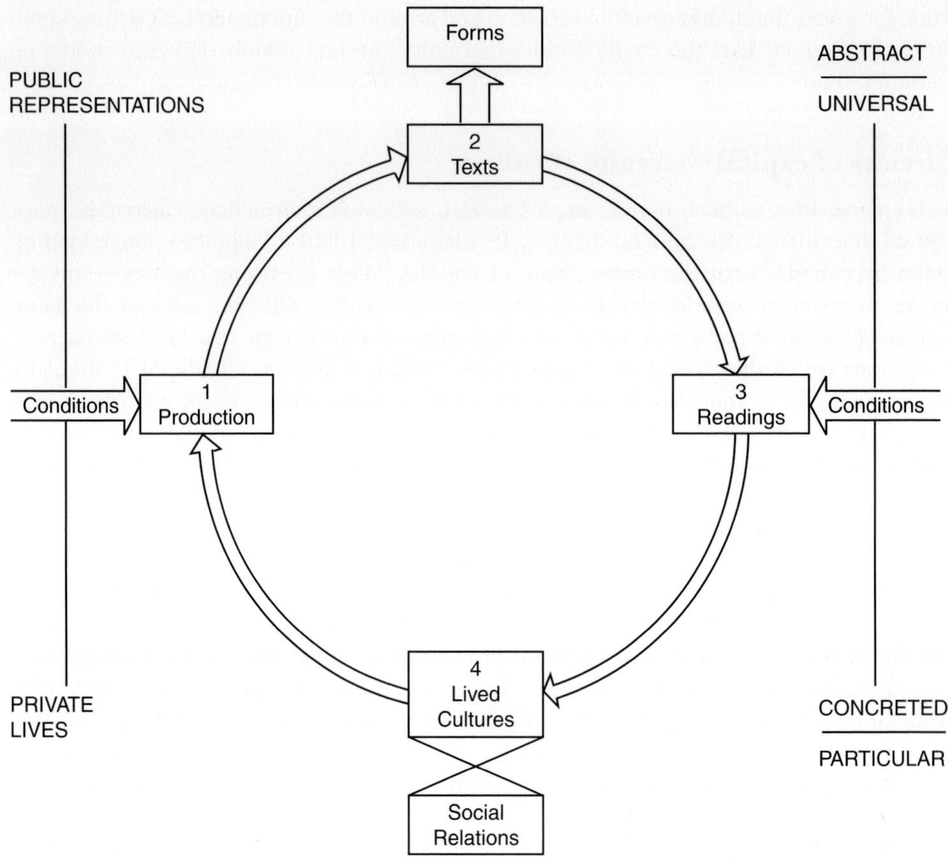

We often call this *mis*understanding or, if we are being very academic, *mis*-readings. But these 'misses' are so common (across the range of a whole society) that we might well call them normal. To understand the transformations, then, we have to understand specific conditions of consumption or 'reading'. These include asymmetries of resources and power, material and cultural. They also include the existing ensembles of cultural elements already active within particular social *milieux* ('lived cultures' in the diagram) and the social relations on which these combinations depend. These reservoirs of discourses and meanings are in turn a raw material for fresh cultural production. They are indeed among the specifically cultural *conditions* of production.

In our societies, many forms of cultural production also take the form of capitalist commodities. In this case we have to supply specifically capitalist conditions of production (see the arrow pointing to moment 1) and specifically capitalist conditions of consumption (see the arrow pointing to moment 3). Of course this does not tell us all there is to know about these moments, which may be structured on other principles as well, but in these cases the circuit is, at one and the same time, a circuit of capital and its expanded reproduction and a circuit of the production and circulation of subjective forms. Some implications of the circuit may be clearer if we take a particular case. We can, for example, whizz a Mini-Metro car around it. I choose the Mini-Metro because it is a pretty standard later twentieth-century capitalist commodity that happened to carry a particularly rich accumulation of meaning.

The Metro was the car that was going to save the British car industry, by beating rivals from the market and by solving British Leyland's acute problems of industrial discipline. It came to signify solutions to internal and external national threats. The advertising campaigns around its launching were remarkable. In one television advert, a band of Mini-Metros pursued a gang of foreign imports up to (and apparently over) the White Cliffs of Dover, whence they fled in what looked remarkably like landing-craft. This was a Dunkirk in reverse with the Metro as nationalist hero. Certainly these are some of the forms – nationalist epic, popular memory of World War II, internal/external threat – that I would want to abstract for further formal scrutiny. But this raises interesting questions too about what constitutes the 'text' (or raw material for such abstractions) in these cases. Would it be enough to analyse the design of the Metro itself as Barthes once analysed the lines of a Citroen? How could we exclude the adverts and garage showroom displays? Shouldn't we include, indeed, the Metro's place in discourses upon national economic recovery and moral renaissance?[30]

Supposing that we answered these questions affirmatively (and gave ourselves a lot more work) there would still be unposed questions. What was *made* of the Metro phenomenon, more privately, by particular groups of consumers and readers? It would be unwise to infer this from the public representations. For one thing, we would expect great diversity of response. Leyland workers, for example, were likely to view the car differently from those who only bought it. Beyond this, the Metro (and its transformed meanings) found some kind of lodgement in the ways of life and subjectivities of those groups for which it had a salience. It became a way of getting to work or picking the kids up from school. But it may also have helped to produce for example orientations towards working life connecting industrial 'peace' with national prosperity. Then, of course, the products of this whole circuit returned once more to the moment of production – as profits for fresh investment, but also as market researchers' findings or 'popularity' (capital's own 'cultural studies'), and as a stock of public and private meanings. The subsequent use, by British Leyland management of similar strategies for selling cars and seeking workers suggests considerable accumulations (of both kinds) from this episode. Indeed the Metro became a little paradigm, though not the first, for a much more diffused ideological form, which we might term, with some compression, 'the nationalist sell'.

Publication and abstraction

So far I have talked rather generally about the 'transformations' that occur around the circuit without specifying any. In so brief a discussion, it is only possible to specify two related changes of form. These are indicated on the left and right hand sides of the circuit. The circuit involves movements between the public and the private but also movements between more abstract and more concrete forms. These two poles are quite closely related, private forms are more concrete, and more particular in their scope of reference; public forms are more abstract but also apply over a more general range. This may be clearer if we return to the Metro and, thence, to different traditions of cultural study.

As a designer's idea, as a manager's 'concept', the Metro remained private. It may even have been conceived in secret. It was known to a chosen few. At this stage indeed, it would have been hard to separate it out from the social occasions at which it was discussed: board-room meetings, chats at the bar, Saturday's game of golf? But as ideas were 'put on paper' it started to take a more objective and more public form. The crunch came when decisions were made to go ahead with 'the concept' and, then again, to 'go public'. Finally, the Metro-idea, shortly followed by the Metro-car, moved into the full glare of publicity. It acquired a more general significance, gathering around it, in fact, some pretty portentous notions. It became a great public issue, or a symbol for such. It also took shape as an actual product and set of texts. In one obvious sense it was made 'concrete': not only could you kick it, you could drive it. But in another sense, this Metro was rather abstract. There it stood, in the showroom, surrounded by its texts of Britishness, a shiny, zippy thing. Yet wo would know, from this display, who conceived it, how it was made who suffered for it, or indeed what possible use it was going to have for the harassed-looking woman with two children in tow, who had just walked into the showroom.

To draw out more general points, three things occurred in the process of publication. First, the car (and its texts) became *public* in the obvious sense: it acquired if not a *universal* at least a more *general* significance. Its messages too were generalised, ranging rather freely across the social surface. Second, at the level of *meaning*, publication involved *abstraction*. The car and its messages could now be viewed in relative isolation from the social conditions that formed it. Thirdly, it was subjected to a process of public *evaluation* ('great public issue') on many different scales: as a technical-social instrument, as a national symbol, as a stake in class war, in relation to competing models etc. It became a site of formidable struggles over meaning. In this process it was made to 'speak', evaluatively, for 'us (British) all'. Note, how, in the moment of consumption or reading, represented here by the woman and her children (who have decided views about cars), we are forced back again to the private, the particular and concrete, however publicly displayed the raw materials for their readings may be.

I want to suggest that these processes are intrinsic to cultural circuits under modern social conditions, and that they are produced by, and are productive of, relations of power. But the most germane evidence for this, lies in some repeated differences in the forms of cultural study.

Forms of culture – forms of study

One major division, theoretical and methodological, runs right through cultural studies. On the one side there are those who insist that 'cultures' must be studied as a whole, and *in situ*, located, in their material context. Suspicious of abstractions and of 'theory', their practical theory is in fact 'culturalist'. They are often attracted to those formulations in Raymond Williams or E.P. Thompson that speak of cultures as 'whole ways of life' or 'whole ways of struggle'. Methodologically, they stress the importance of complex, concrete description, which grasps particularly, the unity or homology of cultural forms and material life. Their preferences are therefore for social-historical recreations of cultures or cultural movements, or for 'ethnographic' cultural description, or for those kinds of writings (e.g. autobiography, oral history, or realist forms of fiction) which recreate socially located 'experience'.

On the other side, there are those who stress the relative independence or effective autonomy of subjective forms and means of signification. The practical theory here is usually 'structuralist', but in a form which privileges the discursive construction of situations and subjects. The preferred method is to treat the forms abstractly, sometimes quite formalistically, uncovering the mechanisms by which meaning is produced in language, narrative or other kinds of sign-system. If the first set of methods are usually derived from sociological, anthropological or social-historical roots, the second set owe most to literary criticism, and especially the traditions of literary modernism and linguistic formalism.[31]

In the long run, this division is, in my opinion, a sure impediment to the development of cultural studies. I will return to its limits and its effects. But it is important first to note the logic of such a division in relation to our sketch of cultural processes as a whole. If we compare, in more detail, what we have called the public and private forms of culture, the relation may be clearer.[32]

Private forms are not necessarily private in the usual sense of personal or individual, though they may be both. They may also be shared, communal and 'social' in ways that public forms are not. It is their particularity or concreteness that marks them as private. They relate to the characteristic life experiences and historically-constructed needs of particular social categories. They do not pretend to define the world for those in other social groups. They are limited, local, modest. They do not aspire to 'universality'. They are also deeply embedded in everyday social intercourse. In the course of their daily lives, women go shopping and meet and discuss the various doings of themselves, their families and their neighbours. Gossip is a private form deeply connected with the occasions and relations of being a woman in our society. Of course, it is *possible* to describe the discursive forms of gossip abstractly, stressing for instance the forms of reciprocity in speech, but this does seem to do a particular violence to the material, ripping it from the immediate and visible context in which these texts of talk arose. An even more striking case is the working-class culture of the shop floor. As Paul Willis has shown there is a particularly close relationship here between the physical action of labour and the practical jokes and common sense of the workplace.[33] The whole discursive mode of the culture is to refuse the separations of manual practice and mental theory characteristic of public and especially academic knowledge forms. In neither case – gossip and shop-floor culture – is there a marked division of labour in culture production. Nor are there technical instruments of production of any great complexity, though forms of speech and the symbolic uses of the human body are complex enough. Nor are the consumers of cultural forms formally or regularly distinguished from their producers, or far removed from them, in time or space.

I would argue that particular forms of inquiry and of representation have been developed to handle these features of private forms. Researchers, writers and all kinds of rapporteurs have adjusted their methods to what have seemed the most evident features of 'culture' in this moment. They have sought to hold together the subjective and more objective moments, often not distinguishing them theoretically, or, in practice, refusing the distinction altogether. It is this stress on 'experience' (the term that prefectly captures this conflation or identity) that has united the practical procedures of social historians, ethnographers and those interested, say, in 'working-class writing'.

Compared with the thick, conjoined tissue of face-to-face encounters, the television programme 'going out on the air' seems a very abstracted, even ethereal product. For one thing it is so much more plainly a representation of 'real life' (at best) than the (equally constructed) narratives of everyday life. It takes a separated abstracted or objective form, in the shape of the programme/text. It comes at us from a special, fixed place, a box of standardised shape and size in the corner of our sitting room. Of course, we apprehend it socially, culturally, communally, but it still has this separated moment, much more obviously than the private text of speech. This separated existence is certainly associated with an intricate division of labour in production and distribution and with the physical and temporal distance between the moment of production and that of consumption, characteristic of public knowledge forms in general. Public media of this kind, indeed, permit quite extraordinary manipulations of space and time as, for example, in the television revival of old movies.

I would argue, again, that this apparent abstraction in the actual forms of public communication underlies the whole range of methods that focus on the construction of reality through symbolic forms themselves – with language as the first model, but the key moment as the objectification of languaguage in text. It would be fascinating to pursue an historical inquiry linked to this hypothesis which would attempt to unravel the relationship between the real abstractions of communicative forms and the mental abstractions of cultural theorists. I do not suppose that the two processes go easily hand in hand, or that changes occur synchronously, but I am sure that the notion of 'text' – as something we can isolate, fix, pin down and scrutinise – depends upon the extensive circulation of cultural products which have been divorced from the immediate conditions of their production and have a moment of suspension, so to speak, before they are consumed.

Public-ation and power

The public and private forms of culture are not sealed against each other. There is a real circlation of forms. Cultural production often involves publication, the making public of private forms. On the other side, public texts are consumed or read in 'private'. A girls' magazine, like *Jackie* for instance,[34] picks up and represents some elements of the private cultures of femininity by which young girls live their lives. It instantaneously renders these elements open to public evaluation – as for example, 'girls stuff', 'silly' or 'trivial'. It also generalises these elements within the scope of the particular readership, creating a little public of its own. The magazine is then a raw material for thousands of girl-readers who make their own *re*-appropriations of the elements first borrowed from their lived culture and forms of subjectivity.

It is important not to assume that public-ation only and always works in dominating or in demeaning ways. We need careful analyses of where and how public representations work to seal social groups into the existing relations of dependence and where and how they have some emancipatory tendency. Short of this detail, we can nonetheless insist on the importance of power as an element in an analysis, by suggesting the main ways it is active in the public–private relationship.

Of course there are profound differences in terms of access to the public sphere. Many social concerns may not acquire publicity at all. It is not merely that they remain private, but that they are actively privatised, *held* at the level of the private. Here, so far as formal politics and state actions are concerned, they are invisible, without public remedy. This means not only that they have to be borne, but that a consciousness of them, as evils, is held at a level of implicit or communal meanings. Within the group a knowledge of such sufferings may be profound, but not of such a kind that expects relief, or finds the sufferings strange.

As often, perhaps, such private concerns do appear publicly, but only on certain terms, and therefore transformed and framed in particular ways. They may be ranked low in public evaluation. The concerns of gossip, for example, do appear publicly in a wide variety of forms, but usually in the guise of 'entertainment'. They appear, for instance, in soap opera, or are 'dignified' only by their connection with the private lives of royalty, stars or politicians. Similarly, elements of shop-floor culture may be staged as comedy or variety acts. Such framings in terms of code or genre may not, as some theorists believe, altogether vitiate these elements as the basis of a social alternative, but they certainly work to contain them within the dominant public definitions of significance.

Public representations may also act in more openly punitive or stigmatising ways. In these forms the elements of private culture are robbed of authenticity or rationality, and constructed as dangerous, deviant, or dotty.[35] Similarly the experiences of subordinated social groups are presented as pathological, problems for intervention not in the organisation of society as a whole, but in the attitudes or behaviour of the suffering group itself. This is 'representation' with a vengeance: representation not as subjects demanding redress, but as objects of external intervention.

If space allowed it would be important to compare the different ways in which these processes may occur across the major social relationships of class, gender, race and age-dependence. But one further general mechanism is the construction, in the public sphere, of definitions of the public/private division itself. Of course, these sound quite neutral definitions: 'everyone' agrees that the most important public issues are the economy, defence, law and order and, perhaps, welfare questions, and that other issues – family life, sexuality for example – are essentially private. The snag is that the dominant definitions of significance are quite socially specific and, in particular, tend to correspond to masculine and middle-class structures of 'interest' (in both the meanings of this term). It is partly because they start fundamentally to challenge these dispositions that some feminisms, the peace movements and the Green parties are amongst the most subversive of modern developments.

I have stressed these elements of power, at the risk of some diversion from the main argument, because cultural studies practices must be viewed within this context. Whether it takes as its main object the more abstracted public knowledges and their underlying logics and definitions, or it searches out the private domains of culture, cultural studies is necessarily and deeply implicated in relations of power. It forms a part of the very circuits which it seeks to describe. It may, like the academic and the professional knowledges, police the public–private relation, or it may critique it. It may be involved in the surveillance of the subjectivities of subordinated groups, or in struggles to represent them more adequately than before. It may become part of the problem, or a part of the solution. That is why as we turn to the particular forms of cultural study, we need to ask not only about objects, theories and methods, but also about the political limits and potentials of different standpoints around the circuit.

From the perspective of production

This is a particularly wide and heterogeneous set of approaches. For I include under this head, approaches with very different political tendencies, from the theoretical knowledges of advertisers, persons involved in public relations for large organisations, many liberal-pluralist theorists of 'public communication' and the larger part of writings on culture within the Marxist and other 'critical' traditions.[36] As between disciplines, it is sociologists or social historians or political economists, or those concerned with the political organisation of culture, who have most commonly taken this viewpoint. Literary approaches have often stopped short at the biography of authors and their 'age'. A more systematic approach to cultural production has been a relatively recent feature of the sociology of literature or art of popular cultural forms.[37] These concerns parallel debates about the mass media which are often carried within political science or political sociology, and were originally deeply influenced by the early experiences of state propaganda under the conditions of the modern media, especially in Nazi Germany. Crossing the more aesthetic and political debates has been the pervasive concern with the influence of capitalist conditions of production and the mass market in cultural commodities on the 'authenticity' of culture, including the popular arts.[38] Studies of production within these traditions have been equally varied: from grandiose critiques of the political economy and cultural pathology of mass communications (e.g. the early Frankfurt School)[39] to empirically very close inspections of the production of news or particular documentary series or soap operas on television.[40] In a very different way still, much modern social history has been concerned with 'cultural production', though this time the cultural production of social movements or even whole social classes. It is important to accept E.P. Thompson's invitation to read *The Making of the English Working Class* from this 'cultural' standpoint, Paul Willis' work, especially *Learning to Labour* representing in many ways the 'sociological' equivalent of this historiographical tradition.[41]

What unites these diverse works, however, is that they all take, if not the viewpoint of cultural producers, at least the *theoretical* standpoint of 'production'. They are interested, first and foremost, in the production and the social organisation of cultural forms. Of course, it is here that Marxist paradigms have occupied a very central place, even where continuously argued against. Early Marxist accounts asserted the primacy of production conditions and often reduced these to some narrowly-conceived version of 'the forces and the relations of production'. Even such reductive analysis had a certain value: culture was understood as a social product, not a matter of individual creativity only. It was therefore subject to political organisation, whether by the capitalist state or by parties of social opposition.[42] In later Marxist accounts, the historical forms of the production and organisation of culture – 'the superstructures' has begun to be elaborated. In Gramsci's writing the study of culture from the viewpoint of production becomes a more general interest with the cultural dimensions of struggles and strategies as a whole. The longstanding and baneful influence of 'high-culture' or specialist definitions of 'Culture' *within* Marxism was also definitively challenged.[43] Gramsci was, perhaps, the first major Marxist theorist and communist leader to take the cultures of the popular classes as a serious object of study and of political practice. All the more modern features of cultural organisation also start to appear in his work: he starts to write of cultural organisers/producers not just as little knots of 'intellectuals' on the old revolutionary or Bolshevik model but as whole social strata concentrated around particular institutions – schools, colleges, the academic specialisms, the law, the press, the state bureaucracies and the political parties. Again, it would be interesting to trace this theoretical movement in its connections with social changes, Gramsci's own location being especially fascinating here, pointing back to the Machiavellian, Jacobin and Bolshevik models and forward to 'the modern Prince'.[44]

Gramsci's work is the most sophisticated and fertile development of a traditional Marxist approach via cultural production. Yet I think that Gramsci remains much more the 'Leninist' than is sometimes appreciated in new left or academic debates in Britain.[45] From the work available in English, it seems to me he was less interested in how cultural forms work, subjectively, than in how to 'organise' them externally. I wonder if I am alone, for example, in feeling real disappointment in his accounts of a possible mass attachment to 'the philosophy of praxis'? He seems here to fall back on a rather mechanical adoption or depends too much on a borrowed and unspecified notion of 'faith'.[46]

Limits of the viewpoint of production

More generally, I find two recurrent limits to looking at culture from this viewpoint. The first difficulty is the familiar one of 'economism', though it is useful, I hope, to restate the problem in a different way. There is a tendency to neglect what is specific to cultural production in this model. Cultural production is assimilated to the model of capitalist (usually) production in general, without sufficient attention to the *dual* nature of the circuit of cultural commodities. In this case, for instance, the conditions of production include not merely the material means of production and the capitalist organisation of labour, but a stock of already existing *cultural* elements drawn from the reservoirs of lived culture or from the already public fields of discourse. This raw material is structured not only by capitalist production imperatives (e.g. commodified) but also by the indirect result of capitalist and other social relations on the existing rules of language and discourse, especially, for example, class and gender-based struggles in their effects on the different social symbols and signs. As against this, Marxist 'political economy' still goes for the more brutally-obvious 'determinations' – especially mechanisms like competition, monopolistic control, and imperial expansion.[47] This is why the claim of some 'semiologies' to provide an alternative 'materialist' analysis does have some force.[48] Many approaches to production, in other words, can be faulted on their chosen ground: as accounts of *cultural* production, of the production of *subjective* forms, they tell us at most about some 'objective' conditions and the work of some social sites – typically of the ideological work of capitalist business (e.g. advertising, the work of the commercial media) rather than that of the political parties, the schools, or the apparatuses of 'high culture'.

The second difficulty is not 'economism' but what we might call 'productivism'. The two are often combined but are analytically distinct. Gramsci's Marxism, for instance, is certainly not 'economistic', but it is, arguably, 'productivist'. The problem here is the tendency to infer the character of a cultural product and of its social use from the conditions of is production, as though, in cultural matters, production determines all. The commonsense forms of this inference are familiar: we need only to trace an idea to its source to declare it 'bourgeois' or 'ideological' – hence 'the bourgeois novel', 'bourgeois science', 'bourgeois ideology' and, of course, all the 'proletarian' equivalents. Most critics of this reduction attack it by denying the connection between conditions of origin and political tendency.[49] I do not myself wish to deny that conditions of origin (including the class or gender position of producers) exercise a profound influence on the nature of the product. I find it more useful to question such identifications not as 'wrong' but as *premature*. They may be true as far as they go, according to the logics of that moment, but neglect the range of possibilities in cultural forms especially as these are realised in consumption or 'readership'. As a matter of fact I do not see how any cultural form can be dubbed 'ideological' (in the usual Marxist critical sense) until we have not only examined its origin in the primary production process, but also carefully analysed its textual forms and the modes of its reception. 'Ideological', unless deployed as a neutral term, is the *last* to use in such analysis, certainly not the first.[50]

I still find the debate between Walter Benjamin and Theodore Adorno about the tendency of mass culture a very instructive example here, even though it is rather a 'set piece'.[51] Adorno swept on in his majestic polemic identifying capitalist production conditions, tracing effects in the 'fetishized' form of the cultural commodity and finding its perfect complement in the 'regressive listening' of fans for popular music. There is a highly deductive or inferential element in his reasoning, often resting on some giant theoretical strides, plotted first by Lukács. The conflations and reductions that result are well illustrated on one of his (few) concrete examples: his analysis of the British brewer's slogan – 'What We Want is Watneys'.

> The brand of the beer was presented like a political slogan. Not only does this billboard give an insight into the nature of the up to date propaganda, which sells its slogans as well as its wares . . . the type of relationship which is suggested by the billboard, by which the masses make a commodity recommended to them the object of their own action, is in fact found again in the pattern of reception of light music. They need and demand what has been palmed off on them.[52]

The first four lines of this are fine. I like the insight about the parallel course of political propaganda and commercial advertising, forced on as it was by the German situation. The reading of the slogan is also quite interesting, showing how advertising works to produce an active identification. But the analysis goes awry as soon as we get to 'the masses'. The actual differentiated drinkers of Watneys and readers of the slogan are assumed to act also as the brewer's ventriloquists' dummy, without any other determinations intervening. Everything specific to the enjoyment of slogans or the drinking of beer is abstracted away. Adorno is uninterested, for example, in the meaning of Watneys (or any other tipple) in the contest of pub sociability, indexed by the 'we'. The possibility that drinkers may have their own reasons for consuming a given product and that drinking has a social use value is overlooked.[53]

This is quite an extreme case of 'productivism' but the pressure to infer effects or readings from an analysis of production is a constant one. It is a feature, for example, of a rich vein of work in cultural studies which has mainly been concerned to analyse particular fields of public discourse. Among CCCS publications *Policing the Crisis* and *Unpopular Education* are cases in point.[54] Both books were analyses of our first two moments – of texts, in this case the fields of discourse about law and order and about public education – and of their conditions and histories of production – law and order campaigns, media *causes célèbres*, the work of 'primary definers' like judges and the police, the role of a new political tendency, 'Thatcherism' etc. Both studies defined and attempted to explain a fundamental sea-change in the whole field of force of public representations. Both studies, but especially *Policing the Crisis*, proved to have considerable predictive value, showing the strengths and the popularity of new right politics before, in the case of *Policing*, Mrs Thatcher's first electoral victory in 1979.[55] Similarly, I believe that *Unpopular Education* contained what has turned out to be a percipient analysis of the fundamental contradictions of social democratic politics in Britain and therefore of some of the agonies of the Labour Party. Yet, as political guides, both studies are incomplete: they lack an account of the crisis of '1945-ism' in the lived culture, of especially, working-class groups, or a really concrete rendering of the popular purchase of new right ideologies. They are limited, in other words, by reliance upon, for the most part, the 'public' knowledges of the media and of formal politics. Something more is required than this, especially if we are to go beyond critique to help in producing new political programmes and movements.

This argument may be capped if we turn to Walter Benjamin. Benjamin certainly took a more open view of the potentialities of mass cultural forms than Adorno. He was excited by their technical and educational possibilities. He urged cultural producers to transform not only their works, but also their ways of working. He described the techniques of a new form of cultural production: Brecht's 'epic theatre'. Yet we can see that all of these insights are primarily the comments of a critic upon the theories of producers, or take the standpoint of production. It is here, still with the creater, that the really revolutionary moves are to be made. It is true that Benjamin also had interesting ideas about the potentiality of modern forms to produce a new and more detached relationship between reader and text, but this insight remained abstract, as optimistic, in the same rather *a priori* way, as Adorno's pessimism. It was not rooted in any extended analysis of the larger experience of particular groups of readers.

Our first case (production) turns out to be an interesting instance of an argument the general form of which will recur. Of course, we must look at cultural forms from the viewpoint of their production. This must include the conditions and the means of production, especially in their cultural or subjective aspects. In my opinion it must include accounts and understandings too of the actual moment of production itself – the labour, in its subjective and objective aspects. We cannot be perpetually discussing 'conditions' and never discussing 'acts'. At the same time, we must avoid the temptation, signalled in Marxist discussions of 'determination'; to subsume all other aspects of culture under the categories of production-studies. This suggests two stages in a more sensible approach. The first is to grant independence and particularity to a distinct production moment – and to do the same for other moments. This is a necessary, negative, holding of the line against reductionalisms of all kinds. But once the line is held in our analysis, another stage becomes quite evident. The different moments or aspects are not in fact distinct. There is, for instance, a sense in which (rather carefully) we can speak of texts as 'productive' and a much stronger case for viewing reading or cultural consumption as a production process in which the first product becomes a material for fresh labour. The text-as-produced is a different object from the text-as-read. The problem with Adorno's analysis and perhaps with 'productivist' approaches in general is not only that they infer the text-as-read from the text-as-produced, but that also, in doing this they ignore the elements of production in other moments, concentrating 'creativity' in producer or critic. Perhaps this is the deepest prejudice of all among the writers, the artists, the teachers, the educators, the communicators and the agitators within the intellectual division of labour.

Text-based studies

A second whole cluster of approaches are primarily concerned with cultural products. Most commonly these products are treated as 'texts'; the point is to provide more or less definitive 'readings' of them.

Again, it would be useful, if space allowed, to trace the evolution of this, the characteristic stance of 'the critic'. Two developments seem especially important: the separation between specialist critics and ordinary readers, and the division between cultural practitioners and those who practise, primarily, by commenting on the works of others. Both developments have much to do with the growth and elaboration of educational and especially academic institutions, but it is interesting that the 'modernisms' which have so deeply influenced cultural studies, had their origins as producers' theories, but are now discussed most intensively in academic and educational contexts. I am thinking particularly of the theories associated with Cubism and Constructivism, Russian formalism and film-making, and, of course, Brecht on theatre.[56] These separations, however, are neither absolute nor permanent, especially if their force is recognised and they are struggled against.

Much of what is known about the textual organisation of cultural forms is now carried in the academic disciplines conventionally grouped together as 'the humanities' or 'the arts'. The major humanities disciplines, but especially linguistic and literary studies, have developed means of formal description which are indispenable for cultural analysis. I am thinking, for example, of the literary analysis of forms of the narrative, the identification of different genres, but also of whole families of 'genre' categories, the analysis of syntactical forms, possibilities and transformations in linguistics, the formal analysis acts and exchanges in speech, the analysis of some elementary forms of 'cultural theory' by philosophers, and the common borrowings, by 'criticism' and cultural studies, from semiology and other structuralisms.

Looking at it from outside, the situation in the humanities and especially in literature seems to me very paradoxical: on the one hand, the development of immensely powerful tools of analysis and description, on the other hand, rather meagre ambitions in terms of applications and objects of analysis. There is a tendency for the tools to remain obstinately technical or formal. The example I find most striking at the moment is linguistics, which seems a positive treasure-chest for cultural analysis but is buried in a heightened technical mystique and academic professionalism, from which, fortunately, it is beginning to emerge.[57] Other possibilities seem perpetually cooped up in the 'need' to say something new about some well-thumbed text or much disputed author. This is sometimes shadowed by a freer-ranging amateurism whose general 'cultural' credentials apparently sanction the liberal application of some pretty commonsense judgements to almost everything. Yet the paradox is that humanities disciplines which are pre-eminently concerned with identifying the subjective forms of life, are already cultural studies in embryo.

The example of certain types of genre category is very revealing here. Forms, regularities and conventions first identified in literature (or certain kinds of music or visual art) often turn out to have a much wider social currency. Feminists working on romance, for example, have traced the correspondences between the narrative forms of popular romantic fiction, the public rituals of marriage (e.g. the Royal Wedding) and, if only through their own experience, the subjective tug of the symbolic resolutions of romantic love.[58] Provoked by this still developing model, a similar set of arguments and researches are developing around conventional masculinity, the fighting fantasies of boy-culture, and the narrative forms of epic.[59] As if on a prompter's cue, the Falklands/Malvinas conflict crystallised both of these forms (and conjoined them) in particularly dramatic and real public spectacle. There is no better instance, perhaps, of the limits of treating forms like romance or epic as merely *literary* constructions. On the contrary, they are among the most powerful and ubiquitous of *social* categories or *subjective* forms, especially in their constructions of conventional femininity and masculinity. Human beings live, love, suffer bereavement and go off and fight and die by them.

As usual, then, the problem is to appropriate methods that are often locked into narrow disciplinary channels and use their real insights more widely, freely. What kinds of text-based methods are most useful? And what problems should we look for and try to overcome?

The importance of being formal

Especially important are all the 'modernist' and 'post-modernist' influences, especially those associated with structuralism and post-Saussurean linguistics. I include the developments in semiology here, but would also want to include, as a kind of cousin-hood, once-removed, some strands in 'Anglo-American' linguistics.[60] Cultural studies has often approached these strands quite gingerly, with heated battles, in particular, with those kinds of text-analysis informed by psychoanalysis,[61] but the fresh modernist infusions continue, and continue to be a source of developments. As someone coming from the other historical/sociological side, I am often surprised and uncritically entranced by the possibilities here. Beyond the dazzle, perhaps there are two main reasons for excitement.

Modern formal analysis promises a really careful and systematic description of subjective forms, and of their tendencies and pressures. It has enabled us to identify, for example, narrativity as a basic form of organisation of subjectivities.[62] It also gives us leads – or more – on the repertoire of narrative forms existing contemporaneously, the actual story-forms characteristic of different ways of life. If we treat these not as 'archetypes' but as historically-produced constructions, the possibilities for fruitful concrete study on a very wide range of materials is immense. For stories obviously come not merely in the form of bookish or filmic fictions but also in everyday conversation, in everyone's imagined futures and daily projections, and in the construction of identities, individual and collective, through memories and histories. What are the recurrent patterns here? What forms can we abstract from these texts most commonly? It seems to me that in the study of subjective forms, we are at the stage in political economy which Marx saw as necessary but primitive: 'when the forms had still to be laboriously peeled out from the material'.[63]

There are a number of inhibitions here. One powerful one is an opposition to abstract categories and a terror of formalism. I think that this is often quite misplaced. We need to abstract forms in order to describe them carefully, clearly, noting the variations and combinations. I am sure that Roland Barthes was right when he argued against the quixotic rejection of 'the artifice of analysis':

> Less terrorized by the spectre of 'formalism', historical criticism might have been less sterile; it would have understood that the specific study of forms does not in any way contradict the necessary principles of totality and History. On the contrary: the more a system is specifically defined in its forms, the more amenable it is to historical criticism. To parody a well-known saying, I shall say that a little formalism turns one away from History, but that a lot brings one back to it.[64]

Admittedly Barthes' 'History' is suspiciously capitalised and emptied of content: unlike Marxism, semiology does not present us with a practice (unless it be Barthes' little essays) for reconstituting a complex whole from the different 'forms'. But I am sure we do end up with better, more explanatory, histories, if we have comprehended, more abstractly, some of the forms and relations which constitute them. In some ways indeed, I find Barthes' work not formal enough. The level of elaboration in his later work sometimes seems gratuitous: too complex for clarity, insufficiently concrete as a substantive account. In these and other semiological endeavours do we mainly hear the busy whirr of self-generating intellectual systems rapidly slipping out of control? If so, however, this is a different noise from the satisfying buzz of a really 'historical' abstraction.

Radical structuralisms excite me for another reason.[65] They are the furthest reach of the criticism of empiricism which, as I suggested earlier, founds cultural studies philosophically. This radical constructivism – nothing in culture taken as given, everything produced – is a leading insight we cannot fall behind. Of course, these two excitements are closely related, the second as a premise of the first. It is because we know we are not in control of our own subjectivities, that we need so badly to identify their forms and trace their histories and future possibilities.

What is a text anyway?

But if text analysis is indispensable, what is a 'text'? Remember the Mini-Metro as an example of the tendency of 'texts' to a polymorphous growth; Tony Bennett's example of the James Bond genres is an even better case.[66] The proliferation of allied representations in the field of public discourses poses large problems for any practitioner of contemporary cultural studies. There are, however, better and worse ways of coping with them. Often, I think, it is a traditional literary solution that is reached for: we plump for an 'author' (so far as this is possible), a single work or series, perhaps a distinctive genre. Our choices may now be popular texts and perhaps a filmic or electronic medium, yet there are still limits in such quasi-literary criteria.

If, for example, we are really interested in how conventions and the technical means available within a particular medium structure representations, we need to work across genres and media, comparatively. We need to trace the differences as well as the similarities, for example, between 'literary romance', romantic love as public spectacle and love as a private form or narrative. It is only in this way that we can resolve some of the most important evaluative questions here: how far, for instance, romance acts merely to seal women into oppressive social conditions, and how far ideologies of love may nonetheless express utopian conceptions of personal relations. We certainly do not *have* to bound our research by literary criteria; other choices are available. It is possible for instance to take 'issues' or periods as the main criterion. Though restricted by their choice of rather 'masculine' genres and media, *Policing the Crisis* and *Unpopular Education* are studies of this kind. They hinge around a basically historical definition, examining aspects of the rise of the New Right mainly from the early 1970s. The logic of this approach has been extended in recent CCCS media-based studies: a study of a wide range of media representations of the Campaign for Nuclear Disarmament in October 1981[67] and a study of the media in a 'post-Falklands' holiday period, from Christmas 1982 to New Year 1983.[68] This last approach is especially fruitful since it allows us to examine the construction of a holiday (and especially the play around the public/private division) according to the possibilities of different media and genres, for example, television soap opera and the popular daily press. By capturing something of the contemporaneity and combined 'effects' of different systems of representations, we also hope to get nearer to the commoner experience of listening, reading and viewing. This form of study, based upon a conjuncture which in this case is both 'historical' (the post-Falklands moment of December 1982) and seasonal (the Christmas holiday), is premised on the belief that context is crucial in the production of meaning.

More generally, the aim is to decentre 'the text' as an object of study. 'The text' is no longer studied for its own sake, nor even for the social effects it may be thought to produce, but rather for the subjective or cultural forms which it realises and makes available. The text is only a *means* in cultural study; strictly, perhaps, it is a raw material from which certain forms (e.g. of narrative, ideological problematic, mode of address, subject position etc.) may be abstracted. It may also form *part* of a larger discursive field or *combination* of forms occurring in other social spaces with some regularity. But the ultimate object of cultural studies is not, in my view, 'the text', but the social life of subjective forms at each moment of their circulation, including their textual embodiments. This is a long way from a literary valuing of texts for themselves, though, of course, the modes in which some textual embodiments of subjective forms come to be valued over others, especially by critics or educators – the problem especially of 'high' and 'low' in culture – is a central question, especially in theories of culture and class. But this is a problem which subsumes 'literary' concerns, rather than reproducing them. One key issue here, for instance, is how criteria of 'literariness' themselves come to be formulated and installed in academic, educational and other regulative practices.

Structuralist foreshortenings

How to constitute 'the text' is one problem; another is the tendency of other moments, especially of cultural production and reading, but more generally of the more concrete, private aspects of culture, to disappear into a reading of the text. Around this tendency, we might write a whole complicated history of formalisms using the term now in its more familiar critical sense.

I understand formalism negatively, *not as abstraction of forms from texts, but as the abstraction of texts from the other moments*. For me this distinction is critical, marking the legitimate and excessive concerns with 'form'. I would explain formalism in the negative sense (if time allowed) in terms of two main sets of determinations: those that derive from the social location of 'critic' and the limits of a particular practice, and those that derive from particular theoretical problematics, the tools of different critical schools. Perhaps it is worth saying that though there is a clear historical association, especially in the twentieth century, between 'criticism' and formalism, there is no necessary connection.

The particular formalisms that interest me most – because there is most to rescue – are those associated with the various structuralist and post-structuralist discussions of text, narrative, subject positions, discourses and so on. I include here, in a necessarily very compressed way, and without many proper distinctions, the whole sequence that runs from Saussure's linguistics and Lévi-Strauss' anthropology to early Barthes and what is sometimes called 'semiology mark 1'[69] to the developments set in train by 'May 1968' in film criticism, semiology and narrative theory, including the complicated intersection of Althusserian Marxism, later semiologies and psycho-analysis. Despite their variations, these approaches to 'signifying practices' share certain paradigmatic limits which I term the 'structuralist foreshortening'. I will describe these briefly, then look at each a little more closely.

They are limited, in a very fundamental way, by staying within the terms of textual analysis. Insofar as they go beyond it, they subordinate other moments *to* textual analysis. In particular they tend to neglect questions of the production of cultural forms or their larger social organisation, or reduce questions of production to the 'productivity' (I would say 'capacity to produce') of the already existing systems of signification, that is the formal languages or codes. They also tend to neglect questions of readership, or subordinate them to the competencies of a textual form of analysis. They tend to drive an 'account' of readership, in fact, from the critic's own textual readings. I want to suggest that the common element in both these limits is a major theoretical lack – the absence of an adquate post-structuralist (or should I say post-post-structuralist) theory of subjectivity. This absence is one that is stressed within these approaches themselves; in fact, it is a major charge against old Marxisms that they lacked 'a theory of the subject'. But the absence is supplied most unsatisfactorily by twinning textual analysis and psycho-analysis in an account of 'subjectivity' which remains very abstract, 'thin' and un-historical and also, in my opinion, overly 'objective'. To sum up the limitations, there is not really an account or accounts here, of the genesis of subjective forms and the different ways in which human beings *inhabit* them.

The neglect of production

This is the easier point to illustrate. It is the difference, for example, between 'cultural studies' in the CCCS tradition, and especially the CCCS appropriation of Gramsci's accounts of hegemony and, say, the main theoretical tendency in the magazine of film criticism associated with the British Film Institute, *Screen*. In the Italian context the comparison might be between the 'pure' semiological and cultural studies traditions. While cultural studies at Birmingham has tended to become *more* historical, more concerned with particular conjunctures and institutional locations, the tendency of film criticism in Britain has been, rather, the other way. Initially, an older Marxist concern with cultural production, and, in particular with cinema as industry and with conjunctures in cinematic production was common both in Britain and in France.[70] But like the French film magazines, *Screen* became in the 1970s, increasingly preoccupied less with production as a social and historical process, and more with the 'productivity' of signifying systems themselves, in particular, with the means of representation of the cinematograpahic medium. This move was very explicitly argued for, not only in the critiques of realist theories of the cinema and of the realist structures of conventional film itself, but also of the 'super-realism' of (honoured) Marxist practitioners like Eisenstein and Brecht.[71] It also formed part of a larger movement which placed increasing emphasis on the means of representation in general and argued that we had to choose between the virtual autonomy and absolute determinacy of 'signification' or return to the consistency of orthodox Marxism.[72] As the elegant, one-sided exaggerations put it, it is the myths that speak the myth-maker, the language which speaks the speaker, the texts which read the reader, the theoretical problematic which produces 'science', and ideology or discourse that produces 'the subject'.[73]

There was an account of production in this work, but a very attenuated one. If we think of production as involving raw materials, tools or means of production and socially-organised forms of human labour, *Screen*'s accounts of film, for instance, focussed narrowly on some of the tools or means of production/representation. I say 'some' because semiologically-influenced theories have tended to invert the priorities of older Marxist approaches to production, focussing only on some of the *cultural* means, those, in fact, which 'political economy' neglects. Film theory in the 1970s acknowledged the 'dual' nature of the cinematic circuit, but was mainly concerned to elaborate cinema as 'mental machinery'.[74] This was an understandable choice of *priorities*, but often pursued in a hyper-critical and non-accumulative way. More serious was the neglect of labour, of the actual human activity of producing. Again this may itself have been an exaggerated reaction against older fashions, especially, in this case *auteur* theory, itself an attenuated conception of labour. The neglect of (structured) human activity and especially of conflicts over all kinds of production seems in retrospect the most glaring absence. Thus, though the conception of 'practice' was much invoked (e.g. 'signifying practice') it was practice quite without 'praxis' in the older Marxist sense. The effects of this were especially important in the debates, which we shall come to, about texts and 'subjects'.

This criticism can be pushed, however, one stage further; no material means of production, no labour, but also a very limited conception of 'means'. In *Screen*'s theory for example, there was a tendency to look only at the specifically cinematographic 'means' – the codes of cinema. The relations between these means and other cultural resources or conditions were not examined: for example, the relation between codes of realism and the professionalism of film-makers or the relation between media more generally and the state and formal political system. If these elements might be counted as means (they might also be thought of as social relations of production) the raw materials of production were also largely absent, especially in their cultural forms. For cinema, like other public media, takes its raw materials from the pre-existing field of public discourses – the whole field that is, not just from the bit called 'cinema' – and, under the kind of conditions we have examined, from private knowledges too. A critique of the very notion of representations (seen as indispensable to the critique of realisms) made it hard for these theorists to pull into their accounts of film any very elaborate recognition of what an older, fuller theory might have called 'content'. Cinema (and then television) were treated as though they were, so to speak, only 'about' cinema or television, only reproducing or transforming the cinematographic or televisual forms, not pulling in and transformning discourses first produced elsewhere. In this way the cinematic text was abstracted from the whole ensemble of discourses and social relations which surrounded and formed it.

There was one further major limitation in much of this work, viewed from the perspective of production. There was a tendency to refuse any explanatory move that went behind the existing means of representation, whether this was the language system, a particular 'signifying practice' or, indeed, the political system. The account was foreshortened to textual means and (just) textual 'effects'. The means were not conceived historically, as having their own moment of production. This was not a local difficulty in particular analyses, but a general theoretical absence, to be found in the earliest influential models of the theory. The same difficulty, for example, haunts Saussurean linguistics; although the rules of language systems determine speech acts, the everyday deployment of linguistic forms appears not to touch the language system itself. This is partly because its principles are conceived so abstractly that historical change or social variation escapes detection, but it is also because there is no true production moment of the language system itself. Crucial insights into language and other systems of signification are therefore foreclosed: that languages are produced (or differentiated), reproduced and modified by socially-organised human practice, that there can be no language (except a dead one) without speakers, and that language is continually fought over in its words, syntax and discursive deployments. It is interesting that in order to recover these insights, students of culture who are interested in language have had to go outside the predominantly French semiological traditions, back to the Marxist philosopher of language, Voloshinov, or aross to particular researches influenced by the work of Bernstein or Halliday.

Readers in texts; readers in society

The most characteristic feature of later semiologies has been the claim to advance a theory of the production of subjects. Initially, the claim was based in a general philosophical opposition to humanist conceptions of a simple unified 'I' or subject, standing unproblematically at the centre of thought or moral or aesthetic evaluation. This feature of structuralism had affinities with similar arguments in Marx about the subjects of bourgeois ideologies, especially about the premises of political economy, and with Freud's anatomisation of the contradictions of human personality.

'Advanced semiology' presents several layers of theorisation of subjectivity which are difficult to unravel.[75] This complicated set of fusions and tangles combines fine leading insights with theoretical disasters. The key insight, for me, is that narratives or images always imply or construct a position or positions from which they are to be read or viewed. Although 'position' remains problematic (is it a set of culture competences or, as the term implies, some necessary 'subjection' to the texts?), the insight is dazzling, especially when applied to visual images and to film. We can now perceive the work which cameras do from a new aspect, not presenting an object merely, but putting us in place before it. If we add to this, the argument that certain kinds of texts ('realism') naturalise the means by which positioning is achieved, we have a dual insight of great force. The particular promise is to render processes hitherto unconsciously suffered (and enjoyed) open to explicit analysis.

Within the context of my own argument, the importance of these insights is that they provide a way of *connecting* the account of textual forms with an exploration of intersections with readers' subjectivities. A careful, elaborated and hierarchised account of the reading positions offered in a text (in narrative structure or modes of address for instance) seems to me the most developed method we have so far within the limits of text analysis. Of course, such readings should not be taken to negate other methods: the reconstruction of the manifest and latent themes of a text, its denotative and connotative moments, its ideological problematic or limiting assumptions, its metaphorical or linguistic strategies. The legitimate object of an identification of 'positions' is the *pressures* or tendencies of subjective forms, the *directions* in which they move us, their *force* – once inhabited. *The difficulties arise* – and they are very numerous – *if such tendencies are held to be realised in the subjectivities of readers, without additional and different forms of inquiry*.

The intoxications of the theory make such a move very tempting. But to slip from 'reader in the text' to 'reader in society' is to slide from the most abstract moment (the analysis of forms) to the most concrete object (actual readers, as they are constituted, socially, historically, culturally). This is conveniently to miss out – but not explicitly as a rational abstraction – the huge number of fresh determinations or pressures of which we must now take account. In disciplinary terms we move from a ground usually covered by literary approaches to one more familiar to historical or sociological competences, but the common new element here is the ability to handle a mass of co-existing determinations, operating at many different levels.

Nor is it merely a question of extra determinations. Also at issue is the availability of materials on which to base an analysis of *any* kind. This is much less of a problem for texts which are publicly available and may circulate, in the case of cinema for example, on a world-wide scale. But the moment of reading is not only relatively more concrete, it is also more private. It is the difference between viewing the film ourselves and grasping its significance for the couple in the back row of the cinema.

It would take us into a long and complicated exploration of 'reading' to try and gauge the full enormity of the leap.[76] There is only room to stress a few difficulties, treating reading, not as reception or assimilation, but as itself an act of production. If the text is the raw material of this practice, we encounter, once again, all the problems of textual boundaries. The isolation of a text for academic scrutiny is a very specific form of reading. More commonly texts are encountered promiscuously; they pour in on us from all directions in diverse, co-existing media, and differently-paced flows. In everyday life, textual materials are complex, multiple, overlapping, co-existent, juxtaposed, in a word, 'inter-textual'. If we use a more agile category like 'discourse', indicating *elements* that cut across different texts, we can say that all readings are also 'inter-discursive'. No subjective form ever acts on its own. Nor can the *combinations* be predicted by formal or logical means, nor even from empirical analysis of the field of public discourse, though of course this may suggest hypotheses. The combinations stem, rather, from more particular logics – the structured life-activity in its objective and subjective sides, of readers or groups of readers: their social locations, their histories, their subjective interests, their private worlds.

The same problem arises if we consider the tools of this practice, or the codes, competences and orientations already present within a particular social *milieu*. Again these are not predictable from public texts. They belong to private *cultures*, in the way that term has usually been used in cultural studies. They are grouped according to 'ways of life'. They exist in the chaotic and historically-sedimented ensembles which Gramsci referred to as 'common sense'. Yet these must determine the longer and shorter-range results of particular interpellative moments, or, as I prefer, the forms of cultural transformation which always occur in readings.

All this points to the centrality of what is usually called 'context'. 'Context' determines the meaning, transformations or salience of a particular subjective form as much as the form itself. 'Context' includes the 'cultural' features described above, but also the contexts of immediate situation (e.g. the domestic context of the household) and the larger historical context or conjuncture.

Yet any account would remain incomplete without some attention to the act of reading itself and an attempt to theorise its products. The absence of action by the reader is characteristic of formalist accounts. Even those theorists (e.g. Brecht, *Tel Quel*, Barthes in S/Z) who are concerned with productive, deconstructive or critical reading ascribe this capacity to types of texts (e.g. 'writable' rather than 'readable' in Barthes' terminology) and not at all to a history of real readers. This absence of production in reading parallels the ascription of productivity to signifying systems which we have already noted. At best particular acts of reading are understood as a replaying of primary human experiences. Just as an older literary criticism sought universal values and human emotions in the text, so the new formalisms understand reading as the reliving of psycho-analytically-defined mechanisms. Analysis of the spectator's game, based on Lacanian accounts of the mirror phase, identify *some* of the motions of the way men use images of women and relate to heroes.[77] Such analyses *do* bridge text and reader. There is a huge potentiality, for cultural studies, in the critical use of Freudian categories, as critical that is, as the use of Marxist categories has become or is becoming. Yet present uses often bridge text and reader at a cost: the radical simplification of the social subject, reducing him or her to the original, naked, infant needs. It is difficult on this basis to specify all the realms of difference which one wishes to grasp, even, surprisingly, gender. At worst the imputations about real subjects come down to a few universals, just as it is only now a few basic features of the text which interest us. There are distinct limits to a procedure which discovers, in otherwise very varied phenomena, the same old mechanisms producing the same old effects.

One lack in these accounts is an attempt to describe more elaborately the surface forms – the flows of inner speech and narrative – which are the most empirically obvious aspect of 'subjectivity'. Perhaps it is thought 'humanist' to pay attention to 'consciousness' in this way? But we all are (aren't we?) continuous, resourceful and absolutely frenetic users of narrative and image. And these uses occur, in part, inside the head, in the imaginative or ideal world which accompanies us in every action. We are not merely positioned by stories we 'read'; we position ourselves by our constant internal story-telling, stories about ourselves, stories about others. We use 'realist' stories about the future to prepare or plan, acting out scenarios of dangerous or pleasurable events. We use 'fictional' or fantastical forms to escape or divert. We tell stories about the past in the form of 'memory' which construct versions of who we presently are. Perhaps all this is simply presupposed informalist analysis, yet to draw it into the foreground seems to have important implications.[78] It makes it possible to recover the elements of self-production in theories of subjectivity. It suggests that before we can gauge the productivity of new interpellations, or anticipate their likely popularity, we need to know what stories are already in place.

All this involves a move beyond what seems to me an underlying formalist assumption: that real readers are 'wiped clean' at each textual encounter to be positioned (or liberated) anew by the next interpellation. 'Post-structuralist' revisions, stressing the continuous productivity of language or discourse as *process*, do not necessarily help here, because it is not at all clear what all this 'productivity' actually produces. It is my own view that there is no real theory of subjectivity here, partly because the *explanandum*, the 'object' of such a theory, remains to be specified. In particular there is no account of the carry-over or continuity of self-identities from one discursive moment to the next, such as a re-theorisation of memory in discursive terms might permit. Since there is no account of continuities or of what remains constant or accumulative, there is no account of structural shifts or major rearrangements of a sense of self, especially in adult life. Such transformations are always, implicitly, referred to 'external' text-forms, for example revolutionary or poetic texts, usually forms of literature. There is no account of what predisposes the reader to use such texts productively or what conditions, other than the text-forms themselves, contribute to revolutionary conjunctures in their subjective dimensions. Similarly, with such a weight on the text, there is no account of how some readers (including, presumably the analysts) can use conventional or 'realist' texts critically. Above all, there is no account of what I would call the subjective aspects of struggle, no account of how there is a moment in subjective flux when social subjects (individual or collective) produce accounts of who they are, as conscious political agents, that is, constitute themselves, politically. To ask for such a theory is not to deny the major structuralist or post-structuralist insights: subjects *are* contradictory, 'in process', fragmented, produced. But human beings and social movements also strive to produce some coherence and continuity, and through this, exercise some control over feelings, conditions and destinies.

This is what I mean by a 'post-post-structuralist' account of subjectivity. It involves returning to some older but reformulated questions – about struggle, 'unity', and the production of a political will. It involves accepting structuralist insights as a statement of the problem, whether we are speaking of our own fragmented selves or the objective and subjective fragmentation of possible political constituencies. But it also involves taking seriously what seems to me the most interesting theoretical lead: the notion of a discursive self-production of subjects, especially in the form of histories and memories.[79]

Social inquiries – logic and history

I hope that the logic of our third cluster of approaches, which focus on 'lived culture', is already clear. To recapitulate, the problem is how to grasp the more *concrete* and more *private* moments of cultural circulation. This sets up two kinds of pressures. The first is towards methods which can detail, recompose and represent complex ensembles of discursive and non-discursive features as they appear in the life of particular social groups. The second is towards 'social inquiry' or an active seeking out of cultural elements which do not appear in the public sphere, or only abstracted and transformed. Of course students of culture have access to private forms through their own experiences and social worlds. This is a continuous resource, the more so if it is consciously specified and if its relativity is recognised. Indeed, a cultural self-criticism of this kind is *the* indispensable condition for avoiding the more grossly ideological forms of cultural study.[80] But the *first* lesson here is the recognition of *major cultural differences*, especially across those social relationships where power, dependence and inequality are most at stake. There are perils, then, in the use of a (limited) individual or collective self-knowledge where the limits of its representativeness are uncharted and its other sides – usually the sides of powerlessness – are simply unknown. This remains a justification for forms of cultural study which take the cultural worlds of others (often reverse sides of one's own) as the main object.

It is important to recognise the specific origins of methods which we have adopted here and the usual problems of transformation that are involved. An adequate history of social inquiry would include the forms of philanthropic or state surveillance of working-class populations which have been a feature of the metropolitan societies at least since the late eighteenth century.[81] I include, in the British case, a whole history of 'moral statistics' and empirical sociological inquiry, from the early nineteenth-century statistical societies to much of post-war 'social science'. These regulative paradigms could be usefully compared with those adopted for the scrutiny of peoples on the imperialised peripheries. But attempts to extend a social self-knowledge have also included folkloric or antiquarian adventures into the past and the modern forms of a culturally-rich social history, the *Annales* strands in France, for example, or the Marxist social history tradition in Britain. Nor could we stop with sociological, anthropological and historical studies. These are often closely allied with literary or artistic traditions of social realism, and with various genres of autobiography, reminiscence, and oral history.[82]

We have to keep a discomforted eye on the historical pedigrees and current orthodoxies of what is sometimes called 'ethnography', a practice of representing the cultures of others. The practice, like the word, already extends social distance and constructs relations of knowledge-as-power. To 'study' cultural forms is already to differ from a more implicit inhabitation of culture which is the main 'commonsense' mode in *all* social groups. (And I mean *all* social groups – 'intellectuals' may be great at describing *other* people's implicit assumptions, but as 'implicit' as anyone when it comes to their own.) To go further than this and render such accounts public, activates those relations of power we have already viewed around the circuit.

Of course, there would be qualitative or political discriminations to make in such a history. I do believe that the early years of new left research in particular – the late 1940s, 1950s and early 1960s – did involve a new set of relations between the subjects and objects of research, especially across class relations.[83] Intellectual movements associated with feminism and the work of some black intellectuals have transformed (but not abolished) these social divisions too. Experiments in community-based authorship have also within limits, achieved new social relations of cultural production and publication.[84] Even so, it seems wise to be suspicious, not necessarily of these practices themselves, but of all accounts of them that try to minimise the political risks and responsibilities involved, or magically to resolve the remaining social divisions. Since fundamental social relations have not been transformed, social inquiry tends constantly to return to its old anchorages, pathologising subordinated cultures, normalising the dominant modes, helping at best to build academic reputations without proportionate returns to those who are represented. Apart from the basic political standpoint – whose side the researchers are on – much depends on the specific theoretical forms of the work, the *kind* of ethnography.

Limits of 'experience'

There seems to be a close association between ethnographies (or histories) based on sympathetic identification and empiricist or 'expressive' models of culture. The pressure is to represent lived cultures as authentic ways of life and to uphold them against ridicule or condescension. Research of this kind has often been used to criticise the dominant representations, especially those influencing state policies. Researchers have often mediated a private working-class world (often the world of their own childhood) and the definitions of the public sphere with its middle-class weighting.[85] A very common way of upholding subordinated cultures has been to stress the bonds between the subjective and objective sides of popular practices. Working-class culture has been seen as the authentic expression of proletarian conditions, perhaps the only expression possible. This relation or identity has sometimes been cemented by 'old Marxist' assumptions about the proper state of consciousness of the working-class. A similar set of assumptions can be traced in some feminist writings about culture which portray and celebrate a distinct feminine cultural world reflective of woman's condition. The term which most commonly indexes this theoretical framework is 'experience', with its characteristic fusing of objective and subjective aspects.

Such frameworks produce major difficulties, not least for researchers themselves. Secondary analysis and representation must always be problematic or intrusive if 'spontaneous' cultural forms are seen as a completed or necessary form of social knowledge. The only legitimate practice, in this framework, is to represent an unmediated chunk of authentic life experience itself, in something like its own terms. This form of cultural empiricism is a dead hand on the most important of cultural studies practices, and is one of the reasons why it is also the most difficult to deliver at all.

There is also a systematic pressure towards presenting lived cultures primarily in terms of their homogeneity and distinctiveness. This theoretical pressure, in conceptions like 'whole way of life', becomes startlingly clear when issues of nationalism and racism are taken into account. There is a discomforting convergence between 'radical' but romantic versions of 'working-class culture' and notions of a shared Englishness or white ethnicity. Here too one finds the term 'way of life' used as though 'cultures' were great slabs of significance always humped around by the same set of people. In left ethnography the term has often been associated with an under-representation of non-class relations and of fragmentations within social classes.[86]

The main lack within expressive theories is attention to the means of signifiation as a specific cultural determination. There is no better instance of the divorce between formal analysis and 'concrete studies' than the rarity of linguistic analysis in historical or ethnographic work. Like much structuralist analysis, then, ethnographies often work with a foreshortened version of our circuit, only here it is the whole arc of 'public' forms which is often missing. Thus the creativity of private forms is stressed, the continuous cultural productivity of everyday life, but not its dependence on the materials and modes of public production. Methodologically, the virtues of abstraction are eschewed so that the separate (or separable) elements of lived cultures are not unravelled, and their real complexity (rather than their essential unity) is not recognised.

Best ethnography

I do not wish to imply that this form of cultural study is intrinsically compromised. On the contrary, I tend to see it as the privileged form of analysis, both intellectually and politically. Perhaps this will be clear if I briefly review some aspects of the best ethnographic studies at Birmingham.[87]

These studies have used abstraction and formal description to identify key elements in a lived cultural ensemble. Cultures are read 'textually'. But they have also been viewed alongside a reconstruction of the social position of the users. There is a large difference here between a 'structural ethnography' and a more ethno-methodological approach concerned exclusively with the level of meaning and usually within an individualistic framework. This is one reason, for instance, why feminist work in the Centre has been as much preoccupied with theorising the position of women as with 'talking to girls'. We have tried to ally cultural analysis with a (sometimes too generalised) structural sociology, centring upon gender, class and race.

Perhaps the most distinctive feature has been the connections made between lived cultural ensembles and public forms. Typically, studies have concerned the appropriation of elements of mass culture and their transformation according to the needs and cultural logics of social groups. Studies of the contribution of mass cultural forms (popular music, fashion, drugs or motor bikes) to sub-cultural styles, of girls' use of popular cultural forms, and of the lads' resistance to the knowledge and authority of school are cases in point. In other words the best studies of lived culture are also, necessarily, studies of 'reading'. It is from this point of view – the intersection of public and private forms – that we have the best chance of answering the two key sets of questions to which cultural studies – rightly – continually returns.

The first set concerns 'popularity', pleasure and the *use value* of cultural forms. Why do some subjective forms acquire a popular force, become principles of living? What are the *different* ways in which subjective forms are inhabited – playfully or in deep seriousness, in fantasy or by rational agreement, because it is the thing to do or the thing *not* to do? The second set of questions concerns the *outcomes* of cultural forms. Do these forms tend to reproduce existing forms of subordination or oppression? Do they hold down or contain social ambitions, defining wants too modestly? Or are they forms which permit a questioning of existing relations or a running beyond them in terms of desire? Do they point to alternative social arrangements? As I suggested near the beginning of this discussion judgements like these cannot be made on the basis of the analysis of production conditions or texts alone; they can best be answered once we have traced a social form right through the circuit of its transformations and made some attempt to place it within the whole context of relations of hegemony within the society.

Future shapes of cultural studies: directions

My argument has been that there are three main models of cultural studies research: production-based studies, text-based studies, and studies of lived cultures. This division conforms to the main appearances of cultural circuits, but inhibits the development of our understandings in important ways. Each approach has a rationality in relation to that moment it has most closely in view, but is quite evidently inadequate, even 'ideological', as an account of the whole. Yet different approaches acquire an independence in the various theoretical paradigms, and are also related to the specialisms of academic disciplines. Each approach also implies a different view of the politics of culture. Production-related studies imply a struggle to control or transform the most poweful means of cultural production, or to throw up alternative means by which a counter-hegemonic strategy may be pursued. Such discourses are usually addressed to institutional reformers or to radical political parties. Text-based studies, focussing on the forms of cultural products, have usually concerned the possibilities of a transformative cultural practice. They have been addressed most often to avant-garde practitioners, critics and teachers. These approaches have appealed especially to professional educators, in colleges or schools, because knowledges appropriate to radical practice have been adapted (not without problems) to a knowledge appropriate to critical readers. Finally, research into lived cultures has been closely associated with a politics of 'representation', upholding the ways of life of subordinated social groups and criticising the dominant public forms in the light of hidden wisdoms. Such work may even aspire to help to give a hegemonic or non-corporate turn to cultures that are usually privatised, stigmatised or silenced.

It is important to stress that the circuit has not been presented as an adequate account of cultural processes or even of elementary forms. It is not a completed set of abstractions against which every partial approach can be judged. It is not therefore an adequate strategy for the future just to add together the three sets of approaches, using each for its appropriate moment. This would not work without transformations of each approach and, perhaps, our thinking about 'moments'. For one thing there are some real theoretical incompatibilities between approaches; for another, the ambitions of many projects are already large enough. It is important to recognise that each aspect has a life of its own in order to avoid reductions, but, after that, it may be more transformative to rethink each moment in the light of the others, importing objects and methods of study usually developed in relation to one moment into the next. I think this will work – and already works in the best practices – because the moments, though separable, are not in fact discrete. We therefore need to trace what Marx would have called 'the inner connections' and 'real identities' between them.

Those concerned with production studies need to look more closely, for example, at the specifically cultural conditions of production. This would include the more formal semiological questions about the codes and conventions on which a television programme, say, draws, and the ways in which it reworks them. But it would have to include too, a wider range of discursive materials – ideological themes and problematics – that belong to a wider social and political conjunture. But already, in the production moment, we would expect to find more or less intimate relations with the lived culture of particular social groups, if only that of the producers. Discursive and ideological elements would be used and transformed from there too. 'Already' then, in the study of the production moment, we can anticipate the other aspects of the larger process and prepare the ground for a more adequate account too.

Similarly we need to develop, further, forms of text-based study which hook up with the reduction and readership perspectives. It may well be, in the Italian context, where semiological and literary traditions are so strong, that these are the most important transformations. It *is* possible to look for the signs of the production process in a text: this is one useful way of transforming the very unproductive concern with 'bias' that still dominates discussion of 'factual' media. It *is* also possible to read texts as forms of representation, provided it is realised that we are always analysing a representation of a representation. The first object, that which is represented in the text, is not an objective event or fact, but has already been given meanings in some other social practice. In this way it is possible to consider the relationship, if any, between the characteristic codes and conventions of a social group and the forms in which they are represented in a soap opera or comedy. This is not merely an academic exercise, since it is essential to have such an account to help establish the text's salience, for this group or others. There is no question of abandoning existing forms of text analysis, but these have to be adapted to, rather than superseding, the study of actual readerships. There seem to be two main requirements here. First, the formal reading of a text has to be as open or as multi-layered as possible, identifying preferred positions or frameworks certainly, but also alternative readings and subordinated frameworks, even if these can only be discerned as fragments, or as contraditions in the dominant forms. Second, analysts need to abandon once and for all, both of the two main models of the critical reader: the primarily evaluative reading (is this a good/bad text?) and the aspiration to text-analysis as an 'objective science'. The problem with both models is that by de-relativising our acts of reading they remove from self-conscious consideration (but not as an active presence) our commonsense knowledge of the larger cultural contexts and possible readings. I have already noted the difficuties here, but want also to stress the indispensibility of this resource. The difficulties are met best, but not wholly overcome, when 'the analyst' is a group. Many of my most educative moments in cultural studies have come from these internal group dialogues about the readings of texts across, for example, gendered experiences. This is not to deny the real disciplines of reading, 'close' in the sense of *careful*, but not in the sense of *confined*. Finally, those concerned with 'concrete' cultural description cannot afford to ignore the presence of text-like structures and particular forms of discursive organisation. In particular we need to know what distinguishes private cultural forms, in their basic modes of organisation, from the public forms. In this way we might be able to specify, linguistically for example, the differential relation of social groups to different media forms, and the real processes of reading that are involved.

Of course, the transformation of particular approaches will have effects on others. If linguistic analysis takes account of historical determinations, for example, or provides us with ways of analysing the operations of power, the division between language studies and concrete accounts will break down. This goes for the associated politics too. At the moment there are few areas so blocked by disagreement and incomprehension than the relationship between avant-garde theorists and practitioners of the arts and those interested in a more grass-roots entry through community arts, working-class writing, women's writing and so on. Similarly, it is hard to convey, in the wake of a lost election, just how mechanical, how unaware of cultural dimensions, the politics of the Labour Party and most left factions remains. If I am right that theories are related to viewpoints, we are talking not just of theoretical developments, but about some of the conditions for effective political alliances too.

Notes

1 This paper is a revised and expanded version of talks given at the Department of English at Instituto Universitario Orientale in Naples and at the University of Palermo in April 1983. I am grateful to colleagues at Naples, Palermo, Pescara and from Bari for fruitful discussions around the themes raised here. In revising this paper, I have tried to respond to some comments, especially those concerning questions about consciousness and unconsciousness – though not, I fear adequately. I am grateful to Lidia Curti, Laura Di Michele and Marina Vitale for encouraging the production of this paper and advising on its form, to the British Council for funding my visit, and to friends and students (not mutually exclusive categories) at Birmingham for bearing with very many different versions of 'the circuit'.

2 There are degrees called 'cultural studies' at the polytechnics of North East London, Portsmouth, Middlesex, and Communications Studies or other degrees with strong cultural studies elements at Sheffield, Sunderland, Bristol, Central London, Wales and Trent. The Open University Popular Culture course team has been another important educational focus.

3 The most interesting journals include *Media Culture and Society*; *Screen* (now incorporating *Screen Education*); *Ideology and Consciousness*; *Block*; *Schooling and Culture*; *Theory, Culture and Society*; *L.T.P. Journal of Literature, Teaching, Politics*; more popular or political magazines with cultural studies interests include *Marxism Today*, *New Socialist* and *Spare Rib*. *History Workshop Journal* is increasingly involved in debates with cultural studies traditions. Among feminist journals, *Feminist Review* and *M/F* have many parallel interests. A Cultural Studies Network currently meets three times a year in different centres; an annual conference is planned. The first issue of a new journal, *Formations*, will appear in September 1983, from Routledge and Kegan Paul.

4 The key texts are Richard Hoggart, *The Uses of Literacy*, Penguin, 1958; Raymond Williams, *Culture and Society*, Penguin, 1958; Raymond Williams, *The Long Revolution*, Penguin 1961.

5 They are reconstructed in the fascinating interviews published as *Politics and Letters*, New Left Books, 1979.

6 See especially Bill Schwarz, ' "The People" in history: The Communist Party Historians' Group' in CCCS, *Making Histories: Studies in History-Writing and Politics*, Hutchinson, 1982, though the whole of this volume is relevant.

7 For a still useful summary of CCCS responses to Althusser see McLennan, Molina and Peters, 'Althusser's Theory of Ideology' in CCCS, *On Ideology*, Hutchinson, 1978.

8 See, for example, Hall, Lumley and McLennan, 'Politics and Ideology: Gramsci' in *On Ideology*. But Gramsci's theorisations are a main presence in much of the empirical work from the Centre from the mid-1970s.

9 See for example the dual debts to Barthes' structuralism and Cicourel's phenomenological sociology in Stuart Hall's early 1970s essays on the media, e.g. 'The "Structured Communication" of Events', CCCS Stencilled Paper, no. 5.

10 For one version see the debate over Edward Thompson's history which began with Richard Johnson, 'Edward Thompson, Eugene Genovese and Socialist-Humanist History' *History Workshop Journal*, No.6. 1978, continued with other contributions in this journal (Nos.7,8, & 9) and ended

with the papers published in Raphael Samuel (ed.), *People's History and Socialist Theory*, Routledge and Kegan Paul, 1981. Also clarifying on 'experience' is the treatment in Perry Anderson, *Arguments within English Marxism*, Verso, 1980. I have learnt a great deal working with Gregor McLennan on these themes, see especially Gregor McLennan, *Marxism and the Methodologies of History*, Verso, 1982.

11 See McLennan, *Methodologies* and Richard Johnson, 'Reading for the Best Marx: History-Writing and Historical Abstraction' in CCCS, *Making Histories*. This is really continuing the 'same' debate, by other means.

12 The most striking instance is the work on sub-cultures. See especially S. Hall and T. Jefferson (eds), *Resistance Through Rituals: Youth Sub-Cultures in Post-War Britain*, Hutchinson, 1976 and D. Hebdige, *Subculture: The Meaning of Style*, Methuen, 1979. And compare Stanley Cohen, *Folk Devils and Moral Panics*, Martin Robertson, 1980, first published 1972.

13 See, for instance, the papers collected as a result of the British Sociological Association's Annual Conference on culture in M. Barrett, P. Corrigan, et al. (eds), *Ideology and Cultural Production*, Croom Helm, 1979.

14 These are difficult to represent bibliographically, but key points are made by CCCS Women's Study Group: *Women Take Issue*, Hutchinson, 1978; CCCS, *The Empire Strikes Back*, Hutchinson, 1982. See also the series on Women and on Race in CCCS Stencilled Papers.

15 This is not a new criticism but given fresh force by the 1970s salience of race. See Paul Gilroy, 'Police and Thieves' in *Empire Strikes Back*, esp. pp. 147–151.

16 Some of these, at an early stage, are discussed in *Women Take Issue*, but there is need for a really full and consolidated account of the transformations in cultural studies stemming from feminist work and criticism. See also Angela McRobbie, 'Settling Accounts with Sub-Cultures', *Screen Education*, No.34, Spring, 1980 and the articles by Hazel Carby and Pratibha Parmar in *Empire Strikes Back*.

17 These moves can be traced, for example, in successive shifts of object and emphasis in media work in the Centre, from work on news and current affairs, to 'Nationwide' (a popular, light, news magazine), to light entertainment, soap opera, situation comedy etc. See, for example, Dorothy Hobson, *Crossroads: Drama of a Soap Opera*, Methuen, 1982, but also (internal) reports from the CCCS Media Group for 1979–81. But this has been a quite general move in media work in the late 1970s in Britain.

18 See, for example, Pierre Bourdieu and Jean-Claude Passeron, *Reproduction in Education Society and Culture*, Sage, 1977; Pierre Bourdieu, 'Cultural Reproduction and Social Reproduction' in R. Brown (ed.), *Knowledge, Education and Social Change*, Tavistock, 1973; Michel Foucault, *The Archaeology of Knowledge*, Tavistock, 1972.

19 Brian Easlea, *Science and Sexual Oppression*, Weidenfeld & Nicolson, 1981; Geoff Whitty and Michael Young, *Explorations in the Politics of School Knowledge*, Netterton, 1976. Thanks also to Maureen McNeil for very interesting discussions on these themes.

20 See, for example, Stuart Hall, 'Some Paradigms in Cultural Studies', *Anglistics*, 1978; Stuart Hall, 'Cultural Studies: Two Paradigms', *Media, Culture and Society*, No.2. 1980 (reprinted in part in Tony Bennett et al. (eds.), *Culture Ideology and Social Process*, Open University and Batsford, 1981) and the introductory essays in Hall, Hobson, Lowe and Willis (eds), *Culture, Media and Language*, Hutchinson, 1980. These essays are highly compressed versions of the MA Theory Course at CCCS which Stuart Hall taught and which comprised a comprehensive theoretical mapping of the field. See also my own attempts at theoretical clarification, much influenced by Stuart's, in, especially, Clark, Critcher and Johnson (eds), *Working Class Culture*, Hutchinson, 1979.

21 It will be important, however, to return to these issues, sometime, to state 'solutions' more formally and fully than is possible here. The more explicitly epistemological issues are tackled, and (for me) in large part resolved, in Johnson, 'Reading for the Best Marx' (cited above, note 11).

22 Raymond Williams, *Culture and Society* and the entry in *Keywords*, Fontana, 1976.

23 *Complete Works*, Lawrence and Wishart, 1976, Vol.5, p. 43.

24 *Capital*, Penguin, 1976, Vol.I, p. 283.

25 See especially the *Paris Manuscripts* of 1844.

26 For a discussion of 'general-historical' abstraction in Marx see, Johnson 'Best Marx', p. 172.

27 For the theme of self-production see the 1844 Manuscripts, but also the description of the labour process in *Capital*, Vol.I: 'Through this movement he acts upon external nature, and in this way he simultaneously changes his own nature' (p. 283). For the bracketing out of the artistic, religious etc. see *Grundrisse*, Penguin, 1972, p. 101.

28 'Introduction' to *A Contribution to the Critique of Political Economy*, Lawrence and Wishart, 1971.

29 The diagram is based, in its *general* forms, on a reading of Marx's account of the circuit of capital and its metamorphoses. For an important and original account of this, and of allied questions (e.g. 'fetishism') see Victor Molina, 'Marx's Arguments About Ideology', M.Litt. Thesis, University of Birmingham, 1982. This thesis is currently being revised for submission as a Ph.D. Also important is Stuart Hall's 'Encoding/Decoding' in *Culture, Media, Language*.

30 I am afraid this illustrative case is largely hypothetical since I have no contacts inside British Leyland Management. Any resemblance to persons living or dead is entirely fortuitous and a pure instance of the power of theory.

31 This is the division between 'structuralist' and 'culturalist' approaches Stuart Hall and I, among others, have already discussed, but now in the form of 'objects' and methods, rather than 'paradigms'. See sources listed in note 20 above and add Richard Johnson, 'Histories of Culture/Theories of Ideology: Notes on an Impasse', in Barrett et al. (eds.), *Ideology and Cultural Production*.

32 My thinking on 'the public and the private' is much influenced by certain German traditions, especially discussions around Jurgen Habermas' work on 'the public sphere'. This is now being interestingly picked up and used in some American work. See Jurgen Habermas, *Strukturwandel der Offentlichkeit*, Neuweid, Berlin, 1962; Oskar Negt and Alexander Kluge, *Offentlichkeit und Erfahrung: Zur Organisationsanalyse von burgerlicher und proletarischer Offentlichkeit*, Frankfurt am Main, 1972. For an extract of Negt and Kluge's work see A. Matterlart and S. Seigelaub (eds), *Communication and Class Struggle*, Vol. 2. The American journal *New German Critique* has translated parts of Habermas' text, not yet available in full in English, and carries discussion of the debate about 'the public sphere'. See also, for a summary of the arguments, and a first application to British cultural forms, Michael Bommes and Patrick Wright, ' "Charms of Residence": the Public and the Past' in CCCS, *Making Histories*.

33 Paul Willis, 'Shop-floor culture Masculinity and the Wage Form' in Clarke, Critcher and Johnson (eds), *Working Class Culture*.

34 The most popular of a number of magazines for teenage girls in Britain. See Angela McRobbie, 'Jackie: An Ideology of Adolescent Femininity' CCCS Stencilled Paper, No. 53.

35 There is a very large sociological literature on these forms of stigmatisation, especially of the deviant young. For a cultural studies development of this work see Stuart Hall et al., *Policing the Crisis: 'Mugging', the State and Law and Order*, Macmillan, 1973. For more subtle forms of marginalisation see CCCS Media Group, 'Fighting over Peace: Representations of the Campaign for Nuclear Disarmament in the Media', CCCS Stencilled Paper, No. 72. For current treatment of the left and the trade unions in the British media see the sequence of studies by the Glasgow Media Group, starting with Glasgow University Media Group, *Bad News*, Routledge and Kegan Paul, 1976. Stanley Cohen and Jock Yong (eds), *The Manufacture of News*, Constable, 1973 was a pioneering collection.

36 There is a great deal of practical knowledge about 'communication' in the writing of professionals in these areas. Critically read, much can be learned from these sources. Allied but not identified with explicitly political concerns with communication are the various schools of liberal-pluralist communications research. For a recent overview of these, which however, is profoundly ignorant of the European traditions, see Shearon Lowery and Melvin L.De Fleur, *Milestones in Mass Communication Research*, Longmans, 1983. Most of the work on 'the media' within the cultural studies tradition has been based on a critique of these predominantly American tendencies. For a predominantly left-ish collection in this field, – illustrating, however, different approaches see James Curran et al., (eds), *Mass Communication and Society*, Arnold/Open University, 1977, and, more recently, Michael Gurevitch et al. (eds), *Culture, Society and the Media*, Methuen/Open University, 1982. Among English representatives of the 'mass communications' schools the work of J. G. Blumler is especially interesting.

37 Raymond Williams' formulations on the nature of cultural production are especially important here as a much fuller account than most structuralist or semiological versions. See for example, Raymond Williams, *Culture*, Fontana, 1981.

38 These debates are interestingly reviewed in Alan Swingewood, *The Myth of Mass Culture*, Macmillan, 1977. See also the first four theoretical review essays in Gurevitch et al., *Culture, Society and the Media*.

39 The best review of the Frankfurt School in English is David Held, *Introduction to Critical Theory*, Hutchinson, 1981, which concentrates on the clear presentation of often 'difficult' theories. See also Phil Slater, *Origin and Significance of the Frankfurt School: A Marxist Perspective*, Routledge and Kegan

Paul, 1977, See also Andrew Arato and Eike Gebhardt (eds), *The Essential Frankfurt School Reader*, Blackwell, 1978.

40 Among the best close studies of this kind are Philip Elliott, *The Making of a Television Series: A Case Study in the Sociology of Culture*, Constable/Sage, 1972; Philip Schlesinger, *Putting 'Reality' Together: BBC News*, Constable/Sage, 1978; Jeremy Tunstall, *Journalists at Work*, Constable, 1971; Dorothy Hobson, *Crossroads: Drama of a Soap Opera*, op. cit.

41 E.P. Thompson, *The Making of the English Working Class*, Penguin, 1963; Paul Willis, *Learning to Labour: How Working Class Kids Get Working Class Jobs*, Saxon House, 1977. Both these books are classics in cultural studies, as I understand it. A reading of them should be compulsory, especially for those working with the more formalist models.

42 The forms of 'political organisation' were often not specified in Marx or in the theorists who followed him, up to and including, in my view, Lenin. For Lenin, it seems to me, cultural politics remained a matter of organisation and 'propaganda' in quite narrow senses.

43 Althusser's exceptions of 'art' from ideology are an instance of the persistance of this view within Marxism. It is interesting to compare Althusser's and Gramsci's view of 'philosophy' here too, Althusser tending to the specialist academic or 'high cultural' definition, Gramsci to the popular.

44 Especially important here are notes collected under 'Education' and 'The Intellectual' in the English selection from the *Prison Notebooks*. Quinton Hoare and Geoffrey Nowell-Smith (eds), *Selections from the Prison Notebooks of Antonio Gramsci*, Lawrence and Wishart, 1971. I find the theme of a history of 'intellectuals' and their political connections especially fascinating in Gramsci, not least his tendency to use the language of the past to describe contemporary realities. Thanks also to Michael Green for very stimulating discussions of these themes.

45 I think the predominant reception of Gramsic in Britain is 'anti-Leninist', especially among those interested in discourse theory. But it may be that CCCS appropriations underestimate Gramsci's Leninism too. I am grateful to Victor Molina for discussions on this issue.

46 I recognise this sense may be based on a narrow reading of Gramsci, limited by available translations.

47 See, for instance, the work of Graham Murdock and Peter Golding on the political economy of the mass media: e.g. 'Capitalism, Communication and Class Relations' in Curran et al. (eds), *Mass Communication and Society*; Graham Murdock, 'Large Corporations and the Control of the Communications Industries' in Gurevitch et al. (eds), *Culture, Society and the Media*; for a more explicitly polemical engagement with CCCS work see Golding and Murdock, 'Ideology and the Mass Media: the Question of Determination' in Barratt et al (eds), *Ideology and Cultural Production*. For a reply see I. Connell, 'Monopoly Capitalism and the Media: Definitions and Struggles' in S. Hibbin (ed), *Politics, Ideology and the State*, Lawrence and Wishart, 1978.

48 These claims have their proximate origin in Althusser's statement that ideologies have a material existence. For a classic English statement of this kind of 'materialism' see Rosalind Coward and John Ellis, *Language and Materialism: Development in Semiology and the Theory of the Subject*, Routledge and Kegan Paul, 1977. This is rather different from Marx's argument that under particular conditions ideologies acquire a 'material force' or Gramsci's elaboration of this in terms of the conditions of popularity.

49 This applies to a wide range of structuralist and post-structuralist theories from Poulantzas' arguments against class reductionist notions of ideology to the more radical positions of Barry Hindess and Paul Hirst and other theorists of 'discourse'.

50 In this respect I find myself at odds with many strands in cultural studies, including some influential ones, which opt for an expanded use of ideology rather in the Bolshevik sense or in the more Leninist or Althusser's (several) uses. Ideology is applied, in the OU's important popular culture course, for instance, to the formation of subjectivities as such. If stretched thus, I would argue that the term loses its usefulness – 'discourse', 'cultural form' etc. would do quite as well. On the whole, I wish to retain the 'negative' or 'critical' connotations of the term 'ideology' in classic Marxist discourse, though not, as it happens, the usual accompaniment, a 'hard' notion of Marxism-as-science. It may well be that all our knowledge of the world and all or conceptions of the self are 'ideological', or more or less ideological, in that they are rendered partial by the operation of interests and of power. But this seems to me a proposition that has to be plausibly argued in particular cases rather than assumed at the beginning of every analysis. The expanded, 'neutral' sense of the term cannot altogether lay to rest the older negative connotations. The issues are

interestingly stated in the work of Jorge Larrain. See *Marxism and Ideology*, Macmillan, 1983 and *The Concept of Ideology*, Hutchinson, 1979.

51 See especially Theodore Adorno, 'On the Fetish Character of Music and the Regression of Listening' in Arato and Gebhardt (eds), *Frankfurt School Reader*, Adorno and Horkheimer, *Dialectics of Enlightenment*, Allen Lane, 1973; Walter Benjamin, 'The Work of Art in an Age of Mechanical Reproduction' in *Illuminations*, Fontana, 1973.

52 'Fetish Character in Music', pp. 287–8. Later he gives slightly more rounded pictures of types of consumption of popular music, but even his fans' dancing resembles 'the reflexes of mutilated animals' (p. 292).

53 For more developed critiques see Dick Bradley, 'Introduction to the Cultural Study of Music', CCCS Stencilled Paper, No. 61; Richard Middleton, 'Reading Popular Music', *OU Popular Culture Course Unit*, Unit 16, Block 4, Open University Press, 1981.

54 CCCS Education Group, *Unpopular Education: Schooling and Social Democracy in England since 1944*, Hutchinson, 1981.

55 The analysis of Thatcherism has continued to be one of Stuart Hall's major concerns. See the very important essays republished in Stuart Hall and Martin Jacques (eds), *The Politics of Thatcherism*, Lawrence and Wishart/*Marxism Today*, 1983. 'The Great Moving Right Show', written before the 1979 election, proved to be especially perceptive.

56 Particularly useful introductions, in English, to these combined impacts are Silvia Harvey, *May 1968 and Film Culture*, BFI, 1980; Tony Bennett, *Formalism and Marxism*, New Accents, Methuen, 1979.

57 See, for instance, the work of a group of critical linguists initially based on the University of East Anglia, especially: R. Fowler et al., *Language and Control*, Routledge and Kegan Paul, 1979; Gunther Kress and Thomas Hodge, *Language as Ideology*, Routledge and Kegan Paul, 1979. I am especially grateful to Gunther Kress, who spent some months at the Centre, and to Utz Maas of Osnabruck University for very fruitful discussions on the relationship of language studies and cultural studies. See also Utz Maas, 'Language Studies and Cultural Analysis', paper for a conference on Language and Cultural Studies at CCCS, December 1982.

58 Much of this work remains unpublished. I very much hope that one of the next CCCS books will be a collection on romance. In the meantime see English Studies Group, 'Recent Developments' in *Culture, Media, Language*; Rachel Harrison, 'Shirley: Romance and Relations of Dependence' in CCCS Women's Studies Group, *Women Take Issue*; Angela McRobbie, 'Working-Class Girls and Femininity', ibid.; Myra Connell, 'Reading and Romance' Unpublished MA Dissertation University of Birmingham, 1981; Christine Griffin, 'Cultures of Femininity: Romance Revisited', CCCS Stencilled Paper, No. 69; Janice Winship, 'Woman Becomes an Individual: Femininity and Consumption in Women's Magazines', CCCS Stencilled Paper, No. 65; Laura di Michele, 'The Royal Wedding', CCCS Stencilled Paper, forthcoming.

59 Much of this work is in connection with the work of the Popular Memory Group in CCCS towards a book on the popularity of Conservative nationalism. I am especially grateful to Laura di Michele for her contribution in opening up these questions in relation to 'epic', and to Graham Dawson for discussions on masculinity, war, and boy culture.

60 Especially those developing out of the work on M.A.K. Halliday which includes the 'critical linguistics' group (note 58) but also feminist linguists influenced by his approach. For Halliday see Gunther Kress (ed.), *Halliday's System and Function in Language*, Oxford University Press, 1976.

61 See especially the long, largely unpublished critique of *Screen* by the CCCS Media Group 1977–78. Parts of this appear in Stuart Hall et al. (eds), *Culture, Media, Language*, Hutchinson, 1980, pp. 157–73.

62 I take this to be the common message of a great range of work, some of it quite critical of structuralist formalisms, on the subject of narrative in literature, film, television, folk tale, myth, history and political theory. I am in the middle of my own reading list, delving into this material from a quite unliterary background. My starting points are theories of narrative in general – compare Roland Barthes' 'Introduction to the Structural Analysis of Narratives' in Stephen Heath (ed.), *Barthes on Image, Music, Text*, Fontana, 1977 and Frederic Jameson, *The Political Unconscious: Narrative as a Socially-Symbolic Act*, Methuen, 1981, but I am most interested in work, at a lesser level of generality, that specifies the types of genres of narrative. Here I have found much stimulus in work on filmic or televisual narratives, see especially the texts collected in Tony Bennett et al. (eds), *Popular Television and Film*, BFI/Open University, 1981, but also on 'archetypal' genre forms – epic,

romance, tragedy etc. – as in Northrop Frye, *Anatomy of Criticism*, Princeton University Press, 1957. My particular concern is with the stories we tell ourselves, individually and collectively. In this respect the existing literature is, so far, disappointing. I am about to start, with others, a programme of Freud readings. Perhaps further developments lie there.

63 *Grundrisse*, '1857 Introduction' (ed. and trans. Martin Nicolaus), Penguin, 1973, p. 85.

64 Roland Barthes, *Mythologies*, Paladin, 1973, p. 112.

65 By which I mean 'post-structuralism' in the usual designation. This seems to me a rather misleading tag since it is hard to conceive of late semiology without early, or even of Foucault without Althusser.

66 Tony Bennett, 'James Bond as Popular Hero', *OU Popular Culture Course Unit*, Unit 21, Block 5; 'Text and Social Process: The Case of James Bond', *Screen Education*, No. 41, Winter/Spring, 1982.

67 'Fighting Over Peace: Representations of CND in the Media', CCCS Stencilled Paper no. 72.

68 This project is not yet completed; provisional title: 'Jingo Bells: The Public and the Private in Christmas Media 1982'.

69 This term has been used to distinguish 'structuralist' and 'post-structuralist' semiologies, with the incorporation of emphases from Lacanian psycho-analysis as an important watershed.

70 The combination of formal and more historical modes of analysis is clear, for example, in many of the earlier essays in *Cahiers du Cinema*, including the famous analysis of John Ford's *Young Mr. Lincoln*. See the collection in John Ellis (ed.), *Screen Reader: Cinema/Ideology/Politics*, Society for Education in Film and Television, 1977.

71 The relation of *Screen*'s theory to Brecht and Eisenstein is rather odd. Characteristically, quotations from Brecht were taken as starting-points for adventures which led to quite other destinations than Brecht's own thinking. See, for example, Colin MacCabe, 'Realism and the Cinema: Notes on Some Brechtian Theses' in Bennett et al. (eds), *Popular Television and Film*.

72 See, for example, the culmination of a long exploration of Marxist heterodoxy in A. Cutler et al., *Marx's* Capital *and Capitalism Today*, 2 Volume, Routledge and Kegan Paul, 1978.

73 The original formulation seems to have been Lévi-Strauss on the subject of myth.

74 'The cinematic institution is not just the cinema industry (which works to fill cinemas, not to empty them). It is also the mental machinery – another industry – which spectators "accustomed to the cinema" have internalised historically and which has adapted them to the consumption of films'. C. Metz, 'The Imaginary Signifier', *Screen*, Vol. 16, No. 2 Summer, 1975, p. 18.

75 What follows owes much to the CCCS *Screen* critique cited above (note 61).

76 There seem to be two rather distinct approaches to reading or 'audiences', the one an extension of litarary concerns, the other more sociological in approach and often growing out of media studies. I find David Morley's work in this area consistently interesting as an attempt to combine some elements from both sets of preoccupations, though I agree with his own assessment that the Centre's early starting-points, especially the notions of 'hegemonic', 'negotiated' and 'alternative' readings were exceedingly crude. See David Morley, *The Nationwide Audience*, BFI, 1980; 'The Nationwide Audience: A Postscript', *Screen Education*, No. 39, Summer, 1981; *Open University Popular Culture Course*, Unit 12, Block 3, 'Interpreting Television'. There is much of value on more literary aspects of reading in the long-delayed CCCS book on English Studies, currently being considered for publication by Methuen.

77 See the famous analysis in terms of 'scopophilia' in Laura Mulvey, 'Visual Pleasure and Narrative Cinema', *Screen*, Vol. 16, No.3, Autumn 1975. See also Colin Mercer, *Open University Popular Culture Course*, Unit 17, Block 4. 'Pleasure'.

78 It is significant, for instance, that Barthes does not mention 'internal' narratives in his view of the omnipresence of the narrative form. *Image-Music-Text*, p. 79. Does this absence suggest a larger structuralist difficulty with inner speech?

79 The ideas of the last few paragraphs are still in the process of being worked out in the CCCS Popular Memory Group. For some preliminary considerations about the character of oral-historical texts see Popular Memory Group, 'Popular Memory: Theory, Politics, Method' in CCCS, *Making Histories*. I have found some of the essays in Daniel Bertaux, *Biography and Society: The Life History Approach in the Social Sciences*, Sage, 1981, useful to argue with, especially Agnes Hankiss, 'Ontologies of the Self: on the Mythological Rearranging of One's Life History'.

80 And some of the best and most influential working cultural studies has been based on personal experience and private memory. Richard Hoggart's *The Uses of Literacy* is the most celebrated example, but, in general, students of culture should have the courage to use their personal experience

more, more explicitly and more systematically. In this sense cultural studies is a heightened, differentiated form of everyday activities and living. Collective activities of this kind, attempting to understand not just 'common' experiences but real adversities and antagonisms, are especially important, if they can be managed, and subject to the caveats which follow.

81 For episodes in this tradition see P. Abrams, *The Origins of British Sociology, 1834–1914*, Chicago University Press, 1968; M.J. Cullen, *The Statistical Movement in Early Victorian Britain*, Harvester Press, 1975; Gareth Stedman Jones, *Outcast London*, Clarendon Press, 1971. The continuities between twentieth-century sociologies and nineteenth-century inquiry is argued in CCCS, *Unpopular Education* where comparisons are also made with new left traditions.

82 George Orwell's social commentaries are very relevant here, as is the contemporary (1930s/40s) project of 'Mass Observation', part 'literary', part 'anthropological'.

83 This is forcefully argued by Paul Jones in an article soon to appear in *Thesis Eleven*, Monash University, Australia, 1983.

84 See Dave Morley and Ken Worpole (eds), *The Republic of Letters: Working Class Writing and Local Publishing*, Comedia, 1982. For a more external and critical view see 'Popular Memory' in *Making Histories*. Also instructive is the debate between Ken Worpole, Stephen Yeo and Gerry White in Raphael Samuel (ed.), *People's History and Socialist Theory*, Routledge and Kegan Paul, 1981.

85 This is associated with the centrality of an experience of social mobility in the origins of post-war sociology and cultural studies, especially in their more radical moments. To Hoggart's book we might add much of Raymond Williams' work and much research in the sociologies of education, deviancy, sub-cultures etc.

86 Some CCCS work is not exempt from this difficulty. Some of these criticisms apply, for instance, to *Resistance Through Rituals*, especially parts of the theoretical overview.

87 What follows is based, in rather too composite a way perhaps, on the work of Paul Willis, Angela McRobbie, Dick Hebdige, Christine Griffin, and Dorothy Hobson and on discussions with other ethnographic researchers in the Centre. See especially, Paul Willis, *Learning to Labour*, Paul Willis, *Profane Culture*, Routledge and Kegan Paul, 1978; Angela McRobbie, 'Working-Class Girls and Femininity' and Dorothy Hobson, 'Housewives: Isolation as Oppression' in *Women Take Issue*; Dick Hebdige, *Subculture*; Christine Griffin, CCCS Stencilled Papers, Nos. 69 and 70. For an all-too-rare discussion of method in this area see Paul Willis, 'Notes on Method' in Hall et al., *Culture, Media, Language*.

Section 4

Grounded studies

Introduction

Founding fieldwork

Johan Fornäs

Intellectual fields emerge and grow through co-operative labour that sometimes becomes hidden in the shadow of a series of brilliant works or underneath grand narratives of transforming paradigms. Fields are cultivated by people interacting in a kind of '*field-work*', but in another sense of the word than the usual ethnographic one. The successful survival of cultural studies has been guaranteed by worldwide efforts motivated by the need to grapple with issues when conventional disciplines and more specialised subfields do not suffice. The work done at the CCCS to ground this field in empirical research delivering useful knowledge was crucial to this success, and is a lasting inspiration for similar efforts later and elsewhere.

Interdisciplinary fields are born between disciplines whose limitations have become problematic. Depending on the kind of deficits met by such fields, their fates vary considerably. Some fields grow and crystallise into new disciplines of their own, like, for example, media studies. Others disappear or are integrated as intellectual currents within ordinary disciplinary structures after having fulfilled their vitalising mission, such as critical theory or cultural sociology. Yet the field of cultural studies stubbornly stays on as an interdisciplinary field. This success is based on a continued need for that kind of crossroads in combination with obstacles preventing either the institutionalisation of the field into a regular discipline or the full reintegration of its main parts into established disciplinary bodies. Some scholars do strive to disciplinarise cultural studies, and the story is yet unfinished, but it mostly remains an intersectional borderland rather than a self-sufficient domain. It certainly is becoming increasingly institutionalised, possessing an increasing set of resources in the form of centres of research, educational programmes, national and international associations and journals, etc. But there are other forms of institutionalisation than disciplinary ones, and there are still sufficiently strong voices that define it as a mixed 'crossroads' field and transgressive intellectual movement rather than a clearly delimited discipline. It is structured around an open set of communicative resources and another open set of key assumptions and preferences, including the focus on contextualised intermedial interpretations of meaning constructions, interdisciplinary studies of intersectional identity formations, and reflexive critique of power practices in culture and research.

British cultural studies emerged as a generational response to the challenges posed to critical intellectuals by a world in rapid transformation. Some of these challenges were typically British, but most were also experienced, albeit differently, in many other regions of the world. There was an erosion and transformation of certain key elements in society that also had implications for the educational system. Redefined colonial structures, expanding (though still stratified) welfare, changing age, class and gender relations and new forms of media and youth culture combined to transform the tasks and conditions of the universities as well. Underprivileged class fractions, women and immigrants entered as young challengers on the academic arena. As Rolf Lindner has shown, there were homologies between the life-forms of these young intellectuals and their thought-forms, i.e. between their experience, taste or habitus and their research perspectives (Lindner 2000). It was no coincidence that they argued for the need for a serious study of media and popular culture, working class cultures, women's cultural practices, youth cultures and immigrant cultures. Cultural studies gave voice to 'the inside outsider' who moved in the margins of academia, in the borderlands between empirical research, theoretical debate and popular culture. Their criticism of the shortcomings of established disciplines lead to innovative experiments with new forms of education and research that crossed petrified borders between disciplines, between theoretical traditions, and between the theory and the practice of culture. These new generations of border scholars were often acutely sensitive to their own position and relation to academia, and contributed stronger political and subjective perspectives as well as a strengthened critical and reflexive self-thematisation. This made them, and cultural studies, useful to cultural research in general, in a late modern period when interpretation, networks and reflexive critique are increasingly needed. The field of cultural studies was thus a moment in the modernisation of cultural research in response to intensified processes of culturalisation, mediatisation, globalisation and reflexivity in society at large.

From their marginal position, cultural studies proponents were able to construct what Tony Bennett has described as a transdisciplinary crossroads with simultaneously critical, reflexive and bridging functions, 'acting as an interdisciplinary clearing-house within the humanities, providing a useful interface at which the concerns of different disciplines, and of other interdisciplinary knowledges, can enter into fruitful forms of dialogue' (Bennett 1998).[1] These 'other interdisciplinary knowledges' include feminist and postcolonial studies, science and technology studies, but also critical theory and cultural sociology.

Similar histories may be written on cultural research in other parts of the world. Labels, emphases and timings vary, but globally there has been a growing need for academic reform related to cultural shifts posing new demands on knowledge production and opening new trajectories for critical young scholars. The worldwide expansion of the field has resulted in a complex interaction between a multitude of regional currents, sometimes working in parallel and combining forces, at other times opposing each other. The name of cultural studies is now widely accepted as an umbrella for these efforts, though wider and more exclusive definitions of the field compete. Together with a set of journals, publishers, programmes and networks around the world, the international Association for Cultural Studies (ACS) and its biennial Crossroads in Cultural Studies conferences belong to the organisational resources whereby this ongoing field-work is today cultivated. Parallel to cultural genres, intellectual fields of a certain age and maturity tend to be *polyfocal*, with competing genealogies, even though the Anglo-Saxon, in this case, has a hegemonic position.

Glocalisation and hybridisation

The foundational works of Richard Hoggart and Raymond Williams in the late 1950s and early 1960s were widely acknowledged, but it was the 1970s and early 1980s working papers and anthologies from the CCCS that made this vitalising stream of thought visible as a coherent 'school'. As influential as its theoretical and methodological contributions have proved to be, its approach to under-researched current issues was the main reason for its global breakthrough. These kinds of texts created a feeling of collective movement based on an ability to make important statements about empirical phenomena that were generally found problematic but remained insufficiently examined by traditional disciplinary approaches. That was why Philip Cohen got a reputation in sociology and social work, Paul Willis' work was appreciated as a valuable new path for social anthropology, Dick Hebdige won fame among radical scholars of popular music and literature, and Angela McRobbie and Janice Winship renewed the agenda of feminist media research.[2]

Yet Birmingham was far from the only place where such issues and phenomena were studied, and there were also other currents for interdisciplinary and critical cultural research that developed fascinating new perspectives in the same period. This was true for French and Italian semiotics, poststructuralism, psychoanalysis, cultural sociology and cultural history, but also for German studies of public spheres, cultural history, literary sociology, youth studies and socialisation research. As the field of cultural studies expanded across national borders, it inevitably had to confront and fuse with other competing regional traditions for critical cultural research. Each such local tradition has added new impulses to the field. As a global field, then, cultural studies must today be understood as having multiple roots and routes. Handel K. Wright has suggested some other locally crucial but less transnationally well known roots in, for instance, African as well as Danish popular education (Wright 1998).

The Swedish context of my own first steps in academic research was influenced by British scholarship – but more so by continental European currents that were particularly important among young critical intellectuals in the 1970s and 80s, including strong influences from several generations of continental critical theory; from Walter Benjamin, Ernst Bloch and Theodor Adorno to Karel Kosík, Henri Lefebvre, Norbert Elias, Jürgen Habermas, Ulrike Prokop, Christa and Peter Bürger, Alfred Lorenzer, Oskar Negt and Thomas Ziehe. The articulation of such inputs with domestic research traditions and institutional settings made Nordic cultural studies distinctly different, though also – as in all regions – internally heterogeneous. The historical form of the Nordic welfare system was one key factor which may be hard for us to correctly evaluate from an inside perspective. Handel Wright referred to the people's high schools that emerged in mid- and late 19th-century Denmark and became important all over Scandinavia as sites of popular education for underprivileged classes, especially in rural areas where urbanisation was relatively slow. There was also a wide spectrum of study associations connected to the various popular – nonconformist, temperance and workers – movements. Between the 20th-century world wars, Clarté was a leftist forum for alternative education and debate where many of the leading radical intellectuals gathered. Funded in 1950, the Nordic Summer University (NSU) has been a vital hotbed for advanced interdisciplinary developments among young scholars exploring the frontlines of critical social and cultural research.

These settings and crossroads inevitably fostered specific currents and connections, whose genealogies remain to be written. For instance, Nordic youth culture research always dealt less with subcultures than with the cultural practices and lifestyles of 'ordinary' young people, inspired by continental theories of socialisation and generation, and nourished by support from educational bodies at several levels. In many other areas as well, Nordic research often had a focus on everyday life, not least in feminist women's studies, with well-organised NGO networks that managed to attract resources from the state and university system, but also in studies of state policy, social movements and working life. One impetus to this profile is the funding structure of research. While university teachers have almost no time for research in their ordinary positions, it has been possible to get state grants for three years of research in funded projects. This is a model that invites senior scholars to continue doing somewhat larger empirical studies; the production of shorter essays so typical of British cultural studies may be a less developed art here. There are internationally strong

Swedish traditions of carefully grounded studies in social anthropology (Ulf Hannerz being perhaps the most internationally well-known), ethnology (Billy Ehn, Barbro Klein, Orvar Löfgren and others), cultural sociology (Rita Liljeström, Johan Asplund, Erling Bjurström, Donald Broady *et al.*) and also social and cultural history in literature and other disciplines (Lars Furuland, Lisbeth Larsson, Johan Svedjedal, Jan Ling, Peter Aronsson and Eva Österberg, among others).

In this general setting, the early CCCS work was received by a small but widening set of young Nordic scholars as a model for radical and self-conscious intervention in academia. The bold (sometimes wild) montage or 'bricolage' of diverse theories was one liberating inspiration, very different from the more closed system building among theoreticians like Pierre Bourdieu or the leading semioticians and psychoanalysts, but with a hidden kinship to the similarly dialogic and multipolar (though far less wild) work of Jürgen Habermas and Paul Ricoeur (Fornäs 1995).

This brave dialogicity and ambitious groundedness invited many young Nordic scholars to do their own work, that had links to Birmingham but was no mere linear derivative of what was done there (Fornäs 1995; Fornäs 2001). This enabled us to develop positions and studies that were in some respects ahead of their time, but were rarely internationally acknowledged since we remained marginal in the strongly Anglocentric world of global publishing.[3] We admired much CCCS work but rarely identified as adherents of the 'Birmingham school'. It actually took a long time before anyone up here felt any need or wish to be located within a field of 'cultural studies'. One reason was that many of us felt a distance to some traits in this tradition. For instance, we couldn't situate ourselves in the line from structuralism to post-modernism that was so dominant in the UK. Re-reading some of the earlier CCCS texts in parallel to our early Swedish critiques of the 1970s subcultural studies in particular makes visible some combined strengths and problems in the foundations of this influential work. Seeing all of this work brought together also makes it possible to understand the limited reception it had at the time, and to discern larger patterns across the various thematic areas. The transnationalisation of cultural studies has made it easier to discern the specific strengths and weaknesses of the field-grounding work made in Birmingham. It is possible today to re-read the CCCS papers at a combined temporal and spatial distance, and it is fascinating to encounter them from both a Swedish and a contemporary perspective.

Looking back at my own intellectual history, three main phases may be discerned in my encounter with the CCCS. (1) From my first reading of Birmingham works in 1977–78 until 1985–86 my focus was on youth culture, where I found subcultural theory fascinating although I myself identified more with critical socialisation and research into modernity. (2) From the mid 1980s to the mid 1990s, continued youth culture research overlapped with a new involvement in media studies, where cultural studies was the unchallenged main label for critical and cultural perspectives. In this sphere no other tradition could compete in empirically grounded reflection and theorisation, and as a media researcher I felt that I more and more belonged to that camp. (3) With the Crossroads in Cultural Studies conferences from 1996 onwards, and my own increasing interaction with colleagues around the globe, I noticed how colleagues in Latin America, East Asia and various parts of Europe took their affiliation with the transnational field of cultural studies for granted. This experience allowed me also to dare to take a seat in this field without feeling obliged to the particular version based in Birmingham. As cultural studies had become a globally polycentric intellectual field there were no more obstacles towards claiming a legitimate place for our own version of Nordic cultural studies, and no necessity to give up anything essential in our own understanding of culture, identity and power. The timing and shape of this trajectory may be my own personal one but on the whole it is not untypical among my generation of Nordic academics, where few – if any – before the mid 1990s identified themselves unambiguously with cultural studies, even though several produced interdisciplinary and critical cultural research and found the CCCS work inspiring.[4]

One key ingredient of the academic fieldwork of cultural studies evident in the 1970s' CCCS papers is indeed the commitment to a kind of *grounded studies*. Groundwork is important in all fields, and in this particular one, three main aspects of groundedness may be discerned.

Empirical grounding in profane culture

The most obvious aspect is the determination to ground theoretical innovations in specific *empirical explorations*, with a particular focus on those *new, low and/or complex* phenomena that tend to be neglected by disciplinary knowledge. Conceptual thinking was carried out in close interaction with particular examples and current issues, and new ideas were born through a close reading of some particular phenomenon of popular culture, rather than through abstract philosophical theorising. This wish was shared by certain other positions, including the school of 'grounded theory' (Glaser and Strauss 1967). But these similarities are only superficial. In grounded theory, theoretical models are not to be confronted with empirical observations but to grow organically from them, from a presumed state of blank openness. Cultural studies also had a respect for the empirical, but did not humbly submit to it. Quite the contrary: there was always an urgent wish to make interventions by offering critical perspectives rather than by faithfully reproducing the informants' ideas and developing theories from there. This difference became even more visible with the 1970s' structuralist turn of Stuart Hall and others who followed Louis Althusser *et al.* in making an epistemological break with commonsense knowledge, playing with concepts that emphatically cut off their grounding in everyday language. This was developed to the extreme by some poststructuralists, but still more so among French and American intellectuals of that time than in the comparatively down-to-earth Birmingham texts. Balancing the (post-)structuralist love for strange abstractions, the best CCCS papers demonstrate an equally strong wish to make real studies out there, among real people, in their everyday life; to make their common, ordinary practices leave traces in theoretical developments, and to anchor analyses in the mundane and vernacular life-worlds of common culture.

This empirical grounding had implications both for the gaze and style of research and for the choice of object areas. There was, in the 1970s' papers, impressive attention paid to *the particular detail*, an eye for small everyday things and practices that were used as vehicles for elaborate insights, through close readings and multidimensional interpretations. The papers in this section by Paul Willis, Dick Hebdige and Janice Winship are good examples, where minute details are made eminently meaningful for grand theoretical and political issues. This attention to the crucial detail connects to Benjamin's and Adorno's respect for the fragment as well as to later feminism, discourse analysis and poststructuralism (Derrida, Foucault, Kristeva, Haraway), where the most tiny element is scrutinised as a key to large societal structures. There is a moral obligation involved in this respect for detail: an honouring of the resisting particular, a pledge for understanding cultural phenomena as localised, for placing them in historical and social contexts, for making contextualising interpretations that produce situated and concretely useful rather than absolute or abstracted knowledge (Haraway 1991: 183ff). But this respect for singularities was never as absolute as in some other positions, since there was no obstacle towards using particulars for building grand and sometimes rather sweeping models. There was no submission to the empirical, but a respectful gesture towards it.

There was, further, a lasting preference for *subaltern object areas*: phenomena that were subordinate, subterranean, subcultural or subversive. Much research focused on *new* phenomena that were not yet ripe for inclusion in more traditional disciplines, but were intensely discussed in current public debates and seemed to have an immediate political relevance. Issues of youth subculture and new media genres often provoked moral panics while being neglected by mainstream research, and these soon became favourite subjects for cultural studies scholars.

Another task was to deal with mixed and hybrid phenomena, too impure ones for single disciplines, and *complex* enough to demand interdisciplinary treatment. Many of these papers mix materials and methods that were elsewhere kept strictly apart, and thus manage to point to crosscurrents between different societal spheres (news journalism, entertainment media, everyday gossip, oppositional movements etc.).

As importantly, '*low*' phenomena of vernacular daily life and forms of 'profane' culture were acknowledged to be at least as worthy of attention as any big political event: mass culture and cultural practices of workers, youth, women and immigrants. Papers by Paul Willis, Janice Winship and Richard Johnson testify to this kind of grounding in cultural materials and social strata, often considered elsewhere to be too low for serious academic attention.

The idea that youth and popular culture could be read through theoretically advanced lenses as seismographic clues to deep societal patterns of transformation was common to the Frankfurt and Birmingham schools, giving us courage to develop similar explorations of popular culture with complex interpretive tools and high theoretical ambitions. However, with a few very notable exceptions, there was a heavy reliance on secondary sources, and a lack of substantial empirical study, for instance in the texts by John Clarke and by Eve Brook and Dan Finn, below. The Nordic tradition for careful empirical analysis of combined qualitative and quantitative, ethnographic and textual, contemporary and historical data was felt to be an antidote to such lofty speculations. The free flight of radical thought could perhaps sometimes demand an arrogant neglect of empirical groundwork in order to really take off and hit the stars, but we felt it necessary to make much more detailed and ambitious grounding. From our horizon, we suspected that the heavy reliance on secondary media sources tended to simplify subcultural forms and underestimate their individual nuances and internal contradictions. Compared to other social research, we thought that the inner social structure, functioning and interaction of youth groups were neglected, as were the psychological subject formations of individuals in these groups. We likewise agreed with Angela McRobbie's internal criticism that the focus on spectacular public performance tended to exclude many female cultural practices.

Looking back, a wealth of empirical studies of diverse cultural phenomena has now accumulated, so the gap between strong assertions and scrupulous anchorage has to some extent been filled, but in some of the early CCCS work it remains open.

Methodological grounding in popular education

A second aspect of grounding at the CCCS concerns *method* rather than empirical object – the 'how' rather than the 'what' of research. There was a politically motivated will to ground academic studies in lived cultures outside academia, and to challenge inherited divisions between universities, radical movements and public life. Theoretical debates about agency and ideology were anchored in an effort to let research interact closely with other social practice, and to make this interaction conscious by critically reflecting on the methods and politics of academic scholarship. Several of the Birmingham 'founding fathers' had roots and commitments to extramural popular education, and the forms of work at the CCCS became a laboratory for developing alternative pedagogic practices and research methods. Qualitative participant observation, interviews and textual readings were favoured over statistical data collection, in order to come closer to ordinary people and their cultural practices. Connections were actively sought to social movements and other radical politics. And teaching and research at the Centre was organised in more egalitarian and collective ways. The working papers give ample testimony to this alternative public sphere for research and transmission, both in forms and contents. In particular, the paper by Richard Johnson on radical education and working-class culture exemplifies and expresses well the crucial connections between pedagogy, culture and media. Its complex analysis is presented in an accessible way, revealing a skilled author who has listened and learned from a wide set of contemporary discussions.

There is an external and an internal side to this point. *Externally* there was a wish to forge links to non-academic movements, organisations and social settings, but also to the general public sphere that depends on mass media. This could be done by action research with disenfranchised social groups, but also by border intellectuals who divided themselves between seminar rooms and various forms of political or cultural publishing in the general press and publishing houses as well as in alternative magazines, radio, television and other media circuits. This was one way to ground studies in the surrounding world and make it relevant for and responsible to the general public.

This intention also had consequences for the *internal* organisation of research and education work. The most obvious example is the collectivity nourished by the 1970s working groups and their stencilled papers. Glancing through them in their original form gives a hint of the oppositional stance in this work. It may today be easy to feel nostalgic towards these hand-produced stencils, where students dared to make their voices heard as co-creators of new knowledge, on an almost equal footing with their senior teachers. There must have been a generous and democratic climate in Birmingham during those years to allow that to happen on such a grand scale and with such fine results. Some individual papers are today of less interest, but for predominantly student work, the level is high, and the bold spirit of exploration and innovation impressive.

In Scandinavia the same could be said of much of the work done in the Nordic Summer University or the more intellectually advanced sections of the New Left, where inspiration also came from German and Italian movements that gave rise to Oskar Negt's ideas of workers' education and counter-public spheres, echoes of which can today also be discerned in the writings of Antonio Negri. In my own research practice, learning from collective movements and constructing alternative public spheres have constantly been an important aspect, for instance in and around the network of Swedish youth culture researchers formed in the late 1980s or in the experimental forms of collective ethnographic fieldwork explored in the Passages Project.

There may be some friction between empirical and the methodological grounding. The reliance on secondary sources in combination with the very small case studies mentioned above as a deficit for empirical grounding can to an extent be defended as part of a pedagogical ambition. Detailed empirical work is not *per se* accessible to a wider audience, and the reworking of such studies in texts that sum up and distil greater lines of thought can fulfil important functions in terms of popularisation and usefulness. Here, the CCCS's ambition paralleled the needs of mass higher education and publishers of textbooks. In the best forms of popular education the bold mixture across disciplines of theories and examples can produce new insights and empower less established young scholars and non-academic knowledge producers to trust their own abilities to discern how meaning, identity and power run together in cultural processes. When it does not succeed there is a risk of such studies developing into unoriginal compilations of derived ideas and superficially understood research. The pedagogical grounding of studies introduce theories in ways that may be questionable but can sometimes be creatively irreverent, in forms of bricolage where concepts borrowed from divergent bodies of thought are put to work in relation to current political issues.

Theoretical grounding in critical perspectives

There was also a third aspect of grounding involved, going in almost the reverse direction of the first one. Empirical analyses tended to be grounded in very strongly politicised, normative perspectives and guided by theoretical work. This aspect broke with all 'positivist' ideals of neutral objectivity. Theory was not to be derived by any unprejudiced encounter with empirical facts, but developed in dialectical movements between theories and observations. Research had to be strongly motivated by emancipatory and empowering interests deriving from a critique of societal systems of power and domination, and it had to be guided by advanced and ambitious theoretical work, finding solid grounds for the interpretations made. This epistemological position actually had much in common with critical hermeneutics as formulated by Paul Ricoeur in dialogue with anthropologist Clifford Geertz, though this was never noted. There was a certain lack of reflexive grounding in this respect, although Willis' notes on method are a notable exception (Willis 1976; 1978: 'Theoretical appendix'; 2000).

The effort to ground theories in empirical studies was thus just half the truth of the early CCCS. It could equally well be described as an effort to ground empirical observations in theoretical work. An intermediary link in this dialectics was provided by textual interpretation. Dick Hebdige's work in particular took decisive steps from sociological-ethnographic fieldwork to a very different kind of study: the theoretically informed reading of media texts. This was part of a poststructuralist turn, where the work of Jacques Derrida was influential, though with a materialist twist, partly derived from Bakhtin's ideas of dialogicism in writing and from Julia Kristeva's ideas of embodied subjects-in-process. Hebdige's paper is almost exhausting in its rapid movements between sources and influences of highly divergent kinds, creating a bricolage of elements linked to different genres (sociology, anthropology, literature, media studies, fiction etc.) that can also be read as a vivid pledge for the value of crossing borders between high and low, cultural texts and social data, fiction and science. This debate continues today, for instance in experiments on the border between artistic and academic work.

This *textual turn* was later criticised by scholars, both inside and outside cultural studies, who saw this as a betrayal of grounding in empirical reality.[5] However, texts are also empirical data and all ethnographic data (including fieldnotes and interviews) are processed and interpreted in textual forms (this is even as true for statistical data). There is a risk that the antitextual reaction that was for a while strong in the field, though motivated in response to some poststructuralist excesses, could throw the baby out with the bathwater and lose the crucial anchorage of cultural studies in interpretations of meanings. The early CCCS papers exemplify the fruitful interplay between social science and humanities perspectives that is needed to understand the dialectics of lived experience and mediated texts. Doing *cultural* studies is to do fieldwork in fields that are *cultural*, encompassing interacting texts, subjects and contexts, and thus inviting not only ethnographic work and institutional analysis but also intertextual and interpretive studies of symbolic artefacts and discourses.

In their best moments, the CCCS papers display a brave openness and curiosity that invites rather than forbids new combinations of ideas that are brought together from highly divergent sources. Still, as a Nordic reader I have always regretted the existence of certain blind spots and theoretical taboos in British cultural studies of the 1970s and 80s. One example is the scapegoat function of the Frankfurt school of critical theory, from Adorno to Habermas. Another is the complete absence of any reference to the critical hermeneutics of Paul Ricoeur. Since then, interesting dialogues and combinations have developed across previously deep divides: an increased traffic between paradigms that first seemed hostile to each other. There have, for instance, been productive encounters and even co-operation between Ricoeur, Habermas, Derrida and Foucault. In many parts of the world, cultural studies is an important agent and arena for such dialogue, which need not imply or lead to any univocality, but presupposes some kind of mutual respect.

Michel Foucault once expressed a regret: 'Now, obviously, if I had been familiar with the Frankfurt School, if I had been aware of it at the time, I would not have said a number of stupid things that I did say and I would have avoided many of the detours which I made while trying to pursue my own humble path – when, meanwhile, avenues had been opened up by the Frankfurt School' (Foucault 1983/1994: 117; see also Fornäs 1995: 66). In much Scandinavian cultural studies *avant la lettre* no such artificial boundary was ever raised, and the same scholars introduced British, French and German critical theories to Swedish readers.[6]

Several working papers are much more diverse and polyphonic than the standard British cultural studies textbooks claim. John Clarke's chapter shows affinities to German work, pointing at hidden influences or unconscious parallels between British and continental social research; affinities that tended to be suppressed and forgotten in later historiographies of cultural studies. Janice Winship's paper on consumption, gender and media is another lasting contribution with a non-sectarian openness to a wide set of leading ideas in social and cultural theory, including Manuel Castells, Louis Althusser, Guy Debord, Herbert Marcuse, Henri Lefebvre, Betty Friedan, Marilyn French, Juliet Mitchell and the Swedish Alva Myrdal! The text offers a rich perspective on contradictions and historical transformations of gender relations and the private/public divide. In these cases one may sense a loss of social and cultural insights, which was one of the costs of bidding farewell to Williams' 'culturalism' in the 1970s' theoretical turn to semiotic structuralism. It is high time to take a step into new borderlands of mediation and leave the hampering theoretical taboos behind.

Cultural studies – an unfinished project

This shows that the 'Birmingham school' was always multifaceted. Continental philosophy, hermeneutics and critical theory that were so central to our own dialectical understanding of meaning, identity and power, as always in process, were also close to the CCCS work we found most inspiring.[7] On other occasions there was a stronger dependence on dualist and structuralist models, even in later, poststructuralist versions: a tendency towards binary dualism and against processual mediation that may possibly have a longer and deeper legacy within Anglo-Saxon thinking, from classical empiricism to analytical philosophy. Dualist conceptions appear in all theorising, but their specific form varies. Polarities like base/superstructure, knowledge/ideology, cognition/emotion, body/mind, politics/aesthetics, real/imagined or material/virtual are recurrent in Western thought. Indeed, some of the most fascinating and challenging Western ideas are contributions to a critical de- and reconstruction of such relations, from Hegel to Nietzsche, Adorno and Derrida. In the kind of dualism intended here, two sides are presented as the opposites of one another, with little effort to scrutinise their interconnections. This may result in a wavering between extreme standpoints. One year, or perhaps at one moment in a specific text, everything is said to be text. The next year, or page, all is instead practice. First, all subjects are predetermined by the symbolic order; next, they appear free to transcend and subvert any such structure. Even Stuart Hall, who so efficiently criticised dichotomising stereotyping in racist thought, himself tended to put structuralist semiotic models of culture side by side with polyphonic, Bakhtinian discourse models, without much discussion of how (or if) they may be linked to each other.[8]

However, this problematic tendency is far from being the only one in the present texts. It is true that there is a certain bias towards structural homologies and continuities, but inner contradictions, ambivalences and transforming dialectics are carefully traced in the best of them, from Willis to Winship. This remains highly inspiring to this very day. It is interesting to see that papers sometimes call for cultural analysis rather than carry it out. For instance, the paper by Eve Brook and Dan Finn points out the need for cultural analysis but does not itself take any constructive steps in that direction. This may be seen as a deficit, but it can also be read as a hopeful promise. What was formulated was more of an outline of a programme for research policy than a solid body of finished work. It challenged other cultural research within a series of disciplines, thereby also modernising and vitalising it.

The field of cultural studies remains an unfulfilled programme. The early Birmingham papers offer a look into a particularly formative phase and site of this field, showing how much remains to be done. They produced some grounding fieldwork and spread some seeds – it is we who must continue cultivating it to make it bloom again. I want to emphasise three inspiring achievements that strike me when reading these papers. (1) First, the fruitfulness of doing cultural interpretations, contextualising readings of symbolic forms and practices, understanding how meanings are produced in interactions between subjects, texts and contexts, approaching the always particular, embodied and situated phenomena on the border between everyday practices, media texts and social institutions. (2) Secondly, the attention to internal contradictions, ambivalences and dialectics that also opens interdisciplinary dialogues with other approaches, disciplinary or otherwise, in order to deal with phenomena that intersectionally combine different dimensions of identity, intermedially cross between different genres and aesthetic modes, and intercontextually involve overlapping sets of societal structures. (3) Thirdly, nourishing a critical reflexivity that continues to develop and explore innovative research methods, problematising power structures in academia and never being sure of the perfection of one's own perspective.

Modernity is an unfinished project.
So is cultural studies.
And for good reasons.

Johan Fornäs is Professor at the Department of Culture Studies (Tema Q) of Linköping University in Norrköping, Sweden, where he also heads the Advanced Cultural Studies Institute of Sweden (ACSIS). He is the Vice Chair of the Association for Cultural Studies (ACS). His background is a PhD in Musicology at Göteborg University and a previous professorship in Media and Communication Studies at Stockholm University. He lives in

Stockholm. His previous studies concern popular music, youth and media culture, with publications such as *Cultural Theory and Late Modernity* (1995), *In Garageland: Rock, Youth and Modernity* (1995), *Digital Borderlands: Cultural Studies of Identity and Interactivity on the Internet* (2002) and *Consuming Media: Communication, Shopping and Everyday Life* (2007).

Notes

1 See also Dahlgren (1997) and Fornäs (1999 and 2001) for various Swedish perspectives on cultural studies and its neighbours.
2 On Willis' reception in the new anthropology of the mid 1980s, see Clifford & Marcus (1986) and Marcus & Fischer (1986).
3 One example is my invention of the term 'late modernity' around 1987, as an alternative to the problematic talk of 'postmodernity' (Fornäs 1987, 1990, 1995). The term was made possible by a typically Swedish cross-reading of German, British and Nordic work, and though itself not unproblematic, it proved useful to escape key problems in the postmodern debate. This was years before Anthony Giddens (1991), often mentioned as its originator. It may have been 'in the air', emerging at different sites roughly at the same time, but there might also be a hidden line of inspiration through Paul Willis (1990), who had visited Stockholm in 1987. For a discussion of marginality and centrality in cultural studies, see Fornäs and Lehtonen (2005).
4 I belong to the generation born in the first half of the 1950s, arriving at the university in the early 1970s. Thanks to Ien Ang for inspiring e-mail discussions of our respective pathways into the field.
5 Highly divergent versions of this antitextual turn are formulated in Ferguson and Golding (1997), McRobbie (1997), Grossberg (1998). For a critique, see Fornäs (2000).
6 For instance, Fornäs *et al.* (1984) presented Willis, Hebdige and McRobbie but also the German youth culture researchers Helmut Hartwig and Thomas Ziehe; and Fornäs *et al.* (1988/1995) combined elements of subcultural theory with Kristeva's and Laplanche's psychoanalysis and Habermas' theories of modernity along paths never trodden in Britain.
7 One example is the influences from Mikhail Bakhtin and Julia Kristeva in texts like Stallybrass and White (1986).
8 For a critique of dichotomisations, see Hall (1992); for a split model of culture, see Hall (1997).

Bibliography

Bennett, T. (1998) 'Cultural Studies: A Reluctant Discipline', *Cultural Studies*, 12:4.

Clifford, J. and Marcus, G. E. (eds) (1986) *Writing Culture: The Poetics and Politics of Ethnography*, Berkeley/Los Angeles/London: University of California Press.

Cohen, P. (1972) 'Subcultural Conflict and Working-Class Community', WPCS 2, Birmingham: CCCS; reprinted in Hall *et al.* (1980).

Cohen, P. (1997) *Rethinking the Youth Question: Education, Labour and Cultural Studies*, London: Macmillan.

Dahlgren, P. (1997) 'Cultural Studies and Media Research', in Storey, J., Schlesinger, P. and Silverstone, R. (eds) *International Media Research: A Critical Survey*, London: Routledge.

Ferguson, M. and Golding, P. (eds) (1997) *Cultural Studies in Question*, London: Sage.

Fornäs, J. (1985) *Tältprojektet: Musikteater som manifestation*, Stockholm/Göteborg: Symposion.

Fornäs, J. (1987) ' "Identity is the Crisis". En bakgrund till kulturella uttrycksformers funktioner för ungdomar i senmoderniteten', in Carlsson, U. (ed.) *Forskning om populärkultur*, Göteborg: Nordicom-Sverige.

Fornäs, J. (1990) 'Popular Music and Youth Culture in Late Modernity', in Roe, K. and Carlsson, U. (eds) *Popular Music Research*, Göteborg: Nordicom-Sverige; also as 'Moving Rock: Youth and Pop in Late Modernity', *Popular Music*, 9:3.

Fornäs, J. (1995) *Cultural Theory and Late Modernity*, London: Sage.

Fornäs, J. (1999) *Advancing Cultural Studies*, Stockholm: JMK (Reports and papers 1999:1).

Fornäs, J. (2000) 'The Crucial in Between: The Centrality of Mediation in Cultural Studies', *European Journal of Cultural Studies*, 3:1.

Fornäs, J. (2001) *Advancing Cultural Studies in Sweden: An Infrastructural Initiative*, Norrköping: Arbetslivsinstitutet (Arbetslivsrapport 2001:1).

Fornäs, J. (2004) 'Intermedial Passages in Time and Space: Contexts, Currents and Circuits of Media Consumption', *Nordicom Review*, 25:1–2.

Fornäs, J., Becker, K., Bjurström, E. and Ganetz, H. (2007) *Consuming Media: Communication, Shopping and Everyday Life*, Oxford: Berg.

Fornäs, J. and Bolin, G. (eds) (1995) *Youth Culture in Late Modernity*, London: Sage.

Fornäs, J. and Lehtonen, M. (2005) 'Between Centres and Peripheries in Transnational Cultural Studies', in Kovala, U., Eskola, K., Jokinen, K., Niinikangas, V. and Sironen, E. (eds) *Tarkkoja siirtoja*, Jyväskylä: Research Centre for Contemporary Culture, University of Jyväskylä (http://tuki.hum.jyu.fi/~julkaisu/lehtonenfornas.html).

Fornäs, J., Lindberg, U. and Sernhede, O. (eds) (1984) *Ungdomskultur: Identitet och motstånd*, Stockholm: Akademilitteratur (later editions Stockholm/Stehag: Symposion).

Fornäs, J., Lindberg, U. and Sernhede, O. (1988/1995) *In Garageland: Rock, Youth and Modernity*, London and New York: Routledge.

Foucault, M. (1983/1994) 'Critical Theory/Intellectual History', Kelly, M. (ed.) *Critique and Power: Recasting the Foucault/Habermas Debate*, Cambridge, MA: MIT Press.

Giddens, A. (1991) *Modernity and Self-Identity: Self and Society in the Late Modern Age*, Cambridge: Polity Press.

Glaser, B. G. and Strauss, A. L. (1967) *The Discovery of Grounded Theory: Strategies for Qualitative Research*, New York: Aldine de Gruyter.

Grossberg, L. (1998) 'The Cultural Studies' Crossroads Blues', *European Journal of Cultural Studies*, 1:1.

Hall, S., Hobson, D., Lowe, A. and Willis, P. (eds) (1980) *Culture, Media, Language*, London: Hutchinson.

Hall, S. (1992) 'The West and the Rest: Discourse and Power', in Hall, S. and Gieben, B. (eds) *Formations of Modernity*, Cambridge/Milton Keynes: Polity Press/The Open University.

Hall, S. (1997) 'The Work of Representation', in Hall, S. (ed.) *Representation: Cultural Representations and Signifying Practices*, London/Milton Keynes: Sage/The Open University.

Haraway, D. J. (1991) *Simians, Cyborgs, and Women*, London: Free Association Books.

Lindner, R. (2000) *Die Stunde der Cultural Studies*, Vienna: WUV.

Marcus, G. E. and Fischer, M. M. J. (1986) *Anthropology as Cultural Critique: An Experimental Moment in the Human Sciences*, Chicago/London: University of Chicago Press.

McRobbie, A. (ed.) (1997) *Back to Reality? Social Experience and Cultural Studies*, Manchester/New York: Manchester University Press.

Stallybrass, P. and White, A. (1986) *The Politics and Poetics of Transgression*, Ithaca, NY: Cornell University Press.

Willis, P. (1976) 'Notes on Method', WPCS 9, Birmingham: CCCS; reprinted in Hall *et al.* (1980).

Willis, P. (1978) *Profane Culture*, London: Routledge & Kegan Paul.

Willis, P. (1990) *Common Culture: Symbolic Work at Play in the Everyday Cultures of the Young*, Milton Keynes: Open University Press.

Willis, P. (2000) *The Ethnographic Imagination*, Cambridge: Polity Press.

Wright, H. K. (1998) 'Dare We De-Centre Birmingham? Troubling the "Origin" and Trajectories of Cultural Studies', *European Journal of Cultural Studies*, 1:1.

28 The motorbike within a subcultural group

Paul Willis

I spent several months during 1969 on a case-study at a motorbike club in the Birmingham area – the Double Zero. The building was a disused church and church hall in a run-down area near the city centre. I was studying with the use of participant observation and recorded group discussions the role of pop music in the motor-bike subculture. However, the motorbike as an object was of such paramount 'symbolic' importance within the culture that it demanded separate attention for itself. The following is a description and analysis of the part played by the motorbike in the small group at the Club with whom I was concerned. It is an extract from a much larger report on my research submitted to U.N.E.S.C.O. as part of their programme on Human Rights as Cultural Rights which is to be published later in the year. It should be clear that the article arises from a report of a specific case study and makes no claims to universal validity. Names and nicknames have been altered here.

The motorbike was one of the main foci of interest in the lives of our group, and most of their activities were based on this interest. A large part of conversation was devoted to the motor cycle, discussing new models or comparing performance, or describing in detail how repair jobs are done. This short extract is from an official report describing a club exercise. Double Zero members had distributed a large number of road safety programmes in the Birmingham area; one of the significant results of the exercise was:

> That there was a livelier conversation in the events of the days of delivery, recounting of experience, of personal oddities, of difficulties in finding places, and of the impact which their presence in certain situations had caused, all leading in fact to an atmosphere and level of conversation which normally does not occur because technical jargon concerning the motor bicycles seems to be the norm.[1]

The club itself acted as an important clearing house for spares and accessories. The group regarded the club as a centre of information and supply. On numerous occasions experts were approached by acolytes for detailed descriptions of mechanical repair jobs, or for a 'professional' diagnosis of mechanical problems. A strange rattle or banging, sluggish acceleration, or bad handling characteristics would send the less knowledgeable enthusiasts running to the acknowledged 'experts'. At first sight a kind of unofficial hierarchy seemed to be based partly on this knowledge, so that individuals with extremely fast motor-bikes, or with recognised diagnostic and mechanical skill were likely to be accorded a special respect and position. A common approach would be to offer the 'expert' a drink or a cigarette as a prelude to asking advice. The advice was given with a weighty and self-confident delivery, that seemed an implicit self-recognition of superior status. Within our group, Rock was awarded a senior position within this unofficial hierarchy. This was interesting, because his mechanical skill was not at an extremely high level, and nor was his motorbike particularly fast. In his case it was more his length of experience and his type of experience. He was older than the rest, had been riding a motor-cycle for longer and, more significantly, had had several accidents. He had been in hospital several times, had broken a number of limbs, and had, as a memento of one of his accidents, a piece of metal in one of his legs holding a weakened bone together. All these experiences he recounted with nonchalance and he seemed to make no special effort to avoid further accidents – rather he seemed to expect further accidents as a matter of course. Status, then, in the light of Rock's case, was accorded not only for technical competence with the motor bike, but also for full citizenship within the *world* of the motorcycle. That sheer technical competence alone was not accorded status within the group is clearly shown by the case of Percy. He had a very advanced technical knowledge of the motorbike, but almost no presence in the world of the motorbike and was accorded very little status. He did not ride his machine fast, except when circumstances maximised the probability of safety, he had never had an accident and did not regard the prospect with excitement. His clothing was within the letter, rather than the spirit, of the motorbike world. It was simply *too* functional and *too* meticulous to seem natural in the larger symbolic world. Physically Percy was one of the group I studied, but he was not a member of it in the sense that he did not conform, and was seen not to conform with the values and norms of the motorbike boys – essentially he was a barely tolerated outsider.

This kind of observation about Percy led to an important insight about the nature of the motor-cycle culture. The dress of Fred-the-Ted, Bobby, Rock and Tony was not primarily a functional exigency of riding a motor cycle. It was more crucially a symbolic extension of the motorbike, an amplification of the qualities inherent within the motorbike. The strict motor-cycle apparel, i.e. that most designed to eliminate the discomforts of riding the motor-cycle, had the opposite effect. It tended to close down and minimise the natural qualities of the motorbike. Thus, the conventional clothing of Percy consisted of a helmet, goggles, a belt around the waist, tightly closed in neck, gloves, and large woollen socks. The helmet clearly protected against head injury in an accident, the goggles prevented eye irritation from dust or high winds. The belted waist and tightly closed in neck prevented wind from entering and ballooning the clothes at high speeds. The gloves protected the hands, and, by overlapping the jacket, prevented wind from travelling up the sleeve. The large woollen socks prevented air from pocketing, and kept the feet warm. Generally, this conventional gear was watertight and warm, to minimise the obvious discomforts of driving in the English climate. Also it was generally free from all but essential accoutrements, and was pulled in tightly without open flaps, so as to minimise wind resistance. Thus, in this conventional dress Percy was tightly packaged in, and given the maximum protection from the inherent dangers and discomforts of the motorbike. The special characteristics of the motorbike, its openness to the elements, its instability, its speed, the free rush of air, were minimised as far as possible, so as to render the motor cycle a neutral form of transport.

The other members of the group, the motor-cycle boys, kept the same basic elements within their style but transformed them by small though crucial modifications. To start with, helmets and goggles were never worn. They knew quite well that helmets were most advisable for safety, if only because a national safety campaign of the time, with posters across the nation, was aimed at encouraging motor-cyclists to wear helmets; the slogan read 'You know it makes sense'. The reason was that helmets and goggles would have significantly limited both the experience and the image of motor-cycling. Helmets and goggles destroy the excitement of the wind rushing into the face and of the loud exhaust beat thumping the ears. The point of fast driving was the experience, not the fact of speed. Sports cars, though of similar speed potential to motorbikes, were despised. For those who have never ridden on a motor cycle, it may not be clear that high speed riding is an extremely physical experience. At high speeds the whole body is blown backwards: it was a common way of communicating speed at the club to say that 'I was nearly blown off'. When even a slight bend is taken at high speed the machine and the driver need to go over at quite an angle in order to compensate the centrifugal force which threatens to throw the rider off, and topple the motor cycle away from the direction of turn. Novices find this an extremely precarious situation to be in, and can panic. The experienced fast motor-cyclist will not take a complete amateur on the back of the motor cycle in case a lean in the wrong direction on a fast bend may upset the precise balance, and send them both hurtling towards the tarmac. The experienced driver becomes part of the motor-cycle and intuitively feels the correct balancing at high speeds. If there is anything wrong it is the motorbike's fault. This is a typical comment from our group made on tape in another connection:

BOBBY: No . . . the motor bike don't frighten you.

FRED THE TED: If the bike handles well, the bike well never beat you, if it handles bad, it frightens you, that's all.

PW: Frightens? What does 'frightens' mean?

FRED THE TED: No, scared, I mean. Like if I've got a bike and it don't handle well, I won't go fast on it, but if it'll do everything you want it to, well that's it you know.

The dangers and the excitement of bodily wind pressure exist of course for the conventional motor-cyclist too, but he is partly removed from the rawness of the experience by the protection of his face and eyes and hands from the wind. He is, in a sense, contained and sealed by his gear, so that he makes decisions, and controls the motor-cycle, at one remove from the direct experiences which make the control necessary. Thus, he must lean with the machine around corners, and he will feel the force of the wind bodily moving him back, but these senses are both blunted and mediated by protective clothing. The clothing is also as streamlined and smooth as possible to prevent unnecessary drag. The experience for the motor-cycle boy such as Rock or Fred the Ted is very different. The absence of gloves, goggles and helmet means that the equivalent of a high gale force wind is tearing into the living flesh. Eyes are forced into a slit and water profusely, the mouth is dragged back into a snarl, and it is extremely difficult to keep the mouth closed. The features are generally flattened and distorted, hands become raw red. There is no disjunction whatsoever between the fact and the experience of speed, and physical consequences are minutely articulated with control decisions of the motorbike. There is no sense in which the rider is protected by a panoply in which there is some calm to make protected decisions about events in the world out there. For the motorbike boy, he is in the 'world out there' and copes with handling his motorbike at the same time as feeling the full brunt of its movement in the natural physical world. Furthermore, they make no attempt to minimise the drag aspect of the wind. Jackets are partly open and are not buttoned down around the throat, belts are not worn to keep the jacket close to the skin, trousers are not tucked away in boots and socks, there is nothing to prevent wind rushing up the sleeves. Adornments of the jacket and free-flowing neckties add, although fractionally, to the total drag, an unnecessary drag that would be avoided by conventional motor-cyclists. Nor is the motor-cycle itself designed for aerodynamic efficiency. All of the motor-cycle boys in the group, except for Percy, had fitted large cattle horn handlebars, which required an upright sitting position with hands and arms level with the shoulders. This considerably increases drag, and ironically limits the top speed of the motor-bike. But it improves handling ability and increases the sensation of speed dramatically. The conventional motor-cyclist interested in speed, or the racing motor-cyclist does exactly the opposite and lowers the handlebars and puts the foot rests further back, so that the body can lie virtually flat along the bike and present the minimum surface for wind resistance; tiny windscreens about the handlebars are often used to protect what little frontal surface area of the rider is visible.

Not only did the motor-cycle boys accentuate the unpleasant physical aspects of high speed, they derived excitement from the threat of danger, and did nothing to minimise the threat of serious injury. Quite apart from the style of riding, which was daring and fast, the clearest evidence of this was the absence of crash helmets. They were universally abhorred and regarded as 'cissy' (that is, effeminate). The possibility of accident was recognised and past accidents were a major topic of conversation. The death rate from motorbike accidents at the club was appalling. This is an excerpt from an official report in early summer 1967:

> This period has brought a number of major disasters to club members, both in terms of personal injuries and deaths on the roads. Four deaths were recorded in August alone, and each brought with it a major shock to the organisation with feelings of hopelessness and despair. This was interpreted by staff, and home visits were made for a period of supportive care. Funerals were attended by large numbers of members wearing ordinary clothes (motor cycling gear etc) and pall bearers were provided from the friends.
>
> Spontaneous collections were made for wreaths and short memorial services were held the evening following the death. These services were very well attended, and a high degree of seriousness surrounded each act of worship.
>
> Parents seem to have been impressed by the sheer supportive interest of the membership, but obviously this was the only response open to the members at a time of total inadequacy, the burden naturally falling on the only ordained member of staff.
>
> The atmosphere and bearing of the whole club was deeply affected by suspicions that we were being punished for some failure, and no persuasion has so far removed this pressing fear, supported by a major series of non-fatal accidents. There is no doubt that the presence of the Church, and a priest has been greatly appreciated by the members at this particular time.
>
> No doubt, as numbers grow this will be an increasing experience within the organisation and there will be no short cut to answering the grieving or the question why. The one hope is in the sheer community that is expressed on these intense occasions of member to member and members to the whole staff and family involved.

Every member of our group knew at least one victim personally. The following is a brief excerpt from one of the transcriptions; our group were discussing how they'd like to die:

BOBBY: No, like Johnny, oh he did fucking hell he did, blood poured from from everywhere, cracked his fucking skull wide open.

TONY: Did he die?

BOBBY: Wouldn't you if you hit the back of a stationary lorry at seventy miles an hour? You should have heard the fucking bang. 'Baaang!' I heard it from the other end of the road, about two hundred yards up the road. He went out like a light.

Death on the motor-cycle as a crucial element in the motorbike sub-culture had been given a kind of formal recognition at the club. On the altar table in the church was a large embossed book lying open all the time with the names and dates of the deaths of past members of the club who had been killed on the road, the pages were turned daily to record exact anniversaries. It was one of the familiar sights around the club, to see past girlfriends or admirers of a particular victim looking at the book in an almost ritualistic fashion, on the anniversary of his death. I myself saw a group of girls around the book, one of them crying profusely, paying a strange kind of homage. The club, which was based on the premises of a discontinued parish church, drew, as David Collyer mentions in that extract, an unusual kind of strength from the Church on these occasions. Normally there was little or no interest in the Church, on other occasions the group under consideration treated the Church with complete disregard. On one occasion before a record listening session (which was held in the church on that evening) they had been noisily playing with a large medicine ball, which they were throwing back and forth to each other down the length of the church, crashing it through chairs, throwing it up onto the altar, without the slightest respect or consideration for the church. That is not to say they were being sacrilegious, they simply treated it as another building, and David Collyer, to his credit, made no attempt to force religion, or even respect for religion, on to the members. Normally, even the book itself was dismissed for its religious position within the formal meaning of the Church. In a more general sense they couldn't accept the religious notion of life beyond death, a belief that the book in the church was taken as symbolising. This is how I first mentioned the book:

PW: I was with Tony in the church earlier on, and I saw that book with the names of the people who had been killed on motor bikes, have you seen it?

GENERAL: Yes.

PW: Just on the left-and side there, what do you think about it?

ROCK: A load of rubbish.

FRED THE TED: About the names or the people who are dead like?

PW: Either.

ANN: Where is that?

PW: In the church.

BOBBY: There's a book you, they shove all the names of the people who've fucking copped it.

FRED THE TED: It's for people who croak out you know, they shove their names in the fucking book, on the bike you know, they're dead.

ROCK: If they're dead, you know that's it, you should forget them, I mean some of these birds come in and they has a look in there, they start blarting, and everything . . . it's ridiculous, I mean once they're dead, you can't do anything for them, so why stick their names up in the book.

BOBBY: Some people are like that you, I don't give a fuck actually, when he's dead, he's dead that's it, you can't get him back, so why put his name in the book . . . No, when you're dead, you're fucking dead, there's no two ways about it.

However, when a member of the club was killed in a motor-cycle crash there was always a very well-attended memorial service in the church. In these particular moments of crisis the motor-cycle boys turned towards the Church, not out of a sense of religion, but out of a sense of marking what they regarded as an important even with formal recognition. Death on the motorbike held a particular awe and even attraction for them, it held a privileged position in the symbolic world of the motor-cycle. Death on the motor-cycle was mentioned several times in our discussions; this is a selection of their comments on this subject, taken mostly from one discussion arising from the book in the church:

FRED THE TED: I think it's the best way. I'll have a bike until I'm about thirty-five you know. I think it's the best way to die . . .

TONY: The thing is . . .

FRED THE TED: Hey, it's me . . . I'd like to go quickly mind you, out like a light, bang . . . fast like about a hundred miles an hour . . . hit a car you know . . . smash straight into something.

PW: What are the chances do you think of having a serious accident?

FRED THE TED: Oh well I'm a nut case you know on a motorbike, it might do, I've had some near misses you know, through crash barriers, and I've had concussion and things like that without a crash helmet.

PW: But did that make you think?

FRED THE TED: No, funnily enough it didn't, everybody else said 'I bet that's made you think' . . . You see that's why I think I may die on a motorbike.

BOBBY: I'd like to die on, I'd like to die on a bike, that's the way I want to go, fucking great, I'd hate to get old.

PW: Why?

TONY: The thing is . . .

BOBBY: Hang on you daft cunt.

TONY: I'd like to . . .

BOBBY: It would be a great sensation to croak out on a bike . . . I'd like a fucking smash, got to be a good one, or I don't want to go.

PW: Tell me why you'd like to croak out on a motorbike then?

FRED THE TED: You'd hate to get old, wouldn't you?

BOBBY: I'd hate to grow old, I see some old people and I think, fuck, if I was like you I'd go under the first bus.

PW: Well, why don't you finish yourself off with drugs and die that way.

BOBBY: Oh bollocks to that, I'd sooner kill myself on the bike any day.

Just blast down the road, giving it almighty stick, and fucking that's it. I don't want to know I was going to die, you know what I mean, but if I was going to die, I wouldn't mind going on a bike, fucking great!

BOBBY: I'd like to die racing down the road, down the bastard, give it almighty stick, give a Jag a go, and then you know, a fucking big lorry comes, 'crunch', that's the end of you . . . nice eh?

FRED THE TED: How about robbing a bank and they're all after you?

BOBBY: Racing coppers.

FRED THE TED: Hoorah – eh

BOBBY: Get two of them behind, all fucking day. Thunderbolts you know, the copper's thunderbolts, and you're fucking pissing away on an export Bonnie or summat, give it almighty stick you know, and you kick a couple of coppers, go fast, smoking, your tyres are set alight you know, and a fucking great big twenty-ton lorry comes across, an artic., and you go up the back.

However, the motorbike boys did not have their own formal and recognised systems for recognising an event of such extreme importance. They did not know what forms of action, in the terms of their own culture, could specifically and deeply enough recognise the subjective meaning and importance of death on a motor-cycle. At these times the Church, and its paraphernalia and rituals, were turned to because they offered ready-made and widely recognised *formal* ways of according significance. It was at the memorial church service that the rider was well and truly recognised as dead, and could stay dead, but also glorified in the mythology of the motor bike sub-culture. It did not matter that the church rituals were not understood, they couldn't have been understood in the way the Church would have wanted them understood. What mattered was the sense of presence, the sense of order, the sense of marking within time of a crucial event. Thus, at these times, there was a very special conjunction of a traditional, received form, and a modern, informal form. The motor-cycle boys, who in so many other circumstances, delighted in the outrage of conventional society, at a certain point within the internal expressive life of their culture – at a point which was both crisis and transcendence – turned to a traditional institution to borrow its solemnity and ritual. It is for these reasons that it was strange to see a group of motor-cycle girls, one in deep grief, clustered around a book on an altar. This regard for death, the fascination in its rituals, the need to push beyond the normal bounds of the sub-culture for these rituals, attest the degree to which death on the motor-cycle, and danger on the motorbike, were an essential ingredient of the motor-cycle culture.

Death and danger on the motor-cycle were glorified in another way. It was said frequently, and with pride within our group, that deaths on motor-cycles were always reported in the local press, whereas deaths on scooters or in motor cars were not reported. The following comments were made in the course of the discussion on death in a motor-cycle accident:

BOBBY: They publish a remembrance in the paper, you can cut it out like, and put it in a scrap book. They always do that when you croak out on a bike, they always put it in the paper you know, no scooters, motorbikes, motorbikes; Johnny – and all them lot, all fucking in the paper.

FRED THE TED: Johnny, that was my mate, I talked to him you know . . .

I did not check whether this was, in fact, true, but the important thing is that it was widely held to be true. Again we see a kind of conjunction with conventional society, where an element of conventional society was able to mark or accord significance to something of importance within the sub-culture. Newspaper items were cut out, and kept, and widely talked about, both at the time and afterwards. Individuals, who in their time had achieved no particular status within the club, soon became heroic mythological figures. The build up of figures in this way owed much of its legitimacy and resonance to the conventional organs of the press and of the Church. Past figures and the manner of their deaths were one of the main topics of conversation within our small group.

Thus the *motor-cycle boys* – that is Rock, Fred the Ted, Bobby, Tony, in contradiction to the conventional *motor-cyclist*, Percy – were concerned to open out the inherent characteristics of the motor-cycle. The clothing and style and riding and acceptance of risk accentuated the physical exhileration of speed, and the gut reaction to danger. However, it was not only in the subjective experience of riding that the motorbike was symbolically extended, it was also in the field of public image. With the conventional motor-cyclist the qualities of the motor-cycle are closed down. The rider is completely impersonalised and hidden from view. No part of his body is visible. The whole outfit is a carefully worked-out, and carefully put together, attempt to negate the effects and characteristics of the motorbike; it is the technological answer to the problems technology has created – uniformity, anonymity, featurelessness encircle the rough roaring, dangerous qualities of the motor-cycle. The motor-cycle boys accepted the motorbike and allowed it to reverberate right through into the world of human concourse. The lack of the helmet allowed long hair to blow freely back in the wind, and this, with the studded and ornamented jackets, and the aggressive style of riding, gave the motorbike boys a fearsome look which amplified the wildness, noise, surprise and intimidation of the motorbike. The motorbikes themselves were modified to accentuate these features. The high cattlehorn handlebars, the chromium-plated double exhaust pipes, the high, exuberant mudguards gave the bikes an exaggerated look of fierce power. More particularly, it was common practice to remove the baffles from the silencer box on the exhaust, in order to allow the straight through thumping of the exhaust gases from the cylinder to carry their explosion directly into the atmosphere. The effect was sometimes startling, with the breathy, loud, slightly irregular, bang and splutter bringing the hardness and power of the metal piston exploding down the metal cylinder and abruptly, and inevitably, reversing up again, with the minutely engineered turn of the crankshaft, bringing this power and impersonal ferocity right out into the vulnerable zone of human sensibilities. An alleway led up the side of the church to the coffeebar of the club. Members often parked their bikes along this narrow passageway, and stood by them talking, starting and revving their bikes, discussing technical matters, or indeed, any matters at all. It could be extremely intimidating to walk up this narrow aisle. The noise was sometimes terrific, and the loud thumping of the motorbike seemed to imply sudden movement and action, but none came, so that one could be unnerved by the continual imagined necessity to take evasive action against some fantasy explosion of movement and aggression. This feeling diminished after a time, but on a summer's evening, on a crowded night, the walk up that thundering passage would always bring some unease.

That response illuminates the crucial aspect of the motor-cycle culture both in its image and experience. Human flesh and sensibilities exist in a very special relationship to the motorbike. Where the conventional motor-cyclist and car driver are, to some extent, shielded from the ferocity of mechanical power, the motorbike boy accepts it, controls it, and attempts to make it his own. There are two things here, one is the flesh wrestling with, and controlling of mechanical power precisely overcoming the unease produced by powerful machines. The other is the appropriation and extension of that power into the human zone of meaning, the symbolic extension of the motorbike into the human world. Essentially then, the motor-cycle was not limited to a functional use within the human world. It was accepted in the rawness of experience, allowed to make its full register on the human senses, then amplified and extended through a meaningful human culture. Mechanical qualities were recognised, appreciated, extended, transformed into human qualities. This is not to posit a view of the relationship between men and machines which could be the beginning of some cybernetic nightmare of machines conditioning man, overriding his specifically human qualities. Rather it is the opposite. It is man's domination of the machine: the motor-cycle has to be controlled, the direct physical consequences of riding accepted, before the 'spirit' of the motorbike can be appropriated and anthropomorphised. When a motor-cycle boy was killed on a motor-cycle, it was not the machine that had killed him, it was not simply the sordid, pointless mechanical murder of the motor car death. It was also the appropriate culmination, the final transcendence, the final coming of identity, within a humanly constructed world of meaning. This is an edited version of a longer section from one of the transcriptions, where Fred the Ted describes his feelings after a friend's death:

> A mate of mine used to have a rocket. He hit a tree and I felt all sorry for him dying. I had a dream about him you know.
>
> Up in Heaven – every good motor-cyclist goes to Heaven if they go on a bike. Up in heaven, St. Peter in there. There's this dirty great whacking road, ever so wide. No bends – nothing the other way, nothing coming this way, you know, just that way. No cars, no scooters or anything like that. Just motorbikes. St. Peter gives you the bike of your choice and it's such a fast bike it never goes wrong. There's a cafe about every fifteen miles. You're hearing music all the time, rock and roll, Bill Haley, Little Richard, all the things you like you know. The coffee's free and there's all blonde virgins waiting for you – All blondes and cups of tea. So it must be great up there honest.

The motor-cycle was not *blamed*, or accorded deadly powers, in a curious way it became the corpse itself, because *its* qualities had been stolen and transformed into the material for the heroic apotheosis of the rider.

This article has been an attempt to present the 'world of the motor-cycle'. As I argued earlier, status, and relative degrees of importance, within the sub-culture were accorded by reference to the motorbike. Mechanical skill and experience were important, but what we called 'citizenship' in the world of the motorbike was most important. Percy had a great deal of knowledge about the motorbike but, as I hope to have shown, in a variety of ways, he betrayed his non-citizen status within the 'world of the motorbike'. Rock had considerable status even though his mechanical knowledge was not particularly outstanding. His qualifications were experience, several accidents and a kind of folk memory about who had been killed at the club. Fred the Ted, who had neither technical knowledge nor a particularly high accident score, also had a high status and was extremely popular in the club. His case demonstrates the symbolic force of the 'motor cycle world', because his status was not based on any concrete activity or achievement; he had developed a kind of prescience and ability to articulate some of the more abstract qualities of the world. In this sense, he belonged in the motor cycle culture much more fully than Percy, even though Percy could have dismantled and rebuilt a motor cycle in the time it would have taken Fred the Ted to think about starting.

Thus the motor-cycle was an essential element of the motor-cycle culture. It was not simply one object in a random collection of objects and alienated activities that occupy the life space of an underprivileged group. External notions of 'culture' might attach no more importance to it, than the table or chair we sit on – a functional object totally lacking in 'culture'. I hope to have shown that there can be a tight construction of meanings and attitudes around apparently functional objects in the normal course of living. Such a distinctive and humanly meaningful construction, such a developed and symbolically extended organisation of experience and feelings of the world and the products of its technology so often thought of as alienating, should be recognised.

Note

1 'Pilot Scheme amongst the City Centre Unattached', David Collyer. This is the 'official report' referred to throughout this article.

29 Football hooliganism and the skinheads

John Clarke

1. Introduction

Before any real consideration of the phenomenon of soccer hooliganism can take place, I feel it is necessary to have a more historical understanding of the nature and importance of football itself. Consequently the first section of this paper is an attempt to explain the relationship between football and working-class life.

2. Football and working-class life

Rather than give a history of football or a cultural analysis of the game's developing relationship with the English working class, both of which are available elsewhere,[1] I have limited myself to a brief review of those factors which account for the central position accorded to football in working-class culture. Basically, I see this position as being due to the reflection in the game of certain central values of that culture, notably those of excitement, physical prowess, local identity and victory.

Elias and Dunning have written of the 'quest for excitement' in advanced societies,[2] arguing that the increased routinization of everyday life has reduced the frequency of extraordinary incident, and has also increasingly demanded restrictions on the expression of emotion in public. There remain, however, a number of leisure activities which satisfy a demand for excitement, and also provide a legitimate setting for the expression of emotion. Football is a sport well-fitted for the provision of excitement. Unlike many games it has an almost continuous flow of action, broken only by a brief interval for half-time, and that action is compressed into a very limited time period, in normal circumstances ninety minutes. Compare this state of events with cricket, for example, where the action is interrupted at regular intervals, between overs, at the fall of wickets, and between innings, and where the whole action is spread, traditionally at least, over three or even five days.

Since the Industrial Revolution large parts of working men's lives have become increasingly subject to the organizational techniques and time discipline of factory work. Football offers an alternative to that routine, but one which also draws on the major role of time in working-class experience. Arthur Hopcraft's description of the atmosphere of a football match catches these points as well as the intensifying effect of a large crowd:

> The sound of a big football crowd baying its delight and its outrage has no counterpart. It is the continuous flow of foot that excites this sustained crescendo . . . In football the action is interrupted only by fouls, which add fiercely to the crowd's responses, and when the ball goes out of play, which is very often in the most hectic of circumstances.

> . . . that sudden, damp silence which falls upon a football ground immediately the last players have left the pitch reflects exhaustion. The expression 'football fever' may have been greatly overused, but it is an accurate description of the condition of the fan at the limit of his excitement.[3]

The excitement on the pitch is heightened by the experience of watching it as part of a densely packed crowd of fellow fans. The physical pressure at the heart of the crowd, and the psychological feeling of being 'at one' with hundreds of others, urging *your* team on is an integral part of the appeal of the game. I know a number of fans, who, while not being 'hard-core' supporters, wholly reject the idea of watching football from a seat in the stands. They claim that 'It's not the same game from up there', complaining of a sense of distance from the game and a lack of involvement.

Football is a game based essentially on physical conflict; nothing can be done without possession of the ball, and although the formal regulation of the game over the years has removed the extremes of violent tackling which accompanied the earlier stages of the game's development, football is still very much about physical challenge and combat. In addition, the skills involved in the game are primarily physical ones: dexterity, control, balance and power. Working-class life placed a high value on physical prowess, partly because the work experience centred round largely physical tasks, whether involving physical strength or manual dexterity; and partly because of the strong cultural emphasis on toughness, masculinity, virility and connected values. There was no place, either in the factory or on the football field for the 'pansy', or the man who couldn't 'take it'.

This brings us to the place of violence in working-class life. Because of the valuation placed on 'hardness', and the harsh demands which life made on them, violence was an accepted part of life for most working men. This is not to say that they were all continually involved in fights, but that violence was seen as something that anyone might become involved in. It was not seen as problematic, or in need of explanation. Hopcraft describes the atmosphere of violence or perhaps potential violence, at football matches in this way:

> The point about the cheap parts of the ground is that there are a lot of men there who do hard, manual work, and an evident readiness to fight is part of the common coin of social survival amongst them. The punch-up is threatened far more often than it occurs, of course, just as is the case on the field; players will shake hands at the end of the grittiest games, and so will rival supporters reciprocally back down from their promises to thump one another. You have to stand in among the crowds to realize what the words and the emotions are which sometimes add a special quality of menace to the general clamour of a match.[4]

Football, as Critcher suggests, reflects very accurately the working-class outlook on violence:

> In this alternative moral universe violence is legitimated as nowhere else in society, but it is also quite clearly limited as if football offered a formalization of the informal attitudes so long held by working men, that it is a normal part of life in which any individual may become periodically involved, but that it is never expected to get out of hand or become a pervasive frame of mind.[5]

There are indeed limits placed on what form and what volume of violence is accepted as 'normal'; similarly Elias and Dunning note that only certain types of emotional expression are condoned in the search for excitement. Nevertheless, it is just that state of excitement in which the routine processes of self-control may become less effective as one becomes less sensitive to the nuances of public expectations, and the expression of emotion spill over into undesired forms. In the opposite direction, if one's own expectations of excitement are frustrated, there exists the temptation to create one's own with whatever materials are at hand.

Next the place of local loyalties in the game. Community and mutual assistance have always been strong themes in working-class life; local identities have been of great importance. Football drew on these local ties (most football grounds are built in the heart of early urban working-class housing areas), but it also gave them greater impetus. It gave a national focus to local rivalries, and allowed for their expression in a largely symbolic conflict. The team were in many senses the 'Saturday representatives' of the local people, 'defending' their home record against the invaders, and themselves going to 'steal' or 'plunder' points from other teams' grounds. In earlier times, before the present rash of weekly transfers, these local bonds were strengthened by the fact that large numbers of players were born and lived locally. There is still a special place reserved in the game's affections for both the local lad 'made good', and for the long serving 'club man'. (This feeling may also underlie some of the verbal rituals which surround transfers; the profession that 'I shall be very sorry to leave, the people here have always been good to me' of the out-going player, and the 'I'm very happy to be coming here, it's a very friendly club, and I've always enjoyed playing here' of the new arrival.) In addition, the players themselves were almost wholly recruited from the working class, and unlike today remained a part of it, both in terms of income and life-style. One saw no pictures of Tommy Lawton or Stanley Matthews posed by their Jaguars with a pin-stripe suit on, and rolled umbrella in hand. This tie between player and class is sensitively caught by Hopcraft's description of Matthews:

> . . . the sadly impassive face, with its high cheek-bones, pale lips and hooded eyes, had a lot of pain in it, the deep hurt that came from prolonged effort and the certainty of more blows. It was a worker's face, like a miner's, never really young, tight against a brutal world even in repose. We admired him deeply urging him on but afraid for him too as he trotted up yet again to show his shins to a big young full-back and invite the lad to make a name for himself by chopping the old Merlin down. The anxiety showed in Matthews too; again like the frail miner's fear of the job which must always be done, not joyfully but in deeper satisfaction, for self-respect. As Matthews said 'It's my living.'
>
> In communicating this frailty and this effort Matthews went to men's hearts, essentially to inconspicuous mild working men's. He was the opposite of glamorous: a non-drinker, non-smoker, careful with his money. . . . He was a representative of his age and of his class, brought up among thrift and the ever looming threat of dole and debt . . . He came from that England which had no reason to know that the twenties were Naughty and the thirties had Style.[6]

Finally we come to the place of victory in working-class life. In a life dominated by the controls, orders, and instructions of Hoggart's 'Them', leisure outlets are one possible way of finding opportunities of freedom of choice. Football, because of the strong local and class ties just described, has always been susceptible to at least a belief in control by the fans. Similarly in a society where opportunities for success are largely prescribed by one's class position, the enclosed world of football offers possibilities of victory dependent for once not on one's social status, but on individual and, perhaps more significantly, collective skill and physical prowess. The criteria of success in football are at odds with those which dominated the life experience of the working class. Thus Hopcraft, talking of football in the 1920s, says:

> To go to the match was to escape from the dark of despondency into the light of combat. Here, by association with the home team, positive identity could be claimed by muscle and in goals. To win was personal success, to lose another clout from life. Football was not so much an opiate of the people as a flag run up against the gaffer bolting his gates and the landlord armed with his bailiffs.[7]

To emphasize the symbolic importance of victory in football, let me cite the case of one of the folk-heroes of my own youth, Derek Dooley. As a schoolboy he played football for a secondary modern school, who, because of a lack of facilities of their own, were forced to use the playing fields of a nearby grammar school. The most crucial game of the year for Dooley's team was when they played the grammar school, and Dooley says of it:

> We wanted to beat them because we knew they were better. They had better facilities, better everything. Throughout my life it's been important to me to win.[8]

The phrase often used about more typically middle-class sports 'Well, it's only a game . . .' has no meaning for football fans, as Hopcraft concludes 'It has not only been a game for eighty years: not since the working classes saw in it an escape route from drudgery and claimed it as their own.'[9]

It is now necessary to make some concluding comments about the contents of this section. The factors discussed above are by no means an exhaustive list of the reasons for football's importance to the working class, they are those which seem to me to be most significant for an understanding of the present topic. Secondly, I feel it is important to point out how the expression of working-class values in football reflects the more general relation between those values and the dominant social order. Football is only partially expressive of working-class values; it is also penetrated by that dominant social order, to which the working class stands in a partly oppositional relationship. Critcher describes this ambivalence which permeates working class culture in this way: the world of football

> at once reflects and contradicts the real world, that it generally shows a remarkable capacity to resist incursion from the outside world, but that there are certain situations inside the game which parallel those outside it.[10]

For example:

> Support for the team might obliquely contradict the right of anyone to impose activities on working men, but the positions of power in a football club have always been held by those holding power outside the game.[11]*

Thirdly, the discussion of these values, although not conducted historically, has been

* Frank Parkin dealing more theoretically with these cultural ambiguities has described the relationship as that between 'a negotiated value system' of a subordinate class and the dominant value system.[12]

largely rooted in the past of the game. In the past twenty years both the game and the working-class life of which it is a part have undergone significant changes. It is the changes within football that I wish to look at next.

3. Changes in the game

The main post-war changes in football may be summarized as those of professionalization, internationalization, and commercialization. I will briefly expand on each of these changes and then attempt to account for them and finally set out their consequences for the game.

Firstly, professionalization refers to an increasingly calculatory awareness in the game of the technical requirements for success. This attitude is manifested in concerns for tactics, scientific methods of training and high demands of physical fitness. Similarly, rapidly rising transfer fees indicate the readiness of clubs to add to their assets in order to assure success or avoid failure.

Secondly internationalization describes the increasing introduction into the game of foreign competition as a supplement to the domestic game. This has taken the form of both cup competitions and friendly fixtures. There have also been a number of attempts to introduce more theatrical additions to the game, such as American style cheer-leaders, and the pre-match release of balloons. (Much of this section draws on the work of Ian Taylor, to which more detailed reference will be made later.)

Finally the commercialization of football is to be found both in the increasing financial concerns of the game, rising transfer fees, entrance prices and gate receipts. These concerns are also to be found in the widespread ground improvements made by football clubs. The improvements to facilities include the creation of more seated accomodation, improved provision of toilet and bar facilities, better refreshment facilities, including restaurants at some grounds, and the creation of social clubs for supporters.

All these changes are tied to the beliefs about the social structure of Britain in the 1950s. This was the age of Affluence, consensus politics, and the emergence of the Classless Society. Football clubs, anticipating the disappearance in this new social order of the traditional cloth-capped football fan, felt they would have to compete for audiences with the providers of alternative types of entertainment, the cinema and television especially. If the traditional fan no longer existed, then neither would traditional loyalties, and they would be competing for the favours of the new classless, rationally selective consumer. Consequently, the game had to be made as exciting and dramatic as possible to appeal to the uncommitted, the spectator had to be made comfortable, and his every whim catered for. Further, the uncommitted were unlikely to come each Saturday to watch an unsuccessful team, therefore greater attention had to be paid to avoiding failure.

Ian Taylor describes the combined effect of these changes as 'Bourgeoisification', which is the process

> which legitimizes previously working class activities for the middle class or more accurately, activities which were previously seen as legitimate only for the working class, such as watching doubtful films or congregating on the Kop.[13]

Taylor symbolizes this audience change by commenting that:

> Clearly to attend the Saturday game is no longer simply an activity of the Andy Capps: the Brian Glanvilles and the Professor Ayers of this world are unashamedly interested.[14]

If English society were becoming classless, then the direction of that move was towards a society of middle class life. The key sociological concept of the period was that of 'Embourgeoisement'. (For a discussion of this thesis, see volume 3 of the Cambridge 'Affluent Worker' studies.[15]) The process of bourgeoisification of football has had one consequence of great significance for the discussion of hooliganism; it has carried with it a changed conception of the football supporter. The 'genuine' supporter is no longer the traditional working man, living for the Saturday game, his own fortunes inextricably linked with those of *his* team, actively participating in the game; instead he is the rational, selective consumer of entertainment who objectively assesses the game from his seat in the stands. In fact, I have overdrawn this distinction. The clubs remain ambivalent about the traditional fan, but their view of him depends on his behaviour at the time. However the distinction I am making is perhaps best summarized as the 'Fan' as opposed to the 'Spectator'.† For me, this is the central point of Taylor's thesis, for it is this change both in those attending football matches, and the public redefinition of who the genuine supporter is, that underlie the definition of the problem of hooliganism. Even though a large number of what we may consider 'traditional' fans continue to attend the game, the changes in the game have taken place with the new Spectator in mind. For example, ground improvements typically involve the replacement of popular standing areas with seating, and the addition of new toilets, bars, restaurants, and social clubs are almost always connected with the seated parts of the ground.

The difference between the two ways of watching football can be illustrated by a passage in Hunter Davies' recent book *The Glory Game*. Davies travelled to Coventry with a trainload of young Spurs fans, and stood with them on the terraces. He says that because of all the singing, shouting, chanting and scarf waving they can't have time to observe the technicalities and niceties of the game:

> It would be too easy to say that they weren't interested in the game, only in the result. But by the very nature of standing physically and precipitously so close together and by making so much noise and raising their scarves and pushing each other, it is hard to believe that they can ever follow the details of the game. Coventry did win, by one goal to nil. Unlike Bill Nicholson, the fans didn't criticize the Spurs players. They didn't even admit that Cyril Knowles had had a bad game, which he had. Cyril was bloody unlucky they all said.[17]

What Davies has missed with his detached observer's viewpoint is the sheer *physical* experience of being part of a large crowd at a football match.

To conclude, changes within football, reflecting beliefs about changes in the wider society, have produced a redefinition of what behaviours are acceptable at football matches.

4. The hooligan: stereotype and reality

Hooliganism seems to have become publicly defined as a serious problem from the middle of the 1960s, and since then commentators have felt that it has escalated, and if left unchallenged, would take on frightening proportions:

† Similar distinctions have been made with respect to other working class leisure activities, for example, the pub, in terms of a distinction between member and customer.[16]

> Ten spectators and three policeman dead in scenes at a football match? It has not happened yet. But it might have happened when Liverpool players protested unjustifiably at a goal by Sheffield Wednesday at Hillsborough. . . . IT WILL happen, if something is not done to eliminate this major evil of modern football.

So Eric Cooper wrote in the Daily Express in 1969, and current comment continues this tradition of doom-laden forecast. Hooliganism, along with the attraction of televised football, is probably the most frequently cited reason, for the falling attendances at football games.

The stereotype of the hooligan is that of the ignorant working class 'yob' who attends football matches as an opportunity to get into a fight, and not from any 'genuine' interest in the game itself. His violence, like the destructive behaviour of the vandal (whom he so closely resembles in stereotype), is perpetually described as 'mindless, senseless, illogical and irrational'. These two themes permeate most of the journalistic comment about hooliganism. To illustrate the persistence of this stereotype, let me quote from a recent article by John Arlott, one of the game's more thoughtful commentators:

> It may be accepted from one who has now twice been forced to defend himself against their mindless violence, that a mob of drunken fifteen or sixteen year-olds is frighteningly illogical, unpredictable, and potentially violent. . . . They are not an age-group, but a social phenomenon. They have taken football merely as a convenient – indeed, inviting – environment. In other circumstances they might have chosen Rugby League, dirt-track racing, boxing or all-in wrestling as their stamping ground.[18]‡

Arlott's repetition of the 'not real supporters' theme comes a mere four years after the Government-appointed Harrington committee had come to this bewildered (and bewildering) conclusion about the sample of hooligans which they had investigated:

> We have been impressed by the amount of knowledge and memory for detail (about football) possessed by fans of limited intelligence and intellectual background.[19]

The stereotype, like most stereotypes, has its basis in reality (see Barthes' 'Mythologies'[20] for a discussion of the relationship between reality and distortion in myths); the hooligan is typically a working-class youth of limited educational background, doing an unskilled or semi-skilled job. He is, in fact, in a direct line of descent from the traditional fan discussed earlier, a part of what Taylor describes as football's 'subcultural rump'. But on this basis of fact are built the distortions of mindlessness and the lack of connection with football.

While the stereotype sees the typical hooligan actions as being those of fighting, throwing dangerous missiles, etc., the typical offences for which youths are actually ejected from football grounds or arrested are those of Pushing and Swearing (almost 70% at grounds in the Metropolitan Police district in 1969).[21] Compare these 'offences' with Hopcraft's description of the typical scene on the Kop:

> The steps are as greasy as a school playground lavatory in the rain. The air is rancid with beer and onions and belching and worse. The language is a gross purple of

‡ In an article subheaded 'John Arlott discusses the significance of hooliganism' the significance which Arlott attributes to it is as a causal factor in falling attendances.

> obscenity. When the crowd surges at a shot or a collision near a corner-flag a man or a boy, or sometimes even a girl, can be lifted off the ground in the crush as if by some massive, soft-sided crane grab and dangled about for minutes on end, perhaps never getting back to within four or five steps of the spot from which the monster made its bite.[22]

Making football respectable for the middle-class audience has involved the redefinition of previously common-place behaviours as no longer acceptable. This is not to say that there has been no increase in violent behaviour at football matches, but that that violence has been made to seem more extensive than its actual incidence would seem to warrant because it has included this previously normal behaviour now defined as deviant. (One suspects that if the police were ever to eject all those pushing and swearing at football matches, the terraces would be almost totally deserted.)

The changing view of the supporter accompanying the changes in the nature of the game has not been lost on the fans themselves. Taylor[23] quotes examples of clubs introducing additions to the pre-match entertainment being met with 'derision and scorn' from the popular terraces. Similarly that the ground improvements have occupied so much of the clubs' finances has prompted the typical reaction; 'What's the use of having a f. . .ing palace for a ground when we haven't got a team.' Among Sheffield Wednesday fans the money spent on the ground improvements, and those who spent it are still held responsible for the club's relegation to the second division three years ago. The fans themselves, as noted before, have benefited very little from the improvements. The fans are bewildered by the club's rejection of them; the Spurs fans interviewed by Davies commented:

> The club call us hooligans, but who'd cheer them on if we didn't come. You have to stand there and take it when Spurs are losing and the others are jeering at you. It's not easy. We support them everywhere, but we get no thanks.[24]

The young fan is caught in an impossible dilemma; his game, his team are being taken over for the bourgeoisie, it is being made respectable and he is disapproved. When he attempts to reaffirm his loyalty to the club through the limited channels open to him (the informal contacts which existed between club and fans have been replaced by more formal and institutionalized relations through such bodies as supporters clubs, as befits the emergence of football as part of the entertainments industry), he 'glorifies' their name by painting it on subway walls, defends them against the insults of opposing fans. However when he acts out his allegiance to the club in these ways they disown him further. The views of football held by the clubs and the fans have drifted apart, and the fans lack the articulacy to bridge the differences through formal channels. Taylor characterizes their response as one of 'desperation', which does not seem to overstate the difficulties of their position.

The fans are engaged in an attempt to perpetuate some of the traditional features of the game which are being lost in its colonization by the bourgeoisie. Thus, they keep alive the traditional rivalries which have become of less importance to the clubs, the territorial 'invasion' symbolized in the away match is now physically enacted in the 'taking' of the home fans' 'end', and also the newer rampage through the away town's city centre.

The nature of the away trip is itself significant in this respect. The all-male working man's day out has long been an occasion for letting 'hair down', and fitting considerable drinking into the day's activities (witness the recent Guinness advert featuring a typical excursion coach linked by a pipe to a large Guinness tanker). The days were also marked by a group assertion of the superiority of their local identity as opposed to the native culture (e.g., the taste of local beer, how good-looking the girls are, etc.), and finally by an air of expectation of excitement. (For an analysis of the relation of the seaside weekend and Mods and Rockers clashes, see Cohen's 'Folk devils and moral panics'.[25])

So far the discussion has largely followed the lines of Ian Taylor's argument; it is now time to take stock of its shortcomings. His papers have performed the vital function of linking the violence with foothall itself, but do not account for why sizeable numbers of teenagers should have this extremely close relationship with the game, especially in an era when the major 'youth cultural' developments have centred around newer developments such as pop. It is to this problem that I want to turn now, and look at the wider social changes which have both affected, and been reflected in, the changes in football. The consideration of these changes will be dealt with in relation to the rise of the Skinheads, for many the epitome of football hooligans.

5. 'Where did they come from?' – Social change and the skins

The skinheads first emerged in the east end of London in 1968, and by the end of that year were becoming visible in large numbers at football grounds around the country. They attracted plenty of public attention and comment as a consequence both of their involvement in football violence, and their highly distinctive 'uniform'. The typical skinhead 'gear' was: large working boots, often with steel toe-caps, denim jeans supported by braces, worn with a gap between the top of the boots and the bottom of the jeans, a coloured or patterned, shaped shirt with a button-down collar. Over this was worn a sleeveless pullover and for colder weather a 'Crombie' overcoat. The outfit was topped with very close cropped hair.

The skinheads emerged against a background of social changes which marked the breakdown of a number of strong patterns in the working-class way of life. Perhaps most important of these is the disruption of the traditional community. This took place in three main ways: firstly, large numbers of houses were sold to 'outsiders' – often to immigrants, the most visible of outsiders, but also to middle-class families in search of cheaper housing. Secondly slum areas in most major cities were redeveloped, usually as 'high-rise' schemes, again with outsiders moving into the new homes. Thirdly, families were moved out to the new estates being developed around the outer suburbs. The effect of these changes was felt by the youths as this statement from a member of the Collinwood gang (one of the first groups of skinheads) shows:

> The particular block of flats that I lived in in Stepney, Ring House, were a complete transfusion of people from a street called Twoin Court. So what you had was the same quality of life in Ring House as you 'ad in Twoin Court, except that now people live side by side and over and under each other. Everyone knew everyone else intimately. Flats are not like that now, flats are not what I remember Ring House being, 'cause they draw people from all over. They don't take a street full of people, who have sort of seen each other and 'elped each other and fought each other, and sort of lived together. They don't take that lot and say bang you lot are gonno live in 'ere. That particular good thing is missed in blocks of flats, because they 'ave taken a person from 'Ackney and another one from Woolwich and so on.[26]

The other consequence of this redevelopment has been the disappearance of communal meeting places. Phil Cohen comments that: 'The first effect of the high density, high rise schemes was to destroy the function of the street, the local pub, the corner shop, as articulations of communal space.'[27] (Cohen's article provides a more extended treatment of the dislocation which accompanied the redevelopment.)

The removal of long-standing meeting places meant that those which remained took on extra significance. One of those which remained was the football ground.

It is noticeable that areas where skinhead gangs became most prominent were typically either new council housing estates or old estates being either redeveloped or experiencing an influx of outsiders. For example, in London they were to be found in the East End, and round the new outer ring estates; in Birmingham the main areas were Northfield, Smethwick, Quinton and Ladywood.[28]

The traditional leisure activities of the working class were also undergoing significant changes. Football has already been discussed; both the pub and the working men's club were becoming more self-conscious providers of entertainment. The modernization of the pub has not been restricted to town centre sites but local pubs have also changed beyond recognition. The clubs have increasingly concerned themselves with supplying professional entertainers for their customers, culminating, one supposes, in the Batley Variety club.

Leisure activities for the young have become increasingly concentrated on town centre facilities, bars, discotheques, night-clubs and cinemas, especially since the closure of large numbers of local cinemas throughout the country. This has further speeded that weakening of local ties previously mentioned. However the point here is not that there are now universally available cultural activities, the television for instance, but rather what patterns of usage there are, and more importantly, what different meanings the activities have for those who participate in them. As the Hunter Davies example cited earlier indicates, the activity may have widely differing meanings for different groups of watchers.

We noted earlier the 1950s beliefs in the arrival of the open, classless and affluent society. The 1960s by contrast, were noticeable for the rediscovery of both poverty and class-conflict. The experience of the lower working-class youths who formed the core of the skinheads hardly fitted the myths of the open society. In the school, the supposed step ladder to the golden age, opportunity has remained structured on largely class-based grounds. Moreover the fact that job selection and promotion have become increasingly based on formal educational qualifications means that a dead-end job or sequence of dead-end jobs follow even more certainly than before on poor school performance. Even the illusion of someday working one's way up through the firm is no longer possible. School remains an alien place to large numbers of working-class young, where Hoggart's 'Them' continue to dictate the pattern of life:

> It (school) is a place where *they* make you go and where *they* tell you to do things, and where they try to make your life unpleasant if you don't do them or don't do them right.[29]

The literature of the sociology of education contains a number of examples of subcultural alienation from the success values of the school which emphasize academic performance.[30] The Collinwood referred to successful kids as 'dummoes', and described the differences between their lives in this way:

> Say they give us homework or say memorize this. So their parents (i.e., the successful

> kids'), as they say when they come to school meetings, 'What I lock 'im up in 'is bedroom and make 'im do 'is 'omework. I let 'im out once a week to watch Spurs.' And that was that, their parents made them do it, made them do it, forced them though some must have had the willpower themselves. Where me, I wouldn't think 'cor, I've got 'istory tomorrow'. I'd be out on the streets. I didn't 'ave no interest. I couldn't be bothered devoting all my life to learning. I wanted to do other things.[31]

It is of course lower working-class youth who encounter the educational-employment complex in its most extreme form. Most of the kids in the Collinwood gang expressed little interest in getting a job with any inherent satisfactions (described in the literature of occupational sociology as 'having realistic expectations'), and many found little assistance in finding a job. Typical comments about the role of the Youth Employment service at this period were:

> The Youth Employment and the Labour, they're just interested, when you come in, in getting rid of you as quick as they can . . . If you're thick they don't wanna know you but if you've got a bit of education, and you go in they can't do enough for you . . . I went up there and they just seemed to pawn me off, they didn't wanna know.[32]

Taken together these experiences mark what Critcher describes as a 'cultural crisis' in the working class, the traditional patterns of working-class life which once provided a secure identity for members of the class have collapsed in the face of the challenge from the new mass entertainments, while for many the typical experiences of working-class life, notably those of education and employment, show no signs of having disappeared.

Since the advent of rock'n'roll and the Teds in the early 1950s young people have attempted to resolve this cultural crisis and the lack of identity which it produces by creating their own cultures, more consonant with their own needs and experiences.§ In the middle 1960s the two mainstream developments of youth culture were the continuation of the 'Mod era', and the growth of the British Underground. Neither of these two styles fitted the experiences of the youths who were to become the skinheads. The Mod style was taken up by large numbers of working-class boys (the typical offender arrested at Margate in 1964 was a semi-skilled manual worker),[33] but those at the heart of the Mod scene, the trend setters were more typically in lower white collar jobs, clerks, office boys and shop assistants; see, for example, Tom Wolfe's description of the clientele of 'Tiles' in 'The Noonday Underground'.[34] More importantly the mod style was that of the affluent consumer; their ethic was that of conspicuous consumption, styles were created, taken up and dropped with amazing rapidity. By the end of the 1960s Mod had become a highly organized commercial enterprise and had become institutionalized. As its styles were increasingly taken over by executives and their wives the mods themselves were driven to wilder flights of fancy to maintain their 'differentness'. The movement's musicians, once the kids' representatives, had become institutionalized 'superstars' (see the discussions by Herman and Fowler[35]). Now, established figures in the world of Rock, they became more concerned with their own problems and their music than with their audience. This has not been lost on the stars themselves; in a recent interview Roger Daltrey of The Who, perhaps *the* mod group, said

§ The reaction of older working-class people to these changes has been mixed; some look nostalgically back to the old days, while others go through the 'Affluent Worker' syndrome of an introspective turn into the family.

that the group had lost 'that working class feeling' on their last L.P. through being too concerned with musical technicalities. By the time the skinheads arrived on the scene the real impetus of the Mods had gone and only the commercial remained. In fact, the skinheads came to define themselves against the Mod image, just as the Mods had defined themselves against the Rockers. This opposition of styles is illustrated in this quotation from Phil Cohen:

> . . . the original mod life style could be interpreted as an attempt to realise, but in an imaginary relation, the conditions of existence of the socially mobile white collar worker. While their argot and ritual forms stressed many of the traditional values of their parent culture, their dress and music reflected the hedonistic image of the affluent consumer . . . [the skinheads'] life style in fact represents a systematic inversion of the mods – whereas the mods explored the upwardly mobile option, the skinheads explored the lumpen.[36]

The skinheads' creation of a style involved a reassertion of the old traditions, a defence of that culture which seemed threatened with contamination by middle-class styles and values. Thus, the skinhead uniform is a highly stylized version of 'working clothes', the inverse of the flash of the Mod styles. Indeed, the whole skinhead style may be seen as a *stylized* re-creation of an *image* of the working class. Everything, the clothes, the haircut, the attitudes and the violence are all overdrawn, as if in a self caricature.

What has been said of the opposition between the Mod and skinhead styles applies even more forcefully to the relation between the skinheads and the Underground. The hippie movement was seen as a middle-class indulgence, being both individualist and intellectualist (especially its music – Pete Fowler said of the skinheads[37] 'nothing is more loathsome to them than the junk of progressive rock'). Against the hippies was mobilized the tradition of working-class puritanism: the hippies were dirty and work shy.

So, because the existing youth cultural options did not fit with their experience of the world, the skinheads created their own, and the inevitable setting for the re-enactment of traditional working-class values was the traditional Saturday meeting place of the class, the football ground. Football hooliganism must therefore be seen not only as an attempt to defend football for the class, but as a microcosmic reflection of an attempt to defend the culture against the encroachment of the bourgeoisie. Their violence, racialism, puritanism, and localism (the reflection of the community in the group, who are bound to stand by each other when trouble threatens) are all part of this re-creation of a way of life.

However, the wider society, just like the football clubs, found this active return to the past unacceptable. Institutionalized nostalgia was all right, *Coronation Street* and *Family at War*, for example, but the actual recreation of the past in the present was not. The skinheads, like the Mods and rockers before them, were roughly treated by the law, e.g. skinheads approaching football matches would have their boots impounded and the belts removed from their trousers. Precautions to avert violence, certainly, but also quite clear attempts at degradation.

To recap more theoretically, this section has been an attempt to illustrate how general social processes, in this case, the 'eclipse of community', greater affluence coupled with persistent, class-structured inequalities can be held responsible for the generation of such different responses as the Mods and the skinheads from within one class. Partly the answer is to be found in the fact that there exists no monolithic working-class consciousness, that the major changes are differently experienced by different groups within the class. Also it is to be found in the fact that the possibilities open to such groups at different moments in history differ. Thus, the Mods emerged at a period in English life when the themes of classlessness and affluence were of considerable significance, whereas the picture had changed significantly by the end of the 1960s and the Mod phenomenon was itself part of the social background in which the skinheads developed.

Conclusion: deviancy amplification or 'who's interested in football?'

The skinheads, like most other youth cultural phenomena, were originally a self-generated movement. The themes of the skinhead movement spread quickly to most major towns in the country through two main channels of cultural diffusion. It spread partly through face to face interaction among the fans at football matches and partly through the extensive attention which the phenomenon received in the press, for example, by the summer of 1969 both the *Sunday Times* and the *Observer* had carried articles on the skinheads, and naturally the warnings of magistrates and police about the dangers of this new form of 'gang warfare' had received wide publicity.

It is possible to identify a number of factors contributing to the 'rising tide of violence' at our football grounds. Initially, the reaction of the clubs was to increase the numbers of police on duty at football matches; this higher rate of organizational activity, as Kitsuse and Cicourel have suggested about official statistics generally, is reflected in higher rates of arrests and ejections from matches. That is to say, there is built into the situation both a higher expectation of the possibility of 'trouble' and a higher organizational capacity to respond to it when it takes place.

The presence of large numbers of police itself heightens the likelihood of action. Brian Jackson says this of the Saturday night police riots in Huddersfield:

> The middle class expects help from the police, the working class experts trouble. When a policeman appears on the steps of the Reform Club it is hardly of any consequence to the members; but when he appears outside a Huddersfield working men's club the air is tense with protective hostility. . . . Police are executants of a law that still remains weighted in favour of the middle classes. Their uniform (how the rioters go for these helmets!) may, to many middle class eyes, be the mark of a servant, as with a hotel commissionaire or a bus conductor. To the working class it announces mastery and threat.[38]

Action taken by, or even inaction on the part of, large numbers of policemen is likely to be greeted with either derision, at the least, or outright hostility from the terraces at a football ground.

We must also recognize that the creation of a popular stereotype of the football hooligan may have the unintended consequence of making the original phenomenon become more like the stereotype. These sorts of changes have already been described in the cases of the Teds and of drugtakers.[39] They occur in two ways: either the original participants may come to identify themselves more closely with the behaviour described in the stereotype (a classic case of the sociological notion of conformity to role expectations), or the stereotype may attract new participants who feel that the behaviours and characters described fit their own experience. That is, the stereotype of the football match as a place where people go to find a fight may attract those who are looking for just such a setting in which to be able to build up a 'rep' or reputation.

Thus the phenomenon tends to become more like the public definition of it, a self fulfilling prophecy takes place through the forcefulness of that public definition. There are indeed now those who attend football matches not out of interest in the football but for the opportunity of fighting, though one suspects these numbers are small (the expense of travelling to away games makes such fights an expensive proposition, when, as one Spurs fan said 'I could get a fight much easier at the pub down the road'), and they are certainly looked on disapprovingly by the core of the skins, who see them (in stereotypical terms) as being 'mad', 'unreliable' or out to prove something.

Notes

1 P. Young 'A history of English football', Stanley Paul 1967; C. Critcher 'Football as popular culture – an outline', unpublished, Centre for Contemporary Cultural Studies.
2 Elias and Dunning: 'The quest for excitement in unexciting societies', paper given at the annual conference of the B.S.A., 1967.
3 A. Hopcraft *The football man*. Penguin 1971, pp. 152–3.
4 Hopcraft, p. 156.
5 Critcher, p. 45.
6 Hopcraft, p. 30.
7 Hopcraft, p. 24.
8 quoted by Hopcraft, p. 53.
9 Hopcraft, p. 12.
10 Critcher, p. 44.
11 Critcher, p. 45.
12 F. Parkin *Class inequality and political order.* Paladin 1972, chapter 3.
13 I. Taylor ' "Football mad": a speculative sociology of soccer hooliganism' in E. Dunning (ed.) 'The sociology of sport.' Cass 1971.
14 Taylor, p. 34.
15 J. Goldthorpe et al. *The affluent worker in the class structure.* Cambridge U.P. 1969
16 Young, Sieveking and Jackman 'The pub as a leisure context.' Unpublished. See also Critcher, final section.
17 H. Davies *The glory game.* Weidenfeld and Nicolson 1972.
18 J. Arlott 'Like dogs through Arab villages.' *Guardian* 5 January 1973.
19 J. A. Harrington et al. 'Soccer hooliganism: a preliminary report to Mr. Dennis Howell, Minister of sport.' J. Wright and Sons, Bristol 1968, p. 16.
20 R. Barthes *Mythologies.* Cape 1972.
21 Dr. M.W. Jones 'Soccer hooliganism in the Metropolitan district.' Metropolitan Police management services department, report no. 8/69.
22 Hopcraft, p. 162.
23 Taylor, p. 365.
24 Davies, p. 101.
25 S. Cohen *Folk devils and moral panics.* Macgibbon and Kee 1972.
26 S. Daniel, P. Doyle and P. McGuire *The Paint House: words from an east end gang.* Penguin 1972, p. 19.
27 P. Cohen 'Subcultural conflict and working class community.' Working papers in cultural studies, vol. 2.
28 D. White 'Brum's mobs.' *New Society* 21 October 1971.
29 J. Holt *How children fail.* Pitman 1964, p. 24, quoted in *The Paint House*, p. 41
30 For example, D. Hargreaves *Social relations in a secondary school.* Routledge Kegan Paul 1967, C. Lacey *Hightown grammar.* Manchester U.P. 1970.
31 *The Paint House.* p. 44.
32 *The Paint House.* p. 61.
33 Barker and Little 'The Margate offenders: a survey.' *New Society* 30 July 1964.
34 T. Wolfe 'The noonday underground.' in *The pump-house gang.* Bantam 1969.

35 G. Herman 'The Who.' Studio Vista 1971; P. Fowler 'Skins rule.' in C. Gillett *Rock File.* New English Library 1972.
36 P. Cohen, p. 24.
37 Fowler, p. 20.
38 B. Jackson *Working class community.* Penguin 1972, p. 124.
39 P. Rock and S. Cohen 'The Teddy Boy.' in V. Bogdanor and R. Skidelsky *The age of affluence.* Macmillan, 1970; J. Young *The drugtakers.* Macgibbon and Kee, 1971.

30 Working class images of society and community studies

Eve Brook, Dan Finn

One of the defining characteristics of sociology, and its sub-disciplines, has been its overwhelming concern with questions of social class, particularly in relation to the working class. Its major encounter with the located experiences of working-class people has been conducted through the medium of community studies and in this article we want to evaluate the impact and development of these studies as a genre. This evaluation is particularly important because the findings of this body of work have provided material, both directly and indirectly, which has been used in the analysis of class imagery and class-based meaning systems. The focus of this article then, is on the way in which working-class imagery has been typified by certain sociologists, and the arguments they have advanced to justify these typifications.

We would argue that the introduction of the term 'ideology' into a discussion of working-class imagery is essential. The main problem seems to be arriving at an operationalised definition of what ideology actually is. For many Marxists it is seen as a systematised form of false consciousness (yet another elastic concept), and here it would be the ideas of the ruling class in their best clothes – formalised theoretical constructions epitomised, for example, in religion. On the other hand, ideologies are seen to arise from the working class itself – trade unionism as a purely defensive force is an instance.

Both of these examples are of national, and even international significance, and perhaps for this reason are often seen as existing 'up there', as ahistorical and controlling forces. Similarly, this is why they are often seen abstractly, as 'general value systems', imposing constraints on human conduct. However, we cannot accept any definition of ideology as existing outside material life. This means that ideologies are not only expressed and based in material life, but that they are also under constant pressure to change, as the conditions of material life change. It follows then, that the first part of our definition would be that it is material life which determines ideology.

The next question, inevitably, is how? We would not disagree that certain aspects of working-class ideology are representations of the interests of the ruling class, though we would take issue with any suggestion that this is done conspiratorily. But even here, the ideas of the ruling class are endorsed, modified, or rejected according to certain material conditions.

These material conditions, of course, exist at the level of everyday class experiences and class practices. These experiences and practices differ, not only between classes, but also within them – generating occupational or local class fractions. Thus, it is not only ruling-class ideas that are put to the test in working-class experience, but just as importantly, we would suggest, class practice generates its own kind of consciousness and culture. Thus, the contradictory nature of working-class consciousness reflects the difference between the real experience of capitalist production and the phenomenal forms of the market, reflected in the superstructure. The collective, lived experience of capitalist production gives alternative sets of practices and organisations embodied in working-class culture. The consciousness generated is ideologically 'commonsense': learning through experience what can and cannot be done in *given* conditions. This is ideological, therefore, because the conditions are *given*, they are not questioned – only the best way of manipulating them to advantage is considered.

Here locality and workplace become extremely important. The material base of sectionalism resides in a labour market differentiated by industry, by variations among firms within industries, and by the division of labour within particular workplaces. While in general terms geographically distinct groups of workers have similar sorts of problems, the problems of any specific group are particular and unique. They are bound in time, revolve around particular people, and are confined to a particular workplace or section within it.

Thus, TV assembly workers do not see their ultimate dependence on the coal miner, and there is no 'commonsense' reason why they should. In these situations class activity is industry- and locality-based. Loyalties are formed across a region, a factory or an occupation, *and in some circumstances these loyalties can become so exclusive as to cover up the ultimate reality of being working class.* The best thing that can happen here is indifference to the struggles of other workers. The worst is outright conflict between sections of the working class, for example, the recent struggle between dockers and transport workers, carefully orchestrated by industrial interests, but displaying that inability to transcend sectional interests. Besides the 'particular' ideologies existing on an occupational basis, they can also exist where the occupation is identical, but the locality is different. Cousins and Brown, in a paper on shipbuilding workers, give an example:

> Favouritism based on localism and residence is a factor in employment in an industry and area where unemployment is a major problem. The 'market' or daily callstand encourage localism. A chargehand from the former Blyth shipyard a little farther up the coast and now closed told us 'with us it was always keep the Tynies out'.
>
> (1975 p. 58)

The material conditions underlying this sectionalism are not hard to spot – long-term unemployment in a depressed industry. But a parochial ideology is the mode of responding to it – attacks are directed at other workers, rather than the owners.

It is the relationship between these local, fractional ideologies and the theoretically developed ideologies generated by national institutions, which has been at the heart of sociology's attempt to understand working-class images of society. In this paper, it is the understanding of these 'images' developed by two central theorists that we wish to consider. Both address themselves to the question of how diverse 'images' are created/determined within those sections of the working class characterised, on the one hand, as privatised and traditional, and on the other hand, as accommodative. They are Lockwood (1975) stressing the primacy of immediate work and community relationships, and Parkin (1971) stressing the ideological dominance of national meaning-systems.

Lockwood's typology distinguishes three different working-class images of society, spontaneously generated through work experience and the values held by the local community. Firstly the traditional proletarian, typified by miners, dockers and shipyard workers. Secondly, the traditional deferentialist, whose defining characteristic is that he is likely to work in rural, or craft-based industry, and have face-to-face relationships with a paternalistic employer. Thirdly, the privatised worker who is 'instrumental' in his attitude to work and 'privatised' in his home life.

Before going on to evaluate the theoretical adequacy of these typifications, we want to pursue a line of investigation suggested by Lockwood, in that it should be possible to examine these types and 'flesh them out' or reject them in terms of the data from community studies. However, as we hope to demonstrate, it is not quite so simple, and to outline our reservations it is necessary to say something about the historical, ideological and methodological development of community studies as a genre – particularly in its social democratic forms. The outline and critique of community studies is lengthy, but we feel this is justified because of its position as the major accredited source of 'qualitative' accounts of working-class culture.

Post-war community studies

Post-war community studies can be seen as a reaction against certain developments in sociology, coupled with apprehensions about the direction of social democracy. As with many other developments in the sociology of the 1950s, they can be seen against the background of the proliferation of 'post-capitalist society' and 'embourgeoisement' theories, which, however unwittingly, added a new dimension to the discussion of class. To summarise a familiar argument, during the 1950s it was commonly asserted that capitalism as such had ceased to exist and had been superseded by 'post-industrial' society. All the theorists with something in common with this thesis held that the old sources of class conflict were being progressively eliminated, or rendered irrelevant, and that Western society was being recast in a middle-class style.

These interpretations rested on three basic assumptions. Firstly, that the liberal and social democracies were pluralistic, power being held by a number of social groups. Secondly, that the substantive inequalities of early capitalism were diminishing and losing their former significance: differentials in income were being eroded and other inequalities were being dealt with by an economy stabilised through the application of Keynesian economic policies; due to nationalisation there was now a mixed economy; and most importantly, the post-1945 implementation of the 1942 Beveridge Report had, through the Welfare State, bridged any remaining inequalities – a process expressed in Britain through social security, council housing, the National Health Service, and State-funded secondary education. Thirdly, for the above and other reasons, radical dissent had been progressively eliminated or weakened as new patterns of living and aspirations cut across older class-bound horizons: amongst manual workers a faith in collective action was being replaced by reliance on individual achievement; the old loyalties of class were being replaced with preoccupations of status – the ethos of the middle class.

The major ideological impact of these developments was the widely held and potent belief that class was 'withering away' or had disappeared. This utopianism was not just complacency but a diagnosis of something real and important in the 1950s: working-class apathy and lack of enthusiasm for collective ends. In fact, the sheer number of writers who espoused the thesis was some sort of evidence that the political apathy of the time was not an illusion – a fact not always recognised by some of its opponents.

The fallacies underlying these conceptions went unchallenged, at least ideologically, until the development of the 'New Left' – arising from disillusionment both with the effectiveness of Labour's social reforms and with the sterility of organised left-wing thought. The thrust of this changing ideological stance was characterised in certain key books – Hoggart's *Uses of Literacy* (1957), Williams' *Culture and Society* (1958). Despite the difference of scope, subject and emphasis, these works stood in one way or another for a favourable evaluation of the meanings of working-class culture. As Hoggart makes clear:

> I think such an impression is wrong if it leads us to construct an image of working class people only from adding together the variety of statistics given in some of these sociological works . . . clearly we have to try to see beyond the habits to what the habits stand for, to see through the statements to see what the statements mean . . ., to detect the differing pressures of emotion behind idiomatic phrases and ritualistic observances.
>
> (1957 p. 17)

In the New Left's interpretation of working-class culture, the idea of 'community' plays a pivotal role. 'Community' is important because it allows the Culture/Society question to be thought through in a number of dimensions. Twenty years on, it is difficult to appreciate the radical implications of this – but what more than anything else distinguished these literary/cultural studies at this time was their attention to 'meaning': how separate texts/rituals/institutions interrelated in a 'whole way of life'. The idea of community necessarily pre-supposed an intellectual commitment to go beyond immediate empiricism, the 'obvious', the isolated text, to interpret cultural phenomena in terms of structural relationships or parts of a whole.

The critical developments of Williams and Hoggart were closely linked with a movement in social administration, in which Titmuss (1958) was the leading figure, which stressed the gaps and inadequacies in welfare services, the extent to which working-class material standards remained below those of the middle class, and argued that political policy rather than individual competence was responsible for these differences.

The theme linking the two areas was the realisation that working-class people had characteristics that were not explicable simply in terms of their financial position; that proposals for change needed to be grounded in a more complex theoretical understanding of working-class life. It is within this context that we find the development of those community studies with which we are centrally concerned (see Appendix). These publications, such as the work of the Institute of Community Studies, were conducted at a time when more than superficial social research was rare, and when sociology as an academic subject had gained footholds in only a few universities.

These community studies in fact very largely ignored the assumptions of the 'post-capitalist' society/'embourgeoisement' thesis; or at most they conceded that higher wages had meant a rise in the standard of living of the working class, but asserted that this had made no real difference to working-class culture. Importantly, then, class was understood primarily as a cultural formation, and not as a phenomenon generated by production. Community studies set out to 'rediscover' class, and in this sense 'community' carried connotations which can only be described as *political.* There was a kind of smuggling process, whereby the idea of 'community' was identified with the central socialist/social democratic preoccupation with class cultures. Not accidentally, we might add, for it was based in part on real anxieties about Labour's electoral base. It is noteworthy in this context that many of the studies researched in the late 1950s had authors with some formal connection with the Labour Party (e.g. Jackson [1968], Young and Wilmott [1962], Dennis, Henriques and Slaughter [1969], Townsend [1957]). The notion of 'community' with its overtones of tradition and oppositional culture had an obvious attraction.

So, whilst we can see that the development of community studies was, in part, a reaction to the more vulgar embourgeoisement thesis and a reflection of the concern generated by the apparent erosion of Labour's electoral base, it is also clear that many of the community studies were specifically aimed at the practice of social policy, or directed towards an illumination of those consensually defined 'social problems'. Thus, for Young and Willmott:

> The assumption was that the policy-makers were . . . insufficiently aware of the needs and views of the working class people who form the bulk of the users of the social services, and we hoped that social research might help to provide a more realistic basis for policy.
>
> (1961 p. 2)

Whereas, with Jackson: 'The communal urge could then have been harnessed for a common good'. He took '. . . the illustration of productivity to show the practical help that can flow from an understanding of the otherness of working class life' (1969 p. 156).

It is important at this point to step back and attempt to understand the position that sociology occupies within bourgeois ideology, and to explain the phenomenal growth of sociology, both as an academic discipline and an applied science, during the late 1950s and 1960s. Sociology, as Gouldner (1971) attempts to point out, arises and assumes that 'social problems' cannot be solved within the framework of bourgeois economics:

> Sociology focuses upon the non-economic sources of social order. Academic sociology polemically denies that economic change is a sufficient or necessary condition for maintaining or increasing social order.
>
> (1971 p. 4)

That is to say, when the social character of capitalist production has become apparent in the oppositional life-style and activities of the chief force of production, the working class, sociology arises as a theory of how to respond to this opposition without abolishing the capitalist mode of production.

Sociology recognises the social character of production – but denies that it has to do with production, which is, after all, the concern of economics. 'Social problems', that is, those activities or phenomena which impinge on the interests of capital, are seen to be the result of 'social' life – not economic contradictions. It is no longer the individual 'problem family' that is at fault, it is a lot of 'problem families' living in a 'problem area'. Thus, for example, in regard to education, we can now see that it is the community which largely determines educational success:

> What is unchallenged, however, is that the concept of community provides us with an illuminating guide to the expectations and requirements of the population of the school catchment areas, as well as the prevailing factors in the behaviour of its pupils and teachers.
>
> (Eggleston 1967 p. 36)

This ideological role is clearly exemplified in the notion of a 'culture of poverty'. This argues that the poor constitute a distinctive culture or community within society; that the experiences, attitudes and values generated in poor communities are passed on from one generation to the next in a never-ending cycle. Thus, this culture is able:

> . . . to perpetuate itself from generation to generation because of its effect on the children. By the time slum children are aged six to seven they have usually absorbed the

> basic attitudes and values of their subculture, and are not psychologically geared to take full advantage of changing conditions, or increased opportunities which may occur in their life-time.
>
> (Lewis 1968 p. 60)

So it is not unskilled, meaningless, irregular employment, or bad housing, or an irrelevant education that is at fault – its their basic attitudes that are wrong.

Thus, within the total context of bourgeois ideology, sociology provides important methodological and empirical data for the social-policy makers. Because it has no understanding of contradications within a total structure it is conceptually limited to understanding class conflict in terms of either cultural or individual deprivation, and its policy formulations boil down to 'tinkering with the machine' – never mind the engine. At one and the same time, sociology is both reformist and repressive. By providing palliatives to real material problems, conceived of in terms of 'social problems', it also, by definition, secures means of social control.

This inability to understand society as a total structure has meant that sociology in general, and community studies in particular, have automatically limited themselves to the appearance of things, never trying to analyse the relationships latent in the things themselves. It is in this area, and for this reason, that community studies have drawn on functionalism, particularly as manifested in the work of social anthropologists. A practice, custom or belief is interpreted in terms of its present and ongoing functions in the surrounding society. But whereas anthropologists within small-scale societies are able to study social life at first hand, sociologists have adopted the same model as if their 'communities' were excused participation in national structures of class or politics.

In practice this approach leads to a concentration on 'normative' facts (to treat social facts as things), so that social structure refers to relations between actual, empirically given social phenomena. These relationships are either given in the facts as directly observed, or arrived at by simple abstraction from the facts. Thus, social structure when used in functional analysis refers to no more than the actual organisation of a given social system.

From within this perspective social behaviour is seen as determined by 'norms', enforced by implicit or explicit sanctions. These structure, in a regular and predictable fashion, the social life and relationships of individuals. Thus, to Young and Willmott, the mother/daughter relationship is one where: 'Though they both derive benefit from the relationship, it is far more than a mere arrangement for mutual convenience. The attachment between them is supported by a powerful moral code' (1962 p. 193).

Thus, many community studies erect a social reality which is taken as given and giving of itself in immediate appearance. We are presented with a single-levelled social totality consisting of attitudes, behaviour, activities and institutions and the relationships between these things. There is little awareness of *process*, or dynamic relations between different forces and groupings; there is no sense of *levels* within the social whole, and in particular no notion of the relations and mediations between the subjective level of experience, ideology and determining material conditions. In general, people are seen as passive, with things happening to them, rather than as showing some attempt to create their lives: there is no dialectic between objective and subjective factors.

The ideological construction of a world which is self-evident, single-layered and functionally interrelated, in which ideas are just there as they have always been, delivers a specific kind of methodological unconsciousness. Since *one* reality is there for the seeing, there is no more than one way in which to see it – why therefore give the groundings or detail of your observations? It is not a reflexive world so why should your methodology be reflexive? The techniques are 'naturalist', direct and unproblematic and usually unrecorded.

With no clear statement of the paradigms in this work; without any information about research techniques, or how respondents see investigators; with no information independently presented both concerning the relationship of the researched to the researcher, and concerning the raw data untreated by theories of the writers – it is impossible for us to *triangulate*, to read back along the lines of the prior theoretic predisposition, to deconstruct and reconstruct, to come to our own principled interpretation of the evidence.

Community studies form the single most massive encounter with the located experience of working-class people, and are the major accredited source of 'qualitative' accounts of working-class culture. As such, they should be demystified and also salvaged as sources for our own, hopefully more reflexive, research procedures. As it is, 'reading back' from community studies is an uncertain exercise. We are dealing with a peculiarly untheorised, naturalised, impacted problematic which methodologically conceals its own tracks.

Thus, if we take it as axiomatic that people are not simply on the 'receiving end' of their objective class position, then it is apparent that their actions are partly projected in terms of creative expectations and definitions. Unfortunately, as we have shown, most of the examination of this semi-autonomous layer of working-class experience has been carried out via the medium of community studies, and it is with this imperfect material that the argument about typifications of working-class imagery and the changes occuring within it have been carried out.

Lockwood: community and the traditional proletarian

In returning to Lockwood's typology we find that he argues that there are two crucial variables in the formation of working-class images of society – work and the local community. He then draws a distinction between two basic models of class imagery: a model based on power, conflict and a dichotomy between classes; and a model based on prestige, status and hierarchy. Lockwood argues that it is the proletarian traditionalist who is likely to endorse a dichotomous model, and thereby he implies that it is this type of worker who is the most class conscious. Consequently, it is on this aspect of Lockwood's analysis that we shall be concentrating in this section.

The proletarian traditionalist is the archetypal subject of community studies, and he is certainly the most colourful, romantic and inaccessible representative of his class. He is inevitably male (?) and usually works in a situation of physical discomfort and danger. Nevertheless, he retains a high degree of job involvement and a strong attachment to his primary work-group. His occupational culture spills over into his leisure, facilitated by the fact that most of this kind of work requires an 'occupational community'.

The classic community study in this field is undoubtedly *Coal is Our Life* (1956). This study has shaped a whole generation of academics' perceptions of the miner. The data for this study was collected in the 1950s and it is avowedly a community study influenced by anthropology. The note of caution this strikes in us seems to be shared by a least one of the authors: Henriques in particular is very sensitive to the implications of his approach and method. In the introduction to the second edition he writes: 'By its focus upon the "community framework" as such, this technique will tend to abstract from the societal framework at every level of social life' (1969 p. 7). His example is that whereas relationships between husband and wife and the nature of leisure activity is:

> Viewed primarily from the standpoint of grasping their *interrelationships* with the forms of activity and social relations *imposed* by the coal mining work upon which the community is based, this emphasis will tend to obscure the fact that each of these particular sets of relationships is extended beyond the community, in both space and time. By itself the community study technique provides no way of measuring the significance of its findings against 'external' factors.
>
> (1969 p. 7)

Ashton miners certainly display a dichotomous class imagery; but whether this conforms to Lockwood's model or not will be discussed subsequently. The question of whether this is spontaneously generated through the social relationships of work is highly debatable. The above extract suggests that Henriques would recognise that miners could be drawing on extra-local factors for their class imagery.

The central features of the community life described by Dennis *et al.* are the recurring conflict and attitudes of the miners to their cultural poverty and isolation, and the oppression of their wives. These are seen as the outgrowth of actual economic relationships and working conditions. From the peculiar class situation and from the work situation (to use Lockwood's terms) of the miner, much else follows. There is certainly a logical connection between the common work experience of the miner and a dichotomous social imagery, but logic never made a fact. One objection is the totally different life experience of women in mining areas. Whilst men have been thrown together by coal, it has exerted the opposite or 'centifrugal' influence on women. There is no paid work for them unless they go outside the area. Nor can they identify very easily through the family: marriage and the family is a battle arena, and seems completely devoid of affection. Men and women are as effectively separated as Eskimos and Africans. In fact, the experience of the sexes is so totally different that one has to make the effort to remember that they live *together* in the same town. Since Lockwood is contending that the work and community experience is crucial in the formation of perceptions of class, it is reasonable to expect that the men's and women's images would be different.

However, voting returns from mining areas (admittedly very partial evidence) tend to show that the women vote the same way as the men, at least partly suggesting they share the same type of class imagery. This interpretation would tend to suggest that far from this imagery being spontaneously generated, people are recognising some kind of national ideology and their acceptance or rejection of it is mediated through their local experience and work.

According to Lockwood, however, the old working-class traditions of community and collective culture are undergoing a major change. The modern tendency is to break up traditional working-class communities – whether 'occupational' or not – and to throw people into low-cost private or council housing estates – the living conditions of the 'privatised worker'. This change, he argues, has been an evolution towards a new 'narrower' kind of collectivism – no longer 'instinctual', based on the kinship ties so beloved of social anthropologists, but 'instrumental', based on a rational calculation of self-interest. But despite its Durkheimian connotations, we see no reason why the second form should be judged as 'narrower' than the first. On the contrary, a 'solidarity' based on kinship, community and locality is itself a 'narrow' form of social consciousness, because of its exclusiveness.

So there are several problems with Lockwood's formulation of the traditional worker. In the first place, since Lockwood's typology is heuristic, it is inappropriate to criticise it on the grounds that in every case it does not coincide with empirical reality. We have tried to avoid this by criticising aspects of the type, rather than whether or not particular groups of workers fit the category. Furthermore, 'traditional' and 'proletariat' seem to us to be contradictory terms when applied to working-class consciousness. We would suggest that some of the factors Lockwood associates with traditional community – the existence of face-to-face emotional interactions at work, the localised labour market, and the high degree of job involvement – inhibit the development of proletarian consciousness rather than support it. Again, as Westergaard points out (1970), the economic developments underlying the cultural response of privatisation are leading to an increasing transparency in the cash nexus – a development not unproblematic for capitalism.

Finally, another problem is the determinist/positivistic idea of consciousness displayed by Lockwood in this particular paper. Consciousness is seen merely as a *reflection* of activity at the base. This is surprising in view of Lockwood's (earlier) Affluent Worker monographs when, in the discussion of embourgeoisement, he insisted that three aspects of working-class activity must be taken into account: the economic, the relational and the normative, all of which had relative autonomy, with the relational acting as a mediation between the other two. In this sense, consciousness could never be just a reflection of what people *do*, since the mediations of *how* they did it, and *with whom*, were crucial. In *Sources of Variation in Working Class Images of Society*, Lockwood seems to collapse the levels of economic and relational, giving us instead a crude base-superstructure formulation with mechanistic determinations. An example of this mechanism is displayed in Lockwood's identification of the proletarian traditionalist as the most class-conscious worker. Here is Lockwood's account of their image of the social structure:

> Shaped by occupational solidarities and communal sociability, proletarian social consciousness, is centred on an awareness of 'us' and 'them'. 'Them' are bosses, managers, white collar workers and ultimately the public authorities of the wider society.
>
> (1975 p. 18)

This characterisation displays a crude simplification of a dichotomous imagery of 'us' and 'them'. Shaped by work and the local community, the proletarian traditionalist sees 'them' as a hierarchy impinging on the activities of work and community, an imputed characteristic of the privatised worker. Fundamentally, a dichotomous conception of 'them' and 'us' reflects a power and class relationship with wider ramifications than those within the local community. This point reflects Westergaard's criticism that Lockwood's schema does not allow for a 'radical class consciousness' that is, one which transcends occupations and localities and becomes generalised to other sections of the working class. Since they are both hierarchical, neither of Lockwood's models displays radical overtones and neither represent a dichotomous *class* imagery.

Lockwood is subsequently reduced to arguing that only when a sense of 'relative deprivation' permeates working-class consciousness, will radical alternatives appear as viable objectives – almost suggesting that mass unemployment is the pre-requisite of revolutionary activity. His inability to draw a distinction between the experience of the labour process, and the experience of the capital relation, compounds his reification of the difference between the privatised worker and the traditional worker.

In political terms the consciousness of Lockwood's traditional proletarian is an 'accommodation' to capitalism – a cultural transcendence rather than a material transformation. Far from engendering a radical class consciousness, the type of community relationships experienced by the traditional proletarian tend to bring about the opposite result – a parochial self-interest. And, as Westergaard has pointed out in numerous articles, localism and parochialism are endemic in the working class and this factor inhibits them in the pursuit of their interests.

Whilst we do agree with Westergaard on the importance of locality- and community-based ideologies, we do find his formulation of this rather bizarre:

> Victorian reformers and critics . . . often explicitly recognised the clash (either actual or potential) between the conservative restraints of localism, on the one hand, and the radical and therefore frightening implications of any breach of those restraints, on the other. I am always reminded on this point of Thomas Chalmers who in his book *The Civic and Christian Economy of Large Towns* in the 1820 advocated a system of 'localism' to break down working class districts of the big cities into small units . . . to stifle any rebellious tendency. His argument was precisely that if working class interests could be turned inward to the locality, then workers would be prevented from forming alliances and loyalties across the restraining boundaries of the locality; and social order would be safeguarded. Divide and rule.
>
> (1975 p. 252)

We find Westergaard's thesis untenable insofar as it suffers from the weakness of all conspiracy theories, in that it attributes far too much power and intelligence to the conspirators. We do find that there is something piquant about Westergaard's intellectual career, mainly built on castigating the ruling class for its stupidity, yet in this article pointing to the fiendishly clever plots they manage to devise to keep the worker in a state of 'false consciousness'.

One thing seems very clear. Workers may not view the class structure in one way, but in different and contradictory ways. This is more understandable in view of the effects on class consciousness and imagery of the educational system and the mass media. Given all the different influences working on the consciousness of workers we would suggest that any kind of coherent 'images of society' would be the exception rather than the rule. If neither the social situation of a particular group of workers, nor the interpretations of these situations are as homogeneous as Lockwood suggests, the way is opened for apparent contradictions between attitude and conduct and also for a considerable variation in the attitudes themselves.

Parkin: national meaning systems and the accommodative worker

In turning to Parkin's categories we find significant differences in the way working-class imagery is typified. Primarily they do not refer to spontaneously generated ideologies, but to national ideologies imposed by some means or another and to which different sections of the working class give allegiance. Firstly, there is the dominant value system, the social source of which is the ruling class. Typically it is accepted by the 'deferential' or 'aspirational' working class. Secondly, the subordinate value system, the social source of which is trade unionism, and into which is collapsed the 'traditional proletarian' and the 'privatised worker' which Lockwood distinguishes. Thirdly the radical value system, which is not the property of the working class, since it is incapable of autonomously generating its own *systematic* critique of capitalism: 'the working class on its own can only develop trade union consciousness'. One is left with the interpretation that individuals rather than whole social groups subscribe to this value system since its only institutional bearer is the 'mass political party', and no conditions are suggested for its social acceptance.

Linked to these categories is a specific political thesis about the nature of trade unionism and the working-class political party, in this case the Labour Party. In the case of the former: 'Collective bargaining does not call into question the values underlying the existing reward structure. Trade unionism could in fact be said to stabilise the modern capitalist order by legitimising further the rules and procedures which govern the allocation of resources' (1972 p. 91). Thus, trade unions are viewed as an accommodative response to inequality.

Furthermore, in the case of the Labour Party, the only source of the radical value system, he points to its post-war revisionism, and argues:

> It seems plausible to suggest that if socialist parties ceased to present a radical, class-oriented meaning system to their supporters, then such an outlook would not persist of its own accord among the subordinate class. Once the mass party of the underclass comes to endorse fully the values and institutions of the dominant class, there remains no major source of political knowledge and information which would enable the subordinate class to make sense of their situation in radical terms.
>
> (1971 p. 98)

Now the basic error that Parkin makes in his analysis of both the trade unions and the Labour Party is to generalise into atemporal categories characteristics peculiar to a particular historical period. In the first place his description of economism, despite his quote from Lenin, is a simple characterisation of the labour movement at a particular juncture. Lenin was describing the limitations of trade unionism as a political and revolutionary force – its relation to political activity. Fundamentally, whatever the degree of reformism of trade union leaders, the very existence of a trade union *ipso facto* asserts the unbridgeable difference between capital and labour in a market society; it embodies the refusal of the working class to become integrated into capitalism on capital's own terms. Trade unionism always has been a direct response to economic forces – a response to a system where workers are forced to sell their labour power as a commodity in the market. As Benyon (1973) points out, this situation has generated a factory class consciousness which understands class relationships in terms of their direct manifestation in conflict between employers and workers within a factory. This consciousness is rooted in the workplace where struggles are fought over the control of the job and the 'rights' of management and workers. Whilst it may be a a 'politics of the factory', the fact that it concerns itself with exploitation and power indicates that it contains definite political elements. Trade unions, therefore, reflect and express a 'working-class consciousness': a consciousness which recognises the validity of the proletariat as a distinct social force, with its own corporate interests in society. This may not be the same thing as a socialist consciousness, but it must be recognised as a necessary precondition for its development.

Furthermore, whilst the 'instrumental collectivism' of workers expresses itself in aggressive economism and defensive shop-floor control, Parkin's articulation of this as purely 'accommodative' is one dimensional. He assumes that economistic demands will consistently be met and that shop-floor control is something which only has to be defended from time to time. Both these implicit assumptions are contentious. Crucially, the delicate balance of bargaining power in modern industry is not determined by any abstract standards of 'fairness'. It is an unstable equilibrium of forces. If one of the forces is weakened, the balance will shift. At the moment it is shifting against the unions. Against a hostile press, which is itself an integral arm of the power structure, unions find themselves constantly under attack. At the same time, under the pressure of a State which is equally subordinated to monopoly power, they find themselves responding to a series of carefully imposed pseudo-choices such as 'either you accept a restrictive incomes policy or high unemployment will result' – in the event, the unions have had to accept both options. At the same time, industry by industry, attempts are made to push back and whittle down the areas of control which local union initiatives have already established over management prerogatives (the most recently publicised example being the case of the 'door-hangers' at Fords in Dagenham). The motive behind all such pressures, of course, is the appreciation of the competitive weakness of British industry, and the need to cut costs accordingly. Similarly, both economistic demands and the system's ability to concede them are subject to change and fluctuations, and this defines limits to the logic of business unionism. Thus, whilst Parkin describes working-class consciousness to an extent, the understanding is superficial, in that there is no appreciation of the tensions and contradictions within the aggressive economism/defensive shop-floor control formula. The cash-nexus of instrumentalism is a 'brittle bond' with shifting and problematic implications for industrial conflict and class consciousness.

Similarly, the development of oligarchy and/or conservatism in unions, with the resulting control of rank and file militancy, must be seen within a particular economic and political context rather than as a result of the dynamics of organisation *per se*. For example, as Lane (1974) has argued, the conciliatory policies of the craft unions in the 1880s have to be seen within the context of the real concessions being made by the State in a particularly favourable economic climate; whereas the more militant tendencies of the 1910s in part represented reactions to real economic and legal threats. And again, within the unions there are counter-tendencies, which confront oligarchic trends, and they must not be lost sight of. Thus, whilst in most unions there is continual opposition to reformist leadership, more importantly, local groups, through a parochial bargaining leverage, are able to take their own initiatives and act as sources of opposition (see Benyon 1973). Thus, in the 1960s sustained unofficial action generated a radicalisation of sections of the trade union bureaucracy and saw the revival of the 'official' strike.

We are not arguing that trade unions constitute a revolutionary base from which an effective assault on capitalist society can be made. Indeed, we recognise that at their core trade unions are defensive organisations built and supported by workers who need protection in the labour market. However, unlike Parkin, we would argue that they involve more than this. Crucially, they are working-class organisations and consequently the numerous conflicts experienced by workers find their expression within the union. As Benyon points out:

> The disjuncture between what has been termed a 'trade union consciousness' and a 'political consciousness' is not a clear one. Politics and a political understanding can be contained implicitly in the way in which workers and activists deal with and come to understand their union and their employers. What is clear though is that while politics is contained within trade unionism, trade unions restrain rather than develop this political awareness . . . Traditionally the British trade union movement has coped with the contradiction of opposing the employer while at the same time recognising him through a dichotomy of the 'industrial' and 'political' wings of the Labour movement. Anything to do with changing society has been hived off to the Labour Party.
>
> (1973 p. 231)

Turning to Parkin's treatment of the Labour Party, we see that, initially, he defines it as the major historical source of the radical value system. He then argues that in the post-war period the Party has been characterised by its acceptance of the status quo, and its consequent abandonment of any policies directed towards a radical alternative. The first point we would make is that to characterise the pre-war Labour Party as 'radical' is misleading – if by it he means a class-conscious radicalism. Labour's fundamental characteristic since its inception has been its overriding commitment to the parliamentary route and to reformism.

Whilst we would accept that the transition from a party of opposition to a party of government has increasingly seen the Labour Party adopt the revisionist role of 'manager' of a mixed economy we would reject Parkin's assertion that this has not only led to a de-radicalisation of the working class, but effectively precludes the working class from developing a radical perspective.

Just as the 1950s can be seen as a period of 'consensus', characterised by working-class quietism, so the 1960s has to be seen as a period of economic conflict, characterised by a developing working-class militancy. It was a period in which capital became concentrated in the hands of fewer and larger corporations. This, combined with the declining rate of profit on domestic capital and an inflationary economy, produced an economic situation against which the notions of 'one country', so prevalent in the 1950s, were beginning to crumble. 'The 1960s brought home the existence of social classes and the class struggle' (Benyon p. 148).

The upsurge in industrial militancy was paralleled by a growing tendency for direct action to spill over into other areas. This was especially marked in housing where there was a rapid growth of associations among corporation tenants. These developments, and others, generated an intense period of extra-parliamentary radical political struggles – in housing and community politics, in women's politics, both personal and economic, in the shop stewards' movement, and so on (for examples, see Bailey 1973; *The Body Politic* (Feminist Books) 1972; Blackburn and Cockburn 1967). Surely not soley reducible to the activities of disaffected students and intellectuals?

Our argument, then is that in Parkin's treatment of trade union activity and radical politics he abstracts particular historical developments from their economic and political context. In this process important contradictions and tensions are submerged and hidden within a one dimensional presentation of a superficially coherent analysis. The suggestion is that the Labour Party, and consequently the working class, is now embarked on an irreversible process of de-radicalisation and that the radical value system will now only 'influence small parties on the political fringe' (1971 p. 101). Do we not detect a note of determinism? Furthermore, class struggle is not a figment of the 'intellectual's' imagination. It is a real dynamic process arising from the contradictory interests of capital and labour. Whilst we accept that in a particular historical period – where an 'orchestrated' consensus excludes the articulation of any socialist options – the traditional parties of the left can become agencies of the status quo, this process is not without contradictions, and this juncture is not fixed for all time.

Having consigned the radical value system to the 'ivory towers', Parkin is left with two meaning systems that characterise working-class imagery – the dominant and subordinate. The subordinate value system he identifies as being generated in the local working-class community:

> Subordinate class communities throw up their distinctive value systems more or less independently of one another: there is no 'national' subordinate value system in the way there is a truly national dominant value system. The similarity in the normative patterns of working-class communities derives largely from the similarity of the conditions they are exposed to. They generate a meaning system which is of purely parochial

> significance, representing a design for living based upon localised social knowledge and face-to-face relationships.
>
> (1971 p. 90)

One of the major conditions to which they are exposed is the dominant value system by way of the educational apparatus, the media and so on. The working class are unable to negate these values, as they lack other sources of knowledge and information, there being no radical party, so their reaction is not to reject these values '. . . and thus create an entirely different normative system, but to negotiate or modify them in the light of their own existential conditions' (1974 p. 92). 'On these grounds it is useful to regard subordinate values as a negotiated form of dominant values' (1971, p. 95).

Within this conception is collapsed both the proletarian traditionalist and the privatised worker. Although we criticised Lockwood's typification, it at least made some reference to history, whereas Parkin has subsumed the whole development of working-class culture within the category 'subordinate value system', its defining characteristic being an accommodative response to inequality. Yet even this value system is merely a negotiation of dominant values, and once again we seem to be in the realm of determinism. For working-class meaning systems are merely a negotiation of dominant values, to fit the prevailing exigencies of the working-class community. We are given no sense of the creative aspect of working-class response to material conditions, nor of the accumulated reservoir of cultural practices and meanings embodied in working-class culture which act as determinants of and tools for the transformation of culture in response both to changing material conditions and to evolving ideological assaults from the bourgeoisie, in the form of education, social security, housing, and so on.

Thus in effect, Parkin has only one value system, and a residual category. The former has a dominant and a negotiated version, whereas the latter is confined to 'free-floating' intellectuals and the 'looney left'.

Conclusion

In the preceding discussion, we have outlined a critique of two conceptual typologies and what we saw as their empirical base. In the case of Lockwood we have argued that almost all workers within capitalism are placed in such a contradictory real situation that it is unlikely that they can develop insulated and cohesive sub-cultures, of the kind he posits. Consequently, we argued that 'images of society' are likely to be contradictory rather than homogeneous, displaying ambiguities in attitudes and behaviour and even contradictory attitudes. Methodologically, we would also argue that the heuristic typologies within which Lockwood's argument is couched are too static to aid the understanding of the essentially dialectical relationship between capital and labour.

Parkin tries to account for these contradictions by arguing that in abstract situations workers will answer in terms of the dominant value system, but in situations involving choice and action they will call upon the negotiated subordinate value system. However, the monolithic and determinist nature of these value systems provides no explanatory power. Reified, abstract value-systems, which blanket the cultural complexity and divergencies of working-class imagery, coupled with a de-historicised political thesis, serve to smother the potential oppositional elements displayed in the contradictory nature of working-class consciousness.

Within both these sociological attempts to understand working-class imagery a homologous relationship between ideas and experience is posited, the difference consisting in the emphasis placed on the different levels – Parkin emphasising ideas, and Lockwood work and community experience. Both typifications, we would argue, degenerate into a crude single-levelled determinism because they collapse both consciousness and ideology into a uniform 'image of society'.

Our basic argument is that in analysing working-class 'images of society', what must be placed at the heart of the analysis is their historical nature. The historical development of the relationship between capital and labour has thrown up specific forms of resistance peculiar to the material conditions and strategies of particular conjunctures. These specific forms can be analysed in terms of the uneven development of capitalism, not just on an international, but also on a intra-national level, thus leading to differences in regional industrial development or even differences within a region. John Foster's book *Class Struggle and the Industrial Revolution* is a useful starting point for this kind of analysis, dealing as it does with the development of different degrees of class consciousness in three towns, ultimately based on different relations between capital and labour and different forms of the labour process. Also methodologically useful are the analyses of Lenin (1960) and Gramsci (1971) on the development of capitalism within Russia and Italy.

Once established, particular forms of resistance achieve institutional expression in, for example, trade unions, working men's clubs, etc. Within these institutions, which are in a constant process of struggle, ideologies are constructed – about the job, about the area, and specific local social relationships – which come to have a great influence on the people they serve and are addressed to.

However, these ideologies are not simply determining; they not only influence but change in accordance with developments in material life. This process is examined sociologically in Stacey's Banbury (1960), which at the time of the study was a small market town with handicraft industry. Stacey's book explores the changes in class composition and class consciousness due to the introduction of modern machinofactures in the shape of a plastics factory. In the book, the author almost sees the inherent contradiction between class and community, but the analysis ultimately fails because there is no examination of the relationship between these ideologies and the real experience of wage labour as mediated through consciousness. It is also this contradictory level which Parkin and Lockwood subsume under 'imagery', and it is this semi-automomous layer of working-class experience which throws up new 'forms' of resistance and defends and adapts old 'forms' to meet new conditions.

Thus, the quest for working-class 'images of society' collapses contradictions in its search for coherence. The coherence established is achieved 'one dimensionally' at a verbal level, at the expense of de-historicising the complex phenomen in question. Crucially, an analysis of the uneven development of capitalism and the labour process with their attendant ideologies – local, occupational and national – is necessary to understand the relations and mediations between the subjective level of experience, ideology and determining material conditions.

References

Bailey, R. (1973) *The Squatters* Penguin

Benyon, H. (1973) *Working for Ford* Penguin

Blackburn, R. and Cockburn, A. (eds) (1967) *The Incompatibles: Trade Union Militancy and the Consensus* Penguin

Cousins and Brown (1975) 'Patterns of Paradox: Shipbuilding Workers' Images of Society' in Bulmer (ed.) *Working Class Images of Society* RKP

Dennis, Henriques and Slaughter (1956) *Coal is our Life*, 2nd edn 1969 Tavistock

Eggleston, S.J. (1967) *The Social Context of the School* RKP
Foster, J. (1974) *Class Struggle and the Industrial Revolution* Weidenfeld & Nicolson
Gouldner, A.W. (1971) *The Coming Crisis of Western Sociology* Heinemann
Gramsci, A. (1971) 'Notes on Italian History' in *Prison Notebooks* Lawrence & Wishart
Hoggart, R. (1957) *The Uses of Literacy* Penguin
Jackson, B. (1968) *Working Class Community* Penguin
Lane, T. (1974) *The Union Makes Us Strong* Arrow
Lenin, V.I. (1960) 'The Development of Capitalism in Russia' in *Collected Works* Moscow
Lewis, O. (1951) *Life in a Mexican Village: Tepoztlan Revisited* University of Chicago Press (1968) *La Vida* Panther
Lockwood, D. (1975) 'Sources of Variation in Working Class Images of Society' in Bulmer *op.cit.*
Parkin, F. (1971) *Class Inequality and the Political Order* Paladin
Stacey, M. (1960) *Tradition and Change: A Study of Banbury* OUP
Titmuss, R. (1958) *Essays on the Welfare State* Unwin
Townsend, P. (1957) *Family Life of Old People* RKP
Westergaard, J.H. (1970) 'The Rediscovery of the Cash Nexus' *Socialist Register* 1970, (1975) 'Radical Class Consciousness' in Bulmer *op.cit.*
Williams, R. (1958) *Culture and Society* Penguin
Young and Wilmott (1961) 'Research Report No. 3: Institute of Community Studies: Bethnal Green' *Sociological Review* July 1961.
1962 *Family and Kinship in East London* Penguin

Appendix

We include this appendix to illustrate how interest among sociologists focussed both on 'community' as an ideology and on community studies themselves in the 1950s. We have included American material as a comparison, since a similar development occurred there in the 1930s.

Allcorn, D.H. (1954) *The Social Life of Young Men in London* Manchester
Arensberg & Kimball (1940) *Family and Community in Ireland* Peter Smith, London
Baltzell, D. (1958) *Philadelphia Gentlemen* Free Press, Glencoe
Bell & Newby (1971) *Community Studies* Allen & Unwin
Bell & Newby (1972) *The Sociology of Local Communities* Allen & Unwin
Birch, A.H. (1959) *Small Town Politics* OUP
Boal, J.W. (1969) 'Territoriality on the Shankhill–Falls Divide, Belfast', in *Irish Geography*.
Bonjean & Olsen (1964) 'Community Leadership: Directions of Research' in Zollschen & Hirsh, *Exploration in Social Change* RKP
Bott, E. (1957) *Family & Social Network* Tavistock
Brennan, Cooney & Pollins (1954) *Social Change in S.W. Wales* Watts
Coates & Silbum (1970) *Poverty: The Forgotten Englishman* Penguin
Coleman, J. (1957) *Community Conflict* Free Press, Glencoe
Collinson, P. (1963) *The Cutteslowe Wells* Faber
Dahl, R. (1961) *Who Governs* Yale U.P.
Davies & Gardner (1944) *Deep South* Chicago U.P.
Davies & Rees (1960) *Welsh Rural Communities* University of Wales Press
Dennis, N. (1970) *People & Planning: The Sociology of Housing in Sunderland*
Dennis, N. (1972) *Public Participation & Planning Blight*
Dennis, Henriques & Slaughter (1957) *Coal is Our Life* Eyre & Spottiswood
Doherty, M. (1955) *A Miner's Son* Lawrence & Wishart
Dollard, J. (1937) *Caste & Class in a Southern Town* Yale U.P.

Durrant, R. (1959) *Watling: A Survey of Social Life on a New Housing Estate* P.S. King

Engels, F. (1969) *The Condition of the Working Class in England* Panther (first English edn. 1892).

Firth & Djamour (1956) *Kinship in South Borough: Two Studies of Kinship in London* Athlone Press

Frankenberg (1957) *Village on the Border* Cohen & West

Frankenberg (1966) *Communities in Britain* Penguin

Gamson, W. (1966) *Rancorous Conflict in Community Politics* A.S R. 31

Gans, H. (1952) 'Urbanism & Surburbanism as a Way of Life' in Rose (ed.) *Human Behaviour and Social Processes* RKP

Gans, H. (1962) *The Urban Villagers* N.Y. Free Press

Gans, H. (1967) *The Levittowners* Allen Lane

Glass, R. (1948) *The Social Background to a Plan: Middlesborough* RKP

Glass, R. (1955) 'Urban Sociology' in *Current Sociology* Vol. IV No. 4 UNESCO

Glass, R. (1966) 'Conflict in Cities' in *Conflict in Society* Churchill

Glass & Frenknel (1946) 'How they lived at Bethnal Green' in *Britain East and West* Contact Books, London

Goldthorpe & Lockwood (1963) 'Affluence & the British Class Structure' in *Sociological Review*

Green, B.S.R. (1968) *Community Decision Making in Georgian City* unpb. Phd. University of Bath

Hatt & Reiss (1957) *Cities & Society* Free Press, Glencoe

Havighurst & Jansen (1967) 'Community Research' in *Current Sociology* 15.2

Hawley, A. (1950) *Human Ecology: A Theory of Community Structure*, Ronald, New York

Hillery, G.A. Jnr. (1955) 'Definitions of Community: Areas of Agreement' in *Rural Sociology* 20

Hodges & Smith (1954) 'The Sheffield Estate' in *Neighbourhood & Community* Liverpool U.P.

Homans, G.C. (1953) 'The Rural Sociology of Medieval England' in *Past & Present.* No.4

Hunter, F. (1953) *Community Power Structure* University of N. Carolina Press

Jackson, B. (1968) *Working Class Community* Penguin

Jeffrys, M. (1964) 'Londoners in Hertforshire' in *London: Aspects of Change*, Urban Studies Report No. 3

Kerr, M. (1958) *The People of Ship Street*, Routledge and Kegan Paul, London

Konig, R. (1968) *The Community* RKP

Kuper, L. (1953) *Living in Towns* Cresset Press, London

Lewis, O. (1965) *Life in a Mexican Village: Tepoztlan Revisited* University of Chicago Press

Lewis, O. (1968) *Children of Sanchez* Penguin

Lloyd, A.L. (1952) *Come All Ye Bold Miners*, Lawrence & Wishart

Loudon, J.B. (1961) 'Kinship & Crisis in S. Wales' BJS Vol. X11 No.4

Lupton & Mitchell (1954) 'The Liverpool Estate' in *Neighbourhood & Community op.cit.*

Lynd, R. & H. (1929) *Middletown: A Study in Contemporary American Culture* Harcourt Brace, N.Y.

Lynd, R. & M. (1937) *Middletown: A Study in Transition* Harcourt Brace

Martindale, D. (1964) 'The Formation and Destruction of Communities'. Zollschan & Hirsch: *Exploration in Social Change* RKP

Maud Report on Local Government (1967)

McKinney & Loomis (1957) 'The Application of Gemeinschaft & Gesellschaft to Other Typologies' in intro. to American ed. Tonnies, *Community & Society* Harper Torchbooks.

Mitchell, G.D. (1951) 'The Parish Council and the Rural Community' in *Rural Administration* Winter 1951

Mitchell, *et al.* (1954) *Neighbourhood and Community op.cit.*

Mitchell, J.C. (1969) *Social Networks in an Urban Situation* Manchester U.P.

Mogey, J.M. (1956) *Family and Neighbourhood: Two Studies in Oxford* OUP

Nisbet, R. (1966) *The Sociological Tradition* Heinemann

Pahl, R. (1966) 'The Rural Urban Continuum' in *Sociologia Ruralis V*

Pahl, R. (1968) *Readings in Urban Sociology* OUP

Peterson, W. (1968) 'The Ideological Origins of Britain's New Towns' in *American Inst. of Planners Journal* Vol. XXXIV.

Plowman, Minchington & Stacey (1962) 'Local Social Systems in England & Wales' in *Sociological Review* 10
Polsby, N. (1963) *Community Power and Political Theory* Vol. X No.2. Yale U.P.
Redfield, R. (1947) 'The Folk Society' AJS 52
Rees, A.D. (1950) *Life in the Welsh Countryside* University of Wales Press
Rex, J. (1968) 'The Sociology of the Zone of Transition' in Pahl, *op.cit.*
Rex, J. (1972) *Race, Community & Conflict* OUP
Robinson, W. S. (1950) 'Ecological Correlations and the Behaviour of Individuals' ASR 50
Rosser & Harris (1961) 'Relationships through Marriage in a Welsh Urban Area' in *Sociological Review* Vol. X.
Schnore, L.F. (1967) 'Community' in Smelser (ed.) *Sociology* Wiley, N.Y.
Seabrook, J. (1971) *City Close Up* Penguin
Seeley *et al.* (1956) *Crestwood Heights* Basic Books
Sjoberg, G. (1965) 'Community' in Gould & Klob, *Dictionary of Sociology* Tavistock
Skeffington Report (1969) *People & Planning*
Spencer, J. (1964) *Stress and Release in an Urban Estate* Tavistock
Stacey, M. (1960) *Tradition and Change: A Study of Banbury* OUP
Stacey, M (1969) 'The Myth of Community Studies', in *BJS*
Stein, M. (1960) *The Eclipse of Community* Princeton U.P.
Sussman, M.B. (1959) *Community Structure and Analysis* Cromwell
Sutton & Kojola (1960) 'The Concept of Community' in *Rural Sociology* 25
Theodorson, G.A. (1961) *Studies in Human Ecology*, Row, Peterson, Chicago
Thrasher, F.M. (1963) *One Thousand Boys' Gangs in Chicago* Chicago U.P.
Townsend, P. (1957) *The Family Life of Old People* RKP
Viditch & Bensman (1958) *Small Town in Mass Society* Princeton U.P.
Viditch *et al.* (1964) *Reflections of Community Studies* Wiley
Walton, J. (1966) 'Substance and Artifact: The Current Status of Research on Community Power Structure' AJS
Warner & Lunt (1941) *The Social Life of Modern Community* (Yankee City)
Warner & Lunt (1942) *The Status System of Modern Community* (YC) Yale U.P.
Warner & Srole (1945) *The Social System of American Ethnic Groups* (YC) Yale U.P.
Warner & Low (1947) *The Social System of a Modern Factory* (YC) Yale U.P.
Warner (1949) *Democracy in Jonesville* (YC) Yale U.P.
Warner (1959) *The Living and the Dead* (YC) Yale U.P.
Warner (1963) *Yankee City* (as one abridged volume) Yale U.P.
Warren, R. (1963) *The Community in America* Rand McNally
Warren, R.L. (1966) *Perspectives on the American Community* Rand McNally
Watson, W. (1964) 'Social Mobility and Social Class in Industrial Communities' in *Closed Systems and Open Minds* Oliver Boyd
Webber, M.L. (1963) 'Order in Diversity: Community without Propinquity' in *Cities and Space* Johns Hopkins Press
Williams, W.M. (1956) *The Sociology of an English Village: Gosforth* RKP
Williams, W.M. (1958) *The Country Craftsman* RKP
Williams, W.M. (1963) *A West Country Village: Ashworthy* RKP
Willmott & Young (1957) *Family and Kinship in East London* RKP
Willmott & Young (1960) *Family & Class in a London Suburb* RKP
Wilson, R. (1963) *Difficult Housing Estates* Tavistock
Wirth, L. (1938) 'Urbanism as a Way of Life' AJS 44
Wolfinger, R. (1960) 'Reputation and Reality in the Study of Community Power' ASR
Wood, R.C. (1958) *Suburbia: Its People and Their Politics* Boston
Zorbough, H.W. (1929) *The Gold Coast and the Slum* Chicago U.P.

31 'Really useful knowledge'

Radical education and working-class culture, 1790–1848

Richard Johnson

Introduction

One of the most interesting developments in working-class history has been the rediscovery of popular educational traditions, the springs of action of which owed little to philanthropic, ecclesiastical or state provision. For a long time these traditions remained hidden, though they appear in some early social histories, especially those written in one period of radical education (1890s to 1920s) about another (1790s to 1840s).[1] But it was not until the 1960s that more fully researched accounts appeared, forming part of the general recovery of early working-class radicalism. In 1960 Brian Simon's *Studies in the History of Education* drew attention to the continuity and the liveliness of independent popular education from Jacobinism to Chartism. In 1961, J.F.C. Harrison's *Learning and Living* examined traditions of adult self-education in one locality. Harold Silver's important book, *The Concept of Popular Education* (1965), looked at 'developments in attitudes to the education of the people' more generally, but focused especially on Owen and Owenism, Thompson's *The Making of the English Working Class* (1963) permitted a fuller contextualization of others' findings, but also stressed the intellectual character of early-nineteenth-century radicalism and the role of 'the articulate consciousness of the self-taught'.[2] These themes have become more explicit in later studies of Owenism and Chartism and of the radical press, the main 'educational' medium.[3] Related to radical traditions, but not yet connected in the historiography, were other educational resources which have been receiving increasing attention from historians – especially the extent and uses of private schools.[4] Some recent studies of Sunday schools have shown the co-existence of schools under popular control with more clearly philanthropic institutions.[5] There is, however, no adequate study of the other important popular educational resource: the working-class family itself.

The radical press remains the obvious route of entry into popular educational practices and dilemmas. It was extremely articulate, indeed talkative, providing a weekly set of commentaries on everyday life and politics. Although it is the main source for what follows, this use is in itself problematic, posing additional questions which must be answered *en route*. For we cannot assume that the attitudes of radical leaders and writers were those of 'the workers' (any more than we can assume that radicalism was 'unrepresentative' or the downwards extension of middle-class 'ideas').[6] For one thing, radicals differed a lot on some essential matters. For another, popular opinion itself was not homogeneous. Moreover, radical leaders were clearly involved in a process that was part mediation or expression of some popular feelings, and part a forming or 'education' of them, an attempt to achieve, from very diverse materials, some unity of will and direction. This necessarily involved fostering some tendencies and opposing others. The image of the educator or 'schoolmaster' is itself interesting here. It was one of the commonest guises adopted by radical journalists.[7] Though it was an identity often adopted jokingly and as a conscious play upon Henry Brougham's populist 'schoolmaster abroad' speeches of the 1820s, it was an image that constructed some distance between 'teachers' and 'pupils', despite the involvement in a common enterprise. It is important, then, to understand the particular position of leaders and journalists within radical movements and, more generally, within the popular classes as a whole. It is necessary, in other words, to face squarely the problem of the 'popularity' of radicalism. This is an especially important question for the concerns of this essay, which puzzles around the relation between various kinds of radicalism, understood as 'educative' or transformative ideologies, and the conditions of existence and lived culture of some of the groups which radicalism addressed. But first it is necessary to describe some salient features of radical education over this period, concentrating, at first, on some common elements. Later we shall look, more discriminatingly, at some internal differences and changes over time.

The radical dilemma

There were four main aspects to 'radical education'. First, radicals conducted a running critique of all forms of 'provided' education. This covered the whole gamut of schooling enterprises from clerically dominated Anglican Sunday schools, through Cobbett's 'Bell and Lancaster work', to the state-aided (and usually Anglican) public day schools of the mid century. It also embraced all the institutes, clubs and media designed to influence the older pupil – everything from tracts to mechanics institutes. Plans for a more centralized state system of schooling were also opposed, a feature to which we will return. This tradition, then, was sharply oppositional: it revolved around a contestation of orthodoxies (and some unorthodoxies too) both in theory and practice. Nor was this critique limited to formally 'educational' institutions. In its later phases radicalism developed a practical grasp and a theoretical understanding of cultural and ideological struggle in a more general sense.

The second main feature was the development of alternative educational goals. At one level these embraced a vision of a whole alternative future – a future in which educational utopias, among other needs, could actually be achieved. At another, radicalism developed its own curricula and pedagogies, its own definition of 'really useful knowledge', a characteristically radical *content*, a sense of what it was really important to know.

Thirdly, radicalism conducted an important internal debate about education as political strategy or as a means of changing the world. Like most aspects of counter-education, this debate was also directed at dominant middle-class conceptions of the relation between education and politics, especially the argument that 'national education' was a necessary condition for the granting of universal suffrage. But it expressed real radical dilemmas too.

Finally, radical movements developed a vigorous and varied educational practice. The distinctive feature was, at first sight, an emphasis upon informing mature understandings and upon the education of men and women as adult citizens of a more just social order. But radicals were also concerned with men and women as educators of their own children and they improvised forms for this task too. It might, however, be truer to say that the child–adult distinction was itself less stressed in this tradition, or in parts of it, than in the contemporary middle-class culture of childhood. This is one reason why, in what follows, no large distinction is made between the education of 'children' and 'adults'. Such a distinction is not found in nature by educators, but has actually, in large part, been constructed.

We can move beyond a rather descriptive listing like this by seeing these elements as aspects of a particular, lived, dilemma. This dilemma was not unique to early nineteenth-century radicals. It is arguable that it represents the *typical* popular educational dilemma under capitalist social conditions. Nineteenth-century radicals, however, certainly experienced it with a particular sharpness. On the one hand, they valued the acquisition of knowledge very highly indeed, often with a quite abstract passion. Knowledge or 'enlightenment' was *generally* sought: it was a good in itself, a use value. This passion can be traced in many working-class autobiographies in which the fervent 'pursuit of knowledge' always looms large, in the language and educational stance of the unstamped press, in the popular reception of quite abstract texts, and in an educational rhetoric as exalted and sometimes as high-flown as the more familiar Broughamite language of middle-class liberals:

> Self-reformation is the only reform that will establish the happiness of mankind. Man must be taught to know what are, as well as what are not his rights; he must learn the dependence of his happiness on the happiness of his fellow-creatures; his mind must be cleansed of all the many and pernicious prejudices, which, when it was too weak to resist their influence, even at the time of its birth, took root around it, and have hitherto choked up its real nature and hidden from it the lights of truth; he must be made to love, instead of fearing – to pity, instead of blaming – to reason, instead of listening – to be convinced, instead of believing – and, above all, he must know his weakness as an individual, and his strength in proportion only as he UNITES and co-operates with others.[8]

At the same time, however, radicals were aware of the poverty of educational resources to hand – a recognition often enforced by personal experience. This was partly a quantitative scarcity – lack of schools, lack of books, lack of energy, lack of time. But there was also a qualitative question involved. In the course of the period some of the quantitative deficiencies were supplied: certainly from the 1830s there was a growth, in real terms, of educational facilities of the provided kind, if not of opportunities for their use. Yet as 'facilities' grew, the dilemma actually deepened. The quality of what was on offer never matched the aspirations. Far indeed from promising liberation, provided education threatened subjection. It seemed at best a laughable and irrelevant divergence (*useless* knowledge in fact); or, at worst, a species of tyranny, an outward extension of the power of factory master, or priest, or corrupt state apparatus. There is a continuity of comment of this kind from Paine's initial warnings on the educational tendencies of hereditary monarchies and established religions to the caveats of the *Northern Star* on government education schemes. Paine taught radicals that monarchy, being based on so irrational a device as inheritance, tended to 'buy reason up' and that priests were employed to keep the people ignorant.[9] Cobbett, the original de-schooler, extended this to cover schools and schoolmasters. Note the industrial and political analogies:

> He is their over-looker; he is a spy upon them; his authority is maintained by his absolute power of punishment; the parent commits them to that power; to be taught is to be held in restraint; and, as the sparks fly upwards, the teaching and restraint will not be divided in the estimation of the boy.[10]

Early radical journalists put each new educational innovation into a place already prepared for it in Painite theory. Schooling was not about 'political education' at all, not about 'rights' and 'liberties'; it was about 'servility', 'slavery' and 'surveillance', about government spies in every parish, about the tyranny of the schoolroom. This theme was elaborated in a hundred ingenious ways: reporting injustice in individual schools, parodying hymns, catechisms and teaching methods, exposing Dr Bell's sinecure, stressing the ideological rationale of schooling by which all evils were ascribed to 'popular ignorance'.[11] By the 1830s new forms of provided education had appeared, especially mechanics institutes, infant schools and the Society for the Diffusion of Useful Knowledge (SDUK), some of which were less obviously 'knowledge-denying' than tracts or monitorial schools. Yet radicals maintained a critical opposition. The SDUK was universally ridiculed: infant schools were attacked by Owenites (as a corruption of Owen's ideals) and parodied in the Chartist press;[12] and mechanics institutes, the most popular of the innovations, were very cautiously evaluated and, on the ground, openly opposed or instrumentally used.[13] *The English Chartist Circular*'s comment on the SDUK was typical:

> Their determination is to stifle inquiry respecting the great principles which question their right to larger shares of the national produce than those which the physical producers of the wealth themselves enjoy.[14]
>
> There was also a host of jokes on all possible variants of the epithet 'useful knowledge'.
>
> In conformity with the advice of Lord Brougham and the Useful Knowledge Society, the Milton fishermen, finding their occupation gone, have resolved to become capitalists forthwith.[15]

'Why', it was asked, 'did not the lass Victoria learn *really* useful knowledge by being apprenticed to a milliner?'[16] 'What' asked the *Poor Man's Guardian*, 'is useful *ignorance*? – ignorance useful to constitutional tyrants.'[17] One editor of the Un-stamped even produced a one-off issue of a little thing called 'The Penny Comic Magazine of an Amorous, Clamorous, Uproarious and Glorious Society for the Diffusion of Broad Grins'.[18]

It was '*really* useful knowledge', then, that was important. But 'education-mongers' offered the opposite. They didn't offer 'education' at all; only, in Cobbett's coinage, 'Heddekashun', a very different thing.[19] So how was really useful knowledge to be got? How were radicals to educate themselves, their children and their class within cramping limits of time, and income? The main answer for the whole of this period was by their own collective enterprise. The preferred strategy was substitutional. They were to do it themselves. A series of solutions of this kind were improvised, all resourceful, though none wholly adequate. Radical education may be understood as the history of these attempts.

Forms

The key feature was *in*formality. Certainly, Owenites and Chartists did found their own educational institutions and even planned a whole alternative system. Secular Sunday schools and Owenite Halls of Science, for instance, represent the most visible, formalized (and best documented) aspects of activity. They remain extremely interesting. Yet to concentrate on counter-institutions would be seriously to misread the character of the radical response and the nature of the transition in the practices of cultural reproduction through which working people were living. There is a danger, too, of separating out 'the educational' and constructing a story parallel to but different from the usual tales of schools and colleges.[20] Radical education was not just different in content from orthodox schooling: its formal principles were different. It was constructed in a wholly different way. There is also a temptation to exaggerate the extent and, especially, the permanence of such institutions in collusion with the invariably euphoric reporting of their activities.

Typically, then, educational pursuits were not separated out and labelled 'school' or 'institute' or even 'rational recreation'. They did not typically occur in purpose-built premises or places appropriated for one purpose. The typical forms were improvised, haphazard and therefore ephemeral, having little permanent existence beyond the more immediate needs of individuals and groups. Educational forms were closely related to other activities or inserted within them, temporally and spatially. Men and women learned as they acted and were encouraged to teach their children, too, out of an accumulated experience. The distinction between 'education' (i.e. school) and not-education-at-all (everything outside school) was certainly in the process of construction in this period, but radicals breached it all the time. As George Jacob Holyoake put it, 'knowledge lies everywhere to hand for those who observe and think'.[21] It lay in nature, in a few much-prized books, but above all in the social circumstances of everyday life.

Radical education cannot be understood aside from inherited educational resources. It rested on this basis but also developed and enriched it. We mean the whole range of indigenous educational resources, indigenous in the sense that they were under popular control or within the reach of some popular contestation. Struggle of some kind was possible, of course, in every type of school or institute but there were also whole areas that were relatively immune from direct intervention or compulsion by capital or capital's agencies. We include, then, the educational resources of family, neighbourhood and even place of work, whether within the household or outside it, the acquisition of literacy from mothers or fathers, the use of the knowledgeable friend or neighbour, or the 'scholar' in neighbouring town or village, the work-place discussion and formal and informal apprenticeships, the extensive networks of private schools and, in many cases, the local Sunday schools, most un-school-like of the new devices, excellently adapted to working-class needs.

On top of this legacy, which in nineteenth-century conditions was very fragile, radicals made their own cultural inventions. These included the various kinds of communal reading and discussion groups, the facilities for newspapers in pub, coffee house or reading room, the broader cultural politics of Chartist or Owenite branch-life, the institution of the travelling lecturer who, often indistinguishable from 'missionary' or demagogue, toured the radical centres, and, above all, the radical press, the most successful radical invention and an extremely flexible (and therefore ubiquitous) educational form.

The product of these two levels of activity may best be thought of as a series of educational networks. 'Network' is a better word than 'system', suggesting a limited availability, fragile existence and a highly contingent use. The ability to use them, even at high points of radical activity, was always heavily dependent on chance individual combinations of more structural features. Accordingly, the working-class intellectual was (and is) a rare creation. The fully educated working man and, still more, working woman was, in Thomas Wright's phrase, 'an accidental being'.[22]

We have, however, many accounts of such people, for they often wrote about their lives. It is worth tracing through a few individual histories, not to present them as representative, but to illustrate the place of the various elements as we have mentioned in a kind of educational progression. It is in autobiographies, besides, that we have the clearest evidence of networks and their use.

Biographies

Parents, relations and friends were a crucial initial influence. Samuel Bamford's parents bestowed on their children 'a sort of daily fireside education'.[23] It was his father – a 'superior man', a weaver, a Painite, once a private schoolmaster – who implanted in the future radical a predisposition towards politics. Bamford, typically, was sure he had learned more at home than at school, regretting only his father's refusal to let him learn Latin.[24] William Lovett's educational experiences commenced with a disciplinarian Methodist mother and a great-grandmother of eighty who taught him to read.[25] Joseph Gutteridge, silk-weaver and amateur scientist, owed much to a schoolmaster uncle, a father who 'always carefully helped me' and the freedom to botanize in the fields and lanes around Coventry.[26] Roland Detroisier, the radical lecturer, was brought up by a Swedenborgian tailor who established his fertile contact with the Sunday schools of that sect.[27] 'My father', wrote John Wood, son of a West Riding weaver, 'being able to read and write a little taught me all he knew.'[28] But, like other lads, John also took lessons, *gratis*, from friends who, for instance, knew more arithmetic than he. We might note, in passing, that something more is suggested in these cases than the generalization that parental influence is enormously important in forming the interests and character of children. More interesting are the historical (and historically changing) conditions in which, say, fathers could quite commonly teach their sons to read, a practice which requires both an inherited literacy and time for its reproduction.

The educational resources of home and neighbours were invariably supplemented by some form of schooling. Schooling was common but took different forms, differently used. Dame schools and private schools, for instance, were quite casually used. When public or charity schools were also included they were used in much the same way, were changed often and were left early. Tutelage under any one schoolteacher in any one school was, in the total sum of educational experiences, usually quite marginal. The major exception here, in some cases, was Sunday schooling, which seems to have been more likely to create an abiding loyalty than any other form of contemporary schooling. Thus, George Jacob Holyoake, after attending dame schools in fits and starts, went to a Methodist Sunday school for five years, later joining John Collins, another Birmingham Chartist and Co-operator, teaching Sunday school at Harborne.[29] Bamford attended several Sunday schools and two different free grammar schools; J. Passmore Edwards, later a radical journalist, learned the three Rs at 3d. a week in a school kept by an injured ex-tin miner.[30] Julian Harney, the revolutionary Chartist, was, exceptionally, educated at the Boys' Naval School at Greenwich in the expectation that he would become a merchant sailor.[31] Gutteridge remembered with affection a Quaker dame who helped him to read newspapers by the age of seven, but suffered under a savage schoolmaster at a local charity school.[32] Lovett's mother sent him off to school after school, strictly enforcing attendance. He went to 'all the dame schools in the town', two private schools with severe, even sadistic masters, and ended up at a local Anglican school.[33] This somewhat experimental approach to schooling was, according to later official reports, a not uncommon one: some respectable working-class parents certainly sought a better school by a process of trial and error.

One of the most interesting aspects of the relation of radicalism and the education of children is the quite pervasive figure of the radical schoolmaster or mistress. The common philanthropic distrust of the intelligent but unsupervised teacher of working-class loyalties undoubtedly had a basis in fact.[34] Schoolmaster was quite a common occupation among prominent radicals.[35] Teaching was indeed an obvious resource for an intelligent, self-educated man or woman especially if he or she had already fallen foul of employers or other authorities. Two examples must suffice to illustrate the way in which such people actually became schoolteachers, either full-time or as a bye-employment.

Mary Smith, radical schoolmistress of Carlisle, was the daughter of a rural artisan, a shoemaker, in a Gloucester village. She could not remember a time when she could not read and her father took pains to provide her with books from second-hand sales.[36] Even so, she went to a string of schools, ending with one of 'higher grade' run by Methodist ladies who stressed deportment and polite accomplishments. Unmarried and with characteristic independence, she left home and, in the 1840s, set up school in Carlisle. Supporting herself by teaching farmers' daughters, she soon developed an alliance with some local workers, sharing many of their political enthusiasms. She attended lectures by James Silk Buckingham and by Henry Vincent, of whom she became an enthusiastic supporter.[37] She rejoiced 'with the best when unkingly kings were uncrowned' in 1848, and later took to freelance, crusading journalism and became involved in the campaign against the Contagious Diseases Act. Violently anti-Tory and not afraid to offend the orthodox religions, she gave secular lectures to working women on Sundays and helped in evening schools.[38] One imagines she had something useful to teach.

Roger Langdon's father was a parish clerk and Sunday school teacher but sent the boy off to work under a brutal ploughman at the age of eight.[39] He ran away and after many wanderings, became a railwayman and eventually, in 1867, a stationmaster. He was a self-taught amateur astronomer, making his own telescopes. He never went to school himself, but 'somehow or other' learnt to write. For most of their married life, he and his wife ran a private school, a practice begun for the education of their own children. His wife taught reading, writing, arithmetic, geography and sewing, while Roger taught scripture, provided scientific apparatus and made the benches for the schoolroom.

> His teaching [recorded his daughter] was unorthodox and advanced, and he always gave us plenty to think about. When later on we went to school at Taunton we found ourselves in most subjects in advance of children who attended schools in the town.[40]

Two main factors seem to have been important in maintaining an educational progression once the influence of parents or schoolteachers came to an end. The passion for reading was sometimes expressed in a catholic appetite for print (as in the famous case of Thomas Cooper) or in the desire to devour, and preferably to possess, a very particular book.[41] But the reading habit itself needed to be supported by some kind of fellowship in the effort to understand. This might be associated with religious questioning, a very common feature in youth, or with accounting for ordinary conditions of life, or might happen in a less self-conscious way in the course of ordinary sociality. For George Howell, for example, who learned his later liberalism within a radical culture, it was discussion with his mates in a shoemaker's workshop which provided the stimulus. The radical press, in this case as very often, furnished texts of debate, bridging a more private educational experience and the more public world of a movement.[42] (Mayhew's typification of London trades by 'intelligence' suggests that an education at the work-place was, where conditions still allowed, quite common.) From this point on 'the educational' becomes indistinguishable from more general currents in radical culture and the approach via individuals distorts a more collective pattern, in which 'living' and 'learning' are hard to disentangle. The most important experiences were those that have been examined by students of the cultural life of 'infidelity', the more heterodox forms of religion and especially Sunday school teaching, the local life of radicalism, Owenism and Chartism. Thus Holyoake, under the influence of the Birmingham Owenites and Unitarians, became a social missionary, while Lovett, Cooper and Harney brought very different attributes to Chartism. Gutteridge, still pondering on nature, read Voltaire, Volney, Paine and Owen and joined a group of free-thinkers. A later generation, following Bamford in many ways, brought a characteristically educational orientation to popular liberalism.

Press

It was, perhaps, the press, in each distinctive phase, that epitomized the forms of radical education. Its general historical importance is now well established. In the first phase it was the main source of unity: '1816–1820 were, above all, years in which popular Radicalism took its style from the hand-press and the weekly periodical.'[43] The unstamped press from 1830 to 1836 was both an educative force, developing much later Chartist theory, and a practical example of the struggle against unjust laws and oppressive government.[44] More recently, it has been established that the press was important within the dynamics of Chartism itself and that 'the establishment of a national newspaper [the *Northern Star*] was a vital prerequisite to the emergence of the Chartist party'.[45]

The political importance of the press was closely linked to its versatility as an educational form. It was a resource that could be used with great flexibility. It could be carefully studied and pondered over, as the more expository parts of, say, the *Poor Man's Guardian* must have been. It could be read aloud in declamatory style in pub or public place as Cobbett's or O'Connor's addresses were.[46] It reached its 'pupils' at different levels of literacy and preparedness for study. The conjunction, it is true, sounds somewhat paradoxical: because of our experience of the modern popular press, we are not used to thinking of a newspaper as an educative medium. An example may convince. We can take the *Northern Star* as the hardest case, the most newspaperly of the radical media and that with the strongest reputation for sheer demagoguery.

The *Star* was certainly a newspaper. It 'could complete with any adversary for coverage', using paid journalists and local correspondents.[47] It remains, as a result, the best source for the study of Chartism everywhere. Yet the *Star* was also saturated with an educational content, even if we interpret 'education' in the most conventional sense. It contained regular advertisements and reviews of radical literature, drew attention to travelling lecturers likely to appeal to popular audiences, noted prosecutions of flogging schoolmasters (presumably to warn readers off such offenders) and published Charles Dickens's exposé of boarding schools from *Nicholas Nickleby*.[48] It gave special attention to Sunday schools, noting the opening of new ones, reporting on meetings of Sunday school teachers and covering the doings of Sunday school unions in Chartist localities. It supported the fund-raising efforts of schools belonging to the more adventurous chapels and sects.[49] It carried reports of Sunday school festivals and outings. In June 1838, for instance, it printed an account of the festival at Keighley, noting a Radical presence in the usual procession through the town: 'the most conspicuous was the Providence, or as it has been charitably denominated by its pious neighbours, the Infidel Sunday School'. The children were preceded by an 'excellent band' and a banner carrying the words 'No Sin to Write'.[50] O'Connor, in his strenuous tours of branches of the National Charter Association, often noted and praised their educational efforts, including those for children.[51] In all these ways, quite aside from its 'teaching', we can certainly see the *Star* as an educational medium. The distinction between 'physical' and 'moral' force Chartism and the tendency to identify O'Connor with the latter has distorted understanding of the *Star* as a newspaper and of O'Connor as a leader.[52] A study of the newspaper itself does not support the contention of R.C. Gammage, Chartism's first historian, that O'Connor 'never sought to raise the Chartist body by enlightening its members'.[53]

Content

Perhaps the phrase 'really useful knowledge' is the best starting point. It was more than just a parody of the Society for the Diffusion of Useful Knowledge. It was a way of distancing working-class aims from some immediate (capitalist) conception of utility and from recreational or diversionary notions. It expressed the conviction that real knowledge served practical ends, ends, that is, for the knower. The insistence on this was unanimous:

> This knowledge will be of the best kind because it will be practical.
>
> [The *Co-operator*, an early Owenite journal]

> All useful knowledge consists in the acquirement of ideas concerning our conditions in life.
>
> [*The Pioneer*, an Owenite/trade union journal]

> It is a wrong use of words to call a man an ignorant man, who well understands the business he has to carry on . . .
>
> [Cobbett]

> What we want to be informed about is – *how to get out of our present troubles.*
>
> [*Poor Man's Guardian*]

> A man may be amused and instructed by scientific literature but the language which describes his wrongs clings to his mind with an unparalleled pertinacity.
>
> [*Poor Man's Guardian*][54]

A concern that knowledge should be relevant to the experienced problems of life was reflected in the criticisms of the SDUK and of the fare of mechanics institutes as trivial and childish.[55] A slightly different criticism was sometimes addressed to lecturers and to the more 'philosophical' of fellow radicals: a criticism of wilful abstractness or abstruseness, of the failure to speak plainly. When a reviewer in the *Pioneer* exhorted his readers 'to call on men of talent to instruct you in the highest branches of science', a fine Cobbett-like editorial, probably by James Morrison, put him in his place:

> No proud, conceited scholar knows the way – the rugged path that we are forced to travel; they sit them down and sigh, and make a puny wail of human nature; they fill their writings full of quaint allusions, which we can fix no meaning to; they are by far too classical for our poor knowledge-box; they preach up temperance, and build no places for our sober meetings . . . but we will make them bend to suit our circumstances.[56]

There is a lot going on in these few pungent sentences. There is a hostility to the scholar and a recognition that his skills may dominate or mystify. There is a moment of self-deprecation ('poor knowledge-box'). But there is also a sense of the idealism or triviality of much 'preaching' and of the absence of that really materialist grasp of conditions which 'we' ourselves (for all our lack of learning) actually possess. There is also a determination to work through the problems politically, to make the 'intellectuals' work *for* us. Very similar themes appear in a running debate within radicalism between those who argued that we remain ignorant and need to get knowledge and those who inverted the intellectual pyramid and argued that 'we' were really wiser than 'they'.

Radicals, however, also argued that their conception of knowledge was wide, much more liberal than philanthropic offerings. Education should be comprehensive in *every* meaning of the word: widely available and extensive in content. The language of universal enlightenment occurs again and again in radical propaganda, the contrast being with the confining of knowledge by monopoly or control. In one of its earthier analogies, the *Poor Man's Guardian* compared knowledge with capital and with manure:

> If manure be suffered to lie in idle heaps, it breeds stink and vermin. If properly diffused, it vivifies and fertilizes. The same is true of capital and knowledge. A monopoly of either breeds filth and abomination. A proper diffusion of them fills a country with joy and abundance.[57]

A fuller formulation was that given in 1853 by Benjamin Warden, a Marylebone artisan, trade unionist, Co-operator and later Chartist.

> Knowledge was very differently understood in its application to the people generally. Brougham and others summed it up as little more than honour and obey the King, and all who are in authority under him. 'You may get practical science', say they, 'but it is only to make you better servants'. Their views expressed a limited range, while our own were founded on all known facts. Mechanics Institutes were not intended to teach the most useful knowledge but to teach only as might be profitable to the unproductive, He trusted, however, we should now get working men to inquire how the produce of their labour was so cunningly and avariciously abstracted from them, and thence go on to the attainment of truth, in order to obtain, before long . . . happiness and community.[58]

The 'practical' and the 'liberal' were not seen as incompatible as they tend to be in modern education debates. For the practical embraced 'all known facts' and 'the attainment of truth'. Despite the stress on a relation to the knower's experience, there is no narrowly *pragmatic* conception of knowledge here. Knowledge is not just a political instrument; the search for 'truth' matters.

Radicals did distinguish, however, between different kinds of knowledge and the practical priorities between them. While a really full or human education, embracing a knowledge of man and nature, would certainly be achieved once the Charter had been won or the New Moral World ushered in, some substantive understandings had a special priority, here and now. Certain truths had a pressing immediacy. They were indispensable means to emancipation. These truths were several simple insights. Once grasped they provided explanations for whole areas of experience and fact. Once these truths were understood, the old world could indeed be shaken.

Because the radical 'theory' of this period is already well known, it is possible to be very brief. There were three main components in what we might term the 'spearhead knowledge' of early-nineteenth-century radicalism. For the radical mainstream, running from Jacobinism through Cobbett and the unstamped and into the Chartist movement, 'political knowledge' maintained its pre-eminence. As a number of studies have now shown, Paine's popular radical liberalism was the most powerful continuing influence on radical political theory.[59] Yet it is important to stress the historical distance that separates Paine's world of the French and American Revolutions from the Britain of the 1830s. The changes had been very great, not least within the British state. This was not just a question of the Reform Act of 1832, the bringing of industrial interests within 'the constitution' and the exclusion of the propertyless. Under Whig auspices after 1832 the state was increasingly employed in a dynamic and transformative manner both to discipline individual capitals and to secure the conditions of capital accumulation as a whole. This involved attacking the customary defences of the poor and handling the hostility which this itself produced, both by coercive means and by modifying the most aggressively forward policies. Radicals schooled in natural right theory and the 'aristocratic' character of state and church had to come to some understanding of Poor Law, Factory Acts, the professionalization of civilian police, the reform of secondary punishments and important changes in the criminal law. Nor was it altogether convincing to attack the educationalists of the 1830s in the same terms as the conservatives of the 1800s like Dr Bell, John Weyland and Patrick Colquhoun.

Something of these changes was grasped in later radical theory, especially in the *Poor Man's Guardian* and the *Northern Star*. While retaining the theory of natural rights as a kind of moral underpinning of the demand for universal suffrage and, certainly, on occasion, speaking of the evils of taxation, the *Guardian* changed Paine's political sociology and developed a more active, interventionist view of 'government'. From the Reform Act, the *Guardian* learnt to draw relations of power (and exploitation) between property as a whole and the working class, not, as in Paine, between 'aristocracy' and 'people'.[60] The *Guardian* was much more interested too in the law and in the actual operations of government: government was an instrument of great power – hence the absolute priority of changing it and the centrality of political solutions:

> From government all good proceeds – and from government – all evils that afflict the human race emanate. There is no power except that of government, that can extensively affect the state of man. How necessary – how important it is – that government should be pure, not alone in its acts but in its constitution – in its construction.[61]

The primary strategic problem was how to secure a 'government of the whole people to protect the whole people'. This once achieved 'the majority' would be in a position to introduce 'Owenism, St. Simonism or any other -ism' that would ensure the well-being of the whole.[62] This was the core of what the *Guardian* called 'knowledge calculated to make you free'.[63]

Like 'political knowledge', the Owenite's 'social science' or 'science of society' incorporated a central ethical notion and a simple principle of social explanation. In advanced versions of 'political knowledge' these were the rights of man and an extreme (political) democracy and the principle of the class nature of the state. Owenism centred on 'community' and a rational altruism and the principle of the educative force of competitive social relationships and institutions. Social co-operation among equals-in-circumstances was the only enduring source of progress and happiness. (It was also 'true Christianity', unlike the priestly kinds.) But why was Society so unlike what Reason prescribed? The explanation hinged on the socializing force of institutions and, in the end, on a fairly mechanical environmentalism. To live in this old immoral world was to become irrational, to have one's character misshapen as competitive, disharmonious and violent, and to learn the great untruth that the fault lay with oneself. The competitiveness of the economic system was reinforced by a whole range of social institutions. There was little indeed which did not, in the Owenite analysis, count as an ideological resource. But it was in relation to three key institutions – the family, the church and the school – that Owenite ideas were most forcibly expressed: in Owenite feminism, in Owenite secularism and in Owenite educational theory.[64] Owenism, then, added whole dimensions to the analysis of privations and a much more rounded view of liberation. It also tended to counter the overwhelmingly conspiratorial view of ruling-class actions promulgated by most of the radical press. The *Crisis*, for instance, spent some time explaining why it was impossible for men like Lords Grey and Brougham or the Duke of Wellington to analyse society rationally. They too were creatures of circumstance:

> The circumstances of an hereditary Earl, of one trained in the profession of law, and especially of English law, and now a Lord, and of a successful soldier of fortune, now a Duke, are the most unlikely to form human beings competent to understand the *real cause* of the errors and evils of society . . .[65]

Or as the *Pioneer* put it, 'Ye are as circumstances made you; nor praise nor blame from us.'[66]

The third main element of spearhead knowledge concerned questions of poverty and exploitation. How was it, in the midst of the production of wealth, that the labourers remained so poor? Economic justice prescribed that the labourer should have the full fruits of his toil; 'labour economics' or 'moral' or 'co-operative political economy' showed how capitalists stole a proportion in the shape of a 'tax' called profit. Though such theories gave a central place to capital, unlike the older notions of poverty through taxation or land theft, the capitalist still tended to be understood in his role as factor, merchant or external organizer of production, and exploitation was still understood as something that happened in exchange. The characteristic solution was to attempt to cut out the middle man from the process altogether and subject production and distribution to communal control.[67]

When radicals spoke of 'really useful knowledge' they usually meant one or other or all of these understandings of existing circumstances. As Patricia Hollis has argued the radical repertoire was built accumulatively not in some simple developmental sequence towards the more 'socialist' elements. Newer insights tended to be expressed in the older rhetoric.[68] Yet these understandings were very powerful. They embraced, after all, a theory of economic exploitation, a theory of the class character of the state and a theory of social or cultural domination, understood as the formation of social character.

'How to do as many useful things as possible'

It is not possible to do justice here to all the elements in radical conceptions of knowledge. Chartism, for instance, was possessed of a rich literary culture. There was a widespread popular interest in the natural sciences, important in some forms of radicalism for its iconoclastic relation to 'Superstition' and 'Church Christianity'. A more complete treatment should also consider the startling modernity of Owenite experiments in the education of children, especially the stress on the child's own activity, the width of the curriculum and the insistence on reasonable adult behaviour towards the young.[69] One more theme must suffice: the relation of knowledge to production, or what is now often summed up (misleadingly) as the question of 'skills'.

Cobbett's approach to this question is particularly interesting.[70] Like all radicals he was concerned with political education. 'I was', he wrote, with typical immodesty and a grain of truth, 'the teacher of the nation: the great source of political knowledge.'[71] But he added a stock of notions about the education of children, attempting to distinguish a real 'education' (a word worth rescuing) from mere 'Heddekashun'. Education meant 'bringing up', 'breeding up' or 'rearing up'. It included the cultivation of 'everything with regard to the *mind* as well as the *body* of the child'.[72] It embraced book-learning where this was useful, but much more besides. One central concern was to teach the child to earn a living, to acquire an economic independence – a 'competence' in both sets of meanings of the word. Such an education should occur almost imperceptibly in the course of play or labour. 'Heddekashun' by contrast was artificial, coercive and divorced from real needs. It involved learning irrelevancies from books. It was a thing quite outside the control of parents and children, resting on alien purposes. It meant 'taking boys and girls from their father's and mother's houses, and sending them to what is called a school . .'[73]

The two most important constituents of 'rearing up' were an emphasis on practical skills and on the educative context of the home. Since Cobbett almost always had in mind the village labourer or small farmer, his prescriptions often have an old-fashioned or 'Tory' ring. He sometimes used the language of a traditionalist squire or farmer, especially when blaming 'Heddekashun' for encouraging artificial social ambitions.[74] Yet the appropriate education of the labourer or small farmer was not particularly limiting. The first priority was to teach the practical skills of husbandry and of 'cottage economy': gardening, rearing animals, making bread, beer, bacon, butter and cheese, tending trees, and, for boys, ploughing, hedging and ditching. Farmers must know how to ride, hunt, shoot and manage accounts. A healthy body and sober habits were also important. Yet more literary skills, as tools, should also be accessible to all. 'Book-learning is by no means to be despised; and it is a thing that may be laudably sought after by persons in all states of life.'[75] So when Cobbett praised the native wisdom of the untutored person, it was not to justify the withholding of literacy, a common argument among 'Tories'.[76] Cobbett was concerned, rather, to stress the value and rootedness of common sense and customary knowledge and to show the inadequacy of purely literary or abstract study. This was most startlingly expressed in a defence of the illiterate.

> Men are not to be called *ignorant* merely because they cannot make upon paper certain marks with a pen, or because they do not know the meaning of such marks when made by others.[77]

By the same rule, those whom the world called wise were often very stupid. Of the editor of the *Morning Chronicle* and of others with a facility for words, he wrote, 'they were extremely enlightened, but they had no knowledge'.[78]

Cobbett's positive evaluation of more literary skills was expressed more fully in his *Advice to Young Men*, and his *Grammar of the English Language*, works which ought to establish his reputation as a conscious educator. These texts were certainly intended for a popular audience, though one that was almost wholly male. *Advice to Young Men* was sub-titled 'and incidentally to Young Women' and addressed to 'every father'; The *Grammar* was intended for 'soldiers, sailors, apprentices and ploughboys'. (Cobbett was indeed the original patriarch, a theme to which we will return.) In the *Grammar* Cobbett sought to democratize the subject and to rescue it from its association with dead languages. He understood the connection between forms of language and social domination and saw the teaching of grammar as a way of protecting the ordinary man 'from being the willing slave of the rich and titled part of the community'.[79] Arithmetic too was a 'thing of everyday utility'.[80] History also was valuable, as a study of 'how these things came'. Cobbett actually wrote his own history book, but he was teaching how these things (tithes, taxes, the National Debt and his whole demonology) came, all the time.[81]

His curriculum, then, had the same feature as other radical versions. Working back from the living situation of adults, he ended with a range of 'competences' that combined the practical and the liberal.

His stress on the educative role of the family was linked to his political suspicion of schools. But we cannot understand this part of his writing without remembering two points made about Cobbett in *The Making of the English Working Class*: his 'personalisation of political issues' and the fact that 'his outlook approximated most closely to the ideology of the small producers'.[82] The central experience in his educational writing is Cobbett the father. Moreover, he actually lived (or envisaged) a situation in which production, domestic labour and the reproduction of skills all remained within the control of the father in the family of the direct producer. In such a situation the natural way for boys or girls to learn was alongside father or mother in the ordinary tasks of the day. All Cobbett's descriptions emphasize such learning situations; learning to make hurdles by helping father at work in a Hampshire copse; learning to manage a farm and read and write letters through the medium of a hamper that passed from family to prison cell; the daring image of the Sandhill, a description of a childhood game to set beside the philanthropic ban on play.[83] His own children were taught 'indirectly'. Things were made available – ink, pens and paper – 'and everyone scrabbled about as he or she pleased'. So 'the book-learning crept in of its own accord, by imperceptible degrees'. Cobbett's conclusions, then, appear equally inevitable:

> What need had we of *schools?* What need of *teachers?* What need of scolding or force, to induce children to read and write and love books?[84]

Cobbett's personalisms were based on rather special circumstances, 'a marvellous concatenation of circumstances such as can hardly befall one man out of a thousand', according to the *Poor Man's Guardian*'s critique.[85] As writer and farmer, engaged (between politics, prison and exile) in two unalienated forms of labour, Cobbett spent much time at home in conditions of economic independence. (One is also curious about the relative roles of Mr and Mrs Cobbett in the 'rearing up' of their children.) If he expressed, in ideal form educational practices appropriate to the small producer household, he expressed them at a time when they were becoming less easy to realize.

Cobbett's ideal united mental and manual labour through the father's control of production. Owenites argued that monopoly or distortion of knowledge was a feature of capitalist industry. Capital seized hold of the secrets of the trades (once reproduced within the labourer's culture) and made of their workers 'unthinking slaves'.[86] Although these themes are everywhere present in the theory and practice of co-operation, they were most elaborately expressed by the 'early Socialist', William Thompson.[87]

Thompson argued that capitalist production tended to divorce labour from a knowledge of productive processes, to divide, in Marx's terms, mental and manual labour, conception and execution. He also argued that 'commercial society' had a more general effect on the production of knowledge itself. There was a direct interest in the development and application of the physical sciences which, by multiplying machinery, would enrich the wealthy. Political and moral sciences, however, were neglected or shaped according to the interests of the rich. In the absence of a knowledge of 'the natural laws of distribution', machinery became a means of oppression. In co-operative activity and ultimately in a new world, mental and manual labour would be reunited and knowledge of man and nature develop in harmony. Co-operative activity was often a conscious living out of these themes. It aimed at re-appropriating the capitalist's control of production and exchange. As the *Birmingham Co-operative Herald* put it:

> Labourers must become capitalists, and must acquire knowledge to regulate their labour on a large and united scale before they will be able to enjoy the whole product of their labour.[88]

The knowledge part of this was important: the Co-operative equivalent of Cobbett's 'how to do as many useful things as possible' was how to repossess the knowledge and skills appropriated by capital. The activity of the collective organization of 'affairs', including affairs of business, was itself an important education:

> They are obliged to exercise their judgement, to weigh and balance probabilities – to count the profit and loss – and to acquire a knowledge of human character. . . . If the mind continues to be occupied in this manner, for a series of years, it will receive a practical education much more improving than the dry lessons of schools, which exercise the memory by rote, without opening and strengthening the understanding. All co-operators will become, to a certain extent, men of business. But they cannot become men of business without becoming men of knowledge.[89]

Popularity

It is difficult, perhaps foolish, to try to weigh the impact of the solutions we have discussed – their 'popularity' – in some simple quantitative sense. We have neither the conceptual means nor the evidence. We do not really know how to 'think' the 'circuit' of such effects: from the conditions from which radical theory arose in the first place, through the educational practices themselves, to success or failure in actually forming people's principles of life and action. The difficulty illustrates the need for an adequate theory of culture/ideology. Empirically, we might begin by establishing what David Jones has called 'the various indices of activity'.[90] We can assess the circulation of the presses, multiplying for collective readership. We can count and place geographically the more formal solutions of schools and halls. We can set this beside the overall geography of the movements themselves and an assessment of the extent to which they moved masses in different places and at different times. Beyond this there are really imponderable questions. How many working men followed Lovett's 'unpopular' advice to economize on drink and spend the surplus on radical journals?[91] How many talked politics with their wives in the spirit of equality advocated by radical women? How common was the practice of Sophia of Birmingham who gave her children a political education by telling them 'all we learn of good' and never shirking difficult questions?[92] How many recipients of tracts conducted this kind of dialogue with the authors?

> When a tract is left me (which is the case almost every Sunday) I examine it, and where I find a blank, there I write some very pithy political or philosophical sentence, and so make them subservient to a purpose diametrically opposed to their intent – namely the diffusion of truth.[93]

How significant a contribution did radical education make to basic attainments – literacy for instance? What kind of effect did radical hostility to provided schooling have on popular patterns of school use?

From existing knowledge something can be said on some of these questions. The indices run very high at peak points of radical activity. The largest ever circulation for a radical paper was that achieved by the *Northern Star* in the summer of 1839 – perhaps 50,000 copies.[94] At such moments radicalism acquired a mass character. Radical ideas and organization could also penetrate into the most unpromising environments, under the noses, for example, of conscientious local paternalists.[95] But even Chartism had marked geographical limits. Whole communities, especially in the countryside and in the south and east, lacked organization, though it is impossible to assess sympathies.[96] (The prior defeat of the southern labourer in 1830 is a crucial unevenness in working-class history.) In the north and Midlands, by contrast, many localities had a continuous history of radicalism throughout the period, often punctuated by major mobilizations. In such areas radical education in its various forms had a continuous and lively history, supported by groups of provincial leaders. It is also clear that radical politics and cultural activity secured, for thousands of individuals, some educational progression, providing a motive for learning. Yet it is certain too that radicalism's more formal solutions did not and could not match the provided forms in extent and solidity. The dream of Lovett and others, of a whole alternative system of education, remained a dream. One might guess, however, that the more democratic institutions had a greater effect on their pupil's consciousness of the social world than a more routine schooling.

It is important to do more work on all these questions, but it may be more useful to approach the broader problem somewhat differently.

As our knowledge of popular movements, especially of Chartism and its antecedents, deepens, much of an older anonymity has been dispersed. It is possible now to identify and name levels of leadership well beyond the kind of national figures discussed in Cole's *Chartist Portraits* and subsequent biographies. For some localities a local leadership has been described quite closely. These were the people whom we have termed, with deliberate looseness, 'radicals' throughout this study. They were the journalists, the demagogues, the lecturers, the national and provincial leaders, the organizers, directors and 'educators' of radical movements. We may refer to many of these people as 'intellectuals'. The value of this term is to mark both the coherence of understanding that was developed and the 'educative' functions that were performed. We might even speak of radicals, and especially Chartists and Owenites, as constituting political parties or proto-parties. In some analyses of party, indeed, the terms party and intellectual are closely connected. For Gramsci, for example, parties were organizations that enabled the production of intellectuals whose experiences and allegiances were, organically, those of the class which they served. Certainly some such distinction – between party and class – between radical 'intellectual' and those whom they addressed – is in this context a useful one. We may then speak of a more or a less 'internal' or 'organic' relation between the two.[97] The question of the 'popularity of radicalism' becomes, then, more qualititive and relational.

There are, of course, great difficulties in answering this question too: it needs to be explored for each movement, each locality and perhaps for each major leader. Edward Thompson's comparison of Owen and Cobbett underlines the importance of individuality:

> If Cobbett's writings can be seen as a relationship with his readers Owen's can be seen as ideological raw material diffused among working-people, and worked up by them into different products.[98]

We might none the less risk the generalization that from 1816 to the early 1840s the relationship between radical leadership and working-class people was extraordinarily close.

One common, but not decisive, test of the organicism of a leadership is its social class origins. It is a common test because it is 'obvious' that people of working-class origin will have a more intimate knowledge of the problems of their class and a stronger sense of loyalty than others. It is not 'decisive' because there seem to have been very many exceptions to this rule: renegades, 'gentleman agitators', 'intellectuals'. The relationship between some of the radicals who were not working class and their working-class 'constituents' seems often to have been peculiarly close – John Fielden, Feargus O'Connor and Bronterre O'Brien are exemplary cases.[99] It would be wrong, however, to regard Chartism or its predecessors as typically led by middle-class people. Perhaps the most important feature of nineteenth-century radicalism was its capacity to produce an indigenous leadership. It is not difficult to understand why this was so, for working people with an inclination towards mental labour *had* to stay within their own class, or occupy positions of great social ambiguity like elementary or private school-mastering or journalism or lecturing. There were few open roads to co-option. At the same time an education and a sort of career were available within radical movements themselves.

The more decisive tests of organicism are those discussed by Gramsci in a 'note' on Italian idealism, though, as usual, the problems of popular communist organization were not far from his mind:

> One could only have had . . . an organic quality of thought if there had existed the same unity between the intellectuals and the simple as there should be between theory and practice. That is, if the intellectuals had been organically the intellectuals of those masses, and if they had worked out and made coherent the principles and the problems raised by the masses in their practical activity. . . . Is a philosophical movement properly so called when it is devoted to creating a specialised culture among restricted intellectual groups, or rather when, or only when, in the process of elaborating a form of thought superior to 'common sense' and coherent on a scientific plane, it never forgets to remain in contact with the 'simple' and indeed finds in this contact the source of the problem it sets out to study and to resolve? Only by this contact does a philosophy become 'historical', purify itself of intellectualistic elements of an individual character and become life.[100]

Early nineteenth-century radicalism did indeed find in the everyday life of the masses 'the source of the problems it set out to study and resolve'. 'Spearhead knowledge' centred, as we have seen, on the experiences of poverty, political oppression and social and cultural apartheid. It gave a wider, more 'historical', more coherent view of everyday life than customary or individual understandings. This was possible, in part, because the commonest inhibitions to such an internal relation were weakly developed. There was nowhere else but contemporary experience from which an appropriate theory could derive: no pre-existing socialist doctrine to be learnt and therefore no danger of the rigidity or autonomy of dogmas. Perhaps there was a tendency of Painite theory to crystallize thus, but, in general, there were simply no historical parallels for the situation of working people in England from which relevant theory might have been derived. A similar argument relates to forms of organization. Though radical groups can be considered parties in a looser Gramscian sense, they were hardly parties on a stricter Leninist model. But organizational looseness had compensations. There were few organizational orthodoxies either, little growth of bureaucracies, little of the more extreme kinds of internal division between 'officials' and 'rank and file' which were to dominate trade union, social democratic and communist politics. The main inhibition to a notably democratic practice was the *amour propre* and charismatic character of some leaders, who, however, could be jettisoned or ignored. In this sense, radicalism had little except its 'popularity' on which to depend. Many of the formal characteristics of its education project stem from this: informality for instance, and the 'practical', 'unintellectualistic' (had we better say unacademic?) character of its 'theory'.

Shifts and differences

The most important shift, over time, was a heightened awareness of the immense difficulty of sustaining radical education. We can, with the benefit of hindsight, see this was the beginning of a longer transformation in working-class educational strategies. From the 1850s and more surely from the later 1860s, the strategy of substitution – of an alternative working-class system – was replaced by the demand for more equal access to facilities that were to be provided by the state. This became the main feature of popular liberal politics and then of the Labour Party's educational stance.[101] Thus while radicals, Chartists and Owenites all opposed 'state education' except as the work of a transformed state, later socialists actually fuelled the growth of state schooling by their own agitations. The consequences of this adaptation were immense: it involved, for instance, accepting, in a very sharp form, the child–adult divide, the tendency to equate education with school, the depoliticization of educational content, and the professionalization of teaching. In all these ways the state as educator was by no means a neutral apparatus.

A study of discussions in the radical press from the later 1830s shows very clearly the preference for, but also the limitations of, a more independent route. Independence remained the central feature of the tradition. Most early radicals had accepted the Godwinian case against every authoritative direction of learning. Cobbett opposed 'national education' right up to his death in 1835. The *Black Dwarf* even opposed the setting up of national libraries on the ground that learning should support itself.[102] Owen himself sometimes, and rather rhetorically, called on government to supply (an Owenite) education: most Owenites probably agreed with Shepherd Smith about 'the folly of looking to governments for aid'.[103] The usual Chartist line was an inversion of that of middle-class reformers: 'national education' could and would follow universal suffrage rather than precede it: any education worth the name was unlikely and would probably be very dangerous beforehand. There was even some debate about the wisdom of a state organization of schooling after the Charter was achieved.[104]

As independence was asserted in still more class-conscious forms, difficulties multiplied. Radicals before the 1830s had tended to see the problem mainly in terms of monopoly. Secular and religious authority kept the people ignorant, ignorant even of the laws they were to obey. The task, then, was to spread knowledge where none had existed before – or only that lack of knowledge which Paine had called 'superstitution': hence that unreasonable faith in reason and in their own presses, legacy in part from their own Enlightenment sources.[105] Besides, as Thompson has stressed, enlightenment seemed to work. But radicals of the 1830s and 1840s, faced by defeats, developed a greater sense of the ideological resources of competitive society, the need to 'un-teach' old associations and the significance, as positive sources of 'error', of institutions like the churches. The Owenite analysis of society's immense ideological weight, which in less sanguine times might have bred a deep fatalism, posed at least the problems of where to start.

The second set of difficulties concerned the material conditions for radical education. There was now much more emphasis on such practical limitations as lack of time, income, rest, and peace and quiet. A sense of these problems seems to have fuelled a move towards more collective and formal solutions, especially for children, different in kind from Cobbett's hearth-based remedies.[106] It was those media with readerships rooted in the industrial north and Midlands – the organs of the factory movement, the Birmingham and union-based *Pioneer* and the *Northern Star* – that seem to have responded most sensitively to new needs.

The factory movement itself is the most obvious example of the newer emphases, for it campaigned on matters of time and the reduction of the working day both for children and adults. It was also the first example of a working-class strategy of pressure on the state to secure well-defined reforms. Of course, the educational content of the movement should not be exaggerated: freedom from excessive toil as a human right or a Christian obligation was also stressed and the factory was attacked as a source of many evils. But the agitation over hours can certainly be read as an attempt to reinstate the educational importance of the family. The need for education was often cited as a motor of the movement and factory reformers put forward their own educational schemes. These sometimes had a Tory or Anglican character but the programme of the Society for Promoting National Regeneration, for instance, put forward a working-class alternative, similar to but more modest than later substitutional schemes.[107]

Working-class difficulties were also often explored in debates with 'education-mongers' – those who saw education as a sufficient remedy for social evils. When Thomas Wyse, a leading educational reformer of the 1830s, commenced his own agitation, he had a series of visits from Robert Owen who gently explained the irrationality of his plans.

> In fact, while the labouring population are kept constantly immersed in pecuniary difficulties, struggling in a whirlpool of evils arising from intermittent employment, and low wages while in employment, the amelioration hoped for by the mere mental reformer can never be achieved.[108]

Similar arguments were repeatedly put by the *Northern Star*. O'Connor himself often wrote on this theme, stressing the indispensability of leisure, the attacks of authority on popular amusements, the perversion of Sunday, the exhaustion produced by 'debasing and life-destroying drudgery', the destruction of physical health and the removal from nature. Working people had little positive incentive to learn or to educate their children. They were shut out from opportunities for economic and political initiatives. The solution was to secure their comforts and political rights first. Once this was done, the people could be trusted to educate themselves.[109] *The Pioneer* put the same argument in more literary form, but with typical concreteness.

> Now mark the toilsome artisan: the bell arouses him from slumber: – soft ease invites him to another nap, but jerk must go to the eyelids, – the half-stretched limbs must spring, – on go the vestments, – up lifts the latch, – and with a hurried step he hastes to work. . . . To work, toil, toil, till strength requires a breakfast – thanks if the cupboard hold one; – a demi-hour allowed to gulp it down. To work again till hunger calls for dinner, – a scanty meal, – and off again to labour until night. Night comes, and now for peaceful leisure. – A book perchance – A book! – A noisy brat to nurse; a scramble for a loaf's small dividend; a cry of pain; a half-a-dozen little feet held up, petitioning for shoes; fit scene for quiet musing. A cluster round the homely hearth, scrambling for scanty rays of heat. A pretty picture, that – fine opportunity for useful training! The mother half worn out, her temper chafed, too busy far to rear the tender thought, – a rap 'o the head more like, eliciting a charming chorus. O, what a wretched catechism is that between a labourer's child and his poor jaded mother! Their little souls grow full of brambles; their health depends on fickle chance; their wanton playfulness has no room to sport in; and *these are but the sweets of poverty*.

Having portrayed family circumstances in this poem of everyday life, the author turns angrily on the charitable:

> Pooh! Cry the rich, it is the lot of poverty – There *must* be rich and poor – the poor are *naturally* ignorant. . . . Wrapped up in vile conceit, and ever ready with the admonition, ye, too, do join the cry, the crafty cry of over abundant wages; the hackneyed slang respecting rights of capital; the enormous wrong of scorning our base origin; the wicked partiality of law; the sordid crippling of light amusements; the maw-worm whine of puffed up charity; the tract, the soup, the caps and tippetts, and little leather breeches . . .

Were conditions equalized – 'just let our noisy brats enjoy a turn or two in your trim nurseries' – there would be no more charges of ignorance and brutishness.[110]

Most of these arguments were directed at targets outside the movement, but they also bore on internal radical debates. The radical enthusiasm for education was composed of several strands, some of them in potential conflict. We began by stressing the dilemma of the desire for education in straightened circumstances, further complicated by the distrust of philanthropy. Counter-education *was* an attempt to solve this dilemma, but it was not *merely* compensatory. Although all radicals saw education as an aspect of equal rights and a goal to be fought for, education was also part of a strategy or method. For Owenites, education (which always included the power of 'institutions', 'writings' and 'discourses' as well as schooling) was the principle means of agitation, but as J.F.C. Harrison has stressed, Owenism was 'not purely a movement to found schools and literary institutes'.[111] Similarly, in the political-radical mainstream, politics and education went together in a complicated web of means-ends relationships. Education without politics was deemed inadequate: it must be allied to some kind of power, some 'physical' or 'moral' force, some purchase on authority. As the *Poor Man's Guardian* put it:

> I may be plundered of my purse by a gang of thieves – I may know *how* they took – *where* they have placed it – *the best way of recovering it;* but, without the means, will this knowledge restore the purse? Certainly not. In England a gang of thieves legislate for the community, and it is not sufficient that we *know* this to be the case, we must possess the means of protecting ourselves from this depredation.[112]

But politics without education was also inadequate. Certain kinds of knowledge were immediate means to the Charter: all sections of the Chartist movement gave to 'intelligence' a key role in mass agitation. This in turn meant that all activity that led to a general raising of levels of literacy and articulacy was to be fostered. There was no division at all in Chartist ranks on this particular theme.

The unity of the compensatory and political aspects of educational enthusiasm did rest, however, on very particular conditions. The whole substitutional strategy was sustained by the belief that sooner or later the Charter or the New Moral World would be secured. Within the terms of this belief, the individual pursuit of knowledge or the general aim of 'improving' the whole class, or the desire to concentrate on the education of children, could all be held together. The task was to prepare for success and speed it. The larger education objectives, utopian indeed in existing circumstances, could be asked to wait. Soon, all would be achieved.

So when political challenges were blunted and hopes of immediate success began to fail, difficult tactical and strategic questions emerged. The commonest response was to hold the existing combination, limit educational ambitions, hope and work for some resolution at other (i.e. political) levels. But the history here is different within the Owenite and Chartist connections. Owenism was a protean movement that met frustrations by once more changing form, stressing yet another aspect of a very fertile repertoire. Chartism faced the problem of power, and had intermediate goals of great clarity (universal suffrage). Setbacks were correspondingly more traumatic, diversions more contentious and battles about strategy more ferocious and debilitating. None the less, somewhat similar debates can be traced within the two movements.

From the perspective of what remained the dominant tendency, the characteristic 'deviation' was to give to education schemes a priority independent of sensible tactical judgement. Since the commonest form of such schemes focused on the education of children, the threat was that radicals would become *merely* school-masters. This was certainly a tendency recurrently feared by the sanest of Owenite theorists: William Thompson up to his death in 1833, James Morrison in the *Pioneer* and Shepherd Smith in the *Crisis*. They warned against the expense, the diversion of effort and the tendency to 'sectarianism'.[113] But the history of Owenism is full of instances of education project-launching. In 1830, John Finch of Liverpool planned a college to provide a 'superior' residential education for hundreds of children of Co-operators.[114] The *Birmingham Co-operative Herald* enlarged this scheme: there should be preparatory schools in every town and country colleges with model farms and small-scale manufactories.[115] In 1833 this plan was revived by two groups. One scheme, proposed by a Mr Reynolds, was supported by Monsieur Philip Baume, a French philanthropist, who offered to lease fourteen acres for a college and give 'everything I possess'.[116] In the same year a group called 'the Social Reformers', meeting in Lovett's Coffee House, planned a boarding school to be supported by 'the intelligent and well-disposed among all classes'.[117] In 1835, an Owenite lecturer called Henderson described a plan for 'a very superior school' before an audience at the Charlotte Street Institute. Children were to board at from £18 to £28 per annum, to study all subjects and, since it had not been positively proved whether Man was 'herbaceous, gramnivorous or carnivorous', they were not to eat too much meat.[118] In 1838 there was a debate in the *New Moral World* about whether to accept £1000 from William Devonshire Saull, a London wine merchant, for educational purposes. The money was eventually used to start an 'Educational Friendly Society', one object of which was to found an 'Educational Community'. At the same time, plans for a Co-operative College were revived.[119] There was more than a hint of education project-building in the programme of the Association of All Classes of All Nations and in the Rational School Movement of 1839 to 1843. In 1839, 'Socius' in the *New Moral World* advocated converting Halls of Science into schools and the setting up of a 'Model Normal School'.[120] The proposal coincided with the debate between church and state over the Whig government's 'Normal School' plan of February 1839.

It was natural that Owenites should wish to found their own schools to show the world how children really could be educated and to avoid using the schools of Church or Dissent. In its more usual forms – more improvised, combining adults and children, and connecting schooling with other activities – Owenite schooling, especially at the level of the local branch, was a widespread and sensible response. But the education projects often bear the mark of the crankier, more philanthropic aspects of the movement and invariably involved middle-class aid and, perhaps, a loss of independence. One might doubt the value of 'superior' residential education to the children of working-class Co-operators or their ability to raise £1 per month per child (the Social Reformer's scheme) or £18 a year (Henderson's).

The equivalent within Chartism was the Lovett/Collins pamphlet of 1840, the ostracism of the 'new movers' in the battle that followed and the swinging of the main Chartist body behind O'Connor and the *Northern Star*.[121] Lovett's plan was to build a comprehensive system of counter-education eschewing the aid of 'irresponsible government' but allowing a role for middle-class sympathizers. The plan bore the stamp of Owenite influence, not least in its ambition: infant, preparatory and high schools in every place, reading rooms, lectures and libraries for adults in newly built district halls, agricultural and industrial schools for orphans, tracts, school-books, and a system for the training of teachers with at least one 'normal school'.[122]

This was less a middle-class scheme, as the O'Connorite criticism went, than an illustration of the ultimate limitations of the strategy of substitution. While mainstream Chartists continued more modest educational work and indeed increased its intensity, Lovett's association became a progressive but not too successful experiment in middle-class philanthropy. The founding of the first day school was delayed till 1848. By this time Lovett himself had actually become a schoolmaster and, under the influence of William Ellis, had entered 'a new epoch in my life'.[123] Ellis, a founder of the Birkbeck Schools, was a militant teacher of political economy.[124]

But the orthodox Chartist route did not constitute a solution either. By the mid 1840s it had reached its limits. In the decades that followed and in the wake of the political defeats, independent working-class education continued; in the better-off sectors it may even have increased. But it took on more individualized forms ('self-education') or lost its connection with politics ('mutual improvement') or became the cultural preserve of the aristocracies. It certainly lost the ambition of being an alternative system, especially with regard to children. At the same time a new kind of educational agitation began to emerge, linked to popular liberalism and the anti-Anglican alliance. Working-class activists began to demand education through the state, even though initially, like the Chartist rump of 1851, they insisted still on some popular control.

Future questions

Explanations of the whole mid-nineteenth-century shift, of which the story of radical education is a part, have tended to focus on material improvements (economic trends of a largely quantitative kind) or on changes in the mode of 'hegemony' or 'social control' understood mainly as occurring within cultural and political relations. There have also been attempts to rework Lenin's theory of 'the aristocracy of labour'.[125] One common tendency, across very different accounts, has been to treat early-nineteenth-century radicalism rather unproblematically as the politics of a class-conscious working class, made or in the making.[126] We now know a great deal about the culture and forms of organization of this period, yet the position of the different groups of working people within economic relations remains surprisingly obscure. The most important questions concern the relations between labour and capital in the actual production of commodities, in what we might call the direct relations of production. What were the forms and degrees of the dependence of labour within production? How far did capital control through the labour process itself, as opposed to more externally or 'formally' through the ownership of materials or a monopoly or exchange? We badly need more exact categories for describing all the transitional forms between the relatively independent small producer and the fully proletarianized worker. The terms derived from contemporary parlance, like 'artisan', remain too loose for serious analytic use.[127]

These questions have tended to be bypassed by social historians though they are present in Marx and in some of the older economic histories. Yet they are crucial for an understanding of the wider questions which now concern our historiography, especially all the questions around 'control', 'hegemony' or 'reproduction' (in the global sense). For capital's control and labour's subordination were formed first and foremost in production. Certainly the forms of the relations there set the terms of what was struggled over elsewhere. But there are other very important questions too. For our educational themes, it is crucial to establish the effects of a deepening subordination of labour in production on the forms of the reproduction of labour, especially, of course, the production of new generations of labourers. The study of forms of the family and of relations between the sexes then becomes very important. The family was a site of reproduction *and* of production of both capitalist and non-capitalist kinds. These latter questions are only now being properly posed. Answering them requires a different sort of research, one that focuses on structure rather than culture. Even so, it is worth ending with some speculations on what structural changes our materials might suggest.

Initially, the independent tradition appears to have drawn on educational resources that could only have existed had capital's control of production and of the reproduction of labour power been relatively loose. Perhaps the most important of these resources lay in various forms of the small producer household, already partially transformed in its relations to capital, but still possessed of a space or autonomy for activities of an educational kind, including the teaching of skills to children. The educational story we have just described (not by any means the whole story of working-class education) corresponds to the economic experience of the small-producer-becoming-proletarian. The main mechanism here seems to have been the curtailment or interruption of the educative or reproductive autonomies of family and community through, primarily, the more complete subordination of labour (male, female and juvenile) in production. This pressure from the sphere of production and the enforcement of capitalist economic relations was reinforced, of course, by direct intervention into the reproductive sphere, of which the growth of state and provided schooling is the most relevant example. At the same time as indigenous educational resources were squeezed, alternative forms were offered or enforced. The erosion of an indigenous educational capacity seems to have occurred in different ways. It happened in a few trades through the concentration of production in the factory and, eventually, the separation of the household and the sphere of capitalist production. The employment of children, often a concomitant of factory production but occurring on an extended scale outside, had, itself, obvious educative effects. But perhaps the most important form of pressure on the family was through a deepening dependence of domestic outwork on the capitalist merchant, factor or middleman and the reduction of margins of time and income through the prolongation of the working day. Low income not only changed the (necessarily educative) relations within the family but also made the family more and more dependent on the labour of the children. But effects such as these would have to be established for particular trades, times and places.[128]

We may understand radical education as an attempt to expand and develop those areas of autonomy and control over reproduction which remained. If this is accurate, it is important to say that it was not a fully 'working-class' phenomenon: it did not rest on fully proletarian conditions of existence. Indeed, the material spaces which it occupied were actually shrinking. This was accentuated by the changing geographical basis of radicalism which was also a changing social basis. The early radical phases rested upon artisans, trades like weaving with relatively recent histories of some independence, and, perhaps, petit bourgeois and lesser professional groups, more modern analogues of the small producer. The spread of the factories, the deepening subordination of the outworkers, the growth of sweated trades, together with the geographic shift northwards in Chartism, gave to radicalism a more fully proletarian base. To such people some of the earlier solutions must have seemed grossly inapplicable. We might compare Cobbett's fatherly idyll with Morrison's poem of everyday life. Perhaps the whole substitutional strategy was inapplicable too: certainly its ambitious Lovettite forms were. Yet it took time to find another route, appropriate to proletarian conditions, and a much longer haul to socialism. The priority, perhaps, *was* to build barriers to capital's appetite for labour and then to its tendency to intensify it. So far as education is concerned the period from the 1790s to the 1830s did *not* see 'the making of the English working class', did not see, that is, the development of the characteristic class strategies of later periods. *This* story really begins, thinly, with the factory movement and continues with the educational strategies of late Chartism, popular liberalism and the early-twentieth-century labour movement.[129]

Notes

This is a much shortened version of a chapter originally intended for a book on early ninteenth-century educational ideologies. A still shorter version was discussed at the Ruskin History Workshop, May 1976, and was published in *Radical Education*, nos. 7 and 8 (winter 1976 and spring 1977).

1 e.g. A.E. Dobbs, *Education and Social Movements, 1700–1850* (Longman, 1919).
2 Brian Simon, *Studies in the History of Education, 1780–1870* (Lawrence & Wishart, 1960); J.F.C. Harrison, *Learning and Living 1790–1960* (Routledge & Kegan Paul, 1961); Harold Silver, *The Concept of Popular Education* (MacGibbon & Kee, 1965); E.P. Thompson, *The Making of the English Working Class* (Gollancz, 1963), especially pp. 711–45. Also important for first opening up many questions was R.K. Webb, *The British Working Class Reader, 1790–1848* (Allen & Unwin, 1955).
3 Especially Patricia Hollis, *The Pauper Press* (Oxford University Press, 1970); Joel H. Wiener, *The War of the Unstamped* (Cornell University Press, 1969); Dorothy Thompson, *The Early Chartists* (Macmillan, 1971); J.A. Epstein, 'Feargus O'Connor and the *Northern Star*', *International Review of Social History*, vol. 21 (1976), part 1, pp. 51–97; Eileen Yeo, 'Robert Owen and radical culture', in S. Pollard and T. Salt (eds.), *Robert Owen: Prophet of the Poor* (Macmillan, 1971); J.F.C. Harrison, *Robert Owen and Owenites in England and America* (Routledge & Kegan Paul, 1969).
4 The importance of private schooling before 1870 has been stressed by those who now favour a return to market principles in education. See especially E.G. West, 'Resource allocation and growth in early nineteenth-century British education', *Economic History Review*, vol. 13, no. 1 (April 1970). For an example of the kind of careful local study that we badly need see John Field, 'Private schools in Portsmouth and Southampton 1950–1870', *Journal of Educational History and Administration*, vol. 2 (1978), pp. 8–14.
5 The major study of Sunday schools – T.W. Laqueur, *Religion and Respectability: Sunday Schools and English Working Class Culture* (Yale University Press, 1976) – argues that Sunday schools as such were working-class institutions, democratically controlled. For an interesting example of a local study which shows the variety of practices under the term 'Sunday school' see Michael Frost, 'Working-class education in Birmingham 1780–1850' (Unpublished M Litt thesis, University of Birmingham, 1978).
6 For the first of these faults see Simon, *Studies*, p. 275; the latter simplifications are commoner in conservative historiography.
7 For Cobbett see page 88 [of original publication]. But Wooller, Carlile, O'Brien and O'Connor among others used this description of themselves or others.
8 *Poor Man's Guardian*, 26 February 1831. The *Guardian* was the longest-lived and intellectually most impressive of the unstamped weeklies in the 1830–6 phase of the radical press.
9 Tom Paine, *The Rights of Man*, ed. Henry Collins (Penguin, 1969), especially p. 163.
10 William Cobbett, *Advice to Young Men* (London, 1906), p. 261.
11 e.g. *Black Dwarf*, 4 March 1818; Cobbett's or Hone's version of the catechism or Cobbett's 'Sunday school hymn'; *Black Dwarf*, 6 October 1819; *Political Register*, 7 December 1833, p. 603.

12 For infants schools see *New Moral World*, 8 July 1837; and *Northern Star*, 7 January 1843. But for a more favourable view see the *Midlands Counties Illuminator* (Thomas Cooper's paper), 20 March 1841.
13 Even the most favourable assessments of the popularity of the mechanics institutes are open to the interpretation that the institutes were used for their 'really useful' content, e.g. the late acquisition of skills of literacy. See for example Edward Royle, 'Mechanics institutes and the working classes 1840–1860', *Historical Journal*, vol. 14 (1971), where it is shown that elementary classes teaching the three Rs were the most popular aspect.
14 *English Chartist Circular*, no. 37, p. 145.
15 *Poor Man's Guardian*, 18 May 1833.
16 *ibid.*, 22 June 1833.
17 *ibid.*, 24 September 1831.
18 Listed in Joel H. Wiener, *A Descriptive Finding List of Unstamped British Periodicals 1830–6* (Bibliographical Society, London, 1970).
19 'Heddekashun' was defined in Cobbett, *Cottage Economy* (London, 1850), p. 4.
20 For a similar argument see Yeo, 'Robert Owen and radical culture', in Pollard and Salt, *Robert Owen: Prophet of the Poor*, p. 108, note 2.
21 G.J. Holyoake, *Sixty Years of an Agitator's Life* (London 1892), vol 1, p. 4.
22 [Thomas Wright], *The Great Unwashed by a Journeyman Engineer* (1868; reprinted Cass, 1970), p. 7.
23 Samuel Bamford, *Early Days*, 2nd ed. (Manchester, 1859), p. 41.
24 *ibid.*, pp. 2, 43–4, 92.
25 William Lovett, *Life and Struggles in Pursuit of Bread, Knowledge and Freedom*, Fitzroy ed., ed. R.H. Tawney (MacGibbon & Kee, 1967), pp. 1–6.
26 Joseph Gutteridge, *Lights and Shadows in the Life of an Artisan* (Coventry, 1893), pp. 7–9.
27 Gwyn A. Williams, *Rowland Detroisier: A Working Class Infidel, 1800–1834* (St Anthony's Press, York, 1965), pp. 5–6, 8.
28 John Wood, *Autobiography* (Bradford, 1881), p. 5.
29 Joseph McCabe, *Life and Letters of George Jacob Holyoake* (London, 1908), vol. 1, pp. 8–10.
30 J. Passmore Edwards, *A Few Footprints* (London, 1905), p. 5.
31 A.R. Schoyen, *The Chartist Challenge: Portrait of Julian Harney* (Heinemann, 1958), p. 3.
32 Gutteridge, *Lights and Shadows*, pp. 6–7, 14–15.
33 Lovett, *Life and Struggles*, pp. 3–6.
34 For this distrust see Richard Johnson, 'Educational policy and social control in early-Victorian England', *Past and Present*, no. 49 (1970), p. 114.
35 See for example, David Jones, *Chartism and the Chartists* (Allen Lane, 1975), pp. 30, 25.
36 Mary Smith, *The Autobiography of Mary Smith, Schoolmistress and Non-conformist* (Carlisle, 1892), pp. 15, 39–40.
37 Asked by a friend whom they should invite as a speaker she replied, 'Send for Henry Vincent. He will please you all.' *ibid.*, p. 148.
38 *ibid.*, pp. 260, 271–2.
39 Roger Langdon, *The Life of Roger Langdon told by Himself* (London, n.d.), pp. 28–41.
40 *ibid.*, p. 68.
41 For example Gutteridge's desire for *Culpepper* – a standard work of botanical reference; or Cobbett's encounter with *A Tale of a Tub*.
42 F.M. Leventhall, *Respectable Radical: George Howell and Victorian Working Class Politics* (Weidenfeld & Nicolson, 1971), pp. 6–9.
43 Thompson, *Making of the English Working Class*, p. 674.
44 For the best account of the unstamped as, itself, a political force see Wiener, *The War of the Unstamped*; for the best account of radical ideology in this phase see Hollis, *Pauper Press*.
45 Epstein, 'Feargus O'Connor and the *Northern Star*', p. 95.
46 For Cobbett see Thompson, *Making*, especially p. 749; for O'Connot see Epstein, 'Feargus O'Connor and the *Northern Star*', p. 84.
47 *ibid.*, p. 79.
48 For lectures see *Northern Star*, 5 May 1838, 2 June 1838, 28 July 1839; for schoolmasters see 25 August 1838; for Dickens see 1838, *passim*.
49 e.g. *Northern Star* 6 and 13 January, 10 and 31 March, 21 and 28 April 1838.
50 *ibid.*, 9 June 1838.

51 *ibid.*, 13 and 20 April 1844, 14 December 1844.
52 For this argument in full see Epstein, 'Feargus O'Connor and the *Northern Star*', *passim.*
53 R.C. Gammage, *History of the Chartist Movement, 1937–1854* (Merlin Press, London, 1969), p. 197.
54 *Co-operator*, 1 January 1830; *Pioneer*, 31 May 1834; *Political Register*, 21 September 1833, p. 731; *Poor Man's Guardian*, 25 October 1834 and 14 April 1834 ('Letter from a "labourer" in Poplar').
55 For a typical attack on this score see *Le Bonnett Rouge* (journal of the neo-Jacobin, Lorymer), 16 February 1833.
56 *Pioneer*, 25 January 1834.
57 *Poor Man's Guardian*, 14 June 1834.
58 *Crisis*, 1 June 1833.
59 e.g. Hollis, *Pauper Press*, p. 219.
60 e.g. *Poor Man's Guardian*, 26 March 1831, leader on the reform bill, and for a more developed version the leader on 14 June 1834.
61 *ibid.*, 26 May 1832.
62 *ibid.*, 30 November 1833.
63 *ibid.*, 14 April 1832.
64 The most 'authoritative' source for Owenite theory was the *New Moral World*, the 'official' journal of the movement. But see Harrison, *Owen and Owenites*, and Thompson, *Making*, pp. 779–807, for the two most interesting contemporary interpretations.
65 *Crisis*, 19 May 1832.
66 *Pioneer*, 16 November 1833.
67 For a fuller account see E. Halevy, *Thomas Hodgskin 1787–1869* (London, 1903); R. Pankhurst, *William Thompson* (1877–1833): *Britain's Pioneer Socialist, Feminist and Co-operator* (Watts, 1954). For their influence on working-class theory see Hollis, *Pauper Press* and Thompson, *Making*.
68 Hollis, *Pauper Press*, p. 225.
69 On Owenite educational ideas see especially Silver, *The Concept of Popular Education*, and Harrison, *Owen and Owenites*.
70 He was not at all the Tory obscurantist that his vote against the education measures of 1833 has sometimes suggested to educational historians.
71 *Political Register*, 10 April 1830.
72 Cobbett, *Cottage Economy*, pp. 9–10.
73 *Political Register*, 7 December 1833, p. 581.
74 e.g. Cobbett, *Cottage Economy*, pp. 10–14. In this way, and with a typical inconsistency, he managed to blame philanthropy both for destroying an old order and trying to maintain it!
75 Cobbett, *Advice to Young Men*, p. 40.
76 For a typical but intelligent argument of the Tory kind see [John Weyland], *Letter to A Country Gentleman on the Education of the Lower Orders* (London, 1808).
77 Cobbett, *Advice to Young Men*, p. 40.
78 Quoted in William Reitzel (ed.), *The Autobiography of William Cobbett* (Faber, 1967), p. 194.
79 Cobbett, *Advice to Young Men*, p. 48.
80 *ibid.*, p. 41.
81 His own history book was *History of the Protestant Reformation*, of which Cobbett boasted: 'unquestionably the book of greatest circulation in the whole world, the Bible only excepted'.
82 Thompson, *Making*, pp. 755 and 759.
83 *Political Register*, 21 September 1833, p. 735; Reitzel, *Autobiography*, pp. 123–5; Cobbett, *Rural Rides* (Penguin, 1967), p. 41.
84 Cobbett, *Advice to Young Men*, pp. 247–55.
85 *Poor Man's Guardian*, 14 September 1833.
86 e.g. Shepherd Smith's lecture on Education, *Crisis*, 31 August 1833.
87 What follows is drawn mainly from *An Inquiry into the Principles and Distribution of Wealth*, but see the similar argument in *Crisis*, 21 April 1832.
88 *Birmingham Co-operative Herald*, 1 June 1829. This is a part-quote from William Thompson, *Labour Defended*.
89 *Co-operator*, 1 January 1830.
90 Jones, *Chartism and the Chartists*, p. 170.
91 *Poor Man's Guardian*, 23 February 1833.
92 *English Chartist Circular*, nos. 22 and 27.

93 *Poor Man's Guardian*, 11 January 1834.
94 Epstein, 'Feargus O'Connor and the *Northern Star*', p. 69, for a discussion of various estimates.
95 e.g. at Benjamin Heywood's Miles Platting or at Crewe. See W.H. Challoner, *The Social and Economic Development of Crewe 1780–1923* (Manchester University Press, 1950), pp. 233–4; Edith and Thomas Kelly (eds.), *A Schoolmaster's Notebook* (Manchester University Press, 1957), pp. 31–2.
96 See the maps of branches of the National Charter Association and the Land Plan in Jones, *Chartism and the Chartists*, for example.
97 For Gramsci's discussion of parties based on the inter-war Italian experience see Quintin Hoare and Geoffrey Nowell-Smith (eds. and trans.), *Selections from the Prison Notebooks of Antonio Gramsci* (Lawrence & Wishart, 1971), *passim*. The distinction between 'organic' and 'traditional' intellectuals is central to Gramsci's discussion of party and working-class culture.
98 Thompson, *Making*, p. 789.
99 On Fielden see Paul Richards, 'The state and the working class 1833–1841' (Unpublished PhD thesis, University of Birmingham, 1975); on O'Connor see Epstein, 'Feargus O'Connor and the *Northern Star*', and 'Feargus O'Connor and the English working-class movement' (Unpublished PhD thesis, University of Birmingham, 1977).
100 Hoare and Nowell-Smith, *Prison Notebooks*, p. 330.
101 This mutation is examined in Dan Finn, Neil Grant and Richard Johnson, 'Social democracy and the education crisis', in CCCS, *On Ideology* (Hutchinson, 1978).
102 *Black Dwarf*, 6 May 1818.
103 *Pioneer*, 21 June 1834 (Senex was Shepherd Smith. See John Saville, 'J.E. Smith and the Owenite Movement', in Pollard and Salt, *Robert Owen: Prophet of the Poor*).
104 Lovett often put the case against state education; O'Brien the case for.
105 See also Thompson, *Making*, especially the discussion of Carlile and 'rationalism'.
106 *The Poor Man's Guardian* compared Cobbett's impracticalities with the enthusiasm with which the Co-operative Congress 'spoke of the formation of schools' (*Guardian*, 14 September 1833).
107 *Pioneer*, 7 and 21 December 1833.
108 *New Moral World*, 16 November 1838.
109 e.g. *Northern Star*, 22 June 1838 and 26 December 1840.
110 *Pioneer*, 16 November 1833.
111 Harrison, *Owen and Owenites*, p. 139. For the distinction between 'education', 'institutions' and 'writing and discourses' see William Thompson, *Inquiry*.
112 *Poor Man's Guardian*, 14 January 1832.
113 Pankhurst, *Thompson*, p. 140; *Pioneer*, 31 May 1834; *Crisis*, 19 April 1834.
114 Silver, *The Concept of Popular Education*, p. 176.
115 *Birmingham Co-operative Herald*, 1 August and 1 September 1830.
116 *Crisis*, 1 and 8 June 1833.
117 *Crisis*, 28 September 1833.
118 *New Moral World*, 1 August 1835.
119 *ibid.*, 10 March and 14 April 1838.
120 *ibid.*, 24 August 1838.
121 Most accounts of this episode are heavily biased in favour of Lovett and the 'new movers'. See M. Howell, *The Chartist Movement* (Manchester University Press, 1966), pp. 230–6. For criticisms of the 'physical force'–'moral force' polarity on which such accounts were based see D. Thompson, *The Early Chartists*, pp. 16–27 and Asa Briggs, 'National Bearings' in Briggs (ed.), *Chartist Studies* (Macmillan, 1965).
122 J. Collins and William Lovett, *Chartism, A New Organisation of the People* (reprinted Leicester University Press, 1969). There is a useful collection of cuttings and other materials on the scheme in the Lovett Collection, City of Birmingham Reference Library.
123 Lovett, *Life and Struggles*, p. 301.
124 For Ellis see W.A.C. Stewart and W.P. McCann, *The Educational Innovators 1750–1880* (Macmillan, 1967), pp. 327–39.
125 Most recently in John Foster, *Class Struggle and the Industrial Revolution* (Methuen, 1977) and R.Q. Gray, *The Labour Aristocracy in Victorian Edinburgh* (Oxford University Press, 1976).
126 A tendency shared, for example, by two very different books – Foster, *Class Struggle*, and T. Tholfsen, *Working-Class Radicalism in Mid-Victorian England* (Croom Helm, 1976). I think this criticism also applies, in the end, to Thompson, *Making*, for reasons to do with the author's conception of class.

127 It is one of the weaknesses of the *Making* that though it deals with just this transition as experienced by 'the artisan', it tends to understand it in terms of 'loss of status' and perhaps 'independence' without an adequate analysis of changing modes of exploitation or subordination. For an interesting opening out of some of these questions see Gareth Stedman Jones, 'England's first proletariat', *New Left Review*, no. 90 (March–April 1975). The categories, 'real' and 'formal' subsumption of labour, however, may not be adequately complex, as they stand, to describe the early nineteenth-century transitions. I am grateful to Bill Schwarz for suggesting this argument.

128 These suggestions are based, of course, on economic and other histories and are not entirely theoretical speculations. There is much in the following sources especially which point to these conclusions: Thompson, *Making*; N.J. Smelser, *Social Change in the Industrial Revolution* (Routledge & Kegan Paul, 1959); Michael Sanderson, 'Literacy and social mobility in the industrial revolution in England', *Past and Present*, no. 56 (August 1972).

129 This is not to deny the recurrent revivals of independent working-class education especially in the 1880s to 1920s. Nor is it to argue that there is nothing to be learnt from the radical experience. It could be said, indeed, that it is precisely the stress on education as an aspect of socialist politics that needs to be revived today. The inhibitions that remain are less material (though to be sure some exist) than ideological and political. They include, centrally, the obsession of British socialists with education of the most formal kind conducted through a system articulated through state or local state agencies. The exhaustion of this social democratic repertoire is very evident today.

32 The Kray twins

A study of a system of closure

Dick Hebdige

> I must create a System, or be enslav'd by another Mans I will not Reason and Compare, my business is to Create.
>
> Blake's *Jerusalem* f.10.20.

> The vampire pursued his ghastly ends with the single-minded determination of a Hitler.
>
> Herbie Brennan in an article on post-war horror comics published in *Mayfair* Vol. 8, No. 12.

> It would seem that the new idols have to take their image to the greatest extremes to satisfy their audiences.
>
> Mick Farren in 'Sex and the Superstars' published in *Fiesta* Vol. 7, No. 11.

The full extent of the burden of personal responsibility in a post-Nietschzian universe, a universe unpopulated by gods and devils, unlimited by divinely ordained absolutes, was, perhaps, only fully appreciated after the two world wars. Several anachronistic notions about the wholesome and inhibiting nature of civilization died alongside the Jews in Hitler's gas-chambers, and it was probably not until the 1960s, as the threat of nuclear war omnipresent since 1945, gradually subsided, that the awful possibilities of life in such a godless universe could once more be explored. During that decade Western man began once more to play in earnest – to extend and elaborate upon his Splendid Alienation, to explore his lawless fantasies, to watch that stunted progeny; the images of a freedom deformed and constricted in the narrow womb of the bourgeois consciousness perform on the television screen, the cinema screen and the stage of an everyday reality less oppressed by the tyranny of work.

It was because the electric media in the 1960s enabled fantasy to find expression with such immediacy, that styles, images, forms and norms could be so speedily transmitted and, at least extrinsically, assimilated. In a technological society 'reality' was, as ever, impregnated with the images of fantasy and was thereby transformed and visibly enlarged. In McLuhan's global village, this impregnation was intensified to the point of bombardment. The process of actualisation was accelerated to such an extent that the boundary between the actual and the potential, the subjective and the objective, the reality and the dream, became increasingly arbitrary. The definitive history of this erosion of the great Cartesian divide lies outside the scope and purpose of this paper, and is beyond this author's capabilities. Such a history would require a complete synopsis of Romantic thought, the development of existentialism, surrealism, relativism, phenomenology, ethnomethodology, would require a study of the literature of the Underground and the Drug Culture and would be incomplete without an assessment of how far these ideas permeated down into the 'popular consciousness' via the mass media. Suffice it to say that the understanding (that is the intellectual appropriation) of the new discoveries was made impossible. Their sheer volume was overwhelming, the apparent spontaneity of their appearance bewildering. Paradoxically, the expansion of the human world, the dictatorship of human forms, was paralleled by the impoverishment of the psychological dimension. Modern man reacted against the apocalyptic potential implicit in his domination of nature by constructing systems of closure; or, borrowing the terms of Barthes's essay on Jules Verne, he sacrificed the 'bateau ivre' (and 'a true poetics of exploration') for the more manageable Nautilus (merely indulging his 'delight in the finite'). I intend in this paper to approach one of the more sensational crimes of the 1960s, the seemingly motiveless or at least 'inadequately motivated' murders perpetrated by the Kray twins as the 'logical' outcome of a system of closure which parodies the aspirations and fantasies of the society in which it was evolved.

But first I shall attempt to interpret the public reaction to the Krays and should like to suggest that the extraordinary interest such cases elicit in the media, the more questionable covert elements in that ambiguous mix of fascination/horror/admiration that such cases perennially provoke are, themselves, evidence of the bourgeois 'delight in the finite' – in a voyage of the Nautilus which will confirm the severe limitations of his own horizons, by taking him to the very edge of his fantasies – to the threshold of what Hunter S. Thompson calls the 'place of definitions' – without exploding or devaluing those fantasies, without actually breaking into that forbidden area.

I shall conclude by indicating how the severe sentences, hysterical editorials et.al. which constitute the final word are merely transparent and clumsy attempts to resolve the guilty contradictions implicit in that original mix which forms the public's interest.

1. Mailer and madness . . . Manson and the manipulated image

To illustrate just how deeply entrenched are bourgeois attitudes to the criminal, the outsider, I have chosen to concentrate on those commentators of the liberal establishment, who, while refusing to make the crasser distortions of their more reactionary colleagues, remain just as limited in their analyses. I shall start with Norman Mailer. In 1957, Mailer wrote that psychopathy is a primitive and positive solution to the problems posed by existentialism, as a kind of magical act of appropriation, was not only a valid response to post-war society but was the one best equipped 'to deal with those mutually contradictory inhibitions upon violence and love which civilization has exacted of us'.

'Psychopathy [he wrote] may indeed be the perverted and dangerous front-runner of a new kind of personality which could become the central expression of human nature before the twentieth century is over.'[1]

Mailer's total identification with his outlaw subject, reminiscent of R.D. Laing's recent simulations of schizophrenia, is unrestrained by ethical considerations. Its commitment is to conclusions. Like Eve in Sartre's 'The Room'[2] the woman who tries pathetically to emulate her husband's madness, to share his delusions, Mailer adopts a logic at once exciting and suspect; an imaginative exercise undertaken in bad faith. The apparent facility with which Mailer subscribes to a policy of exclusive and explicit ego-centricity not only involves his customary endorsement of a tragically limited and inauthentic concept of the Self, it remains ultimately unconvincing, it fails to disguise his principal interest – a somewhat unwholesome fascination in the infinite permutations of his own alienation. It is a stance, a pose, an act of romantic sympathy which provides Mailer with his passport into the night time world of the urban hipster, but his credentials remain forged, his journey into that world illusory, his participation in its action vicarious.

In a recent article by John Grillo, entitled 'An Excess of Nightmare', the playwright attempts to face up to the consequences of this type of bad faith: in the terms of this essay, to reap Mailer's harvest; by examining the meaning of the preoccupation of the post-war avant-garde theatre with images designed to horrify and disturb the audience:

> A number of young writers . . . who are respectable middle-class gentlemen, reserved intellectuals, if not with Convent upbringings at least from good homes, have peopled the theatre with archcriminals, skinheads, necrophiles, hells angels, lunatics, murderers, delinquents, revolutionaries, and flagellants, none of whom live within our immediate social circle. These characters are not studies of complex, multi-faceted individuals but are personifications of underground instinctive fantasies . . .[3]

Grillo illuminates how the liberal artist has, in recent years, subjected certain deviant personalities to a symbolic assault, so intense and unremitting as to actually translate these personalities into mere images to be manipulated. In the section quoted above, then, Grillo admits to directly contributing to the demonology of the dominant society by depicting the outlaw as a mono-dimensional figure in a poetic fantasy; a symbolisation – a catalyst employed to evince a specific response. Characters have been replaced by figments – closed vessels pushed out by the author to explore and extend the limits of his own alienation. And in 1969, after a decade marked by persistent navigation of such murky waters, the boats quite literally came home, in the form of two murders, both so sensationally reported, so extensively speculated upon us to acquire themselves the status of symbolic events. The two killings took place in the States: the first was the murder of a negro by a group of Hell's Angels employed by the Rolling Stones as security guards at their Altamont concert, the second was the murder by Charles Manson's 'family' of Sharon Tate and her houseguests in the Polanskis' Beverley Hills home. Two arch-celebrities, Jagger and Polanski, both highly successful champions of the Permissive Age, both publicists for a greater liberalisation of controls, both loudly professing a 'sympathy for the Devil', both guaranteed maximum exposure by their long accomplished metamorphosis into living news items were publicly forced to face the ideological implications of their common position. The analogy with Pandora and her box proved irresistible to even the Underground Press (though some insisted on adopting Manson as a martyr, a sword-wielding Angel of the Apocalypse) and the apotheosis of the killings into mythical events was automatic. Manson and the Hell's Angels had stepped straight out of Marcuse's antithetical dimension, the twilight zone of the Great Refusal, to discredit and embarrass their radical promoters, to bite the hand that fed them a symbolic value, to deny with force the meanings imposed so enthusiastically upon them. By refusing to fulfil their mystic function as the revolutionary vanguard of a new society, they were relegated to their customary position as folk devils, becoming as Stuart Ewan argues so convincingly in his article on Manson, merely things to frighten the bourgeois with.[4] Altamont and the Sharon Tate killings showed the limitations of the new radical perspective, a perspective as prone to naive distortions as that adopted by the dominant sections of society. It sought, no less than dominant systems, albeit from a diametrically opposed set of motivations, to incorporate the outlaw within a mythology, to gatecrash an impenetrable world where it was quite simply unwelcome, and to claim that world as its own. The premature reification of metaphors of resistance and denial, the substitution of approximate for precise definitions of freedom amounts to a dangerous and irresponsible abridgement of the authentic process of liberation. It is dangerous firstly because it facilitates the convenient collapsing of the categories of politics and crime by the dominant culture (and the consequent generation of moral panics) and secondly because, as at Altamont, the images tend to defy manipulation, to burst from the dream with disastrous effects.

2. Flawed fantasy – a form for the future

The eventual confrontation of Jagger and Polanski with a reality less amenable than the images with which they had conjured reproduces in miniature a much larger historical process. To take Jung's premise that imagination is 'the mother of all possibilities', it follows that metaphor, the expansion of the possible by imaginative synthesis, strives perpetually towards realisation, and hence fantasy begins to acquire a significance far greater than that which is traditionally assigned to it in Western philosophy. Imagination can now be seen to interact creatively with the objective world, to fertilize it, to influence directly if not actually predict its content. To return to specifics, this means that bourgeois fantasy not only reflects the alienation of the society which has produced it, but actually confirms the conditions of its own creation, perpetuates the alienated situation in which it was produced and further exacerbates the tension between man and his universe. And so when we return once more to Manson and the Hell's Angels we can appreciate their peculiar aptness and consequent potency as folk devils, as vessels loaded down with the illicit cargo of a pernicious fantasy, as the predictable products of a society unable to accept responsibility for its own imaginative creations, unwilling to take the consequences of its own actions.

In the last of his 'murder trilogy', *The Order of the Assassins*, Colin Wilson approaches a full recognition of the complexity of the relationship between the public as frightened dreamer and the folk devil as bogeyman[5] when he describes the impact of the Persian Hashini cult on ninth century Persia. He designates such figures as Hassan-i-Sabbah, the notorious founder of the cult, 'creatures of nightmare' and goes on to say: 'Like the minotaur, he is a mythical archetype, he exists because people want him to exist'.

To cite another example this time from a work of fiction – Robert Musil, the German writer concludes his description of the trial of Moosbrugger, whose crime, a sexual murder, haunts the pages of his meandering novel *The Man Without Qualities* by recognising in the defendant's private world 'merely the distorted pattern of our own elements of existence'. As Moosbrugger is led away to the cells, Ulrich the narrator has the starting revelation that 'if mankind could dream collectively it would dream Moosbrugger.'

With the advent of the electric media – a global nervous system, unevenly sensitive it is true, but a system, nonetheless, constantly registering and interpreting the traumatic productions of time, mankind did indeed possess the means with which to dream simultaneously and collectively. It seems wholly appropriate that mankind in the 1960s should dream the Kray twins.

> Hollywood is a town based on the power of visuals . . . In Hollywood you either become what you look like or you don't become at all.
>
> From Andy Warhol's 'Interview'

3. East End villains in a West Side story

Before actually entering the strange world which the Krays came to occupy, before even describing how that world was created I intend to make a few preliminary observations about the seemingly intimate relationship between the screen gangster and his real life counterpart, observations which, in the light of what I have already written, will I hope escape the categories of cliché, truism etc. to which observations of this nature are usually assigned.

In Robert Warshow's excellent essay on the gangster genre – 'The Gangster as Tragic Hero' (where Warshow interprets its meaning and importance as a carrier of 'the no to the Great American Yes which is stamped so big over our official culture') – there appears the following passage:–

> For the gangster there is only the city, he must inhabit it in order to personify it . . . not the real city but that dangerous sad city of the imagination which is so much more important, which is the modern world. And the gangster, though there are real gangsters – is also and primarily, a creature of the imagination. The real city, one might say, produces only criminals, the imaginary city produces the gangster, he is what we want to be and what we are afraid we may become.

The ease with which we can move from the gangster of the films to his real life counterpart and make mutually applicable statements amounts to more than mere speculative analogy. It provides us with an index whereby we can gauge the narrowness of the gangster's world, the degree of limitation in the range of possibilities open to the actor once he has committed himself to his rôle. The close correspondence between actor and gangster has been fully explored in Colin MacArthur's book *Underworld U.S.A.* (primarily concerned with the gangster film). MacArthur cites George Raft and Alain Delon as examples of the actor/gangster whose private and public personae are virtually inseparable, and records Al Capone's legendary offer of $200,000 to Warner Brothers to appear in their 1932 production 'Scarface' as himself. John Baxter in his analysis 'The Gangster Film' argues that a parallel situation invites this kind of fluidity:

> Both in the public eye, both dependent on the projection of charisma to survive in an uncertain world, both doomed to short-lived careers, gangsters and actors seem too close for true separation.

Whether or not the specific points of convergence are relevant, the closeness of the fictional to the real gangster is important because it highlights a whole set of intermediary determinations of an ultimately aesthetic nature which direct and shape lives dramatically at all levels. I have called these determinations 'intermediary' because they are indeed themselves initially dependent upon class – in this case, the acceptability/availability of a criminal career, and the accessibility of a gangster style are related to primary class determinations. These determinations are aesthetic because they are contingent upon the adoption of a role, the convincing presentation of which is itself dependent upon familiarity with a specific form of popular fantasy.

When Warshow concludes his essay by writing that the gangster genre:

> . . . is a more modern genre than the Western because, like much of our advanced art, it gains its effects by a gross insistence on its own narrow logic. But it is antisocial, resting on fantasies of irresponsible freedom.

he is indeed writing as much about the gangster of the real city, as the gangster of the 'dangerous, sad city of the imagination'. The two can no longer be usefully distinguished. Fictional form and lifestyle, both mutually responsive in a society which denies all responsibility, both competing for a more thorough realisation of the possibilities apparent within the limited area of a form, both committed to the relentless working out of those possibilities to their 'logical' conclusions coalesce to produce one shrunken world, one self-perpetuating, self-supportive universe – to produce, in short, a system of closure, which is a parody of the genuine struggle for completion – a tragic and unnatural synthesis.

It is to aesthetic determinations, rather than the apparent motivations of direct financial gain etc. which were stressed by the press (e.g. the *declared* motivations of the screen gangster), that I will turn when attempting to understand the conduct of the Krays – conduct which often appears unreasonable, unprofitable and bizarre, conduct which threatens constantly to lose all credibility and to lapse back once more into its fictional sources, conduct which makes sense only by a 'gross insistence' on the 'narrow logic' of the world in which they came to exist.[7]

4. What seems to have happened

The tentative tone of this section heading is necessitated by the fact that the twins provided nuclei for such a quantity of myths that the bare facts of their lives can scarcely ever be extracted from their legendary wrappings with confidence. To search for the *truth* about the Krays would involve a reduction of the relevant issues quite as facile and probably as unsatisfactory as those undertaken by the Sunday papers. For the Kray twins existed in the 1960s not merely as professional criminals, but as a living complex phenomenon, an organic myth nurtured by press and public alike, until their actions ceased to have any meaning outside the theatre constructed for them. As the illegitimate offspring of sex and violence fantasy the Krays were hastily adopted by the parents of the Permissive Age, the photographers, journalists, socialists and stars who formed what Peter Evans describes as 'the original cast of characters . . . who between them got the show on King's Road'.[8] Appearing simultaneously in David Bailey's 'Box of Pinups' as menacingly attractive incarnations of evil, in the East London Gazette as local boys made good, as 'the sporting brothers' supporting charity, and variously in the national press as leading lights in the new nightworld, as ex-boxers turned 'company directors', as the intimate associates of the rich and famous, as villains and victims of injustice, the Krays became a polysemantic symbol, our own white whale within whom massive contradictions found dark and mysterious resolution. As Nichol Fortune writes in his article 'The East End – After the Krays'[9] 'they were very public figures indeed', permanent news features,[10] ultimately the possessions of the media, (a kind of joint-stock fantasy-factory) determined like all celebrities by the conditions of public performance, by the obligation incumbent upon their exalted position (written into their showbiz contracts, as it were) to fulfil the expectations of their audience, to consult the precedents set in fantasy fiction, to pursue the goals of a bourgeois society (albeit with the profits of crime), and to live out the destructive fantasies of that culture to their bitter and bloody conclusions. The problem of confronting this Frankenstein, determined to ascertain the facts is not helped by our virtual reliance on one text, John Pearson's *The Profession of Violence* published last year by Weidenfeld and Nicolson and out in paperback last month. This book is vastly superior to others written on the twins (Brian McConnell's *The Evil Firm: The Rise and Fall of the Brothers Kray* and Norman Lucas's *Britain's Gangland* are, for instance, poorly written and hysterical in tone) not simply because the writer succeeds in avoiding the pitfalls of generalisation and emotionalism into which his rivals fall immediately, but because he seems to have enjoyed a privileged status with the gangsters and certainly had access to an enormous amount of previously unknown material.[6] I shall therefore, for the most part, merely summarize Pearson's history.

(a) Early days

Ronald and Reginald Kray were born in Bethnal Green in 1933. They seem to have lived fairly typical Eastend boyhoods – any harshness in the physical conditions of existence were compensated by an excess of maternal love. The boys took up boxing on leaving school after rejecting the only other legitimate occupation which offered itself – collecting empty crates at the local fish market. Their early success as boxers was terminated by their call up in 1952, and most of the next two years was spent on the run, absent without leave, or in the military prisons of Shepton Mallett and Colchester. They were dishonourably discharged in 1954 (following in father's footsteps – Mr. Kray was a wartime deserter) and in the same year became the legal tenants of the Regal Billiard Hall in Eric Street, Mile End, in circumstances which can only be described as suspicious (damage to property preceding takeover, a very low rent accepted by owners). The Regal was used as a meeting place for local criminals and a storage ground for stolen goods and thieves' tools. In 1955, they made their first contact with the men who controlled the lucrative rackets in the West End. Jack 'Spot' Comer and Billy Hill, after a long-standing partnership, were fighting for ascendancy in Soho, and the Krays were temporarily enlisted in the ranks of Comer. They accompanied Comer to the 1955 Epsom Spring Meet which provided the criminal underworld with an annual opportunity for a ritualistic display of power and a chance to see how that power was distributed. The tension between the Hill and Comer mobs subsided with Comer's retirement, after his face had been slashed by razors wielded by 'Mad' Frankie Fraser, who was to play an important part in the formation of the Krays' rivals the Richardson gang, and an associate. Comer refused to sanction a proposal for retaliation, put forward by the Krays which involved the use of guns (an expedient no gang, except the Krays had, as yet, seriously considered according to Pearson). Hill also retired at this time but the Kray's entry into the West End was, for the time being, postponed. Meanwhile the Krays were building up a veritable arsenal, developing techniques of intimidation and cultivating a reputation for ruthlessness and violence which was to stand them in good stead for years to come, and which was facilitating the development of what was always to be their principal source of revenue – extortion. Protection was collected regularly from the public houses and illegal gambling clubs of the East End. ('That according to Jim', Nichol Fortune's informant 'was where the bulk of their income always came from'.[11])

(b) Prison

In 1956, a minor feud between the Krays and a gang called the Watney streeters ended in the particularly brutal beating of one Terry Martin, whose evidence was enough to put Ronnie away for three years. While Ronnie was 'away' Reggie and the Krays' elder brother Charlie, opened their first club, the 'Double R' in the Bow Road. The club immediately became a fashionable meeting place for slumming celebrities, socialites and criminals. Ronnie, meanwhile, after being moved from Wandsworth, a straightforward 'nick' in the old style, to Camp Hill, an experimental prison with a more liberal administration, suffered a nervous breakdown and was moved to Long Grove Prison Hospital in 1958. Here he was classified as a paranoid schizophrenic 'quiet, co-operative and mentally subnormal' in the words of his report. The possibility of committal for life made escape imperative, and in this Ronnie was assisted by his twin who helped to confuse identification by appearing on visitors' day wearing an identical suit to Ron's. (This story appears in all accounts of the Krays' lives.) After avoiding arrest for several months, Ronnie surrendered and was not recertified thus achieving his objective, and serving the rest of his sentence in Wandsworth Prison. He was released in the spring of 1959. In the same year, Reggie received an 18 month sentence for attempting with one Daniel Shay to extort £100 from a Swiss Travel Goods Firm in the Edgware Road. While his twin was in prison, Ronnie began showing an interest in the highly profitable prostitution, protection and rent rackets of Notting Hill and Paddington which were making sensational headlines in the press at this time, and Peter Rachman, the notorious slum landlord, found it expedient to hand over his interest in a successful night club called Esmeralda's Barn which was situated in Wilton Place W.1.

(c) The West End weakens

This was the first real foothold the Krays had won in the West End, but it did not take long for the twins to realize how vulnerable the whole world of 'high society', of success and 'straight' business was to their by no means subtle combination of bribery and intimidation. At this time, the twins recruited Leslie Payne into their organisation. Payne had prospered for many years on the doubtfully legal fringes of big business and now took over the Krays' financial affairs. It seemed likely as the Krays became involved in a variety of semi-legitimate virtually undetectable, often unofficially tolerated activities ranging from credit-dealing to large-scale financial swindles and long-firm fraud that they were ready to follow the upwardly mobile pattern set in the United States by the Mafia, gradually extending into wholly legitimate business whilst refining violence into less and less visible (and crudely tangible) forms. Indeed the Krays began negotiating a link up with organised criminals in the U.S. Payne introduced the Krays to Freddie Gore who became their accountant and set up the Curston Group of Companies which served as a front for many of the Kray's illegal businesses. Reggie started investing in radio and television retailers, bought the 625 Centre and took over Dominion Refrigeration Ltd. whilst Ronnie bought the Cambridge Rooms, a plush, over-decorated club on the Kingston Bypass. In a suspiciously half-hearted attempt to check the Krays' rise (were police already on the Kray payroll?), the police charged the twins with 'loitering in the Queensbury Road with intent to commit a felony and of trying the door handles of parked cars'. The Krays made sure this petty charge received all the contempt and ridicule it deserved in the press when they were finally acquitted.

(d) Success and some important snapshots

In 1961, the Gaming Laws were introduced, transforming London's nightlife and heralding in what Samantha Eggar was later to call 'the road show version of the Jazz Age'. In the immortal words of the contemporary press London began 'to swing' to the delight of both the international set and every other criminal organisation in the country. It was at this time that Ronnie first began mixing in what are conventionally described as 'distinguished' circles. The high point of Ronnie's involvement in this world came with the Enugu Scheme. Kray was planning with Ernest Shinwell and Lord Boothby to finance a new township in Nigeria which was to be called Enugu and was to serve as a model for the rest of Black Africa. The scheme fell through and in July 1964 the 'Sunday Mirror' linked the names of Kray and

Boothby in the notorious 'Prominent Peer and Gangster Scandal'. The paper attempted to launch a two pronged attack; simultaneously exposing the sexual indiscretions of people in high places and the growth of gangsterism in Soho (a kind of updated Profumo with homosexuality and just a hint of the Godfather to add man appeal to a rather hackneyed topic of breakfast conversation). The 'Mirror' made extravagant claims for a somewhat unremarkable photograph of the two seated 'together on a sofa', which had passed rather mysteriously 'into [their] possession', which somehow synthesised the two scandals and which they refrained from publishing, Boothby sued, both exposées were dropped and the Krays had received a very useful advance warning that police investigations into their activities were currently underway. When the photograph finally appeared in the *Daily Express* (August 6 1964) it proved to be totally innocuous.

Another episode that concluded happily for the Krays with another cunningly manipulated photograph commenced in January 1965 when a 'business associate' of the Krays attempted to extort money with menaces from Huw McConary, owner of the Hideaway Club in Soho. On 10 January, 'Mad Teddy' Smith, the above mentioned associate, and the three Kray brothers were arrested and charged. On February 28 they were acquitted after a sensational court case which resulted in a legal change in the jury system, as it was widely suspected that some at least of the twelve upright men and true had been got at (unanimity was abandoned in favour of an eleven to one majority decision; one juryman dissenting would no longer secure a retrial). Another precedent had been set – Lord Boothby had asked how long the twins were to remain in custody without trial – thus raising in the House of Lords a question which Viscount Dilhurne claimed had no place being asked there.[12] The twins celebrated their victory by buying the Hideaway on the day of their acquittal and holding a massive party for the press. According to Pearson, Read, the detective who was to finally bring a successful case against the Krays accepted an invitation to drink with Ronald and was immediately photographed in his company. The embarrassing photograph was again used to achieve some measure of freedom from police interference – Read was taken off the case and all police officers were issued with a directive not to fraternize with known criminals.

On April 20 1965, Reggie's marriage to Frances Shea was greeted by the press as the East End Wedding of the Year and David Bailey took the wedding photographs. In the same year, Ronald met Angelo Bruno, New York mafia chief, at the London Hilton and the Krays became the equivalent of London agents for the mafia, handling stolen American securities, and arranging for their resale in Europe. It was in this capacity that the twins met Alan Cooper, an American gold smuggler and banker who henceforth began to take over the functions performed by Leslie Payne, and who was eventually to play an important part in the Krays' conviction.

(e) Gang war hits streets

Meanwhile, internal tensions between the various gangs in London competing for the control of the protection rackets was translating the ever-present possibility of open gang warfare into an unavoidable certainty. The Richardsons posed the only serious threat to the hegemony of the Kray firm. Charles and Eddie Richardson operated from a scrapyard in Brixton and were extremely powerful south of the river – their successful implementation of crude techniques of 'persuasion' in the previously violence-free area of business fraud encouraged them to consider expanding into the protection rackets. By 1966, the two gangs had clashed several times socially and it was luck more than anything which had prevented armed and open hostilities in the past. At this time, however, the ritual insults were passed back and forth across London with increasing frequency and vehemence. Petrol bomb answered petrol bomb, cars were transformed into weapons and used to mow down members of the rival gang; the Widows, a pub frequented by the Krays was symbolically peppered with shotgun pellets. The ritualistic enactment of territorial conflicts followed precisely that pattern set by Capone in the Chicago of the 1920, and recreated with such monotonous regularity in Hollywood by Cagney and Bogart and Edward G. Robinson. Attack followed counterattack in an escalating spiral as automatic and predetermined as a Hollywood script and London gangsters spoke in the language of the American cinema borrowing the iconography of that cinema to make their emphatic statements. In February, the two most explosive and violent personalities in the two gangs: Ronald Kray and 'Mad' Frankie Fraser clashed in the Stork Club. Verbal insults passed audibly and publicly across the room, and war was openly declared. And then, quite suddenly and unexpectedly the necessity for such an inevitably disastrous conflict was abruptly removed by another battle which led to the immediate destruction of the Richardson gang as a criminal force in London. On 7 March 1966, Eddie Richardson, 'Mad' Frankie Fraser and several others were involved in a shooting incident with a local gang at Mr Smith's Club in Catford. Richardson and Fraser were wounded and taken to Lewisham hospital and Ronald Hart, a member of the opposing gang, was killed. The police immediately launched a detailed investigation into the Richardsons' activities and from that night the South London gang ceased to exist as a challenge to the Krays. Nonetheless on the evening of 10 March, 1966 George Cornell, the only gangster of any importance connected with the Richardsons who had not been implicated in the Catford incident was drinking alone in the Blind Beggar public house, Whitechapel, when Ronald Kray entered accompanied by 'Scotch John' Barrie. Kray produced a revolver and shot him once through the head, killing him instantly.

(f) The legendary springing of the mad axemen

It was apparently with an eye to counteracting the adverse publicity this gratuitious killing had given the Krays throughout the underworld, that they engineered the spectacular escape of Frank Mitchell from Dartmoor later in the year. Mitchell, the 'Mad Axeman', was considered by the Home Office to be one of the potentially most dangerous criminals in prison at the time. He was serving an indefinite sentence for robbery with violence and had earned his nickname by threatening an elderly couple with an axe during a previous escape from a mental hospital. At the Krays' trial, it was established that Mitchell could have been of no direct use to the Kray firm – they did not require a bodyguard and Mitchell's low mental capacity disqualified him from holding a higher position in the firm. It was partly the whim of Ronnie who had befriended Mitchell after meeting him in Wandsworth prison in the 1950s; but the escape is best explained as a gesture of defiance, a dramatic exhibition of the Krays' contempt for all law but their own. Mitchell was a huge figure – both physically and metaphorically – he constituted an extremely potent anti-authority symbol (he constantly attacked the enemy 'screws' in prison) and as such was held in awe by the criminal underworld. By keeping their part in Mitchell's escape the worst-kept secret in the East End (Ronnie's execution of Cornell being perhaps, the next most well-known 'mystery'), the Krays stood to gain an enormous amount of prestige in their world.[13] Mitchell was taken to a flat in Barking where 'Mad Teddy' Smith helped him to compose a letter which was sent to the *Daily Mirror* and the *Times* and which was subsequently published in both papers. The letter appealed to the Home Secretary to grant a definite date of release for the Mad

Axeman if he should give himself up. Whilst Mitchell awaited the public announcement that never came Ronnie Kray left his massive and unpredictable charge in the hands of two members of the 'Firm' – Albert Donaghue and George Dixon. As the days passed with no word from the Home Office, Mitchell became increasingly belligerent and unmanageable, threatening to kill the Krays' parents if they didn't procure him a woman. A club hostess was promptly fetched from Soho, promised £100 and, in Reggie's words 'the gratitude of the whole East End', if her client was satisfied, and was installed with the 'Mad Axeman'. She seems to have succeeded in mollifying Mitchell, but the Krays felt he was becoming a security risk which should be tactfully but speedily removed.

On Christmas Eve, 1966, Mitchell was told he was being transferred to Ronnie's country residence and was collected by Donaghue. The girl said at the trial that she heard four loud reports and when Donaghue returned he phoned up Ronnie and said: 'The dog is dead: We gave him four injections in the nut'. Mitchell's body was never recovered and he is still on the Escaped Prisoners list. Thus, another of the Krays' bizarre games was abruptly terminated.

(g) London overrun by 'absurd creatures of the underworld'

The Krays continued to expand the various businesses, systematically taking over the amphetamine, fruit machine and pornography rackets the Richardsons had previously controlled. 1967 was the year in which the Richardson trial exposed Britain's gangland to its first major publicity since the old Spot-Hill feud. As it became apparent that the technological revolution had completely transformed the techniques and potential of crime (a transformation which is succintly expressed in the substitution of the sawn off shotgun for the razor) a moral panic was declared by Britain's press. The famous Richardson 'Torture Trial' acted as a catalyst for police action in much the same way as the Saint Valentine's Day Massacre provoked a clean-up Chicago Campaign in the America of Capone. Inspector Read was recalled to the case and placed in charge of a top-security investigation into the Krays' activities. The elaborate security arrangements accompanying the investigation (Read's headquarters were situated in Tintagel House, the rumour was circulated throughout Scotland Yard that Read was conducting an investigation into police corruption, which, in a way, he was) testify to the Krays' power (if not 'real' power at least the image of power projected through an extremely effective propaganda campaign). The Krays were henceforth treated as though they constituted a unique threat to the security of the state. News of the investigation, despite these intricate safety measures, was soon transmitted to the Krays and Ronnie's incessant paranoid fantasies were at last given some confirmation in the real world. As in previous crises, he began drawing up lists of men he considered needed liquidating. One such was Leslie Payne who had by now been completely superseded by Cooper.

Kray offered a local East End villain, Jack 'The Hat' McVitie £400 to kill Payne. McVitie had been employed by the firm in various minor capacities many times in the past, not always successfully. Thus, when his attempt to carry out this mission misfired miserably, Ronald decided to add McVitie's name to the list of dispensables, and Reggie was appointed executioner. So it was arranged that Reggie should shoot McVitie at the Regency Club on the night of October 11. When the proprietor of the club, Tony Barrie objected, the Kray twins and three other members of the 'firm', Ronald Bender and two young aspiring gangsters, Chris and Tony Lambrianou adjourned to a flat in Evering Road, Stoke Newington, owned by an acquaintance of the Krays known as Blonde Carol. A party was in progress but was immediately transferred to a different house in the same street and the Krays waited for the Lambrianous who had gone to fetch McVitie. As soon as McVitie arrived (expecting a party) Reggie attempted to shoot him, but when the gun jammed he was forced to use the carving knife brought by Bender. McVitie was stabbed repeatedly in the face and stomach and Reggie finally pinned him to the floor through the throat. As with the murder of Cornell, this extraordinarily brutal crime bears little or no apparent relation to the provocation offered by the victim. McVitie was known to have 'slagged the Krays off' referring specifically to the sensitive areas of Ronnie's size and homosexuality (Cornell had also called Ronald 'a fat poof'). Certainly his failure to accomplish the murder of Payne contributed to his selection as a victim, but this selection seems otherwise to have been curiously arbitrary. At the trial a more sinister motivation was disclosed. Since the murder of Cornell, Ronnie had persistently baited his twin, as though his crime had given him extra points in some dark unstated rivalry. After his visit to Nigeria, during the Enugu period, moreover, Pearson claims that Ronald exhibited an interest in the cult of the Leopard men among whom loyalty rituals were extended to the most complete expression possible – murder – forming, as with the Hashini and the Thugs, a secret common bond of the closest possible nature.[14] Certainly remarks like 'I do all the work around here' and 'I did mine, when are you going to do yours?' from Ronnie (reported during the McVitie trial) were known to precipitate extraordinarily intense fraternal hostilities and McVitie appears to have provided a way out for Reggie.

(h) . . . Stranger and stranger . . .

After this episode, the behaviour of the Krays, their projects and their contacts become increasingly bizarre and difficult to verify with any confidence. By 1968, the twins' violent propensities were finding more and more devious channels of expression. Not only do they seem to have literally searched for potential victims, interpreted every trifling insult, real or imagined, as an act of defiance meriting the murder of anyone with whom they had the slightest criminal contact – but also the methods whereby these murders were to be accomplished became increasingly ingenious and fantastic. In this period 'Mad Teddy' Smith and Frost, a chauffeur of the Krays disappeared after minor arguments with the twins, and old friends like Buller Ward, George Dixon and a man called Fields were treated to the most brutal and pointless outbursts of violence. At this time also, Cooper introduced a man called Paul Elvey to the Krays as a professional killer. Elvey was first hired to kill a man who had offended an ally of the Krays. Elvey was supposed to kill this man in the forecourt of the Old Bailey with an injection of cyanide dispensed by a syringe, secreted in a briefcase. It was to be triggered off by a sensitive spring mechanism on contact with the victim. After two failed attempts, George Caruana, who had intimidated another of the Krays' allies, Bernie Silvers, was selected as an alternative victim. A high powered crossbow equipped with telescopic sights was to be used, but this original plan was dropped in favour of a method which incorporated the use of explosives which were to be detonated by remote control. It was as Elvey was boarding a plane at Glasgow airport with the two sticks of gelignite required for this job that he was arrested by Read's men.

(i) Destination reached – the trial and 'an empire collapses'

Cooper was arrested the next day, but after revealing to the police that he had been employed for the previous two years by the United States Treasury, which institution wanted to break the flow of stolen American securities into Europe, as a source of information and as an 'agent provocateur', and this with the endorsement of Scotland Yard (the archaic class-structure of which prevented this information from permeating down to Read) – the investigation took a different line. After failing in an attempt to use Cooper directly in order to gain self-incriminating statements from the twins, Read went forward with the simultaneous arrests of the three Kray brothers and twenty-one of their associates on the night of 8 May 1968. As an index of their power and an indication of how the Krays were following precedents set by its criminals, up to the time of their arrest, the Krays had been showing an interest in the London Docks – attempting to create a labour union racket similar to the type which operates in the States. The twins had offered the services of an organised force of strongarm men firstly to the employers (members of parliament had been approached on this score) and then to the union itself as an additional protection against picket-line breakers. Although these negotiations came to nothing, the fact that they were even possible provides a disturbing reminder of how far the twins had penetrated the soft shell of the world of power. The magnitude of the imagined threat represented by the Krays was reflected in the trial which was conducted on a larger scale than was absolutely necessary. Everything was a little overplayed – on both sides. Security arrangements were intricately planned and vigorously enforced every day of the 139-day trial. The Krays, in their turn, demanded press coverage and played constantly to the public gallery, as usual. I shall analyse the trial more completely in a later section. Here I need only record the verdict – guilty, and the sentences of 30 years which were imposed upon Ronnie and Reggie, and of 15 years which was imposed upon Charlie (the rest of the Firm receiving sentences ranging from 18 months to 20 years).

> For the judge Moosbrugger was a special case; for himself he was a world, and it is very difficult to say something convincing about a world.
>
> From Robert Musil's *The Man Without Qualities* Vol. 1

I have tried in the above account of the criminal careers of the Kray brothers to record the facts in a narrative form as straightforward and free from comment as possible; intending that the introduction which preceded it should prepare the reader to treat these facts as elements within a system of closure – a system which possesses its own internal 'logic', its own exclusive meanings. I shall now attempt to interpret the significance of that world, to examine that logic and explicate those meanings. I wish firstly to turn to the Twins' complicated relationship with the press and related media, touched upon at the beginning of the account, and assess at what points this relationship bore directly on what was to happen.

5. 'Kray is a very dramatic person'

John Dickson appearing as a prosecution witness in Kray trial (reported 'E.S.' Jan. 14 1969).

The Krays were, as I have already indicated, the darlings of the media of the 1960s. Feted and filmed whenever they emerged from the womb of the underworld, they exercised their privileges as celebrities with an adroitness and a sophisticated awareness of the importance of public relations matched only in the image-conscious field of American politics. They brought a style and polish to the projection of good image (morals apart, of course) quite lacking at that time in many of the more conventional areas of public life – summoning press conferences whenever expedient, paradoxically winning by virtue of their constant visibility in the press, some measure of freedom from police interference.[15] As we have seen certain of the Krays' projects, when closely examined, take on a bizarre aspect more appropriate to the theatre than to the rational pursuit of profit by crime. If the Krays were organised criminals there is nothing 'straight' or 'scientific' about organised crime. The sensational springing of Frank Mitchell,[16] an enterprise undertaken apparently in order to symbolically demonstrate the Krays' immunity from the law, as an exercise of power as an end in itself; the much publicised naming of two pet snakes after the two detectives of the Serious Crimes Squad who were heading the investigation into the twins' activities; and even the public execution of George Cornell in the arena of the Blind Beggar public house before witnesses, all indicate the Krays' flair for exploiting the dramatic opportunities offered by the very high profile they habitually maintained in the press.

The degree to which the whole Boothby scandal was manipulated by the Krays to gain the desired freedoms (from police and, in certain sensitive areas, the press) is problematic. We can be in no doubt, however, when we turn to their handling of the Read photograph in 1965, to their use of the favourable publicity guaranteed by their presence (faithfully recorded by the pressman's camera) at local charity functions, or to their skilful stage presentation of the many press conferences, called at timely intervals throughout their career. Each rung of the ladder of success was marked by a well-handled photograph. It was as if the apotheosis of the Krays into visual image was identified by the twins as a means of refining themselves out of existence, of sweeping them to that never-never land of absolute freedom (promised in popular fiction) where, if police did not actually cease to exist, then crime, at least, escaped detection. And thus we can pass from drama to the underlying aesthetic.

6. Bill Sykes or James Bond? Will the real Ronald Kray please be upstanding?

> It is the adventure I really go for . . . with them it's just like being a spy or something in the Underground movement.
>
> Ronnie Hart, a member of the Firm
> quoted in Pearson's *Profession of Violence.*

Much of the behaviour of the Krays: the dramatic gestures and the strange games played with such frequency toward the end of their careers, has no meaning in the terms of orthodox criminology (in the work of Cressey for example) and evades decodification by the more conventional sociologies of deviancy.[17] It is explicable only when we accept the twins' location within that artificial paradise, the bourgeois utopia, their citizenship of what Tom Pocock calls in his article,[18] the 'citadel of imagined total satisfaction of luxury, sex, power . . . and admiration.' Armed with money and power at a time when anarchic ambition was definitely 'in', when traditional power figures had forfeited their credibility along with Profumo, and the ceaseless, critical, witty wearing away of the *That Was The Week That Was* TV satire team, when ruthlessness, often masquerading as brass tacks working-class honesty, possessed a certain chic appeal and was certainly preferable to the hypocrisy of the Old Guard, the Krays, as the favoured forerunners of a social revolution that never really happened, had determined to take that citadel by force.[19] Ultimately and with a minimum of pressure it capitulated, its inhabitants welcoming the East End invaders with open arms. The emptiness of this easy victory, the tension it created between mutually contradictory drives (to respectability, profit inclusion – to personal power, notoriety, adventure, violence, exclusion) accounts for the Krays' awkwardness, their refusal to settle in this alien territory. Ronnie Kray stares moodily from the plethora of photographs he had taken during the mid

1960s in which he poses next to celebrities and politicians as if sullenly aware of the incongruity of his situation. His attitude towards his new circle of acquaintances was always profoundly ambivalent. On the one hand he seemed to extort some real sense of security from their proximity, as a constant confirmation of his success, his having 'made it' to that neon-lit heaven/haven of his dreams. During his trial, Ronnie chanted the names of his influential friends as magical incantations to protect him against the odious accusations of the prosecuting counsel: 'I have some very influential friends . . . some very distinguished people. If I wasn't here now I'd be out drinking with Judy Garland.'

On the other hand: the susceptibility of this world to corruption, its weakness for hypocrisy; those self-same conditions which had granted him access, seem simultaneously to have disgusted and repelled him. Ronald made much of employing a belted earl as a croupier at Esmeralda's Barn, and I believe there is just the faintest touch of irony in the statement he made to the *Daily Express*; (4 Aug., 1964) refuting the allegations concerning his involvement with Boothby: 'He was everything I expected of an English gentleman.'

Ronald Kray's eyes in those photographs carry a vacant expression which, I suspect, conceals the same kind of mixture of disillusionment, and resentment and frustration which the psychiatrist sees every day in the bitter eyes of the bored and neurotic suburban housewife. Like just such a housewife, sitting in her over-equipped kitchen, filled with a mass of spotless, labour-saving devices which somehow never manage to quite fulfil the dream, Ronald Kray sits in his over decorated clubs surrounded by important people who never quite live up to his cinematic expectations, and feels cheated. Trapped in a photographic image, he sits, cheated on celluloid by celluloid.

Once the haven had been reached, the dream fulfilled, the myth of total satisfaction within a bourgeois utopia was exploded and the Krays were left with the prospect of a great, yawning, undefined future, floating in that vacuum which is at the centre of the consumption ethic, which is at the core of the alienated consciousness. The twins, led by Ronald, escaped even further into the paranoid nightmares of popular fiction-fantasy. As 'real life' lost its urgency, its purpose and its meaning (the competition virtually eradicated with the disintegration of the Richardson gang, the club scene taped, a criminal empire established) they seem to turn more desperately to the genres of the thriller, and the spy story to provide an answer, a mould into which the self could once more be poured to re-establish its substantiality, to reaffirm the clarity of the self-image.

It was at the very apex of their conventionally defined success, precisely when unnecessary risks need no longer have been taken, when recklessness was at its lowest premium, when new and untested ventures could be considered calmly and rationally, that we find the Kray twins at their most incautious, and ill-advised, evolving their most fantastic and unprofitable schemes. It was at this time that they finally terminated their contact with Payne and committed themselves wholly to Alan Cooper, whose credibility as a real life character seems to be challenged at every point, by every 'fact' of his existence. He was working for some undefined body, at different times, named as the United States Treasury, Scotland Yard, the Mafia as a kind of 'agent provocateur'. He was a banker, a gold smuggler, a mysterious figure in the field of international finance. He was involved with his father in the illegal manufacture of narcotics and L.S.D. He was also, it was revealed at the Kray trial by the Defence Counsel, a notorious police informer, and known as such throughout the underworld which had derisively nicknamed him 'Silly Bollocks' because of his silly schemes.

This relationship proved to be exciting, and filled with adventure for Ronnie, fulfilling his expectations derived from popular fiction of what crime at the top was really like; but it was, in every other way, a disastrous association. It was their involvement with Cooper which eventually discouraged the real Mafia from making further contacts with the twins, and yet we find Ronnie being taken at this time to the States by Cooper to meet a mock 'Mafia' – an incredible collection of unemployed actors, ex-boxers and has-beens of the Prohibition era which nonetheless succeeded in convincing and impressing Kray (no doubt they conformed more closely to their cinematic archetypes than the authentic mobsters would have done).[20] It was at this time too that Ronnie drew up endless lists of imaginary enemies and exhorted Reggie in the pointless elimination of Jack 'the Hat'.

During this period Cooper introduced the Krays to Paul Elvey, whom he described as a professional liquidator but who was actually a radio engineer. At the trial, he admitted to being 'hopelessly miscast' in the role of hired assassin, and the idea of murdering a victim on the steps of the Old Bailey seemed, he claimed, 'ludicrous. But I had to make some sort of show.'[21] Together they elaborated those complicated and ingenious methods of eliminating victims which I have already described (section 4 – the crossbow, harpoon etc.), methods chosen on grounds of aesthetic appropriateness rather than practical expediency. It was during this period, finally, that Kray introduced for serious consideration by the Firm schemes such as the kidnapping of the Pope, the assassination variously of President Banda of Malawi, Kaunda, and Colin Jordan, an expedition to recover gold buried by mercenaries in the Congo, and the springing of Moise Tshombe from his Algerian gaol (a project which actually reached the stage of negotiations with Tshombe's relatives during which such topics as the availability of helicopters, machine guns and nerve gas were discussed). Such exotic enterprises seem to have sprung straight from the pages of an Ian Fleming fantasy, and when Reggie Kray, obviously embarrassed by the disclosure of these excesses in open court, leapt to his feet in a vain attempt to exorcise the nightmare, to reintroduce a semblance of sanity to the proceedings, exclaiming, 'Is James Bond going to be called as a witness? This is ridiculous'[22] we must acknowledge the unconscious suitability of such an invocation. For the boundaries of Ronnie Kray's world had indeed been fixed in popular fantasies, its content predicted, its meanings defined in just such fictional forms. We should not then be surprised when we learn that Ronald was much impressed by an account of the life of Al Capone, of whom[23] (according to Norman Lucas) he believed himself to be the reincarnation. Nor should we be unduly perturbed when we find Ronnie cultivating a taste for classical music and singers like Gigli in emulation of his 'spiritual forbear', employing a private barber (so many gangsters having been murdered while having their hair cut), building up the traditional costly and extensive wardrobe of suits and silk socks, investing in the electronic gadgetry which so clutters the paranoid world of the modern fantasy-hero (one complete recorder was concealed in an imitation packet of cigarettes, and button hole cameras were issued to members of the Firm so that suspected detectives could be photographed).[24]

At the point then, when the goals of the bourgeois Dream have been achieved, when time, the cherished prize, the pot of gold at the end of the consumer's rainbow, has been won, we find the twins confronted with a crisis, the solution of which involves an intensification of the fantasy element. Time can once more be consumed purposefully in the exploration of fantasies which had originally dictated the shape of that world. With the subsequent refinement of the internal aesthetic of violence the closure of that world is finalised.[25] The completeness of the form which is presented, then, accounts for the attraction it holds for a public which looks for guidance and reassurance to images of confinement. In a culture whose logic demands that matter, if it is to achieve substance, must first find containment, a closed system is a meaningful system; at once more substantial, more tangible and therefore more real than their own open-ended existences. The semblance of order, or everything having its place, of everything occupying a static position on a fixed semantic scale, these are, ironically, the advantages offered by the gangster's narrow world. Its narrowness is tied inextricably to its appeal. The Krays as public enemies then offer a temporary imagined solution to the citizen's private anomie.

I shall now turn back to the nucleus of this system, the family, the supportive and protective framework of which enabled Ronald Kray to make his statements so emphatically and with such confidence.

7. Humble beginnings – the eye of the storm

> Whaddeyou mean by that word "right"? The only thing we're concerned about is what's right for us. We got our own definition of right.
>
> Hell's Angel quoted in Hunter S. Thompson's book *Hell's Angels.*

Reggie and Ronald Kray were born in Bethnal Green and always maintained strong links with the area, returning frequently to their parents' home in Vallance Road, one of the few surviving relics of the old Bethnal Green 'rookery'. As John Pearson writes: 'the twins were very much part of this whole vanishing world of the Dickensian East-end'. The Krays were an archetypal cockney family providing a veritable microcosm of the pre-war East End. All the major immigrant groups which together made up the area had found some representation in the family (the name was Austrian, and the twins had Irish, Romany, and Jewish blood) and much of the East End's cultural complexity was reflected in the wide range of 'characters' it contained. The twins' grandfather, 'Mad' Jimmy Kray was a prodigious drinker and a notorious barfighter. Their maternal grandfather Jimmy Lee, the 'Cannonball Southpaw' was a confirmed teetotaller, and had been a popular music-hall performer and a boxer. Charles Kray, the twins' father was an itinerant gold-buyer, gambler and drinker. The female wing of the family was equally well-stocked with strong, classic cockney personalities. Aunt Rose was a renowned streetfighter, the grandmothers were typical East End matriarchs, and Violet Kray, the twins' mother could always command the extravagent filial respect, even adulation, to which she was traditionally entitled.

The family always claimed the first and last loyalties of its members, and, after the war, as the physical transformation of the East End was accompanied by a parallel cultural transformation,[26] these loyalties were strengthened and valued with a fanaticism born of desperation. The disruption felt in the fabric of traditional working-class life was counteracted by a reassertion of the value of the only institution guaranteeing some measure of continuity, over which the individual had direct control. The old extended family took on a symbolic significance. It epitomized all the values that the new high rise council blocks, the vertical streets with their built-in isolationism, and individualism, were steadily denying and destroying. The family became what the community had ceased to be – a self-sufficient and fiercely exclusive unit supplying its own justifications, its own codes, its own meanings. From such a perspective, the outside world could be defined negatively, its interests disregarded, its opinions dismissed so long as the family's interests were served, so long as the family was satisfied and continued to survive and prosper. The Kray family became the distillation of a culture which was threatened with extinction, and it is perhaps hardly surprising that the pressures contingent upon this position led to the distortion of what were originally positive values formulated out of the experience of a whole community.[27]

The Kray Firm was the more overtly aggressive extension of the family – its more armoured incarnation, evolved to fulfil its purposes, to impose its will on a hostile outside world. The Firm's; structure duplicated the tight, fiercely self-protective familial structure. Indeed the Firm was always and primarily a family business. As soon as possible, the twins invited their older brother, Charles, to join in their activities and, later, incorporated their cousin, Ronnie Hart into the organisation. Weapons were concealed under the floor-boards of their mother's house, which provided a kind of permanent base (nicknamed the Fortress) from which the Krays issued periodically to carry out the Firm's business. Much of the day to day running of the twins' business interests was entrusted to the friends of their childhood and adolescence. Traditional criminal loyalties asserted against the police were strengthened by relationship ties and consolidated the Krays' impregnability. Thus, the 'scientific' connotations of the word 'firm' (suggesting an organised, impersonally directed industry with a primary commitment to the rational pursuit of profit) which have contributed to the development of so many misleading myths about the Krays can be safely ignored. The alternative adjectival definition of 'firm': 'not yielding easily to pressure, solid; fixed, stable; resolute, unwavering, stern; strong and steady'[28] are altogether more appropriate. The profit motive was, I suspect, secondary to the power motive. The 'Firm' does indeed provide a parody of any capitalist enterprise[29] (although the Richardson gang, more thoroughly submerged in the whole world of big business constitutes a more suitable parody, perhaps) extending the amoral ethic implicit in a laissez-faire economic system based on uncontrolled competition, to a point where its origin in violence, and its destructive and irresponsible nature is made visible. But if it caricatures capitalism, it is a specific form of primitive capitalism . . . the archaic family business and not the rationalised technological mode of monopoly capitalism which is so cruelly exposed. It is more relevant, I think, to see the Firm as fundamentally an instrument whereby the family's needs (interpreted exclusively by Ronnie) could be served).[30] At the centre of Ronnie's world, then, we have the strangely competitive, complementary relationship of Ronnie and Reggie, the terrible twins, two distinct and powerful personalities in their own right, coalescing in a virtually indestructible unit, one mutual identity defying separation. This close-knit relationship of interdependency and mutual reinforcement is extended through the kinship network and reconstitutes or formalizes itself as the fiercely exclusive and profoundly aggressive Firm. This system never loses its original egocentricity (it remains Ronnie's system) and anything registering at the centre finds a response at the periphery. A sensitive mechanism operating through the functions of a centralised nervous system, the Firm could never escape the limitations incumbent upon its dependency on Ronnie. His dominant position meant that Ronnie's paranoid fantasies and bizarre schemes (often brilliant, more often simply insane) flourished unchecked, becoming just as important, demanding as positive a reaction as his more mundane, and workable projects.

As it was with Ian Brady,[31] the Moors Murderer, whose fascist mythology was endorsed and supplemented by Myra Hindley, as it was with Mary Bell,[32] the Newcastle 11-year-old who strangled two children, and who found in the older, though more submissive Norma Bell, a willing partner with whom to realize a pre-pubescent nightmare; as it was with Perry Smith, the killer of the Clutter family immortalized in Capote's *In Cold Blood*, who found in Dick Hickock an ally who would immerse himself in his system of fantasy; so it was, also, with Ronnie Kray, one half of a powerful common personality, which found completion in its twin, Reggie. Unlike these others, however (all of whom held the same fascination for the press, a fascination rooted, as I have argued, in a common addiction to systems of closure, completed forms), Ronnie Kray was able to bring a far greater area within the sphere of his influence by the extension of this original relationship through the family and into the Firm.[33]

Once we have recognised the essential conservatism of the Krays manifested in their commitment to the old familial pattern, we can go on to consider the central paradox which lies at the core of their profoundly ambiguous relationship with the larger East-End community. On the one hand, the Krays seemed to have taken seriously their role as protectors of the local community against the inroads of the state. As they accumulated wealth and prestige, the Krays used their considerable power to influence the direction the new East End was to take; to salvage as much of the old culture as possible. Despite the direct profit to be gained from the cultivation of such an image (limited acceptance by the Establishment, freedom from police harassment), their constantly publicised participation in the public affairs of Bethnal Green derived its primary motivation from a less rational area, and leads us back once more to the family. Ronnie and Reggie sought to reintroduce the old cockney values preserved in the Kray family into the transfigured environment of the East End – to literally see the family built back into that environment.

Edward Ross's definition of the 'criminaloid' as 'the champion of the tribal order as opposed to the civil order' is particularly appropriate to the Krays.[34] Certainly they saw themselves as the unofficial representatives of the local community; 'men of respect' benevolently interceding on the behalf of their constituents, believing as 'symbiotic criminals'[35] that the rules can always be bent, fixed or rigged to achieve the desired result. In fact, the ease with which the Krays duplicated in the straight world, their earlier successes in the overtly criminal world, confirmed East Enders in their traditional cynicism towards all forms of institutionally sanctioned power. The East End's long established contempt for the law contributed significantly to the apotheosis of the twins into local superheroes. Lifted above the community by their business interests in the City, by their involvement in the club life of the West End, and by the sensational reports of their frequent trials in the national newspapers; and at the same time, being a very visible part of that community – opening local fêtes, shaking hands with the mayor of Bethnal Green, collecting protection from the old sources, drinking regularly in the local pubs, the Krays were simply larger than life. Sharing a common heritage (valued because threatened), a common accent, a common language and yet ultimately alien and distinct, the Krays became mythical figures, possessing, as Pearson puts it, 'the rare asset of endless credibility'. Thus the Krays' continuing freedom in the face of their well-publicised acts of villainy meant that the twins had won complete immunity from the law, and this, in turn, was transformed through the magical medium of local gossip into the myth of invulnerability. The tenacity with which some East-Enders still cling to their image of the Krays as the aggressive incarnations of the local community, invested with divine powers by which the interests of that community could be magically served, was brought out in Nichol Fortune's article. Fortune quotes a local resident's indignation over the disruption caused by a recently accomplished redevelopment scheme:

> You know the Queen Street development. The twins would have shook that down something rotten. As it was it got put up with no bother at all. Took about eighteen months. The twins would never have stood for it.

On the other hand, if the Krays' beneficent descent into the politics of the East End assisted their translation into tribal gods, their equally spectacular, often brutally violent involvement in the cockney underworld, their extortion of protection money from the shopkeepers and publicans of the area made them simultaneously the local personifications of the devil. To place an inordinate stress on the folk-god aspects of the Krays' public persona at the expense of a negative image which undoubtedly carried equal, if not more, weight, would involve a crucial misrepresentation of the East-End community. For the Krays deliberately exploited the East End's traditional distrust of the police, reinforced it by spreading the rumour (based on fact, no doubt) that they had 'bought their way beyond the law', that Scotland Yard was 'in their pocket', and used it as a means of oppression. The code of silence was respected not simply because the police were traditional enemies but because of a real physical fear of the retribution a statement to the police would invoke. It was because the conviction of the Krays depended upon the testimony of fellow criminals and fellow East-Enders that they were able to operate so openly and for so long.

Throughout the trial, the defence counsel questioned the integrity of the prosecution witnesses whom he described as 'absurd creatures of the underworld' and made repeated accusations against the police, albeit in the veiled language of the courts, implying that deals had been made with potentially useful witnesses serving prison sentences or coming up for trial. Many witnesses were undoubtedly won over by attractive inducements like the reduction of prison sentences, partial treatment from the judge etc., and yet the testimonies betray a sense of alienation from the excessive, often senselessly violent acts of the Krays which (unless due to an unusually effective briefing from the Prosecution Counsel) is remarkable in its consistency.[36] John Dickson's statement is, in this respect, typical: 'someone had got to have the guts to come forward and let the ordinary people know what cruel bastards they were.'

Sylvia Barnard, McVitie's common-law wife implied that the Krays had somehow violated the honourable tradition of the old individualistic East End villain (a tradition nonetheless on its last legs anyway) when she shouted at the defendants: 'It took ten of you bastards to kill him (McVitie) because he was a man and wouldn't bow down to you.'

And she explicitly invoked the collective judgement of the East End to denounce the Krays in an interview given to the *News of the World* (March 9 1969) in which she insisted that her motive transcended a desire for mere personal revenge:

> I'm an East-ender, born and bred, and proud of it. My father was a 'totter', a rag-and-bone scrap-metal man with a horse and cart. Proud he was, like me . . . So's my mum, and she backed me up in my fight against the Krays.

It was because the Krays ruthlessly used the East-Enders' distrust of the law to further the interests of the family that they were eventually denied the womb-like security of the community. What had originally evolved as an expression of solidarity within the community functioning as a collective defence mechanism against a hostile, oppressive and exploitative system had itself been converted by the Krays into an instrument of exploitation. The Krays, not content merely to inhabit that No-Man's Land which lies between the disaffected working-class East-Ender and the dominant social system which claims to serve him, actively sought to extend its boundaries in the struggle for *lebensraum* for the Kray family. The aggressive confidence and assertiveness with which the Krays openly declared this policy of aggrandisement concentrated attention directly upon the state of anomie thus dramatically highlighted. I shall now turn to this anomic situation and attempt to clarify what contributed to its exacerbation during the 1960s. Anomie is a condition with which modern society has grown accustomed but during the last decade a state of emergency has been more or less permanently declared by the champions of law and order. I shall be examining the explanations offered by the law and order lobby within the context of crime as a category which was being perpetually redefined during the 1960s.

8. Train robber heroes – Soho fiends

> Time is required for the public conscience to reclassify men and things; so long as the social forces thus freed (by the changed conditions of life) have not regained equilibrium, their respective values are unknown and so the regulation is lacking for a time.
>
> Emile Durkheim *Anomie and Suicide.*

The 1960s, as I have already indicated, saw a highly dramatised acceleration in the already declining fortunes of the old pre-war Establishment. The Macmillan administration, embarrassed by its disastrous campaign in Suez, retreated in confusion as the prophetic links between sexual indiscretion and the leaking of state secrets were made during the Vassal and Profumo scandals. Simultaneously, in the early years of the decade, the first tentative sightings of a new and visibly 'affluent'[37] youth culture, confident and often articulate in his criticisms of the parent culture coincided with the boom in satire which the *That Was The Week That Was* team had inaugurated. Poses of defiance, fashionable amongst a fairly limited circle of intellectuals and a section of lower working-class youths since the days of the Angry Young Men, the Aldermaston marches and the teddy boys, became quite suddenly all the rage in 1963. Crime, always an important touchstone to the mood of the times, became an area which was particularly sensitive to these transformations. It inevitably attracted attention at a time when the traditional framework of authority seemed to be threatening collapse at any moment.

Certain key cases were used to focus a debate on the whole legal apparatus (the judiciary, the police, the prisons) in the public forum of the media. Capital punishment, brought into disrepute by the ill-advised execution of the innocent Evans in 1950, was eventually suspended in 1965 and finally abolished in 1970, as the guilt of two other executed men, Bentley and Hanratty began to be seriously challenged by later disclosures. The British bobby, popularly depicted as too slow-witted for corruption was discomposed by the investigation which followed the Challenor case.[38] The absolute nature of the courts' decisions was called into question by the unconventional tactics adopted by the ingenious Alfie Hinds to draw attention to his wrongful conviction which, when eventually more or less conceded, threatened to expose the class bias of the whole legal system.[39] And then in 1963 came the crime which was to consolidate public sympathy for the criminal and capture the public imagination as no other crime, probably, will ever succeed in doing again. The Great Train Robbery was accomplished on the night of 8 August with a minimum of violence,[40] and £2½ million in used banknotes was successfully (at least for a time) spirited away by a gang of professional thieves. The working-class reaction was, perhaps, rather humorously typified in the remark of the guard who offered no resistance, refusing to jeopardize his life for what after all was not his in the first place: 'All right, mate. I'm on your side'.[41]

Two issues of the 'Sunday Times Colour Supplement' (14 February, 21 February 1965) carried an article by Peta Fordham about the robbery which exhibits the more restrained and ambiguous middle-class response and which demands closer examination, if we are to keep up with the subtly changing attitudes of the liberal establishment toward crime. Whilst the violence and the corruption of railway employees which were required for the successful implementation of the plan meet immediate and vocal disapproval Fordham makes no attempt to conceal her admiration for the almost militaristic discipline maintained at all times ('it was to be the exact equivalent of a commando raid . . . just as in wartime'), and for the leadership qualities exhibited by Reynolds and the 'wolfishly handsome' Goody who 'like some underworld-distorted picture of the ideal officer' is 'ready to go over the top, fight and die for his leader', who seems to hold a special attraction for the writer ('The voice was steel-hard; eyes fanatically blue') and whose shoes for some strange reason are possessed of such mute eloquence that she returns to them twice! ('Spruce as always . . . even in canvas shoes', 'neat as usual in blue canvas shoes'). Fordham shows willing to adjust to the morality of the situation by condemning the man, responsible through wilful negligence, for the gang's apprehension by the police as a 'Judas':

> Was this the supreme act of treachery which let down a band of brothers who, whatever their objective, had yet behaved to each other throughout the enterprise with commendable loyalty?

The military metaphors are used to resituate the robbery within a framework in which it can be evaluated positively without offending the nice scruples of the respectable reader; the neatness of the operation, its commando-like precision being stressed so that aesthetic considerations predominate over moral ones. The Great Train Robbery, because of the massive sum involved stimulated the public imagination and disarmed of all unpleasantness by its essentially non-violent execution enabled the public to make that sympathetic passage from interest in, to identification with the criminal which had been preparing for years. Deprived of traditional power idols by the drastic reassessments then underway, the alienated observer was ready to turn explicitly to crime for its heroes.[42]

The counter reaction to this tendency is evidenced in the law and order campaign which backed up its case similarly with references to certain specific sensational criminal cases of the latter half of the decade. In 1966, the unprovoked murder of three policemen in Shepherds Bush by three criminals headed by Harry Roberts inaugurated this reverse trend which was to find further corroboration five years later in the murder by Sewell of a Liverpool policeman. Authority-hatred was permissible, it would seem, as long as it was not taken too seriously. This was followed in the spring by the sudden and startling illumination of the dark and private universe of Brady and Hindley whose highly personal belief system, derived from de Sade, neo-Nazism and pornography, had supplied them with the philosophical means with which to justify child murder. 'Freedom' was once more producing Hitlers and the panic was on.[43] 1967 saw the origins of the gangster-scare which commenced in earnest with the revelations concerning the Richardsons on the first day of the 'Torture Trial'. In 1968, the case of Mary Bell appeared to lend substance to the doom-laden prophecies of the anti-permissiveness brigade now capably led by Malcolm Muggeridge and Mrs Mary Whitehouse of the Clean-Up T.V. Campaign. Here was a child steeped in the fantasies of arbitrarily-directed violence fantasy so much a part of television-oriented society. Batman and the Saint were hastily accused of committing two murders by strangulation in Newcastle-Upon-Tyne.[44] And then, at the end of the year the arrest of the Krays triggered off a remarkable barrage of disclosures which mortified the respectable world confirming its most secret fears about the state of the nation. Ancient analogies were revived and the state became once more the diseased head of the Body Politic requiring the immediate administration of powerful medications (longer sentences), if not actual surgery . . . amputations (reintroduction of capital punishment). During the second half of the 1960s, the trends which I isolated in the earlier part of the decade were pursued relentlessly to their conclusions. The romanticisation of crime which the Great Train Robbery invited, provided the Krays with a questionable mystique which guaranteed their acceptance in the most fashionable circles, and contributed to their mythical deification. The court had meanwhile lost its privileged status as a sanctuary, freed by ritual from the normal pressures of personal responsibility. Those who donned the robes and wigs were no longer magically protected by a divinely-conferred authority. In December 1972, a woman produced a shotgun in the West London court and attempted to shoot the judge who was presiding over the trial of her lover 'with a due solemnity'. More typically, courtroom scenes were liable to disintegrate into undignified drama (Real Method acting as opposed to the classical, formalized style of the past) where challenges were openly issued to the judiciary, accusations were made directly against officers present (as in the case of George Ince during the Barn murder trial), and insults were vociferously exchanged across the courtroom. (See Section 12.)

The Kray trial incorporates all these elements, threatening to descend into farce at times, and never far from the theatre of the absurd. This is best demonstrated in the presentation of the Kray trial in the press, where the piquant tidbits offered almost daily in the court reports appear sandwiched between equally freakish items. Certain incidents contemporaneous with the Kray trial and equally perplexing, find inclusion in the *London Evening Standard* and combine to confirm a view of a world gone crazy. In early January 1969 for instance, above a report which describes the elaborate precautions taken at the Old Bailey to ensure the safety of the jurors in the Kray case, we find a report concerning the conviction of a Dr. Christopher Swan who stands accused of plotting to murder 8 key witnesses in his trial for offences contravening the 1964 Drugs Act. Swan, it transpires had been approached by a Detective Sgt. Vaughan, who, masquerading as a 'chopper man' under the assumed name of Sid Green offered his services for £15,000. It had been arranged that the 'liquidator' should contact Swan with the message. 'I hope the date is right. A happy birthday signed Sid Green' when he was ready.

The deportation of George Raft, the closing of the Colony Club and huge banner headlines declaring 'Soho Clubland Blaze kills 3' (18 Feb 1969 – over a story about an accidental fire unrelated to the internal warfare of gangsters and the politics of Clubland, though indeed taking place in Soho) or 'Who killed "Mad" Percy at the Odeon' (Feb. 1969 – over a story once more cynically introduced to bolster up the Kray material – the late 'Mad Percy' of the story being in fact, an innocent old tramp) provide the thematic background against which the Krays' story is played out on the pages of the *Evening Standard*. The fantasy element does not even remain earth bound as the banning of the sinister, conspiratorial Scientology cult, which hovers mysteriously over the uncertain terrain of science fiction, appears a column or two away from the accounts of the Kray case. On 14 January, 1969 as Ronnie and Reggie 'make a scene' on page 6 by refusing to wear numbered placards to facilitate identification during the trial; the last vestiges of the cult of the Great Train Robbers are being offered up for sale on page 3 (everything from cutlery to blood stained overalls are snatched up by the fans, the collectors of the paraphernalia of crookery – the lorry used during the robbery to transport the money worth approximately £30 fetches £1,550).

And so we come finally to the trial itself, to the meaning of the official interpretation of the Krays as a massive threat to the real security of the state, and to an examination of those subterranean motivations which underlie the public exhibition of a paranoia that validates and sanctifies the crusade for law and order.

9. What 'Mafia' means

> I am satisfied that Goody's friends were prepared to launch something in the nature of a full-scale military attack, even to the extent of using tanks, bombs and what the Army

> describes as limited atomic weapons. Once armoured vehicles had breached the main gates, there would be nothing to stop them. A couple of tanks could easily have come through the streets of Durham. Nothing is too extravagant.
>
> Chief Constable of Durham quoted in Laurie Taylor and Stan Cohen's *Psychological Survival.*

When describing the more bizarre involvements of Ronnie's Firm in Section 5 and 6, I challenged those analyses of organised crime which stress the elements of scientific rationalised organised profit-seeking by counterposing the expression of the power drive, through the prearranged forms of totally non-logical bourgeois fantasy. When we examine these analyses more closely we can distinguish those self-same contradictions (more deeply concealed, no doubt) which characterize the alarmist journalism of the sensationalist press. Judge Gerald Sparrow, in his book 'Gang Warfare' offers an analysis, only slightly more level-headed than the frequent gesticulations made by the *News of the World* and the *Daily Mirror* towards a vaguely defined threat, only marginally less 'authoritative' than the thesis proposed so soberly by Donald Cressey in his book *Criminal Organisation*:

> The modern gang leader has rationalised crime. He and his friends are highly organised, highly specialised, and they represent a challenge to society as a whole far more menacing and a great deal more dangerous than any challenge to Law and Order in the past.
>
> Judge Gerald Sparrow in *Gang Warfare.*

The gangster, it is implied, is at once scientific (i.e. craving anonymity) impersonal, almost automated in his violent reflexes *and* highly visible (advertising his presence by his appearance), psychopathic and unpredictable (i.e. a threat to the personal safety of every individual). He personifies that impossible paradox: the rational and efficient madman, the highly specialised Jack of all vile trades which is at the core of all hysteria embedded in the heart of all those unreasonable panics of that undefined fear which is traced along the edge of the known and the familiar. When Edward Heath spoke in March 1966 of 'waging war on the modern highly scientific criminal'[45] he was recommending an attack on that same legendary 'smartly dressed gent in his 60 guinea suits' who the *Sunday Mirror* of 16 July, 1964 depicted running his rackets on 'strict business lines'.

This is the essential meaning of the American mafia myth which is rapidly becoming a metaphorical synonym for every conspiracy theory. Thus Harold Wilson refers smugly to Heath's 'Ministerial Mafia' in a recent speech, and an article published this month (Jan. 5, 1974) in the *Sun* about Arab guerillas is headlined 'The Godfather of World Terror' and is subtitled 'Gadaffi has forged a deadly Mafia out of the fanatics'. For the myth of 'scientific gangsterism' (essentially a contradiction in terms) is effective precisely because it touches a central nerve of urban insecurity. The mafia provides a metaphorical embodiment for those impersonal, external and invisible forces (which we define as malignant) which determine and dictate the individual's actions in a mass society, and which ultimately threaten his identity with extinction (total determination).

By collapsing the categories of rational and non-rational crime, by arranging the unnatural marriage of Goody, the military tactician, the modern 'expert' and Ronald Kray, the imaginative director of a company of talented actor-gangsters, the two great criminal enterprises of the decade (the Great Train Robbery and the Kray protection empire) were united.[46] Two distinct vocabularies of crime were thereby moulded into one monosyllabic utterance which articulates a profoundly modern anxiety. This collapsing is most apparent in the crudest forms of popular journalism, and the most trashy pulp fictions. In *You Nice Bastard*, for instance a novel by G.F. Newman, the author engineers the convergence of an enormous amount of symbolically potent criminal myths to form one gigantic embodiment of the law and order nightmare. Victor Russo, the protagonist, is a half-cockney half-Sicilian gangster who performs the most dastardly deeds of the Krays and the Richardsons (razor-slashing Al Mark (Jack 'Spot' Comer) murdering 'Wild Frankie' Philips (Mad Frankie Frazer) and presiding over brutal torture sessions) whilst managing in the meantime to appropriate the profits of the 'Great Mail bag Robbery' and run a chain of brothels which would have put the Messina brothers to shame.

The convergence of the sub-categories of crime is, of course, less pernicious than the wholesale fusion of politics and crime, accomplished, for instance, by the *Sun* in the article about Gadaffi already mentioned. It does, nonetheless assist the magnification of the subversive potential of crime by presenting the underworld (an amorphous shifting mass of temporary allegiances, and arbitrary convergences,) as a distinct, autonomous and purposeful entity, and hence facilitates the generation of a moral panic.

10. The apple cart almost upset

I have suggested that the imagined threat to the state posed by the Krays originated in a popular law and order myth concerning the specialised and rationalised nature of crime in a Technological Society – I should like to conclude by briefly suggesting that the trial itself, the ritualistic stripping away of the veils of myth in which the twins were clothed, represents an attempt to avoid the implications of their phenomenal success, by erasing the magic runes by which that success was signified. The contempt exhibited by the judge, during his summing-up, for what he described as 'the grotesque respectability' achieved by 'these pathetic products of the criminal underworld' strikes the observer as a transparent attempt at diminishing the Krays' real significance. The Kray trial provided an Establishment, feigning outrage, with a cathartic spectacle, a ceremonial stripping of civic rank which allowed the state to go on functioning, undisturbed. By publicly denying the Twins status, by exiling them once more to the excluded classes of the Cockney and the Criminal the judge was attempting to rewrite history to preserve only official version. But the glorification of the incorruptible Inspector Read and his team (championed by the press, commended by the judge) fails to conceal how completely the Krays demonstrated the real susceptibility of the world of power, money, and success to corruption. The Kray case dramatically illuminated what Sir Joseph Simpson had described in 1964 as 'the declining standards of conduct set by men in responsible positions' and constantly threatened to expose the exploitative system upon which that world was based by uncovering its roots in violence. The Krays advertised their alienation in a spectacular fashion and their sensational careers, so hotly pursued in the press, constitute a parody of the bourgeois success story and threaten to lay bare the faulted structure of bourgeois fantasy, the emptiness of the bourgeois Dream. The Krays then had been admitted to the previously sacrosanct inner chamber of the Capitalist system and had failed to conduct themselves with the proper decorum. They had refused to tread the corridors of power quietly and respectfully, and had instead loudly proclaimed their presence, showing the world just how crooked those corridors actually were. The Kray Twins came very close, in fact, to giving the whole game away.

11. East-end heads and south-side tails: a doppelganger for Mister Kray

> Ten years ago any symmetry with a semblance of order – dialectical materialism, anti-Semitism, Nazism – was sufficient to charm the minds of men. How could one do other than submit to Tlön (a complete fictional world), to the minute and vast evidence of an orderly planet? It is useless to answer that reality is also orderly. Perhaps it is, but in accordance with divine laws – I translate inhuman laws which we never quite grasp. Tlön is surely a labyrinth, but it is a labyrinth devised by men, a labyrinth destined to be deciphered by men.
>
> From 'Tlön, Ugbar, Orbis Terhus' by Jorge Luis Borges.

> Let me have men about me that are arrant knaves. The wicked, who have something on their conscience, are obliging, quick to hear threats, because they know how it's done, and for booty. You can offer them things because they will take them. Because they have no hesitations. You can hang them if they get out of step. Let me have men about me that are utter villains – provided that I have the power, absolute power over life and death. The sole and single leader, whom no one can interfere with. What do you know of the possibilities of evil! Why do you write books and make philosophy, when you only know about virtue and how to acquire it. Whereas the world is fundamentally moved by something quite different.
>
> Herman Göring quoted in *The Inner Circle* by I. Kirkpatrick

A few characteristically succinct lines from Borges elucidate quite adequately the form of the sealed universe in which the Krays came to move and indicate, at once, the origin of that form, its raison d'être, and the compulsive appeal it habitually exerts. Göring speaks from within the form itself and unconsciously diagnoses his own myopia by assigning a specific metaphysical valency (evil) to those 'inhuman laws' which are essentially neutral in moral terms and which are ultimately inaccessible to human terminology itself.[47] He is, by definition, lost in the labyrinth of National Socialism, a system which Joachim C. Fest characterizes by its 'renunciation of ideology for the sake of power'; a system which Göring himself helped to construct, and in which he was inextricably involved.

Perhaps it would be presumptuous to suggest that Ronald Kray could have spoken Göring's words if he had been so inclined and a little more articulate. But we need not resort to hypothesis; the parallels between gangster and fascist are glaringly obvious. Bertolt Brecht's play 'The Rise and Fall of Arturo Ui', which caricatures Nazism by fusing the histories of Hitler and Capone makes all the necessary comparisons. I would maintain that Fest's location of a crude concept of the Darwinian struggle at the very heart of National Socialism, indeed, as an end in itself applies equally well to that world over which the Kray Firm held hegemonic sway during the last decade. Fest writes:

> At its roots National Socialist ideology contained only one tangible idea: the idea of struggle . . . violent struggle was itself an ideology and if it had a goal above and beyond mere self-assertion, it was the power that beckoned at its end.

It should hardly surprise us to find that Fest's observation applies also to the Krays' rivals, the Richardsons, whose eventual removal from the scene ensured the Krays' ascendancy and who, in many ways, merely reflect south of the river, the image which the Krays projected from the East End. Struggle requires two more or less evenly matched opponents and from the late 1950s to the mid 1960s Ronnie and Reggie Kray found an equally resonant echo across the water in Charles and Eddie Richardson.

I shall now attempt to decipher the labyrinth which Charles Richardson created from his scrap-metal yard in Camberwell. So that the basic theme of closure should not translate this paper into an artefact as limited and pernicious as the forms it describes, I shall be placing the Richardsons within the larger context of the world of big business with which they merged at certain crucial times and which always threatened to afford them a permament sanctuary. Thuggery is never far from fascism. Neither can be purposefully isolated from the exploitative and competitive economic system in which they both find origin. Adolf Hitler merely constitutes a charismatic incarnation of the spirit which had moved the Krupps' empire for centuries. And Charles Richardson personified the piratical spirit of primitive capitalism in exactly the same way.

Sadism and the scrap business: a minotaur in the metropolis

> He killed for play
> Out of pure perversity
>
> From a poem written in memory of Lampiao, the Brazilian bandit.

> Richardson is very much a man of our times – stylish until the last.
>
> From an article published in the *Sunday Times* (11 June 1967)

> I can't make it out. It sounds like the Ku Klux Klan.
>
> Charles Richardson refuting allegations made by Laurence 'Johnny' Bradbury in an interview given to the *Sunday Times* (8 May 1966)

> What's Al Capone done then? He's supplied a legitimate demand. Some call it bootlegging. Some call it racketeering. I call it business.
>
> Al Capone quoted in *Al Capone* by F.D. Pasley

Charles William Richardson was born on 18 January, 1934 in Camberwell, South East London. His brother, Edward George was born two years later. Childhood was hardly idyllic. The Great Depression passed away finally, only with the advent of war, which in turn, was followed by the grey years of reconstruction. Unrelieved poverty was punctuated only by the ravages of the bombs and the bulldozers. For Charles and Eddie as for Ronnie and Reggie, bombsites served as playgrounds, but the depressing external conditions were, for the Richardson brothers, unalleviated by the strong, supportive family structure which had nurtured the Krays. Charles was not even permitted the doubtful respite from work and responsibility which school theoretically affords and was forced at the age of fourteen to adopt the role of principal breadwinner for the Richardson family (which also comprised a younger sister) when his father left. In the words of Mrs Eilleen Richardson, the boy's mother: 'Times were pretty hard then',[48] and we can safely assume that severe economic pressures were responsible for Charles' first appearance in juvenile court in May 1948. He was found guilty of stealing a small quantity of lead, valued at £1 and, just a year later, was committed to an approved school, from which he escaped. During 1949 he appeared in juvenile courts another three times for breaking and entering offences.

Richardson himself claimed that his legitimate business career started at this time and grew from the capital he accumulated selling ice-cream and toffee apples. With the money thus saved he began developing a scrap metal business, purchasing a lorry as soon as he was 17. In an interview given to the *Sunday Times* (11 June 1967) his mother says that she had already discerned in her eldest son a single-minded ambition and a fierce independence.

'Charlie always wanted to be his own boss. He didn't care how hard he worked.' An extremely dominant and aggressive personality, Charles had always resented authority at school and resisted incorporation. Predictably then, after being drafted into the army in 1952 (the same year as the twins) we find Charles and Eddie spending most of their service life in military prison (where, according to Pearson, they met and clashed with the Krays for the first time).

In 1956, at the age of 22, Charles formed the Peckford Scrap Metal Company, which, like the Krays' billiard hall in Mile End served as a cover for the Richardsons' operations as receivers of stolen property, and Charles was convicted for receiving in 1957 and 1959. The scrap metal business constituted the original nucleus around which Charles and Eddie (who became a director in 1957) constructed a complex of business (ranging from the purely criminal to the semi-legitimate and the wholly legal) a loosely connected framework of criminal allegiances (the South London equivalent of the Kray Firm) and an elaborate mythology of violence and sadism. Charles and Eddie, deprived of the secure home background which contributed to the Krays' phenomenal power, translated the offices of the Peckford scrap-metal works in New Church Road into a base (both actual and symbolical) and an inviolable castle in much the same way as Ronnie and Reggie apotheosised their mother's house into 'Fort Vallance'. As strongly situated in Camberwell and South London as the Krays were on their Bethnal Green 'manor', the Richardsons remained firmly tied to the scrap yard from whose offices they organised break-ins and business deals, protection and profitable investments overseas; and in which they initiated the notorious torture sessions which provoked such a horrified response from the public gallery during the trial.[49]

From the late 1950s onwards, Richardson began taking an increased interest in the fruits offered by legitimate entrepreneurial activity. Attracted by the impunity which a respectable facade so easily provides, he extended the range of his criminal enterprises by setting up a succession of organisations which served as fronts behind which he could operate unobtrusively and virtually without obstruction from the law. More than this (far more so, perhaps, than the Krays) he threw himself into straight business. Finding a real invisibility (in sharp contrast to the Twins, he rarely appeared in the national press) inside the grey worsted world of the city, he set about engaging in a series of long-firm frauds, and putting into practice the dubious ethic concealed at the core of laissez-faire capitalism. After all, Richardson was singularly equipped to deal with the rigours of life in the rat race. Eventually substituting actual physical violence for the more conventionally acceptable and palatable tactics (outpricing, undercutting etc.) which mean good business and signify a healthy economy he simply applied a literal interpretation to the principle of cut-throat competition.[50]

In 1963, Eddie set up his own very lucrative wholesale chemist's business which soon had branches all over South-East London. Charles became a director of a fancy goods business with premises in Brixton and Camberwell, and rented a railway arch in Bermondsey where he bought and sold office furniture. He was soon entrenched in the fashionable heart of London's whizz-kid world, renting a luxury office in Park Lane. Meanwhile Eddie was quick to capitalise on the gambling boom, opening up with 'Mad Frankie' Frazer a wholesale business in one-armed bandits in Tottenham Court Road, and extorting protection money from the clubs which he supplied with fruit machines.

It is difficult to assess the full extent of the Richardsons' activities from the early 1960s onwards. Shunning the publicity which the Krays seemed to court with such ardour,

Richardson more or less disappeared from public view from 1960 to 1966, when the murder of Thomas Waldeck, a South African mining prospector and the Catford shooting incident refocussed public attention once more. Nonetheless during those years, Richardson was at his most active – and though avoiding a further term in prison until 1967 when he received a 25 year sentence he managed to secure a phenomenal amount of acquittals (14, in fact). To take one example, in 1963 he appeared in court charged with possessing a firearm and 500 rounds of ammunition without a certificate and was given an absolute discharge. As Ronnie Kray began to expand through the militant machinery of the Firm, acquiring (through bribes in the real world, through self-deification in the ideal) the 'invulnerability' which earned him his nickname the 'Colonel', Charles Richardson was simultaneously buying his way above the law (bribing police, corrupting and intimidating witnesses and jurors) and formulating an equally dense personal mythology with himself as prime mover and principle actor. More than this, the two men found, in each other, both an enemy, as potent as firmly located (in a similar local culture) and as determined to win as himself; and an ally. For each found a dangerous confirmation, a double-edged reassurance in the 'reality' of the other. Ronnie Kray needed Charles Richardson in order to prevent the kind of personal collapse he had experienced at the experimental prison, in exactly the same way that we must find a reflection in a mirror in order to preserve some kind of sanity. The preservation of what are primarily adolescent values – a strong sense of territory, the desire for peer-group adulation – was facilitated and made plausible by a parallel retention on the other side of the river. Together cinematic fantasies became realisable and the two gangs were on the point of clashing openly à la Capone when the shooting at Mr. Smith's Club made such a confrontation impossible and unnecessary. Paradoxically then, the gangsters' primary source of self-clarification and potency posed a constant threat to his very survival.

As obsessed with personal power as Ronnie Kray, Charles Richardson declared himself an 'untouchable' and, to all intents and purposes, that, for a time, is exactly what he was. But beyond the fundamental dialectic contained within the struggle as end in itself; beyond the basic terms of the opposition, in which shotgun answered shotgun, and reprisal followed counter-reprisal, the two men diverged considerably, adopting different strategies to realise their common goal. Whilst maintaining a strong financial interest in gambling and drinking clubs (both as owner and as 'protector'), Richardson did not move easily in such surroundings. Neither did he feel comfortable in the expensive suits which were considered a necessary prerequisite for the kind of position he sought to occupy, and, according to an acquaintance, they 'looked better on a coat-hanger'.[51] For the Richardsons, respectability offered anonymity and a semblance of legitimacy. It held no intrinsic appeal and Charles Richardson never suffered from the excessive star-fixations to which his rival was so prone. Needless to say, the Richardsons did not find access to the glamorous circles in which the Krays moved and they never appeared to seek it. The Richardsons, in short lacked the style which was so important to the more subtle, flamboyant and gregarious Krays.

Despite the constant internecine conflict – perhaps even because of it – the Richardsons operated with an ever-increasing confidence never far from 'cockiness' and expanded the range of their business activities at a prodigious rate. The hectic years of the early 1960s which had translated the two vaguely anachronistic, East End criminals into the West End's men of the moment, served the Richardsons equally well. Apart from the proliferation of night-clubs and gaming rooms which, according to an *Observer* article of the time[52] helped to disseminate the criminal way of life, the 1960s as I have suggested favoured the hardheaded working-class opportunist and the Richardson brothers benefited from this unprecedented tolerance. Most of the incidents dealt with in the 1967 trial refer back to this period and the Richardsons were undoubtedly at their most active, their most ambitious, and their most effective during these years. Our information about these activities is restricted to those allegations made by Lawrence 'Johnny' Bradbury, the man convicted for the murder of Waldeck in a statement given to the South African police and to the piecemeal revelations made during the 'Torture Trial'. The Waldeck affair demonstrates most clearly the extent to which the Richardsons had immersed themselves in straight business and illustrates how closely business and violence are related. The facts are themselves sufficiently articulate, I think, and I shall, for the most part, merely summarize Bradbury's statement and subsequent statements made in court by Mrs Connie Waldeck.

In December 1964, Richardson formed a company called Concordia (PTY) Ltd. with a South African mining prospector called Thomas Waldeck in order to exploit certain base mineral rights won by Waldeck in the area, known as the 'Meer'. A similar company was floated in London. Waldeck had been involved in a series of suspect mining deals, and was notorious for his sharp practice. Since 1960, he had become obsessed with the idea of extracting diamonds illegally by winning rights which covered base minerals only. None of the various companies set up for this purpose lasted for long, and a confusing network of mutually contradictory and mutually annulling contracts stretch back over these years. It is fairly certain that Concordia Ltd. and the later Lebombo Mineral Ltd. in which Richardson was to become so passionately involved were also launched in an attempt to realize this ambition.[53]

None of these agreements were legally binding because they contravened the terms of previous contracts undertaken by Waldeck. Furthermore, by May 1965, Richardson had invested at least £200,000 in the venture and had seen no returns. Lawrence Bradbury, who fronted the Bradbury Wholesale Company, a long-firm fraud engineered by the Richardsons was sent to South Africa to evade police enquiries, set up a special company called Orange River Enterprises to buy machinery for the Waldeck venture, and no doubt to report back to Richardson on the state of his affairs in the Meer. Nonetheless, Richardson fired Bradbury on the faulty and, as it later transpired, unfounded evidence supplied by Waldeck accusing Bradbury of misappropriating funds. However, Brian Oseman, another of Richardson's associates who had invested heavily in the perlite scheme confirmed Richardson's earlier reservations concerning Waldeck, after flying out to South Africa and it is probable that by the spring of 1965 Richardson had decided he wanted his partner murdered. In May Waldeck made an application for an additional 20,000 Rand life policy 'to cover anticipated death duties on his enhanced estate'. On June 6, five days after the new policy became effective, rifle shots were fired at Waldeck's home by Bradbury who had returned to South Africa with his family in April. On the night of 29 June, 1965 Waldeck was shot dead when he answered the door of his Parkwood home. Bradbury claimed at his trial that he had merely driven the assassin, a well-known London villain, flown out from London for the purpose to and from the scene of the crime. This was never substantiated and in April 1966, he was convicted of the murder and sentenced to death; the sentence being later commuted to life imprisonment. During the trial Mrs Connie Waldeck claimed that Charles Richardson stood 'at the top of the pile of ruthless London hoodlums', and in subsequent conversations with Chief Inspector Arthur Rees of Scotland Yard, Bradbury made the first sensational allegations against the two brothers which were to lead eventually to the Richardsons' convictions. As the sordid disclosures, the beatings and the knifings, the tales of men nailed to the floor through their knees, of teeth forcibly extracted – began filtering back to England; Richardson agreed to give his first newspaper interview to the *Sunday Times*. In this interview (8 May 1966),

Richardson attempted nervously to refute the allegations with a somewhat misplaced flippancy ('It's so ridiculous, my friends are laughing'), but the document holds a singular interest quite apart from any light it might throw on Richardson's private perversity. Certain oblique references were made in the interview indicating a level of involvement never openly explored in court.

At one point it is hinted that a former C.I.D. officer helped Richardson to negotiate the South African mining deal and such an arrangement would certainly lend substance to the accusations of corruption which Richardson repeatedly levelled at the police. All such accusations were summarily dismissed in court. Furthermore, it was revealed that Concordia's board of directors at various times, included a prominent West End solicitor, a Fleet Street news editor, and an alderman who was associated with Mr. Christopher Soames, former Tory Minister of Agriculture. Once more, evidence indicating a high degree of penetration into the world of legitimated power was never openly discussed and its implications remained unexplored. Needless to say, the obvious connections were not made and respectable names were tactfully forgotten as the more immediately shocking evidence gradually began to accumulate and take precedence. The Waldeck case was never adequately publicised in England (though certain features *did* appear in the *Sunday Mirror*) and it did not feature in the Richardson trial.

The absence of such an investigation does render the ascription of guilt to the obvious villains of the piece somewhat facile and reductive. In the Waldeck case, the line where sharp practice ends and brute force begins is scarcely distinguishable but then again, such vertiginous speculations are not the stuff on which the court thrives.

The evidence accrued in relation to the affray at 'Mr Smith's Club' on the night of 7 March 1966, was far more conducive to judicial debate. The facts of the case were self-evident: two London gangs had clashed in a Catford Club over the right to 'protect' the premises, and the ensuing shoot-out in which several men were wounded, and one was killed, was sufficiently remote from the experience of most of the citizenry to invoke the rhetoric of the prosecuting counsel who compared the scene to that of a Western film ('the picture is . . . rather like a part in a Western film'). Eddie Richardson was sentenced to five years; 'Mad Frankie' Fraser also received five years.

In July 1967, Charles Richardson and Albert Longman were tried on two charges – conspiring to pervert the course of justice by attempting to induce the jurors in favour of Edward George Richardson and conspiring together between 8 March and 28 July, 1966 to pervert the course of justice by suborning witnesses for the prosecution upon the trial of Edward Richardson and others for fighting and making an affray. One prosecution witness had been paid off and a bottle had been thrown through a juror's window. Again we are granted an insight into the strange personal logic which dictated Richardson's erratic behaviour: the bottle contained a note which read: 'Bring them in guilty'. This was apparently designed to frighten and confuse the jurors. Charles Richardson received twelve years for the jury incident and eight years for suborning witnesses. Richardson had been in custody since 30 June, 1966 when he, his common-law wife, Jean, and nine other men were arrested in the co-ordinated dawn raid which was to become a standard Scotland Yard technique for dealing with serious criminals. During May and June 1967, the principal charges connected with the various assaults were dealt with at the Old Bailey – and the 'new wave' of British gangsterism broke on the news media.[54]

The trial suffered from those limitations (the constricting effects of an archaic judicial procedure; the impulse – undeclared of course but perhaps not unconscious – to suppress certain embarrassing facts) which we have seen at work in the Kray trial. It served to illuminate only briefly and unevenly the world which the South London gangsters occupied. The prosecution and the police concentrated on those charges which they felt sure would secure a severe sentence from the judge and a nauseated reaction from an audience, alienated at least in public, by such excesses. Thus we know more than enough about the controlled savagery with which the Richardsons enforced their capricious imperatives. The explicit identification of violence with play was indeed shocking. It was, in fact, designed to shock – to spread that reputation for unpredictable sadism, which was to prove so valuable not only in terms of prestige but in real cash profits as well. Victims were selected more or less at random from among the circle of criminal acquaintances or business contacts compromised by their involvement in various shady deals.

The lesson had no validity for torturer or victim outside the experience itself. The medium was indeed the message. No information seems to have been desperately required; no specific offences demanded such cruel reprisals. Although the initial recipient of the Richardsons' ritualistically formalised violence, Jack Duval, seems to have crossed the Firm in some way (refusing to defraud a company for which he worked through fear of being found out) the later victims were merely acquaintances of the original culprit, supposedly aware and generally ignorant of Duval's whereabouts. Finally Benjamin Coulston, another associate of Richardson's was tortured so badly that he had to spend several days in hospital,[55] for no apparent reason whatsoever. He was accused of swindling two of Richardson's colleagues out of £600 on a consignment of stolen cigarettes; but, after convincing Coulston that he was to be murdered; perpetrating the deceit by wrapping him in a tarpaulin, loudly talking about Vauxhall Bridge and driving the terrified man around the block instead, even Richardson admitted with a smile that he had punished the wrong man.

Victims were often given a roll of banknotes (the sums varying from £30 to £150) as a halfhearted gesture towards some kind of compensation and in contemptuous recognition of their entertainment value (an artiste's fee?). From Duval to Coulston we can chart that movement toward motivelessness or inadequate motivation which I have already noted and related to the Krays' drive to power and their incarceration within bourgeois forms of expression. A certain dubious status was won inside the underworld and certain dubious profits were made from direct extortion as a result of the reputation thus gained. Beyond this, the golf clubs, the barbed wire, the pliers, and the electric generator – the paraphernalia of fascism – became the baroque disguise behind which Richardson sought to conceal his personal deterioration.

I have already described the processes of disintegration and refinement which accompany the final stages of closure when analysing the Kray case, and there is no need to reiterate the argument here. Suffice it to say that the judge expressed in his summing up, a revulsion, genuine enough no doubt, from the deeds of the convicted men. But characteristically he confined his criticisms (rooted in the offended aesthetics of the civilised man) to the *quantity* of violence, and the *manner* in which it was instigated:

> You terrorised those who crossed your path and you terrorised them *in a way* that was vicious, sadistic, and a disgrace to society.
>
> (My emphasis).

And so the judge deplores the method (the 'way') and ignores the meaning. Society had indeed been disgraced but at a level at once too deep and too close to home to be admitted in court. The concentration in the trial itself upon those acts of sadism which enabled the press to abbreviate the case to a conveniently concise and sensational formula 'TORTURE

TRIAL', meant that the full implications of the Richardsons' rise was never drawn out in court (a similar absence was noted in the Kray trial and its treatment in the media).

Richardson's business activities which phase out imperceptibly from the crudely managed small-scale frauds to the less obvious, but no less criminal manipulations of big business and international finance were declared 'sub-judice' after the Richardsons' convictions but later the Attorney-General was to make the somewhat sinister decision (conspiracy theories apart) to drop all outstanding charges on the grounds that the main incidents had been dealt with and a further trial would cost a great deal of public money.

A Polish-born businessman, Bernard Wajcenberg, a man whom the judge said had learned in a war time concentration-camp 'patterns of thought' and 'habits of life' with which the jury would be unfamiliar and who was associated with the Richardsons, described in court how he was confronted by a bruised and bleeding Jack Duval in the Camberwell offices of the Peckford Scrap Metal Company. The shrewd businessman, not unduly scrupulous, but a respectable and useful member of the community nonetheless was thus forced to face the darker side of the system to which he was so firmly committed. He was predictably horrified and said:

> I did not know what this sort of thing was. Business is business, but violence is something different.

Perhaps we are now in a position to dispute that distinction.

It is impossible to draw a paper which deals with organised crime during the 1960s to a satisfactory conclusion. Too much information is still unavailable for any really comprehensive investigation to be made. I have confined myself to studying the history of one particular gang – the Kray Firm; itself, by no means a distinct and self-enclosed unit, which dominated the more publicity prone sectors of the London scene for a number of years. To complete this picture, I then turned to the largest and most prestigious gang (the Richardsons) which for a time, challenged the Krays' hegemony. I should like here to outline subsequent developments in the East-End underworld, to take a cursory glance at three recent highly publicised cases, which, in some way, lead us back into the labyrinth of London's criminal interactions during the last decade. Finally, I shall be suggesting a more obvious matrix for that maze than the one put forward in the earlier sections of this paper, by examining the implications of the Gaming, Betting and Lotteries Act (1960), which, as I have stated, transfigured Soho and the nation's gambling habits.

In the family tradition:

> 'Nothing has gone right since the Twins went into the West End. It got the coppers narked. They didn't mind all the old rackets back in the East End . . . But all this cooking the books in gaming clubs up the other end, was asking for it.'
>
> A Goswell Road resident quoted in the second of Nichol Fortune's articles: 'East End Since the Krays' (Jan 19–25, 1973 issue of *Time Out*.)

> 'My son is as innocent as a new born babe, you bastard!'
>
> The mother of Leon Carlton on hearing the judge pass a 12-year sentence on her son.

In the East End, things unlawful functioned in much the same way as they had before the Kray arrests. Many of the Krays' operations continued to turn over considerable profits virtually without interruption; the business being carried on by various associates. Nonetheless, the traditional East-End pattern, whereby a strong, close-knit family provides a point around which violence and power can accumulate, soon began to reassert itself once more. The Dixons and the Tibbs both attempted to follow in the twins' footsteps during the late 1960s and early 1970s, and neither family got very far.

Changes in the structure and leadership of the Metropolitan Police Force, and a fresh initiative from the Home Secretary, Robert Carr, account for this failure. After the Krays' demise in 1968, the special squad, stationed in Tintagel House, which had led the investigation into the twins' affairs, was retained. 'Nipper' Read was himself promoted; but his successor Chief Superintendent Albert Wickstead (soon nicknamed 'The Gangbuster'), who came himself, from the East End, was quick to prove himself equally dedicated and efficient. This move coincided with the nomination of Robert Mark as Metropolitan Police Commissioner (the only person to whom Wickstead was responsible) and a rigidification of the Home Office line on law and order. From this time onwards, Scotland Yard repeatedly issued directives announcing a more determined and inflexible policy in relation to serious crimes. Armed with the spectre of the Krays, the militant forces of the law proceeded to invade the East End, confident of gaining convictions from a judge and jury, alerted by the recent disclosures, against the dangers of the 'rising tide of crime'.

And so it was that in 1972, George and Alan Dixon appeared in the Old Bailey with several associates, charged with blackmail, conspiracy to assault, conspiracy to cause grievous bodily harm, and conspiracy to blackmail. The Dixons had known the Krays for some years; had mixed in the same circles; had profited from the same sources. But the scale of their operations never approached anything like that achieved by the Krays. Indeed Dixon's counsel contended that the total haul from their activities (as far as was known) amounted to £120; but a precedent had been set and the two brothers were described as 'mini-Krays', and there was talk of 'violence and extortion walking hand in hand'. The conspiracy charges, which automatically increased the seriousness of the original charges (a method of securing longer sentences only recently introduced) mark the new tendency toward rigour and severity which I have dated from this period in Section 8.

The trial bore many resemblances to the Kray trial. The same elaborate security arrangements prevailed and dictated an oppressive atmosphere in court; the integrity of several prosecution witnesses was constantly being questioned by Defence Counsel and the heavy sentences (12 years for the most part) provoked the angry outbursts from the dock, which were to become so familiar two years later, in the trials of George Ince. There were also the accusations of police corruption and bending of evidence which invariably accompany contemporary gangland trials. And Alan Dixon shouted somewhat prematurely: ' "Wickstead's reign is now going to be at an end. We will get you, Wickstead" ', because in late 1972, Wickstead secured the conviction of the four Tibbs brothers (George, Jimmy, Bobby and John), their father James, and four associates. The men were charged with attempted murder, grievous bodily harm, possessing weapons, conspiring to pervert the course of justice and concealment. Again heavy sentences were greeted by violent scuffles in the dock as the convicted men were led away shouting that defendants had been 'verballed-up' by Wickstead. The appeals against the sentences given the Dixons and the Tibbs, together with the allegations of unscrupulous and unlawful police tactics, soon died in the repressive atmosphere of debate which prevailed as the law and order panic began to take a hold.

Buggy, Biggs and the barn murder trial

(i) The nightmare was always defeated by my family's love'.

(George Ince on being found not guilty.)

The Kray name continued to haunt the Central Criminal Court and the occasional headline and it featured quite spectacularly in the Barn murder trial. George Ince, a builder of Manor Park, East London stood trial twice for the murder of Mrs Muriel Patience and the attempted murders of Mr Robert Patience and his daughter, Beverley, in what was to be described by Oliver Martin, Q.C. for John Brook, who was later found guilty of the murder as 'a very strange case' which 'is probably unique in our criminal history'. Once more, the 'facts' are somewhat opaque, the conclusions reached in court unsatisfactory.

It appears that on the night of 4 November 1972, two men broke into the Sun Lido house, the residence attached to the Barn restaurant in Braintree, Essex. After being refused the keys to the safe by the restaurant's owner, Mr Bob Patience, one of the men shot his wife, Muriel, through the head, using a cushion to muffle the blast. The two men left with two bags containing £900 in notes and a quantity of cheques, which were later found burned, leaving Mr Patience and his daughter seriously wounded by further gunshots.

Ince was identified by Beverley Patience from photographs, shown to her by police whilst she was recovering in hospital. She later picked him out of an identification parade and Mr Bob Patience was '100% certain' that Ince was the man who had killed his wife. Ince gave himself up when he heard through underworld sources that an intensive search was underway and that armed police had been authorised to shoot if he resisted arrest. In May, 1973 he angrily protested his innocence before Judge Melford Stevenson, who had presided over the Kray trial in 1968 (a fact which Ince believed would prejudice his chances of acquittal); and succeeded in making the front page more than once by dismissing his lawyer for incompetence and aggressively conducting his own defence, showing scant respect for standard judicial etiquette. He was ordered from the courtroom, on the last explosive day of his 6-day trial, and the jury brought in a 9–3 verdict of guilty after lengthy deliberation. The judge declared a mistrial and the fiasco was suspended until Ince appeared in court a few weeks later on the same charges. The disclosures which were made hardly served to elucidate the matter: Ince claimed throughout that he was caught between a gangland vendetta and a vindictive police hierarchy which resented his association with the Tibbs brothers and the Underworld in general, and were set on a conviction. Rumours began to circulate that Patience was a fence for stolen property, that he had met Ince 15 years previously in this capacity, and that the safe had contained anything between £15,000 and £40,000 on the night of the murder. As the trial progressed, the defence began to rest increasingly on an alibi which for obscure and sinister reasons, would be difficult to substantiate. Tension mounted in the press as veiled references were made to a mysterious woman whose husband was 'out of circulation for the time being', and who, Ince claimed, had spent the night of 4–5 November, 1972 in his company. Eventually, the woman – a Mrs Doris Grey – was compelled to give testimony. Despite an unconvincing attempt at concealing Mrs Grey's identity, certain references to brothers-in-law, and a billiard-hall in Mile End made it obvious that the woman was Charles Kray's wife, Dolly. Her brief appearance was enough to secure an acquittal and, amidst cheers from a public gallery packed with family and friends, the triumphant Ince was led from the dock. A scuffle broke out as he shouted across the court at Chief Superintendent Len White, head of Essex C.I.D.: 'It's your turn now . . . for corruption. You are corrupt.'

As he was being led from the court, the accusations continued: 'You took some money!'

The identity of Mrs Grey was openly disclosed in the newspapers the next day (23 May, 1973) and it was revealed that Ince had been the victim of two attacks by men representing the Krays, one in 1969, when he was shot in the legs, and one in 1971, when an attempt was made to blow his genitals off with a shotgun which had been thrust down his trousers (93 pellets were removed from his left calf).[56]

In September, Ince appeared at the Old Bailey once more and was sentenced to 15 years for his part in a bullion raid that had taken place in 1972 at Mountnessing near Brentwood, Essex, in which £395,000 in silver had been stolen from a security van.

The Barn murder case lapsed yet again into obscurity but was suddenly resurrected by the arrest in January 1974 of John Brook and Michael de Clare Johnson. The trial was greeted with anticipation by a press by now hypersensitive to its sensational potential – and they were not to be disappointed. New headlines progressively more emphatic and astonishing, appeared each day proclaiming the strange goings-on at the Old Bailey: Brook, arrested at a Lake District hotel where he was employed as a porter, admitted that the Biretta discovered in his room (and later found to be the murder weapon) was indeed his, and he pleaded guilty to possessing a firearm without a licence; but he vigorously denied the murder charge, declaring that he had lent the gun to Johnson on the night of 4 November, 1972. Johnson, it was alleged at various times throughout the trial had made a deal with the police to secure preferential treatment and a lighter sentence, and had been present at the murder of Mrs Patience, accompanying another man, possibly Ince. A man called Hanson claimed that Brook had confessed to murdering Mrs Patience when he was sharing a room with the defendant in the Lake District hotel, but on February 1, this testimony was seriously brought into doubt, if not wholly discredited by a man called Trott who declared to the by now bewildered court, that another man called Quinn had approached him (Trott) in Walton prison and had advised him that if he told the authorities that Brook had confessed whilst in prison he (Trott) would get parole. On February 2, Johnson claimed that Brook had gone berserk in the Sun Lido House and had told him not to interfere in what was a family affair.

Finding a way through these confusing and contradictory statements had not been made any easier by the blatant accusations made against Bob Patience by Brook's Counsel. On January 18, he openly accused the appalled and obviously discomposed man of being a 'fence' who had been present when the Mountnessing bullion robbery had been planned and whose unfilled swimming-pool was to be used as a storage-place for a large part of the haul after the crime. It was further suggested that Mr Patience owed Ince money taken in the bullion robbery.[57] Furthermore, a tenuous link between Patience and the Krays was established, and the case became even more complex. It was revealed that 14 years before, when Patience was running another restaurant The Ranch House Club in Ilford, a customer, Richard Coomber, who had attacked him, was later found fatally injured in the car-park. Patience testified that he was bundled into a car by men who were acquainted with the Krays and driven to an East London Engineering Works where the manager advised him to ensure that the 17 witnesses to the incident, all club members, developed 'bad memories'. In a dramatic gesture (dramatic enough to indeed substantiate Patience's statement) a member of the Kray Firm present was said to open a window, produce a gun, and fire one shot into the yard, following this with the cryptic warning: 'It only barks once.'

Eventually on 15 February, 1974, the jury (which had been under close police surveillance since an anonymous threat had been delivered to one of its members urging the jury to bring in a verdict of not guilty for Brook)[58] delivered its verdict of guilty, and Brook received a life sentence three times over. Johnson was given ten years. An enquiry was ordered into the complaints made by Ince into the Essex police force, by the Chief Constable himself. Nonetheless certain questions will most probably never be asked, and we can expect the case to retain its impenetrable mystique.

I have related the events which took place in The Barn murder trial at some length because I think it deserves a detailed treatment. It reflects the complexity of criminal interactions (both with fellow-criminals and the police) and gives us a glimpse of those shifting and unchartable regions which lie between the professional criminal and the police, between crime itself and the law. The court's overt retention of an archaic and reductive morality in which specific individuals are found guilty of committing specific crimes against other individuals in some neutral dimension of pure cause and effect, was rendered absurd as each new witness, whether an ex-prisoner or police officer, restaurant owner or self-confessed criminal declared himself more or less the same shade of grey. The processes of accommodation necessary for the continuance of crime and detection which stood thus exposed, made a comedy of the end result – the judicial process.

(ii) The farcical 'arrest' of the escaped Train Robber, Ronald Biggs, in Brazil, by two intrepid members of British C.I.D. – Detective Chief Superintendent Jack Slipper and Detective Sergeant Peter Jones, played out, for all to see, on the pages of the national newspapers makes similar nonsense of the myth of single-minded police detection by laying bare those self-same processes of accommodation. Ronald Biggs, jailed in 1963 for his part in the Great Train Robbery, escaped from Wandsworth Prison in July 1965. In 1970, reports appeared in Britain that Biggs had been arrested in Australia on a charge of being drunk and disorderly, but had been released before his identity was realised. A home movie purporting to show Biggs swimming off the Australian coast was subsequently shown on British T.V. British police arrived in Melbourne only to find that their man had escaped them by a mere matter of hours. The game of global hide-and-seek was under way and Biggs (as far as the media were concerned) concealed himself successfully for three years in Rio under the alias of Michael Haynes, until the night of 1 February 1974 when he was arrested by two Scotland Yard detectives at the Trocedero Hotel. But despite reports in the *Daily Express* which, in some devious way, had helped to engineer Biggs' reunion with the C.I.D., that Biggs had given himself up, preferring to spend the next 28 years behind bars in order to be near those 'green fields' of England which he missed so desperately, rather than spend a life of exile with a beautiful young girl in Brazil, Biggs seemed reluctant to move. On February 5, the two disconsolate detectives returned to Britain without their charge and there ensued the long diplomatic exchange between England and Brazil which, at the time of writing, has failed to resolve the problematic fate of Ronald Biggs.

Meanwhile certain crucial facts about the circumstances of Biggs' arrest remain remarkably elusive, and these deficiences have invited an enormous amount of conjecture and debate in the press. The simultaneous arrival of two C.I.D. men and a couple of reporters from the *Daily Express* (which had been advertising the life story of Biggs for days) outside Room 909 of the Tracedero Hotel, Rio seemed more like collusion than coincidence. On February 6, Ray Carter, M.P. for Birmingham Northfield tabled a question to Mr Carr, calling for an inquiry into the affair and a statement from the Melbourne police commissioner, Jack Davis, claiming that he had sent detailed information about Biggs' movements to the Yard three years before (this information apparently included the alias under which Biggs was travelling, his route and destination) was published in the national dailies. Rumours began to circulate in the press (though not in the *Express*, of course) that Biggs had been doublecrossed; that 'certain men in England' did not keep their word; and those same swampy ill-lit areas of doubt about the integrity of almost everyone involved began to emerge once more.

At the same time, Brazilian police spokesmen claimed that their part in Biggs' capture had been underplayed by Scotland Yard and that Slipper and Jones had tried to hasten the return of their charge in a manner that was, if not actually high-handed, insensitive in the extreme. The whole affair was indeed clumsily managed and the offended Brazilian authorities demanded an exchange of prisoners, even some kind of bilateral extradition treaty. The political implications of such a treaty would have severe repercussions for the Government at the best of times, but in February, with the election fast approaching, such an incendiary item of foreign policy was automatically taboo, and the debate was played down.

The human interest angle was by no means neglected in the interim. Biggs was pictured in the papers on his arrival at Brasilia airport, waving and smiling at his girlfriend Raimundo de Castro, who in turn was shown alternately blowing kisses and bursting into tears. Uncertainty pervaded Biggs' love-life as much as it did his relations with the law; and the papers made much of Raimunda's loudly proclaimed pregnancy (since discredited – a pregnancy would have guaranteed Biggs Brazilian citizenship and freedom from British law). The same papers dwelt with undisguised relish on the high life of gambling and girls, clubs and red-light districts into which Biggs had been projected by the Great Train Robbery. Here was a man who, despite signs of premature middle-age, kept his love-life at a pitch which could be envied by any commuter with a daydream to spare. Biggs' daylight life as a carpenter with a struggling painting and decorating business was thoroughly eclipsed by the brilliant scenes of Rio night life, sun and swim-suits which served as inspiration for the journalists' rhetorical flourishes. Once more bandit-worship joined forces with the Great Littlewoods syndrome to present a composite picture of a man who had won the pools *his* way – a man who had triumphed on his own terms.

Meanwhile Mrs Charmian Biggs vacillated under the intrusive eye of the camera, proclaiming her resolve to 'stand by Ron' one day, to divorce him the next. On February 4, she explained her decision to remain in Australia without seeing her husband: 'My job is to reassure my children that the world is still stable'. Within a few days a national newspaper had flown her out to Brasilia at its own expense to see what chemical reaction would be provoked by introducing a new element – a deserted wife and family – into the situation. The *Sun* and the *Daily Mirror* carried a photographic record of the couple's first meeting; the holding of hands, the argument, the tears etc. After all, Biggs was a very public person, one of the media's very own, and privacy would be unthinkable at such a mythically crucial moment. Neither did the Brazilian media ignore their illustrious captive. Biggs appeared on a 60-second television interview declaring, in fluent Portuguese, his love for Brazil and his desire to become an honest Brazilian. And of course the native public, traditionally romantic in its attitude towards crime, traditionally reluctant to yield up its suspect refugees, was promptly seduced. Biggs became a national hero overnight and the Brazilian government, by now succumbing to Britain's penitent approaches, was openly embarrassed.

And so, at a somewhat portly 44, Biggs, by maintaining a manifest erotic appeal (still worth fighting for!) confirmed the myth of the bandit-hero and resurrected the Great Train Robbery to its original legendary status. The revival of the Great Train Robbery as a metaphor of the noble crime which was automatically precipitated by Biggs' arrest was further confirmed by the very circumstances of that arrest. In the drama as it was played out on the pages of the national newspapers, Biggs appeared as the duped victim, the harassed fugitive; the little man dragged kicking from his dream by the inhuman and constrictive forces of civil power, which can never be eluded for long. Slipper, on the other hand, appeared as the villain of the piece, collaborating with the press, offending a foreign power, acting dishonourably, spoiling the fun, even, finally, scowling at the cameras, moustachioed and in a white raincoat like some pulp-fiction bad detective. Once more, as in 1965, the Great Train Robbery, shifted by press and public alike into some ideal dimension, became synonymous with all those things conspicuously absent from the lives of ordinary people – riches, sex, leisure time; in a word, Freedom. This was inevitably contrasted against the dull mechanics of apprehension; and the drab monolith of authority which moved slowly but surely towards its prosaic goals; and the contrast was no less effective for being implicit. Caught between three such forces – the Brazilian police; the British police; and the *Daily Express* – Biggs could only smile and wave at the cameras. But by thus establishing a real and immediate link with his audience; by presenting a personality with which they could readily identify (the small man in the tight corner), Biggs was somehow transcending captivity, overshadowing the anonymous official to whom he was handcuffed.

(iii) Biggs and Ince (and Patience for that matter) lead us back into the London underworld of the 1960s. The apprehension in March of two men charged with the murder of 'Scotch Jack' Buggy some time in May, 1967, and the arrest of Bernie Silvers in January on one charge of murder and two charges of incitement to murder (the actual murder took place in 1956, the two incitements are alleged to have taken place in the 1960s) provide even more penetrating inroads into the past.

The bullet-ridden body of 'Scotch Jack' was found floating off the coast at Seaford on 6 June, 1967 and reports of the discovery appeared in the papers the following day next to the announcement of the sentences given the Richardson brothers. Buggy who had disappeared on a night in May, when two slightly different rumours of a shooting in Mayfair began to circulate throughout the underworld, was immediately labelled a victim of a gangland feud 'concerned with gambling club debts or protection rackets in the West End'.[59] He was undoubtedly familiar with the Soho circuit, and had been released the previous December after serving 6 years of a 9 year sentence for shooting a man in Piccadilly. There was talk of £30,000 being peremptorily demanded from Buggy by a notorious protection gang.

Bernie Silver, mentioned more than once in the Kray trial, had been considered, for a number of years, a man whose influence and underworld status bore no relation to his apparent power. Silver declares himself an 'antique-dealer', and is the archetypal man behind the scenes – quietly running strip clubs and undramatically involved in violence.

Needless to say, the circumstances in which these cases have been re-examined are far from clear. Officially, Robert Mark, as part of his crusade against serious crime, has reopened certain files closed by his predecessor. On the other hand, Frank Daniels, the retired bookmaker charged with the murder of Buggy, denies that he was arrested in a Marylebone public house, as was claimed by police, and affirms that he gave himself up voluntarily. The pressure brought to bear on Bernie Silvers (his clubs were closed a week before his arrest), who had operated undisturbed in the West End for several years, coincides with the intensification of police activity in Soho which followed the sensational trial of 'Rusty' Humphreys and the allegations of corruption levelled at police by her husband.

Nonetheless, it does at last seem that light (no matter how shaded) will be thrown for a time on certain areas of the 1960s London Underworld which have, until now, been totally obscured. It would seem that that circus in which the Krays were the clowns is, at last, ready to spotlight some of its more modest performers, and to feature some of its quieter acts.[60]

Clubland cabala, big-shots and bingo

I should like to focus upon a point at which biography and culture, crime and the law, reality and fantasy, all converge in an attempt to effect a fusion of the factual and speculative sections of this paper in some kind of Grand Finale. To accomplish this crucial mediation, I have chosen to concentrate on the Gaming legislation of 1960 and the consequent metamorphosis of the British club scene.

The unprecedented stimulus given to British crime and gangsterism by the Gaming, Betting and Lotteries Act of 1960 (recodified in 1963, without any basic amendments) cannot be overestimated. It performed as vital a function in the evolution of organised crime on this side of the Atlantic, as the Volstead Act did in the America of the 1920s, and inaugurated a similar era of overt violence and spectacular law-breaking. Indeed the already mentioned comparison between the London of the 'Permissive 1960s and the Chicago of the Prohibition (the 'road-show version of the Jazz-Age' etc.) was to prove irresistible. Both pieces of legislation, designed to limit the growth of organised crime, paradoxically had the opposite effect, galvanising a somewhat stagnant gangsterism into frenetic and vigorous activity. In Capone's Chicago, the villains moved in to supply an undiminished though now illegitimate demand. In Kray's Swinging London the criminals emerged from virtual obscurity to openly direct what had formerly been an illegal industry. In both cases the law stood exposed as a transitory artefact as subject to change as man himself, and a mood of irreligious moral relativism prevailed and was popularly applied to other sacrosanct areas of civic life, previously free from moral criticism. In Chicago, where it became necessary, even fashionable to break the law if one was to continue an established life-style, a whole public went subterranean. In London where a healthy disregard for the old restraints became commonplace as a clandestine activity, traditionally associated with crime received the official seal of approval, a whole Underworld turned public.

Betting shops and bingo halls became a part of everyday life, and despite the declared intention of the Act to outlaw professional gambling for individual profit, the bookies thrived visibly. Meanwhile those who played for higher stakes won even greater benefits by opening gambling clubs. The 1960 Act was a legislation of loopholes – its famous clause guaranteeing equally favourable chances to all players ironically legalised *chemin-de-fer*, the game where chances can be held to be equally favourable because the bank passes to each player in turn. In order to comply with this clause, the bank, in craps and roulette, while remaining with the house, was offered to the player (this did not bring him any advantage as the odds in favour of the bank are guaranteed only over a period of time). With the bank's built-in advantages, plus extra money brought in by membership fees, by drinks, and by table charges for *chemin-de-fer*, gambling became very big business indeed.[61] At the Olympics Casino from June 1963 to May 1966, bad debts had reached a phenomenal £1,200,000.

As these developments were not foreseen in the Act, there were no safeguards. There were no licensing requirements for gaming clubs or casinos so the police could not object to men with criminal records opening clubs. There was no police right of entry (except in Manchester under a local Act) and no vetting of personnel. To a large extent, criminals, who had run the racket when gambling was outlawed, merely continued to do so after 1960, under the auspices of the law. Clubs proliferated in every major city throughout the country. London alone contained some 80 casinos in 1966; one of which – the Colony Club – was managed by George Raft, who was being watched by the F.B.I. and was believed to be a 'front man' for the American mafia.[62] Pickings from gambling and protection proved so rich that London was well on the way to becoming a haven for organised crime. The 'underworld way of life' did indeed receive much favourable publicity (the cartoon bookie with a big cigar, the club-owner with his new car, new clothes, new women as the vanguard of the long-prophesied social 'revolution'). The gangsters explored the possibilities within affluence, legging it up the ladder of success and flashily advertising their presence at the top.

And clubs and pubs, the pleasure domes of the working-class, featured constantly in the individual gangster's career, and defined his prospects. They provided platforms on which he could display his worth, his fearlessness ('bottle' in criminal argot), his ability to inspire terror and extort respect. Thus, it should hardly surprise us that clubs and pubs provided the settings for some of the most dramatic confrontations during this era. We need only turn to Ronald Kray's murder of George Cornell in the Blind Beggar, or to the affray at Mr. Smith's Club, or the bombing of the Queen Elizabeth by Tony Lawrence, to confirm their centrality. Quite literally, in a geographical sense the shape of the gangster's world was dictated by the clubs he owned, protected or frequented. They often formed the boundary which enclosed his 'Manor' and his uninvited presence in a club outside his own territory would be interpreted as an act of provocation per se. Business and pleasure, profit and consumption were inextricably entwined in the gaming clubs which provided a new source of revenue: an arena in which the gangster could perform, an area in which he could relax and interact with other criminals. Beyond this, the clubs provide a parameter of the gangster's dream, and define the perimeter of that inner world of aspirations and expectations which I have attempted to describe in this paper. Whether supplying in their dark spaces and furtive corners an objective correlative for his own softly-lit mental states or simply offering an ideal environment (heaven with an extension on the licence) in which to fulfil his dangerous fantasies, the clubs were in every way necessary to men like Ronald Kray. As both the economic base and the superstructure from which depended his private desires, his secret appetites his still-born ideology of struggle, the clubs promised simultaneously satisfaction and excitement, security and challenge, cash and somewhere to spend it. If the Kray twins were actors, with old Hollywood scripts, then clubs like the Colony were the perfect sets on which to play out a vicious dream or two.

In 1968, the amendments to the Gaming Act coincided with the conviction of the Krays and the set was struck as the principal players were led off to Parkhurst. Our own version of the Jazz Age came to an end, like its predecessor, with the grounding of its most flamboyant deities. After Capone's demise, the organisation which he had introduced continued to function with less noise and more subtlety and we can safely surmise that a similar pattern was followed in this country after the Krays' imprisonment. British crime will continue to produce the occasional performances which will entrance and absorb the nation's attention once more. It is doubtful however that it will ever mount a spectacle as brilliant, as dangerous, or of such epic proportions as that mounted by the Krays' in the mid 1960s.

Notes

1 From 'Hitlers' in 'Advertisements for Myself'.

2 From 'Intimacy'.

3 'An Excess of Nightmare' published in *Time Out* 23–9 November1973.

4 'Charlie Manson and the Family' in 'Cultural Studies III'.

5 The awareness of this direct relationship is present in many of the more articulate folk devils who invoke in justification of their actions the correspondence between their violence on a microlevel and the violence perpetrated in the name of society on a macrolevel. During the trial in 1894 of Emile Henry, the French anarchist who had thrown a bomb at the Gare St. Lazare killing one person ('I had hoped for 15 dead and 20 wounded'), the defendant parried the judge's condemnation

('Your hands are covered with blood') by condemning his accuser ('Like your red robes'). Similarly, Susan Atkins, a member of Manson's family, when asked by the judge if the killing of 7 people were not 'a big thing' replied with a question of her own: 'Is one million dead because of napalm, because of your justice a big thing?'

6 It is, of course, characteristic that the Krays should encourage Pearson to write their official biography, and the rumour was published in the *Evening Standard* that they had first tried unsuccessfully to contact Truman Capote, through his London publisher to offer him the first option on the story.

7 A highly imaginative and perceptive depiction of the relationship between the London gangster of the mid-1960s and the Chicago-Hollywood archetype who dictated so much of his style and self-image is found in Nicholas Roeg's film *Performance.* Into the sealed universe of play (Hassan-i-Sabbah's synthetic paradise?) over which the decadent recluse, Turner, presides, bursts Chas the gangster on the run in full possession of the 'demon' which Turner has lost and whose return he so desperately craves. As the self-image of Chas disintegrates under the dual pressures of emancipated sex and an hallucinogenic drug, Turner prepares to absorb the 'demon' as it vacates Chas's body. The first image crucial to Chas's self-perception, to be encountered and discarded (the first card in the pack of his personality to be played), at the beginning of his trip, is the pinstripe-suited, fedorah-hatted gangster. This is the disguise, the fancy dress which Chas adopts for the photograph which is to be included in the forged passport. This passport will take him to the States (a literal interpretation of his inner journey) where he will be safe from the mobsters (his past) who pursue him and seek his death. Harry Flowers, the gang leader, has already hinted at the obsolescence of this image ('You're an old-fashioned boy, Chas, a very old-fashioned boy').

8 Peter Evans and David Bailey: *Goodbye Baby and Amen: A Saraband for the Sixties.*

9 Published in *Time Out,* January 12–18, 1973.

10 They continue to appear with surprising regularity, even now 6 years after the 'collapse of their Empire', in the more sensational papers – 'Krays turn to God' (*Daily Mirror* 1973), 'Ronnie Kray to Marry?' (*News of the World* 1973), 'Krays pay tribute to Italian A1' (*Daily Mirror* 1973), and of course Dolly Kray and George Ince which must run a close second to Mr and Mrs Mark Philips as the media's love affair of 1973 (see Appendix B(ii)).

11 Nichol Fortune *After the Krays.*

12 Reported in Lucas' *Britain's Gangland.*

13 Whether or not this is actually the case remains doubtful. Nichol Fortune's principal source 'Jim' is useful once more, in providing an alternative perspective to Pearson's, 'Jim' claims that Mitchell was slow, likeable but unimpressive, the implication being that the Krays' romantic gesture would be lost on a cynical, and sophisticated Underworld. Nonetheless I am interested here only in what the Krays *believed they were achieving,* and in what they actually *did.* I am interested quite literally in 'THEIR WORLD'.

14 This interest could be confirmed by Norman Lucas's description of Ronnie's Cedar Court flat which seems to have formed a remarkable environment – a small world reflecting the various strains of fantasy which predominated in Ronnie's personal mythology. Apparently oriental and Western kitsch vied for prominence in a startling, characteristically disturbing manner. African tribal art provided one theme in this cacophonous symphony.

15 This freedom must also have been bought in their day to day interactions with the police by actual bribes. Though the extent of this bribing must have been considerable for the Krays to get where they did, it was never disclosed or even touched upon in the press. Perhaps the recent extradition from Holland of Humphreys (the 'Soho Strip King') will result in the promised public disclosure of police corruption.

16 This operation was planned, significantly enough, by 'Mad Teddy' Smith, who described himself as a television scriptwriter and who had, indeed, had a play about a bank robbery recently accepted by the B.B.C.

17 In a later section I intend to analyse the inadequacies of main-stream analyses of organised crime and shall attempt to explain these deficiencies.

18 Printed in *Evening Standard* 6 March, 1969.

19 The new mood of iconoclasm, with its attendant myths reached beyond the trendy world of the pop entrepreneurs, the artists and the actors to infect the sober tradition-bound universe of established industry and politics where Tom Woolfe's mid-Atlantic man, the suburban technocrat was seen as the new Moses, destined to lead Britain into that 'revolutionary' era of no-nonsense

administration, of equal opportunity, and unlimited, general affluence which was to be the next glorious stage in the development of capitalism. (See Anthony Sampson's article 'Changing Anatomy of Britain', *Observer* Colour Magazine 21 March, 1965 for a classic contemporary interpretation of this development.) The 1960s 'revolution' was projected almost exclusively in terms of visual images, styles, 'looks' etc. It was not only a revolution which took place mainly within the media industry itself (benefiting a handful of creative young working-class 'talent') but in the terms dictated by the visual media (e.g. superficial and equivocal pictorial terms which evade a rigorous analysis and a fixed definition). In David Hemmings' words (from 'Only When I Larf' 1968) 'A few poofy East End photographers and a couple of long haired musicians from the North – some bloody revolution.'

20 Cooper also supplied the Krays with a number of faulty weapons (including the gun that failed to kill McVitie).

21 Quoted in the *Evening Standard.*

22 Quoted from court report of *Evening Standard.*

23 This appears to be commonplace among criminals. John McVicar in his articles recently reproduced in the *Sunday Times* Colour Supplement admits to an early predilection for a semi-fictional biography of Capone.

24 Most of this information was gleaned from reports of the trial published in the *Evening Standard* though some is taken from Lucas and Pearson.

25 We can distinguish a similar pattern, though necessarily uncompleted, in the activities of the Richardson gang. Before their arrest they appear to have begun embroidering the edge of violence with the strange and ugly arabesques of pure power fantasies. During their appallingly brutal torture sessions in which the use of electric shock techniques, a variety of blunt instruments, and improvised dental treatment figured largely and which appear to have been games played as ends in themselves, Charlie Richardson presided over the entertainments dressed as a mock-judge in wig and gown. (See Section 11.)

26 Described excellently in Phil Cohen's 'Subcultural Conflicts and Working Class Community' (W.P.C.C.S. II)

27 The primacy of family loyalties contributed to the failure of Reggie Kray's marriage to Frances Shea, and her subsequent suicide, and can, no doubt help to explain Ronnie's homosexuality. More topically, when Charles Kray's wife, Dorothy was subjected to the unwelcome attentions of the media in the recent Barn murder trial, Mrs Violet Kray expressed the family's disapproval of her son's choice in marriage: 'I never liked Charlie's wife, but now I hate her. The family has cut her off completely.'

28 From *The Penguin English Dictionary*.

29 See Section 11 where this metaphor is more fully explored.

30 Ronnie Kray strenuously denied ownership (albeit from a selfish motive i.e. so he could claim legal aid) of an £11,000 Suffolk house, at his trial. Nonetheless, despite the financial considerations, the vehemence with which he insisted 'It's my mother's house' implies her exalted position in the firm/family hierarchy (as if anyone would dare dispossess the matriarch).

31 This relationship is adequately described in Wilson's *The Order of the Assassins.*

32 See *The Case of Mary Bell* by Gitta Sereny.

33 Ronnie's nickname, the 'Colonel' testifies to his ascendancy with the Firm.

34 Edward Allsworth Ross: *The Criminaloid.*

35 A category created by Stan Cohen and Laurie Taylor in their codification of the criminals housed in Durham maximum security prison ('Psychological Survival') it would seem to specifically cover the Krays.

36 Biggs would seem to confirm this disaffection. A man who had met Biggs in Brazil recalls in an article, written for the *Sunday Mirror* (11 Feb., 1974) that Biggs had called the twins 'real swine'.

37 With the emphasis on the visibility: it was a culture 'rich' principally in terms of visual image, style etc.

38 3 Police officers under Sgt. Challenor were jailed for conspiracy to pervert the course of justice. Challenor was found insane and unfit to plead.

39 In 1953, Hinds, an East-Ender, was found guilty of robbery and was sentenced to 12 years' preventive detention. He refused to accept the decision, taught himself law, and conducted his own highly technical and articulate, tightly reasoned appeals going so far as to serve a writ on the Attorney General, took his own case to the House of Lords, and escaped three times from prison to gain

publicity. He eventually brought a successful libel action in 1964 against the senior Scotland Yard detective who had originally arrested him, and generally ran rings round police and lawyers alike winning in the process much public sympathy and admiration.

40 Although this was indeed not inconsiderable – the injuries sustained by the struggling driver were eventually to contribute to his early death.

41 Widely reported at the time and revealed in court to the guards obvious embarrassment.

42 Similar pattern of development of Robin Hood myth characterised by Hobsbawm in *Bandits* and by Norman Lewis in his excellent analysis of he Sicilian mafia *The Honoured Society*.

43 There was, of course, an alternative evaluation to be made of these crimes by those excluded groups, who really did subscribe to a policy of violence in response to existences which continued to remain ugly and impoverished despite the general claims of 'affluence'. The skinhead, for instance, whose words are recorded in 'The Paint House' merely treats the demonology of the Law and Order crusaders to a neat inversion. In a song sung on the terraces of the football ground where the obvious police presence is met with open resentment, for instance:

> Harry Roberts is our mate,
> is our mate
> is our mate
> Harry Roberts is our mate
> he kills coppers

44 See 'The Case of Mary Bell' Gitta Sereny and 'A case of diminished responsibility?' C. Starr in Nova Nov. 1969?

45 Reported in *Daily Mirror* 16 March, 1966.

46 We can, perhaps, formulate the essential difference in status assigned to the Train Robber and the Gangster in the popular consciousness, by applying the terms 'Noble Robber' and 'Avenger' used by Eric Hobsbawm in his analysis of primitive bandit cultures. The Train Robber would correspond to the Noble Robber who effects a redistribution of wealth (albeit on a very small scale indeed); who avoids unnecessary violence; who is admired, helped and supported by his people; and who is captured only through treason. (The models for this type include Robin Hood, Angelo Duca, Pancho Villa and Zelin Khan.) The tabloid press, at least, continues to subscribe to this idealisation. A recent headline in the *Sun* (9 Feb, 1974) reads: 'Biggs the "Robin Hood" Thief may soon go Free in Brazil'. The gangster, on the other hand conforms to the archetype of the Avenger most perfectly represented by Lampiao of Brazil. The avenger symbolises power, and vengeance, inspires fear more than love, emerges in times of rapid social change, and appeals to the public imagination by demonstrating that 'even the poor and the weak can be terrible'.

Lampiao means 'The Captain' and it is sufficient merely to recollect Ronnie Kray's nickname, 'The Colonel', to argue a common source for the two men's mythical potency in a popular 'strong leader fixation'. See Hobsbawm's *Bandits*

47 We can say that Göring has committed the positivist fallacy forcing those precepts which pertain only to the natural sciences into the human sphere where they simply do not apply. It could be argued that Sorel's resolve to create 'an artificial world of order', involves a transposition which is just as suspect, and, perhaps, accounts for that short-lived flirtation with Italian fascism which has caused his Marxist admirers such acute embarrassment.

48 Quoted in *Sunday Times* (11 June 1967).

49 Tony Lawrence, the Fulham scrap merchant, attempted a rather shoddy simulation of the Richardsons' rise to power, complete with shootings, petrol bombings, and a bungled 'liquidation' which resulted in the accidental death of his right-hand man, Terence 'Baa Baa' Elgar. Although achieving a limited notoriety in the press during 1967 and 1968 he remained very small fry indeed never getting further than a somewhat pointless feud with a publican and a rival scrap merchant based in Tooting. John McVicar, the widely respected 'loner' of the London Underworld, in an article written for the *Sunday Times* about his experiences inside Durham's Maximum Security wing, describes Lawrence as a 'mug' and exposes the essentially plagiarist nature of his criminal aspirations. Lawrence, McVicar tells us, idolised Richardson in prison and trailed around rather abjectly after the stronger man. See 'Subcultural conflict and criminal performance' in *CCCS Selected Working Papers Volume 2*.

50 A television series 'Big Breadwinner Hogg' (now discontinued) explored this relationship between business and violence.

51 Which is not to say that the Krays were particularly elegant. Jim, Nichol Fortune's interviewee makes a derogatory remark about the Krays 'flashiness'.

> 'They were cheap, they were flashy, they looked like Italian ice-cream sellers, the pair of them'.

However in spite of the crudity of this image, the Kray's combination of narcissism and nastiness was remarkably successful in the new nightclubs where sophisticates and shotgun-merchants blended in a most disturbing manner.

52 The article by Eric Clark, is entitled 'The Greenfelt Gangsters' (*Observer* 22 May, 1966). The quote comes from Milton R. Wessel, American federal prosecutor and director of a 2-year investigation into organised crime in the U.S. 'If we open the door wider to the spread of gambling we shall accomplish one thing above all others: we shall make the underworld "way of life" more extensive, more secure and almost insusceptible to challenge'. This idea of a criminal 'way of life' firmly entrenched in an expanding clubland is undoubtedly responsible for the genesis of many panics about the scale and cohesiveness of organised crime (mafia – conspiracy and criminal subversion theories). This same article gives some indication of the Richardsons' involvement in protection: the 'South London racketeer' who 'boasts privately that 40 clubs and other enterprises are "under control" ' can only be Charles Richardson.

53 The perlite which was mined was of an inferior quality, and was not commercially viable, being unsuitable for use in the building trade.

54 Finally, in December, 12 men were convicted for operating a fraud at the London Airport car park which had netted them £200,000 in four years. It conspired that during 1965 these men had been approached by the Richardsons and had been compelled to hand over a large proportion of the substantial revenue. Money had continued to arrive in regular payments until November 1966.

55 The struck-off doctor whom Richardson employed to look after his 'mistakes' was unequipped to deal with such severe injuries.

56 The same papers carried a footnote reporting an assault in Parkhurst prison, in which a man had been attacked with a broken bottle. The twins were held responsible and were moved into solitary confinement.

57 These charges were denied on January 19 by a police officer who took the witness stand.

58 Typically, this too is equivocal and ambivalent. It could easily have been an attempt to discredit Brook.

59 Taken from *Birmingham Post*; 7 June, 1967.

60 For instance, the celebrated mystery of 'Ginger' Marks' disappearance from outside the Carpenters Arms, Bethnal Green on the night of 2 January, 1965 might be cleared up. It is widely rumoured that Marks, a 37 year old salesman and haulier, is now helping to prop up Hammersmith Flyover, having been buried beneath one of its supports.

61 This game was known to turn over £10,000 an hour in one big club, when play was going at full-tilt. (Thanks to Eric Clark for much of this information about gambling in his articles on gambling (22 May and 29 May 1966) and a later article 'Crimewave Britain' (*Observer* 18 September, 1966).

62 In 1968, Raft was deported.

Bibliography

General

'The Profession of Violence': John Pearson

'Britain's Gangland': Norman Lucas

'The Evil Firm: the Rise and Fall of the Brothers Kray': Brian McConnell.

'The East End After the Krays': Nichol Fortune published in 2 issues (Jan 12–18, 19–25 1973) of *Time Out*.

Section 1

'Mythologies': Roland Barthes
'Advertisements for Myself': Norman Mailer
'An Excess of Nightmare': John Grillo *Time Out* (Nov 23–9 1973)
'Charlie Manson and the Family': Stuart Ewen W.P.C.C.S. III

Section 2

'Order of Assassins': Colin Wilson
'A Casebook for Murder': Colin Wilson

Section 3

'The Gangster as Tragic Hero': From 'The Immediate Experience': Robert Warshow
'Underworld U.S.A.': Colin MacArthur
'The Gangster Film': John Baxter

Section 4

' "Goodbye Baby and Amen": A Saraband for the Sixties': Peter Evans

Section 6

'Changing Anatomy of Britain': (*Observer* 21 March, 1965)

Section 7

'Subcultural Conflict and Working Class Community': Phil Cohen WPCC.SII
'The Criminaloid': Edward Ross
'Psychological Survival': Stan Cohen and Laurie Taylor

Section 8

'Suicide': Emile Durkheim
'The Case of Mary Bell': Gitta Sereny
'In Cold Blood': Truman Capote
'The Painthouse Gang' – Words From an East End Gang
'How to Steal £2½ million': Peter Fordham in *Sunday Times* Colour Supplement (14 & 21 Feb 1965)
'Bandits': Eric Hobsbawm
'The Honoured Society': Norman Lewis

Section 9

'Gang Warfare': Judge Gerald Sparrow
'Criminal Organisation': Donald Cressey

Appendix A

'The Face of the Third Reich': Joachim C. Fest.

Appendix B

'The Green Felt Gangsters': Eric Clark (*Observer* – 22 May, 1966)
'Gambling: How to Stop the Rot: Eric Clarke (*Observer* – 29 May, 1966)
'Crimewave Britain': " " (*Observer* – 18 Sept, 1966)
The *Evening Standard* was used principally with the Krays, the *Daily Mirror* and the *Sunday Times* with the Richardsons. The *Sun*, the *Daily Mirror*, the *Sunday Mirror* and the *Guardian* were used principally for the sections on Biggs, Buggy and the Barn murder trial.

33 *Jackie*: An ideology of adolescent femininity

Angela McRobbie

These chapters are adapted from a longer study, presented as an MA Thesis in the Centre for Contemporary Cultural Studies, University of Birmingham, on 'Working-Class Girls and the Culture of Femininity'.

Section I: *Jackie*: Cultural product and signifying system

Part 1

> Another useful expression though, is the pathetic appealing look, which brings out a boy's protective instinct and has him desperate to get you another drink/help you on with your coat/give you a lift home. It's best done by opening your eyes wide and dropping the mouth open a little looking (hanging your head slightly) directly into the eyes of the boy you're talking to. Practice this.
>
> *Jackie*, February 15, 1975.

One of the major reasons for choosing *Jackie* for analysis is its astounding success. Since its first appearance in 1964 its sales have risen from an initial weekly average of 350,000 (with a drop in 1965 to 250,000) to 451,000 in 1968 and 605,947 in 1976. This means that it has been Britain's longest selling 'teen' magazine for over ten years. *Boyfriend*, first published in 1959, started off with sales figures averaging around 418,000 but had fallen to 199,000 in 1965 when publication ceased. *Mirabelle*, launched in 1956, sold over 540,000 copies each week, a reflection of the 'teenage boom' of the mid 1950s, but by 1968 its sales had declined to 175,000.[1]

However my aim here is not to grapple with those factors upon which this success appears to be predicated, instead it will be to mount a rigorous and systematic critique of *Jackie* as a system of messages, a signifying system and a bearer of a certain ideology; an ideology which deals with the construction of teenage 'femininity'.

Jackie is one of a large range of magazines, newspapers and comics published by D.C. Thomson of Dundee. [Five newspapers in Scotland, 32 titles in all].

With a history of vigorous anti-unionism, D.C. Thomson is not unlike other large mass communication groups. Like Walt Disney, for example, it produces predominantly for a young market and operates a strict code of censorship on content. But its conservatism is most overtly evident in its newspapers which take a consistently anti-union and 'law and order' line. The *Sunday Post*, with a reputed readership of around 3m. (i.e. 79% of the entire population of Scotland over 15) is comforting, reassuring and parochial in tone. Comprised, in the main, of anecdotal incidents drawn to the attention of the reader in 'couthie' language, it serves as a 'Sunday entertainer' reminding its readers of the pleasure of belonging to a particular national culture.[2]

One visible result of this success has been, at a time of inflation and of crisis, in the publishing world, 'enviably' high profit margins of 20% or more. More than this, D.C. Thomson has expanded into other associated fields, with investments for example in the Clyde Paper Co. (27.15%) and Southern TV (24.8%).[3]

Two points should be made in this context. First, without necessarily adhering to the 'traditional' conspiracy plot thesis, it would be naive to envisage the 'interests' of such a company as being purely the pursuit of increased profits. D.C. Thomson is not, in *Jackie*, merely 'giving the girls what they want'. Each magazine, newspaper or comic has its own conventions and its own style. But within these conventions and through them a concerted effort is nevertheless made to win and shape the consent of the readers to a set of particular values.

The work of this branch of the media involves 'framing' the world for its readers, and through a variety of techniques endowing with importance those topics chosen for inclusion. The reader is invited to share this world with *Jackie*. It is no coincidence that the title is also a girl's name. This is an unambiguous sign that its concern is with 'the category of the subject',[4] in particular the individual girl, and the feminine 'persona'. *Jackie* is both the magazine and the ideal girl. The short, snappy name itself carries a string of connotations: British, fashionable (particularly in the 1960s); modern; and cute; with the pet-form 'ie' ending, it sums up all those desired qualities which the reader is supposedly seeking.

Second, we must see this ideological work as being grounded upon certain so-called natural, even 'biological' categories. Thus *Jackie* expresses the 'natural' features of adolescence in much the same way as, say, Disney comics are said to capture the natural essence of childhood. Each has, as Dorfman and Mattelart writing on Disney point out, a 'virtually biologically captive, predetermined audience'.[5] Jackie introduces the girl into adolescence outlining its landmarks and characteristics in detail and stressing importantly the problematic features as well as the fun. Of course *Jackie* is not solely responsible for nurturing this ideology of femininity. Nor would such an ideology cease to exist should *Jackie* stop publication.

Unlike other fields of mass culture, the magazines of teenage girls have not as yet been subject to rigorous critical analysis. Yet from the most cursory of readings it is clear that they, too, like those more immediately associated with the sociology of the media – press, TV, film, radio, etc. – are powerful ideological forces.

In fact women's and girls' weeklies occupy a privileged position. Addressing themselves solely to a female market, their concern is with promoting a feminine culture for their readers. They define and shape the woman's world, spanning every stage from childhood to old age. From *Mandy*, *Bunty* and *Judy*, to *House and Home*, the exact nature of the woman's role is spelt out in detail, according to her age.

She progresses from adolescent romance where there are no explicitly sexual encounters, to the more sexual world of *19*, *Honey* or *Over 21*, which in turn give way to marriage, childbirth, home-making, child care and the *Woman's Own*. There are no 'male' equivalents to these products. 'Male' magazines tend to be based on particular leisure pursuits or hobbies, motorcycling, fishing, cars or even pornography. There is no consistent attempt to link 'interests' with age (though readership of many magazines will obviously be higher among younger age groups) nor is there a sense of a natural inevitable progression or evolution attached to their readers' expected 'careers'. There is instead a variety of possibilities with regard to *leisure* (a point I take up later) many of which involve active participation inside or outside the home.

It will be argued here that the way *Jackie* addresses 'girls' as a monolithic grouping, as do all other women's magazines, serves to obscure differences, of class for example, between women. Instead it asserts a sameness, a kind of *false* sisterhood, which assumes a common definition of womanhood or girlhood. Moreover by isolating out a particular 'phase' or age as the focus of interest, one which coincides roughly with that of its readers, the magazine is in fact creating this 'age-ness' as an ideological construction. 'Adolescence' and here, female adolescence, is itself an ideological 'moment' whose *connotations* are immediately identifiable with those 'topics' included in *Jackie*. And so, by at once defining its readership vis-à-vis age, and by describing what is of relevance, to this age group, *Jackie* and women's magazines in general create a 'false totality'. Thus we *all* want to know how to catch a man, lose weight, look our best, or cook well! Having mapped out the feminine 'career' in such all-embracing terms, there is little or no space allowed for alternatives. Should the present stage be unsatisfactory the reader is merely encouraged to look forward to the next. Two things are happening here. 1) The girls are being invited to join a close, intimate sorority where secrets can be exchanged and advice given; and 2) they are also being presented with an ideological bloc of mammoth proportions, one which *imprisons* them in a claustrophobic world of jealousy and competitiveness, the most unsisterly of emotions, to say the least.

Part 2

There are several ways in which we can think through *Jackie* magazine as part of the media and of mass culture in general.

The first of these is the traditionalist thesis. In this, magazines are seen as belonging to popular or mass culture, something which is inherently inferior to 'high' culture, or 'the arts'. Cheap superficial, exploitative and debasing, it reduces its audience to a mass of mindless morons,

> the open sagging mouths and glazed eyes, the hands mindlessly drumming in time to the music, the broken stiletto heels, the shoddy, stereotyped 'with it' clothes: here apparently, is a collective portrait of a generation enslaved by a commercial machine.[6]

Alderson, writing explicitly on girls' weeklies, takes a similar position. Claiming, correctly, that what they offer their readers is a narrow and restricted view of life, she proposed as an alternative, 'better' literature, citing *Jane Eyre* as an example.[7]

The problems with such an approach are manifest. 'High' culture becomes a cure for all ills. It is, to quote Willis, 'a repository of quintessential human values',[8] playing a humanising role by elevating the emotions and purifying the spirit. What this argument omits to mention are the material requirements necessary to purchase such 'culture'. And underpinning it is an image of the deprived, working-class youngster (what Alderson calls the 'Newsom girl') somehow lacking in those qualities which contact with the arts engenders. Mass culture is seen as a manipulative, vulgar, profit-seeking industry offering cheap and inferior versions of the arts to the more impressionable and vulnerable sectors of the population. This concept of culture is inadequate because it is ahistorical, and is based on unquestioned qualitative judgements. It offers no explanations as to how these forms develop and are distributed. Nor does it explain why one form has a particular resonance for one class in society rather than another.

The second interpretation has much in common with this approach, although it is generally associated with more radical critics. This is the conspiracy thesis and it, too, sees mass culture as 'fodder' for the masses; the result of a ruling-class plot whose objective it is to keep the working classes docile and subordinate and to divert them into entertainments. Writing on TV, Connell, Curti and Hall describe this approach, 'from this position the broadcaster is conceived of as nothing more than the ideological agent of his political masters'.[9] Orwell, writing on boys' magazines in the 1930s, can be seen to take such a position,

> Naturally, the politics of the *Gem* and *Magnet* are Conservative . . . All fiction from the novels in the mushroom libraries downwards is censored in the interests of the ruling class.[10]

By this logic, *Jackie* is merely a mouthpiece for ruling class ideology, focused on young adolescent girls. Again, mass culture is seen as worthless and manipulative. Not only is this argument also ahistorical, but it fails to locate the operations of different apparatuses in the social formation (politics, the media, the law, education, the family, to name but some) each of which is relatively autonomous, has its own *level* and its own specific material practices. While private sectors of the economy do *ultimately* work together with the State, there is a necessary separation, between them. Each apparatus has its own *uneven* development and one cannot be collapsed with another.

The third argument reverses both of the first two arguments, to the extent that it points to pop music and pop culture as meaningful activities: '. . . for most young people today . . . pop music and pop culture is their only expressive outlet.'[11]

Such a position does have some relevance to our study of *Jackie*. It hinges on the assumption that this culture expresses and offers, in albeit consumerist terms, those values and ideas held by both working-class youth and by sections of middle class youth. Youth, that is, is defined in terms of values held, which are often in opposition to those held by the establishment, by their parents, the school, work, etc. Such a definition does not consider youth's relation to production, but to consumption, and it is this approach which has characterised that huge body of work, the sociology of culture and of youth, subcultural theory, and which includes, too, delinquency theory.

To summarise a familiar argument which finds expression in most of these fields: working-class youth, denied access to other 'higher' forms of culture, and in any case associating these with 'authority' and with the middle class, turns to those forms available on the market. Here they can at least exert some power in their choice of commodities. These commodities often come to be a hallmark of the subcultural group in question but not exactly in their original forms. The group *subverts* the original meaning by bestowing additional implied connotations to the object(s) thereby extending the range of its signifying power. These new meanings undermine and can even negate the previous or established meaning(s) so that the object comes to represent an oppositional ideology linked to the subculture or youth grouping, in question. It then summarises for the outside observer, the group's disaffection from the wider society. This process of re-appropriation can be seen in, for example, the 'style' of the skinheads, the 'mod' suit, the 'rocker' motorbike, or even the 'punk' safety-pin![12]

But this approach, which hinges on explaining the choice of cultural artefacts – clothes, records or motor bikes etc., – is of limited usefulness when applied to teenage girls and their magazines. They play little, if any, role in shaping their own pop culture and their choice in consumption is materially extremely narrow. And indeed the forms made available to them make re-appropriation difficult. *Jackie* offers its readers no active 'presence' in which girls are invited to participate. The uses are, in short, prescribed by the 'map'. Yet, as I have pointed out in some detail elsewhere, this does not mean that *Jackie* cannot be used in subversive ways. Clearly girls *do* use it as a means of signalling their boredom and disaffection, in the school, for example. The point *here* is that despite these possible uses, the magazine itself has a powerful ideological presence as a *form*, and as such demands analysis carried out *apart from* these uses or 'readings'.

The fourth and final interpretation is one most often put forward by media practitioners themselves. Writing on the coverage of political affairs on TV, Stuart Hall *et al.* label this the 'laissez-faire' thesis,

> Programming is conceived, simply, as a 'window' on the campaign; it reflects, and therefore, does not shape, or mould, the political debate. In short, the objectives of Television are to provide objective information . . ., so that they [the public] may make up their own minds in a 'rational' manner.[13]

By this logic, *Jackie*, instead of colouring the way the girls think and act, merely reflects and accurately portrays their pre-existing interests, giving them 'what they want', and offering useful advice on the way.

Part 3

While the argument made here will include strands from the positions outlined above, its central thrust will represent a substantial shift away from them. What I want to suggest is that *Jackie* occupies the sphere of the personal or private, what Gramsci calls 'Civil Society' ('the ensemble of organisms that are commonly called Private').[14] Hegemony is sought uncoercively on this terrain, which is relatively free of direct State interference. Consequently it is seen as an arena of 'freedom', of 'free choice' and of 'free time'. This sphere includes:

> not only associations and organisations like political parties and the press, but also the family, which combines ideological and economic functions[15]

and as Hall, Lumley and McLennan observe, this distinctness from the State has

> . . . pertinent effects – for example, in the manner in which different aspects of the class struggle are ideologically inflected.[16]

Jackie exists within a large, powerful, privately-owned publishing apparatus which produces a vast range of newspapers, magazines and comics. It is on this level of the magazine that teenage girls are subjected to an explicit attempt to win consent to the dominant order – in terms of feminity, leisure and consumption, i.e. at the level of culture. It is worth noting at this point that only three girls in a sample of 56 claimed to read any newspapers regularly. They rarely watched the news on television and their only prolonged contact with the written word was at school and through their own and their mothers' magazines. Occasionally a 'risqué' novel like Richard Allen's 'Skingirl' would be passed round at school, but otherwise the girls did not read any literature apart from 'love' comics.

The 'teen' magazine is, therefore, a highly privileged 'site'. Here the girl's consent is sought uncoercively and in her leisure time. As Frith observes

> The ideology of leisure in a capitalist society . . . is that people work in order to be able to enjoy leisure. Leisure is their 'free' time and so the values and choices, expressed in leisure are independent of work – they are the result of ideological conditions.[17]

While there is a strongly coercive element to those other terrains which teenage girls inhabit, the school and the family; in her leisure time the girl is officially 'free' to do as she pleased. And as we have seen, teenage girls show a marked lack of interest in organised leisure activities, showing instead a preference for dancing or merely 'sitting about'. Otherwise the girls in the sample defined their leisure interests in terms of consumer goods – clothes, make-up magazines, records and cigarettes. It is on the open market then that girls are least constrained by the display of social control. The only qualification here is the ability to buy a ticket, magazine or Bay City Roller T-shirt. Here they remain relatively un-interfered with. It is of no consequence, for example, to the management of the Birmingham Ice Rink that their facilities are used as *the* place for picking up girls by Birmingham's 'pre-pub-going' working-class youth on Sunday afternoons. They have little or no moral interest in youth unlike youth-club leaders who seem to equate adolescent courtship with flagrant immorality, drugs and violence.

Frith[18] notes that there are three main purposes for capital with regard to leisure. 1) The reproduction of labour physically (food, rest, relaxation). 2) The reproduction of labour ideologically (so that the work force will willingly return to work each day). 3) The provision of a market for the consumption of goods, thus the realisation of surplus value.

Now, while the subjects of this study are not yet involved in production, they are already being pushed in this direction ideologically, at school, in the home and in the youth club. *Jackie* as a commodity designed for leisure covers all three of the points noted above. It encourages good health and 'beauty sleep', and it is both a consumer object which encourages further consumption and a powerful ideological force.

So, using *Jackie* as an example, we can see that 'leisure' and its exploitation in the commercial and private sector also provides capital with space to carry out ideological work. Further, it can be argued that the very way in which 'leisure' is set up and defined in capitalist society is itself ideological. Work is a 'necessary evil', possibly dull and unrewarding. But its rationale is to allow the worker to look forward to, as an escape, his or her leisure. That is, leisure is equated with 'free' choice and 'free' time and exists in opposition to 'work', which is associated with 'necessity', 'coercion' and 'authority'. In this sphere of individual self-expression and relaxation, the State remains more or less hidden revealing itself only when it is deemed politically necessary (for example at football matches and rock concerts; through the laws relating to obscene publications and through licensing and loitering laws, etc.).

Commercial leisure enterprises with their illusion of freedom have, then, an attraction for youth. And this 'freedom' is pursued, metaphorically, inside the covers of *Jackie*. With an average readership age of 10 to 14, *Jackie* pre-figures girls' entry into the labour market as 'free labourers' and its pages are crammed full of the 'goodies' which this later freedom promises. *Jackie* girls are never at school, they are enjoying the fruits of their labour on the open market. They live in large cities, frequently in flats shared with other young wage-earners like themselves.

This image of freedom has a particular resonance for girls when it is located within and intersects with the longer and again ideologically constructed 'phase' they inhabit in the present. Leisure has a special importance in this period of 'brief flowering',[19] that is, in those years prior to marriage and settling down, after which they become dual labourers in the home and in production. Leisure in their 'single' years is especially important because it is here that their future is secured. It is in *this* sphere that they go about finding a husband and thereby sealing their fate.

To return to the original point, it is in the interests of capital that leisure be to some extent removed from direct contact with the State, despite the latter's welfare and leisure provisions for youth. Thus a whole range of consumer goods, pop music, pubs, discos and in our case 'teen' magazines occupy a space which promise greater personal freedom for the consumer. *Jackie* exists in this private sphere. The product of a privately owned industry and the prime exponent of the world of the private or personal emotions.

Frith makes the point that:

> The overall result for capital is that control of leisure has been exercised indirectly, leisure choices can't be determined but they do have to be limited – the problem is to ensure that workers' leisure activities don't affect their discipline, skill or willingness to work.[20]

That is, capital needs to provide this personal space for leisure, but it also needs to control it. This is clearly best done through consumption. Hence ultimately State and private spheres do function 'beneath the ruling ideology' but they also have different 'modes of insertion' on a day-to-day basis, which, as pointed out earlier, in turn produce '*pertinent effects*' vis-à-vis their 'handling' of the class struggle.

To put it another way, there is an *unspoken* consensus existing between those ideologies 'carried' in State organised leisure, and those included in *Jackie*. The former is typically blunt in its concern with moral training, discipline, team spirit, patriotism, etc. while the latter is dedicated to fun and romance!

Part 4

What then are the key features which characterise *Jackie*? First there is a 'lightness' of tone, a non-urgency, which holds true right through the magazine particularly in the use of colour, graphics and advertisements. It asks to be read at a leisurely pace indicating that its subject matter is not wholly serious, is certainly not 'news'. Since entertainment and leisure goods are designed to arouse feelings of pleasure as well as interest, the appearance of the magazine is inviting, its front cover shows a 'pretty' girl smiling happily. The dominance of the visual level, which is maintained throughout the magazine reinforces this notion of leisure. It is to be glanced through, looked at and only finally read. Published at weekly intervals, the reader has time to peruse each item at her own speed. She also has time to pass it round her friends or swap it for another magazine.

Rigid adherence to a certain style of lay-out and patterning of features ensures a familiarity with its structures(s). The girl can rely on *Jackie* to *cheer her up*, *entertain her*, *or solve her problems each week*. The 'style' of the magazine once established, facilitates and encourages partial and uneven reading, in much the same way as newspapers also do. The girl can quickly turn to the centre page for the pin-up, glance at the fashion page and leave the problems and picture stories which are the 'meat' of the magazine, till she has more time.

Articles and features are carefully arranged to avoid one 'heavy' feature following another. The black and white picture stories taking up between 2½ and 3 full pages are always broken up by a coloured advert, or beauty feature, and the magazine opens and closes by inviting the reader to participate directly through the letters or the problem pages.

This sense of solidness and resistance to change (*Jackie*'s style has not been substantially altered since it began publication) is reflected and paralleled in its thematic content. Each feature (as will be seen later) comprises workings and re-workings of a relatively small repertoire of specific themes or concerns which sum up the girls' world. These topics saturate the magazine. Entering the world of *Jackie* means suspending interest in the 'real' world of school, family or work, and participating in a sphere which is devoid of history and resistant to change.

Jackie deals primarily with the terrain of the personal and it makes a 'turning inwards' to the sphere of the 'soul', the 'heart', or less metaphorically, the emotions. On the one hand, of course, certain features do change – fashion is itself predicated upon change and upon being 'up to date'. But the degree of change even here is qualified – certain features remain the same, e.g. the models' 'looks', poses, the style of drawing and its positioning within the magazine and so on. All that does change is the length of the hem, shade of make-up, style of shoe, etc.

Above all, *Jackie*, like the girl she symbolises is intended to be 'looked at'. This overriding concern with visuals affects every feature. But its visual appearance and style also reflects the spending power of its readers. There is little of the extravagant or exotic in *Jackie*. The paper on which it is printed is thin without being wafer-thin. The fashion and beauty pages show clothes priced within the girls' range and the adverts are similarly focused at a low budget market featuring, principally, personal toiletries, tampons, shampoos and lipsticks rather than larger consumer goods.

Next, I want to turn to the question of the method of analysis. Instead of drawing on the well-charted techniques of content analysis, I will be using approaches associated with *semiology*, the 'science of signs'. However, this approach offers no fool-proof methodology. As a 'science' it is still in its infancy, yet it has more to offer than traditional content analysis[21] if only because it is not solely concerned with the numerative *appearance* of the content, but with the messages which such 'contents' signify. Magazines are specific signifying systems where particular messages are produced and articulated. Quantification is therefore rejected and replaced with understanding media messages as *structured wholes* and combinations of structures, polarities and oppositions are endowed with greater significance than their mere numerative existence.

Semiological analysis proceeds by isolating sets of codes around which the message is constructured. These conventions operate at several levels, visual and narrative, and include also sets of sub-codes, such as codes (in *Jackie*) of fashion, beauty, romance, personal/domestic life and pop music. These codes constitute the 'rules' by which different meanings are produced and it is the identification and consideration of these in detail that provides the basis to the analysis. Semiology is, in short, concerned with the internal structuring of a text or signifying system, with what Barthes calls 'immanent analysis'.

> The relevance shown by semiological research centres by definition round the signification of the objects analysed: they are examined only in relation to the meaning which is theirs without bringing on – at least prematurely, that is, before the system is reconstituted as far as possible – the other determining factors of these objects (whether psychological, sociological or physical). These other factors must of course not be denied . . .
>
> . . . The principle of relevance evidently has a consequence for the analyst a situation of immanence; one observes a given system from the inside.[22]

How then do we apply such an analysis to *Jackie*? Given the absence of any definitive rules of procedure – an absence which stems from the polysemic qualities of the image ('It is precisely this polysemy which invites interpretation and therefore makes the imposition of one dominant reading among the variants . . . possible')[23] my approach is necessarily exploratory.

First then, I will attempt to locate the more general structural qualities of *Jackie*. Having described the nature and organisation of the codes which hold it together, I then go on to consider these separately in some detail although in practice they rarely appear in such a 'pure' form.

One of the most immediate and outstanding features of *Jackie* as it is displayed on bookstalls, newspaper stands and counters, up and down the country, is its ability to look 'natural'. It takes its place easily within that whole range of women's magazines which rarely change their format and which (despite new arrivals which quickly achieve this solidness if they are to succeed) always seem to have been there! Its existence is taken for granted. Yet this front obscures the 'artificiality' of the magazine, its 'product-ness' and its existence as a commodity. It also obscures the nature of the processes by which it is produced.

Jackie is the result of a certain kind of labour which involves the implementation and arrangement of a series of visual and narrative signs. Its meanings derive from the practice of encoding 'raw material' (or re-encoding already coded material) which results in the creation of new meanings. These new meanings depend upon the specific organisation of different codes all of which in turn involve different kinds of labour – photography, mounting, framing, drawing, headlining etc.

There is nonetheless, a real problem as to what constitutes 'raw material'. It can be argued that any such 'material' by virtue of its existence within a set of social relations is already encoded. But does 'raw material' refer merely to the material existence of 13–15 year old girls? Or does it recognise that they have already been in constant contact with various ideologies since early childhood? That is, does it assume an already existing culture of femininity?

I would argue that it is the latter which is the case. For 'raw material' we can 'read' that pre-existent 'level' of femininity which both working class and middle class girls can hardly avoid. As part of the dominant ideology it has saturated their lives, colouring the way they dress, the way they act and the way they talk to each other. This ideology is predicated upon their future roles as wives and mothers.

In conclusion I want to turn briefly to the codes themselves. Each code combines within it, two separate levels: the denotative – the literal and the connotative. It is this latter which is of greater interest to the semiologist.

> . . . connotative codes are the configurations of meaning which permit a sign to signify in addition to its denotative reference, other additional, implied meanings.[24]

Connotation then, 'refers subjects to social relations, social structures, to our routinised knowledge of the social formation'.[25] And as Barthes comments

> As for the signified of connotation, its character is at once general, global and diffuse; it is if you like a fragment of ideology.[26]

Codes of connotation depend on prior social knowledge on the part of the reader, observer, or audience, they are 'cultural, conventionalised and historical'.[27] A large range of codes operate in *Jackie* (see diagram), but for present purposes I have identified four sub-codes, and organised the study around them.[28] These are (1) the code of romance, (2) of personal/domestic life, (3) of fashion and beauty and (4) or pop music. It is to the first of these that we now turn.

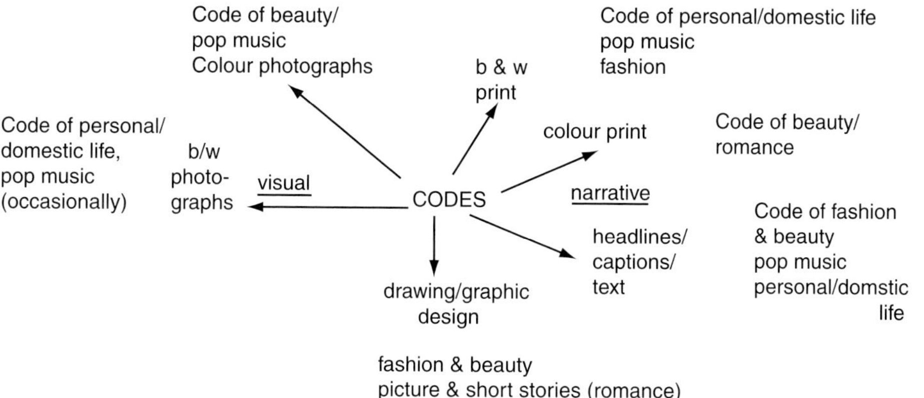

Section II: The code of romance: the moment of bliss

> The hero of romance knows how to treat women. Flowers, little gifts, love letters, maybe poems to her eyes and hair, candlelit meals on moon-lit terraces and muted strings. Nothing hasty, physical. Some heavy breathing . . . Mystery, magic, champagne, ceremony . . . women never have enough of it.[29]

Jackie picture stories are similar *in form* to those comic strips, and tales of adventure, time travel, rivalry and intrigue which regularly fill the pages of children's weeklies. Yet there is something distinctive about these stories which indicates immediately their concern with romance. First the titles clearly announce a concern with 'you', 'me', 'love' and 'happiness'. Romantic connotations are conveyed through the relationship between titles and the names of 'pop' songs and ballads. *Jackie* does not however use the older *Boyfriend* technique of using a well-known pop song and its singer to both inspire the story and give it moral weight!

The tile, then, anchors the story it introduces. In our sample these include: 'The Happiest Xmas Ever', 'Meet Me On The Corner', 'As Long As I've Got You', 'Come Fly With Me', and 'Where Have All The Flowers Gone?'

This concern with romance pervades every story and is built into them through the continued use of certain formal techniques and styles.

For a start, the way the characters look indicates clearly that this is serious, not 'kids stuff'. They are all older and physically more mature than the intended reader. Each character conforms to a well-established and recognisable standard of beauty or handsomeness and they are all smart, fairly sophisticated young adults, rather than adolescents or 'teenagers'.

The most characteristic feature of 'romance' in *Jackie* is the concern with the narrow and restricted world of the emotions. No attempt is made to fill out social events or backgrounds. The picture story is the realm, *par excellence*, of the individual. Each story revolves round one figure and the tiny web of social relationships surrounding him or, usually, her. Rarely are there more than two or three characters in each plot and where they do exist it is merely as part of the background or scenery – in the cafe, at the disco or in the street.

Unlike comic strips, where the subject is fun, excitement or adventure, these stories purport to deal with the more serious side of life – hence the semi-naturalistic style of the drawings and the use of black and white. This, along with the boldness of the drawings, the starkness of stroke and singularity of the figures, conspire to create an impression of 'realism' and seriousness. The form of the stories alone tells us that romance is important, serious and relevant. Yet simultaneously in the content, we are told that it is fun; the essence and meaning of life; the key to happiness, etc. It is this blend which gives the *Jackie* romance its characteristic flavour. In general terms this is nothing new, these stories owe a great deal to popular cinema romances, and to novel ettes. For a start the characters closely resemble the anonymous but distinctive type of the 'film star' – dewy-eyed women and granite-jawed heroes. Their poses are equally soaked in the language of film – the clinch, the rejected lover alone by herself as the sun sets –, the moon comes up – to name but a few. But this cinematic resemblance is based on more than just *association.* The very form of the comic strip has close links with the film. Strung together, in a series of *clips*, set out across and down the page, – the stories 'rise' to a climax and resolution, graphically illustrated in larger images erupting across the page.

From these clips we can see clearly that the emotional life is defined and lived in terms of *romance* which in turn is equated with *great moments* rather than long term processes. Hence the centrality and visual impact of the clinch, the proposal, the wedding day. Together these *moments* constitute a kind of orchestration of *time*; through them the feminine career is constructed. The picture stories comprise a set of visual images composed and set within a series of frames laid out across the page to be 'read' like a text. But these frames communicate *visually*, resemble film-clips and tell the story by 'freezing' the action into sets of 'stills'. Unlike other comics (*Bunty* or *Judy*), *Jackie* stories do not conform to the convention of neatly mounted images set uniformly across the page. Instead a whole range of loose frames indicating different kinds of situations or emotions are used. These produce a greater continuity between 'form' and 'content', so that as the pace of the story accelerates, the visuals erupt *with* the breathless emotional feelings, spilling out over the page.

Each separate image which makes up the story is 'anchored' with sets of verbal messages illuminating the action and eliminating ambiguity. This is necessary since

> all images are polysemic; they imply, underlying their signifiers, a 'floating chain' of signifieds, among which the reader can choose a few and ignore the rest.[30]

But anchorage only refers to one part of the written message accompanying the image in the comic strip, i.e. the caption, title and statement of fact ('the next day', 'later that evening', etc.). The second function of the linguistic message here is 'relay'. Again quoting Barthes:

> words (most often a snippet of dialogue) and image stand in complementary relationship; the words like the images, are thus fragments of a more general syntagm, and the unity of the message occurs at a superior level, the level of the story, anecdote, narrative. . . . The two functions of the linguistic message can co-exist in an iconic group but the dominance of one or the other is not a matter of indifference for the general economy of the work. . . . In some strips which are meant to be read quickly, the narrative is entrusted above all to the word, and the image gathers up the attributive, paradigmatic information (the stereotyped status of persons).[31]

Thus the moment of reading and looking are collapsed into one, and the reader is spared the boredom of having to read more lengthy descriptions; she merely 'takes it in' and hurries on to the next image. The techniques through which this relay operates are well known; – dialogue is indicated by the use of balloons issuing from the mouths of the speakers and filled with words; – and thoughts are conveyed through a series of small bubbles which drift upwards away from the character's mouth – thinking being associated with a 'higher' level of discourse, an 'intellectual' pursuit.

The central and most dramatic incident in each story is specified by the spilling out of one visual image over the page. This image sums up graphically the fraught nature of the moment; the moment when the timid shy heroine catches sight of her handsome boyfriend fascinated by her irresistible best-friend at a party which she stupidly invited her to; or when the girl, let down by her boy rushes out of the coffee bar across the street to be hit by a passing car . . . and so on.

Each frame represents a selection from the development of the plot, and is credited with an importance which those intervening moments are not. Thus the train, supermarket, and office have meaning, to the extent that they represent potential meeting-places where the girl *could well* bump into the prospective boyfriend, who lurks round every corner. It is this which determines their inclusion in the plot; the possibility that everyday life could be transformed into *social life.*

Within the frames themselves the way the figures look, act, and pose contributes also to the ideology of romance. For a start there is very little variation in types of physical appearance. This homogeneity hinges on a blend of modernity and conservatism which typifies the *Jackie* 'look'. The girls are 'mod' but neat and conventional, rarely are they 'way-out'. Boys may look acceptably scruffy and dishevelled by displaying a kind of managed untidiness.

This appearance is matched by language. Deriving seemingly from the days of the teenage commercial boom it has a particularly 50s ring about it.[32] Bereft of accent, dialect, slang or vulgarity it remains the invention of the media – the language of pop, and of Radio I disc jockeys. Distinctly modern it is also quite unthreatening, peppered with phrases like: 'rave', 'yacked', 'zacked', 'scrummy hunk', 'dishy', 'fare', 'comeon, let's blow this place', 'I'm the best mover in town', all of which convey an image of youth 'on the move' of 'a whole scene going' and of 'wowee dig the slick chick in the corner', 'a nice piece of talent', teenagers 'doing their own thing'. But these teenagers are a strangely anonymous and unrecognisable grouping, similar only, perhaps, to the 'Young Generation' seen on TV variety shows or the young people in Coca Cola or Levi Jeans adverts. It is a language of action, of 'action', of 'good times', of enjoyment and of consumerism. The characters in *Jackie* stories and in Coca Cola TV adverts at least seem to be getting things done. They are constantly seen 'raving it up' at discos, going for trips in boyfriends' cars, or else going on holiday. And yet as we shall see, the female and male characters in *Jackie* are simultaneously doing nothing but pursuing each other, and far from being a pleasure-seeking *group* in fact these stories consist of isolated individuals, distrusting even their best-friends and in search of fulfilment only through a partner. The anonymity of the language then parallels the strangely amorphous *Jackie* girls. Marked by a rootlessness, lack of ties or sense of region, the reader is unable to 'locate' them in any social context. They are devoid of history. Bound together by an invisible 'generational consciousness' they inhabit a world where no disruptive values exist. At the 'heart' of this world is the individual girl looking for romance. But romance is not itself an unproblematic category and what I will be arguing here is that its central contradiction is glaringly clear and unavoidable even to the girl herself who is so devoted to its cause. This contradiction is based round the fact that the *romantic moment*, its central 'core', cannot be reconciled with its promise for *eternity*. To put it another way, the code of romance realises, but cannot accept, that the man can adore, love, 'cherish' and he sexually attracted to his girlfriend and simultaneously be 'aroused' by other girls, (in the present of the 'future'). It is the recognition of this fact that sets all girls against each other, and forms the central theme in the picture stories. Hence the girls constant worries, as she is passionately embraced; 'can it last?' or 'how can I be sure his love is for ever?'

Earlier we asserted that *Jackie* was concerned with 'the category of the su subject',[33] with the constitution of the feminine personality. Indeed 'personality' itself forms an important organising category in the magazine. Each week there is some concern with 'your' personality, how to know it, change it or understand those of your friends, boyfriends, families.[34] In the picture stories 'personality' takes on an important role alongside 'looks'. The characters depend for their meaning on well-known stereotypes. That is, to be 'read' correctly the reader must possess previous cultural knowledge of the 'types' of subjects which inhabit his or her social world.

Jackie boys fall into four categories. First there is the fun-loving, grinning, flirtatious boy who is irresistible to all girls; second, the 'tousled' scatterbrained 'zany' youth who inspires 'maternal' feelings in girls; third the emotional, shy, sensitive and even 'arty' type; and fourth, the juvenile delinquent usually portrayed on his motorbike looking wild, aggressive but 'sexy' and whom the girl must 'tame'.

In every case the male figure is idealised and romanticised so that there is a real discrepancy between *Jackie* boys and those boys who are discussed on the Cathy and Claire page. The central point here is that *Jackie* boys are as interested in romance as the girls.

> Mm! I wish Santa would bring me that for Christmas . . . so . . . so how do we get together?

and this, as countless socialogical studies, novels and studies of sexual behaviour indicate, simply does not ring true. Boys in contemporary capitalist society are socialised to be interested in *sex* although this does not mean they don't want to find the 'ideal' girl or wife. (This point is considered in more detail later.)

Female characters, significantly show even less variation in personality. In fact they can be summarised as three opposite or contrasting types. The 'blonde', quiet, timid, loving and trusting girl who either gets her boy in the end or is tragically abandoned; and the wild, fun-loving 'brunette' (often the blonde's best-friend) who will resort to plotting and conniving to get the man she wants. This 'bitch' character is charming and irresistible to men although all women can immediately 'see through' her. Finally there is the non-character, the friendly, open, fun-loving 'ordinary' girl (who may perhaps be slightly 'scatty' or absent-minded). She is remarkable in being normal and things tend to happen *to* her rather than at her instigation. Frequently she figures in stories focusing round the supernatural.

Most of these characters have changed little since the magazine first appeared in 1964. Their 'style' is still rooted in the 'Swinging London' of the mid-1960s. The girls have large, heavily made-up eyes, pale lips and tousled hair, turned up noses and tiny 'party' mouths (à la Jean Shrimpton). They wear clothes at least partly reminiscent of the 60s, hipster skirts with large belts, polo neck sweaters and, occasionally, 'flared' trousers. Despite the fact that several of these girls introduce themselves as 'plain', their claims are contradicted by the accompanying image indicating that they are without exception 'beautiful'. Likewise the men (or boys) are ruggedly handsome, young versions of James Bond (to the extent that some even wear 'shorty' raincoats with 'turned-up' collars). They have thick eyebrows, smiling eyes, and 'granite' jaws.

While some of the stories seem to be set in London, the majority give no indication of 'locale'. The characters speak without an accent and are usually without family or community ties. They have all left school, but 'work' hovers invisibly in the background as a necessary time filler between one evening and the next or can sometimes be a pathway to glamour, fame or romance. Recognisable 'social' backgrounds are rare. The small town, equated with boredom, is signified through the use of strangely anachronistic symbols – the coffee bar, and the motorbike and the narrow street. The country on the other hand, is where the girl escapes *to*, following a broken romance or an unhappy love affair. But when her problems are resolved, she invariably returns to *the city* where things 'really happen'. But it is a city strangely lacking a population that these teenagers inhabit. There are no foreigners, black teenagers, old people or children. No married couples and rarely any families or siblings. It is a world occupied almost solely by young adults on the brink of pairing-up as couples.

The messages which these images and stories together produce are limited and unambiguous, and are repeated endlessly over the years. These are (1) the girl has to fight to *get* and *keep* her man, (2) she can *never* trust another woman unless she is old and 'hideous' in which case she doesn't appear in the stories anyway and (3) despite this, romance, and being a girl, are 'fun'.

No story ever ends with *two* girls alone together and enjoying each other's company. Occasionally the flat-mate or best-friend appears in a role as 'confidante' but these appearances are rare and by implication unimportant. A happy ending means a happy couple, a sad one – a single girl. Having eliminated the possibility of strong supportive relationships between girls themselves, and between people of different ages, *Jackie* stories must elevate to dizzy heights the supremacy of the heterosexual romantic partnership.

This is, it may be argued, unsurprising and predictable. But these stories do more than this. They cancel out completely the possibility of any relationship other than the romantic one between girl and boy. They make it impossible for any girl to talk to, or think about a boy in terms other than those of romance. (A favourite story in both picture form and as a short story, is the 'platonic' relationship which the girl enjoys. She likes him as a friend – but when she is made jealous by his showing an interest in another girl, she realises that it is really love that she feels for him and their romance blossoms.)

Boys and men are, then, not sex objects but romantic objects. The code of romance neatly displaces that of sexuality which hovers somewhere in the background appearing fleetingly in the guise of passion, or the 'clinch'. Romance is about the public and *social* effects of and implications of 'love' relationships. That is, it is concerned with impressing one's friends with a new handsome boyfriend, with being flattered by the attention and compliments lavished by admirers. It is about playing games which 'skirt about' sexuality, and which include sexual innuendo, but which are somehow 'nicer', 'cleaner' and less 'sordid'. Romance is the girls' reply to male sexuality. It stands in opposition to their 'just being after the one thing'; and consequently it *makes* sex seem *dirty*, *sordid*, and *unattractive*. The girl's sexuality is understood and experienced not in terms of a physical need or her own body, but in terms of the romantic attachment. In depicting romantic partnerships, *Jackie* is also therefore constructing male and female roles ensuring that they are separate and as distinct as possible. They are as different as they 'look' different and any interchange between the sexes invariably exudes *romantic* possibilities. What *Jackie* does is to map out all those *differences* which exist between the sexes but to assert that what they do *share* is a common interest, indeed devotion to, 'romance'.

So far, I have outlined in some detail the organising principles around which this discourse (the picture story) is structured. Now, while I would not hold the separation of form and content as being either possible, or necessary for analysis, there are a number of recurring themes which can be identified through a process of extrapolation from both the image and the accompanying text. Thus, temporarily holding constant the formal features of the picture story; the 'balloon' form of dialogue; the action through 'relay'; and the style of illustration – we can go on to deal with the patterns, combinations and permutations of those stock situations which give *Jackie* its characteristic thematic unity.

The stories themselves can be categorised as follows:

(1) the traditional 'love' story,
(2) the romantic adventure serial,
(3) the 'pop' special (where the story revolves around a famous pop star),
(4) the 'zany' tale and
(5) the historical romance.

But those story-types are worked through and expounded by the use of certain conventions or devices and it is through these that the thematic structure can be seen most clearly.

The first of these is the convention of '*time*' or of '*the temporal*'. Under this heading four different modes can be categorised including the *flashback*. Here the opening clips signify 'aloneness' conveyed through images of isolation; a single figure against, say, a rugged, beautiful threatening landscape. Along this same chain of signifieds and following 'aloneness' comes the explanation – that is – 'alone-and-rejected-by-a-loved-one', or 'separated-from-a-loved-one'. Next comes the elucidation; what has caused such a state of unhappiness or misery, and this is classified and expounded upon through the use of the *flashback*. 'I remember only a year ago and it was all so . . .' 'But Dave was different from the others even then.' The reader is transported into the narrator's past and confronted with scenes of love, tenderness, excitement etc. The difference between the past and present state is emphasised by changes of *season*, and particularly by changes of *expression*. Warm weather, for example, goes with smiling, happy faces gazing in mutual pleasure at one another.

From this point onwards different conventions intervene to carry the story along, and it is neatly concluded with a return to the present, and a 'magical' or intentionally un-magical resolution. (The boy reappears, or doesn't, or a new one takes his place –.)

Through this device the reader is invited to interpret her life, past and present, in terms of romantic attachments – her life has meaning through *him*.

The second temporal device is the diary. Again this allows the reader access to the innermost secrets of its writer, sometimes mediated through a plotting, and a guilty best-friend reading her friend's outpourings. But it is the third convention '*History*' which is without doubt the most popular.

By locating the characters in a specific 'period' the scriptwriter and artist are provided immediately with a whole string of easy, and ideologically constructed, concepts with which they can fill out the plot. History *means* particular *styles of clothing, 'quaint' language, strange customs and rituals.*

Thus we have the Victorian heroine connoted through her dress and background dissatisfied with her life and bored by her persistent suitor. When she is transported, magically, into the present she is, however, so horrified by 'liberated' women (policewomen and girls in bikinis) that she is glad to return to her safe and secure environment. Thus, culturally-defined notions of the Victorian period, are used to glamorise the past and criticise the present which is, by implication, bereft of romance. (Bikinis and uniforms don't connote frailty, passivity and fragility.) *At the same time*, this story is incorporating popularised notions of present phenomena which threaten the established order, and in doing so it is thereby diluting and ridiculing them. (This technique has been well documented elsewhere and is also described by Dorfman and Mattelart discussing similar processes in Disney comics.)[35]

Likewise the Edwardian period, again recognisable through costume and this time carrying connotations of more active women, is used to relate a simple story of love, jealousy and reconciliation, with its participants (literally) carrying out their romances on bicycle saddles.

But history is not just novelty, it is also used to demonstrate the intransigence of much-hallowed social values, and 'natural resistance' to change. When a patrician (in the setting of Ancient Rome) falls for a slave girl he can only die for her thereby allowing her to escape with her slave boyfriend; he cannot escape or be paired off with her. Similarly when a flower girl is attracted by a gentleman her thoughts only become romantic when she discovers that he is not *really* a gentleman but rather a bohemian artist. A nineteenth century woman and her child arrive at the doorstep one Christmas but are turned away. Two guests help them and it emerges that the woman is the disinherited daughter of a wealthy man. . . . The messages are clear; love conquers and simultaneously renders unimportant poverty – which at any rate only 'exists' in the past (and is thus contained and manageable). People marry into their own class and their own race. (When a nurse falls for a wounded German prisoner in wartime Britain she knows her love cannot be fulfilled . . . and the prisoner returns to Germany.) Similarly, social class, too 'controversial' an issue to appear in stories set in the present, can be acknowledged as *having* existed in the past.

History then provides the *Jackie* team with a whole set of issues which are more safely dealt with in the past; social problems, social class, foreigners and war. But history also means unchanging *eras* characterised primarily by splendid costumes (the code of fashion), exoticism (language and customs) and adventure. And yet despite this the reader can derive reassurance which lingers on a recognition of the *sameness* which links past and present. Underpinning all the adventures and historical tableaux is *romance*, the young girl in pursuit of it, or being pursued by it. Love, it is claimed, transcends time and is all-important, and history is, again, denied.

The fourth and final temporal device is that of the '*seasons*'. The importance of weather in reflecting 'moods' and creating atmosphere is a feature throughout the stories. 'Love' takes different forms at different times of the year, and holiday romances give way to autumnal 'blues'.

The second set of conventions we will be looking at are those which relate to the exigencies of plot. Thus we have (1) the 'zany' tale where romance is blended with comedy. Here the drawings are less dramatic and are characterised by softer lines. The plots revolve around unusual, unlikely events and coincidences resulting in romantic meetings. At their centre is the 'zany' boy whose bizarre hobbies lead him through a number of disasters until eventually he finds a steady girl who 'tames' him. ('Now they're crazy about each other.')

'Zany' girls of this type are rare. Girls are not really interested in anything outside the confines of femininity, besides which, no girl would willingly make a public spectacle of herself in this way. Often, perhaps instead, animals, always the subject of sentiment, figure strongly in these stories. A camel escapes from the zoo, is caught by a young girl in the city centre who has to await the arrival of the handsome, young, zookeeper. Another favourite centres around the ritual of walking the dog and taking an evening stroll in the local park where numerous handsome, young men are doing the same thing or are willing to be pestered by *her* dog – and so on. 'Hmm, funny names you call your cats.'

Again the message is clear – a 'zany' absent-minded boyfriend is a good bet! He is unlikely to spend his time chasing other girls and is indeed incapable of doing so, he is the lovable 'twit', who needs mothering as well as loving. (Some Mothers Do 'Ave 'Em!)

Second there is the plot which depends on a recognisable social locale. The hospital appears frequently here and carries rich connotations of romance and drama. A girl, for example, is recovering from a throat operation and discovers her boy is going out with someone else, but she overcomes her disappointment by meeting someone new in the hospital.

In another story a dashing young man catches sight of a pretty girl and follows her to her place of work, a bloodbank. Terrified to sign up to give blood he thinks of ways of getting to know her . . .

But hospitals are not the only places where romance can happen; at the bus stop, on the bus, in the park, in the flat downstairs, depending on luck, coincidence or 'stars'. 'He must be on day release . . . he's on the train Mondays and Wednesdays but not the rest of the week'. And there is a moral here, if love strikes, or simply happens 'out of the blue' then all the girl needs to do is look out for it, be alert without actively seeking it. In fact this allows her, once again, to remain passive, she certainly can't approach a young man, only a coincidence may bring them together (though she may work on bringing about such a coincidence). At any rate she certainly can't hang about the bus-stop or street corner waiting to be picked up.

This convention of *place* also, by implication, deems leisure facilities for youth unnecessary. There is no need for them, if *your* boy is on the bus or train each morning. There are no stories set in youth clubs, community centres, even libraries or evening classes, and discos only appear as a backdrop where a girl is taken *to* by her boyfriend. Youth means individuals in search of or waiting for a partner and when this occurs all other leisure needs evaporate.

The third convention takes the idea of luck or coincidence one step further by introducing unambiguously *supernatural* devices. This way the reader is invited to share a fantasy, or 'dream come true'. These include magazines, leprechauns, magic lamps and dreams themselves.

But the dream or fantasy occupies a central place in the girls' life anyway – to an extent *all* the picture stories are fantasies, and escapist. Likewise real-life boys are frequently described as 'dreamy'. Day-dreaming is an expected 'normal' activity on the part of girls, an adolescent phase. But dreaming of this sort is synonomous with passivity – and as we have already seen romance is the language of passivity, *par excellence*. The romantic girl, in contrast to the sexual man is *taken* in a kiss, or embrace. Writing on the development of female sexuality in little girls, Mitchell[36] describes their retreat into the 'Oedipus complex' where the desire *to be loved* can be fulfilled in the comforting and secure environment of the home. Likewise in *Jackie* stories the girl is *chosen*,

> Hmm, this mightn't be so bad after all – if I can get chatting to that little lady later

is taken in an embrace,

> Hmm, I could enjoy teaching you, love . . . very, very much.

And is herself waiting *to be loved.*

> I must be a nut! But I'm really crazy about Jay. If only I could make him care.

Finally there is the convention based round personal or domestic life. Here the girl is at odds with her family and siblings (who rarely appear in person) and eventually is *saved* by the appearance of a boyfriend. Thus we have a twin, madly jealous of her pretty sister, who tries to 'steal' the sister's boyfriend when she has to stay in bed with flu.

> Story of my life! Just Patsy's twin. He doesn't even know my name, I bet. Just knows me as the other one. The quiet one.

Another common theme (echoed in the problem page) is the girl with the 'brainy' family. In one case such a girl is seen reading Shakespeare in the park, by a handsome young man. When he begins to take her out she insists on going to art galleries and museums, but gives herself away when his 'clever' friend shows that she doesn't know what she's talking about. Breaking down she admits to reading cheap romances inside the covers of high-brow drama! Through this humiliation and admission of inferiority (the daughter of another 'clever' family) she wins the true love of the boy. So much for *Jackie*'s anti-intellectualism. All the girl needs is a good personality, 'looks' and confidence. Besides which boys don't like feeling threatened by a 'brainy' girl.

Jackie asserts the absolute and natual separation of sex roles. Girls can take humiliation and be all the more attractive for it, as long as they are pretty and unassertive. Boys can *be* footballers, pop stars, even juvenile delinquents, but girls can only be feminine. The girl's life is defined through emotions – jealousy, possessiveness and devotion. Pervading the stories is an elemental fear, fear of losing your boy, or of never getting one. Romance as a code or a way of life, precipitates individual neurosis and prohibits collective action as a means of dealing with it.

By displacing all vestiges or traces of adolescent sexuality and replacing it with concepts of love, passion and eternity, romance gets trapped within its own contradictions, and hence we have the 'problem page'.

Once declared and reciprocated this love is meant to be lasting, and is based on fidelity and pre-marital monogamy. But the girl knows that where *she*, in most cases, will submit to these axioms, there is always the possibility that her boy's passion will, and can be, roused by almost any attractive girl at the bus-stop, outside the home, etc.

The way this paradox is handled is to introduce terms like resignation, despair, fatalism – it's 'all in the game'. Love has its losers, it must be admitted, but for the girl who has lost, there is always the chance that it will happen again, this time with a more reliable boy. Girls don't, then, fight back. Female 'flirts' always come to a 'bad end'; they are abandoned by their admirers who quickly turn their attention to the quiet, trusting best-friend who had always been content to sit in the background.

Section III: The code of personal life: the moments of anguish

Two sets of features can be categorised under the heading of 'personal life'. These are (1) the 'Cathy and Claire' page and (2) the 'Readers True Experience'. In contrast with fun, fantasy and colour which pervades much of the rest of the magazine, this is the realm, *par excellence*, of realism and of actuality. This is announced clearly in the use of black and white photographs which occupy a prominent position in both these features.

These photographs indicate that the subject being dealt with is 'real life'. They show real, and distinctly unglamorous people in ordinary settings, and they consequently display what

Barthes calls the 'having-been-there'[37] of all photographs. This depends both on the form (black and white, connoting seriousness) and on the content (a couple together or a girl alone). Each figure looks ordinary, unlike the willowy drawings found on the fashion pages. The girl often has long, untidy hair and is heavily made-up. The boy looks even more unkempt in frayed jeans. Their expressions indicate feelings of misery, anxiety or despair except when the photograph belongs to a *past* state when the girl in question *was* once happy.

The problem page itself depends on the dialogue between readers for its impact. They are invited to participate in a personal correspondence with each other as well as with 'Cathy and Claire'. Yet this dialogue is, of course, not so open-ended. The readers are given an address to write to, and are encouraged to share their problems with 'Cathy and Claire', but what appears on the page itself, and what, as a result, constitutes a problem is wholly in the hands of the editors.

The tone is friendly and confidential,

> 'Sorry if this sounds big-headed'
> 'None of them have been serious yet, but I live in hope'.

and the replies, both 'jolly' and supportive.

> 'But seriously love . . .'
> '. . . But we agree it's no joking matter'
> 'You don't want to stop going out with him, love, but you do want to cut down on seeing him so often'.

'Cathy and Claire's' collective image is one of informality. They are neither anonymous editors nor professional problem-solvers (usually introduced by their full names, e.g. Anna Raeburn, or Evelyn Home). They are instead like older sisters; young and trendy enough to understand the girls' problems but also experienced and wise enough to know how to deal with them. This experience is evident in the way they cross-refer between particular problems,

> You'd be surprised at how regularly we get letters like this in our post-bag.

and also their knowledgeable tone,

> unfortunately it's very true that a crowd of girls together tends to get bitchy.

> We know it's an old line, but try to remember looks aren't everything y'know, an attractive personality is just as important.

The problem itself is rooted in and understood in terms of the *personal* even when it is one which is shared by many girls. The situation is invariably an individual one and never involves organisation or discussion between girls. Like the 'letters' page, the problem page is a symbol of women's and in this case, girls' isolation. Frequently they begin with, 'There's nobody I can talk to about this . . .' and the image presented is of the writer *alone* in her bedroom, like the housewife trapped in the home. The page is, then, a sign of women's isolation and separation from each other. And the Cathy and Claire page at once seeks to overcome this isolation through the correspondence and to maintain and nourish it. The personal 'solution' is offered to the readers, regardless of the fact that they may be all experiencing the same problem. That is, the logic which informs the very existence of the problem page depends on problems being individual, not social and their solution likewise revolves round the individual alone, not on girls organising together.

This page depends upon, exploits and offers a magical solution to, the isolation of women. What actually constitutes a problem is never questioned. *In fact* problems, according to this definition, invariably stem from an inability to measure up to some standard or convention either in 'looks', 'popularity' or with 'boys'. The advice which is offered comprises suggestions as to how to avoid or remedy this situation and conform to the 'norm'. For example one girl seeks advice about bringing a partner to a wedding. There is no question of encouraging her to go alone, or with a girl friend!

> You could say something like 'I've been invited to this wedding and I've got to take a partner and I just don't know who to ask'. Then you could look at him and smile sweetly.

However, a whole range of topics, by virtue of their absence are deemed, by implication, either unproblematic or unacceptable as far as this age-group of girls is concerned. These include all references to sexuality as well as more social problems like having nowhere to go in the evening, no privacy at home, no job, prospects or money, etc. (Sexual problems where they do appear are found under the 'Dear Doctor' column and are treated in purely clinical terms. Girls are reassured about irregular periods, pubic hair, weight and so on, but there is no mention of masturbation, contraception or abortion.)

This avoidance of sexuality is quite in keeping with the *Jackie* image. But when 'Cathy and Claire' are confronted with situations which could possibly give rise to promiscuity, their tone quickly becomes one of full-blown moralism. The girl is encouraged, for example, to concede to her parents' demands and stay with an aunt while they go on holiday. Likewise she is persuaded to abandon all plans of going on a youth hostelling holiday with her boyfriend if it is against her parents' wishes.

Three points should be made here. First what Cathy and Claire are distributing is 'really useful feminine knowledge' so that all readers will know how to act, should they find themselves in such a predicament at some point in their teenage years. Second, the discourse, or discussion, is carried out in a tone of secrecy, confidence and intimacy evoking a kind of female solidarity, a sense of mutual understanding and sympathy. But simultaneously the values adhered to are wholly conservative and endorse uncritically the traditional female role. Third, the problem page invariably occupies the same place in all women's magazines, i.e. the inside back page. Comfortably apart from the more light-hearted articles, and set amidst the less flamboyant and colourful small advertisements, it regenerates a flagging interest and also sums up the ideological content of the magazine. It hammers home, on the last but one page, all those ideas and values prevalent in the other sections, but this time in unambiguous black and white.

As with the picture stories, there are a limited number of themes which appear and re-appear in slightly different combinations throughout the problem page and this applies to both questions and answers. Moreover, each page includes a *balanced* cross-section of each type of problem so that the 'one-off' reader gets an opportunity to witness the whole spectrum of issues deemed 'problematic'.

The first of these is, ironically, the *non-problem*. What typifies this category is that, within the definitions set up on the 'Cathy and Claire' page regarding what constitutes a problem, the writer has no *real* problem and knows it. Hence the semi-apologetic tone in which it is written –

> I absolutely hate to admit this, but I'm rather pretty. Now you may think I'm lucky . . .

The purpose of the reply is clearly moral. It is designed to bring the girl 'down to earth', show her that she is lucky, etc., whilst reminding her that 'looks aren't everything'. Under this heading we have the girls whose best friend's brother fancies her, much to her consternation as she is not interested in him. Another girl is worried because, being pretty and attractive, she is accused of being a flirt. In both these cases 'the problem' is 'over-success', and in each case the reply is similar. Be firm, say no, but in a 'friendly' way.

Under this heading comes the 'oddball', the girl worried about *not* having developed an interest in boys, and who is instead devoted to some hobby. The reply to this 'deviation' is reassuring. The girl is encouraged to wait, sooner or later it will happen and she will join that mass of girlhood, united in their pursuit of one goal – a boyfriend! Such an occurrence is so inevitable that there is no *real* problem, she simply has to wait.

> So don't let the opinions of some other school girls upset you. — However there is a danger that you could retreat a bit into your own little world, and cut yourself off from the outside. —

The second category of problems are those dealing with *family life*. This also marks the sole presence of the family in *Jackie* and here it is acknowledged that the girl *will* conceivably have difficulties. 'Cathy and Claire' invariably side with authority and advise either submission, or compromise on the part of the girl.

Dealing with the family, the discussion is couched in the language of sentiment and the girl in question made to feel guilty. When her career (university or college) is posed against the family needing her – she is advised to go to a *local* college or university.

The possibilities that the family throws up for conflict are seemingly endless. One girl's mother reads her diary, another's father acts as though he's jealous – one reader is being confronted with her parents' imminent divorce and doesn't like her prospective step-father and another worries about her parents' extravagance and debt!

It seems that family problems are then a 'natural' part of life and growing up. Yet they do seem to have a *particular* resonance for girls. It is after all they who have to carry the burden of extra housework if 'Mum' is ill, or have to look after younger brothers and sisters. The girls' solid entrenchment in the 'heart' of the family is registered in the extent to which she experiences *its* problems. Moreover it represents the agent of social control, *par excellence*, for the girl, as, say the police do for boys (see next section). As such, in '*Jackie*'s terms, parents are invariably right and their authority is to be bowed to.

Not surprisingly it is then the family which bears the brunt of the girls' rebellion against authority – as *Jackie* eloquently testifies. Year in, year out the 'Cathy and Claire' page is littered with letters from girls who have run away, hitched to London, or have gone to live in a flat. The family in short at least represents an unambiguous point of tension in the girls' lives.

As with the picture stories, every so often juvenile crime figures as a topic in the 'Cathy and Claire' page. The focus of interest here is the rough boyfriend who rides a motorbike, has been in trouble and may even be in Borstal. One writer for example tells how she is frightened that her ex-boyfriend will be 'after' her when he comes out of Borstal, as she is 'going with' someone else.

Although there are no female criminals in the picture stories, they do make an appearance on this page. But their crime is, by definition, less serious than the boys, comprising in the main petty pilfering, shoplifting and stealing out of 'Mum's' purse. No mention is ever made of female violence or of girl gangs.

That said, there is something unwieldy about the way in which *Jackie* 'handles' the subject of crime. The images of the local 'toughie' who 'comes from the wrong side of town', has a typically 50s ring about it:

> My boyfriend comes from a rough area in town and he used to go around in a gang before he met me.

The deviant is the exception, the pathological or 'sick' individual who can't help it. Gangs are mentioned in passing but more often the focus is on the 'rough' individual boy who can lead an innocent girl astray.

The message here is clear; like the family the law must be obeyed. Nonetheless, reverting to the vocabulary of romance, the 'wild' character remains attractive, even irrestible.

> Warning – These Boys Mean Trouble! Bad, Bad, Boys and Why We Love Them.

> your mum and dad don't like him . . . He's mad, bad and dangerous to know . . . but you think he's magnificent. And that's just the beginning of that fatal fascination for a bad boy.

The delinquent has then, something of the appearance of the rebellious pop star. The girl is admiring somebody for doing as he pleased and there is an element of vicariousness in this admiration. There is also a trace of masochism in her interest in such a figure, '. . . the worse he treated me, the more deeply I fell in love with him'. In fact it seems that part of 'his' attraction lies in the threat of sexual violence he represents; another example of the barely disguised rape fantasy so prevalent in *Jackie*. This is clearly illustrated in the way he looks and in the 'violent' objects which surround him – motorbike, leather and so on.

But it is *boyfriend problems* which occupy the dominant position in the 'Cathy and Claire' page each week, and the tensions which arise between 'best-friends' and boyfriends, already documented in the previous section are duplicated here. Under this heading come, for example, the pleas from the girl whose boyfriend is such a flirt, how can she keep him, get him back, or get 'over' him?

And the cry for help from a girl wracked by insecurity and unconfidence, whose boyfriend is so good-looking, attractive and friendly that all girls are after him. How can she overcome her feelings of inadequacy? Finally, there is the girl whose romance is continually being broken off by her indecisive boyfriend.

In each of these cases the girl is plainly powerless and exploited and the stock reply is to become more independent and thus more confident. The girls in question are encouraged to have some 'pride', not to make fools of themselves and thereby become the *more* attractive to boys simply by not being *too* available.

> This should stop his hanky-panky, but if it doesn't, then you must make an effort yourself. Don't submit to his affectionate kisses the next time he comes to see you – he'll soon realise that you mean what you say.

and

Get out with other friends so that you have a life of your own, independent of Jake.

The tone of the answers here are bluntly common-sensical. That is they represent the voice of a true friend, somebody who will tell the 'plain' truth and not deceive the girl as even her best-friend may do. Likewise the girl who is pursued by a married 'bloke' in the office is given short shrift. 'Hands off, he's someone else's property'.

In short the smart girl doesn't run after boys but traps them with more subtlety. The bad relationship, where the girl is clearly being exploited, is worse than no relationship at all; the girl is wasting her time on him, and there are always other boys available. The ideal boy-friend and the one all girls should aim at 'catching' is reliable, attentive, flattering, gallant, undemanding and 'willing to wait'.

But if, as seems the case, this type of boy is unfortunately thin on the ground, true friends are even more scarce. In *Jackie* problems, best-friends continually steal boy-friends, broadcast their friends' inner-most secrets to the outside world, are bitchy and catty, have B.O. or else are so pretty that their friend doesn't have a 'look in' where boys are concerned. In short, real female solidarity doesn't and can't exist. It is up to the girl herself to fight her own battles. If a boy comes along, he takes priority over the best-friend who is relegated to the role of 'girl-friend' and is then seen on a more casual basis one night a week. Friendship makes little demands on the girl, involving only a degree of loyalty and characterised otherwise by convenience and selfishness.

> But now you don't need her so much, now that you're beginning to rebuild your own life.

Finally there are a set of problems which refer to the girls' material situation or her work. These problems are never given priority but simply appear regularly, in one form or another each week.

One girl detests her Saturday job in a supermarket and is encouraged to find something less strenuous like baby-sitting. Several readers have problems affording clothes, make-up and the 'latest' fashion, and there is always the girl who doesn't like her full-time job. This usually stems not from the nature of the work, but from the social relationships of the work-place, for example the bitchiness and cattiness of the office. In one case a girl complains of her workmates' jealousy, the result of her being a relative of the 'boss'. She is encouraged to change jobs where she has no such advantages and thereby is promised the friendship of the other girls. The point here is that work is defined *for* the girl in terms of the agreeable social relationships which surround it and is never seen as problematic in itself.

In conclusion it can be argued that the problem page encourages conventional individual-ism and conformist independence. That is, the girl is channelled towards both traditional female and passive behaviour *and* to having a 'mind of her own'. She is warned of the dangers of following others blindly and is discouraged from wasting time at work, 'dogging off' school or 'gossiping'. Problems are then to do with behaviour; with the individual personality; and with the fact of going through a 'biological phase'. They are never to do with *structures* or with factors arising from social life outside the world of the teenage girl, like for example, class relations.

Operating under the same code as the problems are the 'Cathy and Claire Specials' and the 'Readers' True Experience' features. These latter take the forms of cautionary tales; confessions culminating in an admission of guilt and a warning to other readers. This in fact, allows certain problems to be dealt with in depth, under the guise of the slightly 'spicy' story.

In fact these issues duplicate exactly those dealt with more briefly in the problem page. In 'I Made Him Hate Me' the girl describes how, to keep her boy, she joined in with a group of girls who stole from shops. She then presented him with an expensive birthday present which he realised was stolen. Disgusted by her actions he went off with another girl at his party!

Another 14 year old girl describes how she was tempted into a pub and was seduced by the glamour of drinking bacardi and coke, to be rudely awakened by the arrival of the police.

In 'She's Just Another Run Away' a girl tells how she left home after an argument, hitched to London, got a flat, job and boyfriend. Things went wrong however when her boyfriend arrived drunk one night at her flat demanding entry. Frightened and unhappy she returned home.

Fears based round insecurity and unconfidence also crop up time and time again. In 'She Stole My Boy' a writer, who claims to be, 'quite plain apart from my hair' has her boy stolen, yet again by her best-friend, and in another feature this time a 'pretty' girl tries to grapple with her lack of success with the boys.

> I played every trick I knew in an effort to be the sort of girl boys would rave about.

In the 'Cathy and Claire Specials' the readers have spelt out for them even more clearly, how they should act. In 'Are You Ready For Love' infatuations and crushes are dealt with and girls are encouraged to make a break with dream relationships and look round for more satisfying 'real' romances. Finally, in a feature titled Does He Feel the Same? a boy gives advice to girls about how they should act.

> Don't plan what you're going to say beforehand . . . just make some casual remark.
>
> . . . I don't like girls who are always wanting you to give a big demonstration of how you feel about them, especially when their friends are around.

To sum up, the same themes appear and re-appear with monotonous regularity so that the narrowness of the *Jackie* world and its focus on the *individual* girl and *her own* problems comes to signify the narrowness of the woman's role in general and to pre-figure her later isolation in the home.

Section IV: Fashion and beauty: a girl's best-friend . . . is her mirror

> When I go out without mascara on my eyes I experience myself as I knew myself before puberty. It is inconceivable that any man could desire me sexually, my body hangs together quite differently. Rationally I can see the absurdity of myself. But this does not mean I experience myself in a different way.[38]

So far I have considered the two main sub-codes which operate in *Jackie*, those of romance and of personal and domestic life. I have noted how each grants ascendancy to the boyfriend/girlfriend relationship, and cites as problematic girls' relations with each other. Romance focuses round the 'high points' of the 'affair', emphasising the 'first kiss', the passion, ecstasy and despair. The code of personal life looks at the more long term factors surrounding these relationships. Together these codes throw open for discussion, fill out and eventually 'close' the *Jackie* definition of 'girlhood'.

But there are two other codes which also contribute to this ideology of adolescent femininity in *Jackie*. These are (1) fashion and beauty, and (2) pop music. Again they rarely appear in their 'pure' form; the whole fashion and beauty enterprise is, for example, predicated upon the romantic possibilities it precipitates. Greer quotes from a romantic weekly

> She had a black velvet ribbon round her small waist . . . 'She's going to her first ball' her mother said to me, 'She's wildly excited'.[39]

and adds that

> All romantic novels have a pre-occupation with clothes. Every sexual advance is made with clothing as an attractive barrier.[40]

Likewise pop music centres round, for teenage girls, the pop idol who is the prime embodiment of the 'romantic' hero. But despite this general overlap, each of these codes does occupy its own specific place in *Jackie*. First I want to look at fashion and beauty.

To put it briefly, the central concerns of fashion and beauty are the care, protection and improvement and embellishment of the body with the use of clothing and cosmetics. As signifying systems they each have a powerful existence outside the world of *Jackie* and a few words should be said on these more general cultural meanings.

Firstly, one clear way in which the oppression of women has been expressed is in their aesthetic idealisation by men as objects of physical perfection, to be adorned with beautiful garments, jewellery, perfume and cosmetics. This 'image' is a 'given' of patriarchy and the 'ideal beauty', as a standard towards which all women should strive, is part of the cultural myth of femininity.

But if we look at the more current connotations attached to fashion and beauty we can see that these purely aesthetic dimensions have been somewhat eroded by their cultural connotations as commodities. Like furnishings, cars and other consumer goods, they are socially useful and carry cultural meanings. (Marx called commodities 'social hieroglyphs'.)

Fashion and beauty are not then concerned with the material fact of clothing and servicing the body. As commodities they are cultural signs and as Hall et al. have pointed out, one of the qualities of these signs lies in in their ability to look fixed and 'natural'. This is clearly illustrated in the culture of 'beauty'. The beauty industry is predicated upon women's inability to measure up to male-defined beauty standards without the use of artificial aids. Cosmetics are then designed to compensate for 'natural' deficiencies and as such carry particular, social meanings. Together with clothing they create particular and recognisable images of women.

> In fact, in cultural systems, there is no 'natural' meaning as such. . . . the bowler hat, pin stripe shirt and rolled umbrella do not, in themselves, mean 'sobriety', 'respectability', bourgeois-man-at-work.[41]

The woman wearing her hair in rollers secured to her head with a chiffon scarf embodies different social meanings from the woman wearing a 'Gucci' silk scarf carefully tied under her chin; and the 14 year old pop fan dressed in 'Bay City Roller' outfit similarly connotes different meanings from the public schoolgirl, resplendent in uniform. But to decode these meanings the reader must have prior social knowledge, 'routinised knowledge of the social formation'. Fashion has its own specific language, what Barthes calls the language of the 'garment system'. The fashion industry requires that new clothes are constantly being bought, regardless of 'need'. This is guaranteed at least partly by seasonal innovations and 'style'. Fashion depends on its consumers wanting to be 'up-to-date'; so, for example, the sweater is advertised for autumnal walks; but the language of fashion indicates that it is not for *all* autumnal walks but for this season's rambles in the country. Likewise the same sweater is not designed for *all* Sundays but for *these present* Sundays.

Fashion is then, predicated upon change and modernity ('off with the old and on with the new') and the job of the fashion writer is to continually create a new language to circumscribe what is new in his or her field. This language necessarily negates, and renders redundant what has gone before it, consigning last year's 'look' to oblivion.

But, returning to *Jackie*, we can see that it occupies an anomalous position here. It is not principally a fashion magazine and its fashion pages indicate no uncompromising commitment to the 'latest'. Instead the emphasis is on 'budget buys', good value, economy, and 'ideas'. Similarly its beauty features tend to deal with down-market 'classic' images rather than high fashion beauty styles. In fact the emphasis here is on underplaying the use of make-up to the extent that it is hardly visible. *Jackie* is propagating, in fact, a puritanism as far as make-up is concerned, but this is not incompatible with the continual development and expansion of the beauty market. In fact the beauty pages are quite clearly disguised advertising features, where the image to be achieved ultimately depends on the consumption of certain kinds of goods.

Beauty is, then, announced as a 'fun' feature. The page is set out in highly colourful combinations of photographs, drawings, headlines, captions and texts. Its entertainment value is compounded by the use of puns, proverbs or witticisms which characterise the headlines: 'How Yule Look Tonight', 'Moody Hues', 'Hair Goes', 'Back to the Drawing Board'.

Typically a photograph is at the centre of the page flanked on three sides by text and commanding the immediate attention of the reader. Although the expressions on the models' faces do vary, a distinct pattern can be detected. First there is the 'just-woken-up' look, where the model is at her most 'natural'. This is achieved by the use of an out-of-focus lens and a shot angled so as to be looking down on her face, thus giving the impression of tranquillity, serenity and 'dewiness' (like TV shampoo adverts).

The complex structuring of this kind of image stems from the fact that it holds together a set of contradictions. It provokes the envy and admiration of the reader and offers her the possibility of achieving such beauty by following the instructions. But this involves making-up and the model's beauty here is predicated upon her 'natural' good-looks. At the same time the reader recognises that this 'naturalness' is in itself a 'lie'. It is rather the result of applying make-up in a certain *subtle* way. Make-up is, then, a necessary evil even first thing in the morning. It is as necessary to the woman as her handbag, designed both to make her more desirable and to hide her 'natural' flaws.

The second recurring image on the beauty page is the '*glow*', which emanates from the model's face. Dressed, made-up and ready to go out, she glances nervously at the camera as though it were a mirror. Gratified by what she sees she radiates a glow of happiness, satisfaction and pleasure.

The glow, technically achieved through the use of warm, smudgy colours (reds/pinks/rusts and browns) signifies a kind of calm anticipation. The expression is almost coy, timid, yet happy and excited. The girl is shining with a confidence which allows her to sit back, passively, awaiting praise and admiration.

The message stemming from these images are clear. First if you look good, you feel good and are guaranteed to have a good time. Second, looking as good as this you can expect to be treated as something special, even precious. And third, beauty like this is the girls' passport to happiness and success.

There are of course variations, not all beauty pages are organised around a central, dominant image. Sometimes the page includes several smaller photographs of different parts of the body, and when the subject is 'weight', the location is frequently out-of-doors and the atmosphere is sporty.

In general, however, the emphasis is on two things, the end product (the 'look') and the means of achieving it. The fact that this depends on the consumption of special commodities, is kept well in the background, so that the concept of *beauty* soars high above the mundanity of *consumption.*

The themes around which these features are focused are as predictable as they are also repetitious, including the care and improvement of each part of the body. Often social customs, rituals and events are drawn upon to provide the framework within which the beauty feature of the week operates. Thus we have New Year *beauty* resolutions, or *be-witching* looks for Halloween.

Again there is an emphasis on seasonality, a handy euphemism both for change, for the necessity of continually restocking the 'toilet bag'. (Warm colours in the winter, lighter shades in the summer.) The reader is told, exactly, what to do and what not to do, and much time and effort is spent spelling out what is unattractive and unfeminine. Often a step-by-step procedure, like a do-it-yourself manual, is adopted. Thus one feature on nail-care starts off by showing how to remove stains and old varnish and how to protect the nails. Next it moves on to nail-health and encourages the girl against biting her nails. She is then, finally, shown how to polish them. Only at this point are the latest shades and fashions in nail varnish introduced. The tone adopted by the writer is chatty, friendly yet didactic and imperative. But the assumption upon which all of this *work* is based is that these tricks, routines and rituals are absolutely necessary. Not only romance but even getting a good job, depends on them. It is openly acknowledged that such practices *are* dishonest, and that they are secret rituals carried out in the privacy of the bedroom. Underpinning this is a sense of shame and humiliation that they (women) *have* to resort to artificial aids. But in the beauty page this is 'handled' by adopting a tone of resilience, after all 'all-of-us-girls-are-in-the-same-boat'. The shame and guilt of such an enterprise, which stems from an open acknowledgement that the subject does not 'naturally' measure up to these beauty standards, is disguised by the 'fun' elements of the beauty routine.

Yet even here there is a tone of hesitancy and apologetics 'Unless you're blessed with', 'If you're lucky enough to have large, bright eyes . . .'

The existence and use of make-up is at once a form of female entertainment (staying in at night to experiment with hair dye) and something to be ashamed of. This latter hinges on a recognition that 'men' find the whole idea of make-up distasteful.

The language of the beauty page of course doesn't question *why* women feel ashamed or embarrassed by this 'failing' instead it offers practical solutions.

> Let's face it, no one's going to wink at you if your nose is red with cold and your cheeks are white and pinched.
>
> Don't rely on nature – cheat a little with a foundation.

and indicates how girls can get the best of both worlds by deceiving men into believing they are naturally lovely, whilst subtly hiding their own flaws.

First the authors adopt a tone of sisterly resignation evoking comfort and reassurance from the fact that these are shared problems. 'Most of us have some things we don't like about ourselves.' The next step is *action*, doing something about it 'no-one, but no-one should ever feel they are ugly', and finally transforming this action into 'fun', a 'hobby'. 'Take care of yourself and pamper yourself.'

To put it briefly, the girl is caught in a web of conflicting directives. First she doesn't and can't measure up to the ideal standard expected of her by men. Recognising this, she must set about doing something about it as best she can through the use of cosmetics available to her as commodities on the open market. Nevertheless she must avoid, at all costs, making this obvious since to do this would be to defeat the whole point.

Now, whilst other magazines especially those for older, working girls, handle this dilemma by elevating make-up into the realm of 'style' and bestowing on it an importance equal to that of fashion, *Jackie* comes down unequivocally on the side of compromise and moderation, constantly using phrases like – 'a hint of' – 'the merest touch of' – 'a trace of', and expressing its own position on make-up clearly.

> Most boyfriends (there are few exceptions) hate loads of make-up, they think it goes with a loud, brassy personality and are usually frightened off by a painted face. Ask the majority and they'll say they prefer natural looks and subtle make-up – so that's the way it has to be.

Beauty routines in *Jackie* are then of the greatest importance. Being inextricably linked to the general care and maintenance of the body, and thus with good health (no smoking and plenty of sleep . . .) the girls are encouraged to consider beauty as a full-time job demanding skill, patience and learning. Consequently Beauty Box is a manual and hand-book comprising a feminine education. Here the girls learn how to apply mascara correctly, pluck their eyebrows or shave their legs. Each of these tasks involve *labour* but become fun and leisure when carried out in the company of friends, Besides which when the subject is the self, and when 'self-beautification' is the object, narcissism transforms work into leisure. Nonetheless, this labour, carried out in the confines of the home (bedroom, or bathroom) does contribute, both *directly* and *indirectly* to domestic production, itself the linchpin upon which the maintenance and reproduction of the family depends.

By doing her own washing, mending, by washing her own hair and keeping herself clean, tidy and well-groomed the girl is, in effect, shifting some of the burden of housework from her mother onto herself. By taking responsibility at one level for her own 'reproduction' she in effect lessens the amount of domestic labour the mother would otherwise have to carry out.

It could of course be argued that the girl plucking her eyebrows and manicuring her nails, is not performing necessary labour. But such labour is not absolutely separate or different from the mother knitting or sewing whilst watching TV. Neatness, smartness and good grooming are absolutely necessary when the girl tries to get a job, and this does not simply mean tidy hair, clean face and laundered clothes. It means being well-made-up, having manicured nails, wearing smart clothes and so on.

The girls' invisible work in the home, quite apart from the housework she shares directly with her mother, displays the same ambiguities as her mother's work in this sphere. In each case the sharp distinction between work and leisure is blurred. And, to return to *Jackie*, the insistence on the importance of such labours is relentless. The girl must always have glossy hair, shining skin, clean tights, pressed skirts, laundered shirts and so on. Like housework, it is never 'done', but comprises a set of endless chores, to be repeated daily, weekly or monthly. *Jackie* makes it palatable by describing the romantic prospects it promises and by announcing beauty routines in the language of action 'fun'.

> (a) If you do have a problem with yours, find out what it is and *do* something about it right away.
> (b) When you're all alone you can have a great time making yourself up . . . trying out different hair-styles and see what suits you best.

Far from advocating passivity here, the girl is encouraged to spend her free time working on herself, immersed in self-improvement! Moreover, the same information is given out year in year out so that it, like the advice on the Cathy and Claire page, becomes part of the general currency of female knowledge. *Every* girl knows how to cope with greasy hair, dandruff and rough elbows. Beauty 'know-how' seeps into the larger body of domestic knowledge to be amassed alongside tips on childcare, cookery and 'love'.

Beautification is then, the ideal 'hobby' for girls. Simon Frith has already pointed to the amount of time girls spent engaged in these activities. The important point is that beauty-work assumes that its subjects are house-bound and hence foreshadows yet again the future isolated image of the housewife. And the nature of the work, servicing and caring, directly pre-figures the *kind* of work the girl will later be expected to do for others in the home; from changing her child's nappies to washing her husband's socks.

And so, every moment of the girls' time, not taken up with romance, is devoted to the maintenance and re-upholstery of the self, at least that is how *Jackie* sees it. This 'work' is necessary because on it depends the girls' future success.

* * *

As countless articles and features testify, fashion has been a problematic subject for feminists. Wilson acknowledges the hugely exploitative side to the fashion business and the ways styles express aspects of women's oppression; yet she concludes by referring to the ambiguous relation she still has with clothes.

> So in me at least there survives a secret cultivator of the self, an aesthetic who really did think that style was the most desirable thing in the world. In serious moments I feel I should show her the door – boot her out. Usually I just hope she'll slip away without my noticing.[42]

Jackie fashion fortunately is easier to deal with. The fashion page has little text, its linguistic message merely sets the tone and indicates prices and stockists. Otherwise the whole page, or double page, is covered by the visual images which erupt across it in a mass of colour. The clothes on display are drawn rather than photographed (from this sample only eight issues used photographic models) and as Barthes points out this does have important implications.

> It is therefore necessary to oppose the photograph, a message without a code, to the drawing, which, even when it is denoted, is a coded message. The coded nature of the drawing appears on three levels; firstly to reproduce an object or a scene by means of a drawing necessarily implies a set of rule-governed transpositions; secondly – the denotation of the drawing is less pure than photographic denotation, for there cannot be drawing without style. Finally, like all codes the drawing demands learning.[43]

Each of these points holds true for *Jackie* fashion. In keeping with the rest of the magazine, there is a strong 60s flavour to the drawings. Their style is firmly rooted in the commercial art 'boom' of the mid-1960s and resembles the kinds of art-work which covered the walls of boutiques, discos and coffee shops during this period.

The emphasis is on design rather than on realism and consequently the models can look as bizarre and as exotic as 'Vogue' models for a fraction of the cost. This means that cheap, badly-cut and shoddy clothing can be transformed into 'haute couture' through art-work. In 'real-life' there is nothing very exciting about 'Tesco' clothes, *Jackie* manages to make them look great!

The models are without exception long-legged, boyishly flat chested and huge-eyed; exactly like the Twiggy look of the 60s. They are then, 'safely' asexual, displaying a kind of childlike innocence. Their poses are highly narcissistic, the models are aware of themselves being watched and admired, and are exploiting this position of power. This behaviour is, as feminist writers have pointed out, the essence of femininity.

> A woman is never so happy as when she is being wooed. Then the mistress of all she surveys, the cynosure of all eyes, until that day of days when she sails down the aisle.[44]

And

> She has to develop her threatened narcissism in order to make herself loved and adored. Vanity thy name is woman.[45]

What the clothes and general style of *Jackie* tell us about the code of fashion for young girls is quite straightforward. First; fashion changes with the seasons, second; it changes also with different social events, with the time of day and with its wearer's 'moods'. Third; the girls' wardrobe must continually be replenished, she must make a real attempt to have the latest style. Fourthly; fashion also means neatness, matching colours, 'ideas' and occasionally experiment. It is never 'way-out' or outlandish, instead the desired effect is a kind of stylish conservatism where much emphasis is placed on having matching accessories, well cut hair, carefully applied make-up and freshly laundered tights, shirts etc.

Quite clearly such an expensive wardrobe is well beyond the girls' reach at this moment in their careers. Nonetheless they are here being introduced to and educated into, the sphere of feminine consumption. The message is clear. Appearance is of paramount importance to the girl, it should be designed to please both boyfriend and boss alike and threaten the authority of neither.

Section V: Pop music in *Jackie*: stars and fans

Finally I want to look briefly at the fourth code, that of pop music. In fact this is possibly the most difficult to deal with, not least because its very existence in *Jackie* is problematic. This is because the musical side of pop is pushed into the background and is replaced instead with the 'persona' of the 'pop idol'.

But first it is worth making some general points about pop and 'teen' magazines. Writing in 1964 Hall and Whannel point out that

> It would be difficult to guess, for example, whether an aspiring singer like Jess Conrad pays *Mirabelle* to interview him, or *Mirabelle* pays Jess Conrad, or they both thrive on mutual admiration and goodwill.[46]

Since then various people have commented on the importance of these magazines in 'selling' an act,

> 'Papers like *Jackie* have got an awfully big coverage', says Leslie. 'Imagine how many fans actually see the magazine. We are going for kids and that's what the kids buy.'[47]

Jackie's policy here is quite straightforward. It allots one single and one double page to pop pin-ups each week. Constantly flooded with publicity material, photographs and personal profiles, the *Jackie* team chooses from between these. With its huge weekly sales figures, it is obviously highly sought after by record promoters and hence is able to choose from a vast range of stars. This is evident in the spectrum of stars who appear each week. In this sample they include such diverse figures as 'Queen', 'Sparks' and 'Brotherhood of Man', all of whom are given an opportunity to develop their image or gimmick in these pop features.

The shift here, away from music to the 'star', is a crucial one. It happens basically because it is well-known 'stars' who guarantee high record sales rather than a large range of 'hopefuls'. That is it is always much easier to 'sell' established acts than to promote newcomers. And, as is the case with *Jackie* aspiring teenybopper stars are primarily interested in selling their images. Music itself in fact is credited with little or no importance in the pages of *Jackie*. This is an important point because it marks the one arena where readers *could* be drawn into a real 'hobby'. Instead of being encouraged to develop an interest in this area, or to create their own music, the readers are presented, yet again, with another opportunity to indulge their emotions, but this time on the pop star figure rather than the boyfriend.

The magazine offers its readers little information on pop apart from occasional mentions of 'new releases' or 'forthcoming films'. There is neither critical attention shown to the music itself nor to its techniques and production. The girls are, by implication, merely listeners. Moreover with 'pop', the girls' passivity, as far as *Jackie* is concerned, takes on even larger dimensions. Pop stars are by definition 'dreamy', 'successful' and to be adored in the quiet of the bedroom. The social meaning of the pin-ups hinges then on the *unequal* relationship between adoring fan and star looking down on her.

Turning to look at the pin-up of the pop star unaccompanied by band or group, several points can be made. First it is accompanied by a minimum linguistic message, i.e. simply his name. This starkness points to the overriding importance of the visual element. The star is how he looks. The only additional information needed by the reader is his name. Second, this visual image contains a whole repertoire of signs, one of which can be dealt with under the code of *expression*. These,

> depend on our competence to resolve a set of gestural, non-linguistic features (signifiers) into a specific expressive configuration (signified).[48]

The purpose of the facial expression here is to effect a 'personalising transformation'; a necessary element in the construction of the star who is more than a mere performer of songs. This is done by introducing glimpses of or hints as to the nature of, the star's personality through his expression, so that this personality corresponds to what have already been set up as familiar male character stereotypes in the picture stories.

Thus we have the 'pert cheekiness' of David Essex, the sweet 'babyish' qualities of David Cassidy and the 'pretty poutiness' of Marc Bolan. Not surprisingly, there is a marked absence of aggressive, sexual, 'mean and nasty' rock stars in these pages.

The star's face, the sole male presence in the magazine, looks out of the page, directly into the eyes of the reader, a symbol of male mastery if not outright supremacy. No other character occupies such space in the magazine, even the 'cover girl' has to compete with title, caption, headline and summary of contents, for the reader's attention.

Third, the social meaning of the background and context within which the pop star is often posed is clearly important. David Essex, relaxed and crouching in a garden and with a dog, connotes more meanings than simply his handsomeness and star-like qualities. There is something comforting and reassuring about such an image. It says that rock or pop stars, out of the limelight, are much the same as anybody else. Their lifestyles are not all 'sex'n'drugs' at least certainly not those who appear in *Jackie* pin-ups. Essex's relaxed pose also suggests that this is *his* garden, *his* dog, otherwise, constantly being in the public eye, he would find it difficult to be at such ease. He is thus informing the reader that he is rich, as well as being happy, handsome, famous and so on.

But familiar settings and objects are not the only contexts which crystallise the star's image. They can be even more firmly looked at through the use of another set of non-verbal signs, that is through the gimmick. The tartan armbands and scarves of the Bay City Rollers connote 'Scottishness', a reassuring recognisable image shot through with such noble feelings as patriotism, love of one's country, etc. This 'tartanry' combined with their distinct style of clothing, borrowed from the street style of working-class Scottish boys, compounds their comfortable 'homely' image by reminding their fans that they too are ordinary working-class lads. Both Essex and the 'Rollers' are saying in their own ways, 'Look at me: I am like you.'[49]

Gimmicks, then, eliminate the need for more extended linguistic messages. Through them, the girl is introduced to the 'star', it is his hallmark, the sign through which he is remembered. When he is fully established as a 'superstar', these gimmicks become symbols of allegiance to him, something to be taken up by the fans and worn as a sign of their admiration. Thus we have the typical scene at 'Roller' concerts where the entire audience is decked out in tartan!

These carefully constructed 'images' find fuller expression in the other pop features which appear each week in *Jackie*. These are:

(1) 'Pop Gossip', comprising tit-bits of pop information, each item being accompanied by a small photograph of the star or group in question.
(2) '*Jackie* Pop Specials', usually interviews with the members of a group about forthcoming tours, or films.
(3) '*Jackie* Pop Exclusives' – typically 'in-depth' and personal interviews usually with a 'teenybopper' superstar – 'Donny', David Cassidy or Garry Glitter, for example.

The kind of information which the reader is furnished with here can be categorised under three headings, (1) consumption, (2) family life and (3) personal biography.

First consumption. Dyer has pointed to the ways in which stars are presented to the world and 'rooted' in terms of the objects which their fame allows them to accumulate.

> The Rolls Royce is of course almost of itself suggestive of a different world of being – luxuriant, smoothness, wealth. Anyone who is at home in a Rolls Royce seems almost a different order of person.[50]

The commodity is the most visible sign of the star's success and consequently figures highly in his general presentation.

In one edition of *Jackie*, we, the readers, are invited on a trip round Rod Stewart's mansion. We see him alternately lounging in its luxuriant surroundings and posing formally as 'lord of the manor' by his mantelpiece in what is clearly the main drawing room. Simultaneously, however, the 'seriousness' of this image is fragmented by Rod's own personal appearance. Bizarre and exotic, to the point of being clownish, Rod combines extravagant flowing clothes with a working-class, ex-mod hairstyle and 'tough' facial expression. Several connotations flow from this set of images. First there is the idea of the 'working-class boy made good'; second there is the element of exposition. *Jackie* is momentarily revealing to its readers how the pop star lives. The feature is then voyeuristic allowing the readers a special privilege, a glimpse into the private life of 'Rod'! Third, in Rod's own self-presentation, there is clearly an element of self-parody, and self-mocking. Despite the splendour of his surroundings 'Rod' is, it seems, unchanged and his loyalties remain with his class origins (expressed in other contexts through his accent, appearance and devotion to football).

Other shorter features produce similar kinds of connotations, 'Pop Gossip' in particular pays special attention to the consumer power of pop stars.

> One of the Bay City Rollers has just bought his own cottage
>
> Jim Lea of Slade has recently bought a flat in London
>
> Les McKeown of the Bay City Rollers says he's mad about cars . . . 'The car I'd like to have is an R0.80 . . . its cruising speed is 140 m.p.h.'

The second set of 'personalising' conventions focus around the family, and since the image of so many stars depends on their being unmarried, such references are usually made to their parents. Several idols talk about the pleasures of 'family occasions' and those who no longer need to depend on a 'single and available' image talk animatedly about their wives and children, (included here are Paul McCartney, Jim Lea of Slade and Alvin Stardust). In each case the family serves to normalise the image of the star. It is presented as a protective and comforting environment, the place where the star loves to return after exhausting tours.

The effect of these pieces is, again, to assert a sense of sameness, normality, of sharing certain unshakeable beliefs and ideas about life. Human nature, 'natural' interests, and commitments to certain values mean that less important differences are transcended. We are *all* the same in our love of children, comfort, the family, homeland – and so on. More than this we *all* enjoy the simple things of life, going to a football match on a Saturday afternoon, eating steak and chips, going on holiday . . .

Thirdly, and finally, there is the emphasis on the star's personal biography. Often these comprise anecdotes or witty stories about life 'on the road with the band', at the same time they are both chauvinistic and xenophobic. Again the intention here is to reassure the reader that the star is not *so* alienated from his roots, that he does not feel utterly at ease amongst the 'jet set'. One singer, Don Powell of Slade, tells how nobody could understand his accent in America, and Paul McCartney, discussing the early days of the Beatles, describes how horrified he was to find that German people ate fish for Christmas dinner!

The point is that the star is, at heart, an ordinary lad unused to 'foreign ways'. Frequent references are made to the class origins of certain idols, particularly to David Essex's career as barrow boy in East London. On the one hand it is simply a re-iteration of the rags-to-riches story, on the other it clearly represents an attempt to closen the ties between stars and fan by evoking a sense of shared experiences and of 'normality'. What I am suggesting is that the pop fan/idol relationship is predicated upon distance through hero worship and adulation, but is cemented by what they allegedly have in common.

Conclusion

What, then, are the central features of *Jackie* insofar as it presents its readers with an ideology of adolescent femininity? First it sets up, defines and focuses exclusively on 'the personal', locating it as the sphere of *prime* importance to the teenage girl. It presents this as a totality – and by implication all else is of secondary interest to the 'modern girl'. Romance problems, fashion, beauty and pop mark out the limits of the girl's concern – other possibilities are ignored or dismissed.

Second, *Jackie* presents 'romantic individualism' as the ethos, *par excellence*, for the teenage girl. The *Jackie* girl is alone in her quest for love; she refers back to her female peers for advice, comfort and reassurance *only* when she has problems in fulfilling this aim. Female solidarity, or more simply the idea of girls together – in *Jackie* terms – is an unambiguous sign of failure. To achieve self-respect, the girl has to escape the 'bitchy', 'catty' atmosphere of female company and find a boyfriend as fast as possible. But in doing this she has not only to be individualistic in outlook – she has to be prepared to fight ruthlessly – by plotting, intrigue and cunning, to 'trap her man'. Not surprisingly this independent-mindedness is short-lived. As soon as she finds a 'steady', she must renounce it altogether and capitulate to *his* demands, acknowledging his domination and resigning herself to her own subordination.

This whole ideological discourse, as it takes shape through the pages of *Jackie*, is immensely powerful. Judging by sales figures alone, *Jackie* is a force to be reckoned with by feminists. Of course this does not mean that its readers swallow its axioms unquestioningly. And indeed until we have a clearer idea of just how girls 'read' *Jackie* and encounter its ideological force, our analysis remains one-sided.[51]

For feminists a related question must be how to go about countering *Jackie* and undermining its ideological power at the level of *cultural* intervention. One way of beginning this task would be for feminist teachers and youth leaders to involve girls in the task of 'deconstructing' this seemingly 'natural' ideology; and in breaking down the apparently timeless qualities of girls' and women's 'mags'.

Another more adventurous possibility would be the joint production of an alternative;[52] a magazine where girls are depicted in situations other than the romantic, and where sexuality is discussed openly and frankly; not just contraception, masturbation and abortion, but the *social relations* of sexuality especially the sexism of their male peers. Likewise girls would be encouraged to create their own music, learn instruments and listen to music without having to drool over idols. Their clothes would not simply reflect styles created by men to transform them into junior sex-objects, products of male imaginations and fantasies. But most of all, readers would be presented with an *active* image of female adolescence – one which pervades every page and is not just deceptively 'frozen' into a single 'energetic/glamorous' pose as in the fashion pages and Tampax adverts in *Jackie*.

Notes

1 Figures taken from Appendix IV, C.L. White, *Women's Magazines 1693–1968* (1970) and from British Rate and Data (June 1977).

2 G. Rosei, 'The Private Life of Lord Snooty', in the *Sunday Times* Magazine July 29, 1973, pp. 8–16.
3 Ibid., see also Willing's Press Guide 1977 and McCarthy Information Ltd (June 1977) where it is noted that 'Among the enviably high profit margin firms are Shopfitters (Lancs); Birmingham satchel maker by Ralph Martindale, and "Dandy" and "Beano" published D.C. Thomson – all with profit margins of 20% or more'. See also Extel Card March 1977 for D.C. Thomson.

Year	*Turnover*	*Profit After Tax*
1974	£18,556,000	£2,651,000
1975	£23,024,000	£2,089,000
1976	£28,172,000	£2,092,000

4 L. Althusser, 'Ideology and the State', in *Lenin and Philosophy and Other Essays* (1971) p. 163.
5 A. Dorfman and A. Mattelart, *How to Read Donald Duck* (1971), p. 30.
6 Paul Johnson in the *New Statesman*, 1964
7 C. Alderson, *The Magazines Teenagers Read* (1968), p. 3
8 P. Willis, 'Symbolism and Practice. A. Theory for the Social Meaning of Pop Music'. C.C.C.S. Stencilled paper, p. 2
9 S. Hall, I. Connell, L. Curti, 'The Unity of Current Affairs Television' in *Cultural Studies 9* (1976), p. 51
10 George Orwell, 'Boys Weeklies' in *Inside the Whale and Other Essays* (1969), pp. 187–203, first published in 1939.
11 Paul Willis, *op. cit.*, p. 1.
12 J. Clarke, S. Hall, T. Jefferson, B. Roberts, 'Subcultures, Cultures and Classes' in *Resistance Through Rituals* (1976) p. 55
13 Hall, Connell & Curti, *op.cit.*, p. 53
14 Antonio Gramsci, *Selections from the Prison Notebooks*, quoted in S. Hall, B. Lumley, G. McLennan 'Politics and Ideology: Gramsci' in *On Ideology. Cultural Studies 10* (1977), p. 51.
15 *Ibid.*, p. 51
16 *Ibid.*, p. 67
17 From an unpublished ms. by Simon Frith.
18 *ibid.*
19 Richard Hoggart, *The Uses of Literacy* (1957), p. 51
20 Simon Frith, *op. cit.*
21 B. Berelson defines C.A. as 'a research technique for the objective, systematic and quantitative description of the manifest content of communication'. B. Berelson, *Content Analysis in Communication Research* (1952), p. 18.
22 R. Barthes, *Elements of Semiology* (1967), pp. 95, 96.
23 S. Hall, 'The Determination of News Photographs' in *Cultural Studies* 3 (1972), p. 69.
24 *ibid.*, p. 64
25 *ibid.*, p. 65
26 Quoting R. Barthes, *Elements of Semiology* (1967), p. 91.
27 *ibid.*, p. 66.
28 My analysis based round these codes is by no means exhaustive, nor does it cover every different kind of feature. Absent are advertisements, personality quiz games, on the spot interviews and short stories. However, each of these do fit into the codes outlined, some into more than one. Personality games and on the spot interviews obviously would be examined under the code of personal/domestic life, short stories under romance.
29 G. Greer, *The Female Eunuch* (1970), p. 173
30 R. Barthes, 'The Rhetoric of the Image' in *Cultural Studies 1* (1971), p. 43
31 R. Barthes, *op.cit.*, p. 44
32 The language is remarkably reminiscent of the 'hip' language of commentaries on the 'teenage scene' in the 50s, e.g.

> 'Hey gang – some square's giving Jules trouble' and 'Hey, what you at man? Like, I don't mind sharing my thoughts with all mankind but I draw a line at the furniture, dig?'

33 L. Althusser, 'Ideology and the State', in *Lenin and Philosophy and Other Essays* (1971), p. 163.

34 These take the form of quizzes, articles and features on birth signs, all of which are designed to help '*you*' know '*yourself*'. e.g. The reader is asked to tick, from a selection of possible responses, what she would do, in a number of given situations. Her answers are then tallied up numerically and there is a particular personality profile which allegedly corresponds to her 'total'.

35 A. Dorfman and A. Mattelart. *How To Read Donald Duck*, (1971), p. 56.

> The second strategy is called recuperation; the utilisation of a potentially dangerous phenomena of the social body in such a way that it serves to justify the continued need of the social system and its values, and very often justifies the violence and repression which are part of that system.

36 J. Mitchell, *Psychoanalysis and Feminism* (1974), p. 117.

37 R. Barthes, 'The Rhetoric of the Image', in *Cultural Studies 1* (1971) p. 46.

38 S. Rowbotham, 'Women's Liberation and the New Politics', in *Spokesman Pamphlet No.17*, p. 27.

39 Taken from 'Woman's Weekly', 2.7.69 and quoted in G. Greer, *The Female Eunuch* (1970) p. 171

40 G. Greer, *The Female Eunuch* (1970) p. 179.

41 J. Clarke, S. Hall, T. Jefferson, B. Roberts in 'Subcultures, Cultures and Classes', in *Resistance Through Rituals* (1976), p. 55

42 E. Wilson, 'Clothes' in *Spare Rib* (Sept. 1975), No.39, p. 32.

43 R. Barthes, 'The Rhetoric of the Image' in *Cultural Studies 1* (1971) p. 43

44 G. Greer, *op.cit.*, pp. 185–6

45 J. Mitchell, *Psychoanalysis and Feminism* (1974), p. 116

46 S. Hall & P. Whannel, *The Popular Arts* (1964), p. 295

47 P. Erskin, *New Musical Express* (2.11.74) p. 17

48 S. Hall, 'The Determinism of the News Photograph', in *Cultural Studies 3* (1972), p. 67

49 R. Barthes, *Mythologies* (1972), p. 91

50 R. Dyer, 'The Meaning of Tom Jones', in *Cultural Studies 3* (1972) p. 57.

51 In '*Working-Class Girls and the Culture of Femininity*' (M.A. Thesis, C.C.C.S., University of Birmingham). I look at the general culture of a group of working-class teenage girls – their experience of the home, school, leisure and sexual relations. I did not however have time to examine in detail how they 'made sense of' *Jackie.*

52 Without necessarily attempting to compete nationally with *Jackie*, it would nonetheless be interesting to produce local/community-based or school alternatives to it.

34 Woman becomes an 'individual'

Femininity and consumption in women's magazines 1954–69

Janice Winship

Every house in the street looks the same – but come inside and see the difference. All over the country couples are coming back from Honeymoon to a house that's one of a row. Edith Blair visits three clever brides who show how beautifully individual a room, same size, same shape as the neighbours' can be.

Woman 10/5/58 p. 36

Honey campaign clothes.

Whichever candidate you put in your wardrobe, the cult of the individual is sweeping the country. New young designers with constituencies from the Chelsea Bear to the Cheltenham Ladies Club have something to offer – the promise of fresh young clothes, free opportunities for all to dress on a budget, and the right of all *Honey* readers to a democratic vote for the young, gay and getahead outfits that swing. Turn the pages and elect a candidate dedicated to a policy of raising standards and furthering prettiness.

Honey Oct. 1963 p. 60

Introduction

Tracing the origins of the Women's Liberation Movement in the 1960s,[1] Juliet Mitchell in *Woman's Estate* (1971) discusses the contradiction between the 'active production' of sexuality and its 'passive consumption'. She maintains that in this contradiction lay the potential strength of the 'sexual revolution' whose 'most visible symptom' was 'dress and personal appearance' (ibid p. 141). She writes

> For women . . . the 'sexual revolution' has meant a positive increase in the amount of sexual (and hence social) freedom; it has also meant an increase in their use as sexual objects. The tension produced by the inevitable consequence of the one on the other has, in itself, been a motivating force behind the creation of a Women's Liberation Movement. Illusorily offered the free and glorious expression of ourselves; it turned out to be only a further alienation; turning ourselves into products which are then confiscated for use in a consumer society.
>
> (ibid p. 142)

What I want to do here is explore that contradiction between 'active production' and 'passive consumption' of sexuality. But I want to examine it primarily in its 'most visible symptom' of 'dress and personal appearance' as it is represented in the discourse of *Honey* magazine in the 1960s. The magazine offers through the consumption of personal commodities a contradictory 'individuality' which, manifestly provocatively sexual, strains towards the wider arenas of work and politics. The dress and appearance through which we are 'offered the free and glorious expression of ourselves' become the metaphor and symbolisation of that 'freedom' but crucially it's

> this selective penetration of the family and privatised consumption by the 'new' capitalism.
>
> (1979)

Moreover, although it is a different group of women, it still *continues* to be women who are at the centre of new consumption in the 1960s. (cf. Scott 1976.)

First then, how did consumption change in the 1950s and 1960s? Between 1955–65 Mark Abrams (1966) reckoned that the proportion of car owning families doubled, and there were similar proportional increases in households owning TVs (40–88%), vacuum cleaners (45–82%), and washing machines (20–56%). Additionally there were increases in ownership of refrigerators (10–39%) and lawn-mowers (38–52%). Further, he maintained that a 'good 10% of the decade's additional prosperity has been absorbed by expenditure on women's and infant's clothes (up by nearly 50%) and cosmetics (also up by 50%). There was no comparable advance in spending on men's clothes' (ibid p. 9). The rise in real consumption of food, he comments, showed a shift to 'frozen vegetables, processed meats and instant coffee' (ibid p. 9). Rosemary Scott observes that between 1953–69 the increase in the real value of food purchased per head was 2½% and that 'practically all this gain was in convenience foods' (Scott 1976 p. 20).

Those commentators concerned with the 'greater movements' of capital (cf. Castells 1977, Hobsbawm 1968, Mandel 1975) select the appropriately 'bigger' items of consumption, for example, vacuum cleaners and cars, to indicate changing domestic consumption, but they fail to mention either the substantial and diversified consumption of clothes and cosmetics which has continued to increase right through the 1960s when the 'boom' was over, or the massive expenditure on house contents from furniture to lavatory brushes, which in terms of 'consumer decisions', rather than value, are enormous. (cf. Scott 1976).

It is particularly within these two areas – clothes/make up and household goods that the activity of consumption entailed an increasing proliferation of choice. A cosmetics 'buy does not just mean mascara, eyeshadow, powder, lipstick but for *each* item, say mascara, the selection of one *kind*: liquid, fibre, coloured, waterproof, anti-allergic or . . . similarly the range of 'convenience' household items has magnified far beyond any 1950s' hope. By the end of the 1960s we have: tissues, polythene bags, jeye cloths, tin foil, plastic scourers, non-stick pans etc. plus a multiplication of 'aids' for babycare. Yet all these new items represent a *new work*, even as they relieve the arduousness of some chores. Which should one buy for what purpose, choosing the appropriate specialised cleaner for bath, oven, lavatory . . . not employing one 'old fashioned' abrasive Vim/Ajax.[2] Consequently there is a new work of beauty, domesticity and child care to follow the purchase.

As Scott suggests then,

> In the woman's function as consumer . . . she is indomitable and it is indisputable that the phenomenon of female consumption . . . is marked by two overriding principles: first that it is massive and second that it is both frequent and extensive.[3]
>
> (Scott 1976 p. ix)

Additionally the experience of consumption, from single status through to marriage and motherhood, whether or not women are in paid work, is continuous and cumulative – *unlike* their usual experience of paid work where child bearing marks a disruptive break. (However the relations of consumption and the objects which are consumed of course do markedly alter according to class, age, marital status and motherhood.) For this reason alone an investigation of consumption work is important, central even, to an understanding of women's position, and, moreover, salient, to a feminist politics.

II Relations of consumption: economic, ideological and political

In the post Second World War period women have continued performing their economic and ideological functions in the home as wives and mothers. But while as married women they have increasingly participated in paid work – primarily as part time workers, as *young* women they have entered very particular sectors of expanding employment – shop work and clerical work especially. (Ministry of Labour 1967, Mackie and Pattulo 1977, Bland et al. 1978.) Moreover, 'being at home' and 'going out to work' have both been clearly associated with a consumption of commodities which has contributed to the reproduction of their femininity. Here then it is pertinent to examine the *ideological* relations of consumption for women in the work place and outside, at home and at leisure. That examination shifts us beyond sole attention to the relations of capital to the ways in which capital 'takes over' certain patriarchal relations between women and men; a process which involves as much change for the relations of capital as it does for the relations of femininity and masculinity.

However, such an interest, or posing of the problem, has not been the concern of those who have initiated discussion of consumption. Here I want briefly to consider some of these conceptualisations in order to begin to open up a theoretical space and argue for the necessary attention to the ideological relations of consumption, and further their potential political effect for women. These concerns should, I suggest, be central to *any* study of post war developments in capitalist production of commodities and their consumption, not just those in which the focus is explicitly women.

The specific unfolding of capitalist production in the post war period has generally been considered in its *class* aspects, at both production and consumption 'ends' of the economic circuit. Manuel Castells, for example, defines consumption as 'the social process of appropriation of the product by people, i.e. by social classes' (1977 p. 454). Further the particular relation between capitalist production and consumption which delivered the 'boom' of the 1950s is examined as it affects the *family*, i.e. the working class family, which benefited from the increase in standard of living and, in appearance at least, aligned itself through these material appurtenances, more closely with the middle class. Such analyses (Castells 1977, Hobsbawm 1968, Mandel 1975, Pinto-Duschinsky 1970) tend to disregard the unique role within the family that women play – as consumers and as wage earners. But additionally they also tend to ignore the partly autonomous position of single women outside the family, whose pattern of employment and consumption are *specific* to them. In particular there is an absence of the ways in which consumption is important in the work place itself, i.e. that clothes and make-up are essential to some 'women's jobs'; that women integrate shopping into the working day etc. Where young women are discussed they are often incorporated within the categories of 'youth' or 'teenagers', in effect young *men*, in relation to whom consumption is wholly a *leisure* pursuit, wholly outside of work.[4]

The emphases of 'class', 'family' and 'leisure' outside of work' in Marxist analyses of consumption are partly attributable to Marx's own conceptualisations and assumptions about consumption. Firstly what he terms 'individual consumption' is primarily defined by what it is not: in contrast to 'productive consumption' of machinery, raw materials and labour power which takes place within the process of *social* production itself, individual consumption is *privatised* – *outside* of the production process in its narrow sense. But secondly Marx generally assumes a *male* wage labourer who is a *family* man, equating his individual wages with individual consumption which, as Marx points out, in fact provides subsistence for the *whole* family (cf. Bland et al. 1978, Foreman 1977). Since his analysis is primarily concerned with individual consumption in so far as it reproduces *labour power* as an abstract commodity he does not consider either the *distribution* of the 'family wage' for spending, or the specificity of the commodities which each members of the family buys. Additionally this absence is an outcome of capitalism's under-developed commodity production for the private sphere at the time Marx was writing.

Nevertheless he not only argued for the economic importance of individual consumption to the circuit of capital (cf. Marx 1973 p. 91, p. 676; Marx 1976 p. 718; Marx 1972 p. 77, p. 100) and deduced the mode of its future expansion and diversification (cf. Marx 1973 p. 408–9, p. 419) but also hinted at the ideological implications for the labourer whose 'dependence instead of becoming more intensive with the growth of capital become more extensive' (Marx 1976 p. 769). Harry Braverman has detailed this penetration[5] of commodities into the family describing it as the tendency towards a 'universal market' (Braverman 1974). Sheila Rowbotham focussing specifically on women's oppression has more vehemently castigated the trend as 'the imperialist onslaught into everyday life' which overwhelms even that most intimate area of personal life – sexuality (Rowbotham 1973, Ch. 7). Yet although as Castells maintains 'the process of consumption acquires a decisive place in the reproduction of the mode of production as a whole in its present phase' (Castells 1977 p. 457), there is a paucity of Marxist work in this area, while, for obvious reasons, there is a wealth of market research on the topic (cf. Scott 1976).

The more historically specific analyses of the post Second World War period, for example Hobsbawm 1968, and the Bogdanor and Skidelsky edited collection of essays (1970), examine political and ideological as well as economic determinants which contribute to the pattern of consumption in Britain. Hobsbawm and Pinto-Duschinsky both stress the type of commodity expansion peculiar to Britain: for the home market rather than for export; for 'family consumption' i.e. 'individual consumption' as opposed to an expanded 'productive consumption'. One central aspect of that was the emphasis the Conservative government placed on a house building programme, so that by 1964, when the Conservatives went out of office, 1 family in 4 was in accomodation built while they were in power, and half the population was in owner occupied housing, not rented accomodation, compared to one quarter in 1951.[6] At the level of production such an investment curtailed investment in productive industry 'more fundamental to the reconstruction of the economy' (Hobsbawm 1960 p. 62), but for families who moved into this housing it meant the 'need' to buy certain commodities – as anyone who has recently changed living quarters will well know and therefore further stimulated the consumption of domestic commodities. Hobsbawm argues that domestic purchases marked a move from the public enjoyment of leisure – the pub, the football match – to the privacy of home, a characteristic previously associated with the lower middle class. But perhaps more significantly he suggests

The truth was that a mass-consumption society is dominated by its biggest market which

> in Britain was that of the working class. . . Henceforth it was their demand which took over the task of filling the proletarian world.
>
> (1968 pp. 242–3)

Clearly he neglects to consider that the working class has two sexes. Firstly women's leisure showed no move from public to private. If anything the demand for married women workers in the face of male 'full employment', meant *less* leisure for them. Secondly, and perhaps curiously, it was the consuming housewife whose 'demand dominated commercially' on the basis both of her husband's wage, but particularly of her own wage packet as wife and as single women. (cf. Bland et al. 1978, Seccombe 1975.)

Mandel, though not specifically dealing with Britain (Mandel 1975), more adequately includes women in the analysis and grants them the centrality owing them as *paid workers* in the boom of the 1950s' consumption. Moreover he also points to the tendency towards a displacement of the family as the unit of consumption, in favour of properly individual consumption – in particular the 'teenage market' – but it is not sexually differentiated by him (ibid p. 391n). He argues that the 'accumulation of non-invested surplus capitals' (ibid p. 387) generated, according to him, by the fall of the rate of profit leads to the 'vast penetration of capital into the spheres of circulation, services and reproduction', one feature of which is to extend 'the boundaries of commodity production' i.e. individual consumption and hence create further surplus value (ibid p. 388). The constant contradiction between the need to stimulate new consumption in this area at an ever increasing rate, and the necessity to realise profits, limits the 'breadwinners' wages 'below the level necessary to cover all the new needs of consumption generated by capitalist production itself' (ibid p. 392). Without going into the economic niceties and theoretical differences around these arguments we can note that one recognisable outcome was the 'increased employment of married women' (ibid p. 392). As Hall observes about Britain 'women were being called upon to be both wives-and-mothers – spending homemakers – and (part-time) working women' (Hall 1979). The two are of course integrally related: women's wages often spent by them on precisely those new commodities for home and themselves which capital has to offer. (cf. Seccombe 1975.) It is this relation which Mandel overlooks when he considers women's employment as representing an *undermining* of the patriarchal relations of the family. On the one hand commodities may well replace services and use values for which women were responsible, but there is nevertheless still a *work*-of consumption required for the commodities to be useful; on the other hand at the *ideological* level it is not just labour power which is reproduced in the family, but people as women and men, and hences as *gendered* labourers.

It is consumption as a process, and a work which has ideological purchase, to which Castells, despite his scarce mentions of women, gives us some theoretical access. He conceptualises consumption as a process with different effects at different levels: at the economic level of the production process the practice of consumption reproduces labour power; at the political level consumption is an expression of class relations within distribution; and at the ideological level it reproduces *social relations* as far as the mode of production as a whole is concerned. Thus

> From the point of view of social classes, consumption is both an *expression* and a *means*, realised according to a certain (ideological) content and which concretizes at the level of the relations of distribution the oppositions and struggles determined by the relations of production.
>
> (Castells 1976 p. 455)

While his differentiation of three specific but overdetermined levels is useful, I would argue against the kind of primacy he accords to the relations of production such that all other relations are mere expressions of those. However he writes also

> The material realisation of the process of consumption involves the relating of *products* (or consumer goods) with *agent-consumers*, according to a relatively autonomous social determination.
>
> (ibid p. 455)

Within that 'relatively autonomous social determination' we have leeway to locate patriarchal relations: women are 'agent-consumers' of particular products by virtue of being women; their class position is (perhaps) only secondarily relevant. The distribution of commodities expresses class relations then, only as they are further articulated through patriarchal relations and in a mode which is *unpredictable* by the relations of production themselves, and in turn works back on those productive relations. Consumption is therefore a means of transformation as well of reproduction: the penetration of capitalist consumption into the family mobilises already existing patriarchal relations at both economic and ideological levels, using both, but also transforming both so that although broadly, both patriarchal and capitalist relations are reproduced, yet as we shall see, there are significant changes. Particularly is that the case for women. It is in those transformations and the contradictions to which they give rise, which I shall examine through magazines, that a potential basis for a shift in political consciousness arises for women.[7]

From the representations in women's magazines I want to argue that the articulation of patriarchal and capitalist relations, through women's involvement in the process of consumption (and in paid work) has ideologically constructed them as 'individuals'. As Victor Molina describes in 'Notes on Marx and the Problem of Individuality'

> In capitalist society the individual appears as 'independent' because 'detached from *natural* bonds' . . . this detachment *from* natural bonds is simultaneously a complete attachment *to* objective social bonds.
>
> (Molina 1977 p. 241)

For women the potential movement is detachment *from* patriarchal relations *to* those of capital. However the articulation of the process of consumption with an ideology of femininity renders it only a partial break: woman is a 'feminine' individual whose 'individuality' and implied 'independence' are, in part, recuperated by patriarchal relations. Nevertheless as the Political Economy of Women Group entreat us in relation to the introduction of a political or social reform, so we should ask of a shift in ideology 'what new contradictions it sets up for women, how these affect their consciousness and the ability to organize' not whether it has 'improved the position of women'. (PEWG 1975 p. 30.)

To maintain that the sphere of circulation is the breeding ground of 'the individual' is not an original claim. In *Capital* Marx refers to that sphere as 'a very Eden of the rights of man (sic)' (1976 p. 280), and in the *Grundrisse* he writes

> Out of the act of exchange itself, the individual, each one of them is reflected in himself as its exclusive (determinant) subject. With that, then, the complete freedom of the individual is posited.
>
> (1973 p. 244)

But he undoubtedly considers the exchange of labour power for a wage as the primary exchange which forms the basis for this 'individualism' although the further exchange of money for commodities is theoretically included. For men the one reinforces the other, but for women involvement in the process of consumption may *precede*, and historically has preceded, women's wholesale entry into employment.[8] Even as a wife spending her husband's wage she begins to demarcate an arena of power for *herself*, but comparable to his: he responsibly earns money; she responsibly allocates it.[9] Furthermore consumption is firstly, so *frequent* that the repetition of 'individual' choices is endless (for men as well), and appears as '*choice*' unlike work which more often seems like compulsion; but secondly its products are so *visible*, that for women who have always been judged by their *looks* (cf. John Berger '*men act* and *women appear*' 1972 p. 47) – even if it is the 'looks' of their house – consumption grants them a market access to the construction of an 'individual appearance', but indeed a feminine appearance which *everybody can recognise*. Consumption is therefore the superstructural terrain *par excellence* for the construction of an ideology of individuality in relation to women.[10]

III Women's magazines for consumption

Women's magazines are particularly appropriate for the study of the ideological representation of consumption. Cynthia White maintains that

> The boom in women's periodicals has in fact paralleled the boom in domestic consumption and the vast expansion in advertising which has accompanied it.
>
> (White 1970 p. 201)

Continuing into the 1960s we can see that the appearance of new magazines for young women closely followed the boom in the *personal* consumption for femininity, clothes, make up etc.

Women's magazines are themselves capitalistically produced commodities which must, necessarily, be consumed. But their economic viability relies on two economic exchanges: the sale of space to advertisers whose purpose is to further purvey the sale of commodities, and the sale of the completed magazine to readers – mainly women. From the mid-1950s the balance between these two shifted, with several consequences. Editorial departments were pressured by advertising departments to 'co-operate in stimulating consumption' (White 1970 p. 157) so that there was a closer tie up between editorial and advertising material and hence a narrowing of editorial feature: 'the muffling of intelligent writing' (ibid p. 203). We could say that the *raison d'être* of magazines became consumption. Further since revenue was derived increasingly from ads, rather than cover price and circulation numbers, magazines were geared to readers in terms of their consumer demands.[11] Thus the general and mass women's market which *Woman* and *Woman's Own* together with *Woman's Weekly*, *Woman's Realm* and *Woman's Mirror*, represented in the second half of the 1950s was fragmented into its different consumer groups.

Honey was launched in 1960 as a specific response to research by Abrams on the potential power of young women,[12] and was to provide a colourful shop window for fashion and cosmetics. It would perhaps be apt to credit IPC & *Honey* with the creation of the 'young woman as consumer'. Indeed *Honey* went further than most in its links with consumption. While most magazines have offers: clothes, furniture etc. *Honey* established its own boutiques and hairdressing salons (1965), which carried the *Honey* sign and standards, and were reported on each month in the magazine. Then in October 1968 began the *Honey* Club offering free gifts, special buys and the chance to be invited for a day out and beauty treatment in London.

On the domestic scene *Family Circle* (1964) and *Living* (1966) were clear examples of an attempt to capture a particular consuming audience, 'the young housewife with a full time interest in home-making' (White 1970 p. 150). Uniquely distributed through supermarkets and originally containing no fiction *Family Circle* was, as White describes, 'the most remarkable of the new magazines tailor-made to reach pre-researched markets' (ibid p. 189) and which showed a 'meteoric rise' (ibid p. 193) in its circulation figures. In a slightly different field *Annabel* (1966) appeared designed for the young mum who 'wants to read all about parenthood. And that involves everything from prams and pedal cars, to looking pretty while pregnant' (ibid p. 185).

My study here of ideological representations of consumption, specifically in *Woman*, *Woman's Own* and *Honey* is not arbitrary. *Woman* and *Woman's Own* were *the* magazines of the 1950s selling at their peak around 3 million copies per week (1958), though they were not the magazines which were geared most closely to domestic consumption. (That accolade would perhaps be conferred on *Good Housekeeping* and *Homes and Gardens* with *Woman and Home* the third but lower middle/working class contender.) Moreover they remain, I would maintain, the 'prototype' of women's magazines in terms of their content. (Cf. Winship 1978.) On the other hand *Honey* was not the chief circulation puller of the 1960s, nor was it the earliest magazine for young women. Apart from the pop orientated romance comics of the mid 1950s *She* had blazed its outspoken trail from 1955, and *Vanity Fair* for the 'younger, smarter woman' had appeared in 1949. *She*, however, while its circulation has increased when that of other magazines, including *Woman* and *Honey*, has decreased, has been set apart from other magazines by its format – its concentration of material, black and white photos, and its newsy, jokey style more aligned with *Titbits* and *Weekend* than most women's magazines. *Vanity Fair* might have been for 'younger' women and was certainly a vehicle to sell clothes, but it aped a *Vogue* style of chic, middle class glamour typically for the 'wife of the young-up-and-coming-executive', whereas *Honey* of the 1960s did indeed capture the mood of the period, if not always the reality – the scene of 'Swinging England'. In its presentation of fashion and beauty for the *young*, its emphasis on 'style' of presentation, its declaration of 'fun', it has shaped the appearance of many later magazines, and even *Woman* has not escaped its influence.

IV *Woman* and *Woman's Own* – 1950s

1. *'Home work'*

I would argue generally about the 1950s for women that it was a period of amazing optimism, when it was frequently considered, particularly by middle class women and men, that women had achieved equality, or at the most there remained only a few 'mopping up' operations (cf. 'The Feminists Mop Up' Douglas 1956). However women were represented as 'equal but different' to men. Their 'natural' difference realized through their potential position as mothers remained central but rather than being seen as a source of subordination was transformed, in its glorification, into an attribute of 'equality'. Ideologically there was a struggle to privilege this representation, which, fraught with the contradictions of women's dual role, was impossibly difficult for women themselves to live out. The only resistance to any dissatisfaction they may have felt could, in the face of such privilege bestowed on them, only be expressed in the terrain of the *personal*. (Cf. French 1978, Friedan 1968, Laing and Esterson 1964, Myrdal and Klein 1956.) The problem pages of *Woman* and *Woman's Own* reveal the mere ripples of a serious pool of unhappiness and frustration.

However, it is not the ideology of 'equal but different' in its complexity that I intend to detail here.[13] Instead I want to examine the ideology of consumption, or more precisely the ideology of the *work* of consumption, as it most decisively consolidates the equality through difference, constructing women as individuals with their own specific arena of work operation – primarily in the home. Consumption justifies and augments women's domestic role.[14] In 1951 Evelyn Home had written, in response to a reader's letter complaining about a fiance who had twice jilted her:

> To almost every woman her work comes first too – the work of homemaking and husband tending. He is interfering with your career as a wife and I advise you to tell him so.
>
> (*Woman* 13/1/51 p. 33)

As Mark Abrams, the market researcher, later put it

> Since now home has become the centre of his activity and most of his earnings are spent on or in the home his wife becomes the chooser and spender and gains a new status and control – her taste forms his life.
>
> (Abrams 1959b p. 914)

Or as a feature on 'New Homemakers' in *Woman* describes one particular couple (cf. epigraph).

> . . . Margaret is loving the privacy of this first home of her own. . . . Though Derek wasn't a contemporary fan he had complete faith in Margaret's choice – happy now about the furniture they bought . . .
>
> (*Woman* 1/1/57 p. 27)

This power of consumption decision making for women which establishes them as 'individuals' through the individuality of their homes, does not reside in their having money of their own as wage workers. The evidence that increasing numbers of married women are earning is generally displaced from view and moreover frowned upon. This is Monica Dickens, herself a 'working mother', advising a mother on whether she should return to paid work.

> I hope Mrs. X does not go rushing out to look for a job. She is not cheating the children by staying at home. She is giving them the supreme gift – herself.
>
> (*Woman's Own* 8/3/56 p. 28. Quoted in White 1970 p. 150)

It is an argument she is still rehearsing in 1961 (cf. *Woman's Own* 28/1/61). Woman's 'power' lies in the skill – the knowledge and practice of shopping successfully. Consumption, as work, has its own procedures, rules, planning and measurements of efficiency *in the same way*, it is represented, as the work of production. If men fight their battles and gain their excitement on the shop floor of industry women do so on the shop floor of the local store at sales time.

> This is the time of year when even the most timid shopper feels her fighting spirit come to the fore . . . So before we plunge into the fray . . .
>
> (*Woman* 7/1/56 p. 7)

The whole process of consumption has three stages at each of which there is a certain work to be performed, a work which the magazines aid.[15] First there is the prior knowledge required of particular commodities on the market: on carpets – 'Here's a sample of the wonderful colours available in the new tufted carpets . . . Tufted carpets are made by a new process which gives them a luxury pile at reasonable cost . . . They don't have quite the dirt resistance that wool has . . .' (*Woman's Own* 25/9/57 p. 30). (This is also knowledge gleaned from ads – 'Formica . . . there's a place for Formica in every room, a colour or pattern to suit every scheme . . . won't chip, crack or stain. Resists heat up to 310 °F, stays like new for years . . .' (*Woman* 18/8/56 p. 60)). But a housewife also needs to understand how to arrange a room – which colours it is thought are complementary, which colours clash; which curtains she should buy to tone with a highly patterned carpet etc. Throughout the 1950s Edith Blair persuasively educates housewives – 'a strong all-over patterned wall paper needs plain quiet colours to make a restful room' (*Woman* 10/5/58 p. 36). Or she guides through example – Margaret and Derek's home – 'colour and clever furniture choosing have brought this pleasant old house very much alive without losing any part of its quiet charm' (*Woman* 6/1/57 p. 27). Additionally a wife must know how to set about her shopping. In preparation for the 'sales fray', for example 'this chart gives you the essential statistics you'll need on your list when sales shopping' (ibid p. 24, a list of curtain/bed/kitchen measurements), 'Before you go out take a careful look round the house . . . you'll avoid mistakes' (*Woman's Own* 3/1/57 p. 14). Thus 'Bargain hunting is a dangerous sport for innocents but a rewarding one for those who go armed with real knowledge' (*Woman* 7/1/56 p. 24).

For the second stage of 'shopping' a cool temperament is required. 'First and foremost get your ideas straight . . . keep your head firmly on your shoulders' (ibid p. 12), and 'don't let your heart run away with your head' (*Woman* 28/4/56 p. 24). Nevertheless you do need a lively mind – 'Keep your ideas versatile' (*Woman* 7/1/56 p. 12). There are too, aids to shopping which only the initiated know about – 'Lots of young wives have told us that they find it a bewildering job to search out the best value from a wide range of goods . . . they ask, how can we be sure that a good-looking article will be hard wearing, too? . . . The secret is look for the sign of the kite' (*Woman* 21/6/58 p. 19), i.e. the British Standards sign. But there are also practical skills to acquire – '. . . you can spot the skilled sales shopper by her critical eye, by the list in her hand, her booklet of snippets of furnishing . . . and her inquiring finger and thumb appraising fabric textures . . . The critical eye and thumb-and-finger technique are not difficult to acquire if you go about it in this way. . .' (*Woman* 7/1/56 p. 24), and which are bound to deliver results – 'Joan's practical eye was quick to spot the zip-fasteners on the cushion covers which means it can be taken off for cleaning' (*Woman* 7/4/56 p. 19).

Finally having made an appropriate purchase which is typically 'practical, pretty and versatile', there is likely to be a further work. On the one hand commodities are seen to do 'work by themselves', particularly in ads which conceal all trace of the real labour of domesticity performed by women – 'Tide's in – dirt's out' (*Woman's Own* 13/12/56 p. 76), 'Batchelor's soups make a good meal wonderful' (ibid p. 66). This 'commodity work' often appears as adulation of products – '. . . take a tube for ease and economy . . . light weight, easy to pack . . .' (*Woman* 2/8/58 p. 37). On the other hand the purpose of most purchases is to aid further work, e.g. polishing, or it must be transformed by labour to be of any use.

Especially is the latter the case with sales' buys – 'It's amazing what a spot of paint can do . . .' on a chipped chair (*Woman* 7/1/56 p. 23), and of course with food purchases.[16] New commodities also mean a hitherto unheard of work – 'Give an ugly fireplace a lovely new look with these easy-to-lay tiles says Edith Blair' (*Woman* 7/4/56 p. 22).

Although 'outside' the magazines, as Scott suggests, women view shopping 'ambiguously as a skill and a chore, a pleasure and a duty' (Scott 1976 p. 105), in the magazines we have scarcely a glimpse of these tensions. Perhaps in the reference to sales as an 'adventure . . . lacking in a routine day's shopping' (*Woman's Own* 3/1/57 p. 14), there is at least the hint of a hidden tedium. While assuming 'duty' the magazines contrive to construct a *pleasureable* 'skill' which, once achieved, transforms the 'Chore' through the rewards it brings. (Cf. Derek's pleasure at Margaret's choice; Joan's satisfaction of a 'good' buy.) Women's 'duty' is, of course, centrally constructed in relation to men – their husbands. The process of consumption places women in a *complementary* position to their husbands, but it is a 'balance of power' which, for the sake of marital harmony must not be abused. The role of husband should always be tactfully considered: women are addressed as the 'ones who know', but the choice also *appears* to be his – a woman schemes to gain his co-operation – 'It is a wise wife who starts off carrying the shopping basket when it's empty . . . he will be happier to hump it when it is full if he has not had it all afternoon . . . If she is wise then she will always let him make the final choice. There is pleasure and interest in this for him because the final choice is a blending of taste – his and hers, the way it should be . . .' (*Woman* 10/5/58 p. 11). The construction of a complementary relationship reappears in the final stage of consumption work, the work performed on or with the commodity itself – 'Tackle it together' – a regular *Woman* column generally featuring house improvements.

2. *'Earning compliments'*

It might be thought that there is a world of difference between the fairly obvious work of home making and the other major area of feminine work – beauty.[17]

While commodities are used here with the most finesse; husband/boyfriend relations are at their most fragile; consumption and its work more clearly 'fun' – 'This summer your shoes will be your most glamorous accessories. Have fun choosing them' (*Woman* 28/4/56 p. 24); more *personal* – 'Colour in fashion offers you the most personal way of using colour in your life. The colour of clothes expresses your personality and influences your mood . . .' (*Woman* 12/1/57 p. 16); and *creative* – 'Get friendly with colour, mingle it with an artist's skill to create a brilliant seaside picture . . . to make you the centre of seaside attraction' (*Woman* 1/6/57 p. 36), yet the work of beauty closely *parallels* the work of the home. It confirms your 'individuality', which in home making can only be expressed through the appearance of your home, in your *personal* appearance, but it is similarly a fairly serious business which demands the astuteness needed in any other work. Moreover women are encouraged to look 'pretty' and 'glamorous' not to please themselves in a hedonistic way but to *conform* to the regulations of fashion, to the parameters of femininity in that period,[18] and hence to gain compliments from men. It is your 'duty' as a woman to dress appropriately for the occasion at hand, but by whatever means: men pay attention to your finished appearance, yet know little of the 'deceit' that lies behind it. The aim is to appear 'natural' – 'Choose the fashion and make up that enhance your natural colouring' (*Woman* 12/1/57 p. 36), and to tread the precarious line between discreet and glamorous femininity.

First then you must search out the knowledge – 'It's a fascinating business, beauty – the more we know about it the more there is to learn . . . Sharpen your wits by scanning this page . . . Beauty know-how – make sure you've got it right' (*Woman* 2/8/58 p. 13). You need to plan – 'The girl who is wise about clothes doesn't add – she builds . . . that means patience. Careful, look ahead planning in fact' (*Woman* 5/1/57 p. 32). You must choose discriminatingly – 'To find the perfect accessories means only picking the right shade for the basic colour' (*Woman* 7/1/56 p. 6), knowing the rules – 'With a plain outfit you can wear a fancy show or a plain one . . . But with a print dress you'll choose a plain coloured shoe, picking up one of the colours of the season . . .' (*Woman* 28/4/56 p. 24), while at the same time following 'nature's' contours – 'The rules are simple. Stress a good point, bypass a bad one.' (*Woman* 21/6/58 p. 14), 'Every girl has at least one good beauty point . . . resolve to devote a great deal of your cosmetic budget to enhancing it' (*Woman* 5/1/57 p. 21). However the product will not enhance you alone – you must work at it. 'Glamour is added. Something we can achieve – if we work for it. These cover girls we so much admire have acquired their loveliness the hard way' (*Woman* 3/10/59 p. 38). Nor is there any let up in the work – 'Glamour begins with impeccable grooming. Earmark one evening each month for clothes' maintenance . . .' (ibid p. 38). And what do you receive in return for your work? 'They have earned their glamour. And so can you' (ibid p. 38), 'an allout effort . . . will repay you everyday in compliments' (*Woman* 5/1/57 p. 21).

3. Tensions and contradictions – commodity as 'ogre' and 'saviour'

While consumption is necessary to femininity, women must never abandon themselves to the pursuit of merely material possessions. It is always a finely balanced procedure which clearly poses limits and and tensions for women. As the commodity form invades family relations motherhood slides dangerously into domesticity. Child care features are few compared to the pages devoted to the home. In ads 'good mothering' becomes servicing children with the appropriate commodities. An editorial holding on to the magazines' disappearing 'core' of the motherchild relation therefore has to warn women of this seduction to the value of monetary possessions for their children: 'Children – and adults, if they are wise – don't judge by the price tag . . . often the simplest things give the greatest pleasure' (*Woman* 2/10/54 p. 3). There is also a danger within marriage itself. 'All that you are' a short story (*Woman's Own* 3/1/57 p. 9) tells of a wife's attraction to the 'glitter of material things', and her attempts to push her husband into a better paid job so that *she* could have 'new clothes and a house filled with space, light and air, a house with a garden'. Finally she recognises the folly of her thoughts – 'The glitter of outward things had begun to obsess her, but she realised now that outward things would never be enough. She still in her heart 'wanted that true person who was Tony' and she resolves to love and support him as he is. In the work of 'glamour' too it is not just the commodity that counts but also *personal charm* – '. . . Ina. Besides her good grooming, she has a lot of that other elusive quality: charm. I'd define that charm as a mixture of generosity and awareness . . .' (*Woman* 3/10/59 p. 38). Yet while we are advised to be restrained in our spending there are times when a frivolous spree is encouraged. If you are 'jaded' for example – 'It's no frivolous extravagance to treat yourself to a little fashion present . . . wear it with confidence . . .' (*Woman* 5/1/57 p. 29).

But if there are *boundaries* within particular areas of consumption beyond which women must not pass, there are also *contradictions* within femininity which, not in themselves created by the process of consumption, are nevertheless articulated through certain aspects of consumption and often shaped by them. The three major contradictions represented in the magazines are between motherhood and domesticity; between the femininity of single status, in paid work, and available for marriage, and that of marital status; at home, and sexually possessed; and between the 'wifehood' of motherhood-domesticity and that of a-sexually-attractive-woman-to-husband. In the ads motherhood and domesticity do not conflict; in editorial feature and fiction they often do.

> My 18 month old son will have nothing to do with his toys but adores 'helping' in the house. I find this a trial as I like to get down to my work uninterrupted. Can you suggest any method of keeping Bobby anchored in his pen at least for a few hours a day? REPLY:
>
> > It is natural to want your house to be clean and shining but I'm sure your son's well being is even more important to you. Try to be patient with him over his passion for housework – it is for his own good.
>
> (*Woman* 30/10/54 p. 39)

Single status is seen as the time when women have money to spend on commodities. In fictions the contrast is made between the 'smart', 'glamorous' clothes of such women, and therefore their attraction to men, and the slightly old fashioned, down-at-heel, functional clothes of the wife and mother who fears she has lost her attraction to men. The central contradiction is thus between beauty (which hides beneath it sexuality) the necessary attribute of being a *wife*, and the combination of motherhood and domesticity which constantly renders the task of personal self care a feat for the outstanding only. Yet that personal, individual care *remains the salve of individuality* in the face of marriage and motherhood.

In a story by Rebecca Shallit 'A day in town with the girls' (*Woman* 2/10/54) the 'symbolic' place of consumption is well illustrated: it is certain commodities and consumption itself which features at central moments in the story. It recounts how a young married woman, mother of twin boys, goes to London for the day with 'the girls' – her married women friends, in order to get away from her 'unbearably humdrum' life at home. She first appears in the story, having performed her beauty work – 'hair shining . . . fresh lipstick' – in 'the pink housecoat he had given for her birthday'. This most feminine of garments, which parts 'to reveal a glimpse of her legs', is the personal *commodity* through which her husband asserts marital rights to her sexuality, a sexuality other men may only admire from a distance. 'She could still deserve a wolf whistle anywhere Jim thought with great pride'. Yet Julie herself recognises that marriage and family have lessened the attention she and 'the girls' pay to the cultivation of their sexuality – 'We don't fuss over our hairdoes or manicures any more'. Consequently the anticipated day out, when 'the idea is to give ourselves one completely carefree, unplanned day when we can forget about being wives and mothers and just be – women', necessitates just such personal solicitude. She buys a new hat, that item of 1950s clothing which most neatly summed up women's mode of femininity: frivolous, sober, sensible . . .? In this instance she asks her husband 'Does it do anything for me? You know, make me seem young and gay, not like a wife but somebody a man might look twice at?' 'The silly hat perched on her head' transforms her 'blue suit', so that as she sets off one Saturday morning, Jim notices that she 'looked pretty and young and carefree'. When she's not yet back late that evening he worries, contemplating on what a 'desirable woman she was', that she has gone off with another man. But of course she arrives at last, only having missed her lift and then the train. She takes off her symbol of 'carefree femininity' – the hat, and immediately asks after the children, recounting her day out. She confesses 'I'm afraid I really went on a spending spree darling'. However it turns out that the shopping extravaganza has *not* been for herself but for her husband and children. Even on her day out as a 'woman' she could not forget that she was a 'wife and mother'. Noticing her reluctance to 'let go of the day' and change her clothes – 'the far away look was still in her eyes', Jim casually suggests that she put on her 'pretty housecoat'. She agrees. She disappears upstairs to where Jim also adjourns. He *knocks* at *their* bedroom door, in acknowledgement of her 'separateness' from him, recognising her as an 'individual' and 'independent', not merely an adjunct to him. However as he enters to find her 'dabbing perfume behind her ears', he reasserts his 'control' and 'dominance'. She is indeed wearing *his* present once more, and he pulls 'her down on the bed beside him' – 'the faraway look left Julie's eye and was replaced after a while, by a look of utter contentment'.

The woman here has held onto vestiges of herself outside of her role in the family, even if it is only for one day, and in that way retains her sexuality and her attractiveness to her husband. But a feature by John Deane Potter 'Girl with the dressing gown mind' (*Woman* 26/11/60 p. 25),[19] illustrates both the likely 'fall' from husband's grace and the disintegration of 'individuality' and 'independence', that the struggle to hold together the contradictory strands – the problem of dressing attractively and of maintaining an active mind, while keeping up the standards of motherhood and domesticity – is likely to incur. Here her appearance, whether 'neatly dressed' when single, or in the 'ill-fitting skirt' and 'grey dressing gown' when a wife and mother, is seen to reflect her *mind* – 'intelligent' in her 'bright' secretary days, now succumbing to its 'grey dressing gown' character. Typical of the period she, *personally* is to blame for her 'failure' and her husband's retreat from her.

> . . . She was 32 . . . She wore an ill-fitting, somewhat creased, pleated skirt which seemed to broaden her hips . . . Yet I remember her as one of the brightest secretaries I have encountered . . . She was always neatly dressed, without beribboned fussiness, and was witty and opinionated. . . . Now here she was after seven years with her two nicely behaved children. . . . As she babbled on about domestic details ranging from the children to her kitchen layout, I realized suddenly what she had become – girl in a grey dressing gown. I could visualise her wandering about the house in the early morning with her hair flopping into her eyes, and that warm, serviceable garment roped around her . . .
>
> My wife did not agree when I said that the corny ending might be in sight – that he would look for something a little more glamorous and amusing to compensate for her mental lowliness. No . . . She is a good natured girl and a fine mother and he is not the roving kind. They will live together but drift further and further apart. . . . He will spend more time under the car . . . she will be absorbed in the house, her children and her neighbours. It is the pattern of many marriages. And it will be mostly the wife's fault as she is generally the one who supplies the stimulus.
>
> But the mystery still remained. Why did a girl so intelligent, so eager, suddenly jump off life's bus?

Within the terms of the magazines there really is no answer. Deane Potter falls back on 'magic' – 'not even Black Magic – it was just rather dull, dreary grey'. The magazines have constructed the *possibility* and *success* of 'you' the wife and mother managing the various aspects of femininity, so long as you *work hard enough at it* – and anyway hadn't all those commodities the 1950s' boom brought made the task that much easier?

We must shift to the terrain of femininity '*outside*' of marriage and motherhood for the developments which make any kind of break at all conceivable. Attention to that terrain was pointed to in the 1950s by, among others, Abrams in *The Teenage Consumer.* He wrote of the teenager as 'newly enfranchised in an economic sense' which 'has given him (sic) the chance to be himself and show himself' (1959a p. 3). While *Woman* and *Woman's Own* were extensively read by young women in the 1950s it did not purport to address itself solely to them. It was however, precisely for this group that *Honey* was brought out.

V *Honey* – 1960s

1. *'A girl spends her own money, has fun – and problems'*

The relations of consumption represented in *Honey* are manifestly different from those of *Woman* and *Woman's Own* in the 1950s. While there is a disarticulation of femininity from child care, and primarily a concern with the 'run-up' to marriage itself, consumption is, on the other hand inseparable both from *paid work* and *sexuality*.[20] It is explicitly the wholehearted individual and mainly *personal* consumption of one's own wage. Sexuality provides the reason for the kind of consumption that is indulged in and is constructed by that consumption. The contradiction which Mitchell refers to between the 'active production' and 'passive consumption' of sexuality is built into the consumption process itself. At one and the same time the act of consumption as it is realised in women's appearance, expresses their 'individuality' and 'independence' while providing the means by which patriarchal relations are potentially reaffirmed both by women themselves and by men. Women construct themselves as the unique *woman* attractive beyond all female rivals to *men*. Men construe the 'image' as a 'sexual independence' which can be 'exploited' and abused, or 'recycle' the image to sell the drabber commodities to themselves. Ads directed at women entrench the contradiction by collapsing both sides into one visual/verbal representation. (e.g. 'Come join the freedom lovers' Berlei girdle ad–cf p. 31)

With the same editor – Audrey Slaughter – for most of the 1960s this magazine for the 'young, gay and get ahead' has, despite its appearance of making 'each issue different from the last' (White 1970 p. 173) a coherence which begins to break at the end of the decade. It disintegrates, I would argue, as the contradiction between the 'active production' and 'passive consumption' of sexuality becomes more acute, and because fashion and its discourse no longer has the ideological power to carry with it and, to speak for, the developments in those 'outside' areas of sexuality, work and politics.[21] These contradictory elements are already there at the outset in *Honey* but we need to explore their burgeoning growth to understand their ideological and eventual political impact.

The magazine sets itself up in 1960 with the intimacy between editorial staff and readers which is its hallmark for that period. The people who work on the magazine are not mere photos at the head of a column like they are in *Woman* and *Woman's Own*: they deal with readers' requests and anxieties in what is sometimes a motherly/big sisterly style, but they also become friends whose lives, and especially working lives on the magazine, we learn about. *They* too, often act as the 'guinea pigs' and models for beauty and fashion features, so that we see them 'guilty' of the same bad fashion habits as us. In one sense then, at the level of representation, the division between producer and consumer is dissolved, although the magazine itself, as commodity, is witness to that separation. Such a dissolution is possible because it is assumed that most readers are women in paid work – 'Helen Kayes 20. She works in the fashion department of a famous store . . .', 'Personal assistant in a busy press office, Felicity Wigs is 21 . . .' (Jan 1961 p. 12). *Honey* therefore enters women's lives in a different mode from *Woman* and *Woman's Own*. The latter provide entertainment but in the space of women's work of femininity in the home, a work which must be constructed as work, to 'cover up' women's subordination. The terrain of *Honey's* entertainment is similarly a work of femininity, though a different work – 'catching a man', which precisely because there is that other arena of paid work (to which the magazine is not wholly aligned) need not be constructed *as work*. The upshot of this difference is that the magazine can be more outrageously *fun*, and at the level of representation there is an apparent blurring of 'fantasy' and 'reality' that does not occur in *Woman's Own* and *Woman* of the 1950s where each is clearly demarcated.[22]

'Fun' eminently takes place outside of the family home. As a 'honey' you are assumed to live away from your parents, in flat or bedsit, possibly in a different town, or at the very least to have your own room at home that you've transformed from bedroom to bedsit status. Thus you have established an 'independence' which you mark with your individuality – *your* room: 'It was a room in search of a true individuality but our friend Betsy took it. She had ambitions . . . you see the clever results of her colourful outlook' (Jan 1961 p. 8), and in your appearance: 'stand out in a crowd' (May 1961 p. 17) 'hit an original note' (April 1960, p. 84), 'turn a head' (May 1961 p. 16).

This individuality of appearance is in part made possible by the breakdown of fashion convention and its construction as 'fun'. The seeds of this shift in fashion's seriousness had already been sown in 1957 when, as Christopher Booker describes, the *sack* shocked fashion protocol and 'the waistless Twenties-style Sack dress and the new kneelength "short skirt" were able to sweep away the last remnants of the New Look' (1970 p. 38). Veronica Scott in *Woman* had simply proclaimed – 'It's fun . . . we've been stuck in a fashion rut for years' (*Woman* 19/10/57 p. 13). But now in *Honey* gone too were those other marks of 1950s' fashion: the model hat, the little gloves even for summer, the classic bag to tone and the *red* lipstick. Clothes were 'forward looking' in a way they had not been since the 1920s (and have not been since), i.e. they were not revamped versions of what had already gone before, but were original to the 1960s. In particular the rapid appearance of the mini skirt in 1965, then trouser suits, the convenience of tights and the later outrage of hotpants, summed up that move. But even before those were introduced we had: low heeled and round toed shoes, as opposed to the pointed stilettos of the late 1950s, the design of PVC clothes-in 'op-art' patterns, and brightly coloured stockings. 'Individuality', possible through the plurality of choice is both available and indeed *acceptable*.

But the rigorous effort at individuality is, at least in the early years of *Honey*, still governed by attention to the likes of men, whose opinions in this area are much sought after: 'Bachelor' – 'I don't like seeing a badly dressed girl either in the office or out of it – it annoys me. . . . My job is very exacting, and the girl who looks really wonderful makes me *want* to be in the office – she doesn't distract me, but helps me to work . . .' (April 1960 p. 58). Such arrogant sexism in these early days is fatalistically considered 'natural': honeys accommodate to it – here we have the clothes which meet with that male approval. The blatant 'active pursuit' of men, the attempt at provocation through appearance – 'a dress designed to clinch any budding romance' (May 1961 p. 18), 'Danger, woman at work capturing hearts . . . 'cos a young man's fancy can't help turning in the direction of this brilliant crimson pique dress' (ibid p. 20), brings with it the problem of sex, which is exacerbated by living away from the parental home. 'How to say *No*. Any girl on her own has to learn to master a delicate art . . . the know-how of NO-how' (Jan 1961 pp. 16–17). In *Honey* there is a lag between the 'freedom' that is offered through consumption and the quite conservative pronouncements on virginity which are later fairly reluctantly dropped by the magazine. Yet the two are integrally related. Booker points out 'Mary Quant's constantly quoted reiteration that she wanted clothes she designed above all to be "sexy" ' (Booker 1970 p. 21). But while *Honey* saw fit to illustrate and talk about 'sexy' fashion in the early 1960s it was not able to relax taboos on sex. It was a tension which had continually to be discussed – how far could a *girl go*

> Your most repeated no . . . will be the ever-present problem of necking. You *do* want to say no to more than affectionate kisses. You *do* want to say no to parking, lovers' lanes, to bear hugs. You *don't* want to say no to your beau's place in your life, if he's basically nice and only occasionally crosses the border of good dating sense.
>
> (Jan 1961 p. 16)

And how did you actually cope with it?[23]

> Your words should be something on these lines 'I like you Bob. You're nice, you're fun, you're attractive. But we're both adult enough to know that living for the moment doesn't make sense. Let's keep this evening the kind we'll remember as a good happy one.'
>
> (ibid p. 16)

2. *'Striding out and bouncing back'*

The momentum of 'self-confidence' and 'individuality' gains ground as the 1960s progress and 'the cult of the individual' through fashion proceeds (cf epigraph). In Jan 1965 the theme of the issue was 'How far will you go?' 'What we're really after', wrote Audrey Slaughter in her editorial, 'is the girl who goes far to be an individual'. There were two main aspects to this 'individuality': 'work' and 'fashion', but it is primarily the discourse of fashion that sets the parameters within which 'individuality' is constructed. 'The 1965 girl is the one who realizes the tremendous rewards there are in working at an absorbing job', but also 'She's the girl who thinks fashion is fun, not a dictator. She'll mess about experimenting but she'll carve her own way through the maze of what's new so that she makes everybody wish they'd thought of the precise way of wearing that'. In May 1966 the magazine proclaimed 'Next month we're stepping out of line.'

> We're tired of being told what *not* to do. . . . Who says you can't do anything about the face you were born with. . . . Beauty for the individualist . . . and fashion too. Who says you've got to look like the girl at the next desk? . . . What law ever said you must stick to work that bores you – when the world is full of out-of-line jobs if you've got the guts to find time?
>
> (May 1966 p. 3)

If honeys stride out to take adventurous holidays and jobs in unusual places (if not unusual jobs) it is in their appearance that the 'derring' is most obvious. It is the discourse of fashion which seems to 'speak' on behalf of these movements in other arenas – it encapsulates them. Thus in 1967 Audrey Slaughter asks 'What *is* fashion?' and can answer

> It's an expression of mood, of our age, of political climate, of economic pressures . . . we're hanging onto the shreds of our individuality . . . We've discovered a new confidence, a

> kind of derring-do . . . the current dolly strides in, supremely unconcerned that her outfit is a combination of attic finds, boutique gimmick, Sellotape creation and tin-foil glitter. She'll take on a big job now that previously she would have had to wait years to get . . . and find a job in a faraway place with little to go on except a terrific optimism and faith in her own ability to make out . . . Fashion isn't frivolous, though it's fun (or should be); it's a creative expression of our age . . .
>
> (Jan 1967 p. 3)

However this optimism belies the contradictory relations which construct 'individuality'. Even the 'dolly' herself as modelled in the magazine, with her childlike Twiggy waifness, and wide eyed innocence, is uncertainly bold. Then there is the 'man problem'. The acceptance of men – as they are, with all their faults – in the early 1960s, is quickly challenged, but contradictorily. In the August 1962 issue, 'all about men', there is idolisation of men and still the obsessive concern to attract them with one's looks, but also *acute discontent*. This fictional letter from a 'mother' captures these contradictions.

> Daughter dear, take a long, cool look at the men you're going to meet in your life. They're wonderful and deserve a great deal of us. For example you'll need a high standard of grooming, dressing and beauty, seasoned well with wit and personality, if you're going to be lucky enough to attract one of the creatures for all time. This may mean putting up with giant rollers in your hair each night . . . screwing and scraping to buy clothes and cosmetics . . . keeping abreast with new thought, new books, new talk. Eschew all ideas of splurging cash on cars, good luncheons, nights on the town. Only men can enjoy that sort of thing. In return – what do you get? Darling, *men*, of course! Isn't that enough! . . . Aren't you a lucky girl?
>
> (August 1962 p. 15)

Yet in the same issue a fashion feature on frilly underwear complacently declares 'I'm a girl and by me that's only great' (ibid p. 33). In 1963 the *inequality* between women and men is explicitly voiced

> . . . all this talk about equality is sheer illusion . . . the dice is heavily loaded . . . Just think about it a girl *cannot* be an airline pilot or . . . A girl cannot really have a night out with the girls . . . It is the girls who stay at home with the kids . . .
>
> (Oct 1963 p. 94 – note that it is the same issue as epigraph)

But further the mode of operation of femininity which copes with this is also challenged

> Making herself maddeningly, deliciously feminine as possible, she takes her revenge in all the subtle ways open to her. Realizing she doesn't hold the trump cards, she plays her inferior hand with superlative skill – and if she's really smart she may even take the last trick. This isn't a real solution, of course, because I, for one, don't want to go around being maddeningly feminine *all* the time, but so far I haven't thought of a better answer. Have you?
>
> (ibid p. 74)

The work of beauty which has always been deceitful achieves the ultimate with a battery of commodity 'fakes' behind which 'you' in your 'individuality' are hidden. If clothes declare themselves a mock up in their outrageousness, body beauty apes 'the natural'. Thus this worried honey:

> Help me, *Honey*! I'm a fake; I wear a false hair piece, false eye lashes, falsies to give me a bigger bust, a pantie girdle to give me smaller hips and false nails. Now I'm terrified of being exposed because my boyfriend, who's been fooled so far (and keeps saying how nice and 'natural' I am) wants me to go swimming with him.

The reply displays perhaps surprising insight

> You aren't a fake – you just know how to make the best of yourself and should continue to do so. You can either – keep up your present image with well cut bikinis that have built in tops . . . waterproof eyeliner . . . or you can show him the 'natural' you. But of course the *natural* state has been carefully tended with sun tan preparations, de-fuzzing equipment, deodorants . . . It's all a question of hard work once again, but our only other suggestion is to find a short sighted boyfriend.
>
> (June 1966 p. 40)

Ads endeavour to enshrine women within the commodity, well typified by a Coty ad in which a woman's face is framed by 'Hot lips' lipstick (May 1969 p. 49), though they also offer 'freedom' *through* the commodity – 'Come join the freedom lovers', the caption of a series of ads for Berlei foundation garments, in which women wearing this 'controlling' attire hold the banner which proclaims 'freedom' (ibid p. 72).

3. 'The "individual" as "spectacle"'

Honey presents to the reader a series of 'spectacles' right through from the colourful ads to editorial feature. This visuality, in relation to the verbal material that is its support,[24] manifestly reveals 'the individual' as only mere 'spectacle'! Guy Debord in *The Society of the Spectacle* has argued for the centrality of the 'spectacle' in a consumer society.

> . . . lived reality is materially invaded by the contemplation of the spectacle . . . reality emerges into the spectacle, and the spectacle is real (Paragraph 8).
>
> . . . the world at once and absent which the spectacle *lets us see* is the world of the commodity dominating everything that is lived. (Para 37) The spectacle is the moment when the commodity has achieved the total occupation of social life. Not only is the relation to the commodity visible but it is all one sees: the world one sees is its world (Paragraph 42).
>
> (Debord 1967 No page numbers)

In the context of the magazine it is fashion photography which most clearly 'spectacularises'. The foreign countries which provide the backcloth are emptied of their own reality which is replaced by the fashion models and their clothes. In a similar vein there is the 'Gypsy Caravan . . . a *look* that conjures up flamboyant men and women from hot-blooded lands . . . a defiant look worth chasing on fiery July days. And who better to follow than the gypsies? . . . Your gypsy scene is now . . . The Romany *look*' (July 1968 pp. 62–71, My emphases). The 'look' is indeed all we have of the gypsies whose history and hardships are displaced from view. Their 'look' is transformed by the commodity form and transferred to young English women who create their 'individuality' through that 'look'. It *refers* to a reality it attempts to take over in a process comparable to that explained by Judith Williamson in relation to ads. She suggests that they employ 'hollowed out referent systems' which are 'filled' by the commodity (Williamson 1978 p. 168).

Likewise the fashion item 'Jail break' (May 1966 p. 64) relies on an original meaning with its connotations of excitement and *daring initiative* but 'plays' on it.

> Prisoners take heart! And if you've ever heaved yourself out of your underclothes with a sigh of relief at the end of the day, that means you! So cast off your fetters – tough plastic, bones, pins and other feminine tortures – liberation day is here, underwear is light and mobile as your skin, and coloured that way. Make a run for it.
>
> (Cf Berlei girdle ad p. 31)

The meaning of 'Jail-break' is limited to the use of a particular commodity in a mode which Herbert Marcuse has termed the 'language of operationalism' (Marcuse 1969 p. 78) 'in which opposites are reconciled' (ibid p. 79), and which 'impose themselves with an overwhelming and petrified concreteness' (ibid p. 82). For Marcuse it is such ways of thinking that contribute to a 'one dimensional society'.

> . . . the products indoctrinate and manipulate; they promote a false consciousness which is immune against falsehood. And as these beneficial products become more available to more individuals, in more social classes, the indoctrination they carry ceases to be publicity; it becomes a way of life. It is a good way of life – much better than before – as a good way of life it militates against qualitative change. Thus emerges a pattern of one dimensional thought and behaviour.
>
> (ibid p. 26)

It is what John O'Neill has termed a '*goods* society' (O'Neill 1972 p. 27). But if it is pernicious it is so in the contradictory manner that Marcuse poses of being in fact 'better than before'. This is important for women in a particular way. While commodities have 'invaded' the personal arena, they have also made that arena public (cf Rowbotham 1973 p. 110) so that in a limited way, through commodities, the *masculine* construction of femininity can be turned back into men's faces by women themselves: showing that it is indeed a masculine construction. Thus what Marcuse says here does not quite fit in relation to women.

> The idea of 'inner freedom' . . . it designates the private space in which man may become and remain 'himself'. Today this private space has been invaded and whittled down by technological reality. Mass production and mass distribution claim the entire individual . . .
>
> (Marcuse 1969 p. 25)

Women have never had an 'inner freedom', a 'self', but have been the 'hidden mystery of the female sex', the 'natural' for *men* (cf Brunsdon 1978). In the 1960s women now flaunt to men the visible sexuality hitherto confined to privacy, but it is a sexuality in part constructed by the commodity, ambiguously 'available' to *all* men, but partially controlled by women themselves. O'Neill seems not to understand this point when he remarks

> . . . what is even more shocking to critical reason is that this irrational economic order is

> able to appear quite beneficient through a technique of splitting behaviour and fantasy in the packaging of goods. To consider a trivial example (sic), the girl who is not free to resist the mini-skirt fashion can be sold her sexual or feminine liberation with it in a vicarious fantasy of admiration and conquest which is split off from the everyday mini-scenes in which nothing happens to her or to the men around her.
>
> (O'Neill 1972 p. 51)

While her life may well be a series of 'mini-scenes' yet he does not grasp what Marcuse holds on to, that the mini-skirt *is* liberation for those who wear it – even if it is only the 'look' of liberation. *Not* to wear a mini-skirt may well 'look' better if your legs are podgy, your bottom large, but it is not only to cover up your legs but also to forego the attempt at, and the idea of, an active 'sexuality' and 'freedom'. As young women in that period we all *had* to wear mini-skirts – or be categorised as a failure and a 'frump': old fashioned and asexual.

In granting the 'reality' of the 'freedom' offered by such developments Marcuse refers to the 'absorption of ideology into reality' (Marcuse 1969 p. 26), in which

> the tension between appearance and reality, fact and factor, substance and attribute tend to disappear. The elements of autonomy, discovery, demonstration and critique recede before designation, assertion and imitation. Magical, authoritarian and ritual elements permeate speech and language . . .
>
> (ibid p. 78)

This assignation is partially true of *Honey*, but there is also a way in which the 'absorption of ideology into reality' is also a means of *questioning* the 'real'. The mini-skirt, through the contradictions it throws up, begins to challenge the status of female sexuality for men. If we consider the October 1963 issue from which the epigraph is taken this process becomes more defined. *Honey* takes over the vocabulary and procedure associated with election campaigns, but transfers it to a site not usually considered political – clothes.[25] 'Here's *Honey* girl in action again. This month she's been trailing up and down the country fixing for you to see the Campaign clothes' (Oct 1963 p. 35). The 'candidates' are the various fashion designers. But having exhausted that 'election' the magazine then turns to a further extrapolation.

> Won any good elections lately? I'm not joking. Most of us are being 'elected' for things all our lives – or being beaten in 'elections' we don't even know about. Take jobs for instance . . . Even marriage is a sort of election. Well – it is, isn't it?
>
> (ibid p. 111)

Moreover sandwiched between these 'elections' discussions the three leaders of Britain's major political parties are given a platform to talk about young people. The issue is serious despite its 'fantasy' air: the 'politics' that General Elections are about seem to be completely cut off from the lives which *Honey* readers lead where, indeed, the more personal elections over work, marriage and fashion are the problems and issues of the day. As the introduction comments '. . . we don't feel inspired to join in' (ibid p. 50).

4. Consumption at work – it works too well

If consumption in *Honey* is dependent on having a job, it most frequently also has a place *within* that job. There is little paid work in which it is not expected that a woman should look feminine, and in *Honey* the most often discussed jobs are those in which the reproduction of labour power necessitates the reproduction of a *feminine* labourer: shop assistants, models, actresses, secretaries, *Honey*'s own editorial staff, must all conserve their appearance through the purchase of commodities and the work of beauty. For these women work and consumption mesh neatly together. In Dec 1966 *Honey* there is a primarily visual feature 'Once Upon a Time' (p. 44) which concisely represents in a highly fictionalised form, the relations between paid work, consumption/commodities and love. Ostensibly about a girl who moves from a village shop, to London where she works 'behind the cosmetic counter in a city department store', it describes and illustrates the work she does and her conceptions of it – 'the customers were pleasant', 'it was a novelty to be able to offer a customer choice of no fewer than eight Revlon hair sprays', but it also details these commodities and displays them, as well as some of the clothes she wears. Further it is through the process of selling a young man 'just what he wanted' for his mother that she also succeeds in love. In the July 1968 issue *Honey* announced that it would hold 'career checkpoints' in various towns where *Honey* readers could 'talk to experts about careers from Advertising to Zoology' (p. 76). But additionally and *necessarily* – 'that's not all . . . a Honey team will be advising on fashion and experts from Helena Rubenstein will be giving advice on how to make up for the office' (p. 76).

Marcuse extensively discusses the libidinization of the work place (Marcuse 1969, 1972), yet he fails to differentiate on the basis of gender.

> It has often been noted that advanced industrial civilization operates with a greater degree of sexual freedom – 'operates' in the sense that the latter becomes a market value and a factor of social mores. Without ceasing to be an instrument of labour, the body is allowed to exhibit its sexual features in the everyday work world and in work relations. This is one of the unique achievements of industrial society – rendered possible by the availability of cheap, attractive clothing, beauty culture and physical hygiene; by the requirements of the advertising industry, etc. The sexy office and sales girls, the handsome, virile junior executive and floor walkers are highly marketable conditions.
>
> (Marcuse 1969 pp. 70–1)

To understand this shift we have to consider the development at the consumption 'end' of capitalist production of a 'privatised hedonism'[26] or 'libidinization of consumption' (Hall 1979), as it initially takes place through women's sexuality. As Mitchell describes, women became the 'subject of the most advanced ideological utilization' (1971 p. 143) to sell such hedonism. But they do so because they too are sold commodities for their *personal* consumption – for use on their person precisely because they are already confined to their 'sex' (cf Mitchell 1975 p. 405). Only later has a similar male market been explored – deodorants for men, sexy underwear etc. This commodity production therefore mobilises but transforms already existing patriarchal relations, in a mode which potentially contradicts the social relations of the capitalist work place. What Mitchell calls the shift from a 'production-and-work ethos to a consumption-and-fun ethos' (ibid p. 147) has an articulation in the work place as well as outside. It is women taking their sexuality, in its commodity form, into the work place itself, which allows men a relaxation on this front too. 'Repressive desublimation' (Marcuse 1969 p. 69) in which the 'body is allowed to exhibit its sexual features in the everyday work world and in work relations' is therefore primarily articulated through *women's* sexuality, but via the commodity form.

However the libidinization of consumption and the work place could not have taken place so easily without the contraceptive pill. *Honey's* earnest entreaties to say 'No' finally proved to be of no avail. Between the Scylla of hedonistic consumption with its sexual appeal, and the Charybdis of access to the pill,[27] women were caught in sexual activity. May 1969 *Honey* is a paradise of female nudity and sensuality. It boasts eroticism at visual and verbal levels, with such ads as 'Eros' (swimwear/underwear), 'The "Soflons" inspiration . . . a stroke of genius caressing you in a tender embrace . . .' (tights), 'Hot lips' (lipstick), 'So now you can feel a new sensation' (tights). It is an ambiguous sexuality – often obviously for male consumption, but sometimes a more self-involved narcissism that excludes men.[28] There is too a 'sideways' double spread featuring a sexy shirt – 'Sexeez – stretchies, see throughs, skin tights' (p. 120), a fashion feature on shoes – 'Stop pussyfooting around – this cat's shoes are the cream' (p. 104), and 'plunge into the deep end for the new slinky swimsuits' (p. 98).

It is in this 'sexual environment' that *Honey* carries one of its most serious articles – 'Birth Control and the Single Girl' (p. 122). (In 1966 *Honey* had issued a booklet – Birth Control & the Single Girl). *Honey* accedes to contraception not in a proclamation of sexual enjoyment but at the level of prevention of that 'unlucky, unloved third' (p. 123). On the basis of statistical probability – '67,000 illegitimate children are born each year, and there are roughly 100,000 abortions a year' – that you and your boyfriend are asked to face your responsibility and 'be sure that this sort of tragedy doesn't happen to you' (p. 5). Sex is represented as that 'natural' sometimes uncontrollable animal urge of 'sexual desire' – 'It is undoubtedly true that, once a girl has started indulging in petting, she is in danger of becoming pregnant, simply because of the difficulty of stopping when sexual desire is aroused' (p. 5). The magazine attempts to hold firmly to the respectability of virginity until marriage, showing a puritanism out of keeping with the 'fun' ethic of its fashion features. Nevertheless the following feature – a *personal* view – 'Anyone can marry', seems not to advocate such restraint. Rebecca Greer more openly discusses the options in 'the mating game' – 'on behalf of the single girl' – in terms of what '*you*' will gain from a relationship with a man who need not become your husband. With men as 'friends' and 'lovers' a woman does not lose her 'independence', but 'the price you pay for marriage' is 'relinquishing your freedom to do whatever you want with anyone you please' (p. 136).

Besides the 'break' represented here in sexual relations outside of marriage, there is also a shift signalled in the field of politics. In October 1963 politics entered only at the level of clothes. In March 1966 'the soap boxes' were again 'pulled out on Honey' (p. 3) and this time the representation straddles the 'masculine' and 'feminine' versions of politics. Alongside the serious airing of political views by *Honey*'s editorial team Gillian Cooke, then fashion editor, describes the kind of people they are and chooses the most suitable 'clothes policy' for them; this we see implemented on the fashion pages. We were also greeted with – 'Would you make a good politician's wife?', a flippant quiz and 'Our vote for the big time – James Fox'. By 1969 votes for eighteen year olds are seriously being discussed, but the greater interest the magazine now shows in politics is probably more attributable to the *visibility* of women's issues at the *political* level: as well as abortion and contraception, equal pay and divorce reform in particular, which had been struggled for *outside* the terrain *Honey* was primarily concerned with. The 'Honey Club Opinion Poll' (May 1969 p. 152) was no longer a fashion poll, but a survey of what honeys would do with a 'real' vote now that 'you' have 'a growing interest in politics especially when they are concerned with social affairs which affect your life' (p. 152). Seemingly anomalously it was Enoch Powell who overwhelmingly headed the people honeys would vote for as prime minister, but to 'balance' him in the top ten are Barbara Castle – 'who we've a sneaky feeling collected extra votes just because she's one of us' (p. 152), Jeremy Thorpe, Joe Grimond, Harold Wilson, and Jimmy Saville. Yet the Conservatives still easily won the poll. Was Enoch Powell a 'flash-in-the-pan' or the most 'out-of-the-ordinary' and '*individual*' politician, if strikingly the most racist?[29] In this same issue there is a fashion feature in which black models are used – 'The temperature of yellow fevered fashion – cooled be black and white' (p. 82) – which is an obvious but curious play on race.[30] The Conservatism of honeys which the 'poll' feature revealed is partly outweighed by a critical but 'liberally' positive evaluation of the underground press: *it*, *Oz*, *Black Dwarf* etc. (p. 138), but finally there is an item entitled 'The revolutionary Mr. Sharif' (p. 92), which refutes its contents. Mr Sharif who is playing Che Guevara in a film speaks of his own apoliticism but more particularly displays his lack of a *sexual* politics by the sexism of his remarks – 'I wouldn't object to marrying a woman who has a career, as long as that career was being my wife and that was all . . .' (p. 93). In more appropriate 'Sharif territory' the cover on which we finally close the magazine declares 'Undies to be sold in' – a woman in bra and pants parades her body in front of a gathering of Arab males. (An ad for Triumph International underwear!)

Conclusion

The 'progress' represented by the address to 'you' as the 'individual' woman who actively and responsibly votes, works and has sex is undermined by the address to a 'you' who passively consumes the masculine fantasies of 'your' sexual representations. The 'real', actual individual – you who in 1969 read this magazine – would appear to stand confused or irate at the dislocation of the two. Yet the rebellion of the Women's Liberation Movement does not appear from within *Honey*'s covers although the seeds of the contradictions which feed it are in evidence. Indeed it cannot, for *Honey* is firstly too firmly 'inside' consumption, most particularly in the area of paid work for women. In the May 1969 issue, for example, 'not just a pretty face . . . more of a hard slog' details the work of models for whom a continual appraisal of their feminine appearance is integral to their work. However it is *all* women who are measured by this gender criterion. Thus George Newnes in the *Times* felt justified in asking of *women* bank managers 'Could you ever be sure that inside every bank manager there was not a sex symbol trying to get out?' ('Unfair Comment?' *Times* 31/10/66). This is not *Honey*'s area of concern. Moreover, secondly, the magazine addresses you as young women *without* children. Women's structural subordination on the site of the family where 'motherhood' throws you back into the 'natural' and economic dependence on men is displaced from view. Even the work of domestic consumption that *Woman* and *Woman's Own* ideologically construct to make sense of that place for women need not be discussed.

Yet all women bring to *Honey* or the similar ideological representations of femininity on ad hoardings, TV and popular newspapers, 'images' that they 'already have of themselves, their mothers and women generally' (Cowie 1977 p. 23). Thus for some – primarily middle class and educated – women in the late 1960s the discourse of the magazine as a whole *contradictorily* placed them in relation to the economic and social position they thought they knew and experienced 'outside' – as participators in higher education with men, and as co-workers: 'equal individuals' no less, *not* 'sexual objects'. Nevertheless as Mitchell percipiently notes it was in part through the 'benefits' of an ideology of consumption which offered them 'individuality', that women gained this insight.

> Expanding the consciousness of many (for the sake of expanding consumerism) *does* mean expanding their consciousness . . . The ideologies cultivated in order to achieve

ultimate control of the market (the free choice of the individual of whatever brand of car suits his individuality) are ones which can rebel in their own terms.

(Mitchell 1971 p. 31)

The WLM with its commitment to 'the personal is political' bears witness to that rebellion. Yet as pre-condition to that it is the possibility of 'free choice', implemented *within femininity*, that is pertinent. As Marcuse comments 'slaves must be *free for* their liberation before they can become free' (Marcuse 1969 p. 47). The ideological construction of women as 'individuals' begins to mark out that pre-requisite of 'free for', although there is by no means any automaticity in its transformation beyond femininity to *feminism.* Indeed precisely because it speaks of 'freedom' 'equality', 'choice', 'individuality', it has the power of all ideology: as Althusser describes 'the individual is interpellated as a (free) subject . . . in order that he shall (freely) accept his subjection' (Althusser 1971 p. 169). For woman her individuality is, then, subjected to femininity and patriarchal relations – and importantly that ideological construction is still pervasively at work to-day. And yet I hope I have demonstrated how, paradoxically, even such an oppressive construction – as it was articulated through an ideology of consumption in the 1950s and 1960s – potentially contributed to foundations for a *political* move forwards for women, and didn't just constitute a mere shift in ideological gear.

Acknowledgements

I would like to give my thanks to Charlotte Brunsdon for seeing me through the last few days of producing this – 'servicing me', typing, reading drafts, suggesting amendments and generally keeping me sane.

Notes

1 I have chosen 1954 to begin the period, as the first year of 'unrestrained' spending after the ending of rationing in 1953. I have ended in 1969 because that was the year when the Women's Liberation Movement, which I see as partly arising out of the contradictory developments around consumption, began.

2 Weinbaum and Bridges (1976) would appear to have been the first to coin the term 'consumption *work*'. They interestingly argue how that work has increased for women with the appearance of *self*-service shops: the shopper now has to do the choosing and sometimes the weighing of food which would previously have been performed by an assistant.

3 Scott recounts that it has been estimated that in the 1970s women in Britain and America decide 75–90% of the number of total sales. Faulder (1977) suggests that women spend £80 out of every £100.

4 See Clarke et al. (1975) who discuss 'youth consumption' for this period without mention of women, and see McRobbie and Garber in the same volume for a criticism of this absence. Abrams (1959a) variously differentiates women from men but at certain points discusses them as one grouping.

5 The term 'penetration', with all its sexual connotations, I use advisedly here: it indicates the argument I am making that there is a reinforcement of capitalist *and* patriarchal relations by this extension of the market.

6 Abrams (1966) gives slightly different figures, but the trend is the same.

7 Along somewhat similar lines Weinbaum and Bridges (1976) argue that – 'the work of consumption, while subject to and structured by capital, embodies those needs – material and non-material – most antagonistic to capitalist production; and the contradiction between private production and socially determined needs is embodied in the activities of the housewife'.

8 Working class women have, of course, always been engaged in paid employment in greater or smaller numbers; in the Second World War too large numbers of all women were employed, and

I do not want to underestimate the importance of that. I want merely to emphasize another significant feature of the post war period: the economic and ideological construction of *all* women – across classes – as consumers. Alongside that married women have increasingly entered paid work, but *ideologically* that has been unevenly and contradictorily acceptable, according to class and marital (i.e. childcare) responsibilities.

9 Of a cartoon in *Women's World* where a middle aged, rather large woman stands aggressively by an armchair in which cowers her small husband, and declares: 'You may make the money clever Dick, but *I* have to decide how you're going to spend it!' (Sept 1978 p. 89).

10 Lefebvre (1971) who discusses both 'femininity' and 'consumption' quite extensively nevertheless does *not* make the association of 'individuality' through consumption for women. However he does say on the one hand about an ideology of consumption that it creates 'an image of the "I" consumer fulfilled as such, realizing himself in actions . . .' (p. 90); on the other hand that 'the ideology of femininity . . . is only another form of the ideology of consumption' (p. 96).

11 1963 weeklies offset 67% and monthlies 82% of their costs from ads (White 1970 p. 207).

12 See Abrams 'The Teenage Consumer' (1959). The 'teenager' was defined for consumption purposes as a young person between 15 and 25 years old. Curiously Abrams collates consumption figures for women and men together, although it is clear that the largest section of commodity purchase – women's clothes – must be gender specific. Overall however it is young men who in fact spend the most – 67% of all teenage spending. A curious paradox here? Where were the advertising and magazines addressed to them?

13 For further discussion of the ideology of 'equal but different' see Birmingham Feminist History Group (1979) and Elizabeth Wilson (1980).

14 Long time editor of *Woman* Mary Grieve observes in her autobiography which is primarily about her life with the magazine that – 'A very great part of a woman's life is spent choosing, buying and preparing goods for her own and her family's consumption. . . . An immense amount of her personality is engaged in her function as the selector of goods, and in this she endures many anxieties, many fears. Success in this function is as cheering and vitalising to her as it is to a man in his chosen career, failure as stimulating' (1964 p. 137. Also quoted in White 1970 p. 146).

15 Scott (1976) delimits two stages within consumption: 'shopping' and 'buying', but fails to consider the final stage of what is done with the commodity after it is bought.

16 'Cooking' is another area of 'home making' that I do not consider here. It is however as important and subject to the same rationalisation and ambiguities of being both 'work' and 'fun'. I have briefly discussed it elsewhere (Winship 1978 p. 146).

17 For other discussion of the work of beauty see McRobbie 1977, Winship 1978. There is a third area of work for women – the work of *personal life*, of relationships with children and especially with husband – which, not performed with the aid of commodities, I do not examine here. (See Brunsdon 1978, Zaretsky 1976).

18 The propriety of fashion's usual codes is reflected in a comment on Audrey Hepburn's breaking of the rules. 'Would you have the nerve to wear this outfit without any jewellery but a simple wedding ring?' (*Woman* 10/5/58 p. 6).

19 In 1957 a film, scripted by Ted Willis, directed by J. Lee Thompson was released with the title 'A Woman in a dressing gown'. It concerns precisely such a woman as is discussed here and it would seem that the film which was a great success is probably implicitly being referred to here.

20 In a wider study than this one would have to examine these factors 'outside' *Honey*. Specifically in relation to the eventual appearance of the WLM. Rowbotham (1973) and Mitchell (1971) both discuss these developments.

21 As a sign of this disintegration *Honey*'s circulation dropped between 1969–72 from 201,223 to 178,120 copies per month although[4] began to rise again in 1973. (Audit Bureaux of Circulation).

22 Its 'fun' character must also be associated simply with the fact that it is a magazine for *young* women.

23 Sheila Rowbotham recounts her personal experience of this problem – 'I could never think quickly enough somehow to translate the gametes and zygotes we learned about in biology into information about what *Honey* called "How far to go?" So I would quickly abdicate my theoretical position and say "no" on the rare occasions when physical circumstances made "yes" possible' (1973 p. 13).

24 In comparison the visual aspect of *Woman* and *Woman's Own*, which I did not discuss, seems of marginal importance. However 'visuality' was, in relation to other magazines of the period, their big selling point.

25 October 1963 was the month Macmillan resigned as prime minister through ill health and after the

trials of the 'Profumo affair'. A general election was being discussed although it did not take place until the following October.

26 See Altmann who discusses 'the present requirements of capitalism . . . for privatised hedonism to maintain . . . extensive consumerism', as they relate to being gay. He argues that in such a situation 'homosexuals represent an attractive market rather than a social threat' (1978 p. 5). It would appear that 'women who express their sexuality' are in a similar position.

27 The Family Planning Association opened their clinics to unmarried women in June 1967.

28 See Brooks 1977, Millum 1975 and Williamson 1978 for 'narcissism' in ads.

29 Powell had delivered his 'Rivers of Blood' speech in April 1968.

30 It must be said that the black models are 'discreetly' black, i.e.; they are 'light' skinned do not have Afro hair and are possibly of Asian origin. Their fleeting appearance here has never since 1969, burgeoned into any serious attempt to deal with the problems of black or Asian women: British women's magazines cultivate a white interest with only the 'token' article either featuring black models or discussing the experience of being black.

References

Abrams, Mark 1959a *The Teenage Consumer* London Press Exchange

Abrams, Mark 1959b 'The Home-centred Society' *The Listener* Nov. 26.

Abrams, Mark 1966 'What's changed in 10 years?' *The Observer* Colour Supplement, New Year issue.

Althusser, Louis 1971 'Ideological State Apparatuses' in *Lenin and Philosophy* New Left Books

Altman, Dennis 1978 'The State, Repression and Sexuality' in *Gay Left* No. 6 Summer 1978

Berger, John 1972 *Ways of Seeing* BBC/Penguin

Birmingham Feminist & History Group (1979) 'Feminism as Femininity?' *Feminit & Reviews* No. 3

Bland, Lucy; Brunsdon Charlotte; Hobson, Dorothy; Winship, Janice 1978 'Women "inside and outside" the relations of production' in *Women Take Issue* CCCS/Hutchinson

Bogdanor, Vernon and Skidelsky, Robert 1970 (ed) *The Age of Affluence 1951–1964* Macmillan

Booker, Christopher 1970 *The Neophiliacs – A study of the revolution in English life in the Fifties and Sixties* Fontana/Collins

Braverman, Harry 1974 *Labour and Monopoly Capital* Monthly Review Press New York

Brooks, Rosetta 1977 'Woman visible: Women invisible' *Studio International* Vol. 193 No. 987

Brunsdon, Charlotte 1978 'It is well known . . .' in *Women Take Issue* CCCS/Hutchinson

Butcher, Helen; Coward, Ros; et al. 1974 'Images of Women in the Media' Centre for Contemporary Cultural Studies. Occasional Paper.

Castells, Manuel 1977 *The Urban Question: a marxist approach.* Edward Arnold

Clarke, John; Hall, Stuart; Jefferson, Tony; Roberts, Brian 1975 'Subcultures, cultures and class; a theoretical overview' Working Papers in Cultural Studies 7/8 *Resistance through Rituals* Centre for Contemporary Cultural Studies.

Cowie, Elizabeth 1977 'Women, Representation and the Image' *Screen Education 23* Summer 1977

Debord, Guy 1967 *The Society of the Spectacle* Translated for Practical Paradise Publications 1977

Douglas, J.W.B. 1956 'The Feminists Mop up' *The Economist* Vol. 179 no. 5879

Faulder, C. 1977 'Advertising' in *Is This Your Life?* J. King and M. Scott (eds.) Virago

Foreman, Ann 1977 *Femininity as Alienation* Pluto Press

French, Marion 1978 *The Women's Room* Jonathan Cape

Friedan, Betty 1968 *The Feminine Mystique* Penguin

Grieve, Mary 1964 *Millions Made my Story* Victor Gollancz

Hall, Stuart 1979 'Legislation of Consent' in *Consenting Legislation in the 1960s*, (ed) Macmillan

Hobsbawm, E.J 1968 *Industry and Empire* Weidenfeld and Nicolson

Laing, R.D and Esterson, A. 1964 *Sanity, Madness and the Family* Tavistock

Lefebvre, Henri 1971 *Everyday Life in the Modern World* Allen Lane

Mackie, Lindsay and Patullo, Polly 1977 *Women at work* Tavistock

Mandel, Ernest 1975 *Late Capitalism* New Left Books

Marcuse, Herbert 1969 *One Dimensional Man* Sphere

Marcuse, Herbert 1972 *Eros and Civilisation* Abacus
Marx, Karl 1973 *Grundrisse* Penguin
Marx, Karl 1976 *Capital* Vol.1. Penguin
Marx, Karl 1972 *Capital* Vol.2. Lawrence and Wishart
McRobbie, Angela 1977 *Working Class Girls and the Culture of Femininity* MA Thesis Birmingham University.
McRobbie, Angela and Garber, Jenny 1975 'Girls and Subcultures: an exploration' *Resistance through Rituals* Working Papers in Cultural Studies 7/8. Centre for Contemporary Cultural Studies.
Millum, Trevor 1975 *Images of Women* Chatto and Windus
Ministry of Labour. Manpower Studies No. 6. 1967 *Occupational Changes 1951–61* HMSO
Mitchell, Juliet 1971 *Women's Estate* Penguin
Mitchell, Juliet 1975 *Psychoanalysis and Feminism* Penguin
Molina, Victor 1977 'Notes on Marx and the Problem of Individuality' *Working Papers in Cultural Studies* 10. CCCS.
Myrdal, Alva and Klein, Viola 1956 *Women's Two Roles: Home and Work* Routledge and Kegan Paul
O'Neill John 1972 *Sociology as a Skin trade* Heinemann
Pinto-Duschinsky, Michael 1970 'Bread and circuses? The Conservatives in Office 1951–64' *The Age of Affluence 1951–61* ed. Bogdanor and Skidelsky, Macmillan.
Political Economy of Women Group 1975 'On the Political Economy of Women' Conference of Socialist Economists pamphlet 2. Stage One.
Rowbotham, Sheila 1973 *Woman's Consciousness, Man's World* Penguin
Seccombe, W. 1975 'Domesti labour: reply to critics' *New Left Review* 94 pp. 84–96
Scott, Rosemary 1976 *The Female Consumer* Associated Business Programmes
Weinbaum, Batya and Bridges, Amy (1976) 'The Other Side of the Paycheck: Monopoly Capital and the Structure of Consumption.' *Monthly Review* Vol. 28 no.3
White, Cynthia 1970 *Women's Magazines 1693–1968: A sociological Study*
White, Cynthia 1977 *Royal Commission on the Press, The Women's periodical press in Britain 1946–76*. Working Paper no 4. HMSO
Williamson, Judith 1978 *Decoding Advertisements* Marion Boyars
Wilson, Elizabeth 1980 *Only Half way to Paradise*, Tavistock
Winship, Janice 1978 'A Woman's World: *Woman* – an ideology of femininity' *Women Take Issue* CCCS/Hutchinson
Zaretsky, Eli 1976 *Capitalism, the Family & Personal Life* Pluto

Index

NOTE: Page numbers in bold indicate a paper by an author in this collection.